ILLUSTRATED CATALOGUE

OF

AMERICAN HARDWARE

OF THE

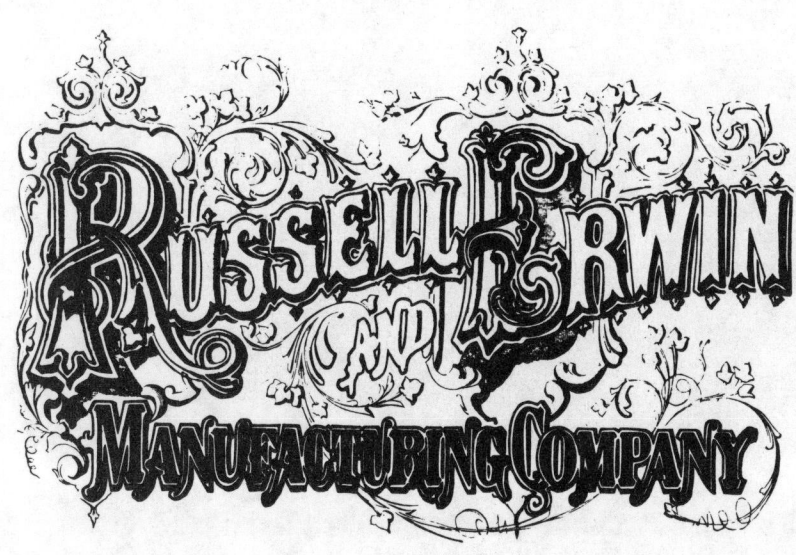

AN UNABRIDGED REPRINT OF THE 1865 EDITION
AND A NEW INTRODUCTION BY LEE H. NELSON, AIA

PUBLISHED BY THE ASSOCIATION FOR PRESERVATION TECHNOLOGY
WITH ASSISTANCE FROM THE FOUNDATION FOR PRESERVATION TECHNOLOGY

First facsimile edition, 1980

Published in the United States of America

ISBN: 0-920476-05-8
Library of Congress Catalog Card Number: 80-67146

PRODUCTION NOTES

This new edition is a reprint of the 1865 catalog in the collection of Russwin, Hardware Division, Emhart Industries, Inc., Berlin, Connecticut. Reproduction proofs, printing and binding was provided by Pub Press, Inc., 200 N. Bentalou St., Baltimore, Maryland. This edition reproduces the catalog in its entirety at a photographic reproduction of 35%. The cover of this edition reproduces the original four color title page in three colors. Overall supervision for the project was provided by H. Ward Jandl. Design for the introduction is by Judy Wagner.

The Association for Preservation Technology (APT) is an association of professionals active in the preservation of historic resources. From its inception in 1968, APT has been a Canadian-American forum for the development of architectural preservation techniques in North America. The reprinting of Russell and Erwin's 1865 catalog of American hardware is APT's first effort outside of its quarterly *Bulletin* to make key documents available to professionals in the field for research and study.

The Foundation for Preservation Technology (FPT) was incorporated in 1975 exclusively for educational, scientific, and charitable purposes to provide financial support for those activities which advance the knowledge of early building practices and preservation technology.

The Association for Preservation Technology gratefully acknowledges the patience and perseverance of Russwin, Hardware Division, Emhart Industries, Inc., in the reprinting of this important catalog from their private library.

INTRODUCTION

Over the years there has been a steady if romantic appreciation for the blacksmith and the products of the forge. There has, however, been scant attention paid to the subject of builders' hardware which has been an important industry since the late eighteenth century. Except for several singularly focused efforts by Donald Streeter and Peter Priess, there has been little written about the subject, whether from the standpoints of function, materials, inventions, and technology or from the standpoint of industrial management, process, and development.

The 1865 Russell and Erwin catalog is impressive evidence of the hardware industry after a century of growth in England and America. Its size and scope reflect, among other things, the changing needs for building hardware; the changing styles imposed upon some relatively constant functions; the changing technologies of casting, rolling, shearing and other aspects of production; the lessening of handwork, and the increasing use of machines. It also reflects the growing competitiveness of the industry and its new approaches to sales, inventory and distribution.

It is clear that many of the needed studies and researches regarding builders' hardware will not occur until there is more basic information available regarding collections of artifacts, business records, and other reference materials. The reprinting of this catalog is a step in that direction and follows several efforts over the years by the Association for Preservation Technology (APT) to include information about hardware in its publications and at its annual meetings. It also follows several important (but unfortunately relatively inaccessible) publications such as the 1971 *Guide for the Description of Building Hardware* by Peter J. Priess, *et al* (National Historic Parks and Sites Branch, Parks Canada, DINA, Ottawa) and the 1976 limited edition publication of Thomas F. Hennessy, *Early Locks and Lockmakers of America* (Nickerson & Collins Publishing Co., Des Plaines, Illinois).

In sum, this catalog is being reprinted as a basic reference—as a dating and research "tool"—because of its inexplicable rarity, because in many respects it represents a "benchmark" of the hardware industry, and because it helps fulfill one of the stated objectives of APT—"to promote the research, collection and publication of technical information in all aspects of historic preservation."

ENGLISH HARDWARE CATALOGS

Hardware catalogs per se seem to have had their beginnings in ". . . the growth of the organized factory as a means of production and distribution, as compared with the earlier limitation of these functions to the efforts of individuals." [1]

Earlier engraved "patterns" go back to the German and Italian goldsmiths of the fifteenth and sixteenth centuries. Pattern "books" for other crafts—lacemakers, ornamenters, jewelers, costumers, and furniture makers—followed in other countries. Gradually, due to the development of the factory system, these books shifted from serving the purpose of providing patterns to the purpose of promoting the sale of such merchandise.

It is difficult to trace the origin of English illustrated hardware pattern books because so few of them can be associated with specific manufacturers; and, in fact, few of them can be dated except in a rather general way. The earliest such catalogs seem to have closely followed the introduction of stamped brass goods in Birmingham, especially those used as brass ornaments for furniture, beginning about 1770; and at least one such catalog from that early period has survived in America. After the Revolutionary War, a number of Birmingham catalogs, encompassing both furniture fittings and building hardware in cast brass, cast iron and wrought iron, began to appear here. These catalogs exhibited an increasing variety of hardware goods in the first decades of the nineteenth century.

The elaborate copper engraved trade catalogs were intended for the use of dealers, who alone seem to have known their provenance, for none of the catalogs has title pages, and few have any evidence of the manufacturer. Some catalogs have dealers' notations that give clues to the maker, as well as the book "number" (for ordering purposes), and notes regarding the amount of discount for brass or iron goods. Many of the books can be dated approximately from the watermarked paper used for the copperplate engravings.

These catalogs often included a mixture of brassfounders' work, ironmongery, and miscellaneous items such as nails, furniture and coffin fittings, fishing reels, etc. They were usually arranged by subject matter: sash pulleys, padlocks, door knockers, thumb latches, bell mechanisms, hinges, etc. The copperplate engravings were usually numbered (later catalogs had an index) and contained labels identifying the item nomenclature, the item number, its size, sometimes its materials, or other references to a "new" pattern or functional use. Some catalogs have been hand-marked with prices for each item. The items were generally delineated full size in a rather crude combination of elevation and perspective. All of the English hardware catalogs from the period observed (1790s-1830s) are in the "album" format, that is, greater in width than in height. Several of the catalogs seem to be enlarged and undated versions of earlier catalogs with the same item numbers, a practice, of course, that continues today. Important collections of hardware "pattern" books are at the Essex Institute, Salem, Massachusetts (of the 100 plus tradebooks there, approximately 18 are of hardware) and at the Victoria and Albert Museum in London. Other categories of early trade books include brass fittings for furniture, clocks, coffins, lighting, and tools.

Among the earliest of the English catalogs to survive in America is one which is said to have belonged to Benjamin Franklin. When accessioned into Philadelphia's Franklin Institute Library in 1890, it was noted as "taken from Dr. Benjamin Franklin's Portfolio." If

so, Franklin might have used it during the period when he added on to his own house and when several other houses were being built for him on lower Market Street in the late 1780s. This particular catalog contains 57 numbered pages of butt hinges, sash pulleys, "skew butts" (self-closing door hinges), dovetail door hinges, thumb latches, door knockers, cast lath nails, padlocks, barrel bolts, bell pulls and quadrants, key escutcheons, and shutter screws (figure 1). This is an important catalog to American historians of building technology since it parallels the *in situ* presence of some items (like dovetail or cast iron butt hinges) in American buildings dating from the last quarter of the eighteenth century, e.g., the Bishop White House in Philadelphia, built in 1786-87 (figure 2). Other items in the "Franklin" catalog, such as the Norfolk thumb latch, have been seen and reported by various preservationists (see John R. Stevens' notes in the APT *Bulletin*, Vol. 1, No. 3, 1969, pp. 11-13). An almost identical catalog preserved in the library of the Essex Institute was mentioned in a 1926 article by George Francis Dow, who claimed it to be a Birmingham catalog, printed on paper watermarked "Finch," probably about 1800. While it is quite likely that many of these catalogs can eventually be dated by schol-

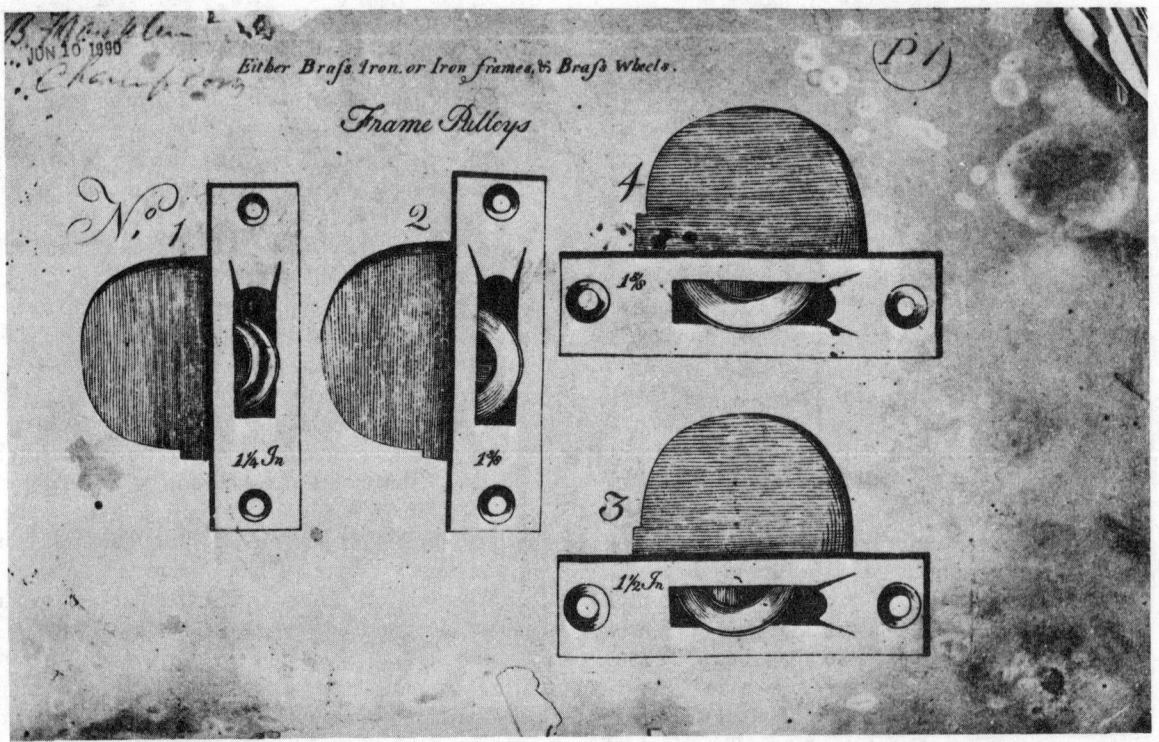

Figure 1. *Window frame pulleys, available in several sizes, with "either brass, iron, or iron frames & brass wheels," illustrated as plate 1 in an anonymous English hardware catalog, circa 1780-1800, said to have been owned by Benjamin Franklin. Franklin Institute Library, Philadelphia.*

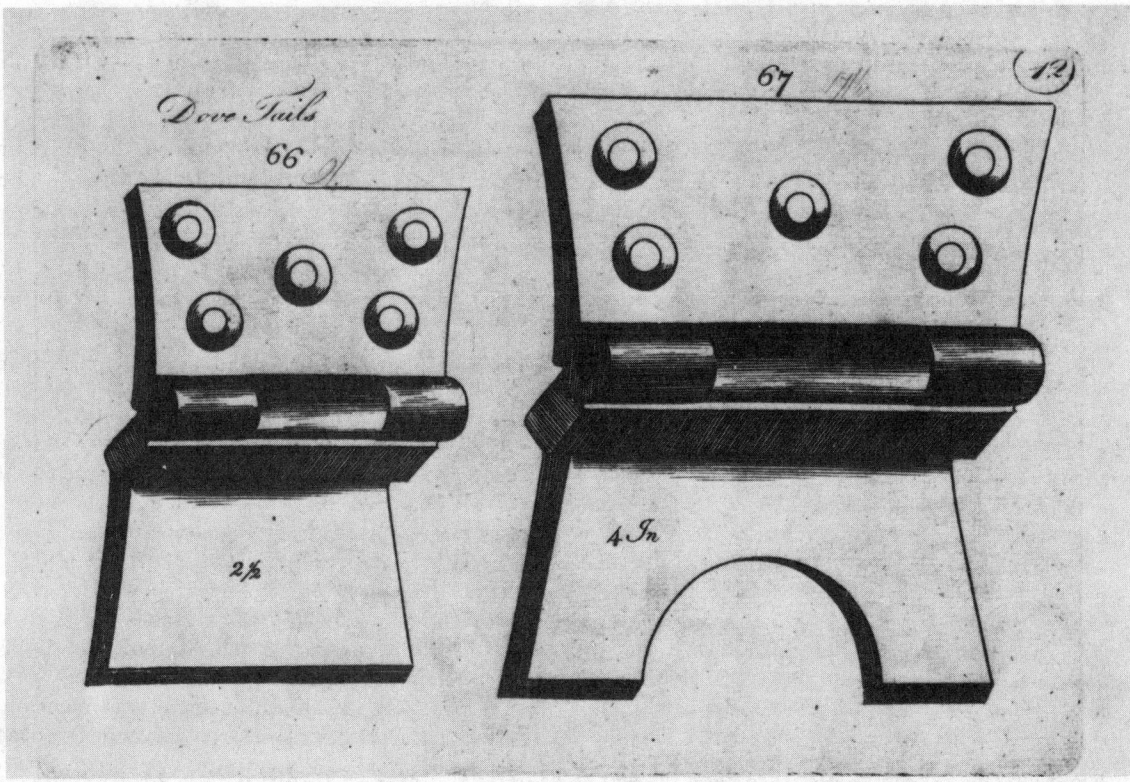

Figure 2. *Another plate from the "Franklin" catalog, showing wrought iron dovetail hinges for doors, available in several sizes and with the self-closing "skew" feature (not seen here). One leaf was screwed to the door jamb; the other leaf was mortised into the edge of the door and secured with wooden wedges. Franklin Institute Library, Philadelphia.*

ars of papermakers, unfortunately a precise date for this and the so-called "Franklin" catalog has yet to be established.[2]

The pioneer compilation of such catalogs is the 1913 publication entitled *Old English Pattern Books of the Metal Trades* (see note 1). In this publication, catalogs were organized under the headings of "Fittings for Furniture and Upholstery," "Ironware," "Horse Furniture," "Coffin Fittings," "Lighting Appliances," "Fancy Articles," "Tools," "Sheffield Plate," and "Carvings." All of those under the first heading were brass founders' and brass stampers' catalogs, though they contained a number of hardware items such as hinges, crank bell fittings, nails, etc.

Of the nearly 50 catalogs described in this 1913 publication, approximately half were in the first two categories, but could be described as being hardware catalogs, i.e., those which include items for buildings, although the emphasis was clearly on furniture fittings. None of the catalogs contains imprints or title pages, and thus none is directly identifiable or datable, except by watermarks or other internal evidence. Of these, about 20 have watermark

dates ranging from 1785 to 1838. About six of the catalogs are dated (by other evidence) before the end of the eighteenth century; since none seems to date before circa 1770, that may well be the beginning date for hardware catalogs.

There does not seem to be any discernible lineage or development of such catalogs, but by the second decade of the nineteenth century, the catalogs had grown in size (a hundred plates or more), with very good quality engravings and a surprising variety of goods in multiple sizes and styles (sometimes up to 30 different sizes of a given item), some items exhibiting ingenious mechanisms and new technology.

Perhaps the most impressive of these English brassfounders' catalogs is one dated circa 1829 (from a watermark) which contains a good many hinges, including butt hinges, card table hinges, clock case hinges, knife case hinges, table hinges, portable desk hinges, rising hinges, tumbler hinges, skew butts, fire screen hinges, French hinges, hollow jointed hinges, etc. It also contains an amazing variety of bell levers and associated hardware, door

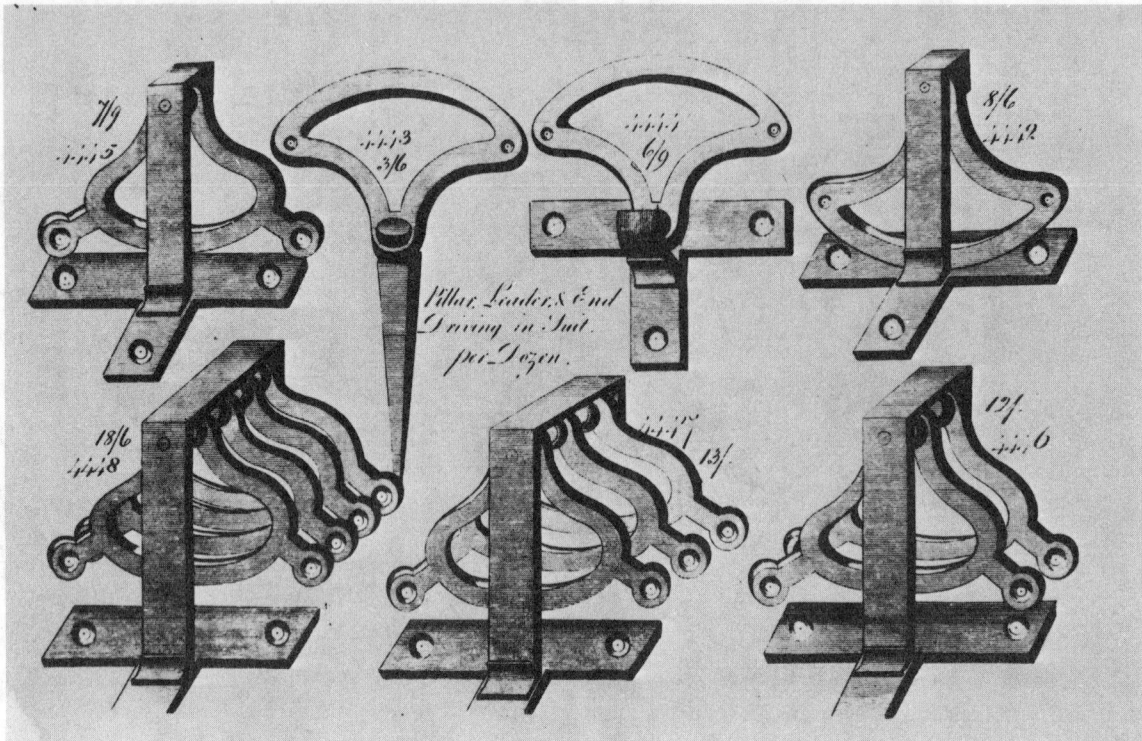

Figure 3. *One of many plates showing a variety of bell crank mechanisms, from a circa 1829 English brassfounder's catalog. Victoria and Albert Museum, accession no. E. 1827-1899.*

knockers, door knobs, sash fasteners, pulleys, screws, and door handles (figure 3). This catalog, in an album format measuring 8½ by 13 inches, has 180 engraved plates, many of which were printed on both sides and some were folded. This catalog, while remarkable in so many ways, shares with all the other surviving English catalogs the aspect of anonymity that is at such odds with the later American business practices that involved a high degree of commercial "identity," with the names of the manufacturers conspicuously displayed on both the merchandise and in the catalogs.

RISE OF AMERICAN HARDWARE MANUFACTURES

It is not possible here to do more than outline the industrial growth that led to the Russell and Erwin catalog of 1865. At the present time, there are many gaps in our understanding of that phenomenal growth; and there are various misconceptions about hardware in early America, especially in the late colonial period and the early decades of the nineteenth century. These misconceptions involve the extent to which hardware was imported vs. that which was made in America or as to when the so-called "Yankee ingenuity" asserted itself, etc.

Actually, these misconceptions and others are not easily resolved because of numerous interrelated factors, most of which are economic rather than technological. These factors include availability of skilled labor, wartime embargoes, tariff and import duties on various goods, economic depressions, building booms, etc. Some of these factors were discussed in the sweeping chronological *History of American Manufactures from 1608 to 1860*, compiled by J. Leander Bishop, and published in Philadelphia in 1868.

Actually, the truth about imported vs. locally made hardware lies somewhere between the misconceptions. First, we must continually bear in mind that the term "hardware" was (and is) a very loose term, one that might be narrowly defined by the maker, but which tended to be broadly defined by the seller. Thus, "hardware" could on occasion range from tools and cutlery, to hinges and nails, to kettles and guns. While our interest may be limited to hinges and locks, for example, it isn't possible to be that restrictive in outlining the growth of American hardware manufactures. In part, this is because the manufacture of hardware involves very different materials and craft specialties. Some hardware came from brassfounders, while others came from forges, or from "furnaces," nail works, locksmiths, whitesmiths, etc. Most of these craft specialties were being practiced well before the American Revolution in cities like Boston, New York, and Philadelphia (and many other cities as well). This is amply demonstrated in newspaper advertisements, especially after about 1760.[3] While such advertisements reveal a surprising variety of craftsmen who were manufacturing and selling, some on a fairly large scale, there were also craftsmen who sold both their own manufactured goods together with imported hardware items, and there were hardware merchants and ironmongers who were entirely in the import-for-sale business and whose advertisements identified the origins of their merchandise as being the "latest" from Birmingham, Sheffield, Bristol, London, etc.

It is also evident that a great deal of building hardware used in the colonies was made locally, especially those items that could be made by blacksmiths, such as the almost infinite varieties of strap hinges, and other items for doors, windows, shutters, as well as rough hardware such as bolts, nails, anchors, etc. Many of these items have been recorded and appreciated by several generations of "collectors," including the 1928 pioneer book by Albert H. Sonn, *Early American Wrought Iron.* There were numerous measured drawings of early American building hardware recorded in the 1930s and which are included in the Historic American Buildings Survey (HABS) in the Library of Congress.

Simply because there seems to have been a continuous coexistence of locally made and imported hardware through most of the colonial period and well into the early years of the Republic and because much hardware was anonymous in either case, it is very difficult to do more than generalize about the state of the "industry." It seems likely that some items seen in the eighteenth century catalogs, such as brass framed window sash pulleys, were seldom used in colonial American buildings. More commonly used were turned wooden pulleys (with iron pins), or wooden pulleys mounted in removable wooden frames, all of which were almost surely locally made. On the other hand, ornamental brass door knockers were more likely to have been imported, although there were brass founders in the larger urban centers. It is also quite likely that the more sophisticated hinges were imported, such as the "skew butts" (self-closing) or the "dovetail" butts (semi-concealed). Such imported hinges were often used on doors in principal rooms of American houses, yet the same houses may have had locally made surface-mounted hinges (such as "H" or "H-L")

on lesser doorways. This "hierarchy" of hardware is a manifestation of the "best-foot-forward" concept, and which was so prevalent in early American buildings.

It is important that this concept be fully understood by preservationists because it affected nearly every aspect of early American buildings (or at least the more substantial buildings). It meant that the best rooms got the best hinges, locks, bell pulls, as well as the best glass, and perhaps the narrowest floor boards, the most elaborate woodwork, mouldings, etc. Thus, it is quite possible to find the mixture of local and imported hardware in a single building as mentioned earlier. On the other hand, the bulk of early American buildings, especially those of less pretentious character or those in rural areas, or those in ethically settled areas, utilized hardware that was entirely locally made, sometimes with an ethnic bias, and sometimes with simple and interesting wooden substitutions for the more conventional iron or brass hardware, especially for doors and windows.

In the final analysis, the provenance of hardware within any given building must be judged individually and compared with other local examples and the English catalogs. Many such studies need to be made before a clearer picture emerges. However, it is evident that beginning about 1810, American made hardware asserted itself and that by 1830 it developed into an industry in the modern sense. This can be seen in the increase in "signed" and attributable hardware (especially in urban areas such as Philadelphia), and in the economic indicators such as the census statistics, business records, city directory listings, patents, and the system of national tariff protection to domestic industry.

For example, the dramatic development of patentable inventions from the 1790s is one index for measuring the growth of the American industry leading up to the Russell and Erwin catalog of 1865. Perhaps the invention and development of cut nails encompassed the most remarkable aspect of one branch of the hardware industry. Between the years 1791 and 1815, there were some 88 patentees of cut nail machines. America seems to have led the English in this aspect.[4]

The almost expotential increase in patents for locks from 1800 to 1850 is a measure of growth for a totally different aspect of the industry. Lock patents for ten year intervals were as follows: 1 from 1800 to 1809; 4 from 1810 to 1819; 14 from 1820 to 1829; 50 from 1830 to 1839; and 100 from 1840 to 1849.[5] Despite the growth indicated by these statistics, however, the British dominated the lock business in the United States until the middle 1830s.

While there were numerous other American hardware inventions (besides nails and locks) during this period, they were seldom significant technologically or in a business sense. They were not inventions upon which fortunes were made (as with cut nails), but they did contribute to the growth of various branches of the industry. Most of the inventions were for door and window fastenings, such as door closers, door latches; items for securing window shutters; numerous devices for hanging and operating Venetian blinds; and many improvements for making wood screws.

There were several "break through" inventions in the 1840s, including the casting of butt hinges in metallic moulds. Instead of a joint pin, according to the patent narrative, "we usually cast the knuckles of one half the hinge with conical depressions, or countersinks, which are to receive conical projections on the knuckles of the other half . . .".[6]

Another important patent was for machinery to make gimlet-pointed screws, an invention that must have gladdened the heart of many a carpenter and cabinetmaker.

Thus, the years following the turn of the nineteenth century saw the establishment of numerous cut nail manufactories, screw-cutting factories, brass foundries, and ironworks; and a few articles of hardware began to be produced in considerable quantities, capitalizing on the growing markets and the new technologies of mass production.

During the first three decades of the nineteenth century, a different kind of hardware catalog emerged on the American scene, one which does not conform to the type being surveyed in this introduction, but which deserves mention as a source of information about hardware during this period. These were catalogs of hardware for sale at auction, primarily by large auction firms in Boston and New York. Some of these were assignee's or sheriff's sales for liquidation purposes (at the store being liquidated), but other auctions appear to have been a method of selling very large quantities of hardware at the auction "house" to dealers in packaged lots. These catalogs are deceptive in several respects. Although they are small in size and unillustrated, they range from 30 to 170 pages, averaging about 25-30 items per page, arranged in columns with "lot" numbers, item descriptions, quantities, and sizes. Sometimes they included a "pattern" number, obviously referring to an illustrated English manufacturer's catalog. Some catalogs include a price

per unit which was extended out for each quantity of items and for the entire lot, all in the English monetary system. It appears that nearly all items sold in this manner were of British manufacture, although there are some references to American made goods.

These catalogs comprise a valuable source of information about marketing practices (and indirectly about manufacturing), but especially about nomenclature and variety, the latter far exceeding anything seen in the illustrated catalogs of British manufactories. For research purposes, these should be used as a supplement to the English catalogs, rather than as a harbinger of American manufacturers' catalogs.[7]

During the mid-1830s there was a noticeable increase in the quantity, variety and quality of domestic production, together with an increase in the number and scope of American hardware dealers. Several important manufactories, especially of locks, were begun in this period, all in Connecticut: the N.C. Sanford and Co. of Meriden in 1828; the F. T. Stanley Co. of New Britain in 1831; Blake Bros. Co. of New Haven in 1833; Lewis, McKee and Co. (later the Eagle Lock Company) of Terryville in 1833; and the F. Baldwin and Co. of Middletown in 1840. The F. T. Stanley Company gradually evolved with changing partners, including Emanuel Russell and Cornelius B. Erwin, to become the Russell and Erwin Manufacturing Co. in 1846. Now known as Russwin, a division of Emhart Industries, this is the oldest surviving name in the hardware industry.

The English type of hardware catalog did not have its counterpart in the United States until the 1850s. Prior to this time there were newspaper advertisements, dealers' price lists, "catalogs" in the form of broadsides, handbills, "books of prices," and the above-mentioned catalogs of hardware to be sold at auction, but without any known exceptions, these were issued by dealers rather than manufacturers. Perhaps the earliest dealer's catalog which specifically identified "American Manufactured Hardware" was one issued by William H. Carr and Co., Philadelphia, in 1838. The catalog included a wide range of "hardware," including tools, cutlery, lamps, hollow wares, locks, builders hardware, and sundries—by some sixty American firms. This catalog unfortunately was not illustrated (figure 4).[9]

Not until the 1850s were there any illustrated hardware catalogs produced American manufacturers. Among the early examples were those by Peck and Walter Manufacturing Co., New Britain, Connecticut, 1853; Pittsburgh Novelty Works, 1855; Sargent and Co.,

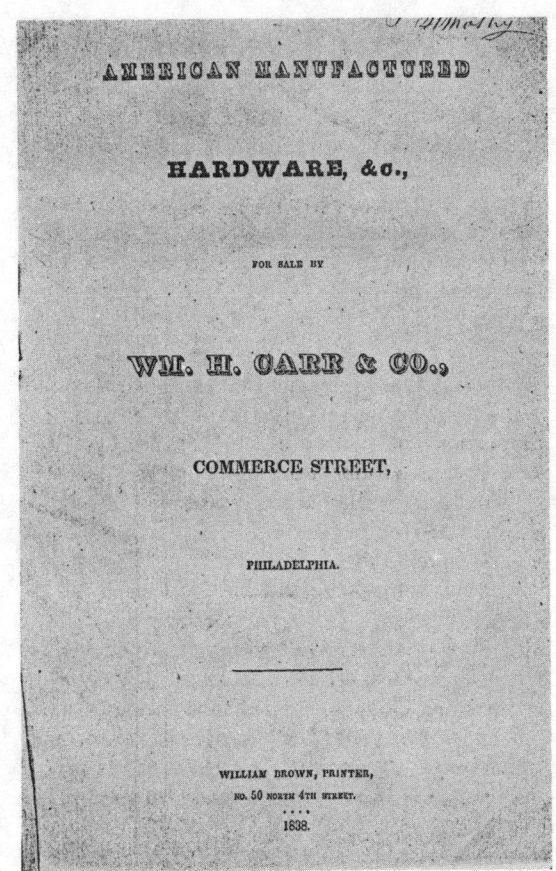

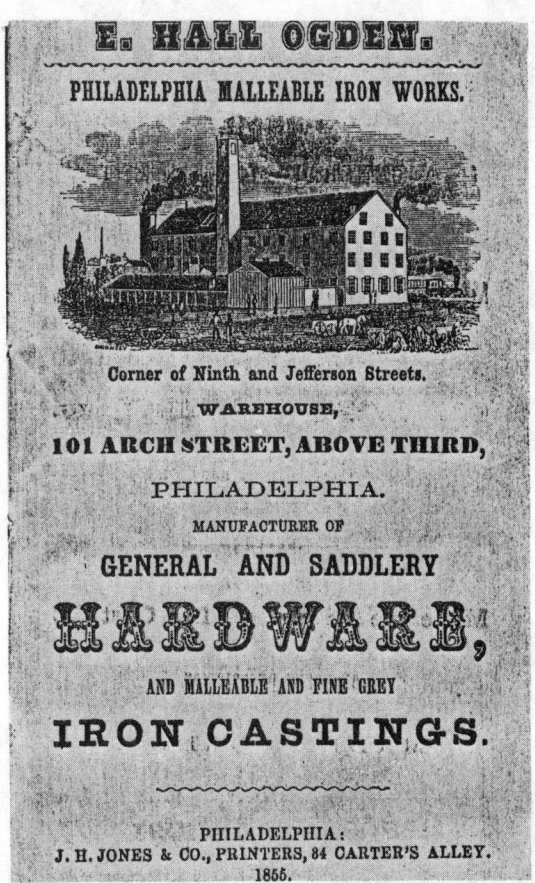

Figure 4. *Title page of unillustrated dealer's catalog (vertical format, 32 pp.) issued by Wm. H. Carr & Co., Commerce St., Philadelphia, 1838, which included mortise locks, patent shutter fasteners, plate locks, spring bolts, etc., all made by identified American manufactories. Eleutherian Mills Historical Library.*

Figure 5. *Title page of 1855 catalog issued by E. Hall Ogden, Philadelphia Malleable Iron Works, unillustrated, 40 pp. with index. Eleutherian Mills Historical Library.*

New Haven, Connecticut, 1852, 1856, 1857; and Hotchkiss and Sons, Sharon Valley, Connecticut, 1859. There were also some unillustrated catalogs by American manufacturers, such as the one by E. Hall Ogden for the Philadelphia Malleable Iron Works, of 1855 (figure 5).

Most of these early American hardware catalogs were quite different from their English antecedents, that is, they were all conspicuously identifiable by maker, place and date; they were small, often pocket size and in a vertical format, utilizing descriptive material set in type with woodcut engravings, and frequently prices were printed in the catalog. Thus, the illustrated American hardware catalogs had their origins, partly from the English prototypes, but mostly to serve an extraordinarily rapid business growth and the then new marketing sample rooms and warehousing practices that served the wholesale commission merchants and jobbers in the United States.

A telling aspect concerning the growth of

the American hardware industry is to compare several catalogs of the period 1855-1860 with the 1865 Russell and Erwin catalog. The E. Hall Ogden catalog of 1855 was unillustrated and consisted of 40 pages and index; the Hotchkiss and Sons illustrated catalog of 1859 had 24 pages with an index; and the James L. Haven Co. (Cincinnati, Ohio) illustrated catalog of 1860 had 59 pages with an index (figure 6). The Russell and Erwin catalog, printed five years later with some 3300 engravings and over 400 pages, represents a remarkable spiralling of manufacturing and technological expertise, combined with business and marketing maturity.

THE 1865 RUSSELL AND ERWIN CATALOG OF AMERICAN HARDWARE

Russell and Erwin had produced several catalogs prior to 1865, including one in 1853;

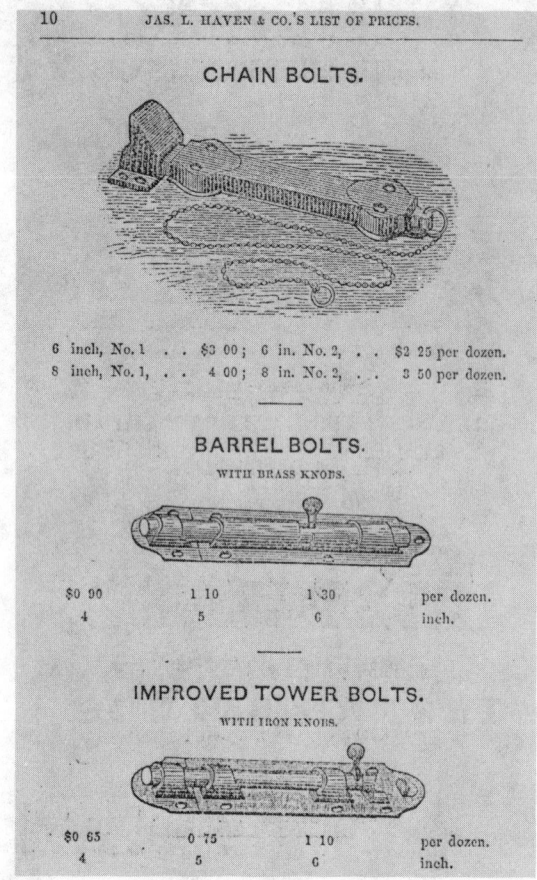

Figure 6. *Various types of sliding bolts, from the illustrated catalog of James L. Haven & Co., "Manufacturers of Butt Hinges, Hardware, and Malleable Castings," Cincinnati, Ohio, 1860. Eleutherian Mills Historical Library.*

their 1864 catalog was in itself an impressive endeavor, consisting of 116 pages of handsome wood engravings, printed in New York, in a vertical format measuring 12 by 17 inches. It set a high standard for the genre, and it was the model for the much larger catalog which followed so soon in 1865. In fact, the first 113 pages of the 436 page catalog of 1865 were almost identical to the 1864 catalog.[10]

The firm published other important catalogs in the last three decades of the nineteenth century, especially in 1887, 1897, and 1899, all of which were catalogs approaching or exceeding 1000 pages, and which probably represent the high point of American hardware catalog production. However, the Russell and Erwin catalog of 1865 is a singular document in several respects, partly because of its size relative to its date, but mostly as an indicator of industrial growth; as an indicator of rapidly changing business practices (away from "commission merchants" to direct sale from "sample" rooms and warehouses); as an indicator of

style (both current and retardataire); as an indicator of inventions, improvements and technology; as an indicator of perceived house and farm needs; and as an example of the engravers' and printers' art.

In 1869, an unabashedly laudatory account of the Company, described this catalog in terms that might seem self-serving, yet from our vantage point it is hard to fault the 1869 praise as being anything but deserved, as follows:

> Without entering further into details regarding the numerous processes of manufacture at this establishment we will here mention the fact that in 1865 the Russell & Erwin Manufacturing Company published a large illustrated catalogue of over four hundred pages, on finely tinted paper, each page 12 by 14 [sic] inches in size, the volume containing 3,300 fine wood engravings representing nearly every article of American Hardware manufactured in the United States. The edition cost many thousand dollars, and the catalogue is used as a standard work of reference by the trade, to whom it is furnished at $25 a copy. It has never been equaled in completeness and beauty by any other commercial handbook in this or any other country. It was designed by this firm to simplify the mode of conducting the hardware business and to assist beginners in learning their business. That the design was successful is shown by the high estimation in which this rare volume is held by the trade.[11]

Certainly a useful aspect of this catalog is the "Table of Contents" with 967 entries, ranging from locks and latches (in profusion), hinges, other door trimmings, bell trimmings, sash hardware, screws, nails, bolts, handles, hooks, carpenter's tools, cooper's tools, tinsmith's tools, blacksmith's and machinist's tools, agricultural implements, scales, bells, silver plated ware, cutlery, lamps, hollow ware, stationer's hardware, traps, sleighs, and coffin trimmings.

Besides the variety of items, the catalog is even more significant for the information it provides to preservationists and to historians of business and technology, such as: information about nomenclature (e.g., "Boston Pattern," "Lull & Porter's Patent"); information about hardware construction (via the illustrations); full information about optional mountings and fittings, packing notations (e.g., with escutcheons, plates and screws); information about materials (e.g., white metal, mineral knobs, bone, cast steel); and references to finishes and technology (e.g., japanned, electro-plated). In addition, there are many clues that other manufacturers' products were being marketed by Russell and Erwin, such as Henry Disston saws, Brown and Sharpe gauges, Fairbanks' Scales, etc.

Of course, looking back to the earlier English catalogs, one finds clues about stylistic evolution and technological change; but it is also striking that some aspects of hardware have changed very little over a century or more! Between these covers, there are many kinds of information that will be useful to architects, archeologists, museum curators, preservationists and educators. It is for these and other persons involved in historic preservation that the Association for Preservation Technology presents the reprint of this rare and valuable catalog. This writer believes that it represents a significant revival of information about the American hardware industry.[12]

– Lee H. Nelson, AIA

NOTES

1. W. A. Young, compiler. *Old English Pattern Books of the Metal Trades*, Victoria and Albert Museum Publication No. 87. London: 1913, p. 6.

2. George Francis Dow, "Old English Pattern Books of Hardware Used in the Building and Cabinet Maker's Trades," *Old Time New England*, vol. XVII, no. 1, July, 1926, pp. 30-41. The Essex Institute and the Franklin Institute catalogs have been compared by National Park Service architect Orville W. Carroll who found them to be identical except that the Essex catalog has several additional plates at the end.

3. See, for example, the compilations by Rita Susswein Gottesman, *The Arts and Crafts in New York, 1726-1776, Advertisements and News Items from New York City Newspapers*. New York: 1938. Subsequent compilations for New York and other cities have also been published.

4. See Greville and Dorothy Bathe, *Jacob Perkins, His Inventions, His Times, and His Contemporaries*. Philadelphia: 1943; and H. R. Bradley Smith, "Chronological Development of Nails," supplement to *Blacksmith's and Farrier's Tools at Shelburne Museum*. Shelburne, Vermont: 1966.

5. See Thomas F. Hennessy, cited earlier, pp. 19, 135-139; and Carole L. Perrault, "Index of Patents for Locks from the Franklin Institute Journals, 1826-1859," *Bulletin* of the Association for Preservation Technology, vol. VIII, no. 2, 1976, pp. 37-69.

6. Patented by Thomas Shepard and Thomas Loving, Southwark (Philadelphia), March 16, 1841, *Franklin Institute Journal*, vol. 33, 1842, p. 339; also see "Priess and Streeter Correspondence on Hinges," *Bulletin* of the Association for Preservation Technology, vol. VI, no. 2, 1974, pp. 24-33.

7. There are 12 such miscellaneous catalogs of hardware sold at auction among the "Inventory of Sample Books," Essex Institute, Salem, Massachusetts, which range in date from 1818-1838, of which seven are from Boston, four from New York City, and one not identified.

8. Many other early lock making companies are listed in Hennessy, *op. cit.*, pp. 143-148.

9. The contents (and manufacturers) of this catalog are listed by Lawrence B. Romaine, *A Guide to American Trade Catalogs*, 1744-1900. New York: 1960, pp. 176 a-b.

10. The Library of Congress has a copy of the 1864 catalog (dated October 1, 1864, on plate 116), brought to my attention by David Look, AIA, Heritage Conservation and Recreation Service.

11. New York *Commercial Path Finder*, November, 1869, brought to my attention by James T. Wollon, Jr., AIA, Havre de Grace, Maryland.

12. In addition to the sources mentioned in the foregoing Introduction, the reader is referred to "Historic Hardware in the United States and Canada," edited by Theodore Prudon, which includes lists of collections, buildings, suppliers, bibliography, trade catalogs and research materials. *Newsletter* of the Association for Preservation Technology, vol. III, no. III, June, 1974.

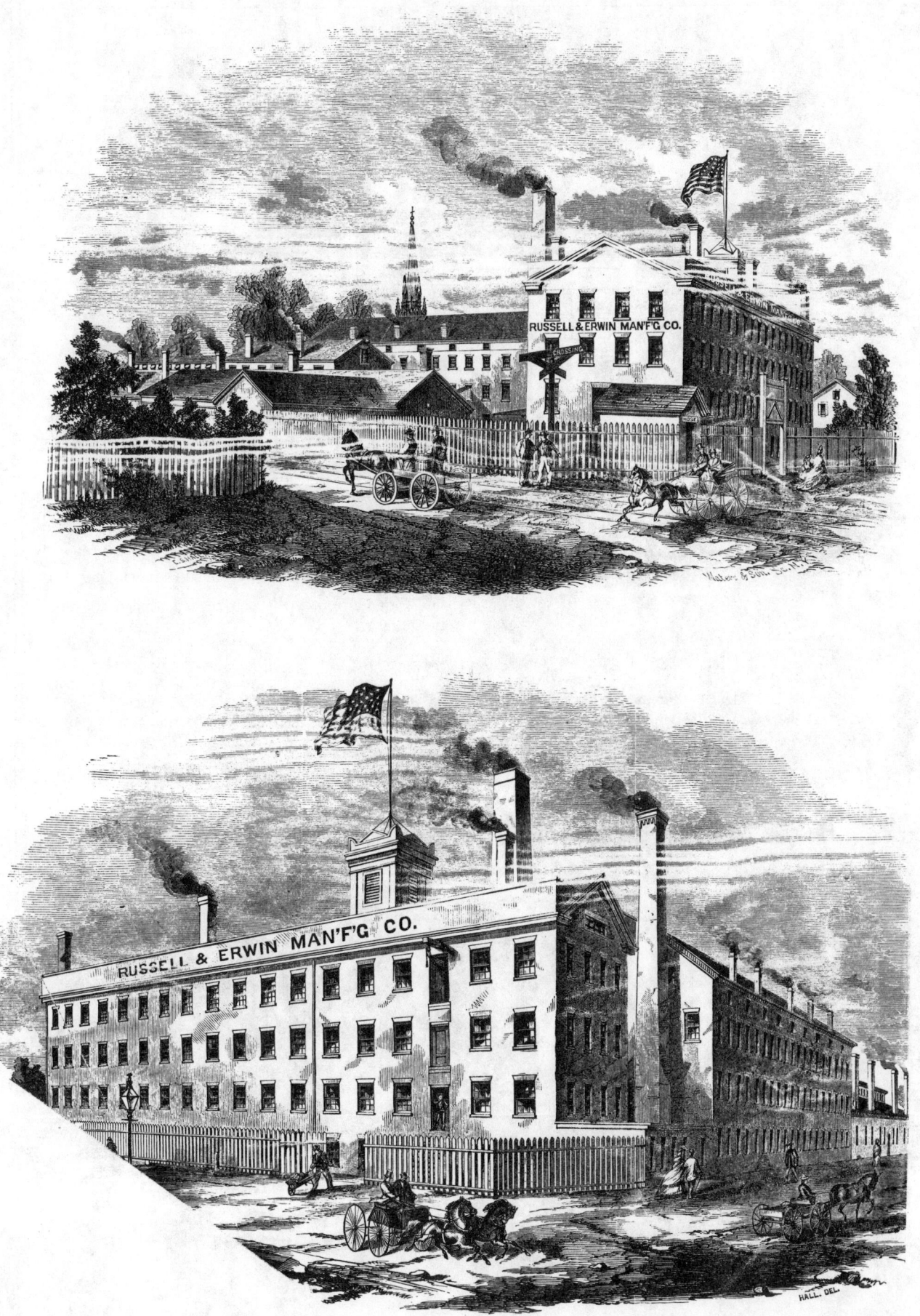

FACTORY BUILDINGS, NEW BRITAIN, CONN.

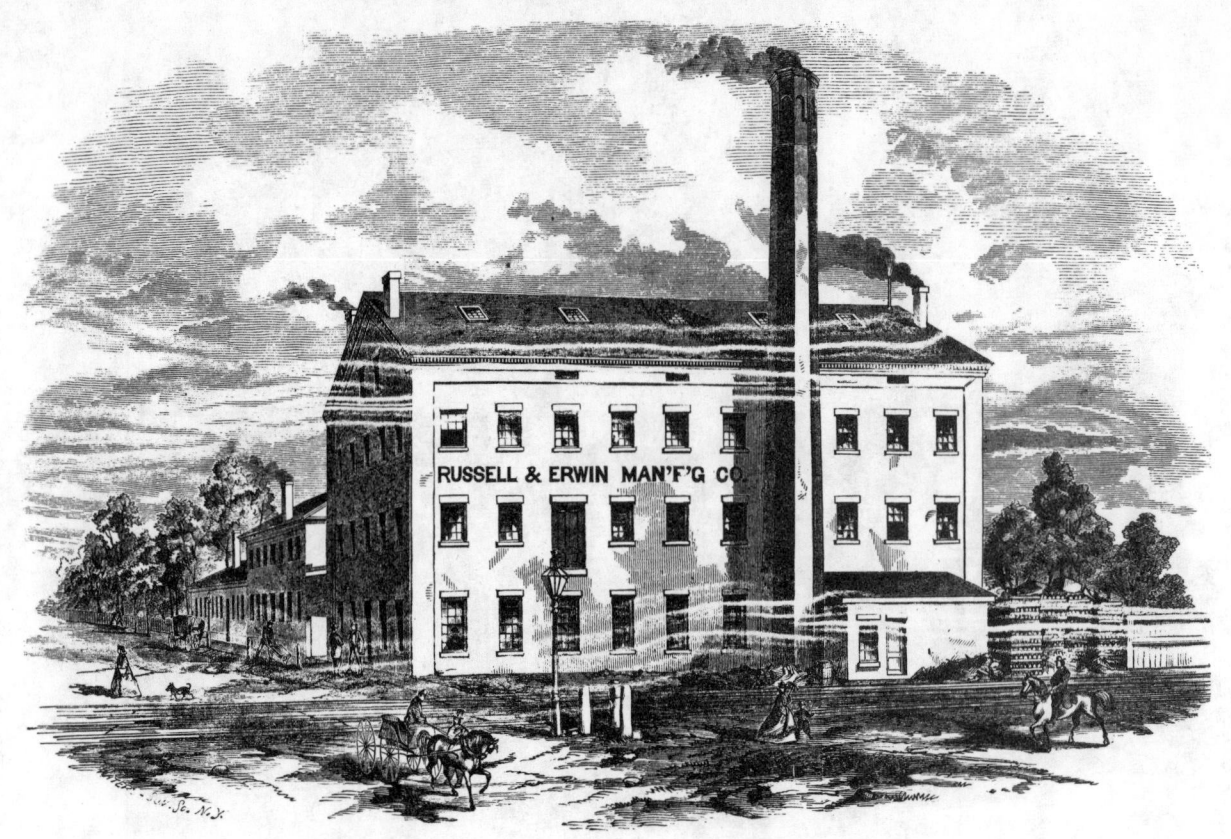

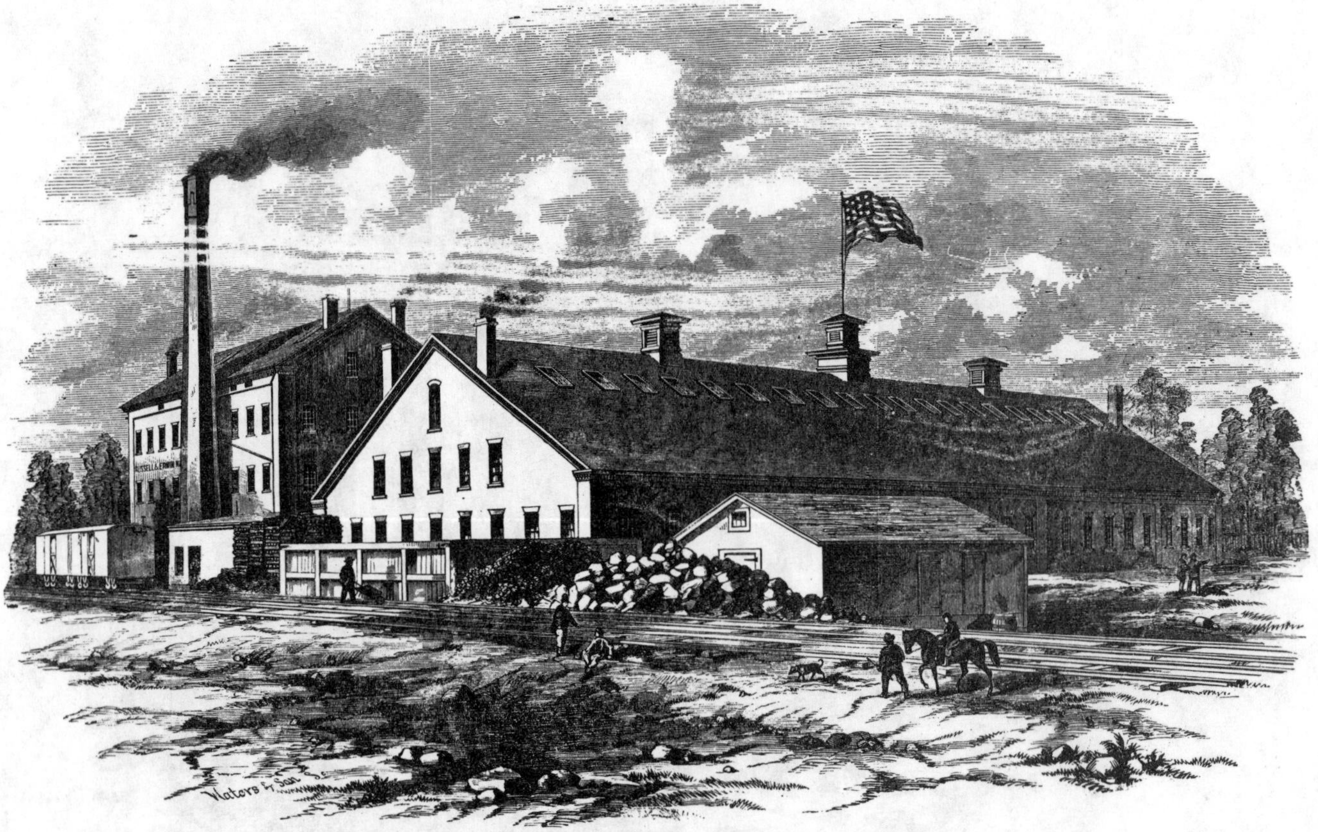

WAREHOUSES.

New-York.

Philadelphia.

San Francisco.

ILLUSTRATED CATALOGUE

OF

AMERICAN HARDWARE

OF THE

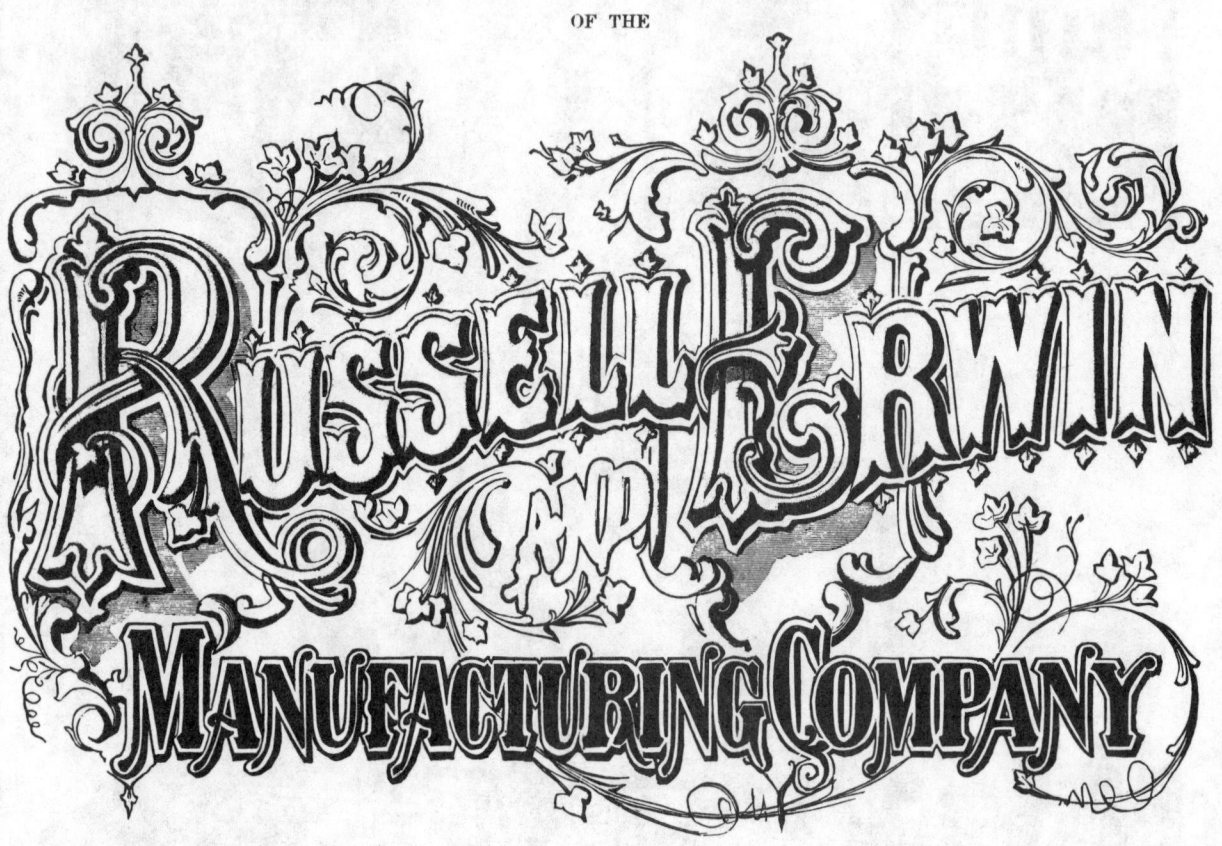

RUSSELL AND ERWIN MANUFACTURING COMPANY

Manufactory, New Britain, Conn.

WAREHOUSES,

NEW-YORK, PHILADELPHIA, BOSTON, SAN FRANCISCO.

1865.

FRANCIS HART & COMPANY, PRINTERS,
63 CORTLANDT STREET, NEW-YORK.

COMPILED BY HENRY E. RUSSELL, 2D.

President :
CORNELIUS B. ERWIN,
New Britain, Conn.

Treasurer :
HENRY E. RUSSELL, - - New Britain, Conn.

Secretary :
LUCIUS WOODRUFF, - - - - - - New Britain, Conn.

Directors :
CORNELIUS B. ERWIN, - - - - - - New Britain, Conn.
HENRY E. RUSSELL, - - - - - - - - "   "   "
HENRY STANLEY, - - - - - - - - - "   "   "
LUCIUS WOODRUFF, - - - - - - - - "   "   "
HORACE EDDY, - - - - - - - - - "   "   "
ISAAC D. RUSSELL, - - - - - - - - New-York City.
JAMES B. OGDEN, - - - - - - - - - "   "

Managers of Warehouses :
New-York - - - - - - { ISAAC D. RUSSELL,
                        { JAMES B. OGDEN,
                        { RICHARD P. BRUFF.
Philadelphia, - - - - - JAMES E. TERRY.
Boston, - - - - - - -
San Francisco, JOSEPH W. STOW.

TABLE OF CONTENTS.

T

HEAVY UPRIGHT RIM KNOB LOCKS,

FOR FRONT OR OUTSIDE DOORS,

WITH NIGHT KEY ATTACHMENT.

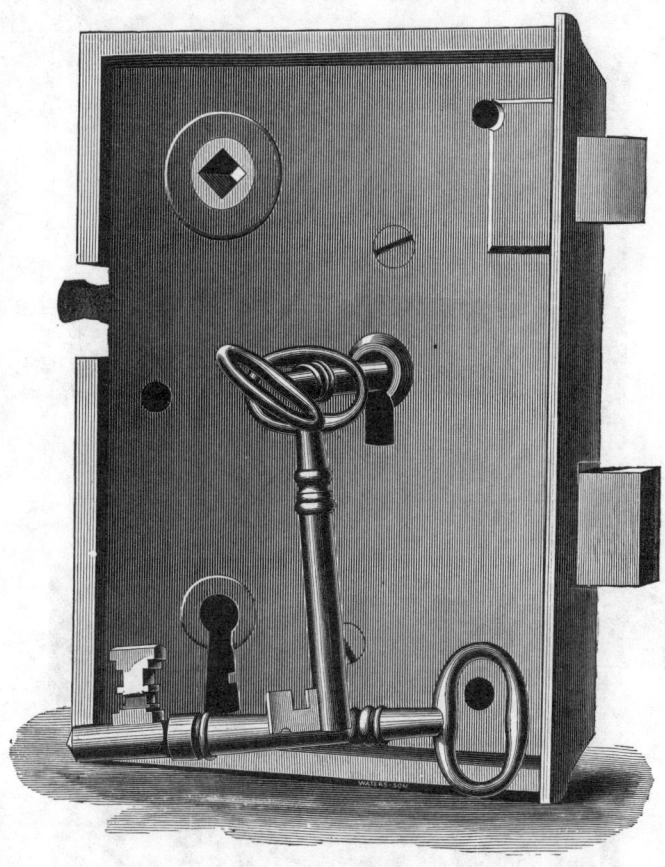

[200.]

No. 200.

SIZE 6¼ × 4½ INCHES.

Beveled Case, one Tumbler, Brass Hub, two Brass Bolts, Brass Key, two Night Keys, Brass Slide Knob—2¼ × 2¼ inch Knobs on Plain Spindles.   (See Plate.)

No. 252.

SIZE 6 × 4½ INCHES.

Beveled Case *Heavy*, 3 Wrought Iron Tumblers, Brass Hub, 2 Heavy Brass Bolts with Wrought Iron Tail, Brass Key, 2 Night Keys, Brass Slide Knob with Stop, 2½ × 2¼ inch Knobs on Plain Spindles.

	Lock No. 200.	Lock No. 252.
	PER DOZ.	PER DOZ.
Without Furniture		
With Mineral Knobs No. 450, Japanned Mountings, Japanned Plate Escutcheons		
" Porcelain Knobs No. 350, Japanned Mountings, Japanned Plate Escutcheons		
" Porcelain Knobs No. 150, Plated Mountings, Plated Plate Escutcheons		
" Porcelain Knobs No. 151, Porcelain Mountings, Porcelain Plate Escutcheons		

No. 201.

SIZE 7 × 4 INCHES.

Square Case, Lever, one Tumbler, Brass Hub, two Brass Bolts, Brass Key, two Night Keys, 2½ × 2¼ inch Knobs on Swivel Spindles.

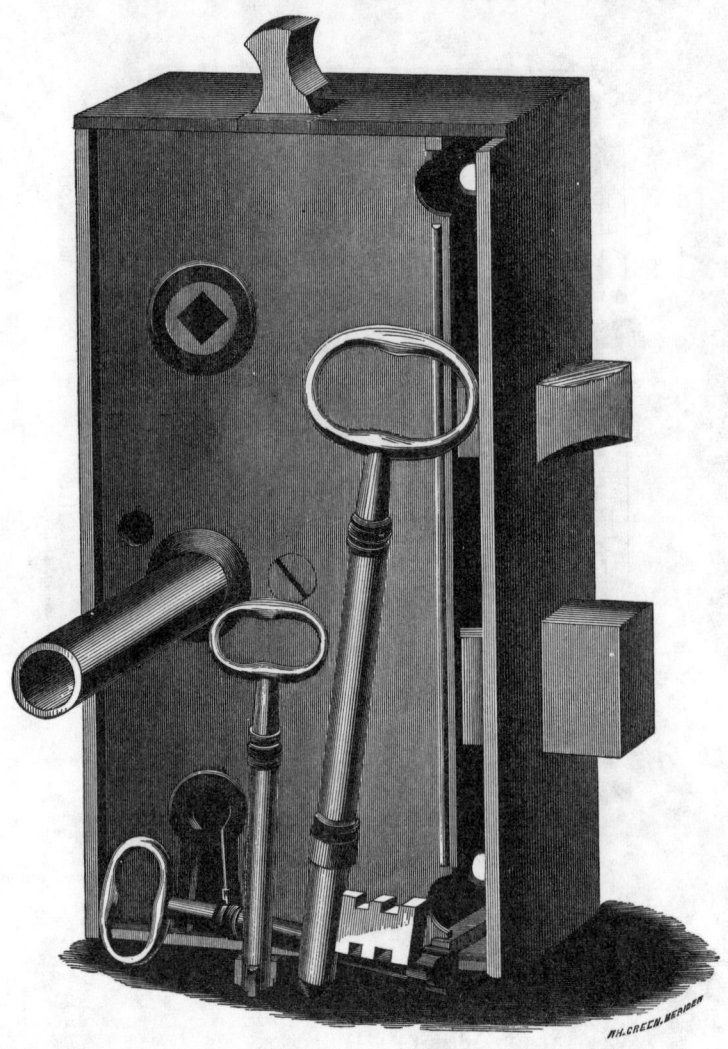

Locks 201 to 204 should be ordered complete with Furniture, as they require a Spindle three-eighths of an inch in diameter, and heavier Knobs than are generally used.

PER DOZ.

Without Knobs or Escutcheons .... $

With Mineral Knobs No. 450, Japanned Mountings and Japanned Drop Escutcheons ....

   " Porcelain Knobs No. 350, Japanned Mountings and Japanned Drop Escutcheons ....

   " Extra Heavy Brass Knobs and Roses, and Brass Drop Escutcheons ....

   " Extra Heavy Brass Knobs outside, and Porcelain Knobs No. 100 inside, and Brass Drop Escutcheons

   " Porcelain Knobs No. 150, Plated Roses, and Plated Drop Escutcheons ....

   " Porcelain Knobs No. 151, Porcelain Roses and Porcelain Drop Escutcheons ....

   " Electro Plated Knobs, Roses, and Electro Plated Drop Escutcheons ....

   " Electro Plated Knobs outside, and Porcelain Knobs No. 100 inside, Electro Plated Drop Escutcheons

   " Hand Plated Knobs, and Hand Plated Drop Escutcheons ....

   " Hand Plated Knobs outside, and Porcelain Knobs No. 100 inside, and Hand Plated Drop Escutcheons

[204.]

No. 202.

SIZE 7½ × 5 INCHES.

O. G. Case, 3 Wrought Iron Tumblers, Brass Hub, 2 Brass Bolts, Brass Key, 2 Night Keys, 2½ × 2¼ inch Knobs on Swivel Spindles.

No. 203.

SIZE 7½ × 5 INCHES.

O. G. Case, 3 Wrought Iron Tumblers, Brass Hub, 2 Brass Bolts, Brass Key, 2 *Extra Safe* Three-Tumbler Bit Night Keys, 2½ × 2¼ inch Knobs on Swivel Spindles. (See Plate.)

No. 204.

SIZE 8 × 5 INCHES.

O. G. Case, 3 Wrought Iron Tumblers, Brass Hub, 2 Brass Bolts, Brass Key, 2 *Extra Safe* Five-Tumbler Bit Night Keys, 2½ × 2¼ inch Knobs, on Swivel Spindles.

	Lock No. 201.	Lock No. 202.	Lock No. 203.	Lock No. 204.
	PER DOZ.	PER DOZ.	PER DOZ.	PER DOZ.
Without Knobs or Escutcheons				
With Mineral Knobs No. 450, Japanned Mountings and Japanned Drop Escutcheons				
" Porcelain Knobs No. 350, Japanned Mountings and Japanned Drop Escutcheons				
" Extra Heavy Brass Knobs and Roses, and Brass Drop Escutcheons				
" Extra Heavy Brass Knobs and Roses outside, and Porcelain Knobs No. 100 inside, and Brass Drop Escutcheons				
" Porcelain Knobs No. 150, Plated Roses and Plated Drop Escutcheons				
" With Porcelain Knobs No. 151, Porcelain Roses and Porcelain Drop Escutcheons				
" Electro-Plated Knobs, Roses, and Electro-Plated Drop Escutcheons				
" Electro-Plated Knobs outside, and Porcelain Knobs No. 100 inside, and Electro-Plated Drop Escutcheons				
" Hand Plated Knobs, and Hand Plated Drop Escutcheons				
" Hand Plated Knobs outside, and Porcelain Knobs No. 100 inside, and Hand Plated Drop Escutcheons				

HEAVY UPRIGHT RIM KNOB LOCKS,
FOR FRONT OR OUTSIDE DOORS,
WITHOUT NIGHT KEYS.

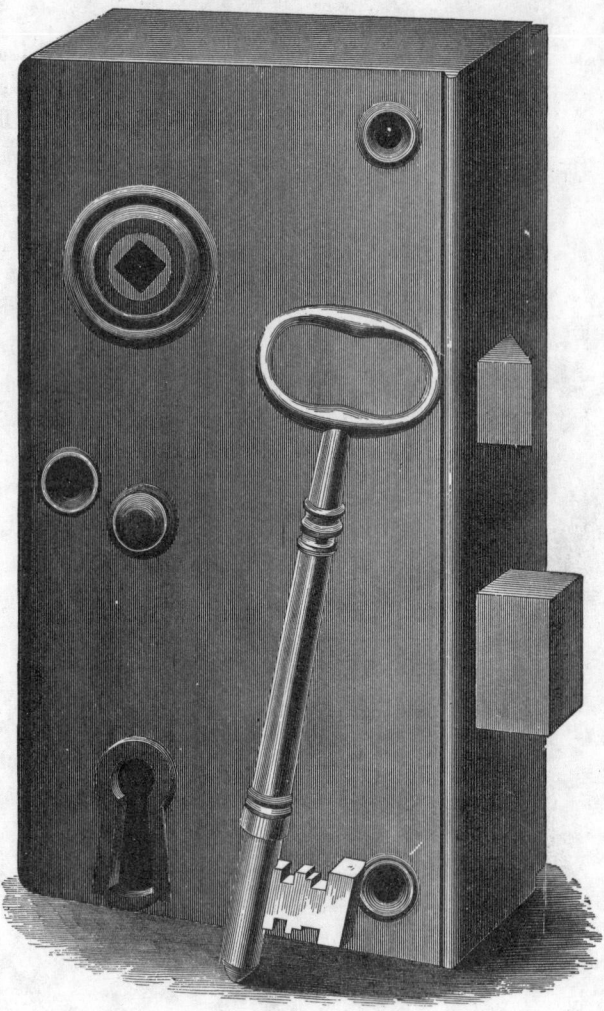

[222.]

Locks 201 to 204 should be ordered complete with Furniture, as they require a Spindle three-eighths of an inch in diameter, and heavier Knobs than are generally used.

No. 220.

Size 6¼ × 4½ Inches.

Beveled Case, 1 Tumbler, Iron Hub, 2 Brass Bolts, Extra Brass Night Bolt, Brass Key, same as No. 532, 2½ × 2¼ inch Knobs on Plain Spindles.   (For Furniture, see opposite page.)

No. 222.

Size 7 × 4 Inches.

Square Case, Lever, 1 Tumbler, Brass Hub, 2 Brass Bolts, Brass Key (see Plate), 2½ × 2¼ inch Knobs on Plain Spindles.   (For Furniture, see opposite page.)

No. 223.

Size 7 × 4 Inches.

Square Case, Lever, 1 Tumbler, Brass 'Hub, 2 Brass Bolts, *Extra Brass Night Bolt*, Brass Key, Case same as No. 222, 2½ × 2¼ inch Knobs on Plain Spindles.   (For Furniture, see opposite page.)

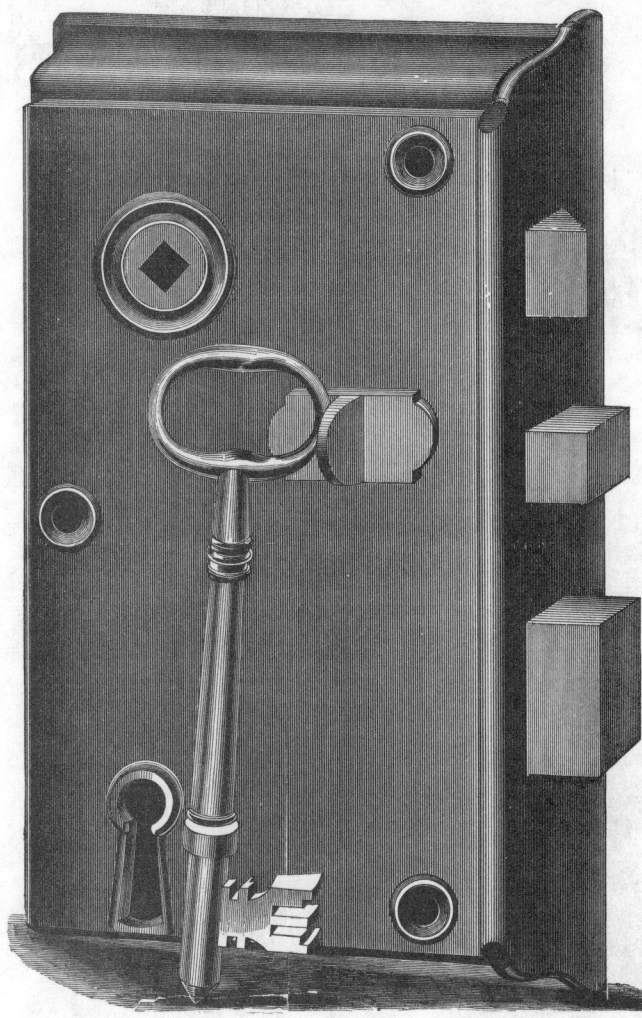

[225.]

No. 224.

SIZE 7½ × 5 INCHES.

O. G. Case, 3 Wrought Iron Tumblers, Brass Hub, 2 Brass Bolts, Brass Key, Case similar to Lock No. 225, 2½ × 2¼ inch Knobs on Plain Spindles.

No. 225.

SIZE 7½ × 5 INCHES.

O. G. Case, 3 Wrought Iron Tumblers, Brass Hub, 2 Brass Bolts, Extra Brass Night Bolt, Brass Key, 2½ × 2¼ inch Knobs on Plain Spindles. (See Plate.)

	Lock No. 220. PER DOZ.	Lock No. 222. PER DOZ.	Lock No. 223. PER DOZ.	Lock No. 224. PER DOZ.	Lock No. 225. PER DOZ.
Without Furniture					
With Mineral Knobs No. 450, Japanned Mountings and Japanned Drop Escutcheons					
With Porcelain Knobs No. 350, Japanned Mountings and Japanned Drop Escutcheons					
With Extra Heavy Brass Knobs and Roses, and Brass Drop Escutcheons					
With Extra Heavy Brass Knobs and Roses outside, and Porcelain Knobs No. 100 inside, with Brass Drop Escutcheons					
With Porcelain Knobs No. 150, Plated Roses and Electro-Plated Drop Escutcheons					
With Porcelain Knobs No. 151, Porcelain Roses and Porcelain Drop Escutcheons					
With Electro-Plated Knobs, Roses, and Electro-Plated Drop Escutcheons					
With Electro-Plated Knobs outside, and Porcelain Knobs No. 100 inside, and Electro-Plated Drop Escutcheons					
With Hand Plated Knobs, and Hand Plated Drop Escutcheons					
With Hand Plated Knobs outside, and Porcelain Knobs No. 100 inside, and Hand Plated Drop Escutcheons					

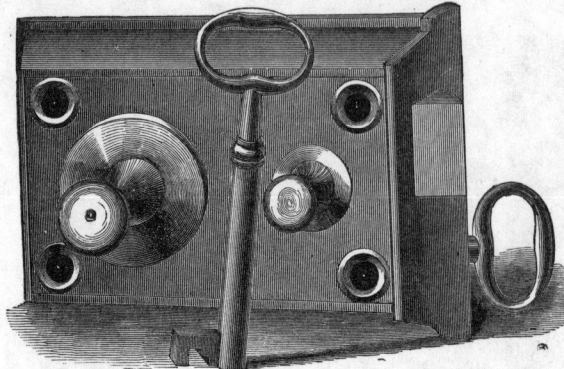

[661.]

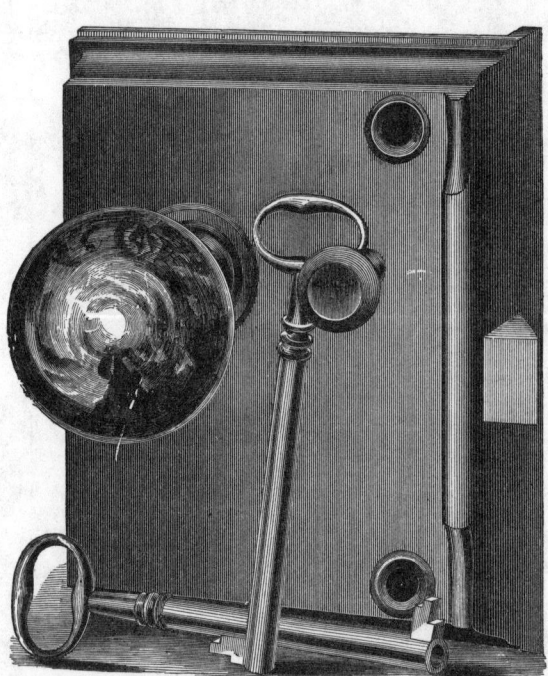

[659½.]

HORIZONTAL
RIM NIGHT LATCHES.

PACKED COMPLETE, TWO KEYS TO EACH.

No. 661.

SIZE 3¾ × 2½ INCHES.   Per Doz.

Rural, Iron Bolt, Malleable Iron Keys, assorted hands, Brass Slide Knob. (See Plate.) --------

No. 659.

SIZE 4 × 3¼ INCHES.

Rural, O. G. Case, Brass Bolt, Malleable Iron Keys, Right or Left Hand, Mineral Knobs, Japanned Furniture, same as No. 659½, differing only in the Knob Furniture --------------------

No. 659½.

SIZE 4 × 3¼ INCHES.

Rural O. G. Case, Brass Bolt, Malleable Iron Keys, Right or Left Hand, Porcelain Knobs, Plated Furniture. (See Plate.)-------------------

No. 660.

SIZE 4 × 3 INCHES.

Square Case, Brass Bolt, Malleable Iron Keys, Right or Left Hand, Mineral Knobs, Japanned Furniture ------------------------------------

No. 660½.

SIZE 4 × 3 INCHES.

Square Case, Brass Bolt, Malleable Iron Keys, Right or Left Hand, Porcelain Knobs, Plated Furniture, same as No. 660, differing only in the Knob Furniture------------------------------------

UPRIGHT SAFE
RIM NIGHT LATCHES.

PACKED COMPLETE, TWO KEYS TO EACH.

No. 664.

SIZE 4¾ × 3¾ INCHES.   Per Doz.

O. G. Case, Heavy Brass Bolt, 3 Wrought Iron Tumblers, Fine Finish and SAFE Mineral Knobs, Japanned Furniture, 2 Key-Metal Keys each. (See Plate.)-------------------------

No. 664½.

SIZE 4¾ × 3¾ INCHES.

O. G. Case, Heavy Brass Bolt, 3 Wrought Iron Tumblers, Fine Finish and SAFE, Porcelain Knobs, Plated Furniture, same as 664, differing only in the Knob Furniture, 2 Key-Metal Keys each-------------------------------------

[664.]

UPRIGHT EXTRA-SAFE RIM NIGHT LATCHES.

PACKED COMPLETE, TWO KEYS TO EACH.

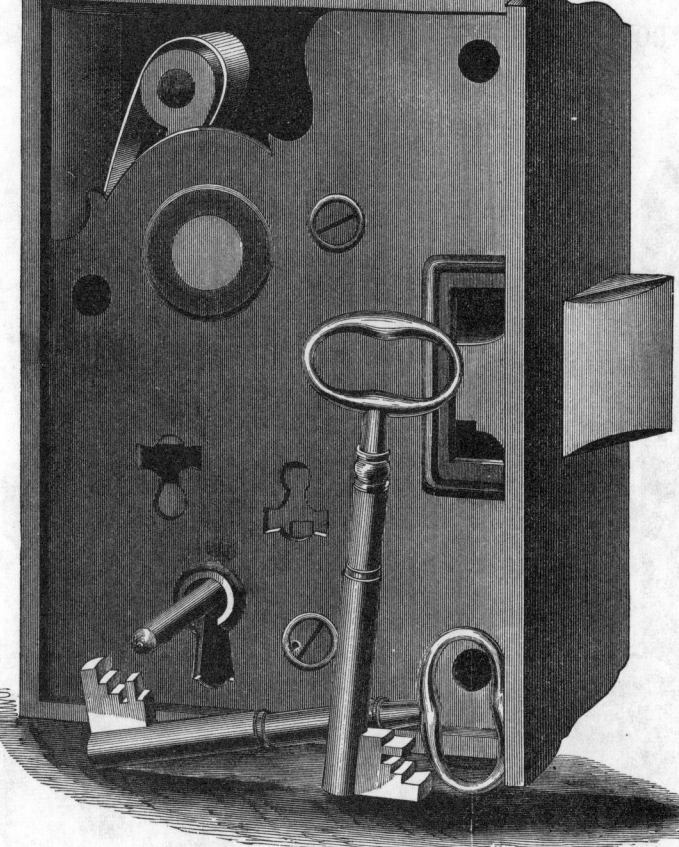

[666.]

No. 666.

SIZE 6 × 5 INCHES.

Heavy O. G. Case, Heavy Brass Bolt, 5 Wrought Iron Tumblers, 2 Key-Metal Keys each, Extra Safe and Strong, Mineral Knobs, Japanned Furniture. (See Plate.)_____

No. 666½.

SIZE 6 × 5 INCHES.

Heavy O. G. Case, Heavy Brass Bolt, 5 Wrought Iron Tumblers, 2 Key-Metal Keys each, Extra Safe and Strong, Porcelain Knobs, Plated Furniture, same as No. 666, differing only in Knob Furniture_____

Per Doz.

Reverse Bevels made to order; also No. 666 and 666½, with Extra (short or long) Keys, Mineral or Porcelain Pull-to Knobs, and Brass or Japanned Concave Keyhole Escutcheons for Engine Houses, Heavy Outside Doors, and Club Rooms.

When ordering these Latches, the thickness of door should be given, as there are two lengths of Keys made, and different escutcheons.

Concave Keyhole Escutcheons for Above.

No. 80, 3¼ inch diam., all Brass____
" 80, 3¼ " " Japanned__
" 81, 4¼ " " all Brass___
" 81, 4½ " " Japanned__
" 82, 5¼ " " all Brass___
" 82, 5¼ " " Japanned__

PATENT CYLINDER RIM NIGHT LATCHES.

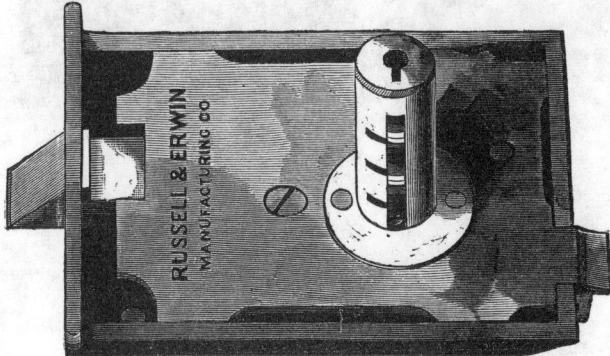

[671.]

No. 670.

SIZE 3½ × 2½ INCHES.

Per Doz.

Rural Japanned Case, Iron Bolt, with 2 Malleable Iron Keys, Extra Safe _____

No. 671.

SIZE 4 × 3 INCHES.

Rural Japanned Case, Brass Bolt, with 2 Brass Keys, Extra Safe_____

No. 672.

SIZE 4½ × 3 INCHES.

Rural Japanned Case, Brass Bolt, 2 Brass Keys, Extra Safe_____

UPRIGHT RIM KNOB LOCKS,

FOR NARROW STILE STORE DOORS.

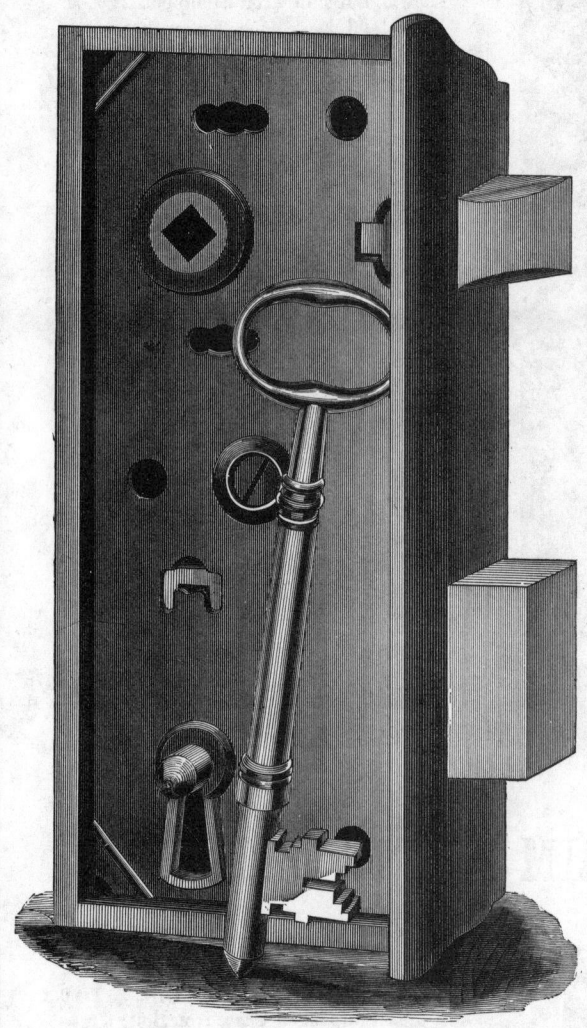

[420.]

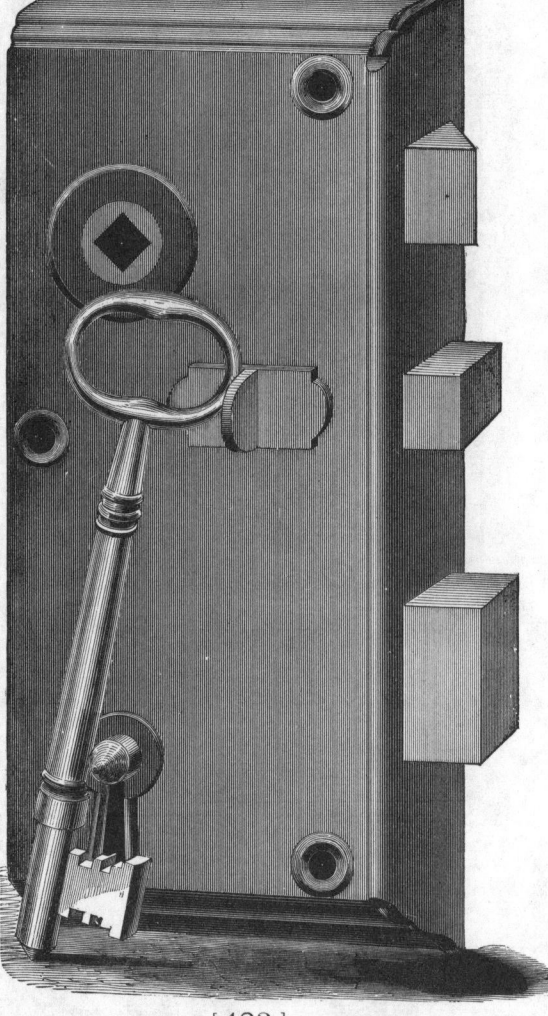

[423.]

No.	Size.		Without Furniture.	Mineral Knobs, Japanned Crank Handles, No. 13 or 13½.	Porcelain Knobs, Plated Crank Handles, No. 14 or 14½.
			PER DOZ.	PER DOZ.	PER DOZ.
422	7½ × 3¾	Fancy Case, 2 Heavy Iron Bolts, 1 Tumbler, Iron Hub, 2 Brass Keys, same style as No. 423			
423	7½ × 3¾	Fancy Case, 2 Heavy Iron Bolts, Extra Slide Bolt, 1 Tumbler, Iron Hub, 2 Brass Keys, see plate			
420	7¼ × 3½	O. G. Case, 2 Heavy Brass Bolts, 5 Wrought Iron Tumblers, Brass Hub, 2 Key-Metal Keys, see plate			
421	5¾ × 2½	O. G. Case, 2 Brass Bolts, 3 Wrought Iron Tumblers, Brass Hub, 1 Key-Metal Key, same style as No. 420, lighter			

HORIZONTAL RIM LEVER KNOB LOCKS,

FOR STORE DOORS,

TWO FINE-FINISHED KEY-METAL KEYS TO EACH.

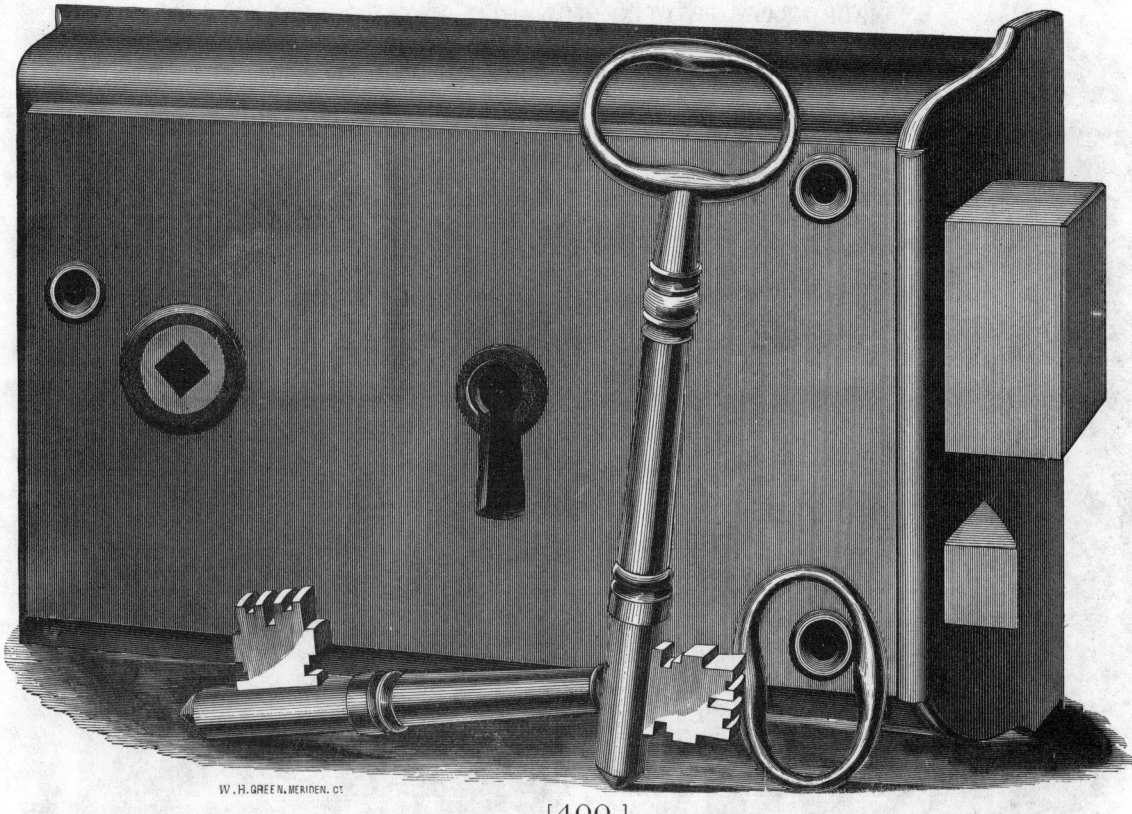

[400.]

To avoid mistakes, it is necessary to order these Locks with Furniture complete, as they require larger Knobs and heavier Spindle (⅜ inch) than the usual size, which are adapted for inside Locks.

No.	Size.		Without Furniture.	2½×2¼ in. No. 450 Mineral Knobs, Japanned Escutcheons.	2½×2¼ in. No. 350 Porcelain Knobs Japanned Escutcheons.	2½×2¼ in. Brass Knobs, Brass Escutcheons.
			PER DOZ.	PER DOZ.	PER DOZ.	PER DOZ.
400	8 × 5	O. G. Case, 2 Heavy Iron Bolts, Brass Hub, 5 Wrought Iron Tumblers, Heavy. (See Plate.)				
401	9 × 6	O. G. Case, 2 Heavy Iron Bolts, Brass Hub, 5 Wrought Iron Tumblers, Heavy, same style as No. 400.				
402	7 × 4½	O. G. Case, 2 Heavy Iron Bolts, Brass Hub, 3 Wrought Iron Tumblers, Heavy, same style of case as No. 400.				
404	8 × 5	Square Case, 2 Iron Bolts, Iron Hub, 1 Tumbler				
405	9 × 5¾	Square Case, 2 Iron Bolts, Iron Hub, 1 Tumbler				
406	10 × 6	Square Case, 2 Iron Bolts, Iron Hub, 1 Tumbler				
407	8 × 5	Square Case, 2 Iron Bolts, Iron Hub, 2 Tumblers				
408	9 × 5¾	Square Case, 2 Iron Bolts, Iron Hub, 2 Tumblers, Bridge Ward				
409	10 × 6	Square Case, 2 Iron Bolts, Iron Hub, 2 Tumblers, Bridge Ward				
412	9 × 6	Square WROUGHT IRON Case, Brass Bushed and Warded, all Brass inside work, 2 Bolts, 1 Tumbler				
413	10 × 6½	Square WROUGHT IRON Case, Brass Bushed and Warded, all Brass inside work, 2 Bolts, 1 Tumbler				
414	9 × 6	Square WROUGHT IRON Case, Brass Bushed and Warded, all Brass inside work, 2 Bolts, 2 Tumblers, Bridge Ward				
415	10 × 6½	Square WROUGHT IRON Case, Brass Bushed and Warded, all Brass inside work, 2 Bolts, 2 Tumblers, Bridge Ward				

UPRIGHT RIM DEAD LOCKS,

FOR NARROW STILE STORE DOORS,

MADE HEAVY, TWO FINE KEY-METAL KEYS TO EACH.

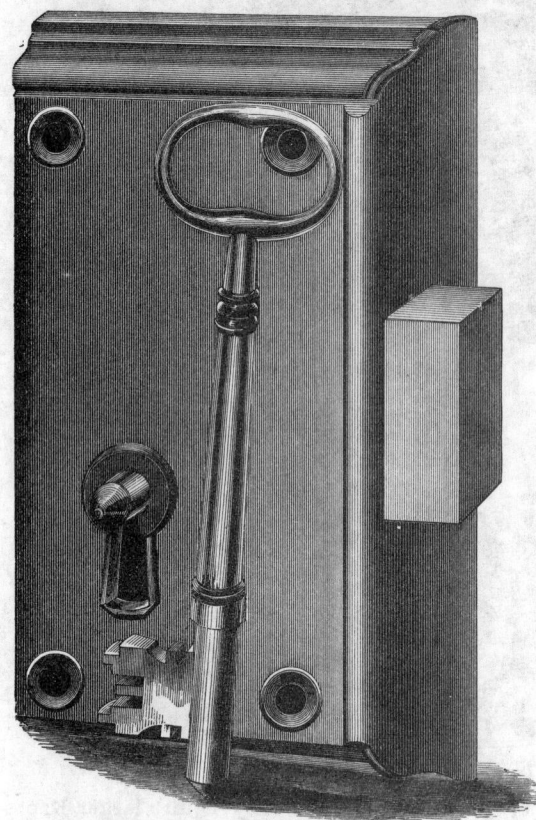

[434.]

[626¼.]

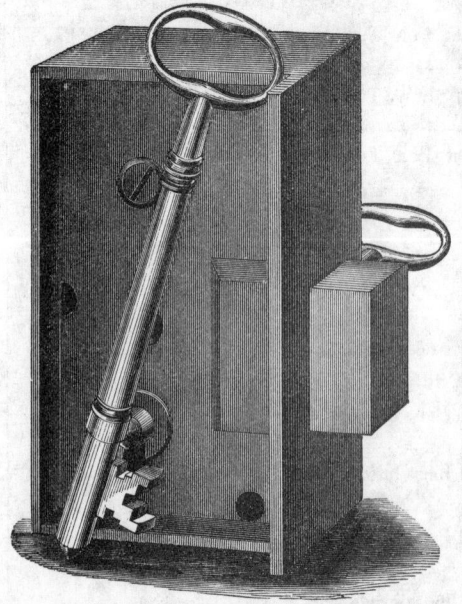

[457.]

No.	Size.		Per Doz.
434	5¾ × 3½	O. G. Case, Brass Bolt, 5 Wrought Iron Tumblers, 2 Keys each. (See Plate.)	
435	5¾ × 3½	O. G. Case, Iron Bolt, 2 Wrought Iron Tumblers, 2 Keys each, Case same as No. 434	
435½	5¾ × 3½	O. G. Case, Iron Bolt, 1 Wrought Iron Tumbler, 2 Keys each, Case same as No. 434	
626	5⅝ × 4	O. G. Case, Iron Bolt, 3 Wrought Iron Tumblers, 1 Key, Case same as No. 626½	
626½	5⅝ × 4	O. G. Case, Iron Bolt, 3 Wrought Iron Tumblers, 2 Keys each. (See Plate.)	
456	4 × 2½	Square Case, Iron Bolt, 1 Tumbler, same Case as No. 457, 2 Keys each	
457	4 × 2½	Square Case, Iron Bolt, 3 Tumblers, 2 Keys each. (See Plate.)	

UPRIGHT RIM DEAD LOCKS,
FOR NARROW STILE STORE DOORS.
(Continued.)

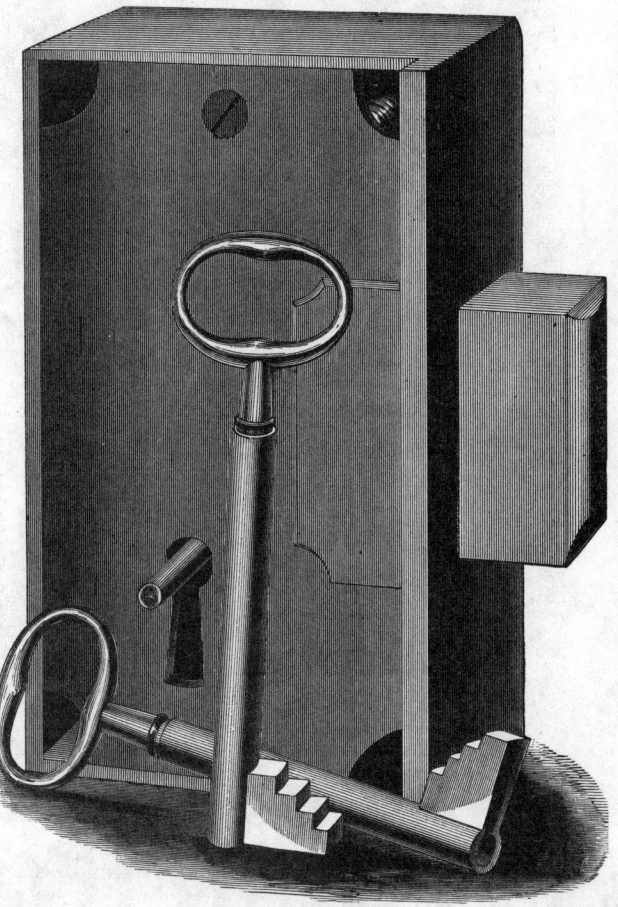

[450.]   [455.]

Per Dozen.

No. 450.
SIZE 7 × 3½ INCHES.
Boston Pattern, Iron Bolt, 1 Tumbler, 2 Keys each. (See Plate.)------------------------

No. 451.
SIZE 7 × 3½ INCHES.
Boston Pattern, Iron Bolt, 2 Tumblers, 2 Keys each, same Case as No. 450------------------

No. 452.
SIZE 7 × 3½ INCHES.
Boston Pattern, Iron Bolt, 3 Tumblers, 2 Keys each, same Case as No. 450 ---- -------- ------- ---------
Locks No. 450, 451, 452, made to order without flanges, for Iron Doors.

No. 453.
SIZE 6¼ × 3⅞ INCHES.
Square Case, Drill Pin Key, Iron Bolt, 1 Tumbler, 2 Keys each, same Case as No. 455-------------------

No. 454.
SIZE 6¼ × 3⅞ INCHES.
Square Case, Drill Pin Key, Iron Bolt, 2 Tumblers, 2 Keys each, same Case as No. 455------------------

No. 455.
SIZE 6¼ × 3⅞ INCHES.
Square Case, Drill Pin Key, Iron Bolt, 3 Tumblers, 2 Keys each. (See Plate.)------- -------------------

HORIZONTAL RIM DEAD LOCKS,

FOR STORE DOORS,

MADE HEAVY, TWO FINE KEY-METAL KEYS TO EACH.

[430.]

W. H. GREEN. D. & S. MERIDEN, Ct.

[448.]

HORIZONTAL RIM DEAD LOCKS,

FOR STORE DOORS,

MADE HEAVY, TWO FINE KEY-METAL KEYS TO EACH.

[479.]

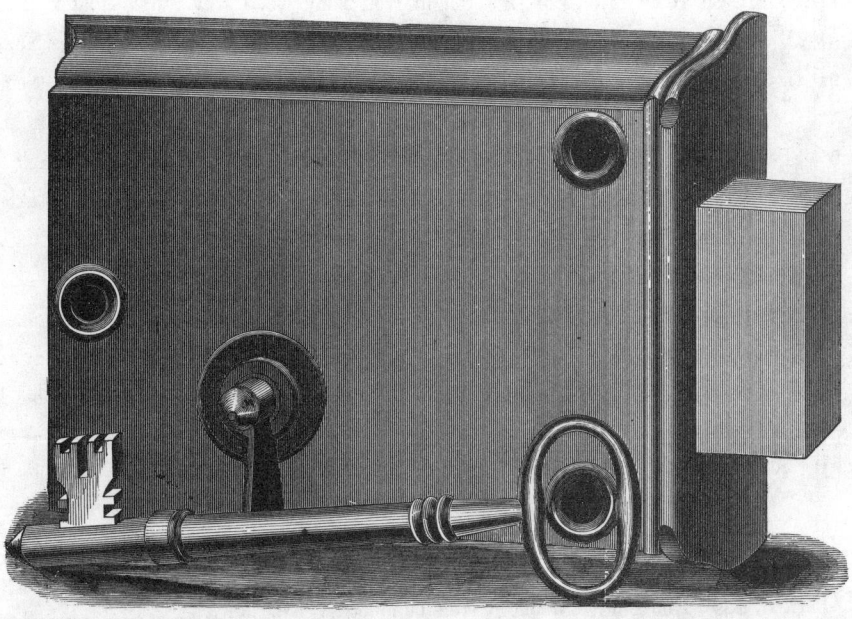

[627½.]

(For Description of Plates on pages 12 and 13 see next page.)

HORIZONTAL RIM DEAD LOCKS,

FOR STORE DOORS.

MADE HEAVY, 2 FINE KEY-METAL KEYS TO EACH.

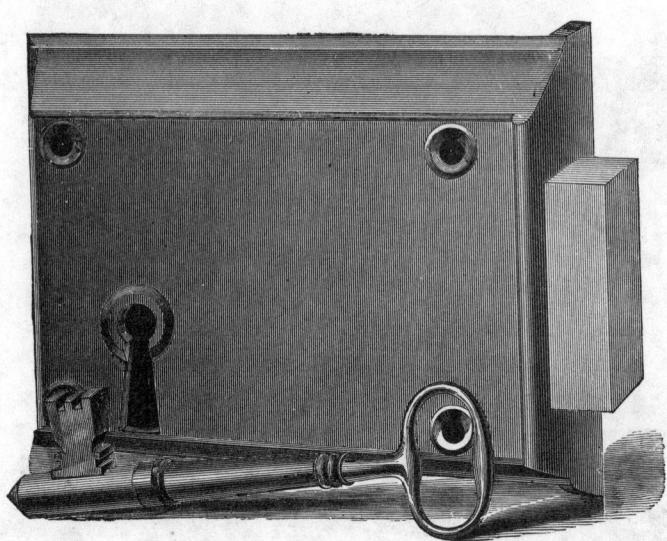

[436.]

No.	Size.		Per Doz.
430	8½ × 5½	O. G. Case, Iron Bolt, 5 Wrought Iron Tumblers, 2 Keys each. (See Plate, page 12.)	
431	9 × 6	O. G. Case, Iron Bolt, 5 Wrought Iron Tumblers, same style as No. 430. 2 Keys each	
432	8½ × 5½	O. G. Case, Iron Bolt, 2 Wrought Iron Tumblers, same style as No. 430. 2 Keys each	
436	5 × 3½	O. G. Case, Heavy Iron Bolt, 2 Wrought Iron Tumblers, 1 Key. (See Plate)	
437	5 × 3½	O. G. Case, Heavy Iron Bolt, 2 Wrought Iron Tumblers, 2 Keys, same style as No. 436	
479	5 × 3½	O. G. Case, Heavy Brass Bolt, DRILL PIN BOTH SIDES, 3 Tumblers, 2 Keys. (See Plate, page 13)	
440	8 × 5	Square Case, Iron Bolt, Single Tumbler, 2 Keys each	
441	9 × 5¾	Square Case, Iron Bolt, Single Tumbler, 2 Keys each	
442	10 × 6	Square Case, Iron Bolt, Single Tumbler, 2 Keys each	
443	8 × 5	Square Case, Iron Bolt, Double Reverse Tumblers, 2 Keys each	
444	9 × 5¾	Square Case, Iron Bolt, Double Reverse Tumblers, 2 Keys each	
445	10 × 6	Square Case, Iron Bolt, Double Reverse Tumblers, 2 Keys each	
446	9 × 5¾	Square WROUGHT IRON Case, Brass Bushed, Brass Bolt, Single Brass Tumbler, Fine Finish, 2 Keys each	
447	9 × 5¾	Square WROUGHT IRON Case, Brass Bushed, Brass Bolt, Double Brass Tumblers, Bridge Ward, Fine Finish, 2 Keys each	
448	9 × 5¾	Square WROUGHT IRON Case, Brass Bushed, Heavy Iron Bolt, Double Reverse Brass Tumblers, Fine Finish, EXTRA SAFE, 2 Keys each. (See Plate, page 12.)	
624	7¼ × 4¼	O. G. Case, Iron Bolt, 3 Wrought Iron Tumblers, 1 Key	
625	7¼ × 4¼	O. G. Case, Iron Bolt, 3 Wrought Iron Tumblers, 2 Keys each	
627	5¾ × 4	O. G. Case, Heavy Iron Bolt, 3 Wrought Iron Tumblers, 1 Key, same as No. 627½	
627½	5¾ × 4	O. G. Case, Heavy Iron Bolt, 3 Wrought Iron Tumblers, 2 Keys. (See Plate, page 13.)	

UPRIGHT RIM KNOB LATCHES,
FOR NARROW STILE STORE DOORS.

Per Dozen.

[460.]

No. 460.

Size 5¾ × 3½ Inches.

O. G. Case, Heavy, Brass Bolt and Hub, (see Plate,) to match Locks 434 or 435, page 10.

Without Knobs_____
With No. 13 or 13½ Mineral Knobs and Japanned Crank Handles_____
With No. 14 or 14½ Porcelain Knobs and Plated Crank Handles_____

No. 461.

Size 4 × 2½ Inches.

Square Case, Lever, Brass Bolt and Hub, to match Locks 456 or 457. (See Plate of Lock 457, page 10.)

Without Knobs_____
With No. 13 or 13½ Mineral Knobs and Japanned Crank Handles_____
With No. 14 or 14½ Porcelain Knobs and Plated Crank Handles_____

UPRIGHT RIM KNOB LOCKS,
PACKED WITH ESCUTCHEON PLATES, AND SCREWS.

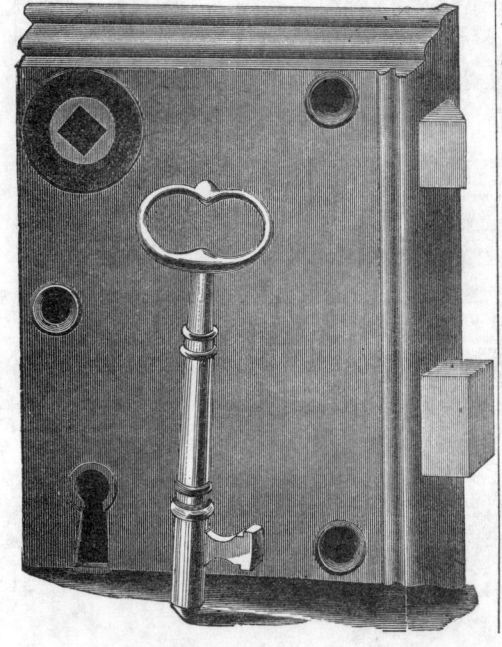

[504.]

No.	Size.		Without Knobs. PER DOZ.	No. 500 Mineral Knobs, Japanned Mount'g. PER DOZ.	No. 300 Porcelain Knobs, Japanned Mount'g. PER DOZ.
210	4½×3½	American, 2 Iron Bolts, *Wrought Iron Inside-work*, Malleable Iron Key, (Coppered)			
212	4½×3½	American, 2 Iron Bolts, *Wrought Iron Inside-work*, Brass Key			
214	4½×3½	American, 2 Brass Bolts, *Wrought Iron Inside-work*, Brass Key, same style of Case as Lock No. 504			
501	5 ×3¾	Western, 2 Iron Bolts, Iron Key			
503	5 ×3¾	Western, 2 Iron Bolts, Iron Key			
504	4½×3½	Western, 2 Iron Bolts, Iron Key. (See Plate.)			
504½	4½×3½	Western, 3 Iron Bolts, Iron Key			
505	5 ×3¾	Western, 2 Iron Bolts, Brass Key			
507	5 ×3¾	Western, 2 Iron Bolts, Brass Key			
508	4½×3½	Western, 2 Iron Bolts, Brass Key			

UPRIGHT RIM KNOB LOCKS,

PACKED WITH ESCUTCHEON PLATES AND SCREWS.

(Continued.)

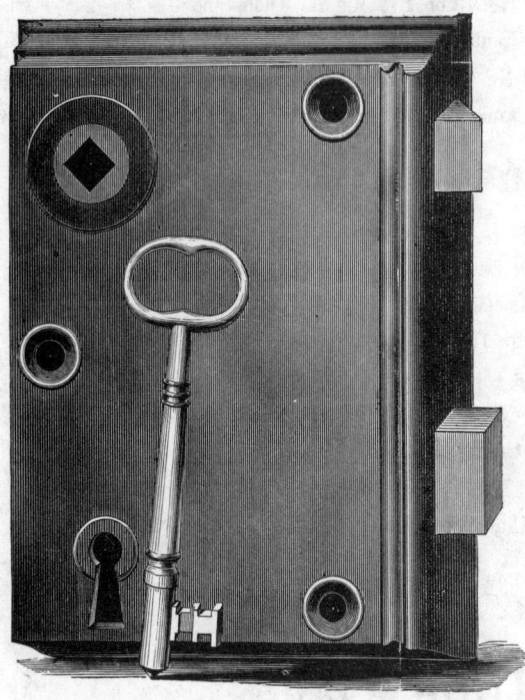
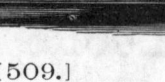

[509.]

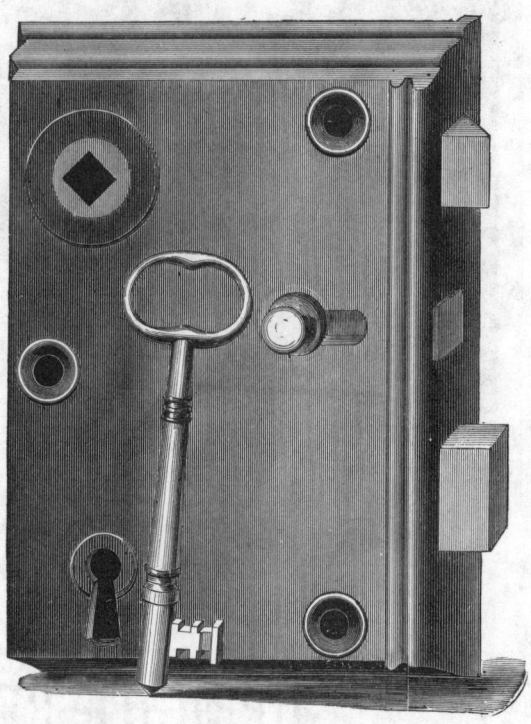

[513.]

No.	Size.		Without Knobs.	No. 500 Mineral Knobs. Japanned Mountings.	No. 300 Porcelain Knobs. Japanned Mountings.
			PER DOZ.	PER DOZ.	PER DOZ.
509	5 × 3¾	Western, 2 Brass Bolts, Brass Key. (See Plate.)			
511	5 × 3¾	Western, 2 Brass Bolts, Brass Key			
512	4½ × 3½	Western, 2 Brass Bolts, Brass Key			
512½	4½ × 3½	Western, 3 Brass Bolts, Brass Key			
513	5 × 3¾	Western, 3 Iron Bolts, Brass Key. (See Plate.)			
514	5 × 3¾	Western, 3 Brass Bolts, Brass Key, same Case and Cap as No. 513, differing only in the Bolts			

Locks No. 501, 505, 509, are 5 inch Solid Front Locks, with a Flange; all have the same Case and Cap, differing only in the Bolts and Keys.

Locks No. 503, 507, 511, are 5 inch Locks; all have the same Case and Cap, differing only in the Bolts and Keys, but are not solid Fronts, the Flange being formed upon the Cap.

Locks No. 504, 508, 512, are 4½ inch Locks, same description as No. 503, 507, 511.

Locks No. 504½ and 512½ are same in style as 504.

UPRIGHT RIM KNOB LOCKS,

(Continued.)

JANUS FACE, WITH REVERSIBLE LATCH, EITHER RIGHT OR LEFT HAND,

PACKED WITH ESCUTCHEON PLATES, AND SCREWS.

Per Doz.

[800.]

JANUS FACE, LIFT-LATCH, WITH CAM FASTENER.

☞ The Cam Fastener secures the latch bolt at pleasure, giving entire protection against opening of the door from outside.

[900.]

No. 800.

Size 4¼ × 3¼ Inches.

Square Case, Reversible Latch, 2 Iron Bolts, Iron Key. (See Plate.)

Without Knobs

With Mineral Knobs and Japanned Mountings

With No. 300 Porcelain Knobs, Japanned Mountings

No. 900.

Size 4¼ × 3¼ Inches.

Square Case, Lift Latch, with Cam Fastener, 2 Iron Bolts, Iron Key. (See Plate.)

Without Knobs

With Mineral Knobs

With No. 300 Porcelain Knobs

No. 901.

Size 4¼ × 3¼ Inches.

Square Case, Lift Latch, with Cam Fastener, 2 Iron Bolts, Brass Key

Without Knobs

With Mineral Knobs

With No. 300 Porcelain Knobs

No. 905.

Size 5 × 3¾ Inches.

Square Case, Lift Latch, with Cam Fastener, 2 Iron Bolts, Iron Key

Without Knobs

With Mineral Knobs

With No. 300 Porcelain Knobs

No. 906.

Size 5 × 3¾ Inches.

Square Case, Lift Latch, with Cam Fastener, 2 Iron Bolts, Brass Key

Without Knobs

With Mineral Knobs

With No. 300 Porcelain Knobs

UPRIGHT RIM KNOB LOCKS,

PACKED WITH ESCUTCHEON PLATES, AND SCREWS.

(*Continued.*)

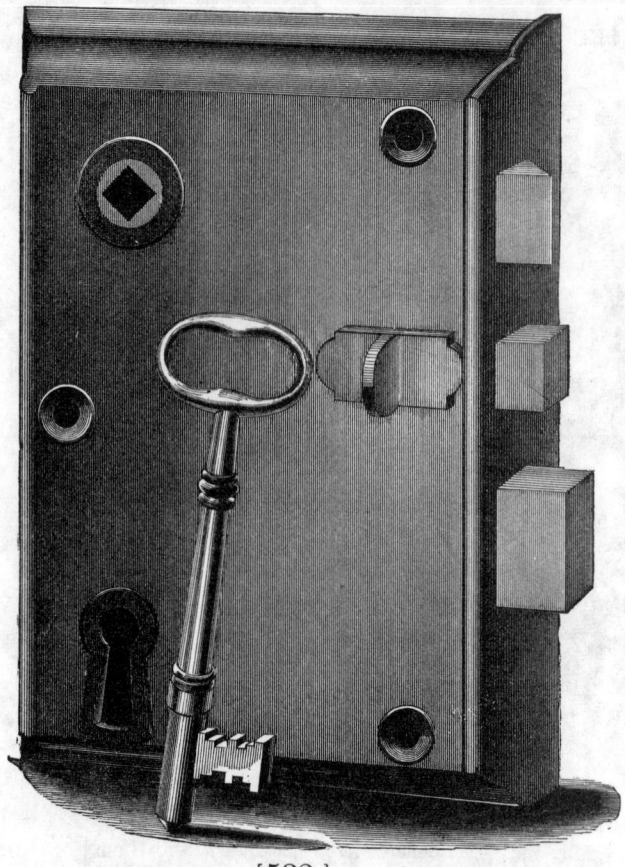

[532.]

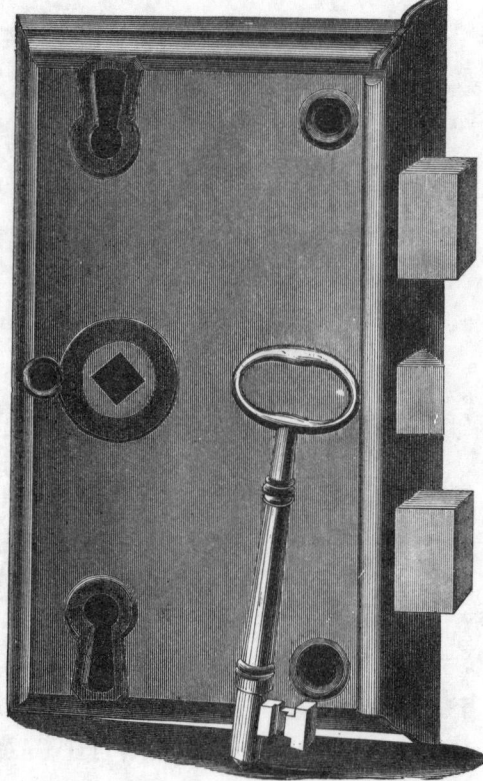

[543.]

No.	Size.		Without Knobs. PER DOZ.	Mineral Knobs, Japanned Mountings. PER DOZ.	No. 300 Porcelain Knobs, Japanned Mountings. PER DOZ.
530	5 × 3¾	Rural, 2 Brass Bolts, Brass Key and Hub, same style of Case as Lock 509. Page 16			
530½	5½ × 3¾	Rural, 2 Brass Bolts, Brass Key and Hub, same style of Case as Lock 509			
531	6¼ × 4½	Rural, 2 Brass Bolts, Brass Key, same style of Case as Lock 532			
532	6¼ × 4½	Rural, 3 Brass Bolts, Brass Key. (See Plate.)			
535	6¼ × 4½	Rural, 2 Iron Bolts, Brass Key, same style of Case as Lock 532			
537	6¼ × 4½	Rural, 2 Iron Bolts, Iron Key, same style of Case as Lock 532			
537½	6¼ × 4½	Rural, 3 Iron Bolts, Iron Key, same style of Case as Lock 532			
539	7½ × 3¾	Heavy Western, 2 Iron Bolts, Brass Key, Drop Escutcheons, same style of Case as Lock 423. Page 8			
540	7½ × 3¾	Heavy Western, 3 Iron Bolts, Brass Key, Drop Escutcheons, same style of Case as Lock 423. Page 8			
543	6 × 3½	Hotel, 3 Brass Bolts, Brass Key, Right or Left Hand, 2 disconnected Keyholes, suitable for Hotel Chambers or Steamboats. (See Plate.)			

UPRIGHT RIM KNOB LOCKS,

PACKED WITH ESCUTCHEON PLATES AND SCREWS.
(*Continued.*)

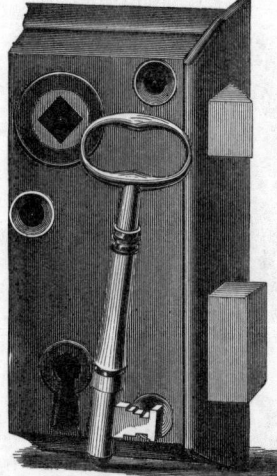

[538.]

Per Doz.

No. 538.

SIZE 3½ × 2 INCHES.

For Venetian Blind Doors, 2 Brass Bolts, Brass Hub, Brass Key. (See Plate.) Reverse Bevels made to order same price.

Without Knobs _____

With No. 39 Mineral Knobs, Japanned Crank Handle, and Japanned Plate Escutcheons _____

With No. 19 Porcelain Knobs, Plated Crank Handle, and Plated Plate Escutcheons _____

[560.]

Per Doz.

No. 560.

SIZE 5 × 3¾ INCHES.

Eagle Improved, 2 Brass Bolts, Brass Hub, Brass Key. (See Plate.)

Without Knobs, Japanned Plate Escutcheons ____

With Mineral Knobs, Japanned Mountings, and Plate Escutcheons _____

With No. 300 Porcelain Knobs, Japanned Mountings, and Plate Escutcheons _____

No. 561.

SIZE 5 × 3¾ INCHES.

Eagle Improved, 3 Brass Bolts, Brass Hub, Brass Key, similar to 560, but with extra Bolt.

Without Knobs, Japanned Plate Escutcheons ____

With Mineral Knobs, Japanned Mountings, and Plate Escutcheons _____

With No. 300 Porcelain Knobs, Japanned Mountings, and Plate Escutcheons _____

UPRIGHT RIM KNOB LOCKS,

PACKED WITH ESCUTCHEON PLATES AND SCREWS.

(Continued.)

[564.]

[565.]

[562.]

No.	Size.		Without Knobs.	Mineral Knobs Japanned Mount'gs.	No. 300 Porcelain Knobs, Japanned Mount'gs.
			PER DOZ.	PER DOZ.	PER DOZ.
562	4½ × 3½	Pioneer, Green Bronze Japanned, [Patented Aug. 10, 1858,] 2 Iron Bolts, Iron Hub, Iron Key. (See Plate.)_____			
563	4½ × 3½	Pioneer, [Patented Aug. 10, 1858] 2 Brass Bolts, Iron Hub, Brass Key_____			
564	5 × 3¾	Emigrant, Green Bronze Japann'd, [Patented Aug. 10, 1858,] 2 Brass Bolts, Iron Hub, Brass Key. (See Plate.)___ _____			
565	5 × 3¾	Village, Green Bronze Japanned, [Patented Aug. 10, 1858,] 2 Brass Bolts, Brass Hub, Brass Key. (See Plate.) _____			

UPRIGHT RIM KNOB LOCKS,

PACKED WITH ESCUTCHEON PLATES AND SCREWS.

(Continued.)

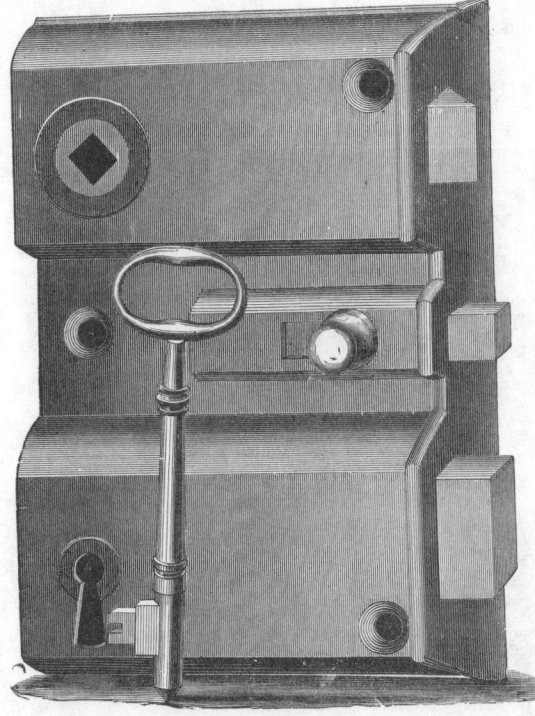

[546.]

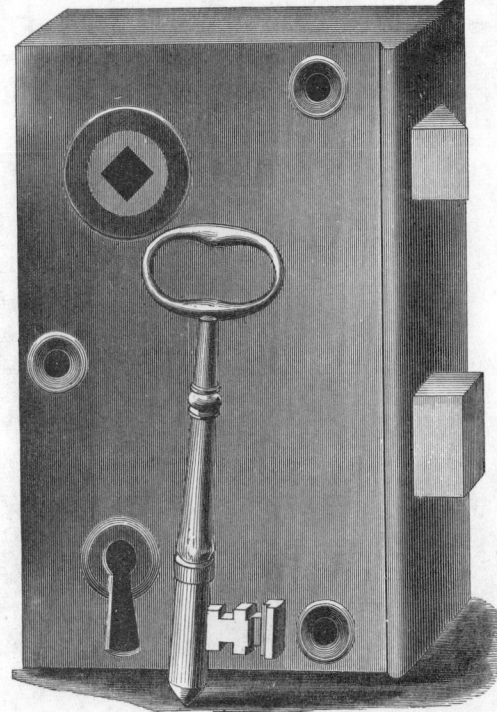

[590.]

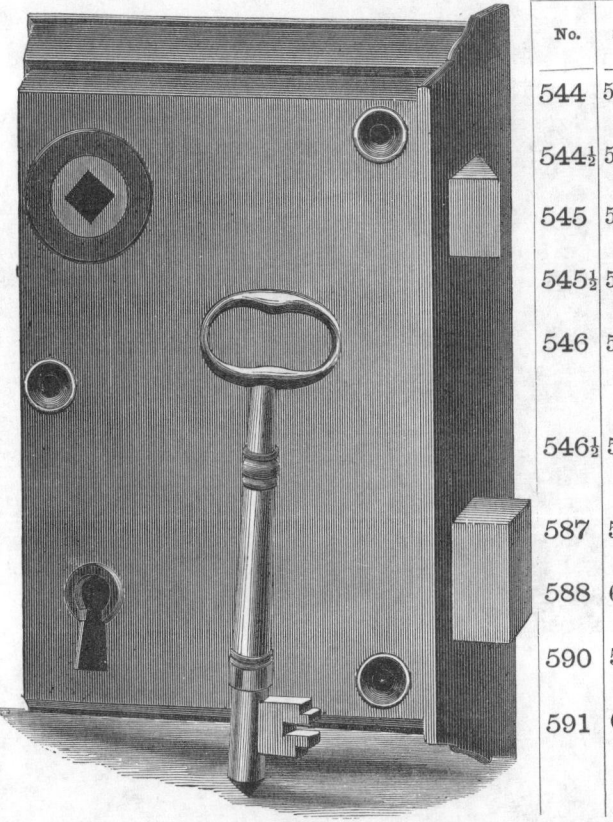

[588.]

No.	Size.		Without Knobs.	Mineral Knobs. Japanned Mount'gs.	No. 300 Porcelain Knobs, Japanned Mount'gs.
			PER DOZ.	PER DOZ.	PER DOZ.
544	5 × 4	Cottage, Improved, 2 Heavy BRASS BOLTS, Brass Hub, Brass Key, 1 Wrought Iron Tumbler, 14 Changes of Keys........			
544½	5 × 4	Cottage, Improved, 2 Heavy Iron Bolts, Brass Hub, Brass Key, 1 Tumbler, 6 Changes of Keys...................			
545	5 × 4	Cottage, Improved, 2 Heavy Brass Bolts, Brass Hub, Brass Key, 3 Wrought Iron Tumblers, 14 Changes of Keys.......			
545½	5 × 4	Cottage, Improved, same as No. 545, but with 2 Heavy Iron Bolts, 14 Changes of Keys........................			
546	5 × 4	Cottage, Improved, 2 Heavy Brass Bolts, Extra Brass Night Bolt, Brass Hub, Brass Key, 3 Wrought Iron Tumblers, 14 Changes of Keys, suitable for Hotels, Steamboats; &c. (See Plate.)...			
546½	5 × 4	Cottage, Improved, same as No. 546, but with 2 Heavy Iron Bolts, Extra Brass Night Bolt, &c., with 14 Changes of Keys.........................			
587	5 × 4	Villa Rim, 2 Heavy Brass Bolts, Brass Hub, Brass Key, 3 Wrought Iron Tumblers, 14 Changes of Keys...........			
588	6 × 4	Villa Rim, 2 Heavy Brass Bolts, Brass Hub, Brass Key, 2 Wrought Iron Tumblers, 14 Changes of Keys. (See Plate.)			
590	5 × 3½	Square Case, Lever, 2 Brass Bolts, Iron Hub, Brass Key, 1 Tumbler, 6 Changes of Keys. (See Plate.)..............			
591	6 × 3¾	Square Case, Lever, 2 Brass Bolts, Brass Hub, Brass Key, 1 Tumbler, 6 Changes of Keys, similar to No. 590..........			

HORIZONTAL RIM LEVER KNOB LOCKS,

"CARPENTER PATTERN,"

PACKED WITH ESCUTCHEON PLATES AND SCREWS.

[518.]

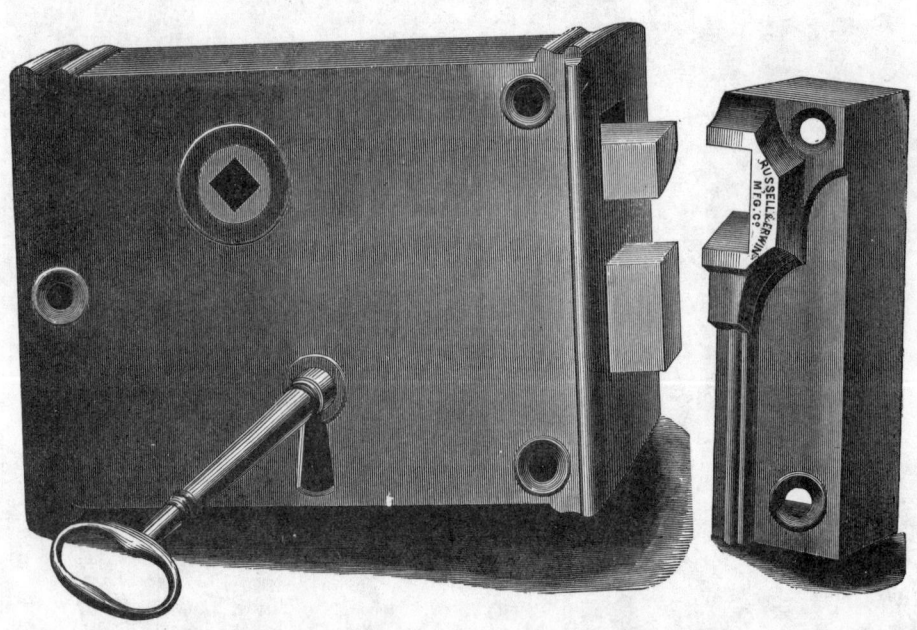

[525.]

[*For description of Plates see Page 24.*]

HORIZONTAL RIM LEVER KNOB LOCKS,

PACKED WITH ESCUTCHEON PLATES AND SCREWS.

(Continued.)

[574.]

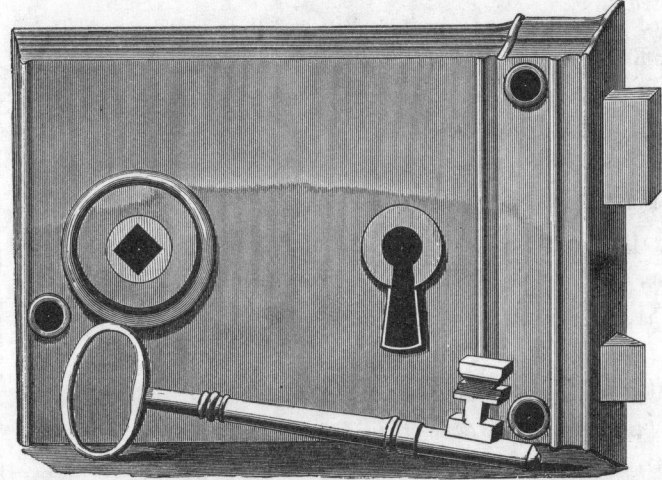

[570.]

[580.]

[*For description of Plates see Page 24.*]

HORIZONTAL RIM LEVER KNOB LOCKS,

PACKED WITH ESCUTCHEON PLATES AND SCREWS.

(Continued.)

No.	Size.		Without Furniture. PER DOZ.	Mineral Knobs, Japanned Mountings. PER DOZ.	No. 300 Porcelain Knobs, Japanned Mountings. PER DOZ.
515	5 × 3¾	Improved Square Case "Carpenter's Pattern," 2 Iron Bolts, Iron Hub, Iron Key, Case same as No. 518			
516	6 × 4	Improved Square Case "Carpenter's Pattern," 2 Iron Bolts, Iron Hub, Iron Key, Case same as No. 518			
517	7 × 4½	Improved Square Case "Carpenter's Pattern," 2 Iron Bolts, Iron Hub, Iron Key, Case same as No. 518			
518	5 × 3¾	Improved Square Case "Carpenter's Pattern," 2 Iron Bolts, Iron Hub, Brass Key, (See Plate, page 22)			
519	6 × 4	Improved Square Case "Carpenter's Pattern," 2 Iron Bolts, Iron Hub, Brass Key, Case same as No. 518			
520	7 × 4½	Improved Square Case "Carpenter's Pattern," 2 Iron Bolts, Iron Hub, Brass Key, Case same as No. 518			
521	8 × 5	Improved Square Case "Carpenter's Pattern," 2 Iron Bolts, Iron Hub, Brass Key, Case same as No. 518			
522	8 × 5	Improved Square Case "Carpenter's Pattern," 3 Iron Bolts, Iron Hub, Brass Key, Case same as No. 518			
525	5 × 3¾	Superior Quality "Carpenter's Pattern," 2 Polished Iron Bolts, Brass Strikes, Hubs and Keys, with Bridge Wards. (See Plate, page 22.)			
526	6 × 4	Superior Quality "Carpenter's Pattern," 2 Polished Iron Bolts, Brass Strikes, Hubs and Keys, with Bridge Wards, Case same as No. 525			
570	5 × 3¼	Rural Case, Heavy, 2 Brass Bolts, Brass Keys, Brass Hub, *Wrought Iron Inside Work.* (See Plate, page 23.)			
571	6 × 3¾	Rural Case, Heavy, 2 Brass Bolts, Brass Keys, Brass Hub, *Wrought Iron Inside Work*, Case same as No. 570			
572	7 × 4	Square Case, 2 Brass Bolts, Brass Key, Brass Hub			
573	8 × 5	Square Case, 2 Brass Bolts, Brass Key, Brass Hub, Drop Escutcheons			
574	5 × 3	Square Case, 2 Brass Bolts, Brass Key, Iron Hub. (See Plate, page 23.)			
575	6 × 3½	Square Case, 2 Brass Bolts, Brass Key, Iron Hub, similar to No. 574			
594	5 × 3	Square Case, " City Pattern," 2 Brass Bolts, Iron Hub, Brass Key, Case same as No. 574			
595	6 × 3½	Square Case, " City Pattern," 2 Brass Bolts, Iron Hub, Brass Key, Case same as No. 575			
580	5 × 3¼	Square Case, A. No. 1, Fine Quality and Finish, Heavy, all Brass Inside Work, and complete Variety of Fine Metal Keys. (See Plate, page 23)			
581	6 × 3¾	Square Case, A. No. 1, Fine Quality and Finish, Heavy, all Brass Inside Work, and complete Variety of Fine Metal Keys, same style as No. 580			
582	7 × 4	Square Case, A. No. 1, Fine Quality and Finish, Heavy, all Brass Inside Work, and complete Variety of Fine Metal Keys, same style as No. 580			
585	5 × 3½	Rural Case, Heavy, Brass Bolts, Hubs and Keys, 2 Wrought Iron Tumblers, Wrought Tails to Bolts, Finely Finished, Case same as No. 570			
586	6 × 4	Rural Case, Heavy, Brass Bolts, Hubs and Keys, 2 Wrought Iron Tumblers, Wrought Tails to Bolts, Finely Finished, Case same as No. 571			

HORIZONTAL RIM CLOSET OR DEAD LOCKS,

PACKED WITH ESCUTCHEON PLATES AND SCREWS.

[606.]

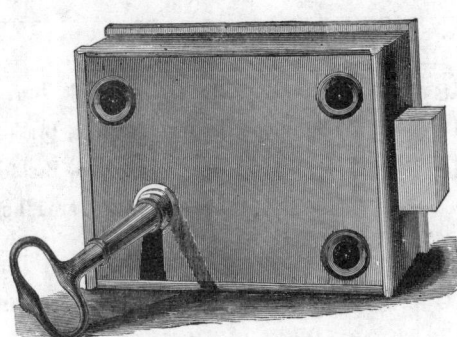

[604.]

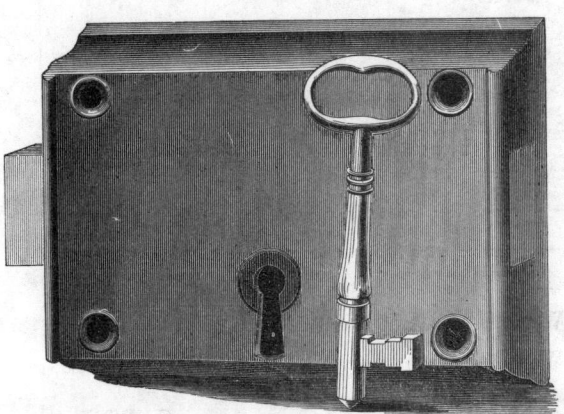

[631.]

[611.]

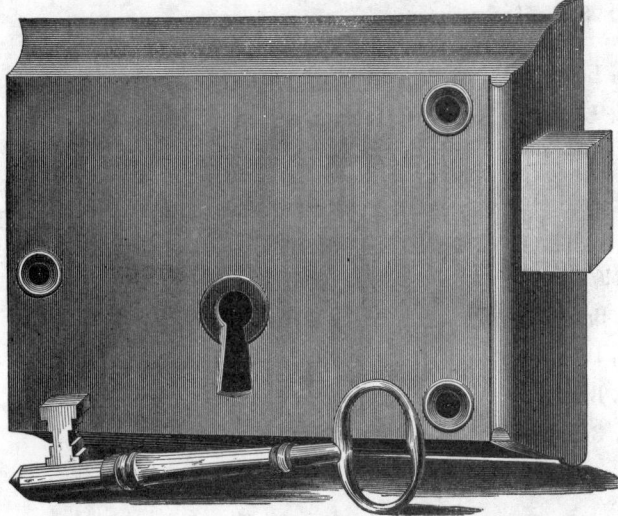

[613.]

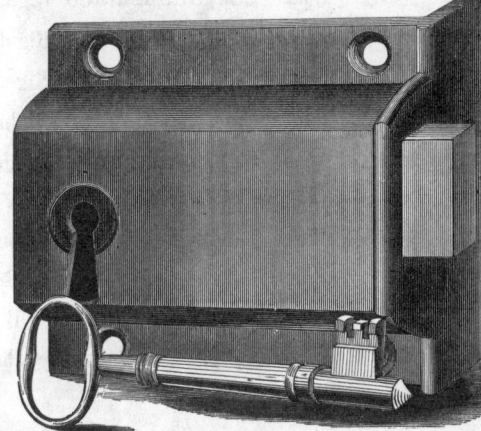

[548.]

For description of Plates, see page 26.

HORIZONTAL RIM CLOSET OR DEAD LOCKS,

PACKED WITH ESCUTCHEON PLATES AND SCREWS.

(Continued.)

No.	Size.		Per Doz.
548	4 × 3	Cottage, Heavy Brass Bolt, Brass Key, 3 Wrought Iron Tumblers. (See Plate, page 25.)	
548½	4 × 3	Cottage, Heavy Iron Bolt, Brass Key, 3 Wrought Iron Tumblers	
548¾	4 × 3	Cottage, Heavy Iron Bolt, Brass Key, 1 Iron Tumbler	
		The Cases of the above are all similar in style, the difference being in the Bolts and Tumblers.	
609	3½ × 2½	Rural, Iron Bolt, Iron Key, 1 Tumbler	
610	3¾ × 2½	Rural, Iron Bolt, Iron Key, 1 Tumbler	
611	3¾ × 2½	Rural, Iron Bolt, Brass Key, 1 Tumbler. (See Plate, page 25.)	
611½	3¾ × 2½	Rural, Brass Bolt, Brass Key, 2 Tumblers	
		The Cases of the above are all similar in style, the difference being in the Bolts, Tumblers and Keys.	
612	4 × 3	Rural, Iron Bolt, Brass Key, 1 Tumbler	
612½	4 × 3	Rural, Iron Bolt, Iron Key, 1 Tumbler	
613	5 × 3⅜	Rural, Iron Bolt, Brass Key, 1 Tumbler. (See Plate, page 25.)	
613½	5 × 3⅜	Rural, Iron Bolt, Iron Key, 1 Tumbler	
614	6 × 3⅝	Rural, Iron Bolt, Brass Key, 1 Tumbler	
614½	6 × 3⅝	Rural, Iron Bolt, Iron Key, 1 Tumbler	
615	7 × 4	Rural, Iron Bolt, Brass Key, 1 Tumbler	
620	5 × 3¼	Rural, Heavy Brass Bolt, Brass Key, 3 Wrought Iron Tumblers	
621	6 × 3¾	Rural, Heavy Brass Bolt, Brass Key, 3 Wrought Iron Tumblers	
622	5 × 3¼	Rural, Heavy Iron Bolt, Brass Key, 3 Wrought Iron Tumblers	
623	6 × 3¾	Rural, Heavy Iron Bolt, Brass Key, 3 Wrought Iron Tumblers	
624	7¼ × 4¼	Rural, Heavy Iron Bolt, Brass Key, 3 Wrought Iron Tumblers	
		The Cases of the above are all similar in style, differing in Bolts, Keys, Tumblers, and Size of Locks.	
604	2¾ × 2	Square Case, **Janus Face**, Right or Left Hand, Iron Bolt, Iron Key. (See Plate, page 25.)	
605	2¾ × 2	Square Case, **Janus Face**, Right or Left Hand, Iron Bolt, Brass Key	
606	3½ × 2½	Square Case, **Janus Face**, Right or Left Hand, Iron Bolt, Iron Key. (See Plate, page 25.)	
607	3½ × 2½	Square Case, **Janus Face**, Right or Left Hand, Iron Bolt, Brass Key	
608	3½ × 2½	Square Case, **Janus Face**, Right or Left Hand, Brass Bolt, Brass Key	
629	3½ × 2½	Cottage, Right or Left Hand, Iron Bolt, Iron Key	
630	3½ × 2½	Rural, Right or Left Hand, Iron Bolt, Brass Key	
630½	3½ × 2½	Rural, Right or Left Hand, Iron Bolt, Iron Key	
631	4 × 3	Rural, Right or Left Hand, Iron Bolt, Brass Key. (See Plate, page 25.)	
632	5 × 3¼	Rural, Right or Left Hand, Iron Bolt, Brass Key	

CUPBOARD LOCKS, RIGHT OR LEFT HAND.

[651.]

[653.]

No.	Size.		Per Doz.
650	3 × 2¼	Rim, Iron Key, Iron Bolt_____	
651	3 × 2¼	Rim, Brass Key, Iron Bolt. (See Plate.) _____	
652	3½ × 2⅛	Straight, Drill Pin, Iron Key, Iron Bolt_____	
653	3½ × 2⅛	Straight, Drill Pin, Brass Key, Iron Bolt. (See Plate.)___	

UPRIGHT RIM KNOB LATCHES,

PACKED WITH SCREWS.

[550.]

No. 550.

SIZE 3¾ × 2½ INCHES.

Rural, [upright,] Iron Bolt, Iron Hub. (See Plate.)_____

No. 550½.

SIZE 3¼ × 2½ INCHES.

Rural, [upright,] Brass Bolt, Iron Hub_____

The above are both similar in style. (See Plate.)

	Without Knobs.	No. 39 Mineral Knobs, Japanned Crank Handle.
	PER DOZ.	PER DOZ.

HORIZONTAL RIM KNOB LATCHES,

PACKED WITH SCREWS.

(Continued.)

Per Doz.

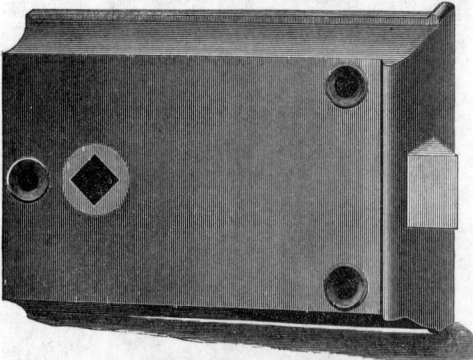

[551.]

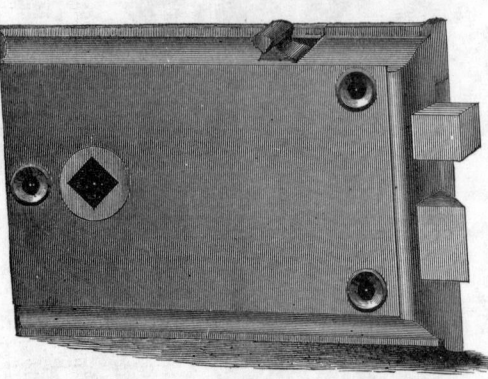

[552.]

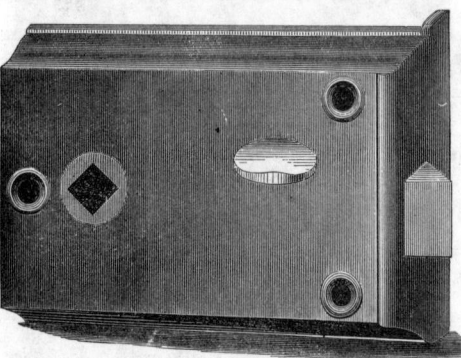

[553.]

[558.]   *See page opposite.*

No. 551.

Size $3\frac{3}{4} \times 2\frac{1}{2}$ Inches.

Rural, Iron Bolt, Iron Hub. (See Plate.)
Without Knobs_____
With Mineral Knobs_____
With No. 300 Porcelain Knobs_____

No. 551½.

Size $3\frac{3}{4} \times 2\frac{1}{2}$ Inches.

Rural, same as No. 551, but with Brass Bolt, Iron Hub.
Without Knobs_____
With Mineral Knobs_____
With No. 300 Porcelain Knobs_____

No. 552.

Size $3\frac{3}{4} \times 2\frac{1}{2}$ Inches.

Rural, Iron Bolt, Iron Hub, Iron Slide Night Bolt.
(See Plate.)
Without Knobs _____
With Mineral Knobs_____
With No. 300 Porcelain Knobs_____

No. 552½.

Size $3\frac{3}{4} \times 2\frac{1}{2}$ Inches.

Rural, same as No. 552, but with Brass Bolt, Iron
Hub, Brass Slide Night Bolt.
Without Knobs _____
With Mineral Knobs_____
With No. 300 Porcelain Knobs_____

No. 1552.

Size $3\frac{3}{4} \times 2\frac{1}{2}$ Inches.

Rural, Coppered Iron Bolt and Slide Bolt,—Case same
as No. 552.
Without Knobs_____
With Mineral Knobs_____
With No. 300 Porcelain Knobs_____

No. 553.

Size $3\frac{3}{4} \times 2\frac{1}{2}$ Inches.

Rural, Improved Stop, Iron Bolt, Iron Hub, Brass
Stop. (See Plate.)
Without Knobs _____
With Mineral Knobs_____
With No. 300 Porcelain Knobs_____

No. 553½.

Size $3\frac{3}{4} \times 2\frac{1}{2}$ Inches.

Rural, Improved Stop, same as No. 553, but with
Brass Bolt, Brass Stop.
Without Knobs _____
With Mineral Knobs_____
With No. 300 Porcelain Knobs_____

No. 554.

Size $3\frac{3}{4} \times 2\frac{1}{2}$ Inches.

Rural, Lock Latch, Iron Bolt, Iron Hub, similar in
style to No. 553, but has a Brass Key instead of the Stop
Without Knobs _____
With Mineral Knobs_____
With No. 300 Porcelain Knobs_____

HORIZONTAL RIM KNOB LATCHES,

PACKED WITH SCREWS.

(Continued.)

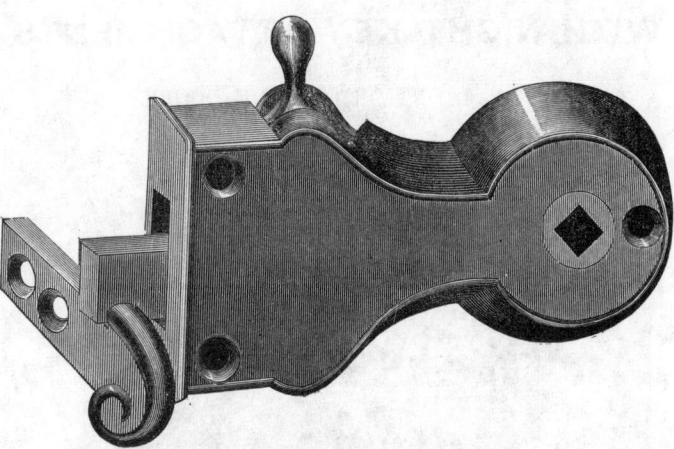

[559.]

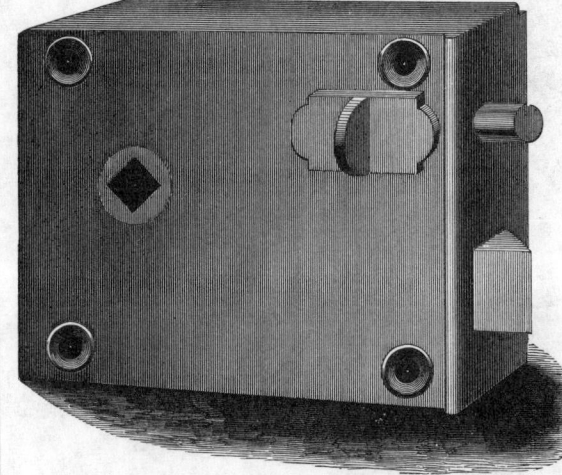

[556.]

[549.]

No.	Size.		Without Knobs. PER DOZ.	Mineral Knobs. PER DOZ.	No. 300 Porcelain Knobs. PER DOZ.
557	$3\frac{1}{2} \times 2\frac{1}{2}$	Western, Iron Bolt, Iron Hub......			
558	$3\frac{1}{2} \times 2\frac{1}{2}$	Western, Stop, Iron Bolt, Iron Hub, Iron Stop. (See Plate, page 28.)			
547	4×3	Cottage, Heavy Brass Bolt, Brass Hub, same as No. 549, without the Brass Stop Knob................			
549	4×3	Cottage Stop, Heavy Brass Bolt, Brass Hub, Brass Stop Knob. (See Plate.)			
555	$4 \times 3\frac{1}{2}$	Heavy Square Case, Iron bolt, Iron Hub......................			
$555\frac{1}{2}$	$4 \times 3\frac{1}{2}$	Heavy Square Case, Brass Bolt, Iron Hub......................			
556	$4 \times 3\frac{1}{2}$	Heavy Square Case, Iron Bolt, Iron Hub, Iron Slide Bolt. (See Plate.)			
$556\frac{1}{2}$	$4 \times 3\frac{1}{2}$	Heavy Square Case, Brass Bolt, Iron Hub, Brass Slide Bolt...........			
		We have substituted a Square Bolt for the Round one represented in the above Plate, and improved the Thumb piece. 555, 555½, and 556½ are all same Style of Case as No. 556.			
$570\frac{1}{2}$	$5 \times 3\frac{1}{4}$	Rural Case, Heavy, Lever, Brass Bolt and Hub, Brass Slide Bolt, Case same as No. 570, page 23........			
$571\frac{1}{2}$	$6 \times 3\frac{3}{4}$	Rural Case, Heavy, Lever, Brass Bolt and Hub, Brass Slide Bolt, Case same as 571, page 24............			
559	$4\frac{1}{4} \times 2\frac{3}{8}$	Hamlet, Stop, Lift Latch, all Iron, Japanned, Right or Left Hand. (See Plate.)			

HEAVY UPRIGHT MORTISE KNOB LOCKS,

WITH NIGHT KEY ATTACHMENTS,

FOR FRONT OR OUTSIDE DOORS.

[100.]

(For Description with Furniture, see pages 34 and 35.)

To avoid trouble in adapting to the door, both the Locks and Knobs, it is desirable that these goods should be ordered complete with Furniture.

HEAVY UPRIGHT MORTISE KNOB LOCKS,

WITH NIGHT KEY ATTACHMENTS,

FOR FRONT OR OUTSIDE DOORS.

(*Continued.*)

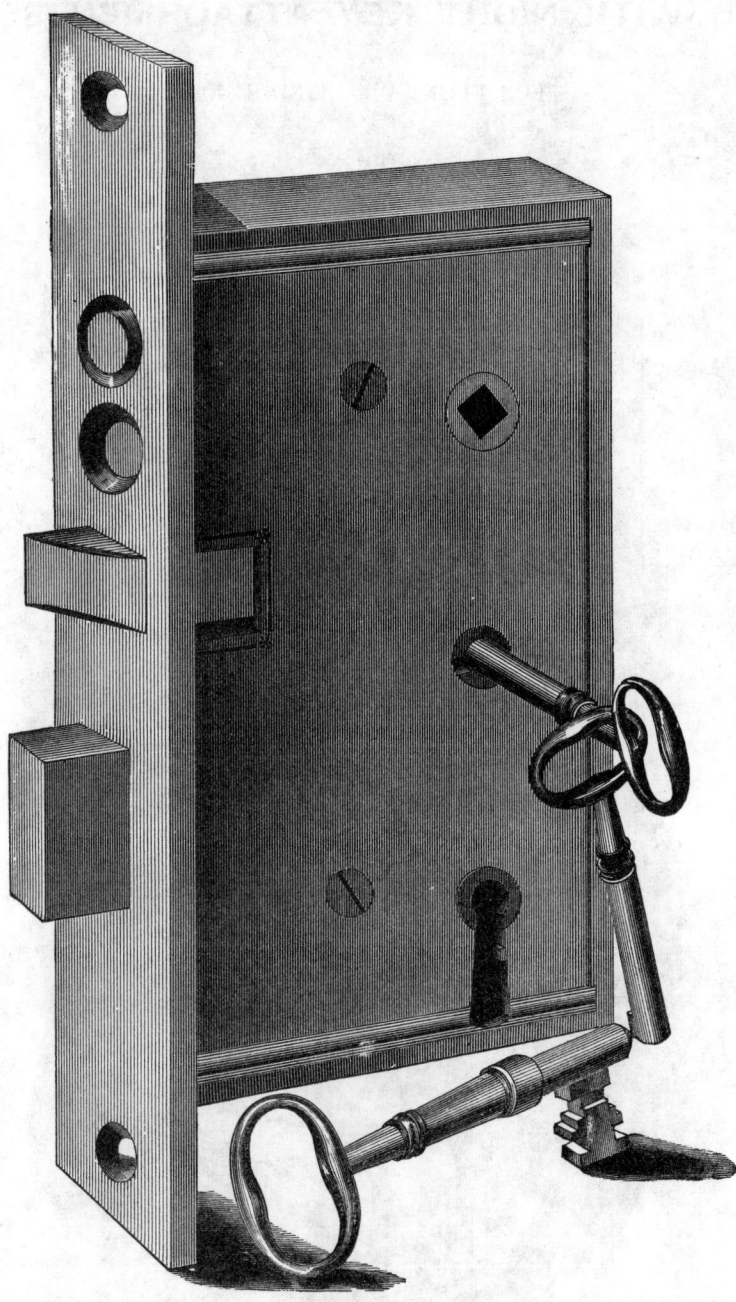

[101.]

Locks No. 101 to No. 135 should be ordered complete with Furniture, as they require a Swivel Spindle three-eighths of an inch in diameter, and heavier Knobs than are generally used.

Many complaints having been made of Locks that were perfect in themselves, but not being properly adjusted to the Door, were unjustly condemned, we would call especial attention to the following Note :

☞ When fitting a door with a Mortise Lock adapted to SWIVEL SPINDLES, care should be taken to place the Lock as near the center as possible, as proper adjustment of the Swivel Spindle requires care and attention so that the working of the Knobs will be perfect. It must be so placed that the Swivel operates exactly in the CENTER of the Lock. The Lock having a double hub, the outer Knob can be shut off or stopped by the lever in the face of the Lock, effectually locking the door, preventing entrance without the aid of a Pass or Night Key, while the inside Knob yet works to open the door from the inside. (For description with Furniture, see pages 34 and 35.)

HEAVY UPRIGHT MORTISE KNOB LOCKS,

WITH NIGHT KEY ATTACHMENTS,

FOR FRONT OR OUTSIDE DOORS.

(Continued.)

[131.]

For Description with Furniture, see pages 34 and 35.

Locks No. 101 to No. 135 should be ordered complete with Furniture, as they require a Swivel Spindle three-eighths of an inch in diameter, and heavier Knobs than are generally used.

(See Note on Page 31.)

HEAVY UPRIGHT MORTISE KNOB LOCKS,

WITHOUT NIGHT KEYS,

FOR FRONT OR OUTSIDE DOORS.

(Continued.)

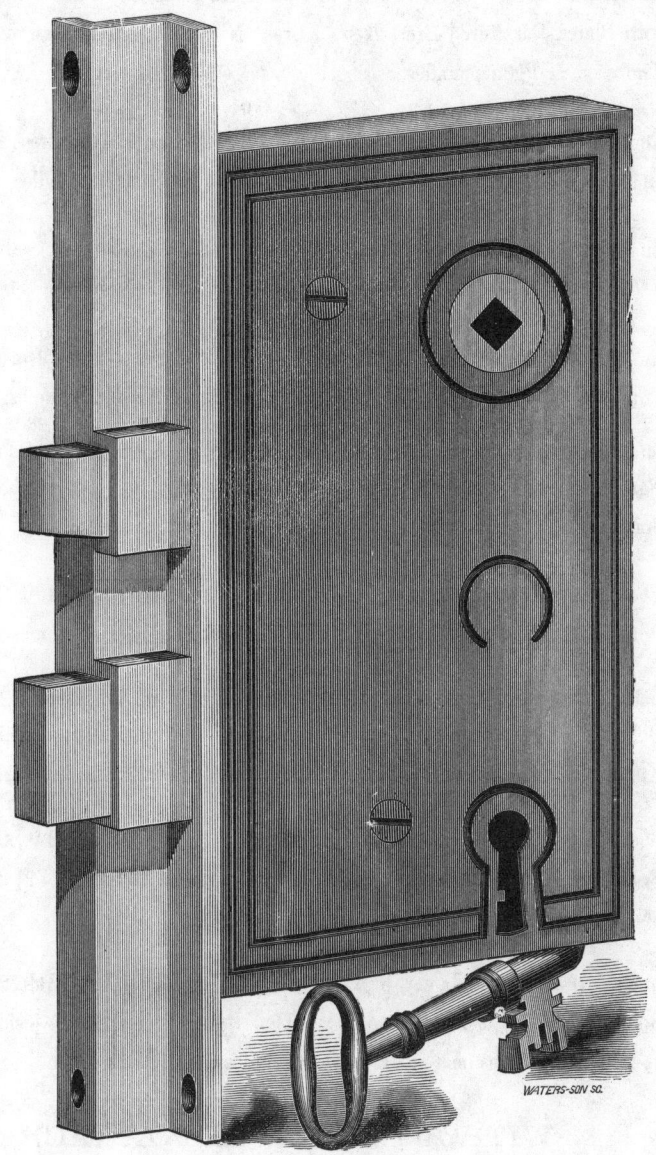

[175.]

(For Description with Furniture, see pages 34 and 35.)

To avoid trouble in adapting to the door, both the Locks and Knobs, it is desirable that these goods should be ordered complete with Furniture.

HEAVY UPRIGHT MORTISE KNOB LOCKS,
WITH NIGHT KEY ATTACHMENTS,
FOR FRONT OR OUTSIDE DOORS.

(*Continued.*)

No.	Size.	
100	$5\frac{1}{2} \times 4\frac{1}{2}$	Plain Brass Front, 2 Tumblers, Brass Hub, 2 Brass Bolts, Brass Draw Back Knob, (Plated when with Plated Furniture,) Brass Key, 2 Brass Night Keys, all Brass inside work, $2\frac{1}{2} \times 2\frac{1}{4}$ inch Knobs on $\frac{5}{16}$ Plain Spindles. (See Plate, page 30.)_____
101	$6 \times 4\frac{1}{2}$	Plain Brass Front, 3 Tumblers, Brass Hub, 2 Heavy Brass Bolts, Brass Key, 2 Bit Night Keys, all Brass inside work, $2\frac{1}{2} \times 2\frac{1}{4}$ inch Knobs on $\frac{3}{8}$ inch Swivel Spindles. (See Plate, page 31.)
121	$6\frac{1}{4} \times 4\frac{1}{4}$	Plain Brass Front, Lever, 3 Wrought Iron Tumblers, Brass Hub, 2 Brass Bolts, Brass Key, 2 *Extra Safe* 3 Tumbler Bit Night Keys, $2\frac{1}{2} \times 2\frac{1}{4}$ inch Knobs on $\frac{3}{8}$ inch Swivel Spindles____
122	$6\frac{1}{2} \times 4\frac{1}{4}$	Plain Brass Front, Lever, 3 Tumblers, Brass Hub, 2 Brass Bolts, Brass Key, 2 *Extra Safe* 5 Tumbler Night Keys, $2\frac{1}{2} \times 2\frac{1}{4}$ inch Knobs on $\frac{3}{8}$ inch Swivel Spindles____
125	$7 \times 4\frac{1}{2}$	Plain Brass Front, Lever, 3 Tumblers, Brass Hub, 2 Heavy Brass Bolts, Brass Key, 2 *Extra Safe* 5 Tumbler Night Keys, all Brass inside work, $2\frac{1}{2} \times 2\frac{1}{4}$ inch Knobs on $\frac{3}{8}$ inch Swivel Spindles____
130	$6\frac{1}{4} \times 3\frac{3}{4}$	Rabbeted Brass Front, Lever, 3 Wrought Iron Tumblers, Brass Hub, 2 Heavy Brass Guarded Bolts, Brass Key, 2 Night Keys, $\frac{1}{2}$ inch Rabbet, $2\frac{1}{2} \times 2\frac{1}{4}$ inch Knobs on $\frac{3}{8}$ Swivel Spindles___
131	$6\frac{1}{4} \times 3\frac{3}{4}$	Rabbeted Brass Front, Lever, 3 Wrought Iron Tumblers, Brass Hub, 2 Heavy Brass Guarded Bolts, Brass Key, 2 *Extra Safe* 3 Tumbler Bit Night Keys, $\frac{1}{2}$ inch Rabbet, $2\frac{1}{2} \times 2\frac{1}{4}$ inch Knobs on $\frac{3}{8}$ inch Swivel Spindles. (See Plate, page 32.) ___
132	$6\frac{1}{2} \times 4\frac{1}{4}$	Rabbeted Brass Front, Lever, 3 Wrought Iron Tumblers, Brass Hub, 2 Heavy Brass Guarded Bolts, Brass Key, 2 *Extra Safe* 5 Tumbler Night Keys, $2\frac{1}{2} \times 2\frac{1}{4}$ inch Knobs on $\frac{3}{8}$ inch Swivel Spindles____
135	7×4	Rabbeted Brass Front, Lever, 3 Wrought Iron Tumblers, Brass Hub, 2 Heavy Brass Guarded Bolts, Brass Key, 2 *Extra Safe* 5 Tumbler Night Keys, all Brass inside work, $\frac{1}{2}$ inch Rabbet, $2\frac{1}{2} \times 2\frac{1}{4}$ inch Knobs on $\frac{3}{8}$ inch Swivel Spindles____

WITHOUT NIGHT KEY ATTACHMENT.

No.	Size.	
173	$5\frac{1}{2} \times 4\frac{1}{2}$	Plain Brass Front, 3 Wrought Iron Tumblers, 2 Brass Bolts, Brass Hub, Brass Strike, Brass Key, with $2\frac{1}{2} \times 2\frac{1}{4}$ inch Knobs on $\frac{5}{16}$ inch Plain Spindles____
174	$6\frac{1}{4} \times 4\frac{1}{4}$	Plain Brass Front, 3 Wrought Iron Tumblers, 2 Heavy Brass Bolts, Brass Hub, Brass Strike, Brass Key, with $2\frac{1}{2} \times 2\frac{1}{4}$ inch Knobs on $\frac{5}{16}$ inch Plain Spindles____
175	$6\frac{1}{4} \times 3\frac{3}{4}$	Rabbeted Brass Front, 3 Wrought Iron Tumblers, 2 Heavy Brass Bolts, Brass Hub, Brass Strike, Brass Key, $\frac{1}{2}$ inch Rabbet, with $2\frac{1}{2} \times 2\frac{1}{4}$ inch Knobs on $\frac{5}{16}$ inch Plain Spindles. (See Plate, page 33.)____

HEAVY UPRIGHT MORTISE KNOB LOCKS,

WITH NIGHT KEY ATTACHMENTS,

FOR FRONT OR OUTSIDE DOORS.

(Continued.)

No.	Without Knobs or Escutcheons.	With No. 450 Mineral Knobs, Japanned Mountings and Escutcheons.	With No. 350 Porcelain Knobs, Japanned Mountings and Escutcheons.	With Extra Heavy Brass Knobs, Brass Escutcheons.	With Extra Heavy Brass Knobs, outside and Porcelain Knobs, No. 100 inside.	With Extra Heavy Brass Knobs outside, and Porcelain Knobs, No. 101 inside.	With No. 150 Porcelain Knobs Plated Roses and Plated Escutcheons.	With No. 151 Porcelain Knobs Porcelain Roses and Porcelain Escutcheons.	With Electro Plated Knobs Roses and Electro Plated Escutcheons.	With Electro Plated Knobs outside and Porcelain. No. 100 inside.	With Hand Plated Knobs, Roses and Escutcheons.	With Hand Plated Knobs outside, and Porcelain No. 100 inside.
	PER DOZ.	PER DOZ.	PER DOZ.	PER DOZ.	PER DOZ.	PER DOZ.	PER DOZ.	PER DOZ.	PER DOZ.	PER DOZ.	PER DOZ.	PER DOZ.
100												
101												
121												
122												
125												
130												
131												
132												
135												
173												
174												
175												

UPRIGHT VESTIBULE MORTISE LATCHES,

WITH NIGHT KEY ATTACHMENTS,

FOR INNER HALL DOORS.

[141.]

(*For Description with Furniture, see opposite page.*)

NOTE.—These Latches are for Inner or Vestibule Doors, intended to be used in connection with Outer or Front Door Locks (pages 34, 35), and are packed in sets with Night Keys to pass. They can also be used on Single Doors as a Pass or Night Latch, when required.

With the description of each variety is shown the Numbers of Front Door Locks they are adapted to. When ordering in *Sets to Match*, it is necessary to so *state*, giving *both* the Numbers of Locks and Latches required, together with the Furniture wanted, this being particularly necessary, as the Trimmings are peculiar to both the Lock and Latch.

UPRIGHT VESTIBULE MORTISE LATCHES,

WITH NIGHT KEY ATTACHMENTS,

FOR INNER HALL DOORS.

(Continued.)

No. 140.

Size $4\frac{3}{4} \times 4\frac{1}{4}$ Inches.

Plain Brass Front, Brass Bolt, Brass Hub, Brass Strike, 2 Night Keys, Knobs on $\frac{3}{8}$-inch Swivel Spindles, to match Lock No. 101.

No. 141.

Size $4\frac{3}{4} \times 4\frac{1}{4}$ Inches.

Plain Brass Front, Brass Bolt, Brass Hub, Brass Strike, 2 Extra Safe 3 Tumbler Bit Night Keys, Knobs on $\frac{3}{8}$-inch Swivel Spindles, to match Lock No. 121.   (See Plate, opposite page).

No. 142.

Size $4\frac{3}{4} \times 4\frac{1}{4}$ Inches.

Plain Brass Front, Brass Bolt, Brass Hub, Brass Strike, 2 Extra Safe 5 Tumbler Night Keys, Knobs on $\frac{3}{8}$-inch Swivel Spindles, to match Locks No. 122 or 125.

No. 160.

Size $4\frac{3}{4} \times 3\frac{3}{4}$ Inches.

Rabbeted Brass Front, Heavy Brass Guarded Bolt, Brass Hub, Brass Strike, 2 Night Keys, Knobs on $\frac{3}{8}$-inch Swivel Spindles, $\frac{1}{2}$ inch Rabbet, to match Lock No. 130.

No. 161.

Size $4\frac{3}{4} \times 3\frac{3}{4}$ Inches.

Rabbeted Brass Front, Heavy Brass Guarded Bolt, Brass Hub, Brass Strike, 2 Extra Safe 3 Tumbler Bit Night Keys, Knobs on $\frac{3}{8}$-inch Swivel Spindles, to match Lock No. 131.

No. 162.

Size $4\frac{3}{4} \times 3\frac{3}{4}$ Inches.

Rabbeted Brass Front, Heavy Brass Guarded Bolt, Brass Hub, Brass Strike, 2 Extra Safe 5 Tumbler Night Keys, Knobs on $\frac{3}{8}$-inch Swivel Spindles, to match Lock No. 132 or 135.

No.	Without Knobs or Escutcheons.	With No. 450 Mineral Knobs, Japanned Mountings and Escutcheons.	With No. 350 Porcelain Knobs, Japanned Mountings and Escutcheons.	With Extra Heavy Brass Knobs, Brass Escutcheons.	With Extra Heavy Brass Knobs outside, and Porcelain Knobs, No. 100 inside.	With Extra Heavy Brass Knobs outside, and Porcelain Knobs, No. 101 inside.	With No 150 Porcelain Knobs Plated Roses and Plated Escutcheons.	With No. 151 Porcelain Knobs Porcelain Roses and Porcelain Escutcheons.	With Electro Plated Knobs Roses and Escutcheons.	With Electro Plated Knobs outside, and Porcelain No. 100 inside.	With Hand Plated Knobs, Roses and Escutcheons.	With Hand Plated Knobs outside, and Porcelain No. 100 inside.
	PER DOZ.	PER DOZ.	PER DOZ.	PER DOZ.	PER DOZ.	PER DOZ.	PER DOZ.	PER DOZ.	PER DOZ.	PER DOZ.	PER DOZ.	PER DOZ.
140												
141												
142												
160												
161												
162												

MORTISE NIGHT LATCHES,

PACKED WITH ESCUTCHEONS.

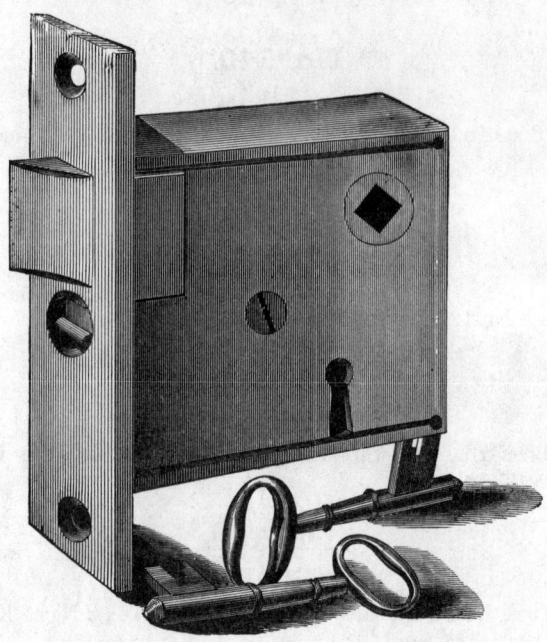

[83.]

No. 83.

SIZE $2\frac{3}{4} \times 3\frac{1}{4}$ INCHES.

Brass Front, Brass Strike, 2 Brass Keys, Brass Bolt, 3 Wrought Iron Tumblers, Safe.   (See Plate.)

Without Knobs, With Japanned Escutcheons..
With Mineral Knobs, Japanned Escutcheons..
  "   Porcelain Knobs, Plated Escutcheons..
  "   Brass Knobs, Brass Escutcheons..
  "   Electro-Plated Knobs, Plated Escutcheons...
  "   Hand-Plated Knobs, Hand-Plated Escutcheons ....
  "   Japanned T Handle No. 1, Japanned Escutcheons..
  "   Bronzed T Handle No. 2, Brass Escutcheons ....
  "   Plated T Handle No. 3, Plated Escutcheons...

No. 84.

SIZE 2×3 INCHES.

Brass Front, Bolt and Strike, 2 Brass Keys, Brass Slide Knob..

Per Doz.

MORTISE LOCKS FOR SLIDING DOORS,

WITH ESCUTCHEONS TO MATCH.

[33.]

[For description, see Page 40.]

MORTISE LOCKS, FOR SLIDING DOORS.

(Continued.)

[35.] [31.]

No.	Size.	
31	4 × 3½	Plain, Iron Front, Dead Lock, Iron Bolt, Iron Strike, Brass Key, for Sliding Barn or Stable Doors. (See Plate above.). Per Doz. $
32	6¼ × 4¼	Plain, Brass Front, Sliding Door Double Locks, to Match, for Doors Sliding in *Flush* with wall, Complete with *Flush Pulls, Flush Escutcheons* and *Keys,* same as No. 33, except Plain Front .... Per Pair. $
32	6¼ × 4¼	Plain, Electro-Plated Front, Sliding Door Double Locks, to Match, as above, with *Electro-Plated Pulls, Escutcheons* and *Keys* .... Per Pair. $
32	6¼ × 4¼	Plain, Hand-Plated Front, Sliding Door Double Locks, to Match, with *Hand-Plated Pulls, Escutcheons,* and *Keys* .. Per Pair. $
33	6¼ × 4¼	Astragal, Brass Front, Sliding Door Double Locks, to Match, for Doors Sliding in Flush, as above, Complete with Flush Pulls, Flush Escutcheons and Keys. (See Plate, page 39.) .... Per Pair. $
33	6¼ × 4¼	Astragal, Electro-Plated Front, Sliding Door Double Locks, to Match as above, with *Electro-Plated Pulls, Escutcheons* and *Keys* .... Per Pair. $
33	6¼ × 4¼	Astragal, Hand-Plated Front, Sliding Door Double Locks, to Match as above, with *Hand-Plated Pulls, Escutcheons* and *Keys* .... Per Pair. $
34	4½ × 3⅜	Astragal, Brass Front, Brass Strike, Japanned Case, Brass Bolts, Brass Hub, Brass Key, without Knobs or Escutcheons, Per Doz. $
35	5¼ × 3⅜	Astragal, Brass Front, Brass Strike, Japanned Case, Brass Bolts, Brass Hub, Brass Key, without Knobs or Escutcheons. (See Plate above.) .... Per Doz. $
36	4¾ × 3¾	Plain, Brass Front, Brass Strike, Japanned Case, Brass Bolts, Brass Hub, Brass Key, without Knobs or Escutcheons, Per Doz. $
37	5¼ × 3¼	Reverse Astragal, Brass Front, Japanned Case, Brass Hub, BOLT LOCK to Match No. 35, without Knobs or Escutcheons, Per Doz. $

RABBETED MORTISE KNOB LOCKS.

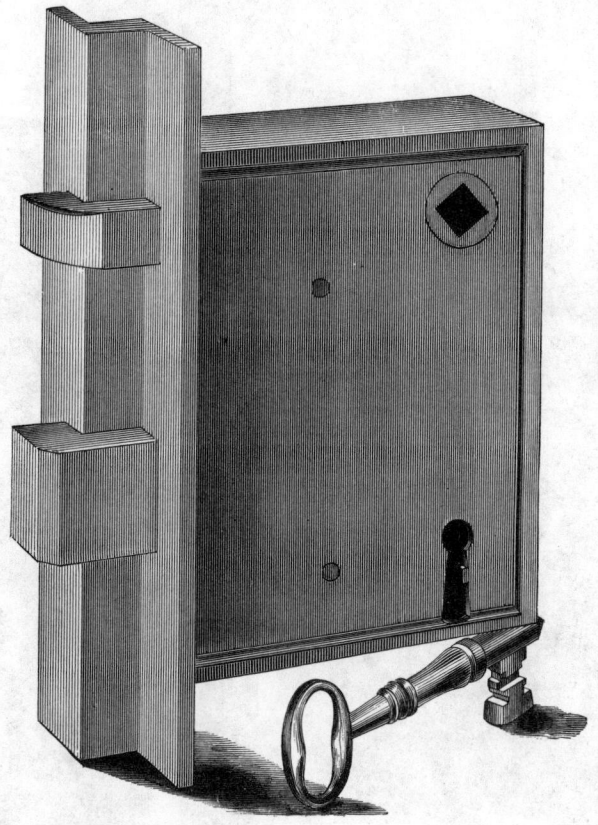

[25½.]

No. 25.

SIZE 5¼ × 3⅜ INCHES.

Brass Front and Strike, Japanned Case, 2 Brass Bolts, Brass Hub and Key, either ½ or ⅝ inch Rabbet, for
Folding Doors

No. 25¼.

SIZE 5¼ × 3⅜ INCHES.

Brass Front, Hub, Strike and Key, Japanned Case, 2 Brass Guarded Bolts

No. 25½.

SIZE 4¼ × 3⅜ INCHES.

Brass Front, Hub, Strike and Key, Japanned Case, 2 Brass Bolts, ½ inch Rabbet. (See Plate above.)

No. 26.

SIZE 3½ × 3 INCHES.

Brass Front, Hub, Strike and Key, Japanned Case, 2 Brass Bolts, ½ inch Rabbet

No. 27.

SIZE 4½ × 3½ INCHES.

Iron Front, Brass Strike, Japanned Case, Brass Hub and Key, 2 Brass Guarded Bolts,

Without
Knobs or
Escutcheons.

PER DOZ.

ROUND EDGE MORTISE LEVER KNOB LOCKS.

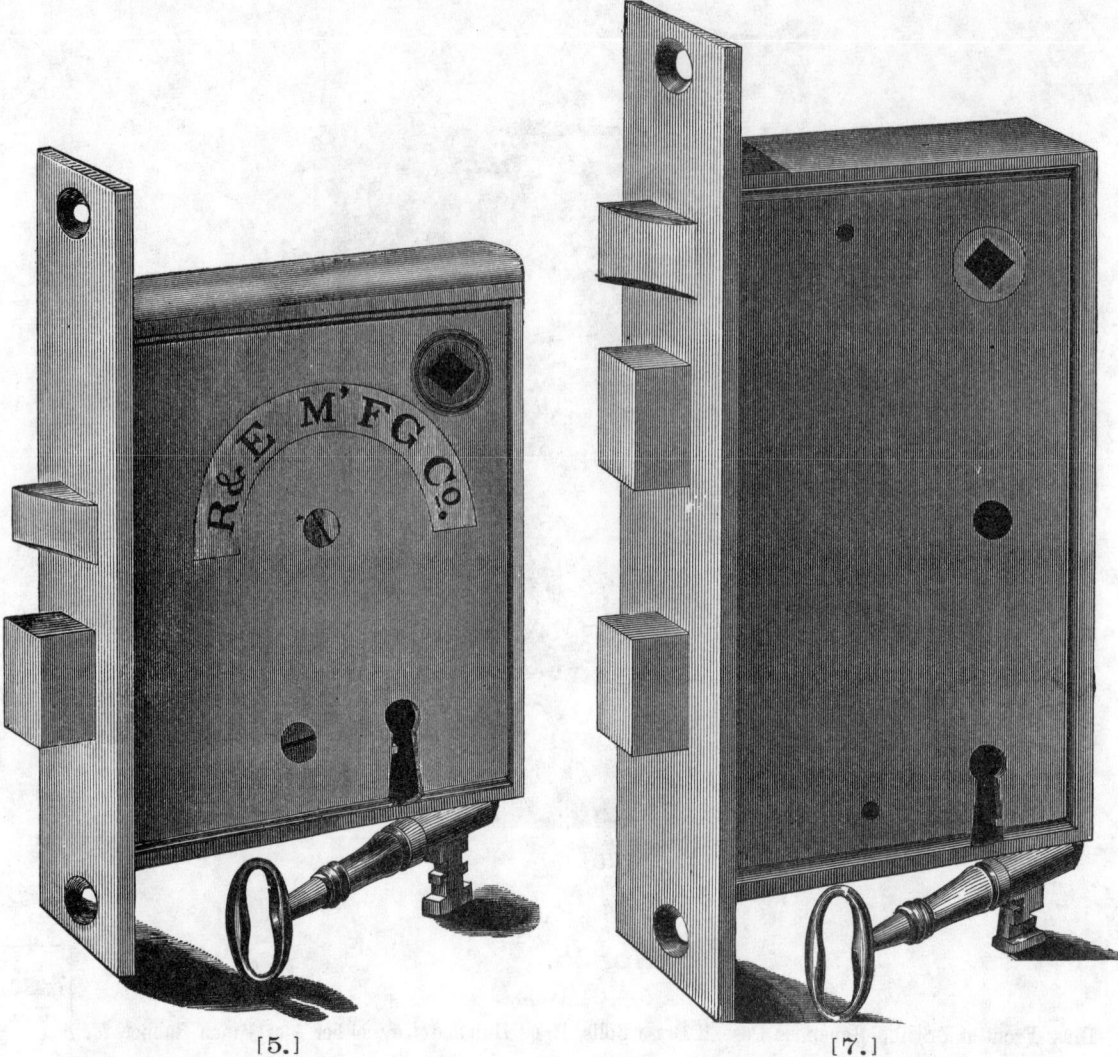

[5.]   [7.]

No.	Size.		Without Knobs or Escutcheons. PER DOZ.
4	$4\frac{1}{4} \times 3\frac{5}{8}$	Polished Brass Front and Strike, Japanned Case, 2 Brass Bolts, Brass Hub and Key	
5	$4\frac{3}{4} \times 3\frac{3}{4}$	Polished Brass Front and Strike, Japanned Case, 2 Brass Bolts, Brass Hub and Key	
6	$5\frac{1}{4} \times 4\frac{1}{8}$	Polished Brass Front and Strike, Japanned Case, 2 Brass Bolts, Brass Hub and Key	
14	$5 \times 3\frac{1}{4}$	*Villa*, Polished Brass Front and Strike, Japanned Case, 2 Brass Bolts, Brass Hub and Key	
15	$5\frac{1}{2} \times 4$	*Villa*, Polished Brass Front and Strike, Japanned Case, 2 Brass Bolts, Brass Hub and Key	
7	$6 \times 3\frac{5}{8}$	*Hotel*, Polished Brass Front and Strike, Japanned Case, 3 Brass Bolts, Brass Hub and Key, 2 Key holes disconnected, dispensing with the necessity for bolts on doors. (See Plate.)	
8	$5\frac{1}{8} \times 3\frac{3}{8}$	*Hotel*—same style as No. 7	
16	4×7	*Horizontal*, Polished Brass Front and Strike, Japanned Case, 2 Brass Bolts, Brass Hub and Key, Heavy, for *Heavy* Doors. (New Orleans Gate Lock and Canada Outside Hall Door Lock)	

[13.]

MORTISE KNOB LOCKS,
ROUND EDGE,
WITH REVERSIBLE LATCH BOLT, RIGHT OR LEFT HAND.

	Without Knobs or Escutcheons.
	PER DOZ.

No. 12.
SIZE 4½ × 3½ INCHES.

Villa, Brass Front and Strike, Japanned Case, Iron Hub, 2 Iron Bolts, Brass Key

No. 13.
SIZE 4½ × 3½ INCHES.

Villa, Brass Front and Strike, Japanned Case, 2 Brass Bolts, Brass Hub and Key. (See Plate.)

No. 13½.
SIZE 4½ × 3½ INCHES.

Villa, Brass Front and Strike, Japanned Case, 2 Brass Bolts, 2 *Tumblers*, Brass Keys *all different*

No. 18½.
SIZE 4½ × 3½ INCHES.

Villa, Brass Front and Strike, Japanned Case, 2 Brass Bolts, Brass Key—same style as No. 13, with Feather Spring Latch Bolt

TUMBLER
MORTISE KNOB LOCKS,
ROUND EDGE.

	Without Knobs or Escutcheons.
	PER DOZ.

No. 18.
SIZE 5 × 3¾ INCHES.

Fine Finish, Polished Brass Front and Strike, Japanned Case, 2 Heavy Brass Bolts, 3 Wrought Iron Tumblers, Brass Hub and Key, *all different*. (See Plate.)

No. 19.
SIZE 5 × 3¾ INCHES.

Fine Finish, Polished Brass Front and Strike, Japanned Case, 2 Heavy Brass Bolts, 3 Wrought Iron Tumblers, Brass Hub and Key, *all different*, with Feather Spring Latch Bolt

No. 20.
SIZE 4 × 3¾ INCHES.

Skeleton, Brass Front and Strike, Japanned Case, 2 Brass Bolts, 3 Wrought Iron Tumblers, Brass Hub and Key, variety of Keys, Right or Left Hand, not liable to bind by swelling or shrinking of Doors. (See Plate, page 44.)

No. 21.
SIZE 4 × 2¾ INCHES.

Skeleton, Brass Front and Strike, Japanned Case, 2 Brass Bolts, 3 Wrought Iron Tumblers, Brass Hub and Key, variety of Keys, Right or Left Hand, not liable to bind by swelling or shrinking of Doors, for narrow Stile Doors

[18.]

ROUND EDGE MORTISE KNOB LOCKS,

WITH PATENT REVERSIBLE LATCH BOLT,

FOR EITHER RIGHT OR LEFT HAND.

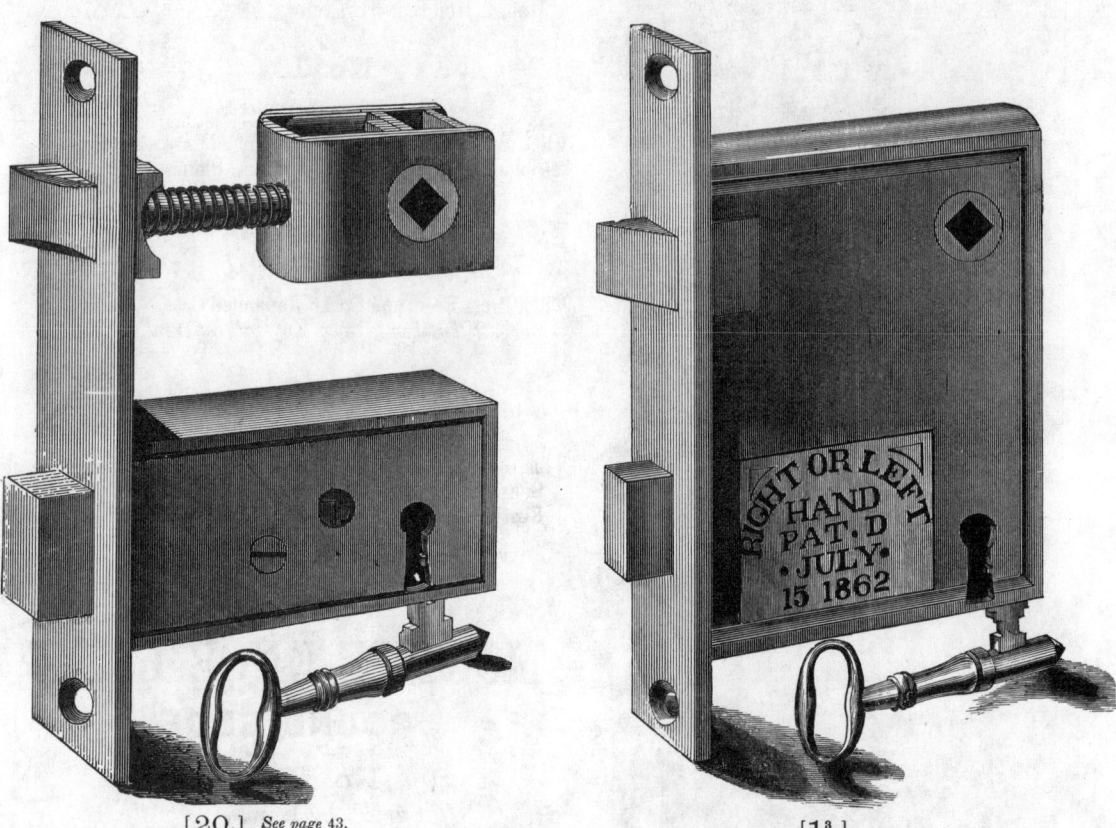

[20.] *See page* 43.   [1¾.]

No.	Size.	Spiral Spring, with Japanned Plate Escutcheons.	Without Knobs. PER DOZ.
0	3½ × 3¼	Lacquered Iron Front and Strike, 2 Iron Bolts, Iron Hub and Key --------------------	
0¼	3½ × 3¼	Lacquered Iron Front and Strike, 2 Brass Bolts, Iron Hub, Brass Key -------------------	
0½	4¼ × 3¼	Lacquered Iron Front and Strike, 2 Iron Bolts, Iron Hub and Key --------------------	
0¾	4¼ × 3¼	Lacquered Iron Front and Strike, Japanned Case, 2 Brass Bolts, Iron Hub, Brass Key --------	
1	3½ × 3¼	Lacquered Brass Front and Strike, Japanned Case, 2 Iron Bolts, Iron Hub, Brass Key --------	
1¼	4 × 3¼	Lacquered Brass Front and Strike, Japanned Case, 2 Iron Bolts, Iron Hub, Brass Key --------	
1½	3½ × 3¼	Lacquered Brass Front and Strike, Japanned Case, 2 Brass Bolts, Iron Hub, Brass Key-------	
1¾	4 × 3¼	Lacquered Brass Front and Strike, Japanned Case, 2 Brass Bolts, Iron Hub, Brass Key. (See Plate above.) --------	
2	4¼ × 3½	Lacquered Brass Front and Strike, Japanned Case, 2 Brass Bolts, Iron Hub, Brass Key --------	
2½	4¼ × 3½	Lacquered Brass Front and Strike, Japanned Case, 2 Iron Bolts, Iron Hub, Brass Key --------	
701	3½ × 3¼	Lacquered Brass Front and Strike, Japanned Case, 2 Iron Bolts, Iron Hub, Brass Key, with 24 Changes --------	
701½	3½ × 3¼	Lacquered Brass Front and Strike, Japanned Case, 2 Brass Bolts, Iron Hub, Brass Key, with 24 Changes--------	
702	4¼ × 3½	Lacquered Brass Front and Strike, Japanned Case, 2 Brass Bolts, Iron Hub, Brass Key, with 24 Changes--------	

MORTISE KNOB LOCKS.

(Continued.)

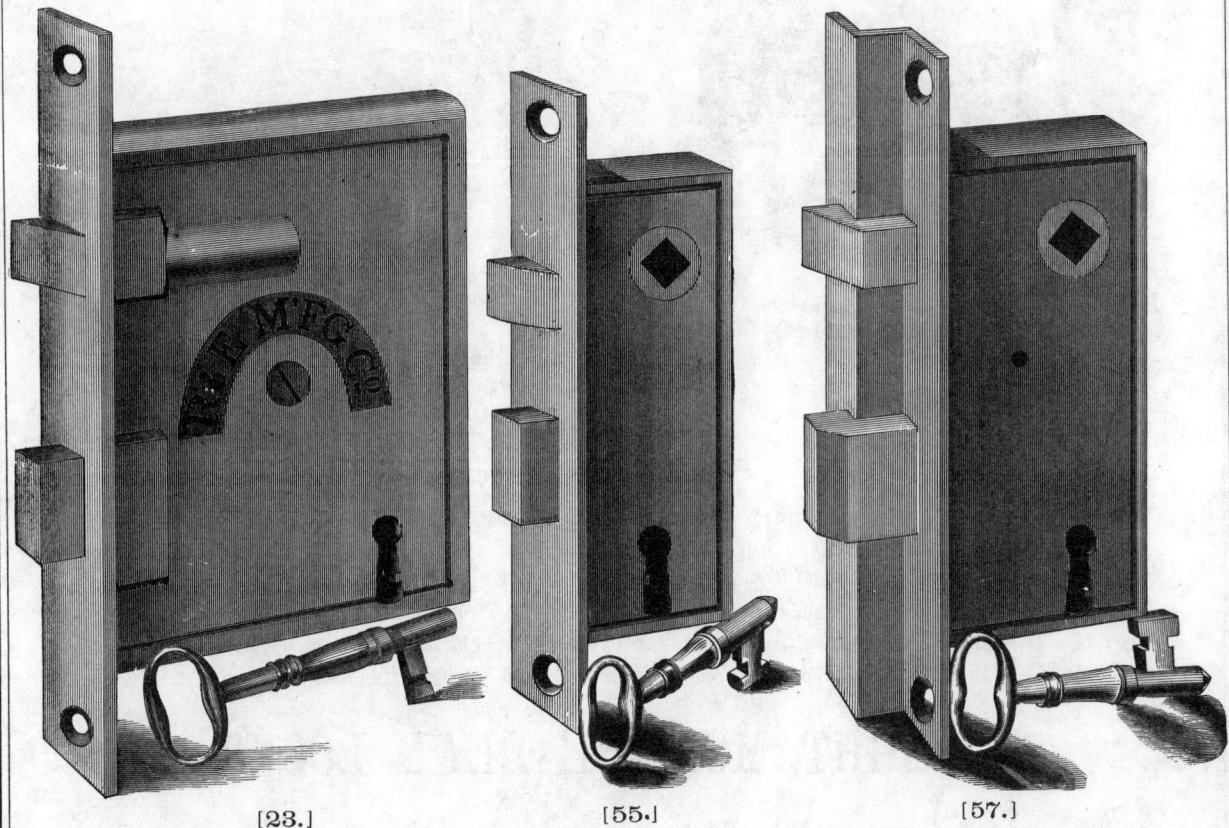

[23.] [55.] [57.]

Without Knobs.

PER DOZ.

No. 9.
SIZE 3½ × 2½ INCHES.

Refrigerator, Lacquered Iron Front, Japanned Case, Brass Bolts, Iron Hub, Brass Key, (see Plate, page 51) packed with Japanned Plate Escutcheons

No. 23.
SIZE 4¼ × 3½ INCHES.

Lacquered Iron Front, Iron Bolt, Japanned Case, Brass Key, *Round Edge*, *Reversible* either Right or Left Hand, ⅜ inch thick for *thin doors*, (see Plate) packed with Japanned Plate Escutcheons

No. 54.
SIZE 3 × 1½ INCHES.

Plain Front, for *French Windows*, or *Narrow Stile Inside Sash Doors*, 2 Brass Bolts, Brass Front, Strike, Hub and Key

No. 55.
SIZE 3¾ × 1⅝ INCHES.

Plain Front, for *French Windows* or *Narrow Stile Inside Sash Doors*, 2 Brass Bolts, Brass Front, Strike, Hub, and Key.   (See Plate.)

No. 57.
SIZE 3¾ × 1⅝ INCHES.

Rabbeted Front, for *French Windows* or *Narrow Stile Inside Sash Doors*, ½ inch Rabbet, Brass Front, Strike, and Key, 2 Brass Bolts. (See Plate.)

HORIZONTAL MORTISE DEAD LOCKS,
ROUND EDGE.

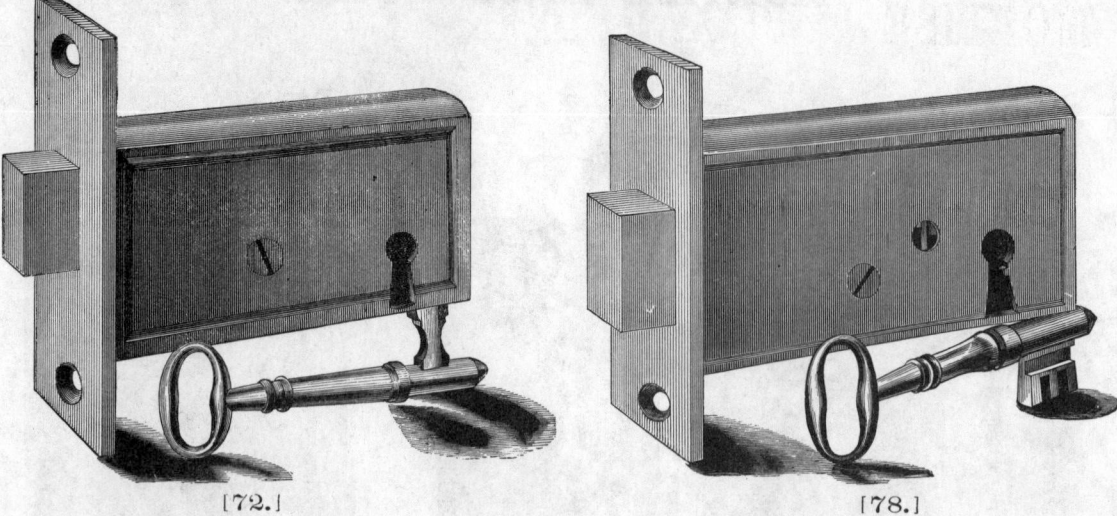

[72.]   [78.]

No.	Size.		Per Doz.
72	$1\frac{3}{4} \times 3\frac{3}{8}$	Iron Front, Bolt and Key, Japanned Case, 1 Tumbler. (See Plate.)	
73	$1\frac{3}{4} \times 3\frac{3}{8}$	Brass Front, Bolt and Key, Japanned Case, 1 Tumbler	
74	$1\frac{3}{4} \times 2\frac{3}{4}$	Iron Front, Bolt and Key, Japanned Case, 1 Tumbler	
77	$1\frac{7}{8} \times 3\frac{3}{4}$	Iron Front and Bolt, Brass Key, Japanned Case, 3 Wrought Iron Tumblers	
78	$1\frac{7}{8} \times 3\frac{3}{4}$	Brass Front and Bolt, Brass Key, Jap'd Case, 3 Wrought Iron Tumblers. (See Plate.)	
79	$1\frac{7}{8} \times 2\frac{3}{4}$	Brass Front and Bolt, Brass Key, Japanned Case, 3 Wrought Iron Tumblers	

UPRIGHT MORTISE DEAD LOCKS.

Per Doz.

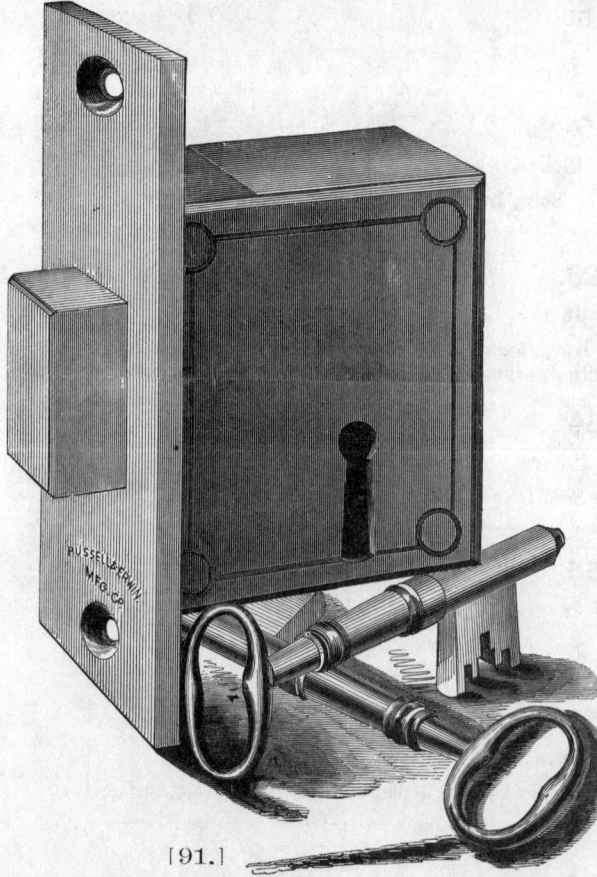

[91.]

No. 90.
Size $2\frac{1}{2} \times 3\frac{3}{4}$ Inches.
Brass Front and Bolt, 2 Brass Keys, 4 Wrought
Iron Tumblers, Heavy, for Store Doors

No. 90½.
Size $2\frac{1}{2} \times 3\frac{3}{4}$ Inches.
Rabbeted, Brass Front and Bolt, 2 Brass Keys,
4 Wrought Iron Tumblers, Heavy, for Store
Doors

No. 91.
Size $3\frac{5}{8} \times 3\frac{3}{8}$ Inches.
Brass Front and Bolt, 2 Brass Keys, 5 Wrought
Iron Tumblers, Variety of Keys for Heavy
Store Doors.   (See Plate.)

No. 91½.
Size $3\frac{5}{8} \times 3\frac{3}{8}$ Inches.
Rabbeted, Brass Front and Bolt, 2 Brass Keys,
5 Wrought Iron Tumblers, Variety of Keys
for Heavy Store Doors

No. 92.
Size $2\frac{3}{4} \times 2\frac{1}{4}$ Inches.
Brass Front and Bolt, 1 Brass Key, 3 Wrought
Iron Tumblers, for Narrow Stile Doors

MORTISE CUPBOARD LOCKS AND LATCHES.

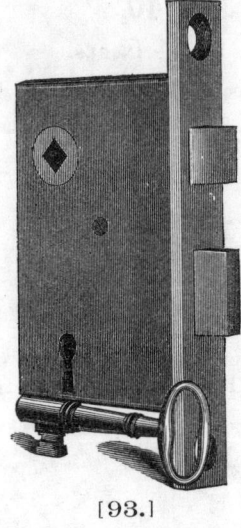

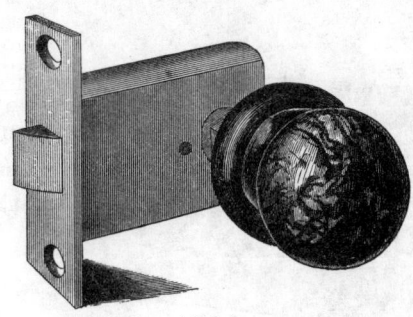

[93.]   [96.]

Per Doz.

No. 93.

SIZE 1¾ × 2¾ INCHES.

Mortise *Lock*, Plain Lacquered Iron Front and Bolts, Round Edge, Japanned Case, Brass Key, with Mineral Cupboard *Knobs* No. 500, Japanned Mountings complete. (See Plate.) Style of Knob same as represented with Latch No. 96_____
　　With Porcelain Cupboard Knobs No. 300, Japanned Mountings complete_____
　　With Porcelain Cupboard Knobs No. 100, Plated Mountings complete_____

No. 94.

SIZE 1¾ × 2¾ INCHES.

Mortise *Lock*, Rabbeted, Lacquered Iron Front and Bolts, Round Edge, Japanned Case, Brass Key, with Mineral Cupboard Knobs No. 500, Japanned Mountings complete_____
　　With Porcelain Cupboard Knobs No. 300, Japanned Mountings complete_____
　　With Porcelain Cupboard Knobs No. 100, Plated Mountings complete_____

No. 96.

SIZE 1⅛ × 1⅞ INCHES.

Mortise Latch, Plain Lacquered Iron Front and Bolt, with Mineral Cupboard Knobs No. 500, Japanned Mountings complete. (See Plate.)
　　With Porcelain Cupboard Knobs No. 300, Japanned Mountings complete_____
　　With Porcelain Cupboard Knobs No. 100, Plated Mountings complete_____

No. 96½.

SIZE 1¾ × 1⅞ INCHES.

Mortise Latch, Rabbeted, Lacquered Iron Front and Bolts, with Mineral Cupboard Knobs No. 500, Japanned Mountings complete_____
　　With Porcelain Cupboard Knobs No. 300, Japanned Mountings complete_____
　　With Porcelain Cupboard Knobs No. 100, Plated Mountings complete_____

No. 80.

SIZE 1¾ × 1¾ INCHES.

Mortise Cupboard or Drawer Lock, Lacquered Iron Front and Bolt, Brass Key_____

No. 81.

SIZE 1¾ × 1¾ INCHES.

Mortise Cupboard or Drawer Lock, Lacquered Brass Front, Bolt and Key_____

MORTISE KNOB LATCHES.

[40.]

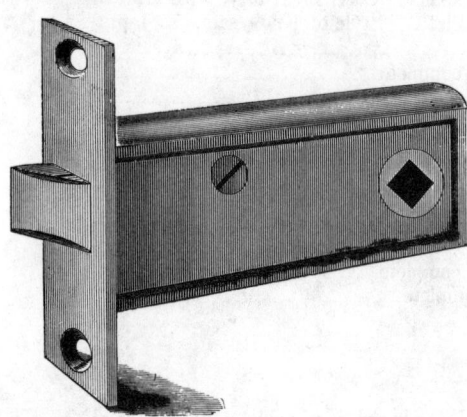

[22.]

[43.]

[44½.]

	Without Knobs.
	PER DOZ.

No. 40.

SIZE 1¼ × 3¼ INCHES.

Round Edge, Lacquered Iron Front and Strike, Japanned Case, Iron Hub and Bolt, for *Inside* Doors. (See Plate.)----------------------------

No. 22.

SIZE 1⅞ × 3½ INCHES.

Round Edge, Lacquered Iron Front and Strike, Japanned Case, Iron Hub, Iron Bolt, ⅜ inch thick, for thin Doors.   (See Plate.)------ -------------

No. 41.

SIZE 1¼ × 3¼ INCHES.

Round Edge, Lacquered Iron Front and Strike, Japanned Case, Brass Bolt, Iron Hub, for *Inside* Doors.

No. 42.

SIZE 1¼ × 3¼ INCHES.

Round Edge, Lacquered Brass Front and Strike, Japanned Case, Iron Hub and Bolt------------- -----------

No. 42½.

SIZE 1¼ × 3¼ INCHES.

Round Edge, Lacquered Brass Front, Strike and Bolt, Iron Hub, Japanned Case --- ----------------------

No. 43.

SIZE 1½ × 3½ INCHES.

Villa, Round Edge, Lacquered Iron Front, Iron Strike, Hub and Bolt, Japanned Case. (See Plate.)----

No. 44.

SIZE 1½ × 3½ INCHES.

Villa, Round Edge, Lacquered Brass Front and Strike, Japanned Case, Iron Hub, Brass Bolt----------

No. 44½.

SIZE 2 × 3¾ INCHES.

Villa, Round Edge, Lacquered Brass Front and Strike, Japanned Case, Iron Hub, Brass Bolt, EXTRA FINISH.   (See Plate.)----------------------

MORTISE KNOB LATCHES.

(Continued.)

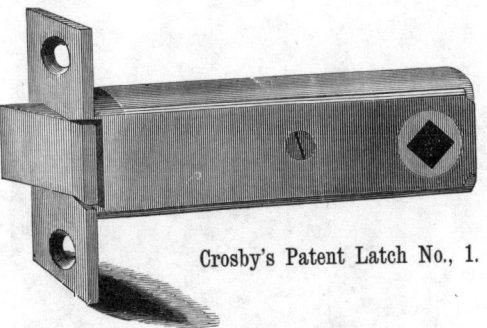

Crosby's Patent Latch No., 1.

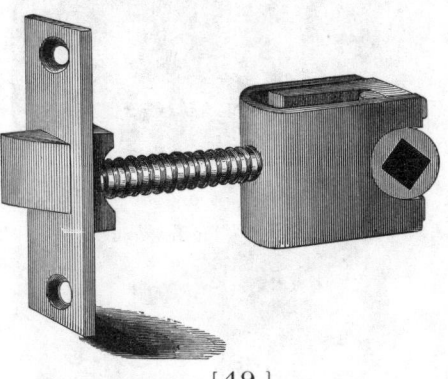

[49.]

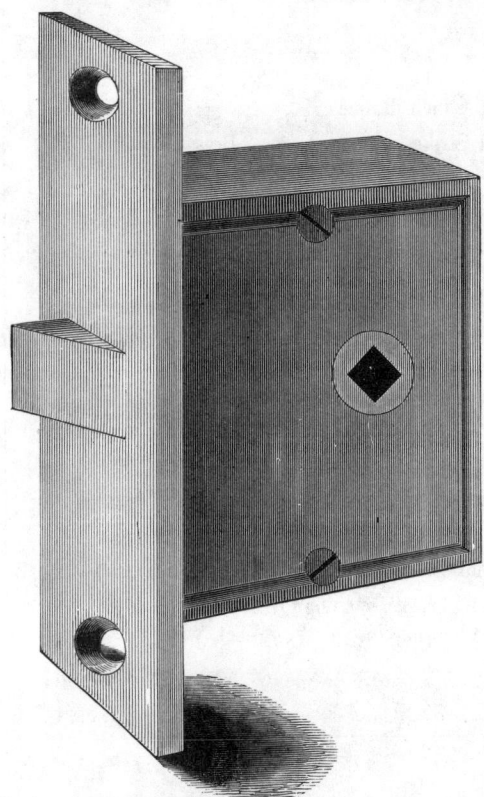

[46.]

	Without Knobs.
	PER DOZ.

No. 1.

SIZE 1 × 3½ INCHES.

Crosby's Patent, Eccentric, Lacquered Iron Front and Strike, Iron Bolt. (See Plate.)............

No. 2.

SIZE 1 × 3½ INCHES.

Crosby's Patent, Eccentric, Lacquered Iron Front and Strike, Brass Bolt.........................

No. 3.

SIZE 1 × 3½ INCHES.

Crosby's Patent, Eccentric, Lacquered Iron Front and Strike, Easy Spring, Iron Bolt.............

No. 4.

SIZE 1 × 3½ INCHES.

Crosby's Patent, Eccentric, Lacquered Iron Front and Strike, Easy Spring, Brass Bolt...........

No. 48.

SIZE 1¼ × 3¾ INCHES.

Wrought Iron Half-Cased, Brass Front, Strike, Hub and Bolt, for Inside Doors, like the Latch to Lock No. 20. (See Plate, page 44.)............

No. 49.

SIZE 1¼ × 3¼ INCHES.

Wrought Iron Quarter-Cased, Iron Front, Strike, Hub, and Bolt, for Inside Doors. (See Plate.)...........

No. 45.

SIZE 2¼ × 4 INCHES.

Square Edge, Brass Front and Strike, Japanned Case, Brass Hub and Bolt, Heavy, for Store Doors, to match No. 90 Mortise Dead Lock. Page 46............

No. 46.

SIZE 3½ × 3¼ INCHES.

Square Edge, Brass Front and Strike, Japanned Case, Brass Hub and Bolt, Heavy, for Store Doors, to match No. 91 Mortise Dead Lock. Page 46. (See Plate.)....

No. 46½.

SIZE 3½ × 3¼ INCHES.

Square Edge, Rabbeted, Brass Front and Strike, Japanned Case, Brass Hub, Guarded Brass Bolt, ⅝ inch Rabbet, Heavy, for Store Doors, to match No. 91½ Mortise Dead Lock. Page 46..........

No. 47.

SIZE 2½ × 2¼ INCHES.

Square Edge, Brass Front and Strike, Japanned Case, Brass Hub and Bolt, Heavy, for Store Doors, to match No. 92 Mortise Dead Lock. Page 46.................

No. 47½.

SIZE 3 × 2⅞ INCHES.

Square Edge, Brass Front and Strike, Japanned Case, Brass Lever Bolt, Heavy, for Store Doors, used with Oblique Store Door Handles. (See Index for Handles.)

MORTISE KNOB LATCHES.

(Continued.)

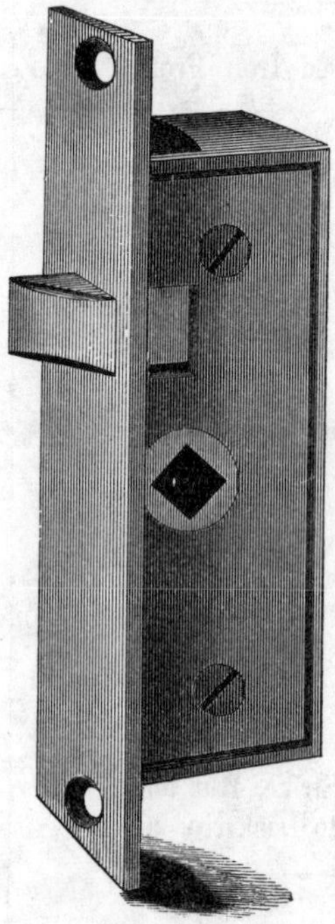

[50.]

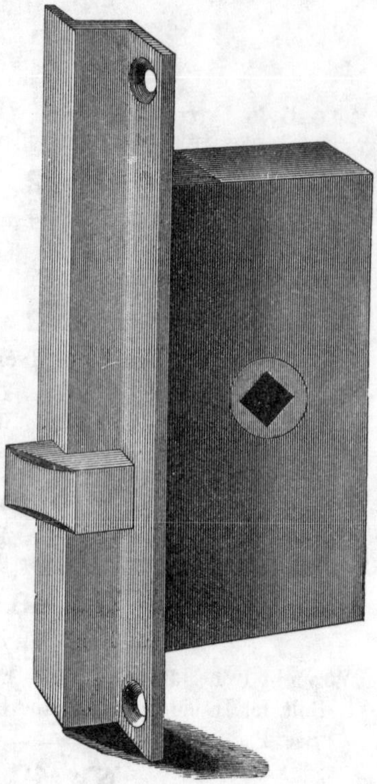

[52.]

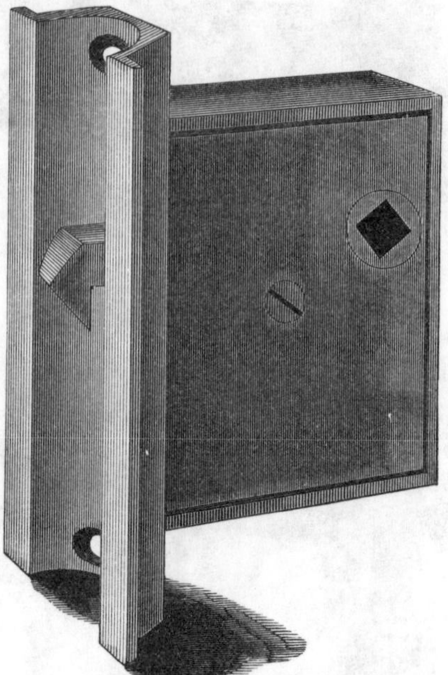

[38½.]

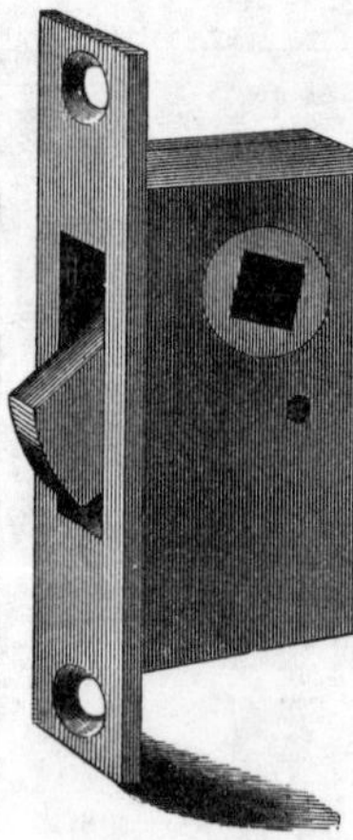

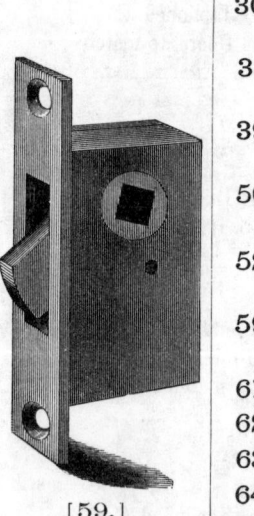

[59.]

No.	Size.		Without Knobs. PER DOZ.
30	$2\frac{1}{4} \times 3$	Rabbeted, Brass Front and Strike, Japanned Case, Brass Bolt and Hub, for Folding Doors, ½ inch Rabbet	
38½	$3\frac{1}{4} \times 3$	Astragal, Brass Front and Strike, Japanned Case, Brass Bolt and Hub, for Sliding Doors. (See Plate.)	
39	$3\frac{1}{4} \times 1\frac{7}{8}$	Plain Brass Front and Strike, Japanned Case, Brass Bolt and Hub, for Sliding Doors	
50	$3\frac{3}{4} \times 1\frac{3}{8}$	Plain Front, for *French Windows* or *Narrow Stile Inside Sash Doors*, Brass Front, Strike, Hub and Bolt. (See Plate.)	
52	$3\frac{3}{4} \times 1\frac{3}{8}$	Rabbeted Front, for French Windows or Inside Sash Doors, ½ inch Rabbet, Brass Front, Strike, Hub and Bolt	
59	$2\frac{1}{8} \times 1\frac{3}{8}$	Turnbuckle, for French Windows, Brass Face, Iron Bolt. (See Plate.)	
61	$2\frac{1}{4} \times 1\frac{7}{8}$	Astragal Front, for Sliding Shutters or Sashes, Brass Face and Bolt	
62	$2\frac{1}{4} \times 1\frac{5}{8}$	Plain Front, for Sliding Shutters or Sashes, Brass Face and Bolt	
63	$1\frac{1}{2} \times 1\frac{3}{4}$	Astragal Front, for Sliding Shutters or Sashes, all Brass, Brass Key	
64	$1\frac{1}{2} \times 1\frac{3}{8}$	Plain Front, for Sliding Shutters or Sashes, all Brass, Brass Key	
67		Espagniolette, Bar or Bolt, a perfect fastening for French Windows, drawing the sash top and bottom close to the rabbet, with	
		Brass Handles	each,
		Bronzed Handles	"
		Electro-Plated Handles	"

REFRIGERATOR
LOCKS, LATCHES, KNOBS AND REGISTERS.

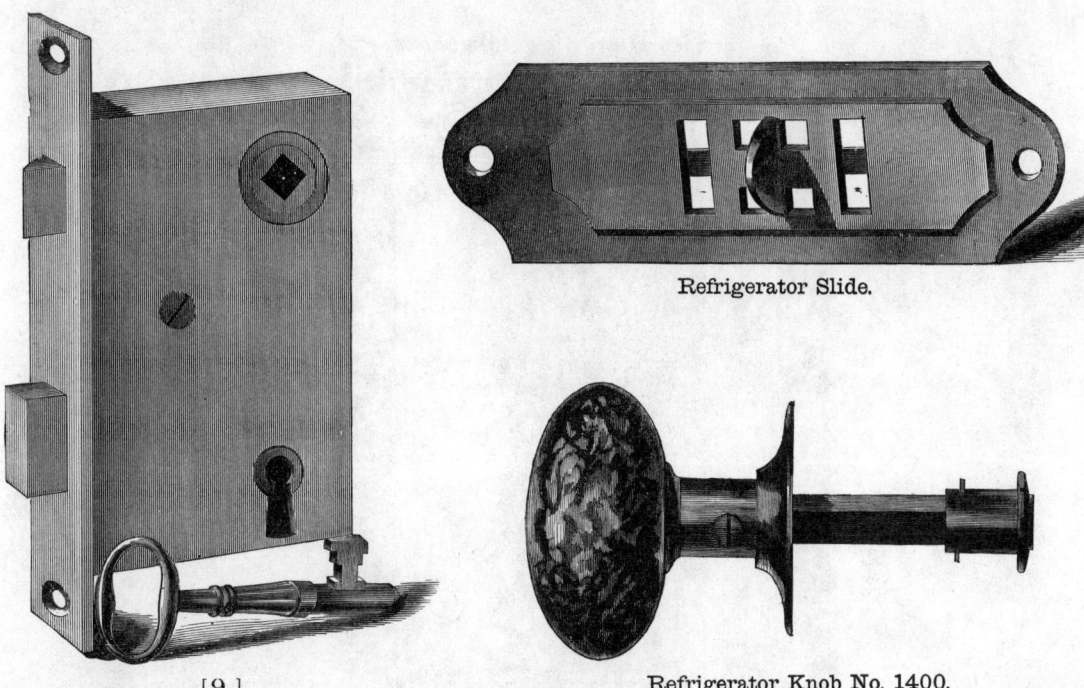

Refrigerator Slide.

[9.]

Refrigerator Knob No. 1400.

No. 9.

SIZE 3½ × 2½ INCHES.

Refrigerator, Mortise Lock, Lacquered Iron Front, Brass Bolts, Japanned Case, Brass Key. (See Plate.)
  Without Knobs
  With No. 1400 Mineral Refrigerator Knobs, Japanned Mountings
  "   No. 1300 Porcelain Refrigerator Knobs, Japanned Mountings

No. 96.

SIZE 1⅛ × 1⅞ INCHES.

Refrigerator, Mortise Latch, Lacquered Iron Front and Bolt.   (See Plate, page 47.)
  With Mineral Cupboard Knobs No. 500, Japanned Mountings
  "   Porcelain Cupboard Knobs No. 300, Japanned Mountings
  "   Porcelain Cupboard Knobs No. 100, Plated Mountings

No. 96½.

SIZE 1¾ × 1⅞ INCHES.

Refrigerator, Mortise Latch, Rabbeted, Lacquered Iron Front and Bolt
  With Mineral Cupboard Knobs No. 500, Japanned Mountings
  "   Porcelain Cupboard Knobs No. 300, Japanned Mountings
  "   Porcelain Cupboard Knobs No. 100, Plated Mountings

No. 80.

SIZE 1¾ × 1¾ INCHES.

Refrigerator, Mortise Dead Lock, Lacquered Iron Front and Bolt, Brass Key

No. 81.

SIZE 1¾ × 1¾ INCHES.

Refrigerator, Mortise Dead Lock, Lacquered Brass Front and Bolt, Brass Key
Refrigerator Knobs No. 1400, Mineral, Japanned Mountings. (See Plate.)
Refrigerator Knobs No. 1300, Porcelain, Japanned Mountings
Refrigerator Register No. 1, 5-inch, Japanned. (See Plate.)
Refrigerator Register No. 2, 7-inch, Japanned

Per Doz.

LOCKS FOR SHIP USE, ALL BRASS.

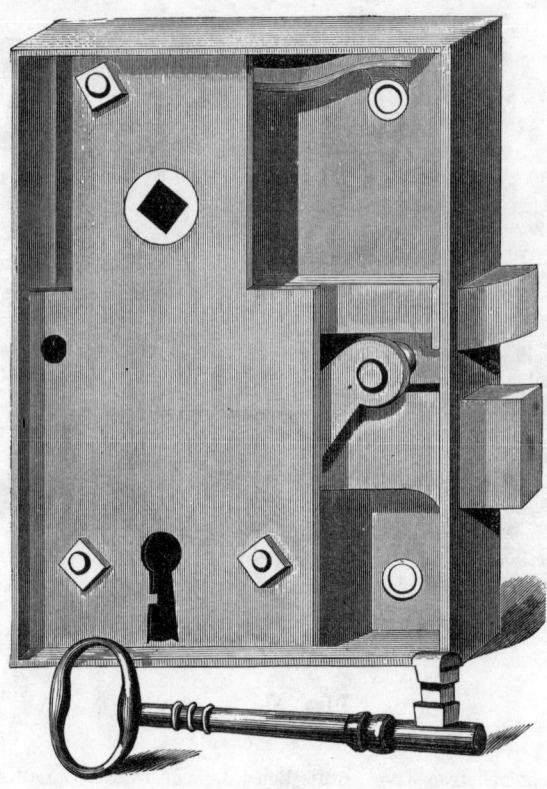

[589.]

No.	Size.		Per Doz.
1	$3\frac{1}{2} \times 3\frac{1}{4}$	Mortise 2 Bolt Lock	
2	$3\frac{3}{4} \times 3\frac{3}{8}$	Mortise 2 Bolt Lock	
$2\frac{1}{2}$	4×3	Mortise 2 Bolt Lock	
13	$4\frac{1}{2} \times 3\frac{1}{2}$	Mortise 2 Bolt Lock, Villa	
$25\frac{1}{2}$	$4\frac{1}{4} \times 3\frac{3}{8}$	Mortise 2 Bolt Lock, Rabbeted Front	
35	$5\frac{1}{4} \times 3\frac{3}{8}$	Mortise 2 Bolt Lock, Astragal Front for Sliding Doors	
70	$3\frac{1}{4} \times 2\frac{3}{4}$	Mortise, Dead Lock, Plain Front, for Sliding Cabin Doors	
530	$5 \times 3\frac{3}{4}$	Rural, Rim Lock and Latch, 2 Bolts	
589	$5 \times 3\frac{1}{2}$	Upright, Rim Lock and Latch, 2 Bolts, "New York City Pattern." (See Plate.)	
590	$5 \times 3\frac{1}{2}$	Upright, Rim Lock and Latch, 2 Bolts	
613	$5 \times 3\frac{3}{8}$	Rural, Rim Closet or Dead Lock, 1 Bolt	
663	3×3	Flush Night Latch, 2 Keys each, for Sliding Doors	

LOCKS FOR SHIP USE, ALL BRASS.

The following named Locks are not usually kept in Stock, but Made to order.

No.	Size.		Per Doz.
3	$4\frac{1}{4} \times 3\frac{1}{2}$	Mortise, 2 Bolt Lock	
$3\frac{1}{2}$	$5 \times 3\frac{1}{2}$	Mortise, 2 Bolt Lock, Lever	
17	$5\frac{1}{4} \times 3\frac{3}{8}$	Mortise, 2 Bolt Lock, "Carpenters" Pattern	
25	$5\frac{1}{4} \times 3\frac{3}{8}$	Mortise, 2 Bolt Lock, Rabbeted Front, for Folding Doors	
26	$3\frac{1}{2} \times 3$	Mortise, 2 Bolt Lock, Rabbeted Front	
36	$4\frac{5}{8} \times 3\frac{1}{4}$	Mortise, 2 Bolt Lock, Plain Front, for Sliding Doors	
38	$3\frac{1}{4} \times 2\frac{1}{8}$	Mortise, Latch, Astragal Front, for Sliding Doors	
40	$1\frac{3}{8} \times 3\frac{1}{4}$	Mortise, Latch	
74	$1\frac{1}{4} \times 2\frac{3}{4}$	Mortise, Closet or Dead Lock	
551	$3\frac{3}{4} \times 2\frac{1}{2}$	Rural, Rim Latch	
552	$3\frac{3}{4} \times 2\frac{1}{2}$	Rural, Rim Latch, with Slide Bolt	
553	$3\frac{3}{4} \times 2\frac{1}{2}$	Rural, Rim Latch, with Stop Knob	
555	$4 \times 3\frac{1}{2}$	Square Case, Rim Latch	
556	$4 \times 3\frac{1}{2}$	Square Case, Rim Latch, with Slide Bolt	
611	$3\frac{3}{4} \times 2\frac{1}{2}$	Rural, Rim Closet or Dead Lock	
612	4×3	Rural, Rim Closet or Dead Lock	
614	$6 \times 3\frac{5}{8}$	Rural, Rim Closet or Dead Lock	
640	$3\frac{3}{4} \times 2\frac{3}{4}$	Square Case, Rim Closet or Dead Locks	
650	$3 \times 2\frac{1}{4}$	Right or Left, Rim Cupboard Lock	
652	$3\frac{1}{2} \times 2\frac{1}{8}$	Right or Left, Straight Cupboard Lock	
654	$3\frac{1}{2} \times 2\frac{1}{8}$	Right or Left, Straight Cupboard Lock, 3 Tumblers	
660	4×3	Rim Night Latch, 2 Keys, Square Case	
661	$3\frac{3}{4} \times 2\frac{1}{2}$	Rim Night Latch, 2 Keys, Rural	

Any description of Knobs, Handles and Escutcheons, furnished with all Brass Locks. (See Index for Knobs, Handles and Escutcheons.)

Locks with Reversed Bevel Latches made to order; also, all Brass Sliding Door Sheaves, $1\frac{3}{4}$, $2\frac{1}{4}$, 3, 4, 5, 6 inch. (See page No. 62.)

Composition Hinges, Hasps, &c.

Composition Hooks, Rings and Staples.

Ship Side Lights, various sizes.

Ship Butt Hinges, various sizes.

NEW PATENT IMPROVED
COMBINATION REVOLVING TUMBLER LOCKS,
FOR STORE DOORS, SAFES, VAULTS, PRISONS, &c. &c.
Burglar and Powder Proof.

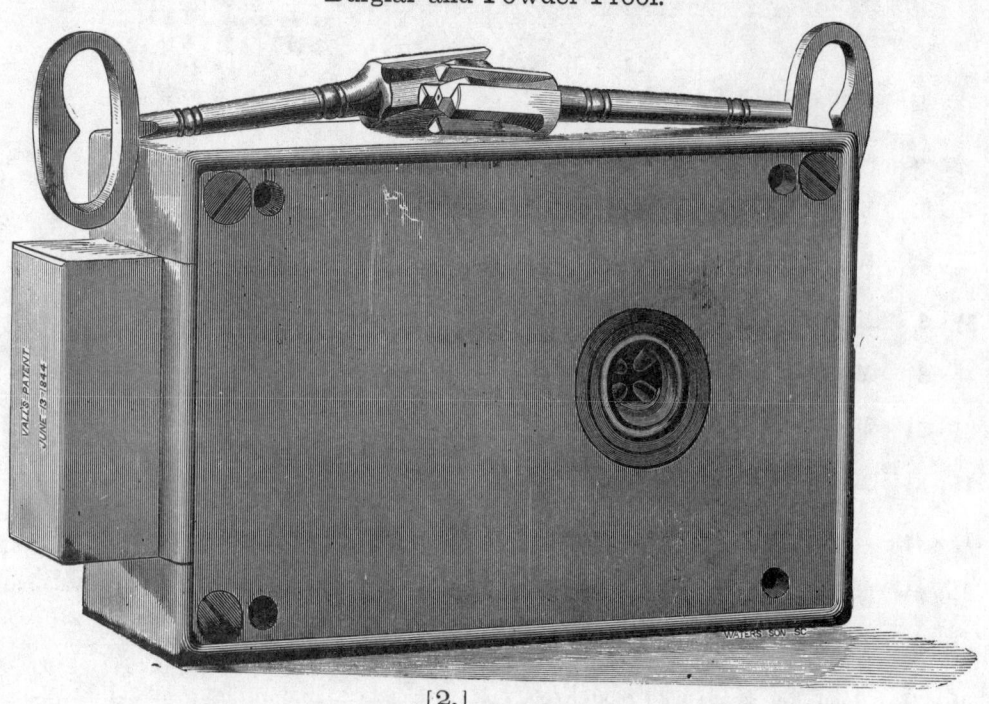

[2.]

No.	Size.	RIGHT OR LEFT HAND.	Each.
1	5 × 7	Horizontal, 2 Steel Keys to each..	
2	4 × 6	Horizontal, 2 Steel Keys to each. (See Plate.)...................	
3	4 × 4	Horizontal, 2 Steel Keys to each..	

BOX STAPLES OR STRIKES,
FOR RIM LOCKS.

Per Doz.

For Locks No. 551 to 554, 557, 558, 610, 611, 629 to 632, 659, 661, 672...................

For Locks No. 210 to 214, 501 to 514, 538, 547 to 549, 555, 556, 560, 561, 574, 575, 594, 595, 612, 613, 660.........

For Locks No. 456, 457, 461, 515, 516, 518, 519, 530, 550, 570, 571, 580, 581, 585 to 587, 614, 615, 620 to 623, 664.

For Locks No. 200, 220, 421 to 423, 440, 443, 450 to 455, 517, 520, 531, 532, 535, 537, 539, 540, 543 to 546, 562 to 565, 572, 573, 582, 588, 590, 591, 624 to 627..............

For Locks No. 201 to 203, 221 to 224, 400, 401, 404, 407, 420, 430 to 435, 460, 521, 522...................

For Locks No. 204, 405, 406, 408, 409, 441, 442, 444, 445, 525, 526, 666...................

FOR MORTISE LOCKS.

For Locks Nos. 22, 40, 41, 43, 49, 74, and for Crosby's Bolts...................

For Locks Nos. 0, 0¼, 0½, 0¾, 9, 23, 72, 73...................

For Locks Nos. 42, 42½, 44, 59...................

For Locks Nos. 39, 83, 84, 99...................

For Locks Nos. 1, 1¼, 1½, 1¾, 2, 2½, 4, 5, 12, 13, 13½, 14, 18½, 44½, 45, 47, 47½, 48, 54, 55, 56, 78, 79, 92, 701, 701½.........

For Locks Nos. 6, 7, 8, 15, 18, 19, 20, 21, 26, 30, 36, 38½, 46, 50, 52, 57, 90...................

For Locks Nos. 25, 25¼, 25½, 25¾, 27, 140, 141, 142...................

For Locks Nos. 90½, 91, 100, 173...................

For Locks Nos. 34, 35, 46½, 101, 121, 122, 125, 160, 161, 162, 174...................

For Locks Nos. 91½, 175...................

For Locks Nos. 130, 131, 132, 135...................

BRASS DOOR KEYS.

(For Classification List see page 59.)

Any Key in one Class will answer for all the Numbers of Locks in the same Class. In ordering Keys, give the number and quantity of each Class required.

☞ Keys furnished to order with Fancy Bows, either Metropolitan Pattern (see Plate below) or such styles as may be desired.

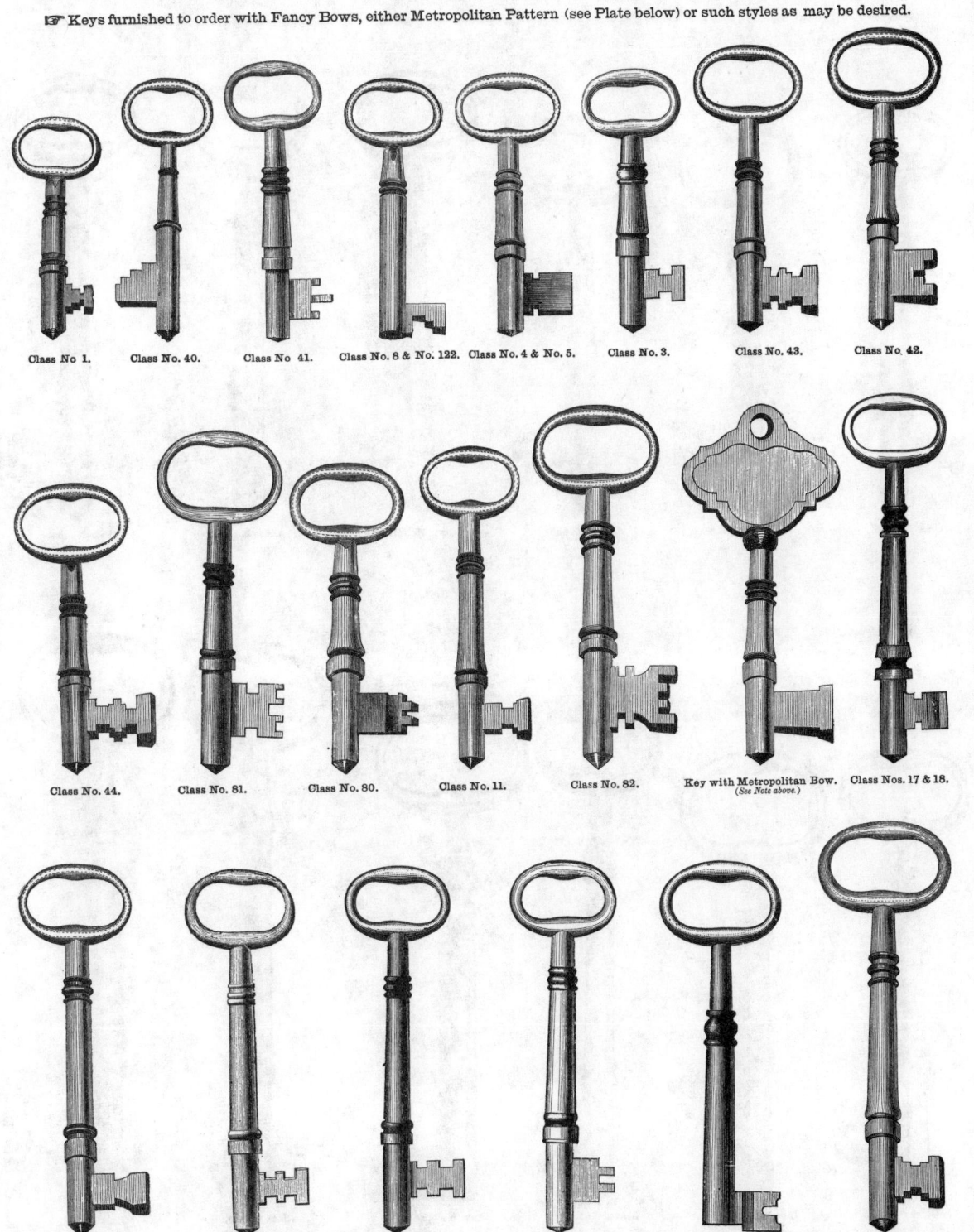

Class No 1. Class No. 40. Class No 41. Class No. 8 & No. 122. Class No. 4 & No. 5. Class No. 3. Class No. 43. Class No. 42.

Class No. 44. Class No. 81. Class No. 80. Class No. 11. Class No. 82. Key with Metropolitan Bow. *(See Note above.)* Class Nos. 17 & 18.

Class No. 16. Class No. 13 & No. 14. Class No. 20. Class No. 25 & No. 47. Class No. 90. Class No. 21.

BRASS DOOR KEYS.

(Continued.)

[*For Classification List see page 59.*]

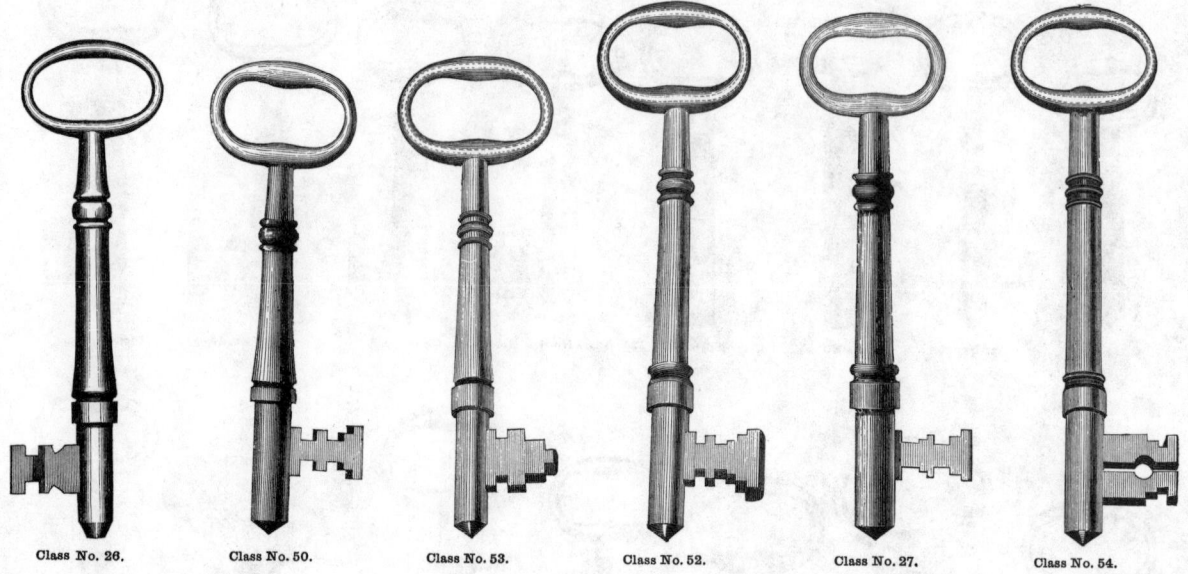

Class No. 26.　　Class No. 50.　　Class No. 53.　　Class No. 52.　　Class No. 27.　　Class No. 54.

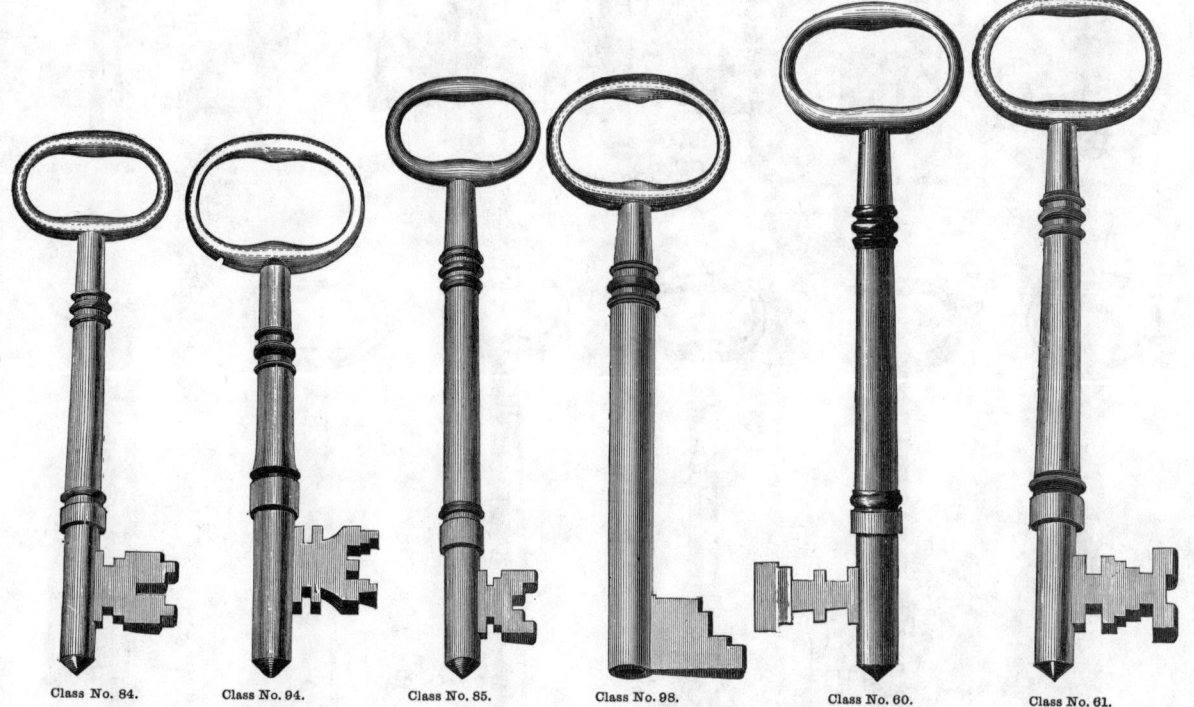

Class No. 84.　　Class No. 94.　　Class No. 85.　　Class No. 98.　　Class No. 60.　　Class No. 61.

BRASS DOOR KEYS.

(Continued.)

[*For Classification List see Page 59.*]

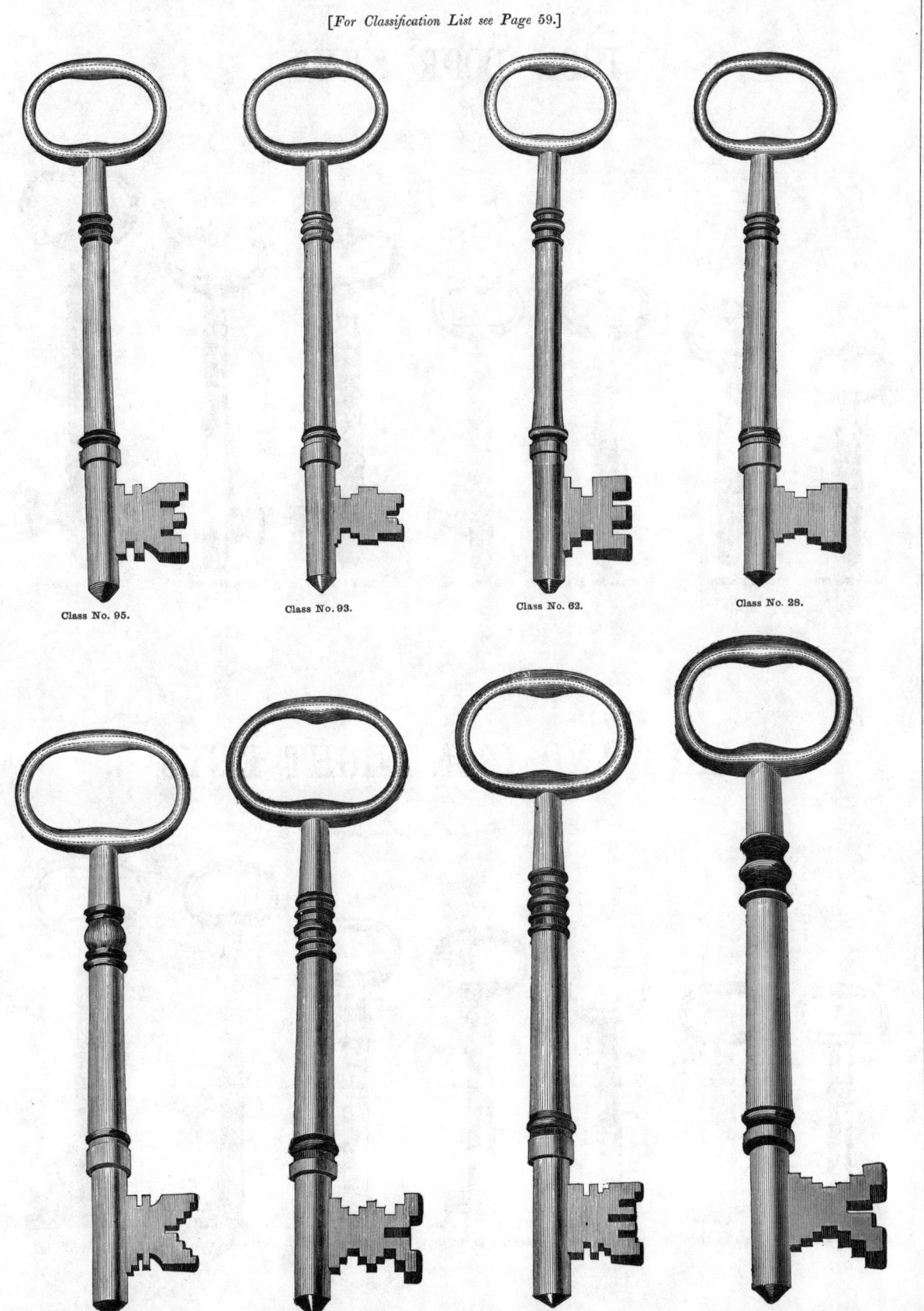

Class No. 95.   Class No. 93.   Class No. 62.   Class No. 28.

Class No. 101.   Class No. 67.   Class No. 103.   Class No. 68.

IRON DOOR KEYS.

(For Classification List see opposite Page.)

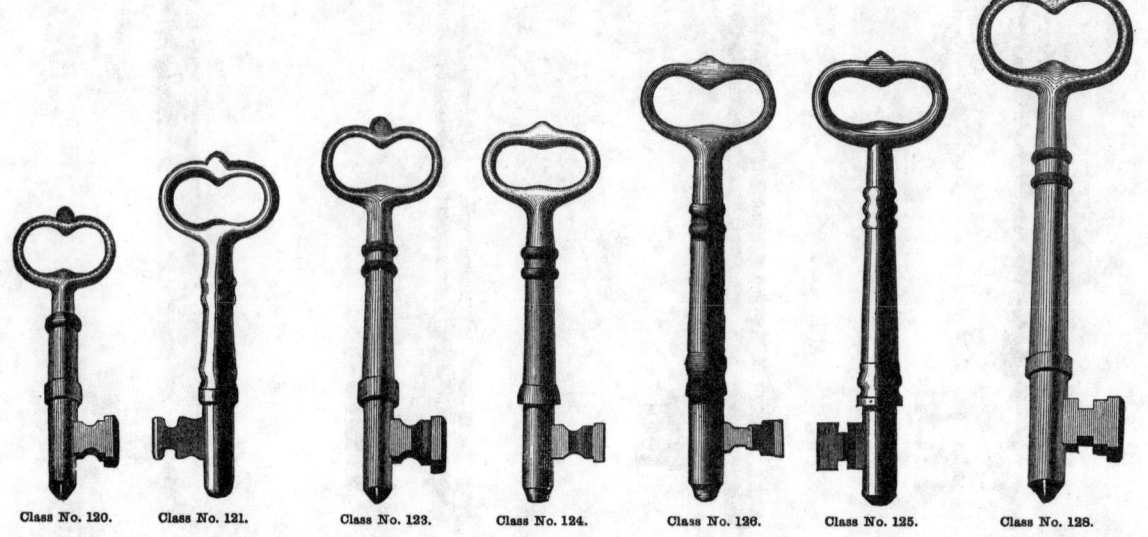

Class No. 120.   Class No. 121.   Class No. 123.   Class No. 124.   Class No. 126.   Class No. 125.   Class No. 128.

BRASS AND IRON NIGHT KEYS.

(For Classification List see opposite Page.)

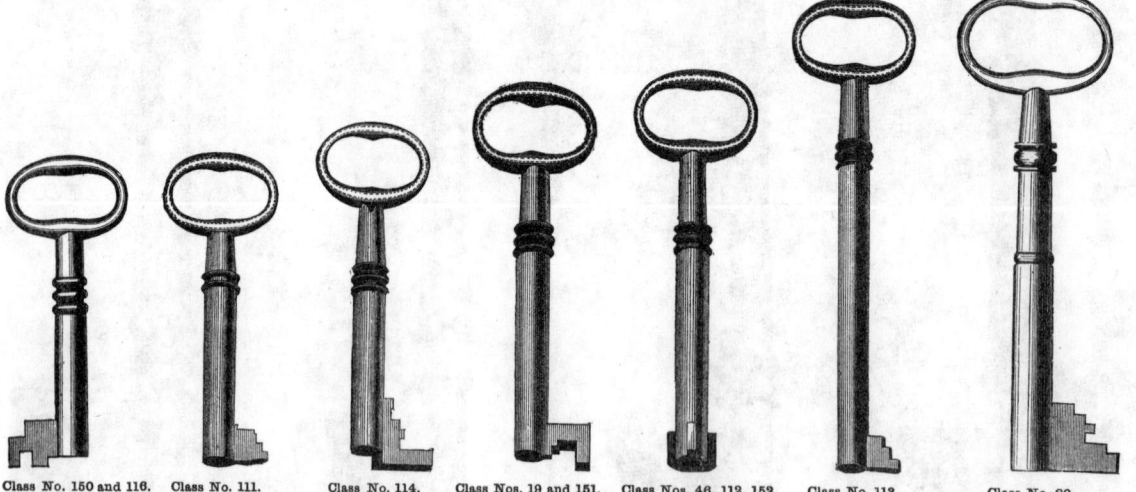

Class No. 150 and 116.   Class No. 111.   Class No. 114.   Class Nos. 19 and 151.   Class Nos. 46, 112, 152.   Class No. 113.   Class No. 89.

BRASS DOOR KEYS.

Any Key in one Class will answer for all the Numbers of Locks in the same Class. In ordering Keys, give the Number and quantity of each Class required.

(For Plates, see pages 55, 56, 57, 58.)

Class No.		Per Dozen.
0	For Locks Nos. 9	
1	For Locks Nos. 54, 80, 81, 93	
2	For. Locks Nos. 84	
3	For Locks Nos. 4, 8, 18½, 26, 27, 55, 56, 57, 58, 701, 701½	
4	For Locks Nos. 0¼, 0¾, 31	
5	For Locks Nos. 1, 1¼, 1½, 1¾, 2, 2½, 12, 73	
6	For Locks Nos. 13	
7	For Locks Nos. 23	
8	For Locks Nos. 653	
9	For Locks Nos. 605, 611, 651	
10	For Locks Nos. 538	
11	For Locks Nos. 554, 607, 608, 630, 631	
12	For Locks Nos. 611½	
13	For Locks Nos. 543, 563, 612, 901, 902	
14	For Locks Nos. 564	
15	For Locks Nos. 613, 614, 632	
16	For Locks Nos. 530½, 560, 561, 565	
17	For Locks Nos. 212, 214, 505, 507, 508, 509, 511, 512, 512½, 513, 514	
18	For Locks Nos. 530	
19	For Locks Nos. 661, 200 Night	
20	For Locks Nos. 574, 575, 594, 595	
21	For Locks Nos. 518, 519, 520, 535, 615	
22	For Locks Nos.	
23	For Locks Nos.	
24	For Locks Nos. 544½, 548¾	
25	For Locks Nos. 620, 621, 622, 623	
26	For Locks Nos. 570, 571	
27	For Locks Nos. 200, 220, 531, 532, 572, 591	
28	For Locks Nos. 422, 423, 539, 540	
40	For Locks Nos. 83	
41	For Locks Nos. 13½	
42	For Locks Nos. 18, 19, 20, 21, 77, 78, 79, 92	
43	For Locks Nos. 5, 7, 14, 25¼, 25½, 25¾, 34, 36	
44	For Locks Nos. 6, 15, 25, 35	
45	For Locks Nos. 654	
46	For Locks Nos. 659, 659½, 660	
47	For Locks Nos. 544, 545, 545½, 546, 546½, 548, 548½, 587	
48	For Locks Nos. 588	
49	For Locks Nos. 589	

Class No.		Per Dozen.
50	For Locks Nos. 580, 16, 16½	
51	For Locks Nos. 581	
52	For Locks Nos. 582	
53	For Locks Nos. 585, 586	
54	For Locks Nos. 525, 526	
55	For Locks Nos. 671, 672	
56	For Locks Nos. 521, 522	
60	For Locks Nos. 404, 573	
61	For Locks Nos. 407	
62	For Locks Nos. 450	
63	For Locks Nos. 451	
64	For Locks Nos. 452	
65	For Locks Nos. 405, 412	
66	For Locks Nos. 406, 413	
67	For Locks Nos. 408, 414	
68	For Locks Nos. 409, 415	
80	For Locks Nos. 100, 173	
81	For Locks Nos. 90, 90½	
82	For Locks Nos. 101, 121, 122, 130, 131, 132, 174, 175,	
83	For Locks Nos. 436, 437	
84	For Locks Nos. 624, 625	
85	For Locks Nos. 421	
86	For Locks Nos. 456	
87	For Locks Nos. 457	
88	For Locks Nos. 125, 135	
89	For Locks Nos. 666, 666½	
90	For Locks Nos. 479	
91	For Locks Nos. 626, 626½, 627, 627½	
92	For Locks Nos. 201, 222, 223, 592	
93	For Locks Nos. 202, 203, 204, 224, 225, 402	
94	For Locks Nos. 91, 91½	
95	For Locks Nos. 420, 434	
96	For Locks Nos. 435	
97	For Locks Nos. 435½	
98	For Locks Nos. 453	
99	For Locks Nos. 454	
100	For Locks Nos. 455	
101	For Locks Nos. 400, 430	
10 2	For Locks Nos. 432	
103	For Locks Nos. 401, 431	

BRASS NIGHT OR PASS KEYS.

(See Plates, opposite page.)

Class No.		Per Dozen.
110	For Locks Nos. 101, 130, 140, 160	
111	For Locks Nos. 121, 131, 141, 161	
112	For Locks Nos. 201, 202	
113	For Locks Nos. 203, 664, 664½	
114	For Locks Nos. 122, 125, 132, 135, 142, 162	
115	For Locks Nos. 204	
116	For Locks Nos. 100	

IRON KEYS.

(See Plates, opposite page.)

Class No.		Per Dozen.
120	For Locks Nos. 74	
121	For Locks Nos. 0, 0¼, 72	
122	For Locks Nos. 652	
123	For Locks Nos. 604, 606, 609, 610, 629, 630½, 650	
124	For Locks Nos.	
125	For Locks Nos. 501, 503, 504, 504½	
126	For Locks Nos. 562, 612½, 900	
127	For Locks Nos. 613½, 614½	
128	For Locks Nos. 515, 516, 517, 537, 537½	
135	(Coppered) Malleable Iron, for Locks No. 210	
140	Malleable Iron Night, for Locks No. 670	
150	Malleable Iron Night, for Locks No. 100	
151	Malleable Iron Night, for Locks Nos. 200, 661	
152	Malleable Iron Night, for Locks Nos. 659, 659½	

SLIDING DOOR TRIMMINGS.

(For Description of Plates see page 62.)

Door Sheave, 3 inch.

Boston Pattern.

Sliding Shutter Sheave, 1⅜ inch.

Cups and T. Handles, for Sliding Doors.

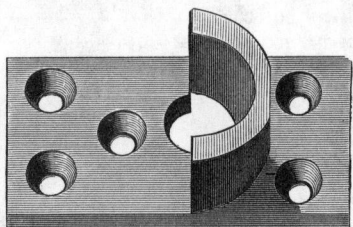

Sliding Door Stop.

Iron Sliding Door Rail.

SLIDING DOOR TRIMMINGS.

(Continued.)

[*For Description of Plates see Page 62.*]

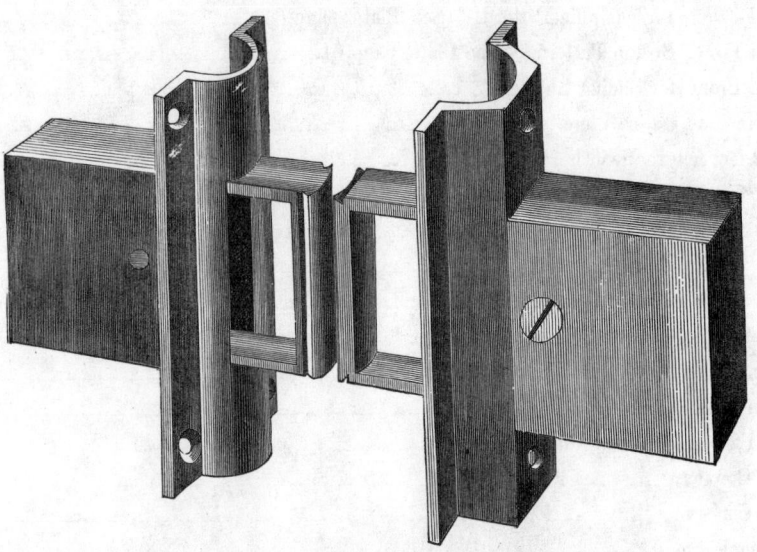

Flush Pulls, Philadelphia Pattern.

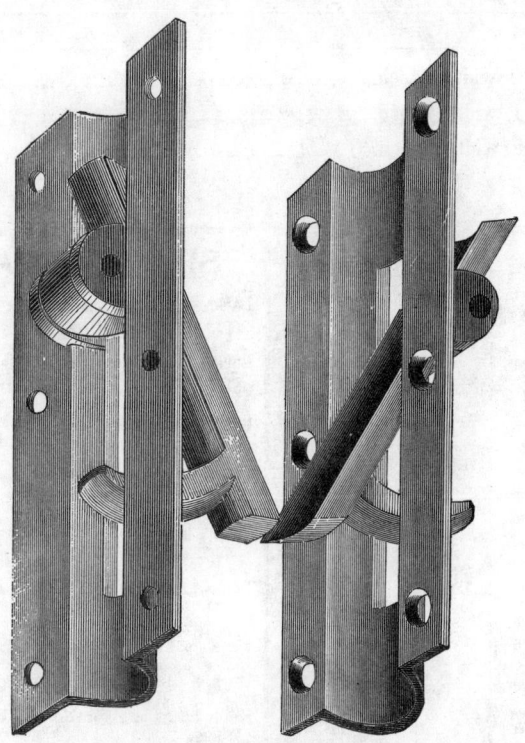

Flush Pulls, Boston Pattern.

SLIDING DOOR TRIMMINGS.

Set

No. 1 consists of 1 Lock each, Nos. 35 and 37, without Furniture, 6 inch Brass Wheel Sheaves, 16 feet

  1¼ inch Cast Brass Rail, 10 feet Wrought Brass Astragal, Brass Stop, Iron Guide Plates and Bolts......per set,

No. 2, same as No. 1, with 4 inch Brass Wheel Sheaves..per set,

No. 3, same as No. 1, with 6 inch Iron Sheaves, and Iron Rail..per set,

No. 4, same as No. 1, with 4 inch Iron Sheaves, and Iron Rail...per set,

Flush Pulls, Astragal Front, Philadelphia Pattern. (See Plate, page 61.)....................................per pair,

Flush Pulls, Astragal Front, Boston Pattern. (See Plate, page 61.)...per pair,

Flush Pulls, Astragal Front, for Sliding Shutters...per dozen pair,

Flush Cups and T. Handles. (See Plate, page 60.)..per pair,

Cast Brass Rail, in 2 feet lengths, width 1 inch..cents per foot,

Cast Brass Rail, in 2 feet lengths, width 1¼ inch...cents per foot,

Cast Brass Rail, in 2 feet lengths, width 1½ inch...cents per foot,

Wrought Brass Rail, width 1 inch..cents per foot,

Wrought Brass Rail, width 1⅛ inch..cents per foot,

Wrought Brass Rail, width 1¼ inch..cents per foot,

Iron Rail, Painted, in 2 feet lengths, width 1¼ inch. (See Plate, page 60.).................................cents per foot,

Iron Rail, Painted, in 2 feet lengths, width 1½ inch...cents per foot,

Iron Rail, Painted, in 2 feet lengths, width 2½ inch...cents per foot,

Cast Brass Astragal, Convex..per foot,

Cast Brass Astragal, Concave...per foot,

Wrought Brass Astragal...per foot,

Wrought Brass Astragal, Bolts and Guide Plates...per set,

Cast Brass Stops. (See Plate, page 60.)...per doz.

Iron Stops..per doz.

Iron Bolts and Guide Plates...per set,

Cast Brass Rail, when soldered,...per foot extra,

Barn Door Rail, Japanned, No. 0, width ½ inch...per foot,

Barn Door Rail, Japanned, No. 1, width ⅝ inch...per foot,

Barn Door Rail, Japanned, No. 2, width ⅞ inch...per foot,

SHEAVES.

	Iron Case, Iron Wheel, with Iron Rivets.	Iron Case, Brass Wheel with Iron Rivets.	All Brass.
1¾ inch, for Sliding Shutters, or Sashes (see Plate, p. 60).per set,			
2¼ inch, for Sliding Shutters, or Sashes................per set,			
		With Brass Rivets.	
3 inch, for Sliding Doors (see Plate, page 60)..............per set,			
4 inch, for Sliding Doors....per set,			
5 inch, for Sliding Doors....per set,			
6 inch, for Sliding Doors....per set,			
3×⅝ inch, for Sliding Doors, Heavy ....per set,			
6×¾ inch, Axle, Extra Heavy, for Heavy Sliding Doors, face 1¾ inches wide...........per set,			
6×¾ inch, Axle, Extra Heavy, for Heavy Sliding Doors, face 2½ inches wide...........per set,			
2¼×½ inch, Boston Pattern, Heavy, for Trap Doors and Hatches (see Plate, page 60)........per set,			
2¾×⅝ inch, Boston Pattern, Heavy, for Trap Doors and Hatches.per set,			

SILVER PLATING.

	Electro Plated.	Hand Plated.
Locks, Front Door Mortise, as Nos. 100, 141, 142, 173, Front and Strike..............per dozen,		
Locks, Front Door Mortise, as Nos. 101, 121, 122, 125, 161, 162, Front and Strike.....per dozen,		
Locks, Rabbeted, Front Door Mortise, as Nos. 130, 131, 132, 135, 175, Front and Strike..per dozen,		
Locks, Plain Front, Inside Mortise, Front and Strike......................per dozen,		
Locks, Rabbeted Front, Inside Mortise, as Nos. 25, 52, Front and Strike..............per dozen,		
Locks, Astragal Front, as Nos. 34, 35, 37, Front and Strike........................per dozen,		
Keys, for Front Door Mortise Locks....per dozen,		
Keys, for Inside Mortise Locks........per dozen,		
Knob and Plate for No. 100 Front Door Mortise Locks.........................per dozen,		
Astragal, for Sliding Doors............per foot,		

SASH, SCREW, SIDE, UPRIGHT AND DUMB-WAITER PULLEYS.

Japanned Screw Pulley, 1¼ inch.

Brass Screw Pulley, 1¼ inch.

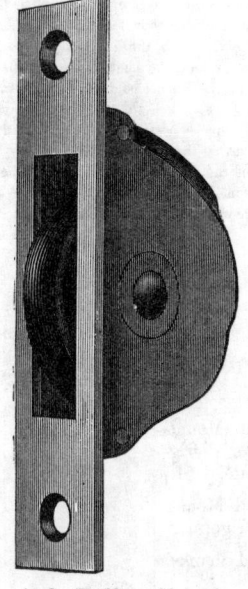

Axle Pulley, 1¾ inch.

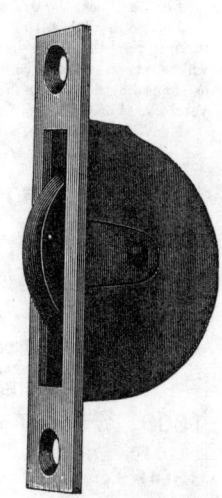

Frame Pulley, 1¾ in.

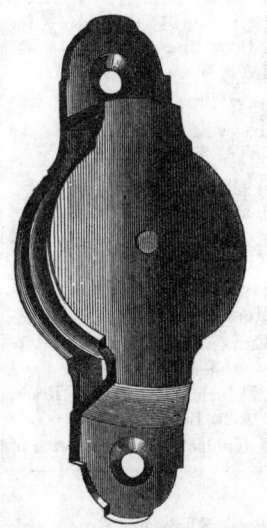

Japanned Side Pulley, 1¾ inch.

Japanned Upright Pulley, 1¾ inch.

Sham Axle, Sash or Frame, 1½ inch _____ per doz.
Sham Axle, Sash or Frame, 1¾ inch. (See
 Plate above.) _____ per doz.
Axle Sash, 1¾ inch. (See Plate above.)___per doz.
Axle Sash, 2 inch _____per doz.
Axle Sash, 1¾ inch, EXTRA strong and good, per doz.
Axle Sash, 2 inch, EXTRA strong and good, per doz.
Axle Sash, 2½ inch, EXTRA strong and good, per doz.
"Judd's Patent Axle, 2 inch, with de-
 tached wheels, for the convenience of
 entering the cords through to the
 weights _____per doz.
Dumb Waiter_____per set.

Brass, Screw. (See plate above.)
 $ per doz.
   ⅝ ¾ ⅞ 1 1¼ 1½ 1¾ 2 inch.
Brass, Screw, EXTRA heavy, for large cord,
  wheel ½ inch thick_____1¾ inch, per doz.
Japanned Screw. (See Plate above.)
 $ per doz.
   1½   1¾   2   2½   3 inch.
Japanned Side. (See Plate above.)
 $ per doz.
   1½   1¾   2   2½ inch.
Japanned, Upright. (See Plate above.)
      $ per doz.
      1¾   2 inch.

DOOR KNOBS.

All Mineral and Porcelain Rim Knobs are spindled to extend half an inch on each spindle, thus: 1½ to 2, 1¾ to 2¼, 2 to 2½, &c.

Mortise Knobs extend ¾ of an inch, thus: 1 to 1¾, 1¼ to 2, 1½ to 2¼, &c.

Silvered Glass Knobs extend 1 inch, and are spindled 1½ to 2½.

Brass and Plated Knobs extend 1 inch, and are spindled 1¼ to 2¼, 1½ to 2½.

Mineral and Porcelain Knobs on swivel spindles, extend, Mortise ¾, Rim ½ inch.

Silvered Glass, Brass and Plated Knobs on swivel spindles, extend, Mortise 2 inch, Rim 1 inch.

Mortise, Crank Handles, extend ½ of an inch, thus: 1 to 1½, 1¼ to 1¾, 1½ to 2, &c. &c.

Rim, Crank Handles, extend ½ of an inch, the same as Door Knobs.

For Rim Locks the thickness of the Lock must be deducted from the length of spindles to get required thickness of the door,

For Mortise Locks the length of the spindle is the thickness of the door. When fitting a door with a Mortise Lock adapted to swivel spindles, care should be taken to place the Lock as near the center as possible. The proper adjustment of the swivel spindle requires care and attention so that the working of the Knobs will be perfect. It must be so placed that the swivel operates exactly in the center of the Lock. The Lock having a double hub, the outer Knob can be shut off or stopped by the lever in the face of the Lock, effectually locking the door, preventing entrance without the aid of a Pass or Night Key, while the inside Knob yet works to open the door from the inside.

Many complaints have been made of Locks that were perfect in themselves, but not being properly adjusted were unjustly condemned.

DOOR KNOBS.

No.	FOR INSIDE DOOR.	Japanned Roses.	Plated Roses.	Porcelain Roses.
	Rim or Mortise Locks.	PER DOZEN.	PER DOZEN.	PER DOZEN.
400	Mineral			
1400	Mineral, Japanned Mountings, especially for Refrigerators. (See Plate, p. 51.)			
1300	Porcelain, Japanned Mountings, &c., for Refrigerators			
300	Porcelain, Japanned Shanks			
100	Porcelain			
100	Porcelain, Hand Plated Shanks and Roses			
101	Porcelain			
	Porcelain, Decorated in Gold,			
	Porcelain, Decorated in Gold and Flowers			
1000	Silvered Glass			
	FOR STORE AND FRONT DOOR.			
	Rim or Mortise Locks.			
	2½×2¼ inch Knob. Spindle ⅜ inch diameter.			
450	Mineral, Extra Finish, Turn-Roses			
350	Porcelain, Japanned Shanks,			
150	Porcelain			
151	Porcelain			
1050	Silvered Glass			

No.	FOR SHIP USE.	Brass Shanks and Roses.	Electro-Plated Shanks and Roses.	Hand Plated Shanks and Roses.
		PER DOZEN.	PER DOZEN.	PER DOZEN.
	Mineral, Brass Spindles			
	Porcelain, Brass Spindles			

CLOSET KNOBS.

No.		Japanned Roses.	Plated Roses.	Porcelain Roses.
		PER DOZEN.	PER DOZEN.	PER DOZEN.
400	Mineral			
300	Porcelain			
100	Porcelain			
101	Porcelain			
	Porcelain, Decorated in Gold			
	Porcelain, Decorated in Gold and Flowers			
1000	Silvered Glass			

BRASS DOOR KNOBS.

	Brass.	Electro-Plated.	Hand Plated.
	PER DOZEN.	PER DOZEN.	PER DOZEN.
1¾ inch, Heavy Brass, for 5 and 6 inch Rim Locks			
2 in. Heavy Brass, for 7 in. Rim Locks			
2¼ and 2 in. Heavy Brass, for 7 in. Front Door and 8 in. Rim Locks			
2½ and 2¼ in. Heavy Brass, for 8, 9 and 10 in. Store Door Rim Locks			
2¾ and 2½ in. Extra Heavy Brass, for 8, 9 and 10 inch Store Door Rim Lock			
2½ and 2¼ inch, Extra Heavy, for Front Door Rim Locks			
1¾ in. Heavy Brass, for Mortise Locks			
2 in. Heavy Brass, for Mortise Locks			
2¼ in. Heavy Brass, for Mortise Locks			
2½ and 2¼ in. Heavy Brass, for Mortise Locks			
2½ in. Heavy Brass, for Mortise Locks			
2¼ in. Extra Heavy Brass, for Mortise Locks			
2½ and 2¼ in. Extra Heavy Brass, for Mortise Locks			
2½ in. Extra Heavy Brass, for Mortise Locks			
2¾ and 2½ inch, Extra Heavy Brass, for Mortise Locks			
CLOSET Knobs, two-thirds price of pairs			

Single Brass Knobs and Roses without Spindles.

$ per dozen,

1¾, 2, 2¼, 2½ inch

Knobs on Swivel Spindles extra, per dozen, $

Brass or Plated Knobs on Brass Spindles, ex. per doz. $

To ascertain the price of Plated Knobs outside, and Porcelain inside, or the price of any other variety not named in list, take half the price of each kind wanted.

HALL DOOR PULL-TO KNOBS.

2½ inch Knobs.	Japanned Shanks and Seats.	Plated Shanks and Seats.	Plated Shanks, Porcelain Seats.
	PER DOZEN.	PER DOZEN.	PER DOZEN.
Mineral			
Porcelain			

CRANKS, HANDLES AND KNOBS.

(For Description of Plates see page 66.)

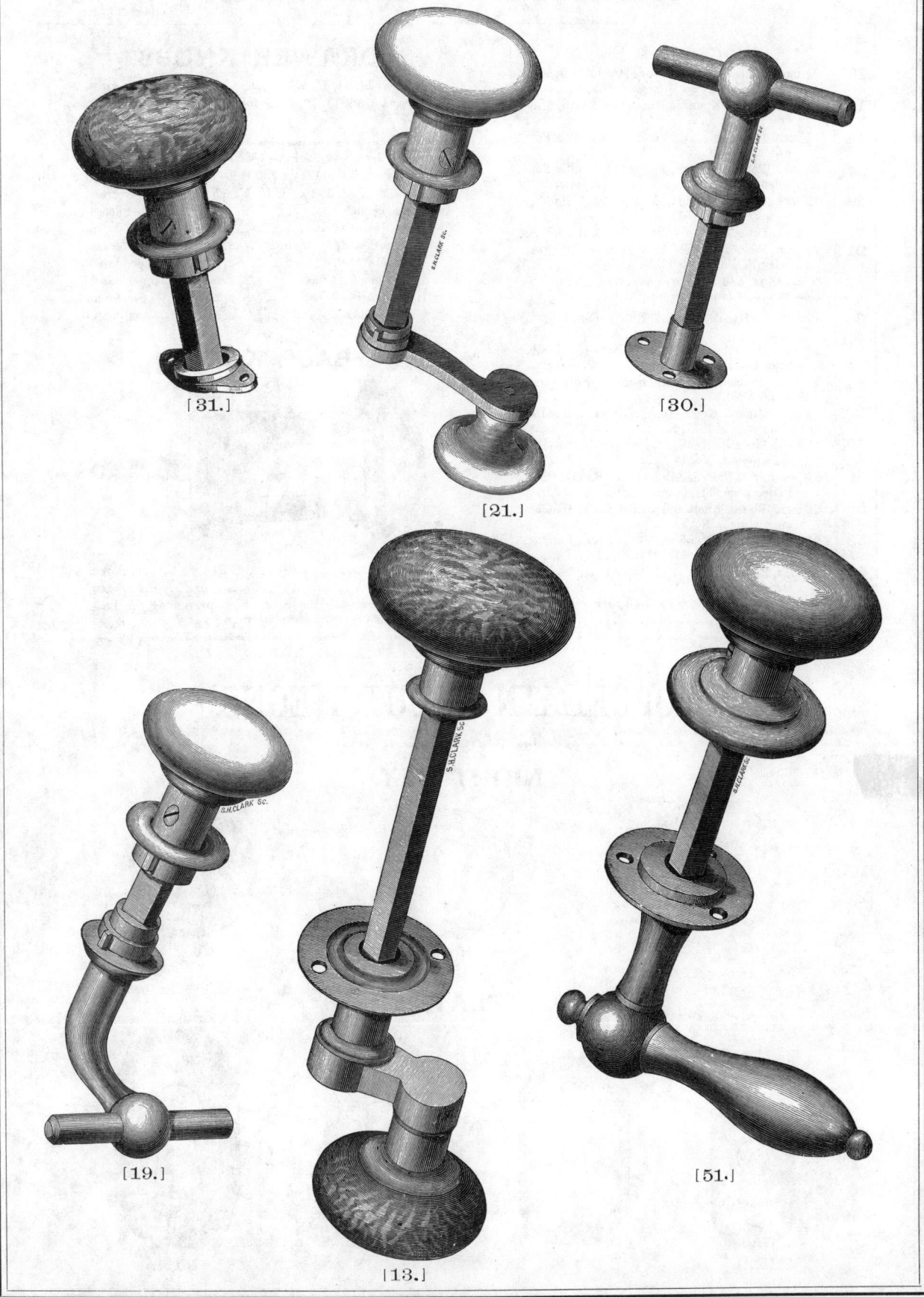

[31.]　　　　　[21.]　　　　　[30.]

[19.]　　　　　[13.]　　　　　[51.]

CRANKS, HANDLES AND KNOBS,

FOR FRENCH WINDOWS, STORE, AND SASH DOORS, ETC.

No.		Per Doz.
13	$2\frac{1}{4}$ inch, Mineral Knob, Japanned Crank with Mineral Knob. (See Plate, page 65)..........	
$13\frac{1}{2}$	2 inch, Mineral Knob, Japanned Crank with Mineral Knob..............................	
14	$2\frac{1}{4}$ inch, Porcelain Knob, Plated Crank with Porcelain Knob..............................	
$14\frac{1}{2}$	2 inch, Porcelain Knob, Plated Crank with Porcelain Knob..............................	
19	$1\frac{3}{4}$ inch, Porcelain Knob, Plated Crank Handle. (See Plate, page 65).....................	
20	2 inch, Porcelain Knob, Plated Crank Handle...	
21	$1\frac{3}{4}$ inch, Porcelain Knob, Plated Crank with Porcelain Knob. (See Plate, page 65)...........	
	Nos. $13\frac{1}{2}$, 14, and $14\frac{1}{2}$, are same style as No. 13.	
	Nos. 19 and 20 are same style.	
30	Plated T Handle, Plated Nut. (See Plate, page 65).....................................	
31	$1\frac{3}{4}$ inch, Mineral Knob, Japanned Nut. (See Plate, page 65)................................	
34	$1\frac{3}{4}$ inch, Porcelain Knob, Japanned Nut, same style as No. 31.........................	
39	$1\frac{3}{4}$ inch, Mineral Knob, Japanned Crank Handle, same style as No. 19.......................	
$39\frac{1}{2}$	$1\frac{3}{4}$ inch, Porcelain Knob, Japanned Crank Handle, same style as No. 19.......................	
51	$2\frac{1}{4}$ inch, Brass Knob and Brass Lever Handle. (See Plate, page 65)	
52	$2\frac{1}{4}$ inch, Plated Knob and Plated Lever Handle, same style as No. 51.......................	
53	$2\frac{1}{4}$ inch, Porcelain Knob and Brass Lever Handle, same style as No. 51.......................	
54	$2\frac{1}{4}$ inch, Porcelain Knob and Plated Lever Handle, same style as No. 51.......................	
5100	Brass Lever Handle, both ends, same style as No. 51	

DRAWER KNOBS.

Mineral, $1\frac{1}{4}$, $1\frac{1}{2}$, $1\frac{3}{4}$, 2, $2\frac{1}{4}$ inch................per gross, $
Porcelain, $1\frac{1}{4}$, $1\frac{1}{2}$, $1\frac{3}{4}$, 2, $2\frac{1}{4}$ inch ....per gross,

SHUTTER KNOBS.

Mineral, $\frac{5}{8}$, $\frac{3}{4}$, 1, $1\frac{1}{4}$, $1\frac{1}{2}$, $1\frac{3}{4}$, 2 inch............per gross, $
Porcelain, $\frac{5}{8}$, $\frac{3}{4}$, 1, $1\frac{1}{4}$, $1\frac{1}{2}$, $1\frac{3}{4}$, 2 inch..........per gross,
Brass, $1\frac{1}{8}$ inch...............................per dozen,
Brass, $1\frac{1}{4}$ inch...............................per dozen,
Electro Plated, $1\frac{1}{8}$ inch..................per dozen,
Electro Plated, $1\frac{1}{4}$ inch..................per dozen,
Hand Plated, $1\frac{1}{8}$ inch.......................per dozen,
Hand Plated, $1\frac{1}{4}$ inch.......................per dozen,
Silvered Glass...............................per dozen,

BASE KNOBS.

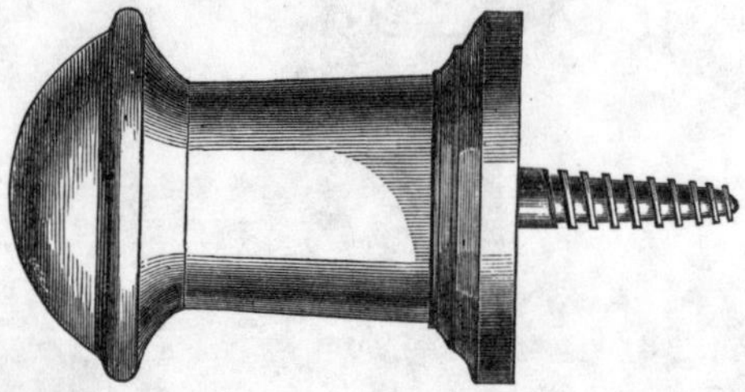

Mineral.......................................per dozen, $
Porcelain ....per dozen,
To screw into the base board, preventing the Lock Knob from injuring the plastering.

PORCELAIN ESCUTCHEONS.

(For Description of Plates, see page 71.)

NIGHT KEY.

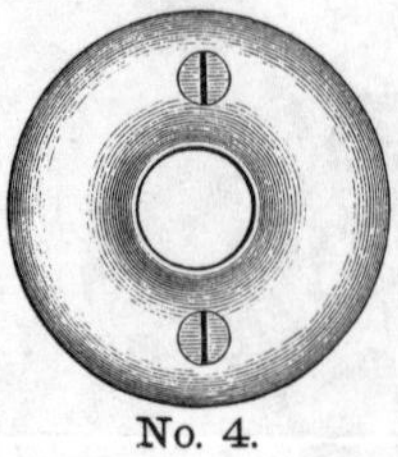

No. 4.

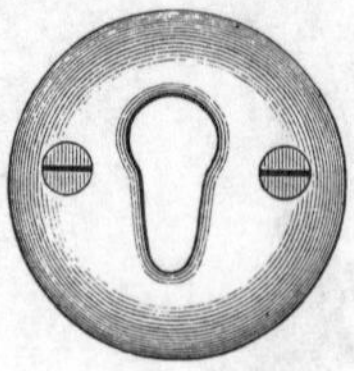

No. 6.

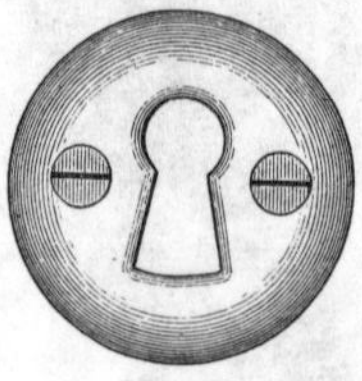

No. 7.

PLATE.

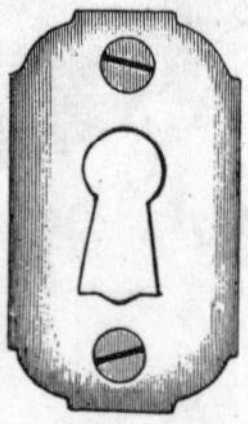

No. 1.

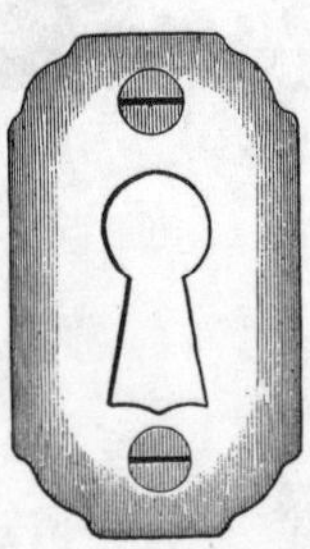

No. 2.

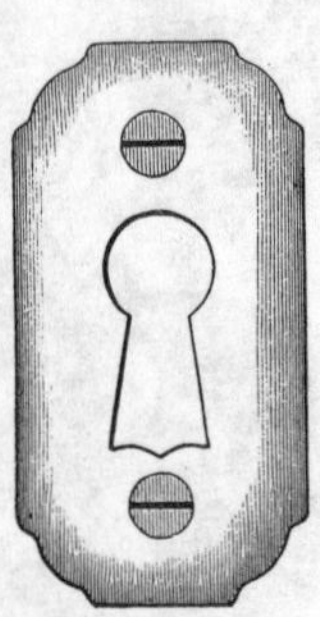

No. 3.

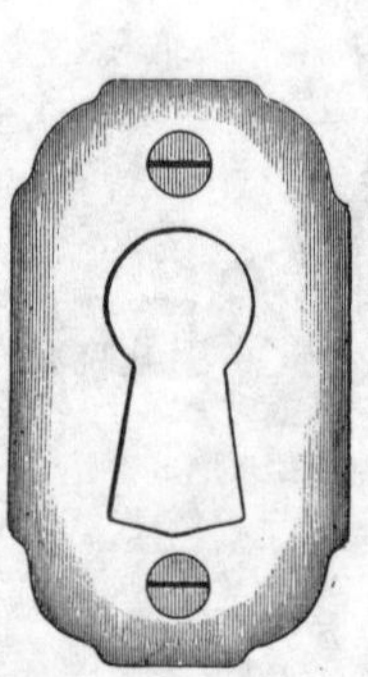

No. 4.

PORCELAIN DROP ESCUTCHEONS.

(For Description of Plates see page 71.)

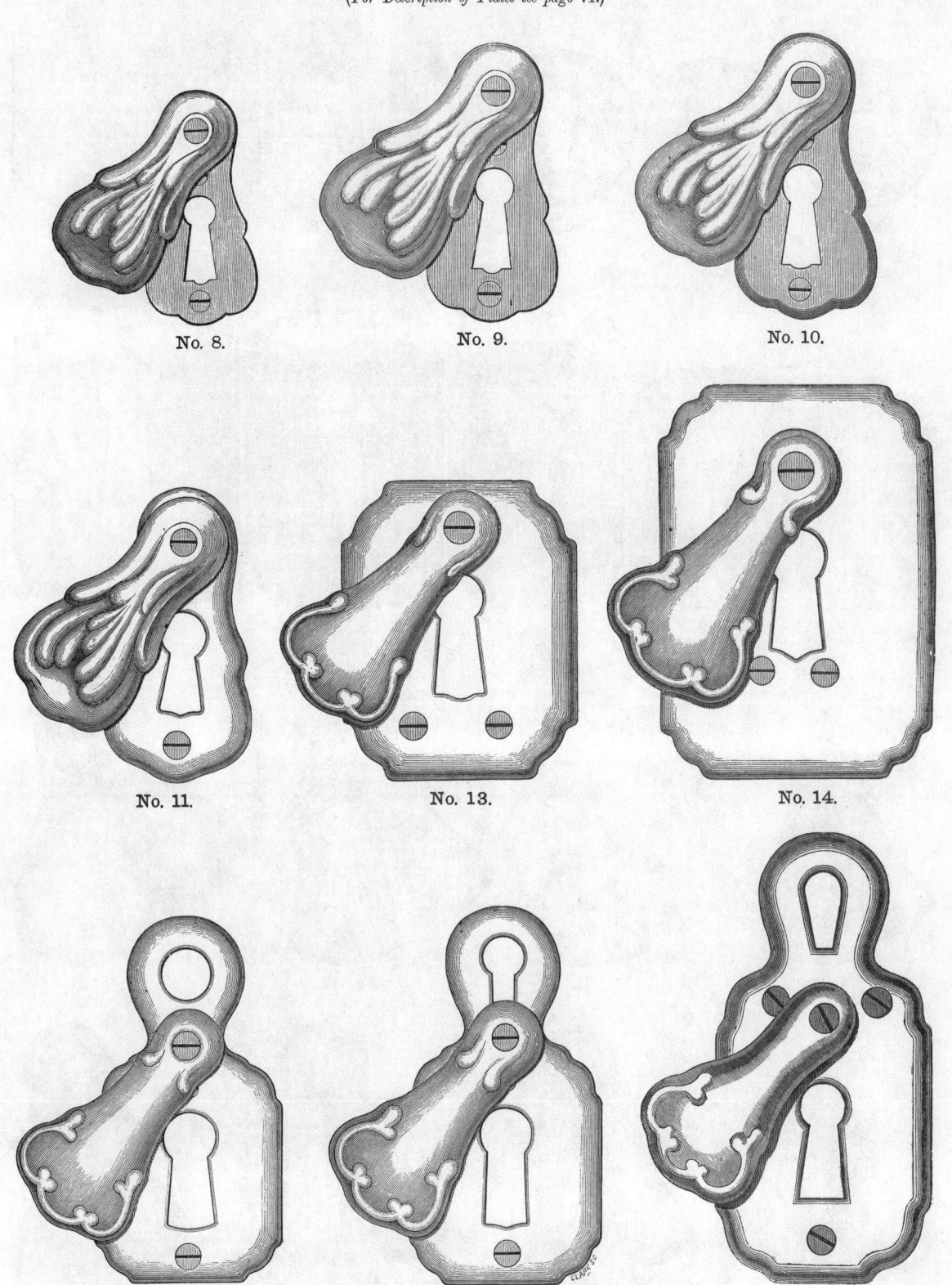

No. 8.   No. 9.   No. 10.

No. 11.   No. 13.   No. 14.

No. 15.   No. 16.   No. 17.

METAL ESCUTCHEONS.

(For Description of Plates see pages 71, 72.)

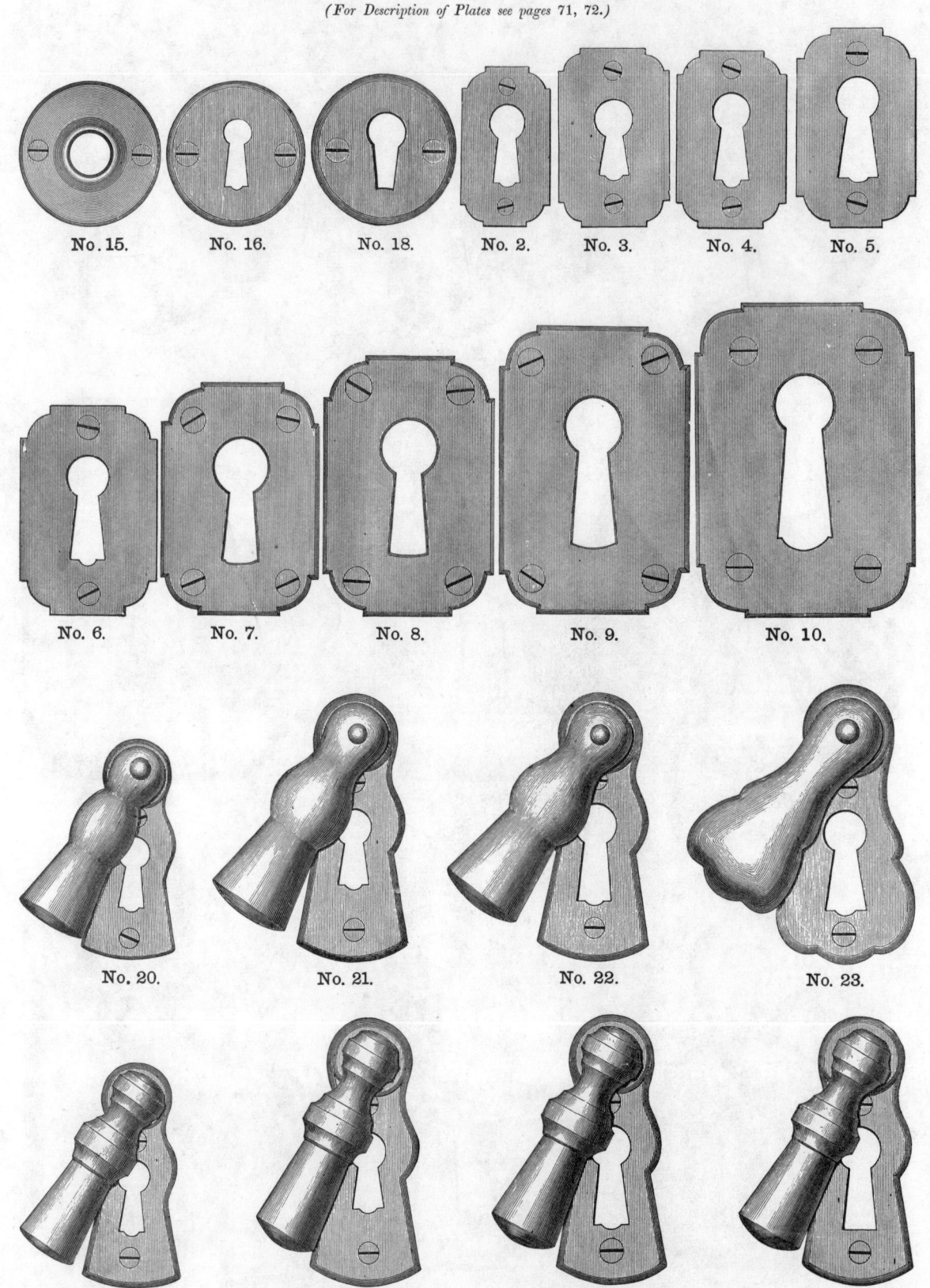

No. 15. No. 16. No. 18. No. 2. No. 3. No. 4. No. 5.

No. 6. No. 7. No. 8. No. 9. No. 10.

No. 20. No. 21. No. 22. No. 23.

No. 25. No. 26. No. 27. No. 28.

METAL DROP ESCUTCHEONS.

(Continued.)

[*For Description of Plates see page 72.*]

No. 30.

No. 31.

No. 32.

No. 40.

No. 41.

No. 42.

No. 43.

No. 50.

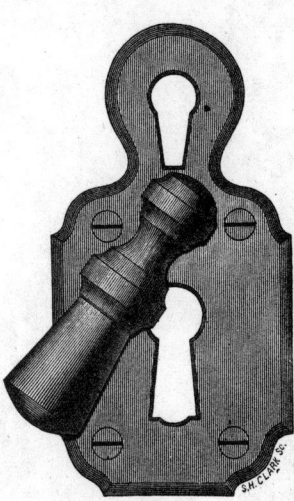

No. 51.

No. 52.

METAL DROP ESCUTCHEONS.

(Continued.)

[For Description of Plates see page 72.]

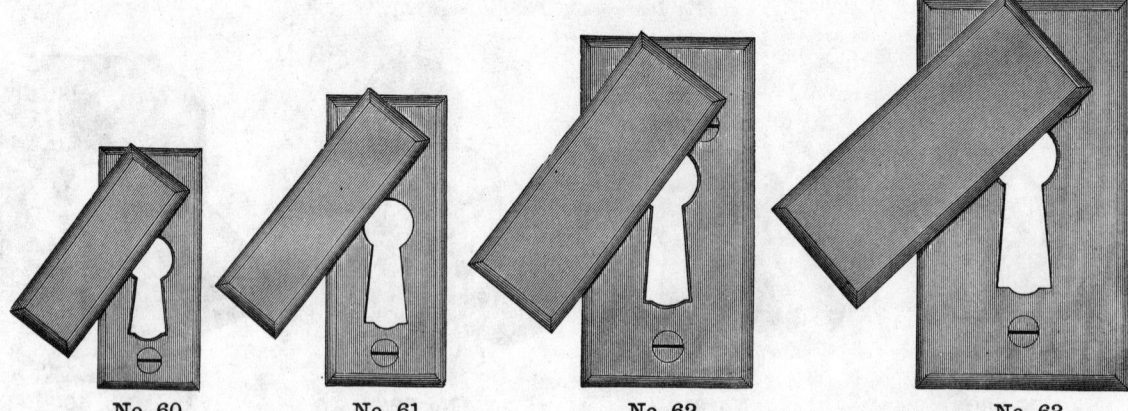

No. 60.   No. 61.   No. 62.   No. 63.

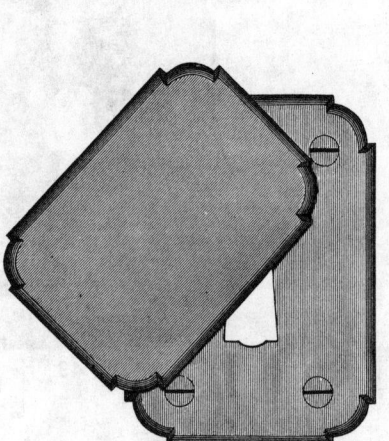

No. 70.

No. 71.

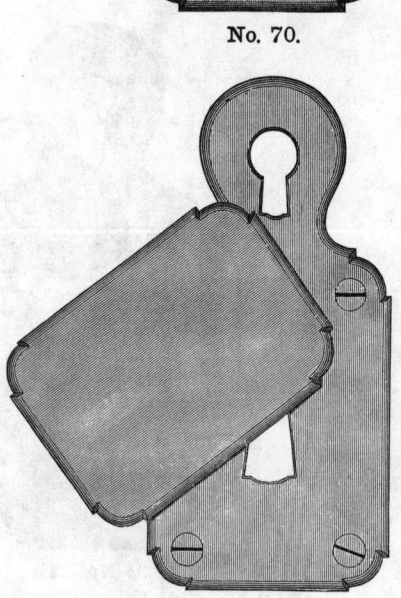

No. 72.

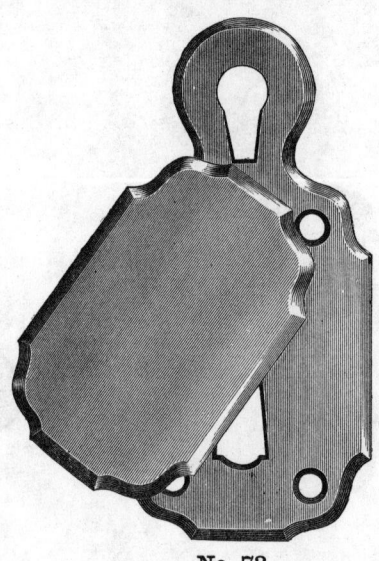

No. 73.

PORCELAIN ESCUTCHEONS.

PACKED WITH SCREWS, PER SINGLE DOZEN.

(See Plates, pages 66, 67.)

No.		Plain Porcelain.	Decorated in Gold	Decorated in Gold and Flowers.
1	Plate, $\frac{3}{4}$ inch Keyhole			
2	Plate, $\frac{7}{8}$ inch Keyhole			
3	Plate, 1 inch Keyhole			
4	Plate, $1\frac{1}{8}$ inch Keyhole			
8	Drop, $\frac{7}{8}$ inch Keyhole, Poppy Shape, Silvered Base			
9	Drop, $1\frac{5}{16}$ inch Keyhole, Poppy Shape, Silvered Base			
10	Drop, $1\frac{5}{16}$ inch Keyhole, Poppy Shape, Raised Plated Base			
11	Drop, $1\frac{5}{16}$ inch Keyhole, Poppy Shape, Porcelain Base			
13	Drop, $1\frac{1}{8}$ inch Keyhole, Fancy Shape, Square Porcelain Base for Front Doors, large,			
14	Drop, $1\frac{1}{8}$ inch Keyhole, Fancy Shape, Square Porcelain Base for Front Doors, extra large			
15	Drop, $1\frac{1}{8}$ inch Keyhole, Fancy Shape, Porcelain Base for Front Doors, Double Keyhole, Round Night Key, for Lock No. 130			
16	Drop, $1\frac{1}{8}$ inch Keyhole, Fancy Shape, Porcelain Base for Front Doors, Double Keyhole, Bit Night Key, for Locks Nos. 101, 121, 131			
17	Drop, $1\frac{1}{8}$ inch Keyhole, Fancy Shape, Double Keyhole, for Locks Nos. 125, 135, and 204			
4	Night Key Escutcheons, Round Keyhole			
6	Night Key Escutcheons, Bit Keyhole			
7	Night Key Escutcheons, Bit Keyhole			

METAL ESCUTCHEONS,

BRASS AND IRON.

(See Plates, pages 68, 69, 70.)

No.	Plates—Per Single Dozen.	Iron Japanned.	Brass.	Electro Plated.	Hand Plated.
2	$\frac{3}{4}$ inch Keyhole, for Locks Nos. 0, 9, 54, 72, 73, 74, 80, 81, 83, 84, 93, 504, 538, 554, 604, 605, 606, 607, 608, 609, 610, 611, $611\frac{1}{2}$, 629, 630, $630\frac{1}{2}$, 631, 650, 651, 652, 653, 800, 801, 802				
3	$\frac{3}{4}$ inch Keyhole, for Locks Nos. $0\frac{1}{4}$, $0\frac{1}{2}$, $0\frac{3}{4}$, 1, $1\frac{1}{4}$, $1\frac{1}{2}$, $1\frac{3}{4}$, 2, $2\frac{1}{4}$, 4, 8, 12, 13, $13\frac{1}{4}$, 18, $18\frac{1}{4}$, 19, 20, 21, 23, $25\frac{1}{4}$, 26, 27, 31, 55, 57, 77, 78, 79, 92, 501, 503, 505, 507, 508, 509, 511, 512, $512\frac{1}{4}$, 513, 514, 530, $530\frac{1}{4}$, 543, 544, $544\frac{1}{4}$, 545, $545\frac{1}{4}$, 546, $546\frac{1}{4}$, 548, $548\frac{1}{4}$, $548\frac{1}{2}$, 560, 561, 562, 563, 564, 565, 587, 588, 612, $612\frac{1}{4}$, 613, $613\frac{1}{4}$, 620, 621, 622, 623, 701, $701\frac{1}{4}$, 702, 900, 901, 905, 906				
4	$\frac{7}{8}$ inch Keyhole, for Locks Nos. 5, 6, 7, 14, 15, 16, 25, $25\frac{1}{4}$, 34, 35, 36, 90, $90\frac{1}{4}$, 515, 516, 517, 518, 519, 520, 535, 537, $537\frac{1}{2}$, 574, 575, 594, 595, 614, $614\frac{1}{4}$, 615, 632				
5	$1\frac{1}{2}$ inch Keyhole, for Locks Nos. 200, 436, 437, 456, 457, 479, 525, 526, 531, 532, 570, 571, 572, 580, 581, 582, 585, 586, 590, 591, 624, 625, 666				
6	1 inch Keyhole, for Locks Nos. 200, 402, 421				
7	$1\frac{1}{4}$ inch Keyhole, for Locks Nos. 402, 434, 435, $435\frac{1}{4}$, 450, 451, 452, 453, 454, 455, 521, 522, 626, $626\frac{1}{4}$, 627, $627\frac{1}{4}$				
8	$1\frac{1}{4}$ inch Keyhole, for Locks Nos. 430, 432, 440, 443				
9	$1\frac{1}{4}$ inch Keyhole, for Locks Nos. 431, 441, 442, 444, 445, 446, 447				
10	$1\frac{1}{8}$ inch Keyhole, for Locks No. 448				

METAL ESCUTCHEONS,

BRASS AND IRON.

(Continued.)

[*For Plates, see pages* 68, 69, 70.]

No.		Iron Japanned.	Brass.	Electro Plated.	Hand Plated.
	Night Key Plates—Per Single Dozen.				
15	Round Keyhole, for Locks Nos. 140, 160, 201, 659, 659½, 660, 660½, 670, 671, 672				
16	Long Keyhole, for Locks Nos. 100, 141, 142, 161, 162, 200, 661, 664, 664½				
17	Round Keyhole, for Locks Nos. 140, 160				
18	Long Keyhole, for Locks Nos. 141, 142, 161, 162				
	Wrought Drops, Raised Wrought Bases—Per Single Dozen.				
20	$\frac{11}{16}$ inch Keyhole, for Locks Nos. 0, 0¼, 0½, 0¾, 1, 1¼, 1½, 1¾, 2, 2½, 12, 13, 13½				
21	¾ inch Keyhole, for Locks Nos. 8, 18, 18½, 19, 20, 21, 23, 25½, 26, 27, 31				
22	$\frac{15}{16}$ inch Keyhole, for Locks Nos. 5, 6, 7, 14, 15, 16, 25, 25½, 34, 35, 36				
23	1 inch Keyhole, for Large Mortise Locks				
	Round Cast Drops, Raised Wrought Bases—Per Single Dozen.				
25	$\frac{11}{16}$ inch Keyhole, for 3½ and 4 inch Mortise Locks				
26	¾ inch Keyhole, for 4½ inch Mortise Locks				
28	1 inch Keyhole for Large Mortise Locks, and for inside of Mortise Locks Nos. 100, 101, 121, 122, 130, 131, 132, 173, 174, 175				
	Round Cast Drops, Cast Bases—Per Single Dozen.				
30	$\frac{11}{16}$ inch Keyhole, for 3½ and 4 inch Mortise Locks				
31	$\frac{15}{16}$ inch Keyhole, for Large Mortise Locks, and for inside of Mortise Locks Nos. 100, 173				
32	1 inch Keyhole, Heavy, for Inside of Front Door Mortise Locks 101, 121, 122, 130, 131, 132, 174, 175				
	NEW YORK PATTERN.				
	Round Cast Drops, Square Bases—Per Single Dozen.				
40	1 inch Keyhole, for Outside of Locks Nos. 100, 173, 174, 175, 220				
41	1⅛ inch Keyhole, for Locks Nos. 201, 222, 223, 224, 225, 539, 540, 573, 420, 422, 423				
42	1¼ inch Keyhole, for Locks Nos. 400, 404, 407				
43	1½ inch Keyhole, for Locks Nos. 401, 405, 406, 408, 409, 412, 413, 414, 415				
	Double Keyholes.				
50	1⅛ inch Keyhole, for 130 F. D. Locks and 202 F. D. Rim				
51	1⅛ inch Keyhole, for Locks Nos. 101, 121, 122, 131, 132, 203				
52	1¼ inch Keyhole, for Locks Nos. 125, 135, 204				
	BOSTON PATTERN.				
	Flat Cast Drops, Square Cast Bases—Per Single Dozen.				
60	¾ inch Keyhole, for Small Mortise Locks				
61	$\frac{15}{16}$ inch Keyhole, for Large Mortise Locks				
62	1¼ inch Keyhole, for Front Door Locks				
63	1⅜ inch Keyhole, for Store Door Locks				
	HEAVY PHILADELPHIA PATTERN.				
	Flat Cast Drops, Cast Bases, Fancy Corners—Per Single Dozen.				
70	1¼ inch Keyhole, for Front Door Rim Locks				
71	1¼ inch Keyhole, for Front Door Locks No. 130				
72	1¼ inch Keyhole, for Front Door Locks Nos. 101, 121, 131				
73	— inch Keyhole, NEW PATTERN, for Locks Nos. 125, 135, 204				
	Concaves or Bowls—Each.				
80	Keyholes to order, 3¼ inches diameter, for No. 666 Latches, to avoid using a LONG KEY				
81	Keyholes to order, 4¼ inches diameter, for No. 666 Latches				
82	Keyholes to order, 5¼ inches diameter, for No. 666 Latches				

ELECTRO-PLATED SCREWS.

On Brass, for Escutcheons, etc.

	$					per gross.
⅜ inch,	No. 3	4	5			
	$					"
½ "	No. 3	4	5	6		
	$					"
⅝ "	No. 5	6	7	8		

	$						per gross
¾ inch.	No. 6	7	8	9	10		
	$						"
1 "	No. 7	8	9	10	11	12	
	$						"
1¼ "	No. 9	10	11	12			

HOUSE BELL TRIMMINGS.

BELL PULLS.

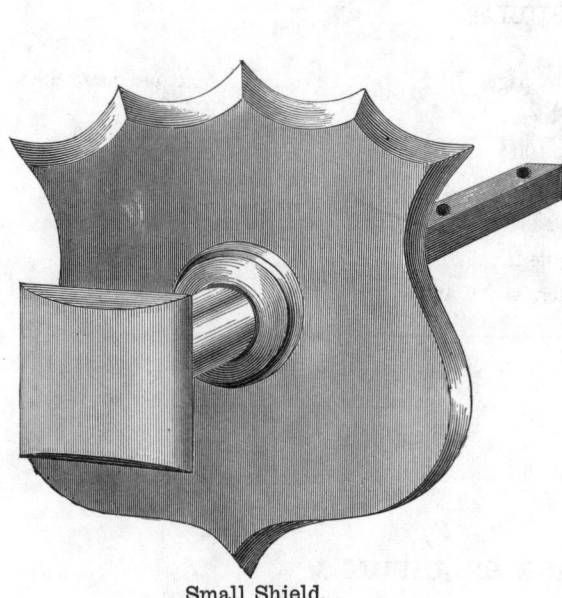

Small Shield.

Name Plate.

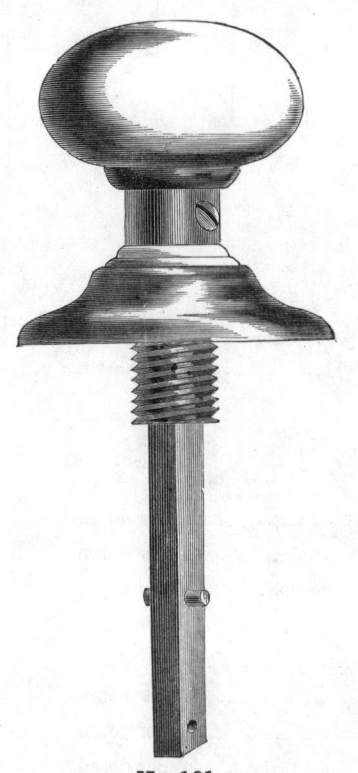

No. 101.

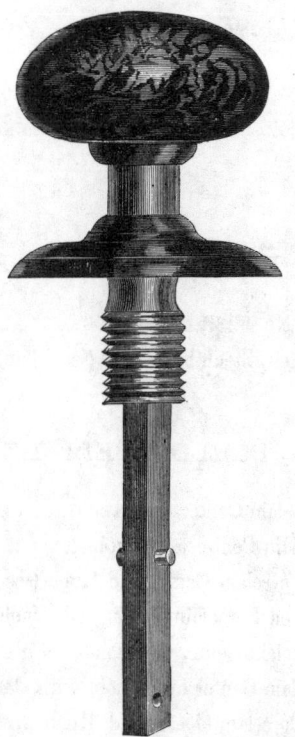

No. 500.

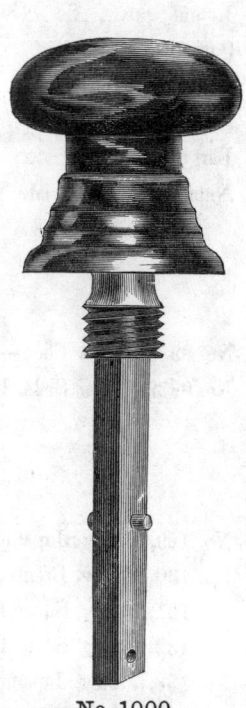

No. 1000.

HOUSE BELL TRIMMINGS.

(Continued.)

BELL PULLS.

No. 500, Mineral, Japanned Shank, Japanned Seat (see plate, page 73)............................per dozen $

No. 99, Porcelain, with Small Knob and Seat for Narrow Stile...⎫
Electro Plated Round Seat—same pattern as No. 100 ⎬............................per dozen

No. 100, Porcelain, Electro Plated Round Seat............................per dozen

No. 101, Porcelain, Electro Plated Shank, Porcelain Seat (see Plate, page 73)............................per dozen

No. 102, Porcelain, with Small Knob and Seat for Narrow Stile............................⎫
Electro Plated Shank, Porcelain Seat—same pattern as No. 101 ⎬............................per dozen

No. 300, Porcelain, Japanned Shank, Japanned Seat............................per dozen

No. 600, Porcelain Knob, Electro Plated Shield Pattern Seat............................per dozen

No. 601, Plated Knob, Electro Plated Shield Pattern Seat............................per dozen

No. 602, Hand Plated Knob, Hand Plated Shield Pattern Seat............................per dozen

No. 1000, Silvered Glass, Electro Plated Seat (see Plate, page 73)............................per dozen

HEAVY CAST BRASS BELL PULLS.

	Cast Brass.	Electro Plated.	Hand Plated.	Extra Hand Plated.
	PER DOZEN.	PER DOZEN.	PER DOZEN.	PER DOZEN.
Round Seat				
Square Seat				
Concave Seat				
Small Shield (see Plate, page 73)				
Large Shield				
Name Plate (see Plate, page 73)				

BELL SLIDES OR PULLS.

No. 9938, Brass Slide—same style as No. 9939............................per dozen $

No. 9939, Brass Slide, Heavy, for Hotels, Steamboats, &c. (see Plate, page opposite)............................per dozen

PARLOR BELL LEVERS.

No. 129, Fancy, Japanned, Plain Porcelain Center and Knob............................per dozen $

No. 130, Fancy, Bronzed, Plain Porcelain Center and Knob............................per dozen

No. 131, Fancy, Silver Plated, Plain Porcelain Center and Knob (see Plate, page opposite)............................per dozen

No. 132, Fancy, Silver Plated, Decorated Porcelain Center and Knob............................per dozen

No. 133, Fancy, Japanned, Plain Porcelain Center and Knob, with Chain............................per dozen

No. 134, Fancy, Bronzed, Plain Porcelain Center and Knob, with Chain............................per dozen

No. 135, Fancy, Silver Plated, Plain Porcelain Center and Knob, with Chain............................per dozen

No. 136, Fancy, Silver Plated, Decorated Porcelain Center and Knob, with Chain............................per dozen

HOUSE BELL TRIMMINGS.

(Continued.)

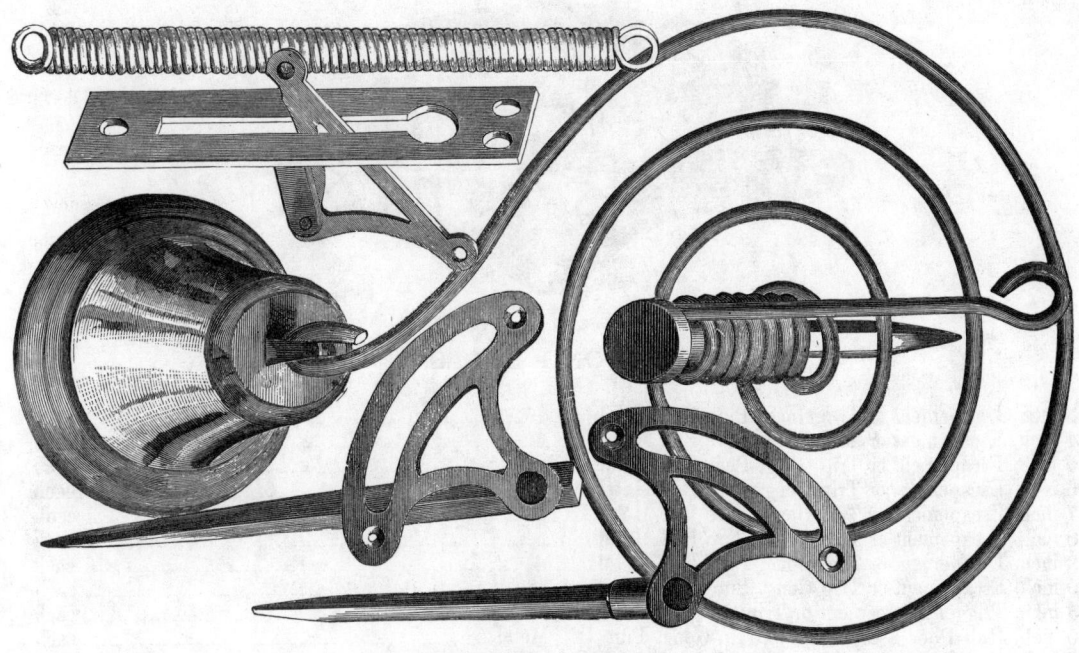

Bell Carriage Complete.
(For description, see page 76.)

Parlor Bell Lever, No. 131.

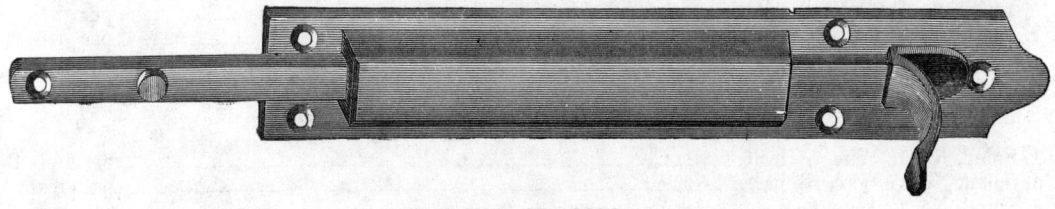

Bell Slide, No. 9939.

HOUSE BELL TRIMMINGS.

(Continued.)

GONG BELLS.

3 inch, Escapement or Trip Gong, Pure Bell Metal...each $

4 inch, Escapement or Trip Gong, Pure Bell Metal...each

5 inch, Escapement or Trip Gong, Pure Bell Metal...each

6 inch, Escapement or Trip Gong, Pure Bell Metal...each

7 inch, Escapement or Trip Gong, Pure Bell Metal...each

8 inch, Escapement or Trip Gong, Pure Bell Metal...each

9 inch, Escapement or Trip Gong, Pure Bell Metal...each

10 inch, Escapement or Trip Gong, Pure Bell Metal...each

3 inch, Trigger Escapement or Trip Gong, Pure Bell Metal...each

5 inch, Hall Door Escapement or Trip Gong, Pure Bell Metal...each

5 inch, Rail Car Escapement or Trip Gong, Pure Bell Metal...each

7 inch, Locomotive Escapement or Trip Gong, Pure Bell Metal...each

HOUSE BELL CARRIAGES,

Consisting of POLISHED BELLS, hung on Japanned Scroll Carriages, with Mortise, Side and End Cranks, Check Springs and Spikes.　(See Plate, page 75.)

No. 1　is a No. 5 Polished Bell, with Trimmings, complete...per dozen sets

No. 2　is a No. 4 Polished Bell, with Trimmings, complete (see Plate, page 75)...per dozen sets

No. 3　is a No. 3 Polished Bell, with Trimmings, complete...per dozen sets

No. 3½ is a No. 2 Polished Bell, with Trimmings, complete...per dozen sets

No. 4　is a No. 4 Polished Bell, on Scroll Carriage, with Spikes only...per dozen sets

No. 5　is a No. 3 Polished Bell, on Scroll Carriage, with Spikes only...per dozen sets

No. 6　Scroll Carriages, with Spikes only...per dozen sets

For House Bells without Trimmings, see Index for House Bells.

BELL CRANKS.

No. 0, Mortise, all Brass...per gross $

No. 1, Mortise, all Brass...per gross

No. 2, Mortise, all Brass...per gross

No. 3, Mortise, all Brass, Heavy...per gross

No. 1, Side, Brass Crank, Malleable Iron Spike...per gross

No. 2, Side, Brass Crank, Malleable, Extra Heavy...per gross

No. 1, End, Brass Crank, Malleable...per gross

No. 2, End, Brass Crank, Malleable, Extra Heavy...per gross

CHECK SPRINGS.

No. 1, Spiral, No. 18 Wire, 5¼ inch...per gross $

No. 2, Spiral, No. 17 Wire, 5¼ inch...per gross

No. 3, Spiral, No. 17 Wire, 6½ inch...per gross

No. 5, Spiral, No. 18 Wire, 7 inch...per gross

SASH FASTENERS.

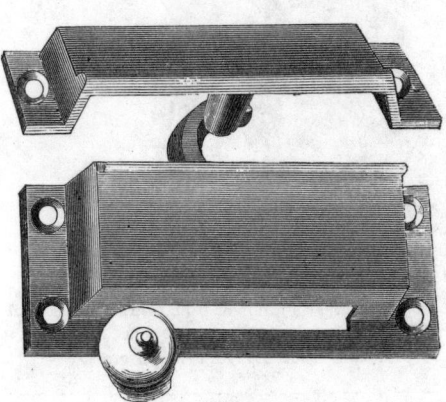

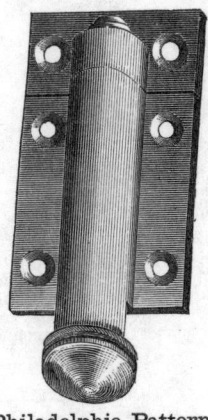

METROPOLITAN PATTERN.

☞ We would call especial attention to this article, as it makes a much neater finish on the window, and is more secure than any fastening in market.

No. 11. Iron Japanned................ per doz. $
" 12. Bronzed, with Porcelain Knob. (See Plate.).................... "
" 13. All Brass, with Porcelain Knob "
" 14. Electro-Plated, with Porcelain Knob..................... "
" 15. Hand Plated, with Porcelain Knob..................... "

PHILADELPHIA PATTERN.

No. 1. All Brass, Screw. (See Plate.).. per doz. $
" 2. All Brass, Screw, for imitation French Windows............. "

Metropolitan Pattern.　　　Philadelphia Pattern.

JUDD'S PATENT.

No. 1.

No. 2.

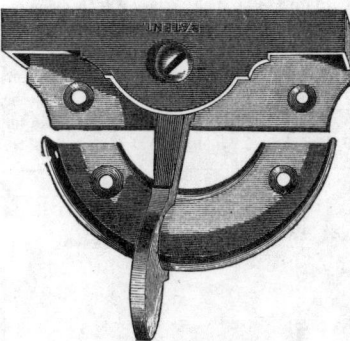

No. 3.

No. 27.

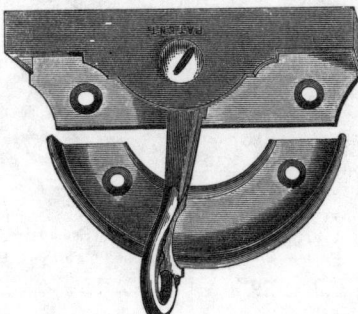

No. 28.

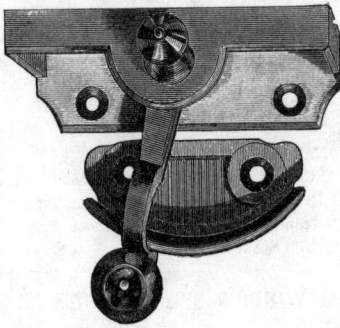

No. 41.

No. 0. Iron, Japanned...................... per gross, $
" 1. Iron, Bronzed, Brass Capped Rivet. (See Plate).......................... "
" 2. Iron, Bronzed, Brass Capped Knob and Rivet. (See Plate.)................. "
" 3. Brass, Plain Lever, Brass Capped Screw. (See Plate.)................. "
" 3½. Brass, Plain Lever, Brass Capped Screw, Porcelain Knob.................. "
" 9. Silver Plated, Plain Lever, Silver Capped Screw, Porcelain Knob, same pattern as No. 3½.
" 10. Heavy Plated and Polished, Plain Lever, Silver Capped Screw, Porcelain Knob.. "

No. 17. Iron, Bronzed, Brass Capped Rivet and Porcelain Knob, Heavy.............. per gross, $
" 27. Iron, Bronzed, Brass Capped Rivet and Porcelain Knob. (See Plate.)......... "
" 28. Brass, Fancy Lever, Brass Capped Screw. (See Plate).................... "
" 28½. Brass, Fancy Lever, Brass Capped Screw, Porcelain Knob.................. "
" 38. Silver Plated, Fancy Lever, Silver Capped Screw...................... "
" 38½. Fancy Lever, Silver Capped Screw, Porcelain Knob.................... "
" 41. Heavy Cast Brass, Polished, Brass Knob Rivet, Brass Knob. (See Plate.)...... "

SASH LIFTS.

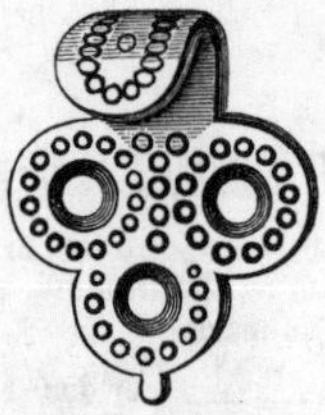

No. 50.

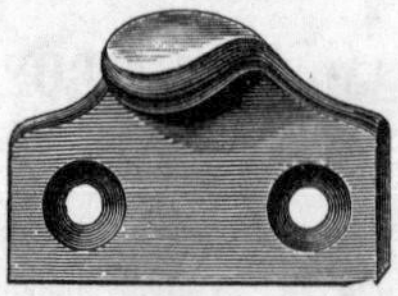

No. 60.

No. 50, Fancy Brass .... per gross, $
" 51, Fancy Plated .... per gross,
" 60, Plain Brass .... per gross,
" 61, Plain Plated .... per gross,
" 62, Plain Hand Plated .... per dozen,

SASH ROLLERS.

Iron Plate, Iron Wheel.

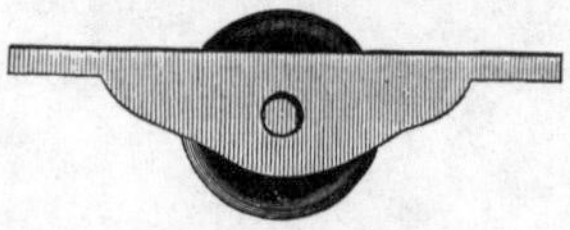

No.		Per Gross.
1,	Plate $1\frac{1}{2}\times\frac{11}{16}$ inch, Wheel $\frac{5}{8}$ inch diameter, $\frac{3}{8}$ inch thick.	$
2,	Plate $1\frac{3}{4}\times\frac{3}{4}$ inch, Wheel $\frac{5}{8}$ inch diameter, $\frac{1}{2}$ inch thick.	
3,	Plate $2\frac{1}{4}\times1$ inch, Wheel $\frac{7}{8}$ inch diameter, $\frac{5}{8}$ inch thick.	
5,	Plate $2\frac{1}{2}\times1\frac{1}{4}$ inch, Wheel 1 inch diameter, $\frac{3}{4}$ inch thick.	
7,	Plate $2\frac{5}{8}\times1\frac{3}{8}$ inch, Wheel 1 inch diameter, $\frac{7}{8}$ inch thick.	
8,	Plate $2\times\frac{7}{8}$ inch, Wheel $\frac{5}{8}$ inch diameter, $\frac{1}{2}$ inch thick.	
9,	Plate $2\times\frac{7}{8}$ inch, Wheel $\frac{3}{4}$ inch diameter, $\frac{1}{2}$ inch thick.	

WINDOW SPRINGS.

Improved.

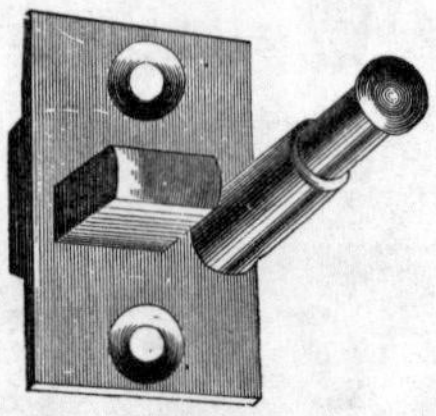

No. 2.

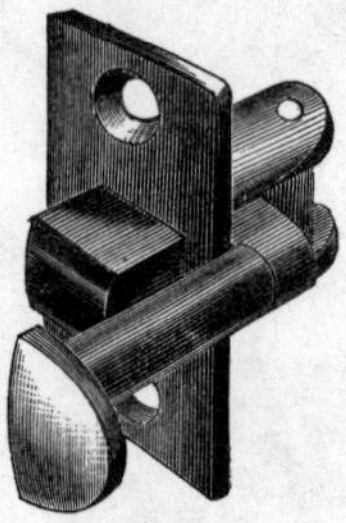

No. 6.

No.		Per Gross.
2,	All Brass (see Plate)	$
3,	Brass Socket, Brass Thumb Piece	
6,	Iron Socket, Brass Thumb Piece, Extra Strong (see Plate),	
11,	Iron Socket, Iron Thumb Piece	
12,	Iron Socket, Brass Thumb Piece	

WINDOW SPRING BOLTS OR SASH CENTERS.

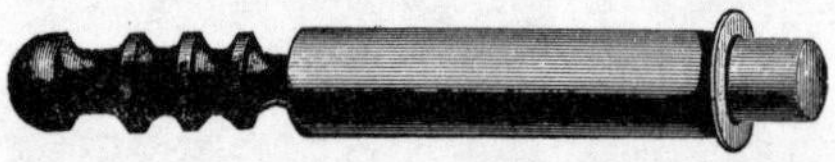

	Per Gross.
Window Spring Bolts, Japanned	$
Window Spring Bolts, Cased, Japanned, for $1\frac{3}{4}$ to $2\frac{1}{4}$ inch Sash (see Plate)	
Window Spring Bolts, Cased, Silver Tip, for $1\frac{3}{4}$ to $2\frac{1}{4}$ inch Sash	

SASH CORD IRONS.

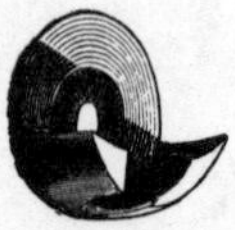

For convenience in attaching and detaching the Cords and Weights to Window Sashes .... per gross,

JONES' SASH LOCKS.

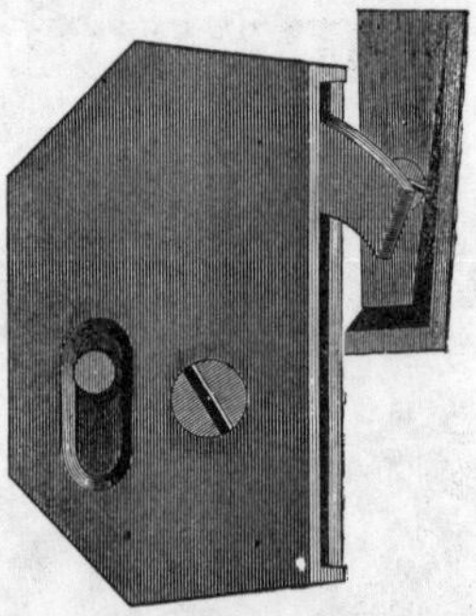

This is one of the most durable, reliable and efficient locks now in use, and is particularly adapted for heavy sash. It is furnished with cast iron stops for upper and lower sash, which prevent all wear upon the window jam.

Not Japanned .... per gross, $

TRUNK ROLLERS.

Iron Plate, Iron Wheel.

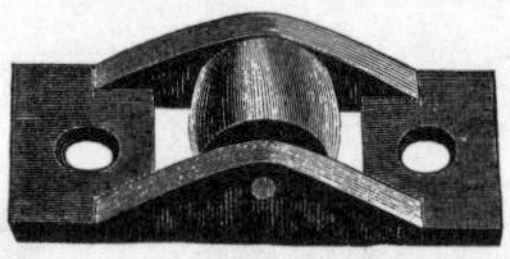

No.		Per Gross.
4,	Plate $2\frac{1}{4}\times1$ inch, Wheel $\frac{7}{8}$ inch diameter, $\frac{5}{8}$ inch thick,	$
6,	Plate $1\frac{7}{8}\times\frac{3}{4}$ inch, Wheel $\frac{11}{16}$ inch diameter, $\frac{1}{2}$ inch thick.	
10,	Plate $1\frac{5}{8}\times1\frac{1}{8}$ inch, Wheel $\frac{1}{2}$ inch diameter, $\frac{5}{8}$ inch thick.	
11,	Plate $1\frac{1}{2}\times1$ inch, Wheel $\frac{1}{2}$ inch diameter, $\frac{1}{2}$ inch thick.	

SASH PROPS.

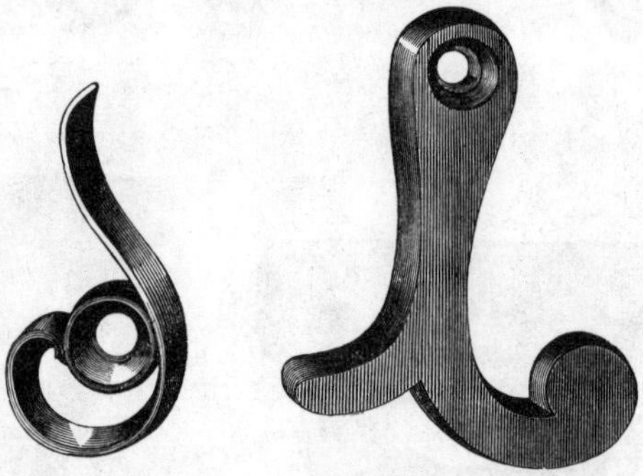

Japanned, Eccentric .... per gross, $
Japanned Y, or Sash Props .... per gross,

BRASS FLUSH RINGS.

For Drawers, &c.

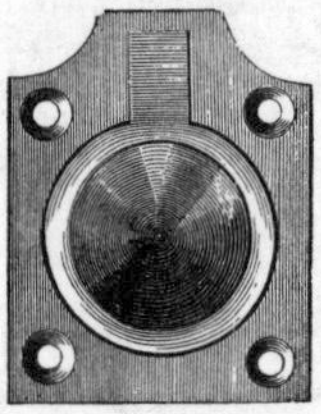

$			per dozen,
1	$1\frac{1}{4}$	$1\frac{1}{2}$ inch,	

WINDOW SHADE FURNITURE.

Brackets No. 00.0

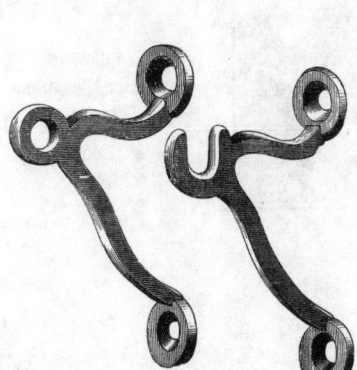

No 1.

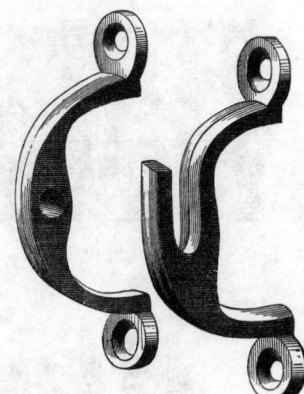

No. 2.

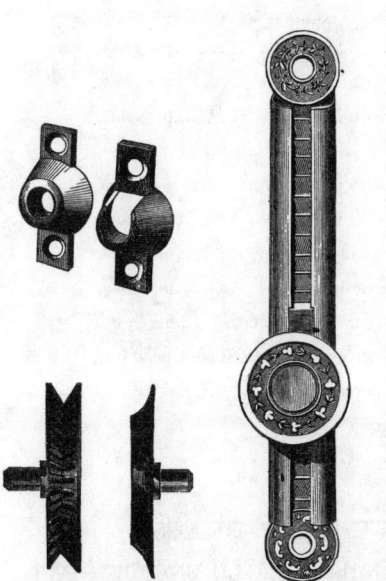

Roller Ends No. 4.   Rack Pulleys No. 230.

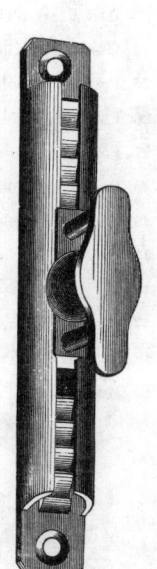

No. 300.

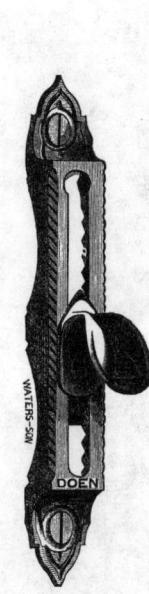

No. 3.

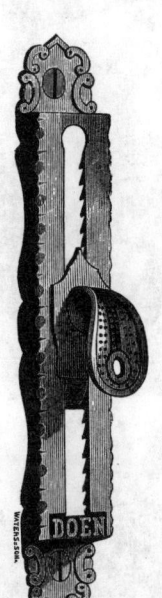

No. 2.

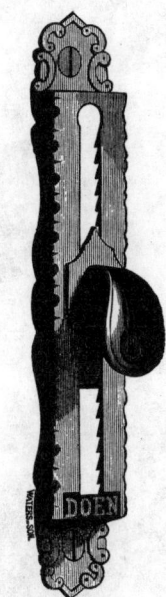

No. 1.

BRACKETS.

No. 00, Iron, Coppered (see Plate).............per gross, $

"   0, Brass.....................................per gross,

"   1, Brass (see Plate).......................per gross,

"   2, Brass, Heavy (see Plate)..............per gross,

ROLLER ENDS.

No. 1, Coppered Iron.........................per gross, $

"   4, Cast Brass (see Plate)..................per gross,

"   5, Cast Brass, for Heavy Shades.........per gross,

RACK PULLEYS.

No. 230, Wrought Brass (see Plate)...........per gross, $

"   234, Wrought Brass, Heavy...............per gross,

"   240, Wrought Brass, Porcelain Knob......per gross,

"   245, Wrought Brass, Wedge, 4 inch.......per gross,

"   250, Wrought Brass, Wedge, 4½ inch.......per gross,

"   260, Wrought Brass, Wedge, Porcelain Knob.per gross,

"   300, Cast Brass, Heavy, Strong Article (see
    Plate) ....per gross,

No. 1, Doens' "Patent," Bronzed (see Plate)....per gross, $

"   2, Doens' "Patent," Bronzed, Brass Holder
    (see Plate)..........................per gross,

"   3, Doen's "Patent," Bronzed (see Plate)....per gross,

CUPBOARD CATCHES.

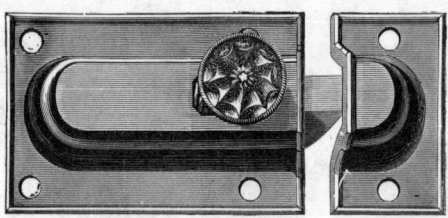

No. 4.

RURAL—IMPROVED.

No 1, Japanned, Cast Brass Knob..............per gross, $

" 2, Japanned, Cast Brass Knob..............per gross,

" 3, Japanned, Cast Brass Knob..............per gross,

" 4, Japanned, Cast Brass Knob (see Plate)....per gross,

———————

RURAL, ALL BRASS, made to order, Plain or Reverse Bevel.

———————

No. 20.

WROUGHT BRASS.

No. 20, Cast Brass Knob (see Plate)............per gross, $

" 21, Cast Brass Knob.......................per gross,

" 22, Cast Brass Knob.......................per gross,

" 23, Cast Brass Knob.......................per gross,

" 24, Cast Brass Knob.......................per gross,

" 25, Porcelain Knob with Brass Base.........per gross,

" 26, Porcelain Knob with Brass Base.........per gross,

" 27, Porcelain Knob with Brass Base (see Plate), per gross,

" 28, Porcelain Knob with Brass Base.........per gross,

" 29, Porcelain Knob with Brass Base.........per gross,

" 45, Mineral Knob, securely attached.........per gross,

" 46, Mineral Knob, securely attached.........per gross,

" 47, Mineral Knob, securely attached........per gross,

" 48, Mineral Knob, securely attached (see Plate), per gross,

" 49, Mineral Knob, securely attached.........per gross,

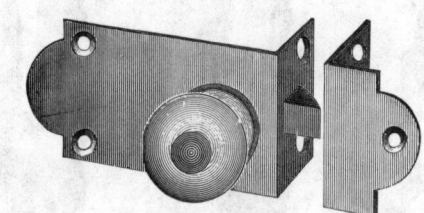
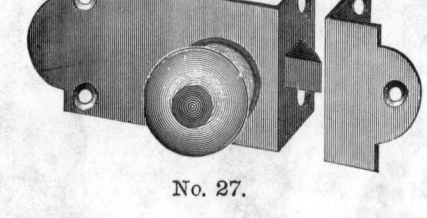

No. 27.

———————

No. 48.

HEAVY CAST BRASS,

Corresponding with the Full OLD ENGLISH PAT-
TERNS, both in size and weight.

No.   0, Brass Bolt, Brass Knob..............per gross, $

"   1, Brass Bolt, Brass Knob..............per gross,

"   2, Brass Bolt, Brass Knob..............per gross,

"   3, Brass Bolt, Brass Knob..............per gross,

"   125, Brass Bolt, Brass Knob, Heavy (see Plate), per gross,

"   15, Brass Bolt, Porcelain Knob with Brass
          Base...............................per gross,

"   16, Brass Bolt, Porcelain Knob with Brass
          Base...............................per gross,

"   17, Brass Bolt, Porcelain Knob with Brass
          Base................. ....per gross,

"   18, Brass Bolt, Porcelain Knob with Brass
          Base...............................per gross,

No. 125.

No. 00.

No. 2.

CUPBOARD TURNS.

No. 151.

No. 150, Mineral Knob, Japanned Base........................per dozen, $
No. 151, Porcelain Knob, Japanned Base (see Plate)..............per dozen,
No. 152, Porcelain Knob, Plated Base........................per dozen,

IMPROVED LATCHES OR CATCHES.

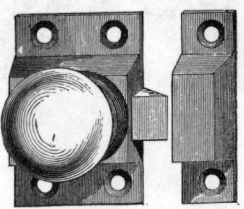

No. 5.

No. 3.

For Show-Cases, Pew Doors, Wardrobes, Cupboards, etc.	Brass. PER DOZEN.	Plated. PER DOZEN.
No. 00, Cast Brass, Mineral Knob (see Plate).................		
" 0, Cast Brass, Mineral Knob with Brass Base.............		
" 1, Cast Brass, Porcelain Knob..........................		
" 2, Cast Brass, Porcelain Knob with Brass Base (see Plate).		
" 3, Cast Brass, Upright Lever Spring, Porcelain Knob, Heavy Cast Brass Base (see Plate)......................		
" 4, Cast Brass, Upright Lever Spring, Mineral Knob, Heavy Cast Brass Base..........................		
" 5, Cast Brass, Spiral Spring, Porcelain Knob for Show Cases, to be used with Bonney's Bolts (see Plate).....		
" 6, Cast Brass Upright, Porcelain Knob, for Show-Cases (see Plate)..		

No. 7.

FLUSH SHOW-CASE CATCHES.

No. 7, Cast Brass, Flat Ring (see Plate)........................per dozen, $
" 8, Cast Brass, Round Ring.................................per dozen,

BONNEY'S PATENT BOLT.

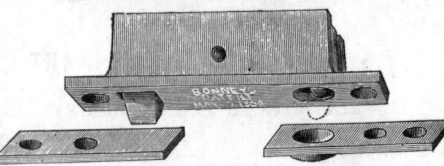

To be used on Book Cases, &c. having double doors, avoiding the use of Bolts or Hooks, at the same time being a perfect fastening.

$

No. 1.   2.

per dozen.

No. 6.

CUPBOARD LATCHES,

DOEN'S PATENT.

No. 1 and No. 15.

No. 2 and No. 16

No. 17.

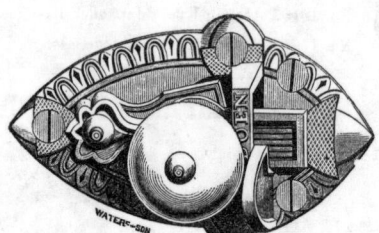

No. 6.

No. 11.

IRON, PLAIN, ACORN PATTERN.

No. 1, Japanned (see Plate) ....per gross, $

" 2, Japanned, Iron Knob (see Plate)........per gross,

No. 3, Japanned, Porcelain Knob................per gross, $

" 4, Japanned, Brass Knob ....per gross,

Put up in boxes of one dozen each, all Right and all Left Hand.

BRASS, FANCY, ACORN PATTERN.

No. 5, Brass Knobs ....per gross, $

" 6, Porcelain Knobs (see Plate) ....per gross,

" 7, Porcelain Knob, Bronzed, and Brass Rivets.per gross,

No. 8, Silver Plated, Porcelain Knobs...........per gross, $

" 9, Extra Heavy Silver Plate, Porcelain Knobs.per gross,

BRASS, LEAF PATTERN.

No. 10, with Brass Knob ....per gross, $

" 11, with Porcelain Knobs (see Plate)........per gross,

" 12, with Porcelain Knob, Bronzed, Brass Rivets ....per gross,

No. 13, Silver Plated, with Porcelain Knobs.....per gross, $

" 14, Extra Heavy Silver Plated, with Porcelain Knobs ....per gross,

Put up in boxes of one dozen each, half Right and half Left Hand.

IMPROVED CUPBOARD LATCHES, PATENTED.

FOR EITHER RIGHT OR LEFT HAND DOORS—ACORN PATTERN.

No. 15, Japanned.........................per gross, $

" 17, Bronzed, Ribbed Acorn Pattern, Porcelain Knob (see Plate).....................per gross,

No. 16, Japanned, Iron Knob (see Plate).......per gross, $

" 18, Bronzed, Ribbed Acorn Pattern, Brass Knob............................per gross,

CUPBOARD BUTTONS.

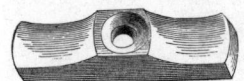

Brass.

Japanned, Flat.

Japanned, Raised.

Japanned.

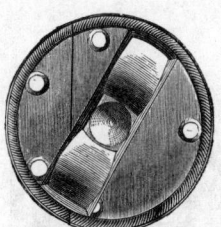

Brass.

Cast Brass, $ per gross.

    1¼   1½   1¾   2 inch.

Japanned, Iron, Raised,

  $ per gross.

    1¼   1½   1¾   2   2¼ inch.

Japanned, Iron, Flat,

  $ per gross.

    1¼   1½   1¾   2   2¼   2½   3 inch.

Cast Brass, on Plates, Loose Pins,

  $ per gross.

    1½ in. No. 2464   1¾ in. No. 2465   2 in. No. 2466

Japanned, Iron, on Plates,

  $ per gross.

    1½   1¾   2   2¼ inch.

SHUTTER OR SASH BARS.

FOR INSIDE SHUTTERS AND LIGHT FRENCH WINDOWS.

New Britain Pattern.

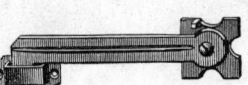

Japanned Iron Shutter Bar.

New York Pattern, 2¼.

Ohio Pattern, Brass.

Philadelphia Pattern.

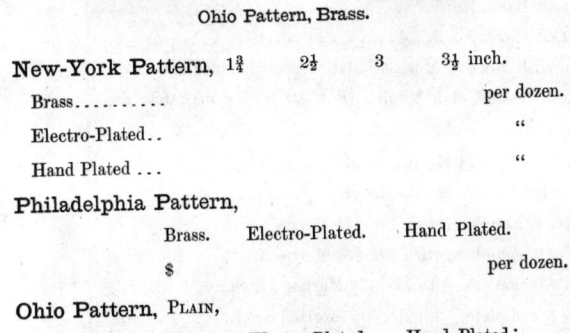

Ohio Pattern, Brass.

New-York Pattern, 1¾   2½   3   3½ inch.

  Brass..........   per dozen.

  Electro-Plated..   "

  Hand Plated ...   "

Philadelphia Pattern,

    Brass.   Electro-Plated.   Hand Plated.

    $ per dozen.

Ohio Pattern, PLAIN,

    Brass.   Electro-Plated.   Hand Plated.

    $ per dozen.

Ohio Pattern, FANCY,

    Coppered.   Brass.   Electro-Plated.

    $ per dozen.

New Britain Pattern,

    Brass.   Electro-Plated.   Hand Plated.

    $ per dozen.

Iron Japanned,

    $ per gross.

    3   4   6 inch.

HANDLES.

FLUSH DRAW HANDLES.

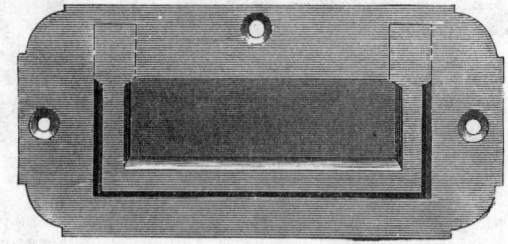

$ per dozen pair. $ per dozen pair.

Cast Brass. No. 1482   1483   1484   Cast Brass. No. 4944   4946

DRAWER PULLS.

No. 2.   No. 3.

No. 2, Japanned (see Plate)..................per dozen, $ No. 3, Coppered (see Plate)..................per dozen, $

" 4, Brass, same pattern as No. 3...........per dozen.   " 5, Plated, same pattern as No. 3...........per dozen,

OBLIQUE HANDLES, FOR STORE DOORS.

	Per Dozen.
Japanned, with Plate, No. 1, Right or Left Hand.......................................	
Japanned, with Plate, No. 2, Right or Left Hand (see Plate).........................	
Japanned, without Plate, No. 3, same pattern as No. 2..............................	
All Brass, Right or Left Hand, No. 1...	
All Brass, Right or Left Hand, No. 2...	
All Brass, Electro-plated, Right or Left Hand, No. 1...............................	
All Brass, Electro-plated, Right or Left Hand, No. 2...............................	
All Brass, Hand-plated, Right or Left Hand, No. 1.................................	
All Brass, Hand-plated, Right or Left Hand, No. 2.................................	
Japanned Handle No. 1, complete, with No. 47½ Mortise Latch, especially made to be used with Handle of this description instead of a Knob. (For description of Latch, see page 49)...	
All Brass Handle No. 1, complete, with No. 47½ Mortise Latch...........................	
All Brass Handle No. 2, complete, with No. 47½ Mortise Latch...........................	
All Brass Handle Electro-plated No. 1, complete, with No. 47½ Mortise Latch............	
All Brass Handle Electro-plated No. 2, complete, with No. 47½ Mortise Latch............	
All Brass Handle Hand-plated No. 1, complete, with No. 47½ Mortise Latch.............	
All Brass Handle Hand-plated No. 2, complete, with No. 47½ Mortise Latch.............	

WARDROBE, COAT & HAT, AND HAT HOOKS.

(For description of Plates see page 87.)

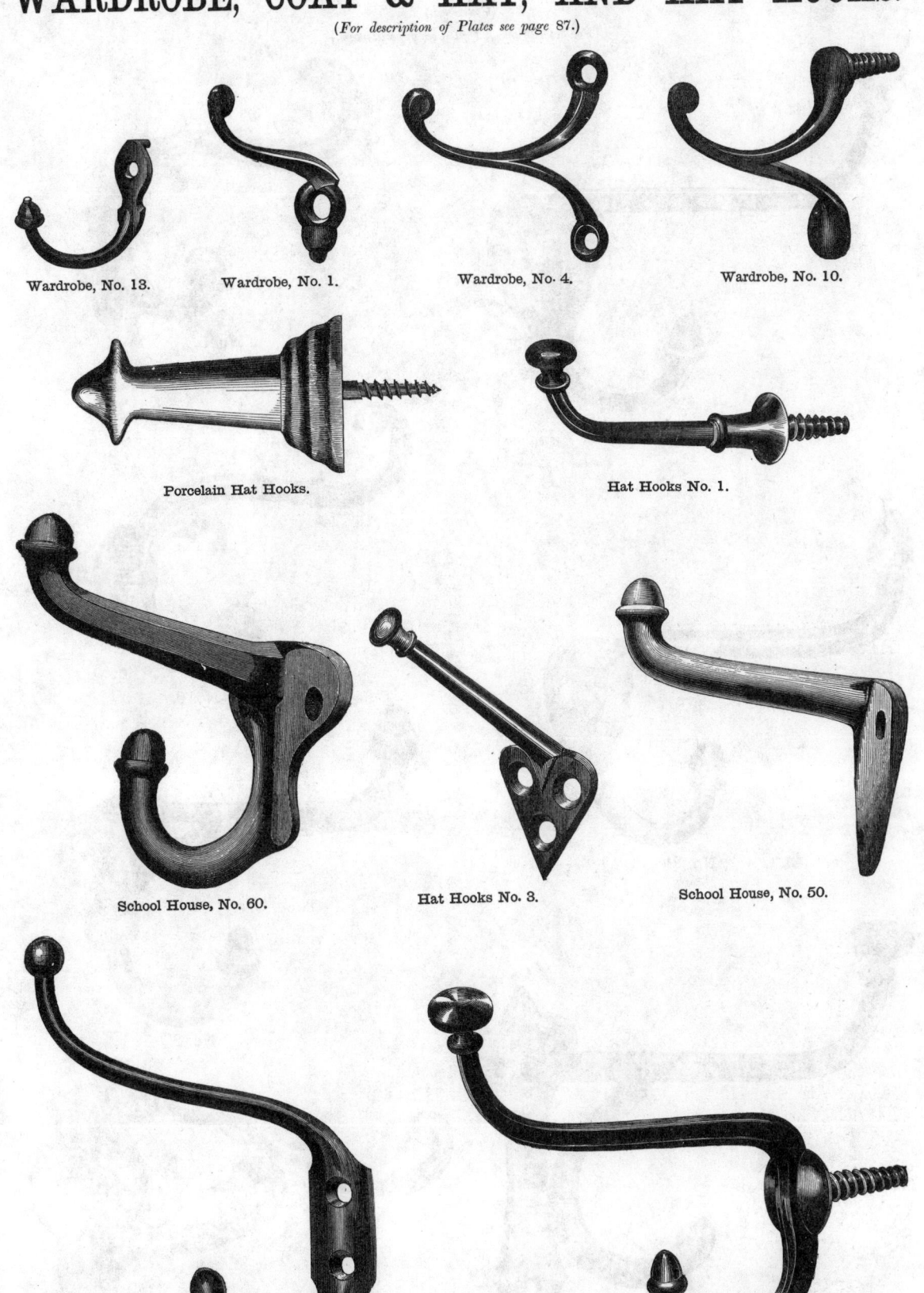

Wardrobe, No. 13.

Wardrobe, No. 1.

Wardrobe, No. 4.

Wardrobe, No. 10.

Porcelain Hat Hooks.

Hat Hooks No. 1.

School House, No. 60.

Hat Hooks No. 3.

School House, No. 50.

Coat and Hat Hooks No. 1.

Coat and Hat Hooks No. 2.

COAT AND HAT HOOKS.

(Continued.)

[For description of Plates, see opposite page.]

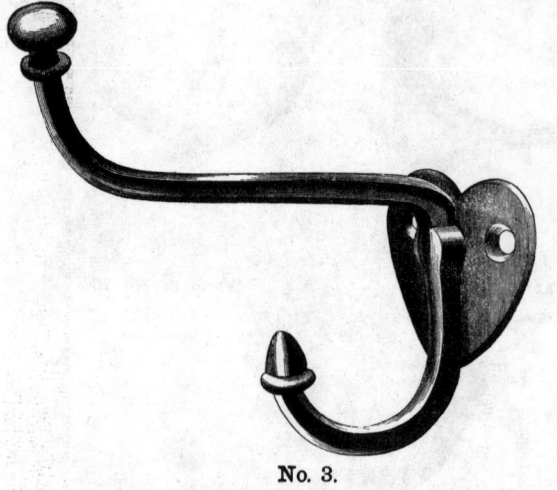

No. 3.

No. 5.

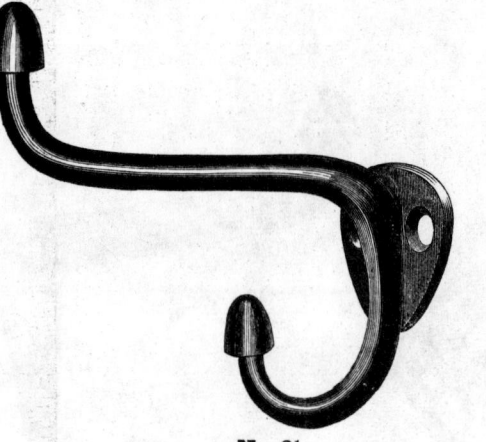

No. 3½.

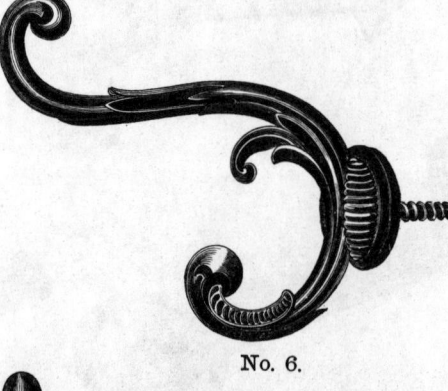

No. 6.

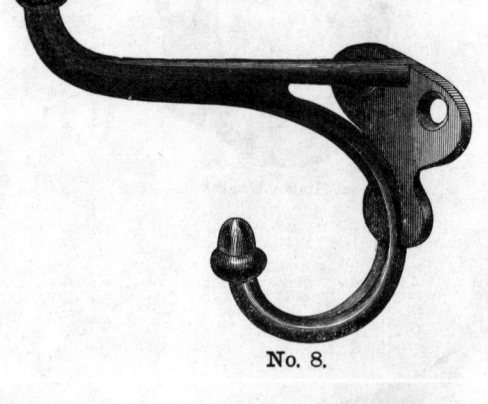

No. 8.

No. 4.

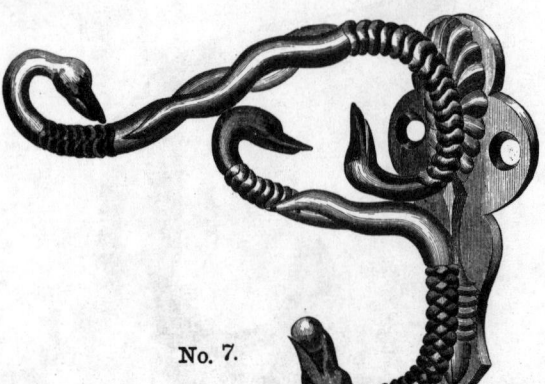

No. 7.

WARDROBE, COAT & HAT, AND HAT HOOKS.

(Continued.)

Harness Hooks, No. 1.

Clothes Line Hooks, No. 1.

Harness Hooks, No. 2.

WARDROBE HOOKS.—See Plates, page 85.

	$					per gross.
Single, Japanned, No. 1	2	3	3½	13	14	15

	$					per gross.
Braced, Japanned, No. 4	5	6	10	11	12	

HAT HOOKS.—See Plates, page 85.

	$			per gross.
Japanned, No. 1	2	3	4

Porcelain, Plain, Fluted or fancy (see Plate, page 85)$ per gross.

SCHOOL HOUSE.—See Plates, page 85.

Japanned, Hat, No. 50.....................per gross, $

Japanned, Coat and Hat, No. 60.............per gross,

COAT & HAT HOOKS.—See Plates, pp. 85, 86.

	$				per gross.
Japanned, No. 1	2	3	3½	4	

	$				per gross.
Japanned, Fancy, No. 5	6	7	8		

	$						per gross.
Bronzed, No. 1	2	3	4	5	6	7	

HARNESS HOOKS.

Japanned, Double, very Heavy, No. 1 (see Plate), per gross, $

Japanned, Double, No. 2........................per gross,

CLOTHES-LINE or HAMMOCK HOOKS.

Japanned, No. 1 (see Plate)...................per dozen, $

Japanned, No. 2 (see Plate)...................per dozen,

JAMB HOOKS.

No. 1.

No. 2.

No. 3.

Japanned, single...............................per doz. pairs, $
Bronzed, single................................per doz. pairs,
Brass, single, No. 1, Heavy (see Plate)..........per doz. pairs,
Brass, single, No. 2, Heavy   "   ....per doz. pairs,
Brass, double, No. 3, Heavy   "   ....per doz. pairs,

PICTURE SPIKES.

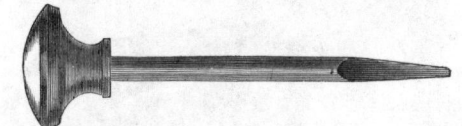

Plain Brass Head, Porcelain Center,

$ per dozen.

No. 1	2	3	4
$2\frac{1}{2}$	3	$3\frac{1}{2}$	4 inch.

Silver Plated Head, Porcelain Center,

$ per dozen.

No. 1	2	3	4
$2\frac{1}{2}$	3	$3\frac{1}{2}$	4 inch.

BRASS OX BALLS.

No. 1.

No. 2.

No. 3.

No. 4.

EXTRA HEAVY.		LIGHT.	
Octagon, Solid, No. 1 ....per gross, $		Octagon, Solid, No. 56 ....per gross, $	
Octagon, Solid, No. 2 ....per gross,		Octagon, Solid, No. 57 ....per gross,	
Octagon, Solid, No. 3 ....per gross,		Octagon, Solid, No. 58 ....per gross,	
Octagon, Solid, No. 4 ....per gross,		Octagon, Solid, No. 59 ....per gross,	

HEAVY CAST BRASS FERRULES.

	$\frac{3}{8}$ inch.	$\frac{1}{2}$ inch.	$\frac{5}{8}$ inch.	$\frac{3}{4}$ inch.	$\frac{7}{8}$ inch.	1 inch.
Rough,......$	$	$	$	$	$	per gross.
Polished, ...$	$	$	$	$	$	per gross.

STORE DOOR SHUTTER TRIMMINGS.

Shutter Screws.

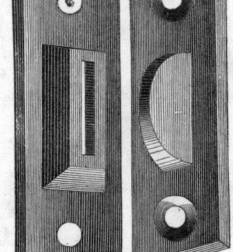

Square.

Round.

Shutter Locks, with three Keys to each dozen..$ per dozen.

Screws, Japanned $ per gross.

       1¾, 2 and 2¼   2½, 2¾ and 3   3½ inch.

Screws, Brass, $ per dozen.

       1¾   2   2¼   2½ inch.

Stubbs and plates, Japanned, SQUARE.

       $ per gross.

Stubbs and Plates, Japanned, ROUND.

       $ per gross.

Shutter Lifts, Flush.

Shutter Lifts. 3 Hole.

Lifts, Japanned, Flush....................$ per gross. | Lifts, Japanned, 3 hole.....................$ per gross.

FLUSH RINGS AND TWINE BOXES.

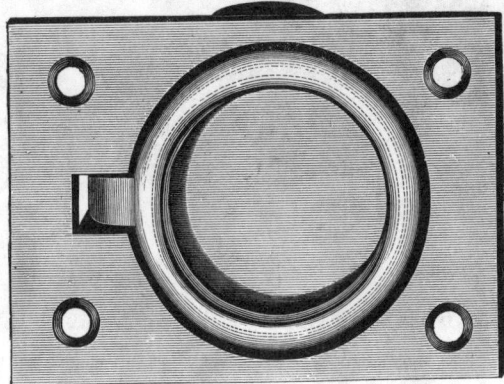

Flush Rings, for Sliding Barn and Trap Doors.

Patent Bivalve Twine Boxes.

    $ per dozen.

    No. 1   2   3

Japanned No. 3.....................$ per dozen.

Bronzed No. 4.....................$ per dozen

BOLTS.

MORTISE BOLTS, FOR INSIDE DOORS.

Crosby's Patent, No. 4.　　　　　　Round Cased, 3 inch.

"CROSBY'S" PATENT ECCENTRIC, FOR INSIDE DOORS.

¾×3, Round Cased, Spring Bolt,

		All Iron.	All Brass.
No. 1, " With Japanned Iron Knobs....per doz.			
No. 2, " With Bronzed Iron Knobs ....per doz.			
No. 3, " With Mineral Knobs, Japanned Roses.................per doz.			
No. 4, " With Porcelain Knobs, Plated Roses (see Plate.).........per doz.			
No. 6, " With Electro Plated Knobs...per doz.			

ALL BRASS, ROUND CASED, MORTISE, ¾ INCH DIAMETER.

3 inch, with Brass Knobs (see Plate.)......per dozen, $
3 inch, with Porcelain Knobs............per dozen,
3½ inch, with Brass Knobs.................per dozen,
3½ inch, with Porcelain Knobs............per dozen
4 inch, with Brass Knobs.................per dozen,
4 inch, with Porcelain Knobs............per dozen,
5 inch, with Brass Knobs.................per dozen,
5 inch, with Porcelain Knobs............per dozen,

No. 99, Mortise Bolt.

No. 99.　Size 1¾ × 2⅞ Inch.

Square Cased, Mortise, Brass Front, Strike, Hub and Bolt, Heavy, for Inside Doors..............per dozen, $
With Mineral Knobs, Japanned Roses...................add per dozen,
With Porcelain Knobs, Plated Roses...................add per dozen,
With Brass Knobs.................................add per dozen,
With Electro Plated Knobs...........................add per dozen,
With Hand Plated Knobs.............................add per dozen,

BOLTS.

(Continued.)

HEAVY BRASS BOLTS, FOR SHIP USE.

[For description of Plates, see page 92.]

Heavy, Flat.

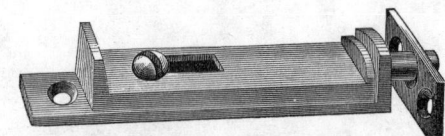

Heavy Cupboard, Straight.

Heavy Cupboard, Necked.

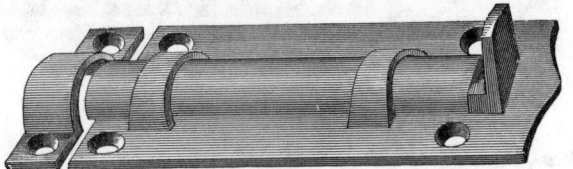

Heavy Half-Round.

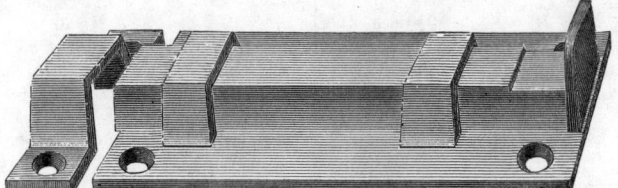

Heavy Square. Straight.

Heavy, Round.

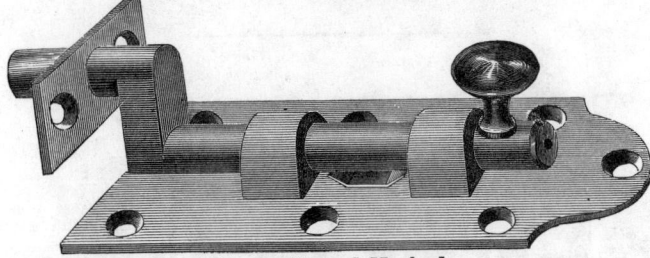

Heavy, Round Necked.

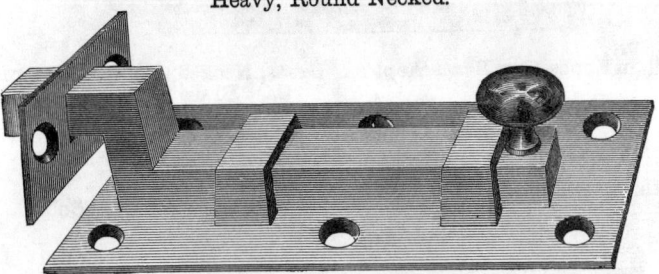

Heavy, Square Necked.

BOLTS.

(Continued.)

HEAVY CAST BRASS BOLTS, FOR SHIP USE.

(See Plates. page 91.)

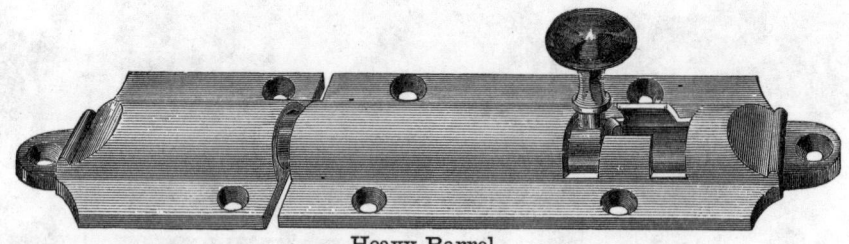

Heavy Barrel.

	$				per dozen.
Brass, **Flat**,.................... 2½			3 inch,		

		$			per dozen.
Brass, **Cupboard, Straight,** 2	2½	3	3½ inch,		

		$		per dozen.
Brass, **Cupboard, Necked,**			3½ inch,	

	$		per dozen.
Brass, **Half Round**........ 4 inch,			

	$				per dozen.
Brass, **Square, Straight**...3	4	5	6 inch,		

	$				per dozen.
Brass, **Square, Necked,** 3	4	5	6 inch,		

	$				per doz.
Brass, **Round, Straight**.2½	3	4	5	6 inch,	

	$		per dozen.
Brass, **Round, Necked**.......5 inch,			

	$					per dozen
Brass, **Barrel**.........3	4	5	6	8 inch,		

LIGHT CAST BRASS BOLTS,

Same Pattern as the Heavy.

	$			per dozen.
Brass, **Square**........ 2½	3		4 inch,	

	$			per dozen.
Square, **Necked**........3		4	5 inch,	

"DOEN'S" PATENT SPRING BOLTS.

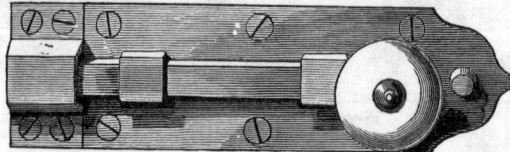

Brass Bolts, with Porcelain Knobs, Cast Brass Staples,

	$			per dozen.
3½	4	4½	5 inch,	

Silver Plated Bolts, with Porcelain or Plated Knobs,

	$			per dozen.
3½	4	4½	5 inch,	

Brass, Necked, Bolts, with Porcelain Knobs, Cast Brass Staples,

	$		per dozen.
4½		5 inch,	

Silver Plated, Necked, Bolts,

	$		per dozen.
4½		5 inch,	

BOLTS.

(Continued.)

"DOEN'S" PATENT SPRING BOLTS.

(Continued.)

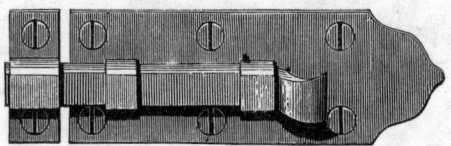

Iron, Wrought Japanned Plate,	Brass Bolts, Wrought Iron Japanned Plate,
$ per doz.	$ per doz.
No. 1, 2, 3, 4, 5, 6.	No. 13, 14, 15, 16, 17, 18.
2½ 3 3½ 4 4½ 5 inch,	2½ 3 3½ 4 4½ 5 inch,
Iron, Wrought Japanned Plate, with Brass Bands,	Brass Bolts, Wrought Brass Plate,
$ per doz.	$ per doz.
No. 7, 8, 9, 10, 11, 12.	No. 19, 20, 21, 22, 23. 24.
2½ 3 3½ 4 4½ 5 inch,	2½ 3 3½ 4 4½ 5 inch,

"DOEN'S" PATENT SPRING NECKED BOLTS.

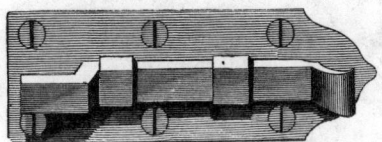

Iron, Wrought Japanned Plate,	Brass Bolts, Wrought Iron Japanned Plate,
$ per doz.	$ per doz.
No. 25, 26, 27, 28, 29, 30.	No. 37, 38, 39, 40, 41, 42.
2½ 3 3½ 4 4½ 5 inch,	2½ 3 3½ 4 4½ 5 inch,
Iron, Wrought Japanned Plate, with Brass Bands,	Brass Bolts, Wrought Brass Plate,
$ per doz.	$ per doz.
No. 31, 32, 33, 34, 35, 36.	No. 43, 44, 45, 46, 47, 48.
2½ 3 3½ 4 4½ 5 inch,	2½ 3 3½ 4 4½ 5 inch,

BOLTS.

(Continued.)

CHAIN BOLTS.

Brass, Plain, 2	3	4	6	8 inch	$ per doz.	Iron Japanned,

| Brass, Fancy, 2 | 3 | | 4 inch | $ per doz. | 3 | 4 | 6 | 8 | 10 inch. | $ per dozen. |

CHAIN DOOR FASTENINGS.

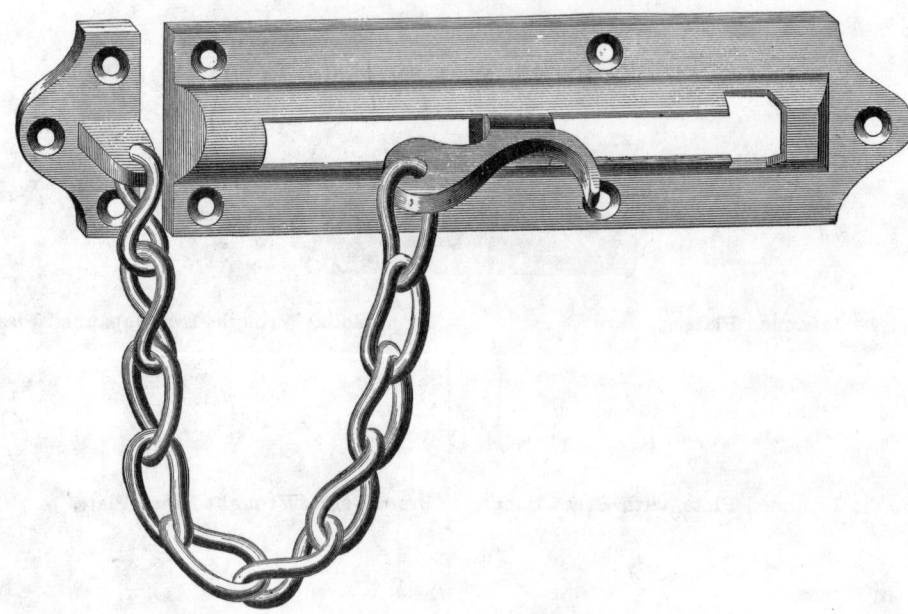

Japanned, 6 inch .... per dozen, $

Brass, 6 inch .... per dozen, $

Silver Plated, 6 inch .... per dozen, $

BOLTS.

(Continued.)

CAST BRASS FLUSH BOLTS.

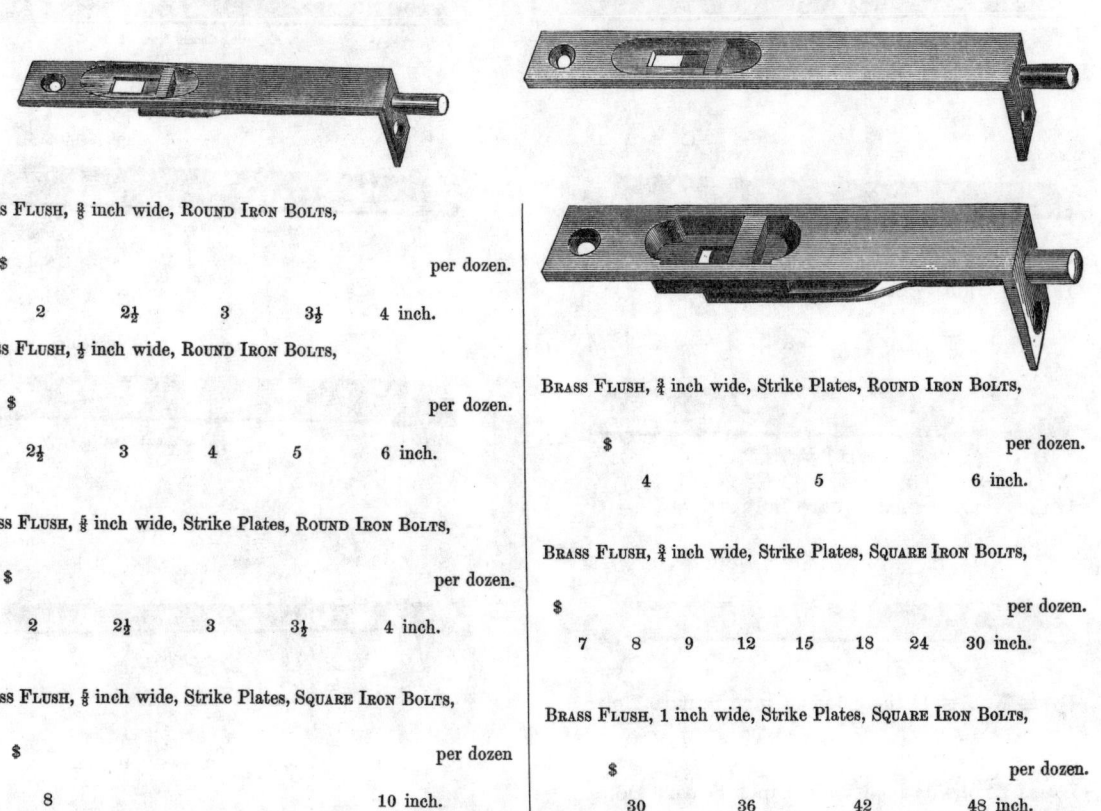

BRASS FLUSH, ⅜ inch wide, ROUND IRON BOLTS,

$ per dozen.

     2   2½   3   3½   4 inch.

BRASS FLUSH, ½ inch wide, ROUND IRON BOLTS,

$ per dozen.

     2½   3   4   5   6 inch.

BRASS FLUSH, ⅝ inch wide, Strike Plates, ROUND IRON BOLTS,

$ per dozen.

     2   2½   3   3½   4 inch.

BRASS FLUSH, ⅝ inch wide, Strike Plates, SQUARE IRON BOLTS,

$ per dozen

     8   10 inch.

BRASS FLUSH, ¾ inch wide, Strike Plates, ROUND IRON BOLTS,

$ per dozen.

     4   5   6 inch.

BRASS FLUSH, ¾ inch wide, Strike Plates, SQUARE IRON BOLTS,

$ per dozen.

    7   8   9   12   15   18   24   30 inch.

BRASS FLUSH, 1 inch wide, Strike Plates, SQUARE IRON BOLTS,

$ per dozen.

    30   36   42   48 inch.

CAST BRASS FLUSH BOLTS,

FOR SHIP USE.

BRASS FLUSH, HEAVY, with BRASS HEAD Bolts, 1¾ × 1½ inch.

                    $ per dozen.

BRASS FLUSH, HEAVY, with BRASS HEAD Bolts, 2 × 1½ inch.

                    $ per dozen.

BRASS FLUSH, HEAVY, ¾ inch wide, with BRASS HEAD Bolts,

$ per dozen.

    2   3   4   5   6 inch.

BRASS FLUSH, HEAVY, 1 inch wide, with BRASS HEAD Bolts,

$ per dozen.

    8   10   12   18   24 inch.

BRASS FLUSH, HEAVY, BULKHEAD, 5 × 2 inch.

                    $ per dozen.

BOLTS.

(Continued.)

WROUGHT IRON FLUSH BOLTS.

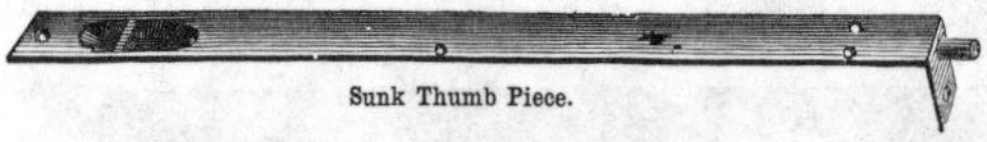

Sunk Thumb Piece. 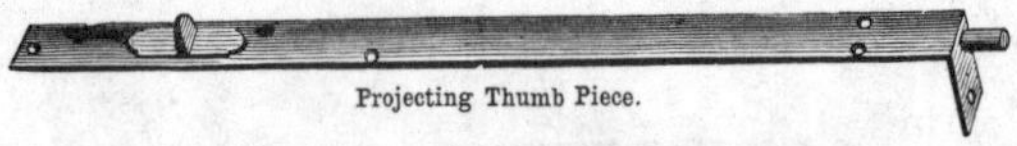　　Projecting Thumb Piece.

¾ inch wide, ¼ inch Round Bolt.

$	6	9	12	15	18	21	24	30	36	42 inch.	per dozen.

Sunk Thumb Piece. 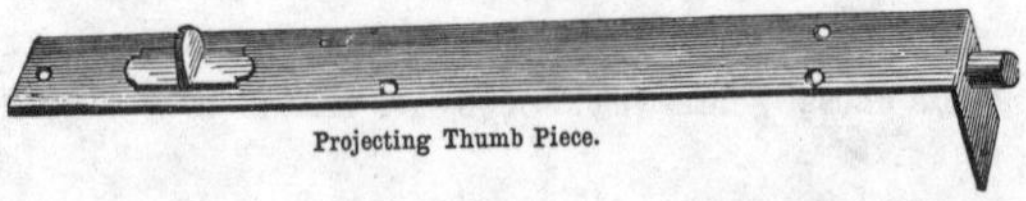　　Projecting Thumb Piece.

1¼ inch wide, 7⁄16 inch Round Bolt.

$	6	9	12	15	18	21	24	30	36 inch.	per dozen.

Sunk Thumb Piece. 　　Projecting Thumb Piece.

1¾ inch wide, ⅝ inch Square Bolt.

$	12	15	18	24	30	36	42	48 inch.	per dozen.

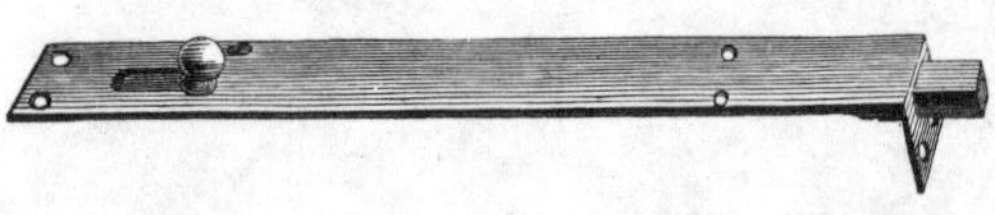

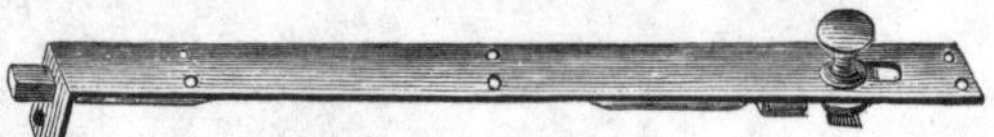

Brass Knobs, 1¼ inch wide, ½ inch Square Bolts.

$	6	9	12	15	18	21	24	30	36	42	48 inch.	per dozen.

Brass Knobs, 1½ inch wide, ½ inch Square Bolts.

$	6	9	12	15	18	21	24	30	36	42	48 inch.	per dozen.

Brass Knobs, Polished Plates, Extra Heavy, 1¼ inch, 9⁄16 inch Square Bolts.

$	6	9	12	15	18	24	30	36	42	48 inch.	per dozen.

☞ Iron Flush Bolts with Silver Plated Knobs furnished to order.

CANADA BOLTS.

Bolts ½ × ¼ in. Iron Plates 1 in. or 1¼ in. as ordered.　1 in. Plates have Staples to drive.　1¼ in. Plates have Staples on Plates to screw.

With Mineral Knobs, Japanned Shanks, Plates and Staples.

$	6	9	12	15	18	21	24	30	36 inch.	per dozen.

With Porcelain or Mineral Knobs, Plated Shanks, Bright Plates and Staples.

$	6	9	12	15	18	21	24	30	36 inch.	per dozen.

With Porcelain Knobs, Japanned Shanks, Plates and Staples.

$	6	9	12	15	18	21	24	30	36 inch.	per dozen.

BOLTS.

(Continued.)

CANADA SASH KNOBS—TO SCREW.

Mineral Knobs, Japanned Shanks,
2 inch........................$ per dozen.

Mineral Knobs, Plated Shanks,
2 inch...........................$ per dozen.

Porcelain Knobs, Japanned Shanks,
2 inch...............................$ per dozen.

Porcelain Knobs, Plated Shanks,
2 inch...............................$ per dozen.

TOWER, AND BRASS KNOB BARREL BOLTS.

Tower Bolts.

Brass Knob Barrel Bolts.

$ per doz. | $ per doz.
4   5   6   7   8   9   10 inch. | 4   5   6   7   8   9   10 inch.

BRASS KNOB SHUTTER, AND STEEL SPRING SQUARE BOLTS.

Brass Knob Shutter Bolts.

Steel Spring Square Bolts.

$ per doz. | $ per doz.
6   8   10   12 inch. | 4   5   6   7   8   9   10   12 inch.

BRASS KNOB CHAMBER BOLTS.

Brass Knob Chamber Bolts.

5 inch...   per dozen.

SQUARE SPRING NECKED BOLTS.

Square Spring Necked Bolts.
WITH BRASS KNOB.

Square Spring Necked Bolts.

$ per dozen. | $ per dozen.
4   5 inch. | 6   7   8   9 inch.

WROUGHT IRON BRASS KNOB BARREL BOLTS.

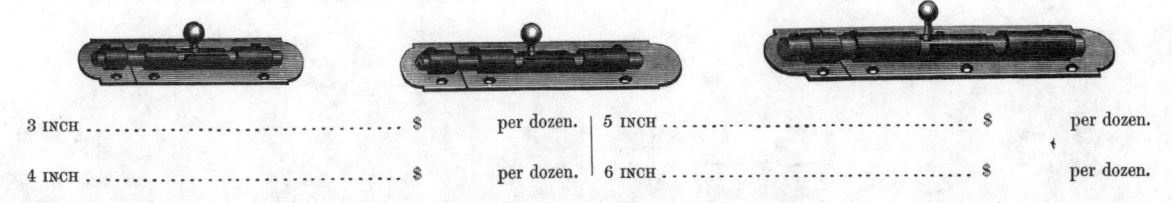

3 INCH.............................$ per dozen. | 5 INCH.............................$ per dozen.

4 INCH.............................$ per dozen. | 6 INCH.............................$ per dozen.

BOLTS.

(Continued.)

COTTAGE, AND HOTEL CHAMBER BOLTS.

Cottage Bolts.	Hotel Chamber Bolts.

$ per dozen | $ per dozen.

4   5   6   7 inch.   4   5 inch.

WROUGHT IRON SQUARE SPRING BOLTS.

Common.	Extra Heavy.

$ per dozen. | $ per dozen

4   5   6   7   8   9   10   12 inch.   4   5   6   7   8   9 inch.

WROUGHT IRON FLAT AND ROUND TAIL BOLTS.

EXTRA QUALITY AND HEAVY.

Wrought Iron Flat Tail Bolts.	Wrought Iron Round Tail Bolts.

$ per dozen. | $ per dozen.

12   15   18   24   30   36   42   48 inch.   12   18   24   30 inch.

Longer sizes made to order.

WROUGHT IRON, AND WROUGHT IRON NECK SHUTTER BOLTS.

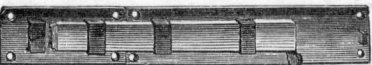

Wrought Iron Shutter Bolts.	Wrought Iron Neck Shutter Bolts.

$ per doz. | $ per dozen.

6   7   8   9   10   11   12   13   14 inch.   6   7   8   9   10 inch.

WROUGHT IRON STORE DOOR, AND CASED SHUTTER BOLTS.

CAST CASE, WROUGHT BOLT.

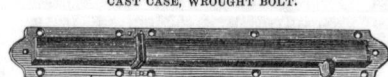

Heavy Wrought Iron Store Door Bolts.	Cased Shutter Bolts.

Bolts ¾ inch square.

$ per dozen. | $ per dozen.

10   12   14 inch.   6   8   10   12 inch.

FLOOR STAPLES FOR SQUARE SPRING BOLTS. | STAPLES FOR SQUARE SPRING BOLTS.

$ $ per dozen. | $ per dozen.

6   7   8   9   10   11   12 inch.   4 & 5   6 & 7   8 & 9   10   12 inch.

SHOVELS AND TONGS.

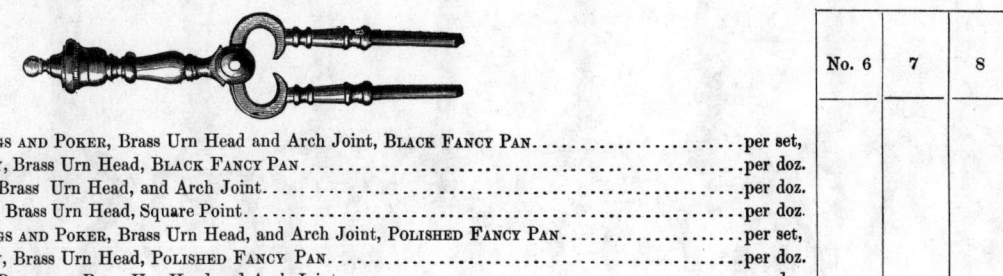

	No. 1	2	3	4	5	6
Shovel and Tongs, All Iron, Solid Head, Improved Square Pan, with 3 Rivets . . per dozen pairs,						
Shovels only, All Iron, Solid Head, Improved Square Pan, with 3 Rivets . . per dozen,						
Tongs only, All Iron, Solid Head. . . . . .per dozen,						
KITCHEN, Shovel and Tongs, All Iron, Solid Head, Improved Square Pan, with 3 Rivets . . . . per dozen pairs,						
KITCHEN, Shovels only, All Iron, Solid Head, Improved Square Pan, with 3 Rivets . . . . .per dozen,						
KITCHEN, Tongs only, All Iron, Solid Head. . . . . .per dozen,						
Brass Head, SHOVEL AND TONGS, Improved BLACK Square Pan, with 3 Rivets . . .per pair,						
Brass Head, SHOVELS ONLY, Improved BLACK Square Pan, with 3 Rivets . . . . . . .per doz.						
Brass Head, TONGS ONLY. . . . . .per doz.						
Brass Head, SHOVEL AND TONGS, Improved POLISHED Square Pan, with 3 Rivets . .per pair,						
Brass Head, SHOVELS ONLY, Improved POLISHED Square Pans, with 3 Rivets . . . .per doz.						
Brass Head, TONGS ONLY, Polished. . . . . .per doz.						

	No. 6	7	8
SHOVEL, TONGS AND POKER, Brass Urn Head and Arch Joint, BLACK FANCY PAN . . . . .per set,			
SHOVELS ONLY, Brass Urn Head, BLACK FANCY PAN. . . . . .per doz.			
TONGS ONLY, Brass Urn Head, and Arch Joint. . . . . .per doz.			
POKERS ONLY, Brass Urn Head, Square Point. . . . . .per doz.			
SHOVEL, TONGS AND POKER, Brass Urn Head, and Arch Joint, POLISHED FANCY PAN . . . . .per set,			
SHOVELS ONLY, Brass Urn Head, POLISHED FANCY PAN. . . . . .per doz.			
TONGS ONLY, POLISHED, Brass Urn Head and Arch Joint. . . . . .per doz.			
POKERS ONLY, Brass Urn Head, Polished Square Point. . . . . .per doz.			

COAL SCOOPS AND SIFTERS.

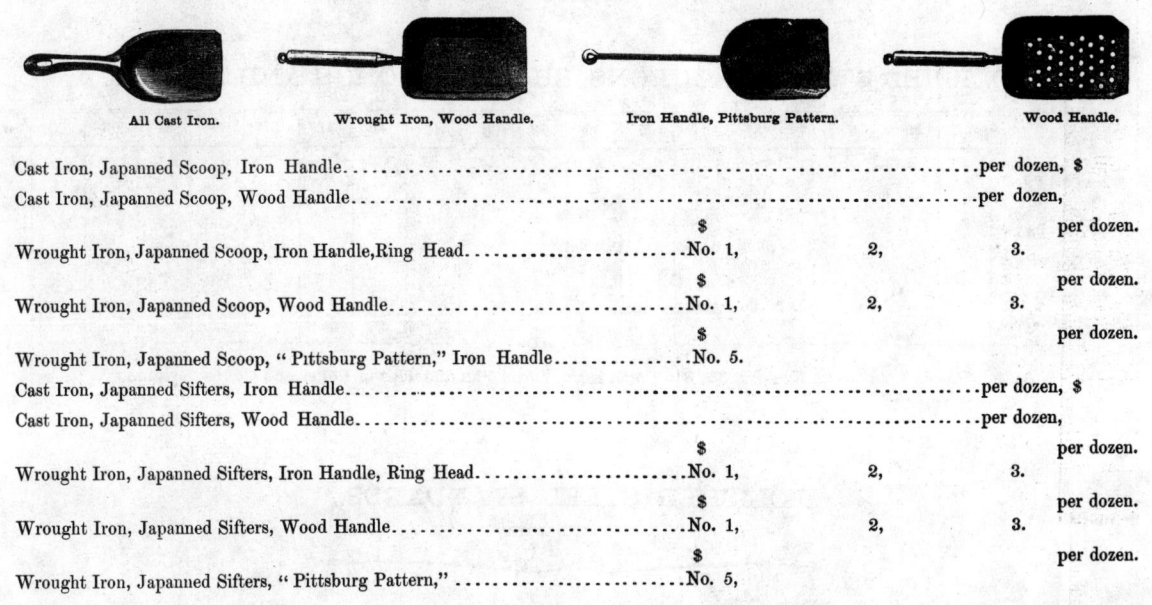

All Cast Iron.   Wrought Iron, Wood Handle.   Iron Handle, Pittsburg Pattern.   Wood Handle.

Cast Iron, Japanned Scoop, Iron Handle. . . . . .per dozen, $			
Cast Iron, Japanned Scoop, Wood Handle. . . . . .per dozen,			
Wrought Iron, Japanned Scoop, Iron Handle, Ring Head. . . . . .No. 1, $ 2, $ 3. per dozen.			
Wrought Iron, Japanned Scoop, Wood Handle. . . . . .No. 1, $ 2, $ 3. per dozen.			
Wrought Iron, Japanned Scoop, "Pittsburg Pattern," Iron Handle. . . . . .No. 5. $ per dozen.			
Cast Iron, Japanned Sifters, Iron Handle. . . . . .per dozen, $			
Cast Iron, Japanned Sifters, Wood Handle. . . . . .per dozen,			
Wrought Iron, Japanned Sifters, Iron Handle, Ring Head. . . . . .No. 1, $ 2, $ 3. per dozen.			
Wrought Iron, Japanned Sifters, Wood Handle. . . . . .No. 1, $ 2, $ 3. per dozen.			
Wrought Iron, Japanned Sifters, "Pittsburg Pattern," . . . . .No. 5, $ per dozen.			

POLISHED STEEL FIRE IRONS.

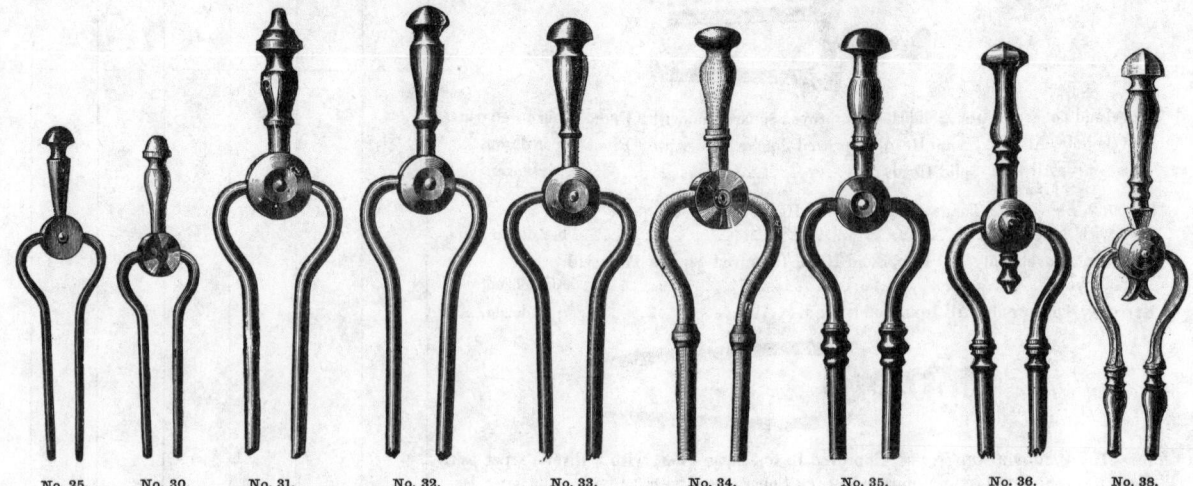

No. 25.   No. 30.   No. 31.   No. 32.   No. 33.   No. 34.   No. 35.   No. 36.   No. 38.

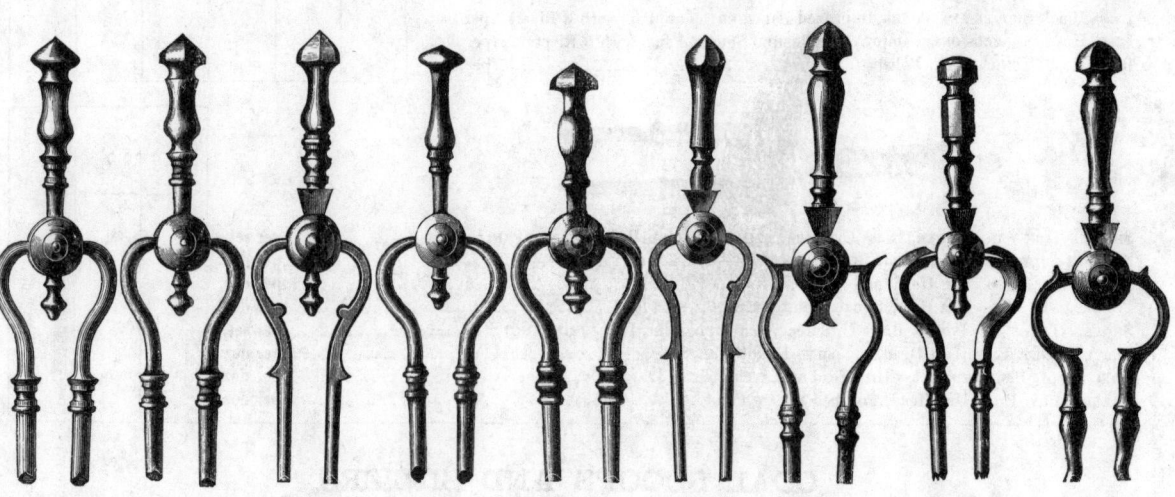

No. 39.   No. 40.   No. 41.   No. 57.   No. 58.   No. 61.   No. 63.   No. 66.   No. 67.

POLISHED STEEL FIRE IRONS, SHOVELS, TONGS AND POKERS.

	No. 25	30	31	32	33	34	35	36	38	39	40	41	42	57	58	61	63	66	67
Shovel, Tongs and Poker ....Per set																			
Shovels and Tongs, Per pair																			
Shovels only.....Per dozen																			
Tongs only ......Per dozen																			
Pokers only......Per dozen																			

All full Polished excepting Nos. 25, 30, 31, which have Shovel Pan and Tips of Poker and Tongs Japanned.

POLISHED STEEL STANDARDS,

TO MATCH ABOVE.

No. 1,   2,   3

$ $ $ each.

PATENT MALLEABLE IRON COAL TONGS.

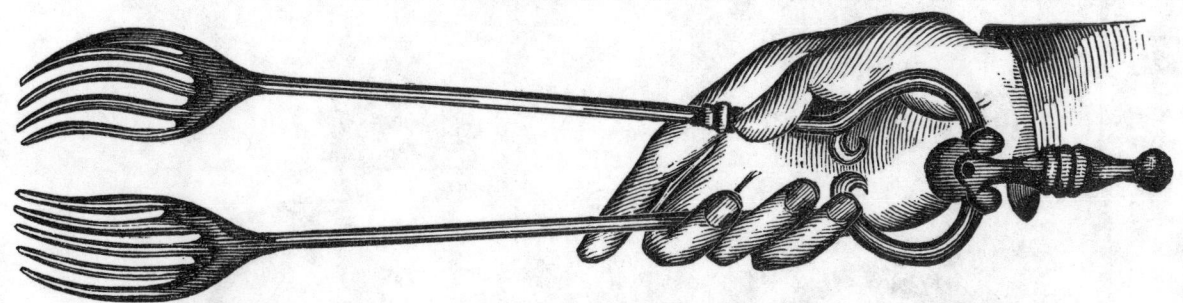

Patent Iron Coal Tongs No. 3.

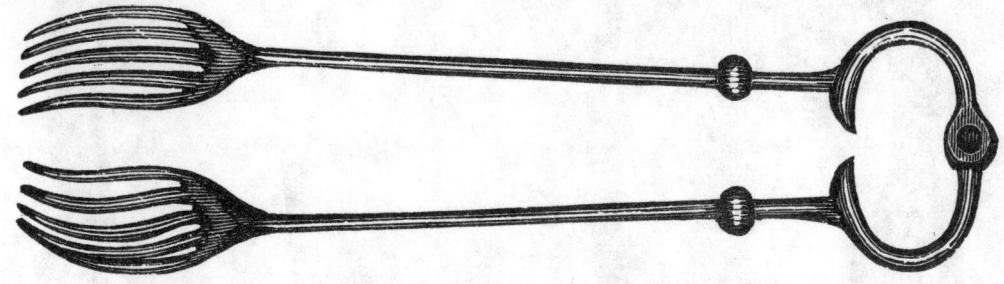

Patent Iron Coal Tongs Nos. 1 and 2.

$	$	$	per dozen.
No. 1,	No. 2,	No. 3,	

POKERS.

☞ We send Bent, unless otherwise ordered. ☜	No. 00	0	1	2	3	4	5	6
All Iron, Bent or Straight Points..........per dozen,								
All Iron, Square Points...........per dozen,								
Brass Head, Bent or Straight Points........per dozen,								
——	No. 1	2	3	4	5	6	7	8
Brass Head, Heavy Square Black Points........per dozen,								
Urn Head, Heavy Square Black Points........per dozen,								
Urn Head, Heavy Square Polished Points........per dozen,								

POKER AND LID-LIFTER COMBINED.

A very useful Kitchen utensil.  Wood Handle, $ per dozen.

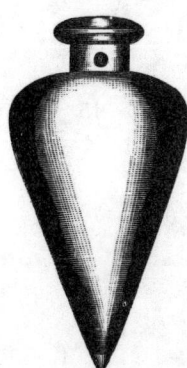

PLUMB BOBS.

	No. 1.	No. 2.
Fine Brass, Steel Pointed..........per dozen, $	$
Lead, Steel Pointed..........per dozen, $	$
Iron, Japanned..........per dozen, $	$

CORK SQUEEZERS.

	No. 1	2	
Japanned..........	$	$	per dozen.

BRASS AND MALLEABLE IRON SPURS.

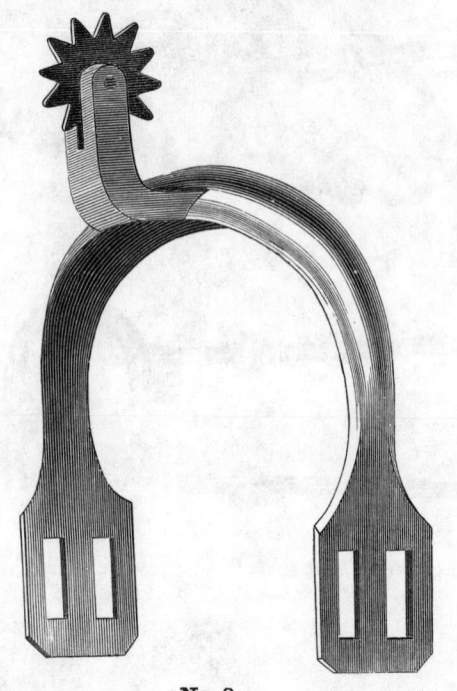

No. 3.

No. 9.

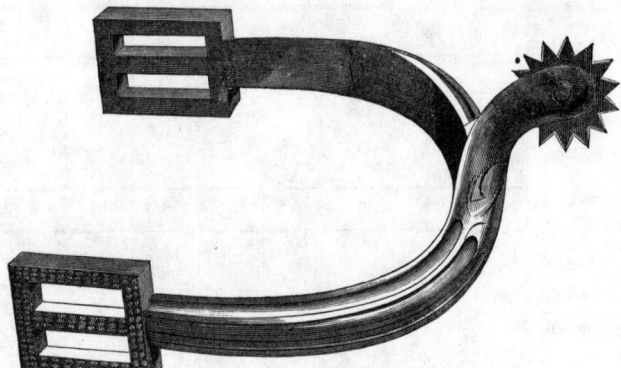

No. 15.

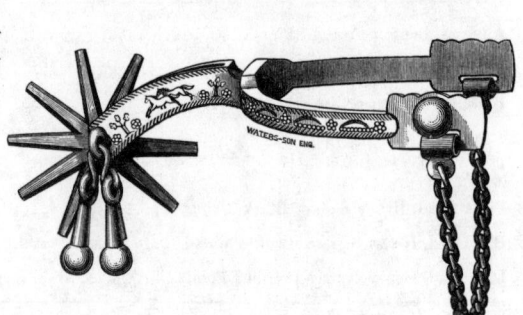

No. 1242.

Fine Brass, Highly Finished	No. 1,	2,	3.
Without Straps, per dozen pairs	$	$	$
With Straps, per dozen pairs	$	$	$
Army Pattern, Gilt Finish	No. 9,	10,	15.
Without Straps, per dozen pairs	$	$	$
With Straps, per dozen pairs	$	$	$
Mexican Pattern, Malleable Iron, Highly Finished	No. 1242,	1244,	1245.
Without Straps, per dozen pairs	$	$	$
With Straps, per dozen pairs	$	$.	$

CAST COW, SHEEP, AND HOUSE BELLS.

PURE BELL METAL.

Cow Bells.

Sheep Bells.

House Bells.

$ per doz.	$ per dozen.
No. 2 3 4 5 6 7 full sizes.	No. 1, 2, full sizes.
	$ per dozen.
	Strapped, No. 1, 2, full sizes.

Nos. 1,   2,   3,   4,   5,   6,   7,   8,

Rough...............per pound, $

Outside Polished........per pound,

(House Bells Mounted with Trimmings complete, see pp. 75, 76)

BORING MACHINES.

With arched Frame, the Spring attached to the Arch, a new and Important Improvement.

No. 0, Machine without Augers................................each, $

No. 0, Machine with Augers................................each, $

No. 1 is a Machine with Turned Journals and Bearings, Gear Polished, Frame Enlarged, the Iron Work Strengthened, and is warranted perfectly accurate in operation, without Augers................each, $

No. 1, With Solid Cast Steel Augers................each, $

BRASS SAW SCREWS.

Flat Head No. 1.   No. 2.   Oval Head No. 1.   No. 2.   Eagle No. 1.   No. 2.

	No. 1.	No. 2.	
Plain, Flat Head	$	$	per gross.
Plain, Oval Head	$	$	per gross.
Fancy, Eagle	$	$	per gross.

MEAT CUTTERS.

"HALE'S PATENT" CUTTER AND STUFFER,

Will cut from 3 to 5 pounds per minute, the quantity varying with the size.

We can without hesitation offer this Cutter as the best article in use for the purpose. It will cut more rapidly (not TEAR the meat), is more simple in construction, having but one knife which is self-sharpening, and easier cleaned than any Cutter made.

$	$	$	per dozen.
No. 11,	12,	13.	
Length of Cylinders, 5 inch,	6 inch,	7½ inch.	

BUTCHERS' MEAT CUTTERS.

 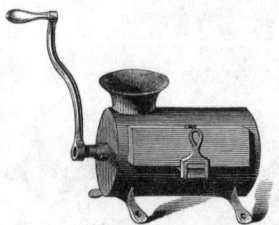

No. 100. Double Cylinder.   No. 5. Single Cylinder.

No. 100. Length of Cylinders 10 inches, with 54 Steel Knives. Can be used with or without power..................each, $ | No. 5. Length of Cylinder 11 inches, with 38 Steel Knives. To be used by hand only...............................each, $

BOOT JACKS.

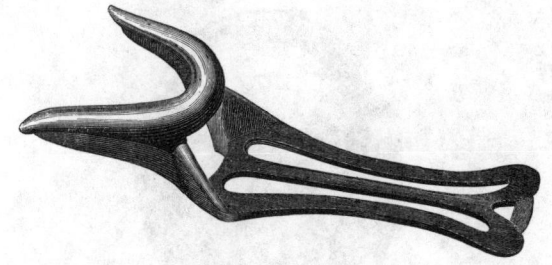

Japanned Boot Jacks, No. 1 .... $ per dozen.

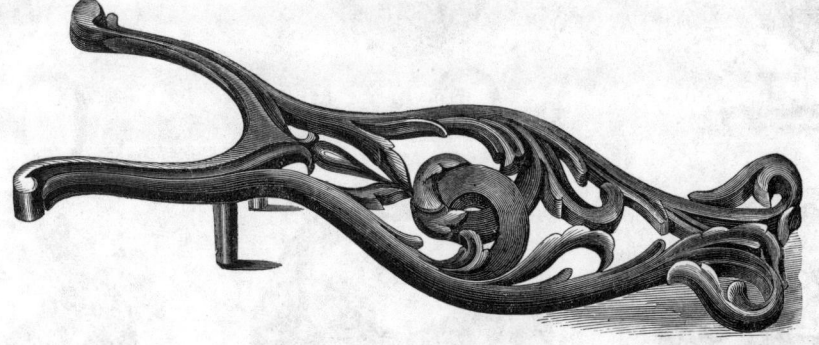

Japanned Boot Jacks, No. 2 .... $ per dozen.

BED KEYS.

Japanned Bed Keys, 3 Socket, and Screw Driver .... $ per dozen.

CAST IRON NAIL HAMMERS, POLISHED AND HANDLED.

$ per dozen.

TUMBLER PADLOCKS,

WITH WROUGHT CASES, SHACKLES AND BOLTS.

(For description of Plates, see page 109.)

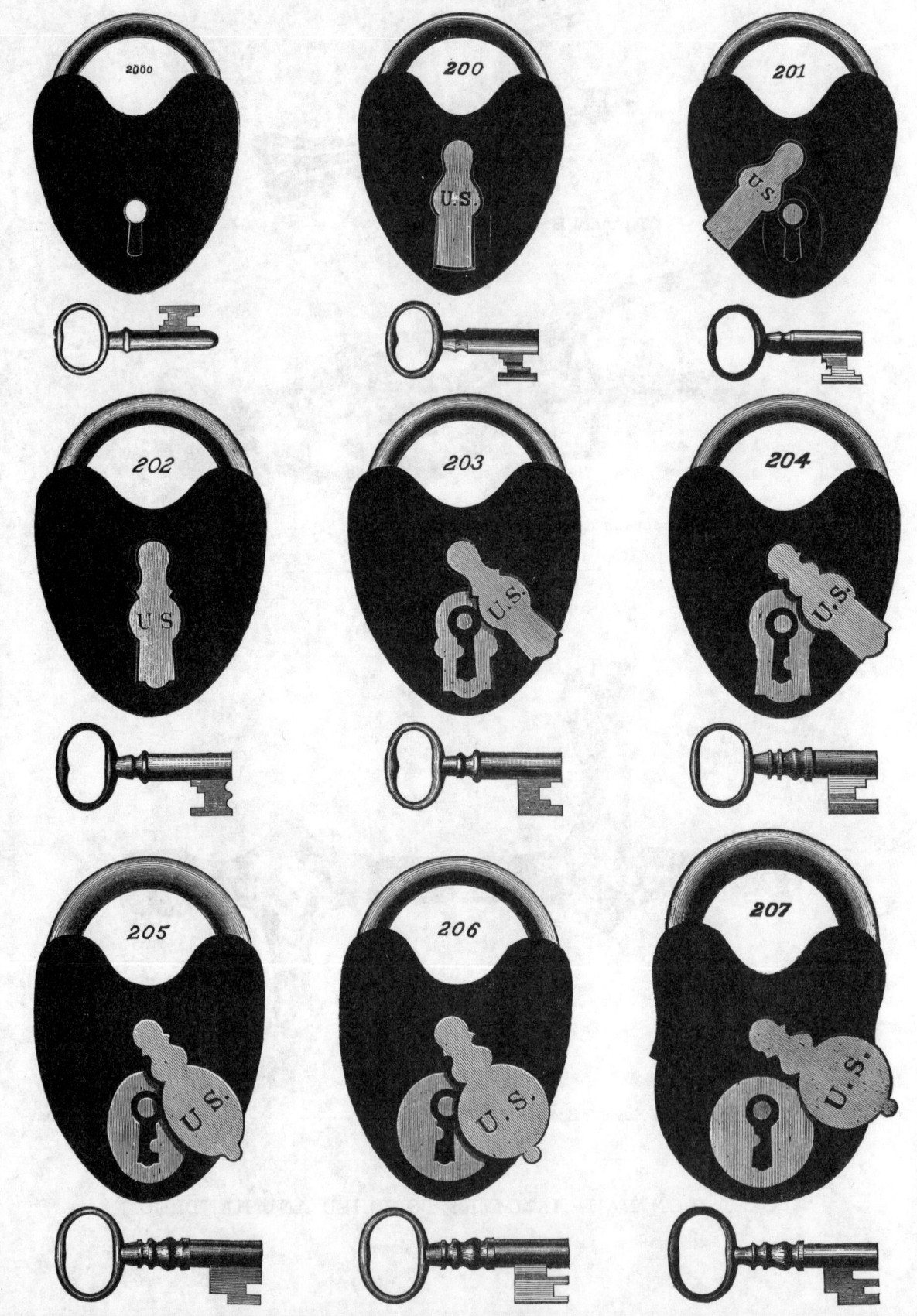

TUMBLER PADLOCKS,

(Continued.)

(For description of Plates see page 109.)

TUMBLER PADLOCKS.

(Continued.)

[For description of Plates, see opposite page.]

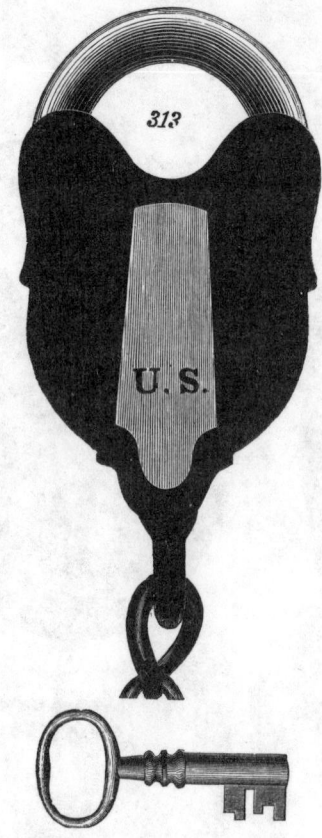 

BRASS SWITCH CIRCULAR PADLOCKS.

[For description of Plates see opposite page.]

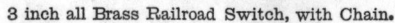

3 inch all Brass Railroad Switch, with Chain.

Circular Padlocks, all Brass.

PADLOCKS.

For Plates, see pages 106, 107, 108.

No.	Inches.	WROUGHT IRON PADLOCKS.	Per Dozen.
2000	2¼	Plain, without Drop	
200	2¼	With Brass Drops	
201	2¼	With Brass Drops and Raised Bushings, with 4 varieties of Keys to the dozen	
202	2½	With Brass Drops	
203	2½	With Brass Drops and Bushings, with 4 varieties of Keys to the dozen	
204	2½	With Brass Drops and Bushings, with 4 varieties of Keys to the dozen	
205	2½	Heavy, with Brass Drops and Bushings, with 6 varieties of Keys to the dozen	
206	2½	2 Wheel and Side Wards, with 12 varieties of Keys to the dozen	
207	2½	2 Wheel and Side Wards, Heavy, with 12 varieties of Keys to the dozen	
208	2¾	2 Wheel, Side and Bridge Wards, with 12 varieties of Keys to the dozen	
209	2½	Solid Brass Wheels, Side and Bridge Wards, with 12 varieties of Keys to the dozen	
210	3	Heavy, with 6 varieties of Keys to the dozen	
211	3	Heavy, Extra Finish, Solid Brass Wheels, Side and Bridge Wards, with 12 varieties of Keys to the dozen	
212	3¼	Heavy, with 6 varieties of Keys to the dozen	
301	2¼	With Chain attached, same style as No. 201	
306	2½	With Chain attached, same style as No. 206	
313	2½	With Chain attached, 3 Tumblers and Bridge Ward, Spring Shackle and Drop, for Railway Cars and Switches	
314	2½	With Chain attached, and Spring Shackle	

ALL BRASS PADLOCKS.

No.	Inches.		Per Dozen.
501	2¼	Same Style as No. 201, Iron Lock	
504	2½	Same Style as No. 204, Iron Lock	
507	2½	Same Style as No. 207, Iron Lock	
509	2½	Same Style as No. 209, Iron Lock	

IRON PADLOCK KEYS.

For Padlocks Nos. 2000 .... per gross, $
For Padlocks Nos. 200, 201, 202, 203, 301 ..... per gross,
For Padlocks Nos. 204 .... per gross,
For Padlocks Nos. 205, 206, 306 .... per gross,
For Padlocks Nos. 207, 208, 209, 210, 212, 314, per gross,
For Padlocks Nos. 211, 313 .... per gross,

BRASS PADLOCK KEYS.

For Padlock No. 501, same Style of Key as No. 201 .. per gross, $
For Padlock No. 504, same Style of Key as No. 204 .. per gross,
For Padlock No. 507, same Style of Key as No. 207 .. per gross,
For Padlock No. 509, same Style of Key as No. 209 .. per gross,

ALL BRASS CIRCULAR PADLOCKS.

Circular—Fine Finish, 2 inch .... per dozen, $
Circular—Fine Finish, 2¼ inch .... per dozen,
Circular—Fine Finish, 2½ inch (see Plate, p. 108) per dozen,
Circular—Fine Finish, 3 inch .... per dozen,
Circular Brass Padlock Keys, for 2, 2¼, 2½, 3 inch Locks,
$ per doz.

ALL BRASS RAILROAD SWITCH AND CAR LOCKS.

Railroad Switch and Car, 3 inch .... per dozen,
Railroad Switch and Car, 3 inch, with Iron
     Chain (see Plate, page 108) .... per dozen,

Brass Railroad Switch Lock Keys .... per dozen,

REVERSE ACTING TUMBLER PADLOCKS,

BRASS AND IRON, WITH DOUBLE-BITTED KEYS.

PYE'S PATENT.

The key is placed in the centre of the tumblers, and moves some in one direction, and others in the opposite direction, the stud in the bolt passing through the tumblers. It is an entirely new and secure Lock cannot be picked, and will not get out of order.

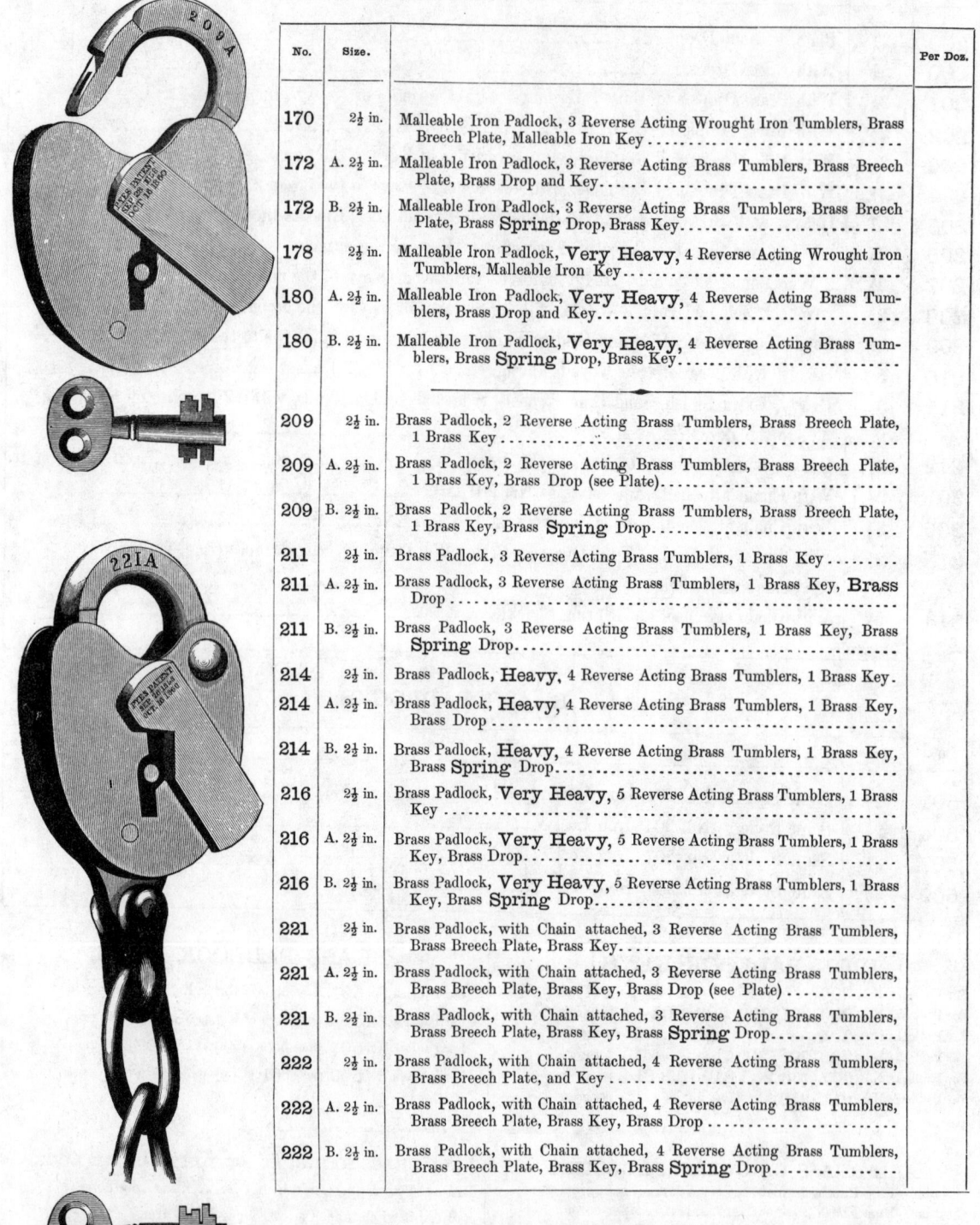

No.	Size.		Per Doz.
170	2½ in.	Malleable Iron Padlock, 3 Reverse Acting Wrought Iron Tumblers, Brass Breech Plate, Malleable Iron Key	
172	A. 2½ in.	Malleable Iron Padlock, 3 Reverse Acting Brass Tumblers, Brass Breech Plate, Brass Drop and Key.	
172	B. 2½ in.	Malleable Iron Padlock, 3 Reverse Acting Brass Tumblers, Brass Breech Plate, Brass **Spring** Drop, Brass Key.	
178	2½ in.	Malleable Iron Padlock, **Very Heavy**, 4 Reverse Acting Wrought Iron Tumblers, Malleable Iron Key.	
180	A. 2½ in.	Malleable Iron Padlock, **Very Heavy**, 4 Reverse Acting Brass Tumblers, Brass Drop and Key.	
180	B. 2½ in.	Malleable Iron Padlock, **Very Heavy**, 4 Reverse Acting Brass Tumblers, Brass **Spring** Drop, Brass Key.	
209	2½ in.	Brass Padlock, 2 Reverse Acting Brass Tumblers, Brass Breech Plate, 1 Brass Key	
209	A. 2½ in.	Brass Padlock, 2 Reverse Acting Brass Tumblers, Brass Breech Plate, 1 Brass Key, Brass Drop (see Plate).	
209	B. 2½ in.	Brass Padlock, 2 Reverse Acting Brass Tumblers, Brass Breech Plate, 1 Brass Key, Brass **Spring** Drop.	
211	2½ in.	Brass Padlock, 3 Reverse Acting Brass Tumblers, 1 Brass Key	
211	A. 2½ in.	Brass Padlock, 3 Reverse Acting Brass Tumblers, 1 Brass Key, **Brass** Drop	
211	B. 2½ in.	Brass Padlock, 3 Reverse Acting Brass Tumblers, 1 Brass Key, Brass **Spring** Drop.	
214	2½ in.	Brass Padlock, **Heavy**, 4 Reverse Acting Brass Tumblers, 1 Brass Key.	
214	A. 2½ in.	Brass Padlock, **Heavy**, 4 Reverse Acting Brass Tumblers, 1 Brass Key, Brass Drop	
214	B. 2½ in.	Brass Padlock, **Heavy**, 4 Reverse Acting Brass Tumblers, 1 Brass Key, Brass **Spring** Drop.	
216	2½ in.	Brass Padlock, **Very Heavy**, 5 Reverse Acting Brass Tumblers, 1 Brass Key	
216	A. 2½ in.	Brass Padlock, **Very Heavy**, 5 Reverse Acting Brass Tumblers, 1 Brass Key, Brass Drop.	
216	B. 2½ in.	Brass Padlock, **Very Heavy**, 5 Reverse Acting Brass Tumblers, 1 Brass Key, Brass **Spring** Drop.	
221	2½ in.	Brass Padlock, with Chain attached, 3 Reverse Acting Brass Tumblers, Brass Breech Plate, Brass Key.	
221	A. 2½ in.	Brass Padlock, with Chain attached, 3 Reverse Acting Brass Tumblers, Brass Breech Plate, Brass Key, Brass Drop (see Plate)	
221	B. 2½ in.	Brass Padlock, with Chain attached, 3 Reverse Acting Brass Tumblers, Brass Breech Plate, Brass Key, Brass **Spring** Drop.	
222	2½ in.	Brass Padlock, with Chain attached, 4 Reverse Acting Brass Tumblers, Brass Breech Plate, and Key	
222	A. 2½ in.	Brass Padlock, with Chain attached, 4 Reverse Acting Brass Tumblers, Brass Breech Plate, Brass Key, Brass Drop	
222	B. 2½ in.	Brass Padlock, with Chain attached, 4 Reverse Acting Brass Tumblers, Brass Breech Plate, Brass Key, Brass **Spring** Drop.	

☞ Any of the above Locks furnished with additional Keys to order. ☜

HINGES,

WITH CAPS COVERING SCREW HOLES, FOR MAHOGANY DOORS, &c.

Size.			Brass.	Electro Plated.	Hand Plated.	Extra Hand Plated.
3½ × 3½	Steel Bushed, Plain Tips	per pair,				
4 × 4	Steel Bushed, Plain Tips	per pair,				
4 × 4½	Steel Bushed, Plain Tips	per pair,				
4½ × 4½	Steel Bushed, Plain Tips	per pair				
4½ × 5	Steel Bushed, Plain Tips	per pair,				
5 × 5	Steel Bushed, Plain Tips	per pair,				
5 × 5½	Steel Bushed, Plain Tips	per pair,				
5 × 6	Steel Bushed, Plain Tips	per pair,				
5 × 7	Steel Bushed, Plain Tips	per pair,				
5½ × 5½	Steel Bushed, Plain Tips	per pair,				
5½ × 6	Steel Bushed, Plain Tips	per pair,				
6 × 6	Steel Bushed, Plain Tips	per pair,				
	Fancy or Acorn Tips,	extra per pair,				

SHUTTER OR BLIND HINGES.

"LULL & PORTER'S" PATENT SELF-LOCKING HINGES, WITH INSIDE FASTENINGS, THE BEST IN USE.

DIRECTIONS.

Select a size so that the Shutter, when open, will leave a space between the wall and the Shutter or Blind, at the Butt, of about one inch. This will give the Blind such a declination as to prevent the wind from closing it.

Set the Hinge flush and square on the Frame and Blind, so that each Hinge has a like bearing; thus set, they will operate smoothly and give entire satisfaction.

Butt Hinge.

Surface Hinge.

Sill Catches.

No. 0 opens 6½ inches...............per dozen pair, $	No. 3 opens 3¼ inches, for Wood.......per dozen pair, $
" 1 opens 5½ inches...............per dozen pair,	" 3½ opens 3¼ inches, for Wood, Heavy.per dozen pair,
" 1½ opens 5 inches...............per dozen pair,	" 4, Surface for Wood...............per dozen pair,
" 2 opens 4¼ inches...............per dozen pair,	" 5, Surface for Brick...............per dozen pair,

Inside Fastenings (or Sill Catches,) only...................$ per dozen.

HINGES.

(Continued.)

LIGHT AND HEAVY STRAP HINGES.

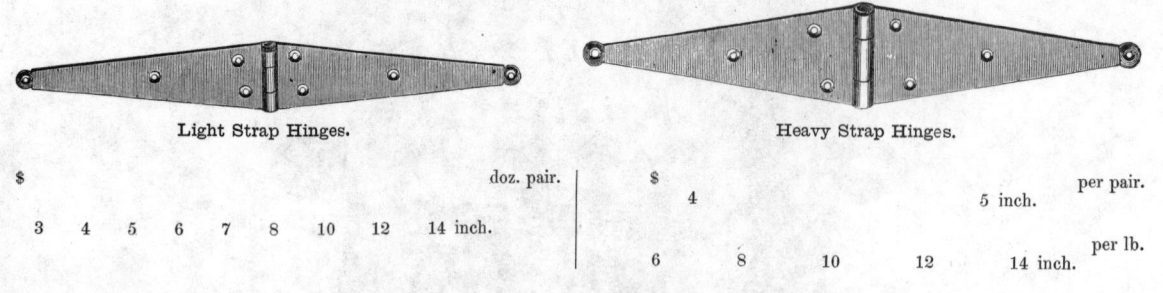

Light Strap Hinges.   Heavy Strap Hinges.

$								doz. pair.		$					per pair.
											4			5 inch.	
3	4	5	6	7	8	10	12	14 inch.							per lb.
										6	8	10	12	14 inch.	

LIGHT AND HEAVY T HINGES.

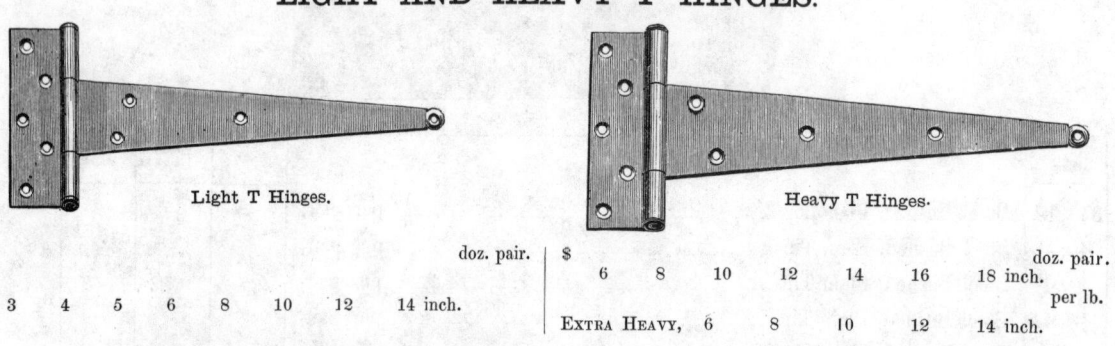

Light T Hinges.   Heavy T Hinges.

$							doz. pair.		$						doz. pair.
										6	8	10	12	14 16 18 inch.	per lb.
3	4	5	6	8	10	12	14 inch.		Extra Heavy,	6	8	10	12	14 inch.	

LONG CHEST, AND BULK, SHUTTER, OR FLASK HINGES.

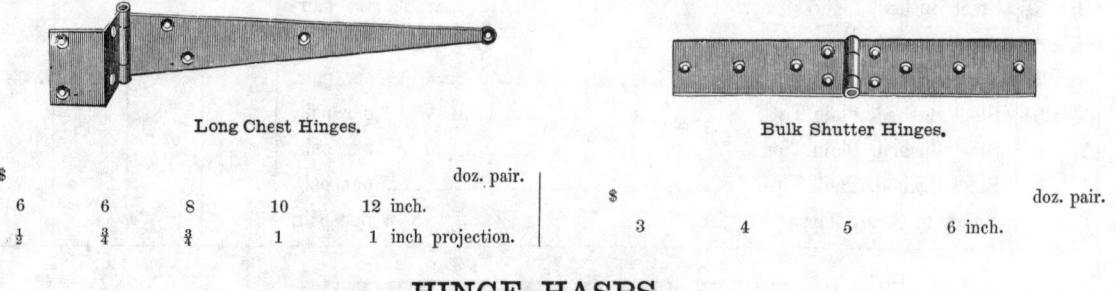

Long Chest Hinges.   Bulk Shutter Hinges.

$				doz. pair.		$				doz. pair.
6	6	8	10	12 inch.						
½	¾	¾	1	1 inch projection.		3	4	5	6 inch.	

HINGE HASPS.

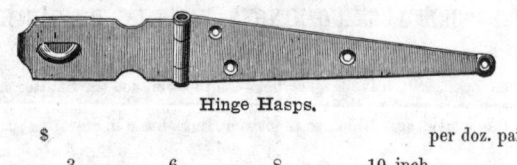

Hinge Hasps.

$			per doz. pair.
3	6	8	10 inch.

ROLLED PLATE, AND ROLLED RAISED HINGES.

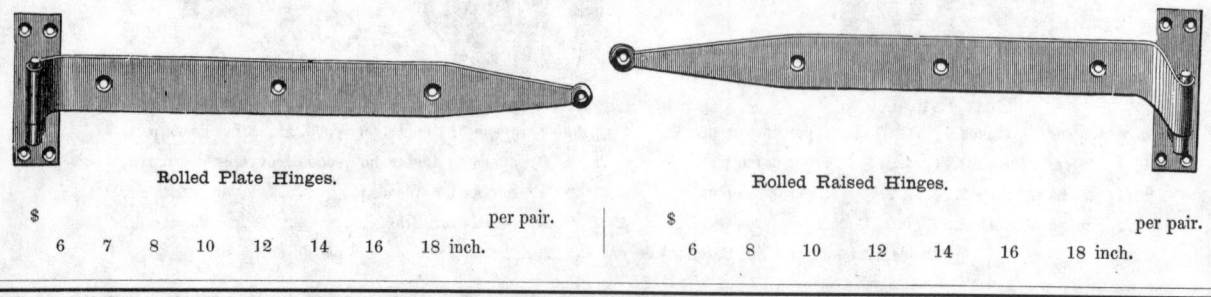

Rolled Plate Hinges.   Rolled Raised Hinges.

$							per pair.		$						per pair.
6	7	8	10	12	14	16	18 inch.			6	8	10	12	14 16 18 inch.	

BLIND HINGES.

(Continued.)

NORWICH PATTERN.

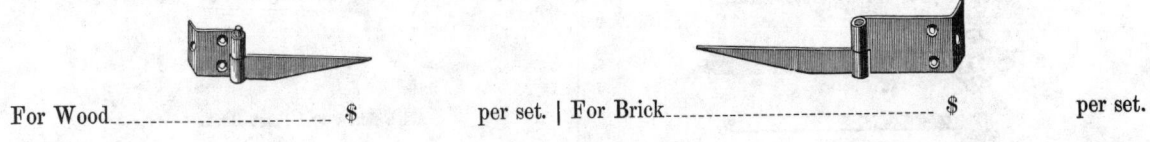

For Wood_____ $ per set. | For Brick_____ $ per set.

ROLLED PLATE, HOOKS TO DRIVE, FOR WOOD.

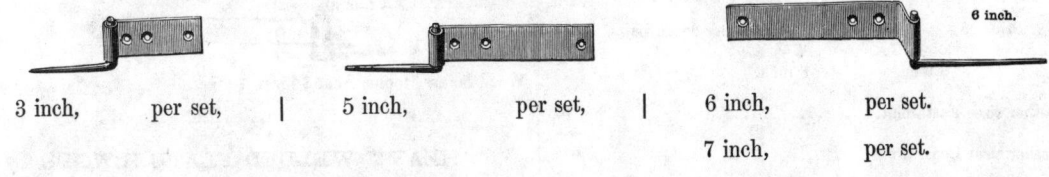

6 inch.

3 inch, per set, | 5 inch, per set, | 6 inch, per set.

7 inch, per set.

ROLLED PLATE, HOOK PLATES TO SCREW, FOR WOOD.

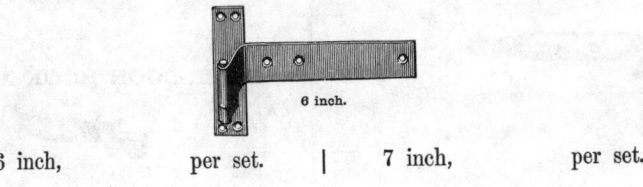

6 inch.

6 inch, per set. | 7 inch, per set.

ROLLED RAISED, HOOKS TO DRIVE, & HOOK PLATES TO SCREW FOR BRICK.

Hooks to Drive for Brick.

6 inch.

Hook Plates to Screw for Brick.

4 inch, per set. | 6 inch, per set.

8 inch, per set.

STEP LADDER JOINTS.

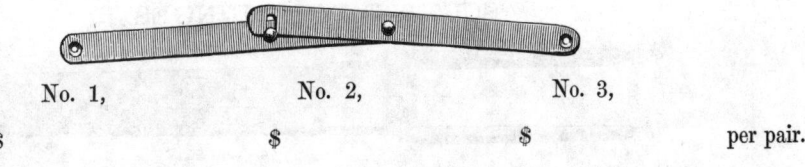

No. 1, No. 2, No. 3,

$ $ $ per pair.

HINGES.

(Continued.)

PROVIDENCE PLATE HINGES.

Straps Tapered and Holes Countersunk.

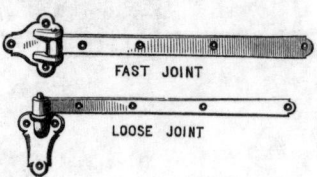

FAST JOINT

LOOSE JOINT

Width of Strap ⅝, ⅝, ¾, ¾, ⅞, 1, 1⅛, 1¼, 1½, 1¾, 2 inch.

Length of Strap 6, 8, 10, 12, 14, 16, 18, 20, 24, 30, 36 inch

     Price, $ per dozen pairs.

       6 inch.   8 inch.

All other sizes Fast Joint.............$ per lb.

All other sizes Loose Joint.............$ "

AMERICAN HOOKS AND HINGES,

ENGLISH PATTERN.

                         per lb.

8   10   12   14   16   18   20   22   24

ROLLED BLIND HINGES,

NEW YORK CITY PATTERN.

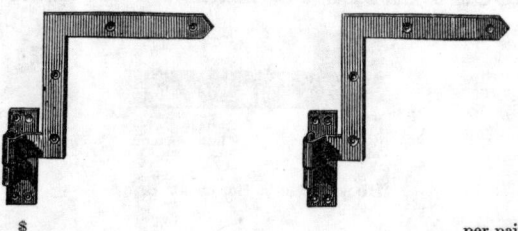

                             per pair.

$

No. 1, for Wood.   No. 2, for Brick.

$ per pair.

No. 3, for Wood or Brick.   No. 4, for Wood or Brick.

HEAVY WELDED HOOK HINGES.

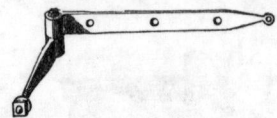

With Screw and Point Hook.

8   10   12   14   16   18   20   24   30 inches to 10 feet.

cents per lb.

HEAVY WELDED HOOK HINGES.

Wood Screw Hooks, from 8 in. to 10 feet,   cts. per lb.

HEAVY WELDED PLATE HINGES.

cents per lb.

HEAVY WELDED RAISED HINGES.

cents per lb.

BARN-DOOR HOOK AND EYE HINGES.

cents per lb.

WELDED, T OR TRAP DOOR HINGES.

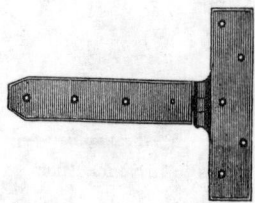

           $ per pair.

Light, $1\frac{3}{16}$ inch Iron, 8   10   12   14   16   18 inch.

          $ pair.

Heavy, ¼ in. Iron, 10   12   14   16   18   20   22   24 in.

SCUTTLE DOOR HINGES.

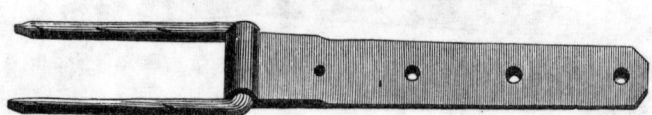

     6   8   10   12 inch.   per lb. $

HINGES,

(Continued.)

WROUGHT IRON BUTTS.

RIVETED PIN AND EASY WORKING JOINT.

NARROW BUTTS, FAST JOINT.

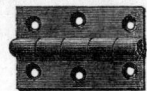

$							doz. pair.
1	1¼	1½	1¾	2	2¼	2½	2¾ inches.
$							doz. pair.
3	3¼	3½	3¾	4	4½	5 inches.	

PEW DOOR BUTTS.

$		doz. pair.
1½	2 inches.	

CHEST HINGES.

$			doz. pair.
1½	2	2½ inches.	

BED HINGES.

$		doz. pair.
2	2½ inches.	

BROAD BUTTS, FAST JOINT.

$					doz. pair.
2×2	2×2½	2½×2½	2½×3	3×2½ inch.	
$					doz. pair.
3×3	3×3½	3½×3	3½×3½	3½×4 inch.	
$					doz. pair.
4×3½	4×4	4×4½	4×5	4½×4½ inch.	
$					doz. pair.
4½×5	5×5	5×6 inch.			

INSIDE BLIND BUTTS.

$	doz. pair.
1⅛	1¼ inch.

LOOSE JOINT DOOR, OR WINDOW BLIND BUTTS.

$					doz. pair.
2×2	2×2½	2½×2	2½×2½	2½×3 inch.	
$					doz. pair.
2½×3½	2½×4	2½×5	2½×6	3×2½ inch.	
$					doz. pair.
3×3	3×3½	3½×4	3×5	3×6 inch.	
$					doz. pair.
3½×3	3½×3½	3½×4	3½×5	3½×6 inch.	
$					doz. pair.
4×3	4×3½	4×4	4×4½	4×5 inch.	
$					doz. pair.
4½×4½	5×5 inch.				

TABLE BUTTS.

$								doz. pair.
¾	1	1⅛	1¼	1⅜	1½	1⅝	1¾	2 inch.

BACK FLAPS.

$								doz. pair.
¾	1	1⅛	1¼	1⅜	1½	1⅝	1¾	2 inch.

SQUARE BACK FLAPS.

$								doz. pair.
¾	1	1⅛	1¼	1⅜	1½	1⅝	1¾	2 inch.

TRUNK HINGES.

$						doz. pair.
¾	⅞	1	1⅛	1¼	1⅜	1½ inch.

UNFINISHED TRUNK HINGES.

$	doz. pair.

In bulk, guage No. 16. 1 inch.

HINGES.

(Continued.)

CAST IRON BUTTS.

NARROW BUTTS, FAST JOINT.

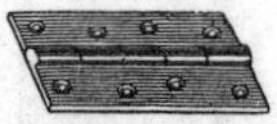

$								doz. pair.
1	1¼	1½	1¾	2	2¼	2½	2¾	3 inch.

$							doz. pair.
3¼	3½	3¾	4	4½	5	5½	6 inch.

BROAD BUTTS, FAST JOINT.

$				doz. pair.
2×2	2×2½	2½×	2½×2½	2½×3 inch.
$				doz. pair.
3×2½	3×3	3½×3	3×3½	3½×3½ inch.
$				doz. pair.
3½×4	4×3½	4×4	4×4½	4½×4 inch.
$				doz. pair.
4½×4½	4½×5	5×4½	5×5	5×5½ inch.
$				doz. pair.
5½×5	5½×5½	5½×6	4×6	4½×6 inch.
$				doz. pair.
6×5½	6×6 inch.			

BROAD BUTTS, LOOSE JOINT.

$				doz. pair.
2×2	2¼×2¼	2×2½	2½×2	2½×2½ inch.
$				doz. pair.
2½×3	3×2½	3×3	3×3½	3½×3 inch.
$				doz. pair.
3½×3½	3½×4	4×3½	4×4	4×4½ inch.
$				doz. pair.
4½×4	4½×4½	4½×5	5×4½	4×6 inch.
$				doz. pair.
5×5	5×5½	5½×5	5½×5½	5½×6 inch.
$				doz. pair.
6×5½	6×6	6×6½	6×7 inch.	

NARROW BUTTS, LOOSE JOINT.

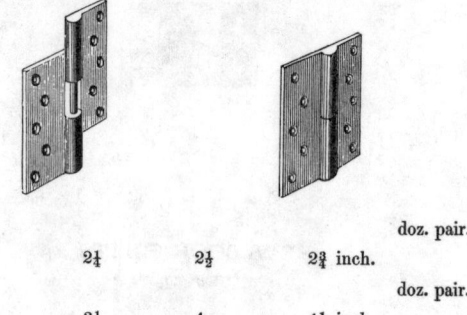

$			doz. pair.
2	2¼	2½	2¾ inch.
$			doz. pair.
3	3½	4	4½ inch.

PARLIAMENT BUTTS, LOOSE JOINTS.

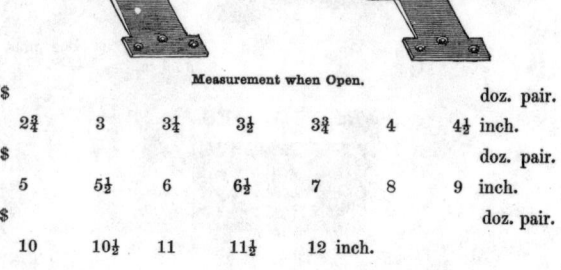

Measurement when Open.

$						doz. pair.
2¾	3	3¼	3½	3¾	4	4½ inch.
$						doz. pair.
5	5½	6	6½	7	8	9 inch.
$					doz. pair.
10	10½	11	11½	12 inch.	

MEYER'S HINGES, LOOSE JOINTS.

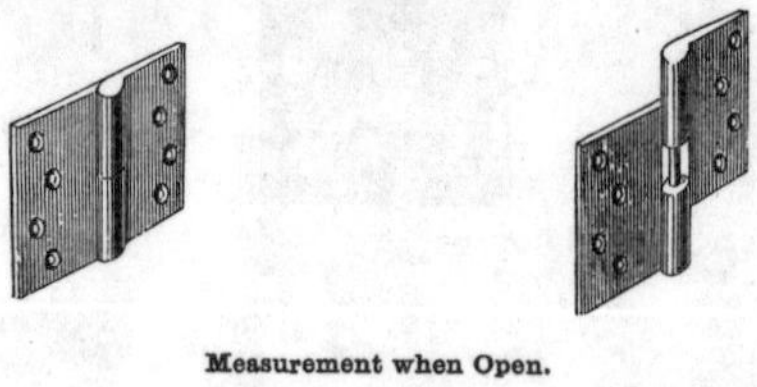

Measurement when Open.

$		doz. pair.
No. 0, 2×3¼	No. 1, 2¼×3½	No. 2, 2½×3¾ inch.
$		doz. pair.
No. 3, 2¾×4	No. 4, 3 ×4¼	No. 5, 3¼×4½ inch.

All of the LOOSE JOINT BUTTS are made with heavy flaps and knuckles and strong wrought iron wires. They are rapidly coming into general use, having decided advantages over Fast Joints, as with them doors can be easily unhung without injury to the paint.

BUTT HINGES of any size and description, not enumerated in the foregoing lists, made promptly to order. Patterns also furnished for the same when desired.

HINGES.

(Continued.)

CAST IRON FANCY BUTTS.

FAST JOINT.

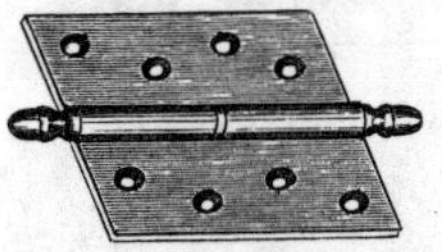

Size of Butts.	Acorn Butts.	Japanned Acorn Butts.	Japanned Butts with Brass Acorns.	Japanned Butts with Silvered Acorns.	With Steel Washers.
3½×3 inches					
3½×3½ "					
3½×4 "					
3½×5 "					
4×3 "					
4×3½ "					
4×4 "					
4×4½ "					
4×5 "					
4½×4 "					
4½×4½ "					
4½×5 "					
4½×5½ "					
5×5 "					
5×7 "					
5½×5½ "					
6×6 "					
6×7 "					

For *Washers* on *Fast* Joint Butts, add $ per doz. to list.

LOOSE JOINT.

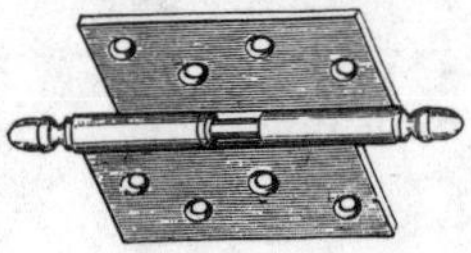

Size of Butts.	Acorn Butts.	Japanned Acorn Butts.	Japanned Butts with Brass Acorns.	Japanned Butts with Silvered Acorns.	With Steel Washers.
3½×3 inches					
3½×3½ "					
3½×4 "					
3½×5 "					
4×3 "					
4×3½ "					
4×4 "					
4×4½ "					
4×5 "					
4½×4 "					
4½×4½ "					
4½×5 "					
4½×5½ "					
5×5 "					
5×7 "					
5½×5½ "					
6×6 "					
6×7 "					

For *Washers* on *Loose* Joint Butts, add $ per doz. to list.

Various out of the way sizes not mentioned above, we have patterns for, and any size ordered will be got up at short notice, and on reasonable terms.

BRONZING any size Butt will add $ to the list price per dozen pair.
BROWNING (or BLACKWALNUT color) any size Butts will add $ to list price per dozen pair.
SCREWS Japanned, BRONZED and BROWNED, will be furnished at small addition to cost of Bright Screws.
For Fancy Butts, all BRASS, ELECTRO-PLATED, and HAND PLATED, see page 111.
Fancy Butts, Loose Joint, furnished to order, either Brass, Electro-Plated or Hand Plated.

HEAVY CAST BRASS BUTTS, FOR SHIP USE.

STOUT, WITH BRASS PINS.

$ doz. pair. 1½×1 1½×1¼ 1¾×1¼ 2×1¼ 2¼×1⅜ inch.

$ doz. pair. 2½×1⅝ 2¾×1¾ 3×2 3¼×2¼ 3½×2⅜ inch.

$ doz. pair. 3¾×2⅝ 4×2¾ 4½×3 5×3¼ inch.

$ doz. pair. 2×1 2×1½ 2×1⅝ 2×1¾ 2×2 inch.

$ doz. pair. 2×2¼ 2×2½ 2¼×1½ 2¼×2 2¼×2¼ inch.

$ doz. pair. 2½×1¼ 2½×1⅞ 2½×2 2½×2¼ 2½×2½ inch.

$ doz. pair. 2½×3 2½×3¼ 2¾×2 3×1½ 3×1¾ inch.

$ doz. pair. 3×2¼ 3×2½ 3¼×1¾ 3¼×2 3½×1¾ inch.

$ doz. pair. 3½×2¼ 3½×2½ 3½×2⅝ 3⅝×2⅝ 4×2 inch.

$ doz. pair. 4×2¼ 4×2⅜ 4×3 4×3¼ 4×3½ inch.

$ doz pair. 4⅜×2½ 4½×1¾ 4½×2½ inch.

HINGES.

(Continued.)

CAST BRASS BUTTS FOR SHIP USE.

FAST JOINT.

Stout, With Brass Pins.

	Zigzag Screw Holes.	Edge Holes and Polished Backs.
3×3 inch, per dozen pair...........		
3×3¼ inch "		
3×3½ inch "		
3×4 inch "		
3¼×3¼ inch "		
3¼×4 inch "		
3½×3 inch "		
3½×3¼ inch "		
3½×3½ inch "		
3½×4 inch "		
3½×4½ inch "		
3½×5 inch "		
4×4 inch "		
4×4½ inch "		
4×5 inch "		
4×6 inch "		
4½×4½ inch "		
4½×5 inch "		
5×5 inch "		

LOOSE JOINT.

Stout, with Brass Pins.

	Zigzag Screw Holes.	Edge Holes and Polished Backs.
1¼×1 inch, per dozen pair...........		
1¾×1½ inch "		
2×1 inch "		
2×1¼ inch "		
2×2 inch "		
2½×1⅝ inch "		
2½×2 inch "		
2½×2½ inch "		
2½×3 inch "		
2¾×2½ inch "		
3×2 inch "		
3×2½ inch "		
3×3 inch "		
3×4 inch "		
3½×2⅜ inch "		
3½×3½ inch "		
4×2¾ inch "		
4×4 inch "		
4½×4 inch "		

FAST JOINT, LIGHT, WITH BRASS PINS.

| 1½ inch, per dozen pair..................$ |
| 1¾ inch " .... |
| 2 inch " .... |
| 2¼ inch " .... |
| 2½ inch " .... |
| 2¾ inch " .... |
| 3 inch " .... |
| 3¼ inch " .... |
| 3½ inch " .... |

SLIP PIN BUTTS.

Add to Price of Narrow Butts.

3 inches long and under, per dozen pair ....$

5 " " to 3 inches, per dozen pair........

Add to Price of Wide Butts.

3½×3½ inches and under, per dozen pair..................

5×5 " " to 3½×3½ inches, per dozen pair...

BRASS FLAP HINGES, WITH BRASS PINS.

| 1⅛×1¾ inch, per dozen pair..................$ |
| 1¼×1⅞ inch " .... |
| 1¼×2¼ inch " .... |
| 1½×2 inch " .... |
| 1½×2½ inch " .... |
| 1½×3 inch " .... |
| 1¾×2½ inch " .... |
| 1¾×3½ inch " .... |
| 2×3 inch " .... |
| 2×4 inch " .... |
| 2×4½ inch " .... |
| 2½×5 inch " .... |

BRASS PARLIAMENT HINGES.

1 ×3 inch, per dozen pair..................$

2⅜×5 inch, " ....

HINGES.

(Continued.)

WROUGHT BRASS SHIP BUTTS, WITH BRASS PINS.

Length and Width, Open.

No. 16, 2 ×3 inches.....................per doz. pairs, $	No. 48, 4½×3 inches.....................per doz. pairs, $
No. 17, 2¼×3 " ...."	No. 53, 3½×2$\frac{7}{16}$ " loose pin.............."
No. 31, 2½×1⅝ " stout ...."	No. 54, 3 ×2 " loose pin.............."
No. 32, 2¾×1⅞ " stout ...."	No. 55, 4½×3 " loose pin.............."
No. 33, 3 ×2 " ...."	No. 59, 4 ×4 " extra stout..........."
No. 34, 3¼×2¼ " ...."	No. 60, 3½×3¼ " extra stout..........."
No. 35, 3½×2⅜ " ...."	No. 61, 3 ×3 " extra stout..........."
No. 36, 3¾×2⅝ " ...."	No. 62, 4½×4½ " extra stout..........."
No. 37, 4 ×2½ " ...."	No. 63, 4½×5 " extra stout..........."
No. 38, 3½×4 " extra stout..........."	No. 64, 4 ×3 " loose pin.............."
No. 39, 2½×2 " stout................."	No. 65, 4 ×3 " extra stout..........."
No. 40, 3 ×2½ " stout................."	No. 66, 1 ×1¼ " ...."
No. 41, 3½×3 " extra stout..........."	No. 67, 2 ×2 " ...."
No. 42, 4 ×3½ " extra stout..........."	No. 68, 2¼×2½ " ...."
No. 43, 2¼×1½ " stout.............."	No. 130, 3½×3½ " ...."
No. 44, 2 ×1⅝ " stout................."	No. 131, 2 ×2 " extra stout..........."
No. 45, 4½×2⅞ " extra stout..........."	No. 132, 1½×1¼ " ...."
No. 46, 1¾×1¼ " ...."	

PATENT WROUGHT BRASS BUTT HINGES.

TRUE IN THE JOINTS.

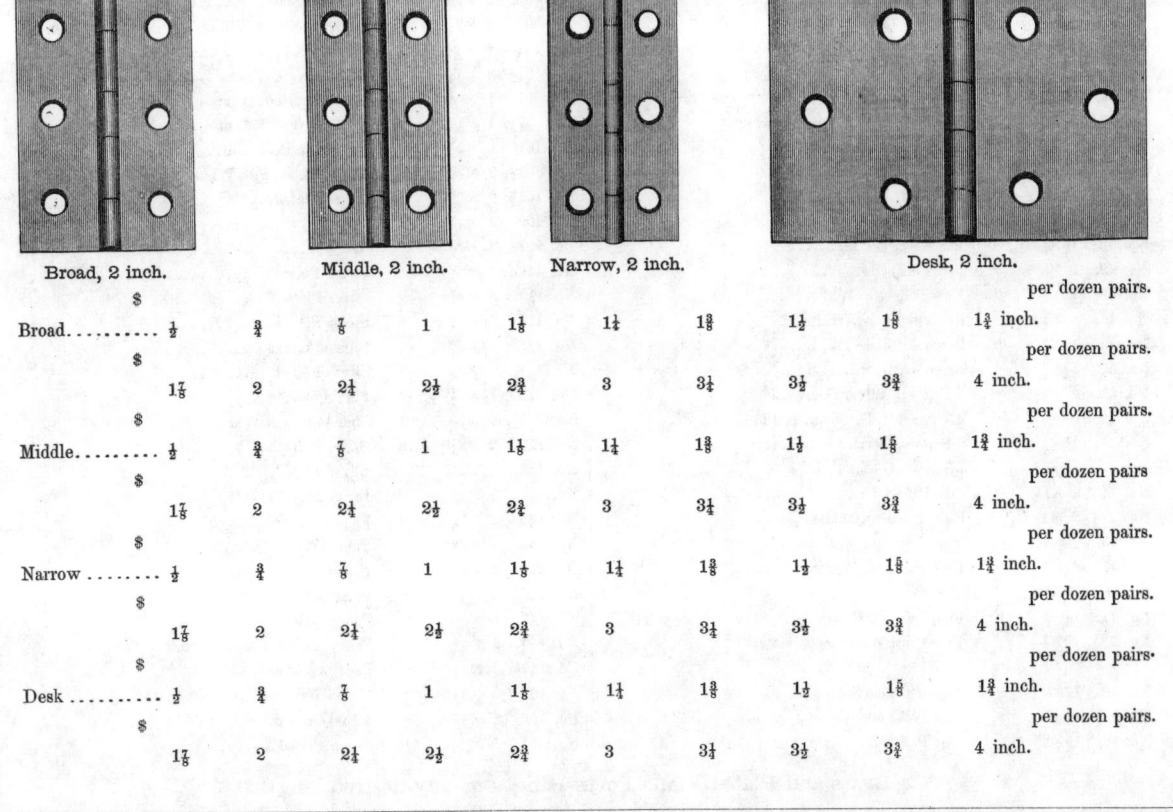

Broad, 2 inch.   Middle, 2 inch.   Narrow, 2 inch.   Desk, 2 inch.

per dozen pairs.

	$									
Broad.........	½	¾	⅞	1	1⅛	1¼	1⅜	1½	1⅝	1¾ inch.

per dozen pairs.

	$									
	1⅞	2	2¼	2½	2¾	3	3¼	3½	3¾	4 inch.

per dozen pairs.

	$									
Middle.........	½	¾	⅞	1	1⅛	1¼	1⅜	1½	1⅝	1¾ inch.

per dozen pairs.

	$									
	1⅞	2	2¼	2½	2¾	3	3¼	3½	3¾	4 inch.

per dozen pairs.

	$									
Narrow........	½	¾	⅞	1	1⅛	1¼	1⅜	1½	1⅝	1¾ inch.

per dozen pairs.

	$									
	1⅞	2	2¼	2½	2¾	3	3¼	3½	3¾	4 inch.

per dozen pairs·

	$									
Desk..........	½	¾	⅞	1	1⅛	1¼	1⅜	1½	1⅝	1¾ inch.

per dozen pairs.

	$									
	1⅞	2	2¼	2½	2¾	3	3¼	3½	3¾	4 inch.

HINGES.

(*Continued.*)

PATENT WROUGHT BRASS BUTT HINGES.

(*Continued.*)

No. 99,	$1\frac{1}{4}\times1\frac{1}{2}$ inches,	Coffin..............$	doz. pair.	No. 109,	3×2 inches, Railroad Car..........$	doz. pair.
No. $99\frac{1}{2}$,	$1\frac{1}{4}\times1\frac{1}{2}$ "	Coffin, White.........	"	No. 110,	$3\frac{1}{4}\times3$ " Lift Joint..............	"
No. 100,	$\frac{7}{8}\times1\frac{3}{8}$ "	Coffin	"	No. 137,	$3\frac{1}{2}\times2\frac{1}{2}$ " Lift Joint.............	"
No. $100\frac{1}{2}$,	$\frac{7}{8}\times1\frac{3}{8}$ "	Coffin, White........	"	No. 103,	$2\frac{1}{4}\times3$ " Coach.................	"
No. 138,	$1\times2\frac{3}{4}$ "	Coffin	"	No. 104,	$2\frac{1}{4}\times4\frac{1}{4}$ " Coach.................	"
No. $138\frac{1}{2}$,	$1\times2\frac{3}{4}$ "	Coffin, White........	"	No. 105,	$2\frac{1}{4}\times2\frac{1}{2}$ " Lift Joint.............	"
				No. 106,	$2\frac{1}{4}\times2\frac{5}{8}$ " Lift Joint.............	"

PIANO FORTE, POLISHED, LACQUERED, WHITENED AND PLATED.

Length and Width, when Open.				Length and Width, when Open.		
No. 11,	$1\frac{3}{8}\times\frac{7}{8}$ inches, 3 Screws................$	doz. pair.	No. $79\frac{1}{2}$,	$1\frac{3}{4}\times1\frac{3}{8}$ inches, Fine Polished, White....$	doz. pair.
No. $11\frac{1}{2}$,	$1\frac{3}{8}\times\frac{7}{8}$ " 3 Screws, White	"	No. 80,	$1\times1\frac{1}{2}$ " Beveled on Both Sides....	"
No. 12,	$2\times2\frac{15}{16}$ " 4 Plain, Loose Pin........	"	No. $80\frac{1}{2}$,	$1\times1\frac{1}{2}$ " Bev. on Both Sides, White.	"
No. $12\frac{1}{2}$,	$2\times2\frac{15}{16}$ " 4 Plain, Loose Pin, White.	"	No. $80\frac{3}{4}$,	$1\times1\frac{1}{2}$ " Crowned	"
No. 13,	$2\times2\frac{15}{16}$ " $4\frac{1}{2}$ Beveled, Loose Pin.....	"	No. 81,	$\frac{7}{8}\times1\frac{3}{8}$ " Beveled on Both Sides....	"
No. $13\frac{1}{2}$,	$2\times2\frac{15}{16}$ " $\frac{1}{2}$ Beveled, Loose Pin, White.	"	No. $81\frac{1}{2}$,	$\frac{7}{8}\times1\frac{3}{8}$ " Bev. on Both Sides, White.	"
No. 15,	$1\frac{1}{2}\times\frac{3}{4}$ " 3 Screws.................	"	No. 83,	$2\times\frac{7}{8}$ "	"
No. $15\frac{1}{2}$,	$1\frac{1}{2}\times\frac{3}{4}$ " 3 Screws, White	"	No. $83\frac{1}{2}$,	$2\times\frac{7}{8}$ " White.................	"
No. 18,	$1\frac{3}{8}\times\frac{3}{4}$ " 3 Screws.................	"	No. $83\frac{3}{4}$,	$2\times\frac{7}{8}$ " Silver Plated............	"
No. $18\frac{1}{2}$,	$1\frac{3}{8}\times\frac{3}{4}$ " 3 Screws, White	"	No. 84,	$\frac{3}{4}$ " Broad Bev. Both Sides....	"
No. 24,	$1\frac{3}{4}\times2\frac{7}{16}$ " 3 Screws, $\frac{1}{2}$ Bevl'd, Loose Pin	"	No. $84\frac{1}{2}$,	$\frac{3}{4}$ " Br'd Bev. Both Sides, White	"
No. $24\frac{1}{2}$,	$1\frac{3}{4}\times2\frac{7}{16}$ " $3\frac{1}{2}$ Beveled, Loose Pin, White	"	No. $84\frac{3}{4}$,	$\frac{3}{4}$ " Br'd, Fine Polished, White	"
No. 25,	$2\times2\frac{15}{16}$ " 3 Screws, Plain, Loose Pin...	"	No. 85,	3×4 " Crown Ends, Loose Pin...	"
No. $25\frac{1}{2}$,	$2\times2\frac{15}{16}$ " 3 Plain, Loose Pin, White....	"	No. $85\frac{1}{2}$,	3×4 " Cr'n Ends, Loose Pin, White	"
No. 26,	$2\times2\frac{15}{16}$ " 3 Screws, $\frac{1}{2}$ Beveled, Loose Pin	"	No. 88,	2×1 " Stout	"
No. $26\frac{1}{2}$,	$2\times2\frac{15}{16}$ " $3\frac{1}{2}$ Beveled, Loose Pin, White	"	No. 90,	$2\times2\frac{1}{2}$ " Unequal Sides...........	"
No. $26\frac{3}{4}$,	$2\times2\frac{15}{16}$ " 3 Screws, $\frac{1}{2}$ Beveled........	"	No. $90\frac{1}{2}$,	$2\times2\frac{1}{2}$ " Unequal Sides, White....	"
No. 27,	$1\frac{3}{4}\times2\frac{7}{16}$ " 4 Screws, Plain, Loose Pin...	"	No. 91,	$2\times1\frac{3}{4}$ "	"
No. $27\frac{1}{2}$,	$1\frac{3}{4}\times2\frac{7}{16}$ " 4 Plain, Loose Pin, White....	"	No. $91\frac{1}{2}$,	$2\times1\frac{3}{4}$ " White.................	"
No. 28,	$1\frac{1}{2}\times\frac{3}{4}$ " 2 Screws	"	No. 97,	$1\times1\frac{1}{2}$ " Face Reversed..........	"
No. $28\frac{1}{2}$,	$1\frac{1}{2}\times\frac{3}{4}$ " 2 Screws, White	"	No. $97\frac{1}{2}$,	$1\times1\frac{1}{2}$ " Face Reversed, White....	"
No. 29,	$1\frac{3}{8}\times1$ " 3 Screws	"	No. 101,	$2\times2\frac{3}{8}$ " $\frac{1}{2}$ Beveled, Loose Pin......	"
No. $29\frac{1}{2}$,	$1\frac{3}{8}\times1$ " 3 Screws, White.........	"	No. $101\frac{1}{2}$,	$2\times2\frac{3}{8}$ " $\frac{1}{2}$ Bev. Loose Pin, White..	"
No. $29\frac{3}{4}$,	$1\frac{3}{8}\times1$ " Reversed Joints, White.....	"	No. $101\frac{3}{4}$,	$2\times2\frac{3}{8}$ " Silver Plated............	"
No. 30,	$1\frac{1}{2}\times\frac{7}{8}$ " 2 Screws	"	No. 102,	$1\times1\frac{1}{2}$ "	"
No. $30\frac{1}{2}$,	$1\frac{1}{2}\times\frac{7}{8}$ " 2 Screws, White	"	No. $102\frac{1}{2}$,	$1\times1\frac{1}{2}$ " White	"
No. 49,	$1\times\frac{7}{8}$ " Fine Polished	"	No. 111,	$1\frac{3}{4}\times\frac{7}{8}$ " Silver Plated............	"
No. $49\frac{1}{2}$,	$1\times\frac{7}{8}$ " Fine Polished, White.......	"	No. 113,	$2\times2\frac{15}{16}$ " Silver Plated............	"
No. $49\frac{1}{4}$,	$1\times\frac{7}{8}$ " Reverse Finish, White......	"	No. 114,	$1\frac{3}{8}\times1\frac{7}{16}$ " Silver Plated............	"
No. $49\frac{3}{4}$,	$1\times\frac{7}{8}$ " Reverse Finish............	"	No. 115,	$1\frac{1}{2}\times\frac{3}{4}$ " Silver Plated............	"
No. 50,	$1\frac{3}{8}\times\frac{7}{8}$ " 3 Screws, G. Silver.........	"	No. 117,	$1\frac{3}{8}\times2\frac{1}{4}$ " Silver Plated............	"
No. 51,	$2\times2\frac{15}{16}$ " 4 Plain, G. Silver, Loose Pin.	"	No. 118,	$1\frac{1}{2}\times1\frac{1}{4}$ " Fine Polished............	"
No. 52,	$2\times2\frac{15}{16}$ " $4\frac{1}{2}$ Beveled, G. Silver, L. Pin	"	No. $118\frac{1}{2}$,	$1\frac{1}{2}\times1\frac{1}{4}$ " Fine Polished, White.....	"
No. 56,	$1\frac{3}{8}\times1$ " 3 Screws, German Silver....	"	No. 126,	$2\times2\frac{15}{16}$ " Silver Plated............	"
No. 57,	$1\frac{3}{8}\times\frac{3}{4}$ " 3 Screws, German Silver....	"	No. 129,	$1\frac{3}{4}\times1$ " Silver Plated............	"
No. 71,	$2\times1\frac{1}{2}$ " Fine Polished	"	No. 142,	$2\times7\frac{3}{8}$ " Fancy Figured, Gilt	"
No. $71\frac{1}{2}$,	$2\times1\frac{1}{2}$ " Fine Polished, White.......	"	No. 143,	$2\times7\frac{3}{8}$ " Fancy Figured, Plated....	"
No. 73,	2×1 " Fine Polished............	"	No. 144,	$2\times7\frac{3}{8}$ " Fancy Plated...........	"
No. $73\frac{1}{2}$,	2×1 " Fine Polished, White.......	"	No. 145,	$2\times7\frac{1}{4}$ " Fancy Plated...........	"
No. $76\frac{3}{4}$,	$\frac{7}{8}\times\frac{7}{8}$ " Fine Polished	"	No. 146,	2×6 " Fancy Plated...........	"
No. 77,	$1\frac{3}{4}\times\frac{7}{8}$ " Fine Polish'd, Revers'd Joints	"	No. 147,	2×6 " Fancy, White...........	"
No. $77\frac{1}{2}$,	$1\frac{3}{4}\times\frac{7}{8}$ " Fine Polish'd, Revers'd Joints, White................	"	No. 149,	$2\times4\frac{3}{4}$ " Fancy Plated............	"
			No. $149\frac{1}{2}$,	$2\times4\frac{3}{4}$ " Fancy, White	"
No. 78,	$1\frac{3}{4}\times2$ " Fine Polished	"	No. 151,	$2\times4\frac{1}{2}$ " 1 End Crowned, White...	"
No. $78\frac{1}{2}$,	$1\frac{3}{4}\times2$ " Fine Polished, White.......	"	No. 152,	$2\times4\frac{1}{2}$ " 1 End Crow'd, Silver Pl't'd	"
No. 79,	$1\frac{3}{4}\times1\frac{3}{8}$ " Fine Polished	"	No. 171,	$2\times1\frac{1}{2}$ " Silver Plated............	"

☞ **Brass and Plated Piano Forte Hinges of any desired length.**

HINGES.

(Continued.)

SECRETARY HINGES, FOR SHIP USE.

$				doz. pair.
	4	4½	5 inch.	

Quadrant Bows..............................doz. pair, $
Quadrant Fasteners......................... "

CARD TABLE HINGES.

Dozen pair............$

PIN, OR CENTRE HINGES, CAST BRASS.

LIGHT.

No. 3, 2 inch...............................doz. pair, $

PIN OR CENTRE HINGES—Continued.

MEDIUM.

2½	3	3½ inch.	
			doz. pair.
No. 4	5	6	

EXTRA HEAVY.

No. 7. Brass, 3 inch.........................doz. pair, $
No. 8, Silver Plated 3 inch................... "

IRON.

	2	2½	3	3	3½	4	4½	5 inch.
								doz. pair.
Round End, No. 9	10	11	12	13	14	15		
								doz. pair.
Square End, No. 16	17	18	19	20	21	22		

PATENT, SPIRAL, SPRING HINGE.

THE BEST AND ONLY RELIABLE SPRING HINGE EVER INTRODUCED.

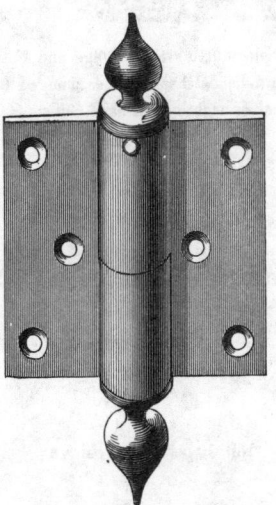
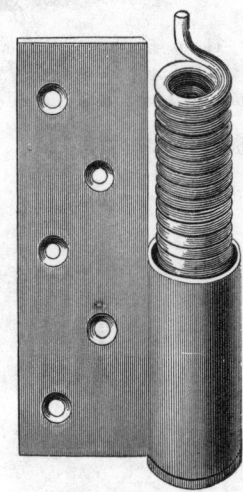

Hinge as seen upon the Door.   Sectional View, showing the Spiral Spring.

Directions.—Place the upper flange of the Hinge on the door, with the revolving cap up. When the door is hung, see that it swings on the Hinges freely. Then place the Lever in one of the holes which are in the revolving cap, turn it towards the jamb of the door, until the power is sufficient to close the door as desired, place the pin in the lower hole which is in the barrel of the Hinge, and it will pass into one of several holes in the cap, and thereby fasten the cap to the upper flange. To remove the pin from the Hinge, so as to hang the door, turn the cap, which will relieve the pressure on the pin.

When the Spring is not required, remove the pin from the barrel of the Hinge, and it then operates as an ordinary Hinge. Do not fasten the door open for any long period of time while the power is on the Spring. They should be oiled, say once in three or four months, and that can be done by removing the pin that regulates the power, and inserting a little oil. It is better not to paint the Hinges, as it clogs up the joints.

$						per pair.
4	5	6	7	8	10	12 inch.

Brass and Silver Plated Hinges made to order.

4 and 5 inch, for Light Inside Doors ; 6 and 7 inch, for Ordinary Inside Doors ; 8, 10 and 12 inch, for Outside Doors, according to size and exposure.

GATE HINGES AND FASTS.

GATE AND BARN DOOR HINGES.

Wrought Pins.

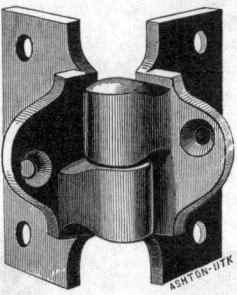

No. 1............................ Per dozen sets, $
No. 2............................ "
No. 3............................ "

☞ These Hinges are extra strong, and the best in use for Gates or Barn Doors.

TOP STATE GATE HINGES.

WROUGHT LOOSE PIN.

Right or Left Hand.

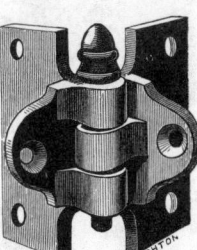

Per dozen sets...................$

HINGES.

(Continued.)

GATE HINGES AND FASTS.

(Continued.)

GATE HINGES AND FASTS.

To Swing Both Ways, and Self-Shutting.

A. ASHTON. UTICA.

Upper Hinge.

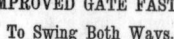

Lower Hinge.

IMPROVED GATE FASTS.

To Swing Both Ways.

Especial attention is directed to this article, as it is the strongest and cheapest Hinge made, and cannot get out of order.

The Improved Gate Fast is more easily put on, and adjusts itself to the sagging of the gate.

No. 1—For Large Gates..............per dozen sets, $

No. 2—For Yard Gates................   "

SELF-SHUTTING GATE HINGES & FASTS

These Hinges have Wrought Iron Pins, and are every way superior to any Self-Shutting Hinge in market.

By reference to the Plate, it will be seen that the Screws are put in at right angles, which prevents them from getting loose or sagging. The Eye or Socket is capped over, so that they will operate in any weather.

No. 1....................................per doz. sets, $

No. 2....................................   "

No. 3....................................   "

SELF-SHUTTING STATE GATE HINGES AND FASTS.

A. ASHTON. UTICA.

The above Plate represents a Self-Shutting Gate Hinge and Fast, with wrought loose pin, cast acorn head, that can be changed by moving the pin so as to work either on right or left hand Gates.

State Gate Hinge.....................per doz. sets, $

RAISING OR SELF-SHUTTING GATE HINGE.

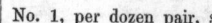

No. 1, per dozen pair, $ No. 2, per dozen pair, $

PLAIN GATE HINGE.

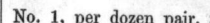

No. 1, per dozen pair, $ No. 2, per dozen pair, $

SELF-SHUTTING GATE HINGES,

New Pattern, Complete with Latch.

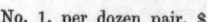

No. 1, per dozen pair, $ No. 2, per dozen pair, $

HINGES.

(Continued.)

CHARLES PARKER'S PATENT BLIND HINGE AND FASTENING.

FOR BRICK BUILDINGS.

No. 5, throws the Blind 3 inches from the casing, per doz. sets, $
No. 6, throws the Blind 3½ inch. from the casing   "
No. 7, throws the Blind 4 inches from the casing   "
No. 8, throws the Blind 4½ inch. from the casing   "

In cases of 4 dozen sets each.

☞ Extra Heavy Hinges of the above sizes made to order.

FOR WOOD BUILDINGS.
For Blinds that Hang on Outside of Casing.

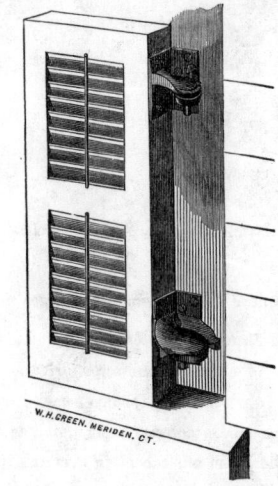

W. H. GREEN, MERIDEN. CT.

These Hinges are warranted not to break in the strongest wind, are easily put on, and the Blind cannot be thrown off in opening and shutting. The large or oblong Eye belongs to the lower Hinge. The Blind may rest on both upper and lower Hinges, but *must* always rest on the lower Hinge, which should be put on first ; the half of the Hinge which has the Pin on, should be put on the Blind with the Pin pointing down.

FOR WOOD BUILDINGS.

No. 1, throws the Blind 1 inch from the casing, per doz. sets, $
No. 2, throws the Blind 1½ inches from the casing   "
No. 3, throws the Blind 2 inches from the casing   "
No. 4, throws the Blind 2½ inches from the casing   "

In cases of 6 dozen sets each.

No. 20, throws the Blind 1 inch from the casing, per doz. sets, $

In cases of 6 dozen sets each.

A. C. PALMER'S PATENT BLIND BUTTS AND FASTS.
WROUGHT IRON PINS.

PALMER'S PATENT BUTTS

The above Plate represents the No. 1, for Wood. It shows the Blind open, with the Lever on the lower Hinge in the position in which it is required to be placed to CLOSE the Blind. There is an Inclined Plane, which raises the Blind while opening, until it reaches the wall,

when it drops and is securely fastened. To close the Blind, it is only necessary to turn the Lever as represented in the Plate, and the Blind will close and fasten on the inside.

Per Doz. Sets.

The Nos. 1½, 2, 3, 5, 6, &c. differ only in length and weight.

No. 1 —For Wood, 1¼ inch Blinds, 3 inches when open....$
No. 1½—For Wood, Heavy Pattern, 3½ inches when open...
No. 1½—For Wood, Light Pattern, 3½ inches when open....
No. 2 —For Brick, 1¼ inch Blinds, 5 inches when open....
No. 3 —For Brick, 1½ to 2 inch Blind, or Plank Shutters, 5½
            inches when open...........................
No. 4 —For Brick, 1¼ to 1¾ inch Blinds, Baltimore Pattern,
            (or Parliament,) 5 inches when open...........
No. 5 —For Brick, 1¼ to 1¾ inch Blinds, 6 inch. when open
No. 6 —For Brick, 1¼ to 1¾ inch Blinds, City Pattern, 6½ in.
            when open...................................
No 11—For Brick and Stone, Extra Heavy, (Canada Pattern)
            8 inches when open..........................
No. 14—For Brick and Stone, Extra Heavy, (Jersey Pattern)
            10 inches when open.........................

☞ A Set is comprised of *two* pairs of Hinges and Fasts complete, or sufficient to hang *one pair* of Blinds.

HINGES.

(Continued.)

NICHOLSON'S PATENT BLIND HINGES.

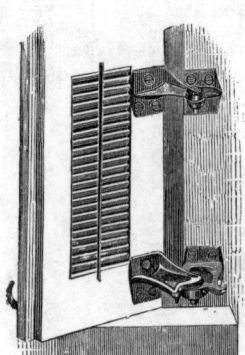

No. 50—for Brick.

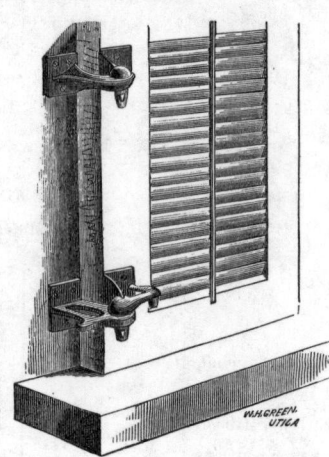

New England Style, No. 60—for Wood.

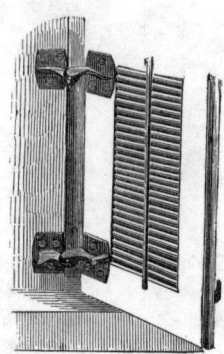

No. 25—for Wood.

These hinges have the following advantages over those of similar construction:

They are Self-Fastening, and can be operated without reaching out of the window. They are strong and cheap, and can be hung simply by the use of a gimlet and screw-driver. The pins are placed in such a position as to cover the sockets, thus obviating the danger of breaking, or rendering them otherwise inoperative by the collection of snow or sleet. A projection has been put on the pin of the upper hinge, and a corresponding notch in the eye, so as to entirely prevent the Blind from blowing off its hinges; and, like Palmer's, cannot be taken off, except in a certain position.

	Per Doz. Sets.		Per Doz. Sets.
No. 25—For Wood, 3 inches, when open.............$		No. 70—For Brick, 6 inches, when open.............$	
No. 50—For Brick, 5 inches, when open............		No. 80—For Brick, 7 inches, when open...........	
No. 60—For Wood, New England Style, 3 in. when open			

☞ A Set comprises *two* pairs of Hinges and Fasts complete, or sufficient to hang *one pair* of Blinds.

LOOSE JOINT BLIND BUTTS.

3 inch............................$ per dozen pairs.

5 inch............................$ per dozen pairs.

JUDD'S BLIND BUTTS.

$
No. 1   2   3   4   6   per dozen pairs.

JUDD'S SURFACE BLIND BUTTS.

$ per dozen pairs.
No. 1   2

MERRIMAN'S BLIND HINGES.

1×14 inch, 1¾ inch turn, 2 to 4 inch Screw Hooks.

1×15 inch, Straight, 2 to 3 inch Screw Hooks.

	Doz. Sets.
1¼×12 in. Straps, for ½ to 2¼ in. turn, 2 to 5 in. Screw Hooks, $	
1¼×12 in. Straps, Straight, 2 to 5 in. Screw Hooks........	
1⅛×13 in. Straps, for ½ to 2¼ in. turn, 2 to 5 in. Screw Hooks,	
1 ×14 in. Straps, for ½ to 2¼ in. turn, 2 to 5 in. Screw Hooks,	
1 ×14 in. Straps, for 1¾ in. turn, 2 to 4 in. Screw Hooks...	
1 ×15 in. Straps, Straight, 2 to 3 in. Screw Hooks........	
Extra Heavy..............per lb. $	

GATE FASTENINGS.

GATE PULLEY, CHAIN, BALL AND FASTENING.

$ per dozen.

GATE FASTENINGS.

Spiral Spring, Riveted......................per dozen sets, $
Spiral Spring, not Riveted................. "

IMPROVED GATE FASTS,
SWING BOTH WAYS.

Per dozen sets..., $

WROUGHT IRON GATE LATCHES ONLY.

per doz.

5   6   7   8   9   10   11   12   14 inches.

WROUGHT IRON GATE LATCHES.
With Staples and Catches, complete.

per doz.

$ 5   6   7   8   9   10   12   14   16 inches.

LATCH CATCHES.

Assorted.............................. cts. per dozen.

LATCH STAPLES.

Assorted.................................. cts. per dozen

HEAVY WROUGHT IRON GATE OR BARN DOOR LATCHES AND HANDLES.

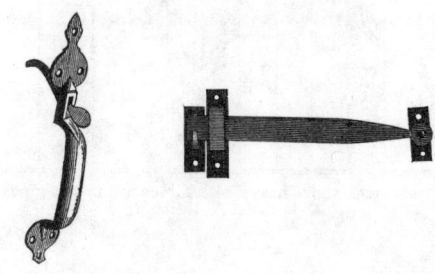

With Latch, Staple and Catch, complete,   cts. each.

IMPROVED BARN DOOR LATCH AND HASP COMBINED.

Barn Door Hasp and Latch Combined, 12 inch....per doz. $
Barn Door Latch,   12 inch.... "

AMERICAN GIMLET-POINT SCREWS,

FLAT, ROUND, OVAL AND FILLISTER HEAD.

Flat Head.

Round Head.

Oval Head.

Fillister Head.

IRON WOOD SCREWS.

Nos.	0	1	2	3	4	5	6	7	8	9	10	11	12	13	14	15	16	17	18	20	22	24	26	28	30
Inches.	Cts.	Cts.	Cts.	Cts.	Cts.	Cts.	Cts.	Cts.	Cts.	Cts.	Cts.	Cts.	Cts.	Cts.	Cts.	Cts.	Cts.	Cts.	Cts.	Cts.	Cts.	Cts.	Cts.	Cts.	Cts.
1/4	29	29	29																						
3/8	..	29	29	29	29	30	32	36	39																
1/2	..	..	29	29	29	30	32	36	39	44	47														
5/8	..	..	30	30	32	33	36	39	44	47	50	53	56												
3/4	..	..	..	..	33	36	39	42	45	48	51	54	57	66	72	84	96								
7/8	..	..	..	..	..	39	41	44	47	50	53	57	62	69	75	87	98								
1	..	..	..	..	..	44	45	48	50	53	56	60	65	72	80	90	102	113	126	174					
1¼	..	..	..	..	..	..	..	56	57	60	65	69	75	83	92	105	120	129	141	176					
1½	..	..	..	..	..	..	..	..	65	68	71	77	83	92	105	119	132	146	158	189					
1¾	..	..	..	..	..	..	..	..	..	78	81	86	95	·105	119	132	146	159	176	201	225	278			
2	..	..	..	..	..	..	..	..	..	..	86	93	107	119	132	146	159	176	189	219	254	338			
2¼	..	..	..	..	..	..	..	..	..	..	..	107	120	134	146	159	177	189	206	236	288	375			
2½	..	..	..	..	..	..	..	..	..	..	..	...	134	146	159	177	189	206	219	254	315	390			
2¾	..	..	..	..	..	..	..	..	..	..	..	...	...	159	176	189	206	233	251	300	369	443			
3	..	..	..	..	..	..	..	..	..	..	..	...	...	...	189	206	233	260	288	342	420	510	570		
3½	..	..	..	..	..	..	..	..	..	..	..	...	...	...	...	...	282	314	351	431	500	554	608		
4	..	..	..	..	..	..	..	..	..	..	..	...	...	...	...	...	...	...	414	519	585	645	720		
4½	..	..	..	..	..	..	..	..	..	..	..	...	...	...	...	...	...	...	480	579	645	720	810		
5	..	..	..	..	..	..	..	..	..	..	..	...	...	...	...	...	...	...	...	675	750	810	900		
6	..	..	..	..	..	..	..	..	..	..	..	...	...	...	...	...	...	...	...	...	...	1013	1163	1358	1575

☞ All sizes above heavy black lines are in ten gross bundles—between lines, five gross bundles—below, single grosses.

BRASS WOOD AND MACHINE SCREWS.

Nos.	1	2	3	4	5	6	7	8	9	10	11	12	13	14	15	16	17	18	20	22	24	26
Inches.	Cts.	Cts.	Cts.	Cts.	Cts.	Cts.	Cts.	Cts.	Cts.	Cts.	Cts.	Cts.	Cts.	Cts.	Cts.	Cts.	Cts.	Cts.	Cts.	Cts.	Cts.	Cts.
3/8	89	89	89	92	96	102	111															
1/2	..	89	89	92	96	102	111	119	129	143												
5/8	..	90	90	93	98	104	113	120	131	144	159	180										
3/4	..	..	..	96	101	107	114	123	135	149	164	180	203	233	270	315						
7/8	..	..	..	..	...	110	119	129	141	156	174	195	228	267	305	345						
1	..	..	..	..	...	114	126	140	155	173	194	218	245	275	308	353	...	413				
1¼	..	..	..	..	...	...	135	146	173	203	233	263	293	323	353	383	413	450	525			
1½	..	..	..	..	...	...	...	188	209	231	258	288	323	363	413	465	525	600	780			
1¾	..	..	..	..	...	...	...	...	245	269	293	324	365	414	473	540	617	702	810	960	1125	
2	..	..	..	..	...	...	...	...	...	300	327	357	416	474	533	591	650	708	834	1050	1200	
2¼	..	..	..	..	...	...	...	...	...	...	...	413	470	531	590	645	705	780	870	1125	....	
2½	..	..	..	..	...	...	...	...	...	...	...	...	...	588	645	695	780	866	1053	1245	1463	
3	..	..	..	..	...	...	...	...	...	...	...	...	...	...	...	843	...	1023	1296	1575	1950	2400

AMERICAN SCREW COMPANY'S
PATENT GIMLET SCREWS.

These Plates represent the exact size of each article.

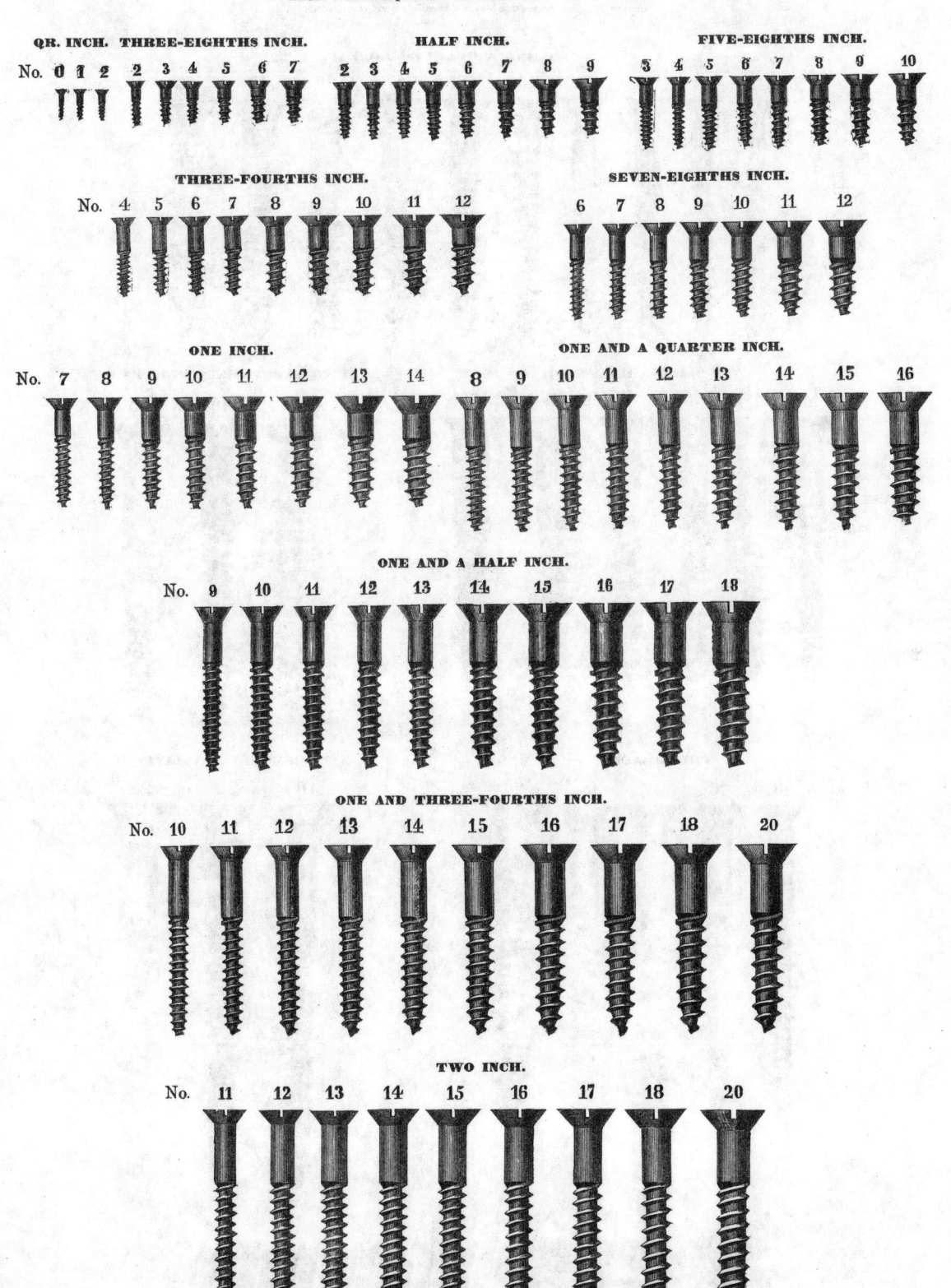

QR. INCH. **THREE-EIGHTHS INCH.** **HALF INCH.** **FIVE-EIGHTHS INCH.**

No. 0 1 2   2 3 4 5 6 7   2 3 4 5 6 7 8 9   3 4 5 6 7 8 9 10

THREE-FOURTHS INCH. **SEVEN-EIGHTHS INCH.**

No. 4 5 6 7 8 9 10 11 12   6 7 8 9 10 11 12

ONE INCH. **ONE AND A QUARTER INCH.**

No. 7 8 9 10 11 12 13 14   8 9 10 11 12 13 14 15 16

ONE AND A HALF INCH.

No. 9 10 11 12 13 14 15 16 17 18

ONE AND THREE-FOURTHS INCH.

No. 10 11 12 13 14 15 16 17 18 20

TWO INCH.

No. 11 12 13 14 15 16 17 18 20

AMERICAN SCREW COMPANY'S
PATENT GIMLET SCREWS.

These Plates represent the exact size of each article.

TWO AND A QUARTER INCH.

No. 11 12 13 14 15 16 17 18 19 20

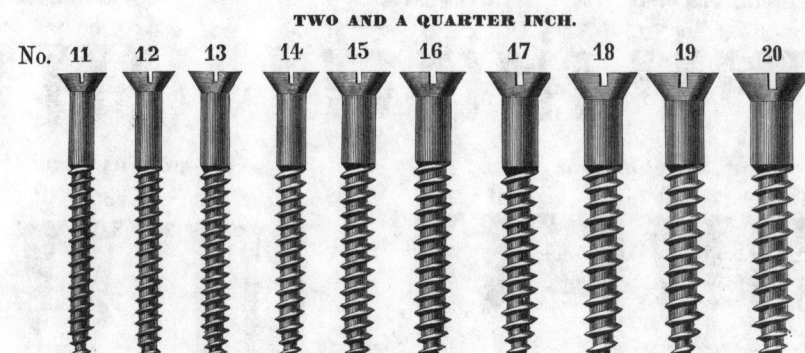

TWO AND A HALF INCH.

No. 14 15 16 17 18 20

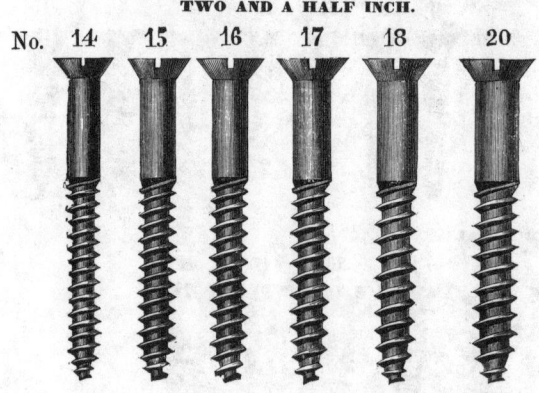

TWO AND THREE-FOURTHS INCH.

16 18 20

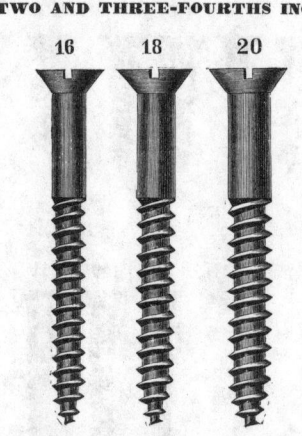

THREE INCH.

No. 15 16 17 18 20

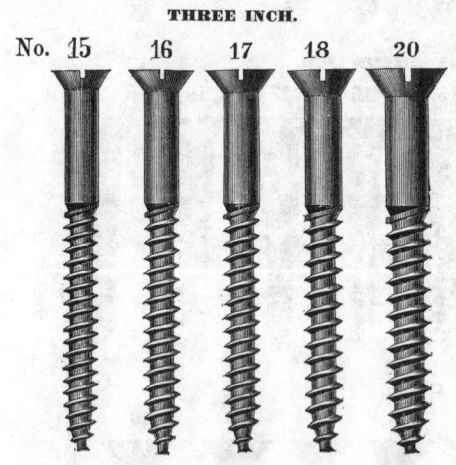

THREE AND A HALF INCH.

18 20 22

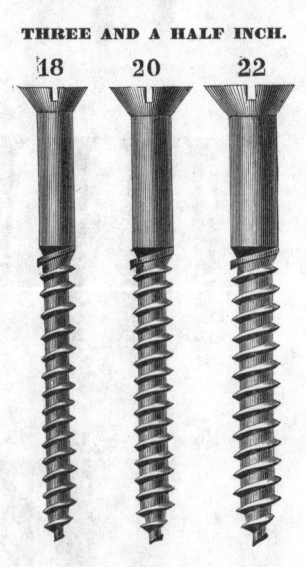

SIX INCH Nº 30

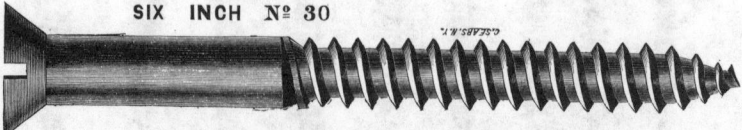

AMERICAN GIMLET-POINT SCREWS.

(*Continued.*)

IRON MACHINE SCREWS.

Nos.	24 and 32 Threads per Inch.			Threads per Inch 20 and 24.		16 and 18 Threads per Inch.			
	6	8	10	12	14	16	18	20	24
Inches.	Cents.	Cents.	Cents.	Cents.	Cents.	Cents.	Cents.	Cents.	Cents.
3/8	68	75	83						
1/2	68	75	83	90	113	135			
5/8		75	83	90	113	135	158	195	
3/4		75	83	98	120	143	173	210	
7/8			90	105	128	150	188	225	
1			98	113	135	165	203	240	300
1 1/4				120	143	180	218	255	330
1 1/2				150	195	233	270	360	

WOOD SCREWS.

FLAT HEAD IRON,..............   per cent. | ROUND HEAD IRON,............   per cent. | FILLISTER HEAD IRON,............   per cent.

FLAT HEAD BRASS,.............   " | ROUND HEAD BRASS,...........   " | FILLISTER HEAD BRASS,...........   "

MACHINE SCREWS.

FLAT HEAD IRON,..............   per cent. | ROUND HEAD IRON,............   per cent. | FILLISTER HEAD IRON,............   per cent

FLAT HEAD BRASS,.............   " | ROUND HEAD BRASS,...........   " | FILLISTER HEAD BRASS,...........   "

PATENT CAPPED GIMLET-POINT SCREWS.

ROUND AND FLAT HEAD SILVER-CAPPED.

1-2 inch.	5-8 inch.	3-4 inch.	7-8 inch.	1 inch.	1 1-4 inch.	1 1-2 inch.	1 3-4 inch.	2 inch.	2 1-4 inch.	2 1-2 inch.	2 3-4 inch.
No. 3 $ .98	No. 3 $ .99	No. 4 $1.06	No. 6 $1.21	No. 6 $1.25	No. 7 $1.48	No. 8 $2.06	No. 9 $2.69	No. 9 $3.13	No.12 $4.54	No.14 $6.46	No.16 $8.40
4 1.01	4 1.02	5 1.11	7 1.31	7 1.38	8 1.60	9 2.30	10 2.95	10 3.30	13 5.17	15 7.09	18 10.38
5 1.06	5 1.08	6 1.18	8 1.42	8 1.54	9 1.90	10 2.54	11 3.22	11 3.61	14 5.84	16 7.64	20 12.92
6 1.12	6 1.14	7 1.25	9 1.55	9 1.70	10 2.23	11 2.84	12 3.56	12 3.92	15 6.49	17 8.58	22 15.51
7 1.21	7 1.24	8 1.35	10 1.71	10 1.90	11 2.46	12 3.16	13 3.92	13 4.57	16 7.09	18 9.50	24 18.77
8 1.31	8 1.32	9 1.48	11 1.91	11 2.13	12 2.89	13 3.55	14 4.55	14 5.21	17 7.75	20 11.58	
9 1.42	9 1.44	10 1.53	12 2.15	12 2.46	13 3.23	14 3.99	15 5.20	15 5.86	18 8.58	22 13.69	**3 inch.**
10 1.57	10 1.58	11 1.80	13 2.50	13 2.69	14 3.55	15 4.54	16 5.94	16 6.50	20 9.57	24 16.09	No.16 $9.27
	11 1.74	12 1.98	14 2.93	14 3.02	15 3.88	16 5.11	17 6.78	17 7.15	22 12.37		18 11.25
	12 1.98	13 2.23	15 3.35	15 3.39	16 4.21	17 5.77	18 7.72	18 7.78	24 14.65		20 14.25
		14 2.56	16 3.79	16 3.88	17 4.54	18 6.60	20 8.91	20 9.17			22 17.32
		15 2.97		17 4.21	18 4.95	20 8.58	22 10.56	22 11.55			24 21.45
		16 3.45		18 4.54	20 5.77		24 12.37				26 26.40

ROUND AND FLAT HEAD BRASS-CAPPED.

1-2 inch.	5-8 inch.	3-4 inch.	7-8 inch.	1 inch.	1 1-4 inch.	1 1-2 inch.	1 3-4 inch.	2 inch.	2 1-4 inch.	2 1-2 inch.	2 3-4 inch.
No. 3 $ 89	No. 3 $ .90	No. 4 $ .96	No. 6 $1.10	No. 6 $1.14	No. 7 $1.35	No. 8 $1.88	No. 9 $2.45	No. 9 $2.85	No.12 $4.13	No.14 $5.88	No.16 $7.70
4 .92	4 .93	5 1.01	7 1.19	7 1.26	8 1.46	9 2.09	10 2.69	10 3.00	13 4.70	15 6.45	18 9.44
5 .96	5 .98	6 1.07	8 1.29	8 1.40	9 1.73	10 2.31	11 2.93	11 3.27	14 5.31	16 6.95	20 11.75
6 1.02	6 1.04	7 1.14	9 1.41	9 1.55	10 2.03	11 2.58	12 3.24	12 3.57	15 5.90	17 7.80	22 14.10
7 1.11	7 1.13	8 1.23	10 1.56	10 1.73	11 2.33	12 2.88	13 3.65	13 4.16	16 6.45	18 8.66	24 17.07
8 1.19	8 1.20	9 1.35	11 1.74	11 1.94	12 2.63	13 3.23	14 4.14	14 4.74	17 7.05	20 10.53	
9 1.29	9 1.31	10 1.49	12 1.95	12 2.18	13 2.93	14 3.63	15 4.73	15 5.33	18 7.80	22 12.45	**3 inch.**
10 1.43	10 1.44	11 1.64	13 2.28	13 2.45	14 3.23	15 4.13	16 5.40	16 5.91	20 8.70	24 14.63	No.16 $8.43
	11 1.59	12 1.80	14 2.67	14 2.75	15 3.53	16 4.65	17 6.17	17 6.50	22 11.25		18 10.23
	12 1.80	13 2.03	15 3.05	15 3.08	16 3.83	17 5.25	18 7.02	18 7.08	24 13.32		20 12.96
		14 2.33	16 3.45	16 3.53	17 4.13	18 6.00	20 8.10	20 8.34			22 15.75
		15 2.70		17 3.83	18 4.50	20 7.80	22 9.60	22 10.50			24 19.50
		16 3.15		18 4.13			24 11.25	24 12.00			26 24.00

SIDE, KNOB SCREWS.

BLUED, IRON.................$ per gross. | BRASS....................$ per gross. | PLATED....................$ per gross.

CABINET LOCKS.

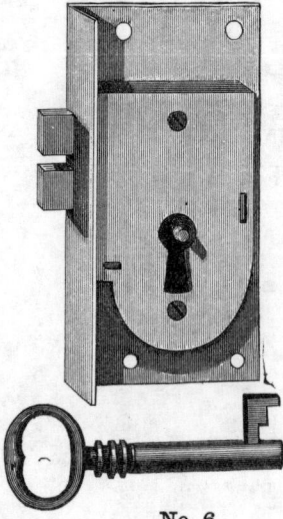

No. 6.

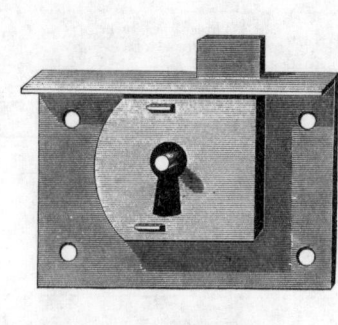

No. 1.

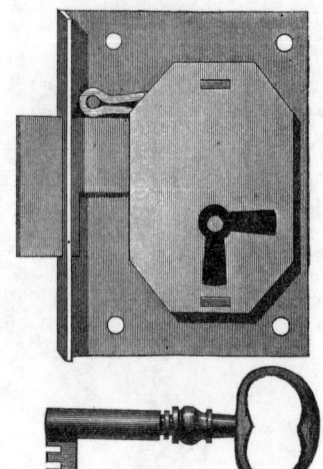

No. 300.

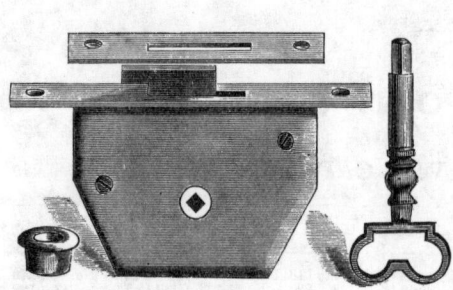

No. 188.

No. 280.

No. 149.

No. 90.

CABINET LOCKS.

(Continued.)

BRASS, TUMBLER CHEST, ENGLISH PATTERNS.

SQUARE SELVEDGE WROUGHT PLATES.

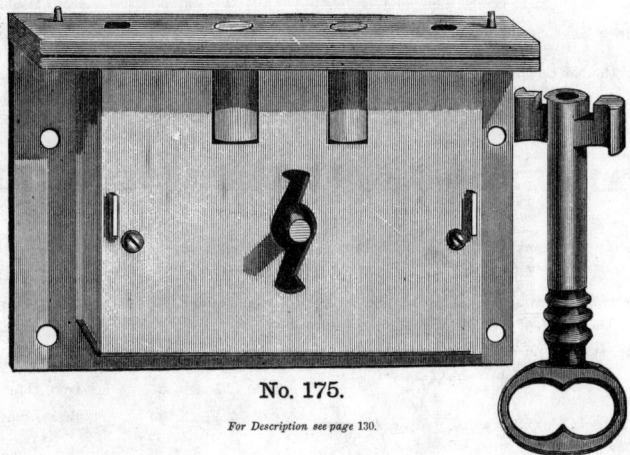

No. 175.

For Description see page 130.

No.	Size.	Price.		No.	Size.	Price.	
250	4 inch, $		Brass, 4 Tumblers, *Detector*, Double Link, Screwed, no two Keys alike, 24 Keyed.	257	3½ inch, $		Brass, 2 Tumblers, Double Link, Screwed, Assorted Keys.
251	4 inch, $		Brass, 4 Tumblers, Double Link, Screwed, no two Keys alike, 24 Keyed.	290	3 inch, $		Brass, 4 Tumblers, Double Link, Screwed, *Square* Selvedge, no two Keys alike.
252	4 inch, $		Brass, 3 Tumblers, Double Link, Screwed, Assorted Keys.	291	3 inch, $		Brass, 3 Tumblers, Double Link, Screwed, *Square* Selvedge, Assorted Keys.
253	4 inch, $		Brass, 2 Tumblers, Double Link, Screwed, Assorted Keys.	292	3 inch, $		Brass, 2 Tumblers, Double Link, Screwed, *Square* Selvedge, Assorted Keys.
254	3½ inch, $		Brass, 4 Tumblers, *Detector*, Double Link, Screwed, no Keys alike, 24 Keyed.	258	2½ inch, $		Brass, 3 Tumblers, Double Link, Screwed, *Square* Selvedge, Assorted Keys.
255	3½ inch, $		Brass, 4 Tumblers, Double Link, Screwed, no two Keys alike, 24 Keyed.	259	2½ inch, $		Brass, 2 Tumblers, Double Link, Screwed, *Square* Selvedge, Assorted Keys.
256	3½ inch, $		Brass, 3 Tumblers, Double Link, Screwed, Assorted Keys.	269	1½ inch, $		Brass, 2 Tumblers, Double Link, Screwed, Assorted Keys.

BRASS AND IRON TUMBLER, CHEST.

No.	Size.	Price.		No.	Size.	Price.	
113	4 inch, $		Brass, Screwed, Assorted Solid Brass Wards, Double Link, every part Brass, Brass Key.	28	2¾ inch, $		Brass, Double Link, 1 Ward, Assorted Fancy Keys.
4	4 inch, $		Iron, Screwed, Assorted Pins and Wards, Double Link.	169	2½ inch, $		Brass, Double Link, 1 Ward, Assorted Keys.
111	4 inch, $		Iron, Screwed, Assorted Solid Wards, Self-Spring, Double Link.	179	2½ inch, $		Brass, Tumbler, Double Link, Solid Wards, for Tin Trunks.
91	4 inch, $		Iron, Screwed, Solid Wards, Double Link, Assorted Fancy Keys.	279	2½ inch, $		Brass, 3 Tumblers, Double Link, Assorted Keys, for Tin Trunks.
2	4 inch, $		Iron, Screwed, Solid Wards, Single Link, Assorted Fancy Keys.	78	2 inch, $		Brass, Double Bolt, Tumbler, for Tin Trunks.
110	3½ inch, $		Brass, Screwed, Solid Brass Wards, Double Link, every part Brass, Fancy Brass Keys, Assorted.	170	2½ inch, $		Iron, Double Link, 1 Ward, Assorted Keys.
				171	2¼ inch, $		Brass, Double Link, 1 Ward, Assorted Fancy Keys.
10	3½ inch, $		Iron, Screwed, Solid Brass Wards, Double Link, Assorted Fancy Keys.	172	2¼ inch, $		Iron, Double Link, 1 Ward, Assorted Fancy Keys.
94	3½ inch, $		Iron, Mortise, Single Link, Warded, for *Refrigerators*.	39	2 inch, $		Brass, Double Link, 1 Ward, Assorted Keys, every part *Brass*, Iron Keys.
20	3 inch, $		Brass, Screwed, Solid Brass Wards, Double Link, Assorted Plain Keys.	134	2 inch, $		Brass, Chronometer, Double Link, 1 Ward, every part *Brass*, Iron Keys.
86	3 inch, $		Iron, Screwed, Solid Brass Wards, Double Link, Assorted Plain Keys.	38	2 inch, $		Brass, Double Link, Assorted Fancy Keys.
				178	2 inch, $		Iron, Double Link, Assorted Fancy Keys.

CABINET LOCKS.

(*Continued.*)

SPRING CHEST, SQUARE SELVEDGE.

No.	Size.	Price.		No.	Size.	Price.	
159	4 inch,	$	Brass, Double Catch, Double Link and Double Bitted Keys, Secret Ward, Brass Escutch's.	175	4 inch,	$	Iron, Double Catch and Link, Assorted Fancy Double Bitted Keys, Warded, Brass Escutcheons, no two Keys alike (see Plate, p. 129.)
114	4 inch,	$	Iron, Double Catch and Link, Double Bitted Keys, Secret Ward, Brass Escutcheons.	9	4 inch,	$	Iron, Double Catch and Link, Double Bitted Keys, Brass Escutcheons.

BRASS AND IRON, BACK SPRING, CHEST AND BOX.

No.	Size.	Price.		No.	Size.	Price.	
92	4 inch,	$	Iron, Double Link, Solid Wards, Screwed, Assorted Fancy Keys.	165	2¾ inch,	$	Brass, Double Link, Warded, Assorted Keys.
182	4 inch,	$	Iron, Single Link, 1 Ward, Taper Keys.	163	2¾ inch,	$	Iron, Double Link, Warded, Assorted Keys.
93	3½ inch,	$	Iron, Double Link, Solid Wards, Screwed, Assorted Fancy Keys.	75	2¾ inch,	$	Brass, Single Link, Warded.
83	3½ inch,	$	Iron, Double Link, 1 Ward, Assorted Fancy Keys.	95	2¾ inch,	$	Iron, Single Link, Warded.
50	3½ inch,	$	Iron, Single Link, Screwed, 2 Wards, Assorted Fancy Keys.	164	2½ inch,	$	Brass, Double Link, Warded, Assorted Keys.
11	3½ inch,	$	Iron, Single Link, 2 Wards, Assorted Fancy Keys.	166	2½ inch,	$	Iron, Double Link, Warded, Assorted Keys.
142	3½ inch,	$	Iron, 1 Ward, Single Link, Taper Key.	29	2½ inch,	$	Brass, Single Link, Screwed, Warded, Fancy Keys.
228	3½ inch,	$	Iron, Single Link, Taper Key, *Circular Cap.*	31	2½ inch,	$	Brass, Single Link, Warded.
7	3½ inch,	$	Iron, Single Link, 1 Ward, Taper Key, Unpolished Cap.	133	2½ inch,	$	Iron, Single Link, Warded, Fancy Keys.
168	3¼ inch,	$	Iron, Double Link, 1 Ward, Assorted Plain Keys.	54	2½ inch,	$	Iron, Single Link, Warded.
154	3¼ inch,	$	Brass, Single Link, 1 Ward, Taper Keys.	105	2¼ inch,	$	Brass, Double Link, Warded.
155	3¼ inch,	$	Iron, Single Link, 1 Ward, Taper Keys.	167	2¼ inch,	$	Iron, Double Link, Warded.
160	3 inch,	$	Iron, Double Link, Warded, Assorted Plain Keys.	126	2¼ inch,	$	Brass, Single Link, Warded, Fancy Keys.
103	3 inch,	$	Brass, Single Link, Warded, Taper Keys.	37	2 inch,	$	Brass, Double Link, Warded.
24	3 inch,	$	Iron, Single Link, 2 Wards, Screwed, Assorted Fancy Keys.	64	2 inch,	$	Iron, Double Link, Warded.
65	3 inch,	$	Iron, Single Link, 2 Wards, Assorted Fancy Keys.	35	2 inch,	$	Brass, Single Link.
141	3 inch,	$	Iron, Single Link, Warded, Taper Keys.	34	2 inch,	$	Iron, Single Link.
226	3 inch,	$	Iron, Single Link, Warded, Circular Cap, Taper Keys.	45	1¾ inch,	$	Brass, Single Link.
8	3 inch,	$	Iron, Single Link, Unpolished Cap, Taper Keys.	139	1¾ inch,	$	Iron, Single Link.
				181	1½ inch,	$	Brass, Double Link, Square Selvedge, Fancy Keys.
				43	1½ inch,	$	Brass, Single Link.
				090	1½ inch,	$	Brass, Single Link, Circular Cap.
				091	1½ inch,	$	Iron, Single Link, Circular Cap.
				55	1½ inch,	$	Iron, Single Link.
				183	1¾ inch,	$	Iron, Mortise, for Pistol Cases, &c.
				42	1¼ inch,	$	Brass, Single Link.

BRASS AND IRON, DESK.

No.	Size.	Price.		No.	Size.	Price.	
91	4 inch,	$	Iron, Double Link, Screwed, Solid Wards, Tumbler, Assorted Fancy Keys.	255	3½ inch,	$	Brass, 4 Tumblers, Double Link, no two Keys alike, 24 Keyed.
92	4 inch,	$	Iron, Double Link, Screwed, Solid Wards, Assorted Fancy Keys.	256	3½ inch,	$	Brass, 3 Tumblers, Double Link, Screwed, Assorted Keys.
250	4 inch,	$	Brass, 4 *Tumblers*, Detector, Double Link, Screwed, no two Keys alike, 24 Keyed.	257	3½ inch,	$	Brass, 2 Tumblers, Double Link, Screwed, Assorted Keys.
251	4 inch,	$	Brass, 4 *Tumblers*, Double Link, Screwed, no two Keys alike, 24 Keyed.	110	3½ inch,	$	Brass, Double Link, Screwed, Solid Wards, Tumbler, Assorted Fancy Keys, every part Brass.
252	4 inch,	$	Brass, 3 *Tumblers*, Double Link, Screwed, Assorted Keys.	10	3½ inch,	$	Iron, Double Link, Screwed, Solid Wards, Tumbler, Assorted Fancy Keys.
253	4 inch,	$	Brass, 2 *Tumblers*, Double Link, Screwed, Assorted Keys.	93	3½ inch,	$	Iron, Double Link, Screwed, Solid Wards, Assorted Fancy Keys.
254	3½ inch,	$	Brass, 4 Tumblers, Detector, Double Link, Screwed, no two Keys alike, 24 Keyed.				

CABINET LOCKS.

(*Continued.*)

BRASS AND IRON, DESK.

(*Continued.*)

No.	Size.	Price.		No.	Size.	Price.	
83	3½ inch,	$	Iron, Double Link, Warded. Assorted Fancy Keys.	24	3 inch,	$	Iron, Single Link, 2 Wards, Screwed, Assorted Fancy Keys.
50	3½ inch,	$	Iron, Single Link, 2 Wards, Screwed, Assorted Fancy Keys.	65	3 inch,	$	Iron, Single Link, 2 Wards, Assorted Fancy Keys.
11	3½ inch,	$	Iron, Single Link, 2 Wards, Assorted Fancy Keys.	296	2½ inch,	$	Brass, *Camp Desk*, Tumbler.
20	3 inch,	$	Brass, Double Link, Solid Wards, Screwed, Tumbler, Assorted Plain Keys.	54	2½ inch,	$	Iron, Single Link, 1 Ward.
86	3 inch,	$	Iron, Double Link, Solid Wards, Screwed, Tumbler, Assorted Plain Keys.	169	2½ inch,	$	Brass, Double Link, Warded, Assorted Fancy Keys.
160	3 inch,	$	Iron, Double Link, Warded.	170	2½ inch,	$	Iron, Double Link, Warded, Assorted Fancy Keys.

BRASS AND IRON TUMBLER, STRAIGHT CUPBOARD AND WARDROBE.

No.	Size.	Price.		No.	Size.	Price.	
100	4 inch,	$	Brass, Screwed, Solid Wards, Thick Pin, Broad Brass Bolt, Assorted Plain Keys, every part Brass.	145	3¼ inch,	$	Brass, Screwed, Square Cast Box, Broad Brass Bolt, 2 Long Keys.
82	4 inch,	$	Iron, Screwed, Solid Wards, Thick Pin, Broad Brass Bolt, Assorted Plain Keys.	245	3¼ inch,	$	Brass, Screwed, Square Cast Box, Broad Iron Bolt, 3 Steel Tumblers, Shoots Right, Assorted Keys.
149	4 inch,	$	Brass, Screwed, Solid Box, Solid Wards, Broad Brass Bolt, Shoots Right and Left, Assorted Keys (see Plate, p. 128.)	246	3¼ inch,	$	Brass, Screwed, Square Cast Box, Broad Iron Bolt, 3 Steel Tumblers, Shoots Right and Left, Assorted Keys.
146	4 inch,	$	Iron, Screwed, Solid box, Solid Wards, Broad Brass Bolt, Shoots Right and Left, Assorted Keys.	247	2½×2½	$	Brass, Screwed, Square Cast Box, Broad Brass Bolt, 3 Brass Tumblers, Assorted Keys.
156	4 inch,	$	Iron, Solid Box, Warded, Shoots Right and Left, Fancy Keys.	248	2 ×2¼	$	Brass, Screwed, Square Cast Box, Broad Brass Bolt, 3 Brass Tumblers, Assorted Keys.
173	4 inch,	$	Iron, Warded, Broad Bolt, Shoots Right and Left.	249	1½×1¾	$	Brass, Screwed, Square Cast Box, Broad Brass Bolt, 3 Brass Tumblers, Assorted Keys.
150	3½ inch,	$	Brass, Screwed, Solid Box, Solid Wards, Broad Brass Bolt, Shoots Right and Left, Assorted Keys, every part Brass.	21	3 inch,	$	Brass Screwed, Solid Wards, Broad Brass Bolt, Assorted Keys.
504	3½ inch,	$	Brass, Warded, Broad Bolt, Shoots Right and Left.	85	3 inch,	$	Iron, Screwed, Solid Wards, Broad Brass Bolt, Assorted Keys.
505	3½ inch,	$	Iron, Warded, Broad Bolt, Shoots Right and Left.	151	3 inch,	$	Brass, Screwed, Solid Box and Wards, Broad Brass Bolt, Shoots Right and Left, Assorted Keys.
147	3½ inch,	$	Iron, Screwed, Solid Box, Solid Wards, Broad Brass, Bolt Shoots Right and Left, Assorted Keys.	148	3 inch,	$	Iron, Screwed, Solid Box and Wards, Broad Brass Bolt, Shoots Right and Left, Assorted Keys.
157	3½ inch,	$	Iron, Solid Box, Warded, Broad Bolt, Shoots Right and Left, Fancy Keys.	158	3 inch,	$	Iron, Solid Box, Warded, Broad Bolt, Shoots Right and Left, Fancy Keys.
174	3½ inch,	$	Iron, 1 Ward, Broad Bolt, Shoots Right and Left.	506	2¾ inch,	$	Brass, Warded, Shoots Right and Left.
500	3½ inch,	$	Iron, 1 Ward, Broad Bolt, Shoots Right and Left.	507	2¾ inch,	$	Iron, Warded, Shoots Right and Left.
84	3½ inch,	$	Iron, Screwed, Solid Wards, Broad Brass Bolt, Assorted Keys.	77	2½ inch,	$	Brass, Broad Bolt, Shoots Right and Left, Fancy Keys.
				76	2½ inch,	$	Iron, Broad Bolt, Shoots Right and Left, Fancy Keys.
				508	2 inch,	$	Brass, Wrought Bolt, Shoots Right and Left.

BACK SPRING, STRAIGHT CUPBOARD.

No.	Size.	Price.		No.	Size.	Price.	
3	4 inch,	$	Iron, Straight, Screwed, Broad Bolts, 2 Wards, Fancy Keys.	88	3 inch,	$	Iron, Straight, Brass Bolt, Screwed, Warded, Fancy Keys.
90	3½ inch,	$	Iron, Straight, Screwed, 2 Wards, Fancy Keys. (See Plate, page 128.)	143	3 inch,	$	Iron, Straight, Warded, Taper Key and Fancy Bow.
152	3½ inch,	$	Iron, Straight, Warded, Taper Key.	153	3 inch,	$	Iron, Straight, Taper Key and Fanch Bows.
87	3 inch,	$	Brass, Straight, Screwed, Warded, Brass Bolt, Taper Keys.	067	3 inch,	$	Iron, Straight, Circular Cap, Taper Key and Fancy Bows.
101	3 inch,	$	Brass, Straight, Warded, Taper Keys.				

CABINET LOCKS.

(Continued.)

TUMBLER, MORTISE AND CUT CUPBOARD.

No.	Size.	Price.	
136	3 inch,	$	Brass Box and Selvedge, Mortise, Screwed, Broad Brass Bolt, Solid Wards, Assorted Keys, Double Keyhole.
121	3 inch,	$	Brass Selvedge, Mortise, Screwed Broad Brass Bolt, Solid Wards, Assorted Keys, Double Keyhole.
221	3 inch,	$	Brass Selvedge, Mortise, Solid Box, Screwed Broad Wrought Bolt, Warded, German Key, Double Keyhole.
6	3 inch,	$	Brass, Cut, Screwed, Solid Wards, Double Brass Bolt, Assorted Keys (see Plate, page 128.)
108	2¾ inch,	$	Brass, Mortise, Solid Wards, Brass Bolt.
107	2¾ inch,	$	Brass, Cut, Solid Wards, Screwed, Double Brass Bolt.
106	2½ inch,	$	Brass, Cut, Solid Wards, Screwed, Double Brass Bolt.
502	2¼ inch,	$	Brass, Tumbler, Brass Bolt, Screwed.
503	2 inch,	$	Brass, Tumbler, Brass Bolt, Screwed.

BACK SPRING CUT CUPBOARD.

No.	Size.	Price.	
22	3 inch,	$	Brass, Double Brass Bolt, Warded.
44	3 inch,	$	Brass, Wrought Bolt, Warded.
104	3 inch,	$	Iron, Double Brass Bolt, Warded.
116	3 inch,	$	Iron, Wrought Bolt, Warded.
61	2¾ inch,	$	Brass, Double Brass Bolt, Warded.
62	2¾ inch,	$	Brass, Double Brass Bolt, Warded, Fancy Keys.
144	2¾ inch,	$	Brass, Wrought Bolt, Warded.
117	2¾ inch,	$	Iron, Wrought Bolt, Warded.
74	2¾ inch,	$	Iron, Wrought Bolt, Warded, Unpolished Cap.
30	2½ inch,	$	Brass, Double Brass Bolt, Warded, Screwed.
32	2½ inch,	$	Brass, Double Brass Bolt, Warded.
137	2½ inch,	$	Brass, Wrought Bolt.
58	2½ inch,	$	Iron, Wrought Bolt.
56	2¼ inch,	$	Brass, Wrought Bolt.
57	2¼ inch,	$	Iron, Wrought Bolt.
501	2 inch,	$	Brass, Wrought Bolt.

PIANO AND SERAPHINE.

No.	Size.	Price.	
109	3 inch,	$	German Silver, Piano, Square Key, Improved Lever.
188	3 inch,	$	German Silver, Piano, Nile's Patent, Square Key (see Plate, page 128.)
190	3 inch,	$	Brass, Piano, Nile's Patent, Square Key.
131	3 inch,	$	Brass, Piano, Square Key, Improved Lever.
196	2¼ inch,	$	Brass, Seraphine, Double Link, Iron Box.
192	3 inch,	$	German Silver, Piano, Hooked Bolt.
193	3 inch,	$	Brass, Piano, Hooked Bolt.
194	3 inch,	$	Iron, Piano, Hooked Bolt.
195	2½ inch,	$	German Silver, Piano, Hooked Bolt.
197	2½ inch,	$	Brass, Piano, Hooked Bolt.
198	2½ inch,	$	Iron, Piano, Hooked Bolt.
295	2 inch,	$	German Silver, Piano, 2 Tumblers, Hooked Bolt, Assorted Keys.
360	2¾ inch,	$	Brass, Mortise Drawer, Tumbler Key, 1 inch from Selvedge.
191	3 inch,	$	German Silver, Mortise Drawer, Square Key.

GERMAN TUMBLER CUT CUPBOARD.

No.	Size.	Price.	
350	3 inch,	$	Brass, Mortise, Cupboard, Tumbler, Keypin 1¼ inch from Selvedge, with Iron Keys.
350	3 inch,	$	Brass, Mortise, Cupboard, Tumbler, Keypin 1¼ inch from Selvedge, with Plated Bow Keys.
351	3 inch,	$	Brass, Mortise Cupboard, Tumbler, Keypin 1¾ inch from Selvedge, with Iron Keys.
351	3 inch,	$	Brass, Mortise Cupboard, Tumbler, Keypin 1¾ inch from Selvedge, with Plated Bow Keys.
330	3 inch,	$	Brass, Broad Bolt, Tumbler and Spring Combined.
340	3 inch,	$	Iron, Broad Bolt, Tumbler and Spring Combined.
700	2¾ inch,	$	Iron, Broad Bolt, Tumbler and Spring Combined.
1010	2¾×2 in.	$	Iron, Broad Bolt, Tumbler, Keypin 1¼ inch from Selvedge, Brass Tube and Selvedge.
331	2¾ inch,	$	Brass, Broad Bolt, Tumbler and Spring Combined.
341	2¾ inch,	$	Iron, Broad Bolt, Tumbler and Spring Combined.
332	2½ inch,	$	Brass, Broad Bolt, Tumbler and Spring Combined.
342	2½ inch,	$	Iron, Broad Bolt, Tumbler and Spring Combined.
333	2¼ inch,	$	Brass, Broad Bolt, Tumbler and Spring Combined.
343	2¼ inch,	$	Iron, Broad Bolt, Tumbler and Spring Combined.

BRASS TUMBLER, CUT CUPBOARD, ENGLISH PATTERNS, SQUARE SELVEDGE.

No.	Size.	Price.	
271	3 inch,	$	Brass, 4 Tumblers, Heavy Bolt, Screwed, Wrought Plates, no two Keys alike.
272	3 inch,	$	Brass, 3 Tumblers, Heavy Bolt, Screwed, Assorted Keys.
273	3 inch,	$	Brass, 2 Tumblers, Heavy Bolt, Screwed, Assorted Keys.
268	2¼ inch,	$	Brass, 3 Tumblers, Heavy Brass Bolt, Straight *Cupboard*, Assorted Keys.

CABINET LOCKS.

(Continued.)

GERMAN TUMBLER DRAWER.

No.	Size.	Price.		No.	Size.	Price.	
307	3½ inch,	$	Brass, Broad Bolt, Tumbler and Spring Combined, Keypin 1¾ inch from Selvedge, *every part Brass.*	309	2½×2,	$	Iron, Tumbler, Keypin 1¼ inch from Selvedge, Brass Selvedge.
308	3 inch,	$	Brass, Broad Bolt, Tumbler and Spring Combined, Keypin 1¼ inch from Selvedge, *every part Brass.*	310	2¼ inch,	$	Iron, Broad Bolt, Tumbler and Spring Combined, Double Keyhole, Keypin 1¼ inch from Selvedge.
300	2¾ inch,	$	Brass, Broad Bolt, Tumbler and Spring Combined, Double Keyhole, Keypin 1¼ inch from Selvedge (see Plate, page 128.)	301	2½ inch,	$	Brass, Broad Bolt, Tumbler and Spring Combined, Double Keyhole, 1 Ward, Keypin 1¼ inch from Selvedge.
1000	2½×4 in.	$	Iron, Tumbler, Keypin 3¼ inch from Selvedge, Brass Tube and Selvedge.	311	2½ inch,	$	Iron, Broad Bolt, Tumbler and Spring Combined, Double Keyhole, 1 Ward, Keypin 1¼ inch from Selvedge.
1000	2½×3 in.	$	Iron, Tumbler, Keypin 2¼ inch from Selvedge, Brass Tube and Selvedge.	122	2½ inch,	$	Iron, Broad Bolt, Tumbler, 1 Ward, Double Keyhole.
1004	2½×2¾,	$	Iron, Tumbler, Keypin 2 inch from Selvedge, Brass Tube and Selvedge.	302	2¼ inch,	$	Brass, Broad Bolt, Tumbler and Spring Combined, Double Keyhole.
1006	2½×2½,	$	Iron, Tumbler, Keypin 1¾ inch from Selvedge, Brass Tube and Selvedge.	312	2¼ inch,	$	Iron, Broad Bolt, Tumbler and Spring Combined, Double Keyhole.
320	2½×2¾,	$	Iron, Tumbler, Keypin 2 inch from Selvedge.	303	2 inch,	$	Brass, Broad Bolt, Tumbler and Spring Combined, Double Keyhole.
321	2½×2½,	$	Iron, Tumbler, Keypin 1¾ inch from Selvedge.	313	2 inch,	$	Iron, Broad Bolt, Tumbler and Spring Combined, Double Keyhole.
322	2½×2,	$	Iron, Tumbler, Keypin 1¾ inch from Selvedge.				

BRASS TUMBLER, MORTISE DRAWER, ENGLISH PATTERNS.

No.	Size.	Price.		No.	Size.	Price.	
284	3 inch,	$	Brass, 4 Tumblers, Detector, Heavy Bolt, Screwed, no 2 Keys alike, Solid Box.	287	3 inch,	$	Brass, 2 Tumblers, Heavy Bolt, Screwed Assorted Keys, Solid Box.
285	3 inch,	$	Brass, 4 Tumblers, Heavy Bolt, Screwed, no two Keys alike, Solid Box.	288	2¾ inch,	$	Brass, Mortise, 3 Tumblers, Heavy Bolt, Screwed, Assorted Keys.
286	3 inch,	$	Brass, 3 Tumblers, Heavy Bolt, Screwed, Assorted Keys, Solid Box.	289	2¾ inch,	$	Brass, Mortise, 2 Tumblers, Heavy Bolt, Screwed, Assorted Keys.

BRASS AND IRON TUMBLER DRAWER, ENGLISH PATTERNS, SQUARE SELVEDGES.

No.	Size.	Price.		No.	Size.	Price.	
280	3 inch,	$	Brass, 4 Steel Tumblers, Heavy Bolt, Screwed, no two Keys alike, 24 Keyed (see Pl. p. 128.)	265	2½ inch,	$	Brass 3 Tumblers, Heavy Bolt, Screwed, no two Keys alike.
281	3 inch,	$	Brass, 3 Steel Tumblers, Heavy Bolt, Screwed, Assorted Keys.	266	2½ inch,	$	Brass, 2 Tumblers, Heavy Bolt, Screwed, Assorted Keys.
282	3 inch,	$	Brass, 2 Steel Tumblers, Heavy Bolt, Screwed, Assorted Keys.	267	2½ inch,	$	Brass, Tumbler, Heavy Bolt, Screwed, Assorted Keys.
260	2¾ inch,	$	Brass, Detector, 4 Tumblers, Heavy Bolt, Screwed, no two Keys alike, 24 Keyed.	0224	2½ inch,	$	Brass, 3 Tumblers, Heavy Bolt, Screwed, Assorted Keys, no two alike.
261	2¾ inch,	$	Brass, 4 Tumblers, Heavy Bolt, Screwed, no two Keys alike, 24 Keyed.	0225	2½ inch,	$	Brass, 2 Tumblers, Heavy Bolt, Screwed, Assorted Keys.
262	2¾ inch,	$	Brass, 3 Tumblers, Heavy Bolt, Screwed, no two Keys alike.	0226	2½ inch,	$	Brass, 1 Tumbler, Heavy Bolt, Screwed, Assorted Keys.
263	2¾ inch,	$	Brass, 2 Tumblers, Heavy Bolt, Screwed, Assorted Keys.	0228	2½ inch,	$	Iron, 3 Tumblers, Heavy Brass Bolt, Screwed, Assorted Keys, no two alike.
264	2¾ inch,	$	Brass, Tumbler, Heavy Bolt, Screwed, Assorted Keys.	0229	2½ inch,	$	Iron, 2 Tumblers, Heavy Brass Bolt, Screwed, Assorted Keys.
0220	2¾ inch,	$	Brass, 4 Tumblers, Heavy Brass Bolt, Screwed, no two Keys alike.	275	2 inch,	$	Brass, 3 Tumblers, Heavy Bolt, Screwed, Assorted Keys.
0221	2¾ inch,	$	Brass, 3 Tumblers, Heavy Brass Bolt, Screwed, Assorted.	276	2 inch,	$	Brass, 2 Tumblers, Heavy Bolt, Screwed Assorted Keys.
0222	2¾ inch,	$	Brass, 2 Tumblers, Heavy Brass Bolt, Screwed, Assorted.	277	2 inch,	$	Brass, 1 Tumbler, Heavy Bolt, Screwed, Assorted Keys.

BRASS AND IRON, TUMBLER DRAWER.

No.	Size.	Price.		No.	Size.	Price.	
115	2¾ inch,	$	Brass, Broad Brass Bolt, Circular Cap, Sham Bramah.	123	2¾ inch,	$	Brass, every part, Screwed, Solid Wards, Broad Brass Bolt, Assorted Keys.
232	2¾ inch,	$	Iron, Broad Brass Bolt, Circular Cap, Sham Bramah, Back Spring.	128	2¾ inch,	$	Brass, Screwed, Solid Wards, Broad Brass Bolt, no two Keys alike.
15	2¾ inch,	$	Brass, Broad Bolt, Square Cap, Sham Bramah.	127	2¾ inch,	$	Iron, Screwed, Solid Wards, Brass Bolt, no two Keys alike.

CABINET LOCKS.

(Continued.)

BRASS AND IRON, TUMBLER DRAWER—*Continued.*

No.	Size.	Price.	
13	$2\frac{3}{4}$ inch,	$	Brass, Screwed, Solid Wards, Broad Brass Bolt, Assorted Fancy Keys.
14	$2\frac{3}{4}$ inch,	$	Iron, Screwed, Solid Wards, Broad Brass Bolt, Assorted Keys.
99	$2\frac{1}{2}$ inch,	$	Brass, Double Brass Bolt, Sham Bramah.
052	$2\frac{1}{2}$ inch,	$	Brass, Screwed, Brass Bolt, Circular Cap, Fancy Keys, no two Keys alike.
129	$2\frac{1}{2}$ inch,	$	Brass, Screwed, Solid Wards, Broad Brass Bolt, no two Keys alike.
130	$2\frac{1}{2}$ inch,	$	Iron, Screwed, Solid Wards, Broad Brass Bolt no two Keys alike.
63	$2\frac{1}{2}$ inch,	$	Brass, Screwed, Solid Wards, Broad Brass Bolt, Assorted Keys.
69	$2\frac{1}{2}$ inch,	$	Iron, Screwed, Solid Wards, Broad Brass Bolt, Assorted Keys.
176	$2\frac{1}{4}$ inch,	$	Brass, Broad Brass Bolt, Screwed, Assorted Fancy Keys.
177	$2\frac{1}{4}$ inch,	$	Iron, Broad Brass Bolt, Screwed, Assorted Fancy Keys.
70	2 inch,	$	Brass, Broad Brass Bolt, Sham Bramah.
79	2 inch,	$	Brass, Broad Brass Bolt, Fancy Assorted Keys.

BRASS AND IRON, BACK SPRING DRAWER.

No.	Size.	Price.	
73	$2\frac{3}{4}$ inch,	$	Brass, Screwed, Double Brass Bolt, 1 Ward.
16	$2\frac{3}{4}$ inch,	$	Brass, Double Brass Bolt, 1 Ward.
12	$2\frac{3}{4}$ inch,	$	Iron, Double Brass Bolt, 1 Ward.
19	$2\frac{3}{4}$ inch,	$	Iron, Double Brass Bolt, 1 Ward, Screwed.
17	$2\frac{1}{2}$ inch,	$	Brass, Screwed, Double Brass Bolt, 1 Ward.
18	$2\frac{1}{2}$ inch,	$	Brass, Double Brass Bolt, 1 Ward.
140	$2\frac{1}{2}$ inch,	$	Brass, Long Broad Bolt, 1 Ward, Keypin $1\frac{5}{8}$ inch from Selvedge, German Key.
161	$2\frac{1}{2}$ inch,	$	Iron, Broad Bolt, Back Spring, 1 Ward.
180	$2\frac{1}{2}$ inch,	$	Iron, Broad Bolt, Back Spring, Warded, Brass Selvedge.
240	$2\frac{1}{2}\times2\frac{3}{4}$,	$	Iron, Broad Bolt, Back Spring, Brass Selvedge, Keypin $1\frac{3}{4}$ inch from Selvedge.
186	$2\frac{1}{2}\times2\frac{1}{4}$,	$	Brass, Broad Bolt, Back Spring, Double Keyhole, Keypin $1\frac{1}{4}$ inch from Selvedge.
187	$2\frac{1}{2}\times2\frac{1}{2}$	$	Iron, Broad Bolt, Back Spring, Double Keyhole, Keypin $1\frac{1}{4}$ inch from Selvedge.
184	$2\frac{1}{2}$ inch,	$	Iron, Long Broad Bolt. Keypin $1\frac{3}{4}$ inch from Selvedge, Round Bow Key.
185	$2\frac{1}{2}$ inch,	$	Iron, Broad Bolt, 1 Ward, Round Bow Key.
66	$2\frac{1}{2}$ inch,	$	Iron, Screwed, Double Brass Bolt, 1 Ward.
67	$2\frac{1}{2}$ inch,	$	Iron, Double Brass Bolt, 1 Ward.
40	$2\frac{1}{4}$ inch,	$	Brass, Broad Brass Bolt, Solid Wards.
89	$2\frac{1}{4}$ inch,	$	Iron, Broad Brass Bolt, Solid Wards.
36	2 inch,	$	Brass, Wrought Bolt, 1 Ward.
71	2 inch,	$	Iron, Wrought Bolt, 1 Ward.
33	$1\frac{3}{4}$ inch,	$	Brass, Wrought Bolt.
138	$1\frac{3}{4}$ inch,	$	Iron, Wrought Bolt.
46	$1\frac{1}{2}$ inch,	$	Brass, Wrought Bolt.
135	$1\frac{1}{2}$ inch,	$	Iron, Wrought Bolt.

IRON TILL LOCKS, KEYED, WROUGHT BOLT.

No. of Lock.	Size.	No. of Keys to each Dozen of Locks. 12 Keyed. per doz.	6 Keyed. per doz.	4 Keyed. per doz.	3 Keyed. per doz.	Description.
49	3 inch.					Capped up, 1 Ward.
162	$2\frac{3}{4}$ "					Capped up, 1 Ward, Screwed, Fancy Keys.
48	$2\frac{3}{4}$ "					Capped up, 1 Ward.
5	$2\frac{3}{4}$ "					1 Ward, Wrought Bolt.
161	$2\frac{1}{2}$ "					Broad Bolt, 1 Ward, German Pattern, Double Keyhole,
180	$2\frac{1}{2}$ "					Broad Bolt, 1 Ward, Tumbler, Double Keyhole.
240	$2\frac{1}{2}\times2\frac{3}{4}$					Back Spring, Iron, Brass Selvedge, Keypin $1\frac{3}{4}$ inch from Selvedge.
187	$2\frac{1}{2}\times2\frac{1}{2}$					Back Spring, Iron, Keypin $1\frac{1}{4}$ inch from Selvedge.
122	$2\frac{1}{2}$ "					Broad Bolt, 1 Ward, Tumbler, Double Keyhole.
81	$2\frac{1}{2}$ "					Capped up, 1 Ward, Screwed, Fancy Keys, Double Keyhole.
$81\frac{1}{2}$	$2\frac{1}{2}$ "					Capped up, 1 Ward, Fancy Keys.
27	$2\frac{1}{2}$ "					Capped up, 1 Ward.
26	$2\frac{1}{2}$ "					1 Ward.
98	$2\frac{1}{2}$ "					1 Ward.
1	$2\frac{1}{2}$ "					1 Ward. See Plates, page 128.
72	$2\frac{1}{2}$ "					1 Ward.
97	$2\frac{1}{4}$ "					Capped up, 1 Ward, Fancy Keys.
51	$2\frac{1}{4}$ "					Capped up, 1 Ward.

BRASS TILL LOCKS, KEYED, WROUGHT BOLT.

No. of Lock.	Size.	No. of Keys to each Dozen of Locks. 12 Keyed. per doz.	6 Keyed. per doz.	4 Keyed. per doz.	3 Keyed. per doz.	Description.
52	3 inch.					Capped up, 1 Ward.
47	$2\frac{3}{4}$ "					Capped up, 1 Ward.
80	$2\frac{1}{2}$ "					Capped up, Screwed, 1 Ward, Fancy Keys.
$80\frac{1}{2}$	$2\frac{1}{2}$ "					Capped up, 1 Ward, Fancy Keys.
25	$2\frac{1}{2}$ "					Capped up, 1 Ward.
23	$2\frac{1}{2}$ "					One Ward, Wrought Bolt.
68	$2\frac{1}{2}$ "					One Ward, Wrought Bolt.
60	$2\frac{1}{4}$ "					Capped up, 1 Ward, Fancy Keys.
53	$2\frac{1}{4}$ "					Capped up, 1 Ward.

MORTISE TILL LOCKS, BRASS SELVEDGE.

No. of Lock.	Size.	No. of Keys to each Dozen of Locks. 12 Keyed. per doz.	6 Keyed. per doz.	4 Keyed. per doz.	3 Keyed. per doz.	Description.
118	3 inch.					Br'd Bolt, Keypin 2 in. from Selv.
119	3 "					Keypin 2 in. from Selvedge.
124	$2\frac{1}{2}$ "					Brass Bolt, Keypin $1\frac{1}{4}$ in. from Selvedge, Double Keyhole.
120	$2\frac{1}{2}$ "					Keypin $1\frac{1}{2}$ in. from Selvedge.
						CIRCULAR CAP TILL LOCKS.
200	$2\frac{1}{2}$ "					Brass, Cap'd up, Double Keyhole.
201	$2\frac{1}{2}$ "					Iron, Cap'd up, Double Keyhole.

TRUNK LOCKS, PATENT CATCH.

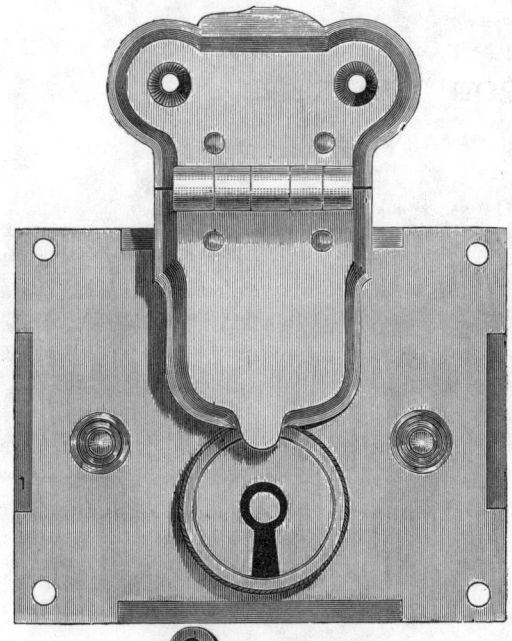

No. 66.

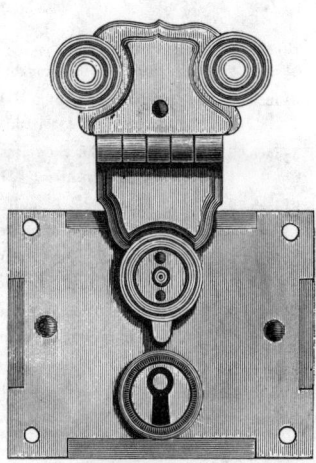

No. 70.

INSIDE LOCKS, BRASS PLATE OUTSIDE, WARDED, ASSORTED FANCY KEYS.

No.	Size.	Price.	
22	3½ inch,	$	Double Catch, with Secret Escutcheons, for Iron Frame Trunks.
1	3½ inch,	$	Double Catch, for Iron Frame Trunks.
23	3½ inch,	$	Double Catch, with Secret Escutcheons, for Wood Frame Trunks.
24	3½ inch,	$	Single Catch, with Secret Escutcheons, for Wood Frame Trunks.
2	3½ inch,	$	Double Catch, for Wood Frame Trunks.
19	3½ inch,	$	Single Catch, for Wood Frame Trunks.
43	3½ inch,	$	Double Catch, with Secret Escutcheons, for Wood Frame Trunks.
49	3½ inch,	$	Single Catch, with Secret Escutcheons, for Wood Frame Trunks.
44	3½ inch,	$	Double Catch, for Wood Frame Trunks.
48	3½ inch,	$	Single Catch, for Wood Frame Trunks.
36	3¼ inch,	$	Double Catch, with Secret Escutcheons, for Wood Frame Trunks.
35	3¼ inch,	$	Single Catch, with Secret Escutcheons, for Wood Frame Trunks.
39	3¼ inch,	$	Double Catch, for Wood Frame Trunks.
38	3¼ inch,	$	Single Catch, for Wood Frame Trunks.
37	3 inch,	$	Brass, Single Catch, Outside, Brass Drop.
32	3 inch,	$	Iron, Japanned, Single Catch, Outside Brass Drop.

BRASS AND IRON TUMBLERS.

No.	Size.	Price.	
50	7 inch,	$	Brass, Secret, Double Stop Hasp, French Pattern, two Keys each, Fancy.
71	5 inch,	$	Brass, Patent Tumbler Catch, Solid Hasp, Secret Ward, two Keys each.
64	5 inch,	$	Brass, Secret Bushed, Extra Large Solid Stop Hasp, Warded, Assorted Keys.
65	5 inch,	$	Brass, Secret Bushed, Extra Large Solid Stop Hasp, Warded, 24 Changes of Keys.
68	5 inch,	$	Brass, Solid Wrought Hasp, in Centre, Warded, 2 Keys each.
62	4 inch,	$	Brass, Solid Stop Hasps, Solid Bush and Drop, Solid Wards Assorted.
63	4 inch,	$	Iron, Solid Stop Hasps, Solid Brass Bush and Drop, Solid Wards, Assorted, Red Japanned.
66	4 inch,	$	Brass, Secret Solid Wrought Stop Hasp in Centre, Warded (see Plate above.)
67	4 inch,	$	Brass, Solid Wrought Hasp in Centre, Warded.
40	4 inch,	$	Brass, Secret Brass Drop, Bushed, Solid Stop Hasp, Solid Wards, Assorted.
41	4 inch,	$	Iron, Polished with Red Japan, Secret Brass Drop, Bushed, Solid Hasp and Wards, Assorted.
72	3½ inch,	$	Brass, Solid Wrought Hasp in Centre, Warded.

TRUNK LOCKS, PATENT CATCH.

(Continued.)

BRASS AND IRON TUMBLERS.

(Continued.)

No.	Size.	Price.		No.	Size.	Price.	
69	3¼ inch,	$	Brass, Solid Wrought Hasp, in Centre, Warded.	55	3 inch,	$	Iron, Solid Stop Hasps, Solid Brass Bush, Drop and Wards, Polished with Red Japan.
60	3½ inch,	$	Brass, Solid Stop Hasps, Solid Bush, Drop and Wards, Assorted.	70	2½ inch,	$	Brass, Solid Wrought Hasp in Centre, Warded (see Plate, page 135.)
61	3½ inch,	$	Iron, Solid Stop Hasps, Solid Bush, Drop and Wards, Assorted, Red Japanned.	73	2½ inch,	$	Brass, Solid Hasp, Patent Tumbler Catch.
33	3½ inch,	$	Brass, Solid Stop Hasps, Solid Wards, Brass Bush and Drop, Assorted.	56	2½ inch,	$	Brass, Solid Stop Hasps, Solid Bush, Drop and Wards, Assorted.
16	3½ inch,	$	Iron, Japanned, Solid Stop Hasp, Brass Bush and Drop, Assorted.	57	2½ inch,	$	Iron, Solid Stop Hasps, Solid Brass Bush, Drop and Wards, Polished with Red Japan.
52	3¼ inch,	$	Brass, Solid Stop Hasp, Solid Bush and Drop, Solid Wards, Assorted.	58	2¼ inch,	$	Brass, Solid Stop Hasp, Solid Bush, Drop and Wards, Assorted.
53	3¼ inch,	$	Iron, Solid Stop Hasps, Solid Brass Bush, Drop and Wards, Red Japanned.	59	2¼ inch,	$	Iron, Solid Stop Hasps, Solid Brass Bush, Drop and Wards, Polished with Red Japan.
54	3 inch,	$	Brass, Solid Stop Hasp, Solid Bush, Drop and Wards, Assorted.				

JAPANNED IRON BACK SPRING.

BRASS DROP, WROUGHT HASP AND BOLT.

No.	Size.	Price.		No.	Size.	Price.	
20	3¾ inch,	$	Iron, Brass Drop, 1 Ward, Fancy.	8	3 inch,	$	Iron, Brass Drop.
15	3½ inch,	$	Iron, Brass Bush and Drop, 1 Ward, Fancy.	4	2½ inch,	$	Brass, Brass Bush and Drop, 1 Ward, Fancy.
17	3½ inch,	$	Iron, Brass Drop, 1 Ward, Fancy.	13	2½ inch,	$	Iron, Brass Bush and Drop, 1 Ward, Fancy.
51	3½ inch,	$	Iron, Brass Solid Stop Hasp, Brass Bush and Drop, Warded.	9	2½ inch,	$	Iron, Brass Drop, Fancy.
14	3¼ inch,	$	Iron, Brass Bush and Drop, 1 Ward, Fancy,	11	2¼ inch,	$	Iron, Brass Bush and Drop, 1 Ward, Assorted.
18	3¼ inch,	$	Iron, Brass Drop, 1 Ward.	6	2 inch,	$	Brass, Brass Drop.
12	3 inch,	$	Iron, Brass Bush and Drop, 1 Ward, Fancy.	5	2 inch,	$	Iron, Brass Drop.

MALLEABLE SOLID HASPS.

No.	Size.	Price.		No.	Size.	Price.	
51	3½ inch,	$	Brass, Solid Stop Hasp, Brass Bush and Drop.	29	3 inch,	$	Iron, Brass Drop, 1 Ward.
30	3¾ inch,	$	Iron, Brass Drop, 1 Ward, Fancy.	28	3 inch,	$	Iron, Brass Bush and Drop, 1 Ward, Fancy.
27	3½ inch,	$	Iron, Brass Bush and Drop, 1 Ward, Fancy.	26	3 inch,	$	Iron, Brass Drop.
25	3¼ inch,	$	Iron, Brass Bush and Drop, 1 Ward, Fancy.				

PATENT CATCH VALISE LOCKS.

No.	Size.	Price.		No.	Size.	Price.	
21	2¼ inch,	$	All Brass, Outside, Double Catch, Brass Solid Hasp, 1 Ward, Highly Finished, Fancy Keys, for Wood or Iron Frame.	45	2½ inch,	$	Iron, Double Catch, Inside, Warded, Assorted Fancy Keys, Secret Escutcheons, for Iron Frame Valises.
3	2½ inch,	$	Iron, Inside, Brass Plate and Drop Outside, Warded, Assorted Fancy Keys, for Iron Frame Valises.	31	2 inch,	$	Brass, Single Catch, Outside, Brass Drop, Fancy Keys.
46	2½ inch,	$	Iron, Inside, Brass Plate and Drop Outside, Warded, Assorted Fancy Keys, for Wood Frame Valises.	42	1¾ inch,	$	Brass, Satchel and Hat Case, Round Plate, Raised Bush.

INDEX—CABINET LOCKS.

Description.	No.	Key'd	Inch.	Price.	Page.
Till........	1	3	2½	$0.46	134
"	1	4	2½	.49	134
"	1	6	2½	.55	134
"	1	12	2½	.72	134
Chest.......	2		4	3.50	129
Cupboard....	3		4	3.00	131
Chest.......	4		4	7.00	129
Till........	5	3	2¾	.70	134
"	5	4	2¾	.74	134
"	5	6	2¾	.82	134
"	5	12	2¾	1.00	134
Cupboard....	6		3	4.00	132
Chest.......	7		3½	1.25	130
"	8		3	1.00	130
"	9		4	8.00	130
"	10		3½	4.50	129
Desk.......	10		3½	4.50	130
Chest.......	11		3½	1.75	130
Desk.......	11		3½	1.75	131
Drawer.....	12		2¾	2.25	134
"	13		2¾	4.50	134
"	14		2¾	3.50	134
"	15		2¾	5.50	133
"	16		2¾	2.38	134
"	17		2½	2.50	134
"	18		2½	2.25	134
"	19		2¾	2.50	134
Chest.......	20		3	4.50	129
Desk.......	20		3	4.50	131
Cupboard....	21		3	4.25	131
"	22		3	2.50	132
Till........	23	3	2½	1.00	134
"	23	4	2½	1.03	134
"	23	6	2½	1.10	134
"	23	12	2½	1.30	134
Chest.......	24		3	1.75	130
Desk.......	24		3	1.75	131
Till........	25	3	2½	1.16	134
"	25	4	2½	1.19	134
"	25	6	2½	1.25	134
"	25	12	2½	1.37	134
"	26	3	2½	.58	134
"	26	4	2½	.61	134
"	26	6	2½	.67	134
"	26	12	2½	.84	134
"	27	3	2½	.70	134
"	27	4	2½	.73	134
"	27	6	2½	.80	134
"	27	12	2½	.95	134
Chest.......	28		2¾	3.00	129
"	29		2½	1.50	130
Cupboard....	30		2½	2.00	132
Chest.......	31		2½	1.20	130
Cupboard....	32		2½	1.75	132
Drawer.....	33		1¾	.95	134
Chest.......	34		2	.75	130
"	35		2	1.00	130
Drawer.....	36		2	1.00	134
Chest.......	37		2	2.25	130
"	38		2	2.67	129
"	39		2	3.50	129
Drawer.....	40		2¼	1.88	134
Chest.......	42		1¼	.75	130
"	43		1½	.75	130
Cupboard....	44		3	1.62	132
Chest.......	45		1¾	.95	130
Drawer.....	46		1½	.75	134
Till........	47	3	2¾	1.60	134
"	47	4	2¾	1.64	134
"	47	6	2¾	1.72	134
"	47	12	2¾	1.87	134
"	48	3	2¾	.84	134
"	48	4	2¾	.87	134
"	48	6	2¾	.92	134
"	48	12	2¾	1.12	134
"	49	3	3	.90	134
"	49	4	3	.94	134
"	49	6	3	1.00	134
"	49	12	3	1.20	134
Chest.......	50		3½	2.00	130
Desk.......	50		3½	2.00	130
Till........	51	3	2¼	.66	134
"	51	4	2¼	.69	134
"	51	6	2¼	.75	134
"	51	12	2¼	.93	134
"	52	3	3	1.85	134
"	52	4	3	1.88	134
"	52	6	3	1.94	134
"	52	12	3	2.12	134
"	53	3	2¼	.84	134
"	53	4	2¼	.88	134
"	53	6	2¼	.92	134

Description.	No.	Key'd	Inch	Price.	Page.
Till........	53	12	2¼	$1.12	134
Chest.......	54		2½	1.00	130
Desk.......	54		2½	1.00	131
Chest.......	55		1½	.68	130
Cupboard....	56		2¼	1.00	132
"	57		2¼	.75	132
"	58		2½	.87	132
Till........	60	3	2¼	.97	134
"	60	4	2¼	1.00	134
"	60	6	2¼	1.04	134
"	60	12	2¼	1.25	134
Cupboard....	61		2¾	2.25	132
"	62		2¾	2.38	132
Drawer.....	63		2½	4.00	134
Chest.......	64		2	1.88	130
"	65		3	1.50	130
Desk.......	65		3	1.50	131
Drawer.....	66		2½	2.12	134
"	67		2½	2.00	134
Till........	68	3	2½	.82	134
"	68	4	2½	.86	134
"	68	6	2½	.94	134
"	68	12	2½	1.10	134
Drawer.....	69		2½	3.25	134
"	70		2	4.25	134
"	71		2	.88	134
Till........	72	3	2½	.40	134
"	72	4	2½	.43	134
"	72	6	2½	.50	134
"	72	12	2½	.66	134
Drawer.....	73		2¾	2.75	134
Cupboard....	74		2¾	1.00	132
Chest.......	75		2¾	1.50	130
Cupboard....	76		2½	2.50	131
"	77		2½	3.00	131
Tin Box.....	78		2¼	3.50	129
Drawer.....	79		2	4.00	134
Till........	80	3	2½	1.60	134
"	80	4	2½	1.65	134
"	80	6	2½	1.75	134
"	80	12	2½	1.87	134
"	80½	3	2½	1.42	134
"	80½	4	2½	1.46	134
"	80½	6	2½	1.54	134
"	80½	12	2½	1.70	134
"	81	3	2½	1.20	134
"	81	4	2½	1.24	134
"	81	6	2½	1.30	134
"	81	12	2½	1.50	134
"	81½	3	2½	.95	134
"	81½	4	2½	.98	134
"	81½	6	2½	1.04	134
"	81½	12	2½	1.20	134
Cupboard....	82		4	5.00	131
Chest.......	83		3½	2.75	130
Desk.......	83		3½	2.75	131
Cupboard....	84		3½	4.00	131
"	85		3	3.25	131
Chest.......	86		3	4.00	129
Desk.......	86		3	4.00	131
Cupboard....	87		3	2.62	131
"	88		3	2.25	131
Drawer.....	89		2¼	1.38	134
Cupboard....	90		3½	2.00	131
Chest.......	91		4	4.75	129
Desk.......	91		4	4.75	130
Chest.......	92		4	4.00	130
Desk.......	92		3½	3.25	130
Chest.......	93		3½	3.25	130
Desk.......	93		3½	3.25	130
Chest.......	94		3½	2.50	129
"	95		2¾	1.10	130
Till........	97	3	2¼	.70	134
"	97	4	2¼	.74	134
"	97	6	2¼	.82	134
"	97	12	2¼	1.00	134
"	98	3	2½	.50	134
"	98	4	2½	.54	134
"	98	6	2½	.62	134
"	98	12	2½	.80	134
Drawer.....	99		2½	5.00	134
Cupboard....	100		4	7.00	131
"	101		3	1.88	131
Chest.......	103		3	1.75	130
Cupboard....	104		3	1.75	132
Chest.......	105		2¼	2.50	130
Cupboard....	106		2½	3.00	132
"	107		2¾	3.25	132
"	108		2¾	3.50	132
Piano.......	109		3	5.50	132
Chest.......	110		3½	6.50	129
Desk.......	110		3½	6.50	130

Description.	No.	Key'd	Inch.	Price.	Page.
Chest.......	111		4	$5.25	129
	112				
Chest.......	113		4	10.00	129
"	114		4	9.00	130
Drawer.....	115		2¾	5.50	133
Cupboard....	116		3	1.25	132
"	117		2¾	1.15	132
Till........	118	3	3		134
"	118	4	3		134
"	118	6	3		134
"	118	12	3		134
"	119	3	3		134
"	119	4	3		134
"	119	4	3		134
"	119	12	3		134
"	120	3	2½	1.16	134
"	120	4	2½	1.19	134
"	120	6	2½	1.25	134
"	120	12	2½	1.37	134
Drawer.....	121		3	4.25	132
Till........	122	3	2½	1.70	134
"	122	4	2½	1.74	134
"	122	6	2½	1.82	134
"	122	12	2½	2.00	134
Drawer.....	123		2¾	5.50	133
Till........	124	3	2½	1.91	134
"	124	4	2½	1.94	134
"	124	6	2½	2.00	134
"	124	12	2½	2.12	134
Chest.......	126		2¼	1.20	130
Drawer.....	127		2¾	4.50	133
"	128		2¾	5.50	133
"	129		2½	5.00	134
"	130		2½	4.00	134
Piano.......	131		3	5.00	132
Chest.......	133		2½	1.12	130
"	134		2	3.00	129
Drawer.....	135		1½	.68	134
"	136		3	5.50	132
Cupboard....	137		2½	1.30	132
Drawer.....	138		1¾	.75	134
Chest.......	139		1¾	.75	130
Till........	140	3	2½	1.80	134
"	140	4	2½	1.84	134
"	140	6	2½	1.90	134
"	140	12	2½	2.10	134
Chest.......	141		3	1.12	130
"	142		3½	1.50	130
Cupboard....	143		3	1.20	131
"	144		2¾	1.50	132
Wardrobe...	145		3¼	10.00	131
"	146		4	6.00	131
"	147		3½	4.75	131
"	148		3	4.00	131
"	149		4	8.00	131
"	150		3½	6.50	131
"	151		3	5.50	131
Cupboard....	152		3½	1.75	131
"	153		3	1.00	131
Chest.......	154		3¼	2.00	130
"	155		3¼	1.25	130
Wardrobe...	156		4	4.75	131
"	157		3½	4.00	131
"	158		3	3.25	131
Chest.......	159		4	13.00	130
"	160		3	2.37	130
Desk.......	160		3	2.37	131
Till........	161	3	2½	1.00	134
"	161	4	2½	1.03	134
"	161	6	2½	1.10	134
"	161	12	2½	1.30	134
"	162	3	2¾	1.32	134
"	162	4	2¾	1.36	134
"	162	6	2¾	1.42	134
"	162	12	2¾	1.62	134
Chest.......	163		2¾	2.25	130
"	164		2½	2.62	130
"	165		2¾	2.75	130
"	166		2½	2.12	130
"	167		2¼	2.00	130
"	168		3¼	2.62	130
"	169		2½	2.87	129
Desk.......	169		2½	2.87	131
Chest.......	170		2½	2.50	129
Desk.......	170		2½	2.50	131
Chest.......	171		2¼	2.75	129
"	172		2¼	2.38	129
Cupboard....	173		4	2.50	131
"	174		3½	2.25	131
Chest.......	175		4	9.50	130
Drawer.....	176		2¼	4.00	134

☞ Gilt or Silver Bow Keys Furnished to any Lock to Order, $2.00 per Dozen Extra.

INDEX—CABINET LOCKS.

DESCRIPTION.	NO.	KEY'D	INCH.	PRICE.	PAGE.	DESCRIPTION.	NO.	KEY'D	INCH.	PRICE.	PAGE.	DESCRIPTION.	NO.	KEY'D	INCH.	PRICE.	PAGE.
Drawer	177		2¼	$3.25	134	Chest	250		4	$25.00	129	Drawer	309	6	2½	2.55	133
Chest	178		2	2.25	129	Desk	250		4	25.00	130	"	309	12	2½	2.85	133
Tin Box	179		2½	5.50	129	Chest	251		4	22.00	129	"	310		2¾	2.62	133
Till	180	3	2½	1.20	134	Desk	251		4	22.00	130	"	311		2½	2.25	133
"	180	4	2½	1.24	134	Chest	252		4	20.00	129	"	312		2¼	2.00	133
"	180	6	2½	1.30	134	Desk	252		4	20.00	130	"	313		2	1.75	133
"	180	12	2½	1.50	134	Chest	253		4	18.00	129	"	320	3	2½	2.30	133
Chest	181		1½	2.25	130	Desk	253		4	18.00	130	"	320	4	2½	2.35	133
"	182		4	1.87	130	Chest	254		3½	24.00	129	"	320	6	2½	2.45	133
Show Case ...	183		1¾	3.00	130	Desk	254		3½	24.00	130	"	320	12	2½	2.75	133
Till	184	3	2½	.70	134	Chest	255		3½	21.00	129	"	321	3	2½	2.20	133
"	184	4	2½	.74	134	Desk	255		3½	21.00	130	"	321	4	2½	2.25	133
"	184	6	2½	.84	134	Chest	256		3½	19.00	129	"	321	6	2½	2.35	133
"	184	12	2½	1.00	134	Desk	256		3½	19.00	130	"	321	12	2½	2.65	133
"	185	3	2½	1.20	134	Chest	257		3½	17.00	129	"	322	3	2½	2.10	133
"	185	4	2½	1.24	134	Desk	257		3½	17.00	130	"	322	4	2½	2.15	133
"	185	6	2½	1.30	134	Chest	258		2½	14.00	129	"	322	6	2½	2.25	133
"	185	12	2½	1.50	134	"	259		2½	12.50	129	"	322	12	2½	2.55	133
"	186	3	2½	1.80	134	Drawer	260		2¾	22.00	133	Cupboard	330		3	3.12	132
"	186	4	2½	1.84	134	"	261		2¾	19.00	133	"	331		2¾	3.00	132
"	186	6	2½	1.90	134	"	262		2¾	17.50	133	"	332		2½	2.75	132
"	186	12	2½	2.10	134	"	263		2¾	15.00	133	"	333		2¼	2.62	132
"	187	3	2½	1.10	134	"	264		2¾	13.00	133	"	340		3	2.50	132
"	187	4	2½	1.14	134	"	265		2½	15.50	133	"	341		2¾	2.37	132
"	187	6	2½	1.20	134	"	266		2½	13.50	133	"	342		2½	2.25	132
"	187	12	2½	1.40	134	"	267		2½	12.00	133	"	343		2¼	2.12	132
Piano	188		3	6.00	132	Cupboard	268		2¼	20.00	132	"	350		3	3.25	132
"	190		3	5.50	132	Chest	269		1½	12.00	129	"	351		3	3.38	132
Drawer	191		3	5.00	132	Cupboard	271		3	19.00	132	Drawer	360		2¾	2.75	132
Piano	192		3	5.50	132	"	272		3	18.00	132	Wardrobe ...	500		3½	2.00	131
"	193		3	4.75	132	"	273		3	17.00	132	Cupboard	501		2	1.00	132
"	194		3	4.25	132	Drawer	275		2	12.00	133	"	502		2¼	6.50	132
"	195		2½	5.75	132	"	276		2	11.00	133	"	503		2	6.00	132
Seraphine ...	196		2¼	2.00	132	"	277		2	10.00	133	Wardrobe ...	504		3½	3.50	131
Piano	197		2½	5.00	132	Cash Box	279		2½	14.00	129	" ...	505		3½	2.25	131
"	198		2½	4.50	132	Drawer	280		3	24.00	133	" ...	506		2¾	3.00	131
Till	200	3	2½	1.10	134	"	281		3	22.00	133	" ...	507		2¾	2.00	131
"	200	4	2½	1.13	134	"	282		3	20.00	133	Cupboard	508		2	3.00	131
"	200	6	2½	1.19	134	"	284		3	20.00	133	"	700		2¾	2.10	132
"	200	12	2½	1.37	134	"	285		3	18.00	133	Drawer	1000		3	4.50	133
"	201	3	2½	.50	134	"	286		3	17.00	133	"	1000		4	4.75	133
"	201	4	2½	.53	134	"	287		3	16.00	133	"	1004		2½	4.37	133
"	201	6	2½	.59	134	"	288		2¾	16.00	133	"	1006		2½	4.25	133
"	201	12	2½	.76	134	"	289		2¾	15.00	133	Cupboard	1010		2¾	4.12	132
Cupboard	221		3	4.75	132	Chest	290		3	20.00	129	Drawer	052		2½	5.00	134
Chest	226		3	1.12	130	"	291		3	18.00	129	Cupboard	067		3	1.00	131
"	228		3½	1.50	130	"	292		3	16.00	129	Chest	090		1½	.75	130
Drawer	232		2¾	3.10	133	"	295		2	13.00	132	"	091		1½	.88	130
Till	240	3	2½	1.50	134	Camp Desk ..	296		2½	2.00	131	Drawer	0220		2¾	16.00	133
"	240	4	2½	1.54	134	Drawer	300		2¾	3.25	133	"	0221		2¾	14.50	133
"	240	6	2½	1.60	134	"	301		2½	3.00	133	"	0222		2¾	13.00	133
"	240	12	2½	1.80	134	"	302		2¼	2.75	133	"	0224		2½	12.00	133
Wardrobe ...	245		3¼	22.00	131	"	303		2	2.50	133	"	0225		2½	11.00	133
" ...	246		3¼	26.00	131	"	307		3½	6.50	133	"	0226		2½	10.00	133
Cupboard	247		2½	18.00	131	"	308		3	6.00	133	"	0228		2½	10.00	133
"	248		2	16.00	131	"	309	3	2½	2.40	133	"	0229		2½	8.50	133
"	249		1½	13.50	131	"	309	4	2½	2.45	133						

INDEX—TRUNK LOCKS.

No.	Price.	In:	P.	No	Price.	In.	P.	No.	Price.	In.	P.	No.	Price.	In.	P.	No.	Price.	In.	P.	No.	Price.	In.	P.
1	$3.25	3½	135	15	$1.62	3½	136	27	$1.65	3½	136	40	$12.00	4	135	53	$5.50	3¼	136	64	$25.00	5	135
2	3.00	3½	135	16	4.50	3½	136	28	1.35	3	136	41	10.00	4	135	54	6.50	3	136	65	28.00	5	135
3	3.00	2½	136	17	1.12	3½	136	29	1.20	3¼	136	42	2.50	1¾	136	55	5.00	3	136	66	13.00	4	135
4	2.50	2½	136	18	1.00	3¼	136	30	1.40	3¾	136	43	4.00	3½	135	56	5.00	2½	136	67	12.00	4	135
5	.88	2	136	19	2.75	3½	135	31	1.50	2	136	44	2.25	3½	135	57	4.00	2½	136	68	16.00	5	135
6	2.00	2	136	20	1.25	3¾	136	32	1.00	3	135	45	4.50	2½	136	58	4.25	2¼	136	69	7.50	3¼	136
8	.88	3	136	21	3.00	2¼	136	33	7.50	3½	136	46	3.00	2½	136	59	3.50	2¼	136	70	5.00	2½	136
9	.88	2½	136	22	7.00	3½	135	35	3.75	3¼	135	48	2.00	3½	135	60	8.50	3½	136	71	16.00	5	135
11	1.25	2¼	136	23	6.50	3½	135	36	4.00	3¼	135	49	3.75	3½	135	61	6.50	3½	136	72	8.00	3½	135
12	1.25	3	136	24	6.00	3½	135	37	1.62	3	135	50	30.00	7	135	62	11.00	4	135	73	6.00	2½	136
13	1.25	2½	136	25	1.60	3¼	136	38	2.00	3¼	135	51	3.50	3½	136	63	9.00	4	135				
14	1.50	3¼	136	26	1.00	3	136	39	2.25	3¼	135	52	7.50	3¼	136								

PRICES OF CABINET KEYS AND BLANKS.

No.	Price per doz.	No.	Price per doz.	No.	Price per doz.	No.	Price per doz.	No.	Price per doz.	No.	Price per doz.	No.	Price per doz.	No.	Price per doz.	No.	Price per doz.	No.	Price per doz.
1	$0.17	21	$0.25	41	$0.17	61	$0.20	81	$0.20	101	$0.20	121	$0.22	141	$0.20	161	$0.25	245	$0.38
2	.31	22	.20	42	.15	62	.20	82	.50	102	.20	122	.20	142	.20	162	.27	250	.38
3	.31	23	.17	43	.15	63	.22	83	.25	103	.20	123	.54	143	.20	163	.25	260	.32
4	.60	24	.20	44	.20	64	.20	84	.31	104	.20	124	.20	144	.20	164	.22	265	.30
5	.20	25	.20	45	.15	65	.20	85	.25	105	.20	125	.20	145	.75	165	.22	275	.25
6	.25	26	.20	46	.15	66	.20	86	.25	106	.20	126	.17	146	.50	166	.22	300	.30
7	.20	27	.20	47	.22	67	.20	87	.20	107	.20	127	.27	147	.31	167	.20	303	.25
8	.17	28	.25	48	.22	68	.15	88	.20	108	.20	128	.27	148	.25	168	.22	7–16	.15
9	.75	29	.20	49	.22	69	.22	89	.17	109	.31	129	.22	149	.75	169	.22	8–16	.17
10	.27	30	.17	50	.25	70	.20	90	.25	110	.62	130	.22	150	.62	170	.22	9–16	.25
11	.25	31	.17	51	.17	71	.15	91	.31	111	.31	131	.31	151	.50	171	.22	10–16	.30
12	.22	32	.17	52	.22	72	.15	92	.31	112		132	.25	152	.20	172	.20	11–16	.34
13	.27	33	.15	53	.17	73	.22	93	.27	113	.75	133	.20	153	.20	173	.44	12–16	.44
14	.25	34	.15	54	.17	74	.20	94	.22	114	.75	134	.20	154	.20	174	.38	13–16	.54
15	.25	35	.15	55	.15	75	.20	95	.20	115	.25	135	.15	155	.20	175	.80	14–16	.60
16	.22	36	.16	56	.17	76	.20	96	.20	116	.20	136	.22	156	.37	176	.22	500	.25
17	.20	37	.20	57	.17	77	.20	97	.20	117	.20	137	.17	157	.31	177	.22	501	.20
18	.20	38	.22	58	.17	78	.20	98	.20	118	.20	138	.15	158	.31	178	.20	507	.20
19	.22	39	.40	59	.20	79	.22	99	.25	119	.20	139	.15	159	.75	179	.40	700	.25
20	.25	40	.17	60	.20	80	.20	100	.75	120	.20	140	.17	160	.22	180	.25	1000	.30

TRUNK KEYS AND BLANKS.

No.	Price per doz.	No.	Price per doz.	No.	Price per doz.	No.	Price per doz.
1	$0.25	21	$0.20	41	$0.50	61	$0.40
2	.25	22	.25	42	.15	62	.50
3	.20	23	.25	43	.20	63	.50
4	.20	24	.25	44	.20	64	.60
5	.12	25	.22	45	.20	65	.60
6	.20	26	.15	46	.20	66	.50
7	.20	27	.22	47	.60	67	.50
8	.15	28	.20	48	.20	68	.50
9	.15	29	.17	49	.20	69	.40
10	.20	30	.17	50	.50	70	.30
11	.20	31	.15	51		71	.50
12	.20	32	.15	52	.40	72	.40
13	.20	33	.40	53	.40	73	.30
14	.22	34	.25	54	.40		
15	.22	35	.17	55	.40		
16	.40	36	.17	56	.30		
17	.17	37	.15	57	.30		
18	.17	38	.17	58	.30		
19	.25	39	.17	59	.30		
20	.17	40	.50	60	.40		

Trunk Lock Keys, ass'd, per Gross, $ Cabinet Lock Keys, ass'd, per Gross, $ Cabinet Lock Blanks, ass'd, per Gross, $

ESCUTCHEONS, SASH AND JAIL LOCKS.

BRASS THREAD ESCUTCHEONS.

$ per gross.
Size, $\frac{3}{8}$ $\frac{1}{2}$ $\frac{9}{16}$ $\frac{5}{8}$ $\frac{11}{16}$ $\frac{3}{4}$, $\frac{13}{16}$ $\frac{7}{8}$ inch.

CIRCULAR ESCUTCHEONS.

Brass................$\frac{9}{16}$ $\frac{5}{8}$ inch.   per gross.

Plated ....$\frac{9}{16}$ $\frac{5}{8}$ inch.   per gross.

WOOD AND BONE ESCUTCHEONS.
Round.

Mahogany....$\frac{5}{8}$ $\frac{3}{4}$ $\frac{7}{8}$ 1 $1\frac{1}{8}$ $1\frac{1}{4}$ inch.   per gross.

Blackwalnut..$\frac{5}{8}$ $\frac{3}{4}$ $\frac{7}{8}$ 1 $1\frac{1}{8}$ $1\frac{1}{4}$ inch.   per gross.

Oak..........$\frac{5}{8}$ $\frac{3}{4}$ $\frac{7}{8}$ 1 $1\frac{1}{8}$ $1\frac{1}{4}$ inch.   per gross.

Rosewood....$\frac{5}{8}$ $\frac{3}{4}$ $\frac{7}{8}$ 1 $1\frac{1}{8}$ $1\frac{1}{4}$ inch.   per gross.

Bone, Plain...$\frac{5}{8}$ $\frac{3}{4}$ $\frac{7}{8}$ 1 $1\frac{1}{8}$ $1\frac{1}{4}$ inch.   per gross.

Bone, Fancy..$\frac{5}{8}$ $\frac{3}{4}$ $\frac{7}{8}$ 1 $1\frac{1}{8}$ $1\frac{1}{4}$ inch.   per gross.

Oval.

Mahogany....$\frac{5}{8}$ $\frac{3}{4}$ $\frac{7}{8}$ 1 $1\frac{1}{8}$ $1\frac{1}{4}$ inch.   per gross.

Blackwalnut..$\frac{5}{8}$ $\frac{3}{4}$ $\frac{7}{8}$ 1 $1\frac{1}{8}$ $1\frac{1}{4}$ inch.   per gross.

Oak..........$\frac{5}{8}$ $\frac{3}{4}$ $\frac{7}{8}$ 1 $1\frac{1}{8}$ $1\frac{1}{4}$ inch.   per gross.

Rosewood....$\frac{5}{8}$ $\frac{3}{4}$ $\frac{7}{8}$ 1 $1\frac{1}{8}$ $1\frac{1}{4}$ inch.   per gross.

Bone, Plain...$\frac{5}{8}$ $\frac{3}{4}$ $\frac{7}{8}$ 1 $1\frac{1}{8}$ $1\frac{1}{4}$ inch.   per gross.

Bone, Fancy..$\frac{5}{8}$ $\frac{3}{4}$ $\frac{7}{8}$ 1 $1\frac{1}{8}$ $1\frac{1}{4}$ inch.   per gross.

PHŒNIX SASH LOCKS.

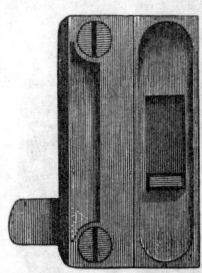

Acting by its own weight without Spring, it is easily applied, efficient in its working, and will not get out of order.

Japanned.......................................per gross, $

Brass Face, with Japanned Slide..............   "

Brass Face, with Brass Slide...................   "

Plated Face, with Japanned Slide..............   "

Plated Face, with Plated Slide.................   "

MINER'S PATENT SASH LOCK.

A very secure and reliable Sash Lock. It will hold the Sash at any point, and securely lock it, whether opened or closed. Are easily put on by means of $1\frac{3}{4}$ inch auger and screw-driver.

No. 1, Plated ....per gross, $

No. 2, Bronzed...............................   "

No. 3, Bronzed, Sunk Thumb-piece.............   "

For Jones' Patent Sash Lock, the *cheapest article made*, see p. 78.

JAIL LOCKS.

Size, $9\frac{1}{2} \times 7$ inches, Rim, Extra Heavy Wrought Iron Square Case, Heavy Wrought Iron Bolt, Drill Pin, Brass Key, Safe, for Jail Doors ....each, $

Size, 12×8 inches, Rim, Extra Heavy Wrought Iron Square Case, Heavy Wrought Iron Bolt, Drill Pin, Brass Key, Safe, for Jail Doors ....each, $

Size, 9×7 inches, Rim, Extra Heavy Cast Iron Square Case, Heavy Wrought Iron Bolt, 6 Pressure Tumblers, Drill Pin, Brass Key, *Extra Safe*, for Iron Gates or Cell Doors..........each, $

JAIL OR SAFE PADLOCKS.

"BUDD'S PATENT."

  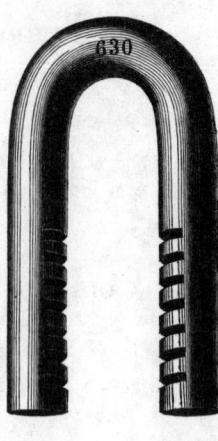

No. 1.   No. 2.

Chilled Iron Case, Case-Hardened Cast Steel Hasp, Drill Pin, 2 Cast Steel Keys to Each, Extra Safe and Strong.

No. 0, Small, 8 Wrought Iron Tumblers _____ each, $
No. 1, Medium, 12 Wrought Iron Tumblers _____ " $
No. 2, Large, 16 Wrought Iron Tumblers _____ " $

LIGHT BRASS AND TUMBLER BRASS PADLOCKS.

LIGHT BRASS PADLOCKS, German Pattern.	FINE FINISH, TUMBLER BRASS PADLOCKS, English Pattern, Polished Keys.
$ per dozen.	$ per dozen.
Size, ¾ 1 1¼ 1½ 1¾ 2 inch.	Size, 1 1¼ 1½ 1¾ 2 inch.

PLATE LOCKS AND KEYS.

PLATE LOCKS.

No. 85.

No. 35, Half Bushed, Fancy Key, 6 to 12 in.....per inch,   cts.
No. 40, Half Bushed, Fancy Key, 5 to 12 in.....   "   "
No. 45, Half Bushed, Fancy Key, 6 to 12 in. Fine
    Broad Bolt, Iron Bound.............   "   "

No. 73, Full Bushed, Fancy Key, 6 to 12 in. Iron
    Bound.............................per inch,   cts.

No. 85, Full Bushed, Fancy Key, 7 to 12 in. Iron
    Bound, Extra Heavy, Brass Face Plate   "   "

Length.	5	6	7	8	9	10	11	12 in.
No.	Price Per Inch.		Price per Dozen.					
35								
40								
45								
73								
85								

POLISHED IRON, PLATE LOCK KEYS.

For Plate Locks, No. 35, 40, 45................per dozen, $
For Plate Locks, No. 73 ....   "
For Plate Locks, No. 85 ....   "

HANDLES.

JAPANNED COFFIN HANDLES.

$ doz. pair.

No. 1   2   3

JAPANNED WINDOW SHUTTER HANDLES.
French Pattern, Wrought Iron Plate.

$ dozen pair.

No. 1   2   3

$ dozen pair.

All Brass   No. 2   3

CHAIN BOLT HANDLES.

$ per dozen.

JAPANNED FLUSH DRAWER HANDLES.

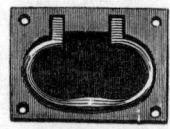

$ per dozen pair.

No. 1   2

JAPANNED FLUSH CHEST HANDLES.

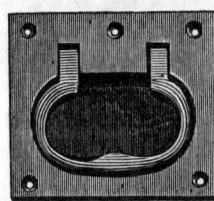

$ per dozen pair.

No. 1   2

WROUGHT JAPANNED TRUNK HANDLES.

$ per dozen pair.

No. 1   2   3

WROUGHT JAPANNED CHEST HANDLES.

$ doz. pair.

No. 1   2   3   4   5   6

IMPROVED LIFTING HANDLES.

$ dozen pair.

Japanned, No. 1   2   3

$ doz. pair.

Plain Brass,   2½   3   3½   3¾   4 inch.

Plain, Silver Plated on Brass,

$ doz. pair.

              2½   3   3½   3¾   4 inch.

Fancy Brass

$ doz. pair.

No. 11   12   13   14   15   16   17

Size 2½   2¾   3   3¼   3½   3¾   4½ inch.

Fancy, Silver Plated on Brass,

$ doz. pair.

No. 11   12   13   14   15   16   17

Size 2½   2¾   3   3¼   3½   3¾   4½ inch.

BRASS DRAWER HANDLES, LIGHT.
For Desk and Bureau Drawers, Small Wood Trunks, &c.

$ doz. pair.

2   2½   2¾   3   3¼   3½   4 inch.

HANDLES.

(Continued.)

TIN TRUNK HANDLES, BRASS,

For Banker's and other Tin Trunks.

$							per gross.
2	$2\frac{1}{2}$	$2\frac{3}{4}$	3	$3\frac{1}{4}$	$3\frac{1}{2}$	4	inch.

WOOD TRUNK HANDLES, BRASS,

With Long Screws, for Fancy Wood Trunks or Drawers.

$							per gross.
2	$2\frac{1}{2}$	$2\frac{3}{4}$	3	$3\frac{1}{4}$	$3\frac{1}{2}$	4	inch.

NEWARK BRASS TRUNK HANDLES,

For Tin or Wood Trunks and Shelf Boxes.

$			per gross.
2	$2\frac{1}{2}$	3	inch.

BOSTON BRASS TRUNK HANDLES.

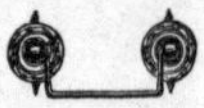

$			per gross.
2	$2\frac{1}{2}$	3	inch.

BRASS SHELF BOX HANDLES,

For Shelf Boxes, Fancy Paper or Wood Trunks, &c.

Filed and Burnished.

$		per gross.
2 inch	$2\frac{1}{2}$	inch.

BRASS RING HANDLES,

For Fancy Trunks, Paper Shelf Boxes, &c.

No. 000, $1\frac{1}{2}$ inch Rosette, Wire Loops.

	$			per gross.
Size of Ring,	$\frac{1}{2}$	$\frac{5}{8}$	$\frac{3}{4}$	inch.

No. 0, $\frac{3}{4}$ inch Rosettes, Sheet Brass Loops.

	$				per gross.
Size of Ring,	$\frac{1}{2}$	$\frac{5}{8}$	$\frac{7}{8}$	1	inch.

BRASS RING HANDLES.

(Continued.)

No. 1, $\frac{7}{8}$ inch Rosette, Pattern as Last.

	$			per gross.
Size of Ring,	$\frac{3}{4}$	$\frac{7}{8}$	1	inch.

No. 2, $1\frac{1}{4}$ inch Rosette.

	$			per gross.
Size of Ring,	1	$1\frac{1}{8}$	$1\frac{1}{4}$	inch.

No. 4, 2 inch Rosette, Heavy Ring.

	$		per gross.
Size of Ring,	$1\frac{1}{4}$	$1\frac{1}{2}$	inch.

DRAWER PULLS.

Nos. 30 to 34. Nos. 200 to 204. Nos. 50 to 54.

No. 30, 4 inch, Japanned.................per dozen, $
No. 31, 4 inch, Copper Bronzed.............. "
No. 32, 4 inch, Gold Bronzed............... "
No. 33, 4 inch, French Bronzed.............. "
No. 34, 4 inch, Brass....................... "
No. 50, 4 inch, Japanned.................... "
No. 51, 4 inch, Copper Bronzed.............. "
No. 52, 4 inch, Gold Bronzed............... "
No. 53, 4 inch, French Bronzed.............. "
No. 54, 4 inch, Brass....................... "
No. 200, $2\frac{1}{2}$ inch, Japanned.............. "
No. 201, $2\frac{1}{2}$ inch, Copper Bronzed.......... "
No. 202, $2\frac{1}{2}$ inch, Gold Bronzed............ "
No. 203, $2\frac{1}{2}$ inch, French Bronzed.......... "
No. 204, $2\frac{1}{2}$ inches, Brass................. "

Nos. 200 to 204, are very neat Pulls for the small drawers of Desks, &c.

Porcelain.

Plain Oval, 4 inch, with or without Lower Rim, per dozen, $
Plain Oval, $2\frac{3}{4}$ inch, with or without Lower Rim, "
Embossed, 4 inch, with or without Lower Rim, "
Embossed, 3 inch, with or without Lower Rim, "

Either pattern decorated to order, any style desired.

For other Drawer Pulls see page 84.

HANDLES, DOOR-KNOCKERS AND FOOT-SCRAPERS.

DOOR HANDLES OR THUMB LATCHES, WITH TURN BUTTONS.

$
Japanned, No. 0 1 2 3 4.   per dozen.

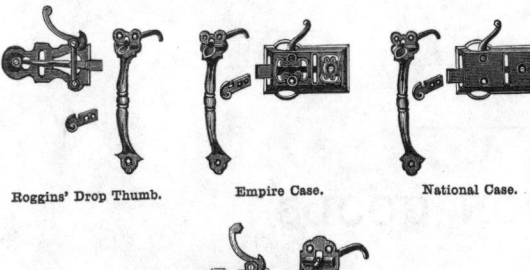

Roggins' Drop Thumb. Empire Case. National Case.

Front Door.

Roggins' Drop Thumb Latches, in cases 6 doz. each, per doz. $

Roggins' Empire Case Latches, in cases 6 doz. each "

Roggins' National Case Latches, in cases 6 doz. each "

Roggins' Front Door Latches, in cases 6 doz. each "

☞ For Oblique Store Door, Gate and Barn Door Handles, see pages 84 & 125.

DOOR PULLS.

Nos. 0 & 1. No. 2. No. 11 & 12. No. 14 & 15.

No. 0, Flat Pattern, Japanned.............per dozen, $

No. 1, Flat Pattern, Japanned............. "

No. 2, Blake's Pattern, Japanned........... "

No. 11, Fancy Brass..................... "

No. 12, Fancy Silvered................... "

No. 14, Plain Brass...................... "

No. 15, Plain Silvered................... "

No. 494, Plain Brass, Heavy............... "

No. 495, Plain Silvered, Heavy............ "

No. 498, Brass, Porcelain Handles, Oblique, Heavy "

DOOR KNOCKERS.

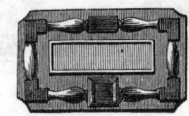

No. 6.

No. 1, Fancy Pattern, Japanned..............per dozen, $

No. 2, Fancy Pattern, Brass Plate, Japanned.... "

No. 3, Fancy Pattern, French Bronzed, copper & green "

No. 4, Fancy Pattern, Brass................... "

No. 5, Square Pattern, Japanned.............. "

No. 6, Square Pattern, Japanned, Brass Plate, see Plate "

No. 7, Square Pattern, French Bronzed........ "

JAPANNED FOOT SCRAPERS—FOR WOOD.

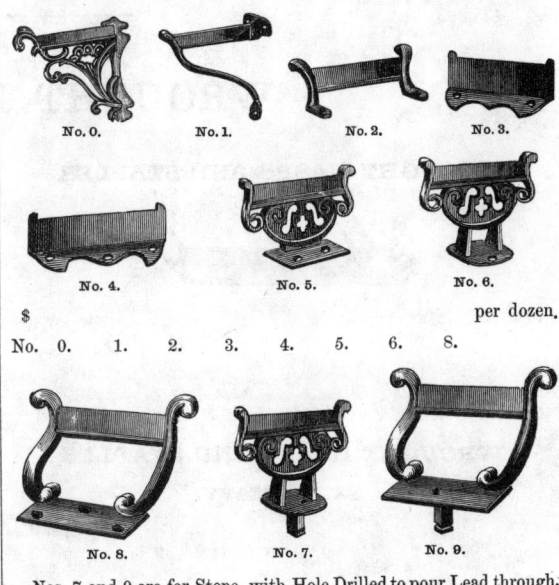

No. 0. No. 1. No. 2. No. 3.

No. 4. No. 5. No. 6.

$ per dozen.

No. 0. 1. 2. 3. 4. 5. 6. 8.

No. 8. No. 7. No. 9.

Nos. 7 and 9 are for Stone, with Hole Drilled to pour Lead through.

$ per dozen.

No. 7.   9.

JAPANNED DISH FOOT SCRAPERS.

No. 20.   No. 25.

$ per dozen.

No. 20.   25.

PATENT REVOLVING BRUSH FOOT SCRAPER AND CLEANER.

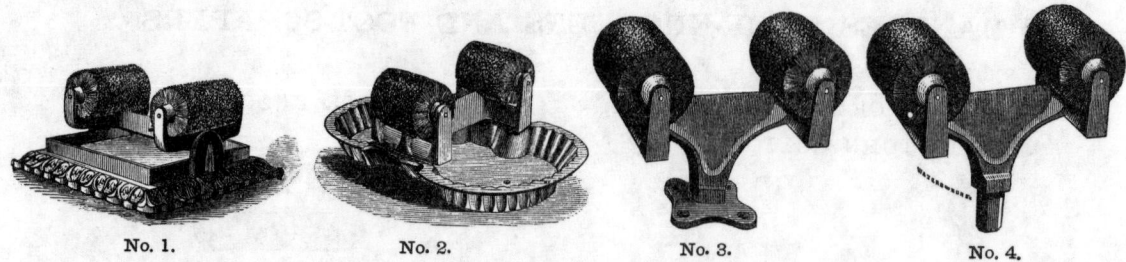

No. 1.   No. 2.   No. 3.   No. 4.

The advantages of this Foot Cleaner over all others, consist in the Revolving Brush, which brushes any part of the boot. By the revolving of the Brush it presents a clean surface continually, as by the friction of the Brush in revolving it cleans itself. New Brushes can be furnished at any time: they can be put in by any person.

No. 1, Japanned Square..per dozen, $
No. 2, Japanned Dish.. "
No. 3, Japanned, for Wood.. "
No. 4, Japanned, for Stone.. "

WROUGHT IRON GOODS.

WROUGHT HASPS AND STAPLES.

cts. per doz.

L'gth, 3   4   5   6   7   8   9   10   11   12 in.

WROUGHT HASPS AND STAPLES,
EXTRA HEAVY.

cts. per doz.

Length, 6   7   8   9   10   11   12 in.

WROUGHT HASPS AND STAPLES, WITH HOOKS,
Either Single or Double Hook, Right or Left Hand.

cts. per doz.

Length, 5   6   7   8   9   10   11   12 in.

EXTRA HEAVY
WROUGHT HASPS AND STAPLES, WITH HOOKS,
Either Single or Double Hook, Right or Left Hand.

cts. per doz.

Length, 6   7   8   9   10   11   12 in.

WROUGHT BENT HASPS AND STAPLES.

cts. per doz.

Length, 5   6   7   8   9   10 in.

BATTEN OR CELLAR DOOR HASPS.

$ per doz.

Length, 8   10   12 in.

WROUGHT STAPLES.

per gross.

Length, 1   1¼   1½   1¾   2   2¼   2½   2¾ in.

per gross.

3   3½   4   4½   5   6 in.

WROUGHT STAPLES.

Assorted, from 1½ to 3 inches,   cents per gross.
Assorted, from 1½ to 3½ inches,   cents per gross.

WROUGHT IRON GOODS.

(Continued.)

WROUGHT HOOKS AND STAPLES.

$
Length, 2   2½   3   3½   4   4½   5   5½   6 in.   per gross.

$
7   8   9 in.   per gross.

WROUGHT GOOSE-NECK HOOKS AND STAPLES,
JAPANNED.

$
Length, 2½   3   3½   4   5   6   7   8 in.   per gross.

WROUGHT HOOKS, WITH PLATE STAPLES,
FOR SCUTTLE DOORS.

$
Length; 3   3½   4   4½   5   6 in.   per gross.

AWNING HOOKS.

$
Length, 1½   1¾   2   2½   3   3½   4   4½ in.   per gross.

$
5   5½   6 in.   per gross.

Assorted,   per gross.

TINNED AWNING HOOKS.

$
Length, 3   3½   4   4½   5 in.   per gross.

WROUGHT AWNING RINGS,
JAPANNED.

$
Diameter, 1   1¼   1½   1¾   2   2½   3 in.   per gross.

IRON MEAT HOOKS, TO DRIVE.

$
No. 0   1   2   3   4   per gross.

TINNED MEAT HOOKS, TO DRIVE.

$
No. 0   1   2   3   4   5   6   per gross.

IRON MEAT HOOKS, TO SCREW ON.

$
No. 1   2   3   4   per gross.

TINNED MEAT HOOKS, TO SCREW ON.

$
No. 1   2   3   4   per gross.

S HOOKS.

Length, 1½   1¾   2   2¼   2½   2¾   3 in.   cts. per doz.

WROUGHT IRON LEADER HOOKS.

2   2½   3   4   5   6 inches.   cents per dozen.

GAS PIPE HOOKS.

$
¼   ⅜   ½   ¾   1   1¼ inch.   per M.

HORSE HOOKS WITH RINGS.

$ per dozen.

WROUGHT IRON GOODS.

(Continued.)

WROUGHT TRAP DOOR RINGS AND STAPLES.

cents per doz.

| 1½ | 1¾ | 2 | 2¼ | 2½ | 2¾ | 3 | 3½ inches. |

WROUGHT TRAP DOOR RINGS.

cents per doz.

| 1½ | 1¾ | 2 | 2¼ | 2½ | 2¾ | 3 | 3½ inches. |

RINGS.

Assorted,   cents per dozen.

RINGS AND STAPLES.

Assorted,   cents per dozen.

LOG RING WEDGES.

Various Patterns and Sizes.

WROUGHT IRON OPEN OR LAP LINKS,

For Mending Chains.

cents per dozen.

No. 0   1   2   3   4

HOLDFASTS.

1 2 3 Holes, Assorted, per gross, $

JAMB OR SIGN HOOKS.

Assorted, per gross, $

POT BALES.

| $ | 6 | 7 | 8 | 9 | 10 | 11 | 12 |

| $ | | | | | | | per dozen. |
| 13 | 14 | 15 | 16 | 17 | 18 inches. |

JOINTED POT BALES, OR HOOKS.

| $ | | | | | | | | per doz. |
| 10 | 12 | 14 | 16 | 18 | 20 | 22 | 24 inches. |

STEP LADDER HOOKS.

| $ | | | | | | | | | per doz. |
| 12 | 14 | 16 | 18 | 20 | 22 | 24 | 26 | 28 | 30 inches. |

LIGHT BAR STAPLES, FOR STORE DOORS.

cts. per pair.

| 2½×1 | 2¾×1¼ | 3×1¼ | 3½×1½ inches. |

HEAVY BAR STAPLES, FOR STORE DOORS.

cts. per pair.

| 3×1¼ | 3½×1¼ | 3×1½ | 3½×1½ | 3½×2 inches. |

LIGHT CORNER IRONS, FOR SHUTTERS.

Edges not Filed.

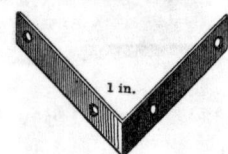

1 in.

cts. doz.

| ¾ | ⅞ | 1 | 1⅛ | 1¼ | 1⅜ | 1½ inch. |

LIGHT CORNER IRONS, FOR SHUTTERS.

Edges Filed.

cts. doz.

| ¾ | ⅞ | 1 | 1⅛ | 1¼ | 1⅜ | 1½ inch. |

HEAVY CORNER IRONS, FOR SHUTTERS.

Edges not Filed.

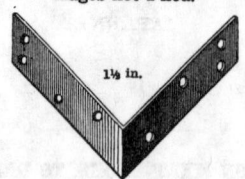

1½ in.

cts. doz.

| ¾ | ⅞ | 1 | 1⅛ | 1¼ | 1⅜ | 1½ inch. |

HEAVY CORNER IRONS, FOR SHUTTERS.

Edges Filed.

cts. doz.

| ¾ | ⅞ | 1 | 1⅛ | 1¼ | 1⅜ | 1½ inch. |

WROUGHT IRON GOODS.

(Continued.)

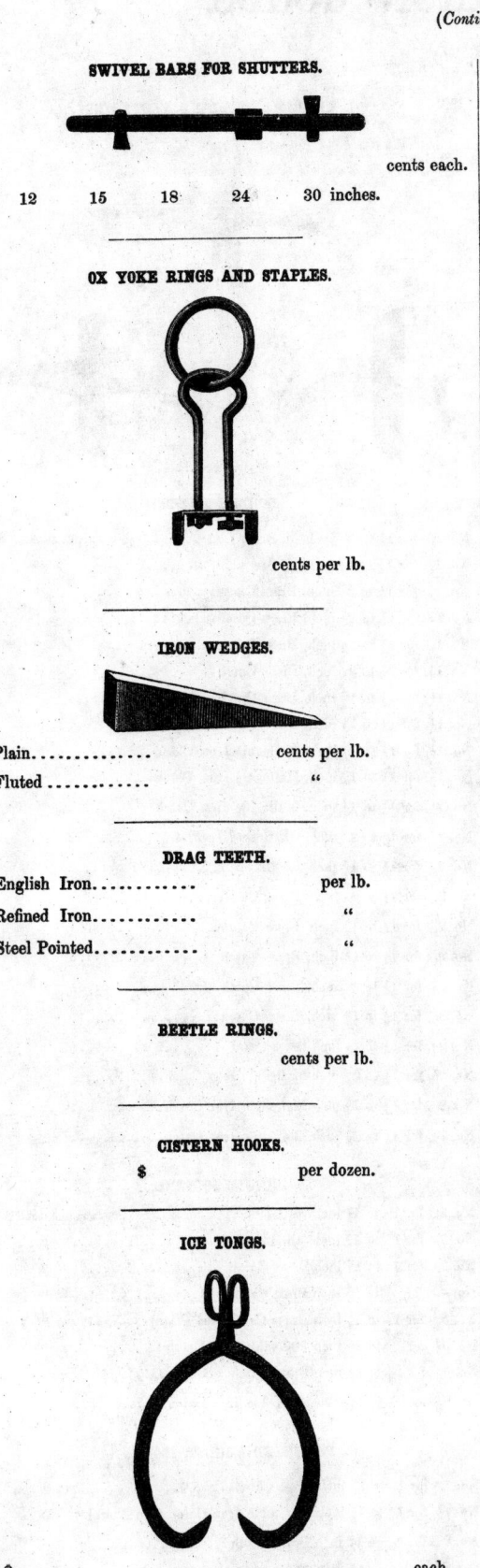

SWIVEL BARS FOR SHUTTERS.

cents each.

12   15   18   24   30 inches.

OX YOKE RINGS AND STAPLES.

cents per lb.

IRON WEDGES.

Plain.............. cents per lb.
Fluted .... "

DRAG TEETH.

English Iron............ per lb.
Refined Iron............ "
Steel Pointed........... "

BEETLE RINGS.

cents per lb.

CISTERN HOOKS.

$ per dozen.

ICE TONGS.

$ each.
No. 1   2   3

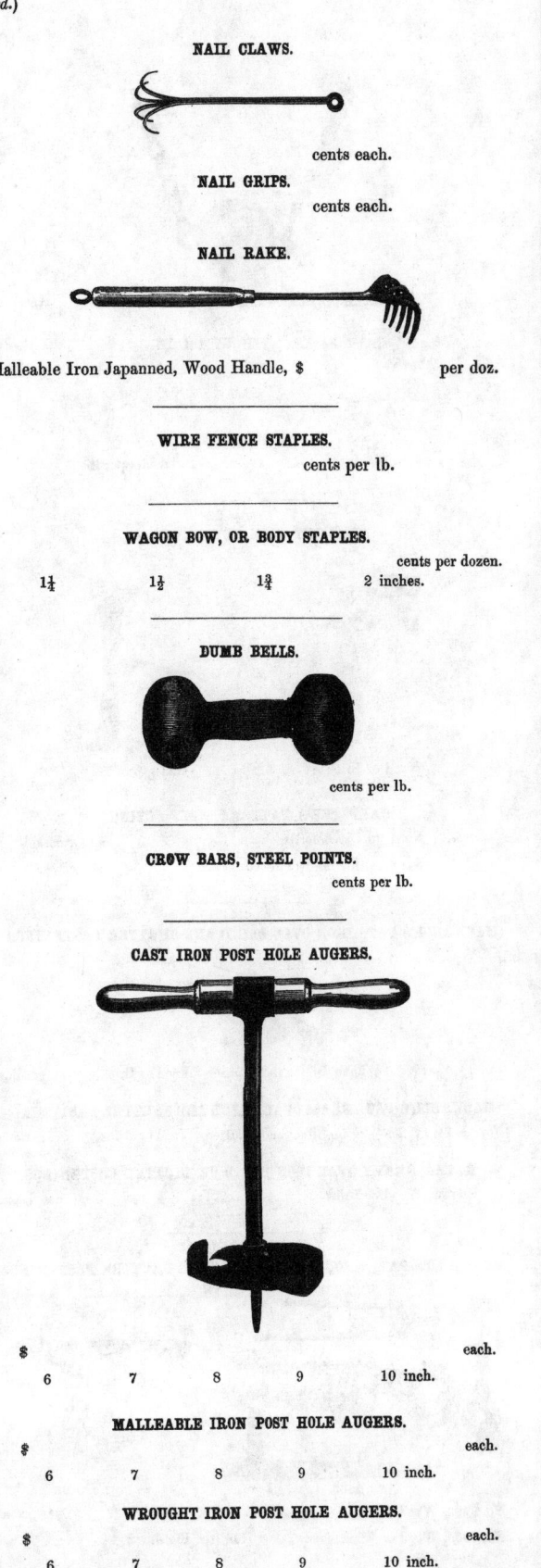

NAIL CLAWS.

cents each.

NAIL GRIPS.

cents each.

NAIL RAKE.

Malleable Iron Japanned, Wood Handle, $ per doz.

WIRE FENCE STAPLES.

cents per lb.

WAGON BOW, OR BODY STAPLES.

cents per dozen.

1¼   1½   1¾   2 inches.

DUMB BELLS.

cents per lb.

CROW BARS, STEEL POINTS.

cents per lb.

CAST IRON POST HOLE AUGERS.

$ each.
6   7   8   9   10 inch.

MALLEABLE IRON POST HOLE AUGERS.

$ each.
6   7   8   9   10 inch.

WROUGHT IRON POST HOLE AUGERS.

$ each.
6   7   8   9   10 inch.

WROUGHT IRON GOODS.

(Continued.)

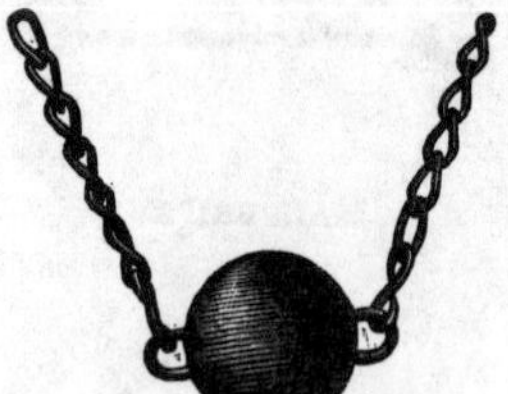

GATE BALLS, WITH CHAIN. cents each.

GATE BALLS, WITHOUT CHAIN. per lb.

QUOITS.

8 to 24 lbs. per set, cents per lb.

WROUGHT IRON TURN BUCKLES.

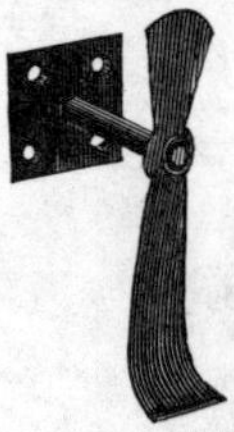

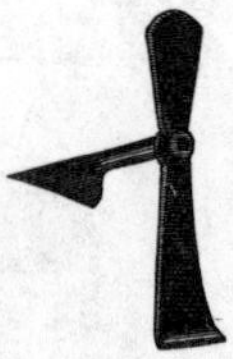

Wood or Brick...... $ per gross.

HARBSTER'S PATTERN, SELF-ACTING.

No. 1, to Drive, for Brick......... $ per gross.

No. 2, with Plate, for Wood...... $ per gross.

(MACKRELL'S PAT.) IRON OVAL BLIND AND SHUTTER FASTENINGS.

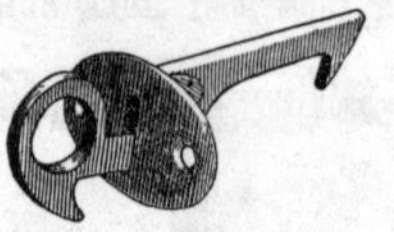

For $1\frac{1}{4}$, $1\frac{1}{2}$, $1\frac{3}{4}$, 2, $2\frac{1}{4}$, $2\frac{1}{4}$ in. Blinds and Shutters, Wood or Brick, per doz.

(MACKRELL'S PAT.) BRASS OVAL BLIND AND SHUTTER FASTENINGS.

For $1\frac{1}{4}$, $1\frac{1}{2}$, $1\frac{3}{4}$, 2, $2\frac{1}{4}$, $2\frac{1}{2}$ in. Blinds and Shutters, Wood or Brick, per doz.

EXTRA HEAVY OVAL IRON BLIND OR SHUTTER FASTENINGS.

All lengths, Wood or Brick.................... $ per dozen.

VAN SAND'S PAT. WROUGHT IRON BLIND OR SHUTTER FASTENINGS.

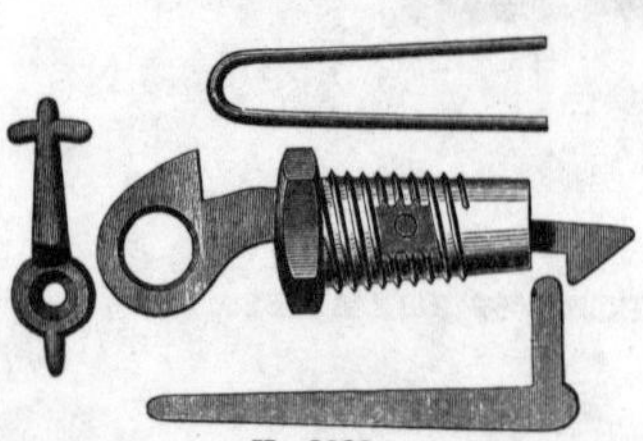

No. 2000.

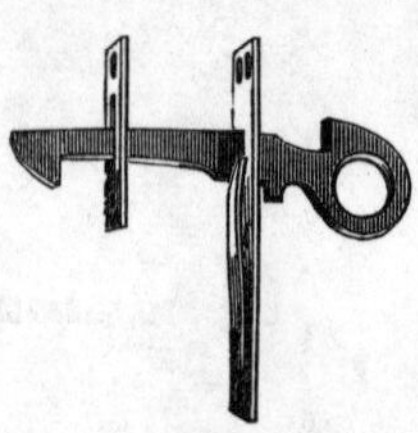

No. 3705.

No. 3705, Wood or Brick (see Plate)................ $ per gross.

No. 2000, Wood or Brick, Screw, Cast Iron (see Plate),. $ "

MERRIMAN'S BLIND FASTENINGS.

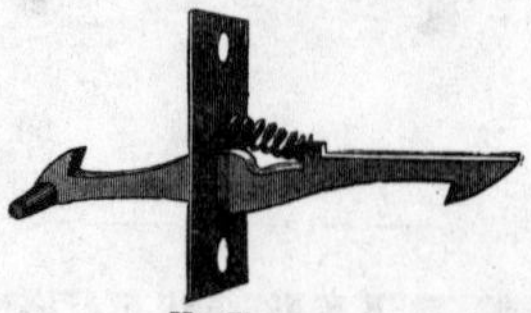

No. $7\frac{1}{2}$.

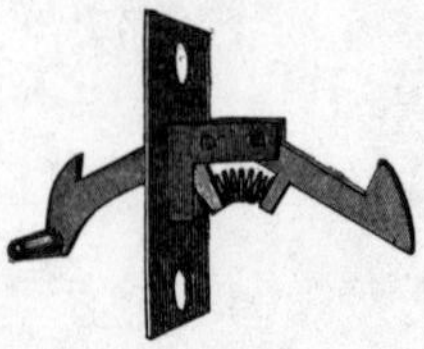

No. 2.

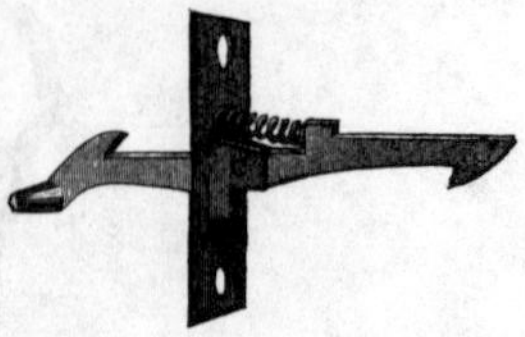

No. 5.

DOUBLE JOINTED.

No. 1, for $1\frac{1}{4}$ to 2 inch, all Brass......................per dozen, $
No. 1, for $1\frac{1}{4}$ to $1\frac{3}{4}$ inch, all Brass.............................. "
No. 1, for $1\frac{1}{4}$ to 2 inch, Brass Catch.............................. "
No. 1, for $1\frac{1}{4}$ to $1\frac{3}{4}$ inch, Brass Catch.............................. "
No. 1, for $1\frac{1}{4}$ to $1\frac{1}{2}$ inch, Brass Catch.............................. "
No. $1\frac{1}{4}$, for $1\frac{1}{4}$ to 2 inch, Brass Catch.............................. "
No. $1\frac{1}{4}$, for $1\frac{1}{4}$ to $1\frac{3}{4}$ inch, Brass Catch.............................. "
No. $1\frac{1}{4}$, for $1\frac{1}{4}$ to $1\frac{1}{2}$ inch, Brass Catch.............................. "
No. $1\frac{1}{2}$, for $1\frac{1}{4}$ to 2 inch, Malleable Iron Catch........... "
No. $1\frac{1}{2}$, for $1\frac{1}{4}$ to $1\frac{3}{4}$ inch, Malleable Iron Catch........... "
No. $1\frac{1}{2}$, for $1\frac{1}{4}$ to $1\frac{1}{2}$ inch, Malleable Iron Catch........... "
No. 2, for $1\frac{1}{4}$ to 2 inch, all Brass (see Plate)............ "
No. 2, for $1\frac{1}{4}$ to $1\frac{3}{4}$ inch, all Brass .... "
No. 2, for $1\frac{1}{4}$ to 2 inch, Brass Catch.............................. "
No. 2, for $1\frac{1}{4}$ to $1\frac{3}{4}$ inch, Brass Catch.............................. "
No. 2, for $1\frac{1}{4}$ to $1\frac{1}{2}$ inch, Brass Catch.............................. "
No. $2\frac{1}{4}$, for $1\frac{1}{4}$ to 2 inch, Brass Catch.............................. "
No., $2\frac{1}{4}$ for $1\frac{1}{4}$ to $1\frac{3}{4}$ inch, Brass Catch.............................. "
No. $2\frac{1}{4}$, for $1\frac{1}{4}$ to $1\frac{1}{2}$ inch Brass Catch.............................. "
No. $2\frac{1}{2}$, for $1\frac{1}{4}$ to 2 inch Malleable Iron Catch........... "
No. $2\frac{1}{2}$, for $1\frac{1}{4}$ to $1\frac{3}{4}$ inch Malleable Iron Catch........... "
No. $2\frac{1}{2}$, for $1\frac{1}{4}$ to $1\frac{1}{2}$ inch Malleable Iron Catch........... "

SINGLE JOINTED.

No. 3, for 1 to $1\frac{3}{4}$ inch, all Brass.............................per doz. $
No. 3, for 1 to $1\frac{5}{8}$ inch, all Brass.............................. "
No. 3, for 1 to $1\frac{3}{4}$ inch Brass Catch.............................. "
No. 4, for $\frac{7}{8}$ to $1\frac{3}{8}$ inch Brass Catch.............................. "
No. 5, for 1 to $1\frac{5}{8}$ inch Brass Catch (see Plate)........... "
No. $5\frac{1}{2}$, for 1 to $1\frac{5}{8}$ inch Malleable Iron Catch........... "
No. 6, for $\frac{7}{8}$ to $1\frac{3}{8}$ inch Brass Catch.............................. "
No. $6\frac{1}{2}$, for $\frac{7}{8}$ to $1\frac{3}{8}$ inch Malleable Iron Catch........... "

PATENTED AUGUST, 1847.

No. 7, for 1 to $1\frac{5}{8}$ inch Brass Catch............................per dozen, $
No. $7\frac{1}{2}$, for 1 to $1\frac{5}{8}$ inch Malleable Iron Catch (see Plate).. "
No. 8, for 1 to $1\frac{3}{8}$ inch Brass Catch.............................. "
No. $8\frac{1}{2}$, for 1 to $1\frac{3}{8}$ inch Malleable Iron Catch........... "

BRASS AND IRON FASTENINGS.

(Continued.)

JAPANNED DROPS AND PINS.

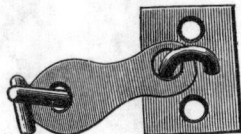

On Plates................$ per gross.
With Staples...............   "

BLIND CATCHES, WOOD OR BRICK.

cents per pair.

BLIND SPRINGS.

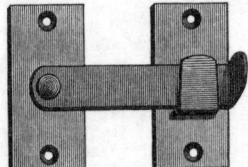

cents per pair.

WROUGHT IRON STEAMBOAT SHUTTER FASTS.

3 inch, Plain.......................................   cts. per dozen.
3 inch, with Brass Knobs.........................   "
3 inch, with Porcelain Knobs.....................   "

HELICAL SPRING SASH FASTENERS—"JUDD'S PATENT."

No. 60 & 61.   No. 66, 67, 68 & 69.

This Sash Fastener is inferior to none in the essential qualities of a Sash Fastener, while the cost of its production is less than others.

No. 60, Japanned ....per gross, $
No. 61, Red Bronzed.................................   "
No. 62, Japanned, with Porcelain Knob.................   "
No. 63, Red Bronzed, with Porcelain Knob.............   "
No. 64, Heavy Brass, Burglar Proof....................   "
No. 65, Heavy Brass, Bronzed, Burglar Proof...........   "
No. 66, Heavy Brass, with Porcelain Knob, Burglar Proof,   "
No. 67, Heavy Brass, Bronzed, with Porcelain Knob, Burglar Proof ....   "
No. 68, Heavy Plated, Burglar Proof ....   "
No. 69, Heavy Plated, Porcelain Knob, Burglar Proof....   "

JUDD'S PATENT STEEL WINDOW SPRINGS,

For Sustaining either the Upper or Lower Sash at any altitude desired.

An excellent substitute for Weights and Pullies—can be easily applied to houses, either new or old.

No. 5, Bronzed Crank and Rosette.....................per gross, $
No. 6, Bronzed Crank and Rosette, Brass Knob.........   "
No. 7, Bronzed Crank and Rosette, Porcelain Knob......   "
No. 1, for Sustaining the Sash only where the Bolt enters..   "

TABLE FASTENERS—ALL BRASS.

$ per dozen pair.
No. 1   2   4.

MERRIMAN'S SPIRAL WINDOW SPRING.

No. 2.

No. 1, all Brass, Finished...............................per gross, $
No. 2, Brass Bolt, Finished Plate (see Plate).............   "
No. 3, Brass Bolt, Unfinished...........................   "
No. 4, Malleable Iron Bolt..............................   "

☞ For Sash Fasts, Lifts, Rollers, Locks, Props, Cord Irons, Window Spring Bolts and Window Springs, see pages 77, 78.

BLIND STAPLES, PACKED IN BOXES OF 10 LBS. EACH.
Common and Fish-hook Patterns.

Common.   Fish Hook.

No. 18, Wire, Length ½, ⅝, ¾, ⅞, 1 inch.....................   per lb.

Patent, "Barbed."

No. 18, Wire, Length ⅜ inch.............................   per lb.
No. 18, Wire, Length ½, ⅝, ¾ inch........................   "

CARRIAGE KNOBS,

SILVERED, BRASS, SILVER CAPPED, JAPANNED WITH ENGLISH FINISH, AND JAPANNED.

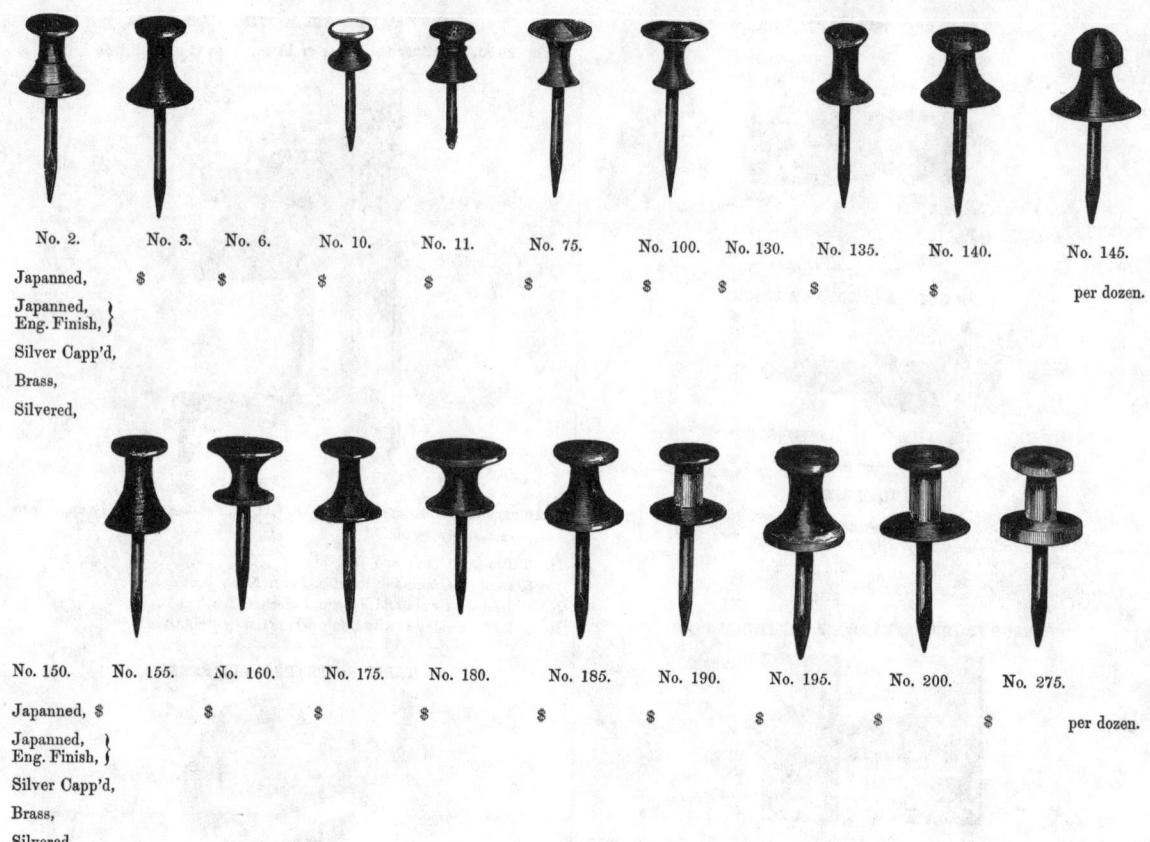

	No. 2.	No. 3.	No. 6.	No. 10.	No. 11.	No. 75.	No. 100.	No. 130.	No. 135.	No. 140.	No. 145.
Japanned,		$	$	$	$	$	$		$	$	per dozen.
Japanned, } Eng. Finish, }											
Silver Capp'd,											
Brass,											
Silvered,											

	No. 150.	No. 155.	No. 160.	No. 175.	No. 180.	No. 185.	No. 190.	No. 195.	No. 200.	No. 275.
Japanned,	$	$	$	$	$	$	$	$	$	per dozen.
Japanned, } Eng. Finish, }										
Silver Capp'd,										
Brass,										
Silvered,										

All our Carriage Knobs have Wrought Shanks. The "Japanned, English Finish," are all turned smooth in a lathe, and Japanned with the best English Japan. Nos. 10 and 11 are very small Knobs for Baby Carriages. Knobs with any desired length of Shank furnished to order.

SASH, SHUTTER, AND PICTURE KNOBS.

SASH KNOBS, SILVERED, BRASS AND JAPANNED.

To Drive, and to Screw.

	$\frac{1}{2}$	$\frac{9}{16}$	$\frac{5}{8}$	$\frac{11}{16}$	$\frac{3}{4}$	$\frac{13}{16}$	$\frac{7}{8}$	1 in.
Brass, Drive, per gross, $								
Brass, Screw, "	$							
Silvered, Drive, "	$							
Silvered, Screw, "	$							
Japanned, Drive, "	$							

JAPANNED SHUTTER KNOBS—TO SCREW.

Nos. 1	2	3	4	5	6
Diameter, $1\frac{3}{16}$	1	$\frac{7}{8}$	1	$\frac{7}{8}$	$1\frac{1}{4}$ inch.
Per gross, $					

For other Shutter Knobs see page 66.

SCREW SUPPORTS OR KNOBS FOR PICTURES, ETC.
Judd's Patent.

No. 1, Bronzed .... per gross, $
No. 2, Bronzed .... "
No. 3, Bronzed, Brass Button .... "
No. 4, Bronzed, Plated Button .... "
No. 5, Brass .... "
No. 6, Plated .... "
No. 7, Bronzed Base, Porcelain Knob .... "
No. 8, Bronzed Base, Porcelain Knob .... "
No. 9, Brass Base, Porcelain Knob .... "
No. 10, Plated Base, Porcelain Knob .... "

The advantage of this support is, it can be used on walls without injuring or cracking the plaster. The base being separate, adjusts itself while screwing the "support" to the wall.

PORCELAIN PICTURE KNOBS.

With Brass Capped Screws through the centre of the Knob, per gross, $
With Silver Capped Screws through the centre of the Knob "

PICTURE NAILS AND FURNITURE KNOBS.

BRASS HEAD PICTURE NAILS.

Brass, Burnished Head, Large Head.

$ per gross.

   1½   2   2½   3   3½   4 inch.

Silver Plated Head,

$ per gross.

   1½   2   2½   3   3½   4 inch.

PORCELAIN CENTRE IRON HEAD PICTURE NAILS—HEAD ON SCREW.

	2½	3	3½	4 inch	
Plain Brass Edge,......	$				per doz.
Fancy Brass Edge......	$				"
Silvered Plain.........	$				"
Silvered Fancy.........	$				"

PORCELAIN CENTRE, LARGE HEAD, FANCY EDGE PICTURE NAILS,
Head on Screw.

No. 974, 2½ inch, Plain Brass.....................per dozen, $

No. 975, 3 inch, Plain Brass...................... "

No. 976, 3½ inch, Plain Brass..................... "

No. 977, 4 inch, Plain Brass...................... "

No. 982, 2½ inch, Fancy Plated................... "

No. 983, 3 inch, Fancy Plated.................... "

No. 984, 3½ inch, Fancy Plated................... "

No. 985, 4 inch, Fancy Plated.................... "

No. 986, 2½ inch, Fancy Olive Green Bronze.......... "

FANCY EDGE PICTURE NAILS—Continued.

No. 987, 3 inch, Fancy Olive Green Bronze..........per dozen, $

No. 988, 3½ inch, Fancy Olive Green Bronze.......... "

No. 989, 4 inch, Fancy Olive Green Bronze.......... "

   For Porcelain Centre Picture Spikes, Brass and Plated Heads, see page 88.

FURNITURE KNOBS.
Common.

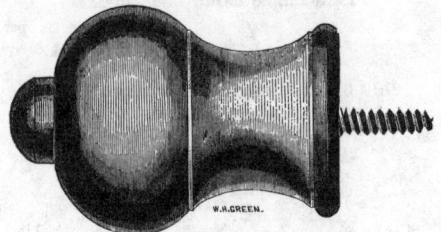

Sizes,	1	1¼	1½	1¾	2	2¼	2½ inch.

Mahogany, for Iron Screws......................per gross, $

Mahogany, with Wood Screws..................... "

Black Walnut, for Iron Screws.................... "

Black Walnut, with Wood Screws................... "

Fancy.

No 0.   No. 9.

No. 0, Varnished, with Wood Screws, all sizes..........per gross, $

No. 8, Varnished, with Wood Screws, (pattern similar to
    Common) all sizes............................ "

No. 9, Varnished, with Wood Screws, all sizes........... "

DOOR STOPS AND FLOOR DOOR FENDER.

PATENT RUBBER DOOR STOP, WITH GIMLET POINT SCREW.

W.H.GREEN.

No. 8.

No. 8, Length 2½ inches (see Plate), Pattern and Finish unexceptionable.

$ per gross.

   Birch,   Blackwalnut,   Mahogany,   Porcelain Enamelled.

No. 9, Length 2½ inches—same Style as No. 8—Tips covered with Reps and
   Plush of various colors, desirable for backs of Sofas, Tete-a-tetes, &c.

$ per gross.

   Blackwalnut and Reps,   Blackwalnut and Plush.

      Packed in Boxes of 3 dozen each.

FLOOR DOOR FENDER,
To Stop a Door at any Point on a Floor.

W.H.GREEN, MERIDEN. CT.

1 Dozen in each Case.................................per dozen, $

BASE KNOBS, OR DOOR STOPS.

Mahogany, with Iron Screws,

$ per gross.

     2½   3   3½ inch.

White Enamelled, 3 inch.............................per gross, $

    For Mineral and Porcelain Base Knobs, see page 66.

BRASS AND IRON HOOKS.

PLAIN BRASS SCREW HOOKS, POLISHED.

$ per gross.
No. 104, ½ ⅝ ¾ 1 1¼ 1⅜ 1½ 1¾ 2 inch.

PLAIN BRASS DRIVE HOOKS, POLISHED.

$ per gross.
No. 104, ½ ⅝ ¾ 1 1¼ 1⅜ 1½ 1¾ 2 inch.

BALL TIP, BENT BRASS SCREW HOOKS, POLISHED.

$ per gross.
No 107, 1 1¼ 1⅜ 1½ 1¾ 2 inch.

ACORN TIP, BRASS SCREW HOOKS, POLISHED.

$ per gross.
No. 107, 1 1¼ 1½ 1¾ 2 2½ 3 3½ 4 inch.

DOUBLE BEND BRASS SCREW HOOKS, POLISHED.

$ per gross.
1 1⅛ 1¼ 1½ 1⅝ 1¾ 1⅞ 2 inch.

BRASS CUP HOOKS, POLISHED.

$ per gross.
¾ ⅞ 1 1¼ 1½ 1¾ inch.

IRON CUP HOOKS, JAPANNED.

$ per gross.
1¼ 1½ 1⅝ inch.

JAPANNED LAMP HOOKS, WROUGHT SCREW.

Plain.

$ per gross.
1¼ 1½ 1¾ 1⅞ 2 2¼ 2½ inch.

Fancy.

$ per gross.
1¼ 1½ 1¾ 1⅞ 2 2¼ 2½ inch.

BRASS LAMP HOOKS, POLISHED.

Plain.—Same Pattern as Japanned.

$ per gross.
1¼ 1½ 1¾ 1⅞ 2 2¼ 2½ inch.

Fancy.—Same Pattern as Japanned.

$ per dozen.
1¼ 1½ 1¾ 1⅞ 2 2¼ 2½ inch.

CHANDELIER HOOKS.

$ per dozen.
Japanned, No. 17 (4 inch Screw), No. 18 (6 inch Screw),
$ per dozen.
Brass, No. 17 (4 inch Screw), No. 18 (6 inch Screw).

BRASS PICTURE AND LOOKING-GLASS HOOKS.

$ per gross.
No. 1, 1¼ inch. No. 2, 1½ inch.

BIRD CAGE HOOKS.

Fancy.

Brass,	$	No. 11, 7 inch.	No. 12, 8 inch.	No. 13, 9 inch. per dozen.
Silvered,	$	No. 14, 7 inch.	No. 15, 8 inch.	No. 16, 9 inch. per dozen.
French Bronzed,	$	No. 17, 7 inch.	No. 18, 8 inch.	No. 19, 9 inch. per dozen.
Gold Bronzed,	$	No. 20, 7 inch.	No. 21, 8 inch.	No. 22, 9 inch. per dozen.
Japanned,	$	No. 23, 7 inch.	No. 24, 8 inch.	No. 25, 9 inch. per dozen.

New Pattern.

With small hook to avoid tipping of cage while being hung.

Brass,	$	No. 111, 7 inch.	No. 112, 8 inch.	No. 113, 9 inch. per dozen.
French Bronzed,	$	No. 117, 7 inch.	No. 118, 8 inch.	No. 119, 9 inch. per dozen.
Japanned,	$	No. 123, 7 inch.	No. 124, 8 inch.	No. 125, 9 inch. per dozen.

Plain.

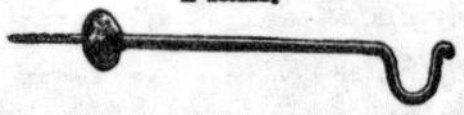

Strengthened by a Wrought Iron Rod running through the whole length.

	7	8	9 inch, per dozen.
Brass.... $			"
Silvered.. $			"

Cottage Bird Cage Hooks.

In Assorted Colors, Green and Blue, Bronze, &c., per dozen, $

PLAIN BRASS CABIN DOOR HOOKS.

$ per dozen.
2 2¼ 3 3½ 4 inch.

SHIP CABIN DOOR HOOKS, EXTRA HEAVY.

With Staples.

$ per doz.
1½ 2 2½ 3 3½ 4 5 6 inch.

With Plates.

$ per doz.
1¼ 2 2½ 3 3½ 4 5 6 inch.

JAPANNED CABIN DOOR HOOKS, PLAIN.

$ per dozen.
2 2½ 3 3½ 4 inch.

FANCY BRASS CABIN DOOR HOOKS.

$ per dozen.
2 2½ 3 3½ 4 inch.

BALE AND BOX HOOKS.

⅞ inch Iron, Japanned.........................per pair, $
¾ inch Iron, Japanned, Double......................"

BARREL AND TIERCE HOOKS.

No. 1, $\frac{7}{16}$ inch Iron, Japanned.........................per pair, $
No. 2, $\frac{9}{16}$ inch Iron, Japanned........................."
No. 3, ⅝ inch Iron, Japanned........................."

BRASS AND IRON HOOKS.

(Continued.)

BRASS WARDROBE HOOKS.

No. 845, Fancy Brass, Lacquered, Braced............per dozen, $
No. 846, Fancy Brass, Silver Plated, Braced.......... "
No. 847, Fancy Brass, Olive Green Bronzed, Braced.... "
No. 848, Fancy Iron, Antique Bronzed, Braced........ "
No. 4, Plain Brass, Lacquered, Braced.............. "
No. 5, Plain Brass, Lacquered, Braced.............. "
No. 6, Plain Brass, Lacquered, Braced.............. "
No. 14, Plain Brass Burnished, Braced.............. "
No. 15, Plain Brass Burnished, Braced.............. "
No. 16, Plain Brass Burnished, Braced.............. "

BRASS COAT AND HAT HOOKS.

No. 1, Plain Brass, Lacquered.................per dozen, $
No. 4, Plain Brass, Lacquered.................. "
No. 5, Fancy Brass, Lacquered.................. "
No. 10, Fancy Brass, Lacquered.................. "
No. 36, Fancy, Solid Brass, with Porcelain Knob, Burnished and Lacquered................ "
No. 37, Fancy, Solid Brass, with Porcelain Knob, Burnished and Lacquered................ "
No 38, Fancy, Solid Brass, with Porcelain Knob, Burnished and Lacquered................ "
No. 39, Fancy, Solid Brass, with Porcelain Knob, Burnished and Lacquered................ "

No. 20, Plain, Solid Brass, with Porcelain Knob, Burnished and Lacquered..............per dozen, $
No. 21, Plain, Solid Brass, with Porcelain Knob, Burnished and Lacquered.............. "
No. 22, Plain, Solid Brass, with Porcelain Knob, Burnished and Lacquered.............. "
No. 23, Plain, Solid Brass, with Porcelain Knob, Burnished and Lacquered.............. "

PATENT COAT AND HAT HOOKS.

No. 45, Solid Brass, Lacquered, with Porcelain Knob....per dozen, $
No. 46, Iron, Japanned, with Porcelain Knob.......... "
No. 47, Iron, Bronzed, with Porcelain Knob.............. "

BRASS SURPLICE PINS, WITH PORCELAIN KNOBS.

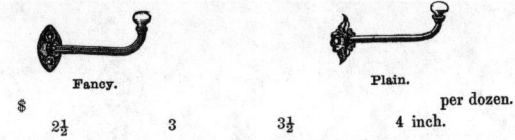

Fancy.   Plain.
                                  per dozen.
2½   3   3½   4 inch.

BRASS HAT HOOKS, WITH PORCELAIN KNOBS.

                                  per dozen.
$ 3   3½   4   4½ inch.

"WALKER'S PATENT CLOTHES RACK."

Patented in the United States March 1st and 22d, 1864.

Hung up for Use.

The most perfect thing of the kind ever invented. It is a full size Clothes Rack, which can be folded up to about the size of your hand and carried in a coat pocket. It is perfectly simple, cannot possibly get out of order, and any one who can drive a nail can put it up. It may be hung on one, two or three nails, and will work well in almost any position. While it is useful everywhere as a permanent fixture, its perfect portability makes it especially convenient for travelers, tourists, frequenters of summer resorts, soldiers in camp, etc. The goods are copper bronzed, and got up in the very neatest manner, each Rack being in a tasty paper box, with brass headed nails complete for putting it up. An India rubber band is around the lower part of each hook, which effectually prevents them from marking the wall or wood-work by swinging against it.

Folded Up.

$ per dozen.

WROUGHT BRASS HOOKS AND EYES.

Right and Left Hand.

Made of Sheet Brass, uniform size and shape, Eyes, Gimlet Pointed.

								gross pairs.
$								
Brass,	1	1¼	1½	1¾	2	2¼	2½ inch.	
$								gross pairs.
Silvered,	1	1¼	1½	1¾	2	2¼	2½ inch.	

HOOKS, WITHOUT EYES.

								gross pairs.
$								
Brass,	1	1¼	1½	1¾	2	2¼	2½ inch.	
$								gross pairs.
Silvered,	1	1¼	1½	1¾	2	2¼	2½ inch.	

BRASS SCREW EYES, GIMLET POINTED.

					per gross.
$					
Brass,	1	2	3	4	

NEW PATTERN, HALF OVAL IRON HOOKS AND EYES.

Polished.

	$					per gross.
Nos.	1	2	3	4	5	
Size,	1½	2	2½	3	3½ inch.	

Japanned.

	$					per gross.
Nos.	6	7	8	9	10	
Size,	1½	2	2½	3	3½ inch.	

Tin Plated.

	$					per gross.
Nos.	11	12	13	14	15	
Size,	1½	2	2½	3	3½ inch.	

HEAVY IRON POLISHED SCREW EYES, WITHOUT HOOKS.

	$			per gross.
Nos.	1	2	3	

BRIGHT WIRE GOODS.

GIMLET-POINTED WROUGHT IRON SCREW EYES.

(For Description of Plates see page 156.)

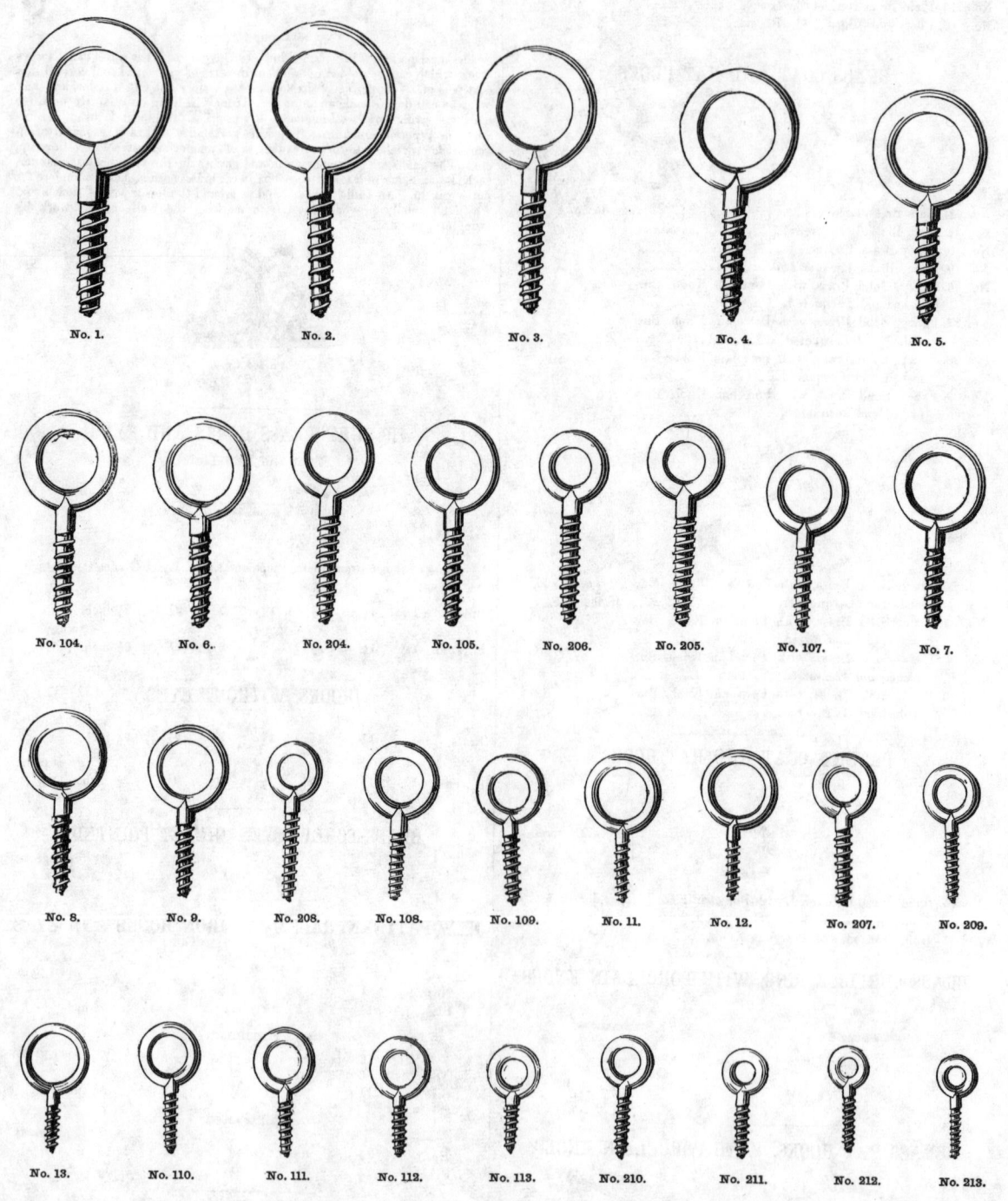

No. 1.   No. 2.   No. 3.   No. 4.   No. 5.

No. 104.   No. 6.   No. 204.   No. 105.   No. 206.   No. 205.   No. 107.   No. 7.

No. 8.   No. 9.   No. 208.   No. 108.   No. 109.   No. 11.   No. 12.   No. 207.   No. 209.

No. 13.   No. 110.   No. 111.   No. 112.   No. 113.   No. 210.   No. 211.   No. 212.   No. 213.

BRIGHT WIRE GOODS.

(Continued.)

GIMLET-POINTED WROUGHT IRON SCREW HOOKS.

[For Description of Plates see page 156.]

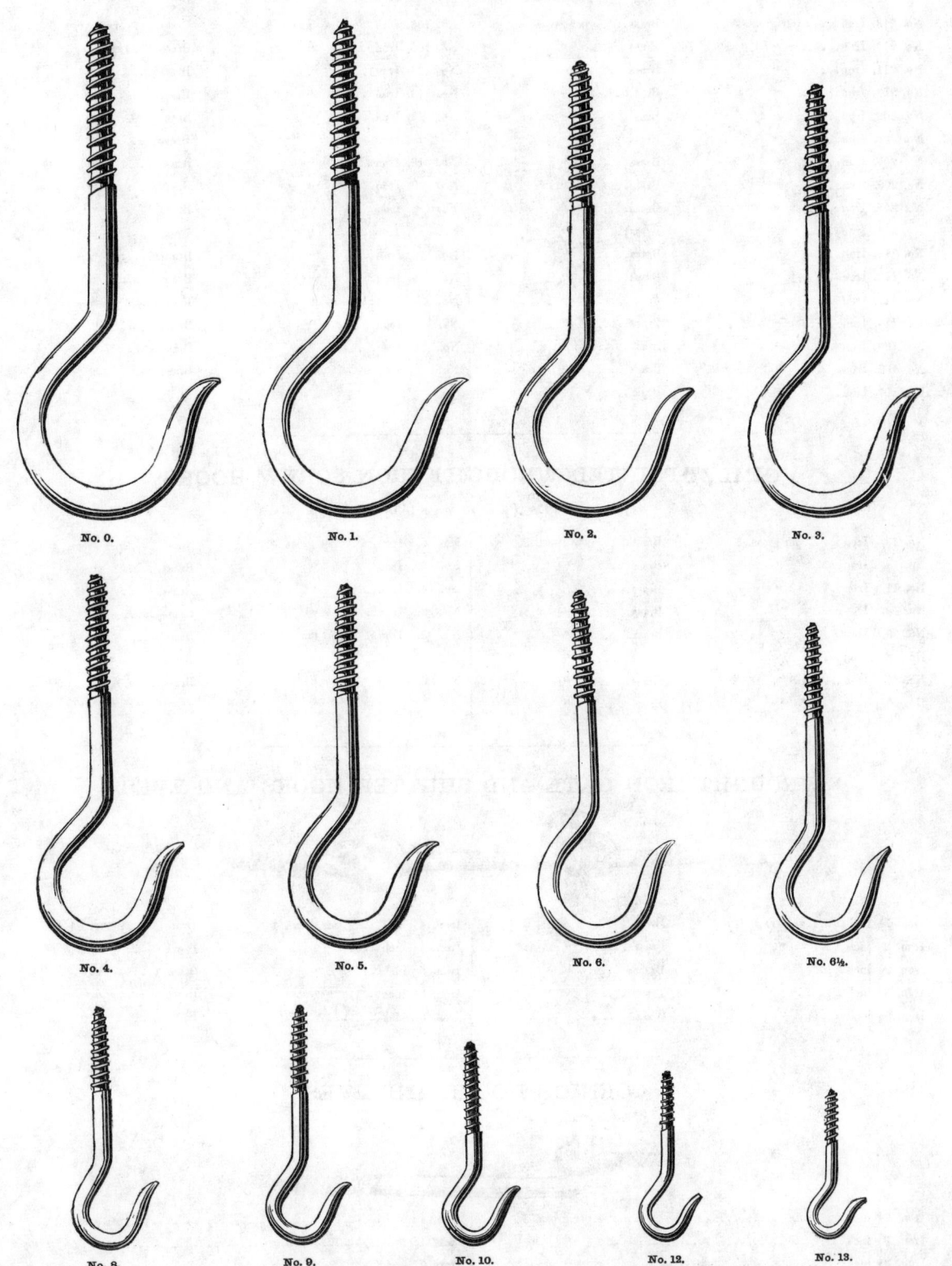

No. 0.   No. 1.   No. 2.   No. 3.

No. 4.   No. 5.   No. 6.   No. 6½.

No. 8.   No. 9.   No. 10.   No. 12.   No. 13.

BRIGHT WIRE GOODS.

(Continued.)

GIMLET-POINTED WROUGHT IRON SCREW EYES.

[*For Plates see page 154.*]

No. 213, Iron......per gross, $	Brass..... per gross, $	No. 106, Iron......per gross, $	Brass......per gross, $
No. 212, Iron...... "	Brass...... "	No. 105, Iron...... "	Brass...... "
No. 211, Iron...... "	Brass...... "	No. 104, Iron...... "	Brass...... "
No. 210, Iron...... "	Brass...... "	No. 13, Iron...... "	Brass...... "
No. 209, Iron...... "	Brass...... "	No. 12, Iron...... "	Brass...... "
No. 208, Iron...... "	Brass...... "	No. 11, Iron...... "	Brass...... "
No. 207, Iron...... "	Brass...... "	No. 10, Iron...... "	Brass...... "
No. 206, Iron...... "	Brass...... "	No. 9, Iron...... "	Brass...... "
No. 205, Iron...... "	Brass...... "	No. 8, Iron...... "	Brass...... "
No. 204, Iron...... "	Brass...... "	No. 7, Iron...... "	Brass...... "
No. 113, Iron...... "	Brass...... "	No. 6, Iron...... "	Brass...... "
No. 112, Iron...... "	Brass...... "	No. 5, Iron...... "	Brass...... "
No. 111, Iron...... "	Brass...... "	No. 4, Iron...... "	Brass...... "
No. 110, Iron...... "	Brass...... "	No. 3, Iron...... "	Brass...... "
No. 109, Iron...... "	Brass...... "	No. 2, Iron...... "	Brass...... "
No. 108, Iron...... "	Brass...... "	No. 1, Iron...... "	Brass...... "
No. 107, Iron...... "	Brass...... "		

GIMLET-POINTED WROUGHT IRON SCREW HOOKS

[*For Plates see page 155.*]

No. 13, Iron......per gross, $	Brass......per gross, $	No. 6, Iron......per gross, $	Brass......per gross, $
No. 12, Iron...... "	Brass...... "	No. 5, Iron...... "	Brass...... "
No. 11, Iron...... "	Brass...... "	No. 4, Iron...... "	Brass...... "
No. 10, Iron...... "	Brass...... "	No. 3, Iron...... "	Brass...... "
No. 9, Iron...... "	Brass...... "	No. 2, Iron...... "	Brass...... "
No. 8, Iron...... "	Brass...... "	No. 1, Iron...... "	Brass...... "
No. 7, Iron...... "	Brass...... "	No. 0, Iron...... "	Brass...... "
No. 6½, Iron...... "	Brass...... "		

WROUGHT IRON GATE AND SHUTTER HOOKS AND EYES.

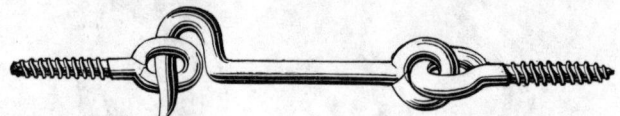

Iron, 1½ inch......per gross, $	Brass......per gross, $	Iron, 4 inch......per gross, $	Brass......per gross, $
Iron, 2 inch...... "	Brass...... "	Iron, 4½ inch...... "	Brass...... "
Iron, 2½ inch...... "	Brass...... "	Iron, 5 inch...... "	Brass...... "
Iron, 3 inch...... "	Brass...... "	Iron, 5½ inch...... "	Brass...... "
Iron, 3½ inch...... "	Brass...... "	Iron, 6 inch...... "	Brass...... "

CORNICE HOOKS AND EYES.

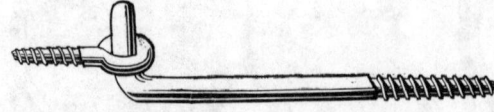

Iron, 2½ inch.................................per gross, $	Iron, 4 inch.................................per gross, $
Iron, 3 inch................................. "	Iron, 4½ inch................................. "
Iron, 3½ inch................................. "	Iron, 5 inch................................. "

TINNED IRON MEAT HOOKS.

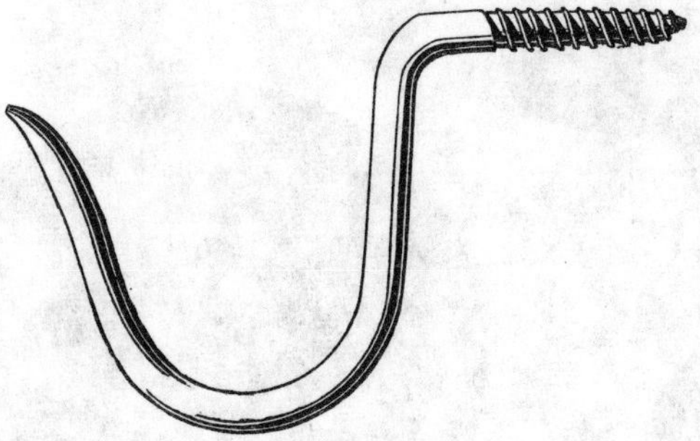

No. 3.

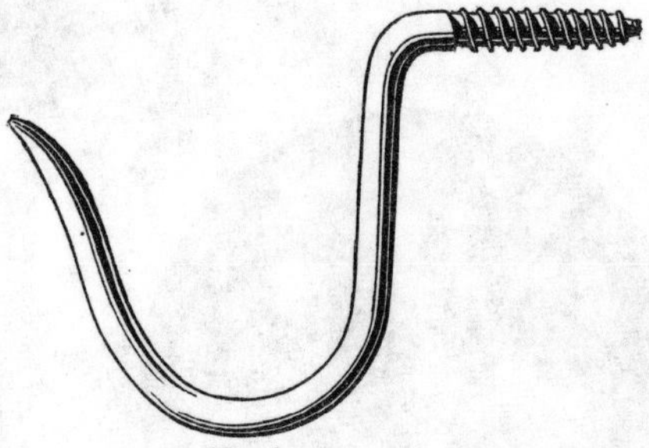

No. 4.

	$			per gross.
No. 3		4	5	

(For other Meat Hooks see page 145.)

WEAVER'S HARNESS HOOKS AND EYES.

Harness Eyes.

No. 11, Iron .... per gross, $
No. 10, Iron .... "
No. 9, Iron .... "
No. 8, Iron .... "
No. 7, Iron .... "
No. 8 and 9, Harness Studs .... "

Guide Wires.

No. 10, Iron ...... per gross, $ Brass ...... per gross, $
No. 9, Iron ...... " Brass ...... "
No. 8, Iron ...... " Brass ...... "

Jack Hooks.

No. 7, Iron .... per gross, $
No. 7, Iron, Jointed .... "
No. 7, Iron, Double .... "

Strap Hooks.

No. 8, for $\frac{3}{4}$ inch Strap, Iron .... per gross, $
No. 8, for $\frac{7}{8}$ inch Strap, Iron, Brazed .... "
No. 8, for 1 inch Strap, Iron, Hook turned Right-angles .. "
No. 8, for $\frac{7}{8}$ inch Strap, Iron, with Screws .... "
No. 8, for 1 inch Strap, Iron, with Screws .... "
No. 8, for 1 inch Strap, Iron, with Screws, open .... "
No. 9, for 1 inch Strap, Iron, with Screws, open .... "
No. 8, for $\frac{1}{2}$ inch Strap, Iron, Square .... "
No. 12, S Hooks .... "

TASSEL CORD HOOKS.

No. 1, Brass Lacquered, Large, Plain .... per gross, $
No. 3, Brass Lacquered, Large, Fancy .... "
No. 5, Brass Lacquered, Fancy .... "
No. 7, Brass Lacquered, Small, Fancy .... "
No. 9, Brass Lacquered, Small, Plain .... "
No. 11, Brass Lacquered, Small, Fancy .... "
No. 2, Silver Plated, Large, Plain .... "
No. 4, Silver Plated, Large, Fancy .... "
No. 6, Silver Plated, Fancy, ... "

TASSEL CORD HOOKS.

(Continued.)

No. 8, Silver Plated, Small, Fancy .... per gross, $
No. 10, Silver Plated, Small, Plain .... "
No. 12, Silver Plated, Small, Fancy .... "

BRASS CURTAIN RINGS.

In. Diam.	No. Wire.	Per Gross.	In. Diam.	No. Wire.	Per Gross.
$\frac{3}{8}$	18	$	1	14	$
$\frac{3}{8}$	19		1	12	
$\frac{7}{16}$	18		$1\frac{1}{8}$	8	
$\frac{1}{2}$	18		$1\frac{1}{8}$	12	
$\frac{1}{2}$	16		$1\frac{1}{4}$	8	
$\frac{9}{16}$	15		$1\frac{1}{4}$	10	
$\frac{5}{8}$	18		2		
$\frac{5}{8}$	16		$2\frac{1}{4}$		
$\frac{5}{8}$	15		$2\frac{1}{2}$		
$\frac{3}{4}$	16		$2\frac{3}{4}$		
$\frac{7}{8}$	16		$3\frac{1}{2}$		

SCREW RINGS.

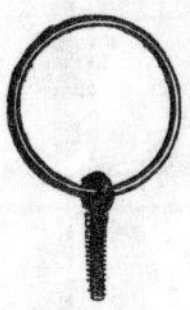

Solid Brazed Rings, Screws Gimlet-pointed.

	$									per gross.
Brass,	$\frac{3}{8}$	$\frac{1}{2}$	$\frac{5}{8}$	$\frac{11}{16}$	$\frac{3}{4}$	$\frac{7}{8}$	1	$1\frac{1}{8}$	$1\frac{1}{4}$	in. diam.
	$									per gross.
Plated,	$\frac{3}{8}$	$\frac{1}{2}$	$\frac{5}{8}$	$\frac{11}{16}$	$\frac{3}{4}$	$\frac{7}{8}$	1	$1\frac{1}{8}$	$1\frac{1}{4}$	in. diam.

CURTAIN PINS.

Fancy Front, $1\frac{1}{2}$ inch Diameter, Patent Head, Porcelain Centre.

	$				per dozen.
Brass	$2\frac{1}{2}$	3	$3\frac{1}{2}$	4 inch.	
	$				per dozen.
Silver Plated	$2\frac{1}{2}$	3	$3\frac{1}{2}$	4 inch.	

GLASS CURTAIN PINS, SILVER LINED.

Engraved.   Plain.   Rose.

No. 0, Diameter 2½ inches, Rose Pattern............per dozen, $ No. 7, Diameter 4½ inches, Plain...................per dozen, $

No. 01, Diameter 2½ inches, Plain...................   "   No. 8, Diameter 4½ inches, Engraved...............   "

No. 02, Diameter 2½ inches, Engraved...............   "   No. 9, Diameter 5 inches, Oval, Rose Pattern.......   "

No. 03, Diameter 3 inches, Rose Pattern...........   "   No. 10, Diameter 2½ inches, Flowers, Red and Green..   "

No. 1, Diameter 3 inches, Plain...................   "   No. 11, Diameter 3 inches, Flowers, Red and Green..   "

No. 2, Diameter 3 inches, Engraved...............   "   No. 12, Diameter 3½ inches, Flowers, Red and Green..   "

No. 6, Diameter 4½ inches, Rose Pattern...........   "   No. 13, Diameter 4 inches, Flowers, Red and Green..   "

JUDD'S PATENT CURTAIN FIXTURES.

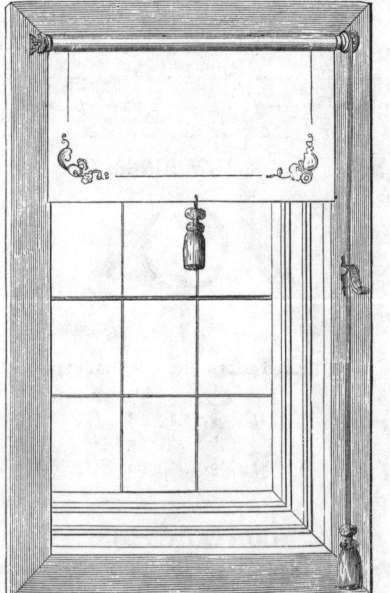

No. 1, Bronzed Holder, Coppered Brackets and Ends, including Rollers and Slats.....................per gross, $

No. 3, Brass Holder, Coppered Brackets and Ends, including Rollers and Slats...................   "

No. 4, Plated Holder, Coppered Brackets and Ends, including Rollers and Slats...................   "

Cotton Tapes for above, either Crimson, Buff, Blue, Drab,
Green or Fancy, *extra* ....per gross yds. $

Two yards of Tape is usually required for one ordinary sized window, the
quantity varying whether larger or smaller.

PUTNAM'S PATENT CURTAIN FIXTURES.

$ per gross.

"Self-Adjusting," Hard Wood Ends, with Rollers and Slats complete,

$ per gross.

Pendulum, Coppered Iron Ends, with Rollers and Slats complete,

Packed in gross and half gross boxes, complete with Rollers and Slats.

Curtain Cord for above, variety of colors, per gross yards, $

Curtain Tassels for above, variety of colors, per doz. yards, $

For other Window Shade Furniture, see page 79.

Packed in cases of half gross each, complete with Slats, Rollers, Brackets,
Ends and Holders.

This is a most complete and simple Curtain Fixture. To be used with a tape
instead of cord.

FURNITURE CASTERS, FULL ORIGINAL SIZES.

SHORT WROUGHT PIVOT.

No. 1   2   3   4   5   6   7

All Iron ....$ per set.
All Iron, Brass Wheel.....   "
All Iron, Wood Wheel.....   "
All Iron, Porcelain Wheel..   "

LONG WROUGHT PIVOT.

No. 1   2   3   4   5   6   7

All Iron ....$ per set.
All Iron, Brass Wheel.....   "
All Iron, Wood Wheel.....   "
All Iron, Porcelain Wheel..   "
Brass Horn and Wheel....   "
Brass Horn, Porcl'n Wheel.   "
Brass Horn, Wood Wheel..   "
Brass Horn, Rubber Wheel.   "
All Brass................   "
All Brass, Porcelain Wheel.   "
All Brass, Wood Wheel....   "
All Brass, Rubber Wheel...   "

SOCKET CASTERS.

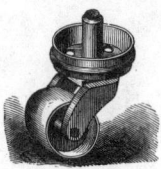

Round Socket.   Square Socket.

Size, $\frac{7}{8}$ 1 $1\frac{1}{8}$ $1\frac{1}{4}$ $1\frac{3}{8}$ $1\frac{1}{2}$ in.

Round Brass............$ per set.
Round Brass, Porcl. Wheel.   "
Round Brass, Wood Wheel.   "
Round Brass, Rubber Wheel   "
Square Brass............   "
Square Brass, Porc. Wheel.   "
Square Brass, Wood Wheel.   "
Square Brass, Rub'r Wheel.   "
Round Beaded,   "   "
Square Beaded,   "   "

PIANO FORTE CASTERS.

No. 1   2

Iron, Turned Wheels ....$ per set.
Iron, Brass Wheels.........................   "

CAST PIVOT, OPEN SOCKET.

No. 6   7

All Iron.......................$ per set.
All Iron, Brass Wheel.................   "

CAST PIVOT, PLATE CASTERS.

$1\frac{1}{4}$ $1\frac{3}{8}$ $1\frac{5}{8}$ in.

All Iron..................$ per set.
Brass Wheel.................   "

SHIP TABLE CASTERS.

No. 1   2

All Iron.......................$ per set.
All Brass............................   "

BED CASTERS.

$1\frac{5}{8}\times1$ $1\frac{5}{8}\times2$ 2×1 2×2 2 in. heavy, $2\frac{1}{2}$ in.

All Iron............   per set.
All Iron, Porc. Wheel   "
All Iron, Wood Wheel   "
All Iron, Lig. Vit. "   "
All Iron, Brass Wheel   "

CASTERS, BED FASTS, HOOKS AND BED KEYS.

GLOBE WHEEL BED CASTERS.

	1⅝	2 in.	
All Iron.....................			per set.
All Iron, Porcelain Wheel...................			"
All Iron, Wood Wheel.....................			"
All Iron, Lignum Vitæ Wheel.............			"
All Iron, Brass Wheel....................			"

BRACKET BED CASTERS.

Size, 3 in.   4 in.   4 in. slanting.   4 in. flange.

All Iron.....................$	per set.
All Iron, Apple Wood Wheel...	"
All Iron, Lignum Vitæ Wheel..	"

DEEP SOCKET CASTERS.

All Brass—No. 21.

$ per set.

Size,   1   1⅛   1¼   1⅜   1½ inch.

Deep Brass Socket, Black Horn, Brass Wheel—No. 10.

$ per set.

Size,   1   1⅛   1¼   1⅜   1½ inch.

Bronzed Iron Socket, Black Horn, Brass Wheel—No. 7.

$ per set.

Size,   1   1⅛   1¼   1⅜   1½ inch.

STORE TRUCK CASTERS.

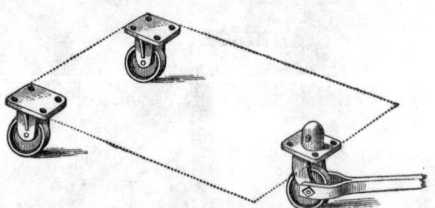

In sets of two Stationary and one Swivel Caster, the latter having a Stump Tongue to which a longer Tongue can be welded. Heavy and strong for any purpose, and ready to fasten to the box. The dotted lines in the Plate represent the bottom of the Box and the position of the Casters.

Per set as per Plate...................................$
The Stationary Casters separately..........................each
The Swivel Casters separately, without Tongue..................
The Swivel Casters separately, with Tongue....................

BED JOINT FASTS.

No. 2, Jenny Lind Pattern..............per set for one Bedstead, $

No. 3, Cottage,....................per set for one Bedstead, $

No. 4, Square.....................per set for one Bedstead, $

No. 5, Hook..........................per set for one Bedstead, $

BED HOOKS,
To Fasten Headboards to the Post.

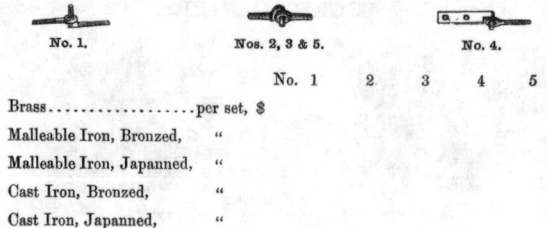

No. 1   Nos. 2, 3 & 5.   No. 4.

No. 1   2   3   4   5

Brass...................per set, $
Malleable Iron, Bronzed,   "
Malleable Iron, Japanned,   "
Cast Iron, Bronzed,   "
Cast Iron, Japanned,   "

JAPANNED BED KEYS.

T Pattern,   Z Pattern,   Z Pattern,   Y Pattern.
One Socket.   Round Shank.   Square Shank.

One Socket, or T ....per dozen, $
Z Pattern, two Sockets, Round Shank, Small...........   "
Z Pattern, two Sockets, Square Shank, Large..........   "
Y Pattern, two Sockets.................................   "

BED SCREWS, HAND RAIL SCREWS AND HANDCUFFS.

<table>
<tr><td valign="top">

MALLEABLE BED KEYS, JAPANNED.

Z Pattern, Square Shank, Large ....per dozen, $

4 Prong, with Screw Driver........................... "

PATENT RATCHET BED KEYS,

For French Bedsteads.........................per dozen, $

☞ For other Bed Keys, see page 105.

AMERICAN BED SCREWS,

Solid Head—Square and Flat.

Square Head.

Flat Head.

⅜ inch Iron, ¾×⅜ inch Nut.

4 inch...................................per gross, $

4½ inch................................... "

5 inch................................... "

5½ inch................................... "

6 inch................................... "

6½ inch................................... "

7 inch................................... "

7½ inch................................... "

8 inch................................... "

⁷⁄₁₆ inch Iron—Nuts ⅞×⅜ inch.

5 inch................................... "

5½ inch................................... "

6 inch................................... "

6½ inch................................... "

7 inch................................... "

7½ inch................................... "

8 inch................................... "

9 inch................................... "

10 inch................................... "

HAND OR STAIR RAIL SCREWS.

One Nut.

No.	$	1	2	3	4	5		per gross.
Length,		4	4½	5	5½ in. dia. ⁵⁄₁₆	6 in. dia. ⅜ in.		

Two Nuts.

No.	$	6	7	8	9	10		per gross.
Length,		4	4½	5	5½ dia. ⁵⁄₁₆	6 dia. ⅜ inch.		

SWELL CENTRE, WROUGHT RAIL SCREWS.

Two Nuts.

No.	$	11	12	13	14	15.		per gross.
Length,		4	4½	5	5½	6 inch. Dia. ⁷⁄₁₆ inch.		

</td><td valign="top">

HAND OR STAIR RAIL SCREWS—Continued.

EXTRA TURNED, MACHINIST'S MAKE.

Two Oblong Nuts.

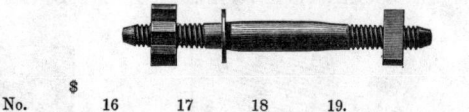

No.	$	16	17	18	19.		per gross.
Length,		4½	5	5½	6 inch. Diam. ½ inch.		

STAIR OR HAND-RAIL BRACES.

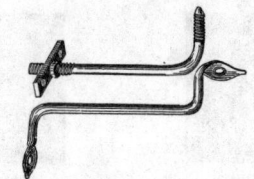

S Braces, Assorted............................. $ per dozen.

Plate Braces, Assorted........................... "

IMPROVED HORSE FETTERS,

For Controlling Vicious and Unruly Horses.

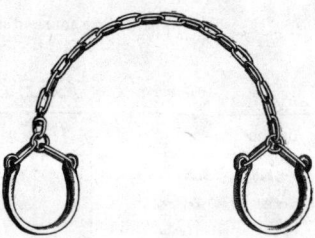

The Chains and Bows are made from the best quality of Iron, and the Springs from Cast Steel. Are easily adjusted, and not liable to get out of order.

Plain.................................. $ per dozen.

Bows covered with Leather............. "

HANDCUFFS OR SHACKLES,

For Controlling Vicious and Unruly Men.

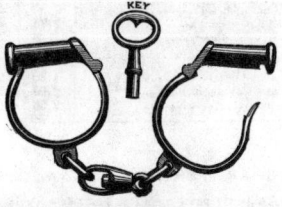

With Keys.

Police Handcuffs (see Plate)............ $ per dozen.

Patent Adjustable Self-Locking.......... "

Ankle Shackles....................... "

</td></tr>
</table>

AMERICAN FILES.

MADE FROM BEST REFINED CAST STEEL, METALLIC TEMPER.

The following Cuts are engraved from Files 12 inches long; if longer than 12 inches, the Cuts will be larger; if smaller, they will be less in proportion.

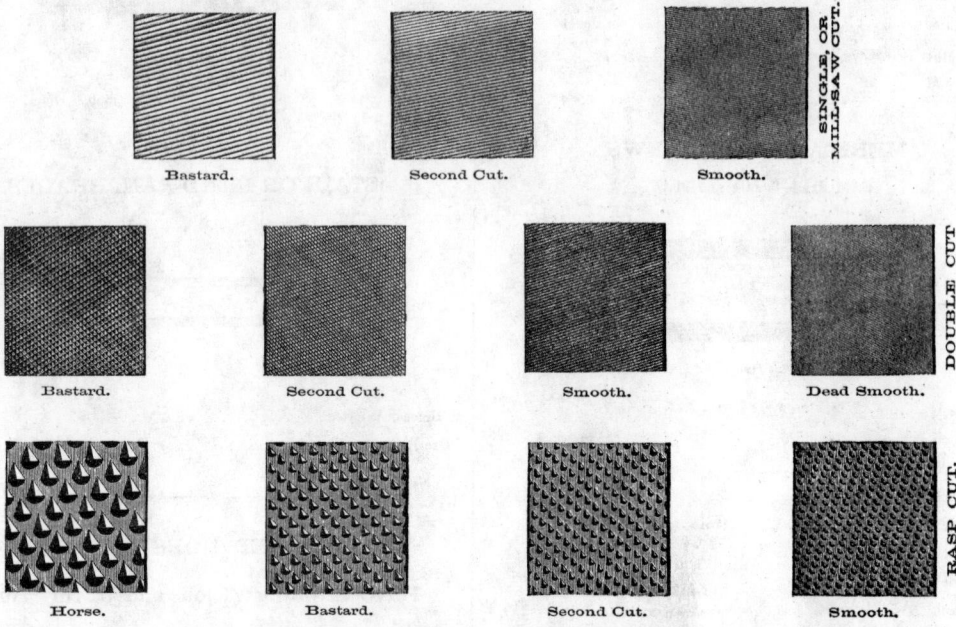

The Prices marked on this List are at the Rate of $5.00 per £ Sterling.

CAST STEEL TAPER FILES.

DESCRIPTION.	3	3½	4	4½	5	5½	6	7	8	9	10	11	12	Inches.
3 Square Taper, 2d Cut, Single............per gross.	$10.00	$10.00	$11.25	$12.75	$14.25	$16.00	$19.50	$25.50	$31.50	$ 37.50	$49.50	$60.00	$72.00	
3 Square blunts, 2d Cut, Single and Tapers, cut to the point.................... "	12.75	12.75	14.25	16.00	19.50	23.25	25.50	31.50	37.50					
Double Cut Tapers, cut to the point, Stubs Pattern.......................... "	14.25	14.25	15.75	18.25	21.75	25.50	27.75	34.50	40.50					
2d Cut Frame or Pit Saw................ "		12.00	13.00	14.50	16.50	19.50	22.50	28.50	36.00					

MISCELLANEOUS FILES.

DESCRIPTION.	3 to 6	7	8	9	10	11	12	13	14	15	16	17	18	Inches.
Mill Saw (Fine Bastard,)..............per dozen.	$1.38	$1.67	$2.00	$2.44	$2.94	$3.44	$4.13	$4.88	5.75	7.13	8.63	10.25	12.00	
Double Cut Mill Files and Wood Rasps.... "	1.50	1.75	2.13	2.62	3.13	3.75	4.63	5.38	6.50	8.00	9.50	11.00	13.00	
Horse and Shoe Rasps.................. "	1.50	1.75	2.13	2.63	3.13	3.75	4.63	5.38	6.50	8.00	9.50			
Flat and Square Bastard................ "	1.38	1.67	2.00	2.44	2.94	3.44	4.13	4.88	5.75	7.13	8.63	10.25	12.00	
Half Round and Round Bastard........... "	1.50	1.75	2.1	2.62	3.13	3.75	4.63	5.38	6.50	8.00	9.50	11.00	13.00	
Hand (Safe edge) do. .... "	1.66	2.00	2.4	2.94	3.44	4.13	4.88	5.75	7.13	8.63	10.25	12.00	13.75	
Flat, Mill Saw and Square, 2d Cut........ "	1.55	1.88	2.38	2.87	3.44	4.12	5.00	6.00	7.00	8.50	10.00	11.75	14.25	
Half Round and Round do. .... "	1.75	2.13	2.62	3.13	3.62	4.50	5.50	6.50	7.50	9.00	10.75	12.75	15.00	
Hand (Safe edge) do. .... "	1.88	2.38	2.87	3.44	4.13	5.00	6.00	7.00	8.50	10.00	11.75	14.25	16.75	
Flat Smooth and Cabinet Files............ "	1.88	2.30	2.70	3.13	3.68	4.38	5.25	6.50	7.50	9.00	11.00	13.50	16.00	
Half Round Smooth and Cabinet Rasps.... "	2.00	2.37	2.88	3.37	4.00	5.00	6.13	7.50	8.50	10.00	12.00	14.50	17.00	
Hand (Safe edge) Smooth................ "	2.30	2.70	3.13	3.69	4.38	5.25	6.50	7.50	9.00	11.00	13.50	16.00	18.50	

Beveled Edge Horse Rasps advance 50 cents per dozen.

Tanged Horse Rasps advance 3 inches on Flat Bastard prices.

Hook Tooth Saw Files advance 2 inches on Half Round 2d Cut.

Double Cut Mill Files, same price as Half Round 2d Cut.

Half Round Shoe Rasps advance one inch in price.

Dead Smooth Files are double the price of Smooth.

Equaling and Parallel Files, of whatever kind, advance 2 inches on their respective descriptions.

Knife Files, advance 3 inches on Half Round price.

Feather Edge, advance 4 inches on Half Round price.

MILL, CROSS CUT, PIT AND TENON SAWS,

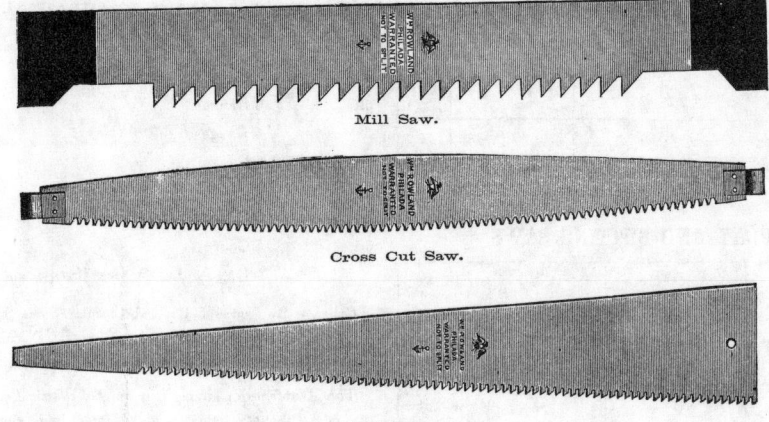

Mill Saw.

Cross Cut Saw.

Pit Saw.

ROWLAND'S ANCHOR BRAND, AMERICAN OR GERMAN STEEL SAWS.

DESCRIPTION.	Ordinary Width.	9 Inches Wide.	9¼ Inches Wide.	9½ Inches Wide.	9¾ Inches Wide.	10 Inches Wide.	10¼ Inches Wide.	10½ Inches Wide.	10¾ Inches Wide.	11 Inches Wide.	11¼ Inches Wide.	11½ Inches Wide.	11¾ Inches Wide.	12 Inches Wide.	12¼ Inches Wide.	12½ Inches Wide.	12¾ Inches Wide.	13 Inches Wide.	13¼ Inches Wide.	13½ Inches Wide.	13¾ Inches Wide.	14 Inches Wide.	
Mill Saws No. 4, 1¼ in.																							Per ft.
" " 5,																							"
" " 6,																							"
" " 7, 3-16																							"
" " 8,																							"
" " 9,																							"
" " 10, 1-8																							"
" " 11,																							"
" " 12,																							"

PIT SAWS.

6 Feet.	6½ Feet,	7 Feet.	7½ Feet.	8 Feet.	8½ Feet.	9 Feet.	9½ Feet.	10 Feet.
$	$	$	$	$	$	$	$	

Pitt Saw Handles, $ per set.

CAST STEEL SAWS.

DESCRIPTION.	Ordinary Width.	9 Inches Wide.	9¼ Inches Wide.	9½ Inches Wide.	9¾ Inches Wide.	10 Inches Wide.	10¼ Inches Wide.	10½ Inches Wide.	10¾ Inches Wide.	11 Inches Wide.	11¼ Inches Wide.	11½ Inches Wide.	11¾ Inches Wide.	12 Inches Wide.	12¼ Inches Wide.	13 Inches Wide.	
Mill Saws No. 4, ¼ in.																	Per Foot.
" " 5,																	"
" " 6,																	"
" " 7, 3-16																	"
" " 8,																	"
" " 9,																	"
" " 10, 1-8																	"
" " 11,																	"
" " 12,																	"

CAST STEEL CROSS-CUT AND TENON SAWS.
$ per doz.

PIT SAWS.

6 Feet.	6½ Feet.	7 Feet,	7½ Feet.	8 Feet.	8½ Feet.	9 Feet.	9½ Feet.	10 Feet.
$	$	$	$	$	$	$	$	$

BUTTING SAWS SAME PRICE AS MILL SAWS.

☞ Saws over 10 feet in length, and any other description not in the above list, furnished at Prices to be agreed upon.

CROSS CUT, CIRCULAR AND HAND SAWS.

CAST STEEL CROSS CUT SAWS.

	Per Foot.	Patent Tabs, Bolts, Per Dozen.	Handles, Per Dozen.	Set and Sharpened, Per Dozen.
Disston, S. S., Extra, No. 1				
Disston, C. S., No. 2				
Keystone, C. S., No. 5				

MILL, MULAY AND BUTTING SAWS.

Disston's C. S., No. 2.	Ordinary Width.	10 In. Wide.	11 In. Wide.	12 In. Wide.	
4 Gauge					Per foot.
5 Gauge					"
6 Gauge					"
7 Gauge					"
8 Gauge					"
9 Gauge					"
10 Gauge					"
11 Gauge					"

Disston's Extra, No. 1, Mill Saws,   cents per foot extra.
Disston's C. S. Pitt Saws,   per foot.

TUTTLE'S PATENT HOOK TOOTH CROSS CUT SAWS.

4 Feet......each, per foot, $ 7 Feet......each, per foot, $

4½ Feet......each,   "   7½ Feet......each,   "

5 Feet......each,   "   8 Feet......each,   "

5½ Feet......each,   "   8½ Feet......each,   "

6 Feet......each,   "   9 Feet......each,   "

6½ Feet......each,   "

DISSTON'S PATENT GROUND CIRCULAR SAWS,
Of Superior Quality.

Terms of Warranty.—Each Saw is warranted perfectly true, and free from flaws and seams ; and, if found to be defective in either of these particulars, a new one will be given in exchange, if returned within *thirty days* from the time of purchasing.

4 inch diam. 19 Gauge, $ For each additional Gauge extra, $

		Each.	
5	"	19 Gauge	" "
6	"	18 Gauge	" "
7	"	18 Gauge	" "
8	"	18 Gauge	" "
9	"	17 Gauge	" "
10	"	16 Gauge	" "
12	"	15 Gauge	" "
14	"	15 Gauge	" "
16	"	14 Gauge	" "
18	"	13 Gauge	" "
20	"	13 Gauge	" "
22	"	12 Gauge	" "
24	"	11 Gauge	" "
26	"	11 Gauge	" "
28	"	10 Gauge	" "
30	"	10 Gauge	" "
32	"	10 Gauge	" "
34	"	9 Gauge	" "
36	"	9 Gauge	" "
38	"	8 Gauge	" "
40	"	8 Gauge	" "
42	"	8 Gauge	" "
44	"	7 Gauge	" "

PATENT GROUND CIRCULAR SAWS—Continued.

			Each.	
46 inch diam.	7 Gauge, $		For each additional Gauge extra, $	
48	"	7 Gauge	"	"
50	"	6 Gauge	"	"
52	"	6 Gauge	"	"
54	"	5 Gauge	"	"
56	"	5 Gauge	"	"
58	"	5 Gauge	"	"
60	"	5 Gauge	"	"

Larger Sizes if required.

Concave Swaged and Beveled Circular Saws for Veneers, Shingles, &c., &c., &c. Veneering Saws in Segments. Circular Saws for Ivory and Metal made to Order, and Circular Saws Repaired.

The Manufacturer having had years of practical experience in the manufacture of the above article, has no hesitation in defying competition as to price, durability, and finish.

CIRCULAR SAW MANDRELS.

Centre Mandrels.

	Dia. of Pulley.	Face of Pulley.	Dia. of Flange.	Length.	Price each.
No. 1,	2 inches.	3 inches.	2 inches.	10 inches.	$
No. 2,	2¼ inches.	3½ inches.	2¼ inches.	12 inches.	
No. 3,	2½ inches.	3½ inches.	2½ inches.	14 inches.	
No. 4,	3 inches.	4 inches.	3 inches.	16 inches.	

Box Mandrels.

	Dia. of Pulley.	Face of Pulley.	Dia. of Flange.	Length.	Price each.
No. 1,	2½ inches.	3½ inches.	2½ inches.	14 inches.	$
No. 2,	3 inches.	4 inches.	3 inches.	16 inches.	
No. 3,	3½ inches.	4½ inches.	3¾ inches.	18 inches.	
No. 4,	4 inches.	5 inches.	4 inches.	20 inches.	
No. 5,	4½ inches.	5½ inches.	4½ inches.	22 inches.	
No. 6,	5 inches.	6 inches.	5 inches.	24 inches.	
No. 7,	5½ inches.	6½ inches.	5½ inches.	26 inches.	
No. 8,	6 inches.	7 inches.	6 inches.	28 inches.	

HAND AND PANEL SAWS, 26 INCH.

No.   Price per doz.

1. Bishop's C. S. Beech Handle, Polished Edges, 4 Rivets.........$

2. Broadwell C. S. Polished Walnut Handles, 5 Raised Iron Screws, up Glazed...

3. Brown, C. S. Beech Handle, Polished Edge, 4 Rivets...........

4. Stamped to Order—C. S. Beech Handle, Polished Edge, 4 Rivets, warranted...

5. Broadwell C. S. Fine Glazed Blade, Polished Mahogany Handle and Raised Brass Rivets.....................................

6. Brown C. S. Fine Glazed Blade, Polished Beech Handle, 4 Raised Iron Screws, Steel Plate...................................

No. 7.

7. Disston C. S. warranted, Beech Handle, Polished Edge, 4 Rivets.

8. Disston S. S. warranted, Apple Handle, Polished Edge, 4 Rivets, warranted equal to Spear & Jackson's.........................

PANEL, RIP AND BACK SAWS.

HAND AND PANEL SAWS—Continued.

No. 16.

No.		Price per doz.

16. Disston London Spring, Cast Steel, warranted, Polished Beech Handle, 4 Raised Brass Screws, Steel Plate, Fine Glazed Blade. *Stamped to Order* .... $

9. Disston Extra C. S., London Spring, warranted, Apple Handle, Polished Edge, 4 Rivets ....

99. Same Saw, selected Blades, Prize Medal Saw. Stamped, Extra Refined London Spring....................................

12. Disston Extra London Spring, warranted, Fine Glazed Blade, Polished Handle, Chased and Steel Plate, 4 Raised Brass Screws....................................

RIP SAWS.

28   30-inch.

Same as No. 3 Hand, per dozen, $

Same as No. 4   "

Same as No. 7   "

Same as No. 8   "

Same as No. 9   "

GENTLEMEN'S PANEL SAWS.

16   18   20   22   24 inch.

Same as Disston's No. 7, per dozen, $

Same as Brown's No. 6,   "

Same as Brown's No. 3,   "

IMPROVED SAWS.

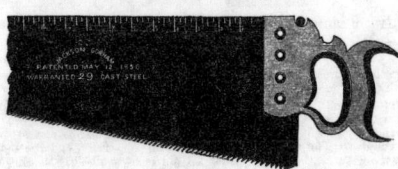

No. 29.

Per dozen,

No. 29, Common Patent Combination Saw, with 24 Inch Square and Rule, Straight Edge and Scratch Awl, Blade as No. 1 .... $

No. 38, Combination Saw, Independent Handle, Blade as No. 3 ....

No. 39, Same Saw, with Plumb and Level....................

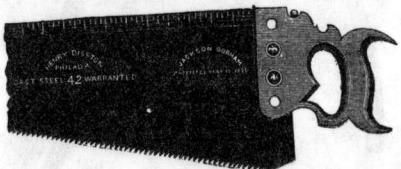

No. 42.

No. 42, Combination Saw, Independent Handle, Blade as No. 7 ....

No. 43, Same Saw, with Plumb and Level....................

IMPROVED SAWS—Continued.

Patent Gauges, for Saws, adapted to Shouldering, Tenoning, Dovetailing, Cog Cutting, Pattern Making, Curfing, or wherever a certain depth is required, put on any Hand or Panel Saw, at an extra charge per dozen of—

For 20 to 24 inches.................................. $

For 26 inches....................................

IMPROVED HALF BACK SAW.

$

14   16   18   20 inch.

IMPROVED MOVABLE STEEL BACK SAWS.

Can be used as an ordinary Saw without the Back, and by replacing the Back, as a Back Saw.

14   16   18   20 inch.

With the Back, per dozen. $

Apple Handle, Polished Edge, $

BUTCHER BOW SAWS.

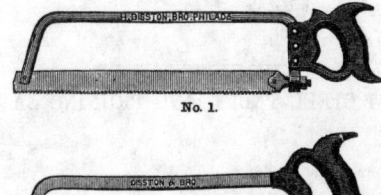

No. 1.

No. 2.

12   14   16   18   20   22   24 inch.

No. 1, Oval,   per dozen, $

No. 2, Common Flat,   "

No. 3, Best New Style,   "

No. 4, Best Old Style,   "

No. 5, Kitchen Saw,   "

BUTCHERS' SAW BLADES.

12   14   16   18   20   22   24 inch.

Per Doz.

No. 1, 1½ wide, $

No. 2, 1¼ wide, $

No. 3 and 4, 2 wide, $

No. 5, ¾ wide, Kitchen Saw Blade, 12 inch, per dozen, $

BACK SAWS.

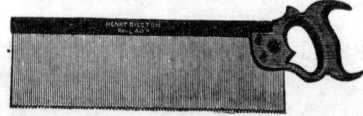

No. 1, Jackson's C. S., Plain Burr, Beech Handle, Polished Edge, Blue Back, per dozen,

$

8   10   12   14   16   18 inch.

BACK, COMPASS, HACK AND WOOD SAWS.

BACK SAWS—Continued.

No. 4, Disston's C. S., Plain Burr, Beech Handle, Polished Edge, Blue Back, per dozen,

$

| 8 | 10 | 12 | 14 | 16 | 18 inch. |

No. 7, Disston's, same Saw as No. 4, with Steel Back, per dozen,

$

| 8 | 10 | 12 | 14 | 16 | 18 inch. |

No. 5, Disston's S. S., Plain Burr, Apple Handle, Polished Edge, Brass Back, per dozen,

$

| 8 | 10 | 12 | 14 | 16 | 18 inch. |

CAST STEEL COMPASS SAWS.

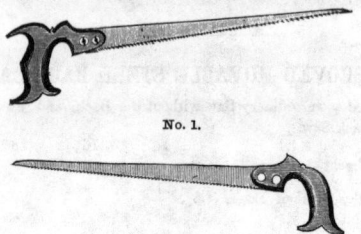

No. 1.

No. 2.

| | 10 | 12 | 14 | 16 | 18 inch. |

No. 1, Old Style, Beech Handle, $ doz.
No. 2, Pistol, Apple Handle, $ "

CAST STEEL TABLE AND PRUNING SAWS.

$

| 14 | 16 | 18 | 20 | 22 | 24 | 26 inch. |

Blind-makers' Saws, per dozen, $
Cast Steel Key-hole Saws, per dozen, $

CAST STEEL HACK SAWS.

$

| 8 | 9 | 10 | 11 | 12 | 14 | 16 inch. |

Framed Complete.—Frame same pattern as Bow Saw No. 1, (p. 165.)

$

| 10 | 12 | 14 inch, per dozen. |

TURNING CHAIR AND FELLOE WEBS.

No. 1, Plain.   Per doz.

$

| 10 | 12 | 14 | 16 | 18 | 20 | 22 |

$

| 24 | 26 | 28 | 30 | 32 | 34 | 36 inch. |

No. 2, Set and Sharpened.

$

| 10 | 12 | 14 | 16 | 18 | 20 | 22 |

$

| 24 | 26 | 28 | 30 | 32 | 34 | 36 inch. |

Felloe Plain.

$

| 10 | 12 | 14 | 16 | 18 | 20 | 22 |

$

| 24 | 26 | 28 | 30 | 32 | 34 | 36 inch. |

TURNING SAWS AND FRAMES, COMPLETE.

$ Per doz.

| 10, | 12, | 14, | 16, | 18 inch. |

Turning Saws in Beech-
    wood Frames . . . . . .   "
Turning Saws, Improved
    Box Handle and Brass
    Collar . . . .   "

CAST STEEL WOOD SAWS.

No. 1. Marshall's Plain,   per dozen, $
No. 2. Marshall's Set,   "
No. 3. Marshall's Set and Sharpened,   "
No. 4. Disston's Cast Steel, Plain,   "
No. 5. Disston's Cast Steel, Set,   "
No. 6. Disston's Cast Steel, Set and Sharpened,   "
No. 7. Disston's Spring Steel, Plain,   "
No. 8. Disston's Spring Steel, Set,   "
No. 9. Disston's Spring Steel, Set and Sharpened,   "
No. 10. Disston's Spring Steel, Extra, (for Wood
        Sawyers), Set,   "

WOOD SAWS, FRAMED, COMPLETE.

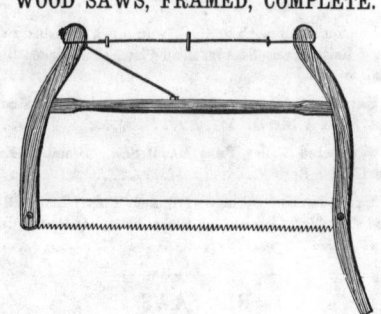

Wood Saws, Framed . . . . per dozen, $
Wood Saws, Framed, Set and Sharpened . . . .   "
Livingston's Patent Framed Wood Saw (see Plate)   "

ROBERT'S "PATENT" FRAMED WOOD SAW.

Fig. 1

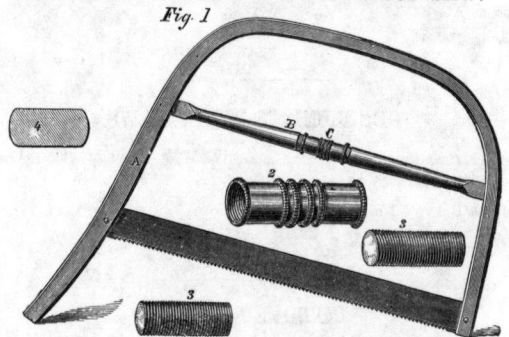

No. 1. Extra, Frame and Saw Complete, Filed and Set, per doz. $
No. 1. Frame and Saw Complete, Filed and Set . . . . .   "

Our engraving represents a new **Saw Frame,** constructed in a different style and superior finish to any heretofore offered to the trade.

DESCRIPTION.—The frame, A, is in one piece; it is bent to the desired conformation and is fitted with a brace, B. This brace has a nut, C, in the centre, which is furnished with a right-and-left thread. When the nut is turned, the frame is sprung apart, and the saw blade extended. The engraving explains itself very fully, and the detached pieces are details of the fixtures, the uses of which are apparent to all—Fig 2 being the nut in an enlarged form, Fig. 3 the screws which work in it, and Fig. 4 a section of the saw frame.

This is a very **Simple, Efficient and Durable Frame,** and will accomplish the desired end fully. It obviates the use of Braces, Wires, or any other appliances of like nature, and completely prevents the racking incident to the ordinary frame.

WOOD SAW FRAMES.

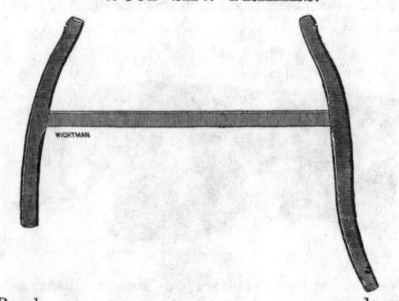

White, Beach . . . . per dozen, $
White, Beach, Extra . . . .   "
Red, Beach, ...   "

SAW RODS, HANDLES, AND SETS.

SAW STRETCHERS OR RODS.

No. 1.

$ .... per gross.

16 to 20 inch,   21,   22,   23,   24,   25 inch.

$ .... per gross.

26,   27,   28,   29,   30,   31,   32 inch.

No. 4.

$ .... per gross.

16 to 20 inch,   21,   22,   23,   24,   25 inch.

$ .... per gross.

26,   27,   28,   29,   30,   31,   32 inch.

SAW BUCKS.

Second Growth Ash, New Pattern..............per dozen, $

Hand Saw Handles.

		$		per dozen.
No. 1. Beechwood,	For Saws,	26	28	inch blade.
		$		per dozen.
No. 3. Beechwood, Pol'd Edges, "		26	28	inch blade.
		$		per dozen.
No. 8. Applewood, Pol'd Edges, "		26	28	inch blade.

Back Saw Handles.

No. 1. Beechwood, Pol'd Ed.,   8, 10, 12,   14, 16 in. blade.

$ .... per dozen.

No. 8. Applewood,   "   8, 10, 12,   14. 16 in. blade.

$ .... per dozen.

Panel Saw Handles.

                              $ per dozen.

No. 3. Beechwood, Polished Edges, For Saws,   18,   20   in. blade.

Saw Pads.

	Large.	Small.
Applewood..........per doz. $		
Rosewood .... "		
Best Impv'd Boxwood. "		
Best Impv'd Ebony... "		

☞ Saw Screws—see page 103.

HAMMER SAW SETS.

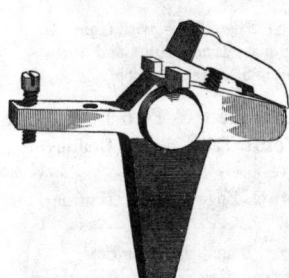

Aiken's Hammer, Genuine, Cast Steel..........per dozen, $

HAMMER SAW SETS—Continued.

Bemis' Hammer, New Pattern,.................per dozen, $

Bemis' Hammer, Light.........................   "

Extra Cast Steel, No. 150 ....per dozen, $

Cast Steel,   No. 151 ....   "

Common,   No. 152 ....   "

LEVER SAW SETS.

Stillman's Patent Lever Saw Set.

Stillman's Lever...............................per dozen, $

Stillman's Lever, Cross Cut....................   "

Bemis' Lever ....per dozen, $

Bemis' Lever, New Pattern.....................   "

Common Lever, Iron Bound.....................   "

Common Lever, Brass Bound...................   "

Lever Mill Saw Sets ....   "

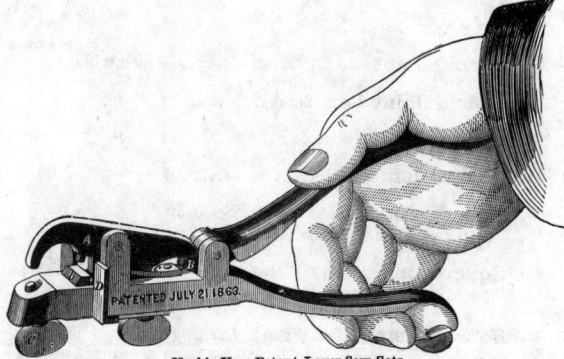

Nash's New Patent Lever Saw Sets.

$ per dozen.

By reference to the engraving the construction of the tool may be seen at a glance. It consists of a frame which has two projections or ears, in which are mounted a short lever A, and a handle, the toe of which, shown at B, acts upon the curved part at the back end of the lever A. There is also a spring c, a movable gauge D, the upper and lower dies a and b, and set screws C, and C'.

In using this tool, first adjust the gauge D, by means of the set screw C', to suit the size and length of the saw teeth, and to ensure the dies acting upon each tooth exactly in the same place; the saw blade is then inserted between the hooked end of the lever A, and the point of the set screw C, the tooth to be set being placed between the dies, with the points of the adjoining teeth in contact with and pressed against the gauge D, the dies giving the set to the tooth when the handles are pressed together, and the degree of set being governed by the set screw C, upon the point of which the saw blade rests. When the hand is relaxed the spring c throws open the set again, and the instrument is shoved along from tooth to tooth until the operation is completed. By means of the gauge D, which is slotted underneath and slides on the set screw C' which secures it to the frame, the teeth may be set from their bases, or near their points, at the pleasure of the operator, while the form of the lower die b, having its face bevelled or inclined backwards, prevents the teeth from being injured at their points.

With the above directions, a few minutes practice will enable any person to set a saw perfectly.

CARPENTERS' RULES.

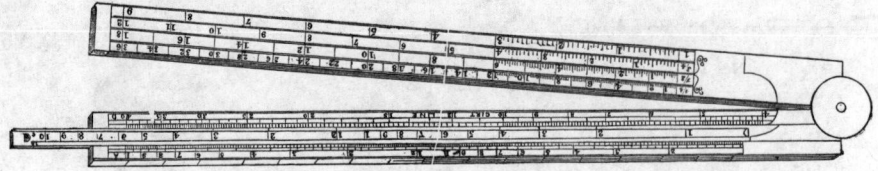

No. 12.

(For Description of Plate see page 169.)

BOXWOOD RULES.

One Foot, Four Fold, Narrow.

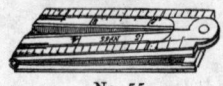

No. 55.

No.		Per dozen.
69,	Round Joint	$
65.	Square Joint	
64,	Square Joint, Edge Plates	
65½,	Square Joint, Bound	
55,	Arch Joint	
56,	Arch Joint, Edge Plates	
57,	Arch Joint, Bound	

Two Feet, Four Fold, Narrow.

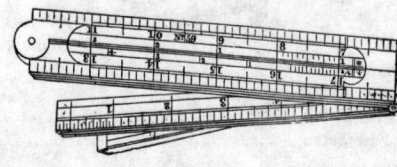

No. 59.

No.			Per dozen.
68,	Round Joint	1 inch wide,	$
	Round Joint, Extra Thick	1	"
1,	Square Joint	1	"
61½	Square Joint	¾	"
63,	Square Joint, Edge Plates, Scale of 10ths on Edge, Drafting Scale	1	"
63½	Square Joint, Edge Plates, Scale of 10ths on Edge, Extra Quality	¾	"
84,	Square Joint, Half Bound, Drafting Scale	1	"
6	Square Joint, Bound, Drafting Scale	1	"
51,	Arch Joint, Drafting Scale	1	"
53,	Arch Joint, Edge Plates, Scale of 10ths on Edge, Drafting Scale	1	"
52,	Arch Joint, Half Bound, Drafting Scale	1	"
54,	Arch Joint, Bound, Drafting Scale	1	"
59,	Double Arch Joint, Drafting Scale	1	"
60,	Double Arch Joint, Bound, Drafting Scale	1	"

BOXWOOD RULES.
(Continued.)
Two Feet, Six Fold.

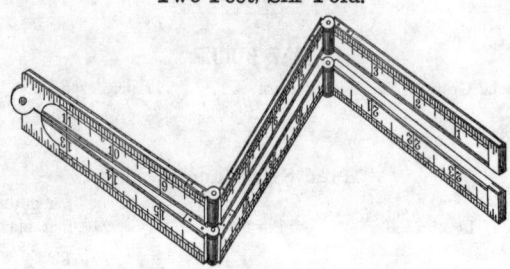

No. 58.

No.			Per dozen.
58,	Arch Joint, Edge Plates	¾ inch wide,	$
58½	Arch Joint, Edge Plates, with Tables for ascertaining the Weights of all sizes of Iron, Steel, Copper, Brass, Lead, &c.	¾	"

Two Feet, Four Fold, Broad.

No.			Per dozen.
67,	Bound Joint	1⅜ inch wide,	$
70,	Square Joint, Drafting Scale	1⅜	"
72,	Square Joint, Edge Plates, Scale of 10ths on Edge, Drafting Scale	1⅜	"
72½	Square Joint, Bound, Scale of 10ths, Drafting Scale	1⅜	"
73	Arch Joint, Drafting Scale	1⅜	"
75	Arch Joint, Edge Plates, Scale of 10ths on Edge, Drafting Scale	1⅜	"
76	Arch Joint, Bound, Scale of 10ths, Drafting Scale	1⅜	"
77,	Double Arch Joint, Scale of 10ths, Drafting Scale	1⅜	"
78,	Double Arch Joint, Half Bound, Scale of 10ths, Drafting Scale	1⅜	"
78½	Double Arch Joint, Bound, Scale of 10ths, Drafting Scale	1⅜	"
83,	Arch Joint, Edge Plates, with Gunter's Slides, 8 Square Lines, 10ths and 12ths of an inch, and 100ths of a foot	1⅜	"

Board Measure, Two Feet, Four Fold.

No.			Per dozen.
79,	Square Joint, Edge Plates, Drafting Scale	1⅜ inch wide,	$
81,	Arch Joint, Edge Plates, Drafting Scale	1	"
82,	Arch Joint, Bound, Drafting Scale	1⅜	"

For any other Boxwood Rule in the List, marked with Board Measure, an extra charge will be made of . . . .

CARPENTERS' RULES.

(Continued.)

BOXWOOD RULES.

(Continued.)

Two Feet, Two Fold.

No.   Per dozen.
29, **Round Joint**......................1⅜ inch wide, $

18, **Square Joint**......................1½   "

22, **Square Joint**, Bitted, **Board Measure**, with 8 Square Lines............1½   "

1, **Arch Joint**, with 8 Square Lines.....1½   "

2, **Arch Joint**, Bitted, with Scale of 10ths and 8 Square Lines..................1½   "

4, **Arch Joint**, Bitted, Extra Thin, Drafting Scale, 8 Square Lines, Extra Finish.1½   "

5, **Arch Joint**, Bound, with 10ths, Drafting Scale, 8 Square Lines............1½   "

Two Feet, Two Fold, Slide.

No.   Per dozen.
26, **Square Joint**, Plain Slide, 10ths and 8 Square Lines,.......................1½ inch wide, $

27, **Square Joint**, Bitted, Gunter's Slide, Drafting Scale, 8 Square Line, 10ths of foot,..............................1½   "

12, **Arch Joint**, Bitted, Gunter's Slide, Drafting Scale, 8 Square Line, 10ths of foot, (see Plate, page 168)............1½   "

15, **Arch Joint**, Bound, Gunter's Slide, Drafting Scale, 8 Square Line, 10ths of inch,..............................1½   "

6, **Arch Joint**, Bitted, Gunter's Slide, Engineering, ...1½   "

16, **Arch Joint**. Bound, Gunter's Slide, Engineering, ...1½   "

We have had prepared a Treatise on the above Gunter's Slide and Engineers' Rules, showing their utility and use; with full and complete instructions, enabling mechanics to make their own calculations. It is also particularly adapted to the use of those having charge of cotton or woolen machinery; 200 pages, bound in Cloth, each, net,..$

CALIPER.

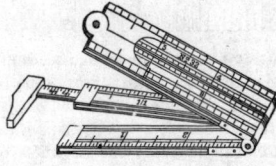

No, 32,

No.   Per dozen,
36, **Square Joint**. 2 Fold, 6 inch,........⅞ inch wide, $

32, **Arch Joint**. 4 Fold, 12 inch, Scale of 10ths,..............................1   "

IVORY RULES.

No,   Per dozen.
93, **Round Joint**, 2 Fold, 6 inch, Brass,.............

93½, **Round Joint**, 2 Fold, 6 inch, German Silver,.......

IVORY RULES.

(Continued.)

One Foot, Four Fold, Narrow.

No.   Per dozen.
90, **Round Joint**, Brass, ...$

92½, **Square Joint**, German Silver,..........⅝ inch wide,

92, **Square Joint**, Edge Plates, German Silver,..............................⅝   "

88½, **Arch Joint**, Edge Plates, German Silver, ⅝   "

88, **Arch Joint**, Bound, German Silver,......⅝   "

91, **Square Joint**, Edge Plates, with 10ths, German Silver,.......................⅞   "

Two Feet, Four Fold, Narrow.

No.   Per dozen.
85, **Square Joint**, Edge Plates, with 10ths on Edge, German Silver,.................⅞ inch wide, $

86, **Arch Joint**, Edge Plates, with 10ths on Edge, drafting Scale, German Silver,.....1   "

87, **Arch Joint**, Bound, Drafting Scale, German Silver,..........................1   "

89, **Double Arch Joint**, Bound, Drafting Scale, German Silver,.................1   "

Two Feet, Four Fold, Broad.

No.   Per dozen.
95, **Arch Joint**, Bound, with Drafting Scale and 10ths, German Silver,..............1⅜ inch wide, $

97, **Double Arch Joint**, Bound, with Drafting Scale and 10ths, German Silver,.....1⅜   "

CALIPER.

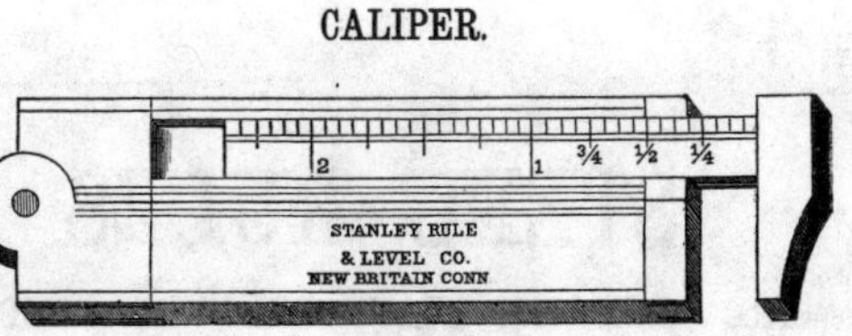

No. 38.

No.   Per dozen.
38, **Square Joint**, 2 Fold, 6 inch, German Silver,..............................⅞ inch wide, $

39, **Square Joint**, 4 Fold, 12 inch, German Silver,..............................⅞   "

40, **Square Joint**, 4 Fold, Bound, 12 inch, German Silver,.......................⅝   "

(Rules with Spanish Measure Made to Order.)

MISCELLANEOUS ARTICLES.

Bench Rules.

No.   Per dozen.
34, **Bench Rules**,......................2 feet, $

35, **Bench Rules**, Board Measure,............2   "

Board Measures.

No.   Per dozen.
46, **Board Stick**, Octagon,..............2 feet, $

47, **Board Stick**, Octagon,..............3   "

43½, **Board Stick**, Flat Hickory, Cast Brass Head and Tip,............................3   "

CARPENTERS' RULES.

(Continued.)

MISCELLANEOUS ARTICLES.

(Continued.)

No.		Per dozen.
49,	**Board Stick**, Flat Hickory, Steel Head, Brazed, Extra Strong,............................3 feet,	$
48,	**Walking Cane**, Octagon, Hickory, Solid Cast Brass Head, and Tip, ¾ inch,.................3	"

Log Measure.

48½,	**Walking Cane**, Octagon, Hickory, Solid Cast Brass Head, and Tip, ¾ inch,.................3	"

Yard Sticks.

33, **Yard Stick**, Polished,...........................

41, **Yard Stick**, Brass Tip, Polished,..................

50, **Yard Stick**, Hickory, Brass Cap and Ends, Polished,.

Wantage and Gauging Rods.

44, **Wantage Rods**,..............................

45, **Gauging Rods**,............................3 feet,

45½, **Gauging Rods, Wantage Tables**.......3 "

Forwarding Sticks.

49½,...5 feet,

Ship Carpenters' Bevels.

42, Boxwood, Double Tongue, marked with inches, one foot,

43, Boxwood, Single   "   "   "   "

Three Feet Yard Rules.

66, **Arch Joint**, Four Fold, Boxwood,.................

STATIONERS' GOODS.

No.		Per dozen.
160,	Rulers, Mahogany, Flat, Plain Finish, Bevel Edge, Assorted, 12 to 15 inches, ...	$
162,	Rulers, Mahogany, Flat, French Polish, Bevel Edge, Assorted, 12 to 15 inches, ...	
164,	Rulers, Mahogany, Octagon, French Polish, Assorted, 12 to 15 inches, ...	
166,	Rulers, Rosewood, Flat, French Polish, Bevel Edge, Assorted, 12 to 15 inches,.........................	
168,	Rulers, Rosewood, Round, French Polish, Assorted, 12 to 15 inches,..	
170,	Rulers, for Scholars' use, Boxwood, Bevel Edge, Extra Finish, Graduated to Eighths and Sixteenths, one foot,	
172,	Drafting Scale, Boxwood, with Scale for Drafting Twelfths and Twenty-fourths of an inch, one foot,....	
174,	Architects' Drafting Scale, Boxwood, with Scale for Drafting for ⅛, ¼, ⅜, ½, ⅝, ¾, ⅞, 1, 1¼, 1½, 1¾, 2, 2¼, 2½, 2¾, 3 inches to the foot,.............................	
176,	Gunter's Scale, Boxwood, ...	
186,	Printers' Rules, Satin Wood, Square, one foot,.........	
188,	Printers' Rules, Boxwood, 4 Fold, 1 Foot,............	
204,	Checkermen, Boxwood, Plain, Assorted Sizes, put up in neat boxes, containing one Set, per gross Set,........	
205,	Checkermen, Boxwood, Polished, Assorted Sizes, put up in neat Boxes, containing one Set, per gross Set,.....	
206,	Dissected Cube, for illustration of Cube Root, Boxwood, per dozen Set,..................................	
208,	Cubical Blocks, 1 inch Square, containing 64 cubical Blocks,..	
210,	Button Gauge, Boxwood,..............................	
212,	Hatters' Rules, Boxwood,.............................	
214,	Watch Glass Gauges,.................................	

STEEL RULES AND WIRE GAUGES.

THE AMERICAN STANDARD WIRE GAUGE.

Adopted by the Brass Manufacturers, January, 1858.

These Gauges are made from the best Steel, and are tempered, adjusted, and warranted accurate.

☞ None genuine unless stamped as in the engraving, with our trade marks.

Prices.	Each.
Round Gauges, sizes, 0 to 36....................	$
Round Gauges, sizes, 5 to 36, (see plate,).......	
Angular Wire Gauges, No. 1, sizes 000 to 20, (see plate).................................	
Angular Wire Gauges, No. 2, sizes 15 to 30, (see plate),	
Angular Wire Gauges, No. 3, sizes 25 to 40, (see plate, p. opposite).................................	
Screw and Wire Gauge Combined, (see plate)........	

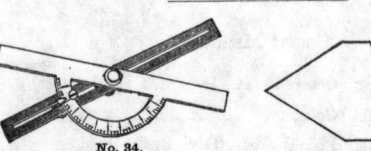

No. 34.
Bevel Protractor, each, $

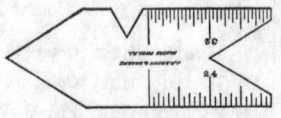

Center Gauge, each, $

STEEL CALIPER RULES.

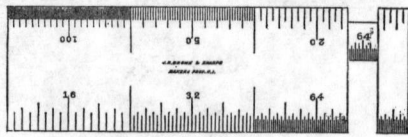

The above cut is a fac-simile of one side of these Rules. The other side is divided to 12ths, 24ths, 48ths, 8ths, 14ths, and 28ths, on the outside, and upon the slide to 32ds and 64ths of inches. When closed they are three inches long. The Caliper can be drawn out to measure two and a half inches. The thickness of the rule is one-tenth of an inch.

The advantages claimed are their superior accuracy and durability.

Price, each,.................. ....$

These Rules are No. 90 of Price List, and are divided in four ways:

No. 90 A, divided on outside like cut, (or like No. 86, p. 172,) on slide to 32ds and 64ths.

No. 90 B, divided on outside like cut, on slide to 64ths or 100ths.

No. 90 C, divided on outside to 8ths, 16ths, 32ds, and 64ths, (or like No. 97, p. 172,) on slide to 32ds and 64ths.

No. 90 D, divided on outside to 8ths, 16ths, 32ds and 64ths; on slide to 64ths and 100ths.

MACHINE DIVIDED
STEEL RULES AND WIRE GAUGES,
UNITED STATES STANDARD.

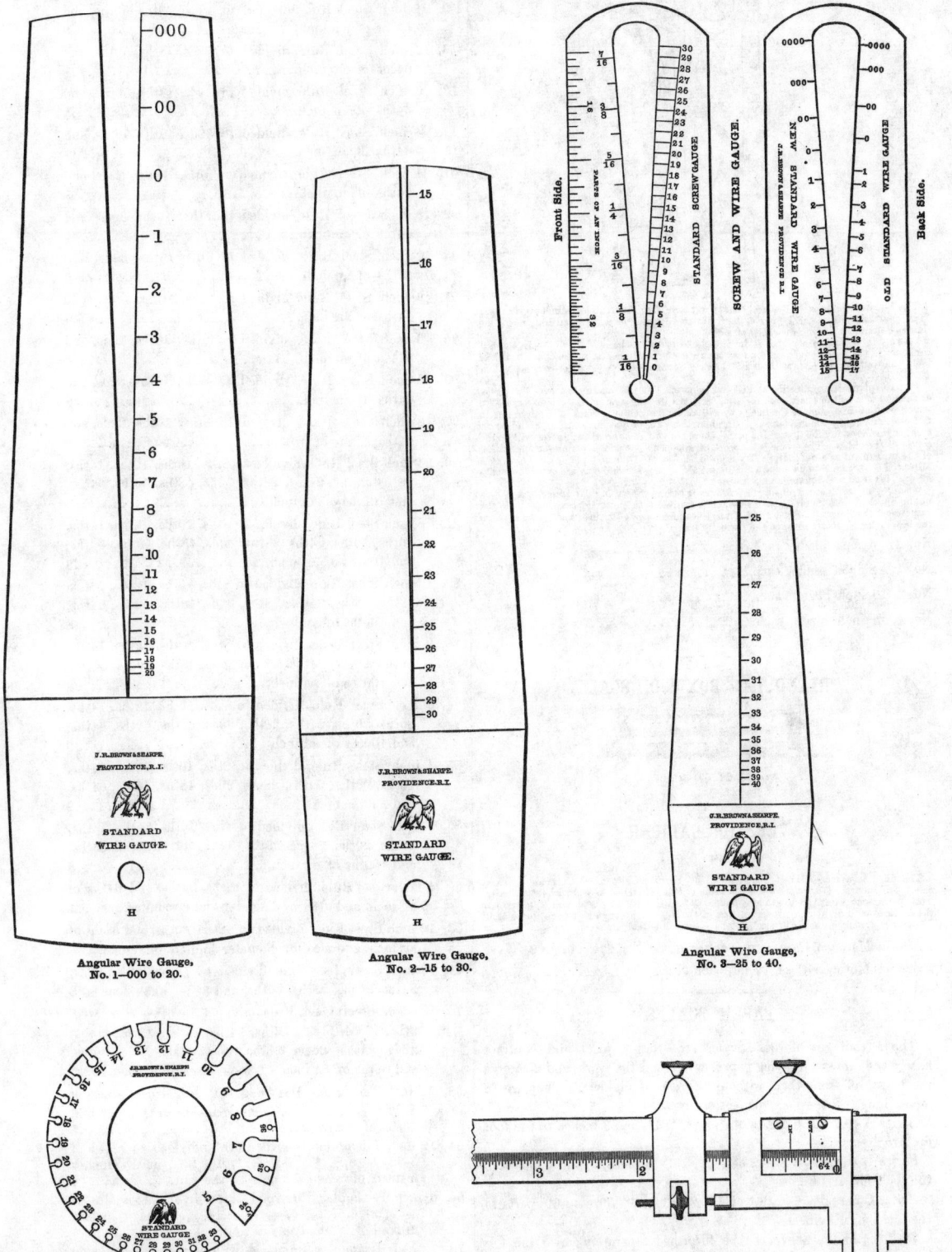

Angular Wire Gauge,
No. 1—000 to 20.

Angular Wire Gauge,
No. 2—15 to 30.

Angular Wire Gauge,
No. 3—25 to 40.

Round Wire Gauge,
No. 5 to 36.

Vernier Calliper. (For Description, see page 172.)

STEEL RULES AND WIRE GAUGES.

(Continued.)

AMES' PATENT UNIVERSAL SQUARE.

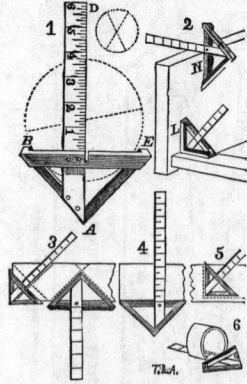

This Square combines, in the most convenient form, five different instruments, viz: the Try Square, the Mitre, the T-Square, the Graduated Rule, and (what is entirely new) the Center Square, for finding the center of a circle.

"As a Center Square alone, it is invaluable to every mechanic. * * * In short, it combines in the most convenient form so many useful instruments, no mechanic's list of tools can well be complete without a Universal Square."—*Scientific American*, September 22, 1855.

Fig. 1 explains its application as a Center Square. Put the instrument over the circle, as the end of a bolt or shaft, with the arms, B A, E A, resting against the circumference, in which position one edge of the rule, A D, will cross the center. Mark a straight line in this position; apply the instrument again to another part of the circumference, and mark another line, crossing the first. The point where the two lines cross each other will be the center of the circle. The whole is the work of a moment. *Fig.* 2 explains the application of the instrument as a carpenter's Try Square, N, and an Outside Square, L. *Fig.* 3 as a Miter. *Fig.* 4, as a T-Square and a Graduated Rule. *Figs.* 5 and 6 as an Outside Square for drawing, and a T-Square for machinists.

The tongue, D A, (Fig. 1,) being fastened, as it is, into the triangular frame, B A E, cannot be knocked from its place, in this respect constituting a great improvement over the carpenters' Try-Square, T-Square and Miter, in common use. The instruments are made of the best material, neatly finished and perfectly true.

No. 1,   6 inch blade, each,.......................... $

No. 2,   8 inch blade, each,..........................

No. 3, 10 inch blade, each,..........................

No. 4, 12 inch blade, each..........................

TRIANGULAR BOXWOOD SCALE.

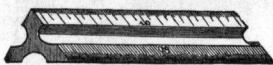

Nos. 63, 64, 65, 73 and 75.

VERNIER CALIPER.

(See Plate, p. 171.)

The plate is a fac-simile of one side of the Vernier Caliper, which reads to thousandths of inches. On the other side are 64ths or 50ths of inches, to read without a vernier. This instrument is furnished with both inside and outside calipers and points, to transfer the distance with dividers. An explanation of the Vernier accompanies each instrument. These instruments are made of steel, and have the points tempered.

Price, in Morocco Case, 6 in., each........................$

Price, in Morocco Case, 12 in., each ....

PAPER SCALES.

The advantages of these Scales are—they expand and contract nearly the same as drawing paper, do not soil the work, and distances can be set off from them without the use of dividers. They are 18 inches long. Price   per set of six.

Series A contains 6 Scales of $\frac{1}{4}$, $\frac{1}{2}$, $\frac{3}{4}$, 1, 1$\frac{1}{2}$, and 3 inches to the foot for Architects.

Series B contains 6 Scales of 3-32, $\frac{1}{8}$, 3-16, 5-16, $\frac{3}{8}$, and $\frac{7}{8}$ inches to the foot, for Architects.

Series C contains 6 Scales of 10, 20, 30, 40, 50, and 60 parts to the inch, for Engineers.

☞ Any of the above can be furnished separately; also the following Scales to the foot, 1$\frac{1}{4}$, 1$\frac{3}{8}$, 1$\frac{1}{8}$, and $\frac{5}{8}$ inches to the foot. Price   cents each.

LIST OF STANDARD RULES AND MACHINISTS' TOOLS.

(The No. will be found before "U. S. St'd," on each Rule.)

No.   Price each.

2,   24 inch Steel Rule, divided to 32ds, 48ths, 50ths, and 64ths of an inch,..............................$

19,   12 inch Steel Rule, divided to 32ds, 48ths, 50ths, and 64ths of an inch,..............................$

13,   6 inch Steel Rule, divided to 32ds, 48ths, 50ths, and 64ths of an inch,..............................$

17,   4 inch Steel Rule, divided to 32ds, 48ths, 50ths, and 64ths of an inch, ...$

91,   24 inch Steel Rule, divided to 8ths, 16ths, 32ds, and 64ths of an inch,..............................$

92,   18 inch Steel Rule, divided to 8ths, 16ths, 32ds, and 64ths of an inch,..............................$

93,   12 inch Steel Rule, divided to 8ths, 16ths, 32ds, and 64ths of an inch,..............................$

94,   9 inch Steel Rule, divided to 8ths, 16ths, 32ds, and 64ths of an inch,..............................$

95,   6 inch Steel Rule, divided to 8ths, 16ths, 32ds, and 64ths of an inch,..............................$

96,   4 inch Steel Rule, divided to 8ths, 16ths, 32ds, and 64ths of an inch,..............................$

97,   3 inch Steel Rule, divided to 8ths, 16ths, 32ds, and 64ths of an inch,..............................$

80,   24 inch Steel Rule, divided to 8ths, 10ths, 12ths, 14ths, 16ths, 20ths, 24ths, 28ths, 32ds, 48ths, 50ths, 64ths, and 100ths of an inch,..........................$

81,   18 inch Steel Rule, divided to 8ths, 10ths, 12ths, 14ths, 16ths, 20ths, 24ths, 28ths, 32ds, 48ths, 50ths, 64ths, and 100ths of an inch,..........................$

82,   12 inch Steel Rule, divided to 8ths, 10ths, 12ths, 14ths, 16ths, 20ths, 24ths, 28ths, 32ds, 48ths, 50ths, 64ths, and 100ths of an inch,..........................$

83,   9 inch Steel Rule, divided to 8ths, 10ths, 12ths, 14ths, 16ths, 20ths, 24ths, 28ths, 32ds, 48ths, 50ths, 64ths, and 100ths of an inch,..........................$

84,   6 inch Steel Rule, divided to 8ths, 10ths, 12ths, 14ths, 16ths, 20ths, 24ths, 28ths, 32ds, 48ths, 50ths, 64ths, and 100ths of an inch,..........................$

85,   4 inch Steel Rule, divided to 8ths, 10ths, 12ths, 14ths, 16ths, 20ths, 24ths, 28ths, 32ds, 48ths, 50ths, 64ths, and 100ths of an inch,..........................$

86,   3 inch Steel Rule, divided to 8ths, 10ths, 12ths, 14ths, 16ths, 20ths, 24ths, 28ths, 32ds, 48ths, 50ths, 64ths, and 100ths of an inch,..........................$

5,   24 inch Steel Rule, divided to 48ths, 50ths, and 64ths of an inch, and also for diameter and circumference, ..$

33,   12 inch Steel Rule, divided to 48ths, 50ths, and 64ths of an inch, and also for diameter and circumference,..$

61,   12 inch Steel Geer Rule, divided to 18ths, 20ths, 22ds, 24ths, 26ths, 28ths, 30ths, and 32ds, whole length, $

78,   12 inch Steel Geer Rule, divided to 6ths, 7ths, 8ths, 9ths, 10ths, 11ths, 12ths, 14ths, 16ths, 18ths, 20ths, 22ds, 24ths, 26ths, 28ths, 30ths, 32ds, 34ths, 36ths, and 38ths of an inch—1 inch in each division,....$

63,   24 inch Triangular Boxwood Rule, divided to scales of $\frac{1}{8}$, $\frac{1}{4}$, $\frac{3}{8}$, $\frac{3}{4}$, $\frac{1}{2}$, 1, 1$\frac{1}{2}$, 2, 3, and 4 inches to the foot and 16ths of inch..................................$

64,   12 inch Triangular Boxwood Rule, divided to scales of 3-32, 3-16, $\frac{1}{8}$, $\frac{1}{4}$, $\frac{3}{8}$, $\frac{3}{4}$, $\frac{1}{2}$, 1, 1$\frac{1}{2}$, 2, 3 and 4 inches instead of 2 and 4 inches to the foot,............$

65,   6 inch Triangular Boxwood Rule, divided to scales of 3-32, 3-16, $\frac{1}{8}$, $\frac{1}{4}$, $\frac{3}{8}$, $\frac{3}{4}$, $\frac{1}{2}$, 1, 1$\frac{1}{2}$, 2, 3 and 4 inches, instead of 2 and 4 inches to the foot,............$

73,   12 inch Triangular Boxwood Rule, divided on one edge to 10ths, 20ths, 30ths, 40ths, 50ths, and 60ths of an inch,..............................$

MACHINISTS' AND CARPENTERS' SQUARES.

LIST OF STANDARD RULES AND MACHINISTS' TOOLS.

(Continued.)

No.   **Each.**

75, 6 inch Triangular Boxwood Rule, divided on one edge to 10ths, 20ths, 30ths, 40ths, 50ths, and 60ths of an inch,.................................$

34, Bevel Protractor, with sliding arm and half circle divided to degrees, with 10 inch sliding arm, (see plate, page 170.)   A very useful article for Machinists...$

90, 3 inch Steel Caliper Rule. (See plate, page 170,)...$

Shrink Rules.

87, 24¼ inch Steel Rule, divided like No. 80, ...$

88, 24¼ inch Boxwood Rule, divided like No. 80,........

STEEL SQUARES, FOR MACHINISTS.

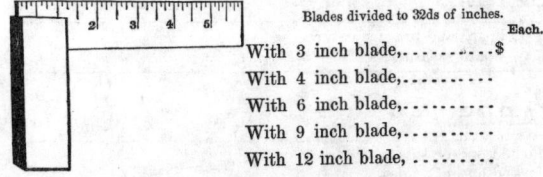

Blades divided to 32ds of inches.

                                            Each.

With 3 inch blade,...........$

With 4 inch blade,...........

With 6 inch blade,...........

With 9 inch blade,...........

With 12 inch blade, ...

No. 1, BEST PLATED TRY SQUARES.

Six Inch.

3 inch, Rosewood, ...per dozen, $

4½ inch, Rosewood,.......................   "

6 inch, Rosewood (see plate,)..............   "

7½ inch, Rosewood,.......................   "

9 inch, Rosewood,......................   "

12 inch, Rosewood,......................   "

15 inch, Rosewood, with Rest, ...   "

18 inch, Rosewood, with Rest, ...   "

The above are warranted Spring Temper, and equal to the best English Try Squares.

No. 2, PLATED TRY SQUARES.

3 inch, Rosewood,.......................per dozen, $

4½ inch, Rosewood,.......................   "

6 inch, Rosewood,.......................   "

7½ inch, Rosewood,.......................   "

9 inch, Rosewood,.......................   "

No. 2 PLATED TRY SQUARES.

(Continued.)

12 inch, Rosewood,.......................per dozen, $

15 inch, Rosewood, with Rests.............   "

18 inch, Rosewood, with Rests.............   "

MITRE SQUARES.

$ per dozen.

     8   10   12   14 inch.

Best Plated.

$ per dozen.

     8   10   12   14 inch.

PLUMB AND LEVEL TRY SQUARES.

No. 1, 12 inch, Rosewood, with Plumb and Level in Handle, with Extra Heavy Mountings, per dozen,.........$

No. 1, 7½ inch, Rosewood, with Plumb and Level in Handle, per dozen, ...$

The above are warranted Spring Temper, and equal to the best English Try Squares.

No. 2, 7½ inch, Rosewood, with Plumb and Level in Handle, per dozen,....................................$

PATENT COMBINATION TRY SQUARE AND BEVEL.

4 inch,........................per dozen, $

6 inch,........................   "

8 inch,........................   "

The Patent Combination Try Square and Bevel will be found a valuable acquisition to Carpenters, Cabinet Makers, Stone Cutters, and others, as it combines within itself a perfect Square and Bevel. The Blade being made by improved machinery, can be relied upon as correct, and can be used either as an inside or outside Square. In using as a Bevel, adjust the blade to any given angle required, by means of the Screw.

CARPENTERS' SQUARES.

STEEL AND IRON SQUARES.

No.	Price.	Names.	Width.	Description.
100		Cast Steel Improved,........	2 inches.	1-16, 1-12, 1-10, $\frac{1}{8}$, $\frac{1}{4}$, with brace, 8 square, 100 scales, and Essex's New Board Measure, giving the feet and inches in full.
1		Cast Steel for drafting,.....	2 inches.	1-16, 1-12, $\frac{1}{8}$, $\frac{1}{4}$, board and brace measure, 8 square and 1-100 scale.
2		Cast Steel finish,..........	2 inches.	1-16, 1-12, $\frac{1}{8}$, $\frac{1}{4}$, board and brace measure, and 8 square scale.
2½		Framing,...................	2 inches.	$\frac{1}{8}$, $\frac{1}{4}$, both sides and edges.
3		Sup. Sup. Extra,..........	2 inches.	1-16, 1-12, $\frac{1}{8}$, $\frac{1}{4}$, board and brace measure. [body.
4		Super Extra,..............	2 inches.	1-12, $\frac{1}{8}$, $\frac{1}{4}$, board and brace measure, extra figures on inner edge of
5		Extra,....................	2 inches.	1-12, $\frac{1}{8}$, $\frac{1}{4}$, board and brace measure.
6		A Brace,.................	2 inches.	$\frac{1}{8}$, $\frac{1}{4}$, board and brace measure.
7		........B,	2 inches.	$\frac{1}{8}$, $\frac{1}{4}$, board measure.
8		Extra,...................	1½ inches.	1-12, $\frac{1}{8}$, $\frac{1}{4}$.
9		Plain,...................	1½ inches.	$\frac{1}{8}$, $\frac{1}{4}$.
10		Extra, 1 foot,...........	1½ inches.	1-12, $\frac{1}{8}$, $\frac{1}{4}$.
11		Plain, 1 foot,.......:....	1½ inches.	, $\frac{1}{4}$.
12		Cast Steel, 1 foot,........	1½ inches.	1-16, 1-12, $\frac{1}{8}$, $\frac{1}{4}$, and 100 scale.

EAGLE SQUARES.

No.	Price.	Names.	Width.	Description.
13		A Brace,................	2 inches.	$\frac{1}{8}$, $\frac{1}{4}$, board and brace measure.
14		........B,	2 inches.	$\frac{1}{8}$, $\frac{1}{4}$, board measure.

IRON SQUARES.

No.	Price.	Names.	Width.	Description.
1		....	1½ inches.	Marked on one side.
2		....	1½ inches.	Marked on both sides.
4		....	2 inches.	Marked on both sides.

Steel Squares packed 4 dozen in a case ; Iron Squares packed 8 dozen in a case.

PLUMBS AND LEVELS.

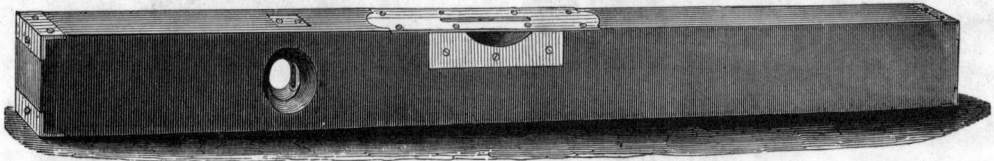

No. 10.

No. 35.

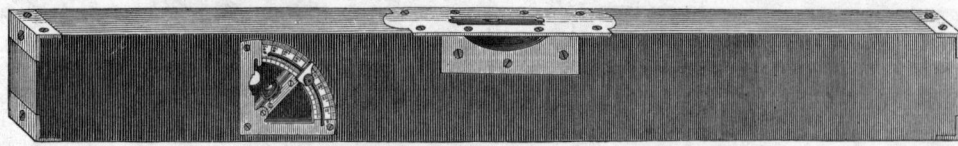

No. 32.

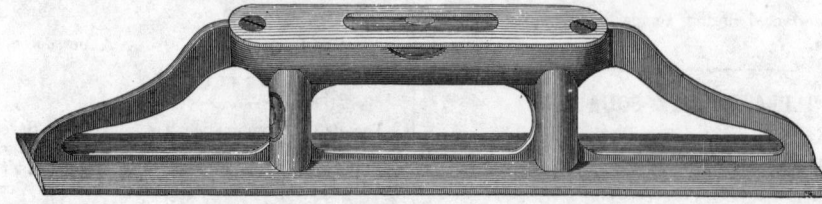

No. 43.

[*For Description of Plates see page 175.*]

PLUMBS AND LEVELS, T BEVELS AND GAUGES.

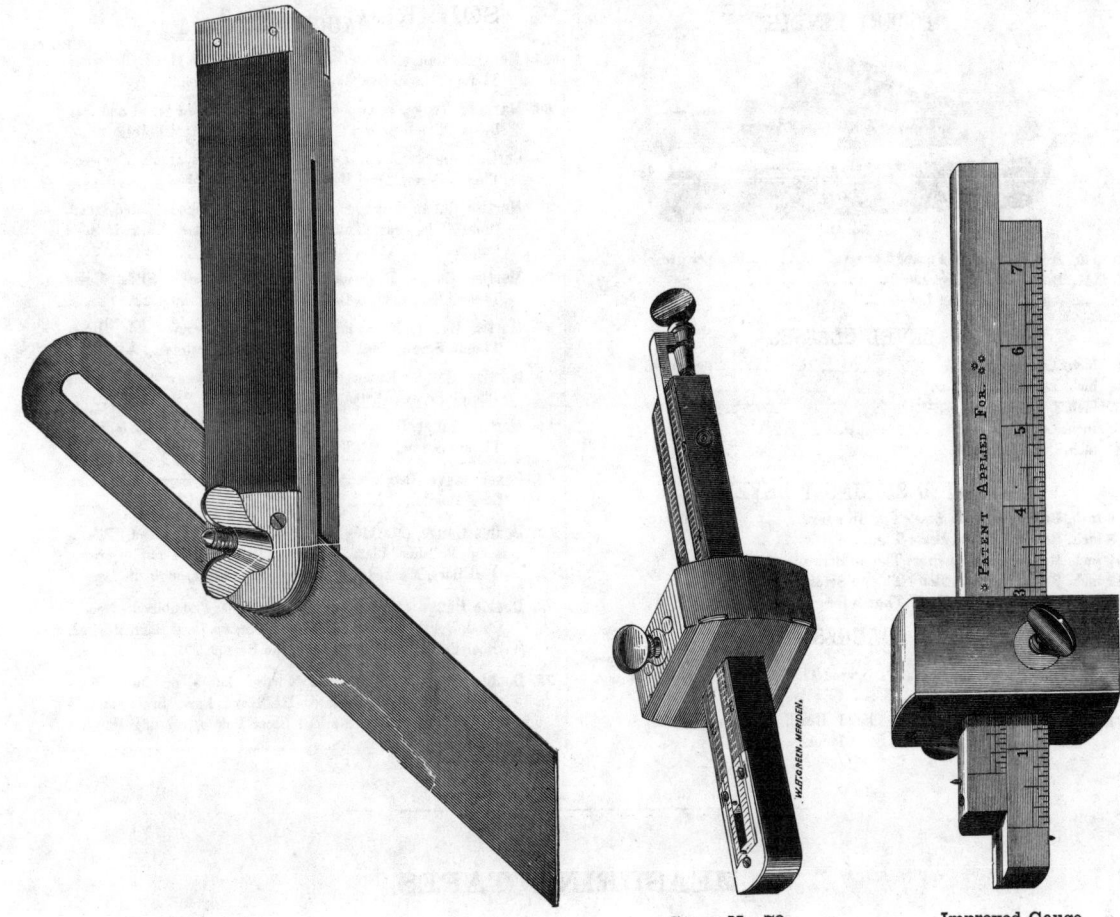

T Bevel, 6 Inch.   Gauge No. 79.   Improved Gauge.

(For Description of Plates see page 176.)

PLUMBS AND LEVELS.

No.		Per dozen.
103,	Levels, Two Side Views, Assorted ....14 to 24 inch,	$
0,	Plumb and Level, Two Side Views, Polished, Assorted ....26 to 30	"
2,	Plumb and Level, Two Brass Lipped Side Views, Polished, Assorted.........................26 to 30	"
4,	Plumb and Level, Two Brass Lipped Side Views, Polished and Tipped, Assorted ....26 to 30	"
5,	Triple Stock, Plumb and Level, Two Brass Lipped Side Views, Polished and Tipped, Assorted ....26 to 30	"
1½,	Mahogany Plumb and Level, Two Side Views, Polished, Assorted ....14 to 24	"
1,	Mahogany Plumb and Level, Two Side Views, Polished, Assorted ....26 to 30	"
6,	Mahogany Plumb and Level, Two Brass Lipped Side Views, Polished, Assorted.............26 to 30	"
9,	Mahogany Plumb and Level, Two Brass Lipped Side Views, Polished and Tipped, Assorted...26 to 30	"
10,	Triple Stock, Mahogany Plumb and Level, Two Extra Brass Lipped Side Views, Polished and Tipped, Assorted, (see plate, page 174)......26 to 30	"
20,	Mahogany Plumb and Level, Improved Double Adjusting Side Views and Top Plates, Polished.....................................	30	"

PLUMBS AND LEVELS.

(Continued.)

No.		Per dozen.
25,	Mahogany Plumb and Level, Improved Double Adjusting Side Views, and Top Plates, Polished and Tipped..........................	30 inch, $
26,	"Brook's" Patent Universal Plumb and Level, Mahogany..............................	
11,	Rosewood Plumb and Level, Two Extra Brass Lipped Side Views, Polished and Tipped, Assorted ....28 to 30	"
11½,	Rosewood Plumb and Level, Two Extra Brass Lipped Side Views, Polished and Tipped	20	"
12,	Machinists' Brass Bound Rosewood Plumb and Level, Two Brass Side Views, Polished......	20	"
32,	Patent Graduating Plumb and Level, Mahogany, (see cut, p. 174,)..........................	28	"
33,	Satinwood Plumb and Level, Two Brass Lipped Side Views, Polished and Tipped, Assorted...28 to 30	"
35,	Mason's Plumb and Level, (see cut, p. 174,) 3¾ inches wide................................	42	"
43,	Iron Plumb and Level, Two Side Views, Brass Top Plates, (see cut, p. 174,)................	9	"
45,	Machinists' Level, all Iron, Brass Top Plate, extra finish................................	9	"

LEVELS AND GAUGES.

POCKET LEVELS.

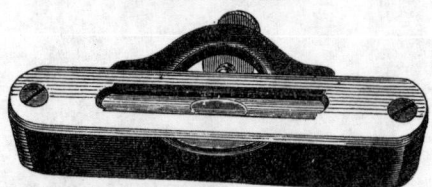

No. 41.

No. 40, Iron, Japanned, Pocket Levels..................per gross, $
No. 41, Brass Top, Pocket Levels.................... "
No. 42, All Brass, Pocket Levels.................... "

LEVEL GLASSES.

2 inch, Level Glasses..................per gross, $
2½ inch, Level Glasses.................... "
3 inch, Level Glasses.................... "
3½ inch, Level Glasses.................... "
4 inch, Level Glasses.................... "

PLATED SLIDING T BEVELS.

6 inch, Rosewood, with Brass Thumb Screw..........per dozen, $
8 inch, Rosewood, with Brass Thumb Screw........... "
10 inch, Rosewood, with Brass Thumb Screw........... "
12 inch, Rosewood, with Brass Thumb Screw........... "
14 inch, Rosewood, with Brass Thumb Screw........... "

GAUGES.

No.   Per dozen.
61, Marking Gauge, Beechwood, Boxwood Thumb Screw, Oval Bar, $
    Marked, Steel Points...................................
64, Marking Gauge, Polished, Plated Head, Boxwood Thumb
    Screw, Oval Bar, Marked, Steel Points...................

GAUGES—Continued.

No.   Per dozen.
65, Marking Gauge, Boxwood, Polished, Plated Head, Boxwood
    Thumb Screw, Oval Bar, Marked, Steel Points...........
66, Marking Guage, Boxwood or Rosewood, Plated Head and Bar,
    Brass Thumb Screw, Oval Bar, Marked, Steel Points.......
70, Cutting Gauge, Mahogany, Polished, Plated Head, Boxwood
    Thumb Screw, Oval Bar, Marked, Steel Points.............
73, Mortise Gauge, Boxwood or Satinwood, Polished, Plated Head,
    Brass Slide, Brass Thumb Screw, Oval Bar, Marked, Steel
    Points...
76, Mortise Guage, Boxwood, Plated Head, Screw Slide, Brass
    Thumb Scrow, Oval Bar, Marked, Steel Points............
78, Mortise Gauge, Rosewood, Plated Head, Screw Slide, Brass
    Thumb Screw, Oval Bar, Marked, Steel Points............
79, Mortise Gauge, Rosewood, Plated Head, Screw Slide, Brass
    Thumb Screw, Plated Bar, Marked, Steel Points.........
80, Mortise Gauge, Boxwood, Full Plated Head, Screw Slide, Brass
    Thumb Screw, Plated Bar, Marked, Steel Points..........
85, Panel Gauge, Beechwood, Boxwood Thumb Screw, Oval Bar,
    Steel Points..
71, Double Gauge, (Marking and Mortise Guage combined,) Beech-
    wood, Polished, Plated Head and Bars, Brass Thumb Screws,
    Oval Bars, Marked Steel Points, running through the Bars..
72, Double Guage, (Marking and Mortise Guage combined,) Beech-
    wood, Polished, Boxwood Thumb Screws, Oval Bars, Marked,
    Steel Points, running through the Bars...................
74, Double Gauge, (Marking and Mortise Gauge combined,) Box-
    wood, Polished, Full Plated Head and Bars, Brass Thumb
    Screws, Oval Bars, Marked Steel Points, running through
    the Bars..

MEASURING TAPES.

BRASS CASE SPRING MEASURING TAPES.

No.   Per dozen.
3002 3 Feet, Plain, Linen Tape, with Stop.............$
3003 5 Feet, Plain, Linen Tape, with Stop.............
3004 3 Feet, Silver Plated, Linen Tape, with Stop......
3005 5 Feet, Silver Plated, Linen Tape, with Stop......

COMMON PATENT LEATHER CASE MEASURING TAPES

With Folding Handles.

No.			Per dozen.
3020	25 Feet,	Union Tape,.....................	$
3021	30 Feet,	Union Tape,.....................	
3023	40 Feet,	Union Tape,.....................	
3026	50 Feet,	Union Tape,.....................	
3027	66 Feet,	Union Tape,.....................	
3028	75 Feet,	Union Tape,.....................	
3029	80 Feet,	Union Tape,.....................	
3030	100 Feet,	Union Tape,.....................	

COMMON ASSES SKIN, BRASS BOUND CASE MEASURING TAPES,

With Folding Handles.

No.			Per dozen.
3040	25 Feet,	Union Tape......................	$
3041	30 Feet,	Union Tape......................	
3042	40 Feet,	Union Tape......................	
3043	50 Feet,	Union Tape......................	
3044	66 Feet,	Union Tape......................	
3045	75 Feet,	Union Tape......................	
3046	80 Feet,	Union Tape......................	
3047	100 Feet,	Union Tape......................	

ROUND EDGE, BEND LEATHER CASE, MEASURING TAPES.

No.			Per dozen.
3500	50 Feet,	Heavy Linen Tape................	$
3600	66 Feet,	Heavy Linen Tape................	
3700	75 Feet,	Heavy Linen Tape................	
3800	100 Feet,	Heavy Linen Tape................	

Tapes marked in 10th and 100th for Engineers and Surveyors.

Lumberman's Tapes.

Tailor's Measures.

CARPENTERS'
BENCH PLANES AND MOULDING TOOLS.

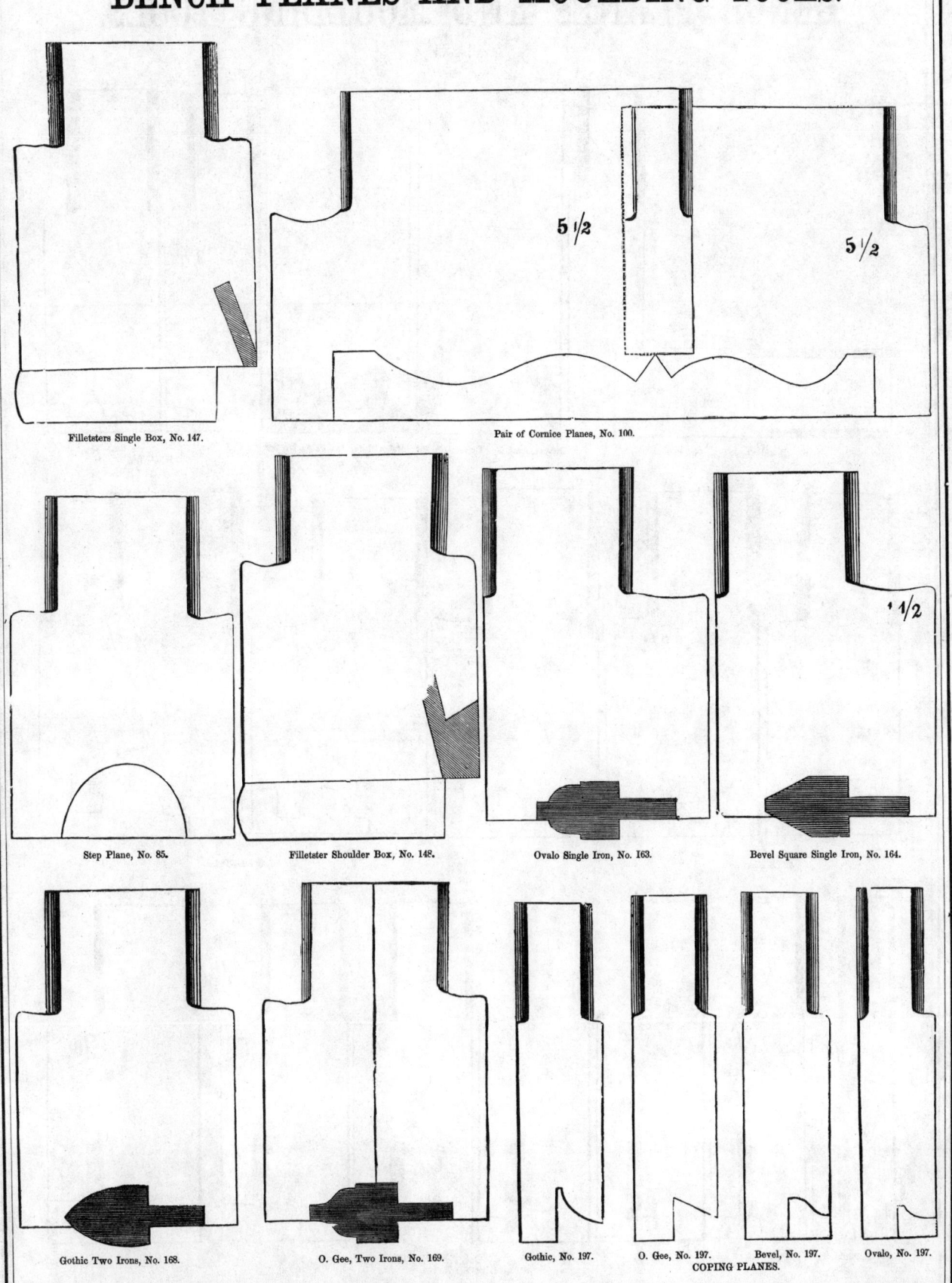

Filletsters Single Box, No. 147.

Pair of Cornice Planes, No. 100.

5 1/2

5 1/2

Step Plane, No. 85.

Filletster Shoulder Box, No. 148.

Ovalo Single Iron, No. 163.

Bevel Square Single Iron, No. 164.

1/2

Gothic Two Irons, No. 168.

O. Gee, Two Irons, No. 169.

Gothic, No. 197.

O. Gee, No. 197.

Bevel, No. 197.

Ovalo, No. 197.

COPING PLANES.

CARPENTERS'
BENCH PLANES AND MOULDING TOOLS.

(Continued.)

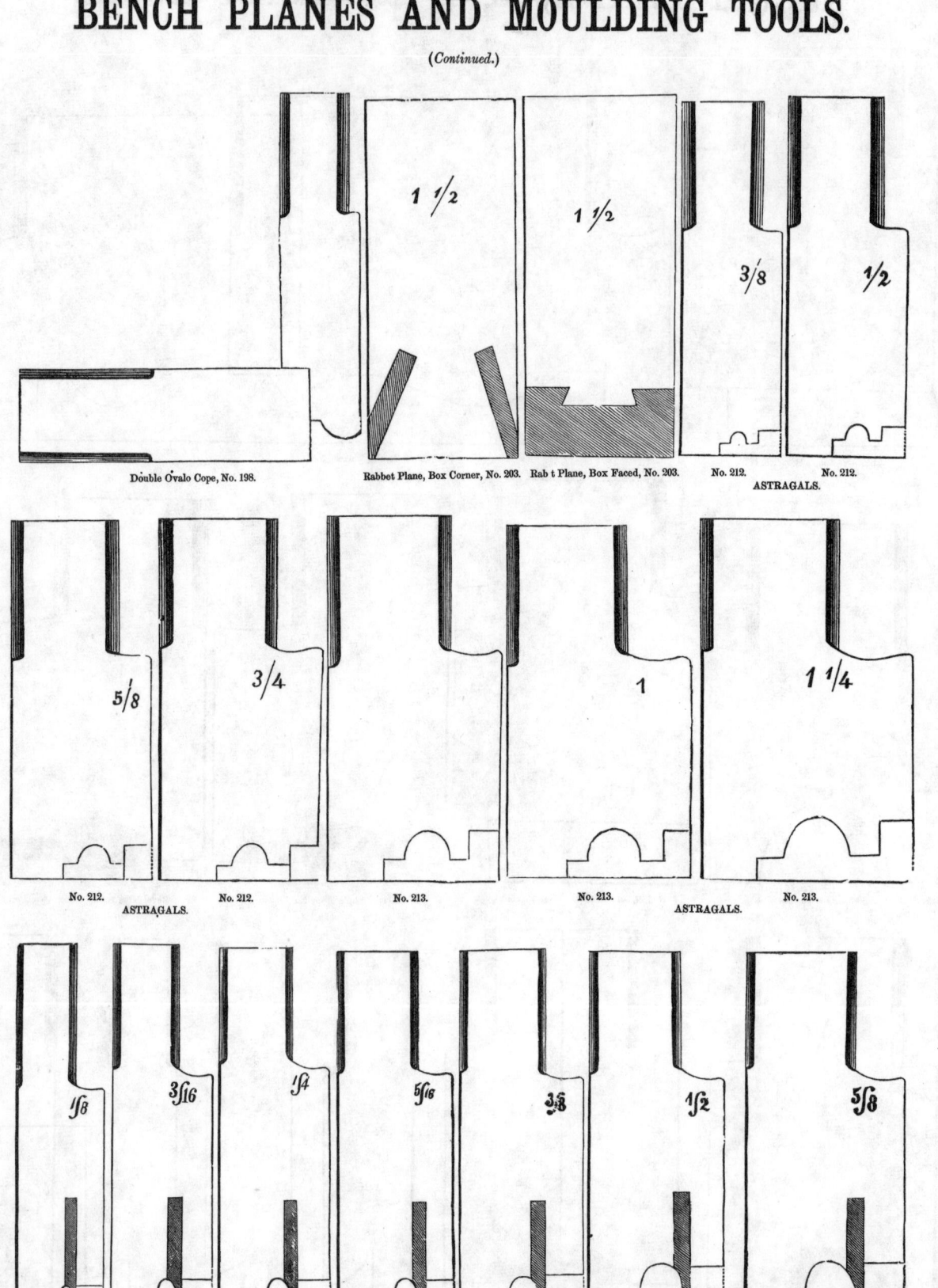

Double Ovalo Cope, No. 198.   Rabbet Plane, Box Corner, No. 203.   Rab t Plane, Box Faced, No. 203.   No. 212.   No. 212.
ASTRAGALS.

No. 212.   No. 212.   No. 213.   No. 213.   No. 213.
ASTRAGALS.   ASTRAGALS.

No. 215.   No. 215.   No. 215.   No. 215.   No. 216.   No. 216.   No. 217.
SINGLE BOX BEADS.

CARPENTERS'
BENCH PLANES AND MOULDING TOOLS.

(Continued.)

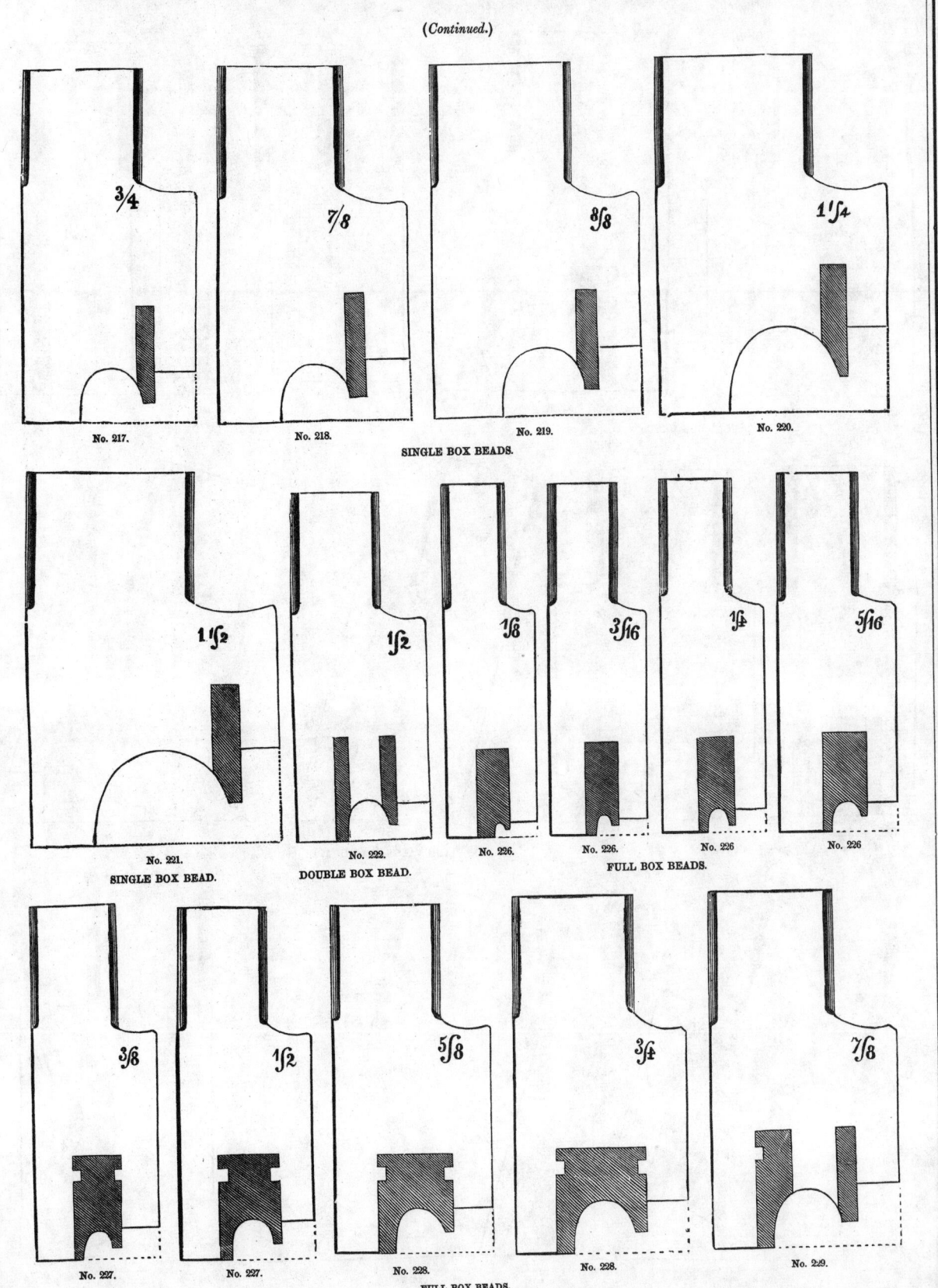

No. 217.   No. 218.   No. 219.   No. 220.

SINGLE BOX BEADS.

No. 221.   No. 222.   No. 226.   No. 226.   No. 226   No. 226

SINGLE BOX BEAD.   DOUBLE BOX BEAD.   FULL BOX BEADS.

No. 227.   No. 227.   No. 228.   No. 228.   No. 229.

FULL BOX BEADS.

CARPENTERS'
BENCH PLANES AND MOULDING TOOLS.

(Continued.)

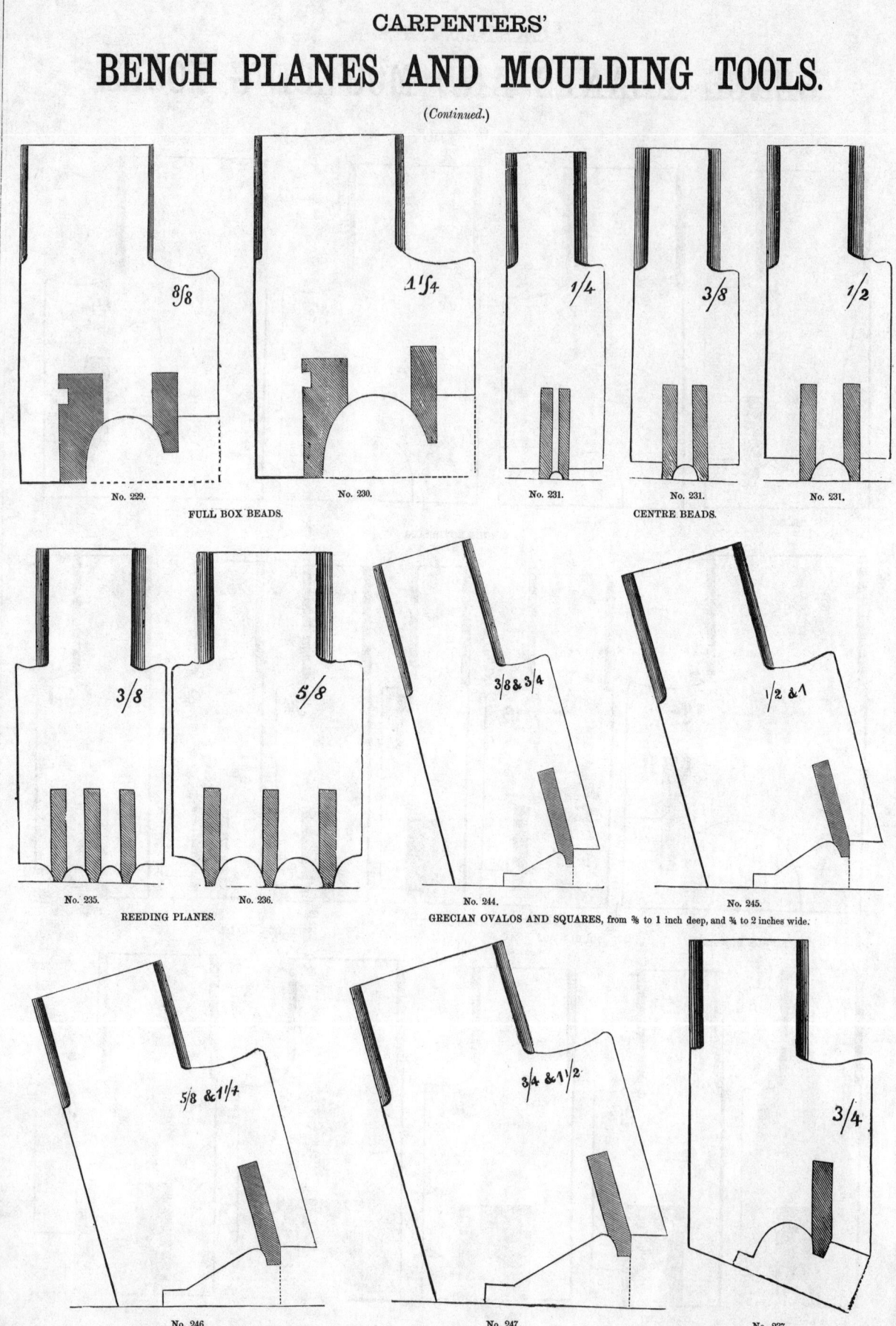

No. 229.   No. 230.   No. 231.   No. 231.   No. 231.

FULL BOX BEADS.   CENTRE BEADS.

No. 235.   No. 236.   No. 244.   No. 245.

REEDING PLANES.   GRECIAN OVALOS AND SQUARES, from ⅜ to 1 inch deep, and ¾ to 2 inches wide.

No. 246.   No. 247.   No. 237.

GRECIAN OVALOS AND SQUARES, from ⅜ to 1 inch deep, and ¾ to 2 inches wide.   TORUS BEAD.

CARPENTERS'
BENCH PLANES AND MOULDING TOOLS.

(Continued.)

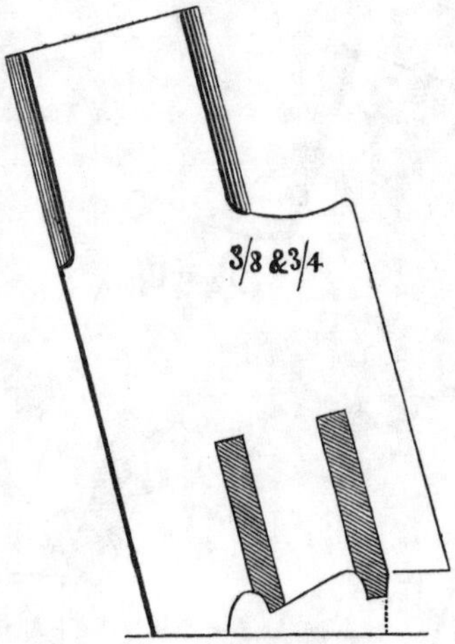

3/8 & 3/4

No. 256.
GRECIAN OVALOS & BEADS, ⅜ to 1 inch deep and ¾ to 2 inch wide.

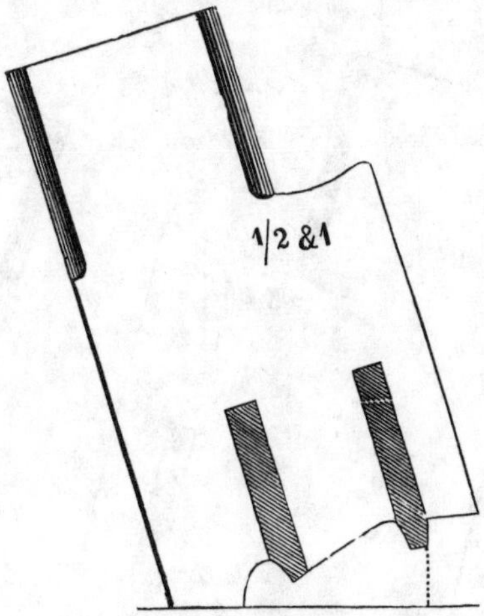

1/2 & 1

No. 257.

5/8 & 1 1/4

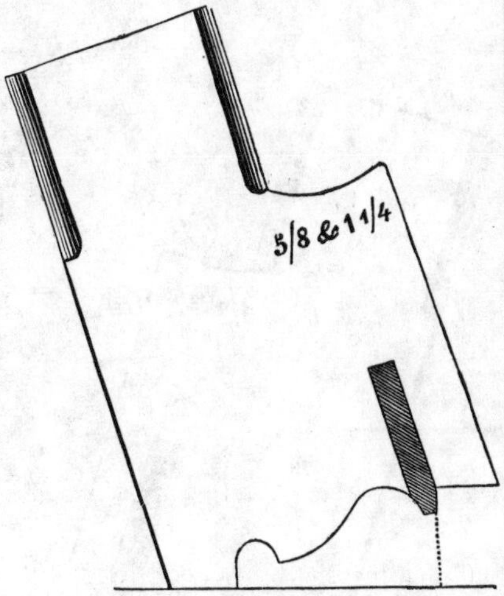

No. 258.
GRECIAN OVALOS & BEADS, ⅜ to 1 inch deep and ¾ to 2 inch wide.

3/4 & 1 1/2

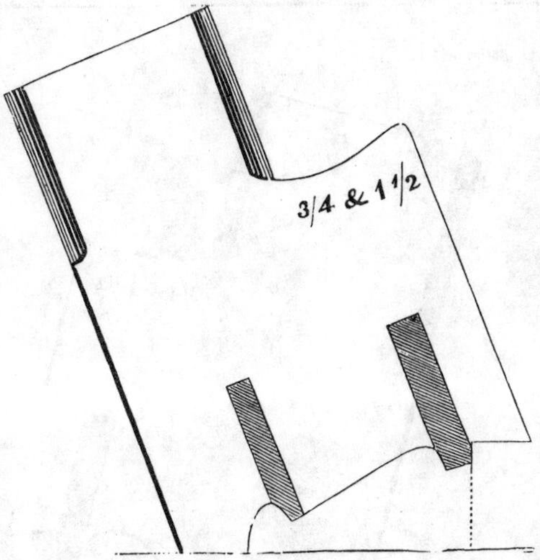

No. 259.
GRECIAN OVALOS & BEADS, ⅜ to 1 inch deep and ¾ to 2 inch wide.

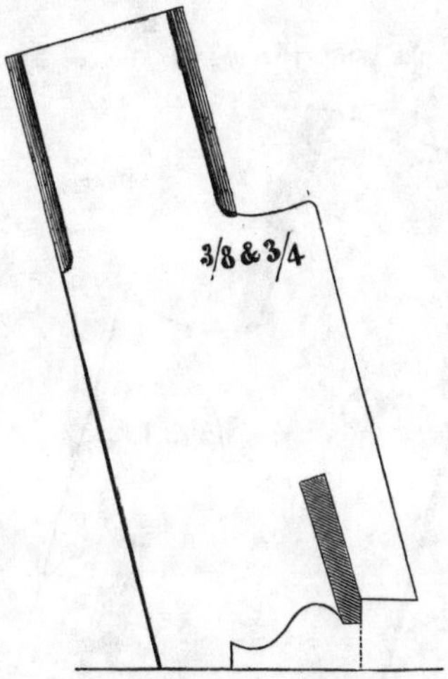

3/8 & 3/4

No. 262.
GRECIAN O. GEES.

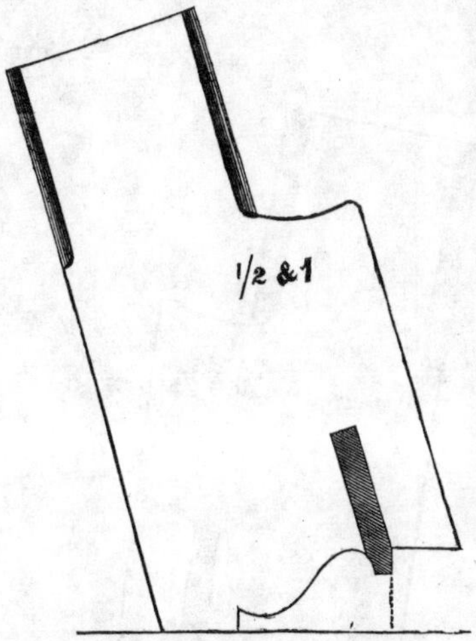

1/2 & 1

No. 263.
GRECIAN O. GEES, from ⅜ to 1 inch deep and ¾ to 2 inches wide.

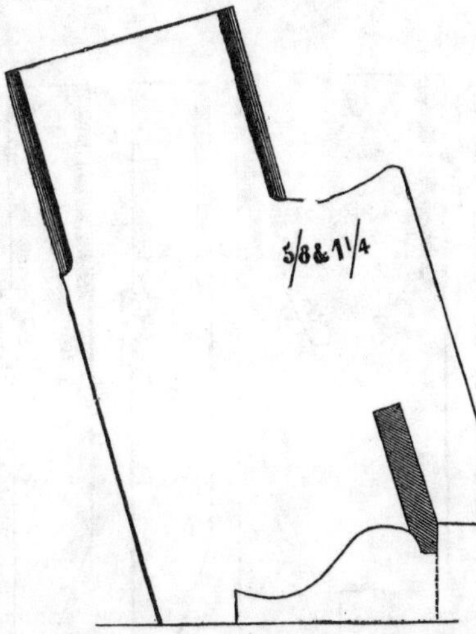

5/8 & 1 1/4

No. 264.

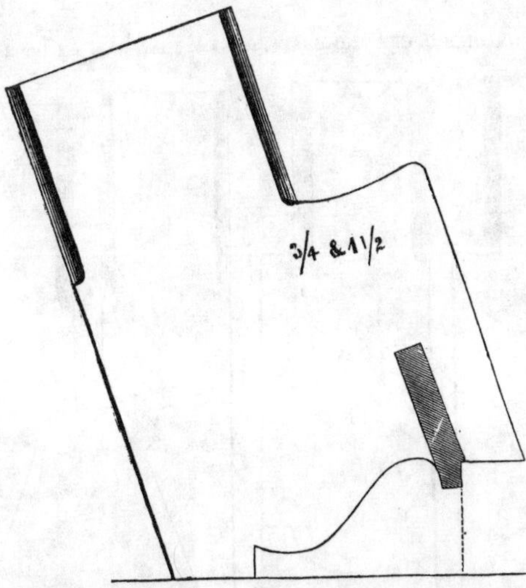

3/4 & 1 1/2

No. 265.
GRECIAN O. GEES, from ⅜ to 1 inch deep and ¾ to 2 inches wide.

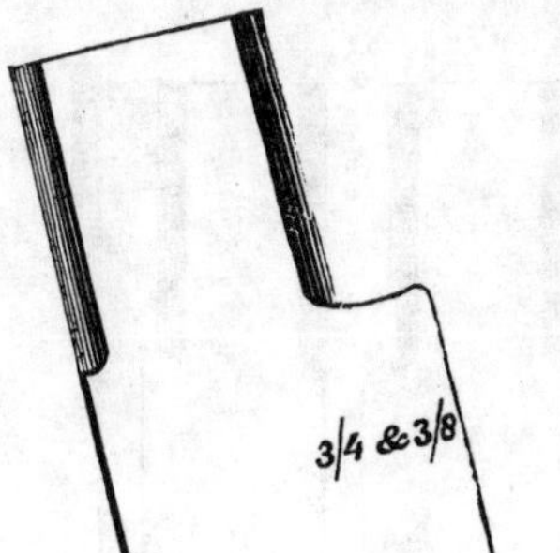

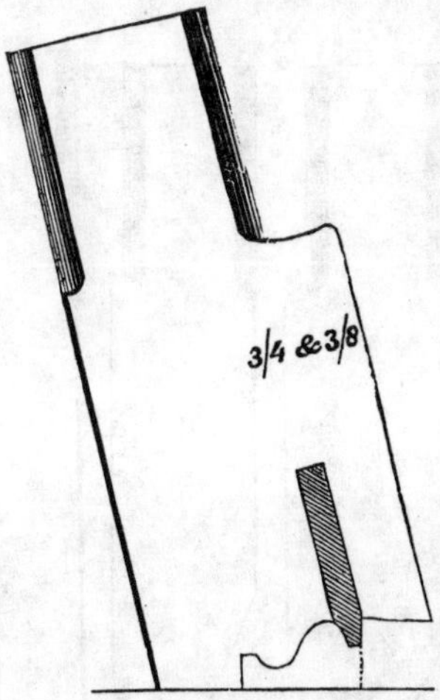

3/4 & 3/8

No. 268.

CARPENTERS'
BENCH PLANES AND MOULDING TOOLS.

(Continued.)

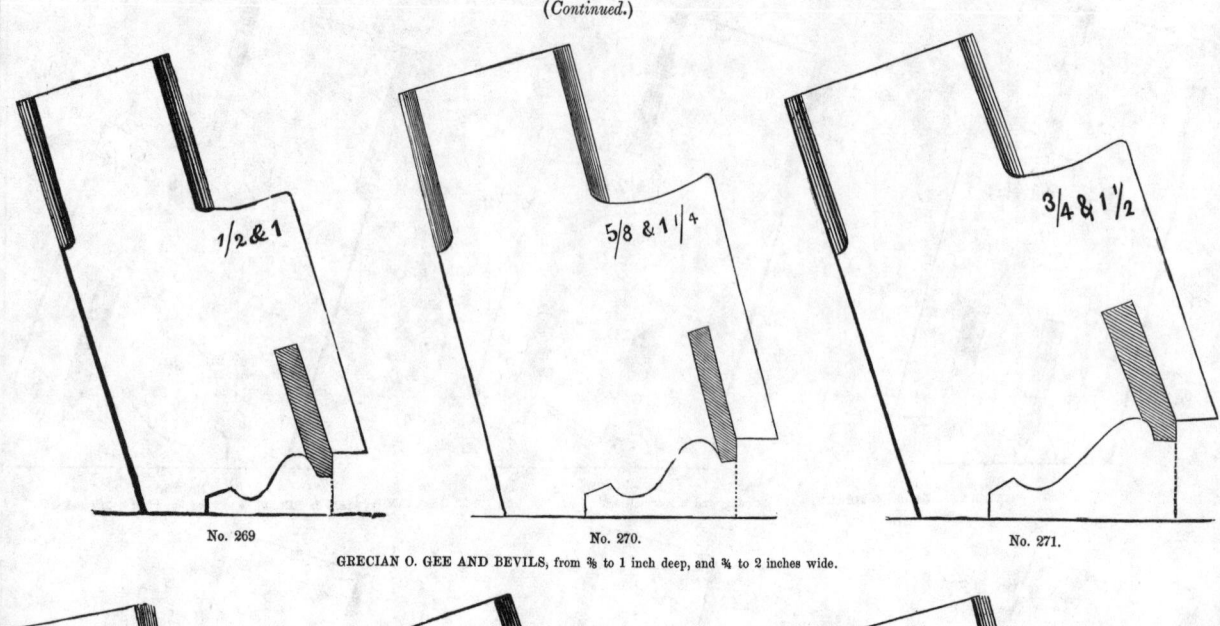

No. 269.   No. 270.   No. 271.

GRECIAN O. GEE AND BEVILS, from ⅜ to 1 inch deep, and ¾ to 2 inches wide.

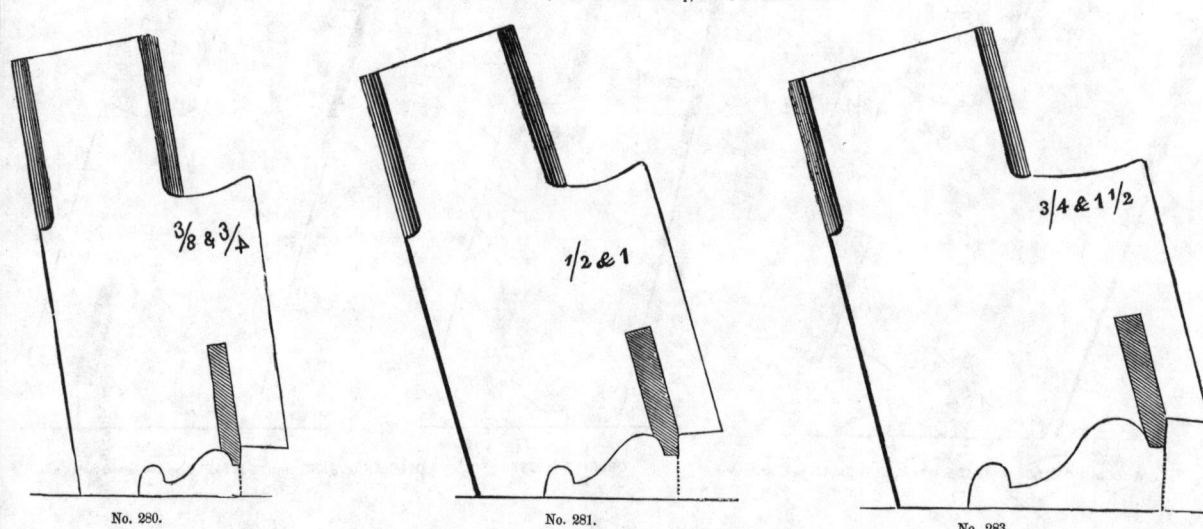

No. 280.   No. 281.   No. 283.

GRECIAN O. GEE AND BEADS, from ⅜ to ¾ inch deep, and 1 to 2 inches wide.

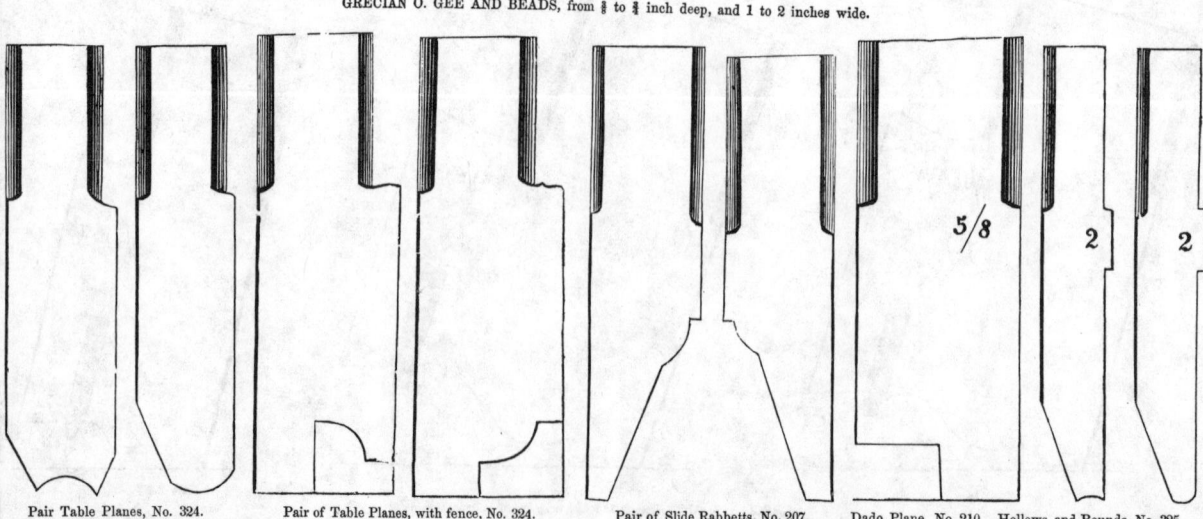

Pair Table Planes, No. 324.   Pair of Table Planes, with fence, No. 324.   Pair of Slide Rabbetts, No. 207.   Dado Plane, No. 210.   Hollows and Rounds, No. 325.

CARPENTERS'
BENCH PLANES AND MOULDING TOOLS.
(Continued.)

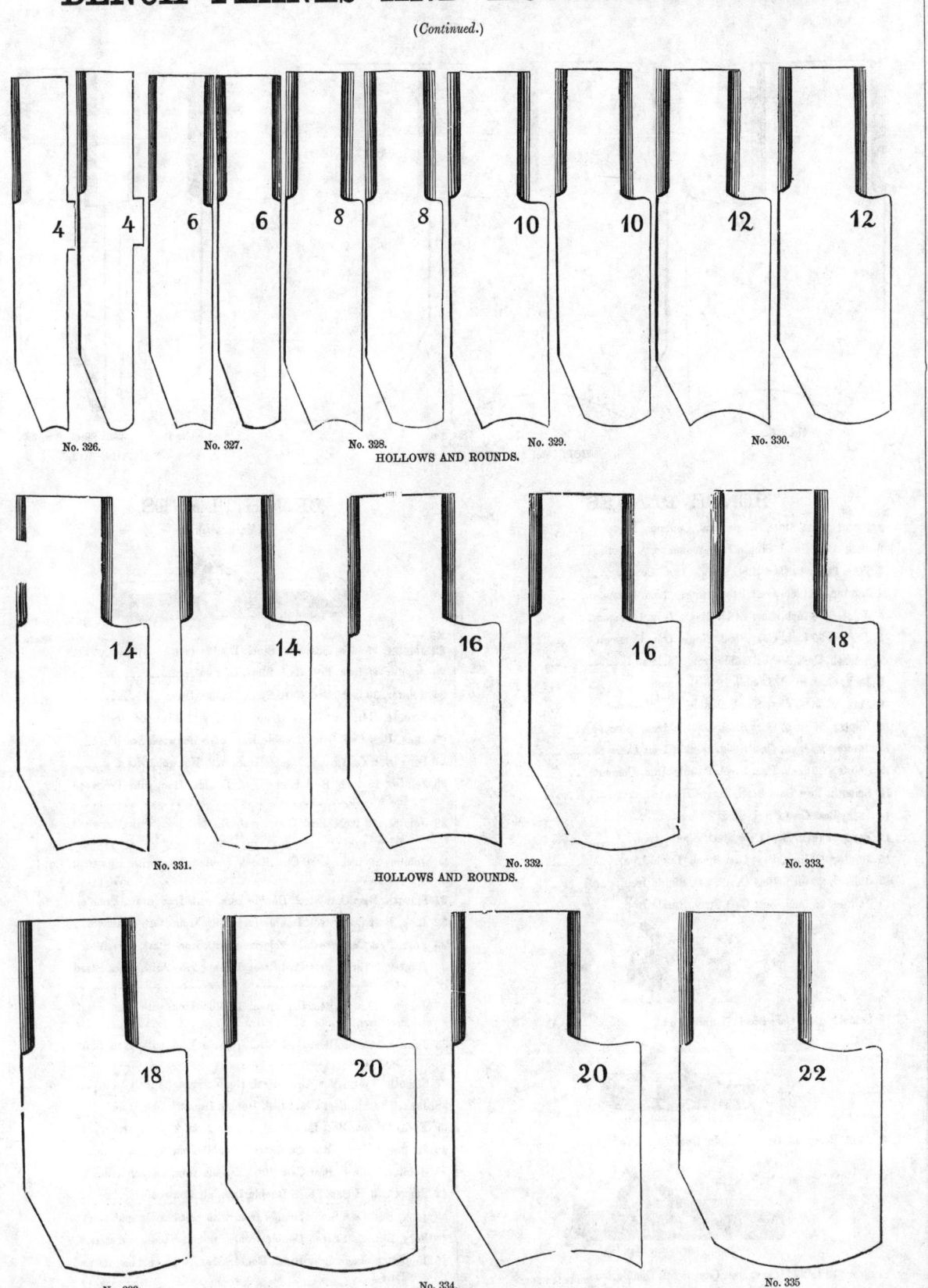

No. 326. No. 327. No. 328. No. 329. No. 330.

HOLLOWS AND ROUNDS.

No. 331. No. 332. No. 333.

HOLLOWS AND ROUNDS.

No. 333. No. 334. No. 335

HOLLOWS AND ROUNDS.

CARPENTERS'
BENCH PLANES AND MOULDING TOOLS.

(Continued.)

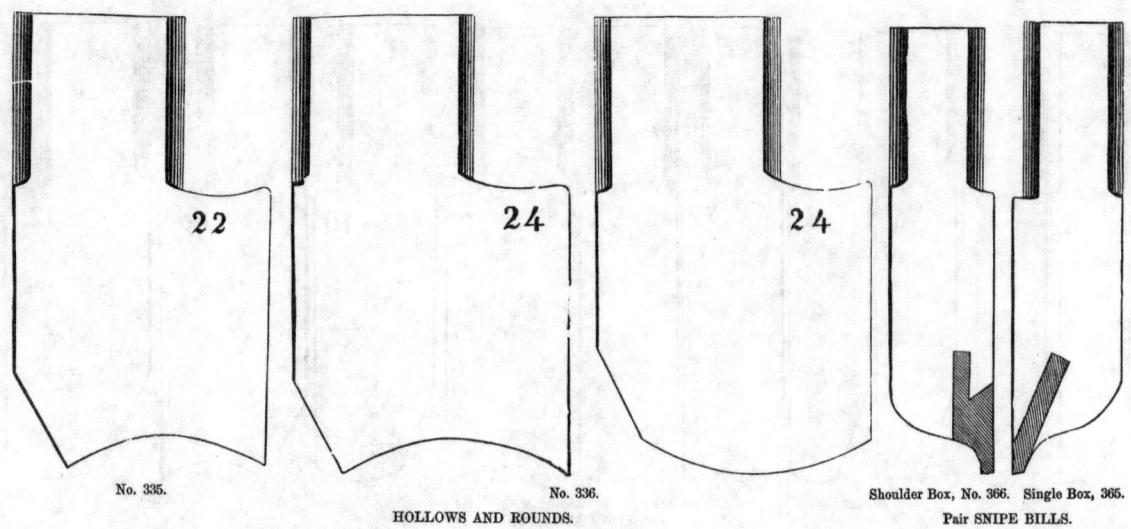

No. 335.

No. 336.

HOLLOWS AND ROUNDS.

Shoulder Box, No. 366.   Single Box, 365.

Pair SNIPE BILLS.

BENCH PLANES.

No.		Each.
1	Smooth, Cast Steel, Single Iron, Common,	$
2	Jack, Cast Steel, Single Iron, Common,	
3	Fore, 22 inch, Cast Steel, Single Iron, Common,	
4	Jointer, 26 inch, Cast Steel, Single Iron, Common,	
5	Jointer, 28 inch, Cast Steel, Single Iron, Common,	
6	Jointer, 30 inch, Cast Steel, Single Iron, Common,	
7	Smooth, Cast Steel, Double Iron, Common,	
8	Jack, Cast Steel, Double Iron, Common,	
9	Fore, 22 inch, Cast Steel, Double Iron, Common,	
10	Jointer, 26 inch, Cast Steel, Double Iron, Common,	
11	Jointer, 28 inch, Cast Steel, Double Iron, Common,	
12	Jointer, 30 inch, Cast Steel, Double Iron, Common,	
13	Smooth, Best Cast Steel, Single Iron,	
14	Jack, Best Cast Steel, Single Iron,	
15	Fore, 22 inch, Best Cast Steel, Single Iron,	
16	Jointer, 26 inch, Best Cast Steel, Single Iron,	
17	Jointer, 28 inch, Best Cast Steel, Single Iron,	
18	Jointer, 30 inch, Best Cast Steel, Single Iron,	

No. 19, Double Smooth Plane.

19	Smooth, Best Cast Steel, Double Iron,	$

No. 20,   Double Jack Plane.

20	Jack, Best Cast Steel, Double Iron,	$

No. 21,   Double Fore Plane.

21	Fore, 18 to 22 inches, Best Cast Steel, Double Iron,	$

BENCH PLANES.

(Continued.)

No. 22.   Double Jointer.

No.		Each.
22	Jointer, 26 inch, Best Cast Steel, Double Iron,	$
23	Jointer, 28 inch, Best Cast Steel, Double Iron,	
24	Jointer, 30 inch, Best Cast Steel, Double Iron,	
25	Smooth, Best Cast Steel, Double Iron, with Boxwood Start,	
26	Jack, Best Cast Steel, Double Iron, with Boxwood Start,	
27	Fore, Best Cast Steel, Double Iron, with Boxwood Start,	
28	Jointer, 26 inch, Best Cast Steel, Double Iron, with Boxwood Start,	
29	Jointer, 28 inch, Best Cast Steel, Double Iron, with Boxwood Start,	
30	Jointer, 30 inch, Best Cast Steel, Double Iron, with Boxwood Start,	
31	Smooth, Best Cast Steel, Double Iron, with Iron Start, Prem'm,	
32	Jack, Best Cast Steel, Double Iron, with Iron Start, Premium,	
33	Fore, Best Cast Steel, Double Iron, with Iron Start, Premium,	
34	Jointer, 26 inch, Best Cast Steel, Double Iron, with Iron Start, Premium,	
35	Jointer, 28 inch, Best Cast Steel, Double Iron, with Iron Start, Premium,	
36	Jointer, 30 inch, Best Cast Steel, Double Iron, with Iron Start, Premium,	
37	Smooth, 9 inch, Best Cast Steel, Double Iron, $2\frac{1}{2}$ inch Iron,	
38	Jack, 18 inch, Best Cast Steel, Double Iron, $2\frac{1}{2}$ inch Iron,	
39	Fore, 20 inch, Best Cast Steel, Double Iron, $2\frac{1}{2}$ inch Iron,	
40	Jointer, 24 inch, Best Cast Steel, Double Iron, $2\frac{1}{2}$ inch Iron,	
41	Jointer, 32 inch, Best Cast Steel, Double Iron, $2\frac{1}{2}$ inch Iron,	
42	Smooth, Best Cast Steel, Double Iron, all Boxwood,	
43	Jack, Best Cast Steel, Double Iron, with bolt handle and start,	
44	Fore, Best Cast Steel, Double Iron, with bolt handle and start,	
45	Jointer, 26 inch, Cast Steel, Double Iron, with bolt handle and Start,	

CARPENTERS'
BENCH PLANES AND MOULDING TOOLS.

(Continued.)

BENCH PLANES.

(Continued.)

No.   Each.

46 Jointer, 28 inch, Cast Steel, Double Iron, with bolt handle and
   start, ... $

47 Jointer, 30 inch, Cast Steel, Double Iron, with bolt handle and
   start, ...

No. 48. Solid Handle Smooth.

48 Smooth, Solid Handle, Best Cast Steel, Double Iron, ...

No. 49. Double Jack, Recess Handle.

49 Jack, Recess Handle, Best Cast Steel, Double Iron, ...

No. 50. Double Fore Plane, Recess Handle.

50 Fore, Recess Handle, Best Cast Steel, Double Iron, ...

51 Jointer, 26 inch, Recess Handle, Best Cast Steel, Double Iron..

No. 52. Boys' Smooth.   No. 53. Boys' Jack.

52 Smooth, Single Iron, for Boys, ...

53 Jack, Single Iron, for Boys, ...

54 Fore, Single Iron, for Boys, ...

55 Smooth, Best Cast Steel, Double Iron, for Boys, ...

56 Jack, Best Cast Steel, Double Iron, for Boys, ...

57 Fore, Best Cast Steel, Double Iron, for Boys, ...

58 Smooth, all Boxwood, Cast Steel, Double Iron, for Boys, ...

59 Smooth, all Boxwood, Cast Steel, Double Iron, for Boys, ...

60 Smooth, Best Cast Steel, Double Iron, for Ship Carpenters, 9 in.,

61 Jack, Best Cast Steel, Dbl. Iron, Recess, for Ship Carpenters, 16 in..

62 Fore, Best Cast Steel, Dbl. Iron, Recess, for Ship Carpenters, 22 in..

63 Jointer, Best Cast Steel, Double Iron, Recess, for Ship Carpenters,
   24 inch, ...

64 Smooth, Upright Iron, Double Cast Steel, for Cabinet Makers,.

65 Jack, Upright Iron, Double Cast Steel, for Cabinet Makers, ...

66 Fore, 20 inch, Upright Iron, Double Cast Steel, for Cabinet
   Makers, ...

67 Jointer, 24 inch, Upright Iron, Double Cast Steel, for Cabinet
   Makers, ...

68 Jointer, 26 inch, Upright Iron, Double Cast Steel, for Cabinet
   Makers, ...

69 Coopers' Jointer, 5 feet long, Single Iron, ...

70 Coopers' Jointer, 5½ feet long, Single Iron, ...

71 Coopers' Jointer, 5 feet long, Double Iron, ...

72 Coopers' Jointer, 5½ feet long, Double Iron, ...

Bench Planes, in iron bound cases, for shipping, consisting of

73 10 each, Double Iron Smooth, Jack and Fore Planes, ...

74 10 each, Single Iron Smooth, Jack and Fore Planes, ...

Bull Planes, ...

BENCH PLANES.

(Continued.)

Premium Planes.

		Each.
Single Smooths, ...	$	
Single Jacks, ...		
Single Fores, ...		
Single Jointers, ...		
Double Smooths, ...		
Double Jacks, ...		
Double Fores, ...		
Double Jointers, ...		

Premium Polished Planes.

Single Smooths, ...

Single Jacks, ...

Single Fores, ...

Single Jointers, ...

Double Smooths, ...

Double Jacks, ...

Double Fores, ...

Double Jointers, ...

Miscellaneous Planes.

No.

75 Compass Plane, Best Cast Steel, Single Iron, ...

76 Compass Plane, Best Cast Steel, Double Iron, ...

MISCELLANEOUS PLANES.

No. 77. Gutter Plane.

77 Gutter Plane ....$

78 Hand Rail Plane, Single Iron ....

No. 79. Hand Rail Plane.

79 Hand Rail Plane, Double Iron ....$

80 Hand Rail Plane, Right and Left, per pair, Short ....

81 Hand Rail Plain, Right and Left, per pair, Handled ....

No. 82. Miter Plane, Square.   No. 83. Miter Plane, Oval Shape.

82 Miter Planes, Single ....$

83 Miter Planes, Single, Smooth Shape ....

84 Block Miter Planes, 2½ inch Iron ....

85 Step Planes, with Handle, Single Iron ....

No. 86. Pump Plane.

86 Pump Planes, 1¼ inches ....

87 Pump Planes, 1½ inches ....

88 Tooth Planes ....

CARPENTERS'
BENCH PLANES AND MOULDING TOOLS.
(Continued.)

MISCELLANEOUS PLANES.
(Continued.)

No. 89. Leveling Plane.

No.		Each.
89	Leveling Planes....................................	$
90	Crows Stocks....................................	
91	Howell Plane and Stock....................................	

No. 92. Raising Jack.

92 **Raising Jack** or Panel Plane, Stop and Cut, 2¼ inches..........$

93 Raising Jack or Panel Plane, Stop and Cut, 2½ inches..........

94 Raising Jack or Panel Plane, Stop and Cut, 3 inches..........

95 Raising Jack or Panel Plane, Stop and Cut, 3½ inches..........

96 Raising Jack or Panel Plane, Stop and Cut, 4 inches..........

No. 97. One Pair Cornice Planes.

97 **Cornice Plane**, per pair, Ogee, 4 inches....................$

98 Cornice Plane, per pair, Ogee, 4½ inches....................

99 Cornice Plane, per pair, Ogee, 5 inches....................

100 Cornice Plane, per pair, Ogee, 5½ inches....................

101 **Cabinet Ogee Plane**, 2½ inches....................

102 Cabinet Ogee Plane, 2¾ inches....................

103 Cabinet Ogee Plane, 3 inches....................

104 Cabinet Ogee Plane, 3½ inches....................

105 Cabinet Ogee Plane, 4 inches....................

106 Cabinet Ogee Plane, 4½ inches....................

107 Cabinet Ogee Plane, 5 inches....................

Grooving Plows.

108 **Slide Arm**, Boxwood Stop, Single Plate, 8 Irons..............$

109 Slide Arm, Boxwood, Iron Foot Stop, Single Plate, 8 Irons....

110 Slide Arm, Boxwood, Screw Stop, Best Plate, 8 Irons....

111 Slide Arm, Boxwood, Screw Stop, Best Box Fence, 8 Irons....

No. 112. Ferruled Arm.

112 **Slide Arm**, Ferruled Screw Stop, Best Plate, 8 Irons..........$

113 Slide Arm, Ferruled Screw Stop, Best Plate, Box Fence, 8 Irons.

114 **Screw Arm**, Boxwood, Iron Foot Stop, Single Plate, 8 Irons...

115 Screw Arm, Boxwood Screw Stop, Single Plate, 8 Irons.......

116 Screw Arm, Boxwood Screw Stop, Single Plate, Plated, 8 Irons.

117 **Screw Boxwood Arm**, Screw Stop, Best Plate, Polished, 8 Irons.

MISCELLANEOUS PLANES.
(Continued.)

No. 118. Screw Arm.   No. 119. Boxwood Screw Arm.   No. 121. All Boxwood Screw Arm.

No.		Each.
118	**Screw Boxwood Arm**, Screw Stop, Best Plate, Polished, all Boxwood Fence, 8 Irons....................	$
119	Screw Boxwood Arm, Screw Stop, Best Plate, 8 Irons.........	
120	Screw Boxwood Arm, Screw Stop, Best Plate, Box Fence, 8 Irons....................	
121	**Screw Arm**, all Boxwood Screw Stop, Best Plate, 8 Irons......	
122	**Screw Arm**, all Rosewood, Screw Stop, Best Plate, 8 Irons.....	
123	Screw Arm, Rosewood Body, Boxwood Fence, Screw Stop, Best Plate, 8 Irons....................	
124	Screw Arm, Solid Handle, Screw Stop, Single Plate, 8 Irons...	
125	Screw Arm, Solid Handle, Screw Stop, Boxed Fence, Single Plate, 8 Irons....................	
126	Screw Arm, Solid Handle, Screw Stop, Boxwood Fence, Single Plate, 8 Irons....................	

No. 127. Solid Handle.   No. 129. All Boxwood Solid Handle, Screw Arm.

127 **Screw Boxwood Arm**, Solid Handle, Screw Stop, Best Plate, 8 Irons..................................$

128 Screw Boxwood Arm, Solid Handle, Screw Stop, Best Plate, Box Fence, 8 Irons....................

129 **Screw Arm**, all Boxwood, Solid Handle, Screw Stop, Best Plate, 8 Irons....................

130 Screw Arm, all Rosewood, Solid Handle Screw Stop, Best Plate, 8 irons....................

131 **Excelsior Plow**, all Box or Rosewood, Polished, 8 Irons.......

Match Planes.

132 **Board Match**....................⅜, ½, ⅝, ¾, ⅞, 1 inch, per pair

No. 133. Board Match, Faced.   No. 134. Solid Handle Match.

133 **Board Match**, Faced, per pair.........................$

134 Board Match, Solid Handles, per pair......................

135 Board Match, Solid Handles, Faced, per pair................

136 Board Match, Double, per pair............................

No. 137. Twin Match, Faced.   No. 139. Plank Match, Faced.

137 **Board Match**, Double Faced, per pair ....$

138 **Plank Match**, from 1¼ to 1½ inch, per pair..................

139 Plank Match, from 1¼ to 1½ inch, Faced, per pair.............

CARPENTERS'
BENCH PLANES AND MOULDING TOOLS.
(Continued.)

MISCELLANEOUS PLANES.
(Continued)

No.
140 Moving Match ....per pair, $
141 Moving Match, Wedge Arm....................per pair,
142 Moving Match, Wedge Arm, Ferruled...............per pair,
143 Moving Match, Screw Arm....................per pair,
144 Moving Match, Box Screw Arm..................per pair,
Extra for Full Box.........................
Extra for Plating.........................

Filletsters.

145 Filletster, Brass Side Stop and Moving Fence...............

No. 146. Filletsters, Side Stop and Cutter.   No. 149. Screw Stop.

No.   Each.
146 Filletster, Brass Side Stop and Moving Fence, and Cutter.... $
147 Filletster, Brass Side Stop and Moving Fence, Single Box....
148 Filletster, Brass Side Stop and Moving Fence, Shoulder Box..
149 Filletster, Screw Stop, Shoulder Box and Cutter............
150 Filletster, all Boxwood, Shoulder Box and Cutter...........
151 Filletster, with Screw Arms, Side Stop and Cutter..........
152 Filletster, with Screw Arms, Side Stop and Cutter, Single
      Boxed.....................................
153 Filletster, with Screw Arms, Side Stop and Cutter, Shoulder Boxed
154 Filletster, with Screw Arms, Side Screw Stop, Shoulder Boxed
155 Filletster, with Screw Wedge Arms, Side Stop and Cutter...
156 Filletster, with Screw Ferruled Arms, Screw Stop and Cutter
157 Sash Filletster or Back Filletster, Wedge Arms, Wood Stop..
158 Sash Filletster, Stop, Ferruled Arms, Brass Stop............
159 Sash Filletster, Screw Arms, Wood Stop...................
160 Sash Filletster, Box Arms, Wood Stop, Brass Stop..........
161 Sash Filletster, Box Arms, Wood Stop, Box Corner.........
162 Sash Filletster, Box Arms, Wood Stop, Box Faced.........

SASH PLANES.

No.
163 Sash Plane, 1 Iron, Ovalo Pattern.....................$
164 Sash Plane, 1 Iron, Bevel Pattern.....................
165 Sash Plane, 1 Iron, Gothic Pattern.....................
166 Sash Plane, 2 Irons, Ovalo Pattern.....................
167 Sash Plane, 2 Irons, Bevel Pattern.....................
168 Sash Plane, 2 Irons, Gothic Pattern.....................
169 Sash Plane, 2 Irons, Ogee Pattern.....................
170 Sash Plane, 2 Irons, Nosing Pattern, Show Case............
171 Sash Plane, 2 Irons, Ovalo Pattern, Iron Fence.............

No. 172. Moving Sash, screw arm, full box.   No. 184. Moving Sash, diamond pad.

No.
172 Sash Plane, Double, Box Screw Arms, Ovalo Pattern,.......$
173 Sash Plane Double, Box Screw Arms, Gothic Pattern,.......
174 Sash Plane, Double, Box Screw Arms, Bevel Pattern,.......
175 Sash Plane, Double, Box Screw Arms, Ogee Pattern, ...
176 Sash Plane, Double, Box Screw Arms, Ovalo, Self-regulating,.
177 Sash Plane, Double, Box Screw Arms, Bevel, Self-regulating,.

SASH PLANES.
(Continued)

No.   Each.
178 Sash Plane, Double, Box Screw Arms, Gothic, Self-regulating,.$
179 Sash Plane, Double, Box Screw Arms, Ogee, Self-regulating,..
180 Sash Plane, Double, Box Screw Arms, Round Brass Pad, Iron
      Screw, Ovalo ....
181 Sash Plane, Double, Box Screw Arms, Round Brass Pad, Iron
      Screw, Bevel ....
182 Sash Plane, Double, Box Screw Arms, Round Brass Pad, Iron
      Screw, Gothic..........................
183 Sash Plane, Double, Box Screw Arms, Round Brass Pad, Iron
      Screw, Ogee..........................
184 Sash Plane, Double, Round Diamond Pad, Iron Screw, Self-
      regulating, Ovalo,..........................
185 Sash Plane, Double, Round Diamond Pad, Iron Screw, Self-
      regulating, Bevel,..........................
186 Sash Plane, Double, Round Diamond Pad, Iron Screw, Self-
      regulating, Gothic,..........................
187 Sash Plane, Double, Round Diamond Pad, Iron Screw, Self-
      regulating, Ogee,..........................
Extra for Single Box in Sash, ...
Extra for Full Box in Sash,..........................
188 Sash Plane, Solid Handle, Single Iron,..................
189 Sash Plane, Double, Solid Handle, 2 Irons,................
190 Sash Plane, Double, Solid Handle, 2 Irons, Double Screw Arm,
191 Sash Plane, Double, Solid Handle, 2 Irons, Self-regulating,....
192 Sash Plane, Double, Solid Handle, 2 Irons, Diamond Pad,....
193 Sash Plane, Double, Solid Handle, 2 Irons, Full Box, ...
194 Sash Plane, Double, Solid Handle, 2 Irons, Screw Arm, Full
      Box,.....................................
195 Sash Plane, Double, Solid Handle, 2 Irons, Self-regulating,
      Full Box,..........................
196 Sash Plane, Double, Solid Handle, 2 Irons, Diamond Pad,
      Full Box,..........................
197 Sash, Coping Planes, single to suit planes,..................
198 Sash, Coping Planes, double to suit planes, ...
199 Bevel, Door Planes, Single,..........................
200 Bevel, Door Planes, Double, with Screw Arms, ...

RABBET PLANES.

No. 201. Rabbet Plane, Skew.   No. 201. Rabbet Plane, Square.

201 To 1 inch, inclusive, Skew or Square, ...$
202 To 1⅛ and 1¼ inch, ...
203 To 1⅜ and 1½ inch, ...
204 To 1⅝ and 1¾ inch, ...
205 To 1⅞ and 2 inch, ...
206 To 2⅛ and 2¼ inch, ...

Handled Rabbet Plane.

Extra for Single Boxed Corners,..........................$

CARPENTERS'
BENCH PLANES AND MOULDING TOOLS.
(Continued.)

RABBET PLANES.
(Continued.)

		Each.
Extra for Shoulder Boxed Corners,	....	$
Extra for Boxed, Faced to $1\frac{1}{2}$ inch,	....	
Extra for Boxed, above $1\frac{1}{2}$ to 2 inch,	....	
Extra for Handles,	....	
Extra for Cutters, each,	....	

No. 207. Pair Side Rabbets.

No.		
207	Side Rabbets, per pair,	....

DADO PLANES.

208	Boxwood Stop, and Side Screw, to 1 inch,	....
209	Boxwood Stop and Side Screw, $1\frac{1}{8}$ to $1\frac{1}{2}$ inch,	....

No. 210. Dado Plane, Screw Stop.

210	Screw Stop to 1 inch,	....
211	Screw Stop $1\frac{1}{8}$ to $1\frac{1}{2}$ inch,	....

MOULDING PLANES.

212	Astragals, $\frac{3}{8}$, $\frac{1}{2}$, $\frac{5}{8}$, $\frac{3}{4}$,	....
213	Astragals, $\frac{7}{8}$, 1,	....
214	Astragals, $1\frac{1}{4}$, $1\frac{1}{2}$,	....

BEADS.

No. 215. Bead.

215	Beads, Single Box, $\frac{1}{8}$, $\frac{3}{16}$, $\frac{1}{4}$, $\frac{5}{16}$,	....
216	Beads, Single Box, $\frac{3}{8}$, $\frac{1}{2}$,	....
217	Beads, Single Box, $\frac{5}{8}$, $\frac{3}{4}$,	....
218	Beads, Single Box, $\frac{7}{8}$,	....
219	Beads, Single Box, 1,	....
220	Beads, Single Box, $1\frac{1}{8}$, $1\frac{1}{4}$,	....
221	Beads, Single Box, $1\frac{1}{2}$, with Handle,	....
222	Beads, Double Box, $\frac{1}{4}$, $\frac{5}{16}$, $\frac{3}{8}$, $\frac{1}{2}$,	....
223	Beads, Double Box, $\frac{5}{8}$, $\frac{3}{4}$,	....
224	Beads, Double Box, $\frac{7}{8}$, 1,	....
225	Beads, Double Box, $1\frac{1}{4}$, $1\frac{1}{2}$,	....
226	Beads, Full Box, $\frac{1}{8}$, $\frac{3}{16}$, $\frac{1}{4}$, $\frac{5}{16}$,	....
227	Beads, Full Box, Dove-tailed, $\frac{3}{8}$, $\frac{1}{2}$,	....
228	Beads, Full Box, Dove-tailed, $\frac{5}{8}$, $\frac{3}{4}$,	....
229	Beads, Full Box, Dove-tailed, $\frac{7}{8}$, 1,	....
230	Beads, Full Box, Dove-tailed, $1\frac{1}{4}$,	....
231	Beads, Center, $\frac{1}{8}$, $\frac{3}{16}$, $\frac{1}{4}$, $\frac{5}{16}$, $\frac{3}{8}$, $\frac{1}{2}$,	....
232	Beads, Center, $\frac{5}{8}$, $\frac{3}{4}$,	....
233	Beads, Cock, $\frac{1}{8}$,	....
234	Beads. Cock, Boxed, $\frac{1}{8}$,	....

MOULDING PLANES.
(Continued.)

No.		Each.
235	Reeding Planes, $\frac{1}{8}$, $\frac{3}{16}$, $\frac{1}{4}$,	.... $
236	Reeding Planes, $\frac{5}{8}$, $\frac{1}{2}$, $\frac{3}{4}$,	....
237	Torus Beads, $\frac{1}{2}$, $\frac{5}{8}$, $\frac{3}{4}$, $\frac{7}{8}$, 1,	....

GRECIAN MOULDING PLANES.

238	Grecian Ovalo, to work, $\frac{3}{8}$ inch × $\frac{3}{4}$ inch,	....
239	Grecian Ovalo, to work, $\frac{1}{2}$ inch × 1 inch,	....
240	Grecian Ovalo, to work, $\frac{5}{8}$ inch × $1\frac{1}{4}$ inch,	....
241	Grecian Ovalo, to work, $\frac{3}{4}$ inch × $1\frac{1}{2}$ inch,	....
242	Grecian Ovalo, to work, $\frac{7}{8}$ inch × $1\frac{3}{4}$ inch,	....
243	Grecian Ovalo, to work, 1 inch × 2 inch,	....

No. 244. Grecian Ovalo and Square.

244	Grecian Ovalo and Fillet, (or Square,) $\frac{3}{8}$ inch × $\frac{3}{4}$ inch,	......
245	Grecian Ovalo and Fillet, (or Square,) $\frac{1}{2}$ inch × 1 inch,	......
246	Grecian Ovalo and Fillet, (or Square,) $\frac{5}{8}$ inch × $1\frac{1}{4}$ inch,	......
247	Grecian Ovalo and Fillet, (or Square,) $\frac{3}{4}$ inch × $1\frac{1}{2}$ inch,	......
248	Grecian Ovalo and Fillet, (or Square,) $\frac{7}{8}$ inch × $1\frac{3}{4}$ inch,	......
249	Grecian Ovalo and Fillet, (or Square,) 1 inch × 2 inch,	......
250	Grecian Ovalo and Astragal, $\frac{3}{8}$ inch × $\frac{3}{4}$ inch,	....
251	Grecian Ovalo and Astragal, $\frac{1}{2}$ inch × 1 inch,	....
252	Grecian Ovalo and Astragal, $\frac{5}{8}$ inch × $1\frac{1}{4}$ inch,	....
253	Grecian Ovalo and Astragal, $\frac{3}{4}$ inch × $1\frac{1}{2}$ inch,	....
254	Grecian Ovalo and Astragal, $\frac{7}{8}$ inch × $1\frac{3}{4}$ inch,	....
255	Grecian Ovalo and Astragal, 1 inch × 2 inch,	....

No. 256. Grecian Ovalo and Bead.   No. 262. Grecian Ogee.

256	Grecian Ovalo and Bead, $\frac{3}{8}$ inch × $\frac{3}{4}$ inch,	....
257	Grecian Ovalo and Bead, $\frac{1}{2}$ inch × 1 inch,	....
258	Grecian Ovalo and Bead, $\frac{5}{8}$ inch × $1\frac{1}{4}$ inch,	....
259	Grecian Ovalo and Bead, $\frac{3}{4}$ inch × $1\frac{1}{2}$ inch,	....
260	Grecian Ovalo and Bead, $\frac{7}{8}$ inch × $1\frac{3}{4}$ inch,	....
261	Grecian Ovalo and Bead, 1 inch × 2 inch,	....
262	Grecian Ogee, to work $\frac{3}{8}$ inch × $\frac{3}{4}$ inch,	....
263	Grecian Ogee, to work $\frac{1}{2}$ inch × 1 inch,	....
264	Grecian Ogee, to work $\frac{5}{8}$ inch × $1\frac{1}{4}$ inch,	....
265	Grecian Ogee, to work $\frac{3}{4}$ inch × $1\frac{1}{2}$ inch,	....
266	Grecian Ogee, to work $\frac{7}{8}$ inch × $1\frac{3}{4}$ inch,	....
267	Grecian Ogee, to work 1 inch × 2 inch,	....
268	Grecian Ogee and Bevel, $\frac{3}{8}$ inch × $\frac{3}{4}$ inch,	....
269	Grecian Ogee and Bevel, $\frac{1}{2}$ inch × 1 inch,	....
270	Grecian Ogee and Bevel, $\frac{5}{8}$ inch × $1\frac{1}{4}$ inch,	....
271	Grecian Ogee and Bevel, $\frac{3}{4}$ inch × $1\frac{1}{2}$ inch,	....
272	Grecian Ogee and Bevel, $\frac{7}{8}$ inch × $1\frac{3}{4}$ inch,	....
273	Grecian Ogee and Bevel, 1 inch × 2 inch,	....
274	Grecian Ogee and Astragal, $\frac{3}{8}$ inch × $\frac{3}{4}$ inch,	....

CARPENTERS'
BENCH PLANES AND MOULDING TOOLS.

(Continued.)

GRECIAN MOULDING PLANES.

(Continued.)

No.		Each.
275	Grecian Ogee and Astragal, ½ inch × 1 inch, ... $	
276	Grecian Ogee and Astragal, ⅝ inch × 1¼ inch, ...	
277	Grecian Ogee and Astragal, ¾ inch × 1½ inch, ...	
278	Grecian Ogee and Astragal, ⅞ inch × 1¾ inch, ...	
279	Grecian Ogee and Astragal, 1 inch × 2 inch, ...	
280	**Grecian Ogee and Bead,** ⅜ inch × ¾ inch, ...	
281	Grecian Ogee and Bead, ½ inch × 1 inch, ...	
282	Grecian Ogee and Bead, ⅝ inch × 1¼ inch, ...	
283	Grecian Ogee and Bead, ¾ inch × 1½ inch, ...	
284	Grecian Ogee and Bead, ⅞ inch × 1¾ inch, ...	
285	Grecian Ogee and Bead, 1 inch × 2 inch, ...	
286	**Grecian Ogee and Plain Ovalo,** ⅜ inch × ¾ inch, ...	
287	Grecian Ogee and Plain Ovalo, ½ inch × 1 inch, ...	
288	Grecian Ogee and Plain Ovalo, ⅝ inch × 1¼ inch, ...	
289	Grecian Ogee and Plain Ovalo, ¾ inch × 1½ inch, ...	
290	Grecian Ogee and Plain Ovalo, ⅞ inch × 1¾ inch, ...	
291	Grecian Ogee and Plain Ovalo, 1 inch × 2 inch, ...	
292	**Torus Cove and Bead,** ⅜ inch × ¾ inch, ...	
293	Torus Cove and Bead, ½ inch × 1 inch, ...	
294	Torus Cove and Bead, ⅝ inch × 1¼ inch, ...	
295	Torus Cove and Bead, ¾ inch × 1½ inch, ...	
296	Torus Cove and Bead, ⅞ inch × 1¾ inch, ...	
297	Torus Cove and Bead, 1 inch × 2 inch, ...	
298	**Reverse Ogee and Bead,** ⅜ inch × ¾ inch, ...	
299	Reverse Ogee and Bead, ½ inch × 1 inch, ...	
300	Reverse Ogee and Bead, ⅝ inch × 1¼ inch, ...	
301	Reverse Ogee and Bead, ¾ inch, × 1½ inch, ...	
302	Reverse Ogee and Bead, ⅞ inch × 1¾ inch, ...	
303	Reverse Ogee and Bead, 1 inch × 2 inch, ...	
304	**Reverse Ogee and Astragal,** ⅜ inch × ¾ inch, ...	
305	Reverse Ogee and Astragal, ½ inch × 1 inch, ...	
306	Reverse Ogee and Astragal, ⅝ inch × 1¼ inch, ...	
307	Reverse Ogee and Astragal, ¾ inch × 1½ inch, ...	
308	Reverse Ogee and Astragal, ⅞ inch × 1¾ inch, ...	
309	Reverse Ogee and Astragal, 1 inch × 2 inch, ...	

Base and all other Moulding Planes, with handles for distance working on, per inch, ...

MISCELLANEOUS.

No.		Each.
310	**Coves,** to ½ inch, ... $	
311	Coves, to 1 inch, ...	
312	**Coves and Bead,** to ½ inch, ...	
313	Coves and Bead, to ¾ inch, ...	
314	Coves and Bead, to 1 inch, ...	
315	**Scotias,** to ½ inch, ...	
316	Scotias, to ¾ inch, ...	
317	Scotias, to 1 inch, ...	

No. 318. Step Plane, Two Irons.

No.		Each.
318	**Step Nosings,** Double Iron, 1¼ inch .... $	
319	Step Nosings, Double Iron, 1½ inch	
320	**Halving Plane**	

MISCELLANEOUS PLANES.

(Continued.)

No.		Each.
321	Halving Plane, with Moving Fences and Stop .... $	
322	**Spar Planes,** Single Iron	
323	Spar Planes, Double Iron	
324	**Table Planes,** per pair	
	Table Planes, per pair, with Fence	
	Table Planes, per pair, Box Faced	
	Gauge Extra	

HOLLOWS AND ROUNDS.

(See Plates, pages 183 & 184.)

No.		Each.
325	**Hollows and Rounds,** 1 pair, No. 2, works ¼ inch circle .... $	
326	Hollows and Rounds, 1 pair, No. 4, works ½ inch circle	
327	Hollows and Rounds, 1 pair, No. 6, works ¾ inch circle	
328	Hollows and Rounds, 1 pair, No. 8, works 1 inch circle	
329	Hollows and Rounds, 1 pair, No. 10, works 1¼ inch circle	
330	Hollows and Rounds, 1 pair, No. 12, works 1½ inch circle	
331	Hollows and Rounds, 1 pair, No. 14, works 1¾ inch circle	
332	Hollows and Rounds, 1 pair, No. 16, works 2 inch circle	
333	Hollows and Rounds, 1 pair, No. 18, works 2¼ inch circle	
334	Hollows and Rounds, 1 pair, No. 20, works 2½ inch circle	
335	Hollows and Rounds, 1 pair, No. 22, works 3 inch circle	
336	Hollows and Rounds, 1 pair, No. 24, works 3½ inch circle	
337	Hollows and Rounds, even Nos., per set, 9 pair, No. 2 to 18...	

No. 338.   One Set Ten Pairs Hollows and Rounds.

No.		Each.
338	Hollows and Rounds, even Nos., per set, 10 pair, No. 2 to 20.. $	
339	Hollows and Rounds, even Nos., per set, 12 pair, No. 2 to 24..	
340	Hollows and Rounds, 1 pair, No. 1, to work ⅛ inch circle ...	
341	Hollows and Rounds, 1 pair, No. 3, to work ⅜ inch circle ...	
342	Hollows and Rounds, 1 pair, No. 5, to work ⅝ inch circle ...	
343	Hollows and Rounds, 1 pair, No. 7, to work ⅞ inch circle ...	
344	Hollows and Rounds, 1 pair, No. 9, to work, 1⅛ inch circle ...	
345	Hollows and Rounds, 1 pair No. 11, to work, 1⅜ inch circle ...	
346	Hollows and Rounds, 1 pair, No. 13, to work 1⅝ inch circle ...	
347	Hollows and Rounds, 1 pair, No. 15, to work 1⅞ inch circle ...	
348	Hollows and Rounds, 1 pair, No. 17, to work 2⅛ inch circle ...	
349	Hollows and Rounds, 1 pair, No. 19, to work 2⅜ inch circle ...	
350	Hollows and Rounds, 1 pair, No. 21, to work 2¾ inch circle ...	
351	Hollows and Rounds, 1 pair, No. 23, to work 3¼ inch circle ...	
352	Hollows and Rounds, per set, 18 pair, from 1 to 18, complete ..	
353	Hollows and Rounds, per set, 20 pair, from 1 to 20, complete..	
354	Hollows and Rounds, per set, 24 pair, from 1 to 24, complete..	
355	**Beads, Left Hand,** ¼ inch	
356	Beads, Left Hand, ⅜ inch	
357	Beads, Left Hand, ½ inch	
358	Beads, Left Hand, ⅝ inch	

CARPENTERS'
BENCH PLANES AND MOULDING TOOLS.

(Continued.)

HOLLOWS AND ROUNDS.

(Continued.)

No.		Each.
359	Beads, Left Hand, ¾ inch	$
360	Beads, Double, Right and Left, ¼ inch	
361	Beads, Double, Right and Left, ⅜ inch	
362	Beads, Double, Right and Left, ½ inch	
363	Beads, Double, Right and Left, ⅝ inch	
364	Beads, Double, Right and Left, ¾ inch	
365	Snipe Bills, Single Box, per pair	
366	Snipe Bills, Shoulder Box, per pair	

PLANE HANDLES.

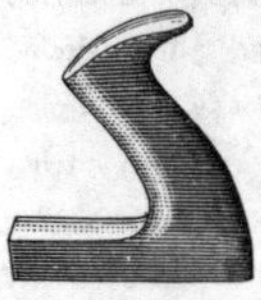

No. 367. Jack Plane Handle.    No. 368. Fore Plane Handle.

367	Jack Plane Handles,	per dozen, $
368	Fore Plane Handles,	"

BAILEY'S PATENT IRON PLANES.

	Each.
Smooth or Veneer Plane, 8 inches in length	$
Jack Plane, 14 inches in length	
Fore Plane, 18 inches in length	
Jointer Plane, 22 inches in length	

BLOCK OR MITRE PLANE.

Carriage Makers' Shoulder or Babbit Plane.....................$

BAILEY'S COMMON IRON PLANES.

Smooth Plane, 8 inches in length	$
Jack Plane, 14 inches in length	
Fore Plane, 18 inches in length	
Jointer Plane, 22 inches in length	
Veneer Scrapers	

These tools are all made of the very best material, and warranted the best in use.

PLANE IRONS.

MANUFACTURED FROM W. & S. BUTCHER'S SUPERIOR REFINED CAST STEEL.

Single.    Cut.    Double.

SINGLE CUT, CAST STEEL, PLANE IRONS.

Per dozen.

$ 1½   1⅝   1¾   1⅞   2   2⅛   2¼   2⅜   2½   2⅝   2¾   3 inches.

Assorted, from 2 to 2½ inches...Per dozen, $

DOUBLE, CAST STEEL, PLANE IRONS.

Per dozen.

$ 1½   1⅝   1¾   1⅞   2   2⅛   2¼   2⅜   2½   2⅝   2¾   3   3¼   3½   3¾   4 inches.

SINGLE, CAST STEEL, PLANE IRONS.

Assorted, from 2 to 2½ inches.. Per dozen, $

CAST STEEL RAISING PLANE IRONS.

Per dozen.

$ 2   2¼   2½   2¾   3   3¼   3½   3¾   4 inches.

CAST STEEL SOFT IRONS.

Per dozen.

$ 2   2⅛   2¼   2⅜   2½   2⅝   2¾   3   3¼   3½   3¾   4 inches.

CAST STEEL SINGLE COOPER'S JOINTER IRONS, 11 Inches Long.

Per dozen.

$ 2¾   3   3¼   3½   3¾   4   4¼   4½ inches.

PLANE IRONS.

(Continued.)

CAST STEEL HOWELLING IRONS.

				Per dozen.
$				
$1\frac{3}{4}$	2	$2\frac{1}{8}$	$2\frac{1}{4}$	$2\frac{1}{2}$ inches.

		Per dozen.
	$	
CAST STEEL TOOTH PLANE IRONS................................2		$2\frac{1}{8}$ inches.

CAST STEEL SOFT MOULDING IRONS.

																Per dozen.
$																
$\frac{1}{4}$	$\frac{3}{8}$	$\frac{1}{2}$	$\frac{5}{8}$	$\frac{3}{4}$	$\frac{7}{8}$	1	$1\frac{1}{8}$	$1\frac{1}{4}$	$1\frac{3}{8}$	$1\frac{1}{2}$	$1\frac{5}{8}$	$1\frac{3}{4}$	$1\frac{7}{8}$	2	$2\frac{1}{8}$	$2\frac{1}{4}$	$2\frac{3}{8}$	$2\frac{1}{2}$ inches.

CAST STEEL RABBET IRONS, SKEW OR SQUARE.

																Per dozen.
$																
$\frac{1}{2}$	$\frac{5}{8}$	$\frac{3}{4}$	$\frac{7}{8}$	1	$1\frac{1}{8}$	$1\frac{1}{4}$	$1\frac{3}{8}$	$1\frac{1}{2}$	$1\frac{5}{8}$	$1\frac{3}{4}$	$1\frac{7}{8}$	2	$2\frac{1}{8}$	$2\frac{1}{4}$	$2\frac{3}{8}$	$2\frac{1}{2}$	$2\frac{5}{8}$ inches.

CAST STEEL GROOVING IRONS, FOR BOARD MATCH.

					Per dozen.
$					
$\frac{3}{8}$	$\frac{1}{2}$	$\frac{5}{8}$	$\frac{3}{4}$	$\frac{7}{8}$	1 inch.

CAST STEEL GROOVING IRONS, FOR PLANK MATCH.

			Per dozen.
$			
$1\frac{3}{4}$	$1\frac{7}{8}$	2 inches.	

CAST STEEL GROOVING PLOW BITTS.

Cast Steel Grooving Plow Bitts, per set...$

CAST STEEL MATCH PLOW BITTS.

				Per dozen.
$				
$\frac{1}{8}$	$\frac{3}{16}$	$\frac{1}{4}$	$\frac{5}{16}$	$\frac{3}{8}$ inch.

	Per dozen.
	$
CAST STEEL FILLETSTER IRONS................................$1\frac{1}{2}$ inch.	

CAST STEEL DADO IRONS.

								Per dozen.
$								
$\frac{3}{16}$	$\frac{1}{4}$	$\frac{5}{16}$	$\frac{3}{8}$	$\frac{1}{2}$	$\frac{5}{8}$	$\frac{3}{4}$	$\frac{7}{8}$	1 inch.

CAST STEEL DADO CUTTERS.

								Per dozen.
$								
$\frac{3}{16}$	$\frac{1}{4}$	$\frac{5}{16}$	$\frac{3}{8}$	$\frac{1}{2}$	$\frac{5}{8}$	$\frac{3}{4}$	$\frac{7}{8}$	1 inch.

FILLETSTER CUTTERS.

Filletster Cutters...per dozen, $

RABBET PLANE CUTTERS.

Rabbet Plane Cutters..per dozen, $

Machine Stave Cutting Knives..from $ to $
Machine Coopers' Heading Knives...................................from $ to $
Machine Shingle Cutting Knives......................................from $ to $

Stave Jointing Knives...from $ to $

Planing Machine Knives...$
Wood Planing Machine Knives..per inch, $

TOOL CHESTS.

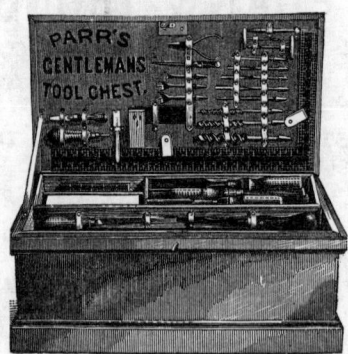

Gentleman's Tool Chest.

MECHANICS' TOOL CHEST.

No. 161, B.   Size, 3 feet 3 inches long, 1 foot 8 inches wide, and 1 foot 7½ inches high.

These Chests are made from the best Cherry and Ash; exterior French Polish, with Brass Trimmings, end Lifting Handles, with Partitions and Drawers to contain each article. The tools are of the best quality, and are sharpened for immediate use. Designed for Mechanics, Amateurs, Planters and Farmers.

LIST OF ARTICLES.

1 Plumb and Spirit Level.
1 40-foot Tape Line.
1 Mason's Trowel.
1 Portable Vice, which can be combined into Monkey Wrench.
1 Double Iron Smooth Plane.
1 Double Iron Jack Plane.
1 Double Iron Jointer Plane.
1 26 inch Cross Cut Saw.
1 26 inch Rip Saw.
1 10 inch Back Saw.
1 Paper 6 ounce Tacks.
1 Paper 8 ounce Tacks.
1 Paper 10 ounce Tacks.
1 Paper 12 ounce Tacks.
1 Paper ⅝ inch Patent Brads.
1 Paper ¾ inch Patent Brads.
1 Paper ⅞ inch Patent Brads.
1 Paper 1 inch Patent Brads.
1 8 inch Keyhole Saw, with handle complete
1 pair 8 inch Carpenters' Nippers.
1 Pocket Tool Chest, with 16 Tools.
1 Pair 4½ inch Flat Nose Plyers.
1 Pair 5 inch Cutting Nippers.
1 Pair 8 inch Compasses.
1 Claw Hammer.
1 C. S. Riveting Hammer.
1 No. 3 Broad Hatchet.
1 Hand Vice.
1 Hammer Saw Set.
1 14 inch Web Saw, or Turning, with Frame, complete.
1 Small Iron Furnace for heating Soldering Iron, to be used with Charcoal.
1 Copper Solder Iron, handled.
1 Stick of Solder.
1 Lot of Resin.
1 Glue Pot to heat and melt glue in above furnace.
1 Glue Brush.
1 Lot of Glue.
1 Small Anvil, weight 15 pounds.
1 Dozen 1½ inch 12 g. p. Screws.
1 Dozen 1¼ inch 10 g. p. Screws.
1 Dozen 1 inch 11 g. p. Screws.
1 Dozen ¾ inch 8 g. p. Screws.
1 Dozen ⅝ inch 4 g. p. Screws.

¼ pound Small Iron Rivets, assorted.
1 10 inch Flat b. File, handled.
1 10 inch ½rd, Cabinet Makers' Rasp.
4 Brad Awls, handled.
1 12 inch C. S. Drawing Knife.
1 Set (6) C. S. Socket Firmer Chisels.
1 Pound 4d Cut Nails.
1 Pound 6d Cut Nails.
1 Pound 8d Cut Nails.
1 Pound 10d Cut Nails.
1 Set C. S. Gouges, each ⅝ and ¾ inches.
1 Set Augurs, ¾, 1, 1¼ and 1¾ inches.
2 Gimlets.
1 Cast Steel Square.
1 Mahogany Stock Try Square.
1 Imp. Augur Handle.
1 Dozen Brace Bits, assorted.
1 Set Spur Augur Bits, each ⅜, 9-16 and ⅞ inches.
1 Ball Brace.
1 2 inch Screw Driver.
1 6 inch Screw Driver.
1 2 foot Rule.
1 Chalk Line Reel, with Awl.
1 Lead Pencil.
1 Marking Gauge.
1 Nail Set.
1 Prick Punch.
1 Round Punch.
1 Oil Stone, in covered box.
1 Oil Can.
1 Square Lignumvitæ Mallet.
1 Mill Saw File, handled.
1 Taper Saw File, handled.
1 Scratch Awl, handled.
1 Extra Heavy Cold Chisel.
2 Pegging Awls, handled.
2 Sewing Awls, handled.
2 Saddlers' Awls, handled.
1 Colton's Patent Adjustable Cam-faced Spoke Shave.
1 Panel Plow, 4 Irons.
1 Pair Hollows and Rounds, No. 16.
1 Pair Hollows and Rounds, No. 4.
1 ⅜ inch Bead Plane.
1 Rabbet Plane, 1½ inch.
1 T Bevel.

Making in the aggregate 128 different Tools, besides the Chest; packed in cases, ready for Shipping. Weight 234 pounds.

Price each,................................$

PLANTERS' TOOL CHEST.

No. 161, A.   Size 2 feet 11 inches long, 1 foot 4 inches wide, and 11 inches high.   Finish and Shape same as the Mechanics' Chest.

LIST OF ARTICLES.

1 Double Iron Smooth Plane.
1 Double Iron Jack Plane.
1 Double Iron Jointer Plane.
1 26 inch Cross Cut Saw.
1 26 inch Rip Saw.
1 10 inch Back Saw.
1 Pair 8 inch Carpenters' Pincers.
1 Pair 4½ inch Flat Plyers.
1 Pair 8 inch Compasses.
1 Claw Hammer.
1 No. 3 Broad Hatchet.

1 12 inch C. S. Drawing Knife.
1 Set (of 6) C. S. Socket Firmer Chisels.
1 Set C. S. Gouges, each ⅝ and ¾ inch.
1 Set Augurs, each ¾, 1, 1¼, and 1¾ inch.
1 Imp. Auger Handle.
1 Ball Brace.
12 Brace Bits, assorted.
1 Set Spur Auger Bits, each ⅜, 9-16, and ⅞ inches.
2 Gimlets.
1 Spoke Shave.

PLANTERS' TOOL CHEST.

(Continued.)

1 Cast Steel Square.
1 Mahogany Stock Try Square.
1 Two Foot Rule.
1 Lead Pencil.
1 Chalk Line and Reel, with Awl.
1 Appletree Brad Set, 20 Tools and Wrench.
1 Marking Gauge.
1 2 inch Screw Driver.
1 6 inch Screw Driver.
1 Handled Scratch Awl.
1 Extra Heavy Cold Chisel.

1 Nail Set.
1 Prick Punch.
1 Round Punch.
1 Mill Saw File, handled.
1 Taper Saw File, handled.
1 Oil Stone, in box, with cover.
1 Oil Can.
1 Square Lignumvitæ Mallet
2 Sewing Awls, handled.
2 Saddlers' Awls, handled.
2 Pegging Awls, handled.

Making in the aggregate, 92 different Tools. Each chest packed in case ready for Shipping. Weight 110 pounds.

Price, each,...............................$

(See Plate.)

GENTLEMAN'S TOOL CHEST.

No. 161.   Size, 2 feet 4 inches long, 1 foot 2 inches wide, and 10½ inches high.   Finish and Shape same as Mechanics' Chest.

LIST OF ARTICLES.

1 Jack Plane, Double Iron.
1 Smooth Plane, Double Iron.
1 Mill Saw File, handled.
1 Pair 8 inch Carpenters' Nippers.
1 Claw Hammer.
1 Oil Can.
1 Chalk Line Reel, with Awl.
1 Rip Saw, 22 inch.
1 Cross Cut Saw, 20 inch.
2 Sewing Awls, handled.
2 Saddlers' Awls, handled.
2 Pegging Awls, handled.
1 Cold Chisel extra heavy.
1 Nail Set.
1 Prick Punch.
1 Round Punch.
1 Pair Compasses, 8 inch.
1 Try Square, 6 inch.
1 Ball Brace.
3 Spur Auger Bits, ⅜, 9-16, and ⅞ inch.

12 Brace Bits, assorted.
1 Pair Plyers, 4½ inch.
1 Wood Gauge.
1 C. S. Drawing Knife.
1 No. 1 Hatchet.
1 2 inch Screw Driver.
1 6 inch Screw Driver.
1 Taper Saw File, handled.
2 Gouges, ⅝ and ¾ inch.
4 Firmer Chisels, ¼, ½, 1, 1½ inch, handled.
1 Oil Stone, in box, with cover.
1 Two Foot Rule.
1 Lead Pencil.
1 Square Lignumvitæ Mallet.
1 Appletree Brad Awl Set, containing 20 Tools and Wrench.
2 Gimlets.
1 Two Foot Iron Square.
1 Scratch Awl, handled.

Making in the aggregate 80 different Tools, besides the Chest; packed in cases ready for shipping. Weight 65 pounds.

Price each,...............................$

YOUTHS' TOOL CHEST.

No. 162.   Size, 1 foot 10¼ inches long, 12¼ inches wide, and 9¾ inches deep.   Finish and Shape the same as Mechanics' Chest.

LIST OF ARTICLES.

1 Single Iron Jack Plane.
1 Single Iron Smooth Plane.
1 Cross Cut Hand Saw, 16 inches.
1 Ball Brace.
1 Chalk Line, with Spool.
1 Square Lignumvitæ Mallet.
1 Gauge.
1 Claw Hammer.
1 0 Hatchet.
1 6 inch Screw Driver.
1 Scratch Awl, handled.
1 Saw File, handled.
3 Firmer Chisels, ¼, ½, and 1 inch, handled.
1 Lead Pencil.
2 Pegging Awls, handled.
2 Sewing Awls, handled.
2 Saddlers' Awls, handled.
1 2 inch Screw Driver.

1 Appletree Brad Awl Set, containing 20 Tools and Wrench.
1 Two Foot Rule.
1 Try Square.
2 Gimlets.
1 Extra Heavy Cold Chisel.
1 Nail Set.
1 Pair Compasses 6 inch.
1 Prick Punch.
1 Round Punch.
1 Screw Driver Bit.
1 Screw Driver Bit, with Slot.
1 Reamer.
2 Spur Auger Bits, ⅝ and ¾ inch.
1 Lip Spoon Bit.
1 Centre Bit.
1 Oil Stone.

Making in the aggregate 62 Different tools, besides the Chest; packed in cases for shipping. Weight 45 pounds.

Price each,...............................$

TOOL CHESTS.

(Continued.)

BOYS' TOOL CHEST.

No. 163. Size, 1 foot 6¾ inches long, 9¼ inches wide, and 8¼ inches deep. Finish and shape the same as Mechanics' Chest.

LIST OF ARTICLES.

1 Jack Plane, 1¾ inch iron.	1 Oil Stone.
1 12 inch Hand Saw.	1 Foot Rule.
1 Claw Hammer.	1 Chalk Line and Reel.
1 Square Hickory Mallet.	1 Scratch Awl, handled.
1 Gauge.	1 Lead Pencil.
1 Pair Compasses.	2 Firmer Chisels, ¼ and ½ inch, handled.
2 Gimlets.	1 Cold Chisel.
1 Try Square.	1 Prick Punch.
1 2 inch Screw Driver.	1 Round Punch.
1 Appletree Brad Set, containing 20 Tools and Wrench.	2 Auger Bits, ¼ and ⅜ inch handled.

Making in the aggregate 44 different Tools, besides the Chest; packed in cases for shipping. Weight, 30 pounds.

Price each, ...$

No. 164. **Gentlemens' Tool Chests,** with Drawers and Partitions for Tools, in case.

Price each, ...$

No. 165. **Youths' Tool Chests,** with Drawers and Partitions for Tools, in case.

Price each, ...$

No. 166. **Boys' Tool Chests,** with Drawers and. Partitions for Tools, in case.

Price each, ...$

JUVENILE TOOL CHESTS.

No. 167. Neatly varnished; with Till, Brass Hinges, Lifting Handles and Lock. A beautiful colored engraving accompanies each chest.

LIST OF ARTICLES.

1 Hand Saw.	1 Gimlet.
1 Plane.	1 Hatchet.
1 Gouge.	1 ¼ inch Firmer Chisel, handled.
1 Try Square.	1 Mallet.
1 Pencil.	1 Brad Awl, handled.
1 12 inch Rule.	1 Chalk Line Reel and Awl.
1 Cold Chisel.	1 Scratch Awl.
1 1 inch Screw Driver.	

Price each, ...$

No. 168.

1 Hand Saw.	1 Gouge.
1 Hatchet.	1 Screw Driver.
1 Mallet.	1 Plane.
1 Gimlet.	1 Pencil.
1 Chisel.	1 Brad Awl, handled.

Price each, ...$

No. 169.

1 Hand Saw.	1 Mallet.
1 Chisel.	1 Gimlet.
1 Hammer.	1 Screw Driver.
1 Gouge.	1 Pencil.

Price each, ...$

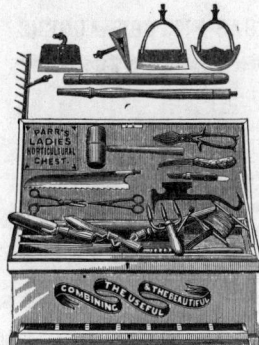

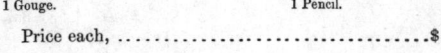
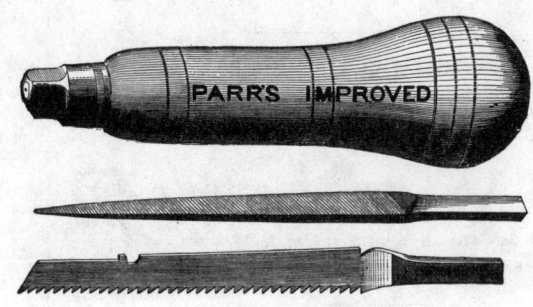

Pocket Tool Chest, No. 161, C.

The increased attention which is being paid to Horticulture by the ladies, and its attractions and benefits, have developed a need of a collected assortment of tools, in a portable receptacle. This Horticultural Tool Chest supplies the want. It is a neat and compact box, with handles, by which it can easily be carried. It contains all the approved gardening implements in ordinary use. Those tools requiring a long handle, such as Grafting Saw, Tree Scraper, Hoes, Rakes, etc., are all made to fit with screws into an improved Screw Jointed Handle; joined in lengths to fit the chest.

LADIES' HORTICULTURAL TOOL CHEST.

No. 161, G. Size, 2 feet 2 inches long, 11¾ inches wide, and 11 inches high. Made from the best Cherry and Ash. Exterior French Polish, with Brass Trimmings and Lifting Handles. Drawers with compartments for Seeds, Garden Gloves, etc.

LIST OF ARTICLES.

1 Shuffle Hoe.	1 Pair Flower Gatherers.
1 Tree Scraper.	1 Lignumvitæ Grafting Mallet.
1 Garden Rake.	1 Strawberry Fork or Flower Weeder.
1 Weeding Hoe.	1 Transplanting Trowel.
1 Pruning Saw.	1 Weeding Trowel.
1 Grass Edger.	1 Garden Line and Reel.
All to fit in one handle, which is jointed.	1 Pair Grass Shears.
1 Grafting Hammer.	1 Pruning Knife.
1 Grafting Chisel.	1 Budding Knife.
1 Pair Pruning Shears.	1 Garden Syringe.
1 Pair Vine Cutters.	

In all 21 Tools. Packed in case for shipping. Weight, 48 pounds.

Price each, ...$

LADIES' GARDEN TOOL CHEST.

No. 161, H. Size, 2 feet 1 inch long, 9¾ inches wide, and 7¾ inches high. With divisions for Seeds, etc. Material and finish same as large size.

LIST OF ARTICLES OF LADIES' GARDEN TOOL CHEST, No. 161, H.

1 Shuffle Hoe.	1 Lignumvitæ Grafting Mallet.
1 Tree Scraper.	1 Strawberry Fork or Flower Weeder.
1 Garden Rake.	1 Transplanting Trowel.
1 Weeding Hoe.	1 Weeding Trowel.
1 Pruning Saw.	1 Garden Line and Reel.
1 Grass Edger.	1 Pruning Knife.
All to fit in one handle, which is jointed.	1 Budding Knife.
1 Grafting Chisel.	1 Pair Pruning Shears.

In all 16 Tools. Packed in case for shipping. Weight, 27 pounds.

Price each ....$

CHILDRENS' SET OF GARDEN TOOLS.

No. 161, I. Consisting of

1 Handled Rake and Hoe, combined.
1 Handled Spade.
1 Handled Fork.

Weight, 3 pounds. Price each, ...$

POCKET TOOL CHEST.

No. 161, C. *(See Plate above.)*

The large cut represents the handle reduced, while the small cuts represent the actual size of the tools. The handle has a cap which unscrews, leaving a hollow space, in which the tools are kept when not in use; making altogether a very useful and complete set of tools, in a very small space.

CONTENTS.

1 Flat Bastard File.	1 Wide Firmer Chisel.
1 3-square Tapered Saw File.	1 Narrow Firmer Chisel.
1 Saw.	1 Scratch Awl.
4 Brad Awls, assorted sizes.	1 Square Reamer.
1 Countersink.	1 Screw Driver.
1 Gouge.	1 Auger Bit.
1 Belt Awl.	1 Wrench.

List Price, per doz., ...$

BORING IMPLEMENTS.

RUSSELL & ERWIN MANUFACTURING CO'S "EXCELSIOR" AUGERS AND BITS.

STEEL CUT AUGERS.

$ per doz.
1/2   5/8   3/4   7/8   1   1 1/8   1 1/4   1 1/2 inch.
$ per doz.
1 3/4   2   2 1/4   2 1/2   3   3 1/2   4 inch.

CAST STEEL CUT BLUED AUGERS.

$ per doz.
1/2   5/8   3/4   7/8   1   1 1/8   1 1/4   1 1/2 inch.
$ per doz.
1 3/4   2   2 1/4   2 1/2   3   3 1/2   4 inch.

SOLID CAST STEEL AUGERS.

$ per doz.
1/2   5/8   3/4   7/8   1   1 1/8   1 1/4 inch.
$ per doz.
1 1/2   1 3/4   2   2 1/4   2 1/2   2 3/4   3 inch.

MILLWRIGHTS' AUGERS.

Millwrights' Solid Cast Steel Augers,

$ per doz.
1/2   5/8   3/4   7/8   1   1 1/8   1 1/4   1 1/2   1 3/4   2 inch.

Assorted in Sets, 41 quarters, 1/2, 5/8, 3/4, 7/8, 1, 1 1/4, 1 1/2, 1 3/4, 2 inch,.... $ per set.
Assorted in Sets, 28 quarters, 1/2, 3/4, 1, 1 1/4, 1 1/2, 2 inch............

LONG BRIGHT AUGERS.

$ per doz.
1/2   5/8   3/4   7/8   1   1 1/8   1 1/4   1 1/2   1 3/4   2 inch.

SHORT BRIGHT AUGERS.

$ per doz.
1/2   5/8   3/4   7/8   1   1 1/8   1 1/4   1 1/2   1 3/4   2 inch.

BORING MACHINE AUGERS.

$ per doz.
1/2   5/8   3/4   7/8   1   1 1/8   1 1/4   1 3/4   2 inch.
In Sets of 18 quarters...................................per set, $

For Boring Machines see page 103.

EYE AUGERS.

Long, Bright Lip, Eye Augers.

$ per doz.
3/8   1/2   5/8   3/4   7/8   1   1 1/8 inch.
$ per doz.
1 1/4   1 3/8   1 1/2   1 5/8   1 3/4   1 7/8   2 inch.

EYE AUGERS—Continued.

Long, Black Lip, Eye Augers.

$ per doz.
3/8   1/2   5/8   3/4   7/8   1   1 1/8 inch.
$ per doz.
1 1/4   1 3/8   1 1/2   1 5/8   1 3/4   1 7/8   2 inch.

Short, Black Lip, Eye Augers.

$ per doz.
3/8   1/2   5/8   3/4   7/8   1   1 1/8 inch.
$ per doz.
1 1/4   1 3/8   1 1/2   1 5/8   1 3/4   1 7/8   2 inch.

CAST STEEL AUGERS.

Assorted, with Patent Handles, in Sets.

$ per set.
1/2   5/8   3/4   7/8   1   1 1/4   1 1/2   1 3/4   2=41 qrs. $
1/2   3/4   1 1/4   1 1/2   2 = 28 qrs. $

SUPERIOR GAS FITTERS' AUGERS.

$ per doz.
1/2   5/8   3/4   7/8   1   1 1/8   1 1/4   1 1/2   1 3/4   2 inch.

CAST STEEL AUGER BITS.

$ per doz.
3   4   5   6   7   8   9   10
$ per doz.
11   12   13   14   15   16   18   20-16ths inch.
In Sets, assorted, 24 quarters...........................per set, $
In Sets, assorted 32 1/2   "   .... "

COOPERS' DOWELLING BITS.

4, 5, 6, 7, 8-16ths, and assorted.....................per dozen, $

IMPROVED HANDLED AUGER BITS.

In dozens, assorted, 2 each, 3, 4, 5, 6, 7, 8-16ths in. Com....per doz. $
In dozens, asst'd, 2 each, 3, 4, 5, 6, 7, 8-16ths in. Cocoa Head, Bright... "

PATENT EXPANSIVE BITS.

Small, With two Cutters, one boring from 1/2 to 7/8 inch, and the other from 7/8 to 1 1/2 inch.........................per doz. $
Large, with two Cutters, one boring from 7/8 to 1 1/2 inch, and the other from 1 1/2 to 3 inches......................... "
Boring Machine, with two Cutters, one boring from 7/8 to 1 1/2 inch, and the other from 1 1/2 to 3 inches................ "

BORING IMPLEMENTS.

(Continued.)

ADJUSTABLE HOLLOW AUGER.
(Stearns' Patent.)

Th s Auger will tenon the following sizes, viz.:

| $\frac{1}{2}$ | $\frac{5}{8}$ | $\frac{3}{4}$ | $\frac{7}{8}$ and 1 inch. |

The advantages of this implement over others consists in its simplicity and easy adjustment. The size of cut is varied by changing the dies and position of the knife, which can be adjusted to cut either light or heavy, to accommodate the size of each bit. The Shank is movable. By changing its position it acts as a gauge and determines the length of the tenon, and at the same time makes a perfect shoulder.

Each, $

SCREW CAP, OR NEW PATTERN HOLLOW AUGERS.

All sizes, with bits complete.

$

| $\frac{3}{8}$ | $\frac{1}{2}$ | $\frac{5}{8}$ | $\frac{3}{4}$ | $\frac{7}{8}$ | 1 | $1\frac{1}{8}$ | $1\frac{1}{4}$ | $1\frac{3}{8}$ | $1\frac{1}{2}$ | per doz. inch. |

SLIDE CUT, OR OLD PATTERN HOLLOW AUGERS.

All sizes, with bits complete.

$

| $\frac{3}{8}$ | $\frac{1}{2}$ | $\frac{5}{8}$ | $\frac{3}{4}$ | $\frac{7}{8}$ | 1 | $1\frac{1}{8}$ | $1\frac{1}{4}$ | $1\frac{3}{8}$ | $1\frac{1}{2}$ | per doz. inch. |

CURRIERS' HOLLOW AUGERS.

All sizes without bits.

| $\frac{3}{8}$ | $\frac{1}{2}$ | $\frac{5}{8}$ | $\frac{3}{4}$ | $\frac{7}{8}$ | inch. |

| 1 | $1\frac{1}{8}$ | $1\frac{1}{4}$ | $1\frac{3}{8}$ | $1\frac{1}{2}$ | inch. | $ | per quarter. |

SNELL'S AUGERS.

Snell's Long Cast Steel Millwright Augers..........per quarter, $

Snell's Long Cast Steel Rafting Augers, with Sockets   "

Snell's Carpenters' Augers, Solid Cast Steel.........   "

Snell's Carpenters' Augers, Polished, Cast Steel Cut..   "

Snell's Carpenters' Augers, Blued, Cast Steel Cut....   "

SNELL'S AUGER BITS.

Snell's "C. S." Auger Bits.

$

| 3 | 4 | 5 | 6 | 7 | 8 | 9 | 10 | 11-16ths. |

SNELL'S AUGER BITS.

(*Continued.*)

Snell's "C. S." Auger Bits.

$

| 12 | 13 | 14 | 15 | 16 | 18 | 20 | 22 | 24-16ths. | per doz. |

Snell's "C. S." Car Bits, 9 inch Twist.

$

| 4 | 5 | 6 | 7 | 8 | 9 | 10-16ths. | per dozen. |

$

| 11 | 12 | 13 | 14 | 15 | 16-16ths. | per doz. |

Snell's "C. S." Car Bits, 12 inch Twist.

$

| 4 | 5 | 6 | 7 | 8 | 9 | 10-16ths. | per doz. |

$

| 11 | 12 | 13 | 14 | 15 | 16-16ths. | per doz. |

BORING MACHINE AUGERS.

Snell's Solid Cast Steel, 18 quarters to the Set.......per quarter, $

Snell's Cast Steel Cut, 18 quarters to the Set, ...   "

Also Machine Augers for power machines, made to order of any required length or size.

Snell's Cast Steel Screw Centre and Double Spur Plug Bits.

6 inch Shanks, twist one inch.......................per quarter, $

Snell's Coopers' Cast Steel Spur Dowelling Bits.

$2\frac{1}{2}$ inch twist, with Shank Square for Brace............per dozen, $

Snell's Boat Builders' Cast Steel Spur Bits.

4 inch twist, 2 inch Shanks.........................per quarter, $

COOK'S AUGERS AND BITS.

	$						
Cast Steel Augers,	$\frac{1}{2}$	$\frac{5}{8}$	$\frac{3}{4}$	$\frac{7}{8}$	1	$1\frac{1}{8}$	
	$1\frac{1}{4}$	$1\frac{3}{8}$	$1\frac{1}{2}$	$1\frac{5}{8}$	$1\frac{3}{4}$	$1\frac{7}{8}$	2	per doz. in.

	$						
Millwright Augers,	$\frac{1}{2}$	$\frac{5}{8}$	$\frac{3}{4}$	$\frac{7}{8}$	1	$1\frac{1}{8}$	
	$1\frac{1}{4}$	$1\frac{3}{8}$	$1\frac{1}{2}$	$1\frac{5}{8}$	$1\frac{3}{4}$	$1\frac{7}{8}$	2	per doz. in.

$

| Auger Bits, | 4 | 5 | 6 | 7 | 8 | 9 | 10 | 11 | 12 | 13 |

$

| 14 | 15 | 16 | 18 | 20 | 22 | 24 | 26 | 28 | 30 | 32-16ths in. | per doz |

$

| Dowell Bits, | 4 | 5 | 6-16ths. in. | per doz. |

Auger Bits in Sets of $32\frac{1}{2}$ quarters.....................per doz. $

In Sets of 24 quarters...............................   "

$

| Car Bits, | 4 | 5 | 6 | 7 | 8 | 9 | 10 |

| 11 | 12 | 13 | 14 | 15 | 16-16ths. in. | per doz. |

BORING IMPLEMENTS.

(Continued.)

EXTENSION LIP AUGER BITS.

Jenning's Patent.

$ per doz.

4   5   6   7   8   9   10   11

12   13   14   15   16-16ths.   "

In Sets, 24 quarters, per set....................................$

In Sets, 32½ quarters, per set....................................

Jenning's Patent Dowel Bits.

$ per doz.

4   5   6-16ths.

PATENT HAMMERED TWIST GIMLET BITS.

Assorted in Sets as Follows.

⅛ to ½ inch, Handled..................................per doz. $

⅛ to ½ inch, not Handled ...."

Pod Gimlet Bits, with Screw......................per gross,

Gimlet Bits, no Screw.

Assorted 1 to 6.............................per gross, $

Extra Large, Assorted, 1 to 6....................."

Gimlet Bits, with Screw.

Assorted 1 to 6.............................per gross, $

Extra Large, Assorted, 1 to 6....................."

Patent Gimlet Bits, Double Cut.

Assorted 1 to 6.............................per gross, $

                               per dozen.

No. $ 1   2   3   4   5   6

Screw Driver Bits.

Assorted in dozens....................................per dozen, $

C. S. Slot Bit, Assorted in dozens ....per dozen, $

GIMLETS.

Cast Steel Nail Gimlets.

Metal Head, common assorted, Nos. 1, 2, 3.............per gross, $

Metal Head, extra assorted, Nos. 2, 3.................."

Wood Head, common assorted, Nos. 1, 2, 3..........."

Wood Head, extra assorted, Nos. 2, 3................."

GIMLETS.

(Continued.)

Cast Steel Excelsior Gimlets.

Metal Head, assorted 1, 2, 3.................per gross, $

Metal Head, assorted, 1, 2, 3, 4.................."

Cocoa Head, assorted, 1, 2, 3.................."

Cocoa Head, assorted, 1, 2, 3, 4.................."

Cast Steel Spike Gimlets.

Metal Head, No. 1.........................per gross, $

Metal Head, No. 2.........................."

Metal Head, No. 3.........................."

Wood Head, No. 1.........................."

Wood Head, No. 2.........................."

Wood Head, No. 3.........................."

Double Extra Metal Head, assorted 1 to 5............."

Double Extra Cocoa Head, assorted 1 to 5..........."

Patent Double Cut Gimlets.

Assorted, 1 to 6 ....per gross, $

$ per hundred.

No. 1   2   3   4   5   6

Pod Gimlets, with Screw, ...per gross, $

TAP BORERS.

$ per doz.

¾   1   1¼   1½   1¾   2   2½   3   in.

CARRIAGE MAKERS' PLUG CUTTERS.

⅜, 7⁄16, ½, 9⁄16, ⅝ inch.............................per dozen, $

CAST STEEL SPOKE TRIMMERS.

Cast Steel...per dozen, $

Stearns' Patent, with Adjustable Knife ...."

COUNTERSINKS.

Flat Countersinks, for Iron, Straw Colored ....per dozen, $

Rose Countersinks, for Brass, Straw Colored.........."

BORING IMPLEMENTS.

(Continued.)

COUNTERSINKS.

(Continued.)

Snail Countersinks, for Wood, Straw Colored .... per dozen, $

Countersink Gouges, for Wood....................... "

Countersink Gouge Bits, for making hole for screw and
head at same time............................ "

REAMERS.

Straw Colored Reamer Bits, Square.................per dozen, $

Straw Colored Reamer Bits, ½ Round .... "

Straw Colored Reamer Bits, 5, 6 and 8 Square........ "

CAST STEEL CHAIR BITS.

	½	⅝	¾	⅞	1 in.	
Flat Shank Black,	$					per doz.
Flat Shank Bright,						"
Flat Shank Scraped out and Bright,						"
Square Shank Black,						"
Square Shank Scraped out and Bright,						"

Brush Bits, black, No. 1 to 3, $ 4 to 16, $ per doz.

Brush Bits, black, No. 17 to No. 21, Wire Gauge, $ per doz.

BRACE BITS IN SETS.—Assorted.

	$					per set.
Straw Colored,.......	24	30	36	42	48	Bits.

CAST STEEL CENTRE BITS.

	$				per doz.
Straw Colored,..........	⅜,	⁷⁄₁₆,	½,	⅝,	inch.

$							per doz.
¾,	⅞,	1,	1⅛,	1¼,	1⅜,	1½,	inch.

Straw Colored, assorted,...........⅛ to 1 inch, $ per doz.

WILSON'S WROUGHT IRON BRACES.

Steel Front Spring, Nos. 1 and 2.

No. 1, 8½ inch Sweep,............................per dozen, $

No. 2, 9 inch Sweep, ... "

Steel Back Spring, Nos. 1½, 2½, 3 and 4½.

No. 1½, 8½ inch sweep.............................per dozen, $

No. 2½, 9 inch sweep .... "

No. 3, 10 inch sweep .... "

No. 4½, 12 inch sweep .... "

WILSON'S WROUGHT IRON BRACES.

(Continued.)

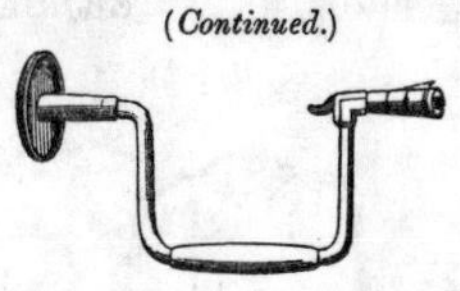

Steel Front Spring, Nos. 4, 5, 5½.

No. 4, 10 inch sweep,............................per dozen, $

No. 5, 12 inch sweep,.............................. "

No. 5½, 14 inch sweep,.............................. "

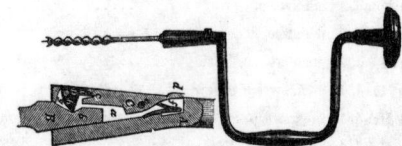

Screw Fastened, Nos. 6, 6½, 7 and 15.

No. 6, Japanned, 8 inch sweep,....................per dozen, $

No. 6½, Japanned, smaller, 8 inch sweep, ... "

No. 7, Polished, 9 inch sweep, ... "

No. 15, Polished ends and centre, 12 inch sweep, ... "

DABOLL'S BRACE.

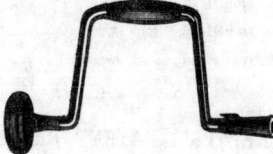

The figure shown above in connection with the Brace, is a section of the pad with the shank of a bit inserted in it.   The bit is secured by a double steel spring.

The invention consists in the improved manner of securing and detaching the bit in and from the socket of the Brace; the catch, D, so operating that any force exerted to withdraw the bit, will bind it tighter in its place, without straining the catch, though a slight pressure upon the thumb lever, combined with the catch, will instantly release it. In using the Brace the greater the strain on the bit, the more securely it will be held in the socket.

No. 22, Double Steel Spring, 9 inch sweep ....per dozen, $

No. 23, Double Steel Spring, 10 inch sweep .... "

No. 25, Double Steel Spring, 12 inch sweep .... "

No. 27, Double Steel Spring, 14 inch sweep .... "

CAST IRON BRACES.

No. 1, 10 inch sweep............................per dozen, $

No. 2, 8 inch sweep.............................. "

BARTHOLEMEW'S BRACES.

No. 0, Iron Head, 7½ inch sweep, Spring..........per dozen, $

No. 1, Iron Head, 9 inch sweep, Spring............ "

No. 2, Iron Head, 10½ inch sweep, Spring............ "

No. 5, Iron Head, 12 inch sweep, Spring............ "

No. 00, Wood Head, 7½ inch sweep, Spring............ "

No. 3, Wood Head, 9 inch sweep, Spring............ "

No. 4, Wood Head, 10½ inch sweep, Spring,............ "

No. 6, Wood Head, 12 inch sweep, Spring, ... "

BORING IMPLEMENTS.

(Continued.)

BARTHOLOMEW'S BRACES.

(Continued.)

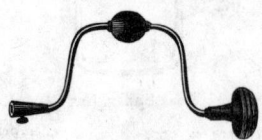

No. 25, Ball Brace, Screw..........................per dozen, $
No. 30, Ball Brace, Screw .... "

WHITE'S WROUGHT IRON BRACES.

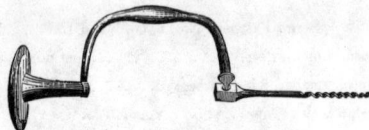

No. 0, Iron Head, 13 inch sweep, Spring............per dozen, $
No. 1, Iron Head, 12 inch sweep, Spring............ "
No. 2, Iron Head, 10 inch sweep, Spring............ "
No. 3, Iron Head, 9 inch sweep, Spring............. "
No. 4, Iron Head, 8 inch sweep, Spring............. "
No. 5, Iron Head, 7½ inch sweep, Spring........... "
No. 0, Iron Head, 13 inch sweep, Screw............ "
No. 1, Iron Head, 12 inch sweep, Screw .... "
No. 2, Iron Head, 10 inch sweep, Screw .... "
No. 3, Iron Head, 9 inch sweep, Screw............. "
No. 4, Iron Head, 8 inch sweep, Screw............. "
No. 5, Iron Head, 7½ inch sweep, Screw............ "

TUCKER'S PATENT BRACES.

A, 1, Wrought Iron, Wood Head, 12 inch sweep ......per dozen, $
A, 2, Wrought Iron, Wood Head, 11 inch sweep ...... "
A, 3, Wrought Iron, Wood Head, 9 inch sweep .... "
A, 4, Wrought Iron, Wood Head, 8 inch sweep .... "
B, 1, Wrought Iron, Iron Head, 12 inch sweep........ "
B, 2, Wrought Iron, Iron Head, 11 inch sweep........ "
B, 3, Wrought Iron, Iron Head, 9 inch sweep........ "
B, 4, Wrought Iron, Iron Head, 8 inch sweep........ "
C, 1, Malleable Iron, Iron Head, 12 inch sweep .... "
C, 2, Malleable Iron, Iron Head, 11 inch sweep .... "
C, 3, Malleable Iron, Iron Head, 9 inch sweep .... "
C, 4, Malleable Iron, Iron Head, 8 inch sweep .... "

STREETER'S PATENT BRACES.

A, 1, Cam and Catch Fastening, Lignumvitæ Head......per dozen, $
A, 2, Cam and Catch Fastening, Lignumvitæ Head...... "
A, 3, Cam and Catch Fastening, Lignumvitæ Head...... "
B, 1, Cam and Catch Fastening, Iron Head .... "
B, 2, Cam and Catch Fastening, Iron Head .... "
B, 3, Cam and Catch Fastening, Iron Head .... "
C, 2, Screw and Catch Fastening, Iron Head .... "
C, 3, Screw and Catch Fastening, Iron Head............ "

STREETER'S PATENT BRACES.

(Continued.)

C, 4, Screw and Catch Fastening, Iron Head...........per dozen, $
Ball, 5, Screw and Catch Fastening, Wood Head .... "
Screw, 3, Screw and Catch Fastening, Wood Head...... "

BEST IMPROVED PLATED BRACES.

Lignumvitæ Head, without bits,........................each, $
Lignumvitæ Head, with 24 straw colored bits .... "
Lignumvitæ Head, with 30 straw colored bits............ "
Lignumvitæ Head, with 36 straw colored bits .... "
Lignumvitæ Head, with 42 straw colored bits .... "
Lignumvitæ Head, with 48 straw colored bits .... "

BEST IMPROVED PLATED ANTI-FRICTION BRACES.

Ebony Head, Brass Neck, without bits...................each, $
Ebony Head, Brass Neck. with 24 straw colored bits...... "
Ebony Head, Brass Neck, with 30 straw colored bits...... "
Ebony Head, Brass Neck, with 36 straw colored bits...... "
Ebony Head, Brass Neck, with 42 straw colored bits...... "
Ebony Head, Brass Neck, with 48 straw colored bits...... "

BOX SCRAPERS.

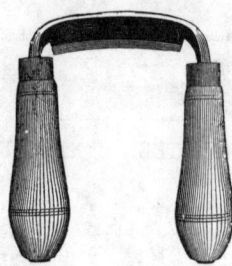

2 Handle C. S.......................................per dozen, $
1 Handle, 3 square, adjustable......................... "
1 Handle, 4 square, adjustable......................... "

CABINET SCRAPERS.

$ per dozen.
4   5   6   inch.

SHIP SCRAPERS.

Cast Steel Blades, Wood Handle....................per dozen, $
Cast Steel Blades, Iron Handle...................... "
Tree Scrapers, Cast Steel Blades.................... "

Plumber's Scrapers ....per dozen. $

LIGHT BOX CHISELS, STEEL FACED.

Polished Iron, 10, 12, and 14 inch......................per doz. $
Japanned Iron, 10, 12, and 14 inch..................... "

AMERICAN CHISELS.

SOCKET FRAMING CHISELS.

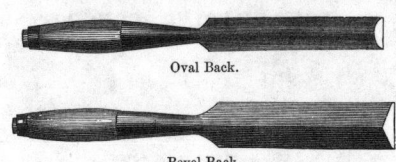

Oval Back.

Bevel Back.

$									per doz.
	$\frac{1}{4}$	$\frac{5}{16}$	$\frac{3}{8}$	$\frac{7}{16}$	$\frac{1}{2}$	$\frac{5}{8}$	$\frac{3}{4}$	$\frac{7}{8}$	1 inch.

$								per doz.
	$1\frac{1}{4}$	$1\frac{1}{2}$	$1\frac{3}{4}$	2	$2\frac{1}{4}$	$2\frac{1}{2}$	$2\frac{3}{4}$	3 inch.

Assorted in sets as follows :　　Per Set.

$\frac{1}{4}$ to 3 inch, 16 Chisels, 1 each—$\frac{1}{4}$, $\frac{5}{16}$, $\frac{3}{8}$, $\frac{1}{2}$, $\frac{5}{8}$, $\frac{3}{4}$, $\frac{7}{8}$, 1, $1\frac{1}{4}$, $1\frac{1}{2}$, $1\frac{3}{4}$, 2, $2\frac{1}{4}$, $2\frac{1}{2}$, $2\frac{3}{4}$, 3 in.,..............................$

$\frac{1}{4}$ to 2 inch, 12 Chisels, 1 each—$\frac{1}{4}$, $\frac{5}{16}$, $\frac{3}{8}$, $\frac{1}{2}$, $\frac{5}{8}$, $\frac{3}{4}$, $\frac{7}{8}$, 1, $1\frac{1}{4}$, $1\frac{1}{2}$, $1\frac{3}{4}$, 2 in.,

$\frac{1}{4}$ to 2 inch, 9 Chisels, 1 each—$\frac{1}{4}$, $\frac{3}{8}$, $\frac{1}{2}$, $\frac{5}{8}$, $\frac{3}{4}$, 1, $1\frac{1}{4}$, $1\frac{1}{2}$, 2 in., ...

$\frac{1}{4}$ to 2 inch, 6 Chisels, 1 each—$\frac{1}{4}$, $\frac{1}{2}$, $\frac{3}{4}$, 1, $1\frac{1}{2}$, 2 in.,.............

SOCKET FRAMING MILLWRIGHTS' CHISELS.

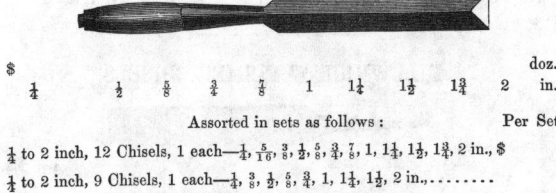

$									doz.
	$\frac{1}{4}$	$\frac{3}{8}$	$\frac{5}{8}$	$\frac{3}{4}$	$\frac{7}{8}$	1	$1\frac{1}{4}$	$1\frac{1}{2}$	$1\frac{3}{4}$　2 in.

Assorted in sets as follows :　　Per Set.

$\frac{1}{4}$ to 2 inch, 12 Chisels, 1 each—$\frac{1}{4}$, $\frac{5}{16}$, $\frac{3}{8}$, $\frac{1}{2}$, $\frac{5}{8}$, $\frac{3}{4}$, $\frac{7}{8}$, 1, $1\frac{1}{4}$, $1\frac{1}{2}$, $1\frac{3}{4}$, 2 in., $

$\frac{1}{4}$ to 2 inch, 9 Chisels, 1 each—$\frac{1}{4}$, $\frac{3}{8}$, $\frac{1}{2}$, $\frac{5}{8}$, $\frac{3}{4}$, 1, $1\frac{1}{4}$, $1\frac{1}{2}$, 2 in.,........

$\frac{1}{4}$ to 2 inch, 6 Chisels, 1 each—$\frac{1}{4}$, $\frac{1}{2}$, $\frac{3}{4}$, 1, $1\frac{1}{2}$, 2 in., ...

CORNER CHISELS.

$				per doz.
	$\frac{3}{4}$	$\frac{7}{8}$	1	$1\frac{1}{8}$　$1\frac{1}{4}$ inch.

CARPENTERS' SLICKS.

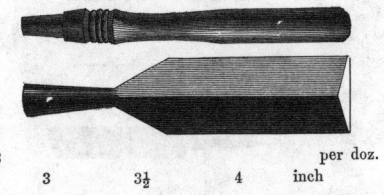

$			per doz.
	3	$3\frac{1}{2}$	4 inch.

SOCKET FRAMING GOUGES.

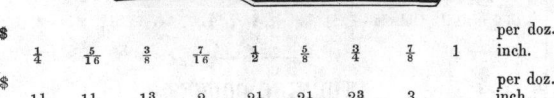

$									per doz.
	$\frac{1}{4}$	$\frac{5}{16}$	$\frac{3}{8}$	$\frac{7}{16}$	$\frac{1}{2}$	$\frac{5}{8}$	$\frac{3}{4}$	$\frac{7}{8}$	1 inch.

$								per doz.
	$1\frac{1}{4}$	$1\frac{1}{2}$	$1\frac{3}{4}$	2	$2\frac{1}{4}$	$2\frac{1}{2}$	$2\frac{3}{4}$	3 inch.

SUPERIOR SOCKET FIRMER GOUGES.

$						per doz.
	$\frac{1}{8}$	$\frac{1}{4}$	$\frac{3}{8}$	$\frac{1}{2}$	$\frac{5}{8}$	$\frac{3}{4}$ inch.

$					per doz.
	$\frac{7}{8}$	1	$1\frac{1}{4}$	$1\frac{1}{2}$	$1\frac{3}{4}$　2 inch.

SUPERIOR SOCKET FIRMER GOUGES.

(Continued.)

Assorted in Sets as follows :　　Per Set.

$\frac{1}{8}$ to 2 inch, 12 Gouges, 1 each—$\frac{1}{8}$, $\frac{1}{4}$, $\frac{3}{8}$, $\frac{1}{2}$, $\frac{5}{8}$, $\frac{3}{4}$, $\frac{7}{8}$, 1, $1\frac{1}{4}$, $1\frac{1}{2}$, $1\frac{3}{4}$, 2 in., $

$\frac{1}{4}$ to 2 inch, 8 Gouges, 1 each—$\frac{1}{4}$, $\frac{1}{2}$, $\frac{3}{4}$, 1, $1\frac{1}{4}$, $1\frac{1}{2}$, $1\frac{3}{4}$, 2 in., ...

SUPERIOR SOCKET FIRMER MILLWRIGHTS' CHISELS.

$						per doz.
	$\frac{1}{8}$	$\frac{1}{4}$	$\frac{3}{8}$	$\frac{1}{2}$	$\frac{5}{8}$	$\frac{3}{4}$ inch.

$					per doz.
	$\frac{7}{8}$	1	$1\frac{1}{4}$	$1\frac{1}{2}$	$1\frac{3}{4}$　2 inch.

Assorted in Sets as follows :　　Per Set.

$\frac{1}{8}$ to 2 inch, 12 Chisels, 1 each—$\frac{1}{8}$, $\frac{1}{4}$, $\frac{3}{8}$, $\frac{1}{2}$, $\frac{5}{8}$, $\frac{3}{4}$, $\frac{7}{8}$, 1, $1\frac{1}{4}$, $1\frac{1}{2}$, $1\frac{3}{4}$, 2 in., $

$\frac{1}{4}$ to 2 inch, 9 Chisels, 1 each—$\frac{1}{4}$, $\frac{1}{2}$, $\frac{5}{8}$, $\frac{3}{4}$, 1, $1\frac{1}{4}$, $1\frac{1}{2}$, $1\frac{3}{4}$, 2 in.,......

$\frac{1}{4}$ to 2 inch, 6 Chisels, 1 each—$\frac{1}{4}$, $\frac{1}{2}$, $\frac{3}{4}$, 1, $1\frac{1}{2}$, 2 in., ...

MILLWRIGHTS' SOCKET FIRMER GOUGES.

$									doz.
	$\frac{1}{4}$	$\frac{3}{8}$	$\frac{1}{2}$	$\frac{5}{8}$	$\frac{3}{4}$	1	$1\frac{1}{4}$	$1\frac{1}{2}$	$1\frac{3}{4}$　2 inch.

Assorted in Sets, as follows :　　Per Set.

$\frac{1}{4}$ to 2 inch, 9 Chisels, 1 each—$\frac{1}{4}$, $\frac{1}{2}$, $\frac{5}{8}$, $\frac{3}{4}$, 1, $1\frac{1}{4}$, $1\frac{1}{2}$, $1\frac{3}{4}$, 2 in.,......$

SUPERIOR COACH-MAKERS' CHISELS.

$								per doz.
	$\frac{1}{8}$	$\frac{1}{4}$	$\frac{3}{8}$	$\frac{1}{2}$	$\frac{5}{8}$	$\frac{3}{4}$	$\frac{7}{8}$	1 inch.

$								per doz.
	$1\frac{1}{8}$	$1\frac{1}{4}$	$1\frac{3}{8}$	$1\frac{1}{2}$	$1\frac{3}{4}$	2	$2\frac{1}{4}$	$2\frac{1}{2}$ inch.

Assorted in Sets, as follows :　　Per Set.

$\frac{1}{8}$ to 2 inch, 12 Chisels, 1 each—$\frac{1}{8}$, $\frac{1}{4}$, $\frac{3}{8}$, $\frac{1}{2}$, $\frac{5}{8}$, $\frac{3}{4}$, $\frac{7}{8}$, 1, $1\frac{1}{4}$, $1\frac{1}{2}$, $1\frac{3}{4}$, 2 in., $

SUPERIOR SOCKET PARING CHISELS.

$						per doz.
	$\frac{1}{8}$	$\frac{1}{4}$	$\frac{3}{8}$	$\frac{1}{2}$	$\frac{5}{8}$	$\frac{3}{4}$ inch.

$					per doz.
	$\frac{7}{8}$	1	$1\frac{1}{4}$	$1\frac{1}{2}$	$1\frac{3}{4}$　2 inch.

Assorted in Sets as follows :　　Per Set.

$\frac{1}{8}$ to 2 inch, 12 Chisels, 1 each—$\frac{1}{8}$, $\frac{1}{4}$, $\frac{3}{8}$, $\frac{1}{2}$, $\frac{5}{8}$, $\frac{3}{4}$, $\frac{7}{8}$, 1, $1\frac{1}{4}$, $1\frac{1}{2}$, $1\frac{3}{4}$, 2 in., $

$\frac{1}{4}$ to 2 inch, 8 Chisels, 1 each—$\frac{1}{4}$, $\frac{1}{2}$, $\frac{3}{4}$, 1, $1\frac{1}{4}$, $1\frac{1}{2}$, $1\frac{3}{4}$, 2 in.,.........

SOCKET FIRMER CHISELS.—No. 1.

$						per doz.
	$\frac{1}{8}$	$\frac{1}{4}$	$\frac{3}{8}$	$\frac{1}{2}$	$\frac{5}{8}$	$\frac{3}{4}$ inch.

$					per doz.
	$\frac{7}{8}$	1	$1\frac{1}{4}$	$1\frac{1}{2}$	$1\frac{3}{4}$　2 inch.

Assorted in Sets, as follows :　　Per Set.

$\frac{1}{8}$ to 2 inch, 12 Chisels, 1 each—$\frac{1}{8}$, $\frac{1}{4}$, $\frac{3}{8}$, $\frac{1}{2}$, $\frac{5}{8}$, $\frac{3}{4}$, $\frac{7}{8}$, 1, $1\frac{1}{4}$, $1\frac{1}{2}$, $1\frac{3}{4}$, 2 in., $

$\frac{1}{8}$ to $1\frac{1}{2}$ inch, 9 Chisels, 1 each—$\frac{1}{8}$, $\frac{1}{4}$, $\frac{3}{8}$, $\frac{1}{2}$, $\frac{5}{8}$, $\frac{3}{4}$, 1, $1\frac{1}{4}$ $1\frac{1}{2}$, in., ...

$\frac{1}{4}$ to 2 inch, 8 Chisels, 1 each—$\frac{1}{4}$, $\frac{1}{2}$, $\frac{3}{4}$, 1, $1\frac{1}{4}$, $1\frac{1}{2}$, $1\frac{3}{4}$, 2 in.,..........

AMERICAN CHISELS.

(Continued.)

SOCKET FIRMER CHISELS.—Extra.

Assorted in Sets, as follows :

Per Set.

$\frac{1}{8}$ to 2 inch, 12 Chisels, 1 each—$\frac{1}{8}$, $\frac{1}{4}$, $\frac{3}{8}$, $\frac{1}{2}$, $\frac{5}{8}$, $\frac{3}{4}$, $\frac{7}{8}$, 1, 1$\frac{1}{4}$, 1$\frac{1}{2}$, 1$\frac{3}{4}$, 2 in., $

$\frac{1}{8}$ to 1$\frac{1}{2}$ inch, 9 Chisels, 1 each—$\frac{1}{8}$, $\frac{1}{4}$, $\frac{3}{8}$, $\frac{1}{2}$, $\frac{5}{8}$, $\frac{3}{4}$, 1, 1$\frac{1}{4}$, 1$\frac{1}{2}$ in.,........

$\frac{1}{4}$ to 2 inch. 8 Chisels, 1 each—$\frac{1}{4}$, $\frac{1}{2}$, $\frac{3}{4}$, 1, 1$\frac{1}{4}$, 1$\frac{1}{2}$, 1$\frac{3}{4}$, 2 in.,..........

SOCKET FIRMER CHISELS.—Common.

Assorted in Sets, as follows :

$\frac{1}{8}$ to 2 inch, 12 Chisels, 1 each—$\frac{1}{8}$, $\frac{1}{4}$, $\frac{3}{8}$, $\frac{1}{2}$, $\frac{5}{8}$, $\frac{3}{4}$, $\frac{7}{8}$, 1, 1$\frac{1}{4}$, 1$\frac{1}{2}$, 1$\frac{3}{4}$, 2 in., $

$\frac{1}{8}$ to 1$\frac{1}{2}$ inch, 9 Chisels, 1 each—$\frac{1}{8}$, $\frac{1}{4}$, $\frac{3}{8}$, $\frac{1}{2}$, $\frac{5}{8}$, $\frac{3}{4}$, 1, 1$\frac{1}{4}$, 1$\frac{1}{2}$ in.,........

$\frac{1}{4}$ to 2 inch, 8 Chisels, 1 each—$\frac{1}{4}$, $\frac{1}{2}$, $\frac{3}{4}$, 1, 1$\frac{1}{4}$, 1$\frac{1}{2}$, 1$\frac{3}{4}$, 2 in.,........

FIRMER CHISELS.

$	$\frac{1}{8}$	$\frac{3}{16}$	$\frac{1}{4}$	$\frac{5}{16}$	$\frac{3}{8}$	$\frac{7}{16}$	$\frac{1}{2}$	$\frac{9}{16}$	$\frac{5}{8}$	$\frac{3}{4}$	per doz. inch.
$	$\frac{7}{8}$	1	1$\frac{1}{8}$	1$\frac{1}{4}$	1$\frac{3}{8}$	1$\frac{1}{2}$	1$\frac{5}{8}$	1$\frac{3}{4}$	1$\frac{7}{8}$	2	per doz. inch.

Assorted in Sets, as follows :

Per Set.

$\frac{1}{8}$ to 1 inch, 8 Chisels—$\frac{1}{8}$, $\frac{1}{4}$, $\frac{3}{8}$, $\frac{1}{2}$, $\frac{5}{8}$, $\frac{3}{4}$, $\frac{7}{8}$, 1 in., ...$

$\frac{1}{8}$ to 1$\frac{1}{4}$ inch, 9 Chisels—$\frac{1}{8}$, $\frac{1}{4}$, $\frac{3}{8}$, $\frac{1}{2}$, $\frac{5}{8}$, $\frac{3}{4}$, $\frac{7}{8}$, 1, 1$\frac{1}{4}$ in., ...

$\frac{1}{8}$ to 1$\frac{1}{2}$ inch, 9 Chisels—$\frac{1}{8}$, $\frac{1}{4}$, $\frac{3}{8}$, $\frac{1}{2}$, $\frac{5}{8}$, $\frac{3}{4}$, 1, 1$\frac{1}{4}$, 1$\frac{1}{2}$ in., ...

$\frac{1}{8}$ to 2 inch, 12 Chisels—$\frac{1}{8}$, $\frac{1}{4}$, $\frac{3}{8}$, $\frac{1}{2}$, $\frac{5}{8}$, $\frac{3}{4}$, $\frac{7}{8}$, 1, 1$\frac{1}{4}$, 1$\frac{1}{2}$, 1$\frac{3}{4}$, 2 in.,.......

$\frac{1}{8}$ to 2 inch, 9 Chisels—$\frac{1}{8}$, $\frac{1}{4}$, $\frac{3}{8}$, $\frac{1}{2}$, $\frac{3}{4}$, 1, 1$\frac{1}{4}$, 1$\frac{1}{2}$, 2 in.,.............

Handling,   per dozen extra.

FIRMER GOUGES.

$	$\frac{1}{8}$	$\frac{3}{16}$	$\frac{1}{4}$	$\frac{5}{16}$	$\frac{3}{8}$	$\frac{7}{16}$	$\frac{1}{2}$	$\frac{9}{16}$	$\frac{5}{8}$	$\frac{3}{4}$	per doz. inch.
$	$\frac{7}{8}$	1	1$\frac{1}{8}$	1$\frac{1}{4}$	1$\frac{3}{8}$	1$\frac{1}{2}$	1$\frac{5}{8}$	1$\frac{3}{4}$	1$\frac{7}{8}$	2	per doz. inch.

Assorted in Sets, as follows :

Per Set.

$\frac{1}{8}$ to 1 inch, 8 Gouges—$\frac{1}{8}$, $\frac{1}{4}$, $\frac{3}{8}$, $\frac{1}{2}$, $\frac{5}{8}$, $\frac{3}{4}$, $\frac{7}{8}$, 1 in., ...$

$\frac{1}{8}$ to 1$\frac{1}{4}$ inch, 9 Gouges—$\frac{1}{8}$, $\frac{1}{4}$, $\frac{3}{8}$, $\frac{1}{2}$, $\frac{5}{8}$, $\frac{3}{4}$, $\frac{7}{8}$, 1, 1$\frac{1}{4}$ in., ...

$\frac{1}{8}$ to 1$\frac{1}{2}$ inch, 9 Gouges—$\frac{1}{8}$, $\frac{1}{4}$, $\frac{3}{8}$, $\frac{1}{2}$, $\frac{5}{8}$, $\frac{3}{4}$, 1, 1$\frac{1}{4}$, 1$\frac{1}{2}$ in.,.............

$\frac{1}{8}$ to 2 inch, 9 Gouges—$\frac{1}{8}$, $\frac{1}{4}$, $\frac{3}{8}$, $\frac{1}{2}$, $\frac{3}{4}$, 1, 1$\frac{1}{4}$, 1$\frac{1}{2}$, 2 in.,.............

$\frac{1}{8}$ to 2 inch, 12 Gouges—$\frac{1}{8}$, $\frac{1}{4}$, $\frac{3}{8}$, $\frac{1}{2}$, $\frac{5}{8}$, $\frac{3}{4}$, $\frac{7}{8}$, 1, 1$\frac{1}{4}$, 1$\frac{1}{2}$, 1$\frac{3}{4}$, 2 in., ...

Beveling inside, in Sets, 1 in.,   ; 1$\frac{1}{4}$ in.,   ; 1$\frac{1}{2}$ in.,   ; 2 in.,

Handling,   per dozen, extra.

LONG THIN PARING CHISELS.

$	$\frac{1}{8}$	$\frac{1}{4}$	$\frac{3}{8}$	$\frac{1}{2}$	$\frac{5}{8}$	$\frac{3}{4}$	$\frac{7}{8}$	1	per doz. inch.
$	1$\frac{1}{4}$	1$\frac{1}{2}$	1$\frac{3}{4}$	2	2$\frac{1}{4}$	2$\frac{1}{2}$	2$\frac{3}{4}$	3	per doz. inch.

Assorted in Sets, as follows :

Per Set.

$\frac{1}{8}$ to 2 inch, 12 Chisels—$\frac{1}{8}$, $\frac{1}{4}$, $\frac{3}{8}$, $\frac{1}{2}$, $\frac{5}{8}$, $\frac{3}{4}$, $\frac{7}{8}$, 1, 1$\frac{1}{4}$, 1$\frac{1}{2}$, 1$\frac{3}{4}$, 2 in., ...$

Handling,   per dozen, extra.

LONG PARING GOUGES.

$	$\frac{1}{8}$	$\frac{1}{4}$	$\frac{3}{8}$	$\frac{1}{2}$	$\frac{5}{8}$	$\frac{3}{4}$	per doz. inch.
$	$\frac{7}{8}$	1	1$\frac{1}{4}$	1$\frac{1}{2}$	1$\frac{3}{4}$	2	per doz. inch.

Assorted in Sets, as follows :

Per Set.

$\frac{1}{8}$ to 1$\frac{1}{2}$ inch, 9 Chisels, 1 each—$\frac{1}{8}$, $\frac{1}{4}$, $\frac{3}{8}$, $\frac{1}{2}$, $\frac{5}{8}$, $\frac{3}{4}$, 1, 1$\frac{1}{4}$, 1$\frac{1}{2}$ in.,......$

$\frac{1}{8}$ to 2 inch, 12 Chisels, 1 each—$\frac{1}{8}$, $\frac{1}{4}$, $\frac{3}{8}$, $\frac{1}{2}$, $\frac{5}{8}$, $\frac{3}{4}$, $\frac{7}{8}$, 1, 1$\frac{1}{4}$, 1$\frac{1}{2}$, 1$\frac{3}{4}$, 2 in.,

Handling,   per dozen, extra.

COACH MAKERS' CHISELS.

$	$\frac{1}{8}$	$\frac{1}{4}$	$\frac{3}{8}$	$\frac{1}{2}$	$\frac{5}{8}$	$\frac{3}{4}$	per doz. inch.
$	$\frac{7}{8}$	1	1$\frac{1}{4}$	1$\frac{1}{2}$	1$\frac{3}{4}$	2	per doz. inch.

Assorted in sets as follows :

Per Set.

$\frac{1}{8}$ to 2 inch, 12 Chisels—$\frac{1}{8}$, $\frac{1}{4}$, $\frac{3}{8}$, $\frac{1}{2}$, $\frac{5}{8}$, $\frac{3}{4}$, $\frac{7}{8}$, 1, 1$\frac{1}{4}$, 1$\frac{1}{2}$, 1$\frac{3}{4}$, 2, in., $

MILLWRIGHTS' FIRMER CHISELS.

$	$\frac{1}{4}$	$\frac{3}{8}$	$\frac{1}{2}$	$\frac{5}{8}$	$\frac{3}{4}$	$\frac{7}{8}$	1	per doz. inch.
$	1$\frac{1}{8}$	1$\frac{1}{4}$	1$\frac{3}{8}$	1$\frac{1}{2}$	1$\frac{3}{4}$	2	per doz. inch.

Assorted in sets as follows :

Per Set.

$\frac{1}{4}$ to 2 inch, 12 Chisels—$\frac{1}{4}$, $\frac{3}{8}$, $\frac{1}{2}$, $\frac{5}{8}$, $\frac{3}{4}$, $\frac{7}{8}$, 1, 1$\frac{1}{4}$, 1$\frac{1}{2}$, 1$\frac{3}{4}$, 2 in., $

MILLWRIGHTS' FIRMER GOUGES.

$	$\frac{1}{4}$	$\frac{3}{8}$	$\frac{1}{2}$	$\frac{5}{8}$	$\frac{3}{4}$	$\frac{7}{8}$	inch. per doz.
$	1	1$\frac{1}{4}$	1$\frac{1}{2}$	1$\frac{3}{4}$	2	in. per doz.

Assorted in sets as Follows :

Per Set.

$\frac{1}{4}$ to 2 inch, 12 Chisels—$\frac{1}{4}$, $\frac{3}{8}$, $\frac{1}{2}$, $\frac{5}{8}$, $\frac{3}{4}$, $\frac{7}{8}$, 1, 1$\frac{1}{4}$, 1$\frac{1}{2}$, 1$\frac{3}{4}$, 2 in., $

TURNING CHISELS.

$	$\frac{1}{8}$	$\frac{1}{4}$	$\frac{3}{8}$	$\frac{1}{2}$	$\frac{5}{8}$	$\frac{3}{4}$	$\frac{7}{8}$	doz.
$	1	1$\frac{1}{8}$	1$\frac{1}{4}$	1$\frac{3}{8}$	1$\frac{1}{2}$	1$\frac{3}{4}$	2 in.	doz.

Assorted in sets as follows :

Per Set.

$\frac{1}{8}$ to 1$\frac{1}{2}$ inch, 9 Chisels—$\frac{1}{8}$, $\frac{3}{8}$, $\frac{1}{2}$, $\frac{5}{8}$, $\frac{3}{4}$, $\frac{7}{8}$, 1, 1$\frac{1}{4}$, 1$\frac{1}{2}$ in., $

$\frac{1}{8}$ to 2 inch, 12 Chisels—$\frac{1}{8}$, $\frac{1}{4}$, $\frac{3}{8}$, $\frac{1}{2}$, $\frac{5}{8}$, $\frac{3}{4}$, $\frac{7}{8}$, 1, 1$\frac{1}{4}$, 1$\frac{1}{2}$, 1$\frac{3}{4}$, 2 in., $

TURNING GOUGES.

$	$\frac{1}{8}$	$\frac{1}{4}$	$\frac{3}{8}$	$\frac{1}{2}$	$\frac{5}{8}$	$\frac{3}{4}$	$\frac{7}{8}$	inch. per doz.
$	1	1$\frac{1}{8}$	1$\frac{1}{4}$	1$\frac{3}{8}$	1$\frac{1}{2}$	1$\frac{3}{4}$	2	inch. per doz.

Assorted in sets as follows :

Per Set.

$\frac{1}{4}$ to 1$\frac{1}{2}$ inch, 9 Gouges—$\frac{1}{4}$, $\frac{3}{8}$, $\frac{1}{2}$, $\frac{5}{8}$, $\frac{3}{4}$, $\frac{7}{8}$, 1, 1$\frac{1}{4}$, 1$\frac{1}{2}$ in., $

$\frac{1}{4}$ to 2 inch, 12 Gouges—$\frac{1}{4}$, $\frac{3}{8}$, $\frac{1}{2}$, $\frac{5}{8}$, $\frac{3}{4}$, $\frac{7}{8}$, 1, 1$\frac{1}{4}$, 1$\frac{1}{2}$, 1$\frac{3}{4}$, 2 in., $

DRAWING KNIVES AND SPOKE SHAVES.

(Continued.)

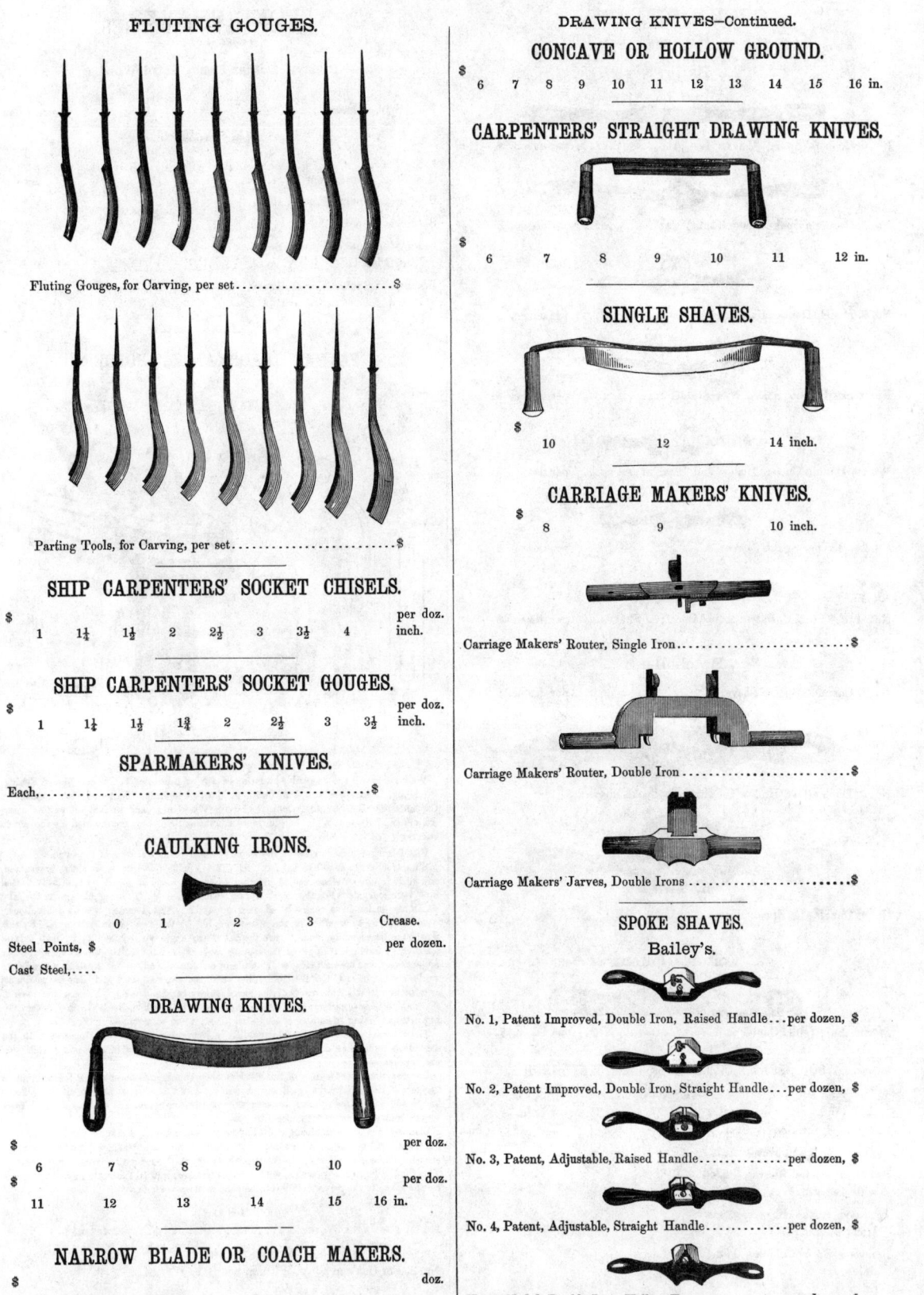

FLUTING GOUGES.

Fluting Gouges, for Carving, per set.........................$

Parting Tools, for Carving, per set.........................$

SHIP CARPENTERS' SOCKET CHISELS.

								per doz.
$								
1	1¼	1½	2	2½	3	3½	4	inch.

SHIP CARPENTERS' SOCKET GOUGES.

								per doz.
$								
1	1¼	1½	1¾	2	2½	3	3½	inch.

SPARMAKERS' KNIVES.

Each..$

CAULKING IRONS.

0	1	2	3	Crease.

Steel Points, $ per dozen.

Cast Steel,....

DRAWING KNIVES.

					per doz.
$					
6	7	8	9	10	
$					per doz.
11	12	13	14	15	16 in.

NARROW BLADE OR COACH MAKERS.

							doz.
$							
6	7	8	9	10	11	12	13	14 in.

DRAWING KNIVES—Continued.
CONCAVE OR HOLLOW GROUND.

$										
6	7	8	9	10	11	12	13	14	15	16 in.

CARPENTERS' STRAIGHT DRAWING KNIVES.

$						
6	7	8	9	10	11	12 in.

SINGLE SHAVES.

$		
10	12	14 inch.

CARRIAGE MAKERS' KNIVES.

$		
8	9	10 inch.

Carriage Makers' Router, Single Iron.............................$

Carriage Makers' Router, Double Iron.............................$

Carriage Makers' Jarves, Double Irons.............................$

SPOKE SHAVES.
Bailey's.

No. 1, Patent Improved, Double Iron, Raised Handle...per dozen, $

No. 2, Patent Improved, Double Iron, Straight Handle...per dozen, $

No. 3, Patent, Adjustable, Raised Handle..............per dozen, $

No. 4, Patent, Adjustable, Straight Handle.............per dozen, $

No. 5, Model, Double Iron, Hollow Face..............per dozen, $

SPOKE SHAVES AND BIT HOLDERS.

SPOKE SHAVES.
(Continued.)
Bailey's.

No. 6, Coopers' Spoke Shave (Heavy)...............per dozen, $

No. 7, Cooper's Spoke Shave (Light)................per dozen, $

No. 8, Model, Double Iron, Spoke Shave............per dozen, $

No. 9, Single Iron Shave, New Style................per dozen, $

No. 10, Double Cutter, Hollow and Straight..........per dozen, $

No. 12, Scraper Spoke Shave........................per dozen, $

Nos. 1, 2, 3, 4, 5, 6, Patent Adjustable Heel Shaves.....per dozen, $

Batcheller's.

No. 1, Common Spoke Shave........................per dozen, $

No. 2, Doub e Cut, Hollow and Straight, Spoke Shave...   "

No. 3, Double Cut Spoke Shave......................   "

Colton's Patent.

Patent, Adjustable, Cam Faced......................per dozen, $

WOOD SPOKE SHAVES, WITH CAST STEEL IRONS.
Boxwood.

	2½	3	3½	4	in.
Boxwood Spoke Shaves, Plain...					per doz.
Boxwood Spoke Shaves, Plated..					"
Boxwood Spoke Shaves, Plated with Ivory.................					"
Boxwood Spoke Shaves, Screw Iron....................					"
Boxwood Spoke Shaves, Plated Screw Iron.................					"

SPOKE SHAVES.
(Continued.)
Ebony, or other Fancy Hard Wood.

	2½	3	3½	in.
Plain Spoke Shaves............				per doz.

Beechwood.

	2½	3	3½	4	in.
Cast Steel Shave Irons.........					per doz
Beechwood Spoke Shaves, Plain.					"
Beechwood Spoke Shaves, Plated,					"
Beechwood Spoke Shaves, Screw Iron, Plated............					"
Beechwood Spoke Shaves, Ivory, Plated.....................					"

PATENT DIAGONAL BIT-HOLDER.

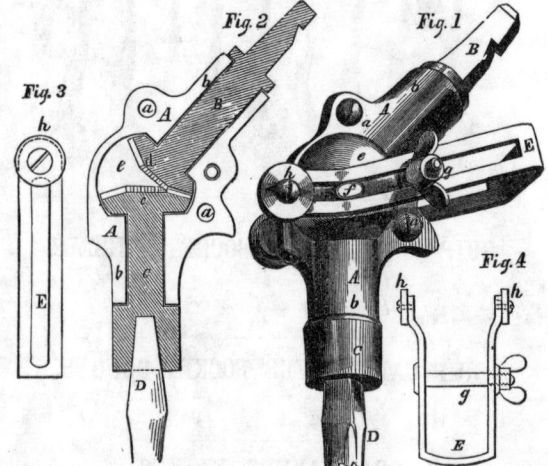

We have to call the particular attention of parties interested in Gas and Steam Fitting, Plumbing, Locomotive and Car Building, Carriage-making, Chair and Cabinet-making, Carpentering, Bell-hanging, Cabin and Ship Work, etc., and in fact all parties using Augers and Bits, to this tool of admirable adaptation, which is represented by the above engraving.

Fig. 1 is a perspective view of the whole. Fig. 2 being a section of the same.

Similar letters refer to like parts in each. A is a hollow casting of the shape represented, and made in two parts, connected together by screws, a. The plane parts of A, indicated by b, form journals. For the shank B, and socket C, a bit D, being shown in C. The shank and socket have each a bevel gear upon the inclosed ends, (as seen in sections,) which work freely together in the space afforded by the swell c, in casting A. By this means the Brace can be made to turn the Bit at any angle with respect to its own axis of rotation, by having the angle of the casting made accordingly. On the swell e, are two projections f, one on each side, which slide in a slot in the adjustable Rest E, a most convenient attachment to the Bit-Holder, but not a necessary adjunct, as it can be used with or without a Rest. This rest is of the shape shown in Fig. 4. Fig 3 being a side view of the same, A, screw and nut g, passes through a hole in A, which holds the Rest to the casting. When boring in corners or awkward places it can be removed.

The compactness and unrivaled durability and cheapness of this tool, together with the ease of operation, has called forth the admiration and approval of all leading architects and mechanics.

One very important feature of this Bit-Holder is, that it is made upon just the right angle to allow of its use with the Bit-Brace close in the corner of a room, and in similar places ; and in addition to many other advantages, the working parts are entirely shielded from contact with any foreign substance, dirt, etc.

It is the most convenient angle Bit-Holder in use, it having a rest to receive a part of the thrust, and can be set at any required distance from the object against which it is operated. There is no other Angle Bit-Holder which has this very important improvement. This Bit-Holder is one by which, with a very slight stoop, in fact scarcely any, the pressure can be given to the perpendicular bit, and the rotation is made easier.

SMALL.

No. 1, For Light Work ....per dozen, $

LARGE.

No. 3, For Gas and Steam Fitting, and Ship Work ...   "

AXES, ADZES AND HATCHETS.

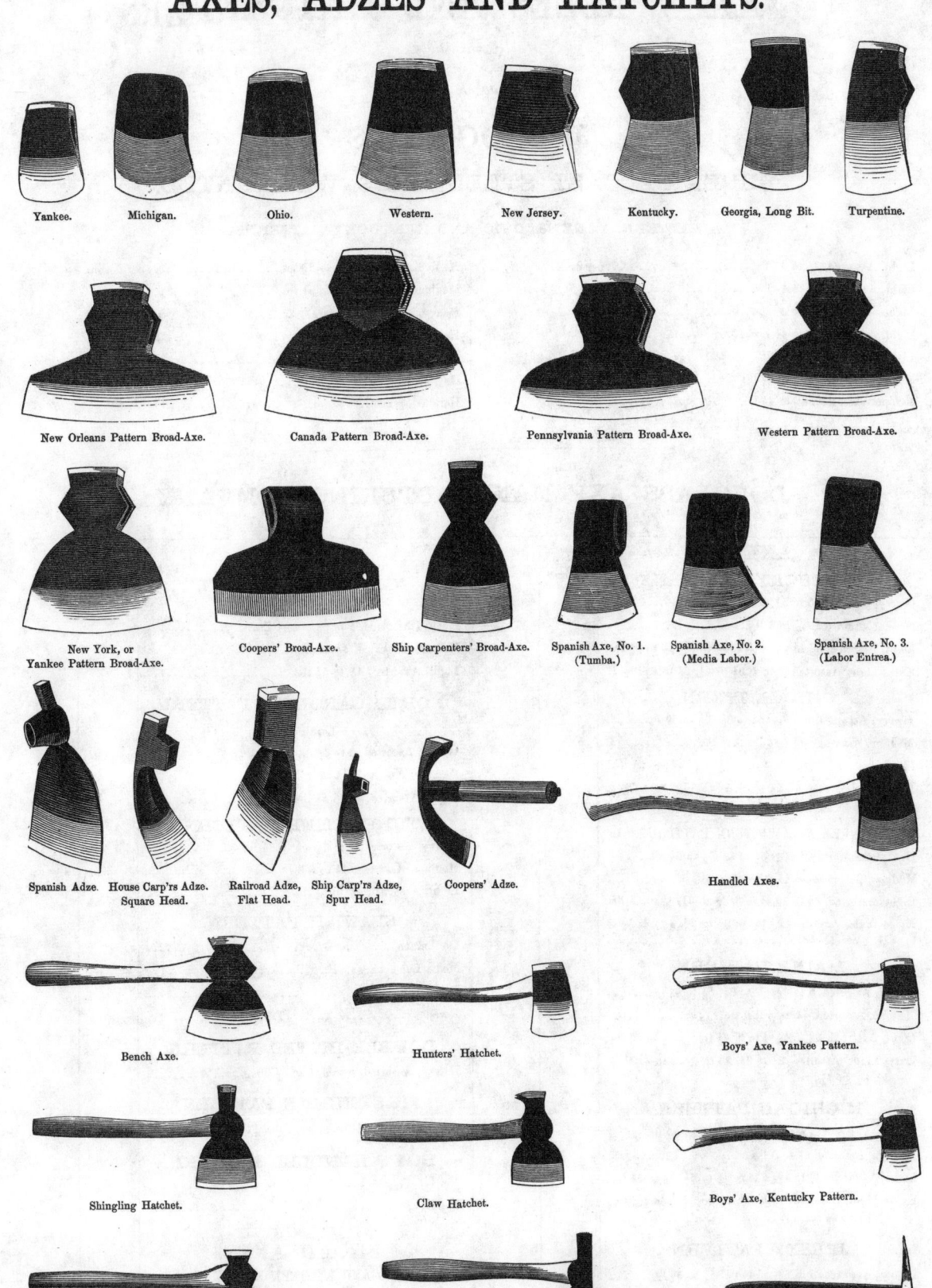

Yankee.   Michigan.   Ohio.   Western.   New Jersey.   Kentucky.   Georgia, Long Bit.   Turpentine.

New Orleans Pattern Broad-Axe.   Canada Pattern Broad-Axe.   Pennsylvania Pattern Broad-Axe.   Western Pattern Broad-Axe.

New York, or Yankee Pattern Broad-Axe.   Coopers' Broad-Axe.   Ship Carpenters' Broad-Axe.   Spanish Axe, No. 1. (Tumba.)   Spanish Axe, No. 2. (Media Labor.)   Spanish Axe, No. 3. (Labor Entrea.)

Spanish Adze.   House Carp'rs Adze. Square Head.   Railroad Adze, Flat Head.   Ship Carp'rs Adze, Spur Head.   Coopers' Adze.   Handled Axes.

Bench Axe.   Hunters' Hatchet.   Boys' Axe, Yankee Pattern.

Shingling Hatchet.   Claw Hatchet.   Boys' Axe, Kentucky Pattern.

Pruning Hatchet.   Lathing Hatchet.   Ice Hatchet.

AXES, ADZES AND HATCHETS.

(*Continued.*)

[*For Plates, see page* 203.]

J. B. OGDEN'S

SUPERIOR CAST STEEL AXES, WARRANTED.

WESTERN, YANKEE, OHIO AND KENTUCKY PATTERNS.

Light, Assorted, 2½ to 4 lbs.	per dozen, $
Light, Assorted, 3 to 4 lbs.	"
Light, Assorted, 3½ to 4 lbs.	"
Light, Assorted, 3¼ to 4¼ lbs.	"
Light, Assorted, 3½ to 4½ lbs.	"
Medium, Assorted, 3¾ to 4¾ lbs.	"
Medium, Assorted, 4 to 4½ lbs.	"
Medium, Assorted, 3½ to 5¼ lbs.	per dozen, $
Medium, Assorted, 4¼ to 5¼ lbs.	"
Heavy, 4½ to 5 lbs.	"
Heavy, 4½ to 6 lbs.	"
Extra Heavy, 4¾ to 5¾ lbs.	"
Extra Heavy, 5 to 6 lbs.	"
Handled, Extra	"

DOUGLASS AXE MANUFACTURING COMPANY.

AXES.	Stamped, W. Hunt. PER DOZEN.	Stamped, D. Sharp. PER DOZEN.
KENTUCKY PATTERN.		
Heavy, Assorted, 5 to 6¼, 5 to 6½, 6 to 7 lbs.		
Medium, Assorted, 4½ to 6 lbs.		
Light, Assorted, 3¾ to 4¾, 4 to 5, 4¼ to 5¼, 4½ to 5½ lbs.		
Extra Light, Assorted, 3 to 4, 3¼ to 4¼, 3½ to 4½ lbs.		
OHIO PATTERN.		
Heavy, Assorted, 5 to 6¼, 5½ to 6½, 5½ to 6¾ lbs.		
Medium, Assorted, 4½ to 6 lbs.		
Light, Assorted, 3¾ to 4¾, 4 to 5, 4¼ to 5¼, 4½ to 5½ lbs.		
Extra Light, Assorted, 2½ to 3½, 2¾ to 3¾, 3 to 4, 3¼ to 4¼, 3½ to 4½ lbs.		
YANKEE AND WESTERN PATTERNS.		
Heavy, Assorted, 5 to 6¼, 5½ to 6½, 5½ to 6¾ lbs.		
Medium, Assorted, 4½ to 6 lbs.		
Light, Assorted, 3¾ to 4¾, 4 to 5, 4¼ to 5¼, 4½ to 5½ lbs.		
Extra Light, Assorted, 2½ to 3½, 2¾ to 3¾, 3 to 4, 3¼ to 4¼, 3½ to 4½ lbs.		
MAINE PATTERN.		
Heavy, Assorted, 5 to 6¼, to 6½, 5½ to 6¾ lbs.		
Medium, Assorted, 4½ to 6 lbs.		
Light, Assorted, 3¾ to 4¾, 4 to 5, 4¼ to , 4½ to 5½ lbs.		
Extra Light, Assorted, 2½ to 3½, 2¾ to 3¾, 3 to 4, 3¼ to 4¼, 3½ to 4½ lbs.		
MICHIGAN PATTERN.		
Heavy, Assorted, 5 to 6¼, 5½ to 6½, 5½ to 6¾ lbs.		
Medium, Assorted, 4½ to 6 lbs.		
Light, Assorted, 3¾ to 4¾, 4 to 5, 4¼ to 5¼, 4½ to 5½ lbs.		
Extra Light, Assorted, 2½ to 3½, 2¾ to 3¾, 3 to 4, 3¼ to 4¼, 3½ to 4½ lbs.		
JERSEY PATTERN.		
Heavy, Assorted, 5 to 6¼, 5½ to 6½, 5½ to 6¾ lbs.		
Medium, Assorted, 4½ to 6 lbs.		
Light, Assorted, 3¾ to 4¾, 4 to 5, 4¼ to 5¼, 4½ to 5½ lbs.		
Extra Light, Assorted, 2¾ to 3¾, 3 to 4, 3¼ to 4¼, 3½ to 4½ lbs.		

AXES.	Stamped, W. Hunt. PER DOZEN.	Stamped, D. Sharp. PER DOZEN.
GEORGIA PATTERN. Long Bits.		
Heavy, Assorted, 5 to 6½, 6 to 7 lbs.		
Medium, Assorted, 4½ to 6 lbs.		
Light, Assorted, 4½ to 5½ lbs.		
NORTH CAROLINA PATTERN. Long Bits.		
Heavy, Assorted, 5 to 6½, 6 to 7 lbs.		
Medium, Assorted, 4½ to 6 lbs.		
Light, Assorted, 4½ to 5½ lbs.		
TURPENTINE PATTERN.		
Heavy, Assorted, 5 to 6¼, 5½ to 6½ lbs.		
Medium, Assorted, 4½ to 6 lbs.		
Light, Assorted, 4½ to 5½ lbs.		
SPANISH PATTERN.		
De Tumba		
Media Labor		
Labor Entera		
Escodas		
DOUBLE BITTED PATTERN.		
Heavy, Assorted, 5 to 6, 5 to 6½ lbs.		
FIRE ENGINE PATTERN.		
Assorted, 4½ to 5½ lbs.		
BOY'S HANDLED PATTERN.		
No. 1		
No. 2		
BROAD AXES. OHIO AND WESTERN PATTERNS.		
Steel Poll, Assorted, 5½ to 8½ lbs.		
Iron Poll, Assorted, 5½ to 8½ lbs.		
Cut of Ohio Pattern, 8½ to 9½ inches.		
Cut of Western Pattern, 10 to 12 inches.		

AXES, ADZES AND HATCHETS.

(Continued.)

[*For Plates see page* 203.]

BROAD AXES.

NEW-ENGLAND PATTERN.	Stamped, W. Hunt. PER DOZEN.	Stamped, D. Sharp. PER DOZEN.
Steel Poll, Assorted, 5½ to 6½ lbs		
Iron Poll, Assorted, 5½ to 6½ lbs		
Cut 8 to 9 inches.		
PITTSBURG PATTERN.		
Steel Poll, Assorted, 6 to 8½ and 9 lbs		
Iron Poll, Assorted, 6 to 8½ and 9 lbs		
Cut 11½ to 12½ inches.		

BROAD AXES.

SHIP PATTERN.	Stamped W. Hunt. PER DOZEN.	Stamped D. Sharp. PER DOZEN.
Steel Poll, Assorted, 5 to 6 lbs		
Iron Poll, Assorted, 5 to 6 lbs		
Cut 6½ to 7½ inches.		
COOPERS' AXES.		
Nos. 1, 2, and 3		

ADZES.

	Stamped W. Hunt. PER DOZEN.	Stamped D Sharp. PER DOZEN.
Railroad, Half Flat Head		
Railroad, Flat Head		
House or Foot, Flat and Half Flat Head		
House or Foot, Spur Poll		
Ship, Flat Head		
Ship, Spur Poll		
Spanish		

ADZES.

	Stamped W. Hunt. PER DOZEN.	Stamped D. Sharp. PER DOZEN.
Coopers', Nos. 1, 2, and 3		
Coopers', Handled and Bolted, extra		
Coopers', Handled, *not* Bolted, extra		
Stirrup Pattern, Handled, No. 283		
Stirrup Pattern, Handled, No. 284		
Adze Hatchets, No. 1		
Adze Hatchets, No. 2		

HATCHETS.

	Stamped W. Hunt. PER DOZEN.	Stamped D. Sharp. PER DOZEN.
Broad, No. 1 per dozen,		
Broad, No. 2 "		
Broad, No. 3 "		
Broad, No. 4 "		
Broad, No. 5 "		
Broad, No. 6 "		
Nos. 1, 2 and 3, packed 2 dozen in case.		
Nos. 4, 5 and 6, packed 1 dozen in case.		
Shingling, No. 1		
Shingling, No. 2		

HATCHETS.

	Stamped W. Hunt. PER DOZEN.	Stamped D. Sharp. PER DOZEN.
Shingling, No. 3		
Packed in 2 dozen or 4 dozen cases.		
Lathing, No. 1		
Lathing, No. 2		
Lathing, No. 3		
Packed in 2 dozen or 4 dozen cases.		
Claw, No. 1		
Claw, No. 2		
Claw, No. 3		
Packed in 2 dozen or 4 dozen cases.		
Axe Pattern		
Packed in 2 dozen or 4 dozen cases.		

BLOOD'S CHOPPING AXES.

Blood's Kentucky Pattern.

Assorted, Light, 4 to 4¾ .... per dozen, $

Assorted, Medium, 4¼ to 5½ } .... "
Assorted, Medium, 4½ to 5¼ }

Assorted, Heavy, 4¾ to 6 } .... "
Assorted, Heavy, 5 to 6 }

Assorted, Extra Heavy, 5½ to 6½ .... "

Assorted, Extra Heavy, 6 to 7 .... "

Assorted, Extra Heavy, 6½ to 7½ .... "

Assorted, Extra Heavy, all 7 lbs .... "

Blood's Ohio or Yankee Pattern.

Assorted, Light, 2¾ to 3¾ }
Assorted, Light, 3 to 4 } .... per dozen, $
Assorted, Light, 3½ to 4¼ }

Assorted, Medium, 3½ to 4½ .... "

Assorted, Medium, 3¾ to 4¾ .... "

Assorted, Medium, 4 to 5 .... "

Assorted, Medium, 4¼ to 5¼ .... "

Blood's Ohio, or Yankee Pattern.

(Continued.)

Assorted, Heavy, 4½ to 5½ .... per dozen, $

Assorted, Heavy, 4¾ to 6 .... "

Assorted, Heavy, 5 to 6¼ .... "

Assorted, Extra Heavy, 5½ to 6½ .... "

Assorted, Extra Heavy, 6 to 7 .... "

Blood's Western Broad Bit.

Weights assorted same as Ohio and Yankee.

Light, ... per dozen, $

Medium .... "

Heavy .... "

Blood's New-Jersey Pattern.

Assorted, 3½ to 4½ .... per dozen, $

Assorted, 4 to 5 .... "

AXES, ADZES AND HATCHETS.

(*Continued.*)

[*For Plates see page* 203.]

BLOOD'S AXES AND HATCHETS.

Silver Steel Axes.

Extra, ... per dozen, $

Handled, Extra .... "

Boys' Axes, Handled—Yankee Pattern.

Assorted Weights, packed in 2 and 3 dozen cases, ... per dozen, $

Kentucky Pattern.

Assorted Weights, packed in 2 and 3 dozen cases ..... per dozen, $

Hunters' Hatchets.

Assorted Weights, and packed in 2, 3 and 4 dozen cases, per doz., $

BROAD AXES.

Canada Pattern.

From 11 to 14 inch on the cut, assorted weight.

$5\frac{1}{2}$ to 8 lb .... per dozen, $

7 to 11 lb .... "

Western Pattern.

From 11 to 13 inch on the cut, assorted weight.

$5\frac{1}{2}$ to 8 lbs .... per dozen, $

Pennsylvania Pattern.

From 11 to 13 inch on the cut, assorted weight.

$5\frac{1}{2}$ to $7\frac{1}{2}$ lbs .... per dozen, $

New Orleans Pattern.

From 11 to 13 inch on the cut, assorted weight.

$5\frac{1}{2}$ to $7\frac{1}{2}$ lbs .... per dozen, $

New York, or Yankee Pattern.

From $8\frac{1}{2}$ to $9\frac{1}{2}$ inch on the cut, assorted weight.

6 to $7\frac{1}{2}$ lbs .... per dozen, $

Ship Carpenters' Broad Axes.

Assorted, ... per dozen, $

House Carpenters' Adze.

Square Head, Assorted .... per dozen, $

Flat Head, Assorted .... "

Ship Carpenters' Spur Head, ... "

Railroad, Flat Head .... "

BLOOD'S HATCHETS.

Bench, No. 4, $5\frac{1}{2}$ inch on the cut .... per dozen, $

Bench, No. 5, 6 inch on the cut .... "

Bench, No. 6, $6\frac{3}{4}$ inch on the cut .... "

Bench, No. 7, $7\frac{1}{2}$ inch on the cut .... "

Bench, No. 8, $8\frac{1}{4}$ inch on the cut .... "

Bench, No. 9, 9 inch on the cut .... "

Pruning, No. 1, $3\frac{1}{2}$ inch on the cut .... "

Pruning, No. 2, 4 inch on the cut .... "

Pruning, No. 3, $4\frac{1}{2}$ inch on the cut .... "

Shingling, No. 1, $3\frac{1}{2}$ inch on the cut .... "

Shingling, No. 2, $3\frac{7}{8}$ inch on the cut .... "

Shingling, No. 3, $4\frac{3}{8}$ inch on the cut .... "

Claw, No. 1, $3\frac{1}{2}$ inch on the cut .... "

Claw, No. 2, $3\frac{7}{8}$ inch on the cut .... "

Claw, No. 3, $4\frac{3}{8}$ inch on the cut .... "

Lathing, No. 1, $2\frac{1}{2}$, inch on the cut .... "

Lathing, No. 2, $2\frac{3}{4}$ inch on the cut .... "

Lathing, No. 3, $3\frac{1}{2}$ inch on the cut .... "

H. COLLINS' "CHOPPING AXES."

Kentucky Pattern, Assorted, $4\frac{1}{2}$ to 5 lbs .... per dozen, $

Yankee Pattern, Assorted, $3\frac{3}{4}$ to $4\frac{1}{2}$ lbs .... "

Yankee Pattern, *Handled*, $3\frac{3}{4}$ to $4\frac{1}{2}$ lbs .... "

HATCHETS.

Stamped "J. Phillips."

Shingling Hatchets, Steel Head.

No. 1. Width of Bit, $3\frac{3}{8}$ inches, Length, $5\frac{3}{4}$ inches .. per dozen, $

No. 2. Width of Bit, $3\frac{7}{8}$ inches, Length, $6\frac{3}{8}$ inches .. "

No. 3. Width of Bit, $4\frac{1}{4}$ inches, Length, $6\frac{3}{4}$ inches .. "

Claw Hatchets, Steel Head.

No. 1. Width of Bit, $3\frac{3}{8}$ inches, Length, $5\frac{5}{8}$ inches .. per dozen, $

No. 2. Width of Bit, $3\frac{5}{8}$ inches, Length, $5\frac{7}{8}$ inches .. "

No. 3. Width of Bit, 4 inches, Length, 6 inches ..... "

HATCHETS.

Stamped "J. Phillips."

Lathing Hatchets, Steel Head.

No. 1. Width of Bit, 2 inches, Length, $6\frac{1}{2}$ inches ... per dozen, $

No. 2. Width of Bit, $2\frac{1}{4}$ inches, Length, $6\frac{7}{8}$ inches .. "

No. 3. Width of Bit, $2\frac{3}{4}$ inches, Length, $7\frac{3}{4}$ inches .. "

Bench or Carpenter's Broad Hatchet, Steel Head.

No. 1. Width of Bit, $4\frac{1}{4}$ inches, Length, $5\frac{3}{4}$ inches ... per dozen, $

No. 2. Width of Bit, $4\frac{5}{8}$ inches, Length, $6\frac{1}{4}$ inches ... "

No. 3. Width of Bit, $5\frac{1}{4}$ inches, Length, $6\frac{3}{4}$ inches ... "

No. 4. Width of Bit, $5\frac{5}{8}$ inches, Length, $7\frac{3}{8}$ inches ... "

No. 5. Width of Bit, $6\frac{1}{4}$ inches, Length, $7\frac{7}{8}$ inches ... "

No. 6. Width of Bit, $6\frac{5}{8}$ inches, Length, $8\frac{1}{4}$ inches ... "

No. 7. Width of Bit, $7\frac{1}{4}$ inches, Length, $8\frac{3}{4}$ inches ... "

Hunter's or Axe Pattern Hatchets, Steel Head.

No. 1. Width of Bit, $3\frac{5}{8}$ inches, Length, $5\frac{1}{2}$ inches ... per dozen, $

AXES, HATCHETS, MATTOCKS AND PICKS.

Boys' Handled Axes.

Stamped "J. Phillips."

No. 1..per dozen, $

No. 2.. "

"M. C. Ogden's"

Lathing Hatchets, all Polished, Adze Eye.

No. 1. Solid Cast Steel..............................per dozen, $

No. 2. Cast Steel Head and Cut..................... "

Maydole's Lathing Hatchets, all Polished.

Solid Cast Steel.....................................per dozen, $

"Caffrey's" Hatchets.

Shingling, No. 1.....................................per dozen, $

Shingling, No. 2..................................... "

Shingling, No. 3..................................... "

Claw, No. 1... "

Claw, No. 2... "

Claw, No. 3... "

H. Collin's Shingling................................ "

Ice Hatchet.

No. 1..per dozen, $

MATTOCKS.

Light Mattock.

Light Mattocks.......................................per dozen, $

Assorted, in 2 or 4 dozen cases.

Large Mattock.

Large Mattock.

Large Mattocks.......................................per dozen, $

Cast Steel Ends, Assorted, 6 to 7 lbs., 3½ to 4 inches Cut, Packed
in 1 and 2 dozen cases.

Pick Mattock.

Pick Mattocks.

Pick Mattocks..per dozen, $

Cast Steel Ends, Assorted, 5 to 6 lbs., 5 inches Cut, Packed in 1
and 2 dozen cases.

Grub Mattock.

Grub Mattock.

Grub Mattock, Assorted Weights....................per dozen, $

PICKS.

Rail Road Pick.

Rail Road Pick.

Assorted, 4 to 5 lbs. ⎫

Assorted, 4¼ to 5¼ lbs. ⎬ Light..................per dozen, $

Assorted, 4½ to 5½ lbs. ⎭

Assorted, 5 to 6 lbs. ⎫

Assorted, 5½ to 6½ lbs. ⎬ Heavy................. per dozen, $

Assorted, 6 to 7 lbs. ⎭

Curved Mining Pick.

Curved Mining Pick.

Curved Mining Pick, Assorted Weights............per dozen, $

California Socket Eye Pick.

California Socket Eye Pick.

California Socket Eye Pick, Assorted Weights......per dozen, $

Washoe Mining Pick.

Washoe Mining Pick.

Assorted, 2½ to 4 lbs...............................per dozen, $

Assorted, 4 to 6 lbs............................ "

Hand or Drifting Pick.

Hand or Drifting Pick.

Assorted, 2 to 3 lbs................................per dozen, $

With Handles, additional........................... "

GRUB HOES.

Grub Hoes.

With Cutter.

Grub Hoe, with Cutter.............................per dozen, $

Oval Eye.

Oval Eye.

No. 1..per dozen, $

No. 2.. "

No. 3.. "

CANE KNIVES AND MACHETES.

GRUB HOES.

(Continued.)

Round Eye.

Round Eye.

No. 1...per dozen, $

No. 2... "

No. 3... "

TURPENTINE TOOLS.

Turpentine Scraper.   Turpentine Puller.   Turpentine Hacker.

Turpentine Scraper.............................per dozen, $

Turpentine Puller............................. "

Turpentine Hacker............................. "

Turpentine Dipper............................. "

(For Turpentine Axes, see pages 203 and 204.)

CANE KNIVES.

Cuba Pattern.

Cuba Pattern....per dozen, $ Louisiana Pattern....per dozen, $ Louisiana Pattern, No. 22....per dozen, $

MACHETES.

No. 1.

No. 3.

No. 4.

No. 9.

No. 21.

No. 37.

No. 76.   No. 110.

$ No. 1	2	3	4	5	6	7	per dozen.
$ No. 8	9	10	15	19	21	22	per dozen.
$ No. 23	29	37	53	63	66	75	per dozen.
$ No. 76	77	86	87	105	207		per dozen.

SCREW DRIVERS AND AWLS.

SCREW DRIVERS.

A No. 1.

Best Cast Steel, Assorted, with Fancy Handles.

| $ | 2 | 3 | 4 | 5 | 6 | 7 | 8 | 10 | 12 | per doz. inch. |

No 1.

Best London Pattern, Cast Steel, Extra Polished Blades, let in strong, Heavy Brass Ferrules.

| $ | 1 | 2 | 3 | 4 | 5 | 6 | per doz. inch. |
| $ | 7 | 8 | 9 | 10 | 11 | 12 | per doz. inch. |

No. 2.

Cast Steel, Plain Flat Blades.

| $ | 1 | 2 | 3 | 4 | 5 | 6 | per doz. inch. |
| $ | 7 | 8 | 9 | 10 | 11 | 12 | per doz. inch. |

No. 3.

Cast Steel Round Blades.

| $ | 2 | 3 | 4 | 5 | 6 | per doz. inch. |

SHOULDERED BRAD AWLS.

Handled.

Shouldered Brad Awls, Beech Handles, ... per gross, $

Shouldered Brad Awls, Assorted, Mahogany, Cocoa, and
Roble Wood Handles . . . . "

SCRATCH AWLS.

Scratch Awls, Assorted, 3½ to 5 inch Beech Handle . . . . per gross, $

Scratch Awls, Assorted, 3½ to 4½ inch Mahogany, Roble
and Cocoa Wood Handles . . . . "

CHALK-LINE REELS AND AWLS.

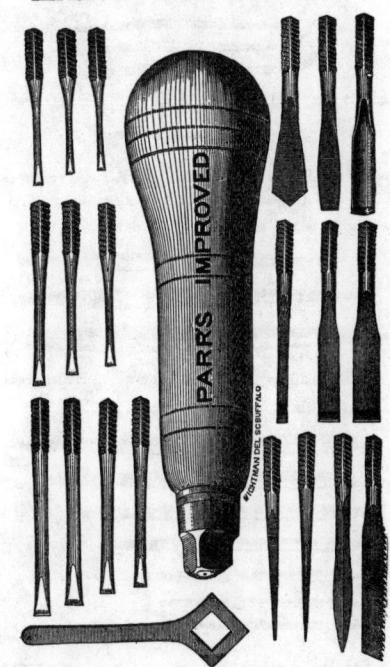

Chalk-Line Reels, Beech . . . . per gross, $

Chalk-Line Reels, Beech, with Awls . . . . "

Chalk-Line Reels, Apple Tree or Laurel . . . . "

Chalk-Line Reels, Apple Tree or Laurel, with Awls . . . . "

Chalk-Line Reels, Boxwood . . . . "

Chalk-Line Reels, Boxwood, with Awls . . . . "

Belt Awls . . . . per dozen, $

IMPROVED BRAD AWL SETS.

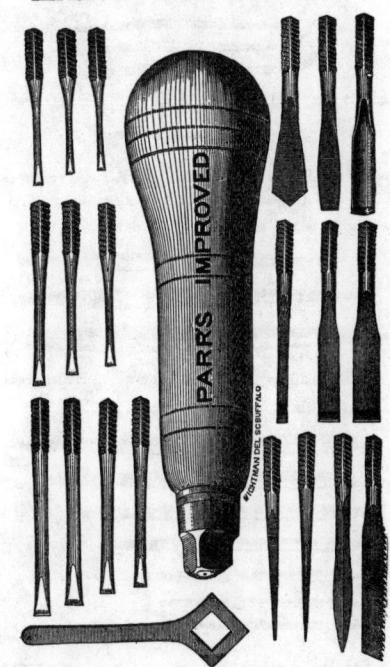

No. 42, Parr's Improved Brad Awl Sets, Apple Tree
Handles, in Sets of 10 Awls . . . . per dozen, $

No. 43, Parr's Improved Brad Awl Sets, Apple Tree
Handles, in Sets of 20 Tools . . . . "

No. 44, Parr's Improved Brad Awl Sets, Rosewood
Handles, in Sets of 10 Awls, ... "

No. 45, Parr's Improved Brad Awl Sets, Rosewood
Handles, in Sets of 20 Tools . . . . "

Brad Awls to fit above Hafts . . . . per gross, $

H. AIKEN'S BRAD AWL SETS.

Improved Brad Awls and Tools, 10 Awls and 10 Tools, per dozen, $

Improved Brad Awls, without Tools, 10 Awls . . . . "

Improved Brad Awls and Tools, on Cards . . . . "

Brad Awls, Assorted, 10 sizes . . . . "

Tools, Assorted, 10 kinds . . . . "

AWLS.

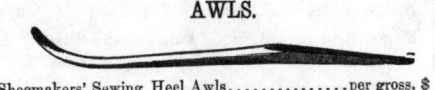

No. 1, Shoemakers' Sewing Heel Awls . . . . per gross, $

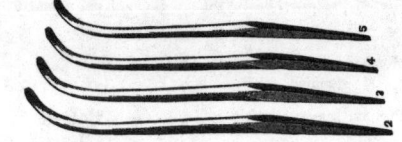

No. 2, 3, 4 and 5, Men's Sewing Awls . . . . per gross, $

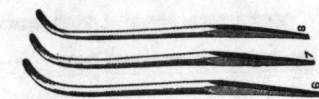

No. 6, 7 and 8, Women's Sewing Awls . . . . per gross, $

SHOEMAKERS' AND CARPENTERS' AWLS.

AWLS.
(Continued.)

No. 9, 10 and 11, Closing Awls .... per gross, $

No. 12, Shoemakers' Round Point Stabbing Awls, ... per gross, $
Oval and Diamond Point same price.
No. 12½, Sewing Awls, reg. assorted, above numbers, ... "

No. 13, 14 and 15, Saddlers' Awls, dirk pattern, ... per gross, $
No. 15½, Saddlers' Awls, dirk pattern, assorted, ... "

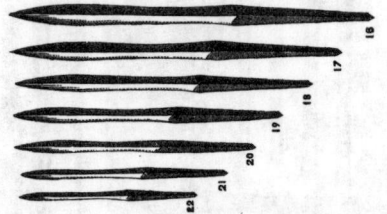

No. 16 to 22, Saddlers' Awls, harness Pattern .... per gross, $
No. 22½, Saddlers' Awls, harness pattern, assorted ..... "

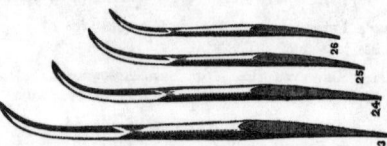

No. 23, 24, 25, 26, American Pattern Sewing Awls, ... per gross, $
No. 26½, American Pattern, assorted, ... "

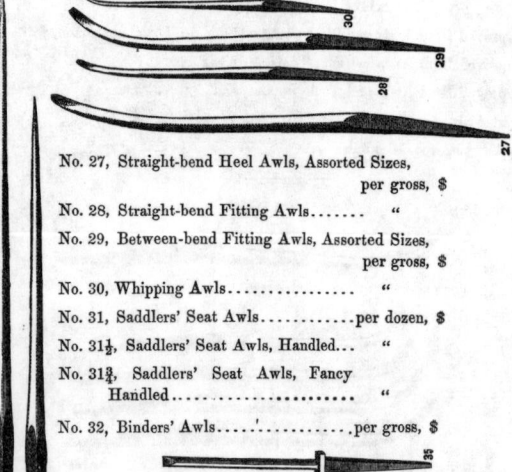

No. 27, Straight-bend Heel Awls, Assorted Sizes,
                      per gross, $
No. 28, Straight-bend Fitting Awls .... "
No. 29, Between-bend Fitting Awls, Assorted Sizes,
                      per gross, $
No. 30, Whipping Awls .... "
No. 31, Saddlers' Seat Awls .... per dozen, $
No. 31½, Saddlers' Seat Awls, Handled... "
No. 31¾, Saddlers' Seat Awls, Fancy
      Handled .... "
No. 32, Binders' Awls ....'........... per gross, $
No. 33, Shouldered Brad Awls .... per gross, $
No. 34, Shouldered Brad Awls .... "

AWLS.
(Continued.)

No. 35, Shouldered Brad Awls .... per gross, $
Larger Sizes, Extra Price.

No. 36, Men's Large Shouldered Pegging Awls .... per gross, $

No. 37, Men's Small Shouldered Pegging Awls ...... per gross, $

No. 38. Women's Large Shouldered Pegging Awls ... per gross, $

No. 39, Women's Small Shouldered Pegging Awls ... per gross, $
No. 39½ Shouldered Pegging Awls, Assorted Sizes .. "

No. 40, Pegging Awls for Patent Hafts, Oval Points, Assorted,
     or any size from 000 to 5 .... per gross, $
(See Patent Hafts, page 216.)

No. 41, Pegging Awls for Patent Hafts, Diamond Points, As-
     sorted, or any size from 000 to 5 .... per gross, $
No. 42, Oval Point Cross Polished Pegging Awls, Assorted, or
     any size from 000 to 5 .... per gross,
No. 43, Diamond Point Cross Polished Pegging Awls, Assorted,
     or any size from 000 to 5 .... per gross,
No. 44, Oval Point Fluted Shank Pegging Awls, Assorted, or
     any size from 000 to 5 .... per gross
No. 45, Diamond Point Fluted Shank Pegging Awls, Assorted,
     or any size from 000 to 5 .... per gross,

No. 46, Square Awls, from 1 to 10, Regularly Assorted, sizes
     same as regular Sewing Awls .... per gross, $

NEEDLES.
Packing.

$	3	3½	4	4½	5	5½	6	per gross. inch.
No. 14	13	12	11	10	9	8		

Sail.

No. 1. 2⅝ inch Tabline .... per gross, $
No. 2. 2¾ inch Oldwork .... "
No. 3. 2⅞ inch Store .... "

DIVIDERS, COMPASSES AND CALIPERS.

SAIL NEEDLES.

(Continued.)

No. 4. 3 inch Headrope . . . . per gross, $
No. 5. 3¼ inch Small Bolt Rope . . . . "
No. 6. 3¾ inch Middle Bolt Rope . . . . "
No. 7. 3⅞ inch Large Bolt Rope . . . . "
No. 8. 4⅛ inch Small Marline . . . . "
No. 9. 4¼ inch Large . . . . "
Mattress Needles . . . . "

SCREW ADJUSTING BENCH HOOKS.

Designed for Cabinetmakers and Joiners. This Hook is adjusted to any desired point by turning the upright screw in the centre.

No. 1 . . . . per dozen, $

Hotchkin's Patent Bench Hook, adjusted by spring on side,
per dozen, $

CAST STEEL DIVIDERS.

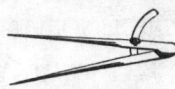

5 Inch . . . . per dozen, $
6 Inch . . . . "
7 Inch . . . . "
8 Inch . . . . "
9 Inch . . . . "
10 Inch . . . . "
12 Inch . . . . "
15 Inch . . . . "
18 Inch . . . . "
24 Inch . . . . "

CAST STEEL COMPASSES.

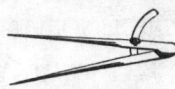

3 Inch . . . . per dozen, $
4 Inch . . . . "
5 Inch . . . . "
6 Inch . . . . "
7 Inch . . . . "
8 Inch . . . . "
9 Inch . . . . "
10 Inch . . . . "
12 Inch . . . . "

PATENT SELF-REGISTERING CALIPERS.

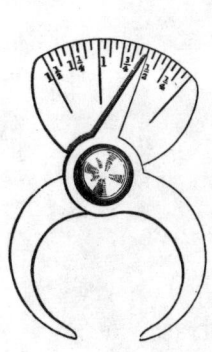

No. 1.

No. 2.

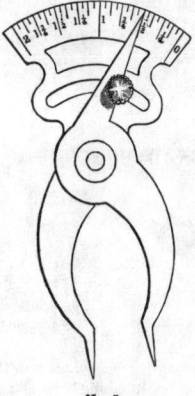

No. 5.

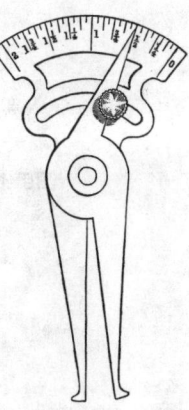

No. 6.

SELF-REGISTERING CALIPERS.

These tools, made of cast steel, and giving the measure without recourse to a rule, will be found the most complete and convenient implement for the use of Machinists, Engineers, Blacksmiths, and Mechanics generally, that have ever been made.

Outside Calipers.

No. 1, 1½ inch, without Set Screw . . . . each, $
No. 2, 2 inch, without Set Screw . . . . "
No. 3, 2 inch, with Set Screw . . . . "
No. 4, 3 inch, with Set Screw . . . . "

Inside Calipers.

No. 6, 2 inch, with Set Screw . . . . each, $
No. 7, 3 inch, with Set Screw . . . . "

Inside and Outside Caliper and Compass Combined.

No. 5, 2 inch, with Set Screw . . . . each, $

CAST STEEL CALIPERS.

6 Inch . . . . per dozen, $
8 Inch . . . . "
10 Inch . . . . "
12 Inch . . . . "
15 Inch . . . . "

Pocket Calipers, 2½ inch, ... per dozen, $
Double Pocket Calipers, 4 inch . . . . "
Double Calipers, 6 inch . . . . "

PUNCHES, PINKING IRONS, & SARDINE KNIVES.

TIMBER SCRIBES.

Per Dozen.. $

PUNCHES.

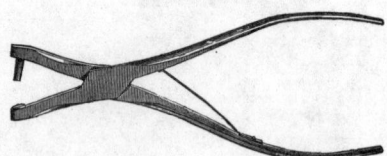

Spring Punches, Assorted Tubes....................per dozen, $
Extra Tubes for the above ....   "
Brass Punches, 3 Tubes............................   "
Conductors' Punches..............................   "

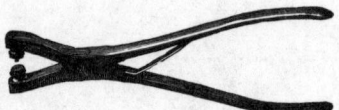

Eyelet Sets, Nos. 1, 2, 3.........................per dozen, $

ROUND OR SADDLERS' PUNCHES, TO DRIVE.

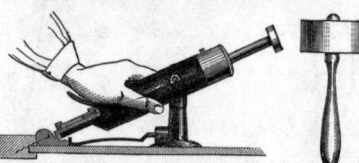

No. 1 to 6 ....per dozen, $
No. 7 to 9.......................................   "
No. 10 to 12.....................................   "
No. 13 to 16.....................................   "
Wad Cutters, Assorted, 10 to 20................   "

THORNDIKE'S BRAD PUNCH.

This Machine, as the cut indicates, is for nailing mouldings into the panels of doors. Its durability and simplicity makes it desirable for all large manufacturers, and the price brings it within the reach of the carpenter who only makes doors for his own business.

                                            Each, $
Brads made especially for this machine, constantly on hand.

PINKING IRONS.

Oval Pattern, Diamond Cut, ⅜, ½, ⅝, ¾, ⅞, 1 inch ......per dozen, $
Oval Pattern, Diamond Cut, 1⅛, 1¼, 1⅜, 1½............   "
Oval Pattern, Diamond Cut, 1¾, 2 ....   "
Oval Pattern, Scolloped Cut, advance,   per dozen.
Straight Pattern, same size and price as Oval.

NAIL SETS.

Solid Cast Steel, unpolished, assorted................per gross, $
Solid Cast Steel, polished, assorted...................   "
Solid Cast Steel, polished, assorted, large.............   "

SARDINE OR CAN KNIVES.

Sardine Knife, Best................................per dozen, $

Sardine Knife, Medium ....   "

Sardine Knife, Small...............................   "
French Sardine Knife ....   "
Improved Sardine Opener...........................   "

Champagne Knife, Best.............................   "
Champagne Knife, Small............................   "

Segar Box Knife ....   "

Sardine Scissors..................................   "
Ham Tryers ....   "

| | $ | | | per dozen. |
| Cheese Tryers | 4 | 5 | 6 | inch. |

| | $ | | | | | | doz. |
| Butter Tryers | 9 | 12 | 15 | 18 | 21 | 24 | inch. |

Flour Tryers, 28 inch...............................per dozen, $
Coffee Tryers, Oval Head...........................   "
Coffee Tryers, Brass Head ....   "
Coffee Tryers, Tunnel Head ....   "

CARPET STRETCHERS.

Steel Points.....................................per dozen, $

OYSTER KNIVES.

No. 52, Boston Pattern Oyster Knives, C. S., Solid
    Octagon Handle...........................per dozen, $

PLYERS, NIPPERS, AND PEG BREAKS.

OYSTER KNIVES.

(Continued.)

No. 53, Boston Pattern Oyster Knives, C. S., Wood Handles,
per dozen, $

No. 54, New York Pattern Oyster Knives, C. S., Flat Solid
Handles................................... per dozen, $

No. 55. Western Pattern Oyster Knives, C. S., Common Solid
Handles...................................per dozen, $

GAS PLYERS.

$					per dozen.
6	7	8	10	12	inches.

Common Round and Flat Nose Plyers.

$					per dozen.
5	5½	6	7	8	inches.

Best Cast Steel Round and Flat Nose Plyers.

$					per dozen.
5	5½	6	7	8	inches.

Best Cast Steel Cutting Nippers.

$					per dozen.
5	5½	6	7	8	inches.

Best Cast Steel Side Cutting Plyers, Flat or Raised.

$					per dozen.
5	5½	6	7	8	inches.

Common Carpenters' Pincers.

$						per dozen.
6	7	8	9	10	11	12	inches.

Carpenters' Pincers, Cast Steel Jaw.

$						per dozen.
6	7	8	9	10	11	12	inches.

All Polished Carpenters' Pincers, Cast Steel Jaw.

$						per dozen.
6	7	8	9	10	11	12	inches.

Cast Steel spring Dividers.

$					per dozen.
6	7	8	9	10	inches.

CAST STEEL SPRING CALIPERS.

$					per dozen.
6	7	8	9	10	inches.

HAND VISES.

$				per dozen.
4½	5	5½	6	inches.

Handled Hand Vises, 5 inch......................per dozen, $

Bench Vises.

1 to 4 lbs..............................per lb., $

1 to 4 lbs., with Anvil............................. "

SHOE PINCERS.

Nos.	00	0	1	2	3	4	per dozen.
$							

PEG BREAKS AND CUTTERS.

No. 162, Peg Breaks, Large Size, C. S.............per dozen, $

No. 163, Peg Breaks, Small Size, C. S............. "

No. 164, Peg Breaks, Shoe Size, C. S............. "

No. 165, Peg Breaks, Large, Case Hardened........ "

No. 166, Peg Breaks, Small, Case Hardened........ "

No. 167, Bow Peg Cutters, C. S...................per dozen, $

No. 168, Bow Peg Cutters, Shoe Size............. "

No. 169, Standard Peg Breaks, D. D. Allen's Patent, per dozen, $

No. 170, Above, with Clinch.................... "

No. 170½, Extra Cutters......................... "

No. 171, Peg Break, Swivel, with Spring..........per dozen, $

No. 172, Round Heel Cutter ....per dozen, $

No. 173, Heel Knife ....per dozen, $

No. 174, Heel Knife, Riveted .... "

PATENT MITRE MACHINE.

For Cutting Mouldings, Picture Frames, &c..........each, $

BENCH, HAND SCREWS AND CLAMP HEADS.

FOOT MORTISING MACHINE.

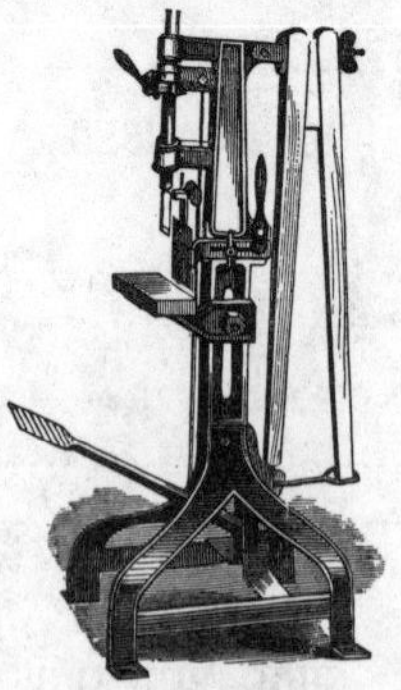

This Machine is adapted for every kind of Mortising, and works easy, is firm and solid, at the same time portable, and is very desirable in working sash, blinds, doors, &c., &c., with three best cast chisels, $\frac{1}{8}$, $\frac{3}{8}$ and $\frac{5}{8}$ inch.

Price.. $

Chisels for same................................per set,

PATENT BLIND SLAT AND ROD WIREING MACHINE.

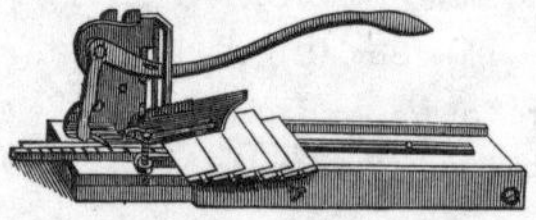

For Driving Wires or Staples into *either* or *both* Slat and Rod, without the necessity of Pricking or Marking........ $

WOOD BENCH SCREWS.

Packed in cases of one dozen.

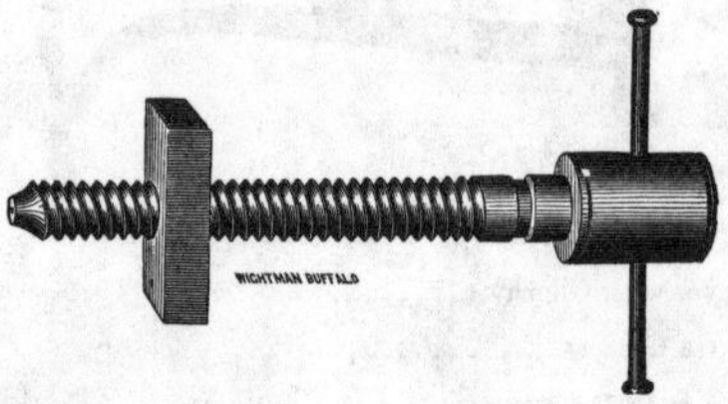

Maple, $2\frac{1}{4}$ inch Screw..............................per dozen, $

Maple, $2\frac{1}{2}$ inch Screw .... "

Hickory, $2\frac{1}{4}$ inch Screw .... "

Hickory, $2\frac{1}{2}$ inch Screw .... "

Beech, $2\frac{1}{2}$ inch Screw .... "

Patent Square Thread, $2\frac{1}{2}$ inch Screw .... "

IRON BENCH SCREWS.

Iron Handles.

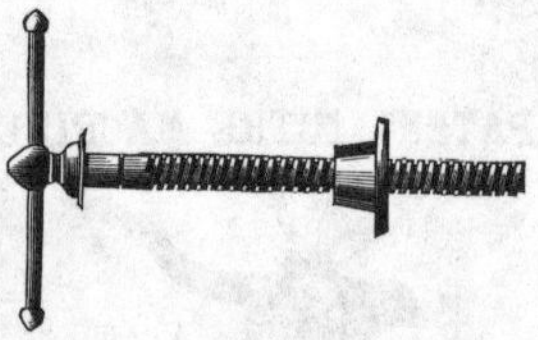

Iron Handle, 1 inch Screw..........................per dozen, $

Iron Handle, $1\frac{1}{8}$ inch Screw.......................... "

Iron Handle, $1\frac{1}{4}$ inch Screw.......................... "

Iron Handle, $1\frac{1}{2}$ inch Screw.......................... "

IRON BENCH SCREWS.

Wood Handles.

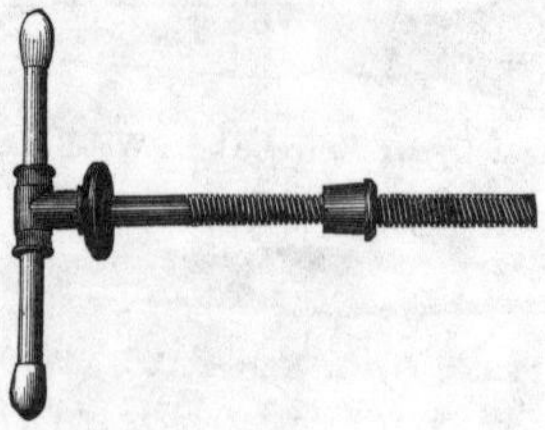

Wood Handle, Movable Collar, 1 inch Screw ....per dozen, $

Wood Handle, Movable Collar, $1\frac{1}{8}$ inch Screw......... "

Wood Handle, Movable Collar, $1\frac{1}{4}$ inch Screw......... "

Wood Handle, Movable Collar, $1\frac{1}{2}$ inch Screw .... "

HAND SCREWS.

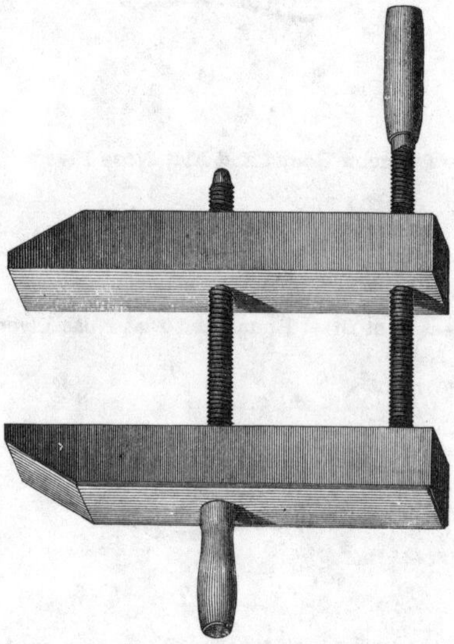

Diameter of Screws.	Length of Screws.	Length of Jaws,	Size of Jaws.	Per Dozen.
$1\frac{1}{4}$ inch......	24 inch......	20 inch......	$2\frac{7}{8}\times2\frac{7}{8}$ inch....	$
$1\frac{1}{8}$ inch......	20 inch......	18 inch......	$2\frac{1}{2}\times2\frac{1}{2}$ inch....	
1 inch......	18 inch......	16 inch......	$2\frac{3}{8}\times2\frac{3}{8}$ inch....	
$\frac{7}{8}$ inch......	16 inch......	14 inch......	$1\frac{7}{8}\times1\frac{7}{8}$ inch....	
$\frac{3}{4}$ inch......	12 inch......	10 inch......	$1\frac{1}{2}\times1\frac{1}{2}$ inch....	
$\frac{5}{8}$ inch......	10 inch......	$8\frac{1}{2}$ inch......	$1\frac{3}{8}\times1\frac{3}{8}$ inch....	

Moulders' Flask Screws made to order.

CARPENTERS' CLAMP HEADS.

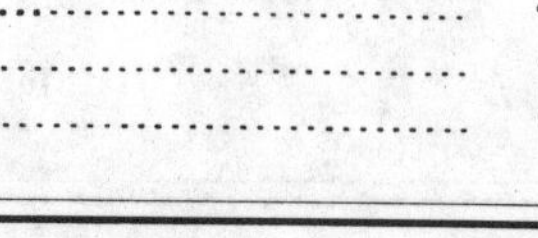

1 inch ....per dozen, $

$1\frac{1}{4}$ inch.. "

$1\frac{1}{2}$ inch.. "

1 inch, Double Nut.................................... "

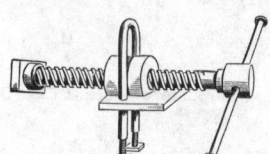

CARPENTERS' CLAMPS, AXE & PICK HANDLES.

IRON BENCH CLAMPS.

$			per dozen.
6	9	12	inch.

CABINET MAKERS' CLAMPS.

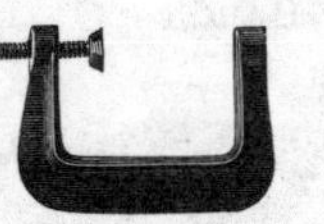

No. 1, Japanned, open, 2¼ inch......................per dozen, $

No. 2, Japanned, open, 2¼ inch, heavy..............   "

No. 3, Japanned, open 4 inch, heavy...............   "

1 inch Clamp Head, with Ratchets and Pawls........per dozen, $

1 inch Clamp Head, with Ratchet and Pawls, on Wood
    Frames....................................   "

RATCHETS AND PAWLS, FOR CLAMPS.

Japanned in Sets.....................................per dozen, $

CARPENTERS' DOOR CLAMPS.

Mounted, or with wood.............................per dozen, $

Plain, or without wood.............................   "

QUILT FRAME CLAMPS.

Same Pattern as Cabinet Makers' Clamp, see plate above.

No. 1, Japanned...................................per dozen, $

No. 2, Japanned...................................   "

CLAMPS FOR SHIP CARPENTERS.

Sliding Jaw.

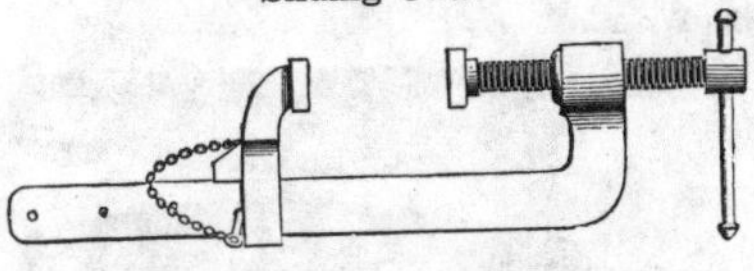

	Size of Bar.	Opening of Clamp.	
1 inch Screw, Comp. Box	2¼×½ inch	18 inch	each, $
1¼ inch Screw, Comp. Box	2¾×⅝ inch	22 inch	"
1½ inch Screw, Wrought Iron Box	3½×¾ inch	26 inch	"

Hook End.

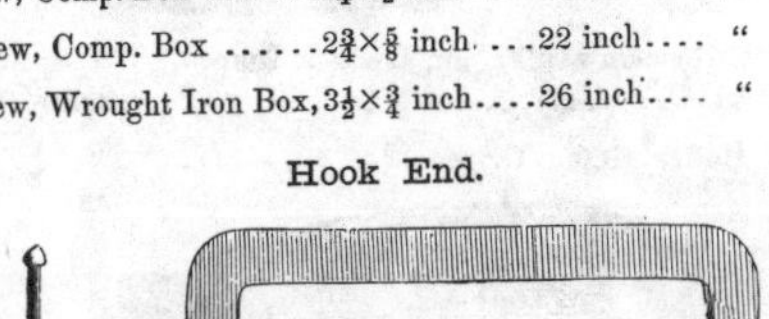

	Size of Bar.	Opening of Clamp.	
1 inch Screw, Comp. Box	2¼×½ inch	16 inch	each, $
1¼ inch Screw, Comp. Box	2¾×⅝ inch	18 inch	"
1½ inch Screw, Wrought Iron Box	3½×¾ inch	20 inch	"
1¾ inch Screw, Wrought Iron Box	3½×⅞ inch	22 inch	"
2 inch Screw, Wrought Iron Box	4 ×1 inch	24 inch	"

PIANO-FORTE STOOL SCREWS.

Cast Iron Plate, ⅞ inch.......................per dozen, $

Cast Iron Plate, 1 inch.......................   "

Cast Iron Plate, 1⅛ inch......................   "

HANDLES.

Boys' Fork Handles................................per dozen, $

Six Feet Hay Fork Handles.......................   "

Seven Feet Hay Fork Handles....................   "

Four and Half Feet Manure Fork Handles, bent.....   "

D Manure Fork Handles, plain...................   "

D Manure Fork Handles, 1 Rivet................   "

D Manure Fork Handles, 2 Rivets...............   "

D Shovel Handles, 1 Rivet.....................   "

D Shovel Handles, 2 Rivet.....................   "

D Shovel Handles, Patent......................   "

Long Shovel Handles...........................   "

Polished, Hickory Quarter Axe Handles, 19 inch....per dozen, $

Polished, Hickory Half Axe Handles, 22 inch.....   "

Polished, Hickory Boy's Axe Handles, 29 inch.....   "

POLISHED HICKORY AXE HANDLES.

	Sizes,	34	36	38	40	42	inch.
No. 1, Extra	per dozen, $						
No. 1,	"						
No. 2,	"						

Polished, Hickory Broad Axe Handles, Right and Left Hand,
    26 inch.....................................per dozen, $

Polished, Hickory, Ship Carpenters' Broad Axe Handles, Right
    and Left Hand, 36 inch.....................per dozen

Polished, Hickory Pick Handles, No. 1, 36 in. Size 2×3 or 2¼×3¼
    inch.......................................per dozen, $

Polished, Hickory Pick Handles, No. 2, 36 in. Size 2×3 or 2¼×3¼
    inch.......................................per dozen,

Polished, Hickory Pick Handles, No. 3, 36 in. Size 2×3 or 2¼×3¼
    inch.......................................per dozen,

Drifting Pick Handle, 32 inch....................per doz. $

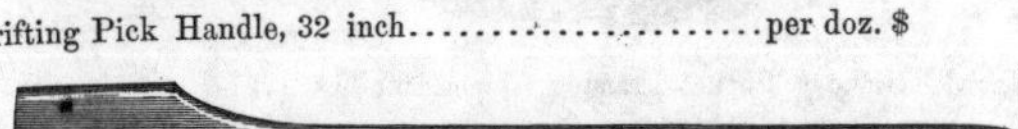

Pole Pick Handle, 32 inch........................per doz, $

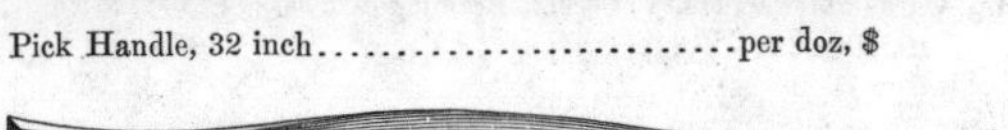

Polished Hickory Adze Handles, No. 1, 32 inch.....per dozen, $

Polished Hickory Adze Handles, No. 2, 32 inch,....   "

Polished Ash Adze Handles, 32 inch..............   "

Polished Ship Carpenters' Adze Handles, No. 1, 32 in.   "

HAMMER HANDLES AND AWL HAFTS.

HANDLES.
(Continued.)

Polished Hickory Hatchet Handles, Shingling.

per dozen.

13   14   15 inch.

Polished Hickory Hatchet Handles, Bench.

per dozen.

16   17   18   19 inch.

Polished Hickory Rivet Hammer Handles.

per dozen.

12   13   14 inch.

Polished Hickory Engineers' Hammer Handles.

per dozen.

12 13 14 15 16 18 20 inch.

Polished Hickory Sledge Hammer Handles.

$

24   28   32   36   inch.

per dozen.

Polished Hickory Auger Handles, assorted............per gross, $

Polished Hickory Augur Handles, extra large......... "

Patent Augur Handles, in sets of two, fitting any size
of Augurs ....per set, $

Tucker's Patent Augur Handle.....................per dozen,

Winslow's Patent Augur Handle.................... "

Polished, Hickory Firmer Chisel Handles, Brass Ferrules,
Assorted Regular............................per gross, $

Polished, Hickory Firmer Chisel Handles, Brass Ferrules, Assorted Extra Large................. "

Polished, Appletree Firmer Chisel Handles, Brass
Ferrules, Assorted Regular.................. "

Polished, Appletree Firmer Chisel Handles, Brass
Ferrules, Assorted Extra Large............. "

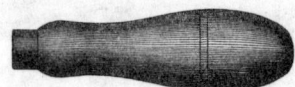

Polished, Hickory Socket Framing Chisel Handles,
Iron Ferrules, Assorted.................... per gross, $

Ship Carpenters' Hickory Socket Framing Chisel
Handles................................... "

File Handles, Soft Wood, Galvanized Iron Ferrules,
Assorted.................................per gross, $

File Handles, Extra Polished, Brass Ferrules, Assorted, "

HANDLES.
(Continued.)

Jewellers' File Handles, Cedar, Brass Ferrules, Assorted
in boxes...................................per gross, $

Brad Awl Handles, Brass Ferrules, Assorted, in boxes, "

Screw Driver Handles, Oval, Improved Pattern.

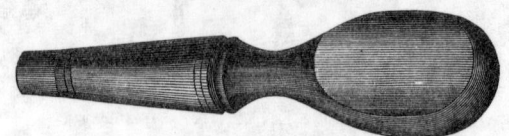

No. 1, Extra Heavy, Brass Ferrule, 4 inches long.....per gross, $

No. 2, Extra Heavy, Brass Ferrule, 5 inches long..... "

No. 3, Extra Heavy, Brass Ferrule, 6 inches long..... "

No. 4, Extra Heavy, Brass Ferrule, 7 inches long..... "

No. 5, Extra Heavy, Brass Ferrule, 8 inches long..... "

No. 6, Extra Heavy, Brass Ferrule, 6 inches long..... "

Assorted................................... "

AWL HAFTS.

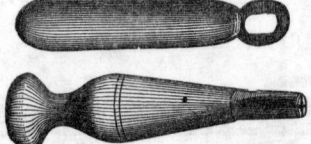

Parr's Improved Patent Sewing Awl Hafts, to hold
any size Awls, Shoemakers' Pattern, with
Wrench................................per dozen, $

Parr's Improved Sewing Awl Hafts, to hold any size
Awls, Saddlers' Pattern, with Wrench....... "

Peg Awl Hafts, Hemminway Patent, Plain Top, with
Wrench................................per dozen, $

Iron Hafts, with Wrench.......................... "

Peg Awl Haft, Hemminway Patent, Leather Topped,
with Wrench...........................per dozen, $

Leather Top Hafts, without Gripes.............. "

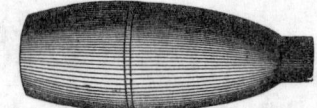

Pegging Awl Hafts, Iron Ferrules.................per gross, $

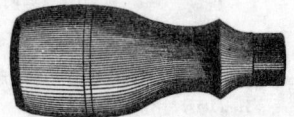

Pegging Awl Hafts, Brass Ferrules.................per gross, $

AWL HAFTS AND MALLETS.

AWL HAFTS.
(Continued.)

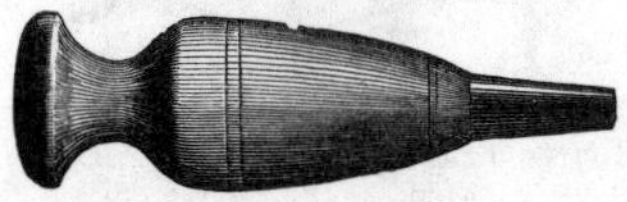

Sewing Pattern.

Sewing Awl Hafts, Iron Ferrules..................per gross, $

Sewing Awl Hafts, Brass Ferrules.................. "

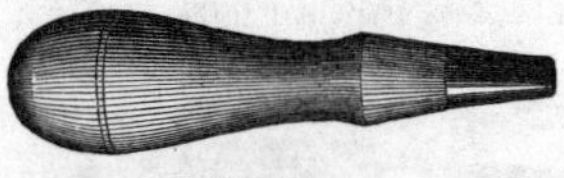

Saddlers' Pattern.

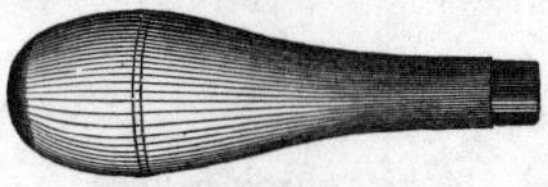

Harness Pattern.

Saddlers' Awl Hafts, for Stitching Harness and Sewing, assorted, or any pattern, polished...............per gross, $

Saddlers' Awl Hafts, Fancy Wood, Roble, Cocoa, Boxwood and Mahogany, for Stitching Harness and Sewing, assorted or any pattern, polished........ "

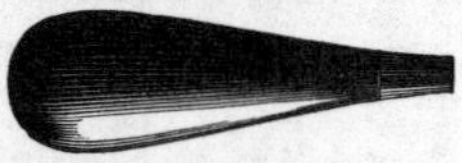

Saddlers' Awl Hafts, oval, new pattern ....per dozen, $

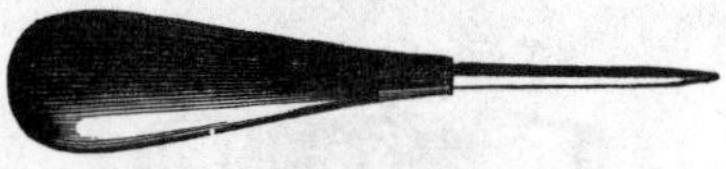

Saddlers' Awl Hafts, oval, new pattern, with Awls, handled for use.............................per dozen, $

MALLETS.

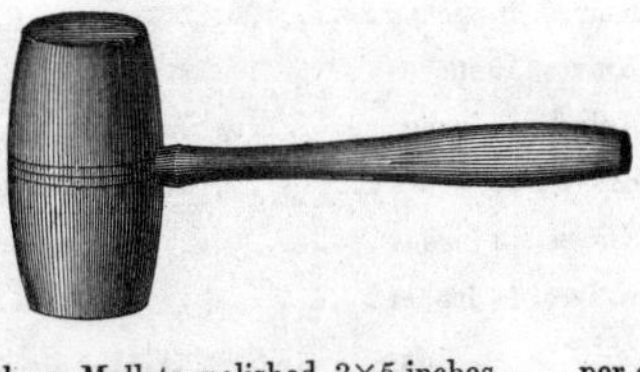

No. 1, Round Hickory Mallets, polished, 3×5 inches.....per doz., $
No. 2, Round Hickory Mallets, polished, 3½×5½ inches.. "
No. 3, Round Hickory Mallets, polished, 4½×6½ inches.. "
No. 4, Round Hickory Mallets, Tinners', polished ...... "
No. 5, Round Lignumvitæ Mallets, polished, 3×5 inches. }
No. 6, Round Lignumvitæ Mallets, polished, 3½×5½ inches, "}
No. 7, Round Lignumvitæ Mallets, polished, 4½×6½ inches, }

Mortice Mallets.

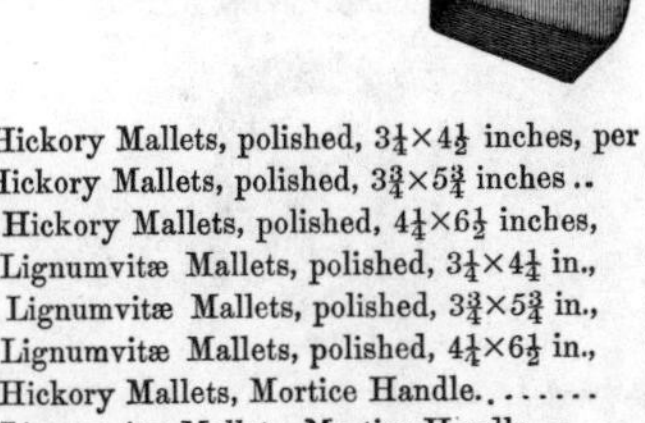

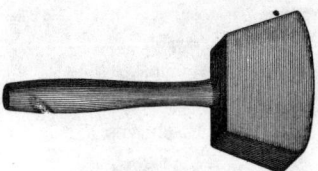

No. 8, Square Hickory Mallets, polished, 3¼×4½ inches, per doz., $
No. 9, Square Hickory Mallets, polished, 3¾×5¾ inches.. "
No. 10, Square Hickory Mallets, polished, 4¼×6½ inches, "
No. 11, Square Lignumvitæ Mallets, polished, 3¼×4¼ in., "
No. 12, Square Lignumvitæ Mallets, polished, 3¾×5¾ in., "
No. 13, Square Lignumvitæ Mallets, polished, 4¼×6½ in., "
Square Hickory Mallets, Mortice Handle....... "
Square Lignumvitæ Mallets, Mortice Handle.... "

MALLETS.
(Continued.)

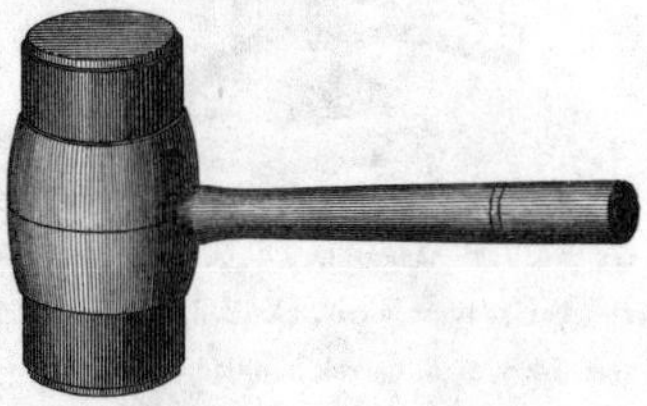

No. 14, Hickory Mallets, polished, heavy iron rings....per dozen, $

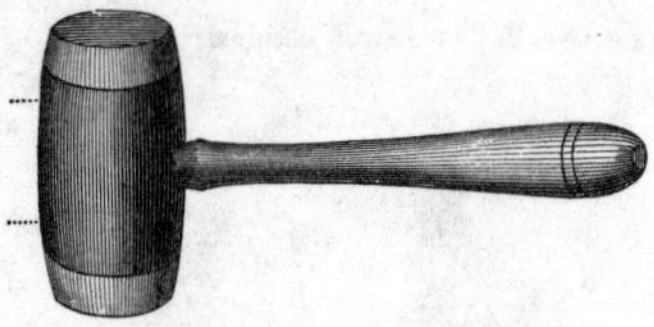

No. 15, Solid Iron Socket Mallets, hickory ends, 2½ inch diam., per doz., $

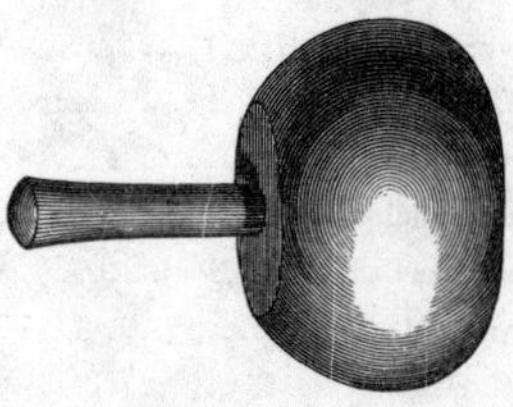

No. 16, Stone Cutters' Hickory Mallets, 3¾×5½ inch ....per doz., $
No. 17, Stone Cutters' Hickory Mallets, 4¾×6½ inch .... "
No. 18, Stone Cutters' Hickory Mallets, 5¾×7½ inch .... "

Caulking Mallets.

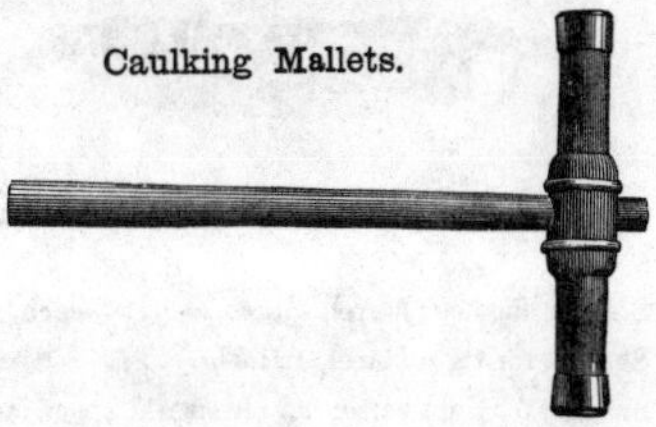

Boxwood, Polished Steel Rings......................per dozen, $
Live Oak, Polished Steel Rings...................... "
Live Oak, Wrought Iron Rings....................... "
Live Oak, Single Iron Rings......................... "

Ice Mallets.

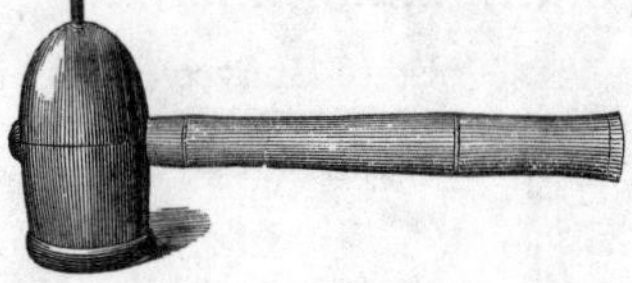

Hickory ....per dozen, $
Lignumvitæ .... "
Ligumvit æ, with Pick in handle.................... "

ICE PICKS.

Wood Head ....per dozen, $
Lignumvitæ Head.................................. "
Iron Head .... "
Griffin's Patent Ice Picks........................... "

WROUGHT IRON OR BRASS FERRULES.

No.			00	0	1	2	
$							per gross.
Size,	1½	1¼	1	15/16	7/8	13/16 inch.	

No.	3	4	5	6	7	8	9
$							per gross.
Size,	3/4	11/16	5/8	9/16	1/2	7/16	3/8

Assorted, $ per gross.

For Cast Brass Ferrules, see page 88.

COOPERS' TOOLS.

Axes.

No.

154 Coopers' Axes, No. 1, tight barrel.............each, $
155 Coopers' Axes, No. 1, tight barrel, handled......   "
156 Coopers' Axes, No. 1, tight barrel, handled, extra.   "
157 Coopers' Axes, No. 2, flour barrel.............   "
158 Coopers' Axes, No. 2, flour barrel, handled......   "
    Coopers' Axes, No. 2, flour barrel, handled, extra.   "

Adzes.

Adzes, Small, No. 3...................each, $
Adzes, Small, No. 2.....................   "
Adzes, Large, No. 1.....................   "
Adzes, Extra Large....................   "
Additional for Checked Head ....   "
Adzes, Improved, No. 2.....................   "
Adzes, Improved, Handled, No. 2.............   "
Adzes, Improved, Handled, Extra, No. 2.......   "
Adzes, Improved, No. 1.....................   "
Adzes, Improved, Handled, No. 1.............   "
Adzes, Improved, Handled, Extra, No. 1........   "

Heading Shaves.

165.

165 Heading Shaves, for flour barrel, 9 inch.........each, $
166 Heading Shaves, for tight barrel, 10 inch........   "
    Heading Shaves, for tight barrel, larger sizes....per inch,
167 Heading Shaves, 9 inches, capped............each, $
    Heading Shaves, 10 inches, capped............   "
168 Heading Shaves, 9 inches, double steel, extra
    and capped..........................   "
    Heading Shaves, 10 inches, double steel, extra
    and capped..........................   "

State Shaves.

169.

169 State Shaves, 7 inch cut.....................each, $
170 State Shaves, 7 inch cut, double steel, extra and
    capped....................................   "

Backing Knives.

Long Handled Backing Knives, 18 to 30 inches between the Handles.

$							per dozen.
6	7	8	9	10	11	12	in. blade.

Short Handled Backing Knives.

$				per dozen.
6	7	8	9	in. blade.

Hollowing Knives.

Hollowing Knives, 6 inches.........................each, $
Hollowing Knives, 7 inches........................   "
Hollowing Knives, 8 inches........................   "
Hollowing Knives, 9 inches........................   "
Hollowing Knives, long Handle, 9 inches............   "

Shave-up.

18 to 30 inches between Handles.

	$							each.
Shave-up,	6	7	8	9	10	11	12	inch blade.

Shave-up, Double Iron.

178.

178 Shave-up, Double Iron............................each, $

Drawing Knives.

Drawing Knives,   6 inches ....each, $
Drawing Knives,   7 inches ....   "
Drawing Knives,   8 inches ....   "
Drawing Knives,   9 inches ....   "
Drawing Knives, 10 inches ....   "
Drawing Knives, 11 inches ....   "
Drawing Knives, 12 inches ....   "
Drawing Knives, 13 inches ....   "
Drawing Knives, 14 inches ....   "

Hoop Shaves.

181.

181 Hoop Shaves.................................each, $
182 Hoop Shaves, over 7 inch cut.................per inch.
183 Hoop Shaves, over 7 inch, capped.............   "
184 Hoop Shaves, over 7 inch, capped, and double
    steel.....................................   "

In-shaves.

185.

185 Coopers' In-Shave, two handles...............each, $
186 Coopers' In-Shave, one handle.................   "

COOPERS' TOOLS.

(Continued.)

Howeling Knives.

Right Hand.

Howeling Knives, No. 1, 3 inches..................each, $

Howeling Knives, No. 2, 3½ inches................. "

Howeling Knives, No. 3, 4 inches................. "

A Right Hand Champer or Howeling Knife is one where the wood handle is in the right hand.

Champering Knives.

187.

187 Champering Knives, for flour barrels, 5 inches...each, $

188 Champering Knives, for tight barrels, 6 inches... "

189 Champering Knives, fancy capped, 5 inches..... "

Champering Knives, fancy capped, 6 inches..... "

Hogshead Champer.

190.

190 Hogshead Champer, 7 inch blade, iron handle....each, $

Keg Champer.

191.

191 Keg Champer...................................each, $

Raising Irons.

192.

192 Raising Irons..................................each, $

Scrapers.

193.

193 Coopers' Scrapers..............................each, $

194 Dowel Bits..................................per dozen, $

V Irons.

195

195 V Irons ....each, $

196 V Howels, for flour barrels........................each,

197 V Howels, for flour barrels, iron block.............. "

198 V Howels, for flour barrels, lignumvitæ face.......... "

199 V Howels, for flour barrels, oak knot or extra lig. board, "

200 V Howels, for flour barrels, Western Pattern......... "

201 Crane's Patent Adjustable V Howels................ "

202 Crane's Patent V Howels, iron block................ "

203 Croze Irons ....per set, $

204 Flagging Irons................................ "

205 Hoops, Flour Barrel, extra, 5 hoops .... "

Hoops, Flour Barrel, No. 1......................... "

Hoops, Flour Barrel, No. 1½........................ "

Hoops, Flour Barrel, No. 2......................... "

Hoops, Flour Barrel, No. 3......................... "

Hoops, Flour Barrel, No. 4......................... "

Hoops, Flour Barrel, ½ barrel...................... "

206 Tight Barrel, 6 hoops, No. 1...................... "

Tight Barrel, 6 hoops, No. 2....................... "

Tight Barrel, half................................ "

207 Tierce .... "

208 Hogshead to 36 inches .... "

209 Hogshead over 36 inches .... "

210 Jointers, Beechwood ....per pair,

211 Coopers' Beech Jointers, Double Irons...........each,

212 Coopers' Beech Jointers, 4½ to 5 feet long, 4×4 ....per pair,

213 Jointers, Apple Tree, long, single iron............ "

Jointers, Apple Tree, long, double iron............ "

Jointers, Apple Tree, short, single iron........... "

Jointers, Apple Tree, short, double iron........... "

Tight Barrel Croze.

214

214 Tight Barrel Croze ....each, $

Hogshead Croze.

215

215 Hogshead Croze...............................each, $

Tight Barrel Croze, with Post.

216

216 Tight Barrel Croze, with post, for all size casks .....each, $

COOPERS' TOOLS.

(Continued.)

Howell, for Tight Barrel.

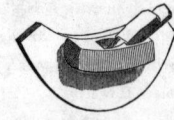

217

217 Howell, for tight barrel, New York pattern............each, $
218 Howell, for tight barrel, Pennsylvania pattern, new style "
219 Crane's Patent Croze, for all size barrels .... "

Levelers.

220

220 Levelers, apple tree................................each, $
221 Levelers, beech, tierce............................. "
222 Levelers, hogshead................................. "

Drivers.

223

223 Drivers, second growth hickory...............per dozen, $
224 Drivers, finished, second growth hickory....... "

Socket Drivers.

Socket Drivers, small...........................each, $
Socket Drivers, medium.......................... "
Socket Drivers, large.......................... "
Socket Drivers with Eye, small.................. "
Socket Drivers with Eye, medium................. "
Socket Drivers with Eye, large.................. "
Long Steel Socket Drivers....................... "
Nantucket Pattern Drivers, small................ "
Nantucket Pattern Drivers, medium............... "
Nantucket Pattern Drivers, large................ "
Nantucket Pattern Drivers, extra large.......... "

Compasses.

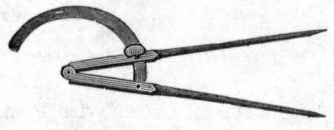

228

228 Compasses, 10 inches ....each, $
Compasses, 12 inches .... "

Hammers.

229

229 Coopers' Hammers, steel faced, handled.............each, $
230 Coopers' Hammers, steel faced, bright, fine polished.... "
231 Coopers' Hammers, solid cast steel .... "

Froes.

232

232 Coopers' Froes ....per inch, $
233 Chime Mauls...............................each,
234 Rivet Set................................... "

Anvils.

235

235 Anvils, cast steel faces, warranted ....per pound, $

Beak Horns.

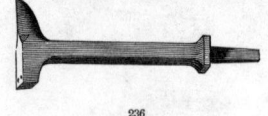

236

236 Beak Horns, cast steel faces, warranted........per pound, $
237 Coopers' Vises ....each,

Adjustable Bung Borer.

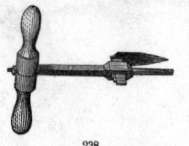

238

238 Adjustable Bung Borer............................each, $
Flagging Irons............................... "
Cold Chisels................................. "
Coopers' Punches .... "

PUMP MAKERS' TOOLS.

248

248 Pump Auger, solid cast steel ....per quarter inch, $

249

249 Pump Rimmers, solid cast steel ....per quarter inch, $

TINSMITHS' MACHINES AND TOOLS.

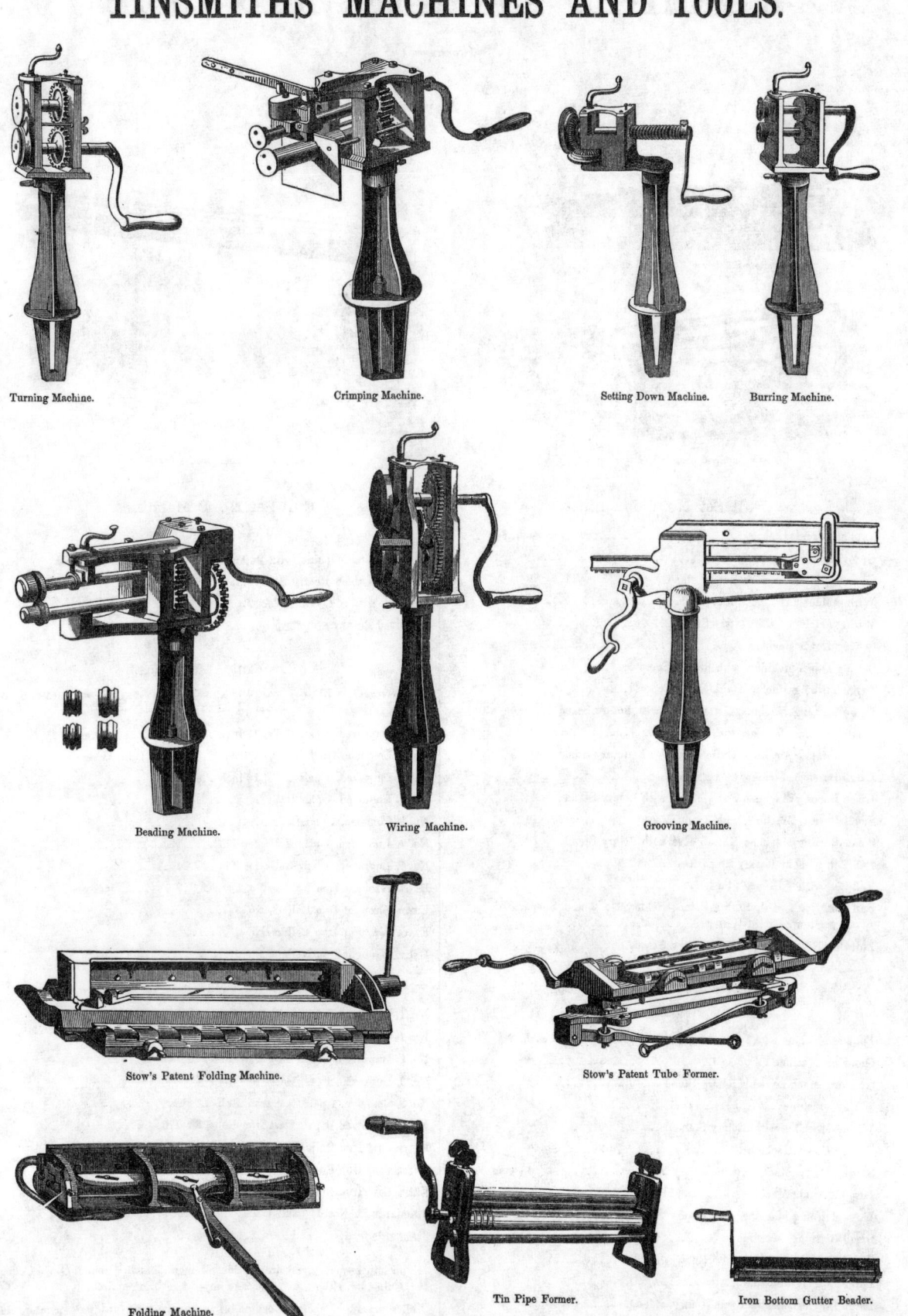

Turning Machine.

Crimping Machine.

Setting Down Machine.

Burring Machine.

Beading Machine.

Wiring Machine.

Grooving Machine.

Stow's Patent Folding Machine.

Stow's Patent Tube Former.

Folding Machine.

Tin Pipe Former.

Iron Bottom Gutter Beader.

TINSMITHS' MACHINES AND TOOLS.

(Continued.)

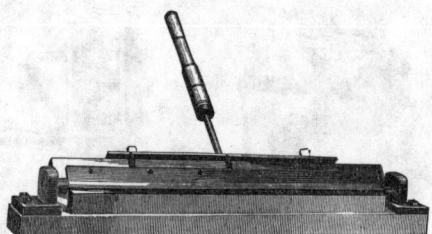

Wood Bottom Sheet Iron Folding Machine.

Stow's Improved Gutter Beader.

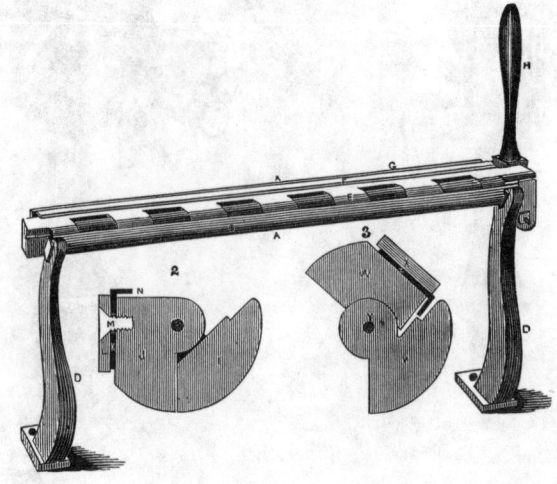

Wright's Patent Sheet Iron Folder.

Full Set No. 1 Machines.

Folding Machine..each, $

Grooving Machine..............................   "

Grooving Machine, with Rotary Stand................   "

Wiring Machine.................................   "

Wiring Machine, with Rotary Stand ....   "

Setting Down Machine...........................   "

Setting Down Machine, with Rotary Stand ....   "

Large Turning Machine, with Extra Faces...........   "

Large Turning Machine, Extra Faces, with Rotary Stand..   "

Small Turning Machine, with Extra Faces...........   "

Small Turning Machine, Extra Faces, with Rotary Stand..   "

Large Burring Machine, with Extra Faces...........   "

Large Burring Machine, Extra Faces, with Rotary Stand...   "

Small Burring Machine, with Extra Faces...........   "

Small Burring Machine, Extra Faces, with Rotary Stand...   "

Full Set, without Rotary Stands..........................$

Full Set, with 7 Rotary Stands.....................

Full Set, No. 1, with Stow's Patent Folder, No. 2, and Shepard   & Stow's Patent Wiring................................

Full Set, No. 1, ditto., with 7 Rotary Stands..................

Full Set No. 2 Machines.

Iron Wheels and Top Plates.

Folding Machine ....each, $

Grooving Machine ....   "

Grooving Machine, with Rotary Stand ....   "

Wiring Machine.................................   "

Wiring Machine, with Rotary Stand.................   "

Setting Down Machine ....   "

Setting Down Machine, with Rotary Stand.............   "

Large Turning Machine ....   "

Large Turning Machine, with Rotary Stand ....   "

Small Turning Machine..........................   "

Small Turning Machine, with Rotary Stand ....   "

Large Burring Machine ....   "

Large Burring Machine, with Rotary Stand.............   "

Small Burring Machine..........................   "

Full Set No. 2 Machines.

(Continued.)

Small Burring Machine, with Rotary Stand ....each, $

Full Set, without Rotary Stands ....   "

Full Set, with Rotary Stands............................   "

Improved Rotary Standards ....   "

Beading Machines.

With Wrought Iron Rollers, converted by a new process to steel, and warranted to be as hard and durable as Cast Steel.

No. 1, Improved, 1 pair Rolls, 13 inch ....each, $

No. 1, Common, 1 pair Rolls, 12 inch ....   "

No. 2, Improved, 1 pair Rolls, 10 inch ....   "

No. 3, Improved, 1 pair Rolls............................   "

No. 3, Common, 1 pair Rolls ....   "

No. 4, Improved, 1 pair Rolls, for Tin ....   "

No. 5, Improved, 1 pair Rolls, for Tin ....   "

Extra Wrought Iron Rollers, No. 1 and 2 ....per pair,

Extra Wrought Iron Rollers, No. 3.....................   "

Extra Wrought Iron Rollers, No. 4 ....   "

Extra Wrought Iron Rollers, No. 5 ....   "

With Cast Iron Rollers, hardened through as hard as steel.

No. 1, Improved, 1 pair Cast Iron Rolls, 13 inch..........each, $

No. 1, Common, 1 pair Cast Iron Rolls, 12 inch...........   "

No. 2, Improved, 1 pair Cast Iron Rolls, 10 inch.........   "

No. 3, Improved, 1 pair Cast Iron Rolls ....   "

No. 3, Common, 1 pair Cast Iron Rolls ....   "

No. 4, Improved, 1 pair Cast Iron Rolls, for Tin..........   "

Extra Cast Iron Rolls, Nos. 1 and 2..................per pair,

Extra Cast Iron Rolls, No. 3..........................   "

Extra Cast Iron Rolls, No. 4..........................   "

Standards for Nos. 1, 2 and 3.......................per pair,

Standards for Nos. 4 and 5..........................   "

The impressions given are 1¼ inch, 1 inch, ⅞ inch, ½ round, O. G., Coffee Pot, Cullender, Elbow, Astragal, and any other form required.

The improved Beading Machine brings the work toward the operator, the common Beaders carry it from him.

TINSMITHS' MACHINES AND TOOLS.

(*Continued.*)

Forming Machines.

No. 00, Extra Large, for Heavy Plate, double geared, 3 inch Rolls 37 inches long . . . . each, $

No. 0, for Cans, etc., 2 inch Rolls, 37 inches long . . . . "

No. 1, Stove Pipe, 2 inch Rolls, 30 inches long . . . . "

No. 2, Stove Pipe, 1¾ inch Rolls, 30 inches long . . . . "

No. 1, Tin Pipe, 1½ inch Rolls, 20 inches long . . . . "

No. 2, Tin Pipe, 1½ inch Rolls, 16 inches long . . . . "

Blacking, Pepper, or Rattle-Box, and Candlestick Former and Beader, Steel Rods . . . . "

Jacket Lamp Former . . . . "

Canister Top . . . . "

Candle Mold and Dipper Handle Former . . . . "

Candle Mold Tip Former . . . . "

Iron Frame, for Stove Pipe . . . . "

Tube Formers.

No. 00, To form Speaking Tubes, 24 inches long . . . . each, $

No. 0, To form Tubes 15 inches long . . . . "

No. 1, For Candle Molds or Ladle Handles, 11 inches long . "

No. 2, For Tea Kettle Spouts, &c., 8 inches long . . . . "

No. 3, For Rattle-Box Handles, 5 inches long . . . . "

No. 4, For Lamp Tubes, 2½ inches long . . . . "

Additional Die Rods and Beds, extra . . . . "

Tin Folding Machines.

No. 1, O. W. Stow's Patent, 22 inches . . . . each, $

No. 2, O. W. Stow's Patent, 17 inches . . . . "

No. 1, Whitney's, 22 inches . . . . "

No. 2, Whitney's, 17 inches . . . . "

Extra Large, 30 inches . . . . "

Large, 20 inches . . . . "

Common, 17 inches . . . . "

No. 1, Walker's Patent, 20 inches . . . . "

No. 2, Walker's Patent, 17 inches . . . . "

Sheet Iron Folding Machines.

No. 1, Wood Bottom, Sheet Iron, 30 inches . . . . each, $

No. 2, Iron Bottom, Sheet Iron, 30 inches . . . . • "

No. 3, Iron Bottom, Sheet Iron, 39 inches . . . . "

No. 000, Wright's Patent, Sheet Iron, 11 inches . . . . "

No. 00, Wright's Patent, Sheet Iron, 9 inches . . . . "

No. 0, Wright's Patent, Sheet Iron, 3½ inches . . . . "

No. 1, Wright's Patent, Sheet Iron, 2½ inches . . . . "

No. 2, Wright's Patent, for Tin, 20 inches . . . . "

Gutter Machines.

No. 0, with 2 Wood Rolls, ⅝ Cast Steel Rod, 20 inches . . . . . each, $

No. 1, with 2 Wood Rolls, ⅝ Cast Steel Rod, 15 inches . . . . . "

No. 2, Iron Bottom, ⅜ or ½ Cast Steel Rod, 20 inches . . . . . "

No. 3, Iron Bottom, ⅜ or ½ Cast Steel Rod, 15 inches . . . . . "

No. 1, O. W. Stow's Improved, 20 inches . . . . "

No. 2, O. W. Stow's Improved, 15 inches . . . . "

No. 1, Steel Gutter Rods, 20 inches . . . . "

No. 2, Steel Gutter Rods, 14 inches . . . . "

Double Seaming Machines.

Savage & Smith's Patent Combination Setting Down and Double Seaming . . . . each, $

Moore's Patent, No. 1, for Heavy Metal . . . . "

Moore's Patent, No. 2, for Common Work . . . . "

Moore's Patent, No. 3, for Common Work . . . . "

Sundry Machines.

Square Box Folding Machine.

No. 0, Wiring, by Steam or Hand Power, for Brass Kettles, &c., Shephard & Stow's Patent . . . . each, $

No. 1, Wiring, Shephard & Stow's Patent . . . . "

No. 1, Wiring, Shephard & Stow's Patent, *with Standard* . . . "

No. 2, Wiring, Shephard & Stow's Patent . . . . "

No. 2, Wiring, Shephard & Stow's Patent, *with Standard* . . "

Wiring, for Brass Kettles and other heavy work by Steam or Hand Power, not Patented . . . . "

Wiring, for Brass Kettles and other heavy work by Steam or Hand Power, not Patented, *with Standard* "

Large Turning, for Brass Kettles and other heavy work, by Steam or Hand Power . . . . "

Large Turning, for Brass Kettles and other heavy work, by Steam or Hand Power, *with Standard* . . . "

Bigelow's Patent Sheet Iron Grooving Machine . . . . . . "

Extra Large Grooving . . . . "

Large Grooving for 20 inch Tin . . . . "

Large Grooving for 20 inch Tin, with Rotary Stand . . "

No. 1, Crimping, for putting Tops and Bottoms on Boxes, Cans, Cups, &c., with Standard . . . . "

No. 2, Crimping, for similar purposes, with Standard . . . . "

Planishing Machine . . . . "

Flanging, for Burring inside of Rim . . . . "

Contracting, for connecting Stove Pipe, No. 1 . . . . . . "

Contracting, for connecting Stove Pipe, No. 1, *with Standard* . . . . "

Contractin , for connecting Stove Pipe, No. 2 . . . . . . "

Contracting, for connecting Stove Pipe No. 2, *with Standard* . . . . "

Elbow, for Stove Pipe, &c. "

Elbow, for Stove Pipe, &c., *with Standard* . . . . "

Pepper-Box or Extra Small Burr . . . . "

Pepper-Box or Extra Small Burr, *with Standard* . . . . "

Wire Spring Former, (or Winder) . . . . "

Square Box Folding Machine, worked by Foot. Accurate and expeditious in its operations (see plate above) "

Box Former and Beader . . . . "

Nippers.

Improved Cutting Nippers.

No. 1, Extra Large Size . . . . each, $

No. 2, Large Size . . . . "

No. 3, Common Size . . . . "

No. 4, Small Size . . . . "

TINSMITHS' MACHINES AND TOOLS.

(Continued.)

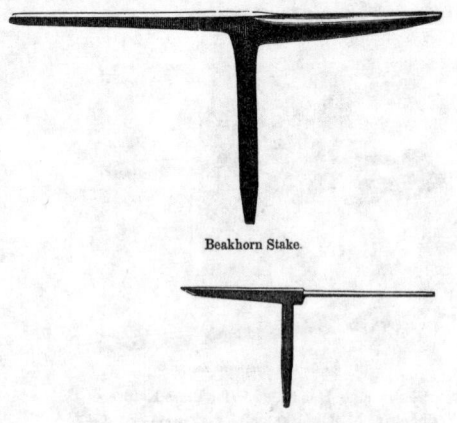

Beakhorn Stake.

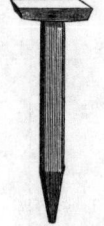

Square Stake.

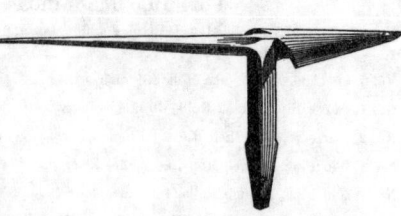

Blowhorn Stake.

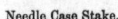

Needle Case Stake.

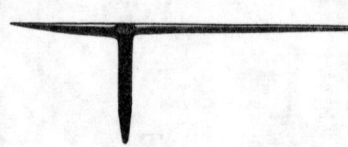

Candle Mold Stake.

Tinman's Full Set of Tools,

Comprised of the following Articles:

1 Large Stake, (or Beak Horn,) No. 1.....................each, $
1 Blow Horn, (or Beak Horn,)........................... "
1 Creasing, (or Beak Horn,)............................. "
1 Square, (or Beak Horn,)............................... "
1 Candle Mold, (or Beak Horn,)......................... "
1 Needle Case, (or Beak Horn,)......................... "
1 Set Hollow Punches, each ½, ¾, 1, 1½, 1¾ inches..... "
1 Set Solid Punches, 4 each do. and 2 Chisels......... "
1 Creasing Swedge..................................... "
1 Cullender Swedge.................................... "
1 Pair Shears, No. 4.................................. "
1 Raising Hammer, each No. 1 and 4................... "
1 Setting Hammer, each No. 2 and 3.................. "
1 Riveting Hammer, No. 5............................ "

The above comprises a full set...................per set, $

Shears.

Bench Shears.

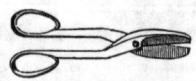

Hand Shears.

No. 00, Bench Shears, Cut, 12 inches...................each, $
No. 0, Bench Shears, Cut, 10½ inches................... "
No. 1, Bench Shears, Cut, 9 inches................... "
No. 2, Bench Shears, Cut, 8⅝ inches.................. "
No. 3, Bench Shears, Cut, 8⅜ inches.................. "
No. 4, Bench Shears, Cut, 8 inches.................. "
No. 5, Bench Shears, Cut, 7 inches.................. "
No. 6, Bench Shears, Cut, 6 inches.................. "
No. 6½, Hand Shears, Cut, 4½ inches.................. "
No. 7, Hand Shears, Cut, 4 inches.................. "

Shears.

(Continued.)

No. 8, Hand Shears, Cut, 3½ inches...................each, $
No. 9, Hand Shears, Cut, 3 inches................... "
No. 10, Hand Shears, Cut, 2½ inches................... "
Circular, Hand Shears, No. 9.......................... "
Circular, Hand Shears, No. 8.......................... "
Elbow Bench.. "
Band Box Bench....................................... "

Hollow Punches.

Hollow Punch.

Set of Solid Punches.

All sizes to and including 1¾ inch diameter, Round.....per inch, $
All sizes above 1¾ inch diameter, Round.............. "
Oval.. "

Wilcox's Pattern, Cast Steel.

All sizes to and including 1⅝ inch diameter............per inch, $
All sizes above 1⅝ inch diameter..................... "
Oval Punches..................................... "

Solid Punches.

Square Cast Steel, No. 0, 1, 2, 3, 4, 5, 6, 7, and Prick......each, $
Round Steel...................................... "

Cast Steel Chisels.

Circular..per inch, $
Lantern, Common Size............................... "
$ each.
Wire, ¼ ½ ¾ 1 1¼ 1½ 1¾ 2 inches.

Bench Plates.

No. 1, Cast Iron.....................................each, $
No. 2, Cast Iron.................................... "

TINSMITHS' MACHINES AND TOOLS.

(Continued.)

Rivet Set and Headers.

Nos. 00 and 0, Cast Steel, Extra.........................each, $

Nos. 1 and 2, Cast Steel, Extra........................ "

Nos. 3 and 4, Cast Steel, Extra........................ "

Nos. 5 and 6, Cast Steel, Extra........................ "

No. 8, Cast Steel, Extra .... "

Grooving Tools.

Nos. 00 and 0...each, $

Nos. 1 and 2... "

Nos. 3 and 4... "

Nos. 5 and 6... "

Nos. 7 and 8... "

Square Pan Tools.

No. 1, Square Pan Turner, 20 inch, Steel.................each, $

No. 2, Square Pan Turner, 15 inch, Steel .... "

Hammers.

Raising.

No. 1, **Raising** ....each, $

No. 2, Raising .... "

No. 3, Raising .... "

No. 4, Raising .... "

Riveting.

No. 0, **Riveting**, Heavy Work, Bright, $1\frac{1}{2}$ inch...........each, $

No. 1, Riveting, Sheet Iron, Bright, Cast Steel, $1\frac{1}{8}$ inch..... "

No. 2, Riveting, Tin, &c., Bright, Cast Steel, 1 inch..... "

No. 3, Riveting, Tin, &c., Bright, Cast Steel, $\frac{7}{8}$ inch..... "

No. 4, Riveting, Tin, &c., Bright, Cast Steel, $\frac{3}{4}$ inch..... "

No. 5, Riveting, Tin, &c., Bright, Cast Steel, $\frac{5}{8}$ inch..... "

No. 0, Riveting, Heavy Work, Black, Cast Steel, $1\frac{1}{2}$ inch..... "

No. 1, Riveting, Sheet Iron, Black, Cast Steel, $1\frac{1}{8}$ inch..... "

No. 2, Riveting, Tin, &c., Black, Cast Steel, 1 inch..... "

No. 3, Riveting, Tin, &c., Black, Cast Steel, $\frac{7}{8}$ inch..... "

No. 4, Riveting, Tin, &c., Black, Cast Steel, $\frac{3}{4}$ inch..... "

No. 5, Riveting, Tin, &c., Black, Cast Steel, $\frac{5}{8}$ inch..... "

Setting.

No. 1, **Setting**, Bright, Cast Steel, $1\frac{1}{2}$ inch.................each, $

No. 2, Setting, Bright, Cast Steel, 1 inch................ "

Hammers.

(Continued.)

No. 3, Setting, Bright, Cast Steel, $\frac{7}{8}$ inch................. "

No. 4, Setting, Bright, Cast Steel, $\frac{3}{4}$ inch................. "

No. 5, Setting, Bright, Cast Steel, $\frac{5}{8}$ inch................. "

No. 1, Setting, Black, $1\frac{1}{8}$ inch................. "

No. 2, Setting, Black,   1 inch................. "

No. 3, Setting, Black, $\frac{7}{8}$ inch................. "

No. 4, Setting, Black, $\frac{3}{4}$ inch................. "

No. 5, Setting, Black, $\frac{5}{8}$ inch................. "

Planishing.................................. per lb. $

Cast Iron Raising, No. 1 .... "

Cast Iron Raising, No. 2 .... "

Cast Iron Raising, No. 3 .... "

Cast Iron Raising, No. 4 .... "

Handled, per dozen, extra.........................$

Swedges.

Creasing Swedge.

Cullender Swedges.

Square Pan Swedge.

Creasing.......................................each, $

Cullender .... "

Square Pan....................................... "

Elbow .... "

Soldering Coppers.

Each,	2	3	4	5	6	7	8	9	10	qrs.
Pair, $										

TINSMITHS' MACHINES AND TOOLS.

(*Continued.*)

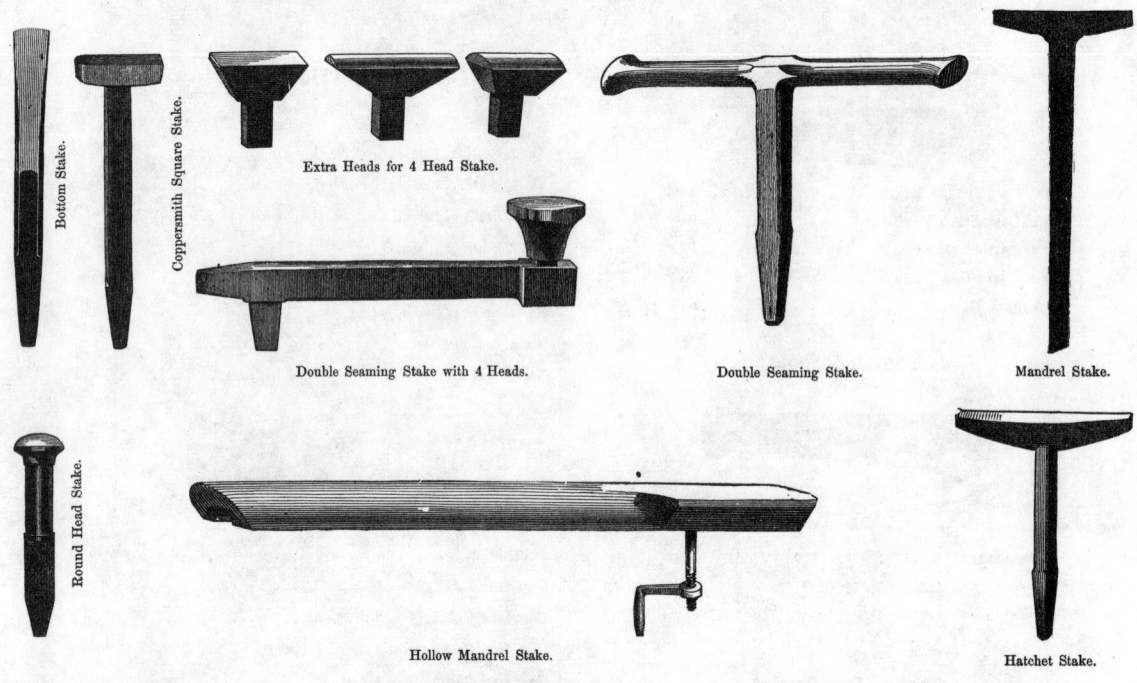

Bottom Stake.

Coppersmith Square Stake.

Extra Heads for 4 Head Stake.

Double Seaming Stake with 4 Heads.

Double Seaming Stake.

Mandrel Stake.

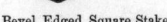

Round Head Stake.

Hollow Mandrel Stake.

Hatchet Stake.

Bevel Edged Square Stake.

Conductor Stake.

Bath Tub Stake.

STAKES.

No. 1, Large (or Beak Horn,) 45 lbs	each, $
No. 2, Large (or Beak Horn,) 40 lbs	"
No. 3, Large (or Beak Horn,) 35 lbs	"
No. 4, Large (or Beak Horn,) 30 lbs	"
No. 1, Double Seaming, large end 16 in., small end 11 in.	"
No. 2, Double Seaming, each end 11 inches	"
No. 0, Conductor, each end 14 inches	"
No. 1, Bevel, Edged Square	"
No. 2, Bevel, Edged Square	"
Common Blowhorn	"
Creasing with Horn	"
Common Creasing	"
Coppersmith Square	"
Common Square	"
Candle Mold	"
Needle Case	"
Small Square	"
Tea Kettle	"
Heads for Kettle	"
Bell Stake or Large Former	"
No. 1, Hatchet, blade 16 inches long	"
No. 2, Hatchet, blade 14½ inches long	"
No. 3, Hatchet, blade 13 inches long	"
No. 4, Hatchet, blade 11 inches long	"
No. 5, Hatchet, blade 9 inches long	"
No. 6, Hatchet, blade 7 inches long	"

STAKES.

(*Continued.*)

No. 1, **Bottom**, width 1¾ inches long	"
No. 2, Bottom, width 1½ inches long	"
No. 3, Bottom, width 1¼ inches long	"
No. 4, Bottom, width 1 inch long	"

Cast Iron.

No. 1, Conductor, Turned	each, $
No. 2, Conductor, Turned	"
No. 00, Mandrel, 5 feet long	"
No. 0, Mandrel, 3 feet four inches long	"
No. 1, Mandrel, 2 feet 10 inches long	"
No. 2, Mandrel, 2 feet 6 inches long	"
No. 3, Mandrel, 2 feet 3 inches long	"
Hollow Mandrel	"
Grooving Mandrel	"
Boiler Mandrel	"
Double Seaming, with 4 Heads	"
Extra Heads for Seaming	"
Common Beak Horn	"
Common Double Seaming	"
Common Double Seaming, Steel Ends	"
Bevel Edged Square	"
Round Head	"
Candle Mold Square	"
Bath Tub	"

TINSMITHS' MACHINES AND TOOLS.
(Continued.)

ROOFING TOOLS.

Double Roofing Seamer.

Roofing Double Seamers, 2 pieces..............per set, $

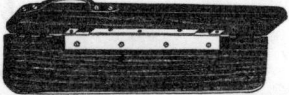

Wood, Roofing Folder.

Roofing Folder, Improved, 20 inch, Iron................each, $
Roofing Folder, Improved, Wood........................ "
Roofing Folder, Common, Wood .... "

ROOFING TOOLS.
(Continued.)

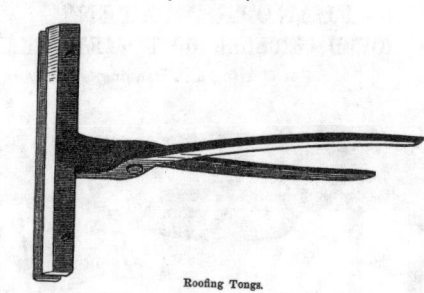

Roofing Tongs.

Roofing Tongs, (Steel,) 2 pairs........................per set, $

SAVAGE'S IMPROVED PATENT COMBINATION ROTARY SHEARS,
WITH BURRING ATTACHMENT OR EDGE TURNER.

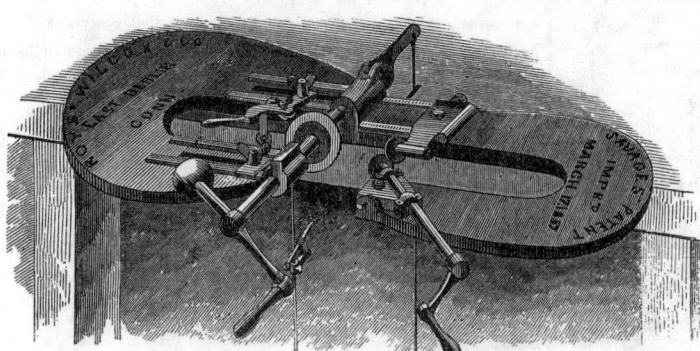

This Machine will cut Circles from Tin and bend (or burr) the same at any desired angle, without extra discs; or with a small additional expense, can be used for bending (or turning) edges at right angles, being more than any other Machine ever invented is capable of doing.

Each.

For Heavy Metal, with Burring Attachment...$

For Light Metal, with Burring Attachment...

For Light Metal, without Burring Attachment.

Extra discs (not exceeding 8 inches diameter) or cutters........................per pair $

Large Rotary Shears, to be driven either by Steam or Water Power, made in a superior manner, expressly for Trimming Boiler Bottoms and Brass Kettles, Oval or Round,

SQUARING SHEARS.

R. & W. CO. PATTERN.
For Cutting Sheet Metals, Paper, &c.

A GREAT LABOR-SAVING MACHINE.

We have no hesitation in recommending the above as the *best Shears* for cutting Sheet Metals into strips, square, or at any angle, that has ever been offered to the public. The operator having *both* hands at liberty to manage the Sheets, can cut more work, with greater accuracy, and much less grinding to keep them in order, than with any other Shears. They are made wholly of Steel and Iron, and are strong and durable, easily worked, (by the foot) and not liable to get out of repair by being worked by inexperienced hands.

STOW'S PATTERN.
For Cutting Sheet Metals, &c

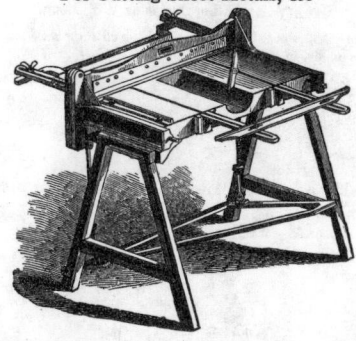

These Shears are arranged with Gauges for squaring, stripping and cutting at any desired angle, without the necessity of marking the sheet, and doing the work much quicker.

No. 0, are for cutting Sheets (30 inches) of Heavy Metal, Steel, Iron, Brass or Copper.

No. 1, are for cutting Sheet Iron, &c.: No. 2, for Tin and other light metals.

No. 0, R. & W. Co. Pattern, with Iron Frame...........each, $
No. 1, R. & W. or P. S. Co. Pattern, with Iron Frame.... "
No. 1, R. & W. or P. S. Co. Pattern, without Iron Frame.. "
No. 2, R. & W. or P. S. Co. Pattern, with Iron Frame.... "
No. 2, R. & W. or P. S. Co. Pattern, without Iron Frame.. "
No. 1, Stow's Pattern, or P. S. Co. Pattern, with Iron Frame "
No. 2, Stow's Pattern, or P. S. Co. Pattern, with Iron Frame "

☞ Lever Shears of any desired length (for cutting straight work) made to order.

TINSMITHS' MACHINES AND TOOLS.

(Continued.)

FLANDERS' PATENT
IMPROVED CIRCULAR OR ROTARY SHEARS,
For Cutting and Bending.

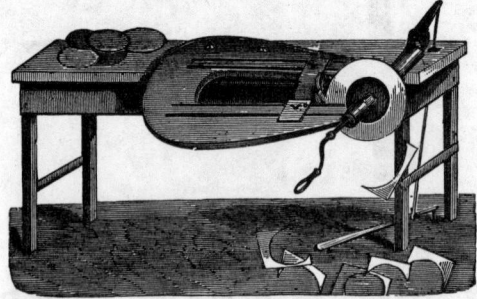

No. 0, For Gas Metres, &c., operated by Steam or Hand Power, with 1 pair 10¼ inch Disc and 1 pair Cutters on Iron Frame....................................each, $

Extra Discs, (average,)..........................per pair,

Extra Cutters..................................

No. 1, Operated by Hand, for Tin, &c., with 4 pair Discs, } each,
1 pair Cutters and Edge Turner.................}

No. 1, Without Edge Turner.........................   "

Extra Discs, (not exceeding 8 inch diam.) or Cutters, per pair,

WALKER'S
PATENT TIN FOLDING MACHINE.

Patent Tin Folding Machine.

This is the most simple, easy, and rapid working Tin Folder ever yet introduced. Many testimonials can be given, all concurring that it is the most convenient, simple, rapid and useful machine made for folding Tin.

Price of No. 1 Machine, 20 inches.........................each, $

Price of No. 2 Machine, 17 inches ....   "

BRUSHES.

PAINT BRUSHES.

Quality A.   Either Twine or Wire Bound.

We furnish five qualities of Paint Brushes, which are all of the same size, the only difference being in the quality of the stock.

	$					per doz.
No.	3	2	1	0	2-0	
	$					per doz.
No.	3-0	4-0	5-0	6-0		

Quality B.   Either Twine or Wire Bound—Star Brand.

Quality B is a brand made especially for shipping and ship use. The handle is fastened in with cement, which makes it very strong.

	$					per doz.
No.	3	2	1	0	2-0	
	$					per doz.
No.	3-0	4-0	5-0	6-0		

Quality C.   Twine Bound—Star Brand.

Quality C is our regular standard Brush, and such as Painters use for all except inside work.

	$					per doz.
No.	6	5	4	3	2	1
	$					per doz.
No.	0	2-0	3-0	4-0	5-0	6-0

Quality D.   Twine Bound.

Quality D is our regular Extra Ground Brush, made from selected bristles, especially for fine inside work.

	$					per doz.
No.	0	2-0	3-0	4-0	5-0	6-0

PAINT BRUSHES.
(Continued.)

Quality E.   Twine or Brass Bound—Star Brand.

Quality E is our Super Extra Brush, made of the best fine *ground* white bristles, the best made.

	$						per doz.
No.	6	5	4	3	2	1	
	$						per doz.
No.	0	2-0	3-0	4-0	5-0	6-0	

Blind Brushes.

Wire Bound—Star Brand.

Made especially for Painting Blinds, the Brush being less in diameter but longer in the Bristles than the ordinary size, and made from the same Bristles as the Super Extra Paint Brushes.

	$		per doz.
No.	1	2	3

Paint or Glue Brushes.

Made from Gray Bristles, with an iron ferrule, especially adapted for Glue Brushes and putting black lead on stoves, or for common Painting—which we term unbleached Paint Brushes.

	$					per doz.
No.	6	8	10	12	14	16

Put up in Boxes 1 dozen, assorted, two of each size.....per box, $

Paint Brushes for Family Use.

Made similar to the unbleached paint brushes, but **extra quality**. White outside.

	$					per doz.
Extra—No.	6	8	10	12	14	16

BRUSHES.

(Continued.)

PAINTERS' TOOLS.

Sash Tools.

Ordinary American Sash Tools, bound with Twine.

$								per doz.
No.	1	2	3	4	5	6	7	8

Extra—Made of French Bristles, **Tin Bound,** which makes a more Solid and strong tool, and Superior to the Sash Brush in general use.

$								per doz.
No.	1	2	3	4	5	6	7	8

Super Extra Sash Tools, made from Extra fine Brushes to correspond with Quality E of Paint Brushes. Usually called French or Lyon's Sash Tools.

$								per doz.
No.	1	2	3	4	5	6	7	8

Varnish Brushes.

Quality A. Twine Bound.

Varnish Brushes of this quality correspond with the same Brand of Paint Brushes, are made of all light colored Bristles, and are a good family Paint or Varnish Brush.

$						per doz.
No.	6	5	4	3	2	1

$						per doz.
No.	0	2-0	3-0	4-0	5-0	6-0

Quality E. Twine Bound—Star Brand.

This brush corresponds in quality with Super Extra Paint Brushes Quality E. As it is ground very fine, the large sizes are used for fine Painting—termed Gloss Brushes.

$						per doz.
No.	6	5	4	3	2	1

$						per doz.
No.	0	2-0	3-0	4-0	5-0	6-0

Flat Varnish.

Quality A.

This Quality of Flat Varnish is made especially for Pasting purposes. Also Mucilage and Common Varnishing, being thinner than the regular Brush.

$					per doz.
	1	1½	2	2½	3 inch.

Quality C. Cedar Handles.

The Second quality is the regular double thick Varnish, is well made and answers for all regular Varnishing.

$						per doz.
	1	1½	2	2½	3	3½	4 inch.

Quality E. Cedar Handles.

This quality corresponds with the Super Extra Varnish Brushes. Warranted in every respect.

$						per doz.
	1	1½	2	2½	3	3½	4 inch.

Camel Hair Varnish or Copying Press Brushes.

$								per doz.
½	1	1½	2	2½	3	3½	4	5 inch.

Thick Badger Hair Varnish.

From 1 to 4 inches.

ARTISTS' BRUSHES.

Fitch Hair Varnish Brushes.

From 1 to 4 inches.

Badger Hair Blenders.

From 2 to 6 inches.

Gilders' Tips.

Camel Hair, 2 inch hair, 4 inch wide................per dozen, $

Badger Hair, 2 inch hair, 4 inch wide................ "

Graining Brushes.

Fine French Bristles, Cedar Handles.

$						per doz.
1½	2	2½	3	3½	4	inch.

Badger Hair Grainers.

From 2 to 4 inches.

Steel Graining Combs.

12 Combs in a set, measuring 36 inches ....per dozen, $

Camel Hair Pencils—Common.

Assorted sizes ¾ inch long.

Camel Hair Pencils—Ordinary.

Assorted sizes in one Box from 1½ inch to 2 inch.

Camel Hair Pencils—Rose.

Assorted sizes in one Box from ½ inch to 2 inch.

Camel Hair Lacquering Brushes.

Round and Oval, assorted from 1 to 6.

Red Sable Lettering and Striping.

Assorted sizes and lengths.

Black Sable Lettering and Striping.

Assorted sizes and lengths.

Red Sable Artists, Cedar Handles.

Assorted from No. 1 to 20.

Marking Brushes.

Ordinary Quality with White Handles, assorted sizes..per gross, $

Extra Quality made with Cedar Handles of very fine Bristles with fine point.

No. 1, 1 inch Bristles ....per dozen, $

No. 2, 1 inch Bristles............................ "

No. 3, 1¼ inch Bristles............................ "

No. 4, 1¼ inch Bristles............................ "

No. 5, 1½ inch Bristles............................ "

No. 6, 1½ inch Bristles............................ "

Assorted, 2 dozen each size in a gross...... per gross, $

Flat Marking.

Same Sizes and Quality.

Camel Hair Marking.

Assorted sizes.

BRUSHES.

(Continued.)

WHITEWASH BRUSHES.

Coach Painters' Brush.

Flat, very fine ground, Cedar Handle.

$	¾	1	1¼	1½	per doz.
					inch.

Bag Marking.

Made flat, very stiff Bristles, for marking Bales and Bags.

$	per dozen.	$	per dozen.
	1 inch		1¼ inch.

Whitewash Brushes.

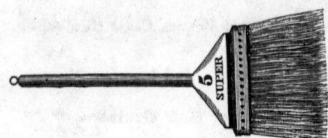

Quality A.

Quality A Whitewash Brushes, corresponds with the same Brand of Paint Brushes. Made from Gray Bristles, and suitable for Fences, Trees, and Cellar Walls.

$						per doz.
No.	4	5	6	7	8	9
$						per doz.
No.	10	11	12	13	14	

Extra Whitewash Brushes.
Quality B.

Second Quality, size of Brush same as the *A*, with pure white Bristles on the outside, makes a good Brush for common use. Each Brush has the size and quality branded on in full.

$						per doz.
No.	4	5	6	7	8	9
$						per doz.
No.	10	11	12	13	14	

3 Rows Whitewash Brushes.
Quality C.

Quality C same as the B, with pure white Bristles on the outside. The Bristles are longer and heavier, with a row in the centre of the Block.

$								per doz.
No.	9	10	11	12	13	14	15	

Whitewash Brushes.
Quality D.

Quality D.—The Block is cut very thin inside of the Bristles, in the wedge shape, which throws the Bristles together and prevents the lime from dropping. A Brush made on this principle will do better work and last longer. Will answer for masons' use. White Bristles on the outside.

$						per doz.
No.	100	200	300	400	500	

Super Whitewash Brushes.
Quality E.

Quality E.—The small sizes are for a good Family Whitewash Brush, and the large for Masons' and Professional Whitewashers' use. They are the best made. They are made of unbleached White Bristles on the outside, and are in every respect a Superior Brush.

$					per doz.
Families', No.	1	2	3	4	
$					per doz.
Masons', No.	5	6	7		

Twyford's Patent Whitewash Brush.

Are bound with Zinc sewed through with Copper Wire, and the Bristles are fastened in with cement, which makes them stronger than when nailed; there is no wood in the centre, so that the Bristles are solid. They answer to paint on a flat surface, and as a Whitewash Brush are unsurpassed. They are pronounced superior to anything made.

$							per doz.
No.	1	2	3	4	5	6	

WHITEWASH HEADS.

Quality A.

Quality A, is the same in quality and quantity of Bristles as the Whitewash Brush of the same brand, except the Blocks are larger on the Medium and larger sizes, the No. 14 Whitewash Heads, being one inch larger than the No. 14 Whitewash Brush.

$							per doz.
No.	4	5	6	7	8	9	
$							per doz.
No.	10	11	12	13	14		

Extra Whitewash Heads.
Quality B.

Quality B is the same size as A, with fine white Bristles on the outside. Each Brush is branded in full each quality and size.

$							per doz.
No.	4	5	6	7	8	9	
$							per doz.
No.	10	11	12	13	14		

3 Rows Whitewash Heads.
Quality C.

Quality C is made on the same size Block as the Extra Head No. 8, 10, 12, 14, 16 and 18, but longer Bristles and much fuller, with a row of Bristles in the centre of the Block.

$							per doz.
No.	100	200	300	400	500	600	

Super Whitewash Heads.
Quality E.

Quality E is the same quality of Bristles and made on the same principle as the Brushes of the same brand, but on a larger Block, either white wood or oak.

$							per doz.
No.	40	50	60	70	80	90	

Super Extra Whitewash Heads.
Quality F.

Quality F is made on the same principle as the Super Whitewash Heads, especially for Practical White-washers, out of White Hair, the same as in the Super Extra Paint Brushes.

$					per doz.
No.	100	105	110	115	

Knotted Whitewash Heads.

$									per doz.
	4	5	6	7	8	9	10	12	knots.

KALSOMINE BRUSHES.

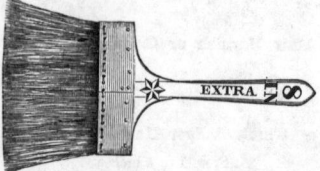

BRUSHES.

(Continued.)

KALSOMINE BRUSHES.

(Continued.)

Quality A.

Made of White Bristles on the Twyford Patent, and warranted in every respect.

	$				per doz.
No.	5	6	7	8	

Extra Kalsomine Brushes,

Are the same in style, but ½ inch longer Hair and more Bristles.

	$				per doz.
No.	5	6	7	8	

Paint Dusters.

	$					per doz.
No.	1	2	3	4	5	

Paste Brushes.

Made on a Block, similar to a W. W. Brush, Handle 8 inches long, white Bristles on the outside, suitable for Paste, Hanging Paper, Painting Roofs, or Varnishing Decks of Vessels.

	$					per doz.
No.	1	2	3	4	5	

Roof Brushes.

Roof Brush or Duplicate Paint Brush. Paint Brushes fastened into a Block with a four foot handle, and are the best article there is for Painting Roofs and Decks or Sides of Vessels.

	$			per doz.
Size	2 knots.	3 knots.	4 knots.	

Stencil Brushes.

Star Brand.

	$						per doz.
No.	1	2	3	4	5	6	
	$						per doz.
No.	7	8	9	10	11	12	

STENCIL BRUSHES.

(Continued.)

Wire Bound **Extra Fine Ground Bristles,** adapted to Shade Makers' use.

Star Brand.

	$						per doz.
No.	1	2	3	4	5	6	

Stove Brushes.

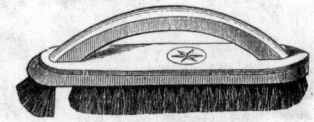

	$						per doz.
No.	11	12	13	14	15	16	17
			$				per doz.
With Bristles on Top.	No.	18	19	20			

Shoe Brushes.

	$						per doz.
No.	40	41	42	43	44	45	
	$						per doz.
No.	46	47	48	50	51	52	

Handled Shoe Brushes.

	$					per doz.
No.	20	21	22	23	24	
	$					per doz.
No.	25	26	27	28	30	

Shoe Top for Applying Blacking.

No. 1......$	per doz.	No. 2...... $	per doz.

Blacking Box Holder.

Holds any Size Box of Blacking.................... $ per doz.

Scrub Brushes.

Bristles.

	$						per doz.
No.	1	2	3	4	5	6	
	$						per doz.
No.	7	8	9	10	11	12	
			$				per doz.
White Tampico,........	No. 50	51	52	53			
			$				per doz.
Gray Tampico,.........	No. 44	45	46	47			

BRUSHES.

(Continued.)

SCRUB BRUSHES.

(Continued.)

Sea Root, ...No. $\begin{array}{cc} \$ \\ 22 & 23 \end{array}$　per doz.

Handled, ...No. $\begin{array}{cc} \$ \\ 62 & 64 \end{array}$　per doz.

Any of the above number handled　　extra per dozen.

Clamp or Deck Scrub Brushes.

With 4 foot Handle.

No. $\begin{array}{cccccc} \$ \\ 5 & 6 & 7 & 8 & 10 & 12 \end{array}$　per doz.

Water Brushes.

No. 1, All Bristles ....per dozen, $

No. 2, All Bristles ....　"

No. 3, Sea Root ....　"

No. 4, Sea Root.....................................　"

No. 5, Whalebone ....　"

No. 6, Whalebone ....　"

Feather Dusters.

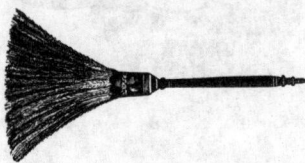

Number.	Size.	Per Dozen.
5	5 inch	$
6	5½	
8	6	
10	7	
12	8	
14	9	
15	10	
16	11	
17	12	
18	13	
19	14	
20	15	
21	16	
22	17	
23	18	
24	19	
25	20	
26	21	
27	22	
28	23	
29	24	
30	25	

DUSTING BRUSHES.

No. $\begin{array}{cccc} \$ \\ 1 & 2 & 3 & 4 \end{array}$　per doz.

Better quality, sizes same as above.

No. $\begin{array}{cccc} \$ \\ 5 & 6 & 7 & 8 \end{array}$　per doz.

Extra Dusting Brushes.

Is a better quality of Bristles, and fuller, cased on the outside with pure white Bristles.

No. $\begin{array}{cccc} \$ \\ 1 & 2 & 3 & 4 \end{array}$　per doz.

Better quality, sizes same as above.

No. $\begin{array}{cccccc} \$ \\ 5 & 6 & 7 & 8 & 9 & 10 \end{array}$　per doz.

Extra Dust Brushes.

Same Size as No. 5, but better Quality.

No. $\begin{array}{cccc} \$ \\ 11 & 12 & 13 & 14 \end{array}$　per doz.

Fancy Dust Brushes.

Ornamented Block.

No. $\begin{array}{ccc} \$ \\ 1 & 2 & 3 \end{array}$　per doz.

Super Extra Dust Brushes.

Made on a Polished Black Walnut Block, of Pure White Bristles.

No. $\begin{array}{cccc} \$ \\ 1 & 2 & 3 & 4 \end{array}$　per doz.

Double Dusters.

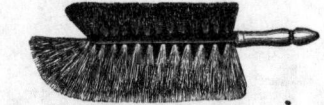

No. $\begin{array}{ccc} \$ \\ 1 & 2 & 3 \end{array}$　per doz.

Factory Dusters.

No. 1......$　per doz.　No. 2......$　per doz.

Toy Dusters.

No. 1......$　per doz.　No. 2......$　per doz.

Furniture Dusters.

Polished White Maple Blocks, made from pure White Bristles, for Dusting Furniture and for Barber use.

No. 1......$　per doz.　No. 2......$　per doz.

Plush Duster.

For cleaning around the Buttons in Sofas and Carriage Cushions, pointed and very stiff in the centre.

No. 1......$　per doz　No. 2......$　per doz.

BRUSHES.

(Continued.)

Hearth Brushes.

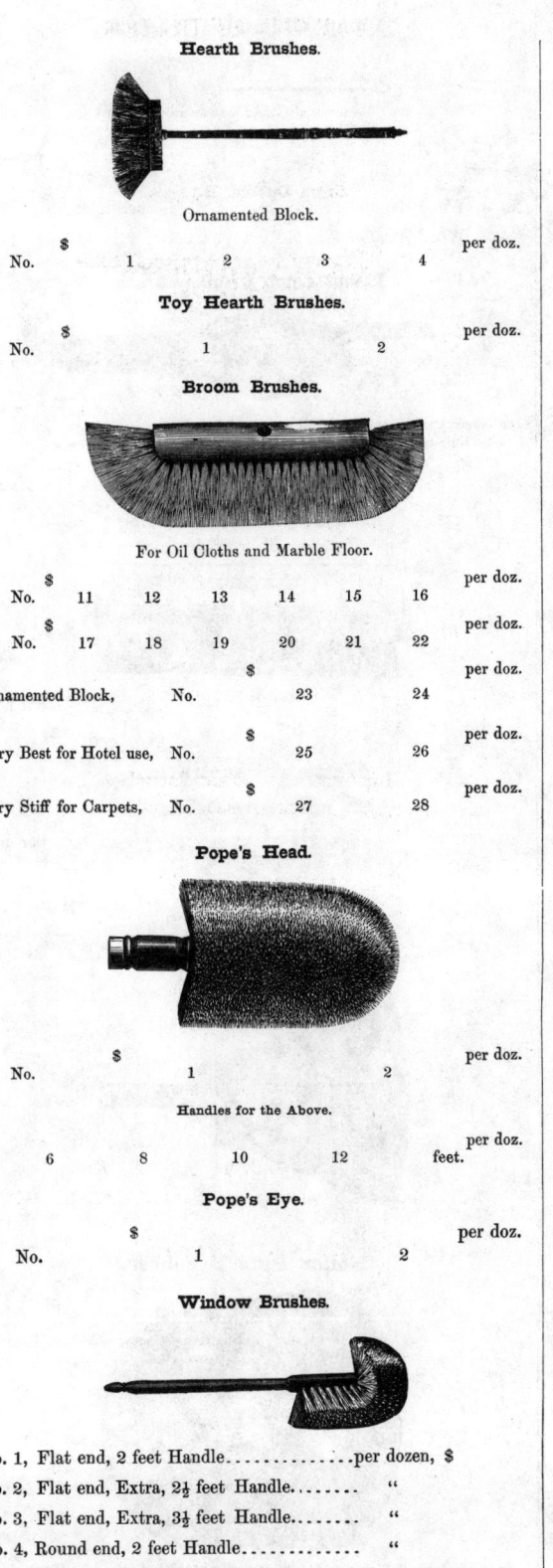

Ornamented Block.

No.	$ 1	2	3	4	per doz.

Toy Hearth Brushes.

No.	$	1	2	per doz.

Broom Brushes.

For Oil Cloths and Marble Floor.

No.	$ 11	12	13	14	15	16	per doz.
No.	$ 17	18	19	20	21	22	per doz.

		$		
Ornamented Block,	No.		23	24	per doz.
Very Best for Hotel use,	No.	$	25	26	per doz.
Very Stiff for Carpets,	No.	$	27	28	per doz.

Pope's Head.

No.	$ 1	2	per doz.

Handles for the Above.

$ 6	8	10	12	feet.	per doz.

Pope's Eye.

No.	$ 1	2	per doz.

Window Brushes.

No. 1, Flat end, 2 feet Handle.............per dozen, $
No. 2, Flat end, Extra, 2½ feet Handle........ "
No. 3, Flat end, Extra, 3½ feet Handle........ "
No. 4, Round end, 2 feet Handle............. "
No. 5, Round end, Extra, 2 feet Handle....... "
No. 6, Round end, Extra, 3½ feet Handle...... "

Crumb Brushes.

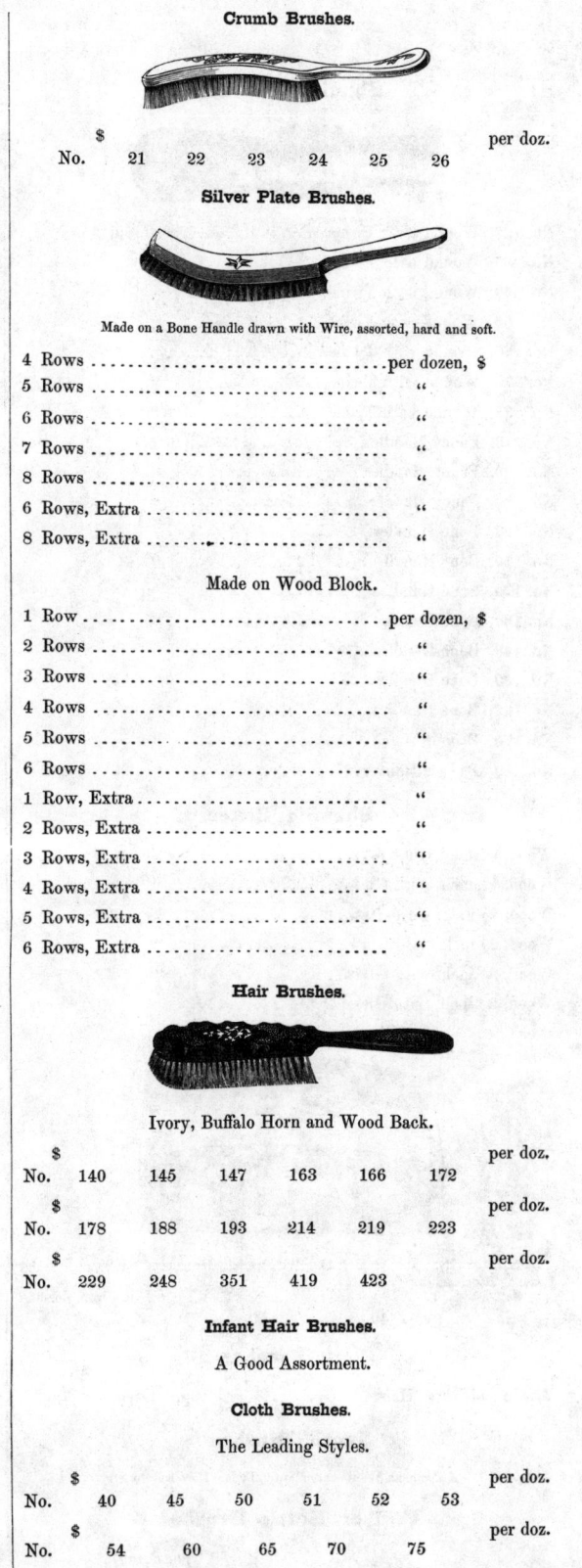

No.	$ 21	22	23	24	25	26	per doz.

Silver Plate Brushes.

Made on a Bone Handle drawn with Wire, assorted, hard and soft.

4 Rows ....per dozen, $
5 Rows .... "
6 Rows .... "
7 Rows .... "
8 Rows .... "
6 Rows, Extra .... "
8 Rows, Extra .... "

Made on Wood Block.

1 Row ....per dozen, $
2 Rows .... "
3 Rows .... "
4 Rows .... "
5 Rows .... "
6 Rows .... "
1 Row, Extra .... "
2 Rows, Extra .... "
3 Rows, Extra .... "
4 Rows, Extra .... "
5 Rows, Extra .... "
6 Rows, Extra .... "

Hair Brushes.

Ivory, Buffalo Horn and Wood Back.

No.	$ 140	145	147	163	166	172	per doz.
No.	$ 178	188	193	214	219	223	per doz.
No.	$ 229	248	351	419	423		per doz.

Infant Hair Brushes.

A Good Assortment.

Cloth Brushes.

The Leading Styles.

No.	$ 40	45	50	51	52	53	per doz.
No.	$ 54	60	65	70	75		per doz.

BRUSHES.

(Continued.)

Hat Brushes.

$

No.	60	61	62	63	64	65	per doz.

Shaving Brushes.

No. 22, Wound with Twine..................per dozen, $
No. 33, Wound with Twine. .... "
No. 44, Wound with Twine.............. "
No. 55, Wound with Twine............. "
No. 66, Wound with Twine............ "
No. 77, Wound with Twine............ "
No. 88, Wound with Twine............. "
No. 10, Fancy Handles................... "
No. 20, Fancy Handles................... "
No. 30, Fancy Handles.................. "
No. 100, Bone Handles................... "
No. 110, Bone Handles.................. "
No. 120, Bone Handles.................. "
No. 130, Bone Handles.................. "
No. 140, Bone Handles.................. "
No. 150, Bone Handles.................. "
No. 160, Bone Handles.................. "
No. 170, Badger Hair.................... "
No. 180, Badger Hair.................... "

Shaving Boxes.

Wood, without Glass......................per dozen, $
Wood, 2 inch, with Glass................. "
Wood, 2½ inch, with Glass................ "
Wood, 2¾ inch, with Glass................ "
Wood, 3 inch, with Glass................. "
Wood, 3 inch, with Glass, Oval........... "

Finger Nail Brushes.

Buffalo Horn, Bone and Wood Back. We especially recommend the Wood Back for Counting Room and Hotel use.

$ per dozen.

No.	40	41	42

Flesh Brushes.

Bristle and Horse Hair.....................per dozen, $

Teeth Brushes.

A Complete Assortment of Ivory, Buffalo Horn and Bone.

Vial or Bottle Brushes.

per dozen, $

Lamp Chimney Brushes.

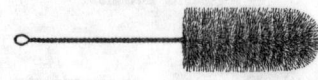

$ per doz.

No.	1	2	3	4

No. 5, Wood Handle....................per dozen, $
No. 6, Wood Handle......................... "

Patent Lamp Chimney Brush.

The Simplest and most Convenient Brush made, for cleaning Kerosene Lamp Chimneys.....................per dozen, $

Hatters' Brushes.

Made especially for Hat Manufacturers' use.

$ per doz.

No.	1	2	3	4

Hatters' Penetrating.

Made from O'katka Bristles.

$ per doz.

No.	1	2

Whist Brooms.

A Complete Assortment.

Boiler Flue Brushes.

From 5 inches to 25 inches, made from either Ratan or Whalebone. The Ratan costing half the price of the Whalebone.

Tube Brushes made of Bristles, on Wood Block, from 2 inches to 6 inches.

BRUSHES.

(Continued)

Whalebone Flue Brushes.

$						per doz.
	1	1¼	1½	1¾	2	2¼	inch diam.
$						per doz.
	2½	2¾	3	3¼	3½	3¾	inch diam.
$						per doz.
	4	4½	5	5½	6		inch diam.

Horse Brushes.

Wood Back.

No. 40, Common Bristles...................per dozen, $
No. 41, Common Bristles.................... "
No. 42, Black Tampico..................... "
No. 43, Black Tampico..................... "
No. 44, Black Tampico..................... "
No. 45, Round Face Tampico .... "
No. 46, Round Face, Mixed .... "
No. 47, Round Face, Mixed .... "
No. 48, Round Face, Mixed .... "
No. 49, Round Face, Mixed .... "
No. 50, Round Face, Mixed .... "
No. 51, Round Face, Mixed .... "
No. 52, Round Facc, Mixed .... "
No. 53, All Bristles .... "
No. 54, All Bristles .... "
No. 55, All Bristles .... "
No. 56, All Bristles .... "
No. 57, All Bristles .... "
No. 58, All Bristles .... "
No. 59, All Bristles .... "
No. 60, All Bristles .... "

Leather Back.

No. 100, Mixed...........................per dozen, $
No. 110, All Bristles .... "
No. 210, All White Bristles .... "
No 220, All White Bristles .... "
No. 230, All White Bristles .... "
No. 240, All White Bristles .... "
No. 250, All White Bristles .... "

Sea Root Horse Brushes.

	$				per doz.
No.	80	81	82	83	

Tar Brushes.

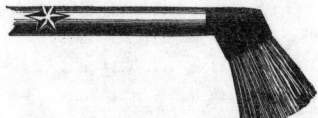

Short Handled Tar Brushes.

	$			per doz.
No.	1	2	3	

Long Handled Tar Brushes.
With Four Feet Handle.

	$			per doz.
No.	1	2	3	

Ship Seam.

No. 1, Horse Hair.........................per dozen, $
No. 2, Bristles............................ "
No. 3, Extra Large......................... "

Lager Beer Cup and Pitcher Brushes.

	$			per doz.
No.	1	2	3	

Tanners' Blacking.

	$		per doz.
No.	1	2	

Tanners' Paste.

	$		per doz.
No.	1	2	

Tanners' Scouring.

7 Rows.................................per dozen, $
8 Rows................................. "

Ratan Street and Stable Brooms.

$			per doz.
12	14	16	inch.

Mane Brushes.

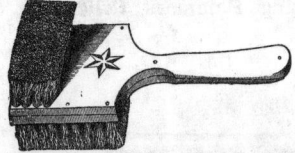

No. 1, All Bristles.........................per dozen, $
No. 2, All Bristles......................... "
No. 3, All Bristles, Double................. "
No. 4, Sea Root............................ "

HAMMERS.

"SELSOR COOK & CO."
Polished Nail Hammers, Solid Cast Steel.

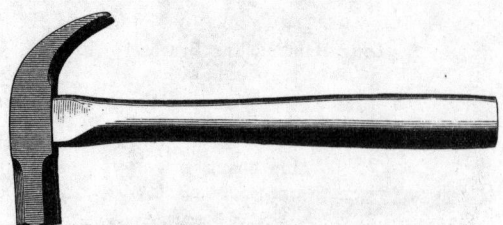

	Weight per single Hammer, including handle.	Diameter of Face.	
No. 0	0 lb........10 oz.	$\frac{3}{4}$ in.	per dozen, $
No. 1	1 lb.........0 oz.	$\frac{7}{8}$ in.	"
No. 2	1 lb.........7 oz.	1 in.	"
No. 3	1 lb........10 oz.	$1\frac{1}{16}$ in.	"
No. 4	1 lb........13 oz.	$1\frac{1}{8}$ in.	"

Polished Nail Hammers, Steel Face and Claw.

	Weight per single Hammer, including Handle.	Diameter of Face.	
No. 0	0 lb........10 oz.	3 in.	per dozen, $
No. 1	1 lb.........0 oz.	$\frac{7}{8}$ in.	"
No. 2	1 lb.........7 oz.	1 in.	"
No. 3	1 lb........10 oz.	$1\frac{1}{16}$ in.	"
No. 4	1 lb........13 oz.	$1\frac{1}{8}$ in.	"

Adze Eye Hammers, Solid Cast Steel.

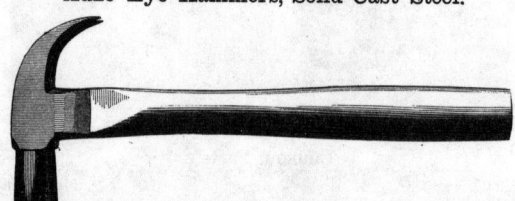

	Weight per single Hammer, including Handle.	Diameter of Face.	
No. 0	0 lb........10 oz.	$\frac{3}{4}$ in.	per dozen, $
No. 1	1 lb.........0 oz.	$\frac{7}{8}$ in.	"
No. 2	1 lb.........5 oz.	$\frac{11}{16}$ in.	"
No. 4	1 lb........10 oz.	$1\frac{1}{4}$ in.	"

Adze Eye Farriers.

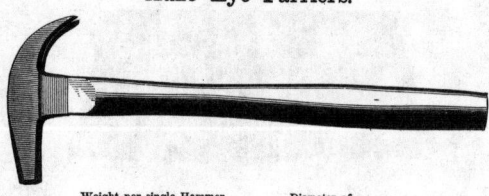

	Weight per single Hammer, including Handle.	Diameter of Face.	
	0 lbs........10 oz.	$\frac{5}{8}$ in.	per dozen, $

Riveting Hammers, Solid Cast Steel.

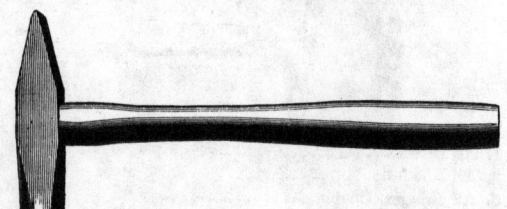

"SELSOR COOK & CO."
Riveting Hammers.
(Continued.)

	Weight per single Hammer, including Handle.	Diameter of Face.	
No. 0	0 lb........6½ oz.	$\frac{5}{8}$ in.	per dozen, $
No. 1	0 lb........9½ oz.	$1\frac{1}{16}$ in.	"
No. 2	0 lb........12½ oz.	$\frac{3}{4}$ in.	"
No. 3	1 lb.........1 oz.	$\frac{7}{8}$ in.	"
No. 4	1 lb........3½ oz.	$\frac{7}{8}$ in.	"
No. 5	1 lb.........6 oz.	$1\frac{5}{16}$ in.	"
No. 6	1 lb.........9 oz.	$1\frac{1}{16}$ in.	"

Riveting Hammers, Steel Face and Pein.

	Weight per single Hammer, including Handle.	Diameter of Face.	
No. 0	0 lb........6½ oz.	$\frac{5}{8}$ in.	per dozen, $
No. 1	0 lb........9½ oz.	$1\frac{1}{16}$ in.	"
No. 2	0 lb........12½ oz.	$\frac{3}{4}$ in.	"
No. 3	1 lb.........1 oz.	$\frac{7}{8}$ in.	"
No. 4	1 lb........3½ oz.	$\frac{7}{8}$ in.	"
No. 5	1 lb.........6 oz.	$1\frac{5}{16}$ in.	"

Engineers' Hammers, Solid Cast Steel.

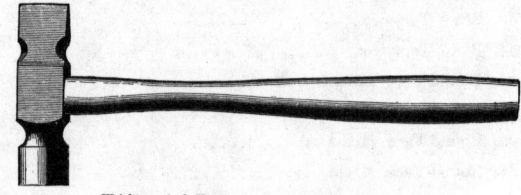

	Weight per single Hammer, including Handle.	Diameter of Face.	
No. 0	1 lb.........2 oz.	$1\frac{1}{8}$ in.	per dozen, $
No. 1	1 lb........13 oz.	$1\frac{1}{4}$ in.	"
No. 2	2 lb.........4 oz.	$1\frac{3}{8}$ in.	"
No. 3	2 lb........11 oz.	$1\frac{1}{2}$ in.	"
No. 4	3 lb.........4 oz.	$1\frac{5}{8}$ in.	"

Blacksmiths' Hammers, Solid Cast Steel.

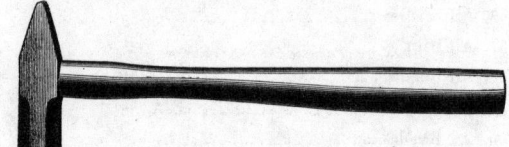

	Weight per single Hammer, including Handle.	Diameter of Face.	
No. 0	1 lb........10 oz.	$1\frac{1}{4}$ in.	per dozen, $
No. 1	2 lb.........4 oz.	$1\frac{3}{8}$ in.	"
No. 2	2 lb........11 oz.	$1\frac{1}{2}$ in.	"
No. 3	3 lb.........9 oz.	$1\frac{5}{8}$ in.	"
No. 4	4 lb.........0 oz.	$1\frac{3}{4}$ in.	"

Double Face.

	Weight per single Hammer, including Handle.	Diameter of Face.	
No. 5	2 lbs........4 oz.	$1\frac{3}{8}$ in.	per dozen, $
No. 6	2 lbs.......11 oz.	$1\frac{1}{2}$ in.	"
No. 7	3 lbs........9 oz.	$1\frac{5}{8}$ in.	"
No. 8	4 lbs........0 oz.	$1\frac{3}{4}$ in.	"

Blacksmiths' Hammers, Steel Face and Pein.

	Weight per single Hammer, including Handle.	Diameter of Face.	
No. 0	1 lb........10 oz.	$1\frac{1}{4}$ in.	per dozen, $
No. 1	2 lbs........4 oz.	$1\frac{3}{8}$ in.	"
No. 2	2 lbs.......11 oz.	$1\frac{1}{2}$ in.	"
No. 3	3 lbs........9 oz.	$1\frac{5}{8}$ in.	"
No. 4	4 lbs........0 oz.	$1\frac{3}{4}$ in.	"

HAMMERS.

(Continued.)

"SELSOR COOK & CO."

Blacksmiths' Hammers.

(Continued.)

Double Face.

	Weight per single Hammer, including Handle.		Diameter of Face.	
No. 5	2 lbs	4 oz	$1\frac{3}{8}$ in.	per dozen, $
No. 6	2 lbs	11 oz	$1\frac{1}{2}$ in.	"
No. 7	3 lbs	9 oz	$1\frac{5}{8}$ in.	"
No. 8	4 lbs	0 oz	$1\frac{3}{4}$ in.	"

Machinists' Cast Steel Chipping Hammers.

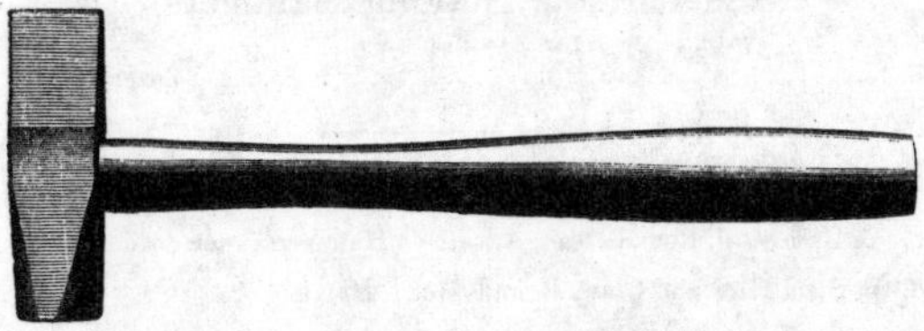

	Weight per single Hammer, including Handle.		Diameter of Face.	
No. 0	1 lb.	4 oz	$1\frac{1}{8}$ in.	per dozen, $
No. 1	1 lb.	12 oz	$1\frac{1}{4}$ in.	"
No. 2	2 lbs	6 oz	$1\frac{3}{8}$ in.	"
No. 3	3 lbs	1 oz	$1\frac{1}{2}$ in.	"
No. 4	4 lbs	8 oz	$1\frac{5}{8}$ in,	"

Veneering Hammers, all Polished.

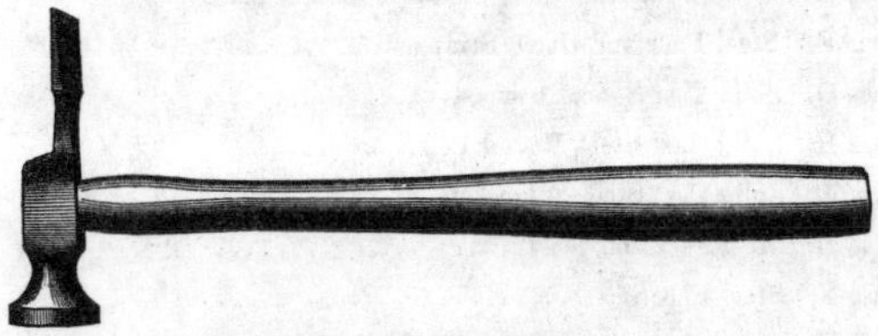

	Weight of single Hammer, including Handle.		Diameter of Face.	
No. 3	0 lbs	6 oz	$1\frac{1}{8}$ in.	per dozen, $
No. 4	0 lbs	9 oz	$1\frac{1}{4}$ in.	"
No. 5	0 lbs	$12\frac{1}{2}$ oz	$1\frac{3}{8}$ in.	"

Coopers' Hammers, Solid Cast Steel.

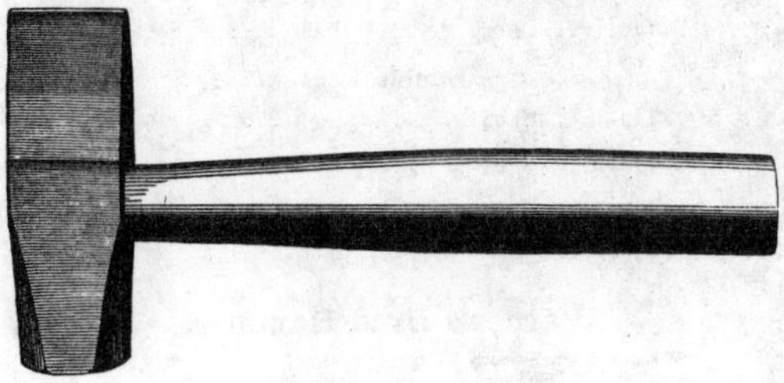

	Weight per single Hammer, including Handle.		Diameter of Face.	
No. 0	1 lb.	9 oz	$1\frac{1}{8}$ in.	per dozen, $
No. 1	2 lbs	1 oz	$1\frac{1}{4}$ in.	"
No. 2	2 lbs	9 oz	$1\frac{3}{8}$ in.	"
No. 3	3 lbs	1 oz	$1\frac{1}{2}$ in.	"
No. 4	3 lbs	10 oz	$1\frac{3}{8}$ in.	"

"SELSOR COOK & CO."

Brick Hammers, Cast Steel Head and Edge.

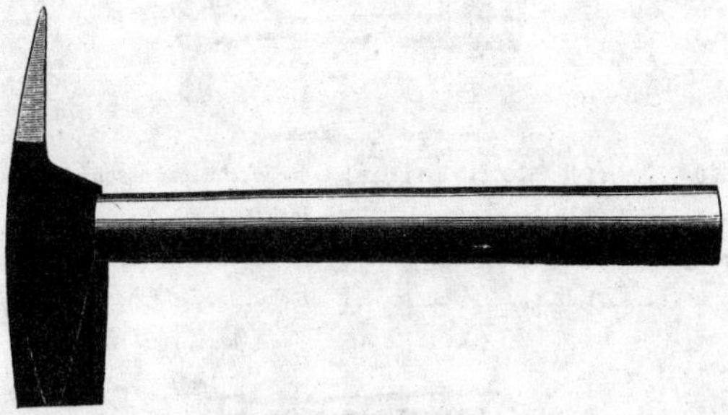

	$			per dozen.
Weight,	$1\frac{1}{2}$	2	$2\frac{1}{2}$	lbs.

Masons' Hammer, Cast Steel Head and Edge.

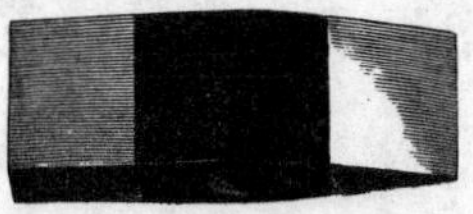

	$						per dozen.
Weight,	3	$3\frac{1}{2}$	4	$4\frac{1}{2}$	5	$5\frac{1}{2}$	lbs.
	$						per dozen.
Weight,	6	7	8	9	10		lbs.

"D. MAYDOLE & CO."

Adze Eye Hammers, Solid Cast Steel.

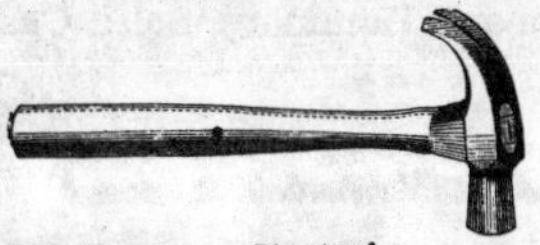

	Weight per Single Hammer including Handle.		Diameter of Face.	
No. 1	1 lb.	8 oz.	$1\frac{1}{8}$ inch	per dozen, $
No. $1\frac{1}{2}$	1 lb.	5 oz.	$1\frac{1}{16}$ inch	"
No. 2	1 lb.	1 oz.	1 inch	"
No. 3	0 lb.	11 oz.	$\frac{3}{4}$ inch	"

Adze Eye, Bell Face Hammers, Solid Cast Steel.

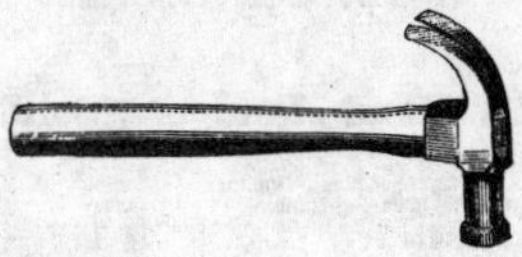

	Weight per Single Hammer, including Handle.		Diameter of Face.	
No. 1	1 lb.	8 oz.	$1\frac{3}{16}$ in.	per dozen, $
No. $1\frac{1}{2}$	1 lb.	4 oz.	$1\frac{1}{8}$ in.	"
No. 2	1 lb.	0 oz	$\frac{15}{16}$ in.	"
No. 3	0 lb.	10 oz.	$\frac{13}{16}$ in.	"

Farriers' Hammers, Solid Cast Steel.

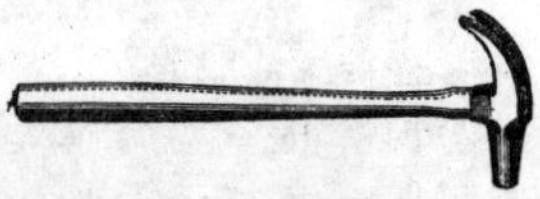

	Weight per Single Hammer including Handle.		Diameter of Face.	
Adze Eye	0 lb.	$10\frac{1}{2}$ oz	$\frac{9}{16}$ inch	per dozen, $
Plain	0 lb.	10 oz	$\frac{5}{8}$ inch	"

HAMMERS.

(Continued.)

"Maydole's" Joiners' Hammers, Solid Cast Steel.

	Weight per Single Hammer including Handle.	Diameter of Face.	
No. 0	1 lb......15 oz	$1\frac{5}{16}$ inch	per dozen, $
No. 1	1 lb......9 oz	$1\frac{3}{16}$ inch	"
No. 1½	1 lb......3 oz	$1\frac{1}{8}$ inch	"
No. 2	1 lb......	1 inch	"

No. 3 (Brad).	0 lb......10 oz	$\frac{13}{16}$ inch	per dozen, $

Joiners' Bell Faced Hammers, Solid Cast Steel.

	Weight per Single Hammer including Handle.	Diameter of face.	
No. 1	1 lb......8 oz	$1\frac{3}{16}$ inch	per dozen, $
No. 1½	1 lb......2 oz	$1\frac{1}{8}$ inch	"
No. 2	1 lb......0 oz	1 inch	"

Engineers' Hammers, Solid Cast Steel.

	Weight per Single Hammer, including Handle.	Diameter of Face.	
No. 1, Riveting Pein	2 lb......9 oz	$1\frac{7}{16}$ in.	per dozen, $
No. 2, Riveting Pein	2 lb......3 oz	$1\frac{3}{8}$ in.	"
No. 1, Ball Pein	2 lb......8 oz	$1\frac{1}{2}$ in.	"
No. 2, Ball Pein	2 lb......2 oz	$1\frac{7}{16}$ in.	"
No. 3, Ball Pein	1 lb......10 oz	$1\frac{5}{16}$ in.	"

Blacksmiths' Hand Hammers, Solid Cast Steel.

	Weight per Single Hammer. including Handle.	Diameter of Face.	
No. 1	3 lbs......7 oz	$1\frac{5}{8}$ in.	per dozen, $
No. 2	2 lbs......14 oz	$1\frac{9}{16}$ in.	"
No. 1, Shoulder Pein	3 lbs......1 oz	$1\frac{11}{16}$ in.	"

Riveting Hammers, Solid Cast Steel.

	Weight per Single Hammer, including Handle.	Diameter of Face.	
No. 0	1 lb......15 oz	$1\frac{1}{8}$ in.	per dozen, $
No. 1	1 lb......7 oz	1 in.	"
No. 2	0 lbs......14½ oz	$\frac{7}{8}$ in.	"
No. 3	0 lbs......10½ oz	$\frac{11}{16}$ in.	"
No. 1, Ball Pein	0 lbs......15 oz	1 in.	"
No. 2, Ball Pein	0 lbs......10 oz	$\frac{7}{8}$ in.	"

Maydole's" Carriage Ironers' Hand Hammers.

	Weight per Single Hammer without Handle.	
No. 1	2 lbs......12 oz	per dozen, $
No. 2	2 lbs......6 oz	"

Machinists' Chipping Hammers.

	Weight per Single Hammer without Handle.	
No. 0	1 lb......12 oz	per dozen, $
No. 1	1 lb......6 oz	"
No. 2	1 lb......2 oz	"

Machine Forgers' Hand Hammers.

	Weight per Single Hammer without Handle.	
No. 1	2 lbs......2 oz	per dozen, $

Machinists' Staving Hammers.

	Weight per Single Hammer without Handle.	
No. 1	2 lbs	per dozen, $

"Cheeney & Lerow's" Nail Hammers.

No. 5, Cast Steel, Round Head, Adze Eye Hammers	per dozen, $
No. 6, Steel Face and Claw, Round Head Hammer	"
No. 22, Steel Faced and Claw, Round Head Hammer	"
No. 23, Wrought Iron, Full Finished	"

Warner's Nail Hammers.

Class A, Solid Cast Steel	per dozen, $
Class B 3, Solid Cast Steel	"
Class B 4, Solid Cast Steel (heavy)	"
Class C, Steel Face and Claw	"
Class D, Steel Face	"
Class E, Steel Face and Claw, Center-braced	"
Class F, Steel Face and Claw, Strapped	"
Class G, Solid Cast Steel, Strapped	"
Class H, Solid Cast Steel, Round Poll	"
Class J, Solid Cast Steel, Adze Eye	"
Class M, Steel Face and Claw	"
Class N, Steel Face	"
Class Union, Steel Face and Claw, Round Poll	"
American Ring Hammer	"

Warner's Solid Cast Steel Blacksmiths' Hammers.

	Weight of Single Hammer, including Handle.	Diameter of Face.	
No. 0	2 lb......0 oz	$1\frac{7}{16}$ inch	per dozen, $
No. 1	3 lb......4 oz	$1\frac{9}{16}$ inch	"
No. 2	3 lb......10 oz	$1\frac{11}{16}$ inch	"
No. 3	3 lb......12 oz	$1\frac{3}{4}$ inch	"
Double Face.			
No. 4	2 lb......10 oz	$1\frac{7}{16}$ inch	"
No. 5	3 lb......0 oz	$1\frac{9}{16}$ inch	"
No. 6	3 lb......10 oz	$1\frac{11}{16}$ inch	"
No. 7	4 lb......6 oz	$1\frac{13}{16}$ inch	"

Warner's Brad Hammers.

	Weight of Single Hammer, including Handle.	Diameter of Face.	
No. 1 (Octagon Face)	5 oz	$\frac{9}{16}$ inch	per dozen, $
No. 2	0 lb......9 oz	$\frac{3}{4}$ inch	"
No. 3	0 lb......11 oz	$\frac{13}{16}$ inch	"
No. 4 (Round Face)	9½ oz	$\frac{13}{16}$ inch	"
No. 5	0 lb......13½ oz	$\frac{14}{16}$ inch	"

Warner's Carpet Hammers, Cast Steel, with Claw, per dozen, $

Bailey's Cast Steel Farriers' Hammers..........per dozen, $

HAMMERS.

(Continued.)

CAST IRON HAMMERS.
Yankee Pattern Nail Hammer.

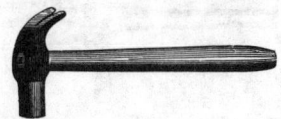

No. 251, Fine Polish ....per dozen, $
No. 250, Half Polish.............................. "
No. 254, Fine Polish.............................. "
No. 58½, Japanned................................. "

Adze Eye Nail Hammers.

				per dozen.
No. $				Fine Polish.
10	20	255	256	

No. 42, Round Face...............................per dozen, $

Yankee Pattern Tack Hammers.

No. 244, Unpolished..............................per dozen, $
No. 245, Polished................................ "
No. 246, Polished................................ "
No. 247, Polished................................ "
No. 252, Fine Polished, Red Handle............... "
No. 253, Red Handle, in boxes.................... "

Carpet Hammers.

No. 45, with Claw ....per dozen, $
No. 48, with Claw, in boxes...................... "
No. 49, with Claw, in boxes...................... "

No. 240, New Pattern Carpet Hammer...............per dozen, $

R. & E. Cast Steel Carpet Hammer, with Claw .....per dozen, $
No. 25, Polished Carpet Hammer, with Claw......... "
No. 1, Magnetic Carpet Hammer, with Claw......... "
No. 2, Magnetic Carpet Hammer, with Claw......... "

Cast Steel Tack Claws............................per dozen, $
R. & E. Steel Tack Claws......................... "

Cast Iron Shoe Hammers.

No. 0, Full Polished ....per dozen, $
No. 67, Half Polished............................. "
No. 67½, Full Extra Fine Polish.................... "
No. 66½, Full Extra Fine, Large................... "
No. 66, Half Polish, Large........................ "
No. 44, Common, Large............................. "
No. 100, Common.................................... "

Allison's Cast Steel Shoe Hammers.

Extra Quality and Polished.

$					per dozen.
No. 0000	000	00	0	1	
$					per dozen.
2	3	4	5	6	

Blacksmiths' Hand Hammers.

Cast Steel Face and Pein, assorted weights ....per lb. $

Stone Hammers.

Assorted weights, all Cast Steel.....................per lb. $
Assorted weights, Iron, Cast Steel Faced................. "

Blacksmiths' Sledges.

Assorted weights, Cast Steel Face and Pein.............per lb. $
Stone Sledges .... "

MAULS.
Stone Mauls.

Assorted, all weights, made of all Cast Steel............per lb. $
Assorted, all weights (Iron), Cast Steel Plug Faced....... "

Ship, Boat or Top Maul.

Assorted weights, Cast Steel Faced.................per dozen, $

BLACKSMITHS' AND MACHINISTS' TOOLS.

Spike or Railroad Maul.

Assorted weights, Cast Steel, Plug Faced..............per lb. $

Horse-shoe Pincers.

$

| 10 | 12 | 14 | each. |
| | | | inches. |

Shoeing Butteris.

Cast Steel, Japanned ....each, $
Cast Steel, Polished ....　"

Twier Irons.

Square Pattern...............................per dozen, $
Duck Nest Pattern..............................　"

Blacksmiths' Tongs.

$

| 18 | 20 | 22 | 24 | 26 | 28 | 30 | each. |
| | | | | | | | inches. |

Box Scrapers.

1 Handle, 3 Square, Adjustable.............$　　per dozen.

For other Box Scrapers see page 198

Geared Braces.

Japanned Wheel ....per dozen, $
Polished Wheel ....　"

Drill Stocks.

Single Geared Stock, Green, with 4 Drills..............each, $
Single Geared Stock, Bright, with 4 Drills.............　"
No. 1, Double Geared Stocks, with 4 Wrought Drills......　"

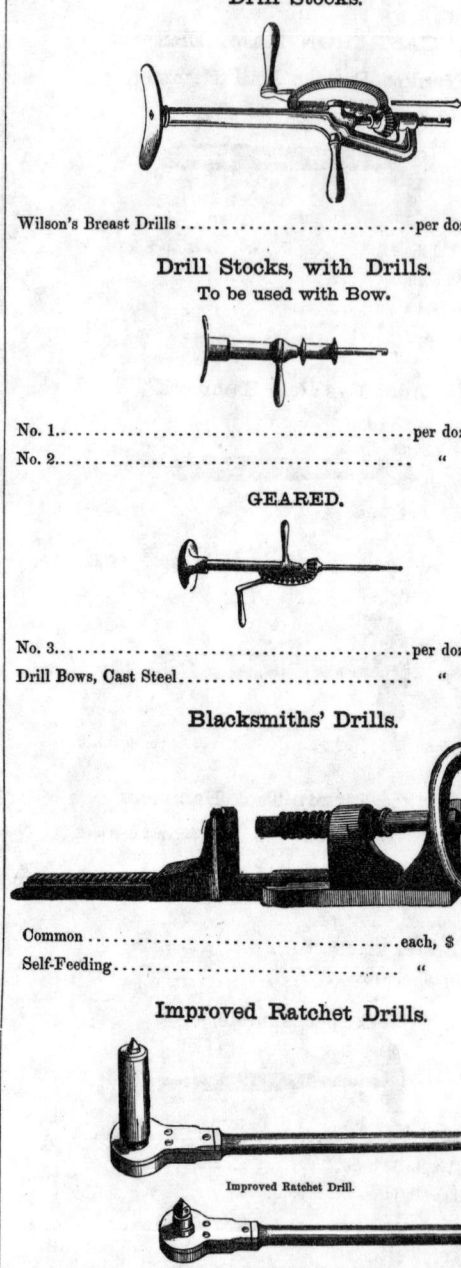

Drill Stocks.

Wilson's Breast Drills ....per dozen, $

Drill Stocks, with Drills.
To be used with Bow.

No. 1...............................per dozen, $
No. 2...............................　"

GEARED.

No. 3...............................per dozen, $
Drill Bows, Cast Steel...........................　"

Blacksmiths' Drills.

Common ....each, $
Self-Feeding ....　"

Improved Ratchet Drills.

Improved Ratchet Drill.

Boiler Ratchet.

The above Cuts represent a new style of Ratchet Drill, which we think will recommend itself to be a *compact, neat and serviceable Tool*.

The Drill Socket, Ratchet, and Feed Screws are forged solid and *case-hardened*. The Steel Pawl is fitted in a groove in the case, and falls into the Ratchet at a right angle, by a spiral spring, partly within the pawl. The working parts are *simple, durable, easily replaced*, and *being within the case*, are well protected from dirt or injury.

$　　　　　　　　　　　　　　　　　　each.

| Sizes, | 8 | 10 | 12 | inch handles. |

Boiler Ratchets, 10 inch handle...................per dozen, $
In Forged Cases, $　　　　　　　　　　　each.

| Sizes, | 12 | 15 | 20 | 24 | inch. |

Boiler Ratchets, 12 inch handle ....each, $

Drills furnished when desired.

BLACKSMITHS' AND MACHINISTS' TOOLS.

(Continued.)

RATCHET DRILLS.

[For Description of Plates see page 242.]

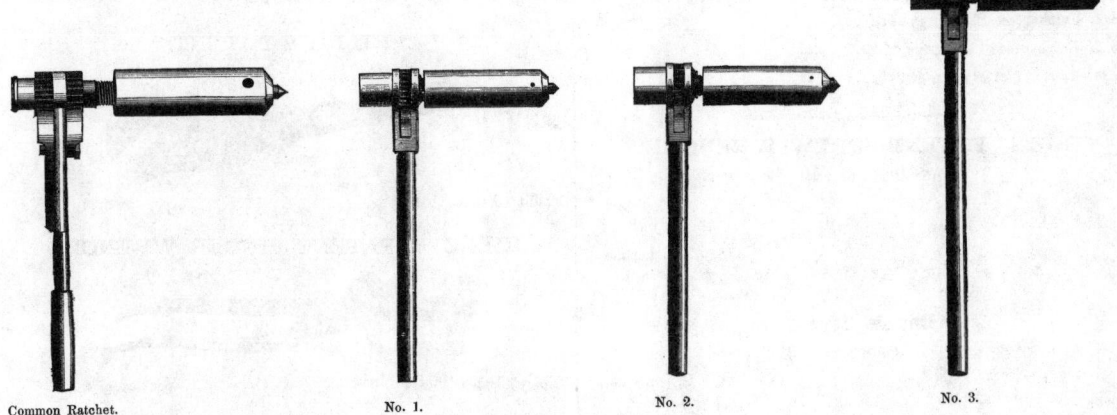

Common Ratchet.   No. 1.   No. 2.   No. 3.

SCREW WRENCHES.

(For Description of Plates see page 242.)

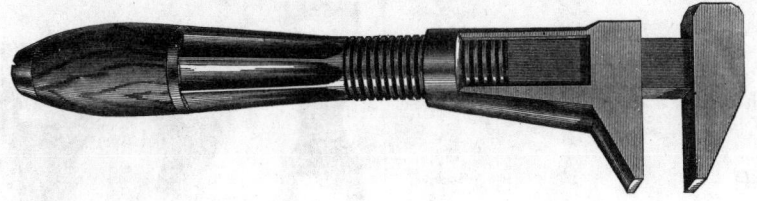

Hewet's Patent.

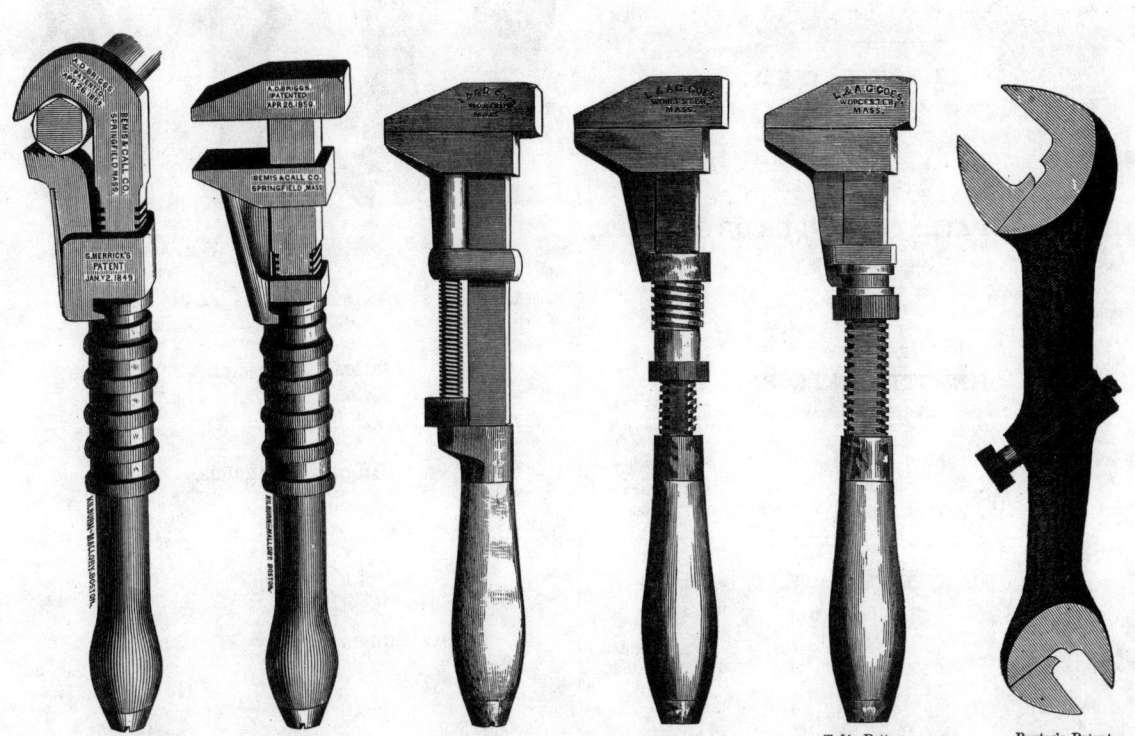

Merrick's Patent.   Briggs' Patent.   Coe's Patent.   Coe's Double Screw.   Taft's Pattern.   Baxter's Patent.

BLACKSMITHS' AND MACHINISTS' TOOLS.

(Continued.)

RATCHET DRILLS.

Common Ratchet (see Plate, page 241)..................each, $
No. 1, Ratchet (see Plate, page 241).................... "
No. 2, Ratchet (see Plate, page 241).................... "
No. 3, Ratchet (see Plate, page 241).................... "

"COE'S" PATENT SCREW WRENCHES.

(See Plate, page 241.)

	$							per doz.
Black,	6	8	10	12	15	18	21	inch.
	$							per doz.
Bright,	6	8	10	12	15	18	21	inch.

Double Screw.

(See Plate, page 241.)

	$					per doz.
Black,	10	12	15	18	21	inch.
	$					per doz.
Bright,	10	12	15	18	21	inch.

Rail Road Pattern.

	$			per doz.
Black,	10	12	15	inch.
	$			per doz.
Bright,	10	12	15	inch.

TAFT'S PATTERN.

(See Plate, page 241.)

	$							per doz.
Black,	6	8	10	12	15	18	21	inch.
	$							per doz.
Bright,	6	8	10	12	15	18	21	inch.

BRIGG'S PATENT.

(See Plate, page 241.)

	$			per doz.
Bright,	10	12	15	inch.

MERRICK'S PATENT CYLINDER OR GAS PIPE.

(See Plate, page 241.)

	$			per doz.
Bright,	10	12	15	inch.

HEWITT'S PATTERN.

(See Plate, page 241.)

	$							per doz.
Black,	6	8	10	12	15	18	21	inch.
	$							per doz.
Bright,	6	8	10	12	15	18	21	inch.

BAXTER'S PATENT.

(See Plate, page 241.)

	$						per doz.
	6	8	10	12	15	21	inch.

SCREW WRENCHES.

(Continued.)

PHILLIP'S PATENT.

Phillip's Patent..................................per dozen, $

RIPLEY'S PATENT PINCER WRENCH.

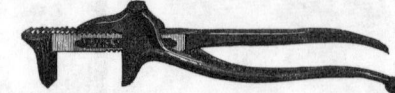

Ripley's Patent Pincer Wrench...................per dozen, $

GRISWOLD'S PATENT
COMBINATION DUPLICATE WRENCHES.

The great demand for a Wrench combining durability and adaptation to various sizes of nuts is met by this. It will out-wear several made from malleable iron, and cost but little more, while it has all the capacity of a Screw Wrench.

It is neat, strong, and cheap, and will recommend itself upon trial.

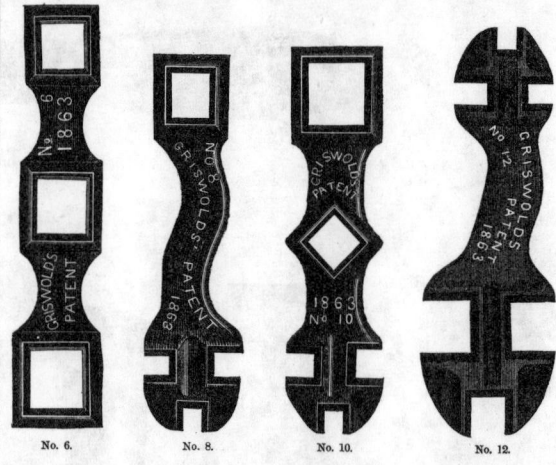

No. 6.	No. 8.	No. 10.	No. 12.

	$				per gross.
No.	6	8	10	12	

Packed in boxes of 3 dozen each size, or 4 dozen assorted
one dozen each size.........................per dozen, $

Malleable Wrenches.

S. Wrenches, assorted sizes..........................per lb. $
Claw Wrenches, assorted sizes......................... "

Buggy Wrenches.

	$					per lb.
No.	1	2	3	4	5	
Size,	$\frac{7}{8}$,	1,	$1\frac{1}{8}$,	$1\frac{1}{4}$,	$1\frac{3}{8}$,	inch.
	$					per lb.
No.	6	7	8	9	10	
Size,	$1\frac{1}{2}$,	$1\frac{5}{8}$,	$1\frac{3}{4}$,	$1\frac{7}{8}$,	2,	inch.

Six Square Buggy Wrenches.

	$			per lb.
Size,	$1\frac{1}{4}$	$1\frac{1}{2}$	$1\frac{5}{8}$	inch.

BLACKSMITHS' AND MACHINISTS' TOOLS.

(Continued.)

Packer's Patent Improved Ratchets.

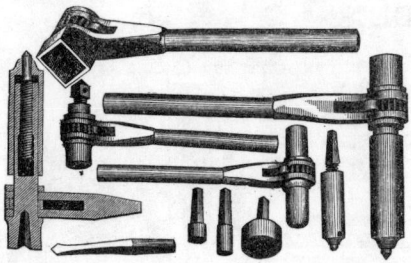

No. 1, 10 inch Handles	per dozen, $	
No. 2, 12 inch Handles	"	
No. 3, 15 inch Handles	"	
No. 4, 17 inch Handles	"	
No. 5, 20 inch Handles	"	

Boiler Ratchets.

No. 1, 10 inch Handles	per dozen, $	
No. 2, 12 inch Handles	"	

Auger Rachets.

No. 1	per dozen, $	
No. 2	"	
Sockets	"	
Screws	"	

"Stiver's" Patent Combination Hand Drilling Machine.

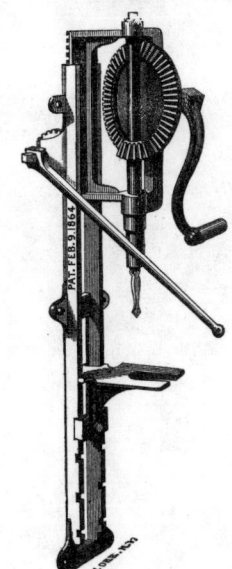

For Blacksmiths, Carriage Smiths, Machinists, and Iron Workers generally.

Its qualities consist, in its cheapness, simplicity, durability, and the ease and facility of putting up, (taking very little room.)

It is made entirely of iron, will work faster than any hand drill made; can be used either horizontal or upright, and with power if necessary.

Each ....$

Gray's Patent Joiners' Clamps.

			per dozen.
$			
Iron........ 6	9	12	inch.

Queen's Patent Portable Forge and Bellows.

1.   2.   3.

☞ The No. 0 Forges are made without slides for closing, and without water-troughs.

Blacksmiths' Forges.

No.	Weight.	Diameter.	Height.	Price.
0 (Army)	95 lbs...1 foot 8 inches....3 feet 8 inches...each, $			
0	95 lbs...1 foot 8 inches....3 feet 10 inches... "			
A	135 lbs...1 foot 9 inches....3 feet 11 inches... "			
1	205 lbs...2 feet............4 feet 2 inches... "			
1½	245 lbs...2 feet 3 inches....4 feet 5 inches... "			
2	335 lbs...2 feet 6 inches....4 feet 8 inches... "			
3	445 lbs...3 feet............4 feet 10 inches... "			

Jewelers' Forges.

No.	Weight.	Price.
0	105 lbs....................each, $	
A	145 lbs..................... "	
1	230 lbs..................... "	
1½	280 lbs..................... "	
2	385 lbs..................... "	

Blacksmiths' Bellows.

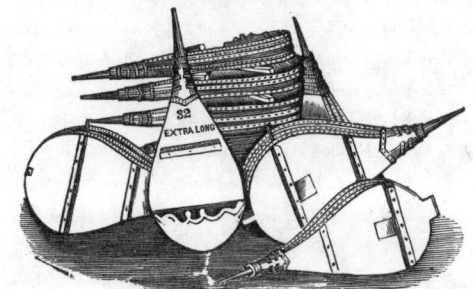

Ordinary Pattern, First Quality.

$									each.
20	24	26	28	30	32	34	36	38	inch.
$									each.
	40	42	44	46	48	50			inch.

Extra Long Pattern.

$						each.
30	32	34	36	38	40	inch.
$						each.
42	44	46	48	50		inch.

Galvanized Bellows for California market, add   per cent.

Iron Founders' Moulding Bellows.

$					each.
10	11	12	13	14	inch.

Hand Bellows.

	$				per doz.
Common,	7	8	9	10	inch.
	$				per doz.
Fancy Flat,	7		8		inch.
	$				per doz.
Fancy Oval,	7		8		inch.

BLACKSMITHS' AND MACHINISTS' TOOLS.

(*Continued.*)

STOCKS AND DIES.

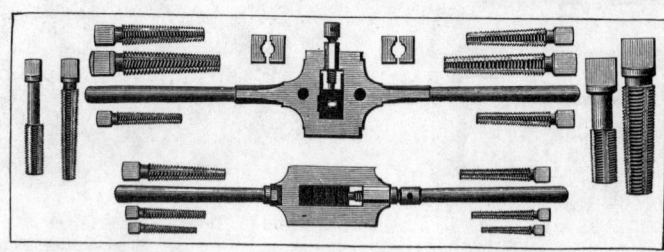

No. 1, 2 inch to 1 inch Left Hand, and 2 inch to 1 inch Right Hand, with 8 Taps and 4 sets of Dies .... each, $60.00

No. 2, 2 inch to $\frac{7}{8}$ inch Right Hand, with 8 Taps and 4 sets of Dies... " 60.00

No. 3, 1$\frac{3}{4}$ inch to $\frac{7}{8}$ inch Left Hand, and 1$\frac{3}{4}$ inch to $\frac{7}{8}$ inch Right Hand, with 8 Taps and 4 sets of Dies .... " 45.00

No. 4, 1$\frac{3}{4}$ inch to $\frac{3}{4}$ inch Right Hand, with 8 Taps and 4 sets of Dies....................................... " 45.00

No. 5, 1$\frac{1}{2}$ inch to $\frac{3}{4}$ inch Left Hand, and 1$\frac{1}{2}$ inch to $\frac{3}{4}$ inch Right Hand, with 8 Taps and 4 sets of Dies .... " 35.00

No. 5$\frac{1}{2}$, 1$\frac{1}{2}$ inch to $\frac{3}{4}$ inch Right Hand, with 8 Taps and 4 sets of Dies.................................. " 35.00

No. 6, 1$\frac{1}{2}$ inch to 1 inch Left Hand, and 1$\frac{1}{2}$ inch to 1 inch Right Hand, with 4 Taps and 2 sets of Dies........ " 16.00

No. 7, 1$\frac{1}{4}$ inch to $\frac{7}{8}$ inch Left Hand, and 1$\frac{1}{4}$ inch to $\frac{5}{8}$ inch Right Hand, with 6 Taps and 3 sets of Dies..... " 12.00

No. 9, 1$\frac{1}{4}$ inch to $\frac{1}{2}$ inch Right Hand, with 6 Taps and 3 sets of Dies................................... " 12.00

No. 11, 1$\frac{1}{4}$ inch to $\frac{7}{8}$ inch Left Hand, and 1$\frac{1}{4}$ inch to $\frac{5}{8}$ inch Right Hand, with 4 Taps and 3 sets of Dies..... " 10.00

No. 13, 1$\frac{1}{4}$ inch to $\frac{5}{8}$ inch Right Hand, with 4 Taps and 3 sets of Dies.................................. " 9.50

No. 15, 1$\frac{1}{4}$ inch to $\frac{1}{2}$ inch Right Hand, with 5 Taps and 3 sets of Dies.................................. " 9.50

No. 17, 1 inch to $\frac{3}{4}$ inch Left Hand, and 1 inch to $\frac{1}{2}$ inch Right Hand, with 6 Taps and 3 sets of Dies...... " 9.00

No. 19, 1 inch to $\frac{3}{8}$ inch Right Hand, with 6 Taps and 3 sets of Dies..................................... " 9.00

No. 21, 1 inch to $\frac{3}{4}$ inch Left Hand, and 1 inch to $\frac{1}{2}$ inch Right Hand, with 4 Taps and 3 sets of Dies...... " 5.75

No. 23, 1 inch to $\frac{3}{8}$ inch Right Hand, with 3 Taps and 3 sets of Dies..................................... " 4.75

No. 25, $\frac{3}{4}$ inch to $\frac{1}{2}$ inch Left Hand, and $\frac{3}{4}$ inch to $\frac{5}{8}$ inch Right Hand, with 6 Taps and 3 sets of Dies..... " 6.50

No. 27, $\frac{3}{4}$ inch to $\frac{3}{8}$ inch Right Hand, with 6 Taps and 3 sets of Dies.................................. " 6.50

No. 29, $\frac{3}{4}$ inch to $\frac{5}{8}$ inch Left Hand, and $\frac{3}{4}$ inch to $\frac{3}{8}$ inch Right Hand, with 4 Taps and 3 sets of Dies..... " 6.00

No. 31, $\frac{3}{4}$ inch to $\frac{3}{8}$ inch Right Hand, with 4 Taps and 3 sets of Dies.................................. " 6.00

No. 32, $\frac{3}{4}$ inch to $\frac{3}{8}$ inch Left Hand, and $\frac{3}{4}$ inch to $\frac{3}{8}$ inch Right Hand, with 4 Taps and 4 sets of Dies..... " 5.00

No. 33, $\frac{3}{4}$ inch to $\frac{1}{2}$ inch Left Hand, and $\frac{3}{4}$ inch to $\frac{1}{2}$ inch Right Hand, with 2 Taps and 2 sets of Dies..... " 3.75

No. 34, $\frac{3}{4}$ inch to $\frac{5}{16}$ inch Right Hand, with 3 Taps and 3 sets of Dies................................. " 4.50

No. 35, $\frac{3}{4}$ inch to $\frac{3}{8}$ inch Right Hand, with 2 Taps and 2 sets of Dies.................................. " 3.75

No. 36, $\frac{5}{8}$ inch to $\frac{1}{2}$ inch Left Hand, and $\frac{5}{8}$ inch to $\frac{5}{16}$ inch Right Hand, with 4 Taps and 3 sets of Dies..... " 4.00

No. 37, $\frac{5}{8}$ inch to $\frac{3}{16}$ inch Right Hand, with 6 Taps and 3 sets of Dies................................. " 4.25

No. 38, $\frac{5}{8}$ inch to $\frac{7}{16}$ inch Left Hand, and $\frac{5}{8}$ inch to $\frac{5}{16}$ inch Right Hand, with 6 Taps and 3 sets of Dies..... " 4.25

No. 39, $\frac{5}{8}$ inch to $\frac{1}{4}$ inch Right Hand, with 4 Taps and 3 sets of Dies.................................. " 4.00

No. 41, $\frac{1}{2}$ inch to $\frac{1}{8}$ inch Right Hand, with 6 Taps and 3 sets of Dies.................................. " 3.25

No. 42, $\frac{1}{2}$ inch to $\frac{5}{16}$ inch Left Hand, and $\frac{1}{2}$ inch to $\frac{3}{16}$ inch Right Hand, with 6 Taps and 3 sets of Dies..... " 3.25

No. 43, $\frac{1}{2}$ inch to $\frac{3}{16}$ inch Right Hand, with 4 Taps and 3 sets of Dies................................. " 3.00

No. 44, $\frac{1}{2}$ inch to $\frac{3}{8}$ inch Left Hand, and $\frac{1}{2}$ inch to $\frac{3}{16}$ inch Right Hand, with 4 Taps and 3 sets of Dies..... " 3.00

No. 45, $\frac{5}{8}$ inch to $\frac{7}{16}$ inch Left Hand, and $\frac{5}{8}$ inch to $\frac{5}{16}$ inch Right Hand, with 6 Taps and 3 sets of Dies..... " 5.50

No. 47, $\frac{5}{8}$ inch to $\frac{1}{4}$ inch Right Hand, with 6 Taps and 3 sets of Dies.................................. " 5.50

No. 49, $\frac{1}{2}$ inch to $\frac{5}{16}$ inch Left Hand, and $\frac{1}{2}$ inch to $\frac{1}{4}$ inch Right Hand, with 6 Taps and 3 sets of Dies..... " 4.50

No. 51, $\frac{1}{2}$ inch to $\frac{3}{16}$ inch Right Hand, with 6 Taps and 3 sets of Dies................................. " 4.50

No. 53, $\frac{5}{16}$ inch to $\frac{1}{16}$ inch Right Hand, with 4 Taps and 4 sets of Dies................................ " 2.75

No. 55, $\frac{5}{16}$ inch to $\frac{1}{16}$ inch Right Hand, with 4 Taps and 3 sets of Dies................................ " 2.50

													$
													each.
Taps,	$\frac{3}{16}$	$\frac{1}{4}$	$\frac{5}{16}$	$\frac{3}{8}$	$\frac{7}{16}$	$\frac{1}{2}$	$\frac{9}{16}$	$\frac{5}{8}$	$\frac{3}{4}$	$\frac{7}{8}$	1	1$\frac{1}{4}$	1$\frac{1}{2}$	inch.

BLACKSMITHS' AND MACHINISTS' TOOLS.

(Continued.)

SCREW PLATES WITH SOLID DIES,

FOR CUTTING SCREWS ON WROUGHT IRON PIPE.

No. 1, Screw Plate, with Right Hand Solid Dies $\frac{1}{8}$, $\frac{1}{4}$, $\frac{3}{8}$, $\frac{1}{2}$ inch...each, $

No. 2, Screw Plate, with Right Hand Solid Dies $\frac{3}{4}$, 1, $1\frac{1}{4}$ inch.. "

No. 3, Screw Plate, with Right Hand Solid Dies 1, $1\frac{1}{4}$, $1\frac{1}{2}$ inch.. "

No. 4, Screw Plate, with Right Hand Solid Dies 1, $1\frac{1}{4}$, $1\frac{1}{2}$, 2 inch.. "

Extra Dies for Right or Left Hand Threads.

| $ | $\frac{1}{8}$ | $\frac{1}{4}$ | $\frac{3}{8}$ | $\frac{1}{2}$ | $\frac{3}{4}$ | 1 | $1\frac{1}{4}$ | $1\frac{1}{2}$ | 2 | inch. | each. |

Taps for Right or Left Hand.

| $ | $\frac{1}{8}$ | $\frac{1}{4}$ | $\frac{3}{8}$ | $\frac{1}{2}$ | $\frac{3}{4}$ | 1 | $1\frac{1}{4}$ | $1\frac{1}{2}$ | 2 | $2\frac{1}{2}$ | inch. | each. |

Drills.

| $ | $\frac{1}{8}$ | $\frac{1}{4}$ | $\frac{3}{8}$ | $\frac{1}{2}$ | $\frac{3}{4}$ | 1 | $1\frac{1}{4}$ | $1\frac{1}{2}$ | 2 | inch. | each. |

IMPROVED GUNSMITHS' STOCK AND DIE.

No. 1.

No. 1, Large, with Handle (see Plate), with 5 Plug Taps and 4 sets of Dies to match, cutting $\frac{2}{16} \times 32$, $\frac{3}{16} \times 28$, $\frac{4}{16} \times 24$, $\frac{5}{16} \times 22$, and $\frac{6}{16} \times 18$...each, $

No. 1, Large, without Handle, Dies same as above.. "

No. 2.

No. 2, Small, with 4 Plug Taps and 2 sets of Dies to match, cutting $\frac{3}{32} \times 48$, $\frac{4}{32} \times 44$, and $\frac{5}{32} \times 36$...each, $

    The improvement in this Stock and Die consists in the easy manner of adjusting the Dies, by swinging the Cap, instead of turning out a long screw, as in the old Stock, and in the facility by which new Dies are fitted by beveling the sides instead of making the V-shaped Die.

    Blank Dies furnished for parties wishing odd Threads.

SCREW PLATES.

| | | | | | | per dozen. |
| $ | 8 | 10 | 12 | 14 | 16 | hole. |

BLACKSMITHS' AND MACHINISTS' TOOLS.

(Continued.)

Grindstone Cranks and Fixtures.

"**Common,**" complete, without Flanges.

| | | $ | | | per dozen. |
| No. | 1 | | 2 | 3. | |

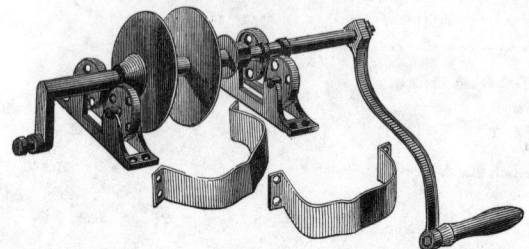

"**Extra,**" with Flanges and all Fixtures complete.

| | $ | | | per dozen. |
| No. | 11 | 12 | 13. | |

With Extra Long Shafts, for Grinding Scythes.

No. 0, Common.................................per dozen, $
No. 10, Extra, with Nut and Flange................ "

GRINDSTONES.

Ship Grindstones.

$						per dozen.
8	9	10	11	12	13	inch.
$						per dozen.
14	15	16	17	18		inch.

Family Grindstones.

| $ | | | | | | | per dozen. |
| 6 | 7 | 8 | 9 | 10 | 12 | 14 | inch. |

Grindstones in Frames.

$						each.
50	60	70	80	90		lb.
$						each.
100	110	120	130	140	150	lb.

Ohio Grindstones................................. cents per lb.
Nova Scotia Grindstones......................... "

Riggers' Screws.

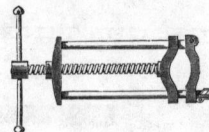

No. 1, $\frac{7}{8}$ inch Screw ....each, $
No. 2, 1 inch Screw .... "
No. 3, 1$\frac{1}{8}$ inch Screw .... "
No. 4, 1$\frac{1}{4}$ inch Screw .... "
No. 5, 1$\frac{3}{8}$ inch Screw .... "

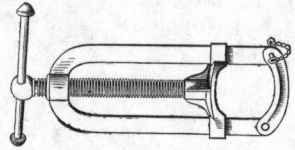

No. 6, 1 inch Screw, Composition Cross Heads..........each, $
No. 7, 1$\frac{1}{8}$ inch Screw, Composition Cross Heads.......... "
No. 8, 1$\frac{1}{4}$ inch Screw, Iron Cross Heads................ "
No. 10, 1$\frac{1}{4}$ inch Screw, Composition Cross Heads.......... "
No. 11, 1$\frac{3}{8}$ inch Screw, Composition Cross Heads.......... "
No. 12, 1$\frac{1}{2}$ inch Screw, Composition Cross Heads.......... "

Ship Augers and Bits, with and without Screw.

Navy Pattern Ship Augers and Bits, $\frac{3}{16}$ to $1\frac{1}{16}$ in. inclusive,   per auger.
Navy Pattern Ship Augers and Bits, $\frac{1}{2}$ to 1$\frac{1}{2}$ in. inclusive,   per quarter.
Navy Pattern Ship Augers .... 1$\frac{5}{8}$ to 2 in. inclusive,   "
Navy Pattern Ship Augers .... 2$\frac{1}{8}$ to 2$\frac{1}{2}$ in. inclusive,   "
Navy Pattern Ship Augers .... 2$\frac{5}{8}$ to 3 in. inclusive,   "
Navy Pattern Ship Augers .... 3$\frac{1}{4}$ and above ......   "
Navy Pattern Ship Augers, with 18 inch twist.................... $\frac{1}{2}$ to 1$\frac{1}{2}$ in. inclusive,   "
Navy Pattern Ship Augers, with 20 inch twist.................... $\frac{1}{2}$ to 1$\frac{1}{2}$ in. inclusive,   "
Navy Pattern Trenail Augers ....   "
Ship Augers with Rings or Sockets, add................   "

☞ It is necessary, in ordering these goods, to state whether they are wanted with or without Screw.

Mill Screws.

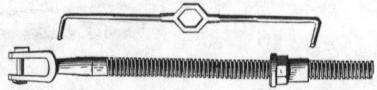

1$\frac{1}{2}$ inch diameter, 3 feet long...........................each, $
1$\frac{3}{4}$ inch diameter, 3 feet 4 inches long.................... "
2 inch diameter, 3 feet 4 inches long.................... "

Marlinspikes.

No. 1, 10 inch, Steel Points, Polished..............per dozen, $
No. 2, 12 inch, Steel Points, Polished................ "
No. 3, 14 inch, Steel Points, Polished................ "

BLACKSMITHS' AND MACHINISTS' TOOLS.

(Continued.)

Jack Screws—Cast Iron Barrel, Bell Bottom.

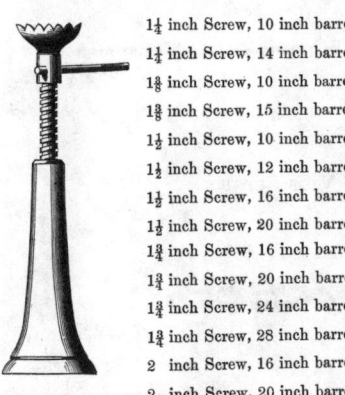

1¼ inch Screw, 10 inch barrel	each, $
1¼ inch Screw, 14 inch barrel	"
1⅜ inch Screw, 10 inch barrel	"
1⅜ inch Screw, 15 inch barrel	"
1½ inch Screw, 10 inch barrel	"
1½ inch Screw, 12 inch barrel	"
1½ inch Screw, 16 inch barrel	"
1½ inch Screw, 20 inch barrel	"
1¾ inch Screw, 16 inch barrel	"
1¾ inch Screw, 20 inch barrel	"
1¾ inch Screw, 24 inch barrel	"
1¾ inch Screw, 28 inch barrel	"
2 inch Screw, 16 inch barrel	"
2 inch Screw, 20 inch barrel	"
2 inch Screw, 24 inch barrel	"
2 inch Screw, 32 inch barrel	"
2¼ inch Screw, 16 inch barrel	"
2¼ inch Screw, 20 inch barrel	"
2¼ inch Screw, 24 inch barrel	"
2½ inch Screw, 10 inch barrel	"
2½ inch Screw, 16 inch barrel	"
2½ inch Screw, 20 inch barrel	"
2½ inch Screw, 24 inch barrel	"

Patent Jack Screws.

Clawed Jack Screw, Iron Box and Wheels, 4 feet long, 10½ × 5 inches square................each, $

Clawed Jack Screw, Iron Box and Wheels, 3 feet long, 8 × 4½ inches square................ "

Clawed Jack Screw, Composition Box and Wheels, 3 feet long, 6½ × 4 inches square................ "

Patent Jack Screws.

(Continued.)

Railroad Clawed Jack Screw, Iron Box and Wheels, 2 feet 9 inches long, 6 × 4 inches square................each, $

Railroad Clawed Jack Screw, Composition Box and Wheels, 2 feet 9 inches long, 6 × 4 inches square............ "

Railroad Jack Screw, Composition Box and Wheels, 3 feet long, 8 × 4¾ inches square................ "

Cotton Jack Screw, Iron Box and Wheels, 4 feet long...... "

Cotton Jack Screw, Iron Box and Wheels, 3 feet long...... "

Cotton Jack Screw, Brass Box and Wheels, 4 feet long..... "

Timber Jacks, Composition Box and Wheels, 3 feet long, 6½ × 4 inches square................ "

Timber Jacks, Riveted, Iron Box and Wheels, 3 feet long, 6½ × 4 inches square................ "

Timber Jacks, not Riveted, Iron Box and Wheels, 3 feet long, 6½ × 4 inches square................ "

Sugar Jack Screws, Riveted, Composition Box and Wheels, 3 feet long, 6½ × 4 inches square................ "

Sugar Jack Screws, Iron Box and Wheels, 3 feet long, 6½ × 4 inches square................ "

Planking Jack Screws, Composition Box and Wheels, and Riveted.

$ each.

Length,   2 ft. 9 in.   3 ft.   3 ft. 3 in.   3 ft. 6 in.   4 ft.

Planking Jack Screws, Iron Box and Wheels, and Riveted.

$ each.

Length,   2 ft. 9 in.   3 ft.   3 ft. 3 in.   3 ft. 6 in.   4 ft.

Eagle Planishing Stakes.

No. 1, size of Faces square, 2 inches	each, $
No. 2, size of Faces square, 2½ inches	"
No. 3, size of Faces square, 3 inches	"
No. 4, size of Faces square, 3½ inches	"
No. 5, size of Faces square, 4 inches	"
No. 6, size of Faces square, 4½ inches	"
No. 7, size of Faces square, 5 inches	"
No. 8, size of Faces square, 5½ inches	"
No. 9, size of Faces square, 6 inches	"

For other Stakes see page 226.

EAGLE ANVIL.

	$										each.
No.	0	1	2	3	4	5	6	7	8	9	
Weight,	10,	15,	20,	30,	40,	50,	60,	70,	80,	90,	lbs.

Anvils, weighing 100 lbs. and over............................per lb. $

BLACKSMITHS' AND MACHINISTS' TOOLS.

(Continued.)

American Star Anvil.

With Tempering Cavity.

	$					per lb. each.
No.	0	1	2	3	4	
Weight,	10	15	20	30	40	lbs.
	$					per lb. each.
No.	5	6	7	8	9	
Weight,	50	60	70	80	90	lbs.

Anvils, weighing 100 lbs. and over....................per lb. $

Eagle Chain Vise.

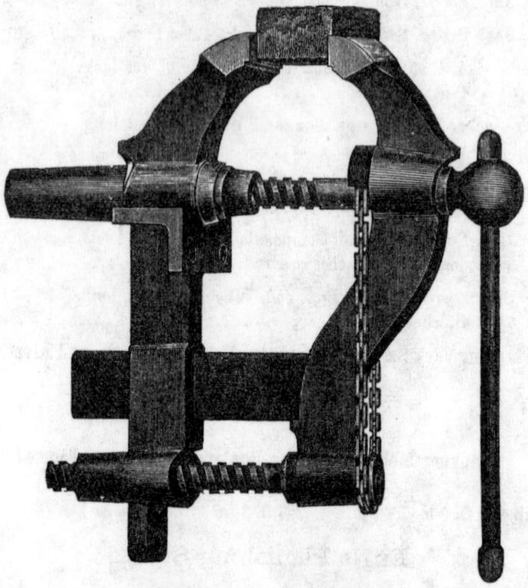

No.	Weight.	Width of Jaw.	Price of each.
1	$11\frac{1}{2}$ lbs	3 inches	$
2	26 lbs	$3\frac{1}{2}$ inches	
3	50 lbs	$4\frac{1}{2}$ inches	
4	80 lbs	5 inches	
5	122 lbs	6 inches	

Vises, Solid Box.

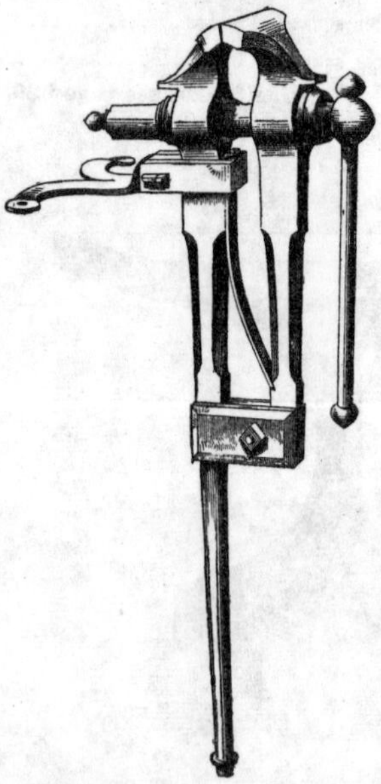

This article is made of the Best Materials, the Box being of first quality **Wrought Iron**, or **Composition**, with the thread *cut out of Solid Metal*, making it in this respect a most reliable article for Machinists and Manufacturers.

Per lb. for Weights of 30 lbs. and upwards, with Wrought Iron Box, $
With Composition Box..

Vises, Solid Box.

(Continued.)

Vises weighing less than 30 lbs. are furnished the following weights:

	20	$22\frac{1}{2}$	25	$27\frac{1}{2}$	lbs.
Composition Box,	$				each.
Wrought Iron Solid Box.	$				each.

Vise Screws.

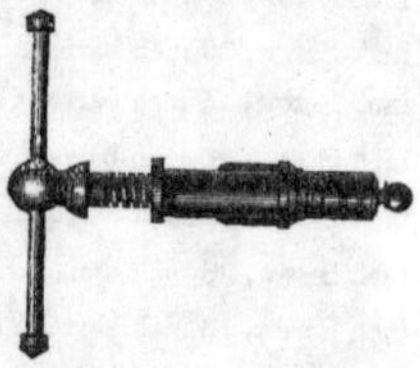

Wrought Iron Box, 1 inch Screw, $1\frac{7}{16}$ in. Diameter Box...each, $
Wrought Iron Box, $1\frac{1}{8}$ inch Screw, $1\frac{11}{16}$ in. Diameter Box... "
Wrought Iron Box, $1\frac{1}{4}$ inch Screw, $1\frac{7}{8}$ in. Diameter Box... "
Wrought Iron Box, $1\frac{3}{8}$ inch Screw, 2 in. Diameter Box... "
Wrought Iron Box, $1\frac{1}{2}$ inch Screw, $2\frac{1}{8}$ in. Diameter Box... "
Wrought Iron Box, $1\frac{5}{8}$ inch Screw, $2\frac{3}{8}$ in. Diameter Box... "
Wrought Iron Box, $1\frac{3}{4}$ inch Screw, $2\frac{1}{2}$ in. Diameter Box... "
Composition Box, 1 inch Screw, $1\frac{7}{16}$ in. Diameter Box... "
Composition Box, $1\frac{1}{8}$ inch Screw, $1\frac{9}{16}$ in. Diameter Box... "
Composition Box, $1\frac{1}{4}$ inch Screw, $1\frac{3}{4}$ in. Diameter Box... "
Composition Box, $1\frac{3}{8}$ inch Screw, $1\frac{13}{16}$ in. Diameter Box... "
Composition Box, $1\frac{1}{2}$ inch Screw, $2\frac{1}{8}$ in. Diameter Box... "
Composition Box, $1\frac{5}{8}$ inch Screw, $2\frac{5}{16}$ in. Diameter Box... "
Composition Box, $1\frac{3}{4}$ inch Screw, $2\frac{1}{2}$ in. Diameter Box... "

Parallel Bench Vises—Oval Slide.

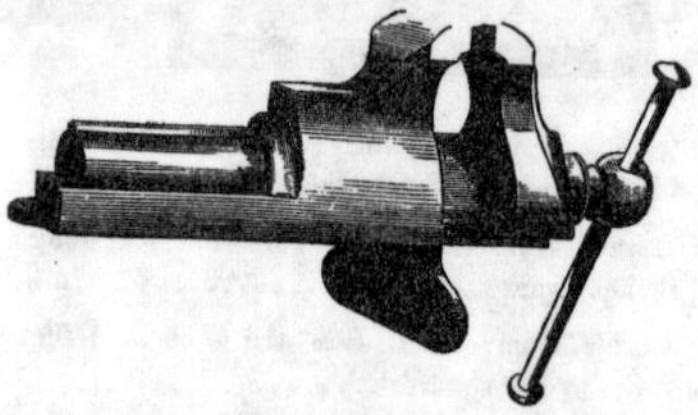

The Jaws of these are faced with the best Steel; Screws made of Wrought Iron, and Box of Composition. They are suited for work on wood, or light work in metal, and are made of the following sizes:

	$						each.
No.	00	0	1	2	3	4	
	$\frac{1}{2}$ in.	$\frac{5}{8}$ in.	$\frac{3}{4}$ in.	$\frac{7}{8}$ in.	1 in.	$1\frac{1}{8}$	inch size of Screws.
	$2\frac{1}{4}$ in.	$2\frac{1}{2}$ in.	3 in.	$3\frac{1}{2}$ in.	4 in.	$4\frac{1}{2}$	inch length of Jaw.

Parallel Bench Vises—Square Slide.

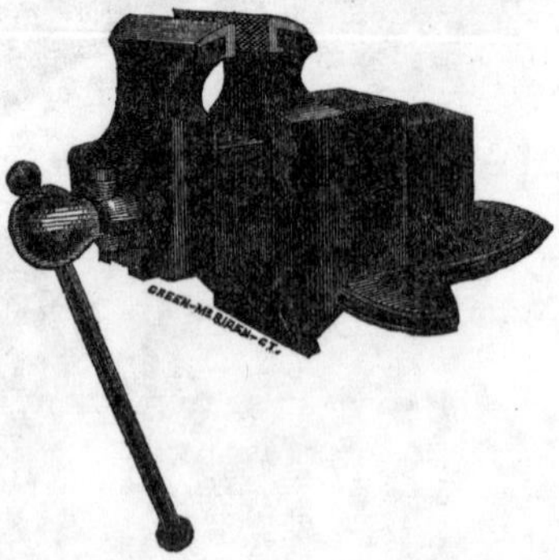

$						each.
No.	1	2	3	4	5	
Length of Jaw,	$3\frac{1}{4}$	$3\frac{5}{8}$	4	$4\frac{1}{2}$	$5\frac{1}{2}$	inch.

BLACKSMITHS' AND MACHINISTS' TOOLS.

(Continued.)

Patent Parallel Swivel Bench Vises.

No.	00	0	1	2	3	each.
Length of Jaw,	2¼	3	3½	4	4¾	inch.

Patent Swivel Jaw Vise.

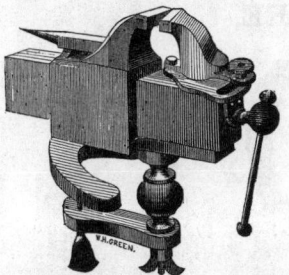

Jewelers' Vise.

Swivel Jaw, Cast Steel Anvil, length of Jaw, 1¾ inches....each, $

This Vise can be swiveled on the bench; the front Jaw can also be swiveled, by which means a wedge can be held firmly, which makes it very desirable for machinists and mechanics.

No. 2, Length of Jaw, 3½ inches..................each, $

No. 3, Length of Jaw, 4 inches.......................   "

Coach Makers' Vise.

Coach Makers' Vise...each, $

Designed expressly for Carriage Makers and Wood Workmen; the Jaws being sharp enables the workmen to use the shave conveniently.

Saw Filers' Vise.

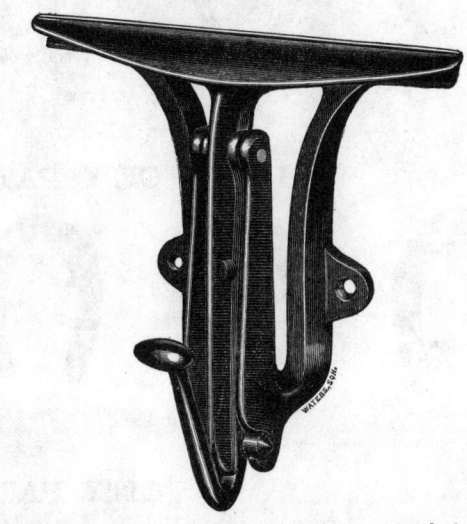

Stearn's Patent...each, $

LATHES.

These Lathes are made with Cast Steel Arbor, and Composition Boxes of best quality; are furnished with Rests, Rest Socket and Bolts suitable for securing them to a frame.

No. 0,	9 inch Swing, without Pulley,	35 lbs	...........each, $
No. 1,	12 inch Swing, without Pulley,	57 lbs	.... "
No. 1½,	13 inch Swing, without Pulley,	89 lbs	.... "
No. 2,	15 inch Swing, without Pulley,	140 lbs	.... "
No. 00,	7 inch Swing, Iron Pulleys,	22 lbs	.... "
No. 0,	9 inch Swing, Iron Pulleys,	37 lbs	.... "
No. 1,	12 inch Swing, Iron Pulleys,	60 lbs	.... "
No. 1½,	13 inch Swing, Iron Pulleys,	97 lbs	.... "
No. 2,	15 inch Swing, Iron Pulleys,	152 lbs	.... "

HORSE SHOES.

GOVERNMENT PATTERN—FORE.

No. 0, 12 oz.   No. 1, 14 oz.   No. 2, 17 oz.   No. 3, 1 lb. 4 oz.   No. 4, 1 lb. 8 oz   No. 5, 1 lb 13 oz.

GOVERNMENT PATTERN—HIND.

No. 5, 1 lb. 10 oz.   No. 4, 1 lb. 6 oz.   No. 3, 17 oz.   No. 3, 17 oz.   No. 2, 13 oz.   No. 1, 11 oz.

Price   cents per lb.

CITY PATTERN—FORE.

No. 6, 2 lb. 12 oz.   No. 5, 2 lb. 6 oz.   No. 4, 2 lb. 1 oz.   No. 3, 1 lb. 11 oz.   No. 2, 1 lb. 8 oz.   No. 1, 1 lb. 4 oz.

CITY PATTERN—HIND.

No. 1, 1 lb. 4 oz.   No. 2, 1 lb. 6 oz.   No. 3. 1 lb. 9 oz.   No. 4, 1 lb. 11 oz.   No. 4, 1 lb. 11 oz.   No. 5, 2 lbs.

Price   cents per lb.

SOUTHERN PATTERN.   LIGHT MULE.

No. 1, 10 oz. No. 2, 12 oz. No. 3, 16 oz.   No. 1, 10 oz. No. 2, 12 oz. No. 3, 15 oz. No. 4, 1 lb. 3 oz.

Price   cents per lb.   Price   cents per lb.

NAILS AND SPIKES.

(For Description of Plates see page 253.)

CUT NAILS.

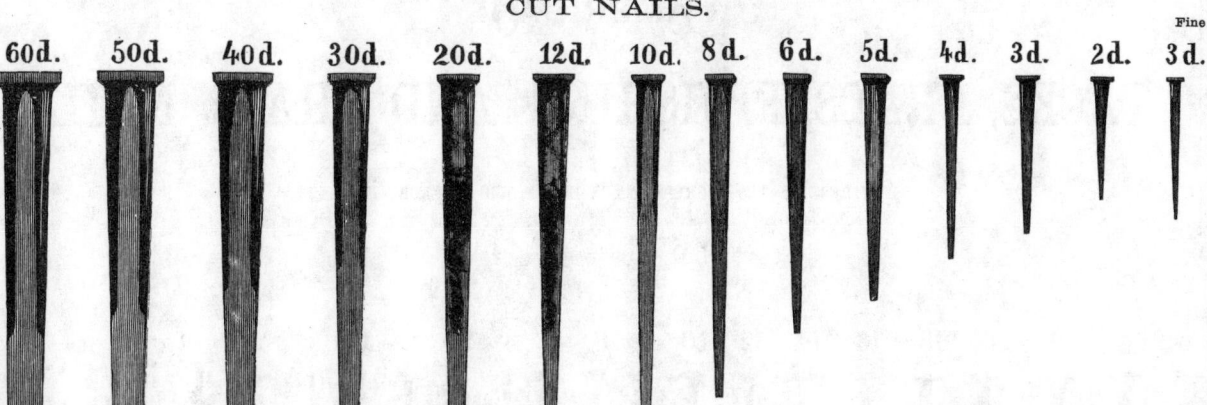

60d. 50d. 40d. 30d. 20d. 12d. 10d. 8d. 6d. 5d. 4d. 3d. 2d. 3d. Fine

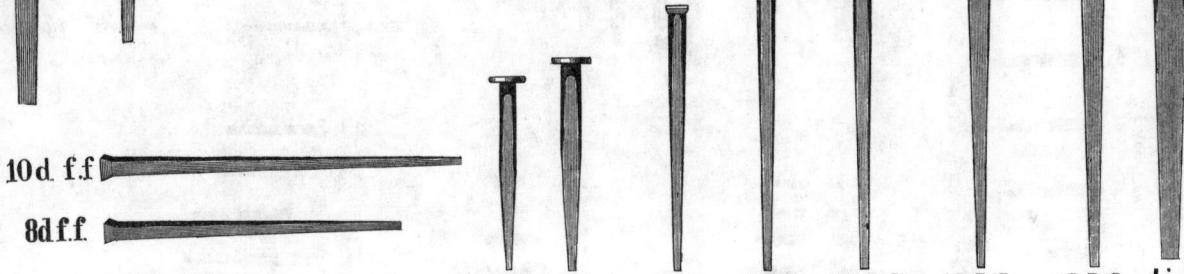

10d. f.f   8d f.f   6d ff
Fine Finishing Nails.

4d. 5d.
Slating Nails.

6d f.   8 d f.   10 d f.   12 d f.   20 d f.   4 in.
Brad Head or Finishing Nails.   Spikes.

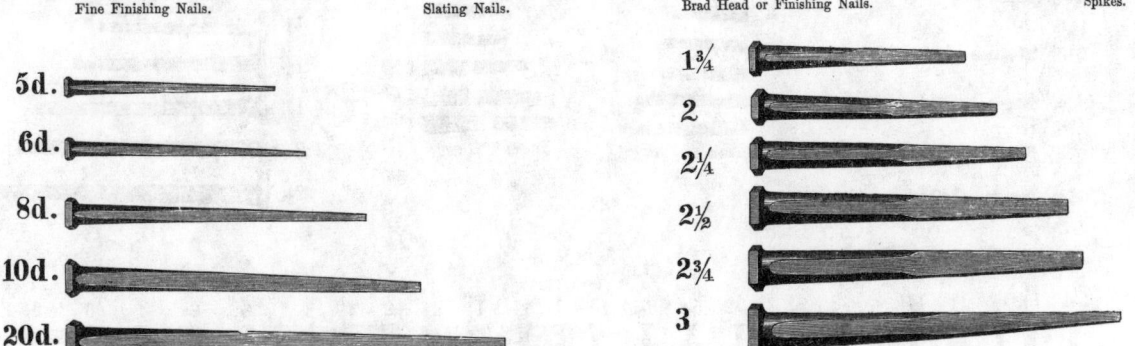

5d.   6d.   8d.   10d.   20d.
Box Nails.

1¾   2   2¼   2½   2¾   3
Sheathing Nails.

Clinch Nails

AMERICAN
TACKS, BRADS, FINISHING AND CHAIR NAILS.

(THESE PLATES REPRESENT THE EXACT SIZE OF EACH ARTICLE.)

[For description see page 254.]

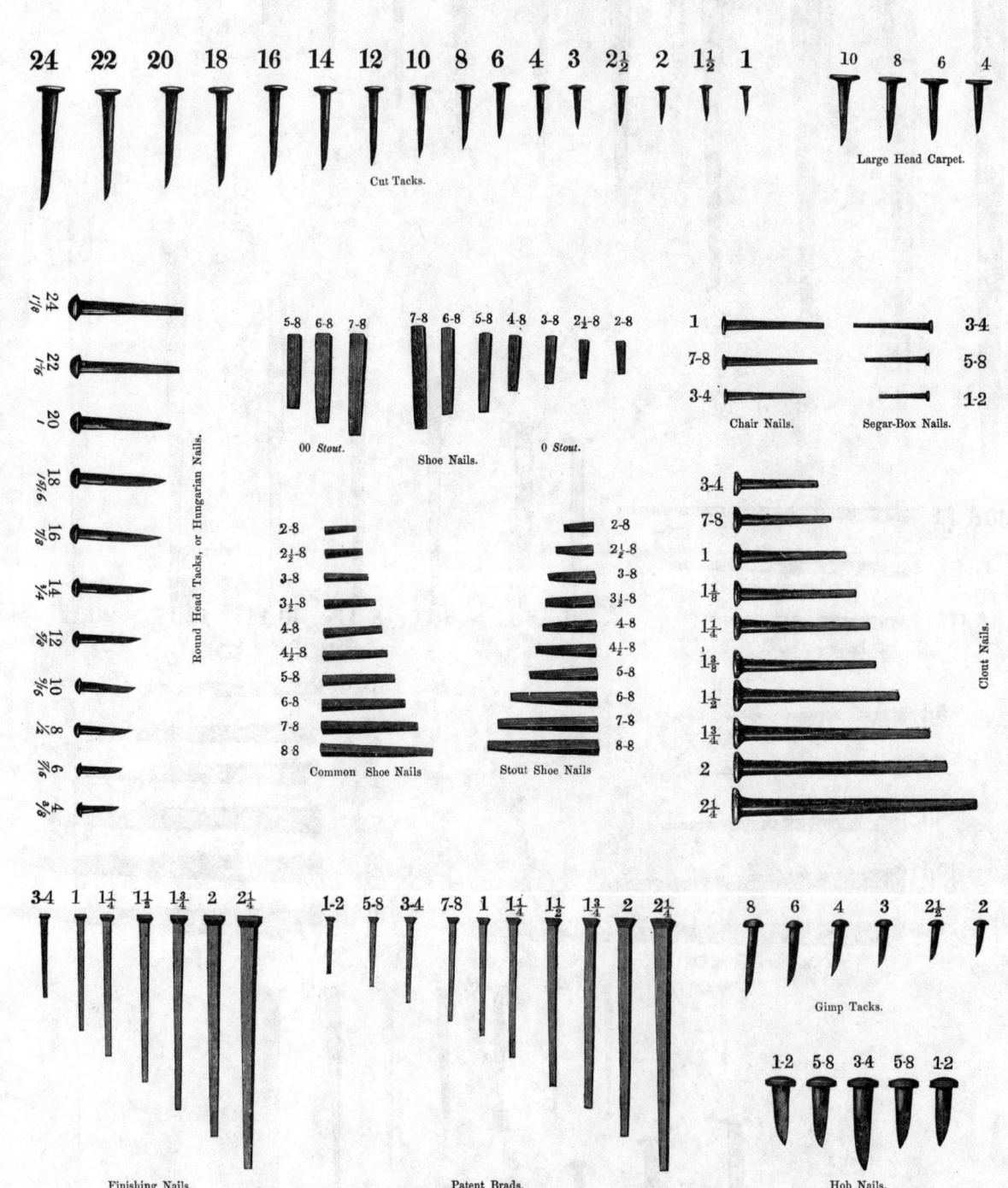

Cut Tacks.

Large Head Carpet.

Round Head Tacks, or Hungarian Nails.

00 *Stout.*

Shoe Nails.

0 *Stout.*

Chair Nails.

Segar-Box Nails.

Common Shoe Nails

Stout Shoe Nails

Clout Nails.

Finishing Nails.

Patent Brads.

Gimp Tacks.

Hob Nails.

NAILS AND SPIKES.

HORSE NAILS.

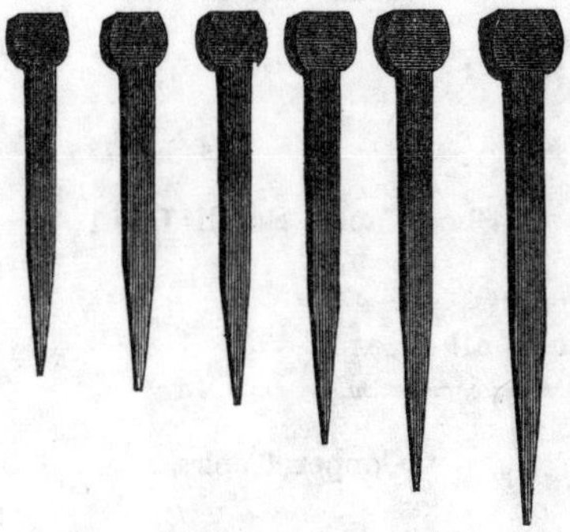

American Pressed Nails.

						cents per lb.
No.	5	6	7	8	9	10

Norway Hammered Nails.

						cents per lb.
No.	5	6	7	8	9	10

Putnam Hammered Horse Nails.

						cents per lb.
No.	5	6	7	8	9	10

CUT NAILS.

(For Plates, see page 251.)

				cents per lb.
2d Fine, 3d Fine.	2d	3d	4d	4½d

					cents per lb.
5d	6d	7d	8d	10d	12d

				cents per lb.
20d	30d	40d	50d	60d

			cents per lb.
Slating Nails,	4d	5d	

Brad Head or Finishing.

						cents per lb.
4d	5d	6d	8d	10d	12d	20d

			cents per lb.
Fine Finishing,	6d	8d	10d

			cents per lb.
Coopers' Nails,	5d	6d	8d

					cents per lb.
Box Nails,	5d	6d	8d	10d	20d

					cents per lb.
Fence Nails,	6d	7d	8d	10d	12d

						cents per lb. / inch.
Sheathing Nails,	1¾	2	2¼	2½	2¾	3

Barrel Nails . . . . .per lb.

SPIKES.

(For Plates, see page 251.)

							cents per lb. / inch.
4	4½	5	5½	6	6½	7	

Wrought Boat Spikes.

			cents per lb. / inch.
2 to 2½,	3 to 3½,	4 to 4½,	5 to 12

Wrought Ship Spikes.

					cents per lb. / inch.
3 to 3½,	4 to 4½,	5 to 5½,	6 to 7½,	8 to 12	

Brad Spikes, 5 inches long and over . . . . .cents per lb.
Countersunk Spikes, 5 inches long and over . . . .   "
Copper Cut Nails, all sizes . . . .   "
Composition Boat and Sheathing Nails . . . .   "

Pressed Clinch Nails.

(For Plates, see page 251.)

Flat Points.

							cents per lb. / inch.
1¼	1½	1¾	2	2¼	2½	2¾	

					cents per lb. / inch.
3	3¼	3½	3¾	4	

Sharp Points.

						cents per lb. / inch.
2	2¼	2½	2¾	3	3¼	

			cents per lb. / inch.
3½	3¾	4	

American Wrought Nails . . . . .cents per lb.

Hinge Nail.   Hinge Rivet.

			cents per lb. / inch
Hinge Rivets and Nails,	3/16	¼	

Forged Wagon Nails, Heavy . . . . .cents per lb.
Forged Wagon Nails, Light . . . .   "
Forged Truss Hoop Nails . . . .   "
Bellows Nails . . . .   "

Wire Nails.

							cents per lb. / inch.
¼	½	⅝	¾	⅞	1	1¼	

							cents per lb. / inch.
1½	1¾	2	2¼	2½	2¾	3	

Brass Nails, Oval Head.

							cents per M.
No.	4	5	6	7	8	9	10

Brass Escutcheon Pins.

Packed in 1 lb. Boxes.

No. 10 to 16 Wire.

						cents per lb. / inch.
¼	⅜	½	⅝	¾	⅞	1

No. 17 and 18 Wire.

						cents per lb. / inch.
¼	⅜	½	⅝	¾	⅞	1

No. 19 and 20 Wire.

						cents per lb. / inch.
¼	⅜	½	⅝	¾	⅞	1

Silver Plated Escutcheon Pins . . . . .extra, per lb.

Lining Nails.

Solid White Metal Oval Head . . . . .per gross,

Silvered Oval Head.

						per paper. / ounce.
3	4	6	8	10	12	

Silvered Flat Head.

						per paper. / ounce.
3	4	6	8	10	12	

Brass Head, assorted sizes . . . . .per paper,
Japanned Head, assorted sizes . . . .   "

NAILS, TACKS AND BRADS.

(Continued.)

Carriage Band Nails.

Brass Head..per paper,

Silvered Head.. "

IRON CUT TACKS.

(For Plates, see page 252.)

7	7	7	8	9	10 cents	per M.
1	1½	2	2½	3	4	ounce.
12	13	15	17	19 cents	per M.	
6	8	10	12	14		ounce.
22	24	26	28	30 cents	per M.	
16	18	20	22	24		ounce.

Per cent. discount from list price, $

Half Weight Tacks, American Iron...... " " "

Full Weight Tacks, American Iron...... " " "

Half Weight Tacks, Swedes Iron........ " " "

Full Weight Tacks, Swedes Iron........ " " "

Miners' Tacks, Full Weight............ " " "

Miners' Tacks, Half Weight............ " " "

In Pound Papers or Bulk, same proportion.

Half Weight Tacks, 100 papers in box, assorted 3 to 12 oz. per box, $

Swedes Iron Tacks, Tinned.

Full Weight.

								per M.
1	1½	2	2½	3	4	6	8	ounce.
								per M.
10	12	14	16	18	20	22	24	ounce.

Half Weight, half Price.

Gimp and Lace Tacks, Tinned.

Full Weight.

								per M.
1	1½	2	2½	3	4	6	8	ounce.
								per M.
10	12	14	16	18	20	22	24	ounce.

Half Weight, half Price.

Carpet Tacks.

(For Plates, see page 252.)

Swedes Iron, Half Weight, Large Head.

						per paper.
6	8	10	12	14	16	ounce.

Swedes Iron, Full Weight, Large Head.

						per M.
6	8	10	12	14	16	ounce.

American Iron, Half Weight, Large Head.

						per paper.
6	8	10	12	14	16	ounce.

American Iron, Full Weight, Large Head.

						per M.
6	8	10	12	14	16	ounce.

Leathered, Full Counts, 6, 8, and 10 ounce........per dozen gross,

Leathered, 100 in a paper, 6, 8, and 10 ounce......per dozen gross,

Gimp and Lace Tacks.

(For Plates, see page 252.)

Full Weight.

							per M.
1	1½	2	2½	3	4	6	ounce.
							per M.
8	10	12	14	16	18		ounce.

Gimp and Lace Tacks.

Half Weight.

							per paper.
1	1½	2	2½	3	4	6	ounce.
							per paper.
8	10	12	14	16	18		ounce.

Shoe Tacks, Small Head.

					per lb.
1	1½	2	2½	3	ounce.

Brush Tacks, all Sizes..............................per M.

In Pound Papers same proportion.

Copper Tacks.

							per M.
1	1½	2	2½	3	4	6	ounce.

8 ounce or ½ inch and upwards..............................per lb.

Cigar Box Nails.

(For Plates, see page 252.)

			per M.
½	⅝	¾	inch.

All Sizes ....per lb.

Chair Nails.

(For Plates, see page 252.)

					per M.
½	⅝	¾	⅞	1	inch.

Common and Patent Brads.

(For Plates, see page 252.)

8	8	9	10	11 cents	per M.
⅜	½	⅝	¾	⅞	inch.
13	16	20	25	30 cents	per M.
1	1¼	1½	1¾	2	inch.

Full Weight Brads, per cent. discount from list price.

Half Weight Brads. per cent. discount from list price.

Iron Finishing Nails.

(For Plates, see page 252.)

							per lb.
¾	1	1¼	1½	1¾	2	2¼	inch.

Finishing Nails, ½ and ⅝ inch, packed in papers of 1000 each, same price as Patent Brads.

Copper Finishing Nails, all sizes.....................per lb.

Trunk and Clout Nails.

(For Plates, see page 252.)

						per lb.
½	⅝	¾	⅞	1	1⅛	inch.
						per lb.
1¼	1⅜	1½	1¾	2	2¼	inch.

Tinned.

						per lb.
½	⅝	¾	⅞	1	1⅛	inch.
						per lb.
1¼	1⅜	1½	1¾	2	2¼	inch.

Shoe Nails.

(For Plates, see page 252.)

American Iron.

										per lb.
2/8	2½/8	3/8	3½/8	4/8	4½/8	5/8	6/8	7/8	8/8	inch.

Charcoal Iron, all sizes..............................per lb.

NAILS, SHEET BRASS AND WIRE.

Shoe Nails.
(Continued)

Swedes Iron, all sizes.................................... per lb.
Zinc, all sizes... per lb.
Copper, all sizes.. per lb.
Common, Stout, 0 Stout, and 00 Stout, all sizes..... .... per lb.
Steel Shoe Nails... per lb.
Steel Shoe Nails... per M.

Hob Nails.
(For Plates, see page 252.)

			per lb.
½	⅝	¾	inch.

Round Head Hungarian Nails.
(For Plates, see page 252.)
Full Weight.

						per M.
4	6	8	10	12	14	ounce.
⅜	7⁄16	½	9⁄16	⅝	¾	inch.

					per M.
16	18	20	22	24	ounce.
⅞	15⁄16	1	1 1⁄16	1⅛	inch.

Half Weight.

						per paper.
4	6	8	10	12	14	ounce.
⅜	7⁄16	½	9⁄16	⅝	¾	inch.

					per paper.
16	18	20	22	24	ounce.
⅞	15⁄16	1	1 1⁄16	1⅛	inch.

All sizes, put up in 1 lb. or ½ lb. papers..................per lb.

Channel Nails.

						per lb.
⅜	3¼	4⁄8	4¾	⅝	5¾	inch.

Glaziers' Points, TIN, in ½ lb. papers.....................per lb.
Glaziers' Points, ZINC, in ½ lb. papers.................... "

ROLLED AND SHEET BRASS.

High Brass.   Per lb.

All Nos. up to No. 30, and widths 14 inches and under ....$
All Nos. up to No. 30 inclusive, and widths over 14 to 20 inches
    inclusive ....
All Nos. up to No. 30 inclusive, and widths over 20 to 30 inches
    inclusive ....

Half cent per lb. advance on each No. above No. 30, to No. 38.

All Brass thinner than No. 38 is Platers' Brass................
Sheets, 24×48 inches, and all other Sheets, cut to particular sizes
    and lengths..
Sheets wider than 30 inches and under 40 inches...............
Sheets wider than 40 inches...................................
Circular Sheets, in diameter 14 inches and under..............
Circular Sheets, in diameter over 14 inches, to 20 inches, inclusive
Circular Sheets, in diameter over 20 inches, to 30 inches, inclusive
Circular Sheets, in diameter over 30 inches, to 40 inches, inclusive
Circular Sheets, in diameter over 40 inches....................
Low Brass 4 cents per lb. more than High Brass.
Gilding Metal 7 cents per lb. more than High Brass.
Platers', or Gold Metal, in Bars..........................per lb. $
Platers' or Gold Metal, Sawed........................ "

Brass over ½ inch to 2 inches in width, 1 cent per lb. advance for slitting.
Brass ½ inch and less in width, 5 cents per lb. advance for slitting.

BRASS AND COPPER WIRE.
High Brass Wire.

								per lb.
No.	0	1	2	3	4	5	6	
No.	7	8	9	10	11	12	13.	per lb.
No.	14	15	16	17	18	19	20	per lb.
No.	21	22	23	24	25	26.		per lb.

Low Brass Wire 4 cents per lb. advance on High Brass.
Copper Wire 10 cents per lb. advance on High Brass.

Brass Tubing.

Plain... per lb.
Fancy... "

German Silver.

Market Metal .... per lb.
Wire.. "

						per lb.
Tubing, No.	4,	6,	9,	12,	15,	18.

Advance   cents per lb. each inch wider than 12 inch.
Advance   cent per lb. each No. thinner than No. 26.

Babbit Metal.

					per lb.
No.	1	2	3	4	5.

IRON AND STEEL WIRE.
Bright and Annealed Market Wire,
(In 63 lb. Bundles.)

	.09	.10	.11	.11½	cents per lb.
Nos.	0000 to 6	7 to 9	10 and 11	12.	
	.12½	.14	.15	.16	cents per lb.
Nos.	13 and 14	15 and 16	17	18.	

Bright and Annealed Weaving, or Stone Wire,
(In 12 lb. Stones.)

	.19	.20	.21	.22	.23	.24	cents per lb.
Nos.	19	20	21	22	23	24.	
	.25	.26	.28	.29	.30	.32	cents per lb.
Nos.	25	26	27	28	29	30.	
	.33	.35	.37	.40	.45	.55	cents per lb.
Nos.	31	32	33	34	35	36.	

Nos. 0000 to 18   per cent.
Nos.   19 to 26   per cent.
Nos.   27 to 36   per cent.

Bright and Annealed Wire, for Hair Work and Special Purposes.

							per lb.
Nos.	37	38	39	40	41	42	43
Nos.	44	45	46	47	48	49	50.

per lb.

Coppered Market Wire............................Market Wire List.
Coppered Bail Wire............................... "
Bright Bail Wire................................. "

Annealed Fence Wire.

					per lb.
Nos	7	8	9	10.	

Fence Wire Staples ....per lb.

Annealed Telegraph Wire.

			per lb.
Nos.	7 to 9	10 and 11.	

Patented Galvanized Telegraph Wire.

			per lb.
Nos.	7 to 9	10 and 11.	

IRON, BROOM AND CAST STEEL WIRE.

Market Tinned Wire.

Nos.	0000 to 6	7 to 9	10 and 11	12			per lb.
Nos.	13 and 14	15 and 16	17	18.			per lb.
Nos.	19	20	21	22	23	24	per lb.
Nos.	25	26	27	28	29	30.	per lb.
Nos.	31	32	33	34	35	36.	per lb.

Bright Broom Wire.

Nos.	19	20	21	22	23	24	25.	per lb.

Tinned Broom Wire.

Nos.	19	20	21	22	23	24	25.	per lb.

Charcoal Wire.

Nos.	0 to 6	7 to 9	10 and 11	12.			per lb.
Nos.	13	14	15	16	17	18.	per lb.

Market Machinery Wire, Drawn Soft for Rivets, &c.

Nos.	0000 to 6	7 to 9	10	11	12	13.	per lb.
Nos.	14	15	16	17	18	19	20.	per lb.

Machinery Wire, Drawn Exactly by Sample or U. S. Standard Gauge,

For Gun Work, and Special Purposes; manufactured from best Swedish Iron.

Nos.	0000 to 9	10	11	12.	per lb.
Nos.	13	14	15	16.	per lb.

Spiral Spring and Flyer Wire, Drawn Hard.

Nos.	00 to 6	7 to 9	10	11.		per lb.
Nos.	12	13	14	15	16	17.	per lb.
Nos.	18	19	20	21	22.	per lb.

☞ Norway and Swedish Rods, in coils or straight lengths, and of any size.

Cast Steel Wire,

Manufactured from best English Cast Steel.

Nos.	0 to 11	12	13	14	15.	per lb.
No.	16	17	18	19	20.	per lb.

Wire Straightened and Cut to any Length required.

For Lengths not less than 20 Inches.

Nos.	0000 to 5	6 to 9	10 and 11.	per lb.
Nos.	12 to 16	17 to 19	20.	per lb.

Iron Wire in Stones, 12 pounds.

No.	Price Per lb.	1 12 lbs.	2 24 lbs.	3 36 lbs.	4 48 lbs.	5 60 lbs.	6 Stones. 72 lbs.
18	16 cts.	1 92	3 84	5 76	7 68	9 60	11 52
19	19	2 28	4 56	6 84	9 12	11 40	13 68
20	20	2 40	4 80	7 20	9 60	12 00	14 40
21	21	2 52	5 04	7 56	10 08	12 60	15 12
22	22	2 64	5 28	7 92	10 56	13 20	15 84
23	23	2 76	5 52	8 28	11 04	13 80	16 56
24	24	2 88	5 76	8 64	11 52	14 40	17 28
25	25	3 00	6 00	9 00	12 00	15 00	18 00
26	26	3 12	6 24	9 36	12 48	15 60	18 72
27	28	3 36	6 72	10 08	13 44	16 80	20 16
28	29	3 48	6 96	10 44	13 92	17 40	20 88
29	30	3 60	7 20	10 80	14 40	18 00	21 60
30	32	3 84	7 68	11 52	15 36	19 20	23 04
31	33	3 96	7 92	11 88	15 84	19 80	23 76
32	35	4 20	8 40	12 60	16 80	21 00	25 20
33	37	4 44	8 88	13 32	17 76	22 20	26 64
34	40	4 80	9 60	14 40	19 20	24 00	28 80
35	45	5 40	10 80	16 20	21 60	27 00	32 40
36	55	6 60	13 20	19 80	26 40	33 00	39 60

Iron Wire in Bundles, 63 pounds.

No.	Price Per lb.	1 63 lbs.	2 126 lbs.	3 189 lbs.	4 252 lbs.	5 315 lbs.	6 Bundles 378 lbs.
0000 a 6	9 cts.	5 67	11 34	17 01	22 68	28 35	34 02
7 a 9	10	6 30	12 60	18 90	25 20	31 50	37 80
10 a 11	11	6 93	13 86	20 79	27 72	34 65	41 58
12	11½	7 24½	14 49	21 73½	28 98	36 22½	43 47
13 a 14	12½	7 87½	15 75	23 62½	31 50	39 37½	47 25
15 a 16	14	8 82	17 64	26 46	35 28	44 10	52 92
17	15	9 45	18 90	28 35	37 80	47 25	56 70
18	16	10 08	20 16	30 24	40 32	50 40	60 48
19	19	11 97	23 94	35 91	47 88	59 85	71 82
20	20	12 60	25 20	37 80	50 40	63 00	75 60

Scale Showing Gauge, Weight, Length and Strength.

Wire Gauge.	Diameter.	Weight of 100 Yards.	Weight of 1 Mile.	Length of 1 Bundle.	Length of 1 Cwt.	DIRECT STRAIN. Area of Section.	DIRECT STRAIN. Breaking Weight.	Wire Gauge.
No.	*Inches.*	*Lbs.*	*Lbs.*	*Yards.*	*Yards.*	*Square Inch.*	*Lbs.*	*No.*
5–0	0·456	161·00	2830	39	70	0·163	13070	5–0
4–0	0·425	140·00	2460	45	80	0·142	11350	4–0
3–0	0·394	120·00	2113	52	93	0·122	9755	3–0
2–0	0·363	102·00	1794	62	110	0·103	8280	2–0
0	0·331	84·72	1490	74	132	0·086	6880	0
1	0·300	68·75	1210	91	162	0·071	5650	1
2	0·280	59·90	1054	105	187	0·062	4930	2
3	0·260	51·65	909	121	215	0·053	4250	3
4	0·240	44·00	775	143	255	0·044	3620	4
5	0·220	37·00	651	170	303	0·038	3040	5
6	0·200	30·56	538	203	361	0·031	2510	6
7	0·185	26·15	461	239	428	0·0265	2220	7
8	0·170	22·10	389	286	509	0·023	1840	8
9	0·155	18·36	323	342	609	0·0195	1560	9
10	0·140	14·97	264	420	747	0·016	1280	10
11	0·125	11·95	211	529	939	0·0125	1000	11
12	0·110	9·24	163	700	1244	0·010	800	12
13	0·095	7·05	124	893	1589	0·0071	568	13
14	0·085	5·51	97	1142	2031	0·0057	456	14
15	0·075	4·29	76	1468	2608	0·0044	352	15
16	0·065	3·22	57	1954	3473	0·0033	264	16
17	0·057	2·48	44	2540	4515	0·0026	208	17
18	0·050	1·91	34	3150	5600	0·0020	160	18
19	0·045	1·55	27	4085	7246	0·0016	128	19
20	0·040	1·22	21	4912	9168	0·0013	104	20
21	0·035	0·94	17	6416	11980	0·0010	80	21
22	0·030	0·69	12	8736	16300	0·0007	56	22

SIZES EXPRESSED IN FRACTIONS OF AN INCH.*

$\frac{15}{32}$ in. = No. 5–0 full.	$\frac{5}{16}$ in. = No. 1 full.	$\frac{1}{8}$ in. = No. 11.
$\frac{7}{16}$ in. = No. 4–0 full.	$\frac{9}{32}$ in. = No. 2.	$\frac{1}{10}$ in. = No. 13 full.
$\frac{13}{32}$ in. = No. 3–0 full.	$\frac{1}{4}$ in. = No. 3½.	$\frac{1}{12}$ in. = No. 14.
$\frac{3}{8}$ in. = No. 2–0 full.	$\frac{7}{32}$ in. = No. 5.	$\frac{1}{16}$ in. = No. 16.
$\frac{11}{32}$ in. = No. 0 full.	$\frac{3}{16}$ in. = No. 7.	$\frac{1}{32}$ in. = No. 22.
	$\frac{5}{32}$ in. = No. 9.	

* The Birmingham "Thick Gauge" (Iron) begins with 3–0 = ⅜ in., and increases $\frac{1}{32}$ in. for each size up to 6–0.

RUSSELL, BURDSALL & WARD'S

BOLTS FOR CARRIAGES, STOVES, RAILROADS,

IRON BUILDINGS, REAPING AND MOWING MACHINES, AGRICULTURAL IMPLEMENTS, SINKS, ELEVATORS, ETC. ETC.

BEVELED HEAD CARRIAGE   COUNTER SUNK CARRIAGE   OVAL HEAD CARRIAGE   BEVELED HEAD CARRIAGE   STOVE   TIRE

COUNTER SUNK CAR'G OR PLOW   SQUARE HEAD PLOW   ROUND HEAD PLOW WITH TEAT

SQUARE HEAD CAR'G

CARRIAGE AND SQUARE-HEAD BOLTS.
With Forged Nuts.

$											per hundred.
Diameter ¼ inch, Length	1¼	1½	1¾	2	2¼	2½	2¾	3	3¼	3½	inch.
$											per hundred.
	3¾	4	4¼	4½	4¾	5	5½	6	6½	7	inch.
$											per hundred.
Diameter ⁵⁄₁₆ inch, Length	1¼	1½	1¾	2	2¼	2½	2¾	3	3¼	3½	inch.
$											per hundred.
	3¾	4	4¼	4½	4¾	5	5½	6	6½	7	inch.
$											per hundred.
	7½	8	8½	9	9½	10					inch.
$											per hundred.
Diameter ⅜ inch, Length	1¼	1½	1¾	2	2¼	2½	2¾	3	3¼	3½	inch.
$											per hundred.
	3¾	4	4¼	4½	4¾	5	5½	6	6½	7	inch.
$											per hundred.
	7½	8	8½	9	9½	10	10½	11	11½	12	inch.

RUSSELL, BURDSALL & WARD'S
BOLTS FOR CARRIAGES, STOVES, ETC.
(Continued.)

CARRIAGE AND SQUARE-HEAD BOLTS, WITH FORGED NUTS.
(Continued.)

$											per hundred.
Diameter $\frac{7}{16}$ inch, Length	1¼	1½	1¾	2	2¼	2½	2¾	3	3¼	3½	inch.
$											per hundred.
	3¾	4	4¼	4½	4¾	5	5½	6	6½	7	7½	inch
$											per hundred.
	8	8½	9	9½	10	10½	11	11½	12	12½	13	14	inch.
$											per hundred.
Diameter ½ inch, Length	1¼	1½	1¾	2	2¼	2½	2¾	3	3¼	3½	inch.
$											per hundred.
	3¾	4	4¼	4½	4¾	5	5½	6	6½	7	7½	inch.
$											per hundred.
	8	8½	9	9½	10	10½	11	11½	12	12½	13	14	inch.
$											per hundred.
Diameter ⅝ inch, Length	1¼	1½	1¾	2	2¼	2½	2¾	3	3¼	3½	inch.
$											per hundred.
	3¾	4	4¼	4½	4¾	5	5½	6	6½	7	7½	inch.
$											per hundred.
	8	8½	9	9½	10	10½	11	11½	12	12½	13	14	inch.

TIRE BOLTS WITH FORGED NUTS.

$											per hundred.
Diameter ¼ inch, Length	1¼	1½	1¾	2	2¼	2½	2¾	3	3¼	3½	4	inch.
$											per hundred.
Diameter $\frac{5}{16}$ inch, Length	1¼	1½	1¾	2	2¼	2½	2¾	3	3¼	3½	4	inch.
$											per hundred.
Diameter ⅜ inch, Length	1¾	2	2¼	2½	2¾	3	3¼	3½	4			inch.

Sleigh Shoe Bolts, with Long Countersunk Heads, same List as Tire Bolts.

PLOW BOLTS WITH FORGED NUTS.
Made with Round or Square Countersunk Heads; Cut Right or Left Hand, as Wanted.
(For Plates see page 257.)

$											per hundred.
Diameter ⅜ inch, Length	1¼	1½	1¾	2	2¼	2½	2¾	3	3¼	3½	3¾	4	inch.
$											per hundred.
Diameter $\frac{7}{16}$ inch, Length	1¼	1½	1¾	2	2¼	2½	2¾	3	3¼	3½	3¾	4	inch.
$											per hundred.
Diameter ½ inch, Length	1¼	1½	1¾	2	2¼	2½	2¾	3	3¼	3½	3¾	4	inch.

PLOW BOLTS IN BULK.

Diameter ⅜ inch, Length 1 inch to 3 inch.. per lb.
Diameter $\frac{7}{16}$ inch, Length 1¼ inch to 4 inch.. per lb.
Diameter ½ inch, Length 1¼ inch to 4 inch.. per lb.

STOVE, RANGE AND FURNACE RODS.

$									per hundred.
Diameter ¼ inch, Length	5	6	7	8	9	10	11	12	13	inch.
$									per hundred.
	14	16	18	19	20	22	24	26	30	inch.
$									per hundred.
Diameter $\frac{5}{16}$ inch, Length	5	6	7	8	9	10	11	12	13	inch.
$									per hundred.
	14	16	18	19	20	22	24	26	30	inch.

Odd sizes furnished to order.

STOVE RODS IN BULK.

										per lb.
Length	5	6	7	8	10	11	13	15	17	18	inches and longer.

RUSSELL, BURDSALL & WARD'S
BOLTS FOR CARRIAGES, STOVES, ETC.

(Continued.)

STOVE BOLTS.

Diameter	$										
Diameter ¼ inch, Length	¾	1	1¼	1½	1¾	2	2¼	2½	2¾	3	per hundred. inch.
Diameter 5/16 inch, Length	¾	1	1¼	1½	1¾	2	2¼	2½	2¾	3	per hundred. inch.

ELEVATOR BOLTS.

Diameter	$				
Diameter 3/16 inch, Length	¾	7/8	1	1⅛	per hundred. inch.

SINK BOLTS.

Diameter	$								
Diameter ¼ inch, Length	1	1¼	1½	1¾	2	2¼	2½	3	per hundred. inch.

DRAWER KNOB SCREWS.

Diameter	$							
Diameter 3/16 inch, Length	1	1¼	1½	1¾	2	2¼	2¾	per hundred. inch.
Diameter ¼ inch, Length	1	1¼	1½	1¾	2	2¼	2¾	per hundred. inch.

MACHINE BOLTS,
With Heavy Heads and Nuts, Designed for Railway Work, Steam Engines and Pipes, and other Machinery.

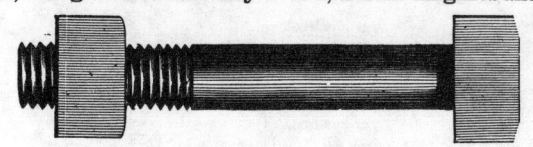

Diameter	$												
Diameter ¼ inch, Length	1½	1¾	2	2¼	2½	3	3½	4	4½	5	5½	6	per hundred. inch.
Diameter 5/16 inch, Length	1½	1¾	2	2¼	2½	3	3½	4	4½	5	5½	6	per hundred. inch.
Diameter ⅜ inch, Length	1½	1¾	2	2¼	2½	3	3½	4					per hundred. inch.
Diameter ⅜ inch, Length	4½	5	5½	6	6½	7	7½	8					per hundred. inch.
Diameter 7/16 inch, Length	1½	1¾	2	2¼	2½	3	3½	4					per hundred. inch.
Diameter 7/16 inch, Length	4½	5	5½	6	6½	7	7½	8					per hundred. inch.
Diameter ½ inch, Length	1½	1¾	2	2¼	2½	3	3½	4					per hundred. inch.
Diameter ½ inch, Length	4½	5	5½	6	6½	7	7½	8					per hundred. inch.
Diameter 9/16 inch, Length	1¾	2	2¼	2½	3	3½	4	4½					per hundred. inch.
Diameter 9/16 inch, Length	5	5½	6	6½	7	7½	8						per hundred. inch.
Diameter ⅝ inch, Length	1¾	2	2¼	2½	3	3½	4	4½					per hundred. inch.
Diameter ⅝ inch, Length	5	5½	6	6½	7	7½	8						per hundred. inch.
Diameter ¾ inch, Length	1¾	2	2¼	2½	3	3½	4	4½					per hundred. inch.
Diameter ¾ inch, Length	5	5½	6	6½	7	7½	8						per hundred. inch.

LARGE SQUARE HEAD BOLTS, FOR BRIDGES, BUILDINGS, SHIPS, &c.

Diameter,	⅜	7/16	½	9/16	⅝	¾	7/8,	1 to 2 inches, Length from 8 to 24 inches.	per lb.

BOLTS, COACH SCREWS, NUTS, WASHERS, ETC.

CARRIAGE OR WAGON SPRING BOLTS.

End Spring Bolt.

Diameter 5/16 inch, Length	$ 1 3/4	2	2 1/4	2 1/2	per hundred. inch.
Diameter 5/16 inch, Length	$ 2 3/4	3	3 1/4	3 1/2	per hundred. inch.
Diameter 3/8 inch, Length	$ 2	2 1/4	2 1/2	2 3/4	per hundred. inch.
Diam. 3/8 in., L'gth	$ 3	3 1/4	3 1/2	3 3/4	4	per hundred. inch.

Center Spring Bolt.

Diameter 5/16 inch, Length	$ 1	1 1/4	1 1/2	1 3/4		per hundred. inch.
Diam. 5/16 inch, L'gth	$ 2	2 1/4	2 1/2	2 3/4	3	per hundred. inch.

COACH SCREWS.

Diameter 5/16 inch, Length	$ 1 1/2	1 3/4	2	2 1/4		per hundred. inch.
Diameter 5/16 inch, Length	$ 2 1/2	2 3/4	3	3 1/2		per hundred. inch.
Diameter 3/8 inch, Length	$ 1 1/2	1 3/4	2	2 1/4		per hundred. inch.
Diameter 3/8 inch, Length	$ 2 1/2	3	3 1/2	4		per hundred. inch.
Diameter 7/16 inch, Length	$ 2 1/2	3	3 1/2	4		per hundred. inch.
Diam. 7/16 in., L'gth	$ 4 1/2	4 3/4	5	5 1/2	6	per hundred. inch.
Diameter 1/2 inch, Length	$ 2 1/2	2 3/4	3	3 1/2		per hundred. inch.

COACH SCREWS.

(*Continued.*)

Diam. 1/2 in., L'gth	$ 4	4 1/2	5	5 1/2	6	per hundred. inch.
Coach Screws in bulk,	7/16	1/2	9/16	5/8	3/4	per lb. in., all lengths.

SET SCREWS.

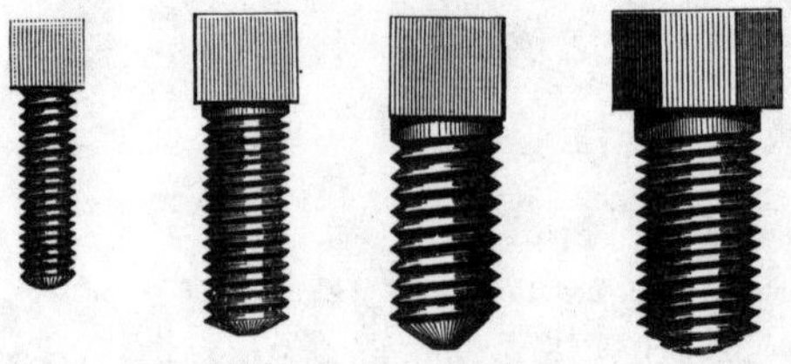

Diam. 1/4 in., L'gth	$ 1 1/2	1 3/4	2	2 1/4	2 1/2	3	per hun. in.
Diam. 5/16 in., L'gth	$ 1 1/2	1 3/4	2	2 1/4	2 1/2	2 3/4	3	per hun. in.
Diam. 3/8 in., L'gth	$ 1 1/2	1 3/4	2	2 1/4	2 1/2	3	per hun. in.
Diam. 7/16 in., L'gth	$ 1 1/2	1 3/4	2	2 1/4	2 1/2	2 3/4	3	per hun. in.
Diam. 1/2 in., L'gth	$ 1 1/2	1 3/4	2	2 1/4	2 1/2	3	per hun. in.
Diam. 9/16 in., L'gth	$ 1 1/2	1 3/4	2	2 1/4	2 1/2	2 3/4	3	per hun. in.
Diam. 5/8 in., L'gth	$ 1 1/2	1 3/4	2	2 1/4	2 1/2	3	per hun. in.
Diam. 11/16 in., L'gth	$ 1 1/2	1 3/4	2	2 1/4	2 1/2	2 3/4	3	per hun. in.
Diam. 3/4 in., L'gth	$ 1 1/2	1 3/4	2	2 1/4	2 1/2	2 3/4	3	per hun. in.

NUTS, WASHERS AND CHAIN LINKS.

SQUARE NUTS,

In Kegs of 150 Lbs. Each.

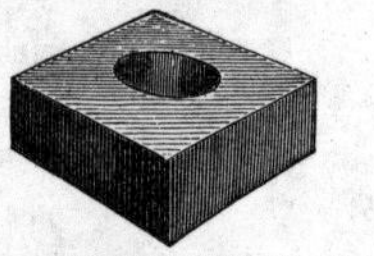

Size Square.	Thickness.	Diameter of Hole.	Size of Bolt.	Price per lb.
1/2 ×	3/16 ×	7/32 for	1/4 in.	
1/2 ×	1/4 ×	7/32 for	1/4 in.	
5/8 ×	1/4 ×	9/32 for	5/16 in.	
5/8 ×	5/16 ×	9/32 for	5/16 in.	
3/4 ×	5/16 ×	11/32 for	3/8 in.	
3/4 ×	3/8 ×	11/32 for	3/8 in.	
7/8 ×	3/8 ×	3/8 for	7/16 in.	
7/8 ×	7/16 ×	3/8 for	7/16 in.	
1 ×	7/16 ×	7/16 for	1/2 in.	
1 ×	1/2 ×	7/16 for	1/2 in.	
1 ×	1/2 ×	1/2 for	9/16 in.	
1 1/8 ×	1/2 ×	1/2 for	9/16 in.	
1 1/8 ×	5/8 ×	9/16 for	5/8 in.	
1 1/4 ×	1/2 ×	9/16 for	5/8 in.	
1 1/4 ×	5/8 ×	9/16 for	5/8 in.	
1 1/4 ×	5/8 ×	5/8 for	11/16 in.	
1 3/8 ×	5/8 ×	5/8 for	11/16 in.	
1 1/2 ×	5/8 ×	11/16 for	3/4 in.	
1 1/2 ×	3/4 ×	11/16 for	3/4 in.	
1 1/2 ×	3/4 ×	3/4 for	13/16 in.	
1 3/4 ×	7/8 ×	3/4 for	7/8 in.	
1 3/4 ×	7/8 ×	13/16 for	7/8 in.	
2 ×	1 ×	7/8 for	1 in.	
2 ×	1 ×	1 for	1 1/16 in.	
2 ×	1 1/4 ×	1 for	1 1/8 in.	
2 1/4 ×	1 1/8 ×	1 for	1 1/8 in.	
2 1/4 ×	1 1/4 ×	1 1/16 for	1 1/4 in.	
2 1/2 ×	1 1/4 ×	1 1/8 for	1 1/4 in.	
2 1/2 ×	1 1/2 ×	1 3/16 for	1 3/8 in.	
2 3/4 ×	1 1/2 ×	1 1/4 for	1 1/2 in.	
3 ×	1 1/2 ×	1 3/8 for	1 5/8 in.	
3 1/2 ×	1 3/4 ×	1 7/16 for	1 3/4 in.	
4 ×	2 ×	1 1/2 for	2 in.	

SIX-SQUARE NUTS,

In Kegs of 150 Lbs. Each.

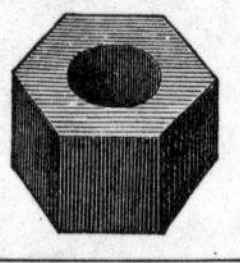

Size Square.	Thickness.	Diameter of Hole.	Size of Bolt.	Price per lb.
1/2 ×	1/4 ×	7/32 for	1/4 in.	
5/8 ×	1/4 ×	9/32 for	5/16 in.	
5/8 ×	5/16 ×	9/32 for	5/16 in.	
3/4 ×	5/16 ×	11/32 for	3/8 in.	
3/4 ×	3/8 ×	11/32 for	3/8 in.	
7/8 ×	3/8 ×	3/8 for	7/16 in.	
7/8 ×	7/16 ×	3/8 for	7/16 in.	
1 ×	1/2 ×	7/16 for	1/2 in.	
1 ×	5/8 ×	7/16 for	1/2 in.	
1 1/8 ×	5/8 ×	1/2 for	9/16 in.	
1 1/8 ×	3/4 ×	1/2 for	9/16 in.	
1 1/4 ×	5/8 ×	9/16 for	5/8 in.	
1 1/4 ×	3/4 ×	9/16 for	5/8 in.	
1 3/8 ×	3/4 ×	5/8 for	11/16 in.	
1 3/8 ×	7/8 ×	5/8 for	11/16 in.	
1 1/2 ×	3/4 ×	11/16 for	3/4 in.	
1 1/2 ×	7/8 ×	11/16 for	3/4 in.	
1 3/4 ×	7/8 ×	13/16 for	7/8 in.	
1 3/4 ×	1 ×	13/16 for	7/8 in.	
2 ×	1 ×	7/8 for	1 in.	
2 ×	1 1/8 ×	7/8 for	1 in.	
2 ×	1 1/4 ×	7/8 for	1 in.	
2 ×	1 1/4 ×	1 for	1 1/8 in.	
2 1/4 ×	1 1/4 ×	1 1/16 for	1 1/4 in.	
2 1/2 ×	1 1/2 ×	1 3/16 for	1 3/8 in.	
2 1/2 ×	1 1/2 ×	1 1/4 for	1 3/8 in.	
2 3/4 ×	1 1/2 ×	1 1/4 for	1 1/2 in.	
3 ×	1 1/2 ×	1 3/8 for	1 5/8 in.	
3 1/2 ×	2 ×	1 7/16 for	1 3/4 in.	
4 ×	2 ×	1 1/2 for	2 in.	

WASHERS,

In Kegs of 150 Lbs. Each.

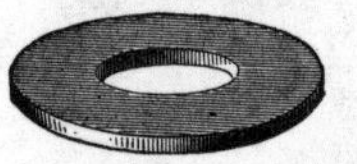

Outside Diameter.	Size of Hole	Thickness Wire Guage.		Price per 100.
1/2 ×	1/4	No. 16 for 3/16	in. bolts	
5/8 ×	5/16	No. 16 for 1/4	in. bolts	
3/4 ×	3/8	No. 15 for 5/16	in. bolts	
7/8 ×	3/8	No. 14 for 5/16	in. bolts	
1 ×	7/16	No. 13 for 3/8	in. bolts	Price per lb.
1 1/8 ×	1/2	No. 13 for 7/16	in. bolts	
1 1/4 ×	9/16	No. 12 for 1/2	in. bolts	
1 3/8 ×	5/8	No. 12 for 9/16	in. bolts	
1 1/2 ×	11/16	No. 11 for 5/8	in. bolts	
1 3/4 ×	3/4	No. 11 for 11/16	in. bolts	
1 3/4 ×	13/16	No. 10 for 3/4	in. bolts	
2 ×	7/8	No. 10 for 13/16	in. bolts	
2 ×	15/16	No. 9 for 7/8	in. bolts	
2 ×	1	No. 10 for 7/8	in. bolts	
2 1/4 ×	1 1/8	No. 9 for 1	in. bolts	
2 1/2 ×	1 1/4	No. 8 for 1 1/8	in. bolts	
2 3/4 ×	1 3/8	No. 7 for 1 1/4	in. bolts	
3 ×	1 1/2	No. 7 for 1 3/8	in. bolts	
3 ×	1 5/8	No. 6 for 1 1/2	in. bolts	
4 ×	1 5/8	No. 7 for 1 1/2	in. bolts	
4 ×	2	No 4 for 1 3/4	in. bolts	

When ordering Nuts and Washers always give the diameter of the hole.

Nuts should be from 1/32 to 1/8 smaller, Washers 1/16 larger, than the bolt for which they are intended.

Joint Bolt, and other Nuts, made to order.

CHAIN LINKS.

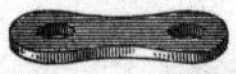

Outside Length.	Price per 100.
3/4	
1	
1 1/8	
1 1/4	
1 3/8	
1 1/2	
1 3/4	
1 7/8	

Larger sizes, per lb.

NUTS, AXLES AND THIMBLE-SKEINS.

Nuts for Iron Axles.

Sizes.

No.	1	2	3	4	5	6	7	8	9	10	
Hole,	$\frac{1}{2}$	$\frac{9}{16}$	$\frac{5}{8}$	$\frac{11}{16}$	$\frac{3}{4}$	$\frac{7}{8}$	1	$1\frac{1}{8}$	$1\frac{1}{4}$	$1\frac{3}{8}$ inch.	
Square,	$\frac{7}{8}$	$\frac{15}{16}$	1	$1\frac{1}{8}$	$1\frac{1}{4}$	$1\frac{3}{8}$	$1\frac{1}{2}$	$1\frac{3}{4}$	2	2 inch.	per lb. $
Flange,	$1\frac{3}{8}$	$1\frac{3}{8}$	$1\frac{1}{2}$	$1\frac{5}{8}$	$2\frac{1}{4}$	$2\frac{1}{2}$	$2\frac{3}{8}$	$3\frac{1}{4}$	$3\frac{1}{2}$	$3\frac{1}{4}$ inch.	

Nuts for Wood Axles.

No.	0	1	2	3	4	5	
Hole,	$\frac{1}{2}$	$\frac{9}{16}$	$\frac{5}{8}$	$\frac{11}{16}$	$\frac{13}{16}$	$\frac{7}{8}$ inch.	
Square,	1	1	1	$1\frac{1}{4}$	$1\frac{1}{4}$	$1\frac{1}{2}$ inch.	per lb. $
Flange,	2	$2\frac{1}{4}$	$2\frac{1}{4}$	$2\frac{5}{8}$	3	3 inch.	

Wagon Axles.

Long Bed, Common.

Long Iron Nut, Half Patent.

Solid Collar, Half Patent.

Swelled Collar, Half Patent.

Solid Collar, Taper.

Swelled Collar, Taper.

Iron Nut, Taper.

Long Bed Common...........................per lb.
Long Bed Common, Chilled Boxes...................per lb.
Long Bed Taper.............................per lb.
Long Bed, Half Patent......................per lb.
Long Bed Express...........................per lb.

	1	$1\frac{1}{8}$	$1\frac{1}{4}$	$1\frac{3}{8}$	$1\frac{1}{2}$ inch.	
Short Bed, Taper, Loose Collar $						per set.
Short Bed, Half Pat't, Loose Collar						per set.
Short Bed, Taper, Solid Collar						per set.
Short Bed, Half Pat't, Solid Collar						per set.
Long Bed, Taper, Solid Collar						per set.
Long Bed, Half Pat't, Solid Collar						

Case Hardening, extra .... per set.

Refined Wrought Iron Axle Clips, with Nuts.

$ per dozen.

No.	0	1	2	3	4	5	
Size,	$\frac{5}{16}\times5\frac{1}{2}$	$\frac{5}{16}\times6\frac{1}{4}$	$\frac{5}{16}\times6\frac{3}{4}$	$\frac{5}{16}\times7\frac{1}{4}$	$\frac{3}{8}\times7\frac{5}{8}$	$\frac{3}{8}\times8\frac{1}{2}$ inch.	

Superior, or Norway Clip, with Forged Nuts, same sizes and Nos. as above.

Axle Grease.

In Barrels or Half Barrels.............................per gallon, $
In Gallon Tins................................per gallon,
In Quart Tins................................per gallon,
Manhattan, in Boxes................................per gross,

Cart and Wagon Boxes.

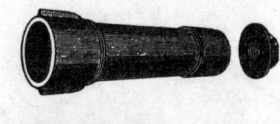

Ground Wagon Boxes (Eight in a Set.)

$								per set.
	2	$2\frac{1}{4}$	$2\frac{1}{2}$	$2\frac{3}{4}$	3	$3\frac{1}{4}$	$3\frac{1}{2}$	inch.
$								per set.
	$3\frac{3}{4}$	4	$4\frac{1}{4}$	$4\frac{1}{2}$	$4\frac{3}{4}$	5		inch.

Ground Cart Boxes (Four in a Set.)

$								per set.
	5	$5\frac{1}{4}$	$5\frac{1}{2}$	$5\frac{3}{4}$	6	$6\frac{1}{2}$	7	inch.

Unground Boxes...per lb.

Thimble Skeins and Pipe Boxes.

2 × $6\frac{1}{2}$ inch, Oval Ends ....per set, $
$2\frac{1}{4}\times$ 7 inch, Oval Ends .... "
$2\frac{1}{4}\times$ $7\frac{1}{2}$ inch, Oval Ends .... "
$2\frac{3}{4}\times$ 8 inch, Oval Ends .... "
$2\frac{3}{4}\times$ $8\frac{1}{2}$ inch, Oval Ends .... "
3 × 9 inch, Oval Ends .... "
$3\frac{1}{4}\times$10 inch, Oval Ends .... "
$3\frac{1}{4}\times$11 inch, Oval Ends .... "
$3\frac{1}{2}\times$12 inch, Oval Ends .... "
$3\frac{3}{4}\times$12 inch, Oval Ends .... "
4 ×12 inch, Oval Ends .... "

CARRIAGE SPRINGS.

MADE OF FIRST QUALITY ENGLISH STEEL, AND EVERY SPRING TESTED.

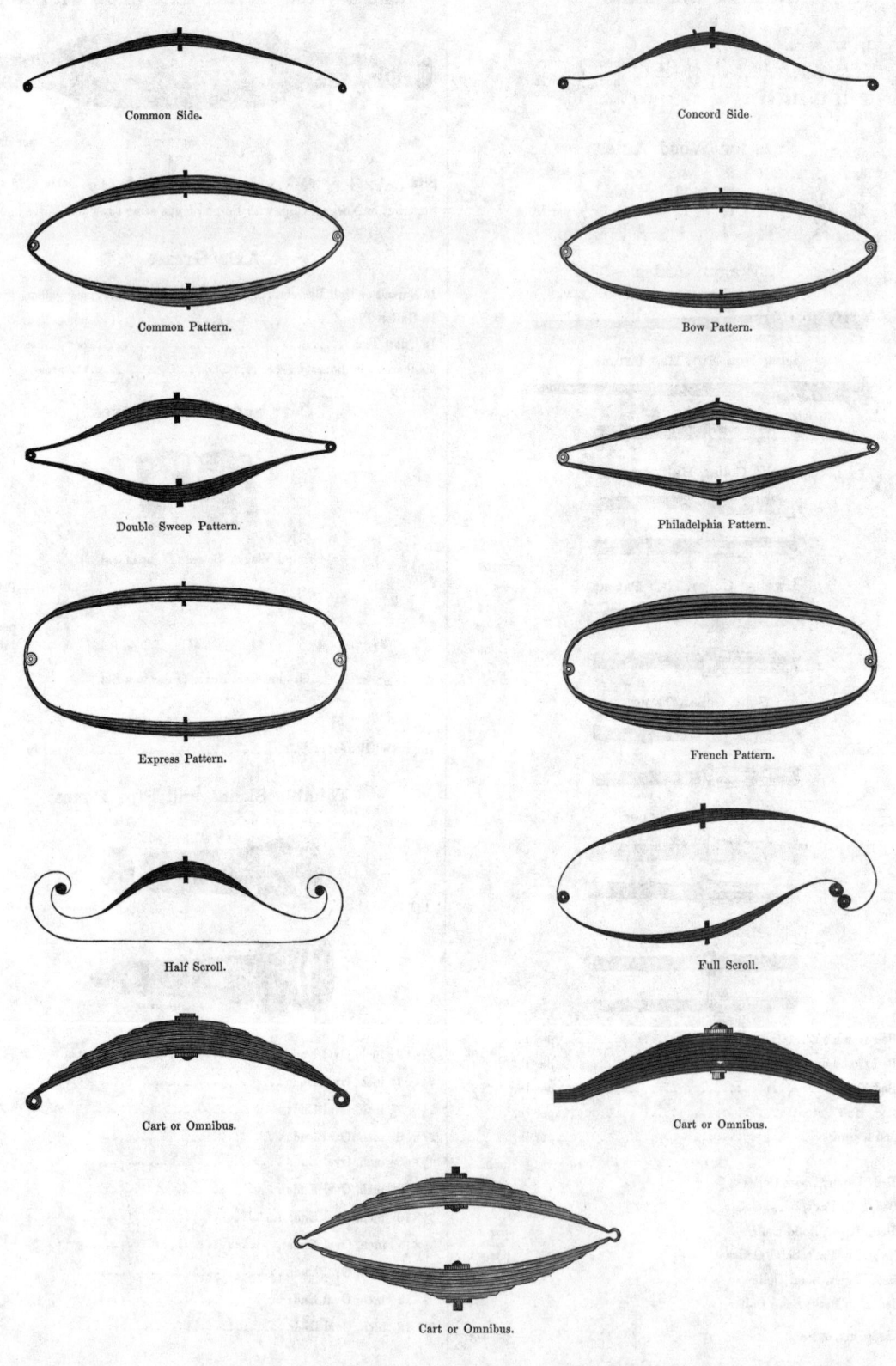

Common Side.

Concord Side.

Common Pattern.

Bow Pattern.

Double Sweep Pattern.

Philadelphia Pattern.

Express Pattern.

French Pattern.

Half Scroll.

Full Scroll.

Cart or Omnibus.

Cart or Omnibus.

Cart or Omnibus.

CARRIAGE SPRINGS, COUPLINGS, ETC.

Carriage Springs.

French Heads without extra charge.

Bright Elliptic Springs 1¼ inch .... per lb. $

Bright Elliptic Springs 1½ inch and larger .... "

Black Elliptic Springs 1¼ inch .... "

Black Elliptic Springs 1½ inch and larger .... "

Bright Elliptic Springs, warranted Tempered, 1¼ inch   "

Bright Elliptic Springs, warranted Tempered, 1½ inch and larger .... "

Bright Elliptic Springs, Oil Tempered, Superior Quality, 1¼ inch .... "

Bright Elliptic Springs, Oil Tempered, Superior Quality, 1½ inch and larger .... "

Bright Scroll Springs, 1¼ inch .... "

Bright Scroll Springs, 1½ inch and larger .... "

Bright Scroll Springs, warranted Tempered, 1¼ inch. "

Bright Scroll Springs, warranted Tempered, 1½ inch and larger .... "

Bright Side Springs, 1¼ inch .... "

Bright Side Springs, 1½ inch and larger .... "

Black Side Springs, 1¼ inch .... "

Black Side Springs, 1½ inch and larger .... "

	$			per pair.
Sulky Springs,	1¼		1½	inch.

Bright Seat Springs, 28 inches and shorter.

	$			per pair.
	1	1¼	1½	inch.

	$			per pair.
Black Seat Springs,	1	1¼	1½	inch.

Cart or Omnibus Springs,   per lb.

Carriage Shackle or Shaft Couplings.

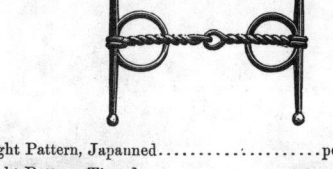

	Black, per doz. pair.	Bright, per doz. pair.
No. 1, Shackle, the Eye or Collar, 1 inch diameter.....		
No. 2, Shackle, the Eye or Collar, ⅞ inch diameter.....		
No. 3, Shackle, the Eye or Collar, 1⅛ inch diameter.....		
No. 1, Pole Eye, to fit No. 1 Shackle.................		
No. 2, Pole Eye, to fit No. 2 Shackle.................		
No. 3, Pole Eye, to fit No. 3 Shackle.................		

Clip Couplings.

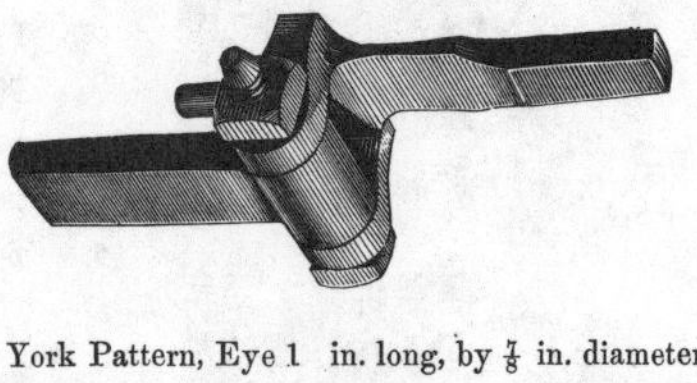

New York Pattern, Eye 1 in. long, by ⅞ in. diameter...

Baltimore Pattern, Eye 1⅛ in. long, by ⅞ in. diameter...

Philadelphia Pattern, No. 1, Eye 1½ in. long, by 1 in. diameter ....

Philadelphia Pattern, No. 2, Eye 1¼ in. long, by 1 in. diameter ....

Pole Eyes for New York Pattern.....................

Pole Eyes for Philadelphia and Baltimore Patterns .....

Stump Joints, First Quality.

	$					per dozen.
Square,	7/16	½	9/16	⅝	¾	inch.

	$					per dozen.
Flat,	⅝×⅜	¾×⅜	⅝×½	¾×½	¾×⅝	inch.

	$				per dozen.
Flat,	⅞×⅝	1×⅝	1⅛×⅝	1¼×⅝	inch.

Felloe Plates.

PHILADELPHIA PATTERN

						per lb.
Plates for	⅞	1	1⅛	1¼	1⅜	1½	inch rim.

Seat Spindles.

	$					per 1000.
A No. 1. Nos.	15	17	19	21	23	

	$					per 1000.
A No. 1. Nos.	25	31	33	41	43	

	$					per 1000.
B No. 2. Nos.	15	17	19	21	23	

	$					per 1000.
B No. 2. Nos.	25	31	33	41	43	

Malleable Iron Harness Rings.

	$					per gross.
	⅝	¾	⅞	1	1¼	inch.
No.	10	9	8	7	6	wire gauge.

	$					per gross.
	1½	1¾	2	2½	3	inch.
No.	5	4	3	2	1	wire gauge.

Wagon Bow or Body Staples.

	$				per dozen.
	1¼	1½	1¾	2	inches.

Twisted Wire Snaffles, with Malleable Iron Cheeks.

No. 1, Light Pattern, Japanned...................per dozen, $

No. 1, Light Pattern, Tinned...................... "

No. 1, Light Pattern, Bright .... "

No. 2, Heavy Pattern, Japanned .... "

No. 2, Heavy Pattern, Tinned.., ... "

No. 2, Heavy Pattern, Bright .... "

Twisted Wire Bradoons, with Malleable Iron Rings.

No. 1, Light Pattern, Japanned...................per dozen, $

No. 1, Light Pattern, Tinned...................... "

No. 1, Light Pattern, Bright .... "

No. 2, Heavy Pattern, Japanned .... "

No. 2, Heavy Pattern, Tinned .... "

No. 2, Heavy Pattern, Bright .... "

Double Mouth Twisted Wire Snaffles.

No. 3, Tinned..........................per dozen, $

No. 3, Japanned .... "

No. 3, Bright .... "

CARRIAGE BANDS.

It will save mistakes in filling orders for Bands, if customers will designate the different styles precisely as they are printed on this List.

Boston Pattern.

		$3\frac{1}{4}$ or under.	$3\frac{3}{8}$	$3\frac{1}{2}$	$3\frac{5}{8}$	$3\frac{3}{4}$	$3\frac{7}{8}$	4	$4\frac{1}{8}$	$4\frac{1}{4}$	$4\frac{3}{8}$	$4\frac{1}{2}$	inch.
Silver Boston.........................$													per set.
Silver Boston, Heavy													per set.
Silver Boston, Extra Heavy													per set.

Concentric.   Concentric Pattern, Boston Edge.

		$3\frac{1}{4}$ or under.	$3\frac{3}{8}$	$3\frac{1}{2}$	$3\frac{5}{8}$	$3\frac{3}{4}$	$3\frac{7}{8}$	4	$4\frac{1}{8}$	$4\frac{1}{4}$	$4\frac{3}{8}$	$4\frac{1}{2}$	inch.
Silver Concentric.....................$													per set.
Silver Concentric,, Heavy													per set.
Silver Concentric, Extra Heavy........													per set.

Philadelphia.   Heavy Philadelphia.   Extra Heavy Philadelphia.

		$3\frac{1}{4}$ or under.	$3\frac{3}{8}$	$3\frac{1}{2}$	$3\frac{5}{8}$	$3\frac{3}{4}$	$3\frac{7}{8}$	4	$4\frac{1}{8}$	$4\frac{1}{4}$	$4\frac{3}{8}$	$4\frac{1}{2}$	inch.
Silver Philadelphia ....$													per set.
Silver Philadelphia, Heavy...........													per set.
Silver Philadelphia, Extra Heavy......													per set.

Concave Heavy.

		$3\frac{1}{4}$ or under.	$3\frac{3}{8}$	$3\frac{1}{2}$	$3\frac{5}{8}$	$3\frac{3}{4}$	$3\frac{7}{8}$	4	$4\frac{1}{8}$	$4\frac{1}{4}$	$4\frac{3}{8}$	$4\frac{1}{2}$	inch.
Silver Concave Heavy.................$													per set.
Silver Concave, Extra Heavy..........													per set.

Rim.   Heavy Rim.   Heavy Rim, with Shoulder.   Roped or Half Roped.

		$3\frac{1}{4}$ or under.	$3\frac{3}{8}$	$3\frac{1}{2}$	$3\frac{5}{8}$	$3\frac{3}{4}$	$3\frac{7}{8}$	4	$4\frac{1}{8}$	$4\frac{1}{4}$	$4\frac{3}{8}$	$4\frac{1}{2}$	inch.
Silver Rim........................$													per set.
Silver Rim, Heavy...................													per set.
Silver Rim, Heavy, with Shoulder.....													per set.
Silver Rim, Extra Heavy, $1\frac{5}{16}$ deep....													per set.
Silver Rim, Extra Heavy, $1\frac{3}{8}$ deep													per set.
Silver Rim, Roped...................													per set.

Excelsior.

		$3\frac{1}{4}$ or under.	$3\frac{3}{8}$	$3\frac{1}{2}$	$3\frac{5}{8}$	$3\frac{3}{4}$	$3\frac{7}{8}$	4	$4\frac{1}{8}$	$4\frac{1}{4}$	$4\frac{3}{8}$	$4\frac{1}{2}$	inch.
Silver Excelsior													per set.
Silver Excelsior, Roped													per set.

Rose Boston Pattern.   Rose Rim Pattern.

		$3\frac{1}{4}$ or under.	$3\frac{3}{8}$	$3\frac{1}{2}$	$3\frac{5}{8}$	$3\frac{3}{4}$	$3\frac{7}{8}$	4	$4\frac{1}{8}$	$4\frac{1}{4}$	$4\frac{3}{8}$	$4\frac{1}{2}$	inch.
Silver Rose Scollop, or Boston Rose.$													per set.
Silver Rose Scollop, Rim													per set.

CARRIAGE BANDS.

(Continued.)

Heavy Reflector Pattern.

3¼ or under.	3⅜	3½	3⅝	3¾	3⅞	4	4⅛	4¼	4⅜	4½	inch.

Silver Reflectors .... $ per set.
Silver Reflectors, Heavy ....   "

Heavy Jersey Mail Pattern.

3¼ or under.	3⅜	3½	3⅝	3¾	3⅞	4	4⅛	4¼	4⅜	4½	inch.

Silver Jersey Mail .... $ per set.
Silver Jersey Mail, Extra Heavy ....   "

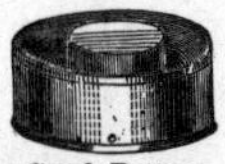

Coach Pattern.

3¼ or under.	3⅜	3½	3⅝	3¾	3⅞	4	4⅛	4¼	4⅜	4½	inch.

Silver Coach .... $ per set.
Silver Coach, Extra Heavy ....   "

Japanned Silver Screw Cap Bands.    Screw Pattern.

3¼ or under.	3⅜	3½	3⅝	3¾	3⅞	4	4⅛	4¼	4⅜	4½	inch.

Silver Japanned Screw .... $ per set.
Silver Boston Screw ....   "

Boston Screw Pattern.    Philadelphia Screw Pattern.

3¼ or under.	3⅜	3½	3⅝	3¾	3⅞	4	4⅛	4¼	4⅜	4½	inch.

Silver Empire Screw .... $ per set.
Silver Philadelphia Screw ....   "

Excelsior Screw Pattern.    Rose Screw Pattern.

3¼ or under.	3⅜	3½	3⅝	3¾	3⅞	4	4⅛	4¼	4⅜	4½	inch.

Silver Excelsior Screw .... $ per set.
Silver Rose Screw ....   "

Champion Pattern.

3¼ or under.	3⅜	3½	3⅝	3¾	3⅞	4	4⅛	4¼	4⅜	4½	inch.

Extra Silver Patent Champion .... $ per set.

Rosette Pattern.    Rose Rosette Pattern.

3¼ or under.	3⅜	3½	3⅝	3¾	3⅞	4	4⅛	4¼	4⅜	4½	inch.

Rosette Pattern .... $ per set.
Rose Rosette Pattern ....   "

CARRIAGE BANDS AND SOCKETS.

SILVER PATENT SAND BANDS.

Silver Patent Sand Bands.

Heavy Sand Bands.

	3 or under.	3¼	3½	3¾	4	4¼	4½	inch.
Silver Patent Sand.....................$								per set.

CLOSE PLATED BANDS.

	3¼ or under.	3⅜	3½	3⅝	3¾	3⅞	4	inch.
On Iron.—Heavy Rim Pattern...............$								per set.
On Brass.—Rim Pattern...................								"
On Brass.—Heavy Rim Pattern.............								"
On Brass.—Heavy Rim Pattern, with Shoulder.								"
On Brass.—Extra Heavy Rim, Medium........								"

BANDS FOR CHILDREN'S CABS.

Cab Bands.

	1¼	1½	inch.
Silver Reflectors...................................$			per pair
Silver Rose...................................			"
Silver Mail...................................			"
Silver Concentric.............................			"
Silver Rim....................................			"
Silver Rim, Roped.............................			"
Silver Sand...................................			"

ELECTRO-PLATED SOCKETS.

Silver Plain Shaft Sockets.

$	⅝	¾	⅞	1	1⅛	1¼	per dozen pair. inch.

Extra Heavy Straight Shaft Sockets.

Plain Pattern, $	⅞	1	1⅛	1¼	1⅜ and 1½	per dozen pair. in. outside measure.

Silver Ball Shaft Sockets.

$	⅝	¾	⅞	1	1⅛	1¼	per doz. pair. inch.

Extra Heavy Ball Shaft Sockets.

$	⅞	1	per dozen pair. in. outside measure.

Octagon Shaft Sockets.

$	¾	⅞	1	per dozen pair. inch.

Philadelphia Ball Shaft Sockets.

$	¾	⅞	per dozen pair. inch.

CLOSE PLATED SOCKETS.

Close Plated Shaft Sockets.

Ball, $	¾	⅞	1	1⅛	1¼	per dozen pair. inch.
Plain, $	¾	⅞	1	1⅛	1¼	per dozen pair. inch.

The two following Patterns are measured outside.

Ball, Extra Heavy, Straight, $	⅞	1			per dozen pair. inch.
Plain, Ex. Heavy, $ Straight,	⅞	1	1⅛	1¼	1⅜	1½	doz. pair. inch.

Pole Sockets.

$	1¼	1⅜	1½	per dozen. inch.

Pole Sockets, Acorn Top.

$	1¼	1⅜	1½	per dozen. inch.

Pole Yoke Sockets.

With Wrought Round Loop, $	¾	⅞	1	per doz. pair. inch.

HAME SOCKETS.

Hame Sockets, Acorn Top.

Hame Sockets, Acorn Top, ¾ inch..............per dozen pair, $

COACH HANDLES, STIRRUPS, ETC.

Express Hame Sockets.

Express Hame Sockets, ⅞ inch...............per dozen pair, $

COACH HANDLES AND APRON HOOKS.
Inside Coach Handles, Electro-Plated on Brass.

No. 1.   No. 2.   No. 3.   No. 5.   No. 6.

$

| No. | 1 | 2 | 3 | 5 | 6. | per doz. pair. |

Outside Coach Handles, Close Plated.

No. 7—Plain Solid.............................$ per doz. pair.

Outside Coach Handles, Electro-Plated on Brass.

No. 8—Plain Solid.............................$ per doz. pair.
No. 9—Plain Solid.............................   "

Apron Hooks.

Brass...$ per gross.
Silver..   "

STIRRUPS, PAD, SYRACUSE & BOLT HOOKS.
Japanned and Polished Stirrups.

No. 30.   No. 35.   No. 65.

No. 66.   No. 45.   Roped.

per doz. pair.

| No. | 30 | 35 | 45 | 65 | 66 | Roped. |

Pad Hooks.

Close Plated.........................$ per dozen.
No. 3   No. 4.

Syracuse Hook.

1½   1¾   inch.

Brass.............................$ per dozen.
Close Plated.........................   "

Silvered Close Plated Bolt Hooks.

Silvered Close Plated....$ per doz.
No. 1   2   3.

TERRETS AND SWIVELS.
Terrets.

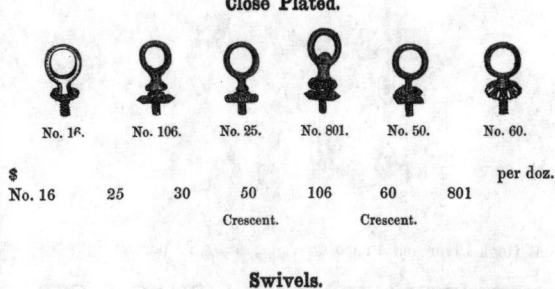

No. 13.   No. 26.   No. 28.   Crown.   Flat Octagon.

| Brass....$ | No. 13 | 26 | 28 | — | — | per doz. |
| | Crescent. | Ring. | Octagon. | Crown. | Flat Octagon. |

Close Plated.

No. 16.   No. 106.   No. 25.   No. 801.   No. 50.   No. 60.

$ per doz.

| No. 16 | 25 | 30 | 50 | 106 | 60 | 801 |
| | | | Crescent. | | Crescent. | |

Swivels.

No. 1.   No. 2.   No. 3.

Brass..........$			per doz.
Close Plated....			"
No.	1	2	3.	

For Spurs, see page 102.

PATENT JOINTED BELT HOOKS.

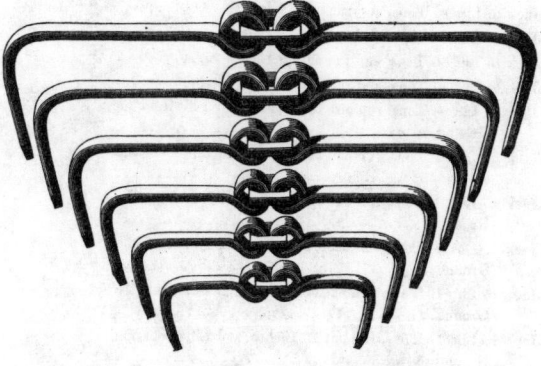

(The Engravings represent the different sizes.)

The advantages of these Hooks over others consist in taking hold of the Belt at greater distances from the ends, thereby preventing the holes from tearing out, and at the same time conform to the circumference of the pulleys while passing over them.

The Belts can be fastened in one half the time it requires with lace leather, and when once fastened need not be disturbed until they require taking up.

$ per gross.

| No. | 11 | 10 | 9 | 8 | 7 | 6 | |
| | 1½ | 2 | 2½ | 3 | 3½ | 4 | inch. |

BELT HOOKS, HYDRAULIC JACKS & PUNCHES.

POINTED BELT HOOKS.

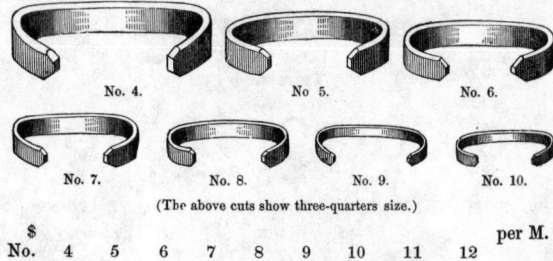

No. 4.   No 5.   No. 6.

No. 7.   No. 8.   No. 9.   No. 10.

(The above cuts show three-quarters size.)

$ per M.

No.   4   5   6   7   8   9   10   11   12

PATENT BELT HOOK PLYER AND PUNCH COMBINED.

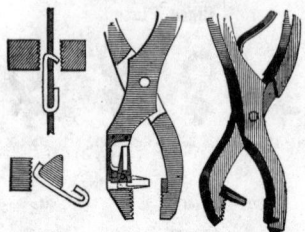

Belt Hook Plyer and Punch..................per dozen, $

PORTABLE HYDRAULIC LIFTING JACKS.

For raising Heavy Weights, such as Locomotives, Boilers, Guns, Heavy Machinery, Wrecking Purposes, or Stationary Pressing.

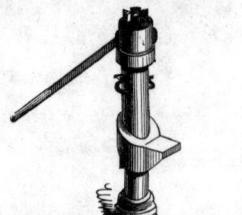 

Jack to Lift   7 Tons, and run out 12 Inches............each, $

Jack to Lift   7 Tons, and run out 24 Inches.............   "

Jack to Lift 10 Tons, and run out 12 Inches.............   "

Jack to Lift 15 Tons, and run out 12 Inches.............   "

Jack to Lift 30 Tons, and run out   9 Inches.............   "

Jack to Lift 60 Tons, and run out   9 Inches............ .   "

Jack to Lift 90 Tons, and run out   7 Inches.............   "

Jack to Lift 4 Tons, run out 12 Inches, and Lift from the Ground...   "

Jack to Lift 4 Tons, run out 24 Inches, and Lift from the Ground...   "

Jack to Lift 7 Tons, run out 12 Inches, and Lift from the Ground...   "

Jack to Lift 7 Tons, run out 24 Inches, and Lift from the Ground...   "

Jack to Lift 10 Tons, run out 12 Inches, and Lift from the Ground...   "

Jack to Lift 15 Tons, run out 12 Inches, and Lift from the Ground...   "

Jack to Lift 7 Tons, and run out 24 Inches, with Wide Base for Locomotive Shops ....   "

Jack to Lift 10 Tons, and run out 12 Inches, with Wide Base for Locomotive Shops ....   "

Jack to Lift 15 Tons, and run out 12 Inches, with Wide Base for Locomotive Shops ....   "

This Jack, or Press, appears to the eye, when depressed, a simple cylinder; and when elevated, one cylinder sliding within another. It is from two to eight or more inches in diameter, according to the power desired, with an enlarged head, (attached to the inner cylinder, which is the ram,) having a socket for the reception of the lever by which the force-pump is worked.

The ram, with its head, contains just so much fluid as is required to fill the vacancy in the cylinder caused by the raising of the ram in the act of lifting; and when this is accomplished, the fluid is returned into its original recess by a valve operated by the lever that

works the pump. The force-pump is contained inside of the ram, and consequently is not seen in the accompanying cuts.

The lever is detached, and may be put on at pleasure. The joints in the head maintain a parallel motion for the force-pump piston, which is the fulcrum of the lever. The ground-lifting attachment is an iron tube, screwed into the lower side of the head, and passing down to the bottom of the press outside of the cylinder, on the lower end of which is a claw that supports the weight to be raised.

These Jacks are light, portable, and of easy application—a Jack to raise four tons not weighing more than 50 lbs. and one to raise sixty tons, not more than 200 lbs. They are all worked by the labor of one man only, who is capable of raising ten tons through a space of one foot in one and a half minutes, or sixty tons the same distance in ten minutes.

DIRECTIONS.

Fill the Jack through the screw in the head with whiskey, in which is a tablespoonful of oil, having the ram quite down; work the lever, pour in the whiskey, until the ram is forced up the number of inches the Jack runs out, which will be the quantity required. Never fill with water. Push the ram down to the bottom of the cylinder, and then put the screw in the head.

Be careful that no dirt gets into the head in filling. Place the head (or if a ground-lifting Jack, the claw or head) under the weight to be raised; put in the lever, on which there is a projection, downward; work it perpendicularly until the weight is at the required height, or the number of inches the Jack runs out. Sometimes it happens that another stroke of the lever would raise the weight too high; then raise the lever a little, and push it down slowly, by which a stroke may be missed. To lower the weight, push the lever to the bottom of the stroke, take it off, turn it with the projection upward, and with a slight pressure of the hand, the weight may be lowered as slow as required, or stopped at any point.

If attempted to lower a weight too fast it will stop. Keep the ram quite down when not used.

If left run out, supporting a weight or otherwise, it may be necessary to slacken the screw in the head, to let out the air with which it becomes filled, before it can be pushed down.

These Jacks may be used standing or at any angle, only that the head should be a little higher than the foot.

In using them for any purpose, one man of ordinary strength can apply all the force on the lever they are designed to stand, and it is intended the lever should bend or break when more than 150 pounds are applied to it.

They should rest fair on the bottom and top in pressing, especially those which raise more than ten tons, and should not be lowered fast and suddenly checked with a heavy weight on them.

HYDRAULIC PULLING JACK,

FOR PULLING, PROVING CHAINS AND ROPES, PULLING STUMPS, SETTING UP RIGGING, &c.

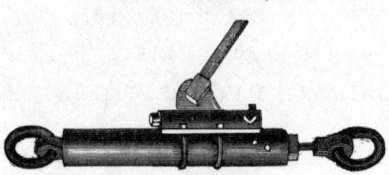

Jack to Pull   6 Tons 2 Feet, without Fleeting............each, $

Jack to Pull   8 Tons 2 Feet, without Fleeting............   "

Jack to Pull 15 Tons 2 Feet, without Fleeting............   "

These Jacks appear like a plain cylinder, with rings at each end, by which to attach to it the body to be moved. It is three or more inches in diameter, and one and a half or more feet long, according to the power required, or the distance it is required to move.

The fluid by which it is worked is all contained in the cylinder, and only changes places from one side of the piston to the other.

It has a force-pump on the outside, worked by a lever, which forces the fluid contained in the cylinder to the opposite side of a piston, to the rod of which one of the rings at the end is attached.

Thus by this operation the Jack is forced together, drawing with it the body to be moved. They will work vertical, horizontal, or at any angle.

Directions.—Fill the Jack through the screw in the side of the cylinder with whiskey and a spoonful of oil. To pull or lift any thing, make it fast to the Jack by chains or ropes through the rings at each end, having first extended it as far as it will go. This is done by giving the thumb-screw in the force-pump two or three turns inward, and pulling out the piston, then turn back the thumb-screw until it stops. Put in the lever, and pump as much as required.

HYDRAULIC PUNCH OR SHEARS.

FOR PUNCHING OR SHEARING IRON, DIE-SINKING, ETC.

Punch for Punching $\frac{3}{8}$ Inch Boiler Iron a $\frac{5}{8}$ Inch Hole .....each, $

Punch for Punching $\frac{1}{2}$ Inch Boiler Iron a $\frac{3}{4}$ Inch Hole .....   "

Punch for Punching $\frac{3}{4}$ Inch Boiler Iron a $\frac{7}{8}$ Inch Hole .....   "

Larger Sizes made to Order.

The well known power of the Hydraulic Press applied in this form to the Punching and Shearing Iron, Die-Sinking, and other purposes, where with a limited movement great power is required, renders this one of the most efficient, convenient, and economical Tools ever offered to the public.

Punches or Presses of this kind, weighing only about 40 lbs., with the power of one man exerted on a lever one foot in length, will give a pressure of 30 tons.

These Presses are simple in their construction, being used entirely without valves or the force-pump in common use in all other Hydraulic Presses.

The Punch for punching through $\frac{3}{8}$ inch boiler iron a hole $\frac{5}{8}$ inch in diameter, with one man to work it, will do as much work as can be done by two men with a common hand-screw punch, besides being applicable in many places where a screw punch could not be used.

Directions.—To fill the Press, push the punch clean back. Take out the screw, and fill with oil; replace or enter the screw; then place under the punch the iron to be punched or sheared, and turn in the screw until the iron is punched. Turn out the screw until the punch will go back the thickness of the iron. Pull back the punch with the claw, and put under another piece, and so on.

WAGON JACKS, CATTLE LEADERS, ETC.

HUSON'S PATENT WAGON JACK.

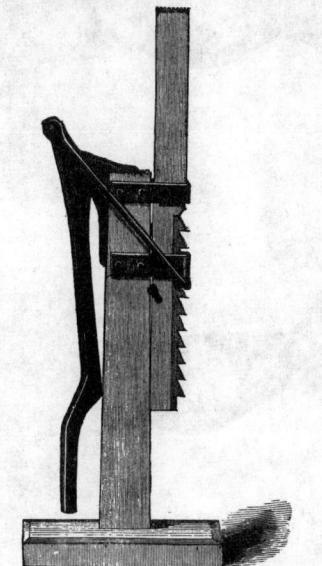

Iron...... .... $ per dozen.
Wood........................   "

BADGLEY'S PATENT WAGON JACK.

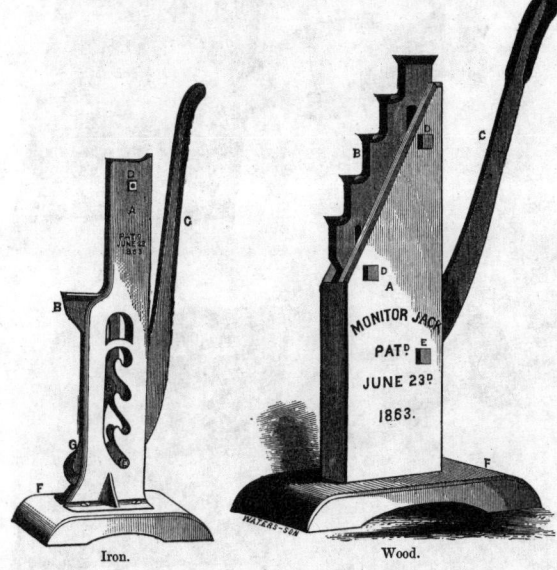

Iron.   Wood.

Iron Jack...each, $
Monitor Wagon, Wood.................................   "
Monitor Carriage, Wood.................................   "

CYLINDER WAGON JACKS.

No. 1, Improved, for Heavy Wagons..............per dozen, $
No. 2, Improved, for Common and Light Wagons ....   "

LANE'S PATENT WAGON JACKS.

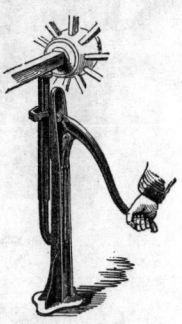

No. 2, Medium ....each, $
No. 3, Large ....   "

IMPROVED CATTLE LEADERS.

No. 1, Small Size.............................per dozen, $
No. 2, Large Size.............................per dozen, $
Welton's Patent, No. 1.......................per dozen, $
Welton's Patent, No. 2... ....per dozen, $

OX BALL WRENCHES.

For Smooth or Octagon Balls.................per dozen, $

SUPERIOR WROUGHT BULL RINGS.

No.	STEEL.		COPPER.		SILVER PLATE.		
No.	1	2	1	2	1	2	
Size,	2½	3	2½	3	2½	3	inch diam'r.
$							per doz.

PATENT OX BOW PINS.

No. 1, for 1¾ inch Bows........................per gross, $
No. 2, for 2 inch Bows........................per gross, $

FITCH'S PATENT CURRY COMBS.

[*For Description of Plates see page 271.*]

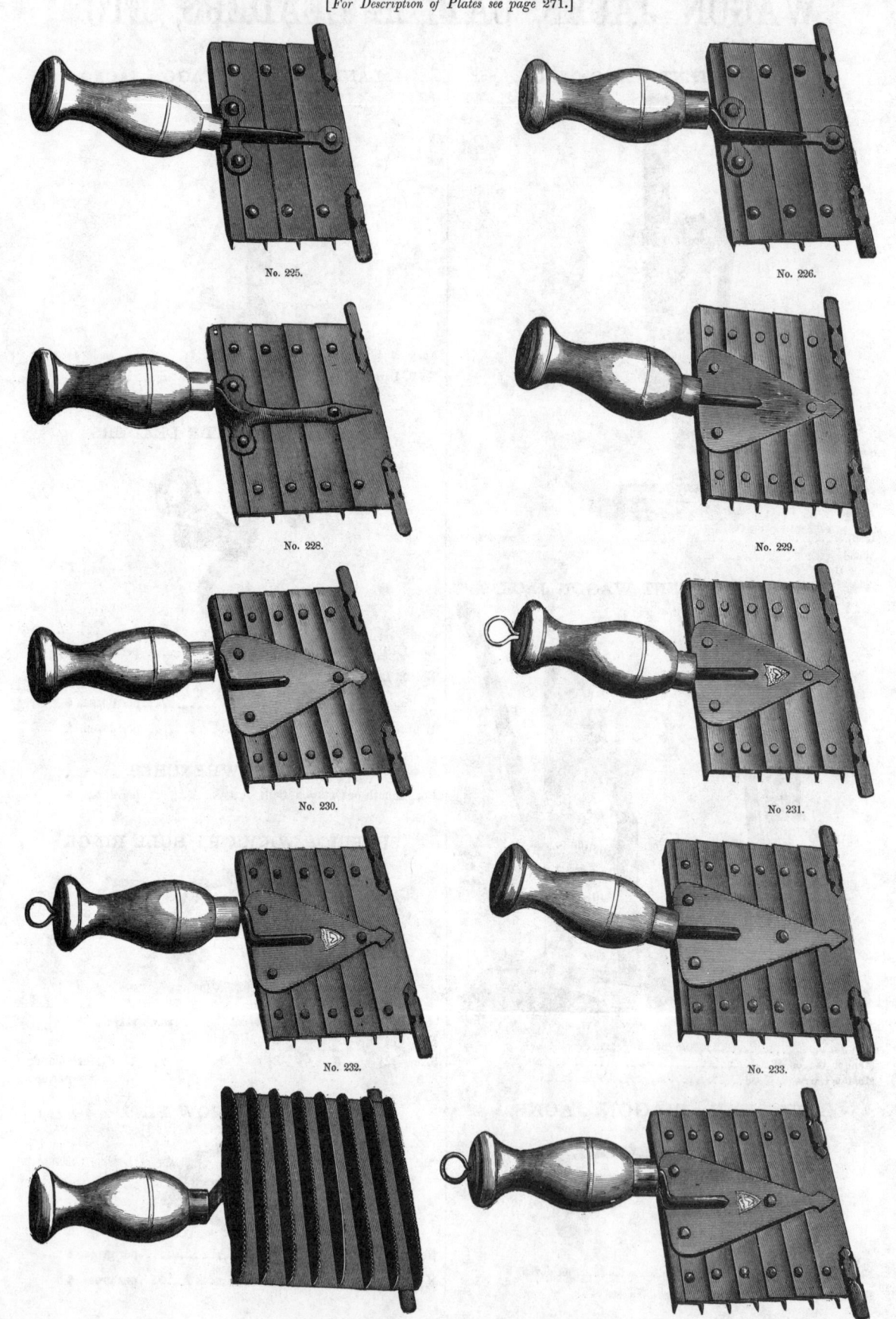

No. 225.

No. 226.

No. 228.

No. 229.

No. 230.

No 231.

No. 232.

No. 233.

No. 234.

No. 236.

CURRY COMBS.

(Continued.)

FITCH'S PATENT CURRY COMBS.

(For Plates see page 270.)

No. 225, 5 Bar, Straight Handle . . . . per doz. $

No. 226, 5 Bar, Crank Handle . . . . "

No. 227, 6 Bar, Straight Handle . . . . "

No. 228, 6 Bar, Crank Handle . . . . "

No. 229, 7 Bar, Straight Handle, Extra Heavy . . . . "

No. 230, 7 Bar, Crank Handle, Extra Heavy . . . . "

No. 231, 7 Bar, Straight Handle, Extra Heavy, Ornamen-
ted Back . . . . "

No. 232, 7 Bar, Crank Handle, Extra Heavy, Ornamented
Back . . . . per doz. $

No. 233, 8 Bar, Straight Handle, Extra Heavy . . . . "

No. 234, 8 Bar, Crank Handle, Extra Heavy, Ornamented
Back . . . . "

No. 235, 8 Bar, Straight Handle, Extra Heavy, Ornamented Back . . . . "

No. 236, 8 Bar, Crank Handle, Extra Heavy, Ornamented
Back . . . . "

WHEELER'S PATENT ALL WROUGHT CURRY COMBS.

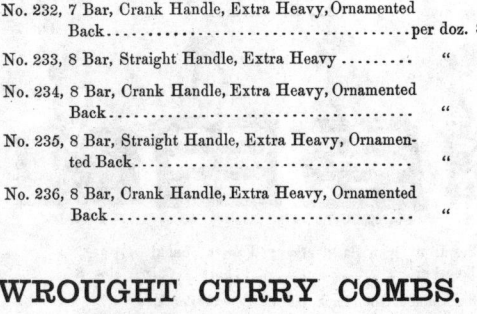

No. 5.   No. 10.

No. 5, 4 Bar, Narrow, Open Back . . . . per doz. $

No. 10, 4 Bar, Narrow, Solid Back . . . . "

No. 20.   No. 30.

No. 20. 6 Bar, Narrow, Open Back . . . . per doz. $

No. 30, 6 Bar, Narrow, Solid Back . . . . "

No. 40.   No. 50.

No. 40, 6 Bar, Broad, Open Back . . . . per doz. $

No. 50, 6 Bar, Broad, Solid Back, Straight Handle . . . . . "

No. 50, 6 Bar, Broad, Solid Back, Crank Handle . . . . . . "

No. 100.   No. 200.

No. 100, 8 Bar, Broad, Open Back . . . . per doz. $

No. 200, 8 Bar, Broad, Solid Back, Straight Handle . . . . . "

No. 200, 8 Bar, Broad, Solid Back, Crank Handle . . . . . . "

No. 300.

No. 300, 8 Bar, Broad, Solid Back, Strap Handle . . . . "

No. 350, 8 Bar, Broad, Solid Back, Cavalry . . . . "

No. 375, 8 Bar, Broad, Solid Back, Straight Handle, Army "

No. 400, 8 Bar, Broad, Solid Back, Crank Handle, Army. "

AMERICAN CURRY COMBS.

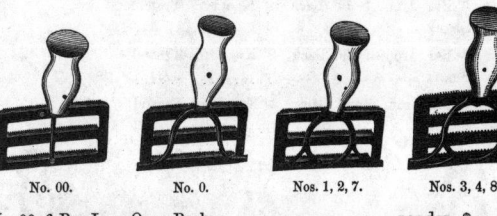

No. 00.   No. 0.   Nos. 1, 2, 7.   Nos. 3, 4, 8.

No. 00, 6 Bar Iron, Open Back . . . . per doz. $

No. 0, 6 Bar Iron, Open Back, 2 Knocker . . . . "

No. 1, 6 Bar Iron, Open Back, 2 Knocker . . . . "

No. 2, 6 Bar Brass, Open Back, 2 Knocker . . . . "

No. 7, 6 Bar Tinned, Open Back, 2 Knocker . . . . "

CURRY COMBS.

(Continued.)

AMERICAN CURRY COMBS.

(Continued.)

No. 3, 8 Bar Iron, Open Back, 2 Knocker ....per dozen, $
No. 4, 8 Bar Brass, Open Back, 2 Knocker .... "
No. 8, 8 Bar Tinned, Open Back, 2 Knocker........... "

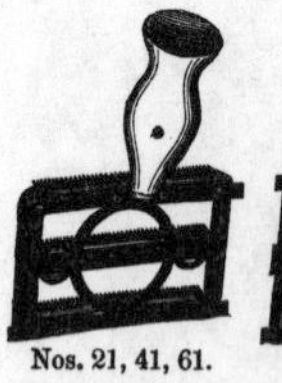

Nos. 21, 41, 61.

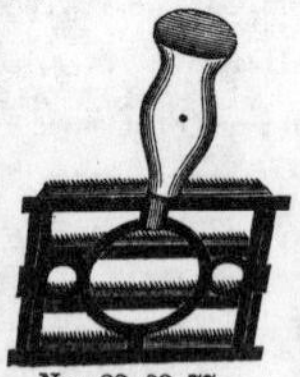

Nos. 22, 23, 77.

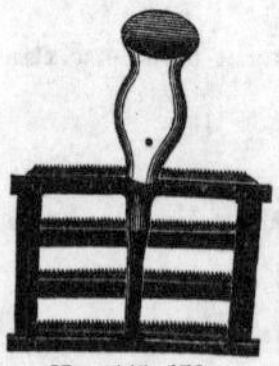

Nos. 145, 150.

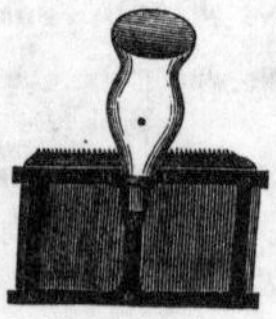

Nos. 135, 140.

No. 21, 6 Bar Iron, Open Back, Heavy Trowel Shank, 4 Knocker..............................per doz. $
No. 41, 6 Bar Tinned, Open Back, Heavy Trowel Shank, 4 Knocker.............................. "
No. 61, 6 Bar Brass, Open Back, Heavy Trowel Shank, 4 Knocker.............................. "
No. 22, 8 Bar Iron, Open Back, Extra Heavy, 4 Knocker "
No. 33, 8 Bar Tinned, Open Back, Ex. Heavy, 4 Knocker "
No. 77, 8 Bar Brass, Open Back, Ex. Heavy, 4 Knocker. "
No. 145, 6 Bar Iron, Open Back, Heavy, 4 Knocker.... "
No. 150, 6 Bar Iron, Open Back, Heavy, 4 Knocker.... "
No. 135, 6 Bar Iron, Solid Back, Heavy, 4 Knocker.... "
No. 140, 8 Bar Iron, Solid Back, Heavy, 4 Knocker.... "

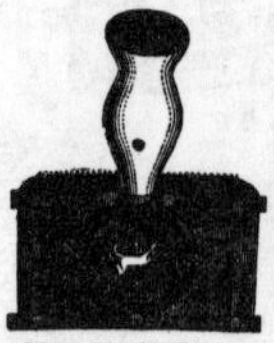

Nos. 31, 51, 71.

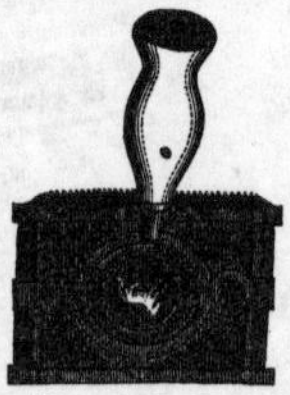

Nos. 44, 66, 88.

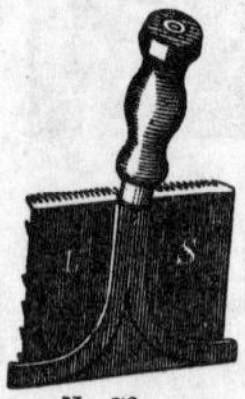

No. 76.

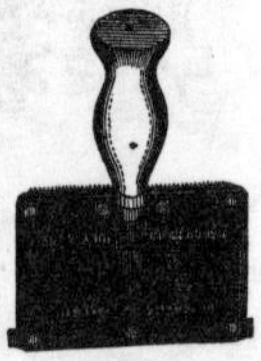

Nos. 110, 120, 130.

No. 31, 6 Bar Iron, Solid Back, Heavy, 4 Knocker, Trowel Shank ....per doz. $
No. 51, 6 Bar Tinned, Solid Back, Heavy, 4 Knocker, Trowel Shank .... "
No. 71, 6 Bar Brass, Solid Back, Heavy, 4 Knocker, Trowel Shank .... "
No. 44, 8 Bar Iron, Solid Back, Heavy, 4 Knocker, Trowel Shank .... "
No. 66, 8 Bar Tinned, Solid Back, Heavy, 4 Knocker, Trowel Shank .... "
No. 88, 8 Bar Brass, Solid Back, Heavy, 4 Knocker, Trowel Shank .... "
No. 76, 8 Bar Cast Steel, U. S. Solid Back, 2 Knocker, Trowel Shank .... "
No. 110, 6 Bar Iron, Solid Back, 2 Knocker, Trowel Shank .... "
No. 120, 6 Bar Iron, Solid Back, 2 Knocker, Trowel Shank .... "
No. 130, 8 Bar Iron, Solid Back, 2 Knocker, Trowel Shank .... "

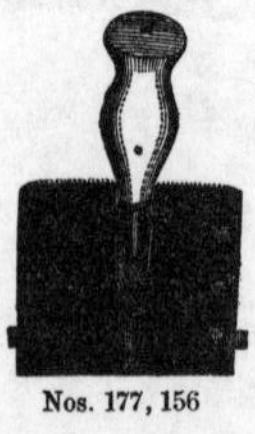

Nos. 177, 156

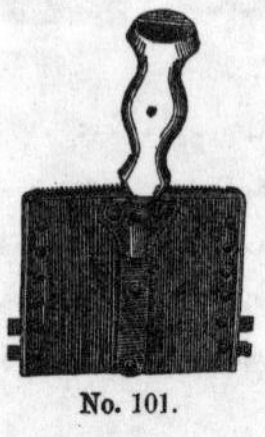

No. 101.

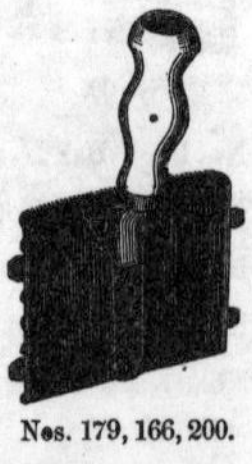

Nos. 179, 166, 200.

AMERICAN CURRY COMBS.

(Continued.)

No. 177, 6 Bar Iron, 2 Knocker, Solid Back, Trowel Shank, English Pattern ....per doz. $
No. 156, 8 Bar Iron, 2 Knocker, Solid Back, Trowel Shank, English Pattern.......................... "
No. 101, 8 Bar Iron, 4 Knocker, Solid Back, Trowel Shank, Forged Bar.......................... "
No. 179, 8 Bar Iron, 4 Knocker, Heavy, Solid Back, Trowel Shank .... "
No. 166, 8 Bar Iron, 4 Knocker, Extra Heavy, Solid Back, Trowel Shank .... "
No. 200, 8 Bar Cast Steel, 4 Knocker, Extra Heavy, Solid Back, Trowel Shank .... "

BEACH'S PATENT CURRY COMBS.

No. 1, 6 Bar, Iron, Open..........................per dozen, $
No. 2, 6 Bar, Iron, Open.......................... "
No. 3, 8 Bar, Iron, Open.......................... "
No. 4, 6 Bar, Iron, Covered.......................... "
No. 5, 6 Bar, Iron, Covered.......................... "
No. 6, 8 Bar, Iron, Covered.......................... "
No. 7, 6 Bar, Brass, Open.......................... "
No. 8, 6 Bar, Brass, Open.......................... "
No. 9, 8 Bar, Brass, Open.......................... "
No. 10, 6 Bar, Brass, Covered.......................... "
No. 11, 6 Bar, Brass, Covered.......................... "
No. 12, 8 Bar, Brass, Covered.......................... "
Rubber Curry Combs.......................... "

HORSE AND CURRY CARDS.

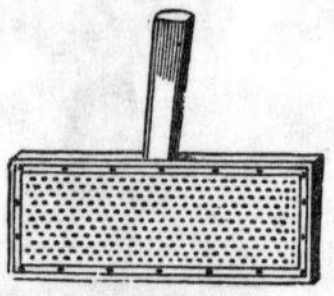

Horse.

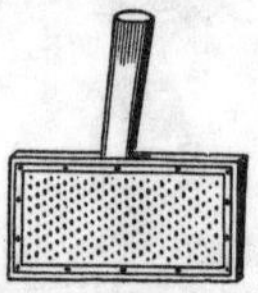

Curry.

Horse Cards, Leathered, Coppered Wire, size $8\frac{1}{4} \times 4$ in..per single doz. $
Horse Cards, Leathered, Brass Wire, size $8\frac{1}{4} \times 4$ in... " "
Curry Cards, Leathered, Coppered Wire, size $5\frac{3}{4} \times 4$ in. " "
Curry Cards, Leathered, Brass Wire, size $5\frac{3}{4} \times 4$ in... " "
Ells Superior Short Curry Cards, Coppered Wire, size $5\frac{1}{4} \times 3\frac{1}{2}$ in.............................. " "
Ells Superior Long Cattle Cards, Coppered Wire, size $5\frac{1}{4} \times 3\frac{1}{2}$ in.............................. " "

COTTON, WOOL AND JIM CROW CARDS.

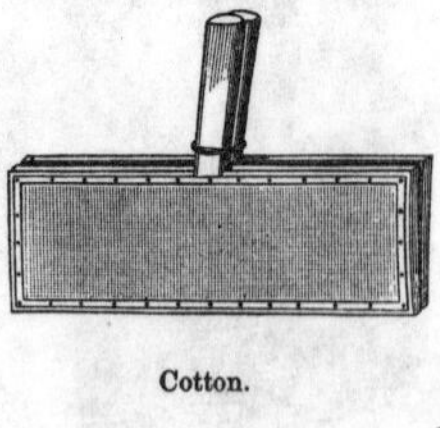

Cotton.

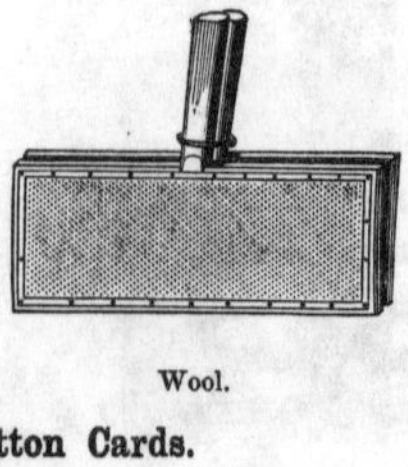

Wool.

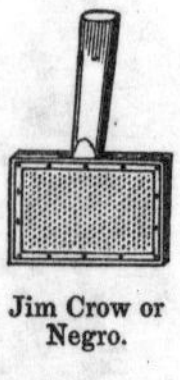

Jim Crow or Negro.

Cotton Cards.

Description.	Letter.	Size.	
No. 10............	A............	$10\frac{7}{8} \times 4\frac{5}{8}$ in.	per doz. pairs, $
No. 10............	1st............	" Successors." in.	" "
No. 10............	B............	$10\frac{7}{8} \times 4\frac{5}{8}$ in.	" "
No. 10............	C............	$10\frac{3}{8} \times 4\frac{3}{8}$ in.	" "

CARDS, COMBS, SNAPS, ETC.

COTTON CARDS.
(Continued.)

Description.	Letter.	Size.				
No. 9	A	$10\frac{3}{8}$	×	$4\frac{3}{8}$	per doz. pairs, $
No. 9	B	$10\frac{3}{8}$	×	$4\frac{3}{8}$	" "
No. 8	A	$9\frac{3}{8}$	×	$4\frac{1}{4}$	" "
No. 8	B	$9\frac{3}{8}$	×	$4\frac{1}{4}$	" "

Wool Cards.

Description.	Letter.	Size.				
No. 8	A	$9\frac{3}{4}$	×	$4\frac{1}{2}$	per doz. pairs, $
No. 8	B	$9\frac{1}{2}$	×	$4\frac{3}{8}$	" "
No. 6	A	$9\frac{3}{4}$	×	$4\frac{1}{2}$	" "
No. 6	B	$9\frac{1}{4}$	×	$4\frac{3}{8}$	" "
No. 4	Virginia	$8\frac{1}{4}$	×	4	" "
No. 5	Virginia	$8\frac{1}{4}$	×	4	" "
No. 4	Canada	$8\frac{3}{4}$	×	$4\frac{3}{4}$	" "
No. 5	Canada	$8\frac{3}{4}$	×	$4\frac{3}{4}$	" "
No. 9	Canada	9	×	$5\frac{1}{2}$	" "

Jim Crow Cards.

Coppered Wire .... per single dozen, $
Iron Wire .... " "
Brass Wire .... " "

STRIPPING CARDS.

$

10   13   16   19   24   31   36   inch.

Machine Card Clothing, at the Lowest Cash Prices.

Metallic .... per dozen, $

$ per dozen.

Horn, Nos.   1   2   3

WROUGHT IRON WIRE SNAPS,
With Improved Spring Fastenings.

| Nos. 8, 9, 10. | No. 6. | Nos. 4, 3, 1, 0, 20. | Nos. 14, 15. |

No. 8, Wire Rein, $\frac{3}{4}$ inch loop, No. 8 Wire .... per gross, $
No. 9, Wire Rein, $\frac{7}{8}$ inch loop, No. 8 Wire .... "
No. 10, Wire Rein, 1 inch loop, No. 7 Wire .... "
No. 6, Wire Halter, $1\frac{1}{4}$ inch loop .... "
No. 4, Wire Breast, $1\frac{1}{2}$ inch loop, No. 3 Wire .... "
No. 3, Wire Breast, $1\frac{3}{4}$ inch loop, No. 3 Wire .... "
No. 1, Wire Breast, $1\frac{3}{4}$ inch loop, No. 1 Wire .... "
No. 0, Wire Breast, $1\frac{3}{4}$ inch loop, No. 0 Wire, **Extra Heavy** .... "
No. 20, Wire Breast, $3\frac{1}{2}$ inch loop, for Back Bands.... "
No. 14, Billet, for Fancy Bridles, with Leathers .... "
No. 15, Billet, for Fancy Bridles, without Leathers.... "

MALLEABLE IRON SNAPS.

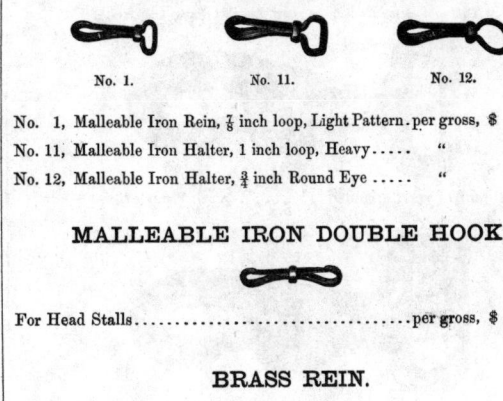

| No. 1. | No. 11. | No. 12. |

No. 1, Malleable Iron Rein, $\frac{7}{8}$ inch loop, Light Pattern. per gross, $
No. 11, Malleable Iron Halter, 1 inch loop, Heavy ..... "
No. 12, Malleable Iron Halter, $\frac{3}{4}$ inch Round Eye ..... "

MALLEABLE IRON DOUBLE HOOK,

For Head Stalls.................................... per gross, $

BRASS REIN.

No. 22 .... per gross, $

JUDD'S PATENT HARNESS SNAPS.

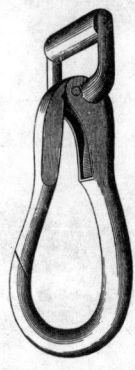

No. 1, Plated, $\frac{7}{8}$ inch Eye .... per gross, $
No. 2, Plated, 1 inch Eye .... "
No. 3, Plated, $1\frac{1}{4}$ inch Eye .... "
No. 4, Plated, $1\frac{1}{2}$ inch Eye .... "
No. 5, Plated, $1\frac{3}{4}$ inch Eye .... "

No. 6, Plated, $\frac{7}{8}$ inch Round Eye .... per gross, $

HULL'S PATENT SNAPS.

REIN, BREAST, TUG, AND HALTER SNAPS.

These plates are intended to show the exact shapes and sizes.

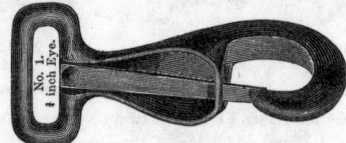

No. 1, ¾ inch Eye, Japanned...................per gross, $

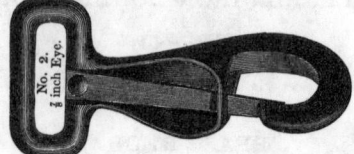

No. 2, ⅞ inch Eye, Japanned...................per gross, $

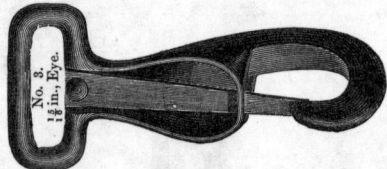

No. 3, 1⅛ inch Eye, Japanned...................per gross, $

HARNESS SNAPS.

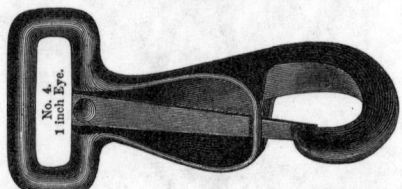

No. 4, 1 inch Eye, Japanned...................per gross, $

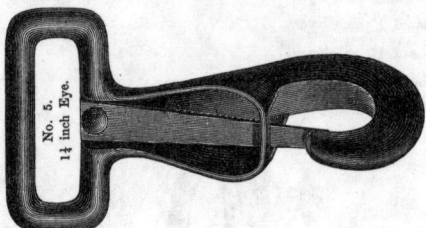

No. 5, 1¼ inch Eye, Japanned...................per gross, $

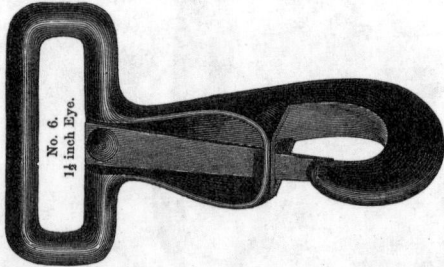

No. 6, 1½ inch Eye, Japanned...................per gross, $

HARNESS AND HALTER SNAPS.

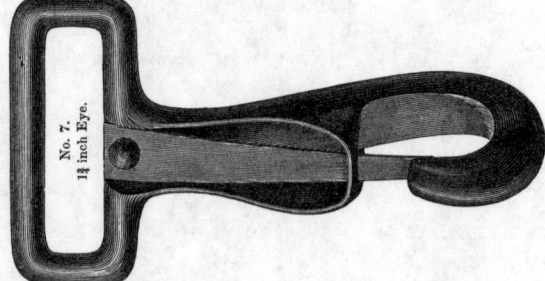

No. 7, 1¾ inch Eye, Japanned...................per gross, $

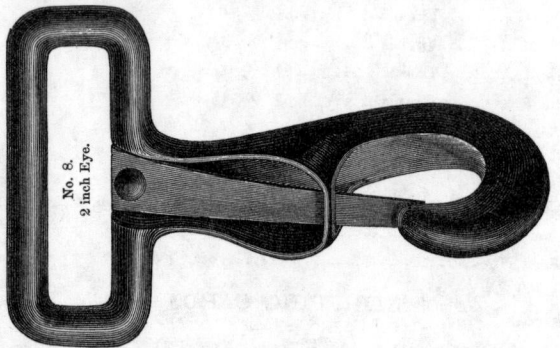

No. 8, 2 inch Eye, Japanned...................per gross, $

No. 20, ⅞ inch Round Eye, Japanned, for Rope
    Halters................................per gross, $

All sizes tinned to order at   advance on list.

PATENT CATTLE TIES.

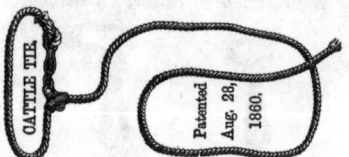

With Rope, ready for use.

No. 17, with 7 feet of ⅝ inch Rope............per dozen, $
No. 18, with 8 feet of ⅝ inch Rope............per dozen, $
No. 19, with 9 feet of ⅝ inch Rope............per dozen, $
    We always send No. 17, unless some other No. is ordered.

Without Rope.

No. 1, Size for (Scant) ⅝ inch Rope............per dozen, $
No. 2, Size for (Full) ⅝ inch Rope............per dozen, $
No. 3, Size for   inch Rope...................per dozen.

BELTING, PACKING, HOSE, ETC.

LEATHER BELTING,
PATENT STRETCHED, CEMENTED AND RIVETED.

								cents per foot.
1	1¼	1½	1¾	2	2¼	2½	2¾	inches wide.
3	3¼	3½	3¾	4	4½	5	5½	cents per foot. inches wide.
6	7	8	9	10	11	12	13	cents per foot. inches wide.
14	15	16	17	18	19	20	22	cents per foot. inches wide.
24	27	30	36	40				cents per foot. inches wide.

Round Belts.

							cents per foot.
⅛	3⁄16	¼	⅜	½	⅝	¾	1	inch.

☞ A full stock of Laced Belts constantly on hand.

Double Belts Double Price.

Lace Leather.

Oil Tanned Patna ....per dozen, $

Bark Tanned Calf Skin .... per lb.

Picker Leather.. per lb.

Leather Hose.

					per foot.
2	2¼	2½	2¾	3	inch diameter.

Rubber Belting—3 Ply.

							cents per foot.
2	3	4	5	6	7	8	inch.
9	10	11	12	13	14		cents per foot. inch.
15	16	18	20	22	24		cents per foot. inch

Rubber Belting—4 Ply.

							cents per foot.
2	3	4	5	6	7	8	inch.
9	10	11	12	13	14		cents per foot. inch.
15	16	18	20	22	24		cents per foot. inch.

Intermediate Widths at Proportionate Prices.

☞ Heavy 5 and 6 ply Belts made to order for purposes where great strength is required, (as a substitute for double leather,) at an advance of twenty-five and fifty per cent. on 4 ply prices.

2 Ply Machine Belting,
For Agricultural Machines and other Light Work.

1 Inch 2 Ply.................................cents per foot,

1¼ Inch 2 Ply................................. "   "

1½ Inch 2 Ply................................. "   "

2 Inch 2 Ply................................. "   "

2½ Inch 2 Ply................................. "   "

3 Inch 2 Ply................................. "   "

3½ Inch 2 Ply................................. "   "

4 Inch 2 Ply................................. "   "

A full roll of Belting Measures from 250 to 300 feet.

STEAM PACKING.

Mixed or Fibrous Packing, in sheets of all thicknesses .... per lb.

Gum Packing, with cloth insertion, in sheets of all thickness .... "

Gaskets, for Man-hole and Hand-hole Plates, Steam Chests, Cylinder Heads, etc., of **Fibrous Packing** .... "

Pure Vulcanized Sheet Rubber, of all thicknesses................................. "

Pure Vulcanized Rubber Valves, for Hot and Cold Water Pumps, Vacuum Pumps, etc...... "

Round Packing, with Duck outside, for Stuffing Boxes, Piston-Rods, etc., from one quarter of an inch to two inches diameter.................. "

Square, Piston and Valve Rod Packing.... "

Pure Vulcanized Rubber Gaskets, Washers, Rings, etc., with or without cloth insertions.. "

Pure Vulcanized Rubber Hinge-Valves· ··· "

☞ Special orders for Gaskets, Valves, etc., of any size or pattern, that we do not keep on hand, can be executed within one week from receipt of order.

Rubber Hose.

The 2 ply Hose, or Conducting Hose, is not calculated to stand much pressure.

The 3 ply Hose, (used for Hydrants, etc,) is made to stand a pressure of 75 lbs. to the square inch.

The 4 ply Hose, (used for Locomotives and for Leading Hose for Fire Engines and other purposes,) is made to withstand a pressure of 150 lbs. to the square inch.

It is furnished in lengths of fifty feet and of any size and strength required. The sizes indicated in the list are the inner diameters, and each size will fully measure what it is marked.

Conducting Hose—2 Ply.

$								cents per foot.
	½	¾	⅞	1	1¼	1½	1¾	inch, internal diam.
$	2	2¼	2½	2¾	3	4		cents per foot. inch, internal diam.
$	5	6	7	8	9	10		cents per foot. inch, internal diam.

Hydrant Hose—3 Ply.

$							cents per foot.
	½	¾	⅞	1	1¼	1½	inch, internal diam.
$	1¾	2	2¼	2½	2¾	3	cents per foot. inch, internal diam.

Engine Hose—4 Ply.

$							cents per foot.
	½	¾	⅞	1	1¼	1½	inch, internal diam.
$	1¾	2	2¼	2½	2¾	3	cents per foot. inch, internal diam.

5 Ply Hose made to order at an advance on prices of 4 Ply.

Suction Hose, on Spiral Brass Wire.

$							cents per foot.
	¾	1	1¼	1½	1¾	2	inch, internal diam.

Larger sizes made to order on Metal Rings, or Flat Galvanized Iron, wound spirally.

BIBBS, COCKS AND COUPLINGS.

For Description of Plates see page 279.

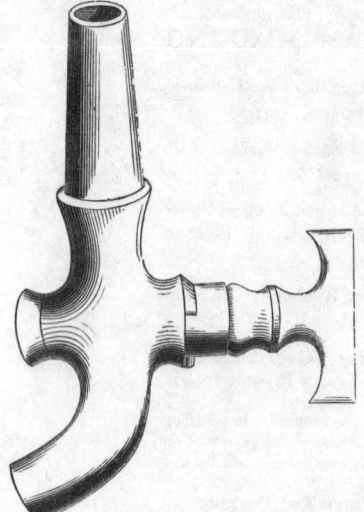

Water or Boiler Cock.

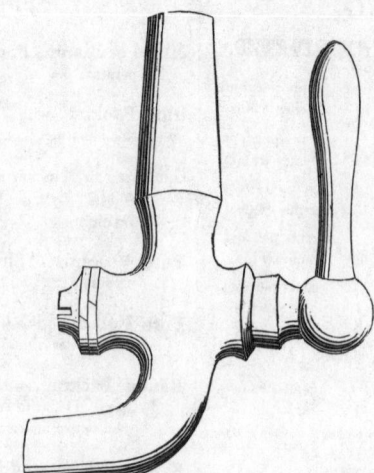

Plain Bibb.

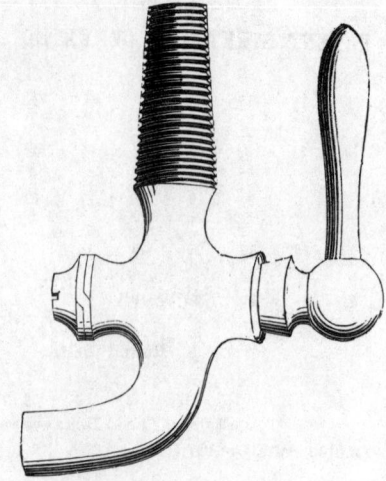

Plain Bibb, Screw Shank.

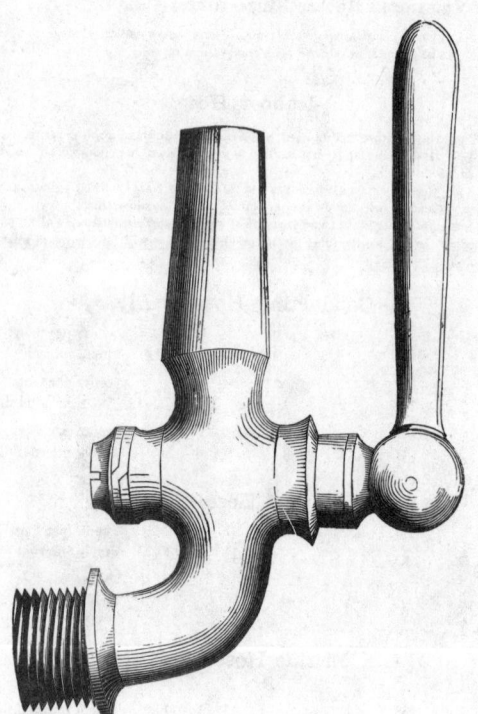

Hose Bibb.

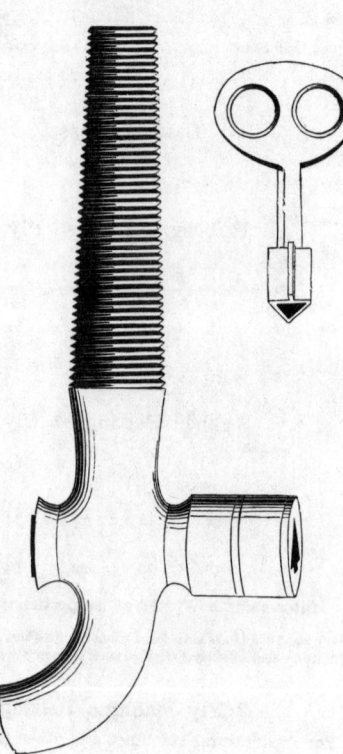

Lock Cock, to Screw.

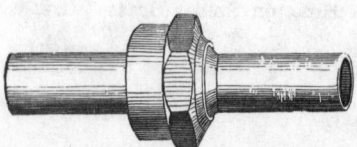

Plain Couplings.

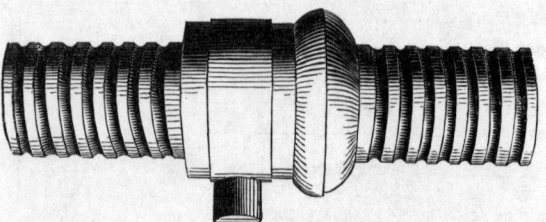

Hose Couplings, for Rubber.

BIBBS, COCKS AND COUPLINGS.

(Continued.)

[*For Description of Plates see page 279.*]

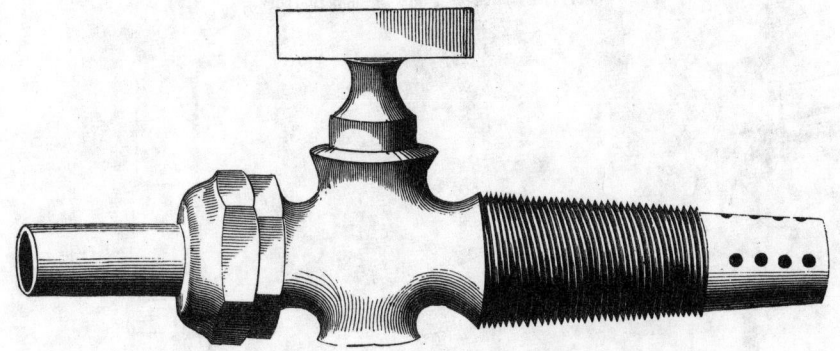

Beer Cock, Rivet Bottom.

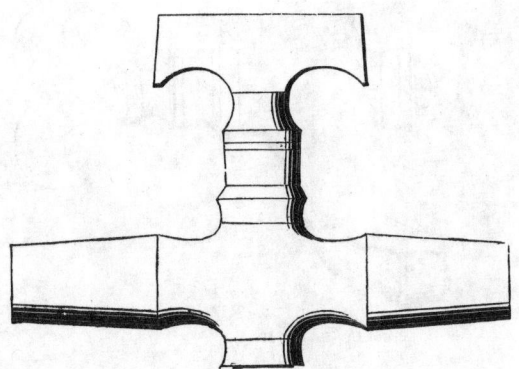

Connecting Cock.

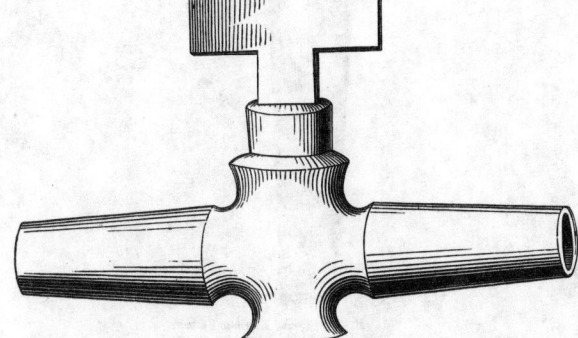

Rough Stop, T Handle.

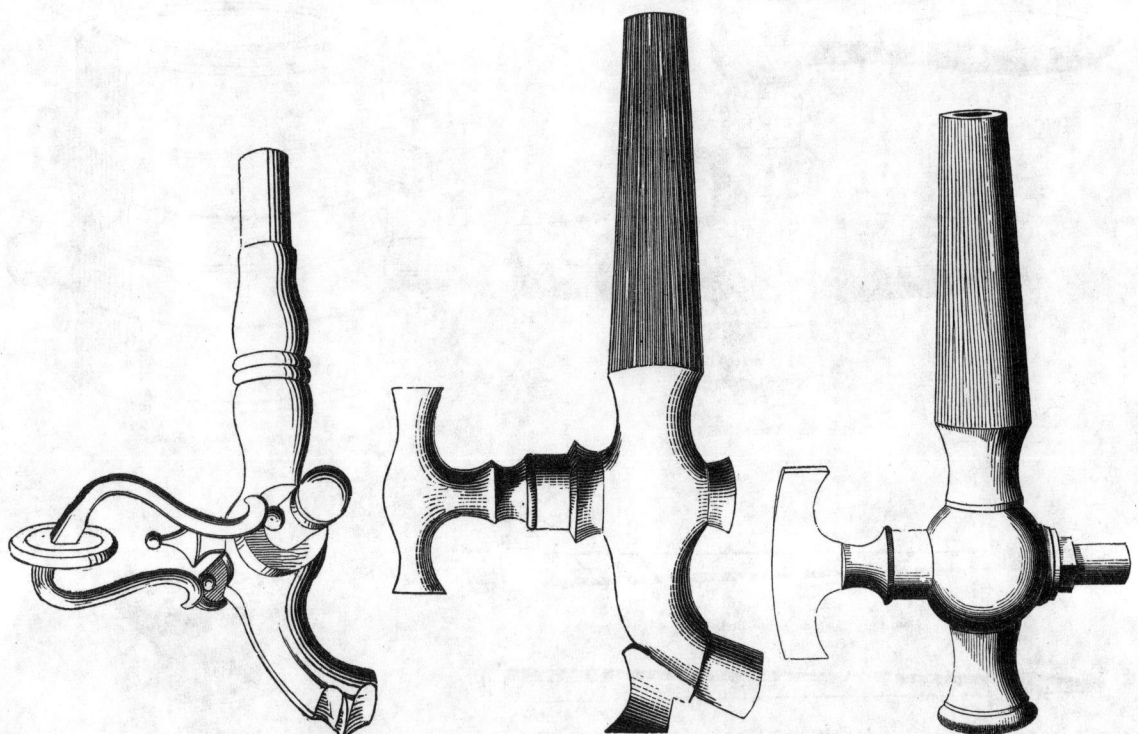

Plated Urn Cock, Loop Handle.   Racking Cock, to Drive.   Lager Beer Cock.

BIBBS, COCKS AND COUPLINGS.

(Continued.)

(For Description of Plates see opposite page.)

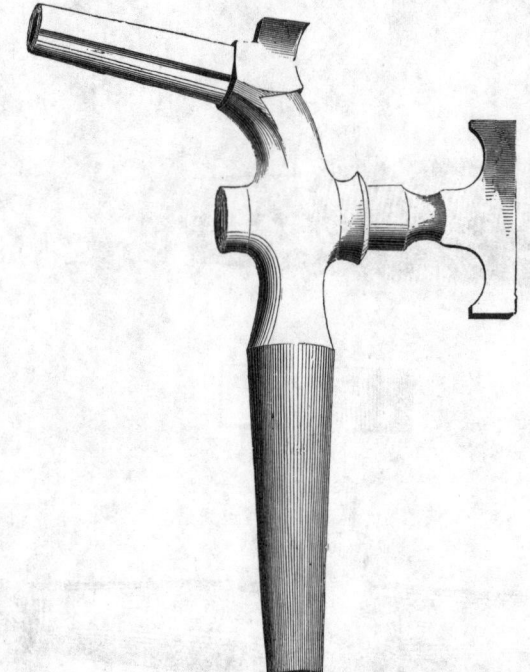

Bottling Cock, English Pattern.

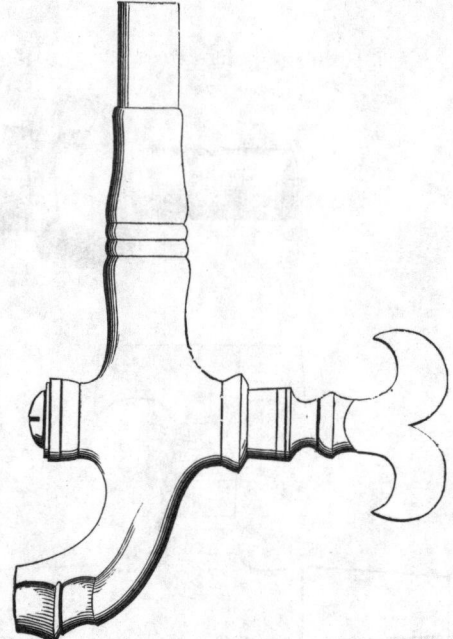

Plated Urn Cock, T Handle.

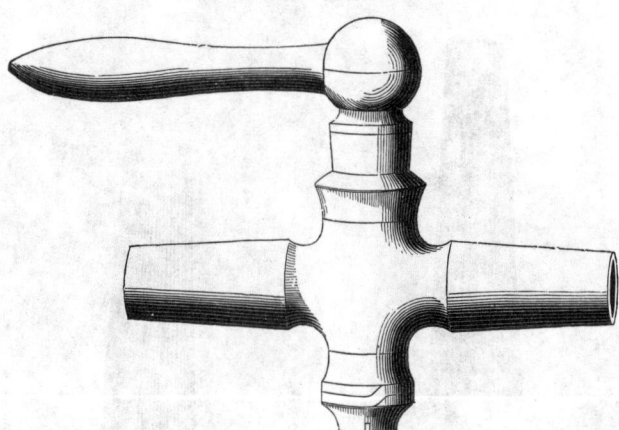

Plain Stop, Lever Handle.

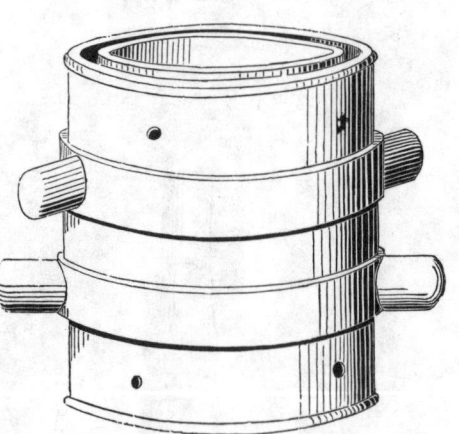

Hose Couplings, for Leather Hose.

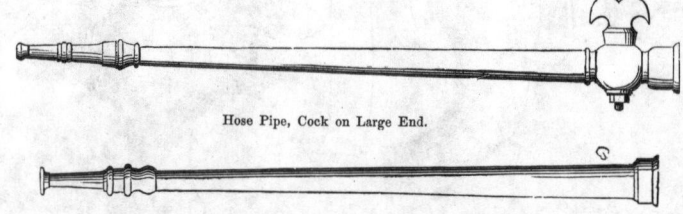

Hose Pipe, Cock on Large End.

Hose Pipes, Screw Tips.

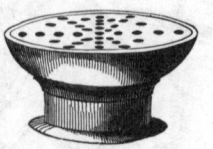

Hose Sprinkler.

BIBBS, COCKS AND COUPLINGS.

(*Continued.*)

[*For Plates, see pages 276, 277, 278.*]

Plain Couplings.

$							per dozen.
Size...	¼	⅜	½	⅝	¾	1	inch.

$							per dozen.
Size...	1¼	1½	1¾	2	2½	3	inch.

Hose Couplings, for Rubber Hose.

$									per dozen.
Size...	½	⅝	¾	⅞	1	1¼	1½	1¾	inch.

$									per dozen.
Size...	2	2¼	2½	3	3½	4	5	6	inch.

Hose Couplings, for Leather Hose.

$								per dozen.
Size...	1	1¼	1½	2	2½	3	3½	inch.

Hose Pipes, Screw Tips.

Size...	¾	1	1¼	1½	1¾	2	inch.
Short..$							per dozen.
Size...	2¼	2½	3	3½	4		inch.
Short..$							per dozen.
Size...	¾	1	1¼	1½	1¾	2	inch.
Long..$							per dozen.
Size...	2¼	2½	3	3½	4		inch.
Long..$							per dozen.

Hose Pipes, Cock on Large End.

Size...	¾	1	1¼	1½	1¾	2	inch.
Short..$							per dozen.
Long..							"

Hose Sprinklers.

Small, fit ¾ and 1 inch Pipes ....per dozen, $

Large, fit 1¼ and 1½ inch Pipes .... "

Plain Bibbs.

Size...	¼	⅜	½	⅝	¾	1	1¼	1½	
Finished......$									per doz.
Rough........									"
Electro-Plated .									"
Size.........	1¾	2	2¼	2½	3	3½	4		
Finished......$									per doz.
Rough........									"
Electro-Plated .									"

Plain Bibbs, Screw Shank.

Size............	¼	⅜	½	⅝	¾	inch.
Finished.......$						per dozen.
Rough..........						"
Size............	1	1¼	1½	1¾	2	inch.
Finished.......$						per dozen.
Rough..........						"

Hose Bibbs.

Size........	½	⅝	¾	1	1¼	1½	inch.
Finished....$							per dozen.
Rough......							"

Plain Stops, Lever Handle.

Stop on Key, $ per dozen extra.

Size..........	¼	⅜	½	⅝	¾	1	1¼	inch.
Finished......$								per doz.
Rough........								"
Size.........	1½	1¾	2	2¼	2½	3		inch.
Finished......$								per doz.
Rough........								"

Rough Stops, T Handle.

Size............	¼	⅜	½	⅝	inch.
Rivet ....$					per dozen.
Springs.........					"
Size............	¾	1	1¼	1½	inch.
Rivet					per dozen.
Springs.........					"

Beer Cocks, with Coupling.

Size..................	½	⅝	¾	inch.
Common, Rivet Bottoms..$				per dozen.
Extra, Spring Bottoms...				"

Lager Beer Cocks.

Add for Grated Ends, $ per dozen.

Style............	Short	Long	Heavy	No. 3.
Rivet Bottoms....$				per doz.
Spring Bottoms...				"

Racking Cocks.

Size....	¼	5/16	⅜	7/16	½	9/16	⅝	¾	⅞	1	in.
To Drive, $											doz.
To Screw											"

Racking Cocks with Lock.

Size....	¼	5/16	⅜	7/16	½	9/16	⅝	¾	⅞	1	in.
To Drive, $											doz.
To Screw											"
New Pat.											"

Add for Grated Ends..........................per dozen, $

Add for Spring Bottoms........................ "

Racking Cocks, Large Sizes.

Size............	1⅛	1¼	1½	2	inch.
To Drive........$					per dozen.
To Screw.......					"

Water and Boiler Cocks, Tinned Ends.

Size....	¼	⅜	½	⅝	¾	⅞	1	inch.
Price...$								per doz.

Connecting Cocks, Tinned Ends.

Size....	¼	⅜	½	⅝	¾	⅞	1	inch.
Price...$								per doz.

Bottling Cocks.

Size.................	⅜	7/16	½	⅝	¾	inch.
English Pattern......$						per doz.
Screw Nozzle, Rivet..						"
Screw Nozzle, Spring.						"

Plated Urn Cocks, Loop Handle.

Size............	No. 21	23	26	
Price.........$				per dozen.

Plated Urn Cocks, T Handle.

Size............	No. 09	07	05	
Price.........$				per dozen.

CORK STOPS AND FAUCETS.

Fenn's Pewter, Albata and Tin Cork Stops and Faucets.

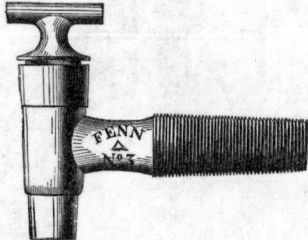

No. 1, Fenn's Cork Stops.........................per dozen, $
No. 2, Fenn's Cork Stops.........................   "
No. 3, Fenn's Cork Stops.........................   "
No. 4, Fenn's Cork Stops.........................   "
No. 5, Fenn's Cork Stops.........................   "
No. 6, Fenn's Cork Stops.........................   "

Fenn's Faucet.

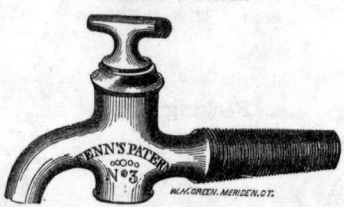

No. 1, Fenn's Faucets.........................per dozen, 8
No. 2, Fenn's Faucets.........................   "
No. 3, Fenn's Faucets.........................   "
No. 4, Fenn's Faucets.........................   "
No. 5, Fenn's Faucets.........................   "
No. 6, Fenn's Faucets.........................   "

Fenn's Keyed Faucet.

No. 1, Fenn's Keyed Faucets ....per dozen, $
No. 2, Fenn's Keyed Faucets ....   "
No. 3, Fenn's Keyed Faucets ....   "
No. 4, Fenn's Keyed Faucets ....   "
No. 5, Fenn's Keyed Faucets ....   "

Fenn's Urn Pattern, Superior Tin, Albata, and Pewter Faucets.

In boxes of ½ dozen.
The **Albata** warranted equal, if not superior to **Tin**.

No.	1	2	3	4	per dozen.
$					

Keyed, Nos.	1	2	3	4	per dozen.
$					

Stearn's Faucets.

No.	$ 1	2	3	4	5½	per dozen.

Frary's Patent Coal Oil Faucet.

Made from Iron Body and Key Bushed, with Brass Bibb Pattern, Lever Handle. Warranted Tight for any Liquid.

No. 5, ⅝ inch, to Screw.........................per dozen, $
No. 6, ¾ inch, to Screw.........................   "

Patent Star and Syphonic Faucets, Pewter, Tin, or Silvered.

In Boxes of ½ dozen.

Pewter.

Star, No.	$ 1	2	3	4	5	per dozen.

Tin or Silvered.

Star, No.	$ 1	2	3	4	5	per dozen.

Syphonic Ventilating and Ordinary Faucet Combined.

Pewter.

No.	$ 1	2	3	4	5	per dozen.

Tin or Silvered.

No.	$ 1	2	3	4	5	per dozen.

Wood Faucets.

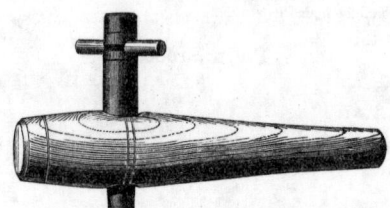

No. 1, 7 inch Barrel, Wood Faucet, Wood Stop ....per hundred, $
No. 2, 9 inch Barrel, Wood Faucet, Wood Stop, Leathered ....   "
No. 3, 6 inch Keg, Wood Faucet, Lignumvitæ Wood Stop, Leathered.........................   "
No. 4, 7 inch Barrel, Wood Faucet, Lignumvitæ Wood Stop, Leathered.....................   "
No. 5, 8 inch Half Hogshead, Wood Faucet, Lignumvitæ Wood Stop, Leathered...........   "
No. 6, 9 inch Hogshead, Wood Faucet, Lignumvitæ Wood Stop, Leathered..................   "
No. 7, 12 inch Wood Faucets, Lignumvitæ Wood Stop, Leathered.........................   "
No. 8, 14 inch Wood Faucets, Lignumvitæ Wood Stop, Leathered.........................   "
No. 9, 7 inch Lignumvitæ Wood Faucets, Lignumvitæ Wood Stop, Leathered ....   "
No. 10, 7 inch Lager Bier Wood Faucets, Wood Stop   "
No. 11, 12 inch Lager Bier Wood Faucets, Wood Stop ....   "
Large Red Faucets, assorted Sizes..............   "

SPIGOTS, OIL AND MOLASSES GATES, ETC.

Patent Cork Lined Wood Spigots.

	$								per dozen.
No.	0	2	3	4	5	6	7	8	

No. 9, Lager Bier Cocks.............................per dozen, $

MOLASSES AND OIL GATES.
Frary's New Patent.

In paper boxes of ½ dozen, in 4 and 6 dozen cases.

No. 5, Crooked Neck ....per dozen, $
No. 6, Crooked Neck .... "
No. 7, Crooked Neck .... "
No. 8, Crooked Neck .... "

Lincoln's.

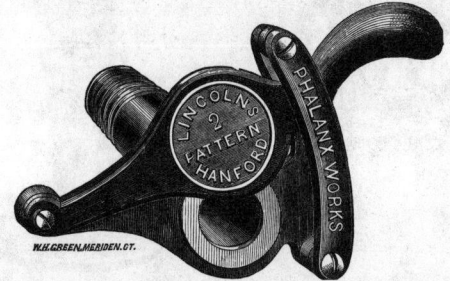

No. 0, Plain, in wood cases of 6 dozen...............per dozen, $
No. 1, Plain, in wood cases of 5 dozen............... "

MOLASSES AND OIL GATES.
(Continued.)
(Lincoln's Patent—*Continued.*)

No. 2, Plain, in wood cases of 4 dozen...............per dozen, $
No. 3, Plain, in wood cases of 3 dozen.............. "
No. 4, Plain, in wood cases of 2½ dozen.............. "
No. 0, Lipped, in wood cases of 5½ dozen............ "
No. 1, Lipped, in wood cases of 4½ dozen............ "
No. 2, Lipped, in wood cases of 3½ dozen............ "
No. 3, Lipped, in wood cases of 2½ dozen............ "
No. 4, Lipped, in wood cases of 1¾ dozen............ "

Carey's (Stebbins' Pattern.)

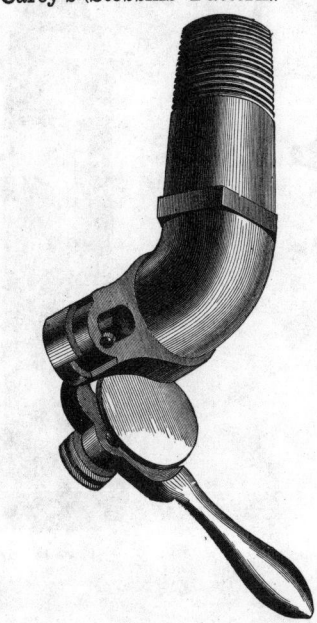

In paper boxes of ½ dozen, wood cases of 4 dozen.

	$				per dozen.
No.		1	2	3	4.

Stebbins' "Patent."

	$					per dozen.
No.	0	1	2	3	4.	

Dudley's Patent.

	$				per dozen.
No.	1	2	3	4.	

Bush's Patent Zinc.

	$			per dozen.
No.	1	2	3.	

Bush's Zinc Water Faucet.

	$		per dozen.
No.	1	2 (Short Tube.)	

FIRE ENGINES, HYDRANTS AND PUMPS.

[For Description of Plates see pages 284, 285, 286.]

Adjustable Standard
Well Pump.

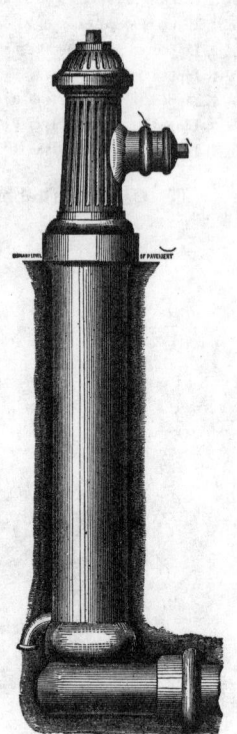

Patent Fire Hydrant.

Patent Fire Hydrant.

Adjustable Standard
Cistern Pump.

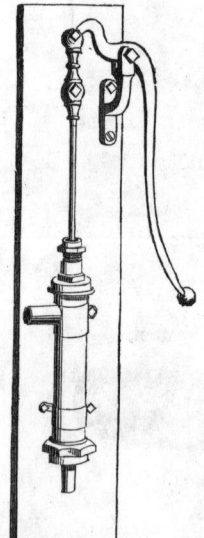

Lift and Force Pump.

Garden, Protection and Fire Engines.

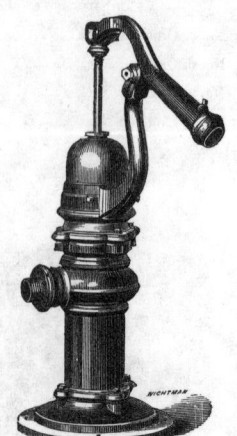

Railroad and Ship Force Pump.

PUMPS, SUCTION PIPES AND SINKS.

(For Description of Plates see pages 284, 285, 286.)

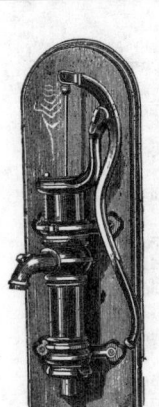
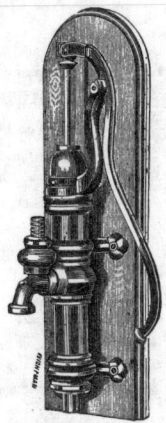

Adjustable Stan'd Side Cistern Pump, Mounted on Black Walnut Plank.

Adjustable Stan'd Side Force Pump, Mounted on Black Walnut Plank.

Adjustable Standard Force Pump.

Adjustable Standard Closed Top Cistern Pump.

Adjustable Standard Vase Top Cistern Pump.

CAST IRON SUCTION PIPE AND ELBOWS.

Length 2 Feet.

Elbow.

Length 1 Foot.

SQUARE AND HALF CIRCLE SINKS.

For Description of Plates see page 288.

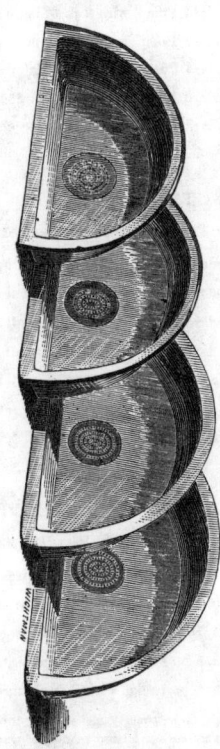

Square Sinks.

Half Circle Sinks.

PUMPS, HYDRANTS, ETC.

AGENTS FOR RACE MATHEWS & CO'S PUMPS, ETC.

(For Plates see pages 282, 283.)

ADJUSTABLE STANDARD "CLOSED TOP" CISTERN PUMPS.

With Heavy Brass Valve Seats, and Combination Plunger.

No. 1, 2¼ inch bore....................................each, $

No. 2, 2½ inch bore... "

No. 3, 2¾ inch bore... "

No. 4, 3 inch bore... "

No. 5, 3¼ inch bore... "

ADJUSTABLE STANDARD "VASE TOP" CISTERN PUMPS.

With Heavy Brass Valve Seats, and Combination Plunger.

No. 1, 2½ inch bore, 5 inch stroke....................each, $

No. 2, 2¾ inch bore, 5½ inch stroke....................... "

No. 3, 3 inch bore, 6 inch stroke....................... "

No. 4, 3¼ inch bore, 6½ inch stroke....................... "

ADJUSTABLE STANDARD SIDE CISTERN PUMPS.

Mounted on Black Walnut Plank.

No. 1, 2¼ inch bore, 6 inch stroke......................each, $

No. 2, 2½ inch bore, 6 inch stroke....................... "

No. 3, 2¾ inch bore, 6 inch stroke....................... "

No. 4, 3 inch bore, 6 inch stroke....................... "

No. 5, 3¼ inch bore, 6 inch stroke....................... "

☞ We warrant the "Vase Top," "Closed Top" and "Side Cistern Pumps" to be superior to any others in market, for strength, durability, elegance of style, and perfection of workmanship.

CISTERN PUMPS WITH IRON SET-LENGTHS.

For Out-door Cisterns and Shallow Wells.

No. 1, Adj. Standard Pump, with 2 ft. of large set-length...each, $

No. 2, Adj. Standard Pump, with 2 ft. of large set-length... "

No. 3, Adj. Standard Pump, with 2 ft. of large set-length... "

No. 4, Adj. Standard Pump, with 2 ft. of large set-length... "

No. 5, Adj. Standard Pump, with 2 ft. of large set-length... "

☞ The above set-length is exclusive of Pump Cylinder.

CISTERN PUMPS WITH IRON SET-LENGTHS.

For Out-door Cisterns and Shallow Wells.

No. 1, Adj. Standard Pump, with 3 ft. of small set-length...each, $

No. 2, Adj. Standard Pump, with 3 ft. of small set-length... "

No. 3, Adj. Standard Pump, with 3 ft. of small set-length... "

No. 4, Adj. Standard Pump, with 3 ft. of small set-length... "

No. 5, Adj. Standard Pump, with 3 ft. of small set-length... "

No. 3, Adj. Spout, Pump, with 4 ft. of small set-length..... "

No. 4, Adj. Spout, Pump, with 4 ft. of small set-length..... "

☞ The above set-length is exclusive of Pump Cylinder.

ADJUSTABLE STANDARD WELL PUMPS, WITH SET-LENGTHS.

For Wells 27 Feet Deep and Under.

No. 6, 3 in. bore, 8 in. stroke, with 3 ft. of iron set-length....each, $

No. 7, 3¾ in. bore, 8 in. stroke, with 3 ft. of iron set-length... "

No. 6, 3 in. bore, 8 in. stroke, with 3 ft. of large iron set-length "

No. 7, 3¾ in. bore, 8 in. stroke, with 3 ft. of large iron set-length "

No. 8, 5 in. bore, 8 in. stroke, with 3 ft. of large iron set-length "

☞ No. 8 is a very large, strongly made Pump, intended expressly for cattle or stock wells, and other purposes where a large quantity of water is used.

☞ All these Pumps are arranged to attach either iron or lead pipe as ordered.

ADJUSTABLE STANDARD DEEP WELL PUMPS, WITH EXTRA SET-LENGTHS.

For Wells 27 to 38 Feet Deep.

No. 7, 3 inch bore, for 27 feet wells, set-length and cylinder, 4 feet long.......................................each, $

No. 7, 3 inch bore, for 28 feet wells, set-length and cylinder, 5 feet long....................................... "

No. 7, 3 inch bore, for 30 feet wells, set-length and cylinder, 7 feet long....................................... "

No. 7, 3 inch bore, for 32 feet wells, set-length and cylinder, 9 feet long....................................... "

No. 7, 3 inch bore, for 34 feet wells, set-length and cylinder, 11 feet long........•........................ "

No. 7, 3 inch bore, for 36 feet wells, set-length and cylinder, 13 feet long....................................... "

No. 7, 3 inch base, for 38 feet wells, set length and cylinder, 15 feet long....................................... "

☞ The above does not include the suction pipe, but sufficient Set-length to place the Pump Cylinder within 23 feet of bottom of well.

The Suction Pipe should be of lead or iron, and of 1¾ or 2 inch bore.

The Cast Iron Suction Pipe, (see page 288,) will be found admirably adapted for this use.

ADJUSTABLE STANDARD DEEP WELL PUMPS.

For Wells any Depth from 20 to 100 Feet.

These Pumps are complete for use, and require no Suction Pipe, the working parts being placed at the bottom of the well.

No. 7, for 20 feet wells, metallic plunger and valves, ground fits...each, $

No. 7, for 25 feet wells, metallic plunger and valves, ground fits... "

No. 7, for 30 feet wells, metallic plunger and valves, ground fits... "

No. 7, for 35 feet wells, metallic plunger and valves, ground fits... "

No. 7, for 40 feet wells, metallic plunger and valves, ground fits... "

No. 7, for 45 feet wells, metallic plunger and valves, ground fits... "

No. 7, for 50 feet wells, metallic plunger and valves, ground fits... "

No. 7, for 60 feet wells, metallic plunger and valves, ground fits... "

No. 7, for 70 feet wells, metallic plunger and valves, ground fits... "

No. 7, for 80 feet wells, metallic plunger and valves, ground fits... "

No. 7, for 90 feet wells, metallic plunger and valves, ground fits... "

No. 7, for 100 feet wells, metallic plunger and valves, ground fits... "

Standard and Cylinder for Deep Well Pump, without Pipe or Rods.. "

Suction Baskets.. "

Large Iron Set-Length and Rods (including couplings)..per foot, $

☞ In ordering the above Pumps, give the exact distance from top of platform to bottom of well, by *actual measurement*, and also the usual depth of water in the well.

BORED OR ARTESIAN WELL PUMPS.

With Brass Pump and Wrought Iron Set Length.

Metallic Plunger and Valves, ground fits.

For 30 feet wells, 3 inch bore or drill....................each, $

For 30 feet wells, 4 inch bore or drill.................... "

For 30 feet wells, 5 inch bore or drill.................... "

Any additional depths, and warranted,...........extra per foot,

Galvanized Pipe,   per foot extra.

PUMPS, HYDRANTS, ETC.

(Continued.)

AGENTS FOR RACE MATHEWS & CO'S PUMPS, ETC.

(For Plates see pages 282, 283.)

ADJUSTABLE STANDARD FORCE PUMPS.

No. 2, with air chamber, double discharge and couplings for hose......each, $

No. 3, with air chamber, double discharge and couplings for hose...... "

No. 4, with air chamber, double discharge and couplings for hose...... "

No. 5, with air chamber, double discharge and couplings for hose...... "

ADJUSTABLE STANDARD FORCE PUMPS.

With Brass Piston Rods and Stuffing Boxes.

No. 2, with air chamber, double discharge and couplings for hose......each, $

No. 3, with air chamber, double discharge and couplings for hose...... "

No. 4, with air chamber, double discharge and couplings for hose...... "

No. 5, with air chamber, double discharge and couplings for hose...... "

Extra Check Valve for Perpendicular Discharge............ "

ADJUSTABLE STANDARD SIDE FORCE PUMPS.

Mounted on Black Walnut Plank.

No. 2, with air chamber, double discharge and couplings for hose......each, $

No. 3, with air chamber, double discharge and couplings for hose...... "

No. 4, with air chamber, double discharge and couplings for hose...... "

No. 5, with air chamber, double discharge and couplings for hose...... "

With Brass Piston Rod and Stuffing Box $ extra.

☞ All the Side Force Pumps have extra Check Valve for Perpendicular Discharge.

ADJUSTABLE STANDARD "BRASS CYLINDER" CISTERN PUMPS, WITH COMBINATION PLUNGER.

Working Parts Entirely of Brass.

No. 1, 2¼ inch bore................................each, $

No. 2, 2½ inch bore.................................. "

No. 3, 2¾ inch bore.................................. "

No. 4, 3 inch bore.................................. "

BRASS CYLINDER SIDE CISTERN PUMPS.

Mounted on Black Walnut Plank.

No. 1, 2¼ inch bore................................each, $

No. 2, 2½ inch bore.................................. "

No. 3, 2¾ inch bore.................................. "

No. 4, 3 inch bore.................................. "

No. 5, 3¼ inch bore.................................. "

BRASS CYLINDER FORCE PUMPS.

With Brass Plunger, Piston Rod and Stuffing Box.

No. 2, with air chamber, double discharge and couplings for hose......each, $

BRASS CYLINDER FORCE PUMPS.

(Continued.)

No. 3, with air chamber, double discharge and couplings for hose......each, $

No. 4, with air chamber, double discharge and couplings for hose...... "

No. 5, with air chamber, double discharge and couplings for hose...... "

BRASS CYLINDER SIDE FORCE PUMPS.

Mounted on Black Walnut Plank.

No. 2, with air chamber, double discharge and couplings for hose......each, $

No. 3, with air chamber, double discharge and couplings for hose...... "

No. 4, with air chamber, double discharge and couplings for hose...... "

No. 5, with air chamber, double discharge and couplings for hose...... "

ADJUSTABLE STANDARD SET-LENGTH FORCE PUMPS.

No. 2, with air chamber, double discharge and couplings for hose......each, $

No. 3, with air chamber, double discharge and couplings for hose...... "

No. 4, with air chamber, double discharge and couplings for hose...... "

No. 5, with air chamber, double discharge and couplings for hose...... "

ADJUSTABLE STANDARD WELL FORCE PUMPS.

No. 7, with air chamber, double discharge and couplings for hose......each, $

Three feet hose and discharge pipe for same.............. "

RAILROAD AND SHIP FORCE PUMPS.

Very Strong, Powerful and Durable, and will not Choke.

No. 9, 5 inch bore, 6 inch stroke, with couplings for hose..each, $

No. 10, 7 inch bore, 6 inch stroke, with couplings for hose.. "

No. 12, Double Action Force Pump, with two 5 inch cylinders, and air chamber, for 2, 4 or 6 men............ "

No. 15, Double Action Force Pump, with two 7 in. cylinders, and air chambers, for 2, 4 or 6 men................ "

☞ The above pumps are designed for Hand or Power, and are unequalled for use in Distilleries, Breweries, Tanneries, Railroad Stations, and for Canal Boats, Ships and Steamboats.

GARDEN AND FIRE ENGINES.

No. 1, Garden Engine, with 3 feet hose and discharge pipe..each, $

No. 2, Garden Engine, extra size pump and box, with 3 feet hose and discharge pipe..................... "

Fitted to attach suction hose, extra................ "

Protection Engine for 2 to 8 men..............each, $ to

Fire Engines for 8 to 16 men.................. "

RACE & MATHEWS' PATENT HYDRANTS

No. 1, Fire Hydrants.............................each, $

No. 2, Fire Hydrants, extra size, with two nozzles........ "

No. 3, Fire Hydrants, with large connection and discharge, 4 inches diameter inside of nozzle, made expressly to supply Steam Fire Engines........................ "

Yard Hydrants.................................... "

Side Walk Hydrants or Pavement Washer................ "

ROTARY AND FORCE PUMPS.

PATENT ROTARY FORCE PUMPS.

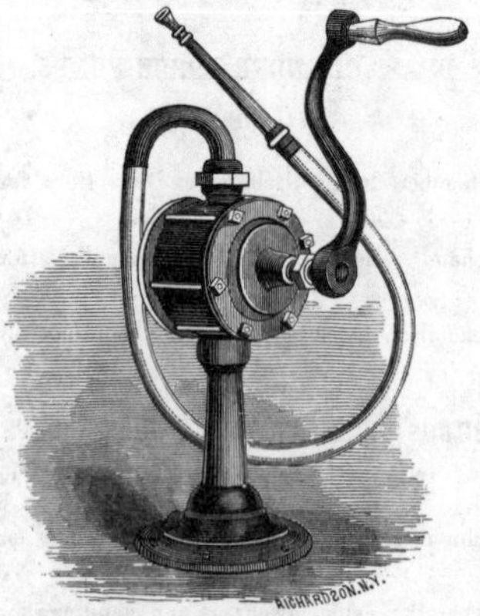

Hand Pump.

These Pumps may be run at from 20 to 200 revolutions per minute, and will do their work in proportion to their velocity. They are built for Hand and Power; of Iron or Brass, and suitable for pumping hot and cold water, tan, liquors, oils, acids, chemicals, &c. &c.

No. 1, Hand Pump, of Iron .... each, $

No. 1, Hand Pump, of Brass .... "

Size of Discharge Pipe ¾ inch.

This Pump is designed for wells, cisterns, &c., and is useful in cases of Fire, it throwing a stream from 50 to 70 feet, and can be used easily with one hand, and will throw from 10 to 12 gallons per minute.

No. 2, Hand Pump, of Iron .... each, $

No. 2, Hand Pump, of Brass .... "

Size of Discharge Pipe ⅞ inch.

This Pump is designed for the same purpose as No. 1, and will throw from 12 to 18 gallons per minute.

No. 3, Hand Pump, of Iron .... each, $

No. 3, Hand Pump, of Brass .... "

Size of Discharge Pipe 1 inch.

This Pump is also designed for same purposes as Nos. 1 and 2, and will throw from 15 to 20 gallons per minute.

No. 4, Hand Pump, of Iron .... each, $

No. 4, Hand Pump, of Brass .... "

Size of Discharge Pipe 1¾ inch.

Of large size, intended for Bilge Pump, for Canal Boats, Vessels and Steamers, throwing from 50 to 60 gallons per minute.

No. 1, Rotary Hand Pump for Barrels .... each, $

No. 2, Rotary Hand Pump for Barrels .... "

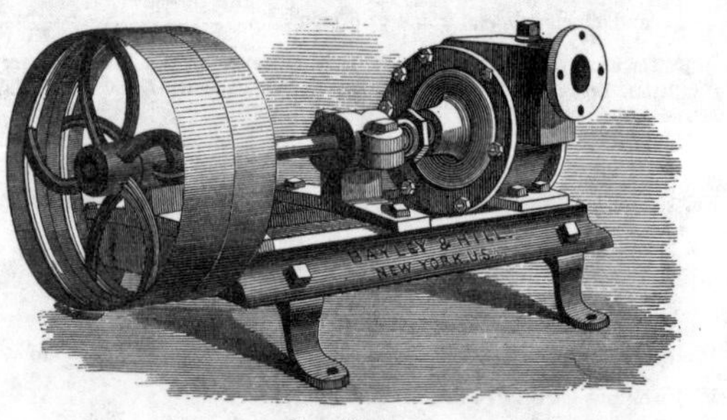

Power Pump.

No. 1, Power Pump .... each, $

Size of Suction and Discharge Pipes, 1¼ inch.
This Pump is used for elevating water. Capacity from 15 to 20 gallons per minute. Pulley, 10×2 inch, and calculated to run from 60 to 80 revolutions per minute.

No. 2, Power Pump .... each, $

Size of Suction and Discharge Pipes, 2 inch.

This Pump will throw from 35 to 40 gallons per minute, running from 80 to 100 revolutions. Pulley 12×2½.

PATENT ROTARY FORCE PUMPS.

(*Continued.*)

No. 3, Power Pump .... each, $

Size of Suction and Discharge Pipes, 2½ inch.

This Pump will throw from 50 to 60 gallons per minute, running from 70 to 80 revolutions. Pulley, 15×4.

No. 4, Power Pump .... each, $

Size of Suction and Discharge Pipes, 3 inch.

This Pump will throw from 70 to 80 gallons per minute, running from 70 to 80 revolutions. Pulley, 18×5.

No. 6, Power Pump .... each, $

Size of Suction and Discharge Pipes, 4 inch.

This Pump will throw from 200 to 225 gallons per minute, running from 100 to 125 revolutions.

This Pump is calculated for raising water, and is also well adapted for a stationary Fire Engine, for Factories, Mills, etc., and will throw two streams with inch Nozzles, equal to any Hand Engine in use, and can be driven with Belt or Geer.

When driven with Bolt, Size of Pulley, 24×6, and when driven by Geers, Coupling is furnished in place of Pulleys.

No. 7, Power Pump .... each, $

Size of Suction and Discharge Pipes, 5 inch. Weight 700 lbs.

Is strong and heavy, intended particularly for fire purposes, in Factories, Mills, &c., and will throw four streams, through 1¼ inch Nozzle, and is the most powerful Fire Engine in use, is driven by Geers, and will throw from 400 to 450 gallons per minute, running 125 revolutions.

No. 10, Power Pump .... each, $

Size of Suction Pipe, 8 inch. Discharge Pipe, 7 inch. Weight 2,000 lbs.

Is sufficiently strong and heavy to bear a pressure of 400 lbs. to the square inch, and is intended for fire and other purposes. It is driven by Geers, and will throw from 800 to 1000 gallons per minute, running 120 to 125 revolutions.

Nos. 1, 2 and 3 Power Pumps have Thimbles, with thread cut to fit proper size pipe, and the larger size connect with flanges. Water Pumps have Rubber Check Valves, and Oil Pumps Metal Check Valves.

LIFT AND FORCE PUMPS—STEAM METAL CHAMBER.

(*For Plate, see* 282.)

Size.....	2	2½	2¾	3	3½	4 inch.
Screw Cap, $						each.
Flange....						"

BEER PUMPS.

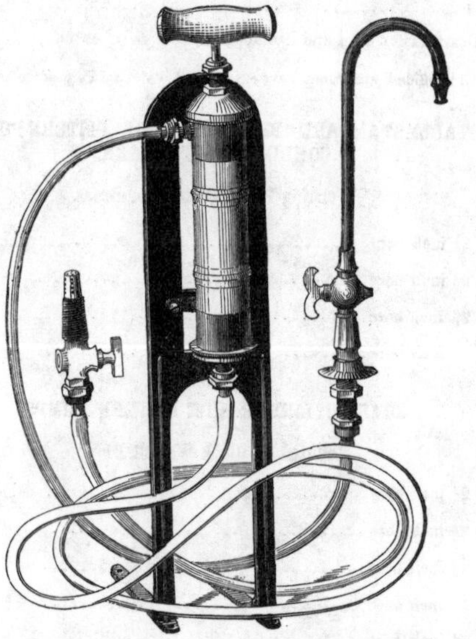

Beer Pumps, (Brass) .... each, $

Beer Pumps, with Brass Cock and Barrel Tap .... "

Beer Pumps, with Plated Cock and Barrel Tap .... "

Beer Pumps, complete, with Lead Pipe and Brass Cock .... "

Beer Pumps, complete, with Lead Pipe and Plated Cock ... "

HYDRAULIC RAMS, WELL CURBS, ETC.

HYDRAULIC RAMS.

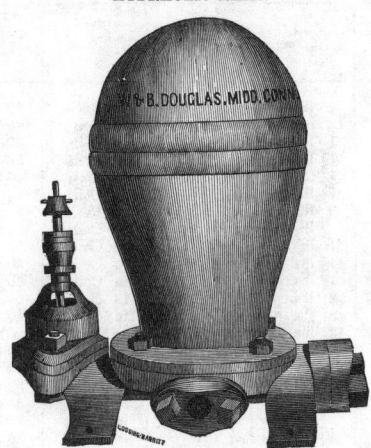

No. 2, Suitable capacity for a Spring or Brook, which furnishes from 3 quarts to 2 gallons per minute ....each, $

No. 3, Suitable capacity for a Spring or Brook, which furnishes from 1½ to 3 gallons per minute .... "

No. 4, Suitable capacity for a Spring or Brook, which furnishes from 3 to 7 gallons per minute .... "

No. 5, Suitable capacity for a Spring or Brook, which furnishes from 6 to 14 gallons per minute .... "

No. 6, Suitable capacity for a Spring or Brook, which furnishes from 12 to 25 gallons per minute .... "

No. 7, Suitable capacity for a Spring or Brook, which furnishes from 20 to 40 gallons per minute .... "

No. 10, Suitable capacity for a Spring or Brook, which furnishes from 25 to 75 gallons per minute .... "

PATENT WELL CURB.
With Self-Filling and Self-Emptying Bucket.

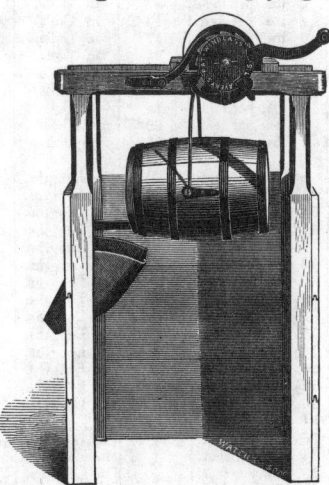

The advantages are, its easy working at all depths, has a simple but powerful brake, and can be managed with ease and safety. The Bucket fills itself by a valve in the bottom, is self-emptying on reaching the spout, and never freezes up.

No. 1, with cover over Roller ....each, $

No. 2, with Roof two pitch .... "

No. 3, with Roof four pitch .... "

Cast Iron Spouts.

For Wooden Curbs for Chain Pumps.....................each, $

For Wooden Curbs for Chain Pumps, Trough Style....... "

Cast Iron Curbs.

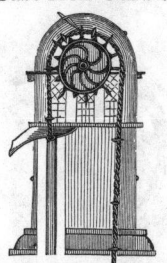

Arranged with Wheel and Crank, complete for Chain Pumps.

No. $ 13   14   15.   each.

Pump Wheels and Fixtures.

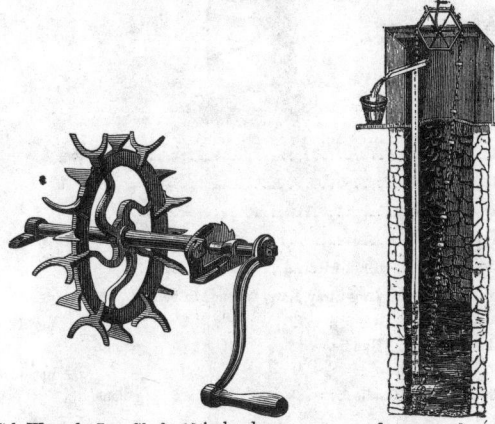

With Wrought Iron Shafts 13 inches long.........per dozen sets, $

With Wrought Iron Shafts 20 inches long......... "

Pump Chain.

Galvanized, with first quality Zinc Buckets from 1½ to 2 in..per lb. $

Wood Tubing for Chain Pumps........................per foot, $

Patent "Aquarius," or Portable Hand Force Pump.

With 2½ feet of Suction, and 3 feet of Discharge Hose, with Brass Discharge Pipe and Sprinkler...............each, $

WELL WHEELS, PIPES, SINKS AND LEAD.

Well Wheels.

$				per dozen.
8	10	12	14	inches.

Oak Well Buckets.

Light .... per dozen, $
Light, Strapped .... "
Heavy .... "
Heavy, Strapped .... "
Heavy, Strapped, with Swivel .... "
Extra Heavy, with long Strap Ears, fastened to bottom "

	$			per dozen.
Without Swivel in Handle,	3	4	5	gallons.
	$			per dozen.
With Swivel in Handle ...	3	4	5	gallons.

CAST IRON SINKS.

(*For Plates see page* 283.)

Square Sinks.

23×15 inches, 5 inches deep, corners slightly rounded ..... each, $
30×18 inches, 6 inches deep, corners slightly rounded ..... "
36×21 inches, 6 inches deep, corners slightly rounded ..... "
42×22 inches, 6 inches deep, corners slightly rounded ..... "
48×23 inches, 6 inches deep, corners slightly rounded ..... "

Half-Circle Sinks.

Back.	Width.	Depth.	
24 inches.	14 inches.	6 inches	each, $
27 inches.	14 inches.	6 inches	"
31 inches.	17 inches.	6 inches	"
27 inches.	15 inches.	8 inches	"

Cast Iron Suction Pipe, Two Feet Lengths.

$						per foot.
$1\frac{1}{8}$	$1\frac{1}{4}$	$1\frac{1}{2}$	$1\frac{3}{4}$	2	$2\frac{1}{4}$	inch bore.
$						per foot.
$2\frac{1}{2}$	$2\frac{3}{4}$	3	$3\frac{1}{4}$	$3\frac{1}{2}$	4	inch bore.

Cast Iron Suction Pipe, One Foot Lengths.

$						per foot.
$1\frac{1}{8}$	$1\frac{1}{4}$	$1\frac{1}{2}$	$1\frac{3}{4}$	2	$2\frac{1}{4}$	inch bore.
$						per foot.
$2\frac{1}{2}$	$2\frac{3}{4}$	3	$3\frac{1}{4}$	$3\frac{1}{2}$	4	inch bore.

Cast Iron Elbows.

$						
$1\frac{1}{8}$	$1\frac{1}{4}$	$1\frac{1}{2}$	$1\frac{3}{4}$	2	$2\frac{1}{4}$	inch bore.
$						
$2\frac{1}{2}$	$2\frac{3}{4}$	3	$3\frac{1}{4}$	$3\frac{1}{2}$	4	inch bore.

Lead Water Pipes for Hydrants, Pumps, Etc.

Size of Calibre.	Weight per foot and rod.	Thickness in 1-100ths of an inch.		Average Length.
$\frac{3}{8}$ inch.	7 lbs. per rod.	6	on Reels.	40 to 60 rods.
$\frac{3}{8}$ inch.	10 oz. per foot.	8	in Coils.	100 to 200 feet.
$\frac{3}{8}$ inch.	1 lb. per foot.	12	in Coils.	60 to 120 feet.
$\frac{3}{8}$ inch.	$1\frac{1}{4}$ lbs. per foot.	16	in Coils.	50 to 100 feet.
$\frac{3}{8}$ inch.	$1\frac{1}{2}$ lbs. per foot.	19	in Coils.	40 to 80 feet.
$\frac{3}{8}$ inch.	$2\frac{1}{2}$ lbs. per foot.		in Coils.	35 feet.
$\frac{1}{2}$ inch.	9 lbs. per rod.	7	on Reels.	30 to 50 rods.
$\frac{1}{2}$ inch.	$\frac{3}{4}$ lb. per foot.	9	in Coils.	90 to 180 feet.
$\frac{1}{2}$ inch.	1 lb. per foot.	11	in Coils.	60 to 120 feet.
$\frac{1}{2}$ inch.	$1\frac{1}{4}$ lbs. per foot.	13	in Coils.	50 to 100 feet.
$\frac{1}{2}$ inch.	$1\frac{3}{4}$ lbs. per foot.	16	in Coils.	70 feet.
$\frac{1}{2}$ inch.	2 lbs. per foot.	19	in Coils.	60 feet.
$\frac{1}{2}$ inch.	3 lbs. per foot.		in Coils.	40 to 74 feet.
$\frac{5}{8}$ inch.	12 lbs. per rod.	8	on Reels.	25 to 45 rods.
$\frac{5}{8}$ inch.	1 lb. per foot.	9	in Coils.	60 to 120 feet.
$\frac{5}{8}$ inch.	$1\frac{1}{2}$ lbs. per foot.	13	in Coils.	40 to 80 feet.
$\frac{5}{8}$ inch.	2 lbs. per foot.	16	in Coils.	50 to 60 feet.
$\frac{5}{8}$ inch.	$2\frac{1}{2}$ lbs. per foot.	20	in Coils.	45 to 50 feet.
$\frac{5}{8}$ inch.	$2\frac{3}{4}$ lbs. per foot.	22	in Coils.	35 to 40 feet.
$\frac{5}{8}$ inch.	$3\frac{1}{2}$ lbs. per foot.		in Coils.	30 to 60 feet.
$\frac{3}{4}$ inch.	16 lbs. per rod.	8	on Reels.	30 to 40 rods.
$\frac{3}{4}$ inch.	$1\frac{1}{4}$ lbs. per foot.	10	in Coils.	50 to 100 feet.
$\frac{3}{4}$ inch.	$1\frac{3}{4}$ lbs. per foot.	12	in Coils.	70 feet.
$\frac{3}{4}$ inch.	$2\frac{1}{4}$ lbs. per foot.	16	in Coils,	45 to 90 feet.
$\frac{3}{4}$ inch.	3 lbs. per foot.	20	in Coils.	35 to 70 feet.
$\frac{3}{4}$ inch.	$3\frac{1}{2}$ lbs. per foot.	23	in Coils.	30 to 60 feet.
$\frac{3}{4}$ inch.	$4\frac{3}{4}$ lbs. per foot.		in Coils.	44 feet.
1 inch.	$24\frac{3}{4}$ lbs. per rod.	10	on Reels.	25 to 30 rods.
1 inch.	2 lbs. per foot.	11	in Coils.	50 feet.
1 inch.	$2\frac{1}{2}$ lbs. per foot.	14	in Coils.	45 feet.
1 inch.	$3\frac{1}{4}$ lbs. per foot.	17	in Coils.	40 feet.
1 inch.	4 lbs. per foot.	21	in Coils.	50 feet.
1 inch.	$4\frac{3}{4}$ lbs. per foot.	24	in Coils.	45 feet.
1 inch.	6 lbs. per foot.		in Coils.	34 feet.
$1\frac{1}{4}$ inch.	2 lbs. per foot.	10	on Reels.	250 to 300 feet.
$1\frac{1}{4}$ inch.	$2\frac{1}{2}$ lbs. per foot.	12	in Coils.	45 feet.
$1\frac{1}{4}$ inch.	3 lbs. per foot.	14	in Coils.	35 feet.
$1\frac{1}{4}$ inch.	$3\frac{3}{4}$ lbs. per foot.	16	in Coils.	30 feet.
$1\frac{1}{4}$ inch.	$4\frac{3}{4}$ lbs. per foot.	19	in Coils.	45 feet.
$1\frac{1}{4}$ inch.	6 lbs. per foot.	25	in Coils.	40 feet.
$1\frac{1}{2}$ inch.	$3\frac{1}{2}$ lbs. per foot.	14	in Coils.	35 feet.
$1\frac{1}{2}$ inch.	$4\frac{1}{4}$ lbs. per foot.	17	in Coils.	30 feet.
$1\frac{1}{2}$ inch.	5 lbs. per foot.	19	in Coils.	22 feet.
$1\frac{1}{2}$ inch,	$6\frac{1}{2}$ lbs. per foot.	23	in Coils.	28 feet.
$1\frac{1}{2}$ inch.	8 lbs. per foot.	27	in Coils.	23 feet.
$1\frac{3}{4}$ inch.	4 lbs. per foot.	13	in Coils.	25 feet.
$1\frac{3}{4}$ inch.	5 lbs. per foot.	17	in Coils.	22 feet.
$1\frac{3}{4}$ inch.	$6\frac{1}{2}$ lbs. per foot.	21	in Coils.	28 feet.
$1\frac{3}{4}$ inch.	$8\frac{1}{2}$ lbs. per foot.	27	in Coils.	22 feet.
2 inch.	$4\frac{3}{4}$ lbs. per foot.	15	in Coils.	30 feet.
2 inch.	6 lbs. per foot.	18	in Coils.	23 to 45 feet.
2 inch.	7 lbs. per foot.	22	in Coils.	20 to 40 feet.
2 inch.	9 lbs. per foot.	27	in Coils.	30 feet.
		inch.		
$2\frac{1}{2}$ inch.	8 lbs. per foot.	$\frac{3}{16}$	in Lengths.	9 to 35 feet.
$2\frac{1}{2}$ inch.	11 lbs. per foot.	$\frac{1}{4}$	in Lengths.	10 to 30 feet.
$2\frac{1}{2}$ inch.	14 lbs. per foot.	$\frac{5}{16}$	in Lengths.	9 to 20 feet.
$2\frac{1}{2}$ inch.	17 lbs. per foot.	$\frac{3}{8}$	in Lengths.	9 to 18 feet.
3 inch.	9 lbs. per foot.	$\frac{3}{16}$	in Lengths.	10 to 20 feet.
3 inch.	12 lbs. per foot.	$\frac{1}{4}$	in Lengths.	10 to 20 feet.
3 inch.	16 lbs. per foot.	$\frac{5}{16}$	in Lengths.	10 to 20 feet.
3 inch.	20 lbs. per foot.	$\frac{3}{8}$	in Lengths.	10 to 16 feet.
$3\frac{1}{2}$ inch.	$9\frac{1}{2}$ lbs. per foot.	$\frac{3}{16}$	in Lengths.	10 to 20 feet.
$3\frac{1}{2}$ inch.	15 lbs. per foot.	$\frac{1}{4}$	in Lengths.	10 to 20 feet.
$3\frac{1}{2}$ inch.	$18\frac{1}{2}$ lbs. per foot.	$\frac{5}{16}$	in Lengths.	9 to 18 feet.
$3\frac{1}{2}$ inch.	22 lbs. per foot.	$\frac{3}{8}$	in Lengths.	13 feet.
4 inch.	$12\frac{1}{2}$ lbs. per foot.	$\frac{3}{16}$	in Lengths.	9 to 18 feet.
4 inch.	16 lbs. per foot.	$\frac{1}{4}$	in Lengths.	7 to 15 feet.
4 inch.	21 lbs. per foot.	$\frac{5}{16}$	in Lengths.	12 feet.
4 inch.	25 lbs. per foot.	$\frac{3}{8}$	in Lengths.	7 to 15 feet.
$4\frac{1}{2}$ inch.	14 lbs. per foot.	$\frac{3}{16}$	in Lengths.	9 to 18 feet.
$4\frac{1}{2}$ inch.	18 lbs. per foot.	$\frac{1}{4}$	in Lengths.	10 feet.
5 inch.	20 lbs. per foot.	$\frac{1}{4}$	in Lengths.	9 feet.
5 inch.	31 lbs. per foot.	$\frac{3}{8}$	in Lengths,	7 feet.

Waste Pipe.

$1\frac{1}{2}$ inch, 2 lbs. .... cents per foot,
2 inch, 3 lbs. .... "
3 inch, $3\frac{1}{2}$ and 5 lbs .... "
4 inch, 5, 6 and 8 lbs. .... "
$4\frac{1}{2}$ inch, 6 and 8 lbs. .... "
5 inch, 8, 10 and 12 lbs .... "

Sheet Lead.

Weight of square foot, $2\frac{1}{2}$, 3, $3\frac{1}{2}$, 4, $4\frac{1}{2}$, 5, 6, 7, 8, 9, 10 lbs. and upwards.

TOBACCO CUTTERS, WHEEL HEADS & RIVETS.

Block-Tin Pipe.

⅜ inch, 5¾, 6 and 8 oz......................... per foot, $
½ inch, 6, 8 and 10 oz.......................... "
⅝ inch, 8 and 10 oz............................ "
¾ inch, 10 and 12 oz........................... "
1 inch, 15 and 18 oz........................... "
1¼ inch, 1¼ and 1½ lbs........................ "
1½ inch, 2 and 2½ lbs......................... "
1 inch, 3 lbs................................. "

Mineral Water Pipe.

Lead Pipe, ₃⁄₁₆, ¼ and ⅜ inch.
Composition, ₃⁄₁₆, ½ and ⅜ inch.

TOBACCO CUTTERS.

Bronzed and Japanned............................. per dozen, $

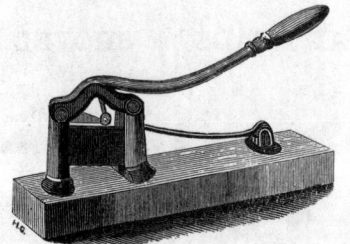

Wood Bottom..................................... per dozen, $

TOBACCO CUTTERS—*(Continued.)*

All Iron.................................... per dozen, $

WHEEL HEADS.

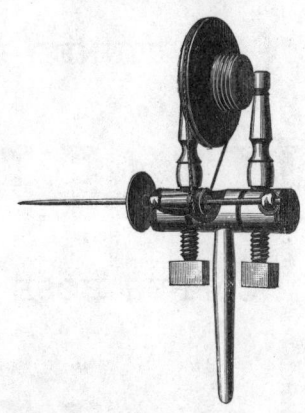

Miner's Patent, Extra Varnished.................. per dozen, $
Miner's Patent, Brass Bushed, Steel Spindle, Varnished   "
Miner's Patent, Improved, Brass Bushed, Steel Spindle,
    Varnished, with Cherry Standards, Brass Bear-
    ings and Side Set Screw....................   "

FLAX WHEELS AND IRONS.

Flax Wheels ....each, $
Spinning Wheels..   "
Flax Wheel Irons...................................per doz. $

HACKLES FOR FLAX.

Hackles for Flax, with 72 Cast Steel Teeth..............each, $
Hackles for Flax, with 111 Cast Steel Teeth.............   "

TRUNK RIVETS.

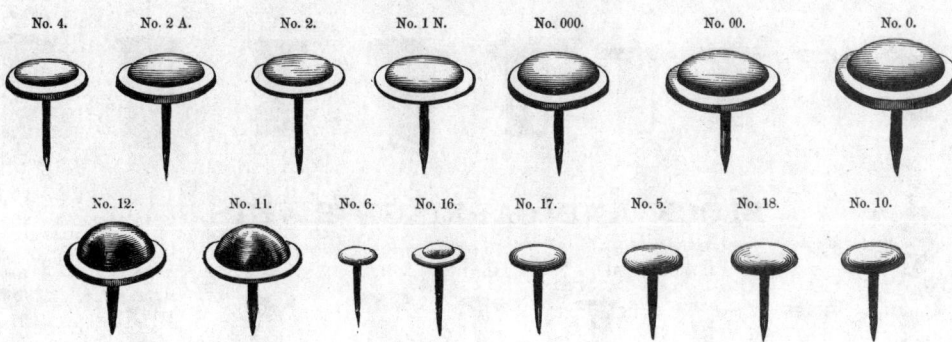

| | | No. 4. | No. 2 A. | No. 2. | No. 1 N. | No. 000. | No. 00. | No. 0. |
| No. 12. | No. 11. | No. 6. | No. 16. | No. 17. | No. 5. | No. 18. | No. 10. |

														cts. per gross.
Trunk Rivets,	No.	0	00	000	1	1 N	2	2 A	4	5	6	16	17	18.
														cts. per gross.
Copper Trunk Rivets, No.		5		6		11		12		16		17		18.

☞ Nails over 1¼ inches long,   extra per gross.

								per M.
Tenter Hooks...................		2		2½		3		3½	4	lbs.

IRON, TINNED AND COPPER RIVETS.

THESE PLATES REPRESENT THE ACTUAL SIZE OF EACH ARTICLE.

BLACK IRON RIVETS.

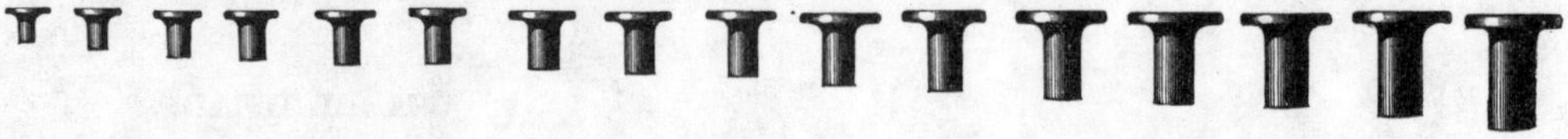
8 oz.
10 oz.
12 oz.
1,
1 1/4,
1 1/2,
1 3/4,
2,
2 1/2.
3,
4,
5,
6,
7,
8,
10 lbs.

TINNED IRON RIVETS AND BURS.

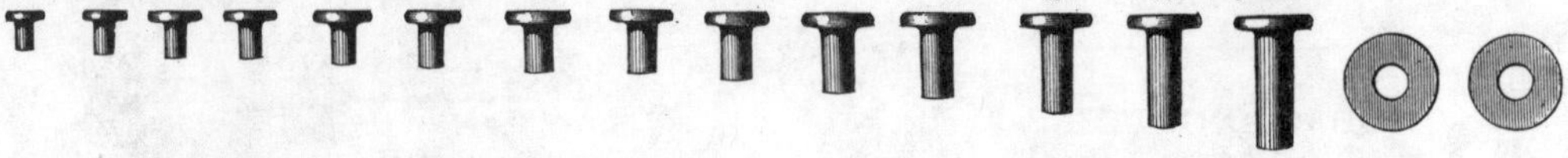
8 oz.
10 oz.
12 oz.
1,
1 1/4,
1 1/2,
1 3/4,
2,
2 1/2,
3,
4,
4 1/2, 7/16,
5, 1/2,
7 lbs. 5/8 inch.
No. 7.
No. 8.

COPPER HOSE AND BELT RIVETS AND BURS.

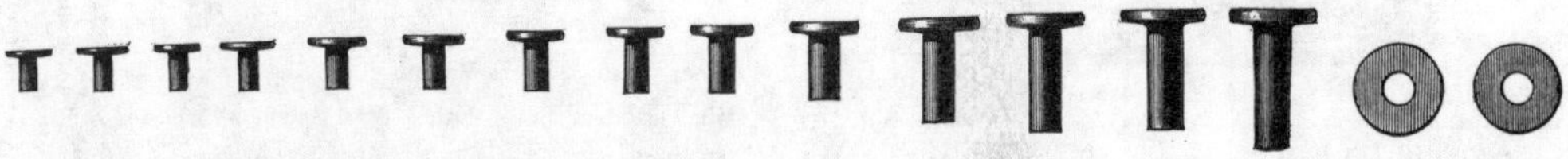
8 oz.
10 oz.
12 oz.
1,
1 1/4,
1 1/2,
1 3/4,
2,
2 1/2,
3 lbs.
7/16, No. 8,
1/2, 8,
1/2, 7,
5/8, 7,
7,
8.

EXTRA LENGTH IRON RIVETS, FLAT AND OVAL HEADS. | SHOVEL RIVETS.

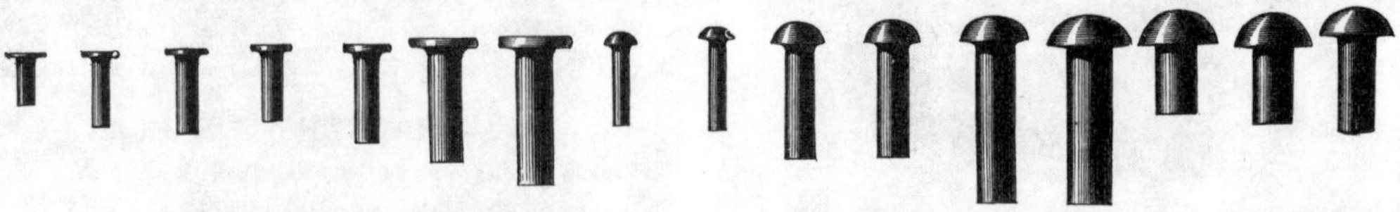
10 oz. 1/4,
1 1/4, 3/8,
1 1/2, 7/16,
2, 3/8,
3, 1/2,
7, 5/8,
9, 3/4,
1 1/2, 7/16,
2, 1/2,
4, 5/8,
6, 5/8,
10 lbs. 7/8 inch.
No. 3, 7/8,
5, 3/8,
5, 7/16,
5 Wire, 1/2 inch.

COOPERS' RIVETS.

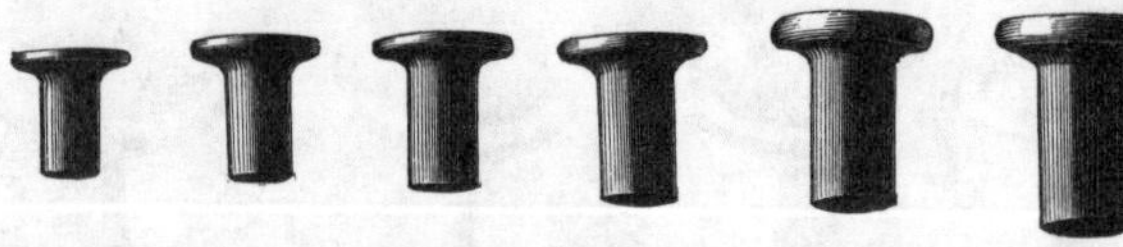
1d,
2d,
3d,
4d,
5d,
6d.

SAFE RIVETS.

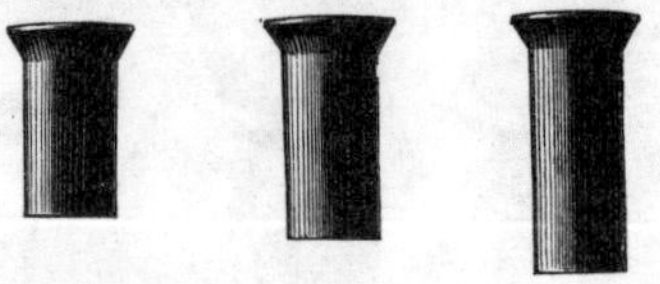
3/8, 3/4,
3/8, 7/8,
3/8 inch Wire. 1 inch long.

BLOCK AND CARRIAGE RIVETS.

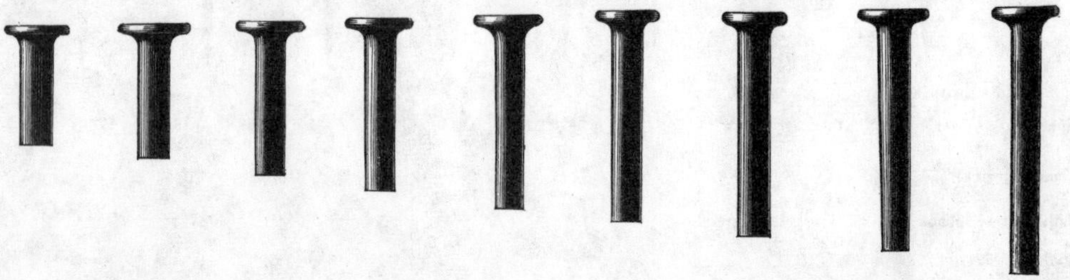
3/4,
7/8,
1,
1 1/8,
1 1/4,
1 3/8,
1 1/2,
1 5/8,
1 3/4 inch.

IRON, TINNED AND COPPER RIVETS.

(Continued.)

(For Plates, see page 290.)

IRON—BLACK.

$																per M.
		8				10				12						ounce.

$																per M.
1	1¼	1½	1¾	2	2½	3	4	5	6	7	8	9	10	12	14	lb.

IRON—TINNED.

$										per M.
		8			10			12		ounce.

$										per M.
1	1¼	1½	1¾	2	2½	3	4	5	6	7	lb.

BLOCK AND CARRIAGE, 100 RIVETS EACH.

	¾	⅞	1	1⅛	1¼	1½	1¾	2	2¼	2½	3	3½	4	inch.
Wire Gauge, No. 3,														cents per hundred.
Wire Gauge, No. 4,														"
Wire Gauge, No. 5,														"
Wire Gauge, No. 6,														"
Wire Gauge, No. 7,														"
Wire Gauge, No. 8,														"

Oval or Countersunk Heads, or extra lengths,   per M additional.

RIVETS IN BULK, PRICES PER POUND.

⅜ Wire, ⅜ to 2 inches long	....	per lb.
5⁄16 to No. 3 Wire, ⅜ to 2 inches long	....	"
¼ to No. 6 Wire, ⅜ to 1¼ inches long	....	"
To No. 7 Wire, ⅜ to 1 inch long	....	"
To No. 8 Wire, ⅜ to 1 inch long	....	"
To No. 9 Wire, ⅜ to 1 inch long	....	"

If shorter than ⅜ inch, or longer than above,   per lb. extra.

Coopers'	2d	3d & 4d	5d & 6d.	per lb.
Ship and Boiler Rivets, all Sizes, and of best quality of Iron	....			per lb.
Oval and Taper Head Tank Rivets	....			per lb.
Safe Rivets	....			per lb.
Shoe Rivets	....			per lb.
Brass Rivets	....			per M.
Burs, Tinned	....			per lb.
Burs, Black	....			per lb.

COPPER RIVETS.

Trunk. 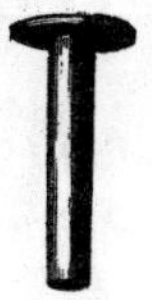   Hose.    Belt. 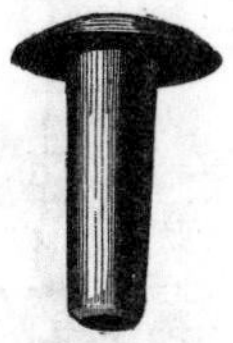   Braziers.

Hose and Belt Rivets and Burs, No.	8	9	10	11	12	13.	per lb.
Braziers' Belt Rivets and Burs	....						per lb.
Oval Head Copper Trunk Rivets	....						"

☞ All sizes of Rivets made to order.

SHOVELS AND SPADES.

[For Description of Plates see pages 294, 295.]

SHOVELS.

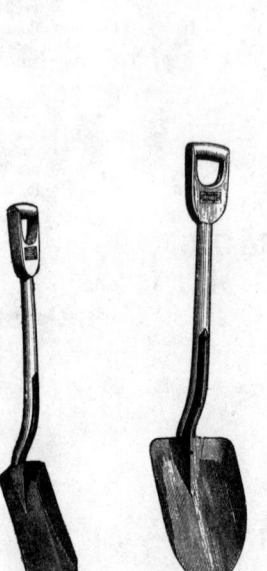

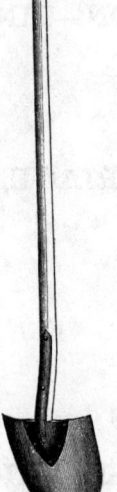

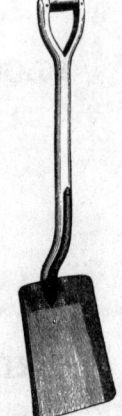

D Handle,
Plain Back,
Steel Edge,
Square Point.

D Handle,
Plain Back,
Steel Edge,
Round Point.

Long Handle,
Plain Back,
Steel Edge,
Round Point.

Long Handle,
Strapped Back,
Cast Steel,
Round Point.

Patent Handle,
Strapped Back,
Cast Steel,
Round Point.

Patent Handle,
Strapped Back,
Cast Steel,
Square Point.

D Handle,
Cast Steel,
Toy, or Boys'.

SPADES.

Cast Steel Toy,
or Boys'.

Cast Steel.

Steel Edge.

No. 1
Drain.

No. 2
Drain.

No. 3
Drain.

No. 4
Drain.

Concave
or Post.

SPADES, SCOOPS, TILE LAYERS, ETC.

(For Description of Plates see pages 294, 295.)

SPADES.   SCOOPS.

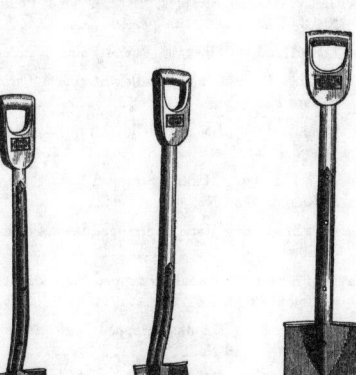
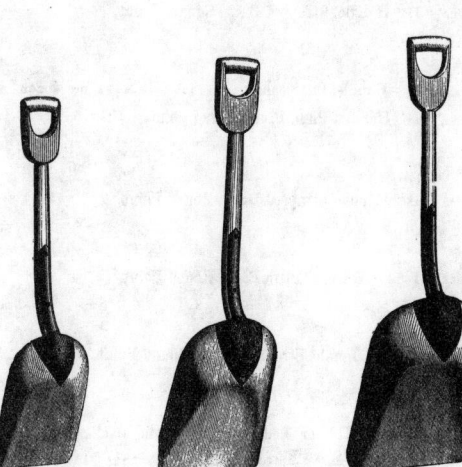

Mining.   Nursery.   Grafting.   Subsoil.   Boys' Cast Steel.   No. 3 Cast Steel.   No. 8 Cast Steel.

TILE LAYER.

FLAT DRAIN CLEANER.

(For Description of Plate see page 294.)

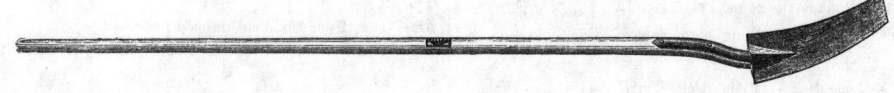

CONCAVE DRAIN CLEANER, TO PUSH.

(For Description of Plate see page 294.)

No. 1.

SHOVELS AND SPADES.

(For Plates, see pages 292, 293.)

Unpolished, Steel Edge Shovels.

Ames' "D" Handle, Plain Back, Square Point,

| $ | | | | | | | | per dozen. |
| Nos. | 0 | 1 | 2 | 3 | 4 | 5 | 6 | 7 |

| $ | | | | | | per dozen. |
| Nos. | 8 | 9 | 10 | 11 | 12 | 13 | 14. |

Ames' "D" Handle, Strapped Back, Square Point,

| $ | | | per dozen. |
| Nos. | 1 | 2 | 3 |

Ames' "D" Handle, Charcoal......................per dozen, $

Ames' "D" Handle, Plain Back, Round Point,

| $ | | | | | | per dozen. |
| Nos. | 1 | 2 | 3 | 4 | 5 | 6 |

Ames' "D" Handle, Strapped Back, Round Point,

| $ | | | | | | per dozen. |
| Nos. | 1 | 2 | 3 | 4 | 5 | 6 |

Ames' "Long" Handle, Plain Back, Round Point,

| $ | | | per dozen. |
| Nos. | 0 | 1 | 2 |

Ames' "Long" Handle, Strapped Back, Round Point,

| $ | | | per dozen. |
| Nos. | 0 | 1 | 2 |

J. B. Ogden's "D" or Long Handle, Plain Back, Square Point, No. 2.........................per dozen, $

J. B. Ogden's "D" or Long Handle, Strapped Back, Square Point, No. 2........................ "

J. B. Ogden's "D" or Long Handle, Plain Back, Round Point, No. 2........................ "

J. B. Ogden's "D" or Long Handle, Strapped Back, Round Point, No. 2........................ "

Rowland's D Handle, Plain Back, Square Point, No. 2.................................... "

Rowland's Long Handle, Plain Back, Round Point, No. 2.................................... "

J. Disston's D or Long Handle, Plain Back, Square Point, No. 2............................... "

J. Disston's D or Long Handle, Plain Back, Round Point, No. 2............................... "

Adams' D Handle, Plain Back, Square Point, No. 2 .. "

Polished Steel Edge Shovels.

Ames' D Handle, Plain Back, Square Point, No. 2....per dozen, $

Ames' D Handle, Plain Back, Round Point, No. 2.... "

Ames' Long Handle, Plain Back, Round Point, No. 2. "

J. B. Ogden's D or Long Handle, Plain Back, Square Point, No. 2 .... "

J. B. Ogden's D or Long Handle, Plain Back, Round Point, No. 2 .... "

Polished Cast Steel Shovels.

"Antrim" D or Long Handle, Patent Welded, Plain Back, Square Point, No. 2 ....per dozen, $

"Antrim" D or Long Handle, Patent Welded, Plain Back, Round Point, No. 2 .... "

Ames' D or Long Handle, Strapped Back, Square Point,

| $ | | | per dozen. |
| Nos. | 1 | 2 | 3 |

Ames' D Handle, Strapped Back, Round Point,

| $ | | | per dozen. |
| Nos. | 1 | 2 | 3 |

Unpolished Steel Edge Shovels.

(Continued.)

Ames' Long Handle, Strapped Back, Round Point, No. 2 ....per dozen, $

Ames' Long Handle, Strapped Back, Round Point, No. 3 .... "

Ames' Long Handle, California, Round Point........ "

J. B. Ogden's D or Long Handle, Strapped Back, Square Point, No. 2.......................... "

J. B. Ogden's D or Long Handle, Strapped Back, Round Point, No. 2 .... "

C. Russell's D or Long Handle, Strapped Back, Square or Round Point, No. 2..................... "

J. Disston's D or Long Handle, Strapped Back, Square or Round Point, No. 2...................... "

R. Naylor's D or Long Handle, Strapped Back, Square or Round Point, No. 2...................... "

M. Clark's D or Long Handle, Strapped Back, Square or Round Point, No. 2..................... "

G. Morse's D or Long Handle, Strapped Back, Square or Round Point, No. 2....................... "

Polished Cast Steel Moulders' Shovels.

"J. Bisbee's," Strapped Back......................per dozen, $

"O. A. Day's," Strapped Back....................... "

"Sanderson's," Strapped Back...................... "

"T. M. Porter's," Plain Back...................... "

Polished Cast Steel Boys' Shovels.

Ames', D Handle.................................per dozen, $

J. Disston's, D Handle .... "

Iron Shovels.

Carr's, D or Long Handle, Unpolished, Square Point..per dozen, $

Carr's, D or Long Handle, Unpolished, Round Point.. "

Carr's, D or Long Handle, Polished, Square Point..... "

Carr's, D or Long Handle, Polished, Round Point...... "

Unpolished Steel Edge Spades.

Ames' D or Long Handle, Plain Back,

| $ | | | | per dozen. |
| Nos. | 1 | 2 | 3 | 4 |

Ames' D or Long Handle, Strapped Back,

| $ | | | | per dozen. |
| Nos. | 1 | 2 | 3 | 4 |

J. B. Ogden's D or Long Handle, Plain Back, No. 2..per dozen, $

J. B. Ogden's D or Long Handle, Strapped Back, No. 2 "

Rowland's D Handle, Plain Back, No. 2............ "

Rowland's D Handle, Strapped Back, No. 2......... "

J. Disston's D Handle, Plain Back, No. 2............ "

Polished Steel Edge Spades.

Ames' D or Long Handle, Plain Back,

| $ | | | per dozen. |
| Nos. | 1 | 2 | 3. |

J. B. Ogden's D or Long Handle, Plain Back No. 2...per dozen, $

J. Disston's D Handle, Plain Back No. 2............ "

SPADES, SCOOPS AND FORKS.

Polished Cast Steel Spades.

(For Plates see pages 292, 293.)

"Antrim" D Handle, Patent Welded, Plain Back No. 2.per dozen, $

Ames' D or Long Handle, Strapped Back,

$ per dozen.

Nos.   1   2   3   4.

J. B. Ogden's D or Long Handle, Strapped Back No. 2..per dozen, $

C. Russell's D Handle, Strapped Back No. 2......... "

J. Disston's D Handle, Strapped Back No. 2.......... "

R. Naylor's D Handle, Strapped Back No. 2.......... "

M. Clark's D Handle, Strapped Back No. 2........... "

G. Morse's D. Handle, Strapped Back No. 2........... "

Ames' D Handle, Subsoil.................... "

Ames' D Handle, Nursery.................... "

Ames' D Handle, Concave or Post.................. "

Ames' D Handle, Clay....................... "

Ames' D Handle, Mining .... "

Ames' D Handle, Peat....................... "

Ames' D Handle, Grafting.................... "

Ames' D Handle, Brick .... "

Polished Cast Steel Boys' Spades.

(For Plates see pages 292, 293)

Ames' D Handle ....per dozen, $

J. Disston's D Handle .... "

Iron Spades.

Carr's D Handle, Unpolished, Strapped Back ....per dozen, $

Carr's Long Handle, Unpolished, Strapped Back...... "

Drainage Tools.

(For Plates see pages 292, 293.)

Ames' D Handle, Steel Edge Drain Spades,

$ per dozen.

Nos.   1   2   3   4.

Ames'. Steel Edge, Concave Drain Cleaner, to Push, No. 1, per doz. $

Ames' Steel Edge, Concave Drain Cleaner, to Draw, No. 2, "

Ames' Steel Edge, Flat Drain Cleaner, to Push, No. 3... "

Ames' Steel Edge, Flat Drain Cleaner, to Draw, No. 4... "

☞ Any variety of Drainage Tools not above, made to order.

Scoops.

(For Plates, see page 293.)

Ames' Polished Cast Steel, with Swede's Iron Straps,

$ per dozen.

Nos.   2   3   4   5   6.

J. B. Ogden's, Polished Cast Steel,

$ per dozen.

Nos.   2   4   6.

$ per dozen.

C. Russell's Half Polished, Cast Steel Nos.   4   6

R. Naylor's Polished Steel, No. 3.................per dozen, $

J. Disston's Half Polished Steel, No. 3............... "

C. Stone's Half Polished Iron, No. 2 .... "

C. Stone's Unpolished, Iron, No. 2................... "

Charcoal or Bark, Polished Cast Steel, Light, No. 8.... "

O. A. Day's, Polished Cast Steel, Light, for Boys..... "

SPADING OR DIGGING FORKS.
Broad, Flat Tine.

No. 67, Four Tine, D Handle, Morticed Ferrule, Riveted
Shank ....per dozen, $

No. 68, Four Tine, D Handle, Strapped Ferrule, Riveted
Shank............................. .... "

Broad, Angular Tine.

No. 70, Four Tine, D Handle, Strapped Ferrule, Riveted
Shank ....per dozen, $

No. 72, Five Tine, D Handle, Strapped Ferrule, Riveted
Shank.....................................per dozen, $

Extra Heavy Street Cleaners' Forks.

No. 62, Four Tine, D Handle, Morticed Ferrule, Riveted
Shank.....................................per dozen, $

No. 63, Four Tine, D Handle, Morticed Ferrule, Riveted
Shank................................... .. "

No. 64, Four Tine, D Handle, Strapped Ferrule, Riveted
Shank.................................. "

No. 65, Five Tine, D Handle, Strapped Ferrule, Riveted
Shank.................................. "

Six Tine Manure and Tanners' Forks.

No. 54, Flat Tine, D Handle, Strapped Ferrule, Riveted
Shank.....................................per dozen, $

No. 58, Eel Tine, D Handle, Strapped Ferrule, Riveted
Shank.................................. "

No. 61, Round Tine, D Handle, Strapped Ferrule, Riveted Shank .... "

No. 64, Diamond Tine, D Handle, Strapped Ferrule,
Riveted Shank .... "

Tanners' Forks, Eight Tine Flat, Strapped Ferrule,
Riveted Shank.......................... "

HAY FORKS.
Polished Ferrule, Riveted Shank, Three Tine.

No. 41, Eel Tine, 6 Feet Handle...................per dozen, $

No. 42, Round Tine, 6 Feet Handle................ "

No. 43, Diamond Tine, 6 Feet Handle.............. "

Two Tine.

No. 45, Eel Tine, 6 Feet Handle.................per dozen, $

No. 46, Round Tine, 6 Feet Handle................ "

No. 47, Diamond Tine, 6 Feet Handle.............. "

Superior Finish Hay Forks.
Long Blued Ferrule, Riveted Shank, Three Tine.

No. 141, Eel Tine, 6 Feet Handle...................per dozen, $

No. 142, Round Tine, 6 Feet Handle............... "

HAY AND MANURE FORKS, ETC.

Superior Finish Hay Forks.
(*Continued.*)
Two Tine.
No. 145, Eel Tine, 6 Feet Handle.................per dozen, $
No. 146, Round Tine, 6 Feet Handle.............. "

Strapped Hay Forks.
Polished Strapped Ferrule, Riveted Shank, Three Tine.

No. 241, Eel Tine, 6 Feet Handle.................per dozen, $
No. 242, Round Tine, 6 Feet Handle............. "

Two Tine.

No. 245, Eel Tine, 6 Feet Handle.................per dozen, $

No. 246, Round Tine, 6 Feet Handle.............per dozen, $
Hay Forks Extra Length of Tines..........per dozen advance,
Hay Forks, Seven Feet Handles ....per dozen advance,

Manure Forks, all Polished, Four Tine.
Flat Tine, D Handles.
No. 101, Strapped Ferrule, Riveted Shank ....per dozen, $
No. 103, Morticed Ferrule, Riveted Shank........... "

Long Handles.
No. 102, Strapped Ferrule, Riveted Shank ....per dozen, $
No. 104, Morticed Ferrule, Riveted Shank .... "

Eel Tine, D Handles.
No. 105, Strapped Ferrule, Riveted Shank ....per dozen, $
No. 107, Morticed Ferrule, Riveted Shank .... "

Long Handles.

No. 106, Strapped Ferrule, Riveted Shank ....per dozen, $
No. 108, Morticed Ferrule, Riveted Shank........... "

Round Tine, D Handles.

No. 109, Strapped Ferrule, Riveted Shank ....per dozen, $
No. 111, Morticed Ferrule, Riveted Shank .... "

Long Handles.
No. 110, Strapped Ferrule, Riveted Shank...........per dozen, $
No. 112, Morticed Ferrule, Riveted Shank........... "

Diamond Tine, D Handles.
No. 13, Strapped Ferrule, Riveted Shank...........per dozen, $
No. 15, Morticed Ferrule, Riveted Shank .... "
No. 17, Morticed Ferrule, Keyed Shank............. "
No. 19, Morticed Ferrule, Keyed Shank (Thomas & Co.) "

Manure Forks, Diamond Tine, Long Handles.
(*Continued.*)
No. 14, Strapped Ferrule, Riveted Shank ....per dozen, $
No. 16, Morticed Ferrule, Riveted Shank .... "
No. 18, Morticed Ferrule, Riveted Shank (Thomas & Co.) "
No. 20, Morticed Ferrule, Riveted Shank .... "

Extra Finish Cast Steel, Long Blued Ferrule.
Riveted Shank, D Handles.

No. A, Eel Tine, New Pattern.....................per dozen, $
No. 55, Eel Tine, Extra Size ....per dozen, $
No. 59, Round Tine, Extra Size .... "

Long Handles.
No. B, Eel Tine, New Pattern.....................per dozen, $
No. 56, Eel Tine, Extra Size .... "
No. 60, Round Tine, Extra Size.................... "

Half Polished Forks of either Flat, Eel or Round Tines   per dozen less than List Price.

Boys' Forks.
No. 49, Eel or Round Tine, 4½ Feet Handle, Polished
    Ferrule.....................................per dozen, $
No. 50, Diamond Tine, 4½ Feet Handle, Polished
    Ferrule .... "

Potato Hooks.

No. 31, Four Tine Oval, 4½ ft. Handle, Keyed Shank.per dozen, $
No. 32, Four Tine Oval, 4½ ft. Handle, Riveted Shank. "
No. 33, Four Tine Oval, 4½ ft. Handle, Riveted Shank. "

Manure Drags.
No. 37, Four Tine Diamond, 6 ft. Handle, Riveted
    Shank ....per dozen, $
No. 38, Four Tine Flat, 6 ft. Handle, Riveted Shank.. "

Leaf or Straw Forks.
No. 16, Four Tine Diamond, Morticed Ferrule, Riveted
    Shank ....per dozen, $
No. 108, Four Tine Eel, Morticed Ferrule, Riveted
    Shank .... "

Handles.
Boys' Fork Handles..............................per dozen, $
Six Feet Hay Fork Handles......................... "
Seven Feet Hay Fork Handles...................... "
Four and Half Feet Manure Fork Handles, Bent..... "
D Manure Fork Handles, Bent, Plain............... "
D Manure Fork Handles, Bent, 1 Rivet............. "
D Manure Fork Handles, Bent, 2 Rivets............ "

Batchellor's, Millard's, or any other make of the above goods furnished to order.

AGRICULTURAL IMPLEMENTS.

SCYTHES.
BLOOD'S GERMAN AND CAST STEEL GRAIN SCYTHES.

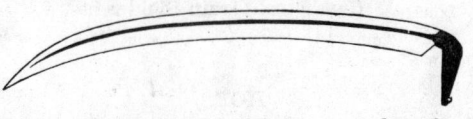

G. S. Corn or Grain Scythes, Full Set, Oiled, Extra Steel Back......................................per dozen, $

G. S. Corn or Grain Scythes, "Waldron Pattern," Oiled, Extra Steel Back.......................   "

G S. Corn or Grain Scythes, Beaded and Painted, Steel Back..............................   "

C. S. Corn or Grain Scythes, Full Set, Polished Backs, Oiled, Extra Steel Back ....   "

C. S. Corn or Grain Scythes, "Waldron Pattern," Oiled, Extra Steel Back.......................   "

BLOOD'S GRASS SCYTHES.

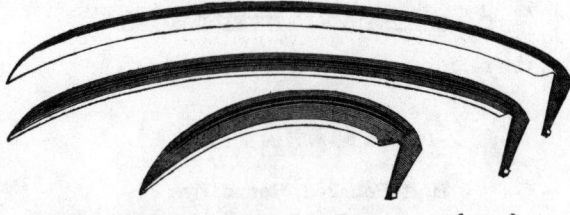

G. S. Grass, Full Set, Oiled, Extra Steel Backs......per dozen, $

G. S. Grass, "Waldron," Oiled, Extra Steel Backs...   "

G. S. Grass, "Black Snake," Oiled, Extra Steel Backs.   "

G. S. Grass, Half Set, Oiled, Extra Steel Backs......   "

G. S. Grass, Beaded and Painted, Steel Backs........   "

C. S. Grass, Full Set, Oiled, Extra Steel Backs.......   "

C. S. Grass, "Waldron," Oiled, Extra Steel Backs....   "

C. S. Grass, Half Set, Oiled, Extra Steel Backs......   "

BLOOD'S GRASS SCYTHES.

S. S. Mirror Blade Grass, Full Set, Extra Extra......per dozen, $

S. S. Grass, Half Set, Oiled, Extra Steel Backs......   "

C. S. Lawn, Full Set, Oiled, Extra Steel Backs.......   "

G. S. Lawn, Full Set, Oiled, Extra Steel Backs.......   "

G. S. Bush or Briar, Beaded and Painted, Steel Backs.   "

HARRIS' GRAIN AND GRASS SCYTHES.

1776 Corn or Grain Scythes, Cast Steel..............per dozen, $

1776 Corn or Grain Scythes, German Steel..........   "

Corn or Grain Scythes, "Waldron Pattern"..........   "

Grass Scythes, "Waldron Pattern"..................   "

Grass Scythes, half and full set Silver Steel..........   "

Grass Scythes, half and full set Cast Steel...........   "

Grass Scythes, half and full set German Steel........   "

Lawn Scythes....................................   "

Bush and Bramble Scythes.........................   "

WATERS' PATENT ROLLED SCYTHES.

Machine Made, with Patent Cast Steel Edges and Steel Backs,

$ per dozen.

No.   1   2.

A full stock of other makes of Scythes constantly on hand.

Wadsworth's Bush Scythes......................per dozen, $

PATENT SCYTHE SNATHS.

No. 0, Wooden Snaths, Hook Bolt Fastening, Brass Ferrule ....per dozen, $

No. 00, Wooden Snaths, Loop Bolt Fastening, Adjustable Plate, Brass Ferrule ....   "

No. 10, Wooden Snaths, Loop Bolt Fastening, Brass Ferrule ....   "

No. 1, Extra, Wooden Snaths, Full Plate, Brass Ferrule   "

No. 1, Wooden Snaths, Slide Socket, Brass Ferrule ..   "

No. 2, Wooden Snaths, Slide Socket, Iron Ferrule ...   "

No. 3, Wooden Snaths, Slide Socket..............   "

No. 4, Wooden Snaths, Slide Socket..............   "

Bush Snaths, 2 Rings.......................   "

Extra charge for Dutch Bend Snaths,   per dozen net.

Extra charge for Jersey Bend Snaths,   "

PATENT GRAIN CRADLES.
Turkey Wing, Patent Wedge.

Turkey Wing.   Grape Vine.

No. 1, Extra, 4 Fingered, Selected.................per dozen, $

No. 1, Extra, 5 Fingered, Selected.................   "

No. 1, Plain, 4 Fingered, Selected..... ....   "

No. 1, Plain, 5 Fingered, Selected..................   "

Grape Vine and Southern Patterns, $ per dozen extra.

Barley Forks, 4 Tined, $ per doz.; 3 Tined, $ per doz.

SCYTHE STONES, SHARPENERS AND RIFLES.
Genuine Cummington Quinebeaug Scythe Stones.

$ per gross.

8   9   10 inch.   Premium.   No. 1 Select.

Plymouth Rock Scythe Stones.

$ per gross.

8   9   10 inch.   Extra.

Genuine Quinebeaug Scythe Stones.

No. 1........$ per gross ; No. 2....$ per gross.

AGRICULTURAL IMPLEMENTS.

(*Continued.*)

Woonsocket Scythe Stones.

$ per gross.
No. 1, Select. 1 2 3.

Indian Pond (Red End) Scythe Stones.

$ per gross.
No. 1, Extra. 1 2.

Blue Rock Scythe Stones.

$ per gross.
8 9 10 inch.

Scythe Rifles.

$ per gross.
Common, 1 2 3 Coats.

$ per gross.
Best, 1 2 3 4 Coats.

Scythe Ticklers..............................per gross, $

Hay Knives.

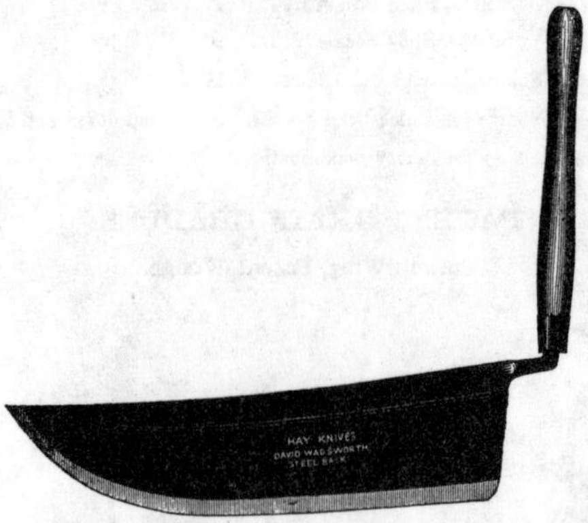

No. 1, Polished Back, 22 to 24 inches, assorted.......per dozen, $
No. 2, Blued Back, 20 to 22 inches, assorted.......... "

Straw Knives.

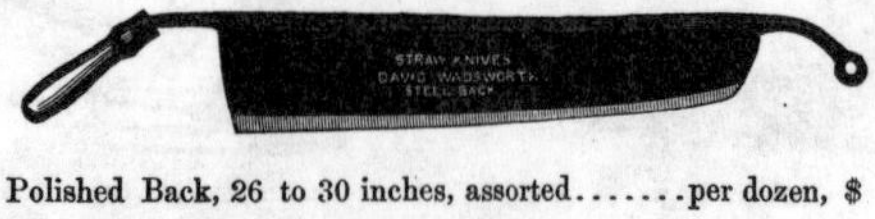

No. 1, Polished Back, 26 to 30 inches, assorted.......per dozen, $
No. 2, Blued Back, 23 to 26 inches, assorted.......... "

German Pattern.

No 1, Polished Back, 26 to 30 inches, assorted........per dozen, $
No. 2, Blued Back, 23 to 26 inches, assorted.......... "

Corn Cutters.

Corn Cutters...per dozen, $

Corn Knives.

Corn Knives..per dozen, $

Cast Steel Grass Hooks.

$ per dozen.
No. 1 2 3 4.

Cast Steel Grain Sickles.

$ per dozen.
No. 2 3 4.

HOES.

Solid Shank, Cast Steel, Goose Neck Hoes, Handled..per dozen, $
Socket Handle, Cast Steel, Goose Neck Hoes, Handled, "
Common Riveted Sheet Steel Hoes, Handled......... "
Polished Cast Steel Planters' Hoes, Handled......... "
Polished Cast Steel Street Hoes, Handled............. "
Polished Cast Steel California Hoes, Handled........ "
Polished Cast Steel, Solid Shank, Ladies' Hoes, Handled "
Polished Cast Steel, Solid Shank, Toy Hoes, Handled. "

CAST STEEL PLANTERS' HOES.

Half Polished, Round Eye.

No. 00, width of Blade $6\frac{1}{2}$ in., size of Eye $1\frac{3}{4}\times1\frac{1}{2}$ in....per dozen, $
No. 0, width of Blade 7 in., size of Eye $1\frac{7}{8}\times1\frac{5}{8}$ in.... "
No. 1, width of Blade $7\frac{1}{2}$ in., size of Eye $1\frac{7}{8}\times1\frac{5}{8}$ in.... "
No. 2, width of Blade 8 in., size of Eye $2\times1\frac{3}{4}$ in.... "
No. 3, width of Blade $8\frac{1}{2}$ in., size of Eye $2\times1\frac{3}{4}$ in.... "
No. 4, width of Blade 9 in., size of Eye $2\frac{1}{8}\times1\frac{7}{8}$ in.... "
No. 5, width of Blade $9\frac{1}{2}$ in., size of Eye $2\frac{1}{8}\times1\frac{7}{8}$ in.... "

Full Polished, Round Eye.

No. 00, width of Blade $6\frac{1}{2}$ in., size of Eye $1\frac{3}{4}\times1\frac{1}{2}$ in..per dozen, $
No. 0, width of Blade 7 in., size of Eye $1\frac{7}{8}\times1\frac{5}{8}$ in.. "
No. 1, width of Blade $7\frac{1}{2}$ in., size of Eye $1\frac{7}{8}\times1\frac{5}{8}$ in.. "
No. 2, width of Blade 8 in., size of Eye $2\times1\frac{3}{4}$ in.. "
No. 3, width of Blade $8\frac{1}{2}$ in., size of Eye $2\times1\frac{3}{4}$ in.. "
No. 4, width of Blade 9 in., size of Eye $2\frac{1}{8}\times1\frac{7}{8}$ in.. "
No. 5, width of Blade $9\frac{1}{2}$ in., size of Eye $2\frac{1}{8}\times1\frac{7}{8}$ in.. "

AGRICULTURAL IMPLEMENTS.

(Continued.)

Heavy or California Hoe.

Half Polished...per dozen, $
Full Polished ....   "

Trowel Top Garden Hoe.

No.   6–0   5–0   4–0   3–0   2–0   per dozen.
$

Cast Steel Garden Rakes.

No. 1, 16 Teeth, Cast Steel, Polished...............per dozen, $
No. 2, 14 Teeth, Cast Steel, Polished...............   "
No. 3, 12 Teeth, Cast Steel, Polished...............   "
No. 4, 10 Teeth, Cast Steel, Polished...............   "
No. 5, 8 Teeth, Cast Steel, Polished...............   "
No. 6, 6 Teeth, Cast Steel, Polished...............   "
Cast Steel Rakes, Black,   less per dozen.

Malleable Iron Garden Rakes,
Ground and Polished.

 6 Teeth, 4 feet Handle, Fitted....................   "
 8 Teeth, 5 feet Handle, Fitted....................   "
10 Teeth, 5½ feet Handle, Fitted....................   "
12 Teeth, 5¾ feet Handle, Fitted....................   "
14 Teeth, 6 feet Handle, Fitted...................per dozen, $
Packed in ½ dozen.   Handles 1 dozen.

Braced.

                    $ per dozen.
No. 9, Handled,   10   12   14   teeth.

Floral Tools, in Sets of 3 Pieces.

Floral Tools, in Sets of 3 Pieces—*(Continued.)*
With Cast Steel Blades.

No. 64, Small Size ....per set, $
No. 65, Large Size..................................   "
No. 66, Small Size, Ex. quality Cherry Handles, Varnished, per set, $
No. 67, Large Size, Ex. quality Cherry Handles, Varnished   "

Children's and Ladies' Garden Sets.

No. 1, Wrought Iron, 3 Pieces.......................per set, $
No. 2, Cast Iron, 3 Pieces ....   "
No. 3, Wrought Iron, 3 Pieces.......................   "

TROWELS.

Boston Pattern.

New Boston Pattern.

	$					per doz.
New Boston Pattern,	6	6½	7	7½	8	inch.

New York Pattern.

Philadelphia Pattern.

London Pattern.

New York, Philadelphia and London Patterns.

$									per doz.
8	8½	9	9½	10	10½	11	11½	12	inch.

Plastering Trowels.

$						per doz.
3×8	3½×9½	4×10	4½×10½	5×11	5½×11½	6×12	inch.

Worrall's Cast Steel Plastering Trowels.

$	21	22	23	24°°				per dozen.
10	10½	11	11½	12	12½	13	inch.

Pointing Trowels—Solid Steel.

$					per dozen.
3	4½	5	5½	6	inch.

Pointing Trowels—Riveted Shanks.

$					per dozen.
3	4½	5	5½	6	inch.

Corner Trowels.

$			per dozen.
5	6	7	inch.

Garden Trowels—Riveted.

$					per dozen.
5	6	7	8	9	inch.

AGRICULTURAL IMPLEMENTS.

(Continued.)

Garden Hoe and Rake.

No. 1 Extra Heavy Malleable and Cast Steel Hoe, Counter Sunk Rivets.

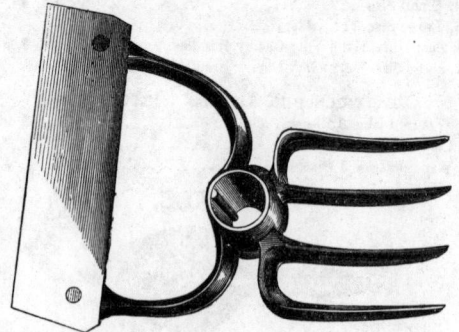

No.   82, 6 Prong and 5 inch Blade..................per dozen, $

No. 401, 4 Prong................................. "

No. 402, 3 Prong .... "

Weeding Hoe and Rake.

No. 1, Polished Cast Steel, 6 Teeth.................per dozen, $

No. 2, Polished Cast Steel, 4 Teeth................. "

No. 1, Cast Iron, with Wrought Iron Hoe, 6 Teeth.... "

No. 2, all Cast Iron, 4 Teeth....................... "

Cast Steel Hoe Rakes.

No. 1, Spade Blade ....per dozen, $

Mountain Ash Handles, made to fit the Hoes, 4 ft. long   "

Mountain Ash Handles, made to fit the Hoes, 5 ft. long   "

Cast Iron Hoe Rakes.

No. 1, 5 Teeth, Handled...........................per dozen, $

No. 2, 6 Teeth, Handled........................... "

FLORAL TOOLS,

All warranted Cast Steel Blades, and put up in Pairs, a Fork and Spade.

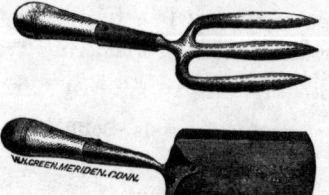

No. 60, 1 Pair Ladies' Transplanting Spade and Fork...per pair, $

No. 61, 1 Pair Ladies' Transplanting Spade and Fork... "

Garden Weeding Forks.

Garden Weeding Forks..........................per dozen, $

Garden Weeding Hoes.

Garden Weeding Hoes.............................per dozen, $

Asparagus Chisel.

Asparagus Chisel ....per dozen, $

Grafting Knives.

Grafting Knives................................per dozen $

Socket Shuffle Hoes.

$ per dozen.

      6   7   8   10   inch.

Edging Knife, Large Size..........................per dozen, $

Edging Knife, Small Size.......................... "

Garden Reel, Large Size........................... "

Pruning Saw and Chisel........................... "

Pruning Shears.

No. 1, Seymour's.................................per dozen, $

No. 2, Seymour's................................. "

No. 3, Seymour's, with Spring......................per dozen, $

Wilcox's Pattern, Cast Steel......................per dozen, $

Garden and Hedge Shears.

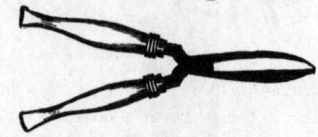

Without Pruning Notch..........................per pair, $

AGRICULTURAL IMPLEMENTS.

(Continued.)

Garden and Hedge Shears.

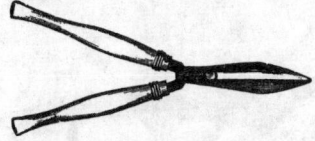

With Pruning Notch................................per pair, $

Lopping or Branch Shears.

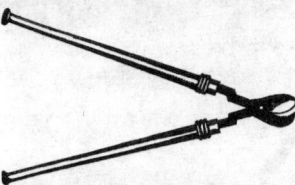

With Short Wood Handles.........................per pair, $
With Long Wood Handles, for cutting large branches.. "

Sliding Pruning Shears.

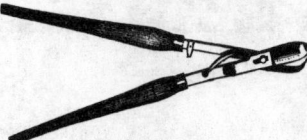

With Movable Center, for making draw-cut............per pair, $

Grass Edging or Border Shears.

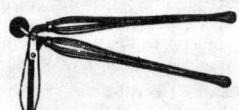

For Trimming Box and Grass Edgings...............per pair, $

Sheep Shears.

Patent American.

No. 10, 3½ inch Blades, Polished........... ......per dozen, $
No. 20, 4 inch Blades, Polished.................. "
No. 30, 4½ inch Blades, Polished................. "
No. 40, 5 inch Blades, Polished.................. "
No. 50, 5½ inch Blades, Polished................. "
No. 60, 6 inch Blades, Polished.................. "
No. 70, 6½ inch Blades, Polished................. "
No. 80, 7 inch Blades, Polished.................. "
No. 90, 7½ inch Blades, Polished................. "
No. 100, 8 inch Blades, Polished................. "
No. 32, 4½ inch Blades, Polished, with Patent Guard
  to prevent Cutting the Skin of the Sheep...... "
☞ Extra Polished Shears furnished to Order.

WILKINSON'S SHEEP SHEARS.

No. H,   16½ Plain, 7 inch Handle, 4½ inch Blade....per dozen, $
No. G, 3766 Plain, 7 inch Handle, 4½ inch Blade... "
No. G, 3767 Plain, 7 inch Handle, 4½ inch Blade.... "
No.   125 Plain, 7 inch Handle, 4½ inch Blade.
  Trowel Shank........................... "
No.   100 B. P. Spring, 7 in. Handle, 4½ in. Blade. "
No. H,   16½ P. Spring, 7 in. Handle, 4½ in. Blade... "
No. G, 3766 P. Spring, 7 in. Handle, 4½ in. Blade... "
No. G, 3767 P. Spring, 7 in. Handle, 4½ in. Blade... "
No.   125 P. Spring, 7 in. Handle, 4½ in. Blade,
  Trowel Shank................. "

German Sheep Shears.

	$		
Half Polished Plain,	11	12	per dozen. inch.
	$		
Full Polished Plain,	11	12	per dozen. inch.
	$		
Full Polished, Patent Spring,	11	12	per dozen. inch.
	$		
Trowel Shank, Patent Spring,	11	12	per dozen. inch.

Bush Hooks.

With Handle, Cast Steel ....per dozen, $
Without Handle, Extra Cast Steel.................. "

Cotton Hooks.

No. 1, New Orleans Pattern, Cast Steel, Black Handle.per dozen, $
No. 2, New Orleans Pattern, Cast Steel, Black Handle. "
No. 3, Red River Pattern, Cast Steel.................per dozen, $
No. 4, Georgia Pattern, Cast Steel.................. "

Ox Yokes and Bows.

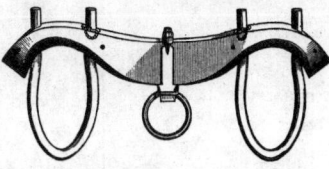

	$					
Ox Yokes, No.	1	2	3	4	5	each.
	$					
Ox Bows,		1¾		2		each. inch.

For Ox Bow Pins, see page 269.

AGRICULTURAL IMPLEMENTS.

(Continued.)

PLOWS.

No. 33, Stubble Plow.

No. X 1, Steel Plow.

PLOWS.

(Continued.)

No. X 4½, Steel Plow.

No. X 8½, Steel Plow.

EAGLE PLOWS.

Kinds.	Nos.	Plain.	Cutter.	Wheel and Cutter.	D. Rod Wheel and Cutter.
Light Horse	14				
Light Horse	14½				
Medium Horse	15				
Small Horse	A 1				
Medium Horse	A 2				
One Horse	1 B				
Two Horse	2 B				
Davis 6 inch Cotton					
Davis 7 inch Cotton					
Rice, Trenching					
One Horse	P. 18				
One Horse	P. 18½				
One Horse	P. 19				
One Horse	P. 19½				
Two Horse	P. 20				
Two Horse	P. 21				
Two Horse	P. 22				

IMPROVED EAGLE PLOWS.

Kinds.	Nos.	Plain.	Cutter.s	Wheel and Cutter.	D. Rod Wheel and Cutter.
One Horse	A				
One Horse	0				
Sod Plow	1				
Sod Plow	1, Coult				
Light Sod	2				
Light Sod	2, Coult				
Large Sod	20				
Large Sod	20, Coult				
Heavy	28, Coult				
Light Sod	36				
Medium Sward	B				
Medium Sward	C				
Medium Coult	D, Coult				
Left Hand	46				
Left Hand	47				

PATENT IMPROVED STEEL PLOWS.

Description.	No.	D. Rod or Scotch Clevis.	Cutter.	Wheel and Cutter.
Stubble or Old Ground Plows.				
Old Ground, Stubble, Furrows 4 to 6 in. deep, 7 to 9 in. wide, right hand, light, one horse..	X 00			
Old Ground, Stubble, Furrows 4 to 6 in. deep, 8 to 10 in. wide, right hand, light, one horse	X 0			
Old Ground, Stubble, Furrows 4 to 6 in. deep, 9 to 10 in. wide, right hand, one horse	X 1			
Old Ground, Stubble, Furrows 4 to 8 in. deep, 10 to 12 in. wide, right hand, light. two horses	X 1½			
Old Ground, Stubble, Furrows 5 to 8 in. deep, 12 to 14 in. wide, right hand, two to three horses	X 4			
Old Ground, Stubble, Furrows 5 to 8 in. deep, 12 to 14 in. wide, right hand, two to three horses	X 4½			
Old Ground, Stubble, Furrows 6 to 9 in. deep, 12 to 14 in. wide, narrow cut, right hand, two to three horses	X 6			
Old Ground, Stubble, Furrows 6 to 9 in. deep, 12 to 14 in. wide, left hand, narrow cut, two to three horses	X 7			
Old Ground, Stubble, Furrows 5 to 10 in. deep, 10 to 12 in. wide, right hand, medium, two horses	X 8			
Old Ground, Stubble, Furrows 5 to 10 in. deep, 12 to 14 in. wide, right hand, medium, two horses	X 8½			
Old Ground, Stubble, Furrows 5 to 10 in. deep, 10 to 12 in. wide, left hand, medium, two horses	X 9			

AGRICULTURAL IMPLEMENTS.

(Continued.)

STEEL PLOWS.
(Continued.)

Description.	No.	D. Rod or Scotch Clevis.	Cutter.	Wheel and Cutter.
Prairie Plows.				
Prairie, Sod, Furrows 4 to 6 in. deep, 12 to 14 in. wide, right hand, two to three horses.	U G 3½			
Prairie, Sod, Furrows 4 to 6 in. deep, 14 to 16 in. wide, left hand, two to three horses.	U G 4			
Prairie, Sod, Furrows 4 to 6 in. deep, 14 to 16 in. wide, right hand, two to three horses.	U G 5			
Lap Sod, Lap Furrows 7 in. deep, 10 in. wide, right hand, for stiff clay soil, two to three horses.	W B 2			
Sod Furrows, 6 to 10 in. deep, 16 in. to 18 in. wide, four horses.	X 6½			

PATENT IMPROVED DEEP-TILLING PLOWS—CAST IRON.

Description.	Nos.	D. Rod or Scotch Clevis.	Cutter.	Wheel and Cutter.
Stubble or Old Ground Plows.				
Old Ground, Stubble, Furrows 4 to 6 in. deep, 8 to 10 in. wide, one horse	No. 30			
Old Ground, Stubble, Furrows 6 to 8 in. deep, 9 to 11 in. wide, small, two horse.	No. 31			
Old Ground, Stubble, Furrows 6 to 8 in. deep, 9 to 11 in. wide, Steel Share, two horse	No. 31½			
Old Ground, Stubble, Furrows suitable for Western and California soils, Steel Share.	No. 31¾			
Old Ground, Stubble, Furrows 6 to 9 in. deep, 9 to 12 in. wide, medium, two horse	No. 32			
Old Ground, Stubble, Furrows 8 to 10 in. deep, 11 to 13 in. wide, large, two to three horses	No. 33			
Old Ground, Stubble, Furrows 9 to 11 in. deep, 12 to 14 in. wide, large, two to three horses	No. 34			
Old Ground, Stubble, Furrows 8 to 12 in. deep, 12 to 15 in. wide, large, three to four horses	No. 35			
Old Ground, Stubble, Furrows 8 to 12 in. deep, 14 to 18 in. wide, three to four horses, is adapted to burying of broom corn	No. 39			

KNOX'S PATENT HORSE HOE.

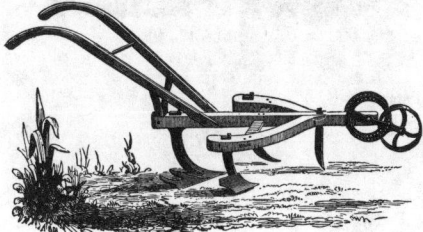

Knox's Patent Horse Hoe.

Horse Hoe, Steel, No. 1 ....$
Horse Hoe, Steel, No. 2 ....
Horse Hoe, Steel, No. 3 ....

	No. 1.	No. 2.	No. 3.
Center Plow, or Tooth, for Horse Hoe			
Two Side Plows, per pair			
Front Tooth,			

HARROWS.

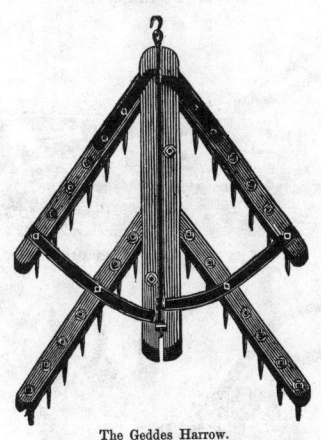

The Geddes Harrow.

Improved Hinge Harrow.

Kinds.	No. of Teeth.	Size of Teeth.	Price.
Geddes	14	¾ in.	$
Geddes	18	¾ in.	
Geddes	22	⅞ in.	
Geddes	22	1 in.	
Geddes	26	⅞ in.	
Geddes	30	⅞ in	
Geddes	30	1 in.	
A	11	¾ in.	
A	13	¾ in.	
A	15	⅞ in.	
A heavy	15	1¼ in.	
A	17	1 in.	
Expanding } Reversible }	20	⅞ in.	
Expanding } Reversible }	20	¾ in.	
Scotch, No. 1	32	¾ in.	
Scotch, No. 2	32	⅞ in.	
Improved Hinge	24	⅞ in.	
Improved Hinge	30	⅞ in.	
Improved Hinge, Steel Teeth,	24	½ in.	
Improved Hinge, Steel Teeth,	24	⅞ in.	
Improved Hinge, Steel Teeth,	30	½ in.	
Improved Hinge, Steel Teeth,	30	⅞ in.	
Sizer's Cotton Harrow			
Cultivator Harrow			

AGRICULTURAL IMPLEMENTS.

(Continued.)

CULTIVATORS.

Knox's Patent Gang Cultivator.

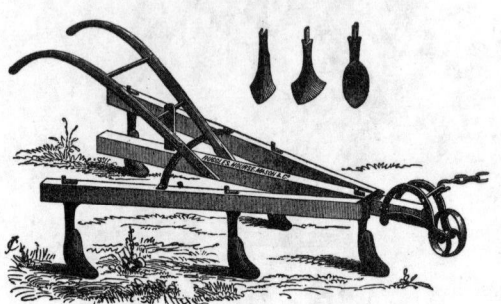

Expanding and Reversible-Tooth Cultivator.

Names.		No. of Teeth.	Clavis.	Wheel.
Old Pattern	Iron,	5		
No. 1 New Pattern	Iron,	5		
Reversible	Iron,	5		
Parallel	Iron,	5		
Parallel	Iron,	3		
Universal	Iron,	5		
Universal, with molds	Iron,	3		
Rogers' Patent	Steel,	5		
No. 2 New Reversible	Steel,	5		
Parallel Reversible	Steel,	5		
Knox's No. 1 Gang	Steel,	4		
Knox's No. 2 Gang	Steel,	6		
Cotton Sweep	......	No. 1		
Cotton Sweep	......	No. 2		

CULTIVATOR TEETH.

Set Cast Cultivator Teeth..$

Set Reversible Cultivator Teeth.............................

Set Reversible Cultivator, Steel Teeth....................

Set Rogers' Patent Steel Teeth............................

Set No. 2 New Reversible Steel Teeth.....................

Hand Hay Rakes.

Bent Handle Hay Rake, 2 Bow, 12 Teeth ....per dozen, $

Bent Handle Hay Rake, 3 Bow, 12 Teeth ....   "

Bent Handle Hay Rake, 3 Bow, 14 Teeth ....   "

Mortice Head Hay Rake...........................   "

Wood Barley Rake................................   "

HORSE HAY RAKES.

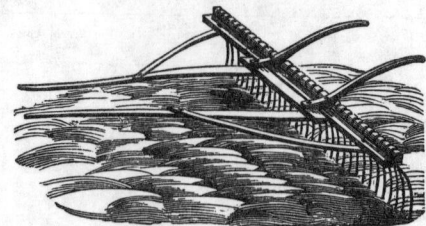

Wire Spring-Tooth Horse Rake.

Wire Spring-Tooth Horse Rake......................each, $

FAN MILLS.

Grant's Patent Fan Mill.

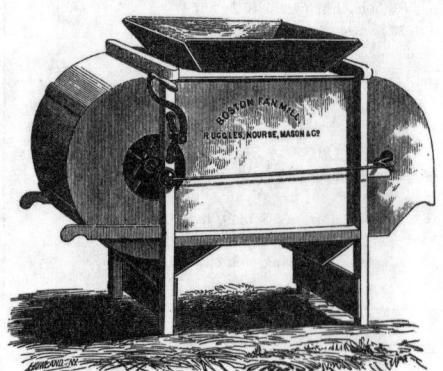

Boston Fan Mill.

	$					each.
Grant's Patent,	1	2	3	4	5	
Extra for Pulley................................each, $
	$					each.
Boston,	1	2	3	4		
Extra for Pulley................................each, $

Yankee..........each, $ Horizontal........each, $

POWER CORN SHELLERS.

Smith's Patent, No. 1......................................each, $

Smith's Patent, No. 2.....................................

Smith's Patent, No. 3.....................................

AGRICULTURAL IMPLEMENTS.

(Continued.)

CORN SHELLERS.

(Continued.)

Southern Sheller.

Armsby's Patent.

Each.

Yankee . . . . $

Yankee Sheller with Separator . . . .

Yankee, extra Wheel . . . .

Boston . . . .

Boston, extra Wheel . . . .

Boston, double . . . .

Boston, double, extra Wheel . . . .

Fitted with Pulley, extra, $

Southern . . . .

Southern, extra Wheel . . . .

Southern, double . . . .

Southern, double, extra Wheel . . . .

Western, No. 1, *single*, without side and inside balance wheels, and outside gearing . . . .

Western, No. 1, *double*, with outside and inside balance wheels, and outside gearing . . . .

Clinton, 1 Wheel . . . .

Clinton, 2 Wheels . . . .

Clinton, double, 2 Wheels . . . .

CHURNS.

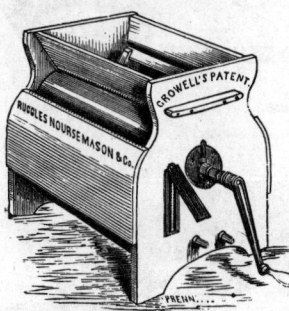

Crowell's Thermometer Churn.

$

No.	0	1	2	3	4	5	$5\frac{1}{2}$	6	each.
	$2\frac{1}{2}$	$4\frac{1}{2}$	6	9	$10\frac{1}{2}$	$14\frac{1}{2}$	20	28	galls.

Extra for Robbin' dash . . . . $

CHURNS.

(Continued.)

Improved Cylinder Churn.

No.	$	1	2	3	4	5	each.
		$2\frac{3}{4}$	4	7	$10\frac{1}{2}$	15 galls.	

STRAW AND HAY CUTTERS.

Daniel's Patent.

Daniels' Patent, 10 inch . . . . each, $

Telegraph.

Telegraph Hay and Fodder Cutter . . . . each, $

National Hay and Fodder Cutter . . . . "

Whittemore's Patent Self-Sharpening Straw and Hay Cutter.

	$						each.
No. of Cutter, ...	00	0	1	2	$2\frac{1}{2}$	3	4
No. of Knives, ...	5	6	7	8	10	6	8
Length of Knives .	$5\frac{3}{4}$	$5\frac{1}{4}$	$5\frac{3}{4}$	$5\frac{3}{4}$	$5\frac{3}{4}$	$6\frac{1}{4}$	$6\frac{3}{4}$ inches.
Length of Cut	$1\frac{3}{4}$	$1\frac{1}{2}$	$1\frac{3}{4}$	$1\frac{1}{4}$	1	$1\frac{1}{2}$	$1\frac{1}{4}$ inches.

	$					each.
No. of Cutter	5	$5\frac{1}{2}$	$5\frac{3}{4}$	6	7	8
No. of Knives	10	12	14	6	8	10
Length of Knives .	$6\frac{3}{4}$	$6\frac{3}{4}$	$6\frac{3}{4}$	$7\frac{1}{4}$	$7\frac{1}{4}$	$7\frac{1}{2}$ inches.
Length of Cut	1	$\frac{3}{4}$	$\frac{1}{2}$	$1\frac{3}{4}$	$1\frac{1}{4}$	1 inches.

AGRICULTURAL IMPLEMENTS.

(Continued.)

STRAW AND HAY CUTTERS.
(Continued.)
Whittemore's Patent—*(Continued.)*

	$							each.
No. of Cutter.....	9	10	11	12	13	14		
No. of Knives....	6	8	10	6	8	10		
Length of Knives.	8½	8½	8½	9½	9½	9½	inches.	
Length of Cut....	1¾	1½	1	1¾	1½	1½	inches.	

Nos. 12, 13 and 14 are fitted for power.

Hovey's Patent Hide Roller Straw and Hay Cutter.

	$							each.
No. of Cutter.....	0	1	1	1	2	2	2	
No. of Knives....	5	6	8	10	6	8	10	

	$						each.
No. of Cutter.....	3	3	3	4	4	4	
No. of Knives....	6	8	10	6	8	10	

	$						each.
No. of Cutter.....	5	5	5	6	6	6	
No. of Knives....	6	8	10	6	8	10	

No 6 Cutter is fitted for power.

WINE AND CIDER MILL.
With Press Combined.

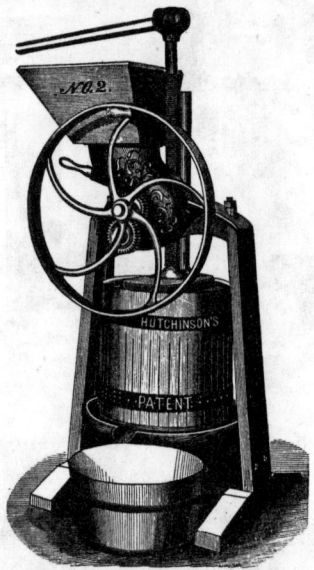

Hutchinson's Patent....................................each, $

This Mill, with the exception of the curb, is made wholly of iron; the parts that come in contact with the Fruit and Juice being prepared by a patent process, so that they do not affect it. It occupies less than two feet square space on the floor, weighs less than 160 pounds, and is easily handled. It has a large balance wheel, and can be worked by hand or power, as desired. It will grind from six to eight bushels of Apples or ten to twelve bushels of Grapes, Currants or other like Fruits, per hour. For simplicity, compactness, strength and economy of power, it is decidedly superior to anything in market.

STORE TRUCKS.

Plain.

	$						each.
No.	1	2	3	4	5	6	

STORE TRUCKS—Continued.
Strapped.

	$						each.
No.		2	3	4	5	6	

Barrel.

	$						each.
No.	1	2	3	4	5	6	

WHEEL BARROWS.

Canal Barrows, 1¼ inch tire..............................each, $
Canal Barrows, extra, 1½ inch tire...................... "
Canal Barrows, Iron Tray............................... "
No. 1 Garden Barrows, Boys' (Painted or Varnished)...... "
No. 2 Garden Barrows, (Painted or Varnished)........... "
No. 3 Garden Barrows, (Painted or Varnished)........... "
Stone Barrows.. "
Ore Barrows.. "
Small Coal Barrows..................................... "
Large Coal Barrows..................................... "

CYLINDER MEAT CUTTERS.

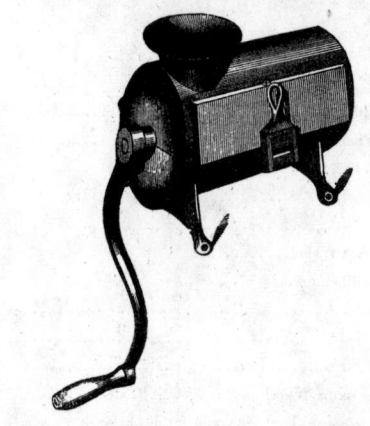

	$				per dozen.
No.	1	2	3	4.	

SAUSAGE STUFFERS.

Stow's Patent.

No. 0, for Butchers' use........................... per dozen, $
No. 1, for Family use............................. "

Railroad Pattern.

Railroad Pattern......................................per dozen, $

For Hale's Patent Meat Cutter and Stuffer, the best article made, see page 104.

BRASS AND IRON CHAIN.

JACK CHAIN.

These Plates represent the Exact Sizes.

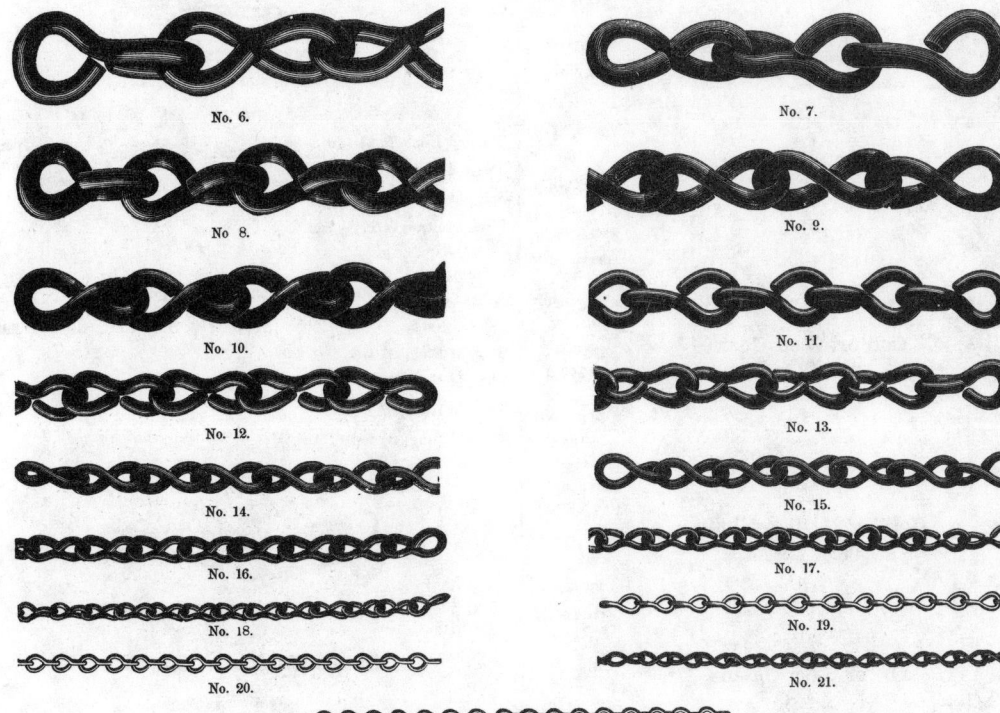

No. 6.   No. 7.

No. 8.   No. 9.

No. 10.   No. 11.

No. 12.   No. 13.

No. 14.   No. 15.

No. 16.   No. 17.

No. 18.   No. 19.

No. 20.   No. 21.

No. 22.

DOUBLE CHAIN.   SAFETY CHAIN.

No. 13.   No. 14, Safe.

No. 14.   No. 3.

No. 15.   No. 2.

No. 17   No. 1.

JACK CHAIN.

	$																	
Iron, Nos.	5	6	7	8	9	10	11	12	13	14	15	16	17	18	19	20	21	22.	per doz.
Brass, Nos.	$ 8	9	10	11	12	13	14	15	16	17	18	19	20	21	22.				per doz.
Silvered, Nos.	$ 12	13	14	15	16	17	18	19	20	21	22.								per dozen.

DOUBLE CHAIN.

	$					
Brass, Nos.	13	15	17	19	20.	per dozen.
Iron, Nos.	$	15		19		per dozen.
Silvered, Nos.	$ 13	15	17	19	21.	per dozen.

SAFETY CHAIN.

	$			
Brass, Nos.	1	2	3.	per dozen.
Silvered, Nos.	$ 1	2	3.	per dozen.

HALTER, COIL, BREAST AND TRACE CHAINS.

Halter Chain.
Regular Length, 4 1-2 feet.

$						per dozen.
Nos.	000	00	0	1	2	3
Nos.	5	6	7	8	9	10	wire gauge.
$						per dozen.
Nos.	4	5	6	7	8	
Nos.	12	13	14	15	16	wire gauge.

Extra Length, 6 feet.

$						per dozen.
Nos.	000	00	0	1	2	3
Nos.	5	6	7	8	9	10	wire gauge.
$						per dozen.
Nos.	4	5	6	7	8	
Nos.	12	13	14	15	16	wire gauge.

Coil or Well Chain.

$					per 100 ft.
Nos.	000	00	0	1	2
Nos.	4	5	6	8	9	wire gauge.
$					per 100 ft.
Nos.	3	4	5	6	
Nos.	10	11	12	13		wire gauge.

Coil or Cable Chain.
Self-Colored or Black.

$\frac{3}{16}$	$\frac{1}{4}$	$\frac{5}{16}$	$\frac{3}{8}$	$\frac{7}{16}$	$\frac{1}{2}$	$\frac{9}{16}$	$\frac{5}{8}$	$\frac{3}{4}$	$\frac{7}{8}$	1	inch.
Straight,											cts. per lb.
Twisted,											"

Ox or Log Chains.

Bright, 8 to 12 feet   per lb.

$\frac{5}{16}$	$\frac{3}{8}$	$\frac{7}{16}$	$\frac{1}{2}$	inch.

Binding or Fifth Chains.

Two Hooks, 9 to 11 feet   per lb.

$\frac{5}{16}$	$\frac{3}{8}$	inch.

Breast Chains.

Single . . . . per dozen pair, $
Double or Star . . . . "

Stay Chains.

No. 2, Twist, 12 link . . . . per dozen, $

Tongue Chains.

No. 2, Straight, 12 link . . . . per dozen, $
No. 3, Twist, 14 link . . . . "

Trace Chains.

No.	1	2	3	
	10, 12	10, 12, 14, 16	10, 12, 14	link.

Straight Hook, 6½ feet, $	per pair.
Straight Hook, 7 feet,	"
Straight Ring, 6½ feet,	"
Straight Ring, 7 feet,	"
Twisted Hook, 6½ feet,	"
Twisted Hook, 7 feet,	"
Twisted Ring, 6½ feet,	"
Twisted Ring, 7 feet,	"

Stage Traces.

No.	3	4	
	12, 14	12, 14	link.

Twisted Hook T, 3½ feet, $	per pair.
Twisted Straight T, 3½ feet,	"
Straight Hook T, 3½ feet,	"
Straight Straight T, 3½ feet,	"

Butt Chains or Half Traces.

No. 2,	12	14	16	link.

Straight Ring, 3½ feet, $	per pair.
Straight Hook, 3½ feet,	"
Twisted Hook, 3½ feet,	"
Twisted Ring, 3½ feet,	"

Stretcher Chains.

No. 1, 10 link, 3 feet . . . . per dozen, $

Cattle Chains or Cow Ties.

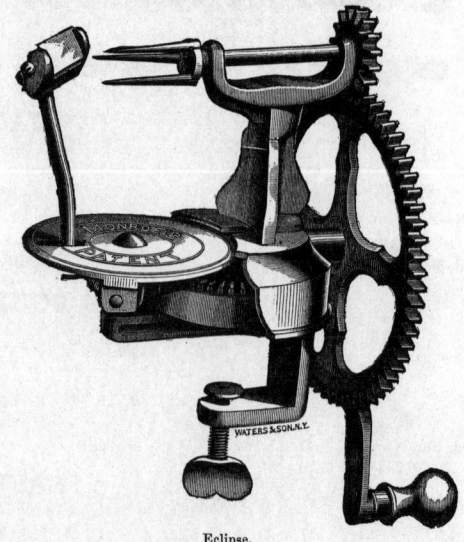

Closed Ring, Light, 5 inch . . . . per dozen, $
Closed Ring, Heavy, 5 inch . . . . "
Open Ring, Light, 6 inch . . . . "
Open Ring, Heavy, 6 inch . . . . "
Straight T and Center Ring . . . . "
Straight T and Center Triangle . . . . "

APPLE PARERS.

Eclipse.

Eclipse Apple Parer . . . . per dozen, $

APPLE PARERS, PAINT AND COFFEE MILLS.

APPLE PARERS.
(Continued.)

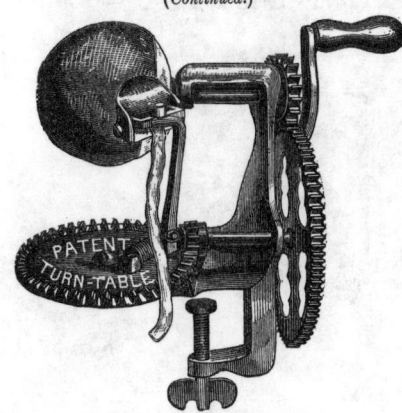

Turn Table.

Turn Table Apple Parers........................per dozen, $

Conqueror.

Conqueror Apple Parers........................per dozen, $
Sargent & Foster's Patent Apple Parers..............   "

HORIZONTAL PAINT MILLS.
Adams' Patent.

No. 0.   No. 1.   No. 2.

No. 0, Geared Mill, 2, in a Box....................per dozen, $
No. 1, 2, in a Box.................................   "
No. 2, 6, in a Box ....   "

IMPROVED CONICAL OR SPIRAL PAINT MILLS.
Adams' Patent.

No. 5.

IMPROVED CONICAL PAINT MILLS.
(Continued.)

No. 4.   No. 3.

The Spiral Mill is of later introduction than the Horizontal; its chief properties are greater speed in grinding, with at least equal excellence and durability.

No. 3, packed 6 in a Box, 65 lbs.................per dozen, $
No. 4, packed 6 in a Box, 70 lbs....................   "
No. 5, packed 2 in a Box, 65 lbs....................   "

Harris' Patent.

No. 1, Power Mill................................each, $
    Pulleys for Power Mill...........................   "
No. 2, Medium Mill...............................   "
    Pulleys for Medium Mill..........................   "
No. 3, Small Mill................................   "
No. 4, Small Polish Mill.........................   "
No. 5, Medium Polish Mill........................   "
No. 6, Large Polish Mill, with Fly Wheel..............   "

Glaziers' Diamonds.

Glaziers' Diamonds, Common.....................each, $
Glaziers' Diamonds, with Guard......................   "

COFFEE MILLS.
Selsor, Cook & Co's Cast Steel.

No. 40.

No. 10, Friction, Iron Hopper ....per dozen, $
No. 15, Friction, Britannia Hopper..................   "
No. 20, Friction, Britannia Hopper..................   "
No. 25, Anti-Friction, Britannia Hopper ....   "
No. 30, Anti-Friction, Cherry Box, Britannia Hopper .   "
No. 40, Anti-Friction, Cherry Box, Britannia Hopper .   "

WILSON'S GENUINE COFFEE MILLS.
Wrought Iron Cranks.

No. 1, with Covers...............................per dozen, $
No. 2, with Covers...............................   "
No. 3, with Covers...............................   "
No. 4, with Covers...............................   "
No. 5, with Covers...............................   "
No. 11, all Iron, new Pattern.......................   "

COFFEE MILLS.

PATENT PLANTERS' MILL.

Planters' Mill . . . . per dozen, $

This Mill is especially adapted for Planters, Hotels, Steamboats, Boarding Houses and Family use.

PATENT UNION MILLS

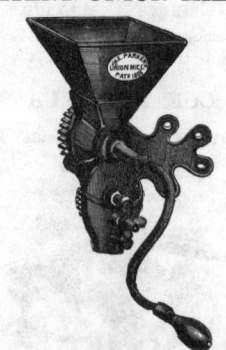

No. 10, all Iron . . . . per dozen, $

No. 15, Wood Back . . . . per dozen, $

No. 20, Wood Back . . . . per dozen, $

PATENT UNION MILLS—(Continued.)

No. 30, Wood Back . . . . per dozen, $

PATENT UNION BOX MILL.

Three Styles, all of One Size.

No. 25, with Iron Hoppers, in half-dozen boxes . . . . . . per dozen, $

No. 35, with Britannia Hoppers, in half-dozen boxes . . .   "

No. 45, with Britannia Hoppers, with nice Cherry or

     Black Walnut Boxes, in half-dozen boxes . . . .

NOTE. The Box, in the above illustration, is cut away upon one corner, to show the working part of the Mill.

PATENT EAGLE COFFEE MILLS.

No.	$				per dozen.
	50	60	70	80	

The peculiar advantage this Mill possesses over the ordinary Board Mills is that the regulating screw is on the front of the Mill, and the bearing of the Runner or Grinder is at both ends, doing away with the guard teeth, and so arranged that it cannot clog or fill up, so as to prevent grinding.

COFFEE MILLS AND ROASTERS.

WOOD BACK COFFEE MILLS.

California, Extra Large Size, in boxes of ⅓ dozen each .per dozen, $

No. 0, in boxes of ⅔ dozen each .... "

No. 1, Large Size, in boxes of ½ dozen each .... "

No. 2, Medium Size, in boxes of 1 dozen each .... "

No. 3, Smallest Size, in boxes of 1 dozen each .... "

Imitation Wilson Size of No. 3, in boxes of 1 doz. each. "

No. 1, Rough and Ready, in boxes of 1 dozen each... "

No. 2, Rough and Ready, small, in boxes of 1 doz. each. "

BOX COFFEE OR SPICE MILL.

In Half Dozen Boxes.

No. 1, Britannia Hoppers .... per dozen, $

No. 2, Britannia Hoppers .... "

No. 3, Britannia Hoppers .... "

No. 1, Iron Hoppers .... "

No. 2, Iron Hoppers .... "

No. 3, Iron Hoppers .... "

With Mineral Knobs, per dozen, extra............... "

SWIFT'S PATENT COFFEE MILLS.

No. 0, Family Post Mill .... per dozen, $

No. 1, Family Post Mill .... "

No. 2, Family Post Mill .... "

No. 3, Frame Mill, with Fly Wheel .... each, $

No. 4, Frame Mill, with Fly Wheel .... "

Drug Mill .... "

Hand and Horse Grain Mill.

Hand and Horse Grain Mill .... each, $

Sugar Mills.

Box Sugar Mill.

No. 1, for Barrel .... each, $

No. 1, with Box or Legs .... "

No. 2, with Box or Legs .... "

No. 3, with Box or Legs .... "

No. 4, with Box or Legs .... "

Butterfield's .... "

Sugar Cane Crushers.

No. 1, Improved, 3 Rollers .... each, $

No. 2, Improved, 3 Rollers .... "

COFFEE ROASTERS.

Hyde's Patent Coffee Roaster.

No. 1, Diam. of Cover 8½ inches, Capacity ¼ to 2 lbs .... each, $

No. 2, Diam. of Cover 11 inches, Capacity ½ to 4 lbs .... "

No. 3, Size 11×22 inches, Capacity 1 to 10 lbs .... "

This Roaster is made in the form of a stove cover, with a revolving cylinder attached, in which are patent propellers acting on the principle of a screw, that agitate the coffee and force it from end to end, thereby insuring a uniform roast. By means of a hollow journal, the substance to be roasted is put into the cylinder. A patent tryer closes the orifice in the journal, by using which the operator can at any moment see the state of the substance he is roasting, without stopping the motion of the cylinder. When roasted, the coffee can be discharged through the same opening by lifting the cylinder with the handle.

COFFEE ROASTERS, STRAINERS, ETC.

Hyde's Patent Coffee Roaster and Stove Combined, for Hotels and other Use.

No. 1, Stove and Roaster, Capacity from 20 to 35 lbs.......each, $

No. 2, Stove and Roaster (Hand or Power), Capacity from 40 to 70 lbs.................................... "

No. 3, Stove and Roaster (for Power), Capacity from 80 to 140 lbs..................................... "

No. 4, Stove and Roaster (for Power), Double, Capacity 150 to 280 lbs.................................... "

Cylinder Coffee Roasters.

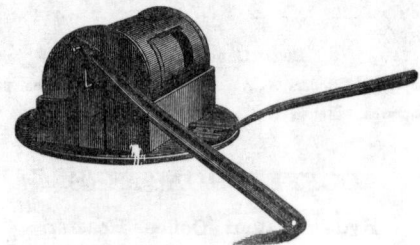

Cast Iron Frame, Russia Iron Cylinder.

No. $ 1   2   3.   per dozen.

Patent Globe Coffee Roasters.

7 Inch...per dozen, $

9 Inch... "

PATENT WIRE GAUZE STRAINERS.
Tea or Coffee Strainers.

Tin Plated, 1¾ inch.................................per dozen, $

Silver Plated, Solid Rims, 1¾ inch.................. "

Urn or Faucet Strainers.

No. 1, 1¾ in.   No. 2, 2⅛ in.

Tin Plated.........................$ per doz.

Silver Plated, Wire Strengthened Rims   "

Silver Plated, Solid Rims ....   "

Handle Strainers.

TWO SIZES.

No. 1, 2½ inch.   No. 2, 3¼ inch.

Tin Plated, Spoon Handle....$ per doz.

Tin Plated, Twisted Handle..   "

Silver Plated, Twisted Handle   "

For Straining Nursery and Fancy Drinks, Starch, Yeast, Blanc Mange, Custards, Gravies, Syrups, Jellies, and for Sifting Sugar upon Fruit, Cakes and Pies.

FOSTER'S STRAIGHT SPRING BALANCE.

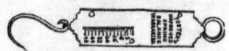

With Hook.

24 lbs., Hook, Extra Light.........................per dozen, $

24 lbs., Hook, Light................................. "

24 lbs., Hook, Heavy................................ "

48 lbs., Hook, Heavy................................ "

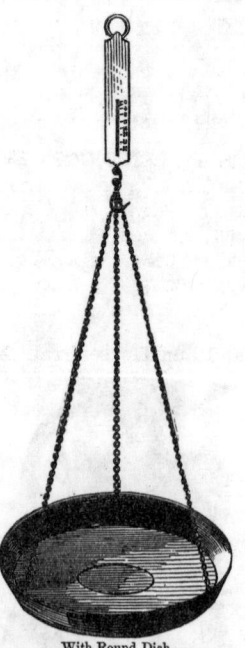

With Round Dish.

24 lbs., Round Dish, Light.........................per dozen, $

24 lbs., Round Dish, Heavy......................... "

48 lbs., Round Dish, Heavy......................... "

SPRING BALANCES.

(*Continued.*)

FOSTER'S STRAIGHT SPRING BALANCE.
(*Continued.*)

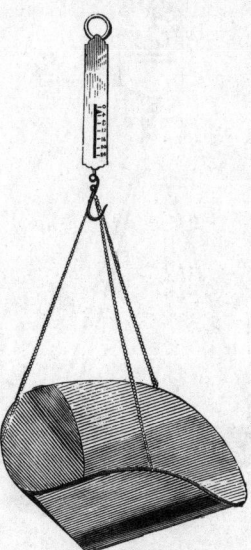

With Scoop.

24 lbs. by ½ lb., Light.............................per dozen, $
24 lbs. by ½ lb., Heavy.............................   "
48 lbs. by 1 lb., Heavy.............................   "

Best Improved Spring Balance.
Warranted equal in quality to any in Market.

With Hook.

12 lbs. by ¼ lb...........................per dozen, $
24 lbs. by ¼ lb...........................   "
30 lbs. by ½ lb...........................   "
40 lbs. by ½ lb...........................   "
50 lbs. by 1 lb...........................   "
60 lbs. by 1 lb...........................   "
80 lbs. by 1 lb...........................   "
100 lbs. by 1 lb...........................   "
125 lbs. by 1 lb...........................   "
200 lbs. by 2 lbs., Ice Balance...........................   "
300 lbs. by 2 lbs., Ice Balance...........................   "

With Round Dish.

12 lbs. by ¼ lb...........................per dozen, $
24 lbs. by ½ lb...........................   "
30 lbs. by ½ lb...........................   "
40 lbs. by ½ lb...........................   "
50 lbs. by 1 lb...........................   "
60 lbs. by 1 lb...........................   "
80 lbs. by 1 lb...........................   "

With Scoop.

12 lbs. by ¼ lb...........................per dozen, $
24 lbs. by ½ lb...........................   "
30 lbs. by ½ lb...........................   "
40 lbs. by ½ lb...........................   "
50 lbs. by 1 lb...........................   "

IMPROVED SPRING BALANCE.
(*Continued.*)

With Square Dish.

24 lbs. by ½ lb.............................per dozen, $
30 lbs. by ½ lb.............................   "
40 lbs. by ½ lb.............................   "
50 lbs. by 1 lb.............................   "
60 lbs. by 1 lb.............................   "
80 lbs. by 1 lb.............................   "
100 lbs. by 1 lb.............................   "
120 lbs. by 1 lb.............................   "

Round Balance.

With Hook.

24 lbs. by ½ lb.............................per dozen, $

With Round Dish.

24 lbs. by ½ lb.............................per dozen, $

With Scoop.

24 lbs. by ½ lb.............................per dozen, $

Frary's Family Balance.

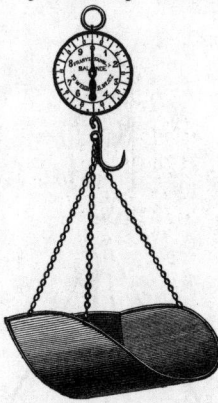

With Hook.

10 lbs. by 1 ounce.............................per dozen, $
20 lbs. by 2 ounces.............................   "

With Round Dish.

10 lbs. by 1 ounce.............................per dozen, $
20 lbs. by 2 ounces.............................   "

With Scoop.

10 lbs. by 1 ounce.............................per dozen, $
20 lbs. by 2 ounces.............................   "

SPRING BALANCES.

(Continued.)

Best Improved Circular Spring Balance.

With Hook.

30 lbs. by 1 oz..................................per dozen, $
60 lbs. by 2 oz..................................   "
120 lbs. by 4 oz..................................   "

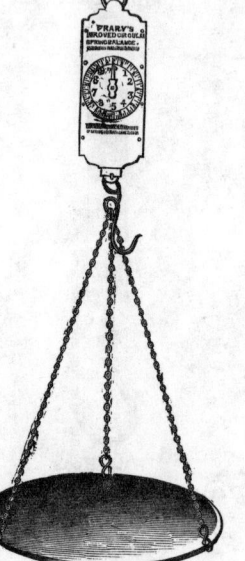

With Round Dish.

30 lbs. by 1 oz..................................per dozen, $
60 lbs. by 2 oz..................................   "
120 lbs. by 4 oz..................................   "

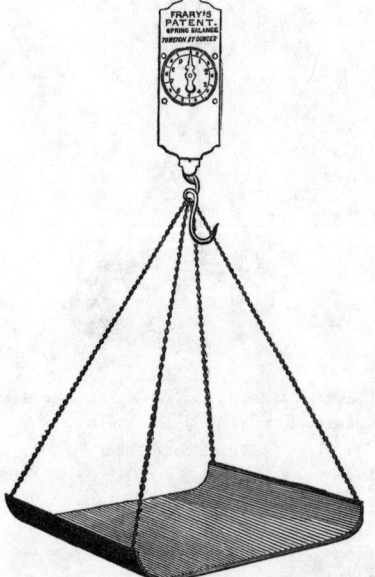

With Square Dish.

30 lbs. by 1 oz..................................per dozen, $
60 lbs. by 2 oz..................................   "
120 lbs. by 4 oz..................................   "

Best Improved Circular Spring Balance.

(Continued.)

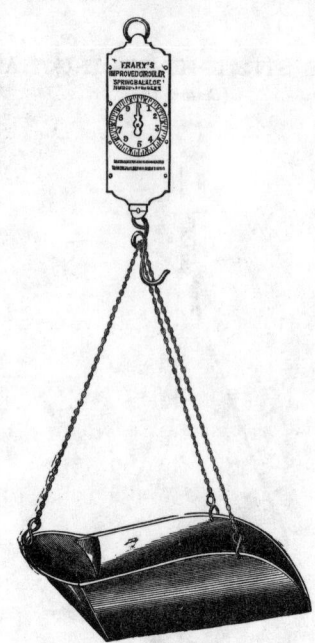

With Scoop.

30 lbs. by 1 oz..................................per dozen, $
60 lbs. by 2 oz..................................   "

Butcher's Circular Spring Balance.

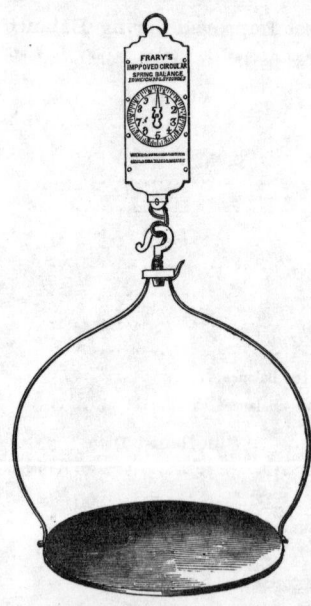

30 lbs. by 1 oz., Tin Pan, Brass Bows..............per dozen, $

60 lbs. by 2 oz., Tin Pan, Brass Bows..............   "

120 lbs. by 4 oz., Tin Pan, Brass Bows..............   "

30 lbs. by 1 oz., Brass Pan, Brass Bow and Swivel....   "

60 lbs. by 2 oz., Brass Pan, Brass Bow and Swivel....   "

120 lbs. by 4 oz., Brass Pan, Brass Bow and Swivel....   "

Extra Heavy.

30 lbs. by 1 oz., Brass Pan, Brass Bow and Swivel....   "

60 lbs. by 2 oz., Brass Pan, Brass Bow and Swivel....   "

120 lbs. by 4 oz., Brass Pan, Brass Bow and Swivel....   "

SPRING BALANCES AND STEELYARDS.

Tubular Locomotive Balances.

50 lbs., Figured to order...............................each, $

75 lbs., Figured to order.............................. "

80 lbs., Figured to order.............................. "

84 lbs., Figured to order.............................. "

100 lbs., Figured to order.............................. "

150 lbs., Figured to order.............................. "

200 lbs., Figured to order.............................. "

Spiral Springs, and Spring Balances made to order.

Turkish, Chinese, Portuguese, French, Russian, Japanese and Spanish Weight Balances made to order.

STEELYARDS.

Improved English Pattern.

Made from superior stock, with great care, and sealed, and warranted to weigh correct.

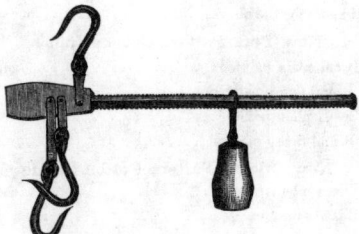

50 lbs., Improved English Pattern...................per dozen, $

100 lbs., Improved English Pattern.................. "

150 lbs., Improved English Pattern.................. "

200 lbs., Improved English Pattern.................. "

250 lbs., Improved English Pattern.................. "

300 lbs., Improved English Pattern.................. "

400 lbs., Improved English Pattern.................. "

500 lbs., Improved English Pattern.................. "

Farmers' Steelyards.

Are equal to the English Pattern for durability and correctness, and are sealed and warranted to weigh correct.

50 lbs..................................per dozen, $

100 lbs.. "

150 lbs.. "

200 lbs.. "

250 lbs.. "

300 lbs.. "

400 lbs.. "

500 lbs.. "

Butchers' and Planters' Steelyards.

Are extra heavy goods, made with very heavy bars, clevs and pivots, and with two hooks on the long clev. They are designed more particularly for Butchers' use; not liable to be broken or get out of order, and warranted a perfect weighing Steelyard.

50 lbs..................................per dozen, $

100 lbs.. "

150 lbs.. "

50 lbs., extra finish.............................. "

100 lbs., extra finish.............................. "

150 lbs., extra finish.............................. "

Steelyards—(Continued.)

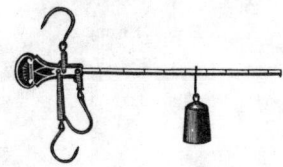

50 lbs., Common....................per dozen, $

50 lbs., Imitation.............................. "

50 lbs., Steel Bar.............................. "

100 lbs., Steel Bar.............................. "

150 lbs., Steel Bar.............................. "

200 lbs.. Steel Bar.............................. "

250 lbs., Steel Bar.............................. "

300 lbs., Steel Bar.............................. "

50 lbs., Steel Bar, extra heavy.............................. "

100 lbs., Steel Bar, extra heavy.............................. "

150 lbs., Steel Bar, extra heavy.............................. "

200 lbs., Steel Bar, extra heavy.............................. "

250 lbs., Steel Bar, extra heavy.............................. "

300 lbs., Steel Bar, extra heavy.............................. "

50 lbs., Steel Bar, extra polish.............................. "

50 lbs., Steel Bar, Collins' pattern.............................. "

100 lbs., Steel Bar, Collins' pattern.............................. "

Hammond's Patent Balance Head.

Solid Steel, all Polished Steelyards.

50 lbs., *with* stop, plain.........................per dozen, $

50 lbs., *without* stop, plain.............................. "

50 lbs., *with* stop, extra finish.............................. "

50 lbs., *without* stop, extra finish.............................. "

100 lbs., *with* stop, extra finish.............................. "

150 lbs., *with* stop, extra finish.............................. "

200 lbs., *with* stop, extra finish.............................. "

225 lbs., *with* stop, extra finish.............................. "

250 lbs., *with* stop, extra finish.............................. "

300 lbs., *with* stop, extra finish.............................. "

350 lbs., *with* stop, extra finish.............................. "

400 lbs., *with* stop, extra finish.............................. "

500 lbs., *with* stop, extra finish.............................. "

600 lbs., *with* stop, extra finish.............................. "

Weighmasters' Beams and Frames.

Iron Beams.

Price estimated for the beam and weights alone by the 100 lbs. capacity, from 300 lbs. upward. All of less capacity rated the same as 300 lbs.

Best Polished Beams.....................per 100 lbs. capacity, $

Best Japanned Beams................... "

SCALE BEAMS AND COUNTER SCALES.

Weighmasters' Beams and Frames.

(Continued.)

Brass Beams.

Capacity.	With Brass Poises.	With Zinc Poises.	With Iron Poises with Brass Hooks.
100 lbs..............each, $		$	$
150 lbs.............. "			
200 lbs.............. "			
300 lbs.............. "			
400 lbs.............. "			
500 lbs.............. "			
600 lbs.............. "			
800 lbs.............. "			
1,000 lbs.............. "			
1,200 lbs.............. "			
1,500 lbs.............. "			
2,000 lbs.............. "			
2,500 lbs.............. "			
3,000 lbs.............. "			

New York Pattern Cotton Beam.

Notched.

	With Iron Poises.	With Brass Poises.
Polished Beam, weighing 640 lbs. on each side....each, $		$
Polished Beam, weighing 800 lbs. on each side.... "		
Japanned Beam, weighing 640 lbs. on each side.... "		
Japanned Beam, weighing 800 lbs. on each side.... "		

New Orleans Pattern Cotton Beam.

Smooth Top.

	With Two Brass Poises.
Polished Beam, weighing 640 lbs. on each side............each, $	
Polished Beam, weighing 800 lbs. on each side............ "	
Japanned Beam, weighing 640 lbs. on each side............ "	
Japanned Beam, weighing 800 lbs. on each side............ "	

Frames for Weighmasters' Beams.

Capacity.	Single lever, plain painted.	Single lever, fancy painted. extra finish.	Double lever, plain painted.	Double lever, fancy painted. extra finish.
800 lbs. and under, each, $		$	$	$
1,000 lbs. and under, "				
1,200 lbs. and under, "				
1,500 lbs. and under, "				
2,000 lbs. and under, "				
2,500 lbs. and under, "				
3,000 lbs. and under, "				
4,000 lbs. and under, "				
5,000 lbs. and under, "				
6,000 lbs. and under, "				

Chain down-hauls for the above......................per set, $

New York Pattern Cotton Frame.

For 640 lbs. Beam, plain painted...........................each, $
For 640 lbs. Beam, fancy painted........................... "
For 800 lbs. Beam, plain painted........................... "
For 800 lbs. Beam, fancy painted......................... "

New Orleans Pattern Cotton Frame.

For 640 lbs. Beam, plain painted.........................each, $
For 640 lbs. Beam, fancy painted......................... "
For 800 lbs. Beam, plain painted .... "
For 800 lbs. Beam, fancy painted .... "

TURNBULL'S PATENT COUNTER SCALES.

No. 10.

No. 50.

No. 10, Capacity ½ oz. to 8 lbs., with Tin Scoop..........each, $
No. 11, Capacity ½ oz. to 8 lbs., with Tin Scoop, Glass Sash, "
No. 12, Capacity ½ oz. to 8 lbs., with Brass Scoop, Glass Sash, "
No. 20, Capacity ½ oz. to 16 lbs., with Tin Scoop..........
No. 21, Capacity ½ oz. to 16 lbs., with Tin Scoop, Glass Sash, "
No. 22, Capacity ½ oz. to 16 lbs., with Brass Scoop, Glass Sash, "
No. 23, Capacity ½ oz. to 16 lbs., with Tin Scoop, Platform and Poise.......................... "
No. 24, Capacity ½ oz. to 16 lbs., with Tin Scoop, Platform and Poise, Glass Sash.......................... "
No. 25, Capacity ½ oz. to 16 lbs., with Brass Scoop, Platform and Poise, Glass Sash.......................... "

No. 27, Capacity 1 oz. to 32 lbs., with Tin Scoop..........each, $
No. 28, Capacity 1 oz. to 32 lbs., with Tin Scoop, Glass Sash, "
No. 29, Capacity 1 oz. to 32 lbs., with Brass Scoop, Glass Sash, "
No. 30, Capacity 1 oz. to 32 lbs., with Tin Scoop, Platform and Poise .... "
No. 31, Capacity 1 oz. to 32 lbs., with Tin Scoop, Glass Sash, Platform and Poise........................ "
No. 32, Capacity 1 oz. to 32 lbs., with Brass Scoop, Glass Sash, Platform and Poise....................... "
No. 40, Capacity 2 oz. to 64 lbs., with Tin Scoop, Platform and Poise................................. "

COUNTER SCALES.

(Continued.)

No. 33, 32 lb. Butchers' Scale.

Turnbull's Patent Counter Scales.

(Continued.)

No. 41, Capacity 2 oz. to 64 lbs., with Tin Scoop, Glass
Sash, Platform and Poise........................each, $

No. 42, Capacity 2 oz., to 64 lbs., with Brass Scoop; Glass
Sash, Platform and Poise....................... "

No. 50, Capacity 1 oz. to 32 lbs., in Scoop, ½ lb. to 256 lbs.
on Platform, with Tin Scoop, Glass Sash (see plate,
opposite page)............................... "

No. 51, Capacity 1 oz. to 32 lbs. in Scoop, ½ lb. to 256 lbs.
on Platform, with Tin Scoop, Glass Sash.......... "

No. 26, Capacity ½ oz. to 16 lbs., Marble Slab, Glass Sash.. "

No. 33, Capacity 1 oz. to 32 lbs., Marble Slab, Glass Sash
(see plate).................................... "

No. 43, Capacity 2 oz. to 64 lbs., Marble Slab, Glass Sash.. "

Hatch's Counter Scales.

No. $ 1   2.   per dozen.

Packed, one in a case.

Hatch's T Scales.................................per dozen, $

Packed, six in a case.

Family Scales.

With Tin Scoop, Fancy Painted.

No. $ 1   2   3   4   each.

Union or Family Scale.

Capacity ½ oz. to 240 lbs., Iron Bearings.............each, $

Capacity ½ oz. to 244 lbs., Steel Bearings............... "

Howe's Union Family Scales.

To weigh from ½ an oz. to 240 lbs., with single or double beam, each, $

To weigh from ½ an oz. to 240 lbs., single or double beam,
with Brass Scoop................................. "

Howe's Grocers' Scale.

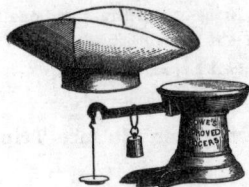

To weigh from ½ an oz. to 62 lbs., with single or double beam, each, $

To weigh from ½ an oz. to 62 lbs., with single or double beam,
with Brass Scoop................................. "

To weigh from ½ an oz. to 36 lbs......................each, $

FAIRBANKS' SCALES.

(Continued.)

Even Balances.

With Weights Complete.

	Capacity.	With Tin Scoop.	With Brass Scoop.
No. 1 Even Balance.................	½ oz. to 10 lbs.	$	$
No. 1 Even Balance, with balance beam,	½ oz.		
No. 2 Even Balance.................	½ oz. to 6 lbs.		
No. 3 Even Balance.................	½ oz. to 4 lbs.		

Butchers' Even Balance Trip Scales.

Scale with Square Marble Slab and Iron Plate.

No. 1, capacity, ¼ oz. to 20 lbs., without weights...........each, $
No. 2, capacity, ¼ oz. to 12 lbs., without weights.......... "
No. 3, capacity, ¼ oz. to 4 lbs., without weights............ "

Scale with Square Tin or Porcelain Pan and Iron Plate.

No. 1, capacity ¼ oz. to 20 lbs., without weights...........each, $
No. 2, capacity, ¼ oz. to 12 lbs., without weights........... "
No. 3, capacity, ¼ oz. to 4 lbs., without weights............ "

Butter Scales with Balance Beam.

Scale with tw oIron Plates.

No. 1, capacity, ¼ oz. to 20 lbs., without weights...........each, $
No. 2, capacity, ¼ oz. to 12 lbs., without weights........... "
No. 3, capacity, ¼ oz. to 4 lbs., without weights............ "

Scale with one Brass or Porcelain and one Iron Plate.

No. 1, capacity, ¼ oz. to 20 lbs., without weights...........each, $
No. 2, capacity, ¼ oz. to 12 lbs., without weights........... "
No. 3, capacity, ¼ oz. to 4 lbs., without weights............ "

Scale with two Brass or one Brass and one Porcelain Plate.

No. 1, capacity, ¼ oz. to 20 lbs., without weights..........each, $
No. 2, capacity, ¼ oz. to 12 lbs., without weights........... "
No. 3, capacity, ¼ oz. to 4 lbs., without weights............ "

Druggists' Even Balance Trip Scales.

Scale with Iron Pan and Iron Plate, Plainly Painted.

No. 1, ¼ oz. to 20 lbs., without weights..................each, $
No. 2, ¼ oz. to 12 lbs., without weights.................. "
No. 3, ¼ oz. to 4 lbs., without weights.................. "
No. 4, ¼ oz. to 2 lbs., without weights.................. "

Scale with Brass, Copper or Porcelain Pan and Iron Plate, Fancy Painted.

No. 1, ¼ oz. to 20 lbs., without weights..................each, $
No. 2, ¼ oz. to 12 lbs., without weights.................. "

Druggists' Even Balance Trip Scales.

(Continued.)

No. 3, ¼ oz. to 4 lbs., without weights..................each, $
No. 4, ¼ oz. to 2 lbs., without weights.................. "

Scale with Brass, Copper or Porcelain Pan and Brass Plate, Fancy Painted.

No. 1, ¼ oz. to 20 lbs., without weights..................each, $
No. 2, ¼ oz. to 12 lbs., without weights.................. "
No. 3, ¼ oz. to 4 lbs., without weights.................. "
No. 4, ¼ oz. to 2 lbs., without weights.................. "

Scale with Two Cast Iron Plates, Plainly Painted.

No. 1, ¼ oz. to 20 lbs., without weights..................each, $
No. 2, ¼ oz. to 12 lbs., without weights.................. "
No. 3, ¼ oz. to 4 lbs., without weights.................. "
No. 4, ¼ oz. to 2 lbs., without weights.................. "

Standing Even Beam Druggists' Scales.

With Brass Beams, Pans and Bows.

No.	Length of Beam.	Diameter of Pan.	With Heavy Painted Iron Column.	With Polished Brass Column.	With Round Marble Column.	With Octagon Marble Column.
1	30 in.	15 in.	each, $	$	$	$
2	24 in.	12 in.	"			
3	21 in.	10 in.	"			
4	18 in.	9 in.	"			
5	15 in.	8 in.	"			
6	12 in.	7 in.	"			

Standing Even Beam Druggists' Scales.

With Light Painted Iron Column, Brass Beam, Pans, and Bows

No.	Length of Beam.	Diameter of Pan.	
4	18 inches	9 inches	each, $
5	16 inches	8 inches	"
6	14 inches	7 inches	"

Wholesale Druggists' Scales.

Description.	No.	Length of Beam.	Diameter of Pan.	Capacity.	
Iron Column, Brass Beam, Brass Pans, Suspended by Brass Chains.	1	30 in.	14 in.	50 lbs.	each, $
	2	24 in.	12 in.	30 lbs.	"
	3	21 in.	10 in.	25 lbs.	"
	4	18 in.	9 in.	20 lbs.	"

FAIRBANKS' SCALES.

(Continued.)

Standing Even Beam Grocers' Scale.

With Light Iron Column.

No.	Length of Beam.	With Tin Scoop and Plate, without Weights.	With Brass Scoop and Plate, without Weights.
4	18 inches	each, $	$
5	16 inches	"	
6	14 inches	"	

Jewelers' and Brokers' Scales.

Description,	No.	Diameter of Pans.	Length of Beam.	Length of Box.	Weights.	
Brass Column, Brass	0,	4 in	7 in	12 in	8 oz.,	each, $
Beam, Brass Pans	1,	4½ in	8 in	13½ in	8 oz.,	"
and Chains, and Ma-	2,	5 in	9 in	15 in	16 oz.,	"
hogany Box with	3,	6 in	10 in	17½ in	32 oz.,	"
drawer, sealed Troy	4,	7½ in	12 in	20 in	32 oz.,	"
Cup Weights, dwts,	5,	8 in	15 in	24 in	64 oz.,	"
and grs. complete.	6,	9 in	18 in	31 in	96 oz.,	"

Grocers' Scale.

Capacity, ½ oz. to 62 lbs., with Tin Scoop................each, $
Capacity, ½ oz. to 62 lbs., with Brass Scoop............ "

With Double Beam and Scoop.

Capacity, ½ oz. to 62 lbs., with Tin Scoop................each, $
Capacity, ½ oz. to 62 lbs., with Brass Scoop............ "

Counter Scale.

Capacity, ½ oz. to 36 lbs., with Tin Scoop................each, $
Capacity, ½ oz. to 36 lbs., with Brass Scoop............ "

Druggists' Scale.

Capacity, 1 drachm to 8 lbs., with Tin Scoop..........each, $
Capacity, 1 drachm to 8 lbs., with Brass Scoop............ "

Improved Letter Balance.

Arranged so that it may be used for other weighing than letters.

Capacity, ½ oz. to 8 oz.................................each, $
Capacity, ¼ oz. to 8 oz................................. "
Capacity, ½ oz. to 34 oz................................. "

Portable Platform Scales.

Without Wheels.

No. 7, capacity, 2,000 lbs. Platform, 30 × 23 inches.....each, $
No. 8, capacity, 1,600 lbs. Platform, 30 × 23 inches..... "
No. 9, capacity, 1,400 lbs. Platform, 28 × 21 inches..... "
No. 10, capacity, 1,200 lbs. Platform, 28 × 20 inches..... "
No. 10½, capacity, 900 lbs. Platform, 26 × 17 inches..... "
No. 11, capacity, 600 lbs. Platform, 25 × 16 inches..... "
No. 11½, capacity, 400 lbs. Platform, 21 × 15 inches..... "

With Wheels.

No. 7, capacity, 2,000 lbs. Platform, 30 × 23 inches......each, $
No. 8, capacity, 1,600 lbs. Platform, 30 × 23 inches...... "
No. 9, capacity, 1,400 lbs. Platform, 28 × 21 inches...... "
No. 10, capacity, 1,200 lbs. Platform, 28 × 20 inches...... "
No. 10½, capacity, 900 lbs. Platform, 26 × 17 inches...... "
No. 11 capacity, 600 lbs. Platform, 25 × 16 inches...... "
No. 11½ capacity, 400 lbs. Platform, 21 × 15 inches...... "

With Heavy Wheels and Drop Lever.

No. 2, capacity, 3,000 lbs. Platform, 39 × 30 inches......each, $
No. 7, capacity, 2,500 lbs. Platform, 30 × 23 inches...... "
No. 8, capacity, 2,000 lbs. Platform, 30 × 23 inches...... "
No. 9, capacity, 1,500 lbs. Platform, 28 × 31 inches...... "
No. 10 capacity, 1,200 lbs. Platform, 28 × 20 inches...... "
No. 10½ capacity, 1,000 lbs. Platform, 26 × 17 inches . ... "

FAIRBANKS' SCALES.

(Continued.)

Rolling Mill or Iron Scales, with Rubber Spring Platform.

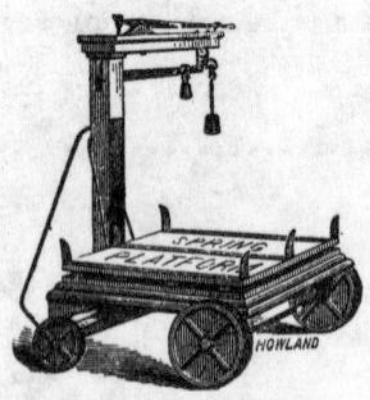

1st Size....Capacity, 4,000 lbs....Platform, 39×30 in....each, $

2d Size....Capacity, 2,500 lbs....Platform, 30×23 in.... "

Wheelbarrow Scales.

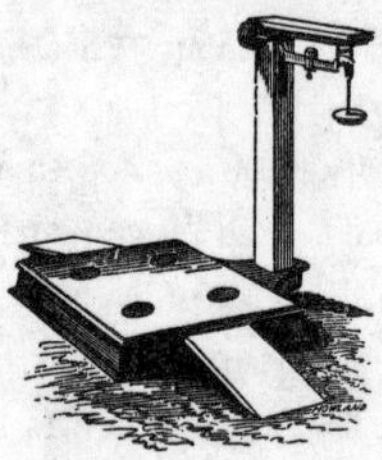

Platform, 2½×3½ feet......Capacity, 1,000 lbs............each, $

Same Scale, with Wheels............................ "

Millers' and Grain Dealers', or Pork Scale.

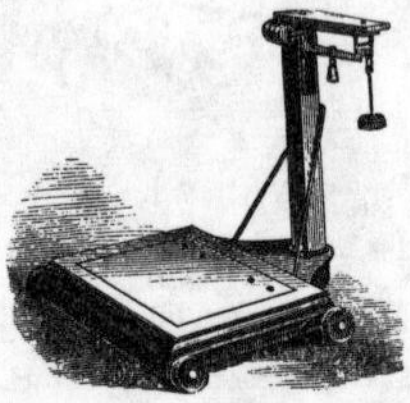

Capacity, 1,000 lbs....Platform, 42×30 in., with wheels....each, $

Capacity, 1,000 lbs....Platform, 42×30 in., without wheels. "

Portable Warehouse Scales.

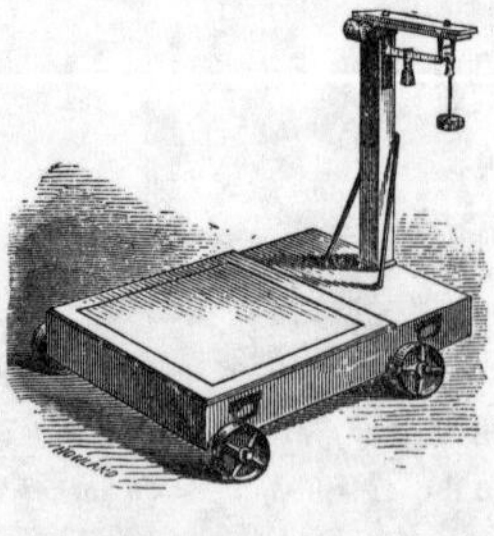

No. 1, Capacity, 5,000 lbs. Platform, 48×48 in., with wheels...each $

No. 1, Capacity, 5,000 lbs. Platform, 48×48 in., without wheels "

No. 4, Capacity, 3,500 lbs. Platform, 41×43 in., with wheels... "

No. 4, Capacity, 3,500 lbs. Platform, 41×43 in., without wheels "

No. 5, Capacity, 2,500 lbs. Platform, 30×36 in., with wheels... "

No. 5, Capacity, 2,500 lbs. Platform, 30×36 in., without wheels "

Dormant Warehouse Scales, with Drop Lever.

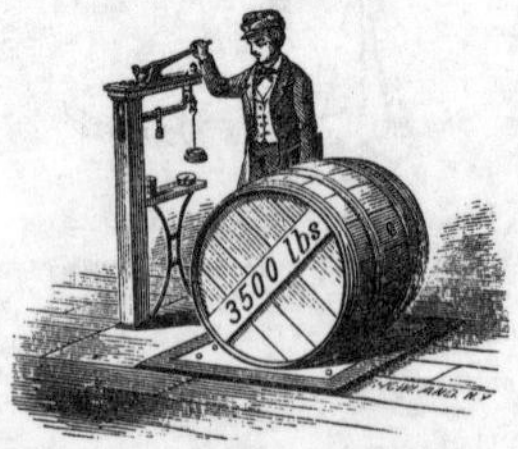

No. 1, Capacity, 5,000 lbs......Platform, 48×48 in.......each, $

No. 4, Capacity, 3,500 lbs......Platform, 41×43 in....... "

No. 5, Capacity, 2,500 lbs......Platform, 30×36 in....... "

No. 7, Capacity, 2,000 lbs......Platform, 24×30 in....... "

No. 9, Capacity, 1,500 lbs......Platform, 28×21 in....... "

Dormant Warehouse Scales, with Two Iron Pillars and Sliding Poise Beam.

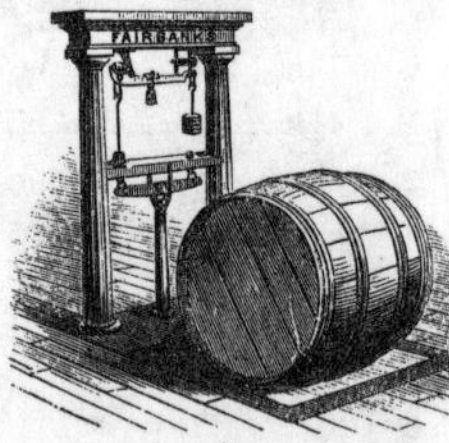

No. 1, Capacity, 5,000 lbs......Platform, 48×48 in.......each, $

No. 4, Capacity, 3,500 lbs......Platform, 41×43 in....... "

Hay and Stock Scales.

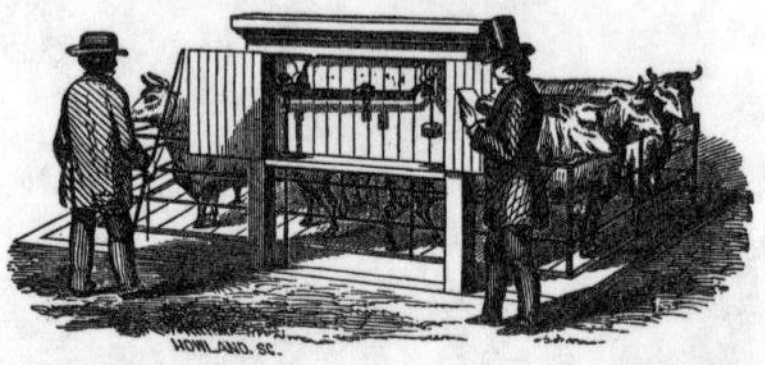

Capacity. Tons.	Description.	Length of Levers. Feet.	Length of Connections. Feet.	Length of Connections. Inches.	Size of Platform. Feet.	Size of Platform. Inches.	Distance from edge of Platform to Beam Rod. Feet.	Distance from edge of Platform to Beam Rod. Inches.	Each.
10..	Hay or Stock Scale.	15	4	6	14×9 or 16×8	 8¼	4 4	11 8½	$
10..	Hay or Stock Scale.	12	4	6	13×8 or 14×8	8 5¼	2 2	1¼ ½	
6..	Hay or Stock Scale.	15	4	6	14×9 or 16×8	 8¼	4 4	11 8½	
6..	Hay or Stock Scale.	12	4	6	13×8 or 14×8	8 5¼	2 2	1¼ ½	
5..	Hay or Stock Scale.	11	4	6	13×8 or 14×8	4 ½	1 1	3 2¼	
4..	Hay or Stock Scale.	12	4	6	13×8 or 14×8	7¼ 4¼	2 2	2 1	
3..	Hay or Stock Scale.	11	4	6	13×8 or 14×8	4 ½	1 1	3 2¼	
2..	Hay or Stock Scale.	10	4	....	13×7 or 14×6	2¼ 10¼	1 1	1¾ 1	
6..	Portable Hay or Stock Scale Requires no Pit.	12	4	6	13×8 or 14×8	7⅛ 4¼	2 2	2 1¼	
5..	Portable Hay or Stock Scale Requires no Pit.	11	4	6	13×8 or 14×8	4 ¼	1 1	3 2¼	
4..	Portable Hay or Stock Scale Requires no Pit.	11	4	6	13×8 or 14×8	4 ½	1 1	3 2¼	
3..	Portable Hay or Stock Scale Requires no Pit.	10½	4	....	13×7 or 14×7	4 1	1 1	7½ 6½	
2..	Portable Hay or Stock Scale Requires no Pit.	10	3	4	12×6	4¼	2	4½	

☞ The above prices are exclusive of the cost of timber and foundation, which is to be paid by purchaser.

SCALES, ETC.

Folding Coffee Bottom.

1st Size, 6 feet 2 inches long, 2 feet 4 inches wide........each, $

2d Size, 5 feet 10 inches long, 2 feet 2 inches wide........ "

Plain Coffee Bottom.

1st Size, 6 feet long, 2 feet 4 inches wide ....each, $

2d Size, 5 feet 8 inches long, 2 feet 2 inches wide......... "

Standing Bottom.

1st Size, 30×36 inches, suitable for 2,500 to 3,000 lbs. beam. each, $

2d Size, 27×33 inches, suitable for 1,500 to 2,000 lbs. beam. "

3d Size, 24×27 inches, suitable for 1,000 to 1,200 lbs. beam. "

4th Size, 22×26 inches, suitable for 600 to 800 lbs. beam. "

5th Size, 20×24 inches, suitable for 300 to 500 lbs. beam. "

Round Bottom, for Pork and Hams, Hung with Chains.

1st Size, 5 feet Diameter ....each, $

2d Size, 4½ feet Diameter .... "

3d Size, 4 feet Diameter .... "

Square Bottom, Hung with Chains.

1st Size, 4 feet Square..............................each, $

2d Size, 3½ feet Square.............................. "

3d Size, 3 feet Square.............................. "

Hide Bottoms, with Folds.

1st size, 4 feet long, 3 feet 2 inches wide ....each, $

2d size, 3½ feet long, 2 feet 2 inches wide .... "

Pig Iron Cradle.

Capacity, ½ a ton.......................................each, $

Capacity, 1 ton.. "

Cotton Hooks.

Large size...each, $

Common pattern....................................... "

Hogshead Hooks.

1st size, heavy, with swivels........................each, $

1st size, heavy, without swivels...................... "

2d size, light, without swivels...................... "

Sliding Can Hooks .... "

Barrel Hooks.

Ordinary size..each, $

Box Hooks.

Large size, with chain...............................each, $

Common pattern,...................................... "

Tobacco Hooks.

Of Steel, suitable for Tobacco Boxes...................each, $

Tea Hooks.

Of Steel, suitable for chests of Tea...................each, $

Hay Hooks.

Suitable for bales of Hay.............................each, $

WEIGHTS AND SLEIGH BELLS.

Nest Weights.

Capacity.	Sealed Iron.	Sealed Zinc.	Cased Brass.	Solid Brass.
8 lbs. down....per nest, $	$	$	$	
4 lbs. down.... "				
2 lbs, down.... "				
1 lb. down .... "				

Ring Weights.

7 lbs..each, $		
14 lbs.. "		
28 lbs.. ".		
50 lbs.. "		

Brass Cup Weights, Troy.

Capacity, 32 oz. down ....per set, $	
Capacity, 16 oz. down............................. "	
Capacity, 8 oz. down............................. "	
Capacity, 4 oz. down............................. "	

Brass Cup Weights, Troy—(Continued.)

Capacity, 2 oz. down ....per set, $	
Capacity, 1 oz. down .... "	
Capacity, ½ oz. down.............................. "	
Troy pennyweights................................. "	
Scruples and drachms.............................. "	
Grain Weights .... "	

Brass Weights in Block, Avoirdupois.

Capacity.	With open Block.	With covered Block.
4 lbs to ¼ oz,.............................per set, $	$	
2 lbs to ¼ oz............................. "		
1 lb. to ¼ oz,............................. "		

Brass Weights in Block, Troy.

Capacity.	With open Block.	With covered Block.
500 ounces down.............................per set, $	$	
300 ounces down..................... "		
200 ounces down..................... "		
100 ounces down..................... "		
50 ounces down..................... "		
30 ounces down..................... "		
20 ounces down..................... "		
10 ounces down..................... "		
5 ounces down..................... "		

SLEIGH BELLS.

Round Sleigh Bells—Rough.

								per doz.
	$							
Nos.	00	0	1	2	3	4	5	
	$							per doz.
Nos.	6	7	8	9	10	11	12	
	$							per doz.
Nos.	13	14	15	16	17	18		

Round Sleigh Bells, Solid Shanks—Rough.

							per doz.
	$						
Nos.	00	0	1	2	3	4	
	$						per doz.
Nos.	5	6	7	8	9		
	$						per doz.
Nos.	10	·11	12	13	14		

Round Sleigh Bells—Polished.

								per doz.
	$							
Nos.	00	0	1	2	3	4	5	
	$							per doz.
Nos.	6	7	8	9	10	11	12	
	$							per doz.
Nos.	13	14	15	16	17	18		

Round Sleigh Bells, Solid Shanks—Polished.

							per doz.
	$						
Nos.	00	0	1	2	3	4	
	$						per doz.
Nos.	5	6	7	8	9		
	$						per doz.
Nos.	10	11	12	13	14		

Round Sleigh Bells—White Metal.

								per doz.
	$							
Nos.	00	0	1	2	3	4	5	
	$							per doz.
Nos.	6	7	8	9	10	11	12	
	$							per doz.
Nos.	13	14	15	16	17	18		

Round Sleigh Bells, White Metal, Solid Shanks.

							per doz.
	$						
Nos.	00	0	1	2	3	4	
	$						per doz.
Nos.	5	6	7	8	9		
	$						per doz.
Nos.	10	11	12	13	14		

SLEIGH BELLS, ETC.

(Continued.)

Round Sleigh Bells, Solid Shank.
Diamond Rim, Extra Polished.

$
Nos.   0   1   2   per doz.

White Metal Bells—York Eye.

$
Nos.   1   2   3   4   per doz.

Round Sleigh Bells, Drilled Shank.
Extra Polished and Burnished.

$
Nos.   00   0   1   2   3   4   5   per doz.

Round Sleigh Bells, Drilled Shank.
White Metal, Extra Burnished.

$
Nos.   00   0   1   2   3   4   5   per doz.

Round Sleigh Bells, Drilled Shank.
Extra Silver Plated.

$
Nos.   00   0   1   2   3   4   5   per doz.

Open Sleigh Bells—Extra Polished.

$
Nos.   00   0   1   2   3   4   5   6   per doz.

Open Sleigh Bells—Extra White Metal.

$
Nos.   00   0   1   2   3   4   5   6   per doz.

Open Sleigh Bells—Extra Silver Plated.

$
Nos.   00   0   1   2   3   4   5   per doz.

Body Straps.
Polished Bells—Two Rows.

No. 1, 48 No. 0 Round Bells on back, and 11 Round Bells, assorted, for belly...............................each, $

No. 2, 48 No. 0 Round Bells on back, and 11 Open Bells, assorted, for belly.............................   "

No. 3, 48 No. 1 Round Bells on back, and 11 Open Bells, assorted, for belly.............................   "

No. 4, 48 No. 1 Round Bells on back, and 11 Round Bells, assorted, for belly........................ ..   "

No. 5, 40 No. 1 Round Bells on back, and 11 Round Bells, assorted, for belly.............................   "

No. 6, 40 No. 1 Round Bells on back, and 11 Open Bells, assorted, for belly.............................   "

Polished Bells—One Row.

No. 7, 24 No. 0 Round Bells on back, and 11 Round Bells, assorted, for belly...........................each, $

No. 8, 24 No. 0 Round Bells on Back, and 11 Open Bells, assorted, for belly.............................   "

No. 9, 20 No. 1 Round Bells on back, and 11 Round Bells, assorted, for belly.............................   "

No. 10, 20 No. 1 Round Bells on back, and 11 Open Bells, assorted, for belly.............................   "

No. 11, 24 No. 1 Round Bells on back, and 11 Open Bells, assorted, for belly.............................   "

No. 12, 24 No. 1 Round Bells on back, and 11 Round Bells, assorted, for belly.............................   "

No. 13, 20 No. 2 Round Bells on Back, and 11 Round Bells, assorted, for belly.............................   "

No. 14, 20 No. 2 Round Bells on back, and 11 Open Bells, assorted, for belly.............................   "

White Metal Bells—Two Rows.

No. 15, 48 No. 0 Round Bells on back, and 11 Round Bells, assorted, for belly...........................each, $

No. 16, 48 No. 0 Round Bells on back, and 11 Open Bells, assorted, for belly.............................   "

Body Straps—(Continued.)
White Metal Bells—Two Rows.

No. 17, 48 No. 1 Round Bells on back, and 11 Open Bells, assorted, for belly.....................each, $

No. 18, 48 No. 1 Round Bells on back, and 11 Round Bells, assorted, for belly.........................   "

No. 19, 40 No. 1 Round Bells on back, and 11 Round Bells, assorted, for belly.........................   "

No. 20, 40 No. 1 Round Bells on back, and 11 Open Bells, assorted, for belly.........................   "

White Metal Bells—One Row.

No. 21, 24 No. 0 Round Bells on back, and 11 Round Bells, assorted, for belly.....................each, $

No. 22, 24 No. 0 Round Bells on back, and 11 Open Bells, assorted, for belly.........................   "

No. 23, 20 No. 1 Round Bells on back, and 11 Round Bells, assorted, for belly.........................   "

No. 24, 20 No. 1 Round Bells on back, and 11 Open Bells, assorted, for belly.........................   "

No. 25, 24 No. 1 Round Bells on back, and 11 Open Bells, assorted, for belly.........................   "

No. 26, 24 No. 1 Round Bells on back, and 11 Round Bells, assorted, for belly.........................   "

No. 27, 20 No. 2 Round Bells on back, and 11 Round Bells, assorted, for belly.........................   "

No. 28, 20 No. 2 Round Bells on back, and 11 Open Bells, assorted, for belly.........................   "

Polished Bells—One Row.

No. 29, 48 No. 0 Round Bells..........................   "

No. 30, 36 No. 0 Round Bells..........................   "

No. 31, 48 No. 1 Round Bells..........................   "

No. 32, 42 No. 1 Round Bells..........................   "

No. 33, 36 No. 1 Round Bells..........................   "

No. 34, 36 No. 2 Round Bells..........................   "

No. 35, 30 No. 2 Round Bells..........................   "

No. 36, 36 No. 3 Round Bells..........................   "

No. 37, 30 No. 3 Round Bells..........................   "

No. 38, 24 No. 3 Round Bells..........................   "

No. 39, 24 No. 4 Round Bells..........................   "

No. 40, 28 No. 3 Round Bells, on Patent Leather.......   "

White Metal Bells—One Row.

No. 41, 48 No. 0 Round Bells.........................each, $

No. 42, 36 No. 0 Round Bells..........................   "

No. 43, 48 No. 1 Round Bells..........................   "

No. 44, 42 No. 1 Round Bells..........................   "

No. 45, 36 No. 1 Round Bells..........................   "

No. 46, 36 No. 2 Round Bells..........................   "

No. 47, 30 No. 2 Round Bells..........................   "

No. 48, 36 No. 3 Round Bells..........................   "

No. 49, 30 No. 3 Round Bells..........................   "

No. 50, 24 No. 3 Round Bells..........................   "

No. 51, 24 No. 4 Round Bells..........................   "

No. 52, 28 No. 3 Round Bells, on Patent Leather........   "

Neck Straps, with Polished Bells.

No. 53, 24 No. 00 Round Bells........................each, $

No. 54, 21 No. 00 Round Bells........................   "

No. 55, 18 No. 00 Round Bells........................   "

No. 56, 12 No. 0 Round Bells........................   "

No. 57, 18 No. 0 Round Bells........................   "

No. 58, 15 No. 0 Round Bells........................   "

No. 59, 18 No. 1 Round Bells........................   "

No. 60, 15 No. 1 Round Bells........................   "

No. 61, 12 No. 1 Round Bells........................   "

SLEIGH BELLS, ETC.

Neck Straps, with Polished Bells.
(Continued.)

No. 62, 18 No. 2 Round Bells........................ each, $
No. 63, 15 No. 2 Round Bells........................   "
No. 64, 12 No. 2 Round Bells........................   "
No. 65, 12 No. 3 Round Bells........................   "
No. 66, 15 No. 3 Round Bells........................   "

Neck Straps with White Metal Bells.

No. 67, 24 No. 00 Round Bells...................... each, $
No. 68, 21 No. 00 Round Bells......................   "
No. 69, 18 No. 00 Round Bells......................   "
No. 70, 12 No. 0 Round Bells......................   "
No. 71, 18 No. 0 Round Bells......................   "
No. 72, 15 No. 0 Round Bells......................   "
No. 73, 18 No. 1 Round Bells......................   "
No. 74, 15 No. 1 Round Bells......................   "
No. 75, 12 No. 1 Round Bells......................   "
No. 76, 18 No. 2 Round Bells......................   "
No. 77, 15 No. 2 Round Bells......................   "
No. 78, 12 No. 2 Round Bells......................   "
No. 79, 12 No. 3 Round Bells......................   "
No. 80, 15 No. 3 Round Bells......................   "

Back Straps, with Polished Bells.

No. 81, 24 No. 00 Round Bells...................... each, $
No. 82, 21 No. 00 Round Bells......................   "
No. 83, 18 No. 00 Round Bells......................   "
No. 84, 12 No. 0 Round Bells......................   "
No. 85, 18 No. 0 Round Bells......................   "
No. 86, 18 No. 1 Round Bells......................   "
No. 87, 15 No. 1 Round Bells......................   "
No. 88, 12 No. 1 Round Bells......................   "
No. 89, 15 No. 2 Round Bells......................   "
No. 90, 12 No. 2 Round Bells......................   "

Back Straps with White Metal Bells.

No. 91, 24 No. 00 Round Bells...................... each, $
No. 92, 24 No. 00 Round Bells......................   "
No. 93, 18 No. 00 Round Bells......................   "
No. 94, 12 No. 0 Round Bells......................   "
No. 95, 18 No. 0 Round Bells......................   "
No. 96, 18 No. 1 Round Bells......................   "
No. 97, 15 No. 1 Round Bells......................   "
No. 98, 12 No. 1 Round Bells......................   "
No. 99, 15 No. 2 Round Bells......................   "
No. 100, 12 No. 2 Round Bells.....................   "

Neck Straps, with Polished Open Bells.

No. 101, 15 No. 00 Open Bells...................... each, $
No. 102, 12 No. 00 Open Bells......................   "
No. 103, 15 No. 0 Open Bells......................   "
No. 104, 12 No. 0 Open Bells......................   "
No. 105, 12 No. 1 Open Bells......................   "
No. 106, 10 No. 1 Open Bells......................   "
No. 107, 10 No. 2 Open Bells......................   "
No. 108, 9 Open Bells, assorted, 00 to 3...........   "
No. 109, 11 Open Bells, assorted, 00 to 4...........   "
No. 110, 13 Open Bells, assorted, 00 to 5...........   "

Neck Straps, with White Metal Open Bells.

No. 111, 15 No. 00 Open Bells...................... each, $
No. 112, 12 No. 00 Open Bells......................   "
No. 113, 15 No. 0 Open Bells......................   "
No. 114, 12 No. 0 Open Bells......................   "
No. 115, 12 No. 1 Open Bells......................   "
No. 116, 10 No. 1 Open Bells......................   "
No. 117, 10 No. 2 Open Bells......................   "
No. 118, 9 Open Bells, assorted, 00 to 3...........   "
No. 119, 11 Open Bells, assorted, 00 to 4...........   "
No. 120, 13 Open Bells, assorted, 00 to 5...........   "

Martingale Straps, with Polished Bells.

No. 121, 30 No. 0 Round Bells...................... each, $
No. 122, 36 No. 0 Round Bells......................   "
No. 123, 30 No. 1 Round Bells......................   "
No. 124, 36 No. 1 Round Bells......................   "
No. 125, 36 No. 2 Round Bells......................   "
No. 126, 30 No. 2 Round Bells......................   "
No. 127, 30 No. 1 Open Bells.......................   "
No. 128, 24 No. 1 Open Bells.......................   "
No. 129, 20 No. 0 Round and 5 No. 00 Open.........   "
No. 130, 24 No. 0 Round and 5 No. 00 Open.........   "
No. 131, 20 No. 1 Round and 5 No. 00 Open.........   "
No. 132, 24 No. 1 Round and 5 No. 00 Open.........   "
No. 133, 20 No. 0 Round and 7 No. 2 Open.........   "
No. 134, 20 No. 2 Round and 7 No. 2 Open.........   "
No. 135, 24 No. 1 Round and 7 No. 2 Open.........   "
No. 136, 20 No. 1 Round and 7 No. 2 Open.........   "

Martingale Straps, with White Metal Bells.

No. 137, 30 No. 0 Round Bells...................... each, $
No. 138, 36 No. 0 Round Bells......................   "
No. 139, 30 No. 1 Round Bells......................   "
No 140, 36 No. 1 Round Bells.......................   "
No. 141, 36 No. 2 Round Bells......................   "
No. 142, 30 No. 2 Round Bells......................   "
No. 143, 30 No. 1 Open Bells.......................   "
No. 144, 24 No. 1 Open Bells.......................   "
No. 145, 20 No. 0 Round, and 5 No. 00 Open........   "
No. 146, 24 No. 0 Round, and 5 No. 00 Open........   "
No. 147, 20 No. 1 Round, and 5 No. 00 Open........   "
No. 148, 24 No. 1 Round, and 5 No. 00 Open........   "
No. 149, 20 No. 0 Round, and 7 No. 2 Open........   "
No. 150, 20 No. 2 Round, and 7 No. 2 Open........   "
No. 151, 24 No. 1 Round, and 7 No. 2 Open........   "
No. 152, 20 No. 1 Round, and 7 No. 2 Open........   "

Heavy Neck Straps, Rough, Lined.

No. 153, 11 Bells, 3 to 8 assorted large........... each, $
No. 154, 11 Bells, 4 to 9 assorted large...........   "
No. 155, 11 Bells, 5 to 10 assorted large...........   "
No. 156, 11 Bells, 6 to 11 assorted large...........   "
No. 157, 11 Bells, 7 to 12 assorted large...........   "
No. 158, 13 Bells, 3 to 9 assorted large...........   "
No. 159, 13 Bells, 4 to 10 assorted large...........   "
No. 160, 13 Bells, 5 to 11 assorted large...........   "
No. 161, 13 Bells, 6 to 12 assorted large...........   "
No. 162, 15 Bells, 2 to 9 assorted large...........   "
No. 163, 15 Bells, 3 to 10 assorted large...........   "

SLEIGH BELLS, ETC.

Heavy Neck Straps, Rough, Lined.
(Continued.)

No. 164, 15 Bells, 4 to 11 assorted large ....each, $
No. 165, 15 Bells, 5 to 12 assorted large .... "
No. 166, 15 Bells, 6 to 13 assorted large .... "
No. 167, 17 Bells, 2 to 10 assorted large .... "
No. 168, 17 Bells, 3 to 11 assorted large .... "
No. 169, 17 Bells, 4 to 12 assorted large .... "
No. 170, 17 Bells, 5 to 13 assorted large .... "
No. 171, 19 Bells, 2 to 11 assorted large .... "
No. 172, 19 Bells, 3 to 12 assorted large .... "
No. 173, 19 Bells, 4 to 13 assorted large .... "
No. 174, 21 Bells, 3 to 13 assorted large .... "
No. 175, 21 Bells, 4 to 14 assorted large .... "
No. 176, 23 Bells, 2 to 13 assorted large .... "
No. 177, 23 Bells, 3 to 14 assorted large .... "
No. 178, 15 Bells, 7 to 14 assorted large .... "

Heavy Neck Straps, Polished, Lined.

No. 179, 11 Bells, 3 to 8 assorted large................each, $
No. 180, 11 Bells, 4 to 9 assorted large................ "
No. 181, 11 Bells, 5 to 10 assorted large................ "
No. 182, 11 Bells, 6 to 11 assorted large................ "
No. 183, 11 Bells, 7 to 12 assorted large................ "
No. 184, 13 Bells, 3 to 9 assorted large................ "
No. 185, 13 Bells, 4 to 10 assorted large................ "
No. 186, 13 Bells, 5 to 11 assorted large................ "
No. 187, 13 Bells, 6 to 12 assorted large................ "
No. 188, 15 Bells, 2 to 9 assorted large................ "
No. 189, 15 Bells, 3 to 10 assorted large................ "
No. 190, 15 Bells, 4 to 11 assorted large................ "
No. 191, 15 Bells, 5 to 12 assorted large................ "
No. 192, 15 Bells, 6 to 13 assorted large................ "
No. 193, 17 Bells, 2 to 10 assorted large................ "
No. 194, 17 Bells, 3 to 11 assorted large................ "
No. 195, 13 Bells, 2 to 8 assorted large................ "
No. 196, 15 Bells, 7 to 14 assorted large................ "
No. 197, 17 Bells, 4 to 12 assorted large................ "
No. 198, 17 Bells, 5 to 13 assorted large................ "
No. 199, 19 Bells, 2 to 11 assorted large................ "
No. 200, 19 Bells, 3 to 12 assorted large................ "
No. 201, 19 Bells, 4 to 13 assorted large................ "
No. 202, 21 Bells, 3 to 13 assorted large................ "
No. 203, 21 Bells, 4 to 14 assorted large................ "
No. 204, 23 Bells, 2 to 13 assorted large................ "
No. 205, 23 Bells, 3 to 14 assorted large................ "

Neck Straps, Assorted from No. 1.
Rough, Lined.

No. 206, 9 Bells, 1 to 5....................each, $
No. 207, 11 Bells, 1 to 6........................ "
No. 208, 13 Bells, 1 to 7........................ "
No. 209, 15 Bells, 1 to 8........................ "
No. 210, 17 Bells, 1 to 9........................ "
No. 211, 19 Bells, 1 to 10....................... "

Polished, Lined.

No. 212, 19 Bells, 1 to 10....................each, $
No. 213, 17 Bells, 1 to 9........................ "

Neck Straps, Assorted from No. 1.
(Continued.)
Polished, Lined.

No. 214, 15 Bells, 1 to 8..................each, $
No. 215, 13 Bells, 1 to 7...................... "
No. 216, 11 Bells, 1 to 6...................... "
No. 217, 9 Bells, 1 to 5...................... "

Polished, Unlined,

No. 218, 9 Bells, 1 to 5..................each, $
No. 219, 11 Bells, 1 to 6...................... "
No. 220, 13 Bells, 1 to 7...................... "
No. 221, 15 Bells, 1 to 8...................... "
No. 222, 17 Bells, 1 to 9...................... "

Rough, Unlined.

No. 223, 17 Bells, 1 to 9..................each, $
No. 224, 15 Bells, 1 to 8...................... "
No. 225, 13 Bells, 1 to 7...................... "
No. 226, 11 Bells, 1 to 6...................... "
No. 227, 9 Bells, 1 to 5...................... "

Neck Straps, Assorted from No. 0.
Rough, Unlined.

No. 228, 9 Bells, 0 to 4..................each, $
No. 229, 11 Bells, 0 to 5...................... "
No. 230, 13 Bells, 0 to 6...................... "
No. 231, 15 Bells, 0 to 7...................... "
No. 232, 17 Bells, 0 to 8...................... "
No. 233, 19 Bells, 0 to 9...................... "

Polished, Lined.

No. 234, 19 Bells, 0 to 9..................each, $
No. 235, 17 Bells, 0 to 8...................... "
No. 236, 15 Bells, 0 to 7...................... "
No. 237, 13 Bells, 0 to 6...................... "
No. 238, 11 Bells, 0 to 5...................... "
No. 239, 9 Bells, 0 to 4...................... "

Polished, Unlined.

No. 240, 9 Bells, 0 to 4..................each, $
No. 241, 11 Bells, 0 to 5...................... "
No. 242, 13 Bells, 0 to 6...................... "
No. 243, 15 Bells, 0 to 7...................... "
No. 244, 17 Bells, 0 to 8...................... "
No. 245, 19 Bells, 0 to 9...................... "

Rough, Unlined.

No. 246, 19 Bells, 0 to 9..................each, $
No. 247, 17 Bells, 0 to 8...................... "
No. 248, 15 Bells, 0 to 7...................... "
No. 249, 13 Bells, 0 to 6...................... "
No. 250, 11 Bells, 0 to 5...................... "
No. 251, 9 Bells, 0 to 4...................... "

Fancy Body Straps.
Patent and Enameled Leather, Bound Edges, Extra Silver Plated Bells.

No. 252, 36 No. 3 Plated Bells ....each, $
No. 253, 30 No. 3 Plated Bells.................. "
No. 254, 36 No. 2 Plated Bells.................. "
No. 255, 30 No. 2 Plated Bells.................. "
No. 256, 48 No. 1 Plated Bells.................. "
No. 257, 42 No. 1 Plated Bells.................. "

SLEIGH AND HAND BELLS.

Fancy Body Straps—(Continued.)

No. 258, 36 No. 1 Plated Bells.......................each, $
No. 259, 30 No. 1 Plated Bells....................   "
No. 260, 60 No. 0 Plated Bells....................   "
No. 261, 48 No. 0 Plated Bells....................   "
No. 262, 42 No. 0 Plated Bells....................   "
No. 263, 72 No. 00 Plated Bells...................   "
No. 264, 60 No. 00 Plated Bells...................   "

Fancy Martingale Straps.
Patent and Enameled Leather, Bound Edges, Extra Silver Plated Bells.

No. 265, 36 No. 2 Plated Bells.......................each, $
No. 266, 30 No. 2 Plated Bells....................   "
No. 267, 36 No. 1 Plated Bells....................   "
No. 268, 30 No. 1 Plated Bells....................   "
No. 269, 36 No. 0 Plated Bells....................   "
No. 270, 20 No. 2, and 6 Open Plated Bells...........   "
No. 271, 20 No. 1, and 6 Open Plated Bells...........   "
No. 272, 20 No. 0, and 6 Open Plated Bells...........   "

Fancy Body Straps.
Stitched Edges, Not Bound.

No. 273, 36 No. 1 Extra White Metal Bells..............each, $
No. 274, 30 No. 1 Extra White Metal Bells..............   "

Fancy Back Straps.
Patent and Enameled Leather, Bound Edges, Extra Silver Plated Bells.

No. 275, 24 No. 2 Plated Bells........................each, $
No. 276, 20 No. 2 Plated Bells....................   "
No. 277, 24 No. 1 Plated Bells....................   "
No. 278, 20 No. 1 Plated Bells....................   "
No. 279, 30 No. 0 Plated Bells....................   "
No. 280, 24 No. 0 Plated Bells....................   "

Fancy Neck Straps.
Patent and Enameled Leather, Bound Edges, Extra Silver Plated Bells.

No. 281, 18 No. 0 Plated Bells........................each, $
No. 282, 18 No. 1 Plated Bells....................   "
No. 283, 15 No. 1 Plated Bells....................   "
No. 284, 18 No. 2 Plated Bells....................   "
No. 285, 15 No. 2 Plated Bells....................   "

Fancy Neck Straps.
Patent and Enameled Leather, Bound Edges, Extra Silver Plated Open Bells.

No. 286, 12 No. 0 Open Plated Bells...................each, $
No. 287, 15 No. 0 Open Plated Bells...................   "
No. 288, 12 No. 1 Open Plated Bells...................   "
No. 289, 15 No. 1 Open Plated Bells...................   "
No. 290, 12 No. 2 Open Plated Bells...................   "

Fancy Body Straps.
Patent and Enameled Leather, Bound Edges, Extra White Metal Bells.

No. 291, 36 No. 3 White Metal Bells...................each, $
No. 292, 30 No. 3 White Metal Bells...................   "
No. 293, 36 No. 2 White Metal Bells...................   "
No. 294, 30 No. 2 White Metal Bells...................   "
No. 295, 48 No. 1 White Metal Bells...................   "
No. 296, 42 No. 1 White Metal Bells...................   "
No. 297, 36 No. 1 White Metal Bells...................   "
No. 298, 30 No. 1 White Metal Bells...................   "

Fancy Body Straps—(Continued.)

No. 299, 60 No. 0 White Metal Bells...................each, $
No. 300, 48 No. 0 White Metal Bells...................   "
No. 301, 42 No. 0 White Metal Bells...................   "
No. 302, 72 No. 00 White Metal Bells...................   "
No. 303, 60 No. 00 White Metal Bells...................   "

Fancy Neck Straps.
Patent and Enameled Leather, Bound Edges, Extra White Metal Bells.

No. 304, 18 No. 0 White Metal Bells...................each, $
No. 305, 18 No. 1 White Metal Bells...................   "
No. 306, 15 No. 1 White Metal Bells...................   "
No. 307, 18 No. 2 White Metal Bells...................   "
No. 308, 15 No. 2 White Metal Bells...................   "

Fancy Martingale Straps.
Patent and Enameled Leather, Bound Edges. Extra White Metal Bells

No. 309, 36 No. 2 White Metal Bells...................each, $
No. 310, 30 No. 2 White Metal Bells...................   "
No. 311, 36 No. 1 White Metal Bells...................   "
No. 312, 30 No. 1 White Metal Bells...................   "
No. 313, 36 No. 0 White Metal Bells...................   "
No. 314, 20 No. 2 and 6 Open White Metal Bells.........   "
No. 315, 20 No. 1 and 6 Open White Metal Bells.........   "
No. 316, 20 No. 0 and 6 Open White Metal Bells.........   "

Fancy Back Straps.
Patent and Enameled Leather, Bound Edges, Extra White Metal Bells.

No. 317, 24 No. 2 White Metal Bells...................each, $
No. 318, 20 No. 2 White Metal Bells...................   "
No. 319, 24 No. 1 White Metal Bells...................   "
No. 320, 20 No. 1 White Metal Bells...................   "
No. 321, 30 No. 0 White Metal Bells...................   "
No. 322, 24 No. 0 White Metal Bells...................   "

Light Hand Bells, Fine Polished.

No.	0	1	2	3	4	5	6	$ per doz.
No.	7	8	9	10	11	12	13.	$ per doz.

Light Hand Bells, Extra White Metal.

No.	1	2	3	4	5	6	7	$ per doz.
No.	8	9	10	11	12	13.		$ per doz.

Heavy Hand Bells, Mahogany Handles.

No.	0	1	2	3	4	5	$ per doz.
No.	6	7	8	9	10.		$ per doz.

TEA, CALL AND GONG BELLS.

Tea Bells.

	$				per doz.
Yellow Metal, Fine Polished, No.	1	2	3		
	$				per doz.
Yellow Metal, Bronzed......No.	1	2	3		
	$				per doz.
White Metal............No.	1	2	3		
	$				per doz.
Silver Plated............No.	1	2	3		

Silver Plated Tea Bells.

No. 050, Pear Shape.............................per dozen, $

No. 060, Gong Shape.............................   "

No. 070, Pear Shape.............................   "

Silver Plated Call Bells, with Spring.

No. 200.   No. 300.   No. 400.

Marbleized Iron Base.

No. 500.   No. 700.   No. 800.

Marbleized Iron Base.

No. 1100. White Marble Base.

No. 100, Plain Base.............................per dozen, $

No. 200, Fancy Base.............................   "

No. 300, Black Marbled Base.....................   "

No. 400, Plain Base.............................   "

No. 500, Fancy Base.............................   "

No. 700, Plain Base.............................   "

No. 800, Black Marbled Base.....................   "

No. 900, Fancy Base.............................   "

No. 1100, White Marble Base.....................   "

No. 1200, Plain Beaded Base.....................   "

Without Spring.

No. 1,300, Plain Beaded Base....................per dozen, $

No. 1,400, Same Base as No. 300.................   "

No. 1,500, Same Base as No. 200.................   "

Silver Plated Call Bells—(Continued.)
Without Spring.

No. 1,600, Plain Base................................per doz., $

No. 1,700, Fancy Base............................   "

No. 1,800, Fancy Base............................   "

No. 1,900, Black Base............................   "

No. 1,900, Black and Gold Base...................   "

No. 1,900, Black and Pearl Base..................   "

No. 2,000, Black Base............................   "

No. 2,000, Black and Gold Base...................   "

No. 2,100, White Marble Base.....................   "

No. 2,200, White Marble Base.....................   "

No. 2,400, Hotel, Black and Gold Base............   "

No 2,400, Hotel, White Marble Base..............   "

PATENT GONG BELLS.
Patent House Bells, Double or Single Trip.
Bronzed Steel.

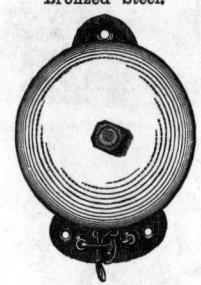

	$								per doz.
Size...	3	4	5	6	7	8	10	12	inch.

Polished Bell Metal.

	$								per doz.
Size...	3	4	5	6	7	8	10	12	inch.

Silver White.

	$								per doz.
Size...	3	4	5	6	7	8	10	12	inch.

Patent Street Car Bell, with Pulley.

Polished Bell Metal................................per dozen, $

Patent Alarm Door Bells.

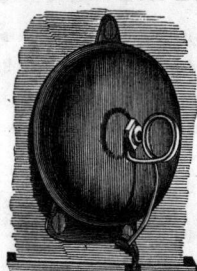

Bronzed Steel....................................per dozen, $

Polished Bell Metal..............................   "

Silver White.....................................   "

TAYLOR'S
PATENT GONG HOUSE BELLS.

The best House Bell made. No wires are required, can be attached to any door, and detached in five minutes, and is never out of repair.

(These Plates represent half the actual size.)

This Plate represents the Bell taken off so as to show the mechanical arrangement.

This Plate represents the Bell complete.

Name Plate Handle.

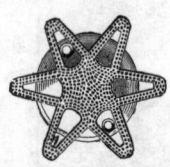

Star Handle.

Plated Handle.

Japanned Handle.

House Bell No. 1—Diameter of Bell 5 inches.

House Bell No. 1, with Japanned Crank Handle...$ per dozen.

House Bell No. 1, with Silver Plated Crank Handle...   "

House Bell No. 1, with Silver Plated Star Handle ....   "

House Bell No. 1, with Hand Plated Name Plate Handle ....   "

House Bell No. 2.—Diameter of Bell 3½ inches.

House Bell No. 2, with Japanned Crank Handle...$ per dozen.

House Bell No. 2, with Silver Plated Crank Handle...   "

House Bell No. 2, with Silver Plated Star Handle..   "

House Bell No. 2, with Hand Plated Name Plate Handle ....   "

Office Bells, with Japanned Frame...$ per dozen.

Office Bells, with Plated Frame ....   "

For other House Bell Trimmings see pages 74 and 75.

HOUSE, SHEEP AND COW BELLS, ETC.

Common Metal House Bells.

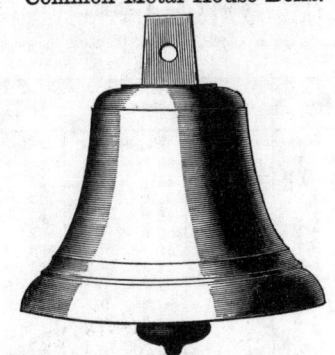

Nos.	1	2	3	4	5	6	7	8
Rough								per lb., $
Outside Polished								per lb.,

(For Pure Metal House Bells, see page 103.)

Sheep and Cow Bells.

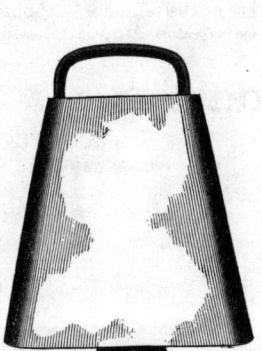

Sheep Bells.   Cast Cow Bells.

	$				per doz.
Not Strapped, Nos.	1		2	3	
	$				per doz.
Strapped, Nos.	1		2	3	

(For Pure Metal Sheep Bells, see page 103.)

Cast Cow Bells.

	$					per doz.
Nos.	1	2	3	4	5	
	$					per doz.
Nos.	6	7	8	9	10	

(For Pure Metal Cast Cow Bells, see page 103.)

Wrought Cow Bells.
Common Pattern.

	$						per doz.
Nos.	0	1	2	3	4	5	6
	$						per doz.
Nos.	7	8	9	10	11	12	

Western or Yaw's Pattern.

	$					per doz.
Nos.	1	2	3	4	5	
	$					per doz.
Nos.	6		7	8	9	

Kentucky or Dodge's Pattern.

	$							per doz.
Nos.	1	2	3	4	5	6	7	

Mountain Forest Pattern.

	$							per doz.
Nos.	0	1	2	3	4	5	6	7

Improved Pattern.

	$					per doz.
Nos.	22	23	24	25	26	
	$					per doz.
Nos.	27	28	29	30	31	

Cow Bell Straps.

	$				per doz.
Nos.		2	4	6	

Factory, Academy and Depot Bells.

☞ From 100 lbs. to 400 lbs. in weight; hung with "Hildreth's Patent Rotary Yoke," which prevents the Bell from being broken in ringing; Iron Wheel and Standards, timber frame and Steel Springs being as full hangings in every respect as for Church Bells, except the Tolling Hammer and wrench.

First Quality ....per lb., $

Second Quality ....per lb., $

Weight.	Diameter.	Size of Frame.	Price of Hangings.	Weight.	Diameter.	Size of Frame.	Price of Hangings.
100	17 in.	26 in Sq.	$	225	23 in.	33 in. Sq.	$
125	18 "	27 " "		250	24 "	34 " "	
150	19 "	28 " "		300	25 "	35 " "	
180	20 "	31 " "		350	26 "	36 " "	
200	22 "	33 " "		375	26 "	36 " "	

Steamboat Bells.

☞ From 100 lbs. to 700 lbs., hung with Revolving Yoke and Crank complete.

Yoke and Crank for Bells weighing

$							each.
	100	150	180	200	250	300	lbs.
$							each.
	350	400	450	500	600	700	lbs.

First Quality ....per lb., $

Second Quality ....per lb., $

Locomotive Bells,

Also, Plantation and Hose Carriage Bells, weighing from 60 to 150 lbs. with Yoke and Sparrow Tail, or turned and finished without mounting.

Locomotive Bells cast with shank of any desired shape, without extra charge.

Bells of less than 100 lbs. are usually furnished with a Yoke and Sparrow Tail only.

First Quality ....per lb., $

Second Quality .... "

Yoke and Tail for Bells weighing

$					each.
	15	20	25	30	40	lbs.
$					each.
	50	60	80	90	100	lbs.

Amalgam Farm Bells.

	$						per lb.
No.		1	2	3	3½	4	5
Weight about		40	50	60	80	100	160	lbs. each.

CHURCH BELLS AND COFFIN TRIMMINGS.

Small Engine Bells,
Polished, from 1 to 15 lbs. Each.

Nos.	$ 4	5	6	7	8	per lb.
Nos.	$ 9	10	12	13	14	per lb.

Church Bells.

First Quality......................per lb., $
Second Quality.................... "

List of Church Bells.

With particulars as to Weight, Keys, Diameter, Hangings, &c.

Weight of Bell.	Keys.	Diameter.	Size of Frame.	Diameter of Wheel.	Price of Hangings.
400 lbs.	C to E	27 inches.	38 in. Square.	48 inches.	$
500 "	B♭ " D	29 "	38 " "	48 "	
600 "	B♭ " C♯	31 "	43 " "	53 "	
700 "	A " C	33 "	43 " "	53 "	
800 "	A " C	34 "	48 " "	63 "	
900 "	A♭ " B	36 "	50 " "	63 "	
1000 "	A♭ " B	38 "	51 " "	66 "	
1100 "	G " B♭	40 "	53 " "	69 "	
1200 "	G " B	41 "	53 " "	69 "	
1300 "	F♯ " A	42 "	53 " "	69 "	
1400 "	F " A	43 "	55 " "	78 "	
1500 "	F " G♯	44 "	58 " "	78 "	
1600 "	F " G♯	44 "	58 " "	78 "	
1800 "	E " G	45 "	64 " "	84 "	
2000 "	E♭ " G	46 "	64 " "	84 "	
2200 "	E♭ " G	48 "	67 " "	84 "	
2300 "	E♭ " F♯	49 "	67 " "	84 "	
2500 "	D " F	50 "	72 " "	90 "	
2800 "	D " F	52 "	72 " "	90 "	
3000 "	D " F	53 "	72 " "	90 "	
3300 "	D♭ " E	54 "	75 " "	90 "	
3500 "	D♭ " E	56 "	77 " "	96 "	
4000 "	C " E♭	58 "	77 " "	96 "	
4500 "	C " E♭	60 "	82 " "	102 "	
5000 "	B " D	62 "	82 " "	102 "	

☞ Bells will be found in most instances to vary somewhat from the exact weights given in the above table, as it is impossible to cast them with *entire* accuracy as to weight.

COFFIN TRIMMINGS.

COFFIN PLATES.

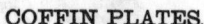

No. 1 M.   No. 2 M.   No. 3 M.

No. 4 M.   No. 5 M.   No. 6 M.

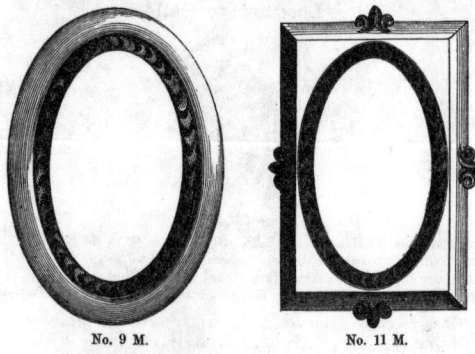

No. 9 M.   No. 11 M.

No. 12 M.   No. 13 M.

COFFIN PLATES.

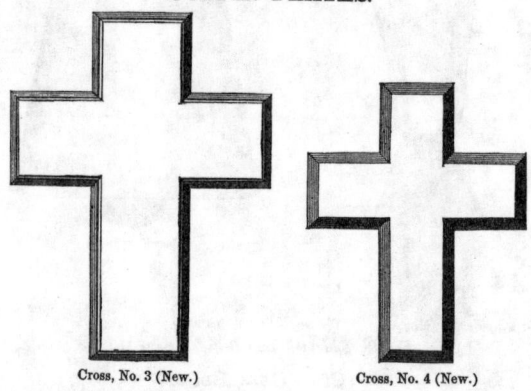

Cross, No. 3 (New.)   Cross, No. 4 (New.)

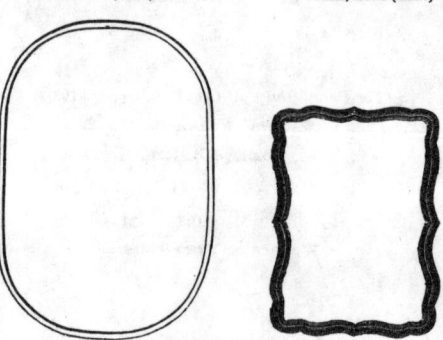

D.   F.

Fine White Metal Coffin Plates.

No.	1,	2,	3,	4,	5,	6,	7,	8.	
M Style									per doz.
D Style									"
F Style									"
Cross ..									"
Olive...									"

COFFIN TRIMMINGS.

(Continued.)

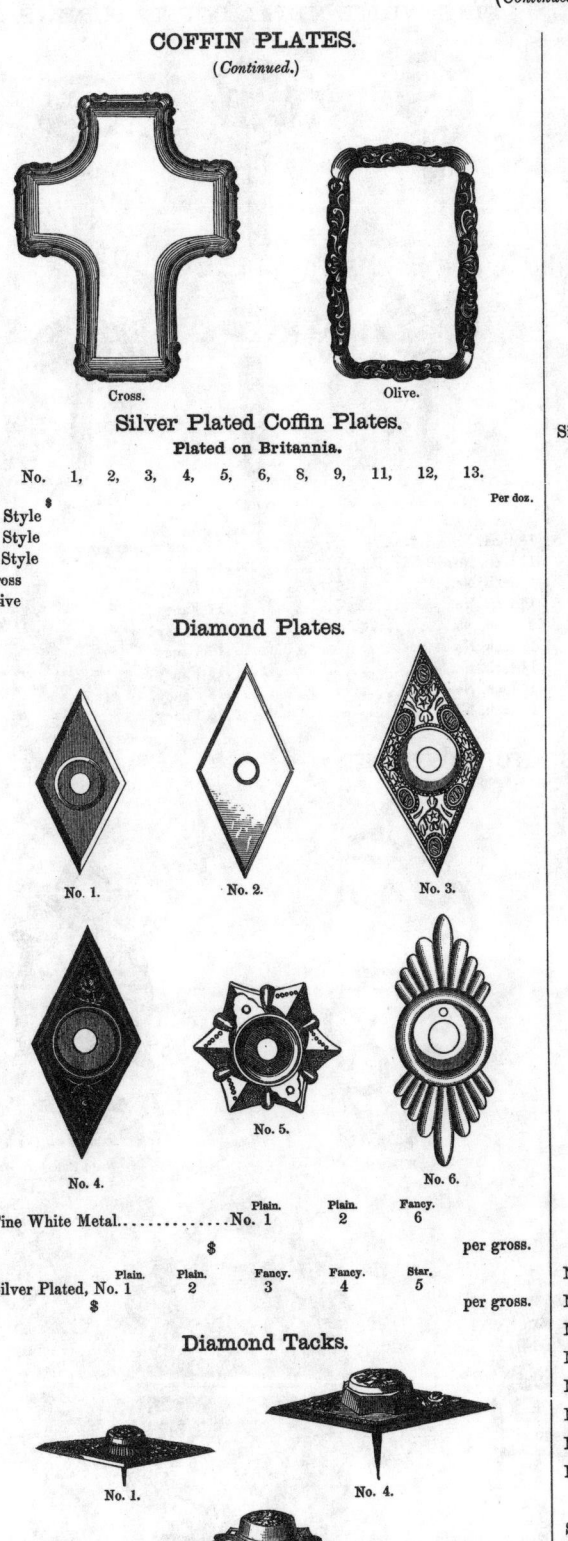

COFFIN PLATES.
(Continued.)

Cross.   Olive.

Silver Plated Coffin Plates.
Plated on Britannia.

No. 1, 2, 3, 4, 5, 6, 8, 9, 11, 12, 13.

$ Per doz.

M Style
D Style
F Style
Cross
Olive

Diamond Plates.

No. 1.   No. 2.   No. 3.

No. 4.   No. 5.   No. 6.

	Plain.	Plain.	Fancy.
Fine White Metal..............No. 1	2	6	

$ per gross.

	Plain.	Plain.	Fancy.	Fancy.	Star.
Silver Plated, No. 1	2	3	4	5	

$ per gross.

Diamond Tacks.

No. 1.   No. 4.

No. 5.

	Fancy.	Fancy.	Star.
Silver Plated..................No 1	4	5	

$ per gross.

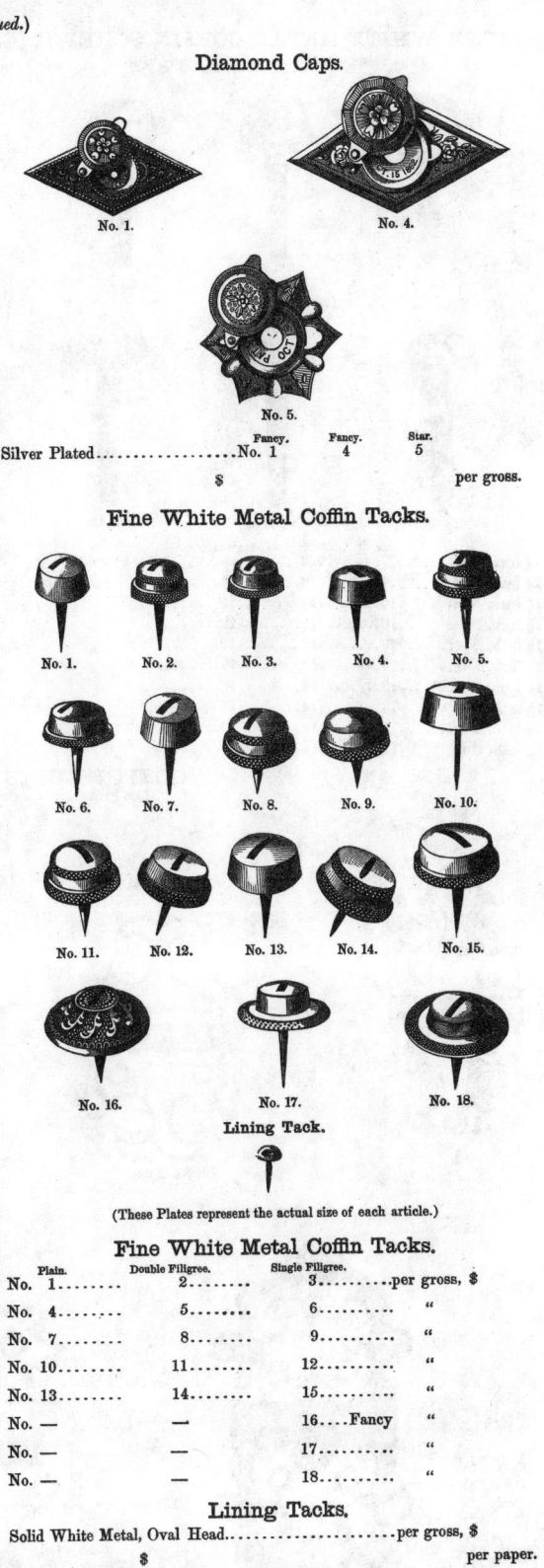

Diamond Caps.

No. 1.   No. 4.

No. 5.

	Fancy.	Fancy.	Star.
Silver Plated..................No. 1	4	5	

$ per gross.

Fine White Metal Coffin Tacks.

No. 1.   No. 2.   No. 3.   No. 4.   No. 5.

No. 6.   No. 7.   No. 8.   No. 9.   No. 10.

No. 11.   No. 12.   No. 13.   No. 14.   No. 15.

No. 16.   No. 17.   No. 18.

Lining Tack.

(These Plates represent the actual size of each article.)

Fine White Metal Coffin Tacks.

Plain.	Double Filigree.	Single Filigree.	
No. 1........	2........	3..........per gross, $
No. 4........	5........	6..........	"
No. 7........	8........	9..........	"
No. 10........	11........	12..........	"
No. 13........	14........	15..........	"
No. —	—	16....Fancy	"
No. —	—	17..........	"
No. —	—	18..........	"

Lining Tacks.

Solid White Metal, Oval Head......................per gross, $				
$				per paper.
Silvered, Flat Head... 4	6	8	10	12 ounces.
$				per paper.
Silvered, Oval Head... 4	6	8	10	12 ounces.
Brass, Assorted.................................per paper, $				
Japanned, Assorted.................................				"

COFFIN TRIMMINGS.

(Continued.)

FINE WHITE METAL COFFIN SCREWS.
(These Plates represent the actual size of each article.)

No. 7.   No. 8.   No. 9.

No. 10.   No. 11.   No. 12.

FINE WHITE METAL COFFIN SCREWS.
(Continued.)

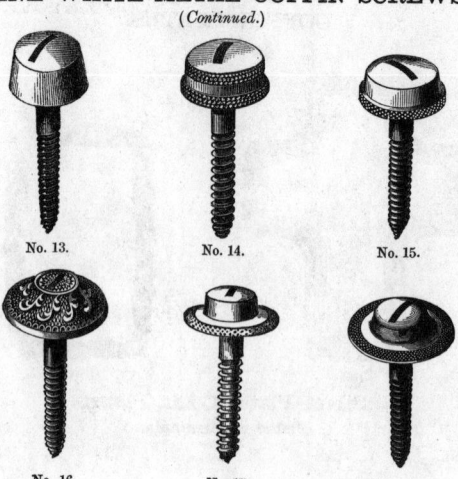

No. 13.   No. 14.   No. 15.

No. 16.   No. 17.   No. 18.

	Plain.	Double Filligree.	Single Filligree.	
1¼ inch, Nos	7	8	9	per gross, $
1½ inch, Nos	7	8	9	"
1¼ inch, Nos	10	11	12	"
1½ inch, Nos	10	11	12	"
1¾ inch, Nos	10	11	12	"
2 inch, Nos	10	11	12	"
1¼ inch, Nos	13	14	15	"
1½ inch, Nos	13	14	15	"
1¾ inch, Nos	13	14	15	"
2 inch, Nos	13	14	15	"

	Single Filligree.	
1½ inch, No	16 Fancy	per gross, $
1¼ inch, No	17 Fancy	"
1½ inch, No	17 Fancy	"
1¾ inch, No	17 Fancy	"
2 inch, No	17 Fancy	"
1¼ inch, No	18 Fancy	"
1½ inch, No	18 Fancy	"
1¾ inch, No	18 Fancy	"
2 inch, No	18 Fancy	"

COFFIN BUTTS AND DOWELLS.
(These Plates represent the actual size of each article.)

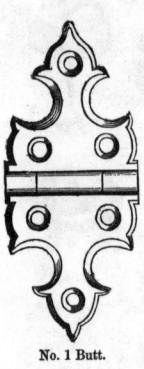
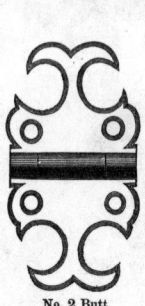
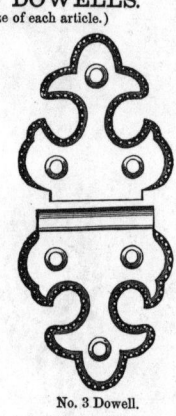

No. 1 Butt.   No. 2 Butt.   No. 3 Dowell.   No. 4 Butt.

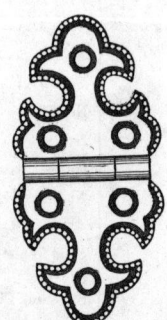

No. 5 Butt.   No. 6 Butt.   No. 7 Dowell.

Fine White Metal Coffin Butts and Dowells.							
$							per doz. pairs.
No.	1	2	3	4	5	6	7

Silver Plated Coffin Butts and Dowells.							
$							per doz. pairs.
No.	1	2	3	4	5	6	7

COFFIN HANDLES.

Coffin Handles, Plain.

(These Plates represent half the size of each article.)

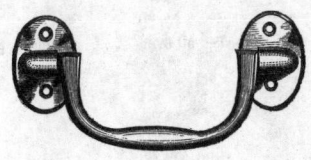

No. 10.

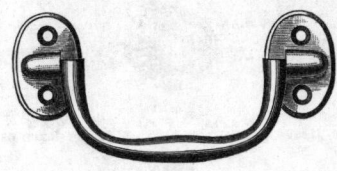

No. 12.

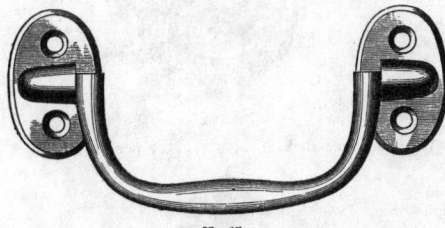

No. 15.

Fancy.

No. 13.

No. 14.

Coffin Handles, Fancy Sockets.

(These Plates represent half the size of each article.)

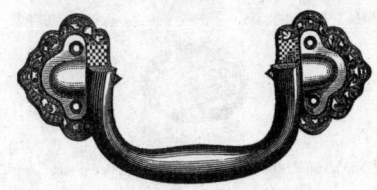

No. 113.

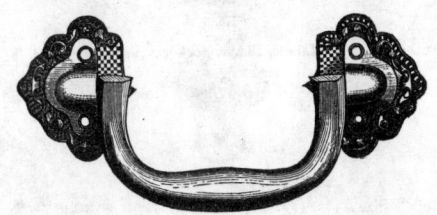

No. 114.

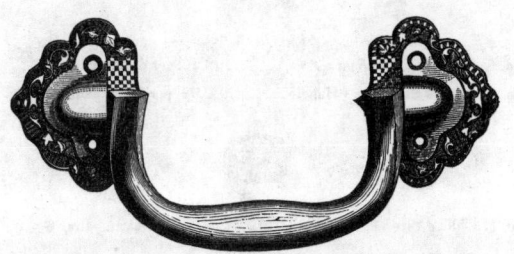

No. 116.

Fancy.

No. 16, Fancy.

Fine White Metal, Coffin or Lifting Handles.

	$			per dozen pairs.
Plain, No.	10	12	15	
	$			per dozen pairs.
Fancy, No.	13	14	16	
		$		per doz. pairs.
Plain, with Fancy Sockets, No.	113	114	116	

Silver Plated, Coffin or Lifting Handles.

	$			per dozen pairs.
Plain, No.	10	12	15	
	$			per dozen pairs.
Fancy, No.	13	14	16	
		$		per doz. pairs.
Plain, with Fancy Sockets, No.	113	114	116	

COFFIN HANDLES.

(Continued.)

Heavy Silver Plated on Brass.

No. 1.

No. 1, Full Size, Stationary .... per dozen pairs, $

No. 2.

No. 2, Full Size, Drop Handle, Patent Socket... per dozen pairs, $

No. 3.

No. 3, Full Size, Drop Handle, Patent Socket... per dozen pairs, $

No. 4.

No. 4, Child's Size...................... per dozen pairs, $

No. 5.

No. 5, Full Size, Stationary .... per dozen pairs, $
No. 6, Child's Size, Drop Handle.............. per dozen pairs, $

No. 7.

No. 7, Child's Size........................ per dozen pairs, $

No. 10.

No. 10, Extra Large, Patent Socket............ per dozen pairs, $

Nos. 11 to 18.

$ per doz. pairs.

No.	11	12	13	14	15	16	17	18	
Size,	$2\frac{1}{2}$	$2\frac{3}{4}$	3	$3\frac{1}{4}$	$3\frac{1}{2}$	$3\frac{3}{4}$	$4\frac{1}{4}$	$4\frac{3}{4}$	inch.

No. 20.

No. 20, Full Size .... per dozen pairs, $

No. 23.

No. 23, Full Size, Patent Socket .... per dozen pairs, $

Heavy Silver Plated on Brass.

(Continued.)

No. 27.

No. 27, Extra Heavy, Burnished all over....... per dozen pairs, $

No. 32.

No. 32, For Metallic Caskets .... per dozen pairs, $

No. 33.

No. 33, Masonic, Heavy.................... per dozen pairs, $

No. 36.

No. 36, Very Large and Rich................. per dozen pairs, $

No. 50.

No. 50, Extra Large, Patent Socket .... per dozen pairs, $

No. 55.

No. 55, Full Size, Heavy .... per dozen pairs, $

No. 56.

No. 56.................................. per dozen pairs, $

No. 57.

No. 57, Full Size .... per dozen pairs,

No. 60.

No. 60, Large and Rich..................... per dozen pairs, $

COFFIN HANDLES.

(Continued.)

Heavy Silver Plated on Brass.

(Continued.)

No. 85, Military, Patented.

No. 85, Very Heavy, Solid Plate, richly Chased,
Burnished......................per dozen pairs, $

No. 115.

No. 115, Rose Pattern.....................per dozen pairs, $

No. 116.

No. 116, Heart Pattern....................per dozen pairs, $

Nos. 125 and 126.

No. 125, Heavy and Strong.................per dozen pairs, $
No. 126, Extra Heavy and Strong...........per dozen pairs,

Nos. 135 and 136.

No. 135.....................................per dozen pairs, $
No. 136.....................................per dozen pairs,

Nos. 145 and 146.

No. 145.....................................per dozen pairs, $
No. 146.....................................per dozen pairs,

No. 232. Masonic, Patented.

No. 232, Masonic Centerpiece and Handle......per dozen pairs, $

No. 234, Plain Burnished Center, with Masonic
Handle...............................per dozen pairs,

No. 236. Patented.

No. 236, Plain Burnished Center, Book with Star
on Handle............................per dozen pairs, $

No. 238. Patented.

No. 238, Plain Burnished Center, Book with Cross
on Handle............................per dozen pairs, $

Heavy Silver Plated on Brass.

(Continued.)

No. 240. Patented.

No. 240, Cross on Burnished Center, Book with
Cross on Handle......................per dozen pairs, $

No. 252. Military, Patented.

No. 252, Design of the Plate is Stars and Stripes.per dozen pairs, $

No. 360.

No. 360, Very rich Plate, 7 inches wide, with fixed
chased Handle.....................per dozen pairs, $

No. 3600.

No. 3600, Very Heavy, Chased and Burnished..per dozen pairs, $

No. 36000.

No. 36000, Large and Heavy fixed Handle......per dozen pairs, $

Silver Plated on White Metal.

Nos. 700, 700½, 710 and 710½.

No. 700, Full Size, rich.....................per dozen, pairs, $
No. 700½, Full Size, rich, light plate.............   "
No. 710, Extra Large, rich....................   "
No. 710½, Extra Large, rich, light plate.........   "

Nos. 1140, 1160 and 1200.

No. 1140, Medium............................per dozen pairs, $
No. 1160, Large.............................   "
No. 1200, Extra Large.......................   "

Nos. 1410 to 1414.

No. 1410, Plain Handle, Fancy Socket........per dozen pairs, $
No. 1411, Plain Handle, Fancy Socket........   "
No. 1412, Plain Handle, Fancy Socket........   "
No. 1413, Plain Handle, Fancy Socket........   "
No. 1414, Plain Handle, Fancy Socket........   "

COFFIN HANDLES.

(Continued.)

White Metal Coffin Handles.

Nos. 400, 401 and 402.

No. 400, Very Large, full burnished............per dozen pairs, $

No. 401, Very Large, full burnished............   "

No. 402, Full Burnished......................   "

Nos. 70 and 71.

No. 70, Full Size and rich, White Metal........per dozen pairs, $

No. 71, Extra Large and rich...................   "

Bronzed Coffin Handles.

Nos. 191 and 1191.

No. 191, Black and Gold Bronzed............per dozen pairs, $

No. 1191, French Bronzed...................per dozen pairs, $

Nos. 19 and 119.

No. 19, Extra Heavy, Black and Gold Bronzed..per doz. pairs, $

No. 119, Extra Heavy, French Bronzed.........per doz. pairs, $

The Handles of Nos. 19 and 119 are cast into and through the Socket, and cannot be detached.

Nos. 400 and 4000.

Bronzed Plates with Silver Plated Rings.

No. 400, Child's Size, Black and Gold Bronzed..per doz. pairs, $

No. 4000, Child's Size, French Bronzed.........per doz. pairs, $

Japanned Coffin Handles.

No. 8.

No. 8, Stationary.....................per dozen pairs, $

No. 91.

No. 91, Drop Handle.....................per dozen pairs, $

No. 9.

No. 9, Drop Handle, Extra Heavy............per dozen pairs, $

Nos. 40 and 40½.

No. 40, Child's Size, Japanned, with Silver Plated Ring,
                        per dozen pairs, $

No. 40½, Child's Size, with Japanned Ring.....per dozen pairs, $

Nos. 51, 52, 53.

No. 51, Japanned, 3 inch.....................per dozen pairs, $

No. 52, Japanned, 3½ inch...................per dozen pairs, $

No. 53, Japanned, 4 inch.....................per dozen pairs, $

Silver Coffin Lace.

In Pieces of 7½ yards, 12 Pieces in a Package.

No.	144	145	146	
$				per piece.
Width	¼	⅝	½ inch.	

SILVER PLATED WARE.

PLATED KNIVES,
Plated on Nickel Silver.

Olive Knives. Hollow Handle.

Beaded Tea or Fruit Knives.

Plain Blades, with Case.....................per dozen, $

Engraved, with Case........................per dozen, $

Without Case...........................less, per dozen, $

PLATED KNIVES.

(Continued.)

Olive or Oval Threaded Tea Knives.

Flat Handle, with Case.....................per dozen, $

Flat Handle, without Case....................per dozen, $

Oval Threaded Knives.

Hollow Handle Dessert, with Case............per dozen, $

Hollow Handle Table, with Case..............per dozen, $

Without Case...........................less, per dozen, $

Olive Knives.

(See Plate.)

Hollow Handle Dessert, with Case............per dozen, $

Hollow Handle Table, with Case..............per dozen, $

Without Case...........................less, per dozen, $

SILVER PLATED WARE.

(Continued.)

TEA SETS,

PLATED ON WHITE METAL, CHASED, ENGINE TURNED OR PLAIN.

5 half pint Tea.　　Slop.　　Sugar.　Coffee.　　Cream.　　6 half pint Tea.

No. 3100, Chased.

No.	Set of 6 Pieces.	Coffee.	6 half pint Tea.	5 half pint Tea.	Sugar.	Cream.	Slop.
Chased 3100	$	$	$	$	$	$	$
Chased *3200							
Engine *3200							
Plain *3200							

* Same shape as No. 3100.　　　　Set with Gilt Cream and Slop, $　　extra.

5 half-pint Tea.　　Sugar.　　Coffee.　Slop.　　　Cream.　6 half pint Tea.

No. 1861, Engine Turned.

No.	Set of 6 Pieces.	10 half pint Coffee.	6 half pint Tea.	5 half pint Tea.	Sugar.	Cream.	Slop.
Chased 1861							
Engine 1861							
Plain 1861							

Set with Gilt Cream and Slop, $　　extra.

SILVER PLATED WARE.

(Continued.)

CASTERS, PLATED ON WHITE METAL.

No. 2100.

No. 1658.

No. 2530.

No. 584.

No. 1644.

No. 1642.

No. 1660.

No. 1964.

COFFEE URNS, PLATED ON WHITE METAL.

Coffee Urns.

No. 3100, Chased....16 half pint......each, $

*No. 3200, Chased....16 half pint...... "

*No. 3200, Engine....16 half pint...... "

*No. 3200, Plain.....16 half pint...... "

*No. 4200, Chased....16 half pint...... "

*No. 4200, Plain.......16 half pint...... "

*No. 5100, Chased....16 half pint...... "

*No. 5200, Plain.......16 half pint...... "

* Same shape as No. 3100, but with trimmings, etc., of sets they are intended to match.

Table Casters, Plated on Nickel Silver.

Number of Rings.	Number of Caster.	Prices Each. With Best Cut Bottles.
6	1670	$
6	1685	
6	1976	
7	1975	
6	1970	
4	1970	
3	1980	

No. 3100. Chased.

Table Casters, Plated on White Metal.

Number of Rings.	Number of Frame.	With Best Bottles.	With No. 70 Bottles.	With No. 2½ or No. 1 Bottles.
6	1860	$	$	$
7	1657			
7	1658			
6	1659			
7	582			
6	581			
7	Engine, 1			
6	Engine, 2			
7	Engine, 3			
6	44			
6	33			
6	22			
6	12			
6	11			

SILVER PLATED WARE.
CASTERS, PLATED ON WHITE METAL.
(Continued.)

TABLE CASTERS.

Number of Rings.	Number of Frame.	With Best Bottles.	With No. 70 Bottles.	With No. 2½ or No. 1 Bottles.	Number of Rings.	Number of Frame.	With Best Bottles.	With No. 70 Bottles.	With No. 2½ or No. 1 Bottles.
6	2500	$	$	$	6	2620	$	$	$
6	2510				6	55			
6	2520				6	580			
6	2530				5	580			
6	2540				6	585			
6	2580				5	585			
6	2590				6	590			
6	2100				5	590			
6	2300				6	579			
8	*76				5	579			
7	1700				6	589			
6	1700				5	589			
6	1656				6	†578			
6	1814				6	1642			
6	99				5	1642			
6	1660				6	187			
6	88				5	187			
6	77				6	167			
6	66				5	167			
6	13				6	155			
6	18				5	155			

Number of Rings.	Number of Frame.	No. 3 Bottles.	No. 53 Bottles.	No. 70½ Bottles.
6	19			
6	1744			
6	1743			
6	1742			
6	2600			
6	2610			
5	584	$	$	$
6	584			

* Hotel.　† Engine.

TABLE AND BREAKFAST CASTERS.

Table Casters.

Number of Rings.	Number of Frame.	With No. 70 Bottles.	With No. 2½ No. 3, or No. 1 Bottles.	With No. 2½ or No. 40 Bottles.
6	577	$	$	$
5	577			
6	576			
5	576			
6	575			
5	575			
6	574			
5	574			
6	573			
5	573			
6	572			
5	572			
6	571			
5	571			
6	570			
5	570			
6	560			
5	560			
6	165			
5	165			
6	464			
5	464			
6	162			
5	162			
5	147			
4	147			
5	145			
4	145			
5	142			
4	142			

Breakfast Casters.

Number of Rings.	Number of Frame.	With Best Bottles.	With No. 70 Bottles.	With No. 2½ No. 2 & No. 3 Bottles.
4	2600	$	$	$
4	2610			
4	1900			
3	1900			
4	1960			
3	1960			
4	1962			
3	1962			
3	1961			
4	*1963			
2	*1963			
4	*1964			
4	*1990			
2	*1990			

* Salt.

Custard or Ice Cream Stand.

No.	Engine.	Plain.
1	$	$

Egg Stands.

Number of Cups.	Number of Stand.	Engine.	Plain.
12	50	$	$
4	60		

Wine Casters.

	Number of Rings.	Number of Frame.	With Best Colored Bottles.	With Best White Bottles.	With Cheaper Colored Bottles.
With Glass Goblets........	3	30	$	$	$
With White or Gilt Goblets.	3	30			
With Gilt Chased Goblets...	3	30			
	3	10			
	3	20			
	3	40			
With Chased or Engine Frame	3	40			
	3	050			
Wine Waiter		060			
Wine Waiter		070			
Pitcher Waiter		060			
Pitcher Waiter		070			

Pickle Casters.

	Number of Bottles.	Number of Frame.	With Best Cut Bottles.	With Pressed Bottles.
Open	2	5	$	$
Plain	2	10		
Plain	2	20		
Oval	1	15		

Toast Rack, Plated on White Metal.

No. 10.

Toast Rack, No. 10 .... each,

Cake Baskets, Plated on White Metal.

No. 1610.

Cake Basket, No. 1610 .... each, $

SILVER PLATED WARE.
(Continued.)

CAKE BASKETS, PLATED ON WHITE METAL.

No. 1615.　Each $　　　　No. 1675.　Each $　　　　No. 1678, Engine.　Each $

BERRY OR PRESERVE DISHES AND BASKETS,
PLATED ON WHITE METAL.

No. 1949.　　　　　　No. 1965.　　　　　　　　No. 1967.

No. 1949, with Ruby Glass Linings ....each, $
No. 1949, with Green or Blue Glass Linings .... "
No. 1950, with Ruby Glass Linings...................... "
No. 1950, with Green or Blue Glass Linings............... "
No. 1965, with Ruby Glass Linings .... "

No. 1965, with Blue Glass Linings ....each, $
No. 1967, with Blue Glass Linings .... "
No. 1967, with Ruby Glass Linings...................... "
No. 1967, with Light Green Glass Linings................ "

BUTTER DISHES, WAITERS AND NUT PICKS.

Butter Dishes, Plated on White Metal.

No. 3300.　　　　　　No. 5000, Revolving.
Each, $　　　　　　　　Each, $

No. 1 Waiters, Plated on first quality Nickel Silver.
Double Plate.

Scroll Pattern.

	$						each.
First Quality,	10	12	14	16	18	20 inches.	
	$						each.
First Quality,	22	24	26	28		30 inches.	

No. 2 Waiters, Plated on German Silver.
Regular Plate.

	$						each.
Second Quality,	10	12	14	16	18	20 inches.	
	$						each.
Second Quality,	22	24	26	28		30 inches.	

Nut Picks.

Nut Picks, including Case.........................per dozen, $

Pitchers, Plated on White Metal.

No. 75, Delevan, without Cover.

No. 75, Chased ....each, $
No. 75, Engine ....each, $
No. 75, Plain..each, $

SILVER PLATED WARE.

(Continued.)

DOUBLE WALL PATENT VALVE ICE PITCHERS,

PLATED ON WHITE METAL.

No. 3, Engine Turned.

No. 3, N, Plain.

No. 3, Engine Turned...each, $

No. 3, N, Plain...each, $

SILVER PLATED TABLE WARE.

PLATED WITH PURE SILVER ON FIRST QUALITY ALBATA METAL AND GERMAN SILVER.

Plain and Tipped Spoons and Forks, &c.

Plain Spoon.

Tipped Fork.

Plain and Tipped Patterns.	Heavy Plate.	Double Plate.	Treble Plate.	Quadruple Plate.
	Per Dozen.	Per Dozen.	Per Dozen.	Per Dozen.
Tea Spoons, Plain..................	$	$	$	$
Tea Spoons, Tipped.................				
Dessert Spoons, Plain.............				
Dessert Spoons, Tipped...........				
Table Spoons, Plain..............				
Table Spoons, Tipped.............				
Dessert Forks, Tipped............				
Medium Forks, Tipped.............				
Table Forks, Tipped..............				
Oyster Forks, Tipped, Two Tines...				
Beef, or Child's Forks...........				
Pickle Forks.....................				
Salt Spoons, Plain...............				
Salt Spoons, Tipped..............				
Salt Shovels, Tipped.............				
Mustard Spoons, Tipped...........				
Bar Spoons, Small................				
Bar Spoons, Large................				
Sugar Shells.....................				
Sugar Sifters....................				
Sugar Tongs......................				
Sugar Shovels....................				
Cream Ladles.....................				
Gravy Ladles.....................				
Butter Knives, Spoon Handle.......				
	Each.	Each.	Each.	Each.
Oyster Ladles....................				
Soup Ladles......................				
Fish Knives, Engraved............				

Threaded Spoons and Forks, &c.

Threaded Spoon.

Threaded Fork.

Threaded Butter Knife, Spoon Handle.

Threaded Pattern.	Heavy Plate.	Double Plate.	Treble Plate.	Quadruple Plate.
	Per Dozen.	Per Dozen.	Per Dozen.	Per Dozen.
Tea Spoons.........................	$	$	$	$
Dessert Spoons.....................				
Table Spoons.......................				
Dessert Forks......................				
Medium Forks.......................				
Table Forks........................				
Salt Spoons........................				
Salt Shovels.......................				
Mustard Spoons.....................				
Sugar Shells.......................				
Sugar Sifters......................				
Sugar Shovels......................				
Butter Knives, Spoon Handle........				
Cream Ladles.......................				
Gravy Ladles.......................				
Oyster Ladles......................	Each.	Each.	Each.	Each.
Fish Knives, Engraved..............				
Pie Knives, Engraved...............				
Cake Knives, Engraved..............				

SILVER PLATED TABLE WARE.

PLATED WITH PURE SILVER ON FIRST QUALITY ALBATA METAL AND GERMAN SILVER.

(Continued.)

Oval Threaded Spoons and Forks, etc.

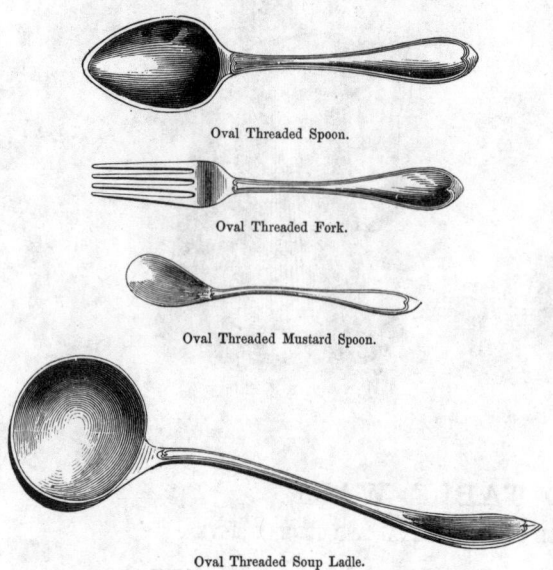

Oval Threaded Spoon.

Oval Threaded Fork.

Oval Threaded Mustard Spoon.

Oval Threaded Soup Ladle.

Oval Threaded Cake Knife.

Oval Threaded Cake Knife.

Olive Spoons and Forks, etc.

Olive Spoon.

Olive Fork.

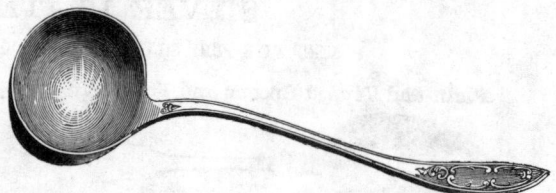

Olive Soup Ladle.

Oval Threaded Pattern.	Heavy Plate.	Double Plate.	Treble Plate.
	Per dozen. $	Per dozen. $	Per dozen. $
Tea Spoons			
Dessert Spoons			
Table Spoons			
Dessert Forks			
Medium Forks			
Table Forks			
Oyster Forks, Two Tines			
Beef or Child's Forks			
Pickle Forks			
Salt Spoons			
Salt Shovels			
Mustard Spoons			
Egg Spoons			
Bar Spoons, Small			
Bar Spoons, Large			
Sugar Shells			
Sugar Sifters			
Sugar Tongs			
Sugar Shovels			
Butter Knives, Spoon Handle			
Butter Knives, Melon Pattern			
Cream Ladles			
Gravy Ladles			
Oyster Ladles	Each.	Each.	Each.
Soup Ladles,			
Fish Knives, Engraved			
Pie Knives, Engraved			
Cake Knives, Engraved			
Ice Cream Knives, Engraved			
Crumb Knives, Engraved			
Asparagus Tongs, Pierced			
Ice Tongs, Pierced			

Olive Pattern.	Heavy Plate.	Double Plate.	Treble Plate.
	Per dozen. $	Per dozen. $	Per dozen. $
Tea Spoons			
Dessert Spoons			
Table Spoons			
Dessert Forks			
Medium Forks			
Table Forks			
Oyster Forks			
Beef or Child's Forks			
Pickle Forks			
Salt Spoons			
Salt Shovels			
Mustard Spoons			
Egg Spoons			
Sugar Shells			
Sugar Sifters			
Sugar Tongs			
Butter Knives, Spoon Handle			
Cream Ladles			
Gravy Ladles			
Oyster Ladles	Each.	Each.	Each.
Fish Knives, Engraved			
Pie Knives, Engraved			
Cake Knives, Engraved			
Ice Cream Knives, Engraved			
Crumb Knives, Engraved			
Asparagus Tongs, Pierced			
Ice Tongs			

SILVER PLATED TABLE WARE.

(Continued.)

Brunswick Spoons and Forks, &c.

Brunswick Spoon.

Brunswick Fork.

Brunswick Sugar Shell.

Brunswick Pattern.	Heavy Plate.	Double Plate.	Treble Plate.	Quadruple Plate.
	Per dozen. $	Per dozen. $	Per dozen. $	Per dozen. $
Tea Spoons				
Dessert Spoons				
Table Spoons				
Dessert Forks				
Medium Forks				
Table Forks				
Oyster Forks, Two Tines				
Beef, or Child's Forks				
Pickle Forks				
Salt Spoons				
Salt Shovels				
Mustard Shovels				
Sugar Shells				
Sugar Sifters				
Sugar Tongs				
Sugar Shovels				
Butter Knives, Spoon Handle				
Cream Ladles				
Gravy Ladles				
	Each.	Each.	Each.	Each.
Oyster Ladles				
Soup Ladles				
Fish Knives, Engraved				
Pie Knives, Engraved				
Cake Knives, Engraved				

Beaded or Mayflower Spoons and Forks, &c.

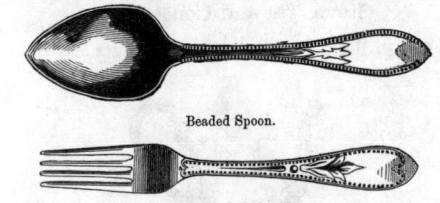

Beaded Spoon.

Beaded Fork.

Beaded or Mayflower Pattern.	Heavy Plate.	Double Plate.	Treble Plate.	Quadruple Plate.
	Per Dozen. $	Per Dozen. $	Per Dozen. $	Per Dozen. $
Tea Spoons				
Dessert Spoons				
Table Spoons				
Dessert Forks				
Medium Forks				
Table Forks				
Beef or Child's Forks				
Salt Spoons				
Salt Shovels				
Mustard Spoons				
Sugar Shells				
Sugar Sifters				
Sugar Tongs				
Butter Knives, Spoon Handle				
Butter Knives, New Pattern				
Butter Knives, Flat Handle				
Cream Ladles				
Gravy Ladles	Each.	Each.	Each.	Each.
Oyster Ladles				
Soup Ladles				
Fish Knives, Engraved				
Pie Knives, Engraved				
Cake Knives, Engraved				

German Silver Spoons.

Plain Table	per gross, $	
Tipped Table	"	
Plain Dessert	"	
Tipped Dessert	"	
Plain Teas	"	
Tipped Teas	"	

CANDLESTICKS, PLATED ON WHITE METAL.

No. 2.	No. 3.	No. 93. With Extinguisher.	No. 9.	No. 11.

per pair.

$

Nos.	2	3	4	5	8	9	10	11	45	55	90	91	92	93	102	103	104	105

BRITANNIA WARE.

Stove, Tea and Coffee Pots,
With Tin Bodies and Britannia Tops, Spouts and Handles.

No. 40.

Nos.	$ 30	40	50	60	70	80	90	per doz.

Rolled Metal Tea and Coffee Pots,

No. 910.   No. 1105.

$									per dozen.
Nos.	900	910	920	930	940	1100	1105	1110	1115
	3½	4	7½	9	11	3½	4	8	10	pints.

$					per dozen.
Nos.	1990	7000	7100	7200	7300
	10	3½	4	8	10	pints.

Plated Tip.

$					per doz.
Nos.	615	616	617	618	619

Rolled Metal Caster Frames, without Bottles.

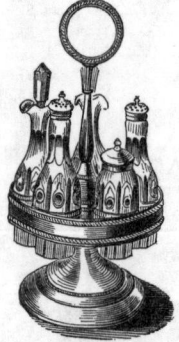 

No. 572.   No. 574.

No. 100, 5 and 6 Ring, Open Band..................per dozen, $
No. 100, 5 and 6 Ring, Engraved...................   "
No. 105, 4 and 5 Ring ....   "
No. 110, 4 and 5 Ring ....   "
No. 115, 4 and 5 Ring ....   "
No. 116, 4 and 5 Ring ....   "
No. 125, 4 and 5 Ring ....   "
No. 140, 4 and 5 Ring ....   "

Rolled Metal Caster Frames, without Bottles
Continued.

No. 141, 4 and 5 Ring ....per dozen, $
No. 142, 4 and 5 Ring ....   "
No. 145, 4 and 5 Ring ....   "
No. 146, 4 and 5 Ring ....   "
No. 147, 4 and 5 Ring ....   "
No. 162, 5 and 6 Ring ....   "
No. 165, 5 and 6 Ring ....   "
No. 167, 5 and 6 Ring ....   "
No. 187, 5 and 6 Ring ....   "
No. 200, 5 and 6 Ring, Open Band...............   "
No. 200, 5 and 6 Ring, Plain Band ....   "
No. 250, 5 and 6 Ring, Open Band ....   "
No. 300,   6 Ring, Open Band ....   "
No. 300,   6 Ring, Engraved Band.............   "
No. 464, 5 and 6 Ring ....   "
No. 550, 4 and 5 Ring ....   "
No. 560, 5 and 6 Ring ....   "
No. 570, 5 and 6 Ring ....   "
No. 571, 5 and 6 Ring ....   "
No. 572, 5 and 6 Ring ....   "
No. 573, 5 and 6 Ring ....   "
No. 574, 5 and 6 Ring ....   "
No. 576, 5 and 6 Ring ....   "
No. 577, 5 and 6 Ring ....   "

Soup Ladles.

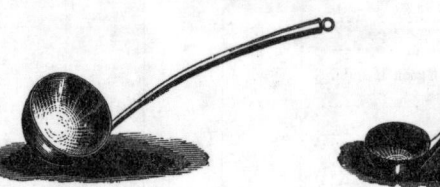

No. 7.   No. 10.

No. 2, Flat Handle.........................per dozen, $
No. 7, Tin   "   ....   "
No. 9, Wire   "   ....   "
No. 10, Britannia Handle, Sauce Tureen.........   "

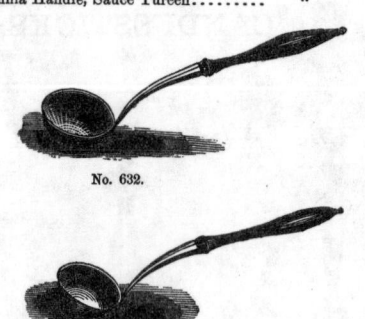

No. 632.

No. 633.

No. 631, Wood Handle ....per dozen, $
No. 632,   "   "   ....   "
No. 633,   "   "   ....   "

BRITANNIA AND TINNED IRON WARE.

BRITANNIA CANDLESTICKS.

No. 92.

$							per doz.
Nos.	1	2	3	3½	4	5	5½	8
	7	9¼	9½	4½	10	11	3	13 inches high.

$							per doz.
Nos.	10	12	45	50	60	70	80
	4½	5	7½	6½	8	9	10 inches high.

$							per doz.
Nos.	90	91	92	93	100	102	103
	4½	4½	4½	6	6	7½	9½ inches high.

$			per doz.
Nos.	104	105	200
	10½	11½	5 inches high.

BRITANNIA SPOONS.

Table Spoons.	Tea Spoons.
No. 2600 . . . . . . per gross, $	No. 1080 . . . . . . per gross, $
No. 2730 . . . . . . "	No. 2110 . . . . . . "
No. 2920 . . . . . . "	No. 2520 . . . . . . "
No. 2950 . . . . . . "	No. 2550 . . . . . . "

BRITANNIA SPOONS—(Continued.)

Figured Patterns.

Table Spoons.	Tea Spoons.
No. 4680, Fr. Tip'd. per gross, $	No. 2340, Fr. Tip'd. per gross, $
No. 5660, Beaded . . "	No. 2830, Beaded . . "
No. 6580, Albata . . "	No. 3290, Albata . . "
No. 6960, Brunsw'k "	No. 3480, Brunsw'k "

Cheap Metal.

| No. 340 . . . . . . per gross, $ | No. 340 . . . . . . per gross, $ |

Metallic Strengthened.

No. 1 . . . . per gross, $	No. 1 . . . . per gross, $
No. 2 . . . . "	No. 10 . . . . "
No. 10 . . . . "	No. 12 . . . . "
No. 12 . . . . "	

Wire Strengthened.

No. 3 . . . . . per gross, $	No. 30 . . . . . per gross, $
No. 20 . . . . "	No. 50 . . . . "
No. 40 . . . . "	No. 70 . . . . "
No. 60 . . . . "	
No. 80 . . . . . . : "	
No. 90 . . . . "	

Plated Britannia, or Argentine Spoons.

Tipped Pattern . . per gross, $	Tipped Pattern . . per gross, $
Beaded " . . "	Beaded " . . "
Brunswick " . . "	Brunswick " . . "

TINNED IRON WARE.

Patent Round Handle Iron Spoons.

No. 85, Tea Spoons . . . . per gross, $
No. 160, Table Spoons . . . . "
No. 170, Table Spoons . . . . "
No. 180, Table Spoons . . . . "

Patent Flat Handle Iron Spoons.

No. 2 Tea Spoons . . . . per gross, $
No. 1 Table Spoons . . . . "
No. 2 Table Spoons . . . . "
No. 3 Table Spoons . . . . "

Patent Bevel Handle Iron Spoons.

No. 02 Tea Spoons . . . . per gross, $
No. 01 Table Spoons . . . . "
No. 02 Table Spoons . . . . "
No. 03 Table Spoons . . . . "

Patent Threaded Spoons.

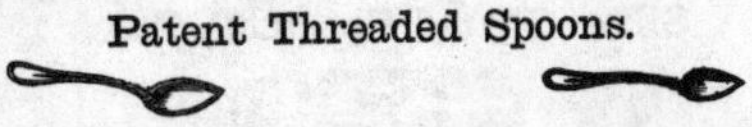

No. 30 Solid Tea Spoons . . . . per gross, $
No. 31 Solid Tea Spoons . . . . "
No. 20 Solid Table Spoons . . . . "
No. 21 Solid Table Spoons . . . . "
No. 22 Solid Table Spoons . . . . "
No. 23 Solid Table Spoons . . . . "
No. 26 Solid Table Spoons . . . . "

Concave Strengthened Tin Spoons.

Tea Spoons.

$				per gross.
No.	1	2	3	4

Table Spoons.

$				per gross.
No.	4	5	6	7

Patent Round Handle Basting Spoons.

$					per gross.
8	10	12	14	16	18 inches.

Patent Flat Handle Basting Spoons.

$					per gross.
8	10	12	14	16	inches.

Patent Bevel Handle Basting Spoons.

$				per gross.
10	12	14	16	inches.

Patent Threaded Solid Basting Spoons.

$					per gross.
10	12	14	16	18	inches.

Patent Wood Handle Preserve Spoons.

$			per gross.
10	12	15	inches.

Patent Heavy Tinned Iron Forks.

No. 850, Table Forks, Four Tined . . . . per gross, $
No. 851, Table Forks, Four Tined, Medium . . . . "

Patent Threaded Forks.

No. 24, Tinned Table Forks . . . . per gross, $

Iron Handle Flesh Forks,

Two Pronged, 13 inch . . . . per dozen, $
Two Pronged, 16 inch . . . . "
Three Pronged, 13 inch . . . . "
Three Pronged, 16 inch . . . . "

CAKE TURNERS, LADLES, TOBACCO BOXES, ETC.

Wood Handle Flesh Forks.

Two Pronged......13 inch.........................per dozen, $
Two Pronged......16 inch........................   "
Three Pronged......13 inch.......................   "
Three Pronged......16 inch.......................   "

Tinned Iron Wash Bowls.
Extra Quality, Double Plated.

	$				per dozen.
No.	24	26	28	30	

Tinned Iron Sauce Pans, Extra Quality.

	$					per dozen.
No.	14	16	18	20	22	

Patent Cake Turners.

No. 1, Russia Iron, square..........................per dozen, $
No. 2, Russia Iron, square, Ferruled Handle ....   "
No. 3, Cast Steel, square, Ferruled Handle ....   "
No. 5, Iron Handle ....   "
No. 10, Wood Handle ....   "

Patent Egg Turners.
No. 4, Iron Handle..............................per dozen, $
No. 8, Wood Handle.............................   "

Patent Wood Handle Ladles.

	$				per doz.
Nos.	1	2	3	4	
	3	3½	4	4½	inch.

Patent Flat Iron Handle Ladles.

	$				per doz.
Nos.	5	6	7	8	
	3	3½	4	4½	inch.

Patent Round Iron Handle Ladles.

	$				per doz.
Nos.	9	10	11	12	
	3	3½	4	4½	inch.

Patent Iron Handle Ladles, Light.

	$				per doz.
Nos.	13	14	15	16	

Patent Perforated Ladles.

No. 2, Iron Handle..............................per dozen, $
No. 4, Wood Handle ....   "

Patent Handle Skimmers.

No. 1, Flat Iron Handle.........................per dozen, $
No. 2, Round Iron Handle ....   "
No. 3, Wood Handle ....   "

Patent Cook's Dippers.
No. 1, Iron Handle..............................per dozen, $
No. 2, Iron Handle.............................   "
No. 3, Wood Handle.............................   "
No. 4, Wood Handle.............................   "

Patent Wood Handle Cook's Scoops.

	$			per doz.
Nos.	1	2	3	

Solid Tin Army Cups.

No. 1, Extra Quality ....per dozen, $
No. 2, Extra Quality ....   "

Planished Tin, Silver Finished Tobacco Boxes.

No. 22, Plain Top and Bottom, Plain Band.
No. 22. Holds one-eighth pound or 2 papers.........per gross, $

No. 20.
No. 20, Plain Top and Bottom.....................per gross, $

No. 81.
No. 81, Figured Top, Plain Bottom.................per gross, $
No. 82, Figured Top, Figured Bottom..............   "

Silver Plated Tobacco Boxes, on German Silver.
No. 300, O. G. Shield.............................per doz., $

Planished Tin, Silver Finished Spectacle Cases.

No. 20.
No. 20, Plain Top and Bottom, Short..............per gross, $

No. 25.
No. 25, Medium, Plain Top and Bottom.............per gross, $

No. 30.
No. 30, Plain Top and Bottom, for Long Spectacles....per gross, $

No. 40.
No. 40, Figured Top, Short.......................per gross, $
No. 50, Figured Top and Bottom, Short.............per gross, $
Planished Cases, all lined with Colored Plush.

Silver Plated Spectacle Cases.

No. 200.
No. 200, Silver Plated, O. G. Shield...............per doz., $
No. 201, Silver Plated, O. G. Shield, Medium..........   "
No. 202, Silver Plated, O. G. Shield, Long.............   "

No. 210.
No. 210, Silver Plated, Fancy Top.................per doz., $
No. 211, Silver Plated, Fancy Top, Medium...........   "
No. 212, Silver Plated, Fancy Top, Long.............   "
These Cases are all lined with Fine Velvet.

Silver Plated Spectacles.

Wide Slide Bows.	Narrow Slide Bows.	Long Single Bows.

	$				per doz.
Nos.	A 1 Extra	1 Extra	1	3	

Either Wide, Narrow, or Long Bows.

RUSSELL'S AMERICAN TABLE CUTLERY.

(For Description of Plates, see pages 356, 357, 358.)

These Plates Represent the Exact Size of Each Article.

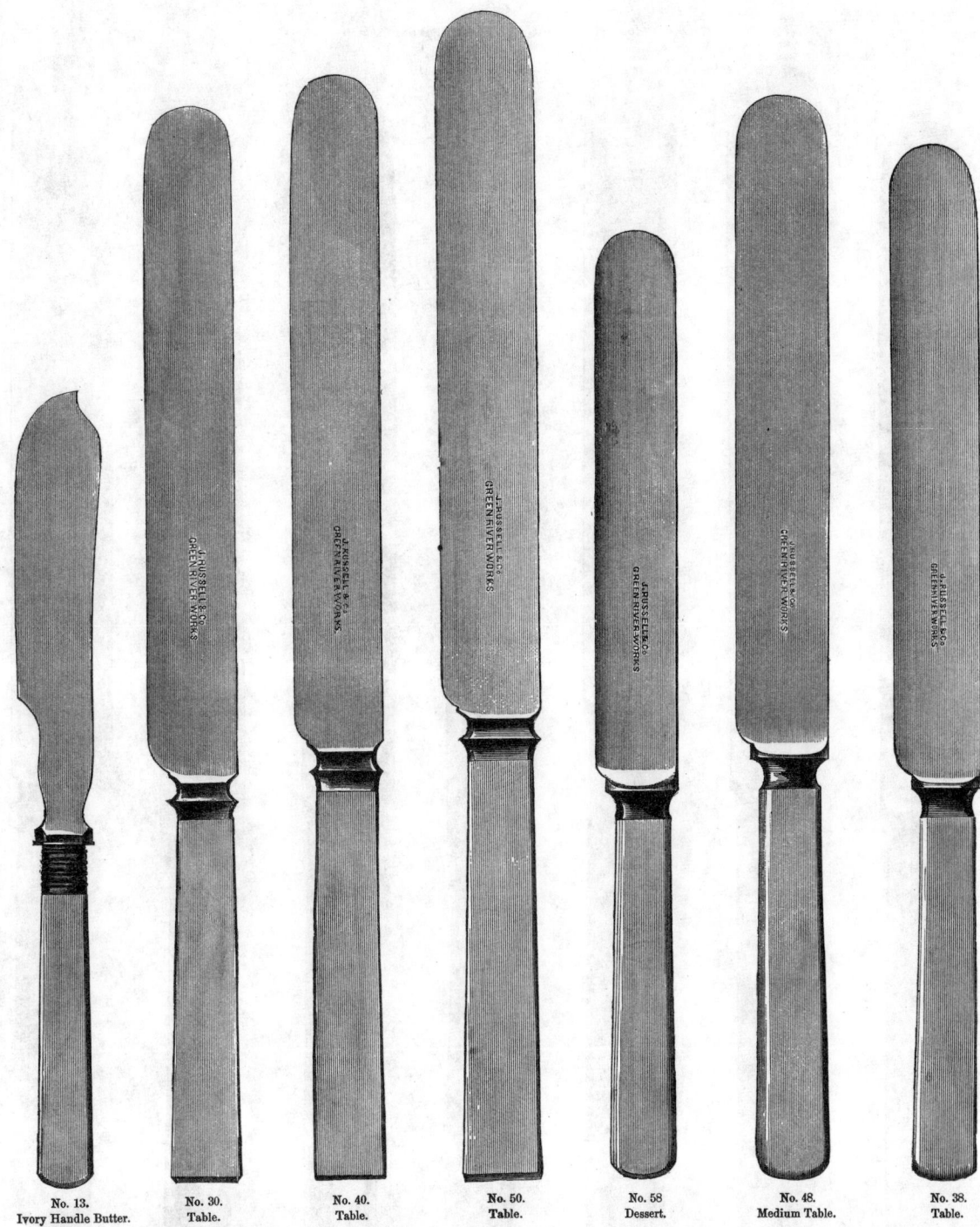

No. 13.	No. 30.	No. 40.	No. 50.	No. 58.	No. 48.	No. 38.
Ivory Handle Butter.	Table.	Table.	Table.	Dessert.	Medium Table.	Table.

RUSSELL'S AMERICAN TABLE CUTLERY.

(Continued.)

(For Description of Plates see pages 356, 357, 358.)

These Plates Represent the Exact Size of Each Article.

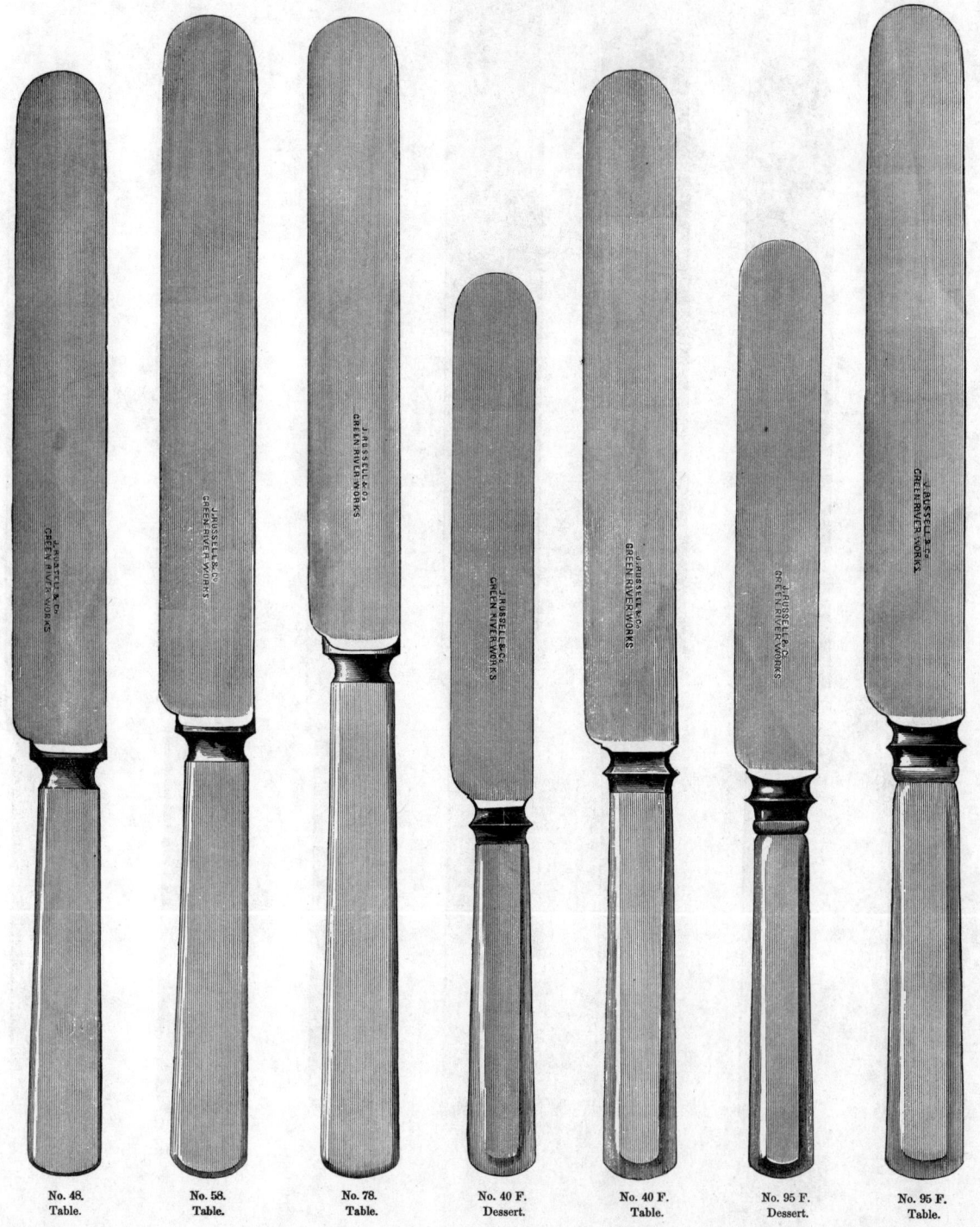

| No. 48. | No. 58. | No. 78. | No. 40 F. | No. 40 F. | No. 95 F. | No. 95 F. |
| Table. | Table. | Table. | Dessert. | Table. | Dessert. | Table. |

RUSSELL'S AMERICAN TABLE CUTLERY.

(Continued.)

[For Description of Plates see pages 356, 357, 358.]

These Plates Represent the Exact Size of Each Article.

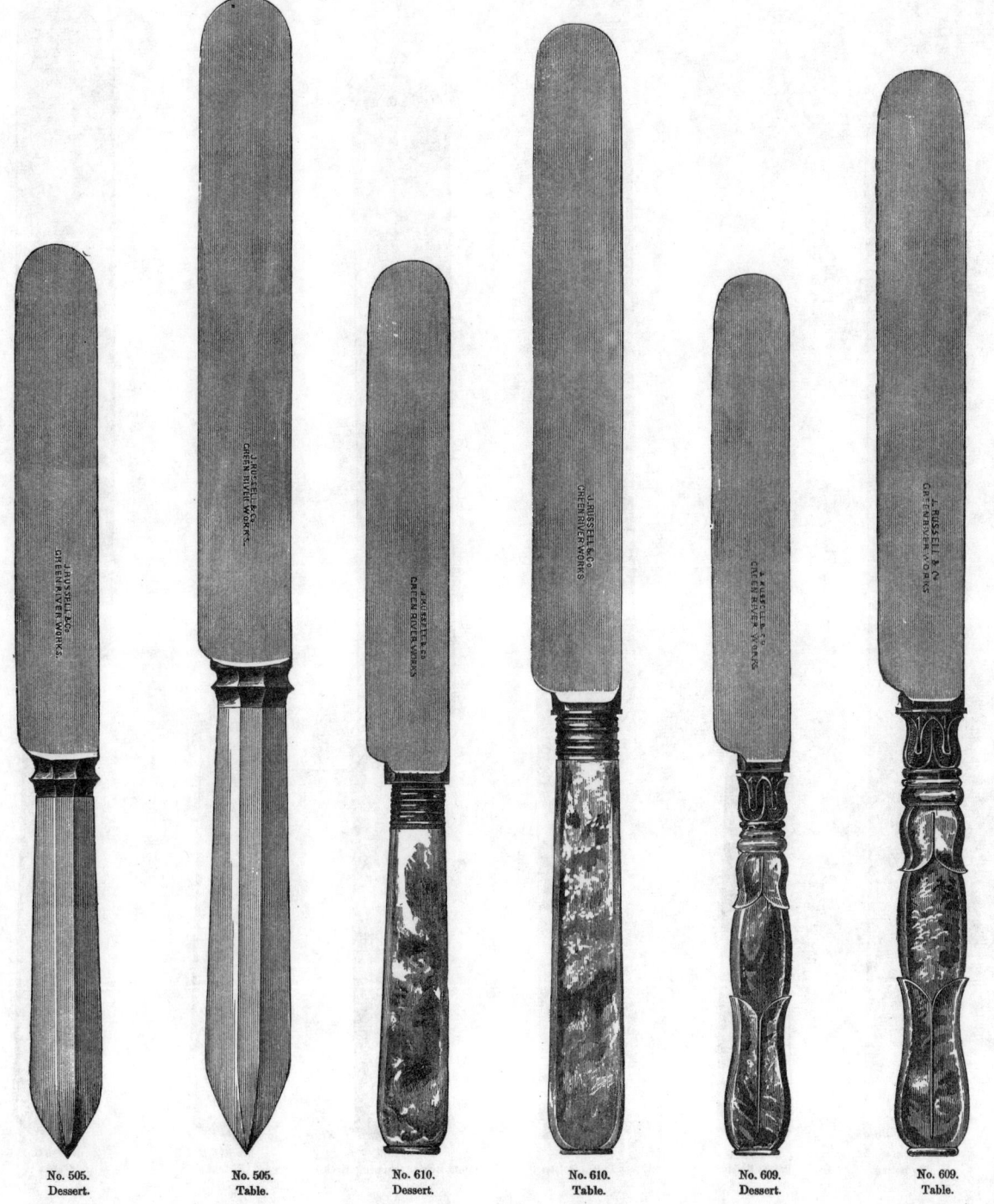

| No. 505. Dessert. | No. 505. Table. | No. 610. Dessert. | No. 610. Table. | No. 609. Dessert. | No. 609. Table. |

RUSSELL'S AMERICAN TABLE CUTLERY.

(Continued.)

(For Description of Plates see pages 356, 357, 358.)

These Plates Represent the Exact Size of Each Article.

No. 1006.	No. 01016.	No. 01016.	No. 1016.	No. 1085 N.	No. 1085.
No Bolster.	Patent Bolster.	Patent Bolster.	Patent Bolster (showing Back.)	Patent.	Table.

RUSSELL'S AMERICAN TABLE CUTLERY.

(Continued.)

(For Description of Plates see pages 356, 357, 358.)

These Plates Represent the Exact Size of Each Article.

No. 0831.	No. 869 N.	No. 863 N.	No. 863.	No. 1649 N.	No. 1506.
Self Tip, Patent Bolster.	Self Tip Handle.	Self Tip Handle.	Table.	Ebony.	No Bolster.

RUSSELL'S AMERICAN TABLE CUTLERY.

(Continued.)

(For Description of Plates see pages 356, 357, 358.)

These Plates Represent the Exact Size of Each Article.

| No. 15060. | No. 15060.
No Bolster. | No. 1049 N.
Patent. | No. 1049 N.
Table. | No. 01503.
Patent Bolster. | No. 1531.
Patent Bolster. | No. 01531.
Patent Bolster. |

RUSSELL'S AMERICAN TABLE CUTLERY.

(Continued.)

(For Description of Plates, see pages 356, 357, 358.)

These Plates Represent the Exact Size of Each Article.

| No. 1569 N. | Putty Knife. | Patent Pallet Knife. 6 inch. | Patent Pallet Knife. 3 inch. | Patent Bolster Hunting Knife. Checked Handle. | Patent Bolster Hunting Knife (showing Back.) |

RUSSELL'S AMERICAN TABLE CUTLERY.

(Continued.)

(For Description of Plates see pages 356, 357, 358.)

These Plates Represent the Exact Size of Each Article.

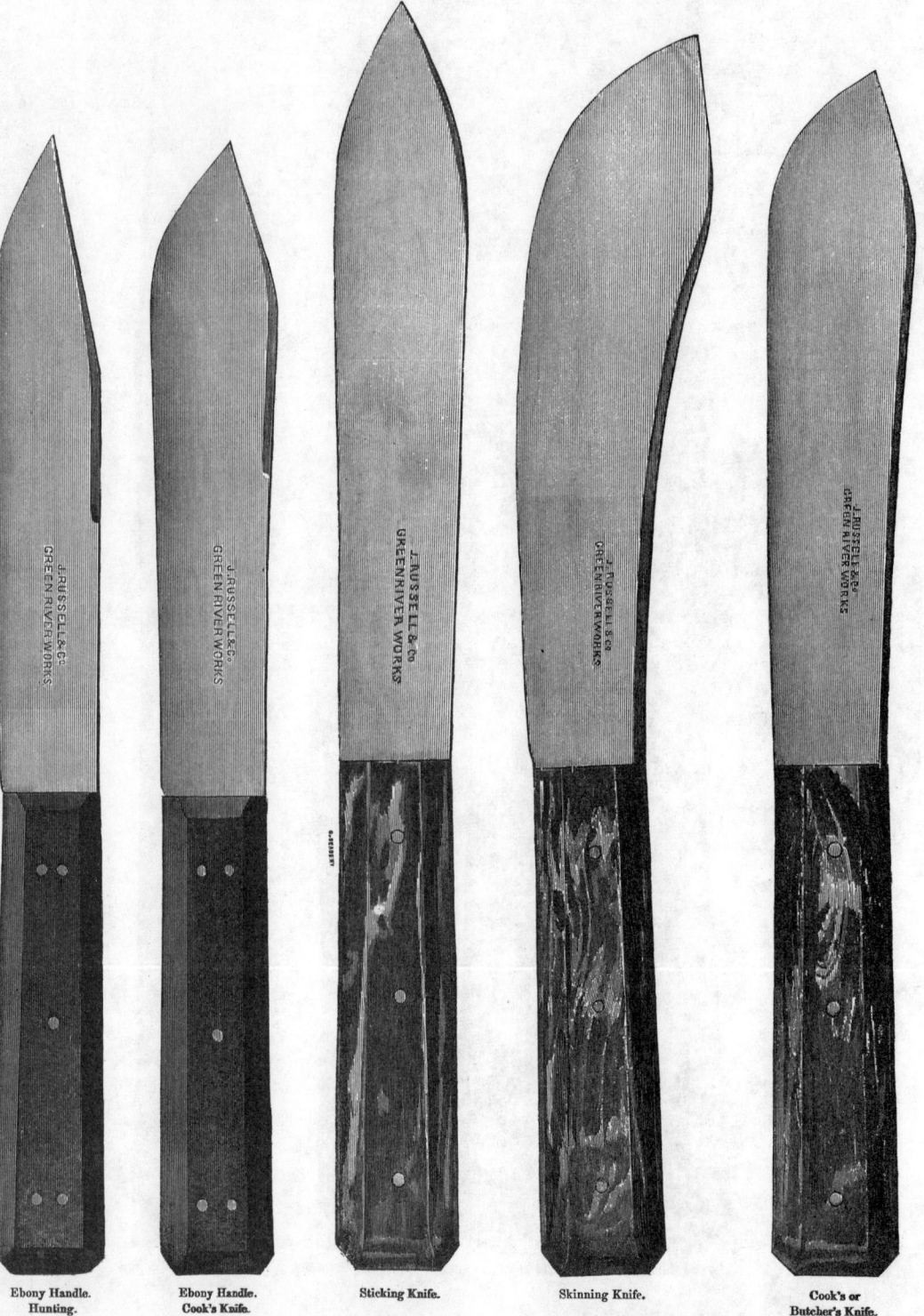

| Ebony Handle. Hunting. | Ebony Handle. Cook's Knife. | Sticking Knife. | Skinning Knife. | Cook's or Butcher's Knife. |

RUSSELL'S AMERICAN TABLE CUTLERY.

(Continued.)

[*For Description of Plates see pages* 356, 357, 358.]
These Plates Represent the Exact Size of Each Article.

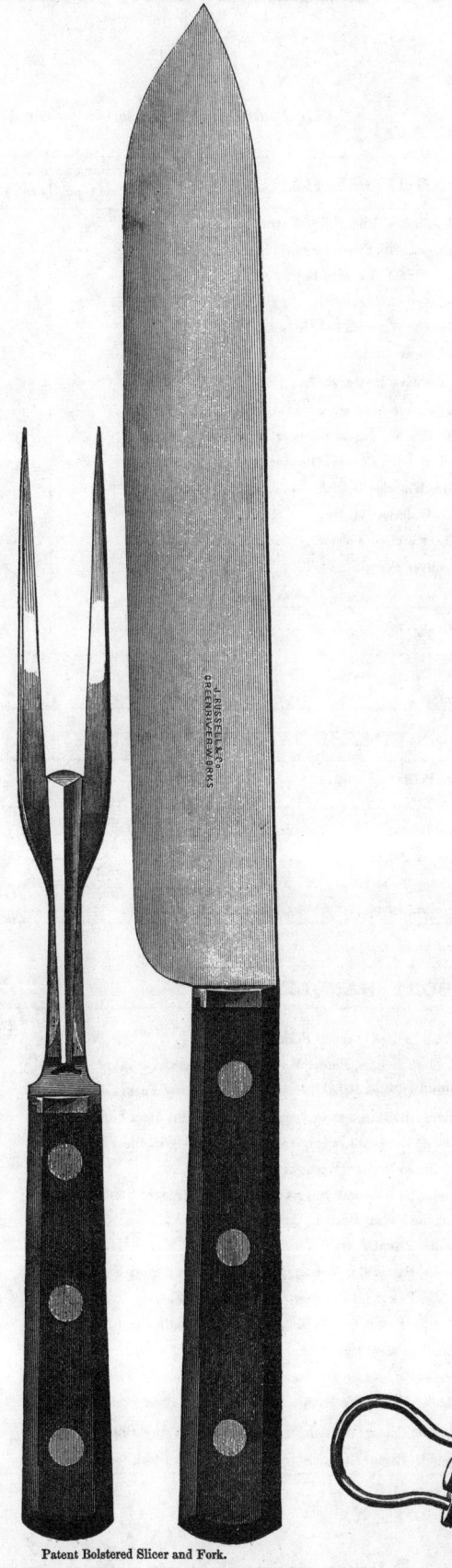

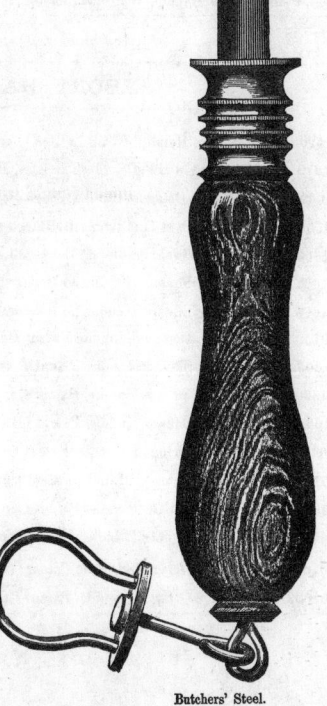

Beef Slicer, French Pattern.   Patent Bolstered Slicer and Fork.   Butchers' Steel.

RUSSELL'S AMERICAN TABLE CUTLERY.

(Continued.)

[*For Plates, see pages 347 to 355 inclusive.*]

FINE PEARL AND IVORY HANDLES.	Table Knives. Per Dozen,	Dessert Knives. Per Dozen,	Beef Carvers. Per Pair,	Game Carvers. Per Pair,	Steels. Per Dozen,	Butter Knives. Per Dozen,
No. 609, Pearl, Double Tulip Handle, Beaded End, Silver Ferrule	$	$	$	$	$	$
No. 610, Pearl Oval Handle, Cambridge Head, Silver Ferrule						
No. 505, Ivory, Octagon Pointed End, Fluted Waterloo Bolster						
No. 95, F, Ivory, Fluted Oval Handle, Waterloo Bolster						
No. 40, F, Ivory, Fluted Square Handle, Waterloo Bolster						
No. 78, Ivory, Plain Oval Handle, Concave Bolster						
No. 58, Ivory, Plain Oval Handle, Concave Bolster						
No. 48, Ivory, Plain Oval Handle, Concave Bolster						
No. 48 Medium. Ivory, Plain Oval Handle, Concave Bolster						
No. 38 Medium. Ivory, Plain Oval Handle, Concave Bolster						
No. 50, Ivory, Plain Square Handle, Waterloo Bolster						
No. 40, Ivory, Plain Square Handle, Waterloo Bolster						
No. 30, Ivory, Plain Square Handle, Waterloo Bolster						
No. 13, Ivory, Plain Oval Handle, Silver Ferrule						
No. 85, Ivory, Plain Oval Handle						

Nut Picks, Oval Handle .... per dozen, $

Nut Picks, Square Handle .... per dozen, $

COARSE IVORY HANDLES.		Table Knives.	Dessert Knives
No. 482, Plain Oval Handle, Concave Bolster	per dozen,	$	$
No. 85, Plain Oval Handle, Concave Bolster	"		
No. 84, Plain Oval Handle, Concave Bolster	"		
No. 402, Plain Square Handle, Waterloo Bolster	"		
No. 302, Plain Square Handle, Waterloo Bolster	"		
No. 303, Plain Square Handle, Waterloo Bolster	"		

EBONY HANDLES.	Table Knives and Forks. Per Gross.	Dessert Knives and Forks. Per Gross.	Carvers. Per Pair.	Steels. Per Dozen.	Jones' Carvers. Per Pair.
No. 1520, Solid Square Handle, Flush Bolster, French Fork	$	$	$	$	$
No. 1679 N, Solid Octagon Handle, Flush Bolster, Patent Wrought Steel Fork					
No. 1649 N, Scale Tang, Octagon Handle, Flush Bolster, Patent Wrought Steel Fork					
No. 16060, Scale Tang, Oval Handle, no Bolster, 3 cap rivets, Patent Wrought Steel Fork					
No. 16050, Scale Tang, Oval Handle, no Bolster, 3 cap rivets, 2 prong, Pat't Wr't Steel Fork					
No. 1606, Scale Tang, Square Handle, no Bolster, Wrought Steel Fork					
No. 1605, Scale Tang, Square Handle, no Bolster, 3 cap rivets, 2 prong, Wrought Steel Fork					
No. 01603, Scale Tang, Octagon Handle, Patent Bolster, Wrought Steel Fork					
No. 1603, Scale Tang, Square Handle, Patent Bolster, Wrought Steel Fork					
No. 1630, Scale Tang, Square Handle, Patent Cap Bolster, 2 prong, Wrought Steel Fork					
No. 1631, Scale Tang, Square Handle, Patent Cap Bolster, Wrought Steel Fork					
No. 01630, Scale Tang, Octagon Handle, Patent Cap Bolster, 2 prong, Wrought Steel Fork					
No. 01631, Scale Tang, Octagon Handle, Patent Cap Bolster, Wrought Steel Fork,					
No. 1632, Scale Tang, Square Handle, Patent Cap Bolster, Brass, 2 pr'g, Wrought Steel Fork					
No. 1633, Scale Tang, Square Handle, Patent Cap Bolster, Brass, Wrought Steel Fork					
No. 01632, Scale Tang, Octagon Handle, Patent Cap Bolster, Brass, 2 pr'g, Wrought Steel Fork					
No. 01633, Scale Tang, Octagon Handle, Patent Cap Bolster, Brass, Wrought Steel Fork					

RUSSELL'S AMERICAN TABLE CUTLERY.

(Continued.)

(For Plates see pages 347 to 355 inclusive.)

HORN HANDLES.	Table Knives and Forks.	Dessert Knives and Forks.	Carvers.	Steels.	Jones' Carvers.
	Per Gross.	Per Gross.	Per Pair.	Per Dozen.	Per Pair.
No. 863 N, Solid Square Balance Handle, Waterloo Bolster, Patent Wrought Steel Fork........	$	$	$	$	$
No. 858 N, Solid Oval Balance Handle, Concave Bolster, Wrought Patent Steel Fork..........					
No. 869 N, Solid Octagon Balance Handle, Flush Bolster, Patent Wrought Steel Fork.........					
No. 1059 N, Scale Tang, Octagon Handle, Flush Bolster, Patent Wrought Steel Fork.........					
No. 806, Scale Tang, Square Handle, no Bolster, Wrought Steel Fork....................					
No. 805, Scale Tang, Square Handle, no Bolster, 2 prong, Wrought Steel Fork...........					
No. 0803, Scale Tang, Octagon Handle, Patent Flush Bolster, Wrought Steel Fork..........					
No. 803, Scale Tang, Square Handle, Patent Flush Bolster, Wrought Steel Fork...........					
No. 830, Scale Tang, Square Handle, Patent Cap Bolster, 2 prong, Wrought Steel Fork......					
No. 831, Scale Tang, Square Handle, Patent Cap Bolster, Wrought Steel Fork............					
No. 0830, Scale Tang, Octagon Handle, Patent Cap Bolster, 2 prong, Wrought Steel Fork.....					
No. 0831, Scale Tang, Octagon Handle, Patent Cap Bolster, Wrought Steel Fork............					
No. 0832, Scale Tang, Octagon Handle, Patent Cap Bolster, Brass, 2 pr'g, Wrought Steel Fork.					
No. 0833, Scale Tang, Octagon Handle, Patent Cap Bolster, Brass, Wrought Steel Fork.......					

BONE HANDLES.	Table Knives and Forks.	Dessert Knives and Forks.	Carvers.	Steels.	Jones' Carvers.
	Per Gross.	Per Gross.	Per Pair.	Per Dozen.	Per Pair.
No. 1079 N, Scale Tang, Octagon Handle, Flush Bolsters, Patent Wrought Steel Fork........	$	$	$	$	$
No. 1006, Scale Tang, Square Handle, No Bolsters, Wrought Steel Fork					
No. 1005, Scale Tang, Square Handle, No Bolsters, 2 prong Wrought Steel Fork.............					
No. 01003, Scale Tang, Octagon Handle, Patent Flush Bolsters, Wrought Steel Fork					
No. 1003, Scale Tang, Square Handle, Patent Flush Bolsters, Wrought Steel Fork.........					
No. 1015, Scale Tang, Square Handle, Patent Cap Bolsters, 2 prong Wrought Steel Fork.....					
No. 1016, Scale Tang, Square Handle, Patent Cap Bolsters, Wrought Steel Fork............					
No. 01015, Scale Tang, Octagon Handle, Patent Cap Bolsters, 2 prong Wrought Steel Fork....					
No. 01016, Scale Tang, Octagon Handle, Patent Cap Bolsters, Wrought Steel Fork...........					
No. 1017, Scale Tang, Square Handle, Patent Cap Bolsters, Brass, 2 prong Wrought Steel Fork					
No. 1018, Scale Tang, Square Handle, Patent Cap Bolsters, Brass, Wrought Steel Fork.......					
No. 01017, Scale Tang, Octagon Handle, Patent Cap Bolsters, Brass, 2 prong Wrought Steel Fork					
No. 01018, Scale Tang, Octagon Handle, Patent Cap Bolsters, Brass, Wrought Steel Fork.......					

COCOA HANDLES.	Table Knives and Forks.	Dessert Knives and Forks.	Carvers.	Steels.	Jones' Carvers.
	Per Gross.	Per Gross.	Per Pair.	Per Dozen.	Per Pair.
No. 1515, Solid Square Handle, Flush Bolster, French Fork...................	$	$	$	$	$
No. 1569 N, Solid Octagon Handle, Flush Bolster, Patent Wrought Steel Fork...............					
No. 1049 N, Scale Tang, Octagon Handle, Flush Bolster, Patent Wrought Steel Fork..........					
No. 15060, Scale Tang, Oval Handle, No Bolster, 3 cap rivets, Steel Fork.................					
No. 15050, Scale Tang, Oval Handle, No Bolster, 3 cap rivets, 2 prong Steel Fork					
No. 1506, Scale Tang, Square Handle, No Bolster, Wrought Steel Fork....................					
No. 1505, Scale Tang, Square Handle, No Bolster, 2 prong Wrought Steel Fork............					
No. 01503, Scale Tang, Octagon Handle, Patent Flush Bolster, Steel Fork.................					
No. 1503, Scale Tang, Square Handle, Patent Flush Bolster, Wrought Steel Fork...........					
No. 1530, Scale Tang, Square Handle, Patent Cap Bolster, 2 prong Wrought Steel Fork......					
No. 1531, Scale Tang, Square Handle, Patent Cap Bolster, Wrought Steel Fork.............					
No. 01530, Scale Tang, Octagon Handle, Patent Cap Bolster, 2 prong Wrought Steel Fork.....					
No. 01531, Scale Tang, Octagon Handle, Patent Cap Bolster, Wrought Steel Fork...........					
No. 1532, Scale Tang, Square Handle, Patent Cap Bolster, Brass, 2 prong Wrought Steel Fork					
No. 1533, Scale Tang, Square Handle, Patent Cap Bolster, Brass, Wrought Steel Fork.......					
No. 01532, Scale Tang, Octagon Handle, Patent Cap Bolster, Brass, 2 prong Wrought Steel Fork					
No. 01533, Scale Tang, Octagon Handle, Patent Cap Bolster, Brass, Wrought Steel Fork......					

RUSSELL'S AMERICAN TABLE CUTLERY.

(*Continued.*)

(*For Plates see pages 347 to 355 inclusive.*)

BUTCHERS', COOKS', PALLET, PUTTY KNIVES, &c.

Russell's Pressed and Cocoa Butchers' and Cooks' Knives.

Size..   4½   4¾   5   5½   6   6½   7   8   9   10   11   12   13   14   15   16   17   18   per doz. inch.

Pressed and Cocoa Butchers' and Cooks' Knives, stamped "J. Ward."

Size..   4½   4¾   5   5½   6   6½   7   8   9   10   11   12   13   14   15   16   18   20   per doz. inch.

Russell's Ebony Handle Swaged Cooks' and Hunters' Knives.

Size..   5   5½   6   6½   7   8   9   10   11   12   13   14   15   16   17   18   per doz. inch.

Bolster Hunting and Cooks' Knives —Ebony Handles.

Size..   5   5½   6   6½   7   8   9   10   11   12   per doz. inch.

Bolster Hunting and Cooks' Knives—Ebony Handles, Checked.

Size..   5   5½   6   6½   7   8   9   10   11   12   per doz. inch.

Russell's Beech Butchers' and Cooks' Knives.

Size..   5   5½   6   6½   7   8   9   10   11   12   13   14   per doz. inch.

Beech Handle Butchers' and Cooks' Knives, stamped "J. Ward."

Size..   5   5½   6   6½   7   8   9   10   11   12   per doz. inch.

Skinning and Sticking Knives 5   5½   6   6½   7   per doz. inch.

Butchers' Steels 8   9   10   12   14   per doz. inch.

Black Handle Shoe Knives, Round and Square Points .... per dozen, $

White Handle Shoe Knives, Scale Tang 4   4½   5   per doz. inch.

Putty Knives, Round and Square Points .... per dozen, $

Pallet Knives 3   4   5   6   7   8   9   10   11   12   per doz. inch.

Pallet Knives, Balance Handle .... extra per dozen,

Hacking Knives .... per dozen,

MISCELLANEOUS.

No. 1040, Scale Tang Carving Knives, 10 inch, 5 pins, Cocoa Handle........................... per dozen, $

No. 1040, Scale Tang Large Forks, to match .... "

No. 1041, Scale Tang Carving Knives, 10 inch, 5 pins, Ebony Handle........................... "

No. 1041, Scale Tang Large Forks, to match........................... "

French Beef Slicers, Ebony Handle................ }
English Slicers, same sizes and prices as French...... }   8   9   10   12   14   16   per dozen. inch.

Patent Bolster Beef Slicers 7   8   9   10   11   12   14   16   per dozen. inch.

French Slicer Forks, large size........................... per dozen, $

French Slicer Forks, small size........................... "

Patent Slicer Forks, large .... "

Patent Slicer Forks, small........................... "

Solid Handle Ebony Bread Knives........................... "

Scale Tang, Cocoa Bread Knives, 8 inch........................... "

Scale Tang Cocoa Bread Knives, stamped "J. Ward," 7 inch........................... "

Scale Tang Cocoa Bread Knives, stamped "J. Ward"........................... "

Butter Knives, Horn Tip........................... "

Butter Knives, Cocoa or Ebony........................... "

AMERICAN POCKET CUTLERY.

(NORTHFIELD KNIFE COMPANY.)

These Plates Represent the Exact Size of Each Article.

ONE BLADE.

No. 52.

No. 50, Pearl Handles, German Silver Bolster, Brass Lined...per dozen, $

No. 51, Shell Handle, German Silver Bolster, Brass Lined.. "

No. 52, Ivory Handle, German Silver Bolster, Brass Lined (see Plate).. "

No. 48.

No. 48, Ivory Handle, German Silver Bolster, Brass Lined...per dozen, $

No. 49, Buffalo Handle, German Silver Bolster, Brass Lined... "

TWO BLADES.

No. 110.

No. 109, Pearl Handle, Polished Blades, Brass Lined...per dozen, $

No. 110, Shell Handle, Polished Blades, Brass Lined.. "

No. 351.

TWO BLADES.

No. 320, Pearl Handle, German Silver Bolster, Sunk Joint, Polished Blades, Brass Lined.................per dozen, $

No. 321, Shell Handle, German Silver Bolster, Sunk Joint, Polished Blades, Brass Lined.................... "

No. 322, Ivory Handle, German Silver Bolster, Sunk Joint, Polished Blades, Brass Lined.................... "

No. 323, Pearl Handle, German Silver Bolster, Sunk Joint, Polished Blades, Fancy Back, Brass Lined........ "

No. 324, Shell Handle, German Silver Bolster, Sunk Joint, Polished Blades, Fancy Back, Brass Lined........ "

FOUR BLADES.

No. 340, Pearl Handle, German Silver Bolster, Sunk Joint, Polished Blades, Brass Lined.................per dozen, $

No. 341, Shell Handle, German Silver Bolster, Sunk Joint, Polished Blades, Brass Lined.................... "

No. 342, Ivory Handle, German Silver Bolster, Sunk Joint, Polished Blades, Brass Lined.................... "

No. 343, Pearl Handle, German Silver Bolster, Sunk Joint, Polished Blades, Fancy Back, Brass Lined........ "

No, 344, Shell Handle, German Silver Bolster, Sunk Joint, Polished Blades, Fancy Back, Brass Lined........ "

FIVE BLADES.

No. 350, Pearl Handle, German Silver Bolster, Sunk Joint, Polished Blades, Fancy Back, Brass Lined.......per dozen, $

No. 351, Shell Handle, German Silver Bolster, Sunk Joint, Polished Blades, Fancy Back, Brass Lined (see plate)................... "

No. 270.

TWO BLADES.

No. 268, Pearl Handle, German Silver Bolster, Polished Blades, Brass Lined, Nail Blade.................per dozen, $

No. 269, Shell Handle, German Silver Bolster, Polished Blades, Brass Lined, Nail Blade.................... "

No. 270, Ivory Handle, German Silver Bolster, Polished Blades, Brass Lined, Nail Blade.................... "

AMERICAN POCKET CUTLERY.

(Continued.)

(NORTHFIELD KNIFE COMPANY.)

No. 298.

TWO BLADES.

No. 271, Pearl Handle, German Silver Bolster, Polished Blades, Brass Lined..per dozen, $

No. 272, Shell Handle, German Silver Bolster, Polished Blades, Brass Lined. .... "

No. 273, Ivory Handle, German Silver Bolster, Polished Blades, Brass Lined .... "

No. 112, Ivory Handle, Shadow Bolster, Polished Blades, Brass Lined... "

THREE BLADES.

No. 296, Pearl Handle, German Silver Bolster, Polished Blades, Brass Lined, Nail Blade ....per dozen, $

No. 297, Shell Handle, German Silver Bolster, Polished Blades, Brass Lined, Nail Blade.................................... "

No. 298, Ivory Handle, German Silver Bolster, Polished Blades, Brass Lined, Nail Blade (see plate) .... "

No. 280.

TWO BLADES.

No. 274, Pearl Handle, German Silver Bolster and Shield, Polished Blades, Brass Lined...per dozen, $

No. 275, Shell Handle, German Silver Bolster and Shield, Polished Blades, Brass Lined....................................... "

No. 276, Ivory Handle, German Silver Bolster and Shield, Polished Blades, Brass Lined....................................... "

THREE BLADES.

No. 278, Pearl Handle, German Silver Bolster and Shield, Polished Blades, Brass Lined, Nail Blade.............................per dozen, $

No. 279, Shell Handle, German Silver Bolster and Shield, Polished Blades, Brass Lined, Nail Blade............................ "

No. 280, Ivory Handle, German Silver Bolster and Shield, Polished Blades, Brass Lined, Nail Blade (see plate)..................... "

FOUR BLADES.

No. 282, Pearl Handle, German Silver Bolster and Shield, Polished Blades, Brass Lined, Nail Blade.............................per dozen, $

No. 283, Shell Handle, German Silver Bolster and Shield, Polished Blades, Brass Lined, Nail Blade............................ "

No. 284, Ivory Handle, German Silver Bolster and Shield, Polished Blades, Brass Lined, Nail Blade............................ "

No. 533.

FOUR BLADES.

No. 531, Pearl Handle, German Silver Bolster, Polished Blades, Brass Lined, Nail Blade...per dozen, $

No. 532, Shell Handle, German Silver Bolster, Polished Blades, Brass Lined, Nail Blade....................................... "

No. 533, Ivory Handle, German Silver Bolster, Polished Blades, Brass Lined, Nail Blade (see plate)................................ "

No. 533½, Buffalo Handle, German Silver Bolster, Polished Blades, Brass Lined, Nail Blade................................. "

No. 531½, Stag Handle, German Silver Bolster, Polished Blades, Brass Lined, Nail Blade...................................... "

AMERICAN POCKET CUTLERY.

(*Continued.*)

(NORTHFIELD KNIFE COMPANY.)

No. 102.

TWO BLADES.

No. 102, German Silver Handle, Polished Blades..per dozen, $

No. 757.

TWO BLADES.

No. 757, Buffalo Handle, German Silver Bolster and Shield, Polished Blades, Brass Lined.....................per dozen, $

No. 758, Ivory Handle, German Silver Bolster and Shield, Polished Blades, Brass Lined........................... "

No. 759, Shell Handle, German Silver Bolster and Shield, Polished Blades, Brass Lined........................... "

No. 760, Pearl Handle, German Silver Bolster and Shield, Polished Blades, Brass Lined........................... "

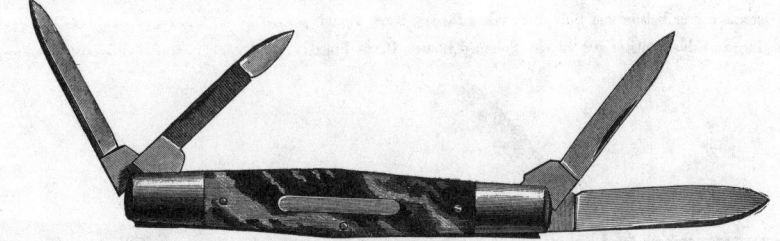

No. 255.

TWO BLADES.

No. 246, Pearl Handle, German Silver Bolster and Shield, Polished Blades, Brass Lined..........................per dozen, $

No. 247, Shell Handle, German Silver Bolster and Shield, Polished Blades, Brass Lined........................ "

No. 248, Ivory Handle, German Silver Bolster and Shield, Polished Blades, Brass Lined........................ "

No. 249, Buffalo Handle, German Silver Bolster and Shield, Polished Blades, Brass Lined........................ "

THREE BLADES.

No. 250, Pearl Handle, German Silver Bolster and Shield, Polished Blades, Brass Lined, Nail Blade...............per dozen, $

No. 251, Shell Handle, German Silver Bolster and Shield, Polished Blades, Brass Lined, Nail Blade............ "

No. 252, Ivory Handle, German Silver Bolster and Shield, Polished Blades, Brass Lined, Nail Blade............ "

No. 252½, Buffalo Handle, German Silver Bolster and Shield, Polished Blades, Brass Lined, Nail Blade......... "

No. 253, Stag Handle, German Silver Bolster and Shield, Polished Blades, Brass Lined, Nail Blade............ "

FOUR BLADES.

No. 254, Pearl Handle, German Silver Bolster and Shield, Polished Blades, Brass Lined, Nail Blade..............per dozen, $

No. 255, Shell Handle, German Silver Bolster and Shield, Polished Blades, Brass Lined, Nail Blade........... "

No. 256, Ivory Handle, German Silver Bolster and Shield, Polished Blades, Brass Lined, Nail Blade........... "

No. 256½, Buffalo Handle, German Silver Bolster and Shield, Polished Blades, Brass Lined, Nail Blade......... "

No. 257, Stag Handle, German Silver Bolster and Shield, Polished Blades, Brass Lined Nail Blade............ "

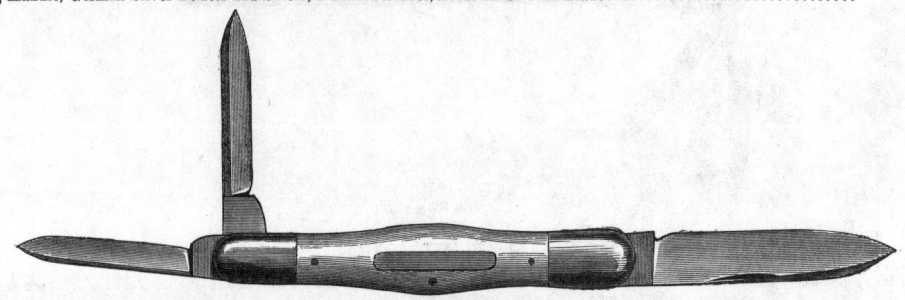

No. 753.

TWO BLADES.

No. 754, Pearl Handle, German Silver Bolster and Shield, Polished Blade, Brass Lined..........................per dozen, $

No. 754½, Shell Handle, German Silver Bolster and Shield, Polished Blades, Brass Lined....................... "

No. 755, Ivory Handle, German Silver Bolster and Shield, Polished Blades, Brass Lined....................... "

No. 756, Buffalo Handle, German Silver Bolster and Shield, Polished Blades, Brass Lined....................... "

AMERICAN POCKET CUTLERY.

(NORTHFIELD KNIFE COMPANY.)

(*Continued.*)

These Plates Represent the Exact Size of Each Article.

THREE BLADES.

No. 751, Pearl Handle, German Silver Bolster and Shield, Polished Blades, Brass Lined..per dozen, $

No. 752, Shell Handle, German Silver Bolster and Shield, Polished Blades, Brass Lined............. ....   "

No. 753, Ivory Handle, German Silver Bolster and Shield, Polished Blades, Brass Lined ....   "

No. 750, Buffalo Handle, German Silver Bolster and Shield, Polished Blades, Brass Lined...............................   "

No. 287.

TWO BLADES.

No. 288, Buffalo Handle, German Silver Bolster, Brass Lined...per dozen, $

No. 286, Ivory Handle, German Silver Bolster and Shield, Polished Blades, Brass Lined.....................................   "

No. 287, Buffalo Handle, German Silver Bolster and Shield, Polished Blades, Brass Lined.................................   "

No. 294.

FOUR BLADES.

No. 292, Pearl Handle, German Silver Bolster and Shield, Polished Blades, Brass Lined, Nail Blade................................per dozen, $

No. 293, Shell Handle, German Silver Bolster and Shield, Polished Blades, Brass Lined, Nail Blade...............................   "

No. 294, Ivory Handle, German Silver Bolster and Shield, Polished Blades, Brass Lined, Nail Blade...............................   "

No. 295, Buffalo Handle, German Silver Bolster and Shield, Polished Blades, Brass Lined, Nail Blade.......:...............   "

No. 307, Stag Handle, German Silver Bolster and Shield, Polished Blades, Brass Lined, Nail Blade.................................   "   •

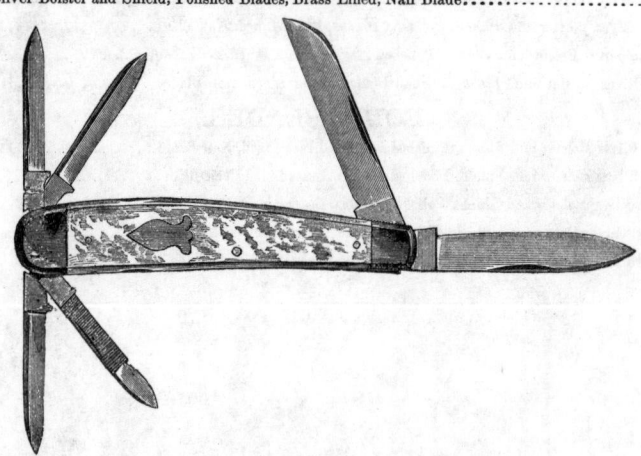

No. 537.

THREE BLADES.

No. 534, Pearl Handle, German Silver Bolster and Shield, Polished Blade, Fancy Back, Brass Lined, Nail Blade ....per dozen, $

No. 535, Shell Handle, German Silver Bolster aud Shield, Polished Blade, Fancy Back, Brass Lined, Nail Blade.....................   "

No. 536, Ivory Handle, German Silver Bolster and Shield, Polished Blade, Fancy Back, Brass Lined, Nail Blade...................   "

SIX BLADES.

No. 537, Pearl Handle, German Silver Bolster and Shield, Polished Blades, Fancy Back, Brass Lined, Nail Blade (see plate)...........per dozen, $

No. 538, Shell Handle, German Silver Bolster and Shield, Polished Blades, Fancy Back, Brass Lined, Nail Blade.....................   "

AMERICAN POCKET CUTLERY.

(NORTHFIELD KNIFE COMPANY.)

(*Continued.*)

These Plates Represent the Exact Size of Each Article.

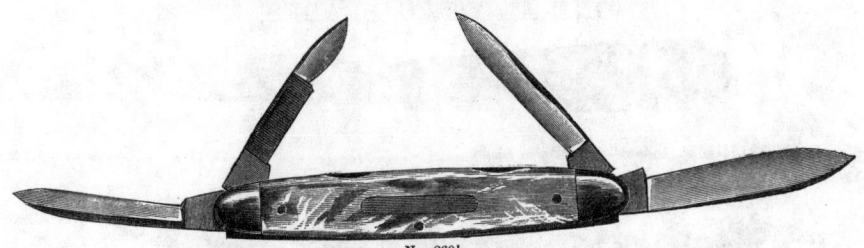

No. 260½.

TWO BLADES.

No. 264, Pearl Handle, German Silver Bolster and Shield, Polished Blades, Brass Lined......................................per dozen, $

No. 265, Shell Handle, German Silver Bolster and Shield, Polished Blades, Brass Lined.................................... "

No. 266, Ivory Handle, German Silver Bolster and Shield, Polished Blades, Brass Lined.................................... "

No. 267, Buffalo Handle, German Silver Bolster and Shild, Polished Blades, Brass Lined.................................... "

THREE BLADES.

No. 260, Pearl Handle, German Silver Bolster and Shield, Polished Blades, Brass Lined......................................per dozen $

No. 261, Shell Handle, German Silver Bolster and Shield, Polished Blades, Brass Lined.................................... "

No. 262, Ivory Handle, German Silver Bolster and Shield, Polished Blades, Brass Lined.................................... "

No. 263, Buffalo Handle, German Silver Bolster and Shield, Polished Blades, Brass Lined.................................... "

FOUR BLADES.

No. 260½, Pearl Handle, German Silver Bolster and Shield, Sunk Joint, Polished Blades, Brass Lined, Nail Blade...................per dozen, $

No. 261½, Shell Handle, German Silver Bolster and Shield, Sunk Joint, Polished Blades, Brass Lined, Nail Blade.................per dozen, $

TWO BLADES.

No. 934, Pearl Handle, Octagon, German Silver Bolster and Shield, Sunk Joint, Brass Lined, Nail Blade, Polished Blades............per dozen, $

No. 935, Shell Handle, Octagon, German Silver Bolster and Shield, Sunk Joint, Brass Lined, Nail Blade, Polished Blades............ "

No. 936, Ivory Handle, Octagon, German Silver Bolster and Shield, Sunk Joint, Brass Lined, Nail Blade, Polished Blades............ "

FOUR BLADES.

No. 931, Pearl Handle, Octagon, German Silver Bolster and Shield, Sunk Joint, Brass Lined, Nail Blade, Polished Blades............per dozen, $

No. 932, Shell Handle, Octagon, German Silver Bolster and Shield, Sunk Joint, Brass Lined, Nail Blade, Polished Blades............ "

No. 933, Ivory Handle, Octagon, German Silver Bolster and Shield, Sunk Joint, Brass Lined, Nail Blade, Polished Blades............ "

The Pattern Handle of Nos. 931 to 936 inclusive is the same as Plate No. 260½, with the exception they are *all* Octagon Handle and *all* Sunk Joint.

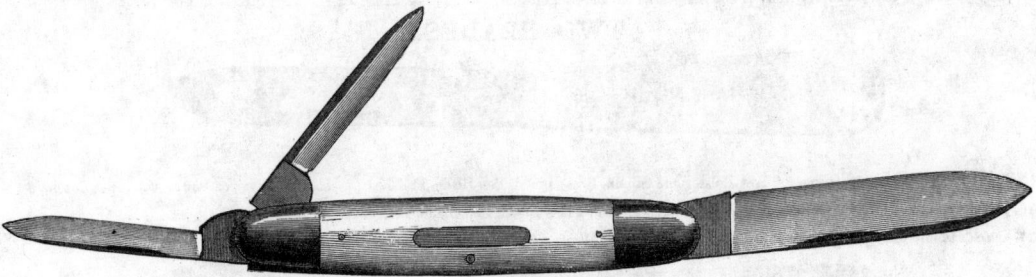

No. 502.

TWO BLADES.

No. 504, Ivory Handle, German Silver Bolster and Shield, Polished Blades, Brass Lined..per dozen, $

No. 505, Buffalo Handle, German Silver Bolster and Shield, Polished Blades, Brass Lined......................................per dozen, $

THREE BLADES.

No. 502, Ivory Handle, German Silver Bolster and Scale, Polished Blades, Brass Lined ....per dozen, $

No. 503, Buffalo Handle, German Silver Bolster and Scale, Polished Blades, Brass Lined......................................per dozen, $

ONE BLADE.

No. 53.

No. 53, Cocoa Handle, Iron Bolster, Iron Lined, Spear Blade...per dozen, $

AMERICAN POCKET CUTLERY.

(*Continued.*)

(NORTHFIELD KNIFE COMPANY.)

ONE AND TWO BLADES.

No. 54.

No. 54, Imitation Stag, Patent Iron Handle, Hollow Bolster, Spear Blade .... per dozen, $

No. 138½.

No. 142,   Cocoa Handle, Iron Bolster, Iron Lined, Spear Blade, *One Blade* .... per dozen, $

No. 142½, Cocoa Handle, Iron Bolster, Iron Lined, Spear Blade, *Two Blades* .... "

No. 138,   Ivory Handle, German Silver Bolster, Brass Lined, *One Blade* .... "

No. 139,   Buffalo Handle, German Silver Bolster, Brass Lined, *One Blade* .... "

No. 139½, Buffalo Handle, German Silver Bolster, Brass Lined, 2 Blades, Pen Blade, Polished .... "

No. 138½, Ivory Handle, German Silver Bolster, Brass Lined, 2 Blades, Pen Blade, Polished .... "

No. 528.

No. 134,   Ebony Handle, Iron Bolster, Iron Lined, 1 Blade, Spear Blade .... per dozen, $

No. 135,   Cocoa Handle, Iron Bolster, Iron Lined, 1 Blade, Spear Blade .... "

No. 135½, Cocoa Handle, Iron Bolster, Iron Lined, 1 Blade, *Sheep Foot* Blade .... "

No. 136,   Ebony Handle, Iron Bolster, Iron Lined, 2 Blades, Spear Blade .... "

No. 137,   Cocoa Handle, Iron Bolster, Iron Lined, 2 Blades, Spear Blade .... "

ONE BLADE.

No. 228, Ivory Handle, German Silver Bolster, Brass Lined .... per dozen, $

No. 229, Buffalo Handle, German Silver Bolster, Brass Lined .... "

No. 230, Cocoa Handle, German Silver Bolster, Brass Lined .... "

No. 231, Buffalo Handle, German Silver Bolster, Brass Lined, Pricking .... "

TWO BLADES.

No. 528, Ivory Handle, German Silver Bolster, Brass Lined, Pen Blade, Polished .... per dozen, $

No. 529, Buffalo Handle, German Silver Bolster, Brass Lined, Pen Blade, Polished .... "

No. 530, Cocoa Handle, German Silver Bolster, Brass Lined, Pen Blade, Polished .... "

TWO BLADES.

No. 815.

No. 815, Ivory Handle, Octagon, German Silver Bolster and Shield, Brass Lined, Pen Blade, Polished .... per dozen, $

No. 816, Buffalo Handle, Octagon, German Silver Bolster and Shield, Brass Lined, Pen Blade, Polished .... "

No. 817, Cocoa Handle, Octagon, German Silver Bolster and Shield, Brass Lined, Pen Blade, Polished .... "

No. 125.

ONE BLADE.

No. 122,   Ebony Handle, Iron Bolster and Scale, Spear Blade .... per dozen, $

No. 122½, Ebony Handle, Iron Bolster and Scale, Sheep Foot Blade .... "

No. 123,   Cocoa Handle, Iron Bolster and Scale, Spear Blade .... "

No. 123½, Cocoa Handle, Iron Bolster and Scale, Sheep Foot Blade .... "

TWO BLADES.

No. 124,   Ebony Handle, Iron Bolster, Iron Lined, Spear Blade .... per dozen, $

No. 124½, Ebony Handle, Iron Bolster, Iron Lined, Sheep Foot Blade .... "

No. 125,   Cocoa Handle, Iron Bolster, Iron Lined, Spear Blade .... "

No. 125½, Cocoa Handle, Iron Bolster, Iron Lined, Sheep Foot Blade .... "

AMERICAN POCKET CUTLERY.

(*Continued.*)

(NORTHFIELD KNIFE COMPANY.)

ONE BLADE.

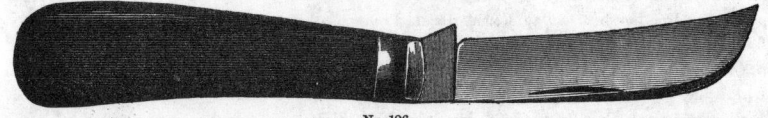

No. 126.

No. 126, Ebony Handle, Small Pruner, Iron Bolster, Iron Lined..per dozen, $
No. 127, Cocoa Handle, Small Pruner, Iron Bolster, Iron Lined.. "

No. 930.

No. 930, Imitation Stag, Patent Iron Handle, Hollow Bolster, Spear Blade......................................per dozen, $

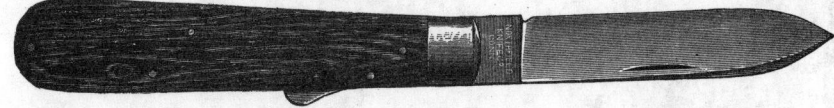

No. 145.

No. 145, Buffalo Handle, Lock Knife, Iron Bolster, Iron Lined, Spear Blade......................................per dozen, $
No. 146, Cocoa Handle, Lock Knife, Iron Bolster, Iron Lined, Spear Blade... "

No. 425.

ONE BLADE.

No. 130, Ebony Handle, Iron Bolster, Iron Lined, Spear Blade..per dozen, $
No. 131, Cocoa Handle, Iron Bolster, Iron Lined, Spear Blade.. "
No. 131½, Cocoa Handle, Iron Bolster, Iron Lined, Sheep Foot Blade.. "
No. 130 B, Bone Handle, Iron Bolster, Iron Lined, Spear Blade... "

TWO BLADES.

No. 132, Ebony Handle, Iron Bolster, Iron Lined, Spear Blade..per dozen, $
No. 133, Cocoa Handle, Iron Bolster, Iron Lined, Spear Blade.. "
No. 132 B, Bone Handle, Iron Bolster, Iron Lined, Spear Blade... "

ONE BLADE.

No. 225, Ivory Handle, German Silver Bolster and Shield, Brass Lined, Spear Blade, Long Polished Swage.........per dozen, $
No. 225 B, Bone Handle, German Silver Bolster and Shield, Brass Lined, Spear Blade, Long Polished Swage......... "
No. 226, Buffalo Handle, German Silver Bolster and Shield, Brass Lined, Spear Blade, Long Polished Swage........ "
No. 227, Cocoa Handle, German Silver Bolster and Shield, Brass Lined, Spear Blade, Long Polished Swage......... "

TWO BLADES.

No. 425, Ivory Handle, German Silver Bolster and Shield, Brass Lined, Spear Blade, Pen Blade, Polished.........per dozen, $
No. 425 B, Bone Handle, German Silver Bolster and Shield, Brass Lined, Spear Blade, Pen Blade, Polished......... "
No. 426, Buffalo Handle, German Silver Bolster and Shield, Brass Lined, Spear Blade, Pen Blade, Polished........ "
No. 427, Cocoa Handle, German Silver Bolster and Shield, Brass Lined, Spear Blade, Pen Blade, Polished......... "

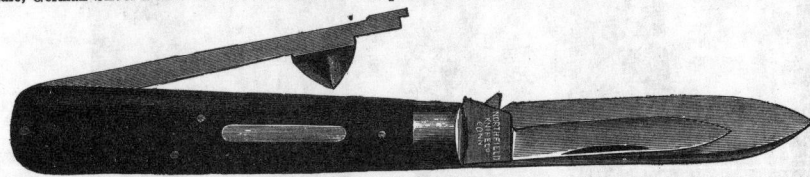

No. 428.

No. 428, Buffalo Handle, German Silver Bolster and Shield, Brass Lined, *Fleam*, Spear Blade, Pen Blade, Polished.................per dozen, $

ONE BLADE.

No. 223.

No. 222, Ebony Handle, Iron Bolster, Iron Lined, Spear Blade..per dozen, $
No. 222½, Ebony Handle, Iron Bolster, Iron Lined, Sheep Foot Blade.. "
No. 223, Cocoa Handle, Iron Bolster, Iron Lined, Spear Blade.. "
No. 223½, Cocoa Handle, Iron Bolster, Iron Lined, Sheep Foot Blade.. "

AMERICAN POCKET CUTLERY.

(NORTHFIELD KNIFE COMPANY.)

(*Continued.*)

These Plates Represent the Exact Size of Each Article.

ONE BLADE.

(*Continued.*)

No. 143, Cocoa Handle, Iron Bolster, Iron Lined, *Pruner* .... per dozen, $

No. 408, Cocoa Handle, Iron Bolster, Iron Lined, Brass Cap, Round Handle *Pruner*.............................. "

No. 405, Buffalo Handle, Lock Knife, German Silver Bolster, Spear Blade, Iron Lined .... "

No. 406, Cocoa Handle, Lock Knife, German Silver Bolster, Iron Lined, Spear Blade .... "

No. 403, Buffalo Handle, Lock Knife, German Silver Bolster, Iron Lined, Clip Point Blade .... "

No. 404, Cocoa Handle, Lock Knife, German Silver Bolster, Iron Lined, Clip Point Blade .... "

ONE BLADE.

No. 666, Buffalo Handle, Lock, Knife, German Silver Bolster and Cap, Brass Lined............................ per dozen, $

No. 667, Cocoa Handle, Lock Knife, German Silver Bolster and Cap, Brass Lined............................... "

No. 670, Buffalo Handle, Lock Knife, with German Silver Guard, German Silver Bolster and Cap, Brass Lined.................... "

No. 670.   No. 666.   No. 404.   No. 405.   No. 408.   No. 143.

PRICE LIST OF

NORTHFIELD KNIFE CO'S

AMERICAN POCKET CUTLERY.

No.	Handle.	Blades.	Price per Dozen.	No.	Handle.	Blades.	Price per Dozen.	No.	Handle.	Blades.	Price per Dozen.
48	Ivory	1	$3.00	252½	Buffalo	3	$11.50	425 B	Bone	2	$8.25
49	Buffalo	1	3.00	253	Stag	3	12.00	426	Buffalo	2	8.00
50	Pearl	1	3.25	254	Pearl	4	16.50	427	Cocoa	2	7.75
51	Shell	1	3.25	255	Shell	4	16.50	428	Buffalo	3	12.00
52	Ivory	1	2.50	256	Ivory	4	12.50	502	Ivory	3	15.00
53	Cocoa	1	2.00	256½	Buffalo	4	12.00	503	Buffalo	3	14.25
54	Iron	1	1.75	257	Stag	4	12.50	504	Ivory	2	11.00
102	German Silver.	2	7.00	260	Pearl	3	17.00	505	Buffalo	2	10.00
109	Pearl	2	5.00	260½	Pearl	4	20.00	528	Ivory	2	7.25
110	Shell	2	5.00	261	Shell	3	16.00	529	Buffalo	2	6.75
112	Ivory	2	6.00	261½	Shell	4	20.00	530	Cocoa	2	6.50
122	Ebony	1	3.00	262	Ivory	3	12.50	531	Pearl	4	14.00
122½	Ebony	1	3.00	263	Buffalo	3	12.00	531½	Stag	4	11.50
123	Cocoa	1	3.00	264	Pearl	2	12.00	532	Shell	4	14.00
123½	Cocoa	1	3.00	265	Shell	2	12.00	533	Ivory	4	11.50
124	Ebony	2	5.00	266	Ivory	2	9.50	533½	Buffalo	4	11.00
124½	Ebony	2	5.00	267	Buffalo	2	9.00	534	Pearl	3	18.00
125	Cocoa	2	5.00	268	Pearl	2	9.25	535	Shell	3	18.00
125½	Cocoa	2	5.00	269	Shell	2	9.25	536	Ivory	3	15.00
126	Ebony	1	3.25	270	Ivory	2	8.00	537	Pearl	6	30.00
127	Cocoa	1	3.25	271	Pearl	2	9.50	538	Shell	6	30.00
130	Ebony	1	3.75	272	Shell	2	9.50	666	Buffalo	1	17.00
130 B	Bone	1	4.75	273	Ivory	2	7.25	667	Cocoa	1	16.00
131	Cocoa	1	3.75	274	Pearl	2	12.00	670	Buffalo	1	22.00
131½	Cocoa	1	3.75	275	Shell	2	12.00	750	Buffalo	3	12.00
132	Ebony	2	5.75	276	Ivory	2	10.50	751	Pearl	3	16.00
132 B	Bone	2	6.75	278	Pearl	3	16.00	752	Shell	3	16.00
133	Cocoa	2	5.75	279	Shell	3	16.00	753	Ivory	3	12.50
134	Ebony	1	3.00	280	Ivory	3	13.00	754	Pearl	2	12.00
135	Cocoa	1	3.00	282	Pearl	4	16.50	754½	Shell	2	12.00
135½	Cocoa	1	3.00	283	Shell	4	16.50	755	Ivory	2	10.50
136	Ebony	2	5.00	284	Ivory	4	13.50	756	Buffalo	2	10.00
137	Cocoa	2	5.00	286	Ivory	2	7.50	757	Buffalo	2	9.50
138	Ivory	1	4.75	287	Buffalo	2	7.00	758	Ivory	2	10.00
138½	Ivory	2	6.50	288	Buffalo	2	6.00	759	Shell	2	12.00
139	Buffalo	1	4.25	292	Pearl	4	16.50	760	Pearl	2	12.00
139½	Buffalo	2	6.00	293	Shell	4	16.50	815	Ivory	2	7.50
142	Cocoa	1	2.50	294	Ivory	4	12.50	816	Buffalo	2	6.75
142½	Cocoa	2	4.50	295	Buffalo	4	12.00	817	Cocoa	2	6.50
143	Cocoa	1	6.00	296	Pearl	3	13.50	930	Iron	1	2.75
145	Buffalo	1	6.50	297	Shell	3	13.50	931	Pearl	4	21.00
146	Cocoa	1	6.00	298	Ivory	3	11.00	932	Shell	4	21.00
222	Ebony	1	4.25	307	Stag	4	13.25	933	Ivory	4	16.00
222½	Ebony	1	4.25	320	Pearl	2	11.00	934	Pearl	2	14.00
223	Cocoa	1	4.25	321	Shell	2	11.00	935	Shell	2	14.00
223½	Cocoa	1	4.25	322	Ivory	2	9.50	936	Ivory	2	12.00
225	Ivory	1	7.00	323	Pearl	2	12.00	937			
225 B	Bone	1	5.75	324	Shell	2	12.00	938			
226	Buffalo	1	5.50	340	Pearl	4	16.00	939			
227	Cocoa	1	5.25	341	Shell	4	16.00	940			
228	Ivory	1	5.25	342	Ivory	4	13.00	941			
229	Buffalo	1	4.50	343	Pearl	4	18.00	942			
230	Cocoa	1	4.25	344	Shell	4	18.00	943			
231	Buffalo	1	4.50	350	Pearl	5	24.00	944			
246	Pearl	2	11.00	351	Shell	5	24.00	945			
247	Shell	2	11.00	403	Buffalo	1	10.00	946			
248	Ivory	2	9.50	404	Cocoa	1	9.50	947			
249	Buffalo	2	9.00	405	Buffalo	1	9.50	948			
250	Pearl	3	16.00	406	Cocoa	1	9.00	949			
251	Shell	3	16.00	408	Cocoa	1	10.00				
252	Ivory	3	12.00	425	Ivory	2	9.50				

AMES' KNIVES.

Ames' Butcher, Skinning and Sticking Knives.

Butcher Knife, 4½ to 7 inches.

Butcher Knife, 8 to 15 inches.

Skinning Knife.   Sticking Knife.

Beech Handle.

$						per doz.
4½	4¾	5	5½	6	6½	inch.

$						per doz.
7	8	9	10	11	12	inch.

Cocoa Handle.

$					per doz.
4½	4¾	5	5½	6	inch.

$					per doz.
6½	7	8	9	10	inch.

$					per doz.
11	12	13	14	15	inch.

Sanger's Butcher, Skinning and Sticking Knives.

Beech Handle.

$						per doz.
4¾	5	5½	6	6½	7	inch.

$					per doz.
8	9	10	11	12	inch.

Cocoa Handle.

$						per doz.
4½	4¾	5	5½	6	6½	inch.

$					per doz.
7	8	9	10	11	12	inch.

Ames' Swaged Cooks' and Hunting Knives.

Swaged Cooks' Knife.

Hunting Knife.

Ebony Handle.

$					per doz.
5	5½	6	6½	7	inch.

$					per doz.
8	9	10	11	12	inch.

Ames' Bread Knives.

Cocoa Handle.

$			per doz.
7	8	9	inch.

Silver Steel Bread Knives...................per doz., $

Silver Steel Bread Knives, Capped Rivets.

$			per doz.
1	2	4	caps.

Ames' Shoe Knives.

Square Point.   Round Point.

Black Handles, Cast Steel.

		$				per doz.
Square Points........	No. 1		2	3	4	
Round Points........	No. 1		2	3	4	
Sharp Points........	No. 1		2	3		
Narrow Points........	No. 1		2	3		
Skivers...............	No. 1		2			

Ferruled Handle, Silver Steel.

Square Point.

		$				per doz.
Square Points........	No. 1		2	3	4	
Round Points........	No. 1		2	3	4	
Sharp Points........	No. 1		2	3		

Skiver.

No. 1, Skiver.................................per doz., $
No. 2, Skiver................................. "
No. 1, Crooked Skiver......................... "
No. 2, Crooked Skiver......................... "

Paring.

Nos. 1 and 2, Paring..........................per doz., $
Nos. 1 and 2, Clicker.........................per doz., $

Hawk Bill.

No. 1, Hawk Bill..............................per doz., $
No. 2, Hawk Bill..............................per doz., $

Sanger's Black Handle Shoe Knives.

		$				per doz.
Square Points, No. 1			2	3	4	
Round Points........	No. 1		2	3		
Skivers..............	No. 1		2			

Kitchen or Paring Knives.............per doz., $
Patent Vegetable Knives............... "
Beech Handle Saw Knives............. "

SEYMOUR'S SHEARS, TRIMMERS, ETC.

Straight Trimmers.

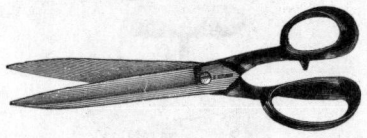

$					per doz.
No.	1	2	3	9	10	
Length	13	12	11	6½	7	inches.
$					per doz.
No.	11	12	13	14	16	
Length	7½	8	8½	9	10	inches.

Bent Trimmers.

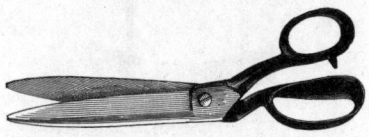

$							per doz.
No.	0	1	2	3	3½	4	5	
Length	13	13	12	11	10	9	8½	inches.

Ladies' Scissors.

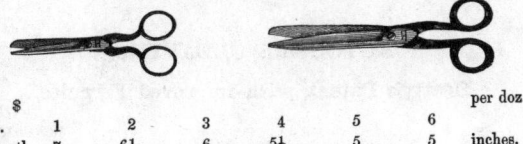

$						per doz.
No.	1	2	3	4	5	6	
Length	7	6½	6	5½	5	5	inches.

Pocket Scissors.

$			per dozen.
No.	1	2	3	
Length	4	4½	5	inches.

Barbers' Scissors.

Plain.

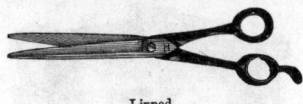

Lipped.

$			per dozen.
Plain, No.	1	2	3	
Length	8	8½	9	inches.
$			per dozen.
Lipped, No.	1	2	3	
Length	8½	9	9½	inches.

Tailors' Points.

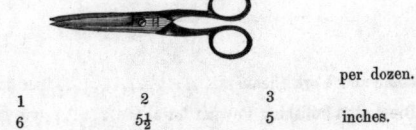

$			per dozen.
No.	1	2	3	
Length	6	5½	5	inches.

Tailors' Shears.

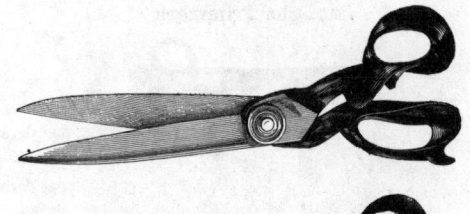

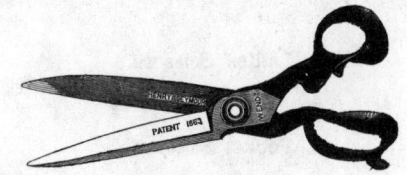

New Patent Tailors' Shears.

$					per pair.
No.	3	4	5	6	7	
Length	11½	12	12½	13	13½	inches.
$					per pair.
No.	8	9	10	11	12	
Length	14	14½	15	15½	16	inches.

Bankers' Shears.

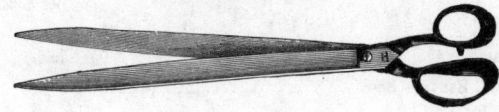

$							per pair.
No.	00	0	1	2	3	4	5	
Length	21½	20	19	18	17	16	15	inches.
$							per pair.
No.	6	7	8	9	11	12	13	
Length	14	13	12	11	10	9	8	inches.

Tinners', Jewellers' and Daguerrean Snips.

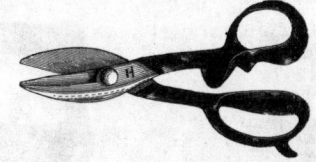

Tinners' Snips.

Daguerrean or Jewellers' Snips.

{					per dozen.
No.	1	2	3	4	5	
Length of Cut	4	3½	3	2¾	1½	inches.

Shears with Silver Plated Handle......................extra, $

Button Hole Cutters.

No. 2, with Punch...............................per dozen, $

No. 3...per dozen, $

Lamp Shears.

Phare's Patent Lamp Shears....................per dozen, $

SHEARS, SCISSORS, MINCING KNIVES, ETC.

RUSSELL & ERWIN MANUFACTURING CO'S CAST STEEL SHEARS.

Straight Trimmers.

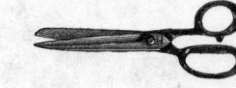

$					per dozen.
6½	7	7½	8	8½	inches.
$					per dozen.
9	9½	10	11	12	inches.

Ladies' Scissors.

$							per dozen.
4	4½	5	5½	6	6½	7	inches.

Pocket Scissors.

$			per dozen.
4	4½	5	inches.

Barbers' Scissors.

	$					per dozen.
Plain,	8	8½	9	9½	10	inches.
	$					per dozen.
Lipped,	8	8½	9	9½	10	inches.

☞ For Pruning and Sheep Shears, see pages 300, 301.

Cast Iron Shears.

	$					per dozen.
No.	0	1	2	3	4.	
Length,	4½	6	7	8	9½	inches.

No. 5, Bankers' Shears........................per dozen, $

MINCING KNIVES.

No. 1.

No. 2.

No. 3. Double Blade.

No. 13. Solid Steel.

Cast Steel.

	$			per dozen.
No.	1	2	3	13.

Extra Solid Cast Steel.

No. 0, Double Shank........................per dozen, $
No. 1, Double Shank........................   "
No. 2, Single Shank........................   "

Common Riveted.

Single Shank.

Single Shank............................per dozen, $

MINCING KNIVES.
(Continued.)

Braced Shank.

Braced Shank.............................per dozen, $

Double Shank.

Double Shank.............................per dozen, $
Round, Unpolished.........................   "
Round, Polished..........................   "

BUTCHERS' CLEAVERS.
Beatty's Patent, with Improved Ferrules.

	$							per dozen.
No.	0	1	2	3	4	5	6.	
Size of Bit,	7	8	9	10	11	12	13	inches.

Western Pork, Iron Handle..................per dozen, $

BUTCHERS' CHOPPERS.

	$				per dozen.
No.	00	0	1	2.	
Size of Bit,	7	8	9	10	inches.

Butchers' Cleavers.........................per dozen, $
Mincing Cleavers...........................   "

BRACKETT'S PATENT KNIFE AND FORK CLEANERS.

Knife and Fork Cleaners....................per dozen, $
Brackett's Polishing Powder for above.......per gross, $
Bath Brick................................per dozen, $

LANTERNS, ETC.

No. 1½, Egg, Ring Top. No. 2, Flanged Egg, Ring Top. No. 3, Egg, Bail Top. No. 1, Globe, Ring Top. No. 2, Flanged Globe, Ring Top. No. 3, Globe, Bail Top.

TIN LANTERNS—OIL.

Egg Pattern—Wire Bail Handle.

$ per dozen.

No.   1   1½   2   3

Egg Pattern—Tin Ring Handle.

$ per dozen.

No.   1   1½   2   3

Globe Pattern—Wire Bail Handle.

$ per dozen.

No.   1   2   2½   3   4

Globe Pattern—Tin Ring Handle.

$ per dozen.

No.   1   2   3

No. 1, Square Japanned.....................per dozen, $
No. 5, Square Japanned.....................per dozen, $

TIN LANTERNS—KEROSENE.

No. 2,   Egg Pattern, Wire Bail Handle, Long
          Bottom.....................per dozen, $

No. 2½,   Globe Pattern, Wire Bail Handle, Long
          Bottom.....................per dozen, $

No. 3,   Globe Pattern, Wire Bail Handle, Long
          Bottom.....................per dozen, $

No. 4,   Globe Pattern, Wire Bail Handle, Long
          Bottom.....................per dozen, $

No. 2,   Egg Pattern, Wire Bail Handle, Am-
          brose.....................per dozen, $

Clark's Patent, Egg, Wire Bail Handle.......per dozen, $

Breckenridge Patent, Egg, Wire Bail Handle..per dozen, $

Sargent's Patent, Egg, Wire Bail Handle.....per dozen, $

WOODWARD'S PATENT
SELF-ADJUSTING COMBINATION LANTERNS—KEROSENE.

per dozen.

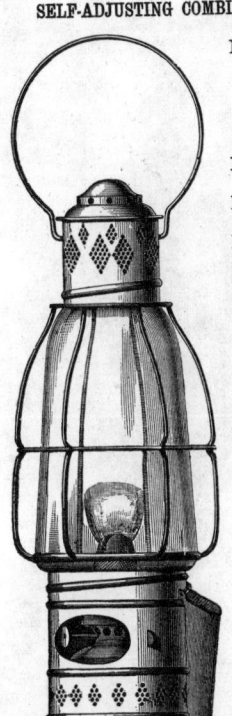

Savage & Co's
No Chimney Burner.

No. 1, with Match Box and Patent Slide and opening for lighting, regulating and extinguishing flame, without removing the Lamp, and Savage & Co's no Chimney Burner No. 2,.....$
No. 2, same as No. 1, without Wire Guard.................$
No. 5, same as No. 1, without Match Box..................$
No. 6, same as No. 2, without Match Box..................$
No. 9, same as No. 1, shorter at the base, and without Match Box and opening in Band, with Savage & Co's No. 3 No-chimney Burner.................$
No. 10, same as No. 9, without Guard......................$
Savage & Company's No-chimney Burner (see Plate).........$

PATENT CONVEX REFLECTOR LANTERN,
FOR BURNING COAL OIL OR KEROSENE WITHOUT A CHIMNEY.

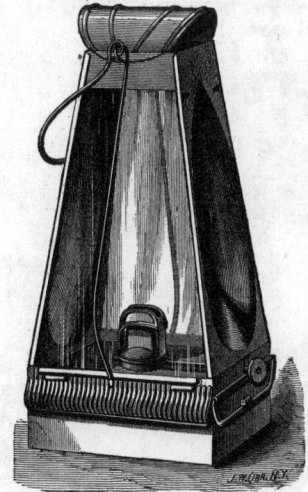

It gives a pure white light, without the use of a chimney, and the flame can be regulated from the outside. It is neat and compact in form, and stands quick motion in any direction. By means of convex reflectors, the force of the flame is greatly increased, while they at the same time serve for the purpose of shades to the eyes.

Convex Reflector Lanterns.....................per dozen, $

Burners for same.............................per dozen, $

LANTERNS, ETC.

(Continued.)

TIN LANTERNS, OIL, COLORED GLASS.

No. 2, Egg Pattern, Wire Bail Handle, Red Glass, per dozen, $

No. 2, Globe Pattern, Wire Bail Handle, Red Glass .... "

No. 2, Egg Pattern, Wire Bail Handle, Green and Blue Glass .... "

No. 2, Globe Pattern, Wire Bail Handle, Green and Blue Glass .... "

Tin Lanterns, with Flanges .... per dozen extra, $

Japanned Police Lanterns.

$　　　　　　　　　　　　　　　per dozen.

Small.　　　　Medium.　　　　Large.

Brass Lanterns, Oil.

No. 2, Egg Pattern, Bail Handle .... per dozen, $

No. 3, Egg Pattern, Bail Handle .... "

No. 1½, Egg Pattern, Ring Handle .... "

Brass Lanterns, Oil.

(Continued.)

No. 2, Egg Pattern, Ring Handle .... per dozen, $

No. 3, Egg Pattern, Ring Handle .... "

No. 2½, Globe Pattern, Bail Handle............ "

No. 3, Globe Pattern, Bail Handle............ "

No. 1, Globe Pattern, Ring Handle .... "

No. 2, Globe Pattern, Ring Handle .... "

No. 3, Globe Pattern, Ring Handle .... "

Fancy Brass Lanterns for Conductors—Oil.

No. 2, Egg Pattern, Spun Ring Handle......... per dozen, $

No. 2, Egg Pattern, Bail Handle .... "

No. 2, Globe Pattern, Spun Ring Handle....... "

No. 2, Globe Pattern, Bail Handle............. "

No. 2, Egg Pattern, Spun Ring Handle, for Fire Department .... "

Brass Lanterns, Flanged .... per dozen extra, $

JAPANNED STATION HOUSE LANTERNS—KEROSENE.

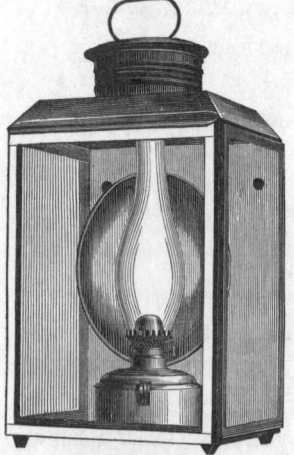

Station Lantern, Square Top.

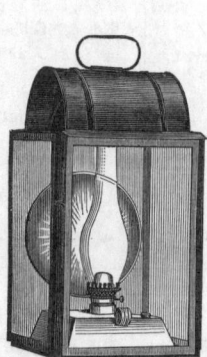

Station Lantern, Bow Top.

Boat Lantern.

Sexagon Sugar House Lantern.

Square Sugar House Lantern.

Street Lantern.

8×12 in. Square Flat Top, with Glass Reflector and Chimney, each $

10×14 in. Square Flat Top, with Glass Reflector and Chimney, "

12×16 in. Square Flat Top, with Glass Reflector and Chimney, "

9×13 in. Square Bow Top, with Glass Reflector and Chimney, "

9×13 in. Square Boat Lanterns, Looking Glass Wings...... "

Six-sided Sugar House Lanterns, Top Reflector.............. "

Square Sugar House Lanterns, Top Reflector................ each, $

7×9 in. Square Japanned Street Lanterns .... per doz. $

5½ inch Square Japanned Street Lanterns, Plain .... "

Triangular Lanterns, Green Glass, for Oil.................. "

Triangular Lanterns, Green Glass, for Kerosene............ "

☞ Signal, Ship, and all other kinds of Lanterns furnished to order.

CANDLESTICKS, SNUFFERS AND TRAYS, ETC.

CANDLESTICKS.

Japanned.

	$			per gross.
Common, No.	1	2	3.	

	$			per gross.
Deep, No.	1	2	3.	

Planished.

	$			per gross.
B, Upright, No.	0	1	2.	

	$		per gross.
D, Dish Bottom, No.	1	2.	

D, Dish Bottom with Handle,

	$			per gross.
No.	3	3 extra	4	4 extra.

Brass.

	4½	5	5½	6	inches.
No. 1, $				per dozen pairs.
No. 2, $				"
No. 3, $				"

AMERICAN SNUFFERS AND TRAYS.
Snuffers.

No. 1, Japanned, without Spring.............per gross, $
No. 2, Tinned, without Spring............... "
No. 3, Japanned, with Spring............... "
No. 4, Tinned, with Spring............... "
No. 5, Plain Brass, with Spring............... "
No. 6, Ornamented Brass, with Spring........ "
No. 7, Plain Silver Plate, with Spring........ "
No. 8, Ornamented Silver Plate, with Spring... "

Trays.

No. 1, Plain Tin.............................per gross, $
No. 2, Japanned Tin............... "
No. 3, Ornamented Tin................... "
No. 4, Brass .... "
No. 5, Silver Plated........................ "

MATCH SAFES.

Twin. Pocket.

Pocket..................................per gross, $
Twin .... "
Combination................. "

MATCH SAFES—*Continued.*
Patent Self-Closing Match Safes.

Nos.	0	1	2.	per dozen.
Size,	2×3¼	2⅜×3¾	3×5¼	inches.

AMERICAN TEA TRAYS—SUPERIOR FINISH.

	10	12	14	16	20	24	28	inches.
No. 24, $								per doz.
No. 1870, $								"
No. 2020, $								"
No. 2060, $								"

PASTE JAGGERS.

Brass....................................per gross, $
Plated...................................... "

FRY PANS.

Burnished Pan.

	$									per doz.
No.	0	1	2	3	4	5	6	7	8	

Tinned Pan.

	$									per doz.
No.	0	1	2	3	4	5	6	7	8.	

GRIDIRONS—HOLLOW BARS.

$						per dozen.
	9	10	11	12	13	14	Bars.

BREWSTER'S PATENT GRIDIRONS.

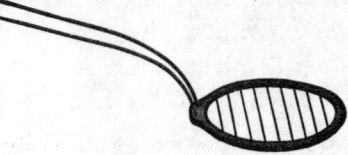

Brewster's Patent Gridiron.................per dozen, $

SOAP STONE GRIDIRONS.
Oval.

$					each.
9×16	9×18	10×20	11×22	12×24	inches.

Round.

	$				each.
Diameter,	10	12	14	16	inches.

Wire Oyster Broilers.

	$			per dozen.
No.	1	2	3.	
Size,	10	12	14	inches.

Stove-Lid Lifter.

Japanned Socket, Wood Handle.............per dozen, $
For Lid Lifter and Poker Combined, see page 101.

MEAT BROILERS, FRUIT JARS, ETC.

LORD'S PATENT MEAT BROILER.

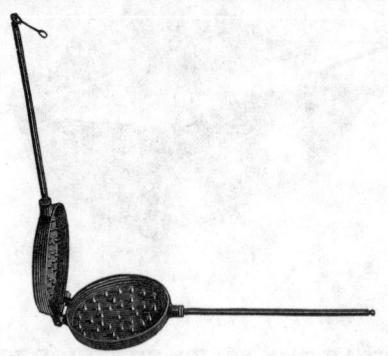

	$			per dozen.
Round, No.	1	2	3	
	8	10	12	inches.
	$			per dozen.
Oblong, No.	1	2	3	4
	$5\frac{3}{4} \times 7$	$6 \times 8\frac{1}{2}$	6×9	$8 \times 10\frac{1}{2}$ inches.

Square, 8 × 12 inches ....per dozen, $

MEAT MAULS.

Dick's Patent Meat Hammer....................per dozen, $

Porcelain Beef Mauls..........................per dozen, $

LEMON SQUEEZERS.

Porcelain Cup and Top........................per dozen, $

PORCELAIN HEAD MUDDLERS.

No. 1, Small Size, Common Wood Handle......per dozen, $

No. 2, Large Size, Common Wood Handle....... "

No. 1, Small Size, Fancy Wood Handle........ "

No. 2, Large Size, Fancy Wood Handle........ "

PORCELAIN HEAD POTATO MASHERS.

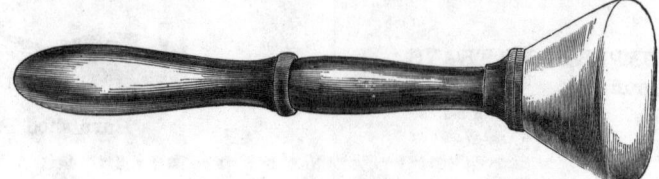

Plain Handles ....per dozen, $ Fancy Wood Turned Handles.................per dozen, $

LYMAN'S PATENT SELF-SEALING FRUIT JARS.

LYMAN'S PATENT.

One Pint...................................per gross, $

One Quart................................... "

Two Quarts................................. "

One Gallon................................. "

Packed in cases of half gross each. Not less than a case sold at a time.

DIRECTIONS FOR PUTTING UP FRUIT.

Fill the jar with fruit, make a syrup of sugar (find the amount of sugar below), pour it into the jar before the fruit is cooked at all, fill the jar with the syrup half-way up the swell in the neck of it. Now take the rubber off the neck of the jar, put on the cover, then set the jar in a kettle of cold water up to the neck of it. Now put a cover on the kettle, and boil according to directions below. Then take the jar out of the kettle, put on the rubber with the smooth side to the glass, now fill the jar full with boiling water, and seal up immediately as follows: force a pin up the air groove between the rubber and the glass, and let it remain until the cover is forced down firmly with the hand; and while the cover is forced down as far as it can be, withdraw the pin and the jar is sealed. After standing a day, set them away in a dark, cool place. The jars are liable to break, if they stand flat on the bottom of the kettle while boiling. To avoid that, put a bit of wire or nail under each jar. Select only sound fruit for preserving. Pears and peaches should be dropped into cold water after paring, to prevent their changing color.

DIRECTIONS FOR PUTTING UP FRUIT—Continued.

Boil Cherries moderately...... 8 minutes.		Boil Bartlett Pears in halves....20 minutes.
Boil Raspberries moderately...10 "		Boil Peaches in halves........10 "
Boil Blackberries moderately..10 "		Boil Peaches whole...........20 "
Boil Plums moderately........12 "		Boil Pineapple slic'd ⅜ in. thick.15 "
Boil Strawberries moderately..12 "		Boil Sib'n or Crab Apple, whole.25 "
Boil Whortleberries...........10 "		Boil Sour Apples, quartered....15 "
Boil Pie Plant, sliced..........15 "		Boil Ripe Currants...........10 "
Boil Small Sour Pears, whole..30 "		Boil Wild Grapes.............15 "

The Amount of Sugar to a quart jar should be :

For Cherries .... 6 ounces.		For Peaches................. 6 ounces.
For Raspberries.............. 6 "		For Bartlett Pears........... 6 "
For Lawton Blackberries...... 8 "		For Pine Apples............. 8 "
For Field.................... 6 "		For Siberian or Crab Apples... 8 "
For Strawberries............. 8 "		For Plums................... 8 "
For Whortleberries .... 5 "		For Pie Plant...............10 "
For Quince..................10 "		For Sour Apple, quartered... 8 "
For Small Sour Pear, whole... 8 "		For Ripe Currants........... 8 "
For Wild Grapes............. 8 "		

Quinces should be scalded in clear water, in a covered vessel, until tender, then put them into the jar with care (to prevent them from falling to pieces). Fill up the jar immediately with boiling syrup, and seal as above. Prepare the jars, before putting in hot fruit, by filling them with warm water.

Any one can know whether the jar is perfectly sealed or not by the eye (which is not the case with any other jar) in a few hours after the jar is sealed. If the sealing is perfect, the cover will be concave or dishing. If not perfect, it will be flat.

To unseal the jar, force a pin up the groove in the neck of it, between the jar and rubber, which admits air into the jar, and relieves the outside pressure on the cover. Then with a knife, or something of the kind, the cover is easily pryed off.

TOMATOES.—Skin, slice, or fill them into the jar whole, pack them in tight up to the swell in the neck of the jar. Then boil the whole twenty minutes, take them out of the kettle, fill from one jar into the rest, so as to have them full, and seal up as above.

GLASS FRUIT JARS AND DOOR SPRINGS.

"KLINE'S PATENT."
[Glass Stopper.]

"WILLOUGHBY'S PATENT."

KLINE'S PATENT.

It combines with safety, neatness, quickness, and convenience.

To Close the Jar.—Place the gum over the small end of the Stopper, insert it into the mouth of the Jar, the gum resting on the shoulder (if the mouth of the Jar is wet the Stopper should also be wet); then by screw motion force the Stopper down. Immediately after closing the Jar, force a pin down between the Stopper and the gum, for the escape of the air compressed, occasioned in putting in the Stopper. Withdraw the pin in a few seconds.

To Open the Jar.—Force a pin down, as in closing, which admits the air into the Jar. Apply warm water around the gum, when the Stopper will be easily withdrawn.

☞ Examine the Jar an hour after closing. If the Stopper has sunk in deeper than at closing, the Jar is air tight.

DIRECTIONS FOR PUTTING UP FRUIT.

Fruit can be put up without any Sugar. Fill the Jar with Fruit, make a cold syrup of one pound of sugar to four quart Jars of Fruit. Fill the Jar half full of the syrup, and set it in a vessel of cold water, to the neck of the Jar, and boil until the Fruit becomes thouroughly heated. (In this Jar the gum may be taken off and the Stopper placed in the Jar while boiling.) Fill the Jar with boiling water, take the Jar out of the kettle, and seal it up according to directions. Put a plate, or a little straw, in the bottom of the kettle for the Jar to rest on while boiling. After standing a day, put them away in a cool, dark place.

Peaches and Pears should be dropped into cold water, after paring, to prevent them from changing color.

Pints...per gross, $
Quarts...per gross,
Half Gallon.......................................per gross,

WILLOUGHBY'S PATENT.

The manner of closing is by simply putting the Stopper into its place and screwing it until the gum is sufficiently compressed to mal an air-tight joint. When the Fruit in the Jar becomes cold, the screw should again be tightened. To open the Jar, apply warm water around the gum ring, partially unscrew, and draw out the Stopper.

Pints...per gross, $
Quarts...per gross,
Half Gallon.......................................per gross,

DOOR SPRINGS.

DOOR SPRINGS.

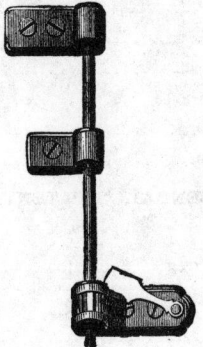

Torrey's Patent Wire Rod Spring........ ... .per dozen, $
India Rubber, complete...............................per dozen,

Barnard's Door Springs.

No. $ 2   4   5.   per dozen.

DOOR SPRINGS.

(*Continued.*)

Wescott's Patent Railway Door Springs.

No. 0, for Largest Size Doors.......................per dozen, $
No. 1, for Large Size Doors..........................   "
No. 2, for Medium Size Doors.......................   "
No. 3, for Common Size Doors.......................   "

EGG BEATERS, NUT CRACKERS, ETC.

EGG BEATERS.

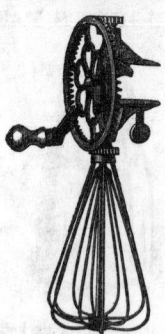

Monroe's Patent.

No.   1   2   3   4   per dozen.

No. 5, Extra Large, for Bakers, Restaurants, &c. per dozen, $

Liquor Whip .... per dozen, $

Ashley's Patent.

No. 1, Large.............................. per dozen, $

No. 2, Small, or Toddy.................... per dozen, $

Egg Whip, all Wire, Spoon Shape............ per gross, $

Egg Whip, Wood Handle, Spoon Shape........ "

Egg Skimmers .... "

NUT CRACKERS.

Table Nut Cracks, Plain, Bright................ per dozen, $

Table Nut Cracks, Plain, Extra Polished........ "

Table Nut Cracks, Fancy, Extra Polished....... "

Table Nut Cracks, Silver Plated............... "

Blake's Patent Nut Cracks.................... "

CORN POPPERS.

Square .... per dozen, $

Round .... per dozen, $

SLAW CUTTERS.

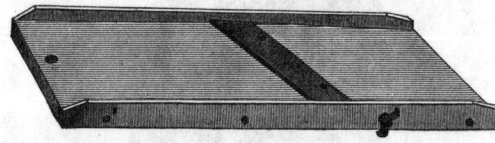

Slaw Cutters................................ per dozen, $

COCOA DIPPERS.

Plain...................................... per dozen, $

Rimmed .... "

MOP STICKS.

Jones' Patent, Common...................... per dozen, $

Taylor's Patent, Best .... per dozen, $

THERMOMETERS.

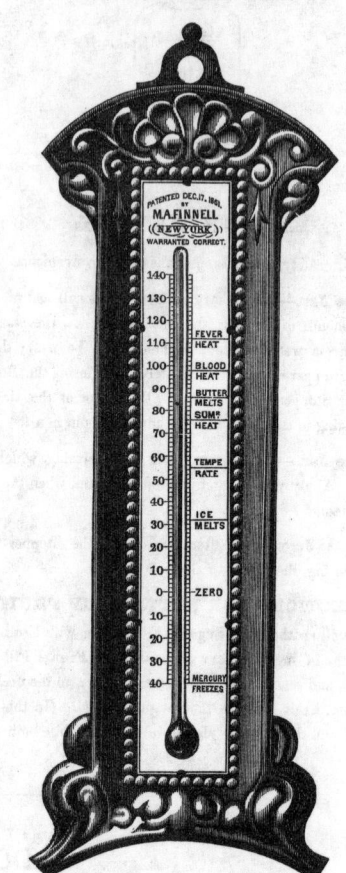

Finnel's Patent, Ruby Tube.

7 inch, on Cards .... per dozen, $

9 inch, on Cards .... "

8 inch, Tin Case, Japanned .... "

10 inch, Tin Case, Japanned .... "

7 inch, Fire Gilt Case....................... "

10 inch, Fire Gilt Case...................... "

KENDALL'S PATENT.
Tin Case.

$ per dozen.

Plain,   7   8   10   12   inch.

Standard Tin Case.

Single Degree, 10 inch....................... per dozen, $

Half Degree, Smithsonian, 12 inch .... per dozen, $

Fancy Case.

| | $ | | | per dozen. |
Mahogany, Plain,   8   12   inch.

| | $ | | | per dozen. |
Mahogany, Ruby Tubes,   8   10   inch.

Rosewood, Plain, 10 inch .... per dozen, $

Rosewood, Ruby Tubes, 10 inch.............. per dozen, $

KEY RINGS, CORK SCREWS, ETC.

THERMOMETERS, KENDALL'S PATENT.

(*Continued*.)

Union Case.

$ per dozen.

6   8   10   inch.

Barometers for Farmers' Use.........................each, $

KEY RINGS.

$ per gross

No.   1   2   3

Assorted on Cards...........................per gross, $

CAST STEEL CORK SCREWS,

With Rosewood and Cocoa Handles.

No. 6.   No. 10.

No. 7.   No. 4.

$ per dozen.

Spiral Coil, No.   0   2   4   6   7

$ per dozen.

Convex Twist, No.   9   10

No. 11.

$ per dozen.

Pocket, No.   11   13   14   15   16

CORK SCREWS—*Continued*.

No. 12, Long Cork Screws.....................per dozen, $

Skater's Pocket Gimlet No. 1..................per dozen, $

CLARK'S AMERICAN CAST-STEEL CONVEX TWIST CORK-SCREWS.

	Boxwood Handles.	Cocoa Handles.
	PER DOZ.	PER DOZ.
No. 4, Plain Handles.....................		
No. 5, Plain Handles.....................		
No. 6, Plain Handles.....................		
No. 4, Extra Handles.....................		
No. 5, Extra Handles.....................		
No. 6, Extra Handles.....................		
No. 4, Plain Handles, with Brush............		
No. 5, Plain Handles, with Brush............		
No. 6, Plain Handles, with Brush............		
No. 4, Extra Handles, with Brush...........		
No. 5, Extra Handles, with Brush...........		
No. 6, Extra Handles, with Brush...........		

Clark's Pocket Cork Screws.

No. 4.......................................per dozen, $

No. 5 ....   "

No. 6 ....   "

Skate Gimlets................................   "

Chinnock's Patent.

Japanned, Iron Guard.......................per dozen, $

Polished, Iron Guard.......................per dozen, $

Rubber Pocket Cork Screws.

$ per dozen.

No.   1   2   3   4

STAIR RODS.

STAIR RODS—BRASS, PLATED, AND GERMAN SILVER.

LENGTH. INCHES.	21	22	23	24	25	26	27	28	29	30	31	32	33	34	35	36	37	38	39	40
INCH.																				
$\frac{5}{8}$, Oval																				
$\frac{3}{4}$, Oval																				
$\frac{7}{8}$, Oval																				
1, Oval																				
$\frac{3}{4}$, Oval, Hollow																				
$\frac{7}{8}$, Oval, Hollow																				
1, Oval, Hollow																				
$1\frac{1}{8}$, Oval, Hollow																				
$1\frac{1}{4}$, Oval, Hollow																				
1, Octagon or Fluted, Hollow																				
$1\frac{1}{8}$, Octagon or Fluted, Hollow																				
$1\frac{1}{4}$, Octagon or Fluted, Hollow																				
1, Silver Plated, Oval, Hollow																				
$1\frac{1}{8}$, Silver Plated, Oval, Hollow																				
$1\frac{1}{4}$, Silver Plated, Oval, Hollow																				
1, Silver Plated, Octagon or Fluted, Hollow																				
$1\frac{1}{8}$, Silver Plated, Octagon or Fluted, Hollow																				
$1\frac{1}{4}$, Silver Plated, Octagon or Fluted, Hollow																				

☞ All Rods made of Solid Metal, $ per dozen extra.   German Silver Rods, $ per dozen less than Plated.

PLAIN ROUND.
Brass.
$
Length,   27   30   36   40   inch.   per dozen.

Plated.
$
Length,   27   30   36   40   inch.   per dozen.

HEXAGON.
Brass.
$
Length,   27   30   36   40   inch.   per dozen.

Plated.
$
Length,   27   30   36   40   inch.   per dozen.

GOLD LACQUERED FRENCH RODS.
NO. 1, ROUND.
Brass.
$
Length,   27   30   36   40   inch.   per dozen.

Plated.
$
Length,   27   30   36   40   inch.   per dozen.

NO. 1, CONCAVE.
Brass.
$
Length, $1\frac{1}{4}$×27   30   36   40   inch.   per dozen.

GOLD LACQUERED FRENCH RODS—*Continued.*
NO. 1, CONCAVE.
Plated.
$
Length, $1\frac{1}{4}$×27   30   36   40   inch.   per dozen.

NO. 2, HOLLOW.
Brass.
$
Length, $1\frac{1}{4}$×27   30   36   40   inch.   per dozen.

Plated.
$
Length, $1\frac{1}{4}$×27   30   36   40   inch.   per dozen.

NO. 3, OCTAGON.
Brass.
$
Length, $1\frac{1}{4}$×27   30   36   40   inch.   per dozen.

Plated.
$
Length, $1\frac{1}{4}$×27   30   36   40   inch.   per dozen.

NO. 3, FLAT HOLLOW.
Brass.
$
Length, $1\frac{1}{4}$×27   30   36   40   inch.   per dozen.

Plated.
$
Length, $1\frac{1}{4}$×27   30   36   40   inch.   per dozen.

STAIR RODS, CLOTHES WRINGERS, ETC.

GOLD LACQUERED FRENCH RODS.
(Continued.)

NO. 4, FLAT HOLLOW.
Brass.

$				per dozen.
Length, 1×27	30	36	40	inch.

Plated.

$				per dozen.
Length, 1×27	30	36	40	inch.

ROPE, ROUND.
Brass.

$				per dozen.
Length, 27	30	36	40	inch.

Plated.

$				per dozen.
Length, 27	30	36	40	inch.

DIAMOND ROPE.
Brass.

$				per dozen.
Length, 27	30	36	40	inch.

Plated.

$				per dozen.
Length, 27	30	36	40	inch.

HALF ROPE.
Brass.

$				per dozen.
Length, 27	30	36	40	inch.

Plated.

$				per dozen.
Length, 27	30	36	40	inch.

ROUND BRONZED.
Brass Tips.

$				per dozen.
Length, 27	30	36	40	inch.

Plated Tips.

$				per dozen.
Length, 27	30	36	40	inch.

ROUND PLATED GOLD TIPS.

$				per dozen.
Length, 27	30	36	40	inch.

STAIR ROD FASTENINGS.
Buttons for Hollow Rods.

$						per gross.
⅝	¾	⅞	1	1⅛	1¼	inch.

Loops for Oval Rods.

$						per gross.
⅝	¾	⅞	1	1⅛	1¼	inch.

Bands for Oval Rods.

$						per gross.
⅝	¾	⅞	1	1⅛	1¼	inch.

Eyes for Round Stair Rods.

No. 1, Small . . . . per gross, $

No. 2, Large . . . . per gross, $

CLOTHES WRINGERS.

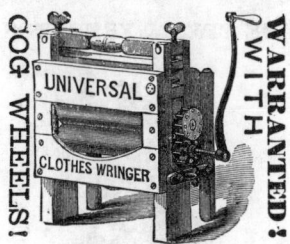

Universal.

No. 1, Large Family Wringer, with Cogs, Warranted, each, $

No. 2, Medium, with Cogs, Warranted . . . . "

No. 2½, Medium, without Cogs, not Warranted . . . . . . "

No. 3, Small, without Cogs, not Warranted . . . . "

No. 8, Large Hotel, with Cogs, Warranted . . . . "

No. 18, Medium, (to run by steam,) with Cogs, Warranted . . . . "

No. 22, Large Laundry, (to run by steam,) with Cogs, Warranted . . . . "

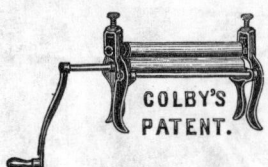

No. 1 Wringer, 10 inch Rollers . . . . each, $

No. 2 Wringer, 8½ inch Rollers . . . . each, $

Whitney's Patent.

No. 2 Wringer, 9 inch Roller . . . . each, $

No. 3 Wringer, 10 inch Roller . . . . each, $

CLOTHES PINS.

Whittled . . . . per gross, $

Spiral Spring, "Patent" . . . . per gross, $

FLY TRAPS.

Patent Revolving . . . . each, $

ICE CREAM FREEZERS, COAL HODS, ETC.

ICE CREAM FREEZERS.

Torrey's Patent.

$	1	2	3	4	6	8	14	23	each. quarts.

BARTLETT'S PATENT POLAR REFRIGERATOR,
With Filter and Water Cooler Combined.

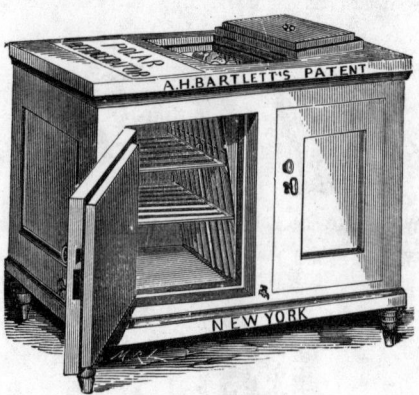

$										each.
No.	0	1	2	3	4	5	6	7	8	9	
Length	27	36	39	42	46	49	53	59	65	71	inches.
Depth	21	21	22	23	24	25	26	27	28	29	inches.
Height	34	34	36	38	40	42	44	46	48	50	inches.

COAL HODS.

Japanned Square Front.

$	12	13	14	15	16	per dozen. inch.
$	17	18	19	20		per dozen. inch.

COAL HODS—*Continued.*

Galvanized Square Front.

$	14	15	16	17	18	per dozen. inch.

Patent Cast Bottom—Japanned, Square.

$	14	15	16	17	18	per dozen. inch.

Patent Cast Bottom—Galvanized, Square.

$	14	15	16	17	18	per dozen. inch.

SAD IRONS.

Round Point.   Sharp Point.

Best Sad Irons, Wrought Handles Assorted, Round and sharp.

No. 4, 5, 6, 7, 8, 9 ....per lb. $

Webster's Patent Smoothing Iron.

Webster's Patent..........................per dozen, $

Polishing Irons.

McCoy's Patent......................per dozen pairs, $

Mrs. Cook's Patent....................per dozen pairs, $

Laundry Irons.

No. 70, with Fine Polished Face............per dozen, $

No. 71, Extra Fine Finish...................per dozen, $

Planed and Polished Tailors' Irons.

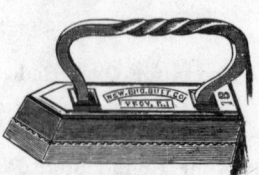

Sizes—9, 12, 15, 18, 21, 24, 27 lbs..........per lb. $

SAD IRONS, KETTLE EARS, ETC.

PATENT SELF-HEATING IRONS.

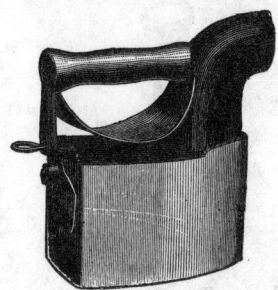

With Shield.

Self-Heating Irons, Plain.................per dozen, $

Self-Heating Irons, with Shield............per dozen, $

Self-Heating Tailors' Iron................per dozen, $

Toy Sad Irons.

Fancy Duck Pattern Toy Sad Irons and Stands.

Painted in four colors, put up in boxes.

A, A, with Stands....................per dozen, $

A, with Stands....................   "

B, with Stands....................   "

C, with Stands....................   "

D, with Stands....................   "

E, with Stands....................   "

Plain, without Stands.

	$					per dozen.
No.	109	0	0½	1	2	3.

Toy Sad Iron Stands.

	$					per dozen.
No.	109	0	0½	1	2	3.

SAD IRON STANDS.

No. 1.   No. 2.   No. 3.

	$			per dozen.
No.	1	2	3.	

Japanned Sad Iron Stands.

Polished on Top Surface, same Patterns as above.

	$			per dozen.
No.	11	12	13.	

COFFEE POT STANDS.

Japanned...........................per dozen, $

FLUTING IRONS.

Two Prong...........................per dozen, $

Three Prong.........................per dozen, $

KETTLE EARS—BLACK.

	$								per gross.
No.	1	2	3	4	5	6	7	8.	

Kettle Ears, Tinned.

	$								per gross.
No.	1	2	3	4	5	6	7	8.	

Kettle Ears, Tin.

	$								per gross.
No.	1	2	3	4	5	6	7	8.	

FIRE DOGS, ETC.

TEA-KETTLE EARS— *Continued.*
Tea Kettle Ears, Tinned.

No.	$ 4	5	6.	per gross.

STEP-LADDER SOCKETS.
[Patent applied for.]

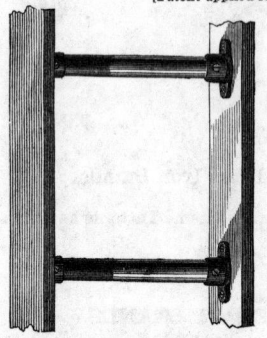 

A useful invention, whereby a Ladder may be made one-half the usual weight, and of equal strength. To make a Ladder with these Sockets, the rounds are made of equal length, fitted in, and wedged; then screw the Sockets to the Ladder Strips.

A broken round may be replaced, without taking the Ladder apart, by unscrewing the Sockets attached to the broken round.

Diameter of hole, 1 inch . . . . per hundred, $

FIRE DOGS.

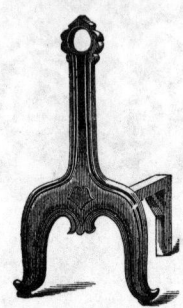

Common Dogs, Japanned.

No. 1, 10 inch Back . . . . per lb. $
No. 2, 15 inch Back . . . .   "
No. 3, 14 inch Back . . . .   "
No. 4, 12 inch Back . . . .   "

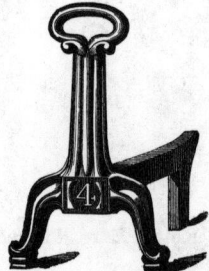

New Pattern Heavy Dogs, Japanned.

No. 1, 18 inch Back . . . . per lb. $
No. 2, 16 inch Back . . . .   "
No. 3, 14 inch Back . . . .   "
No. 4, 12 inch Back . . . .   "

FIRE DOGS— *Continued.*

Ring Top Bronzed Dogs.

No. 0, 16   inch Back . . . . per pair, $
No. 1, 14   inch Back . . . .   "
No. 2, 12½ inch Back . . . .   "
No. 3, 11   inch Back . . . .   "

Brass Top Bronzed Dogs.

No. 1, 15 inch Back . . . . per pair, $
No. 2, 14 inch Back . . . .   "
No. 3, 12 inch Back . . . .   "

BRASS ANDIRONS.
Globe Pattern.

$								per pair.
No.	0	1	2	3	4	5	6 7	

Urn Pattern.

$								per pair.
No.	0	1	2	3	4	5	6 7	

BRASS ANDIRONS.

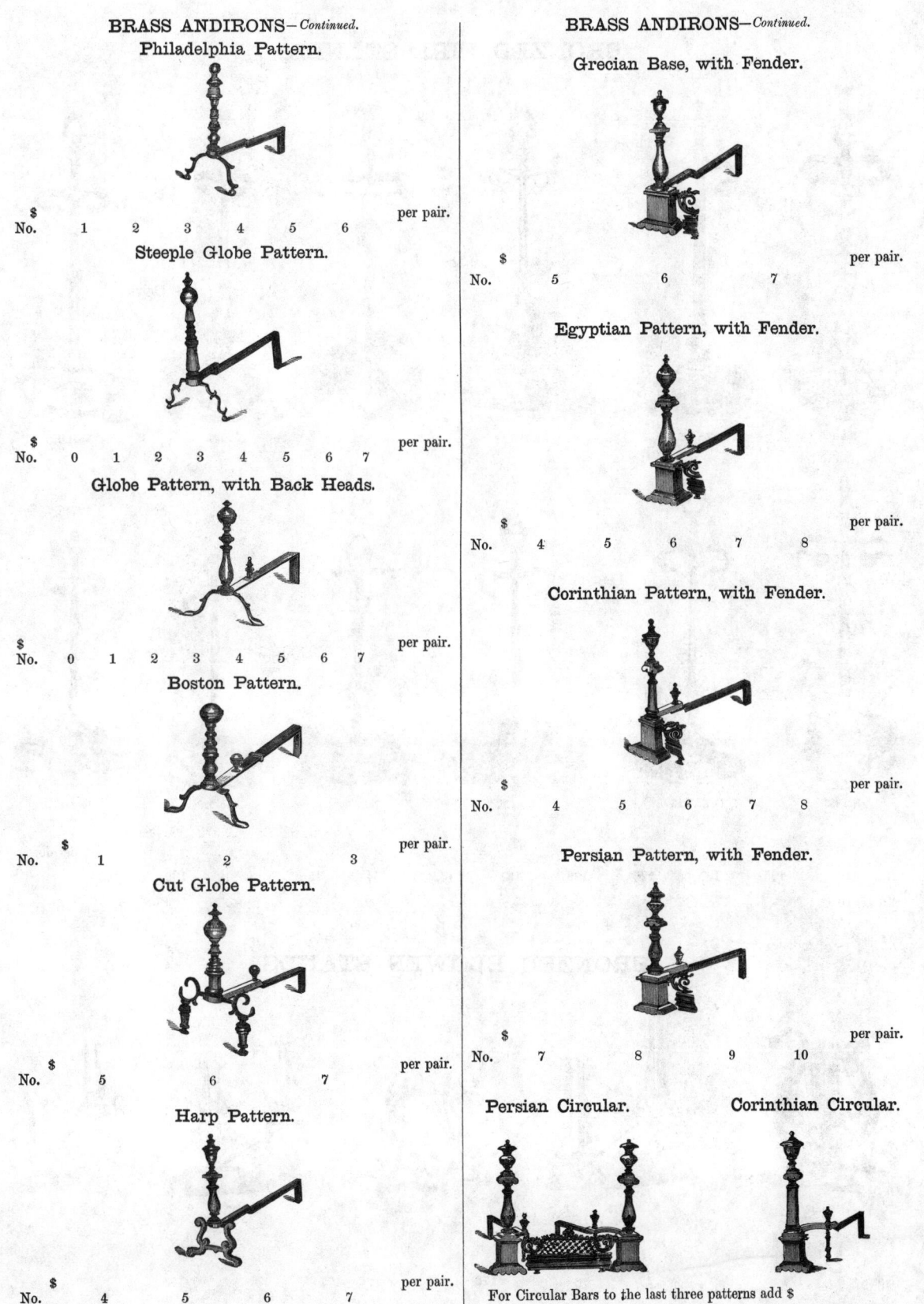

BRASS ANDIRONS—*Continued.*
Philadelphia Pattern.

$
No.   1   2   3   4   5   6   per pair.

Steeple Globe Pattern.

$
No.   0   1   2   3   4   5   6   7   per pair.

Globe Pattern, with Back Heads.

$
No.   0   1   2   3   4   5   6   7   per pair.

Boston Pattern.

$
No.   1   2   3   per pair.

Cut Globe Pattern.

$
No.   5   6   7   per pair.

Harp Pattern.

$
No.   4   5   6   7   per pair.

BRASS ANDIRONS—*Continued.*
Grecian Base, with Fender.

$
No.   5   6   7   per pair.

Egyptian Pattern, with Fender.

$
No.   4   5   6   7   8   per pair.

Corinthian Pattern, with Fender.

$
No.   4   5   6   7   8   per pair.

Persian Pattern, with Fender.

$
No.   7   8   9   10   per pair.

Persian Circular.   Corinthian Circular.

For Circular Bars to the last three patterns add $

BRONZED FIRE AND BLOWER STANDS.

BRONZED FIRE STANDS.

No. 125.    No. 126. 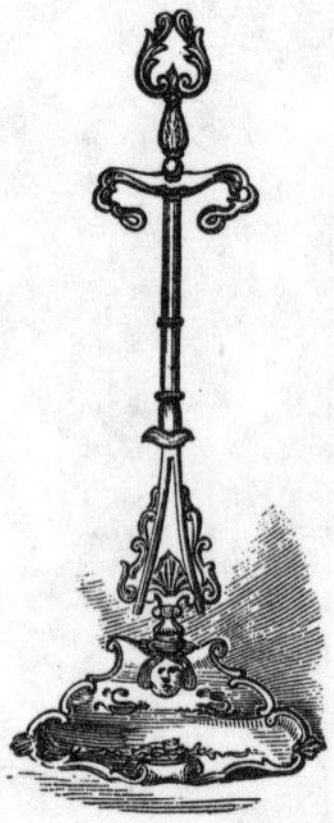   No. 127.    No. 128. 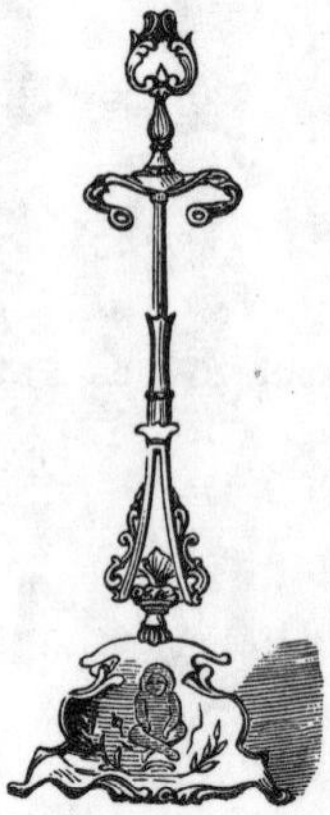   No. 129.    No. 131.

No. 133. 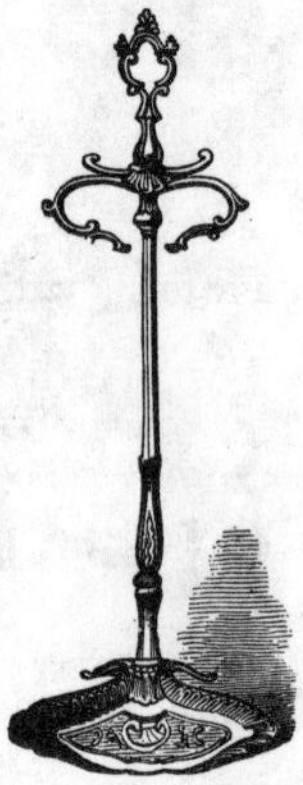   No. 134.    No. 136.    No. 138. 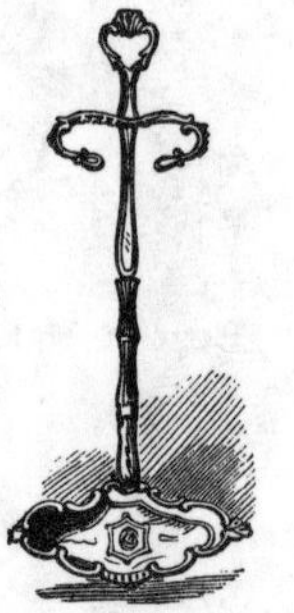   No. 139. 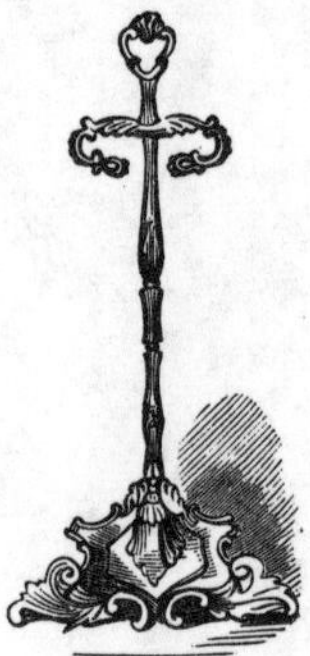   No. 142.

											per dozen.
$											
No.	125	126	127	128	129	131	133	134	136	138	139	142

BRONZED BLOWER STANDS.

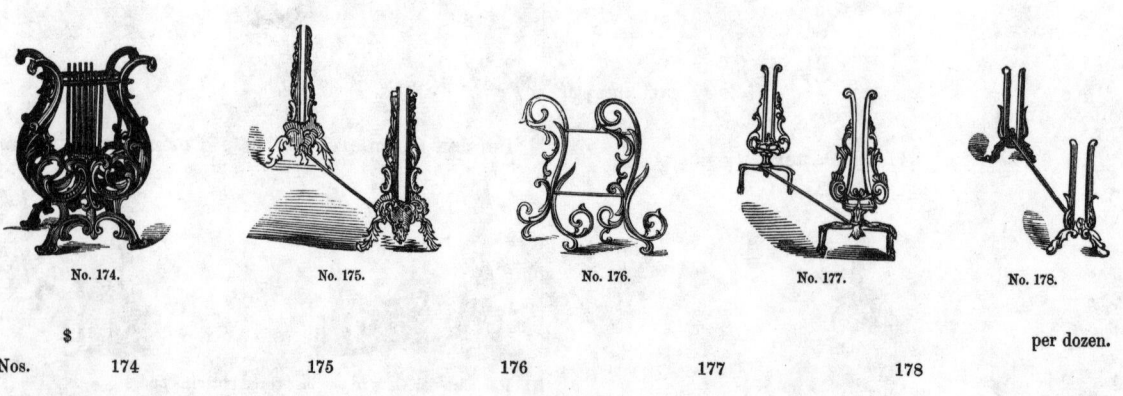

No. 174.   No. 175.   No. 176.   No. 177.   No. 178.

					per dozen.
$					
Nos.	174	175	176	177	178

FANCY IRON HAT STANDS.

No. 64. No. 65. No. 67. No. 68.

No. 70. No. 73. No. 74. No. 77.

$ each.

No.	64	65	67	68	70	73	74	77

UMBRELLA STANDS, IRON CHAIRS, ETC.

FANCY UMBRELLA STANDS.

No. 80.   No. 82.   No. 84.

No. 85.   No. 89.   No. 93.

No.	$	80	82	84	85	89	93	each.

FANCY IRON CHAIRS.

No. 23, Morning Glory Chair.

No. 35, Hall Chair.

No. 29, Grape Chair.

PATENT FLOWER STAND

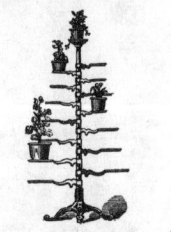

each.

No. 1, arranged for 7 Pots, $
No. 2, arranged for 10 Pots, $
No. 3, arranged for 13 Pots, $
No. 4, arranged for 15 pots, $

No.	$	23	29	35	each.

FANCY IRON SHELF BRACKETS.

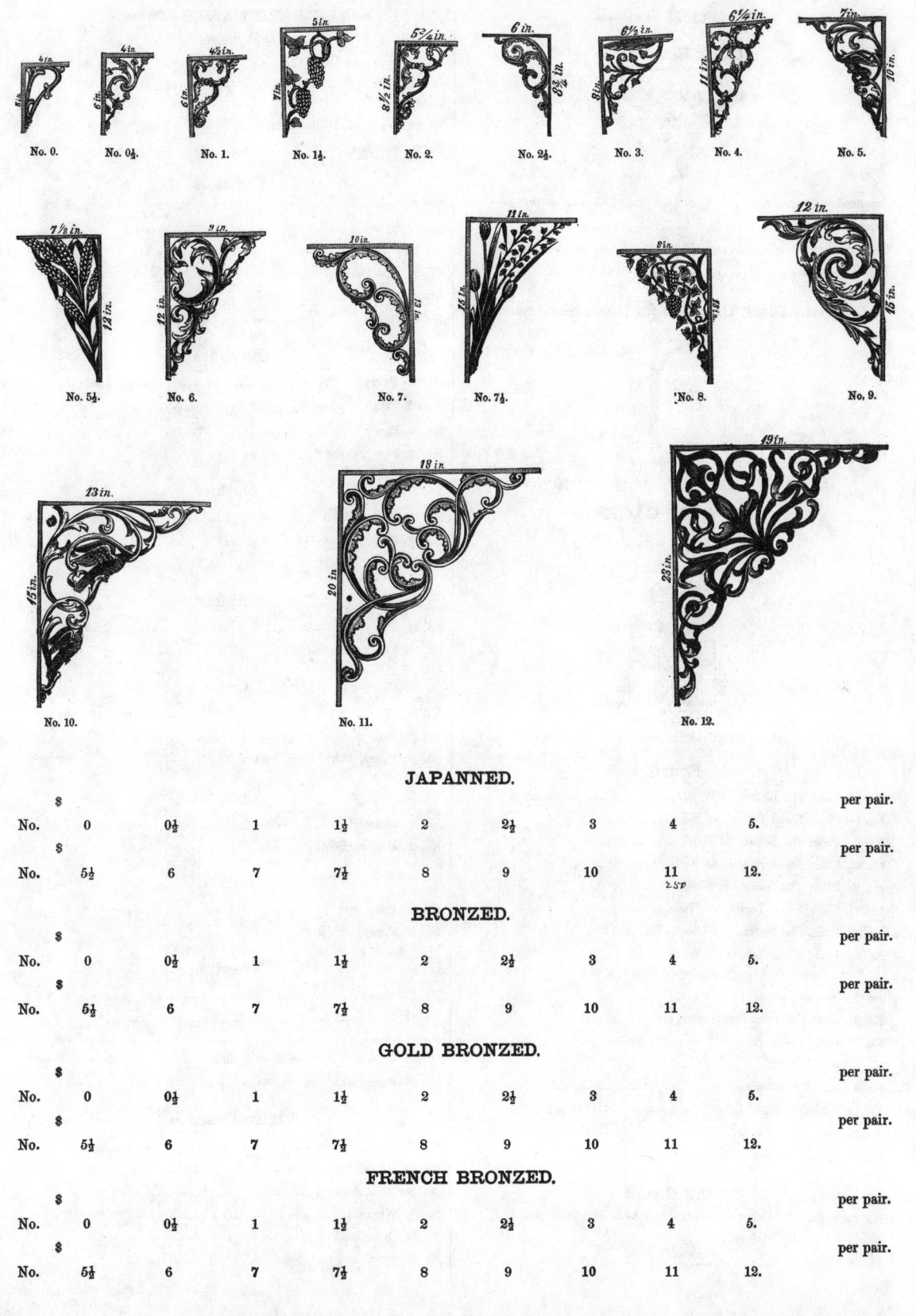

No. 0. No. 0½. No. 1. No. 1½. No. 2. No. 2½. No. 3. No. 4. No. 5.

No. 5½. No. 6. No. 7. No. 7½. 'No. 8. No, 9.

No. 10. No. 11. No. 12.

JAPANNED.

No.	0	0½	1	1½	2	2½	3	4	5.	per pair.
$										per pair.
No.	5½	6	7	7½	8	9	10	11	12.	

BRONZED.

No.	0	0½	1	1½	2	2½	3	4	5.	per pair.
$										per pair.
No.	5½	6	7	7½	8	9	10	11	12.	

GOLD BRONZED.

No.	0	0½	1	1½	2	2½	3	4	5.	per pair.
$										per pair.
No.	5½	6	7	7½	8	9	10	11	12.	

FRENCH BRONZED.

No.	0	0½	1	1½	2	2½	3	4	5.	per pair.
$										per pair.
No.	5½	6	7	7½	8	9	10	11	12.	

BRACKETS, BIRD CAGES, ETC.

BRACKETS—*Continued.*

Clock Brackets.

6 in.

10 in.

Japanned..each,	
Bronzed..	"
Gold Bronzed..	"
French Bronzed.....................................	"

Plain Black Brackets for Store Shelves.

$								per pair.
4	6	8	10	12	15	18	20	inch.

TIN BIRD CAGES.

Round.

No. 1, Plain, Flat Bottom, 40 Wires................per dozen, $	
No. 1½, Plain, Stand Bottom, 40 Wires..............	"
No. 2, Plain, Flat Bottom, 44 Wires....................	"
No. 2½, Plain, Stand Bottom, 44 Wires.............	"
No. 3, Plain, Flat Bottom, 48 Wires....................	"
No. 3½, Plain, Stand Bottom, 48 Wires.............	"
No. 4, Plain, Flat Bottom, 52 Wires....................	"
No. 4½, Plain, Stand Bottom, 52 Wires.............	"
Or $ per doz. Nests of Nos. 1, 2, 3, 4.	
No. 5, Scollop Bottom....................	"
No. 6, Scollop Bottom, Cornucopia..................	"
No. 7, with Wreath......................	"
No. 8, with Wreath......................	"
No. 9, Six-sides Bottom....................	"
No. 10, Six-sides Bottom....................	"
No. 11, Gallery Bottom....................	"
No. 12, Eagle Bottom....................	"

Half Round.

No. 13, Plain, with Gallery....................per dozen, $	
No. 14, Plain, with Gallery........................	"
No. 15, Fancy..................................	"

TIN BIRD CAGES—*Continued.*
Square.

No. 16, Open.....................................per dozen, $	
No. 17, Open..	"
No. 18, Open..	"
No. 19, Flat Back, Rising Sun.....................	"
No. 20, Flat Back...................................	"

Cottages.

No. 21, Open.....................................per dozen, $	
No. 22, Open..	"
No. 23, Open..	"
No. 24, Flat Back...................................	"
No. 25, Flat Back...................................	"
No. 26, Open..	"

Six-Sides.

No. 27, Fancy....................................per dozen, $	
No. 28, Fancy......................................	"
No. 29, Fancy......................................	"
No. 30, Fancy, Brass Stand........................	"

Gothic.

No. 31, Plain Bottom.............................per dozen, $	
No. 32, Plain Bottom...............................	"
No. 33, Fancy Bottom..............................	"

Chinese.

No. 34, Fancy....................................per dozen, $	
No. 35, Fancy, with Bells..........................	"

Oval.

No. 36, Plain....................................per dozen, $	
No. 37, Plain.......................................	"
No. 38, Fancy, with Flower Pots....................	"

Aquarias.

No. 39, Plain Globe..............................per dozen, $	
No. 40, Double Globe...............................	"

Balloons.

No. 41, Plain, with Boat.........................per dozen, $	
No. 42, Fancy, with Boot...........................	"

Breeding.

No. 43, Plain....................................per dozen, $	
No. 44, Plain.......................................	"
No. 45, Plain.......................................	"
Or $ per Nest of three.	
No. 46, Fancy, with Partition......................	"

Miscellaneous.

No. 47, Round, Fancy.............................per dozen, $	
No. 48, Round, Brass Stand........................	"
No. 49, Eight-sides.................................	"
No. 50, Windmill....................................	"
No. 51, Cathedral...................................	"
No. 52, Six-sides, Brass Stand.....................	"

BIRD CAGES, SIEVES, WIRE CLOTH, ETC.

PARROT CAGES.
Plain Bottoms.

No. 1, for Paroquets ....per dozen, $
No. 2, for Parrots, 34 Wires........................   "
No. 3, for Parrots, 37 Wires........................   "
No. 4, for Parrots, 43 Wires........................   "
        Or $ per Nest of four.

Japanned or Polished Bottoms.

No. 1, for Paroquets ....per dozen, $
No. 2, for Parrots, 31 Wires........................   "
No. 3, for Parrots, 37 Wires........................   "
        Or $ per Nest of four.

WHEEL CAGES,
With Draw Bottoms and Partitions.
Plain.

No. 1, for Mice......................................per dozen, $
No. 2, for Rats and Flying Squirrels.................   "
No. 3, for Squirrels.................................   "
No. 4, for Squirrels.................................   "

Japanned.

No. 1, for Mice......................................per dozen, $
No. 2, for Rats and Flying Squirrels.................   "
No. 3, for Squirrels.................................   "
No. 4, for Squirrels.................................   "

TRAVELLING CAGES.

For Canaries ....per dozen, $

WOODEN BREEDING CAGES.

A Nest of three......................................each, $

ROSEWOOD MOCKING BIRD CAGES.

A Nest of three......................................each, $

SUNDRIES.

Extra Feed Cups......................................each, $
Bathing Cups, two sizes..............................   "
Glass Bottles for Wood Cages.........................   "
Feed Cups for Parrots and Mocking Birds..............   "
Bird Nests, Willow...................................   "
Bird Nests, Wire.....................................   "
Perches, per 100 feet................................   "

Hanging Flower Baskets.

                $ each.
No.   101   102   103   104

FLOUR OR MEAL SIEVES.
Iron Wire.

         $ per dozen.
No.   14   16   18   20   22   24   30   mesh.

Plated Wire.

         $ per dozen.
No.   18   20   24   mesh.

Brass Wire.

         $ per dozen.
No.   18   20   24   mesh.

"SHAKER" FLOUR OR MEAL SIEVES.

No. 24 Mesh, Iron, Extra Heavy and Large Size......per dozen, $
    ☞ All Flour and Meal Sieves in 2 dozen Bundles.

Oat Sieves.

14 inch...per dozen, $
16 inch...per dozen,

Riddles.

Nos. 2 and 3, Iron, Assorted, 18 and 20 inch..........per dozen, $
Nos. 4 to 20, Iron, Assorted, 18 and 20 inch..........   "
Nos. 4 to 20, Brass, Assorted, 18 and 20 inch.........   "

Coal Sifters.

Square, 3 in a Nest.................................per dozen, $

Sand Screens.

No. 1, 5 feet 6 inches × 1 foot 11 inches ....each, $
No. 2, 5 feet 10 inches × 2 feet 3 inches ....each,

Toasting Forks.

Plated Wire, 4 Prong................................per dozen, $
Swing Toaster, Wood Handle, Plated Wire........per dozen,

Wire Cloth.

Iron Wire Cloths, in widths of 14, 16, 18, 20, 21 and 24 inches.
Nos. 2 and 3, Wire..................................per square foot, $
Nos. 4 to 24, Wire..................................   "
Fanning Mill Cloth, Square and Twist Mesh.....   "
Rice Cloth, Nos. 9 to 16 Wire.................   "
Locomotive Bonnet Cloth.......................   "

Copper Wire Cloth.

Copper Wire Cloth..................................per square foot, $

Brass Wire Cloth.

For Rosin Strainers............................per square foot, $
For Milk Strainers.............................   "
For Safes ....   "

Plated Wire Cloth.

For Safes...per square foot, $

Dog Muzzles.

Coppered Wire ....per dozen, $

Ox Muzzles.

Ox Muzzles ....per dozen pair, $

Wire Rat Traps.

No. 1, Square, 11 inch..............................per dozen, $
No. 2, Square, 12 inch..............................   "
No. 3, Square, 13 inch..............................   "
No. 5, Square, Double Doors ....   "
No. 6, Square, Double Doors ....   "
No. 7, Square, Double Doors ....   "
No. 1, Round, 12 inch...............................   "
No. 2, Round, 14 inch...............................   "

Patent Revolving Rat Traps.

Self-Setting ....per dozen, $

TRAPS, BRASS KETTLES AND BAKE PANS.

WIRE MOUSE TRAPS.

No. 1, Square, Bright Wire ....per gross, $
No. 1, Square, Coppered Wire....................... "
No. 1, Round, Bright Wire......................... "
No. 1, Round, Coppered Wire...................... "
No. 2, Round, Coppered Wire...................... "

Wood Mouse Traps.

$ 1   2   3   4   5   6   per dozen. holes.

BRASS KETTLES.

Brass Kettles.................................per lb. $

Diameter,	7	8	9	10	11	12	13	14	inches.
Weight,	1	$1\frac{1}{2}$	$2\frac{1}{4}$	$2\frac{3}{4}$	$3\frac{1}{2}$	$4\frac{1}{4}$	5	$5\frac{3}{4}$	lbs.
Capacity,	$\frac{1}{2}$	1	$1\frac{1}{2}$	2	$2\frac{1}{4}$	3	4	5	gallons.
Diameter,	15	16	17	18	19	20	21		inches.
Weight,	$6\frac{1}{2}$	$7\frac{3}{4}$	9	$10\frac{1}{2}$	12	14	$16\frac{1}{2}$		lbs.
Capacity,	6	$7\frac{1}{2}$	9	$10\frac{1}{2}$	12	$14\frac{1}{2}$	17		gallons.
Diameter,	22	23	24	25	26	27	28		inches.
Weight,	$19\frac{3}{4}$	23	$26\frac{1}{2}$	29	31	33	36		lbs.
Capacity,	20	23	26	30	33	37	42		gallons.

Brass Maslin Kettles.

6 to 24 inches in Diameter.........................per lb. $

WATERMAN'S PATENT CAST IRON BAKE PANS.

For Baking Graham Cakes, Wheaten Biscuit, Rolls, &c., these are superior to any other pans for the purpose.

Being of Cast Iron, and thick, without square corners, they retain the heat uniformly, and brown without burning the cakes.

They will bake better after a little use than when new.

No. 4.

DIRECTIONS FOR USE.

For Graham Cakes—Heat and butter the pans, and put in the batter or dough, while the pans are hot, and bake in a very hot oven.

Recipe for "Gem" Graham Cakes—1 pint Milk ; $\frac{1}{2}$ pint Graham Flour ; $\frac{1}{2}$ pint Wheat Flour ; 1 teaspoonful Salt ; 2 Eggs. Mix thoroughly.

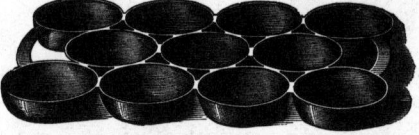

Nos. 1 & 2.

No. 7.

No. 3.

No. 8.

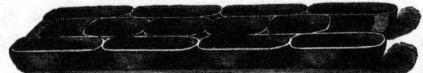

No. 6.

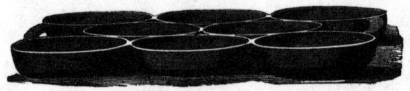

No. 5.

No. 1, 11 Round Pans, Small ....per dozen sets, $
No. 2, 11 Round Pans, Large................... "
No. 3, 11 Round Pans, for Frying Eggs.......... "
No. 4, 8 Oval Pans, for French Rolls .... "
No. 5, 8 Oval Pans, Large .... "

No. 6, 12 Oblong Pans, Small...................per dozen sets, $
No. 7, 8 Oblong Pans, Large.................. "
No. 8, 11 Oval Pans, Small .... "
No. 9, Deep Round Pans, Quite Small........... "

☞ **Each Plate represents one Set.**

HOLLOW WARE.

FLAT-BOTTOM ROUND BOILERS.

With Heavy English Style Covers.

Enameled.

$		1		1½		2		3	each. pints.
$	2		2½		3	4	5	6	7	each. quarts.
$	2	2½	3	3½	4	5	6	7	8	each. gallons.

Tinned.

$		1		1½		2		3	each. pints.
$	2		2½		3	4	5	6	7	each. quarts.
$	2	2½	3	3½	4	5	6	7	8	each. gallons.

Turned.

$		1		1½		2		3	each. pints.
$	2		2½		3	4	5	6	7	each. quarts.
$	2	2½	3	3½	4	5	6	7	8	each. gallons.

FLAT-BOTTOM OVAL BOILERS.

With Heavy English Style Covers.

Enameled.

| $ | 1 | 1½ | 2 | 2½ | 3 | 3½ | each. gallons. |
| $ | 4 | 5 | 6 | 7 | 8 | 10 | each. gallons. |

Tinned.

| $ | 1 | 1½ | 2 | 2½ | 3 | 3½ | each. gallons. |
| $ | 4 | 5 | 6 | 7 | 8 | 10 | each. gallons. |

TEA KETTLES—ENGLISH PATTERN.

With English Bails and Lids, Brass Knobs.

Enameled.

| $ | 3 | 4 | 5 | 6 | 7 | each. quarts. |

Tinned.

| $ | 3 | 4 | 5 | 6 | 7 | each. quarts. |

FLAT-BOTTOM BELLIED SAUCEPANS.

With Heavy English Style Covers.

Enameled.

$		1		1½		2		3	each. pints.
$	2	2½	3	4	5	6	7	each. quarts.
$	2	2½	3	3½	4	each. gallons.

Tinned.

$		1		1½		2		3	each. pints.
$	2	2½	3	4	5	6	7	each. quarts.
$	2	2½	3	3½	4	each. gallons.

UPRIGHT SAUCE PANS.

With Lips and Covers.

Enameled.

| $ | 1½ | 2 | 3 | each. pints. |
| $ | 2 | 3 | 4 | each. quarts. |

Tinned.

| $ | 1½ | 2 | 3 | each. pints. |
| $ | 2 | 3 | 4 | each. quarts. |

SHALLOW FRENCH STEW PANS,

With Covers.

Enameled.

| No. | $ 1 | 2 | 3 | 4 | 5 | 6. | each. |
| No. | $ 7 | 8 | 9 | 10 | 11 | 12. | each. |

Tinned.

| No. | $ 1 | 2 | 3 | 4 | 5 | 6. | each. |
| No. | $ 7 | 8 | 9 | 10 | 11 | 12. | each. |

HOLLOW WARE,

(Continued.)

MASLIN KETTLES,

English Pattern.

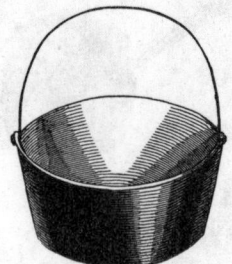

Enameled.

$								each.
No.	1	2	3	4	5	6	7	8.
	2½	3	3½	4½	5½	6	7	8	pints.

$								each.
No.	9	10	11	12	13	14	15	16.
	5	6	7	8	10	12	16	18	quarts.

SCOTCH BOWLS.

Enameled.

$					each.
No.	2	3	4	5	6.

YANKEE BOWLS.

Enameled.

$					each.
No.	2	3	4	5	6.

FISH KETTLES.

Enameled.

$						each.
No.	1	2	3	4	5	6.
Length,	16	18	20	22	24	26	inches.

Tinned.

$						each.
No.	1	2	3	4	5	6.
Length,	16	18	20	22	24	26	inches.

GLUE POTS.

Enameled.

$										per dozen.
No.	000	00	0	1	2	3	4	5	6.

Tinned.

$										per dozen.
No.	000	00	0	1	2	3	4	5	6.

BROWN'S PATENT GLUE POTS.

Galvanized.

$					per dozen.
No.	2	3	4	5.

POLISHED DRUG OR SPICE MORTARS.

Japanned.

½ Pint	each, $
1 Pint	"
1 Quart	"
2 Quarts	"
1 Gallon	"
2 Gallons	"

DEEP OVENS.

No.	1	1½	2	2½	3	3½	4	5	6	
	8	9	10	11	12	13	14	16	18	inch.

Per Ton of 2240 lbs.. $

HOLLOW WARE.

(*Continued.*)

SHALLOW OVENS.

No.	1	1½	2	2½	3	3½	4	5	6	
	8	9	10	11	12	13	14	16	18	inch.

Per Ton of 2240 lbs.............................. $

ROUND POTS.

No.	1	2	3	4	5	6	7	8	
	½	1	1½	2	2½	3	4		5 gallons.
No.	9	10	11	12	13	14	15		
	6	8	10	15	20	25	30		gallons.

Per Ton of 2240 lbs............................. $

HEAVY STAMPED SHEET IRON POT COVERS.

With Ring Handles.

	$					per dozen.
No.	1	2	3	4	5	
	6	7½	8¼	9½	10¼	inches.
	$					per dozen.
No.	6	7	8	9	10	inches.
	11	12	13	14	15¼	

CAULDRONS.

Philadelphia Heavy Pattern.

	$						each.
No.	1	2	3	4	5	6	
	10	20	30	45	60	90	gallons.

New-York Pattern.

	$							each.
No.	1	2	3	4	5	6	7	8	
	16	22	32	45	60	75	90	120	gallons.

SUGAR PANS OR BOILERS.

30 Gallons, 40 inches Diameter, 12 inches Deep..........each, $

40 Gallons, 44 inches Diameter, 14 inches Deep.......... "

60 Gallons, 51 inches Diameter, 16 inches Deep...... "

80 Gallons, 57 inches Diameter, 17 inches Deep.......... "

100 Gallons, 60 inches Diameter, 19 inches Deep.......... "

WASH KETTLES.

$						each.
No.	1	2	3	4	5	6
	8	10	15	20	25	30 gallons.

POT HOOKS.

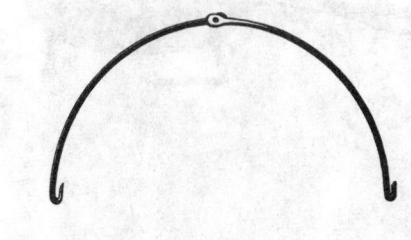

$					per dozen.
No.	1	2	3	4	5

BAKE SPIDERS,

With Lids.

	$						each.
Light— No.	0	1	2	3	4	5	
	13	12	11	10	9	8	inches.
	$						each.
Medium—No.	0	1	2	3	4	5	
	13	12	11	10	9	8	inches.

HOLLOW WARE.

(Continued.)

BISCUIT SPIDERS,

With Lids.

Light— No.	$ 1	2	3	each.
	13	12	11	inches.
Medium—No.	$ 1	2	3	each.
	13	12	11	inches.

LIPPED FRYING SPIDERS.

Light— No.	$ 1	2	3	4	each.
	12½	11	9½	8	inches.
Medium—No.	$ 1	2	3	4	each.
	12½	11	9½	8	inches.

PLAIN CAKE SPIDERS.

Light— No.	$ 1	2	3	4	each.
	12½	11	9½	8	inches.
Medium—No.	$ 1	2	3	4	each.
	12½	11	9½	8	inches.

REVOLVING GRIDIRONS.

No. 1, 12 inches . . . . per dozen, $

REVOLVING GRIDDLES.

No. 1, 12 inches . . . . per dozen, $
No. 2, 11 inches . . . . per dozen,

LONG-HANDLED GRIDDLES.

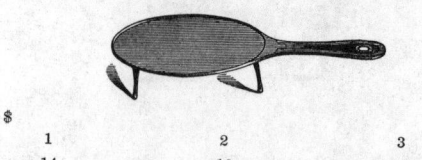

No.	$ 1	2	3	each.
	14	12	10	inches.

GRIDDLES, WITH BAILS.

No.	$ 1	2	3	4	each.
	18	16	14	12	inches.

ROUND GRIDDLES, WITH HANDLES.

No.	$ 1	2	3	each.
	16	14	12	inches.

GRIDIRONS.

No. 1 . . . . per dozen, $
No. 2 . . . . per dozen,

EGG FRYERS,

Or Fancy Cake Bakers.

$			per dozen.
4	6	8	hole.

WAFFLE IRONS, FURNACES, & SASH WEIGHTS.

WAFFLE AND WAFER IRONS.

Heavy English Pattern Waffle Irons, Long Handles.

No. 1, 3 Cake..................................per dozen, $

No. 3, 1 Cake.................................. "

No. 4, Large 1 Cake.............................. "

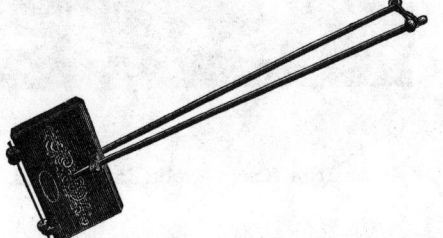

Heavy English Wafer Irons....................per dozen, $

Common Long Handle Waffle Irons.

No. 1, 4 Cake..................................per dozen, $

No. 2, 2 Cake.................................. "

No. 3, 1 Cake.................................. "

Patent Square Revolving Waffle Irons.

No. 1, $ per dozen.   No. 2, $ per dozen.

Patent Round Revolving Waffle Irons.

per dozen.

No.	1	2	3	4

WAFFLE IRONS.
(Continued.)

Stove Waffle Irons—New Pattern.

$ per dozen.

No.	1	2	3	4

PORTABLE SUMMER FURNACES.
For Chips or Charcoal, with Bails.

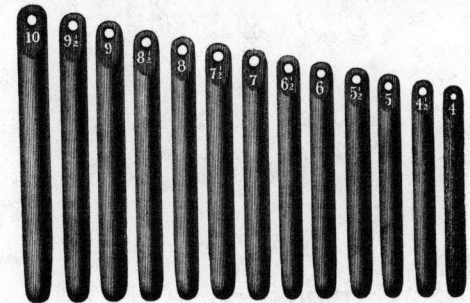

$ each.

No.	0	1	2	3	
	15	13	11½	10	inches.

IMPROVED SOLID EYE SASH WEIGHTS.

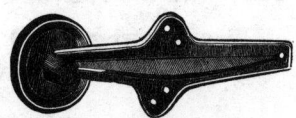

Sash Weights..............................per lb. $

These Weights are made of the following sizes :

3, 4, 4½, 5, 5½, 6, 6½, 7, 7½, 8, 8½, 9, 9½, 10, 10½, 11, 12, 13, 14, 15, 16, 17, 18 lbs.

☞ Larger sizes made to order.

BARN DOOR HANGERS.

Round Groove.

per pair.

$	2½	3	4	5	6	8	10	
								inches.

BARN-DOOR ROLLERS, HANGERS AND BOLTS.

BARN DOOR ROLLERS.

Round Groove.

$							per pair.
	4	6	8	10	12	16	inches.

BARN DOOR RAIL.

No.	$	0		1		2	per pair.
		½		⅝		¾	inches.

BARN DOOR HANGERS.

Square Groove.

No.	$	1	2	3	4	per pair.
Diameter,		3	4	5	6	inches.

BARN DOOR RAIL—TOP.

For No. 1 and 2 Square Groove Hangers.............per foot, $

For No. 3 and 4 Square Groove Hangers.............per foot,

BROWN'S PATENT BOLTS.

Iron.

$					per dozen.
	3	3½	4	4½	inches.

Brass.

$					per dozen.
	3	3½	4	4½	inches.

UNION CHAIN BOLTS.

No.	$	1	2	3	4	per dozen.
Length,		9	8	7	5½	inches.

UNION FOOT BOLTS.

No.	$	1	2	3	4	per dozen.
Length,		9	8	7	5½	inches.

UNION SIDE LOCK BOLTS.

No.	$	1	2	3	per dozen.
Length,		8	6	4	inches.

BUSH'S PATENT CHAIN BOLTS.

	$				per dozen.
No.		0	1	2	3	
Length,	12	10	8	6	inches.

BUSH'S PATENT LEVER BOLTS.

	$					per dozen.
No.		0	1	2	3	5
Length,	12	10	8	6	3	inches.

NEW FANCY CAST IRON SQUARE BOLTS,
With Steel Springs.

	$				per dozen.
Length,	4	6	8	10	inches.

NEW FANCY CAST IRON BARREL BOLTS,
With Brass Knobs—Solid End Staples.

	$			per dozen.
Length,	4	5	6	inches.

With Iron Knobs—Solid End Staples.

	$			per dozen.
Length,	4	5	6	inches.

NEW FANCY ROUND CHAMBER BOLTS,
With Wrought Bolt and Brass Knob.

4 inch Round Chamber Bolt...............per dozen, $

5 inch Round Chamber Bolt...............per dozen, $

NEW PATTERN CHAIN BOLTS.

	$				per dozen.
Length,	4	6	8	10	inches.

PADLOCKS, LATCHES, PULLEYS, ETC.

AMERICAN SMALL BRASS PADLOCKS,
English Pattern.

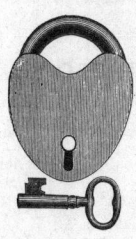

				per dozen.
$				
No.	1	2	3	
	⅝	1	1¼	inches.

YALE'S PATENT NIGHT LATCH.

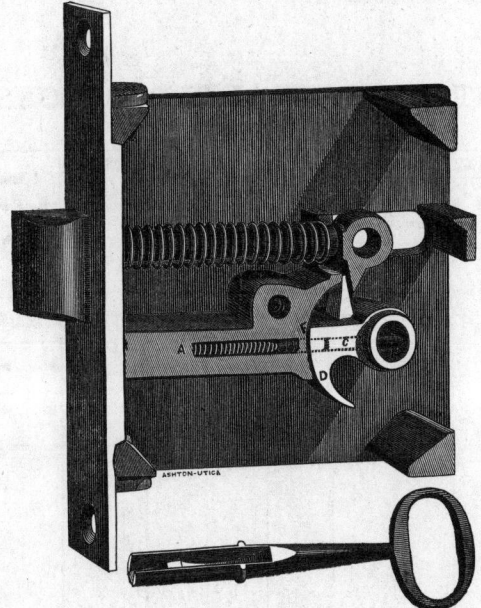

(No. 2.)

		$			per dozen.
Rim,	No.	1	2	3	
		$			per dozen.
Mortice, No.		1	2	3	

YALE'S PATENT DEAD LOCKS.

	$		per dozen.
No.	1	2	

Yale's Patent Drawer Locks.......................per dozen, $

JAPANNED CUPBOARD LATCH, BRASS KNOB.
Either Right or Left Hand.

☞ The Simplest and Cheapest Article in Use. $ per gross.

BRASS FACE AXLE PULLEYS.

	$				per doz.
Brass Face, Iron Wheels,	1¾	2	2¼	2½	inches.
	$				per doz.
Brass Face, Brass Wheels,	1¾	2	2¼	2½	inches.
All Brass,..............	1¾ inch		per dozen, $		

NOISELESS AXLE PULLEYS.

Diameter of Wheel, 2 inches, Brass Rivets, $\frac{5}{16}$ .per dozen, $
Diameter of Wheel, 2½ inches, Brass Rivets, $\frac{5}{16}$.   "
Diameter of Wheel, 3 inches, Brass Rivets, $\frac{3}{8}$.   "
For other Axle Pulleys, see page 63.

JAPANNED YARD OR CLOTHES LINE PULLEYS.

$		per dozen.
2½	3	inch wheel.

Clothes Line Reels, Japanned.....................each, $

HOT HOUSE PULLEYS.

$				per dozen.
1¾	2	2¼	2½	inch single.
$				per dozen.
1¾	2	2¼	2½	double.

2 inch treble..............................per dozen, $

TACKLE BLOCKS.

Brass, Fast Ring.

	$		per dozen.
Single......	1½	1¾	inches.
	$		per dozen.
Double.....	1½	1¾	inches.

Brass, Fast or Swivel Hook.

	$							per dozen.
Single,	2	2¼	2½	2¾	3	3¼	3½	inches.
	$							per dozen.
Double,	2	2¼	2½	2¾	3	3¼	3½	inches.

Iron, Fast Ring.

	$				per dozen.
Single,	1½	1¾	2¼	2¾	inches.
	$				per dozen.
Double,	1½	1¾	2¼	2¾	inches.

BLOCKS, ETC.

BEARDSLEY'S PATENT.

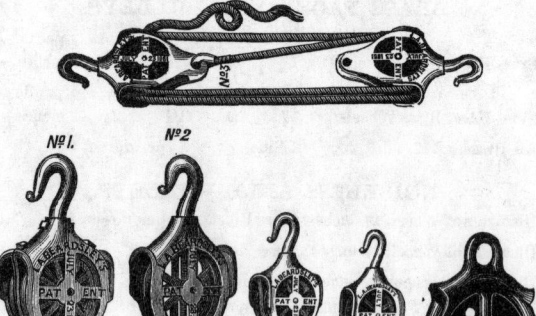

Nº1.   Nº2.   Nº3.   Nº4.

No. 1, Large, Single, Hook and Bale.........per dozen, $

No. 2, Large, Double, Hook and Bale........per dozen,

BEARDSLEY'S PATENT—*Continued*

No. 3, Small, Double Hook and Eye.........per dozen, $

No. 4, Large, Single, with Eye..............   "

No. 5, Large, Single, with Hook.............   "

ROPE STRAPPED BLOCKS.

2 to 3½ inches................................each, $

4   inches................................each,

4 to 4½ inches, Iron Bushed.................per foot, $

5 to 10 inches, Iron Bushed.................   "

11 to 12 inches, Iron Bushed.................   "

13 to 14 inches, Iron Bushed.................   "

4 to 12 inches, Roller Bushed..............per inch, $

13 to 14 inches, Roller Bushed..............per inch,

Strapping, Additional...................................$

Double Blocks, Double Price.

WATERMAN & RUSSELL'S PATENT IRON-STRAPPED BLOCKS.

Size	IRON BUSHED.			ROLLER BUSHED.			IRON BUSHED.			ROLLER BUSHED.			Heavy Tackles.			SNATCH BLOCKS		Lignumvitæ Dead Eyes, Hearts, &c. 7 inch and under, cents per inch.	
	Single.	Double.	Triple.	Single.	Double.	Triple.	Single Swivel.	Double Swivel.	Triple Swivel.	Single Swivel.	Double Swivel.	Triple Swivel.	Single.	Double.	Triple.	Size.	Price.	Size.	Price.
4																6			
5																7			
6																8		7½	
7																9		8	
8																10		8½	
9																12		9	
10																14		9½	
11																16		10	
12																18		10½	
13																20		11	
14																22		11½	
15																24		12	

BLOCKS.

	DOCK BLOCKS.	
	Size.	Price.

Composition Sheaves, Roller Bushed, 6 inches and under.............................   cents per inch.

Lignumvitæ Shells, Iron Bushed, 6 to 8 inches......................................   " | 20 |

Lignumvitæ Shells, Iron Bushed, 9 & 10 inches.....................................   " | 16 |

Lignumvitæ Shells, Roller Bushed, 6 to 8 inches....................................   " | 14 |

Lignumvitæ Shells, Roller Bushed, 9 & 10 inches....................................   " | 10 |

☞ Iron Blocks, Mast Hoops, Hanks, Belaying Pins, Hand Spikes, Hand Pumps, Galvanized Hanks, &c.

☞ Straps Galvanized when Required. ◂

CORDAGE, TWINE, THREAD, LINES, ETC.

OAKUM.

Navy...per lb. $
American Navy....................................   "
Best American Navy...............................   "

ROPE CORDAGE.

Manilla Rope, 6 and 9 Thread.................per lb. $
Manilla Rope, Larger Sizes.......................   "
Manilla Hay Rope ....   "
Manilla Bolt Rope................................   "
Manilla Tarred Rope.............................   "
Russia Tarred Rope...............................   "
American Tarred Rope (assorted sizes)............   "
Marline, Houseline, &c...........................   "
Spun Yarn..   "
Italian Packing..................................   "
Russia Packing ....   "
American Packing................................   "
Jute Packing.....................................   "
Jute Rope (assorted sizes).......................   "
Jute Wrapping Twine..............................   "
Jute Wool Twine..................................   "
Jute Bed Cords, 72 feet.....................per dozen, $
Sisal Bed Cords, 72 feet....................per dozen,
American Hemp Sash Cord......................per lb. $
Patent Sash Cord.............................per lb.

WOOL TWINE.

Jute, Balls or Skeins.........................per lb. $
Hemp, Balls or Skeins ....   "
Hemp, Superior, Balls or Skeins.................   "
Garden Twine.....................................   "
Seaming Cord, for Bag Strings....................   "

SHOE THREAD.

No. 3, H. B., in 3 lb. Packages.............per lb. $
No. 10, H. B., in 3 lb. Packages.................   "
No. 12, H. B., in 3 lb. Packages.... ....   "

BROOM TWINE, VARIOUS COLORS.

Sewing ....per lb. $
Winding......................................per lb.

LINES.
Fish Lines.

No. 1, 15 feet, Imitation Grass............per gross, $
No. 2, 15 feet, Imitation Grass............   "
No. 3,   7 feet, Light......................   "
No. 4, 12 feet, Light......................   "
No. 5, 20 feet, Light......................   "
No. 6, 20 feet, Medium.....................   "
No. 7, 30 feet, Medium.....................   "
No. 8, 30 feet, Heavy......................   "
No. 9, 40 feet, Medium.....................   "
No. 10, 20 feet, Heavy......................   "
No. 11, 20 feet, Extra Heavy ....   "

FISH LINES—*Continued*.

No. 12, 30 feet, Heavy.....................per gross, $
No. 13, 30 feet, Extra Heavy ....   "
No. 14, 40 feet, Heavy.....................   "
No. 15, 60 feet, Light ....   "
No. 16, 60 feet, Medium ....   "

Trot Lines.

No. 17, 52 feet.............................per dozen, $
No. 18, 78 feet............................   "
No. 19, 105 feet............................   "

Lay-Out Lines.

No.   210 feet............................per dozen, $
No. 20, 20 feet, Light ....per gross,

Chalk Lines.

No. 21, 20 feet, Medium....................per gross, $
No. 22, 20 feet, Heavy.....................   "
No. 23, 30 feet, Medium....................   "
No. 24, 30 feet, Heavy.....................   "

Masons' Lines.

No. 26, 22 feet ....per gross, $
No. 27, 100 feet ....   "
No. 28, 50 feet ....   "
Cork Floats ....   "

Packed in Paper Boxes, and of the Best Quality.

BREED'S COTTON AND LINEN LINES.
Cotton.

$	0000	000	00	0		per dozen.
No.	$15\frac{7}{8}$	$15\frac{7}{8}$	$15\frac{7}{8}$	$15\frac{7}{8}$	$15\frac{7}{8}$	
$						per dozen.
No.	$15\frac{3}{4}$	$15\frac{1}{2}$	$15\frac{1}{4}$	15		
$						per dozen.
No.	$14\frac{3}{4}$	$14\frac{1}{2}$	$14\frac{1}{4}$	14	$13\frac{3}{4}$	
$						per dozen.
No.	$13\frac{1}{2}$	$13\frac{1}{4}$	13	$12\frac{3}{4}$		
$						per dozen.
No.	$12\frac{1}{2}$	$12\frac{1}{4}$	12	$11\frac{7}{8}$	$11\frac{3}{4}$	
$						per dozen.
No.	$11\frac{5}{8}$	$11\frac{1}{2}$	$11\frac{3}{8}$	$11\frac{1}{4}$		
$						per dozen.
No.	$11\frac{1}{8}$	11	$10\frac{3}{4}$	$10\frac{1}{2}$	10	
$						per dozen.
No.	$9\frac{3}{4}$	$9\frac{1}{2}$	$9\frac{1}{4}$	9		

Linen.

$	000000	00000	0000	000	00	per dozen.
No.	20	20	20	20	20	
$	0					per dozen.
No.	20	20	$20\frac{1}{4}$	$20\frac{1}{2}$	$20\frac{3}{4}$	
$						per dozen.
No.	21	$21\frac{1}{4}$	$21\frac{1}{2}$	$21\frac{3}{4}$	22	
$						per dozen.
No.	$22\frac{1}{4}$	$22\frac{1}{2}$	$22\frac{3}{4}$	23		
$						per dozen.
No.	$23\frac{1}{4}$	$23\frac{1}{2}$	24	$24\frac{1}{2}$	25	
$						per dozen.
No.	$25\frac{1}{2}$	26	$26\frac{1}{2}$	27		

COPYING PRESSES, CASH BOXES, ETC.

COPYING PRESSES.

No. 3. Dolphin Arch.

No. 3, Dolphin Arch, weighs 56 lbs., Top Plates 9 ×12 in., each, $

No. 4, Dolphin Arch, weighs 64 lbs., Top Plates 9½×13 in., "

No. 5, Dolphin Arch, weighs 70 lbs., Top Plates 10 ×13 in., "

No. 7, Dolphin Arch, weighs 90 lbs., Top Plates 10½×16 in., "

No. 3, Plain Arch,   weighs 56 lbs., Top Plates 9 ×12 in., "

No. 4, Plain Arch,   weighs 64 lbs., Top Plates 9½×13 in., "

No. 5, Plain Arch,   weighs 70 lbs., Top Plates 10 ×13 in., "

No. 7, Plain Arch,   weighs 90 lbs., Top Plates 10½×16 in., "

No. 9, Plain Arch,   weighs 100 lbs., Top Plates 11 ×18 in., "

Railroad, Extra Heavy, weighs 225 lbs., Top Plates 16½×22½ in................................ "

No. 6, Short Arch, weighs 75 lbs., Top Plates 10½×16 in.. "

No. 10, Short Arch, weighs 115 lbs., Top Plates 14 ×18 in.. "

No. 5, Extra, Brass Finish, weighs 90 lbs., Top Plates 10×13 in.................................. "

No. 7, Extra, Brass Finish, weighs 115 lbs., Top Plates 10½×15 in.................................. "

No. 9, Extra, Brass Finish, weighs 125 lbs., Top Plates 11×18 in.................................. "

Embossing Presses.....................................each, $

Seal Presses .... "

CASH BOXES.

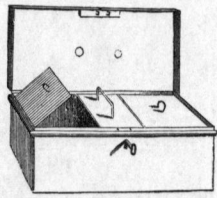

For the purpose of conveniently keeping money and papers of value. Money trays detached, with apartments and covers (to fit the first five sizes). They are made of best quality of Tin, Tumbler locks, and well japanned.

$						per dozen.
No.	1	2	3	4	5	
Length......	8½	9½	11	12½	13½	inches.
Width	6½	6½	7	9	9½	inches.
Heighth	4	4½	4½	6	6	inches.

With Inside.

$						per dozen.
No.	1	2	3	4	5	
Length, with Inside..	8½	9½	11	12½	13½	inches.
Width, with Inside..	6½	6½	7	9	9½	inches.
Heighth, with Inside.	4	4½	4½	6	6	inches.

HASP, OR DEED BOXES.

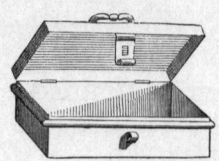

$						per dozen.
No.	1	2	3	4	5	
Length........	8	10	11½	13½	15	inches.
$						per dozen.
No.	1	2	3	4	5	
Width	5½	6½	8	9	10	inches.
$						per dozen.
No.	1	2	3	4	5	
Heighth.......	2¾	3½	4	5	6	

POST OFFICE BOXES.

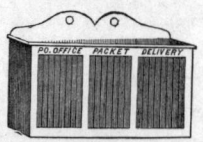

No. 3.

No. 1, One Apartment, for "Post Office"......per dozen, $

No. 2, Two Apartments, for "Post Office" and "Delivery,"........................... "

No. 3, Three Apartments, for "Post Office," "Packet" and "Delivery,"............. "

ENVELOPE CASES.

No. 3.

No. 1, 13½ in. high, by 9 in. wide ....per dozen, $

No. 2,   8 in. high, by 5½ in. wide .... "

No. 3,   6 in. high, by 4½ in. wide .... "

No. 5,   9½ in. high, by 4½ in. wide .... "

BANK NOTICE BOXES.

No. 1, 6½ in. long, by 3 in. wide, glass end ....per doz., $

No. 1, 6½ in. long, by 3 in. wide, without glass end   "

No. 2, 5 in. long, by 2½ in. wide, glass end...... "

No. 2, 5 in. long, by 2½ in. wide, without glass end   "

STATIONERS' HARDWARE.

CALENDARS.

Excelsior Pattern.

Excelsior, Printed in Colors, on Fine Paper ...per dozen, $

No. 1, Showing the Day of the Month only.... "

No. 2, Showing the Month and Day of the Mo. "

No. 2, Showing the Month, Day of the Week and Day of the Month................. "

No. 3, Showing the Month, Day of the Week and Day of the Month................. "

No. 4, Fancy, Showing the Month, Day of the Week and Day of the Month........... "

INK STANDISH.

Japanned, with Glass Inkstands and Conveniences for Holding Pens, Pencils, Wax, &c.

Ink Standish.............................per dozen, $

PEN RACKS.

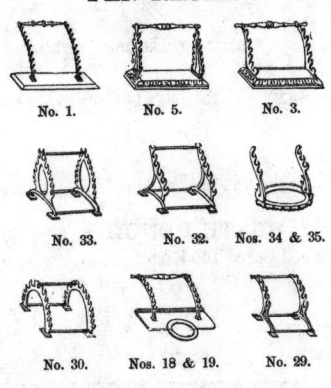

No. 1.   No. 5.   No. 3.

No. 33.   No. 32.   Nos. 34 & 35.

No. 30.   Nos. 18 & 19.   No. 29.

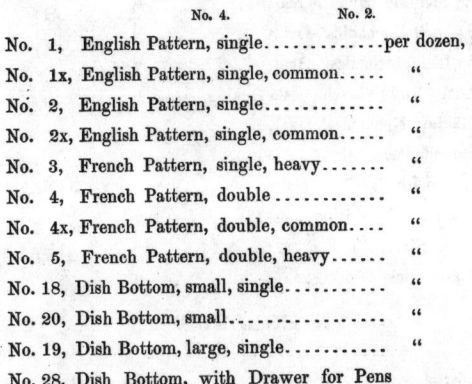

No. 4.   No. 2.

No. 1, English Pattern, single.............per dozen, $

No. 1x, English Pattern, single, common..... "

No. 2, English Pattern, single............. "

No. 2x, English Pattern, single, common..... "

No. 3, French Pattern, single, heavy....... "

No. 4, French Pattern, double............. "

No. 4x, French Pattern, double, common.... "

No. 5, French Pattern, double, heavy...... "

No. 18, Dish Bottom, small, single........... "

No. 20, Dish Bottom, small................. "

No. 19, Dish Bottom, large, single........... "

No. 28, Dish Bottom, with Drawer for Pens and Pins..................... "

PEN RACKS—*Continued.*

No. 29, Light French Pattern, for Pens.......per dozen, $

No. 30, Light French Pattern, double........ "

No. 31, Light French Ring Pattern, single.... "

No. 32, New French Pattern, single.......... "

No. 33, New French Pattern, double......... "

No. 34, New Fancy French Pattern, single.... "

No. 35, New Fancy French Pattern, single.... "

Nos. 18 and 19 adapted for ordinary Inkstands.

Nos. 31, 34 and 35 for Whitney's or Draper's large and small Inkstands.

DESK WEIGHTS.

No. 8.   No. 7.   No. 9.   No. 11.

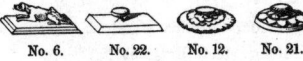

No. 6.   No. 22.   No. 12.   No. 21.

No. 14.   No. 15.   No. 23.   No. 24

No. 6, Dog, oblong, 5 ×2½ in..............per dozen, $

No. 7, Dog, oblong, 4 ×2¼ in.............. "

No. 8, Stag, oblong, 5¼×2¾ in.............. "

No. 9, Joan of Arc, oblong, 4×2¼ in........ "

No. 11, Oblong, light, 4½×2¼ in., plain....... "

No. 12, Round, light, 4 inches in diameter, ornamented.................... "

No. 14, Round, light, 2½ inches in diam., plain. "

No. 15, Round, light, 2¼ inches in diam., ornamented.................... "

No. 21, Round, heavy, 4 inches in diam., ornamented.................... "

No. 22, Oblong, heavy, 4¾×3 inches, plain English Pattern.................... "

No. 23, Round, heavy, 3½ inches in diameter, plain English Pattern............. "

No. 24, Oblong, heavy, 7¾×3 inches, plain English Pattern.................... "

BILL HEAD CASES.

No. 1, With 3 Apartments, one each for whole and half-sheet, quarter-sheet, and sixth-sheet Cap Bill Heads.................per dozen, $

No. 2, With 3 Apartments, two inches shorter than No. 1..................... "

No. 3, Two Apartments, for quarter and sixth-sheet Bill Heads.................. "

No. 4, One Apartment..................... "

No. 5, Three Apartments, with Envelopes.... "

STATIONERS' HARDWARE.

(Continued.)

PAPER FOLDERS AND CHECK CUTTERS.

Japanned Tin, 2, 2¼, 2½, 2¾, 3, 3¼, 3½, 3¾, and 4 inches wide....................per dozen, $

Japanned Iron, 2, 2¼, 2½, 2¾, 3, 3¼, 3½, 3¾, and 4 inches wide.................... "

CARD CASES.

	$					per dozen.
No.	1	2	3	4	5	
	4½	4	3¾	3½	3¼	inches.

BILL FILES.

Spear File.

Slide File.

Harp File.

Spear Files, Octagon, Bottoms Metal........per dozen, $

Spear Files, Oblong, Metal Bottoms.................. "

Spear Files, Oblong, Metal Bottoms, 2 wires. "

Spear Files, Octagon, Metal Bottoms, heavy brass wires........................ "

Hook Slide Files, with sheathed wires for removing papers without displacing others on the File.......................... "

Straight Slide Files, with sheathed wires for removing papers without displacing others on the File.......................... "

Hanging Files, Harp Pattern, large.........per gross, $

Hanging Files, Harp Pattern, small......... "

SAND BOXES.

Round....................................per gross, $

Octagon .... "

Fluted..................................... "

LETTER CLIPS.

No. 60, Brass...............................per gross, $

No. 60, Plated.............................. "

No. 60, Bronzed .... "

No. 65, Brass............................... "

No. 66, Plated.............................. "

No. 67, Bronzed .... "

No. 70, Plain Bronzed .... "

No. 71, Plain Bronzed .... "

LETTER CLIPS—*Continued.*

No. 72, Plain Bronzed ....per gross, $

No. 80, Sheaf Pattern .... "

No. 81, Sheaf Pattern .... "

No. 82, Sheaf Pattern .... "

SLATES.

School Slates, Square Frame.

$							per dozen.
4×6	5×7	6×9	6½×10	7×11	8×12	9×13	inches.
$							per case.
24	18	12	12	10	8	6	dozen in case.

Contents of Assorted Cases.

	5×7	6×9	6½×10	7×11	8×12	9×13	inches.
No. 1,	1½	2	2	2	3	0	doz., per case, $
No. 2,	3	2	2	2	½	½	doz., "

School Slates, Oval Frame.

$						per dozen.
5×7	6×9	6½×10	7×11	8×12	9×13	inches.
$						per case.
18	12	12	10	8	6	dozen in case.

Contents of Assorted Cases.

	5×7	6×9	6½×10	7×11	8×12	9×13	inches.
No. 1,	0	0	4¼	3	2	1	doz., per case, $
No. 2,	2	2	2	3	1	1	doz., "

Counting House Slates.

$						per dozen.
7×11	8×12	9×13	6½×14	7×15	8×16	inches.

Log Slates.

$						per dozen.
7×11	8×12	9×13	6½×14	7×15	8×16	inches.

SLATE PENCILS.

Common, in Wood Boxes, 100 Each.............per M, $

	$			per M.
Soap Stone,	4	5	6	inches.

ROPES'

ARTISTS' AND MECHANICS' LEAD PENCILS.

No. 10, 13 Inch Mechanics', Oval............per gross, $

No. 11, 13 Inch Mechanics', Oval............ "

No. 12, 8½ Inch Mechanics', Oval............ "

No. 13, 8½ Inch Mechanics', Oval............ "

No. 15, 6½ Inch Mechanics,' Oval............ "

No. 16, Large Ruling Mechanics', Oval....... "

No. 17, Medium Mechanics', Oval............. "

No. 51, Round Black Gilt .... "

No. 52, Round Black Gilt Drawing .... "

No. 53, Plain Black Writing................. "

No. 54, Plain Black Writing................. "

No. 55, Plain Black Writing................. "

PEN HOLDERS.

Fluted......................................per gross, $

Accommodation...............................per gross, $

CRAYONS, CARPENTERS' CHALK AND OIL CANS.

BLACKBOARD CRAYONS.

White, in one gross Boxes . . . . .per gross, $

Red, in one gross Boxes . . . .   "

Assorted Colors, in one gross Boxes . . . .   "

PREPARED CHALK FOR CARPENTERS.

White, in half gross Boxes . . . . .per gross, $

Red, in half gross Boxes . . . .   "

Blue, in half gross Boxes . . . .   "

SPRING BOTTOM OIL CANS.

Tin.

| | $ | | | | per dozen. |
| No. | 0 | 1 | 2 | 3 | |

Tin, with Brass Bottom.

| | $ | | | per dozen. |
| No. | 1 | 2 | 3 | |

Zinc.

| | $ | | | | | | per dozen. |
| No. | 00 | 0 | 1 | 2 | 3 | 4 | 5 |

New Pattern Zinc.

| | $ | | | | per dozen. |
| No. | 1 | 2 | 3 | 4 | |

Brass and Copper.

| | $ | | | | | | per dozen. |
| No. | 00 | 0 | 1 | 2 | 3 | 4 | 5 |

New Pattern Brass and Copper.

| | $ | | | | per dozen. |
| No. | 1 | 2 | 3 | 4 | |

FANCY COPPER OIL CANS, FOR ENGINEERS.

No. 1, One Pint, Short Tube . . . . .per dozen, $

No. 2, One Pint, Long Tube . . . .   "

No. 3, One Quart, Short Tube . . . .   "

No. 4, One Quart, Long Tube . . . .   "

PATENT VALVE OIL CANS, FOR LOCOMOTIVES.

Patent with Valves.

Brass, No. 1, One Pint . . . . .per dozen, $

Brass, No. 2, One Quart . . . .   "

Brass, No. 3, Three Pints . . . .   "

Tin, No. 1, One Pint . . . .   "

Tin, No. 2, One quart . . . .   "

Tin, No. 3, Three Pints . . . .   "

Without Valves.

Brass, No. 1, One Pint . . . . .per dozen, $

Brass, No. 2, One Quart . . . .   "

Brass, No. 3, Three Pints . . . .   "

Tin, No. 1, One Pint . . . .   "

Tin, No. 2, One Quart . . . .   "

Tin, No. 3, Three Pints . . . .   "

OIL STONES, SAND PAPER, SOFA SPRINGS, ETC.

OIL STONE.

	$		per lb.
Hindoostan Stone, No.	1	2	

Hindoostan Slips................................per lb. $

Hindoostan Axe Stone..........................per lb. $

	$			per lb.
Washita Stone, No.	1	2	3	

	$			per lb.
Washita Slips, No.	1	2		

Washita Axe Stone.............................per lb. $

SAND STONE.

Sand Stone.....................................per lb. $

BORAX.

Best Refined...................................per lb. $

STOVE POLISH.

Dixon's Carburet of Iron.....................per gross, $

Gautier's Carburet of Iron...................per gross, $

British Lustre...............................per gross, $

BLACK LEAD CRUCIBLES.

	$						each.
No.	1	2	3	4	5	6	

No. 8 and upward to No. 100.................per No. $

    All above No. 100, made to order only.

SHOE BLACKING.
Mason's.

$				per gross.
Small,	Medium,	New Medium,	Large.	

R. & E. Manufacturing Co's.

	$			per gross.
No.	1	2	3	

SAND PAPER.

R. & E. Manufacturing Co's, all Numbers......per ream, $

Excelsior, all numbers .... "

Star, all numbers............................. "

	$							per ream.
Baeder's Flint, No. 0	0½	1	1½	2	2½	3		

	$							per ream.
Emery Paper, No. 0	0½	1	1½	2	2½	3		

SUPERIOR EMERY CLOTH.

    Nos. 60, 70, 80, 90, 100, 120, F, FF, and Crocus.

Size, 7× 9 inches ....per ream, $

Size, 9×12 inches ....per ream, $

EMERY.

R. & E. M'f'g Co's...........................per lb. $

Diamond......................................per lb. $

GLUE.

Common.......................................per lb. $

Medium.......................................per lb. $

Best...per lb. $

HIDE WHIPS.

	$			per gross.
Painted, No.	1	1½	2	

	$			per gross.
Varnished, No.	1	1½	2	

SOFA SPRINGS.
Galvanized Wire.

	$						per lb.
No.	1	2	3	4	5	6	
Weight,	20	26	42	50	65	75 lbs.	per gross.
Height,	5	6	7	8	9	10 inches.	

Galvanized Wire, Knotted.

	$						per lb.
No.	1	2	3	4	5	6	
Weight,	20	26	42	50	65	75 lbs.	per gross.
Height,	5	6	7	8	9	10 inches.	

SAFETY FUSE.

Common Tape.........................per M. feet, $

Single Waterproof........................... "

Double Waterproof........................... "

Treble Waterproof........................... "

TOY, BICKFORD & CO'S PATENT SAFETY FUSE.

Common Hemp.........................per M. feet, $

Common Cotton .... "

Imperial Mining .... "

Single Tape, Water......................... "

Double Tape, Water......................... "

Triple Tape, Water......................... "

RAZOR STROPS.
Emerson's Genuine, Oval.

Medium Size.................................per dozen, $

Large Size................................... "

Barbers' Size................................ "

Emerson's Imitation .... "

Atwell's Draw Strop......................... "

Torrey's Square Strop .... "

Torrey's Flat Strop......................... "

Torrey's Small Flat Strop................... "

Torrey's Draw Strop......................... "

Chapman's Magic Strop.

No. 81, Small Size, Leather Case, with Hone, Pockets
    on Side for Pair of Razors...................per dozen, $

No. 82, Small Size, Morocco Paper Case, with Hone... "

No. 84, Large Size, Morocco Paper Case, with Hone... "

No. 85, Small Size, Leather Case, with Hone......... "

No. 86, Small Size, Leather Case, with Hone......... "

No. 90, Small Size, Morocco Paper Case, without Hone, "

Rough and Ready, Smallest Size, Paper Case, Common,
    with Hone................................. "

Mead's, Smallest Size, Black Paper Case, better quality,
    with Hone................................. "

RAZOR STROPS, WHIFFLETREE HOOKS, ETC.

RAZOR STROPS—*Continued.*

Conger's, Small Size, Fancy Paper Case, still better, with Hone..............................per dozen, $

Alford's, Small Size, Morocco Paper Case, good quality, with Hone.................................... "

Raper's, Small Size, Morocco Paper Case, good quality, with Hone.................................... "

Walter's, Small Size, Morocco Paper Case, good quality, with Hone, gilt label..................... "

Ryer's, Small Size, Morocco Paper Case, good quality, with Hone .... "

Union, Small Size, Morocco Paper Case, good quality, Round Handle, with Hone..................... "

Finger's, Large Size, Morocco Paper Case, good quality, with Hone.................................... "

Roger's, Small Size, Leather Case, good quality, with Hone, gilt label.................................... "

Franconi's, Large Size, Morocco Paper Case, good quality, with Hone, gilt label................. "

Old English, Small Size, Leather Case, good quality, Round Handle, with Hone..................... "

Sheffield, Small Size, Leather Case, good quality, Rosewood Handle, with Hone..................... "

Barnum's, Large Size, Leather Case, good quality, with Hone, gilt label............................. "

Rowland's, Large Size, Leather Case, good quality, with Hone, gilt label............................. "

PATENT BOOT JACKS.

Japanned ....per dozen, $

Bronzed .... "

Plated... "

For other Boot Jacks, see page 105.

HOG SCRAPERS.

Hog Scrapers.....................................per gross, $

WHIFFLETREE HOOKS.

Fig 1

No. 1, Newman, Whitcomb & Co's Patent ....per dozen, $

No. 2, Newman, Whitcomb & Co's Patent .... "

No. 3, Newman, Whitcomb & Co's Patent .... "

SCREW COCKEYES.

$ per dozen.

$1\frac{1}{4}$ $1\frac{1}{2}$ $1\frac{3}{4}$

MULE AND HORSE HAMES.

Common Red, 1 Ring, Mule or Horse...........per dozen pairs, $

Common Red, 2 Rings, Mule or Horse.......... "   "

Root, Varnished, 1 Ring, Mule or Horse... ...... "   "

Root, Varnished, 2 Rings, Mule or Horse.......... "   "

Root, Blue, Round Top, Black Tipped, Mule or Horse .... "   "

COMMON POWDER FLASKS.

No.	Oz.	Pattern.	Top.	Per Dozen.
101	2	Bush	Common Spring	$
110	2	Oak Leaf	Common Spring	
114	4	Dog	Common Spring	
115	4	Dog	Common Spring (Navy)	
125	6	Fighting Cock	Common Spring	
126	6	Fighting Cock	Common Spring (Navy)	
130	8	Elk	Common Spring	
132	8	Elk	Patent Inside Spring	
140	8	Ass'd Shell and Rabbit	Common Spring	
168	8	Ass'd Shell and Rabbit	Patent Inside Spring	
200	2	Eagle	Common Spring	
210	4	Eagle	Common Spring	
220	6	Fighting Cock	Common Spring	
230	8	Wreath and Deer	Common Spring	
231	8	Shell	Common Spring	
235	8	Ass'd Shell and Rabbit	Common Spring	
250	8	Wreath and Deer	Patent Inside Spring	
251	8	Rabbit	Patent Inside Spring	
260	8	Ass'd Shell and Rabbit	Patent Inside Spring	
265	10	Shell	Common Spring	
266	10	Shell	Patent Inside Spring	
270	12	Shell	Common Spring	
275	12	Shell	Patent Inside Spring	
280	16	Man and Dog	Common Spring	
285	16	Man and Dog	Patent Inside Spring	

MEDIUM QUALITY COPPER POWDER FLASKS.

No.	Oz.	Pattern.	Top.	Per Dozen.
299	1	Colt's	Common Spring	$
300	2	Eagle	Common Spring	
303	2	Colt's	Common Spring	
310	4	Wreath, Dog and Birds	Common Spring	
311	4	Wreath, Dog and Birds	Common Spring (Navy Charger)	
315	4	Rifle, Man, Dog and Gun	Common Spring	
317	4	Rifle	Patent Inside Spring	
320	6	Rifle, Partridges	Common Spring	
322	6	Rifle, Partridges	Patent Inside Spring	
325	6	Coat of Arms	Common Spring (Navy Charger)	
330	8	Fluted	Common Spring	
332	8	Fluted	Patent Inside Spring	
333	8	Shell	Common Spring	
335	8	Shell	Patent Inside Spring	
340	8	Dead Game	Common Spring	
342	8	Dead Game	Patent Inside Spring	
350	10	Dog and Birds	Common Spring	
352	10	Dog and Birds	Patent Inside Spring	
360	12	Dead Game	Common Spring	
362	12	Dead Game	Patent Inside Spring	
370	16	Man and Deer	Common Spring	
372	16	Man and Deer	Patent Inside Spring	

POWDER FLASKS.

FINE BRONZED COPPER POWDER FLASKS.

No.	Oz.	Pattern.	Top.	Per Dozen.
410	1	Shell	Common Spring	$
420	1	Fluted	Common Spring	
400	1	Colt's	Common Spring	
430	1	Pl'n Ball & Cap Charger.	Common Spring	
431	1	Pl'n Ball & Cap "	Common Spring, unscrew	
432	1	Pl'n Ball & Cap "	Patent Inside Spring	
440	1	Fluted Ball & Cap "	Common Spring	
441	1	Fluted Ball & Cap "	Common Spring, unscrew	
442	1	Fluted Ball & Cap "	Patent Inside Spring	
450	1	Oak L'f Ball & Cap "	Common Spring	
451	1	Oak L'f Ball & Cap "	Common Spring, unscrew	
452	1	Oak L'f Ball & Cap "	Patent Inside Spring	
460	2	Pl'n Ball & Cap "	Common Spring	
461	2	Pl'n Ball & Cap "	Common Spring, unscrew	
462	2	Pl'n Ball & Cap "	Patent Inside Spring	
470	2	Fluted Ball & Cap "	Common Spring	
471	2	Fluted Ball & Cap "	Common Spring, unscrew	
472	2	Fluted Ball & Cap "	Patent Inside Spring	
480	2	Oak L'f Ball & Cap "	Common Spring	
481	2	Oak L'f Ball & Cap "	Common Spring, unscrew	
482	2	Oak L'f Ball & Cap "	Patent Inside Spring	
490	2	Shell	Common Spring	
491	2	Shell	Common Spring, unscrew	
492	2	Shell	Patent Inside Spring	
500	2	Colt's	Common Spring	
501	2	Colt's	Common Spring, unscrew	
502	2	Colt's	Patent Inside Spring	
510	2	Fluted	Common Spring	
511	2	Fluted	Common Spring, unscrew	
512	2	Fluted	Patent Inside Spring	
530	3	Shell	Common Spring	
531	3	Shell	Common Spring, unscrew	
532	3	Shell	Patent Inside Spring	
540	3	Fluted	Common Spring	
541	3	Fluted	Common Spring, unscrew	
542	3	Fluted	Patent Inside Spring	
550	4	Shell	Common Spring	
560	4	Fluted	Common Spring	
570	6	Shell	Common Spring	
580	6	Fluted	Common Spring	
590	6	Coat of Arms, N'vy Cha'gr.	Com. Spring	$

Rifle Flasks.

No.	Oz.	Pattern.	Top.	Per Dozen.
600	4	Plain	Common Spring	$
601	4	Plain	Common Spring, unscrew	
602	4	Plain	Patent Inside Spring	
603	4	Plain	Patent Outside Spring	
610	4	Fluted	Common Spring	
611	4	Fluted	Common Spring, unscrew	
612	4	Fluted	Patent Inside Spring	
613	4	Fluted	Patent Outside Spring	
620	6	Plain	Common Spring	
621	6	Plain	Common Spring, unscrew	
622	6	Plain	Patent Inside Spring	

Rifle Flasks—*Continued.*

No.	Oz.	Pattern.	Top.	Per Dozen.
623	6	Plain	Patent Outside Spring	
630	6	Fluted	Common Spring	
631	6	Fluted	Common Spring, unscrew	
632	6	Fluted	Patent Inside Spring	
633	6	Fluted	Patent Outside Spring	

Powder Flasks.

No.	Oz.	Pattern.	Top.	Per Dozen.
640	8	Plain	Common Spring	$
641	8	Plain	Common Spring, unscrew	
642	8	Plain	Patent Inside Spring	
643	8	Plain	Patent Outside Spring	
650	8	Shell	Common Spring	
651	8	Shell	Common Spring, unscrew	
652	8	Shell	Patent Inside Spring	
653	8	Shell	Patent Outside Spring	
660	8	Wreath and Shield	Common Spring	
661	8	Wreath and Shield	Common Spring, unscrew	
662	8	Wreath and Shield	Patent Inside Spring	
663	8	Wreath and Shield	Patent Outside Spring	
670	8	Shell and Wreath	Common Spring	
671	8	Shell and Wreath	Common Spring, unscrew	
672	8	Shell and Wreath	Patent Inside Spring	
673	8	Shell and Wreath	Patent Outside Spring	
680	8	Fluted	Common Spring	
681	8	Fluted	Common Spring, unscrew	
682	8	Fluted	Patent Inside Spring	
683	8	Fluted	Patent Outside Spring	
730	8	Dead Game	Common Spring	
731	8	Dead Game	Common Spring, unscrew	
732	8	Dead Game	Patent Inside Spring	
733	8	Dead Game	Patent Outside Spring	
740	8	Dead Game both sides	Common Spring	
741	8	Dead Game both sides	Common Spring, unscrew	
742	8	Dead Game both sides	Patent Inside Spring	
743	8	Dead Game both sides	Patent Outside Spring	
760	8	Gun Stock	Common Spring	
761	8	Gun Stock	Common Spring, unscrew	
762	8	Gun Stock	Patent Inside Spring	
763	8	Gun Stock	Patent Outside Spring	
780	10	Shell	Common Spring	
781	10	Shell	Common Spring, unscrew	
782	10	Shell	Patent Inside Spring	
783	10	Shell	Patent Outside Spring	
790	10	Fluted	Common Spring	
791	10	Fluted	Common Spring, unscrew	
792	10	Fluted	Patent Inside Spring	
793	10	Fluted	Patent Outside Spring	
830	12	Plain	Common Spring	
831	12	Plain	Common Spring, unscrew	
832	12	Plain	Patent Inside Spring	
833	12	Plain	Patent Outside Spring	
840	12	Shell	Common Spring	
841	12	Shell	Common Spring, unscrew	
842	12	Shell	Patent Inside Spring	
843	12	Shell	Patent Outside Spring	

POWDER FLASKS AND SHOT POUCHES.

Powder Flasks— *Continued.*

No.	Oz.	Pattern.	Top.	Per Dozen.
850	12	Fluted	Common Spring	$
851	12	Fluted	Common Spring, unscrew	
852	12	Fluted	Patent Inside Spring	
853	12	Fluted	Patent Outside Spring	
880	16	Plain	Common Spring	
881	16	Plain	Common Spring, unscrew	
882	16	Plain	Patent Inside Spring	
883	16	Plain	Patent Outside Spring	
890	16	Shell	Common Spring	
891	16	Shell	Common Spring, unscrew	
892	16	Shell	Patent Inside Spring	
893	16	Shell	Patent Outside Spring	
900	16	Fluted	Common Spring	
901	16	Fluted	Common Spring, unscrew	
902	16	Fluted	Patent Inside Spring	
903	16	Fluted	Patent Outside Spring	

☞ Powder Flasks of size from 8 ozs. to 16 ozs. have charges graduated from 2 to 2⅔ drams, except those with 16 oz. Fine Patent Tops, which have charges graduated from 3 to 4 drams. When Flasks are ordered with charges of unusual sizes, per dozen extra will be charged for size of 3 to 4 drams, and per dozen extra for size of 4 to 6 drams.

MOROCCO COVERED FLASKS,
With Brass Tops.

No.	Oz.	Top.	Per Dozen.
1203	8	Common Spring	$
1204	8	Common Spring, unscrew	
1205	8	Patent Inside Spring	
1206	8	Patent Outside Spring	
1207	10	Common Spring	
1208	10	Common Spring, unscrew	
1209	10	Patent Inside Spring	
1210	10	Patent Outside Spring	
1211	12	Common Spring	
1212	12	Common Spring, unscrew	
1213	12	Patent Inside Spring	
1214	12	Patent Outside Spring	
1215	16	Common Spring	
1216	16	Common Spring, unscrew	
1217	16	Patent Inside Spring	
1218	16	Patent Outside Spring	

HOG SKIN COVERED FLASKS,
With Brass Tops.

No.	Oz.	Top.	Per Dozen.
1350	8	Common Spring	$
1351	8	Common Spring, unscrew	
1352	8	Patent Inside Spring	
1353	8	Patent Outside Spring	
1354	10	Common Spring	
1355	10	Common Spring, unscrew	
1356	10	Patent Inside Spring	
1357	10	Patent Outside Spring	
1358	12	Common Spring	
1359	12	Common Spring, unscrew	
1360	12	Patent Inside Spring	
1361	12	Patent Outside Spring	
1362	16	Common Spring	

Hog Skin Covered Flasks with Brass Tops— *Continued.*

No.	Oz.	Top.	Per Dozen.
1363	16	Common Spring, unscrew	$
1364	16	Patent Inside Spring	
1365	16	Patent Outside Spring	
1400	8	Common Spring	
1401	8	Common Spring, unscrew	
1402	8	Patent Inside Spring	
1403	8	Patent Outside Spring	
1404	10	Common Spring	
1405	10	Common Spring, unscrew	
1406	10	Patent Inside Spring	
1407	10	Patent Outside Spring	
1408	12	Common Spring	
1409	12	Common Spring, unscrew	
1410	12	Patent Inside Spring	
1411	12	Patent Outside Spring	
1412	16	Common Spring	
1413	16	Common Spring, unscrew	
1414	16	Patent Inside Spring	
1415	16	Patent Outside Spring	

With German Silver Tops.

No.	Oz.	Top.	Per Dozen.
1502	8	Patent Inside Spring	$
1503	8	Patent Outside Spring	
1506	10	Patent Inside Spring	
1507	10	Patent Outside Spring	
1510	12	Patent Inside Spring	
1511	12	Patent Outside Spring	
1514	16	Patent Inside Spring	
1515	16	Patent Outside Spring	

☞ Any of the foregoing Flasks, with extra large Hole for quick Loading, $ per dozen extra.

MEDIUM QUALITY RUSSET LEATHER SHOT POUCHES.

The regular graduate size of Lever Chargers is from 1¼ to 1½ oz.; but by special order, Pouches and Belts can be supplied with Chargers of a capacity of 1 to 1¼ oz., and also 1¾ to 2 oz. For the latter size, $ extra per dozen will be charged.

No.	Size.	Pattern.	Charger.	Per Dozen.
420	2½ lbs.	Plain	Irish	$
421	2½ lbs.	Dead Game	Irish	
422	2½ lbs.	Plain	Irish	
423	2½ lbs.	Dead Game	Irish	
424	2½ lbs.	Dead Game	Patent	
425	2½ lbs.	Dead Game	Lever	
430	2½ lbs.	Wreath and Stag	Lever	
431	2½ lbs.	Fluted	Lever	
432	2½ lbs.	Wreath and Stag	Lever, Outside Cone	
436	3 lbs.	Dead Game	Irish	
437	3 lbs.	Dead Game	Patent	
438	3 lbs.	Dead Game	Lever	
439	3 lbs.	Plain, Pistol	Lever	
440	3 lbs.	Dead Game	Lever	
441	3 lbs.	Boar and Stag	Lever	
442	3 lbs.	Fluted	Lever	
443	3 lbs.	Plain, Pistol	Lever, (Steel)	
444	3 lbs.	Dead Game	Lever, (Steel)	

SHOT BELTS AND DRAM FLASKS.

MEDIUM QUALITY RUSSET LEATHER SHOT POUCHES—*Continued.*

No.	Size.	Pattern.	Charger.	Per Dozen.
445	3 lbs.	Wreath and Deer	Lever, (Steel)	
446	3 lbs.	Fluted	Lever, (Steel)	
450	3 lbs.	Dead Game	Lever	
452	4 lbs.	Fluted	Lever	
453	4 lbs.	Fluted, Pistol	Lever, Outside Cone	
454	4 lbs.	Dead Game	Lever, Outside Cone	
455	4 lbs.	Fluted	Lever, Outside Cone	
458	4 lbs.	Dead Game	Lever, (Steel)	
460	5 lbs.	Wreath and Deer	Lever	
462	5 lbs.	Fluted	Lever	

FINE RUSSET LEATHER SHOT POUCHES,
With Fine Brass Lever Chargers.

No.	Size.	Pattern.	Per Dozen.
2000	2½ lbs.	Wreath and Stag	$
2010	3 lbs.	Stags	
2012	3 lbs.	Stork	
2013	3 lbs.	Pistol, Dead Game	
2021	4 lbs.	Man and Gun	
2022	4 lbs.	Stork	
2023	4 lbs.	Pistol	
2030	5 lbs.	Indian and Buffalo	
2031	5 lbs.	Birds	
2040	6 lbs.	Dog and Birds	
2100	2½ lbs.	Wreath and Stag	
2110	3 lbs.	Stags	
2112	3 lbs.	Stork	
2113	3 lbs.	Pistol, Dead Game	
2121	4 lbs.	Man and Gun	
2122	4 lbs.	Stork	
2123	4 lbs.	Pistol	
2130	5 lbs.	Indian and Buffalo	
2131	5 lbs.	Birds	
2140	6 lbs.	Dog and Birds	

COMMON RUSSET SHEEP SKIN SHOT BELTS.

No.	Description.	Charger.	Per Dozen.
590	Single	Irish	$
600	Single	Irish	
601	Single	Fast Patent	
602	Single	Fast Patent	
603	Single	Screw-off	
604	Single	Lever	
606	Single	Lever	
595	Double	Irish	
610	Double	Irish	
596	Double	Fast Patent	
597	Double	Screw-off	
598	Double	Lever	
612	Double	Fast Patent	
613	Double	Screw-off	
614	Double	Lever	
615	Double	Lever	
619	Double	1 Lever, 1 Patent	
620	Double	2 Levers	

RUSSET LEATHER SHOT BELTS.

No.	Description.	Charger.	Per Dozen.
650	Single	Patent Screw-off	$
651	Single	Lever	
660	Double	Patent Screw-off	
661	Double	Lever	
662	Double	Lever	
663	Double	Patent Screw-off	
664	Double	Lever	
670	Double Oregon	1 Lever, 1 Patent	
671	Double Oregon	2 Levers	
674	Double Oregon	1 Lever, 1 Patent	
675	Double Oregon	2 Levers	
676	Double Oregon	2 Levers	
700	Single	Patent Screw-off	
709	Single	Screw-off, Double Spring	
701	Single	Lever	
702	Single Oregon	Lever	
720	Double	Patent Screw-off	
721	Double	Lever	
722	Double	Lever (German Silver)	
723	Double	Lever (Steel)	
740	Double Oregon	1 Lever, 1 Patent	
741	Double Oregon	2 Levers	
743	Double Oregon	1 Lever, 1 Patent	
762	Double Oregon	1 Lever, 1 Double Spring Patent.	
744	Double Oregon	2 Levers	
747	Double Oregon	1 Lever, 1 Patent	
753	Double Oregon	2 Levers (German Silver)	
754	Double Oregon	2 Levers (Steel)	
756	Double Oregon	2 Levers	

HOG SKIN SHOT BELTS,

No.	Description.	Charger. (Fine.)	Per Dozen.
850	Double	1 Lever, 1 Patent	$
851	Double	2 Levers	
852	Double	2 Levers (German Silver)	
853	Double	2 Levers (Steel)	

COMMON CHEAP DRAM FLASKS.

No.	Size.	Description.		Per Dozen.
1000	½ Pint	Covered with Sheep Skin	No Cup	$
1001	¾ Pint	Covered with Sheep Skin	No Cup	
1002	1 Pint	Covered with Sheep Skin	No Cup	
1013	½ Pint	Half Covered with Sheep Skin	With Cup	
1014	¾ Pint	Half Covered with Sheep Skin	With Cup	
1015	1 Pint	Half Covered with Sheep Skin	With Cup	

DRAM FLASKS.
Strong Glass, Half Covered, with Britannia Tops, Caps, and Drinking Cups.

No.	Size.	Description.	Per Dozen.
920	¼ Pint	Covered with Brown Leather	$
921	½ Pint	Covered with Brown Leather	
922	¾ Pint	Covered with Brown Leather	
923	1 Pint	Covered with Brown Leather	
924	1¼ Pint	Covered with Brown Leather	
930	¼ Pint	Covered with Morocco	
931	½ Pint	Covered with Morocco	
932	¾ Pint	Covered with Morocco	
933	1 Pint	Covered with Morocco	
934	1¼ Pint	Covered with Morocco	
935	¼ Pint	Covered with Hog Skin	
936	½ Pint	Covered with Hog Skin	
937	¾ Pint	Covered with Hog Skin	
938	1 Pint	Covered with Hog Skin	
939	1¼ Pint	Covered with Hog Skin	

DRAM FLASKS, PERCUSSION CAPS, PISTOLS, ETC.

FINE BRITANNIA METAL DRAM FLASKS.

No.	Size.		Per Dozen.
950	¼ pint		$
951	½ pint		
952	¾ pint		
953	1 pint		
954	1½ pint		

DOG CALLS.

No. 1, Britannia Metal .... per dozen, $
No. 2, Britannia Metal .... "
No. 3, Britannia Metal .... "

CAP PRIMERS.

No. 7 .... per dozen, $

PERCUSSION CAPS.

G. D. & S. B. Plain, Full Count, Stamped .... per M. $
G. D. (85) Short Count, Stamped .... "
S. B. Ribbed, (60) Stamped .... "
Hat, Full Count .... "
Hat, Full Count, Water-proof .... "

Ely's Percussion Caps, in Tin Boxes.

E. B. .... per M. $
F. L. .... "
Double Waterproof in ¼ M .... "
Double Waterproof in 1/10 M .... "
Colt's Pistol, Metal Lined .... "

GUN WADDING.

Miller's Artificial Leather, Elastic Indented.

Nos. 10 to 18, in Boxes of 250 .... per dozen boxes, $

Baldwin's Indented.

Nos. 8 to 30, in Boxes of 250 .... per dozen boxes, $

Ely's Indented.

Nos. 8 to 30, Cloth, with Black Edges, in Boxes
of 250 .... per dozen boxes, $
Nos. 8 to **30**, White Cloth, Chemically Prepared,
Pink Edges, in Boxes of 250 .... "
Nos. 8 to 30, Felt, in Boxes of 250 .... "
Nos. 8 to 30, Felt, in Bags of ½ lb .... per lb. $

MELTING LADLES.

	$								per dozen.
No.	1	2	3	4	5	6	7	8	
	2½	3	3½	4	4½	5	6	7	inches.

Monroe's Patent .... per dozen, $

NATIONAL REVOLVER.

¾ Cartridge.

No. 1, Blued Barrels and Cylinder, Plated Frame and Walnut
Stock, Weight, 14 ozs.; Extreme Length, 7 inches;
Ball, 33/100ths .... each, $
No. 1, With Silver Plated Barrels and Cylinders .... "

ITS ADVANTAGES ARE:

1st. It is loaded with perfect ease and safety, without removing the cylinder, (or any part of it,) at the fore end, and can be carried when loaded without the slightest danger.
2d. The cylinder never fouls; is made from solid steel, bored; and cannot get out of repair, or clog, as cylinders made of many parts will do.
3d. The carriage is made on an improved plan; the fulminate is concentrated in one place, which insures sure fire ; is METALLIC, CENTRAL FIRE, AND WATER PROOF.
4th. Its peculiar model makes it the most desirable Pocket Revolver ever made.

NATIONAL REVOLVER.

(Continued.)

DIRECTIONS FOR LOADING:

Set the hammer at half cock to relieve the cylinder, throw open the *Gate* on right hand side of barrel, just forward of the cylinder, insert the cartridge teat downward, so that the flange sinks to its place in the cylinder—close the gate, and the arm is loaded.
To eject the Cartridge Shell after explosion, set hammer at half cock, and open the gate as above, and with the small rod start the Shell through the opening at rear of abutment and cylinder, when the Shell will fall out.
This arm can be carried safely, when loading, with hammer at half cock, or resting on cylinder between the cartridges.

WHITNEY'S REVOLVERS.

	$				each.
	3½	4	5	6	inches.
Navy					each, $

SMITH AND WESSON'S REVOLVERS.

	$		each.
No.	1	2	

Cartridges.

Smith & Wesson's Nos. 1 and 2 .... per 100, $
National Revolver .... per 100,

TOY CANNON—IRON.

Artillery Pattern on Wheels, Mounted.

	$				per dozen.
No.	5¾	6	7	8	9

Mounted, with Swivel.

	$						per dozen.
No.	10	11	12	13	14	15	

BRASS BARRELS.

Mounted, Japanned or Bronzed Iron Carriages.

	$				per dozen.
No.	1	2	3	4	
Length of Barrel,	4½	5½	6	6½	inches.

Brass Barrels not Mounted same Sizes as Mounted.

	$				per dozen.
No.	1	2	3	4	

FRARY'S PATENT TORPEDO AND FIRE CRACKER PISTOL.

No. 2, In Boxes of 1 dozen. Cases of 2 dozen .... per gross, $

FRARY'S IMPROVED TOY AIR PISTOL.

No. 3, Bronzed,   in Cases of 24 dozen .... per gross, $
No. 2, Bronzed,   in Cases of 24 dozen .... "
No. 1, Bronzed,   in Cases of 12 dozen .... "
No. 3, Silver Plated, in Cases of 24 dozen .... "
No. 2, Silver Plated, in Cases of 24 dozen .... "
No. 1, Silver Plated, in Cases of 12 dozen .... "

FISH HOOKS, FISH LINES, AND CORK FLOATS.

FISH HOOKS.

Genuine Hollow Point, Limerick Salmon.

						per 100.
Nos. $	10–0	9–0	8–0	7–0	6–0	
Nos. $	5–0	4–0	3–0	2–0	1–0	per 100.

Genuine Hollow Point, Limerick Trout.

Nos. 1 to 16................................per 100, $

Limerick Hooks, Flatted.

						per 100.
Nos. $	10–0	9–0	8–0	7–0	6–0	
Nos. $	5–0	4–0	3–0	2–0	1–0	per 100.

Nos. 1 to 16................................per 100, $

Limerick Hooks, Bowed.

						per 100.
Nos. $	10–0	9–0	8–0	7–0	6–0	
Nos. $	5–0	4–0	3–0	2–0	1–0	per 100.

Nos. 1 to 16................................per 100, $

Superfine Kirby Salmon.

						per 100.
Nos. $	3–0	2–0	1–0	1	2	3
Nos. $	4	5	6	7	8	per 100.

Kirby Trout Hooks, Flatted.

						per 100.
No. $	4–0	3–0	2–0	1–0	1	
No. $	2	3	4	5	6	per 100.

Kirby Fish Hooks, Flatted.

No. 1 to 16................................per 100, $

Kirby Fish Hooks, Bowed.

					per 100.
No. $	10–0	9–0	8–0	7–0	6–0
No. $	5–0	4–0	3–0	2–0	1–0

No. 1 to 12................................per 100, $

Kirby Sea Hooks, Flatted.

							per 100.
No. $	2–0	1–0	1	2	3	4	5
No. $	6	7	8	9	10	11	12	per 100.

Kirby Sea Hooks, Tinned.

						per 100.
No. $	1	2	3	4	5	6
No. $	7	8	9	10	11	12	per 100.

Black Fish Hooks.

							per 100.
No. $	0	1	2	3	4	5	6
No. $	7	8	9	10	11	12	per 100.

Virginia Hooks.

						per 100.
No. $	1	2	3	4	5	6
No. $	7	8	9	10	11	12	per 100.

HOOKS ON SNELLS.

Genuine Limerick Salmon on Gimp.

					per 100.
No. $	10–0	9–0	8–0	7–0	6–0

No. 5–0 to 10 ....per 100, $

HOOKS ON SNELLS,
(*Continued.*)

Superfine Kirby Salmon on Gimp.

				per 100.
No. $	3–0	2–0	1–0	

No. 1 to 5................................per 100, $

Genuine Limerick Salmon on Twisted Gut.

					per 100.
No. $	10–0	9–0	8–0	7–0	6–0

No. 5–0 to 1–0................................per 100, $

Superfine Kirby Salmon on Twisted Gut.

				per 100.
No. $	3–0	2–0	1–0	

No. 1 to 5................................per 100, $

Limerick Salmon on Gut.

No. 5–0 to 1–0................................per 100, $

Limerick Hooks on Gut.

No. 1 to 12................................per 100, $

Kirby Salmon on Gut.

No. 1 to 8................................per 100, $

Kirby Hooks on Gut.

No. 1 to 12................................per 100, $

ARTIFICIAL FLIES.

Trout Flies, assorted................................per dozen, $
Superfine Trout Flies, for all seasons................per dozen,

SILK LINES.

Waterproof Silk Lines, 100 yards...................per yard, $
Waterproof Silk Lines, 200 yards...................per yard,
Plaited Silk Lines, Assorted Colors, 20 to 200 yards....per yard,
Plaited Silk Lines, Large............................per gross, $
Plaited Silk Lines, Extra Large......................." "
Cable Laid Silk Lines, Large........................." "
Cable Laid Silk Lines, Extra Large..................." "
Chinese Cable Laid Grass Lines, Small..............." "
Chinese Cable Laid Grass Lines, Medium............." "
Chinese Cable Laid Grass Lines, Large..............." "
Silk Lines, Furnished with Hooks and Floats complete.per dozen, $
Linen Lines, Furnished with Hooks and Floats complete.per doz.

LINEN LINES.

Trolling Lines, 84 Feet in Coils.

				per coil.
No. $	1	2	3	4

Black Fish Lines, 84 Feet in Coils.

				per coil.
No. $	1	2	3	4

Cod Lines, 84 Feet in Coils.

			per coil.
No. $	1	2	3

Fancy Linen Lines, in Boxes.

				per gross.
No. $	0	1	2	
Length,	18	18	24	feet.

CORK FLOATS.

Bound Cork Floats, Egg Shape.

						per dozen.
No. $	03	3	4	12	13	14

Unbound Cork Floats, Egg Shape.................per dozen, $
Bound Cork Floats, Assorted Small................per dozen,
Unbound Cork Floats, Assorted Small..............per dozen,

SUPERIOR STEEL TRAPS.

NEWHOUSE'S GENUINE ONEIDA STEEL TRAPS.

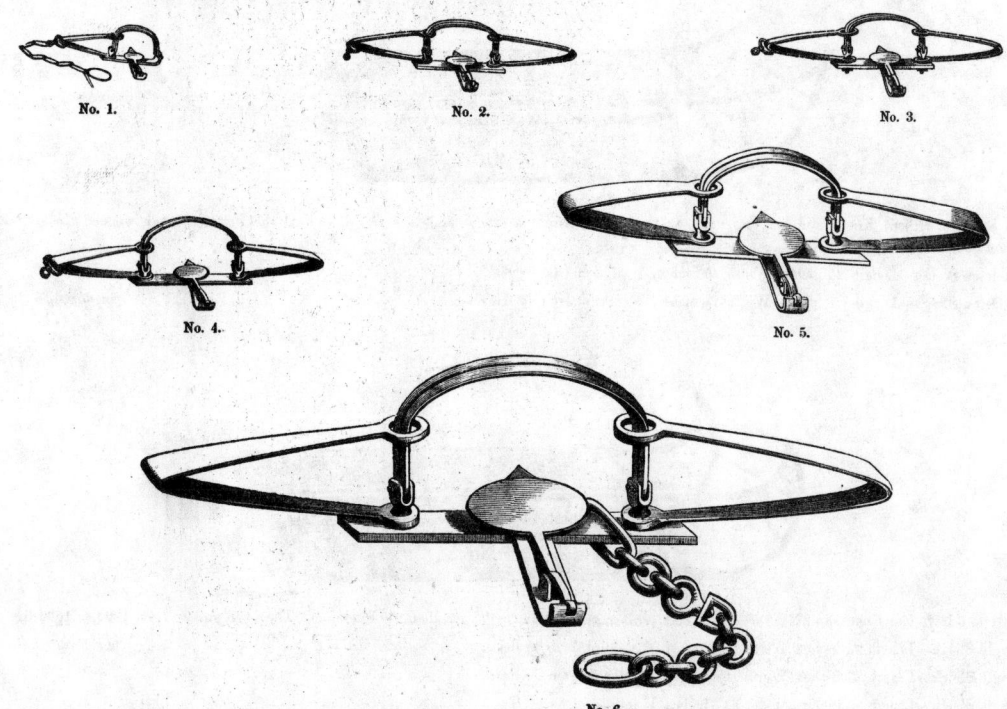

No. 1.   No. 2.   No. 3.

No. 4.   No. 5.

No. 6.

No. 1, Muskrat or Mink Trap, Single Spring; spread of Jaws, 4 inches; of sufficient strength to hold a Fisher or Fox..............per dozen, $

No. 2, Fox Trap, with Double Spring; spread of Jaws, 4½ inches; strong enough to hold an Otter.............................per dozen, $

No. 3, Otter Trap, Double Spring; spread of Jaws, 5½ inches..per dozen, $

*No. 4, Beaver or Wolf Trap, Double Spring; spread of Jaws, 6½ inches..per dozen, $

    *For this Trap we have extra sets of Jaws with Teeth, adapted to trapping Deer, which can be had separately, or inserted in the Trap in place of the ordinary Jaws, as may be desired.

No. 5, Bear Trap; spread of Jaws, 11½ inches; weight of each Spring, 2 lbs. 10 oz.; weight of Trap, 17 lbs.—suitable for taking the common
    Black Bear..each, $

No. 6, Bear Trap—Large Size; spread of Jaws, 16 inches; weight of each Spring, 6 lbs.; weight of the Trap, with Chain, 40 lbs.—strong
    enough to hold the Moose or Grizzly Bear...each, $

ONEIDA PATTERN.		UNION PATTERN.	
No. 1, 3½ inch Single Spring.................per dozen, $		No. 1, 5 inch Single Spring.................per dozen, $	
No. 2, 4½ inch Single Spring................. "		No. 2, 6 inch Single Spring................. "	
No. 3, 4½ inch Double Spring................. "		No. 3, 6½ inch Single Spring................. "	
No. 4, 5 inch Double Spring................. "		No. 4, 5 inch Double Spring................. "	
No. 5, 6 inch Double Spring................. "		No. 5, 6 inch Double Spring................. "	
Chains and Rings, extra................. "		No. 6, 7 inch Double Spring................. "	
		No. 7, 7½ inch Double Spring................. "	
		No. 8, 12 inch Double Spring................. "	

BLAKE'S PATENT TRAPS.

No. 1.   No. 2.   No. 3.

per dozen.

No.	1	2	2¼	3	4
$					

HAND SLEIGHS.

SKELETON.

This style is without Knees, and has less work on the boards than the others, and is designed to take the place of cheap wooden Sleds.　They will sustain from 500 to 800 lbs. each.

No. 1, Skeleton Sleigh—Length 25 inches, Width 10 inches, Weight of Iron 3½ lbs..per dozen, $

No. 2, Skeleton Sleigh—Length 28 inches, Width 11 inches, Weight of Iron 4½ lbs..per dozen, $

EAGLE.

Nos. 1 to 5 have four Knees, and No. 6 has six Knees, with more work on the boards than the Skeleton.　They will sustain from 1200 to 1500 lbs. each.

No. 1, Eagle Sleigh—Length 24 inches, Width　9　inches, Weight of Iron 4½ lbs..per dozen, $

No. 2, Eagle Sleigh—Length 27 inches, Width 10　inches, Weight of Iron 5　lbs...　　"

No. 3, Eagle Sleigh—Length 29 inches, Width 11　inches, Weight of Iron 6　lbs...　　"

No. 4, Eagle Sleigh—Length 32 inches, Width 11½ inches, Weight of Iron 7　lbs...　　"

No. 5, Eagle Sleigh—Length 36 inches, Width 12　inches, Weight of Iron 8　lbs...　　"

No. 6, Eagle Sleigh—Length 39 inches, Width 12½ inches, Weight of Iron 9　lbs...　　"

UNION.

The Running and Rail is composed of one piece of Iron, it has four Knees.　Will sustain from 1200 to 1500 lbs. each.

No. 1, Union Sleigh—Length 33 inches, Width 11½ inches, Weight of Iron 8 lbs..per dozen, $

No. 2, Union Sleigh—Length 38 inches, Width 12　inches, Weight of Iron 9 lbs...　　"

MONITOR.

Designed for coasting, and constructed with a view to great fleetness and strength.　It is very strong, and will sustain from 1500 to 2000 lbs. each.　No. 3 has six Knees.

No. 1, Monitor Sleigh—Length 31 inches, Width　9　inches, Weight of Iron 7 lbs..per dozen, $

No. 2, Monitor Sleigh—Length 36 inches, Width　9½ inches, Weight of Iron 8 lbs...　　"

No. 3, Monitor Sleigh—Length 42 inches, Width 10　inches, Weight of Iron 9 lbs...　　"

HAND SLEIGHS.

(Continued.)

CLIPPER.

No. 1, Clipper Sleigh, Length 42 inches, Width 11   inches, Weight of Iron 9 lbs.............................per dozen, $

No. 2, Clipper Sleigh, Length 48 inches, Width 11½ inches, Weight of Iron 10 lbs.............................per dozen, $

LADIES'

No. 1, Ladies' Sleigh, Length 42 inches, Width 12 inches, Weight of Iron 10 lbs.............................per dozen, $

SWAN.

No. 1, Swan Sleigh, Length 44 inches, Width 14 inches, Weight of Iron 12 lbs.............................per dozen, $

LADIES' ICE SLED.

Ladies' Ice Sled...each, $

TOY SLEIGHS.—Assorted, Three Sizes...per gross, $

GENTLEMEN'S AND LADIES' SKATES.

GENTLEMEN'S SKATES.

No. 20—8 to 10 inches.

No. 20, German Pattern, Red Wood ....per pair, $

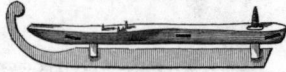

No. 24—9 to 11 inches.

No. 24, Cast Steel, Runner..........................per pair, $

No. 40—8 to 11 inches.

No. 40, Improved American Pattern, Solid Posts, Varnished Wood................................per pair, $

No. 42—9 to 11 inches.

No. 42, English Pattern, Best Silver Steel, Brass Mountings, Apple Tree Wood.....................per pair, $

No. 60—9 to 11 inches.

No. 60, Broad Strap, Solid Blade, English Pattern......per pair, $

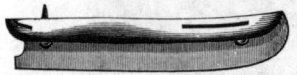

No. 80—10 to 11 inches.

No. 80, Best Silver Steel, Apple Tree Wood, French Polished, Brass Mountings ....per pair, $

LADIES' SKATES.

No. 27—8 to 9½ inches.

No. 27, Wide Steel Blades, Steel Posts...............per pair, $

No. 38—8½ to 9½ inches.

No. 38, English Pattern ....per pair, $

LADIES' SKATES,
(*Continued.*)

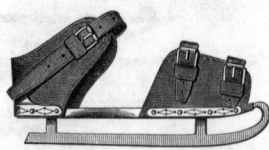

No. 44—8 to 10 inches.

No. 44, Improved American Pattern ....per pair, $

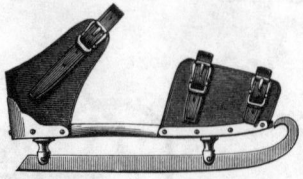

No. 50—8 to 10 inches.

No. 50, Superior Cast Steel, Brass Posts ....per pair, $

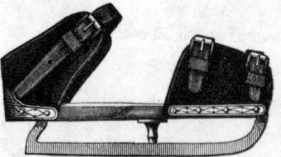

No. 83—9 to 10 inches.

No. 83, The Central Park Favorite, Best Cast Steel....per pair, $

No. 85—8 to 10 inches.

No. 85, Solid Silver Steel Blades, Silver Plated Bolsters, French Polished Wood ....per pair, $

☞ The above Ladies' Skates are all trimmed with Black or Russet Leather, Brass Plates and Round Head Screws.

MAYDOLE'S PATENT BEST CAST STEEL SKATES.

Socket Heels, Adjustable Slide.

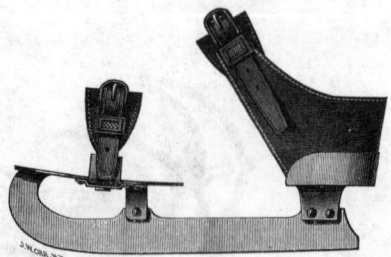

Trimmed with Patent Leather and Stitched.

Ladies' Skates.

No.	$ 2	3	4	5	6	7	per pair.
	8	8½	9	9½	10	10½	inches.

SKATES, SKATE STRAPS, ETC.

MAYDOLE'S PATENT CAST STEEL SKATES,

(*Continued.*)

Gentlemens' Skates.

							per pair.
	$						
No.	6	7	8	9	10	11	
	10	10½	11	11½	12	12½	inches.

Trimmed with Plain Black or Russet Leather.

Ladies' Skates.

							per pair.
	$						
No.	2	3	4	5	6	7	
	8	8½	9	9½	10	10½	inches.

Gentlemens' Skates.

							per pair.
	$						
No.	6	7	8	9	10	11	
	10	10½	11	11½	12	12½	inches.

Hook Heels, Adjustable Slide and Strap in Front.

Gentlemens' Skates.

						per pair.
	$					
No.	2	3	4	5	6	
	7½	8	8½	9	9½	inches.
	$					per pair.
No.	7	8	9	10	11	
	10	10½	11	11½	12	inches.

LOVATT'S PATENT SKATE.

8 to 11½ inches....................................per pair, $

☞ This Skate dispenses with the use of straps, being fastened to the feet by means of clamps or catches. It is adapted to any size boot or shoe and is decidedly the best self-fastening skate made.

American Parlor or Floor Skates.

							per pair.
	$						
No.	1	2	3	4	5	6	7
Length of foot plate,	7	7¾	8¼	9	9¾	10¼	11¼ inches.

Heel Screws and Nuts.

Heel Screws and Nuts.......................per 100, $

SKATE STRAPS.

No. 5, Loop Heel Bands......................	per dozen, $	
No. 6, Short (30 inch Strap)......................	"	
No. 6, Long (36 inch Strap)......................	"	
Broad Toe, 2 and 2¼ inches......................	"	
Broad Toe, 2½ inches......................	"	
English, 3 hole......................	"	
Patent Short (30 inch Strap)......................	"	
Patent Long (36 inch Strap)......................	"	
Toe Straps, 30 inches......................	"	
Toe Straps, 36 inches......................	"	

Skate Straps furnished with Fogg's Patent Buckles.

MONROE'S SNOW SHOVELS.

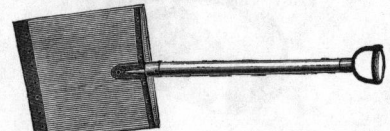

Wood Blade and Handle, with Malleable Iron Japanned
Trimmings.....................................per dozen, $

FOGG'S PATENT DOUBLE-ACTION LEVER BUCKLES.

Skate Buckles.

Brass, with Rivets, ⅝ inch...........................per 100, $

Japanned Iron, with Rivets, ⅝ inch................... "

Shoe Buckles.

Brass, with Roller, ½ inch...........................per 100, $

Plated, with Roller, ½ inch........................... "

Japanned Iron, with Roller, ½ inch................... "

Brass, with Leather, ⅝ inch........................... "

Japanned Iron, with Leather, ⅝ inch................... "

DARRAH'S PATENT UNIVERSAL SHOE-TIE.

Will fasten Shoe and Corset Lacers or any strings which it is customary to tie in knots in half the time that is usually required; and when fastened is perfectly secure, never getting into "hard knots" or coming untied, yet when desired, can be unfastened in an instant. It is an article that has long been needed and is cheap, useful, ornamental and durable. The above cut represents a section of the shoe, showing the position of the tie when in use.

Brass...per gross, $

Plated... "

SHEATHS, PALMS, AND BURGLAR-PROOF SAFES.

SHEATHS AND BELTS.

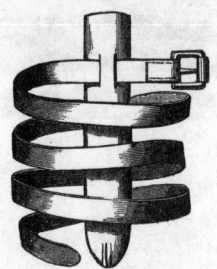

Common Sheaths and Belts........................per dozen, $
Regular Sheaths and Belts......................... "
Best Sheaths and Belts........................... "
Common Belts only............................... "
Regular Belts only.............................. "
Best Belts only................................. "
Common Sheaths only............................ "
Regular Sheaths only........................... "
Best Sheaths only.............................. "

SAILORS' PALMS.

Best Hide and Brass................................per dozen, $
Regular Hide and Brass........................... "
Common Hide and Brass........................... "
Plain Brass and Hide............................ "

Navy.

Seaming..per dozen, $
Roping...per dozen,

DOG COLLARS.
Leather.

No. $
  1   2   3   4   5   6   per dozen.

No. $
  7   8   9   10   11   12   per dozen.

Brass.

Plain Brass, Assorted Sizes.......................per dozen, $

Plain Brass, Leather Lined.

$
  3 to 5   4 to 6   7 to 8   per dozen.
                                     inches.

Fancy Brass, Leather Lined.

$
  3 to 5   4 to 6   7 to 8   per dozen.
                                     inches.

LILLIE'S CELEBRATED CHILLED IRON SAFES, LOCKS, AND VAULT DOORS.

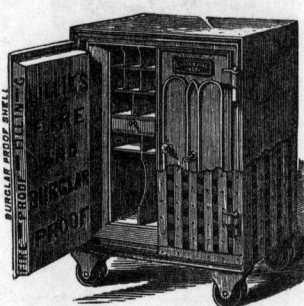

Showing the Net Work of Wrought Iron Bars

LILLIE'S CELEBRATED CHILLED IRON SAFES, LOCKS, AND VAULT DOORS,

(Continued.)

Fireproof Safes, Folding Doors, No. 1 and 2 Lock.

No.	OUTSIDE			INSIDE			Price.
	Heighth.	Width.	Depth.	Heighth.	Width.	Depth.	
	In.	In.	In.	In.	In.	In.	
1	68	52	34	54½	39	18	$
1½	59	50	26	48	39	15	
2	53	44	27	42½	33	16	

No. 2 LOCKS.

3	50	42	27	40	32	16	$
4	46	42	27	36	32	16	
4½	38	46	27	28	36	16	
5	42	38	27	31½	27½	15	

SINGLE DOORS AND No. 2 LOCK.

6	38	35	26	27½	23½	15	$
7	34	31	26	24	21	14	
8	31	28	24	21	18	13	
9	30	24	24	21	15	12	
10	26	22	22	19½	13½	12	
11	24	20	18	17	11½	10	

These Safes are fastened by Lillie's Duodecagon Bank and Monitor Safe Locks.

National Bank, with 3 Locks and Inside Safe.

No.	OUTSIDE			INSIDE			Price.
	Heighth.	Width.	Depth.	Heighth.	Width.	Depth.	
	In.	In.	In.	In.	In.	In.	
1	68	52	34	55	39	18	$

BANK VAULT SAFE, No. 1 LOCK.

1	53	48	25	51	44	20	$
2	54	32	24	50	28	20	
3	42	36	22	38	32	18	
4	36	31	20	32	27	16	
5	30	24	18	26	20	14	

BANK VAULT DOORS AND FRAMES, No. 1 and 2 LOCKS.

No.	Heighth Clear.	Width Clear.	Depth Adjustable.	Weight.	Price.
	In.	In.	In.	lbs.	
1	72	27	20	3000	$
2	72	27	20	1500	

COAL OIL LAMPS AND FIXTURES.

No. 371.
Height 4¼ in.

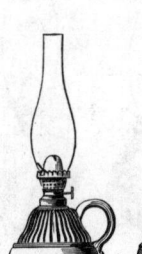
No. 532.
4¾ in.

No. 522.
4½ in.

No 332.
4¾ in.

No. 302.
4¾ in.

No. 312.
5 in.

Monitor Lamp.
No. 353.

Adlam Lamp.
No. 253.

No. 683.
Height 9 in.

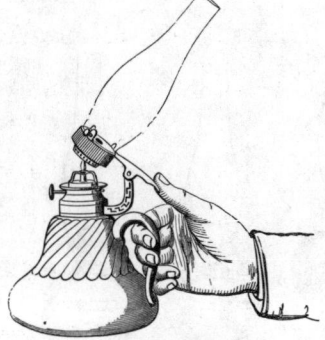
No. 503.   Tom Thumb Lamp.

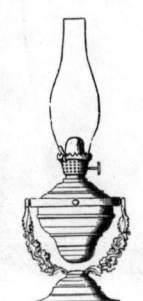
No. 5301. Ship Lamp.
7¼ in.

No. 322.
4½ in.

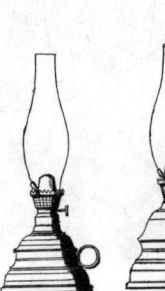
No. 382.
4¼ in.

No. 392.
4¾ in.

No. 674.
9¼ in.

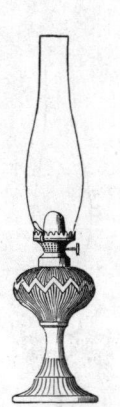
No. 602.
Height 7¼ in.

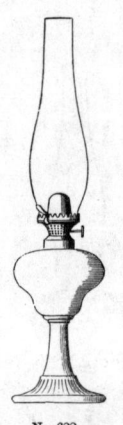
No. 622.
8½ in.

No. 612.
7¾ in.

No. 633.
9¼ in.

No. 693.
9 in.

No. 643.
9 in.

No. 623.
9¼ in.

No. 653.
10 in.

No. 974.
9¼ in.

COAL OIL LAMPS AND FIXTURES.

(Continued.)

No. 924.
Height 11 in.

No. 934.
10½ in.

No. 925 A.
10¼ in.

No. 755.
10¼ in.

No. 844.
11 in.

No. 865.
10½ in.

No. 724.
11 in.

No. 835.
11½ in.

No. 854.
11¼ in.

No. 735.
Height 11½ in

No. 764.
12 in.

No. 734.
12 in.

No. 756.
11¼ in.

No. 746.
12½ in.

No. 944.
10 in.

No. 994.
10 in.

No. 794.
10½ in.

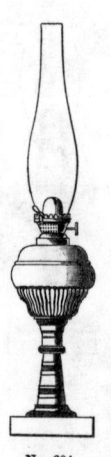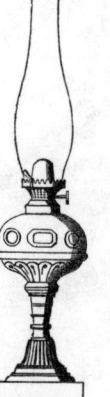

No. 614.
Height 10½ in.

No. 604.
9¾ in.

No. 953.
10½ in.

No. 983.
10 in.

No. 925.
10½ in.

No. 598.
11 in.

No. 9631.
10¾ in.

No. 919.
10½ in.

COAL OIL LAMPS AND FIXTURES.

(Continued.)

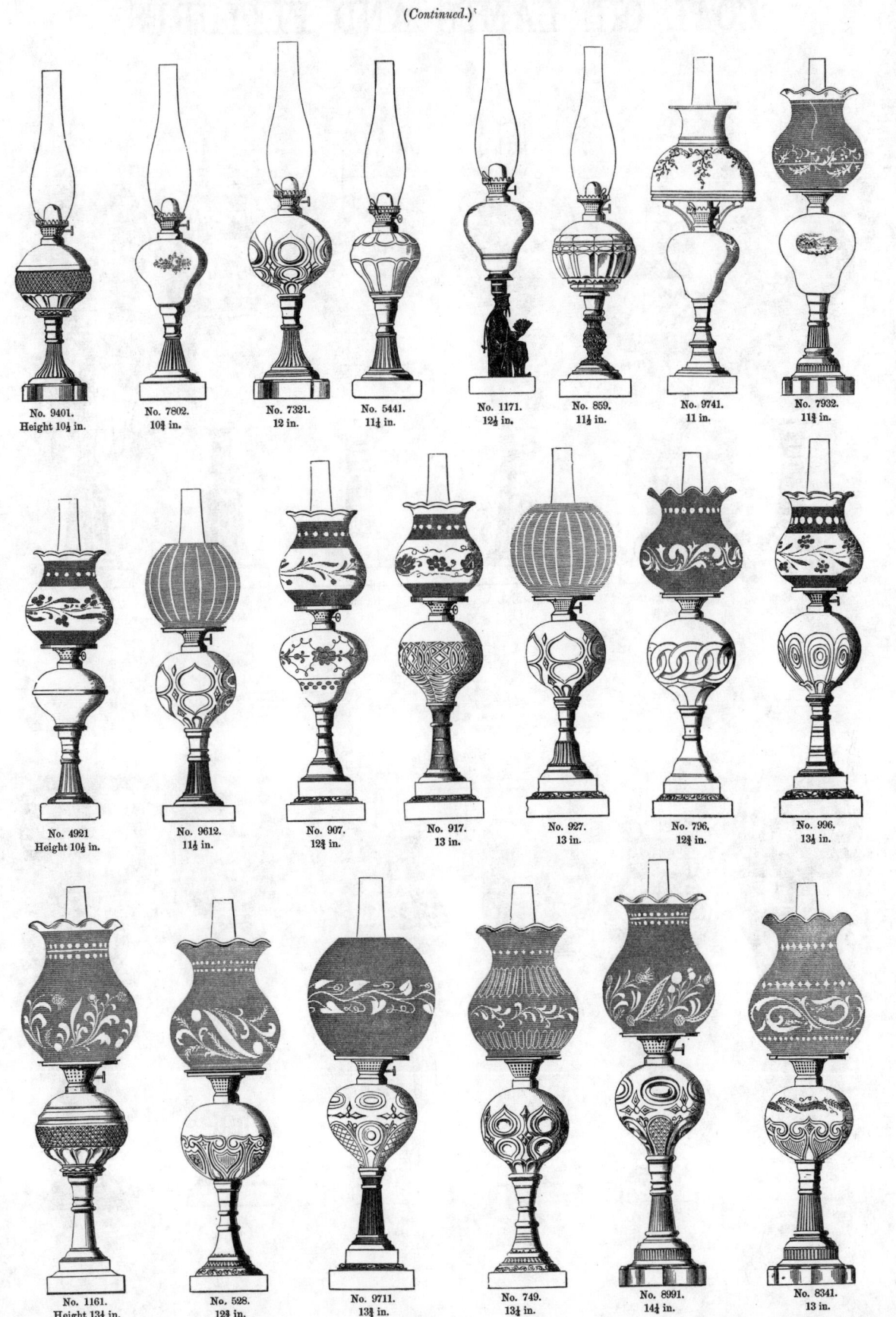

No. 9401.
Height 10¼ in.

No. 7802.
10¾ in.

No. 7321.
12 in.

No. 5441.
11¾ in.

No. 1171.
12½ in.

No. 859.
11½ in.

No. 9741.
11 in.

No. 7932.
11¾ in.

No. 4921
Height 10½ in.

No. 9612.
11½ in.

No. 907.
12¾ in.

No. 917.
13 in.

No. 927.
13 in.

No. 796,
12¾ in.

No. 996.
13¾ in.

No. 1161.
Height 13¼ in.

No. 528.
12¾ in.

No. 9711.
13¾ in.

No. 749.
13¾ in.

No. 8991.
14¼ in.

No. 8341.
13 in.

COAL OIL LAMPS AND FIXTURES.

(Continued.)

No. 4022.
Height 16 in.

No. 8781.
13¼ in.

No. 9161.
16¾ in.

No. 8591.
15¾ in.

No. 8981.
15¼ in.

No. 8202.
16 in.

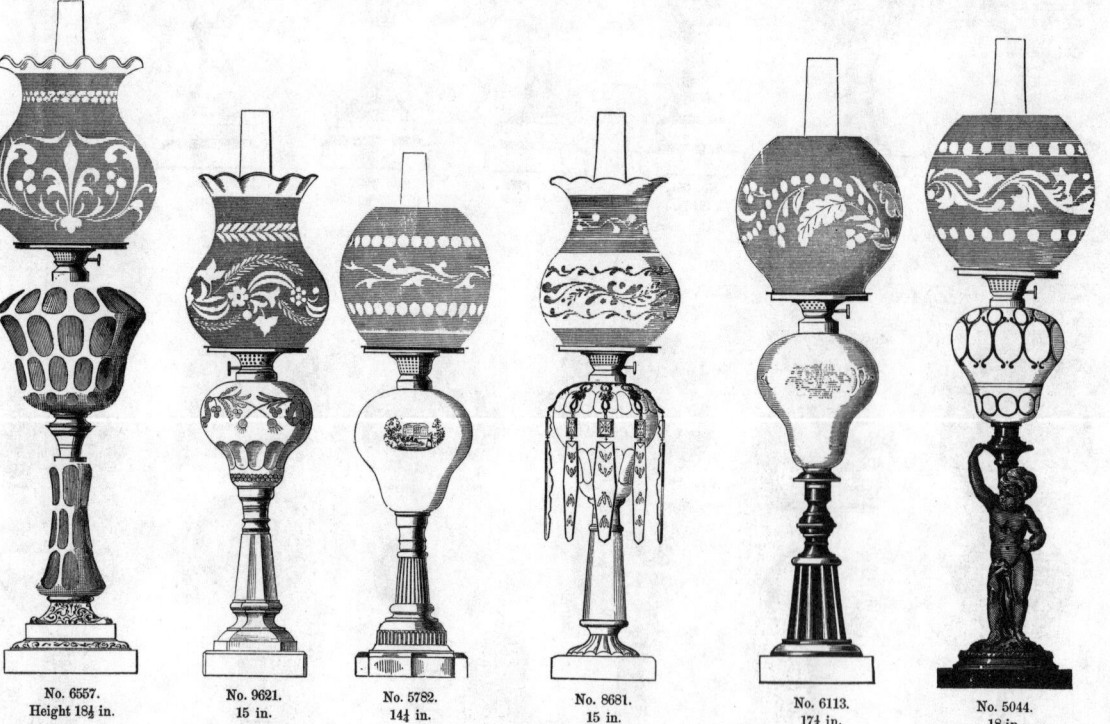

No. 6557.
Height 18¼ in.

No. 9621.
15 in.

No. 5782.
14¼ in.

No. 8681.
15 in.

No. 6113.
17¼ in.

No. 5044.
18 in.

COAL OIL LAMPS AND FIXTURES.

(Continued.)

No. 21 P.
Height 21 in.

No. 5164.
18 in.

No. 22 P.
16½ in.

No. 5334.
15½ in.

No. 3 P.
Height 15¾ in.

No. 10 P.
15⅜ in.

No. 15 P.
Reading Lamp.

No. 18 P.
16 in.

No. 20 P.
17 in.

COAL OIL LAMPS AND FIXTURES.

(Continued.)

No. 4 P.
Height 12 in.   No. 6 P.   No. 8 P.   No. 14 P.
10¾ in.   No. 1 P. Bracket.

No 5 P. Bracket.   No. 6 P. Bracket.   No. 199. Bracket.
Length 14½ in.   No. 579. Bracket.
12 in.

No. 587. Bracket.
Length 12½ in.   No. 5251. Bracket.
16¼ in.   No. 234. Bracket.
7½ in.   No. 516. Bracket.
8½ in.

COAL OIL LAMPS AND FIXTURES.

(Continued.)

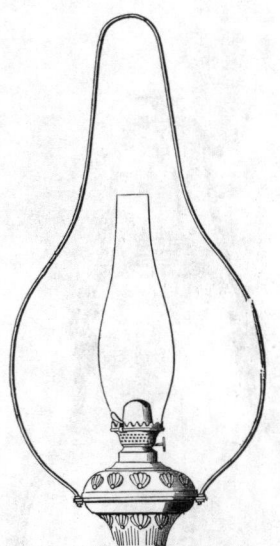

No. 536. Hanger.
Height 26 in.

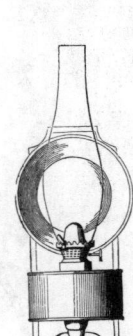

No. 214. Side Lamp.

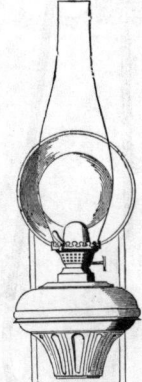

No. 596. Side Lamp.

No. 564. Side Lamp.

No. 999. Hanger.
25½ in.

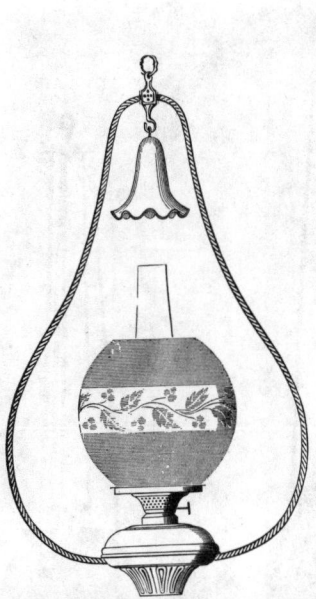

No. 5111. Hanger.
Height 26½ in.

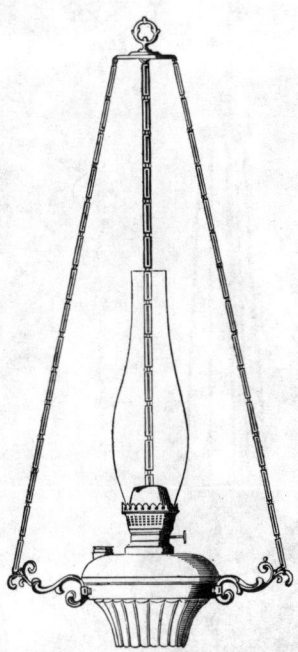

No. 2241. Hanger.
30 in.

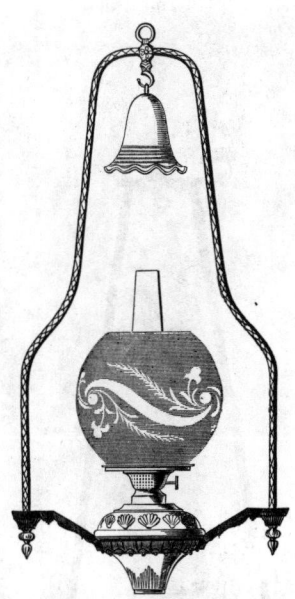

No. 6 P. Hanger.
23½ in.

COAL OIL LAMPS AND FIXTURES.

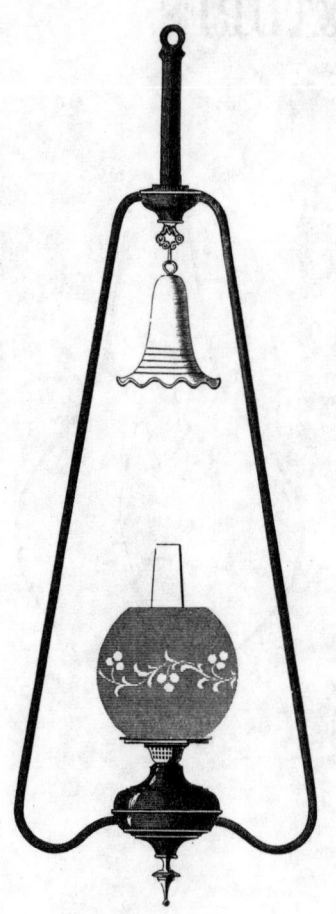

No. 627 P. Hall Light.
Height 41½ in.

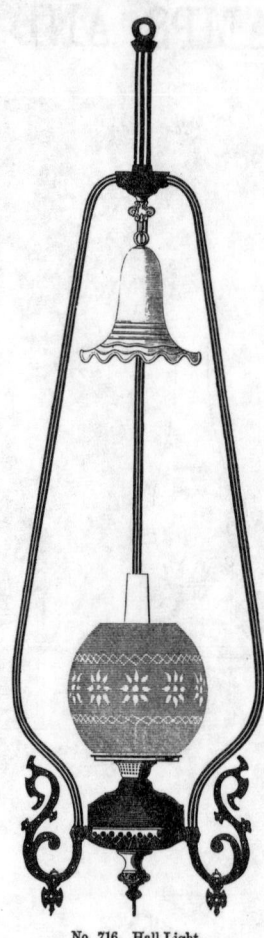

No. 716. Hall Light.
43 in.

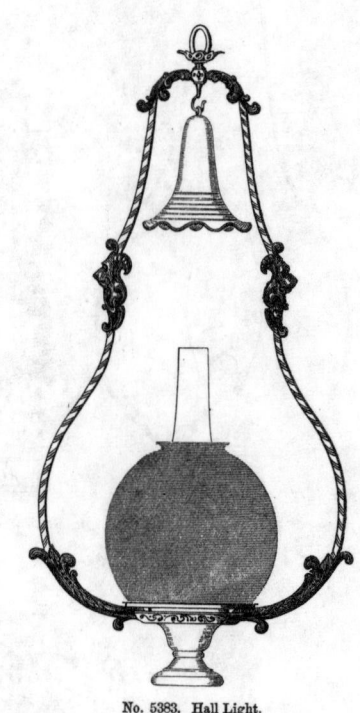

No. 5383. Hall Light.
31½ in.

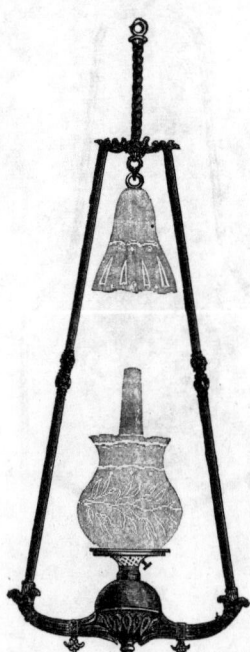

No. 610 P.
Hall Light.

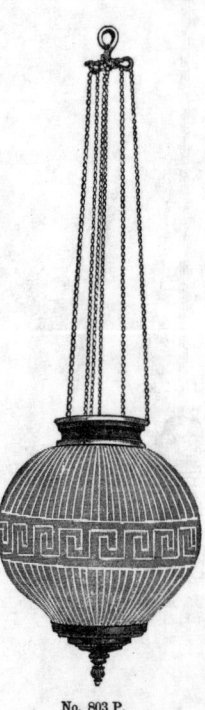

No. 803 P.
Sliding Hall Light.

No. 802 P.
Sliding Hall Light.

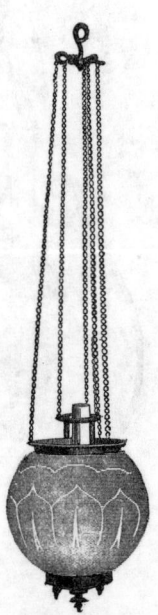

No. 801 P.
Sliding Hall Light.

COAL OIL LAMPS AND FIXTURES.

(Continued.)

No. 875, Height 34 inches.   No. 644, Height 34 inches.

No. 1027½ P.

No. 543 P, Height 3 feet.

COAL OIL LAMPS AND FIXTURES.

(Continued.)

No. 554 P.

No. 704.   34 inch.

COAL OIL LAMPS AND FIXTURES.

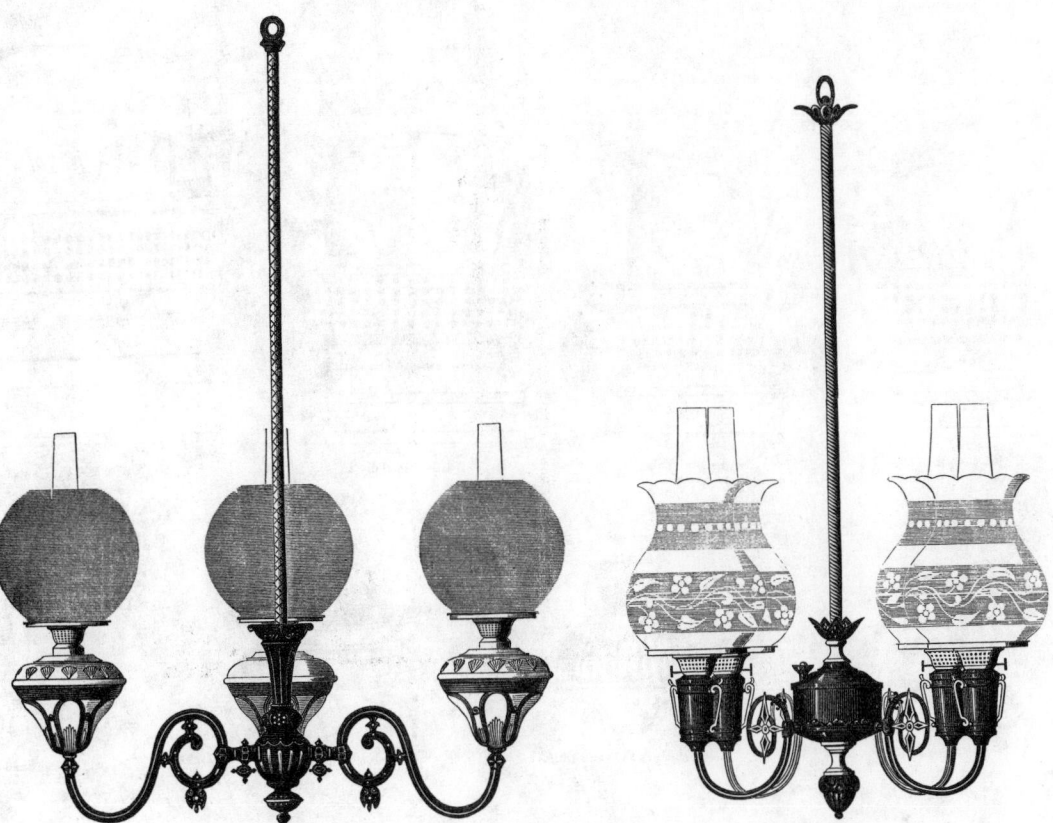

No. 664, Height 38¾ inches.

No. 457, Height 35 inches.

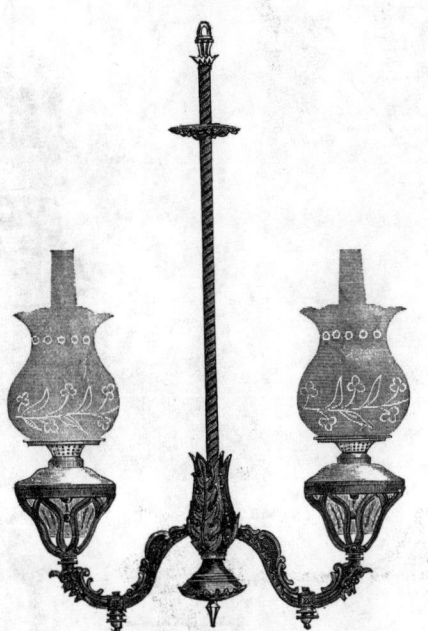

No. 1071 P, Height 36 inches.

No. 539 P, Height 3 feet.

COAL OIL BURNERS, SHADES, CLASPS, ETC.

(Continued.)

No. 0—½ in. Tube.   No. 1—⅞ in. Tube.   No. 2—1 in. Tube.   No. 3—1¼ in. Tube.

Paper Shade.

Porcelain Shade and Ring.

Large Shade Clasp.

Small Shade Clasp.

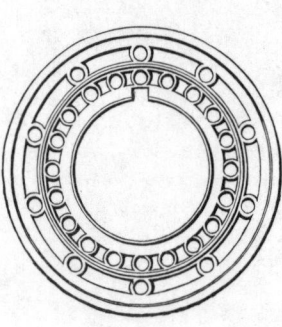

4 in. Globe Ring.

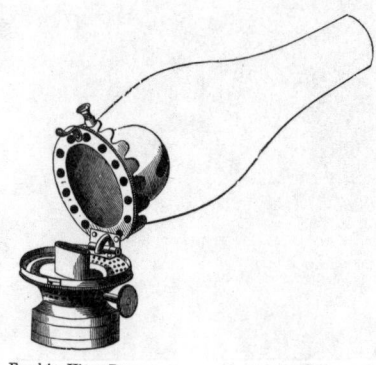

Excelsior Hinge Burner.

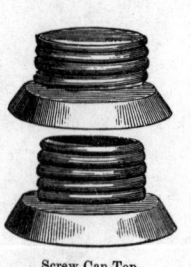

Screw Can Top.

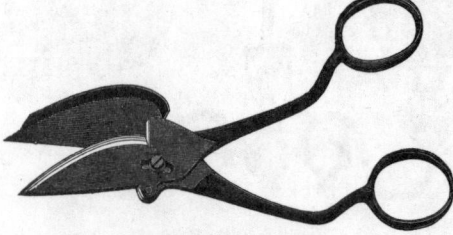

Phare's Patent Trimming Scissors.

No. 1 Gas Cup.

No. 2 Gas Cup.

COAL OIL LAMPS AND FIXTURES.

(Continued.)

LAMPS.

Page 417.

No.	Size of Burner.	Description.	Per dozen.
371	No. 0,	Flint Glass..............................$	
532	No. 0,	Flint Glass.............................	
522	No. 0,	Flint Glass.............................	
332	No. 0,	Flint Glass.............................	
302	No. 0,	Flint Glass.............................	
312	No. 0,	Flint Glass.............................	
353	——	Flint Glass, Round Wick, Monitor Burner.....	
253	——	Flint Glass, Adlam Lamp....................	
683	No. 1,	Marble Base, Brass Column, Flint Font, A, B, C and D.............	
503	——	Flint Glass, Round Wick, Tom Thumb Burner..	
5301	No. 1,	Brass, Double Swing Ship Lamp..............	
322	No. 0,	Tin, Bronzed..............................	
382	No. 0,	Brass, Omula and Bronzed....................	
392	No. 0,	Brass, Omula and Bronzed....................	
674	No. 1,	Flint Glass..............................	
602	No. 1,	Flint Glass, A, B, C and D..................	
622	No. 1,	Flint Glass.............................	
612	No. 1,	Flint Glass.............................	
633	No. 1,	Flint Glass.............................	
693	No. 1,	Marble Base, Brass Column, Flint Font, A, B, C and D.....................	
643	No. 1,	Marble Base, Brass Column, Flint Font, A, B, C and D.....................	
623	No. 1,	Marble Base, Brass Column, Flint Font, A, B, C and D.....................	
653	No. 1,	Marble Base, Brass Column, Flint Font, A, B, C and D.....................	
974	No. 1,	Alabaster Stand, Flint Font..................	

Page 418.

No.	Size of Burner.	Description.	Per dozen.
924	No. 1,	Marble Base, Brass Column, Flint Font.......$	
934	No. 1,	Marble Base, Brass Column, Flint Font.......	
925 A	No. 1,	Opal Base, Brass Column, Flint Font.........	
755	No. 1,	Opal Stand, Engraved Font....................	
844	No. 1,	Marble Base, Brass Column, Engraved Font...	
865	No. 1,	Opal Stand, Brass Column, Flint Font........	
724	No. 1,	Marble Base, Brass Column, Flint Font.......	
835	No. 1,	Opal Stand, Flint Font.....................	
854	No. 1,	Marble Base, Brass Column, Flint Font.......	
735	No. 1,	Marble Base, Brass Column, Flint Font.......	
764	No. 1,	Marble Base, Brass Column, Flint Font.......	
734	No. 1,	Marble Base, Brass Column, Flint Font.......	
756	No. 1,	Opal Stand, Engraved Font..................	
746	No. 1,	Marble Base, Brass Column, Flint Font.......	
944	No. 1,	Marble Base, Brass Column, Flint Font.......	
994	No. 1,	Marble Base, Brass Column, Flint Font.......	
794	No. 1,	Marble Base, Brass Column, Flint Font.......	
614	No. 1,	Marble Base, Brass Column, Flint Font, A, B, C and D.....................	
604	No. 1,	Marble Base, Brass Column, Flint Font, A, B, C and D.....................	

LAMPS.

Page 418—*Continued.*

No.	Size of Burner.	Description.	Per dozen.
953	No. 1,	Marble Base, Brass Column, Flint Font.......	
983	No. 1,	Marble Base, Brass Column, Flint Font.......	
925	No. 1,	Marble Base, Brass Column, Flint Font......	
598	No. 1,	Alabaster, Gilt Stand, Flint Font, Gilt Band, **Assorted Colors**......................	
9631	No. 1,	Alabaster, Gilt Stand, Gilt Font, **Assorted Colors**.................................	
919	No. 1,	Alabaster, Gilt Stand, Gilt Flint Font..........	

Page 419.

No.	Size of Burner.	Description.	Per dozen.
9401	No. 1,	Alabaster, Gilt Stand, Flint Font, Gilt Band...$	
7802	No. 1,	Alabaster, Gilt Stand, Opal, Gilt and Painted Font....................................	
7321	No. 1,	Alabaster, Gilt Stand, Gilt Flint Font.........	
5441	No. 1,	Alabaster, Gilt Stand, Gilt Font, **Assorted Colors**...................................	
1171	No. 1,	Marble Base, Bronze Figure, Gilt Font, **Assorted Colors**..............................	
859	No. 1,	Marble Base, Bronze Column, Flint Font......	
9741	No. 1,	Alabaster, Gilt Stand, Flint Gilt Font, **Assorted Colors**..............................	
7932	No. 1,	Glass Stand, **Assorted Colors**, Alabaster, Painted and Gilt Font.....................	
4921	No. 1,	Alabaster, Gilt Stand, Flint Gilt Font, **Assorted Colors**..............................	
9612	No. 1,	Alabaster, Gilt Stand, Flint Gilt Font.........	
907	No. 1,	Marble, Double Base, Brass Column, Eng'd Font	
917	No. 1,	Marble, Double Base, Brass Column, Flint Font.	
927	No. 1,	Marble, Double Base, Brass Column, Flint Font.	
796	No. 1,	Marble, Double Base, Brass Column, Flint Font.	
996	No. 1,	Marble, Double Base, Brass Column, Flint Font.	
1161	No. 2,	Alabaster, Gilt Stand, Flint Gilt Font.........	
528	No. 2,	Marble Base, Brass Column, Flint Font.......	
9711	No. 2,	Marble, Double Base, Bronze Column, Flint Font	
749	No. 2,	Marble Base, Brass Column, Flint Font.......	
8991	No. 2,	Alabaster Gilt Stand, Flint Gilt Font.........	
8341	No. 2,	Alabaster Double Base, Gilt Flint Engr'd Font.	

Page 420.

No.	Size of Burner.	Description.	Per dozen.
4022	No. 2,	Alabaster Gilt Stand, Fine Engraved Font....$	
8781	No. 2,	Marble Double Base, Gilt or Bronzed Column, Flint Cut and Gilt Font...................	
9161	No. 2,	Marble Base, Gilt or Bronzed Column, Flint Font, A, B and C.........................	
8591	No. 2,	Opal Double Base, Gilt Fine Cut Flint Font...	
8981	No. 2,	Marble Base, Bronze or Gilt Column...........	
8202	No. 2,	Marble Base, Bronze or Gilt Column, Flint Cut Font..................................	
6557	No. 2,	Marble Base, Rich Plated and Cut **Assorted Colors**.................................	
9621	No. 2,	Alabaster Stand, Fine Cut and Engraved Font.	

COAL OIL LAMPS AND FIXTURES.

(Continued.)

LAMPS.

Page 420—*Continued.*

No.	Size of Burner.	Description.	
5782	No. 2,	Alabaster Gilt Stand, Rich Painted and Gilt Alabaster Font	$
8681	No. 2,	Marble Base, Glass Column, **Assorted Colors,** Plated and Cut Fonts, **Assorted Colors**	
6113	No. 2,	Marble Base, Bronze or Gilt Column, Opal Gilt Painted Peg	
5044	No. 2,	Black Marble Base, Fine Cut Cast Bronze Stand, Fonts Plated and Cut, **Assorted Colors**	

Page 421.

No.	Size of Burner.	Description.	Per dozen.
21 P	No. 2,	Rich Cast Bronze in **Relief**	$
5164	No. 2,	Fine Cast Bronze, Marble Base	
22 P	No. 2,	Marble Base, Fine Cast Bronze in **Relief,**	
5334	No. 2,	Fine Cast Bronze	
3 P	No. 2,	Marble Base, Fine Cast Bronze	
10 P	No. 2,	Fine Cast Bronze, Marble Base	
15 P		Bronze and Gilt, Adjustable, **Reading Lamp**	
18 P	No. 2,	Fine Cast Bronze, Marble Base	
20 P		Bronze and gilt in **Relief**	

Page 422.

No.	Size of Burner.	Description.	Per dozen.
4 P	No. 2,	Marble Base, Fine Cast Bronze in **Relief**	$
6 P		Bronze and Gilt, for Halls	
8 P		Bronze and Gilt in **Relief**	
14 P	No. 1,	Marble Base, Fine Cast Bronze in **Relief**	

BRACKETS.

No.		Description.	
1 P		Bronze and Gilt, with Basket, Flint Font	$
5 P		Bronze and Gilt, with Basket, Flint Font	
6 P		Bronze and Gilt, Plain	
199	No. 2,	Bronzed, Relief **Bracket**, Flint Font	
579	No. 2,	Bronze in Relief, Basket **Bracket**, Flint Font	
587	No. 2,	Bronzed, Relief **Bracket**, Flint Font	
5251	No. 3,	Bronze and Relief, **Mammoth Bracket**, Flint Font	
234	No. 1,	Black, Iron **Bracket**, Flint Font	
516	No. 2,	Black, Iron **Bracket**, Flint Font	

Page 423.

SIDE LAMPS.

No.	Size of Burner.	Description.	Each.
214	No. 1,	Bronzed, Tin, **Side Lamp**	$
596	No. 2,	Bronzed, Tin Back, Flint Font, **Side Lamp**	
564	No. 1,	Bronzed, Tin Back, Flint Font, **Side Lamp**	

HANGERS.

No.		Description.	
536	No. 1,	Bronzed Wire, Flint Font	$
536	No. 2,	Bronzed Wire, Flint Font	
536	No. 3,	Bronzed Wire, Flint Font	
999	No. 1,	Bronzed Wire, Flint Font, with Feeder	
999	No. 2,	Bronzed Wire, Flint Font, with Feeder	

HANGERS.

Page 423—*Continued.*

No.	Size of Burner.	Description.	Each.
999	No. 3,	Bronzed Wire, Flint Font, with Feeder	$
5111	No. 2,	Fine Brass Rope, Flint Font	
2241	No. 1,	Brass Chain, Flint Font	
2241	No. 2,	Brass Chain, Flint Font	
2241	No. 3,	Brass Chain, Flint Font, with Feeder	
6 P		1 Light, Bronze and Gilt, Brass Font	

Page 424.

HALL LIGHTS.

No.	Size of Burner.	Description.	Each.
627 P		1 Light, Bronze and Gilt, Bronze Font	$
716	No. 2,	Fine Bronze and Relief, Bronze Font	
5383	No. 2,	1 Light, Cast Bronze Ornaments, Gilt Foot Fonts	
610 P		1 Light, Hall Fixture, Bronze and Gilt	
803 P		12 inch Globe, Sliding Hall Light	
803 P		12 inch Globe, Extra Cut, Sliding Hall Light	
802 P		10 inch Globe, Sliding Hall Light	
802 P		10 inch Globe, Extra Cut, Sliding Hall Light	
801 P		8 inch Globe, Sliding Hall Light	

Page 425.

CHANDELIERS.

No.	Size of Burner.	Description.	Each.
875	No. 2,	Fine Bronze and Relief, Center Font	$
644	No. 2,	Fine Bronze and Relief, Foot Font	
1027½ P		2 Lights, Gilt and Bronze, Brass Fonts	
1027½ P		3 Lights, Gilt and Bronze, Brass Fonts	
1027½ P		4 Lights, Gilt and Bronze, Brass Fonts	
1027½ P		6 Lights, Gilt and Bronze, Brass Fonts	
543 P		2 Lights, Gilt and Bronze, Rings for Fonts	
543 P		3 Lights, Gilt and Bronze, Rings for Fonts	
543 P		4 Lights, Gilt and Bronze, Rings for Fonts	

Page 426.

No.	Size of Burner.	Description.	Each.
554 P		2 Lights, Gilt and Bronze, Brass Fonts	$
554 P		4 Lights, Gilt and Bronze, Brass Fonts	
704	No. 2,	Fine Bronze and Relief, Foot Font	

Page 427.

No.	Size of Burner.	Description.	Each.
664	No. 2,	Fine Bronze and Relief, **Iron**, Flint Font	$
457	No. 2,	Fine Bronze and Relief, Center Font	
1071 P		2 Lights, Gilt and Bronze, Baskets for Fonts	
1071 P		3 Lights, Gilt and Bronze, Baskets for Fonts	
1071 P		4 Lights, Gilt and Bronze, Baskets for Fonts	
539 P		2 Lights, Gilt and Bronze, Brass Fonts	
539 P		3 Lights, Gilt and Bronze, Brass Fonts	
539 P		4 Lights, Gilt and Bronze, Brass Fonts	

COAL OIL LAMPS AND FIXTURES.

(Continued.)

MISCELLANEOUS ARTICLES.

Burners.

No. 0, Jones' Combination Spring .... per dozen, $

No. 1, Jones' Combination Spring .... "

No. 2, Jones' Combination Spring .... "

No. 3, Jones' Combination Spring .... "

No. 0, Screw .... "

No. 1, Screw .... "

No. 2, Screw .... "

No. 3, Screw .... "

No. 1, Deck Spring .... "

No. 0, Excelsior Hinge .... "

No. 1, Excelsior Hinge .... "

No. 2, Excelsior Hinge .... "

Round Wick Burners.

Tom Thumb .... per dozen, $

No. 0, Union .... "

No. 1, Union .... "

No. 0, Union Hinge .... "

Ne Plus Ultra .... "

No Chimney Burners.

No. 0, Miller's .... per dozen, $

No. 1, Miller's .... "

No. 0, Ambrose Lantern .... "

No. 1, Ambrose Lantern .... "

No. 2, Merrill's Lantern .... "

No. 1, Savage's Lantern .... "

No. 1, Billing's Lantern .... "

No. 2, Billing's Lantern .... "

Globes.

3 inch, Oregon Roughed and Engraved .... per dozen, $

3½ inch, Oregon Roughed and Engraved .... "

4 inch, Oregon Roughed and Engraved .... "

5 inch, Oregon Roughed and Engraved .... "

6 inch, Oregon Roughed and Engraved .... "

3 inch, Round Rough Cut .... "

3½ inch, Round Rough Cut .... "

4 inch, Round Rough Cut .... "

5 inch, Round Rough Cut .... "

6 inch, Round Rough Cut .... "

4 inch, Solar Fine Cut .... "

5 inch, Solar Fine Cut .... "

6 inch, Solar Fine Cut .... "

Globe Holders or Rings.

(See plate, page 428.)

3 inch, No. 1 Burners .... per dozen, $

3½ inch, No. 1 Burners .... "

4 inch, No. 2 Burners .... "

MISCELLANEOUS ARTICLES.

(Continued.)

Dithridge's Royal and Patent Oval Lamp Chimneys.

Manufactured of XX Flint Glass.

The superior quality Glass, combined with the new patent process of annealing, render it almost impossible to crack them with the heat of the flame.

Petit Oval and Royal, Short Size of No. 0, for No. 0 Burner .... per dozen, $

No. 0, Oval and Royal, for No. 0 Burner .... "

No. 1, Oval and Royal, for No. 1 Burner .... "

No. 1, Oval and Royal, Short, for No. 1 Burner ...... "

No. 1, Oval and Royal, Nut Cracker, Very Heavy, 6½ oz., for No. 1 Burner .... "

No. 2, Oval and Royal, for No. 2 Burner .... "

No. 3, Oval and Royal, for No. 3 Burner .... "

Chimneys.

No. 0, Flint Glass .... per dozen, $

No. 1, Flint Glass .... "

No. 2, Flint Glass .... "

No. 3, Flint Glass .... "

No. 0, Flint Glass, Extra Heavy Annealed .... "

No. 1, Flint Glass, Extra Heavy Annealed .... "

No. 2, Flint Glass, Extra Heavy Annealed .... "

No. 3, Flint Glass, Extra Heavy Annealed .... "

No. 0, Flint Glass, Moulded Oval .... "

No. 1, Flint Glass, Moulded Oval .... "

No. 2, Flint Glass, Moulded Oval .... "

No. 3, Flint Glass, Moulded Oval .... "

No. 1, Flint Glass, Ground .... "

No. 2, Flint Glass, Ground .... "

No. 0, Flint Glass, Tom Thumb .... "

No. 0, Flint Glass, French .... "

No. 1, Flint Glass, French .... "

No. 2, Flint Glass, French .... "

Flint Glass, Ne Plus Ultra .... "

Flint Glass, Monitor .... "

Reflectors—Glass.

5 inch, Tin or Iron Backs .... per dozen, $

6 inch, Tin or Iron Backs .... "

7 inch, Tin or Iron Backs .... "

8 inch, Tin or Iron Backs .... "

9 inch, Tin or Iron Backs .... "

10 inch, Tin or Iron Backs .... "

11 inch, Tin or Iron Backs .... "

12 inch, Tin or Iron Backs .... "

Reflectors—Metal, Silvered.

5 inch, Tin Backs .... per dozen, $

7 inch, Tin Backs .... per dozen,

Reflectors—Planished Tin.

5 inch, Tin Backs .... per dozen, $

7 inch, Tin Backs .... "

10 inch, for Harps and Chain Hangers .... "

LAMP FIXTURES AND LADIES' LANTERNS.

MISCELLANEOUS ARTICLES.
(*Continued.*)

Shades Paper.
(*See plate, page 248.*)

White, Printed ....per dozen, $
Green, Printed............................   "
Transparent, Assorted Colors and Patterns.....   "

Shades—Porcelain.
(*See plate, page 428.*)

5 inch, Ribbed ....per dozen, $
6 inch, Ribbed, or Plain ....   "
6½ inch, Ribbed, or Plain ....   "

Shade Rings.
(*See plate, page 428.*)

5 inch, for Porcelain Shade ....per dozen, $
6 inch, for Porcelain Shade ....   "
6½ inch, for Porcelain Shade ....   "

Shade Clasps.
(*See plate, page 428.*)

No. 0, Miniature....................per dozen, $
No. 1, Small ....   "
No. 2, Large ....   "

MISCELLANEOUS ARTICLES.
Continued.

Wick.

No. 0, 8 inches long, width ⅜ in....................per gross, $
No. 1, 8 inches long, width ⅝ in ....   "
No. 2, 8 inches long, width 1 in....................   "
No. 3, 8 inches long, width 1½ in....................   "
Tom Thumb, Round.....................per package, $
Fluid, Round............................per package,

Gas Cups.
(For Altering Gas Chandeliers.)

Brass Fonts, with Sockets, No. 1...................each, $
Brass Fonts, with Sockets, No. 2...................   "
Brass Cups, (for Fonts,) No. 1...................   "
Brass Cups, (for Fonts,) No. 2...................   "
Basket Cups, (for Fonts,) No. 2...................   "
Smoke Bells, (for Chandeliers, &c.)................   "

Can Tops—Zinc and Screw.

¾ inch ....per gross, $
1 inch ....   "
1¼ inch ....   "
1½ inch ....   "

Can Tops—Patent Excelsior.

No. 1..................................per gross, $
No. 2..................................per gross, $
Phare's Patent Trimming Shears .....per dozen, $

WOODWARD'S SELF-ADJUSTING SMALL OR LADIES' LANTERN.

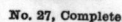

No. 27, Complete.   No. 27, Cap and Hand Lamp Detached.

Can be instantly removed, same as No. 1 (see page 371), is more convenient and complete (as it can be used either as a Hand Lamp or Lantern) than any made.

Woodward's Self-Adjusting, Small or Ladies' Lantern, per doz. $

☞ Extra Glasses for Woodward's Patent Lanterns Furnished to Order.

For other Lanterns, see pages 371, 372.

CALLENDER'S NO-CHIMNEY BURNER, FOR LAMPS AND LANTERNS.

Warranted not to Smoke, Smell, Char the Wick, or Heat the Lamp.

Callender's No-Chimney Burner No. 1.......per dozen, $
Callender's No-Chimney Burner No. 2.......per dozen, $

MORTISING MACHINES, COFFEE ROASTERS, ETC.

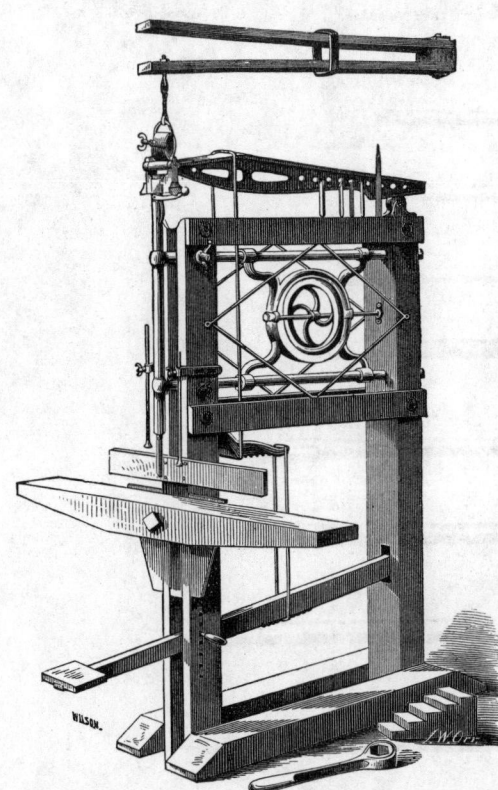

LARGE FOOT MORTISING MACHINE.

The merits of this Machine having been fully tested, it is recommended as the best Machine for the use of Carpenters, Joiners, Sash and Blind Makers, Car Builders, and Cabinet Manufacturers.

The following additional tools and articles apply to this Machine :

The Double Chisel for Sash Work.—It has two edges, with a V shape between. It is pressed into the sash-bar a little more than half way through, when the bar is turned, and, by an impression on the opposite side, the mortise is made.

The Blind Slat Chisel, is used for making the groove for the blind-slat in the stile, the length of which being less than the width of stile, and corresponding with the width of the slat. The slat enters this groove, and is by it confined in its place without mouldings or brads.

These chisels are made with one, two or three pairs of cutters of such length and thickness as may be wanted.

The Pin-tool and Pointer makes both hard and soft wood pins for Sash, Blinds, Doors, &c., varying in size from a quarter to three-eighths of an inch. Pine pins are pointed in the pointer by one blow from a hammer.

Standard Rolls, for door stiles and larger work, are made to play into a small iron frame, from which extends a bolt which is passed through a slat in an upright joist, about three and a half inches square, and by a thumb nut on the end of the bolt the iron frame is confined to the upright, at an elevation corresponding with the level of the *rest* of the machine on which the piece to mortise is placed, and by these rolls is easily moved as the chisel cuts away.

The Extra Rest, to mortise through from one side, is confined to the *main rest* by a single bolt, and has a piece of very hard wood standing endwise, which receives the edge of the chisel after it has passed through the blind-stile. This rest is made to move endwise on the main rest, so that when one place becomes worn by the long continued action of the edge of the chisel, it is changed to the extent of the width of the endwise piece. The mortising of blind-stiles is the most suitable work to be done in this way.

Staple-punch for Blind Rods and Slats.—This tool is inserted in the machine in place of the chisel, and by the pressure of the foot two holes are made for the small staple.

Large Foot Mortising Machine, with 1/4, 3/8, 7/16, 1/2, 5/8 inch Chisels.................................each, $

Extra Chisels 1/8 to 1 inch......................... "

Extra Chisels over 1 inch......................... "

Double Sash Chisels.............................. "

Pin Tools and Pointer............................ "

Blind Slat Chisels, Single Cutters................. "

Blind Slat Chisels, Double Cutters...............each, $

Blind Slat Chisels, Treble Cutters............... "

Standard Rolls..........................per pair, $

Extra Rests to Mortise through.................each, $

Staple Punch for Slats.......................... "

Hub Apparatus................................. "

PATENT SELF-STIRRING COFFEE ROASTING MACHINE.

This Machine runs by Clockwork, requires no tending, and is especially intended for Family use.

It roasts Coffee or any substitute for Coffee, and is well adapted for Popping corn.

Self-Stirring Coffee Roasting Machine...each, $

IMPROVED GUNSMITHS' STOCKS AND DIES.

(For Cuts see Page 245.)

No. 1, 3 Taps, 3 sets of Dies, 1/16, 3/32, 1/8.........each, $

No. 2, 3 Taps, 3 sets of Dies, 3/32, 1/8, 5/32......... "

No. 3, 3 Taps, 3 sets of Dies, 1/8, 5/32, 3/16......... "

No. 4, 3 Taps, 3 sets of Dies, 5/32, 3/16, 1/4......... "

No. 5, 6 Taps, 6 sets of Dies, 1/16, 3/32, 1/8, 3/32, 3/16, 1/4. "

No. 6, 4 Taps, 4 sets of Dies, 3/32, 3/16, 1/4, 5/16..... "

No. 7, 5 Taps, 5 sets of Dies, 3/32, 3/16, 1/4, 5/16, 3/8.... "

Mo. 8, 3 Taps, 3 sets of Dies, 1/4, 5/16, 3/8..........each, $

No. 9, 3 Taps, 3 sets of Dies, 5/16, 3/8, 7/16......... "

No. 10, 3 Taps, 3 sets of Dies, 3/8, 7/16, 1/2......... "

No. 11, 5 Taps, 5 sets of Dies, 1/4, 5/16, 3/8, 7/16, 1/2..... "

Tap Wrenches, No. 1......................per dozen, $

Tap Wrenches, No. 2......................per dozen, $

SAIL AND PACKING NEEDLES, ETC.

These Plates Represent the Exact Size of the Needles.

(See page 210.)

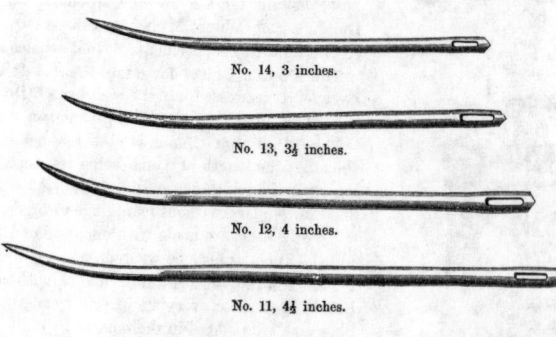

No. 14, 3 inches.

No. 13, 3½ inches.

No. 12, 4 inches.

No. 11, 4½ inches.

No. 10, 5 inches.

No. 9, 5½ inches.

No. 8, 6 inches.

No. 7, 7 inches.

No. 6, 7½ inches.

Flat Seam.	Small Bolt Rope.
Tabline.	Middle Bolt Rope.
Old Work.	Large Bolt Rope.
Store.	Small Marline.
Head Rope.	Large Marline.

Square Corn Poppers—*(See page 376.)*　　　Round Corn Poppers—*(See page 376.)*

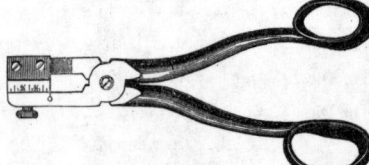

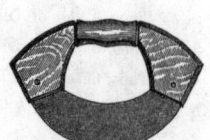

Button Hole Cutters—*(See page 369.)*　　　Taylor's Patent Mop Sticks—*(See page 376.)*　　　Round Mincing Knife—*(See page 370.)*

FISH HOOKS.

THESE PLATES REPRESENT THE EXACT SIZE OF THE VARIOUS KINDS OF HOOKS.

(See Page 410.)

Limerick Hooks, Genuine Hollow Points.

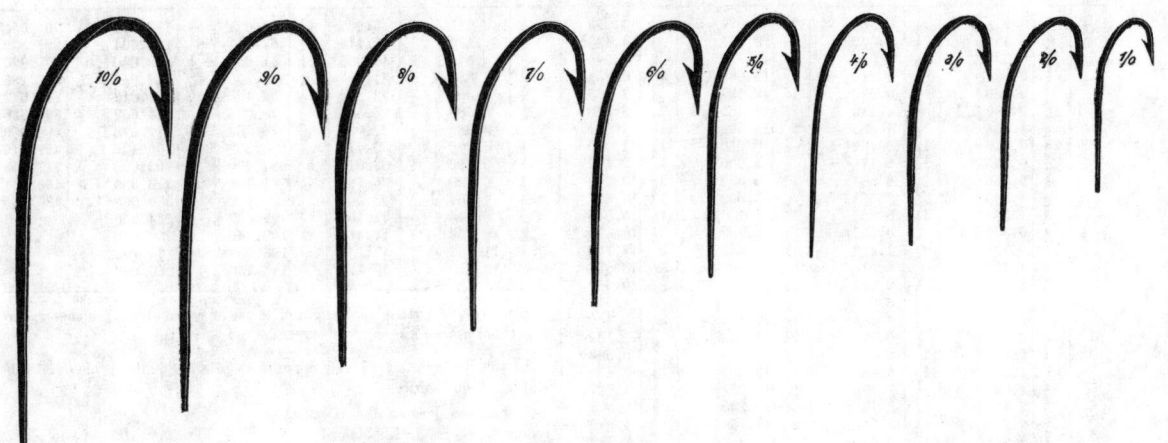

Kirby Trout, Flatted.

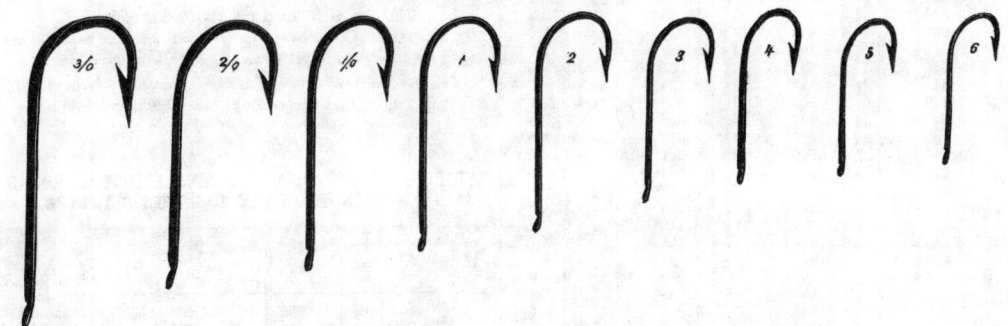

Limerick Hooks, Genuine Hollow Points.

Kirby Fish, Flatted.

TABLES.

EXHIBITING THE WEIGHT OF A LINEAL FOOT OF FLAT BAR IRON, IN LBS., FROM ½ TO 3 INCHES IN BREADTH, AND ⅛ TO 2¾ INCHES IN THICKNESS.

Breadth in Inches	Thickness in Inches	Weight in Pounds
½	⅛	0.211
	¼	0.422
	⅜	0.634
⅝	⅛	0.264
	¼	0.528
	⅜	0.792
	½	1.056
¾	⅛	0.316
	¼	0.633
	⅜	0.950
	½	1.265
	⅝	1.584
⅞	⅛	0.369
	¼	0.738
	⅜	1.108
	½	1.477
	⅝	1.846
	¾	2.217
1	⅛	0.422
	¼	0.845
	⅜	1.267
	½	1.690
	⅝	2.112
	¾	2.534
	⅞	2.956
1⅛	⅛	0.475
	¼	0.950
	⅜	1.425
	½	1.901
	⅝	2.375
	¾	2.850
	⅞	3.326
	1	3.802
1¼	⅛	0.528
	¼	1.056
	⅜	1.584
	½	2.112
	⅝	2.640
	¾	3.168
	⅞	3.696
	1	4.224
	1⅛	4.752
1⅜	⅛	0.580
	¼	1.161
	⅜	1.742
	½	2.325
	⅝	2.904
	¾	3.484
	⅞	4.065
	1	4.646
	1⅛	5.227
	1¼	5.808
1½	⅛	0.633
	¼	1.266
	⅜	1.900
	½	2.535
	⅝	3.168
	¾	3.802
	⅞	4.435
	1	5.069
	1⅛	5.703
	1¼	6.337
	1⅜	6.970
1⅝	⅛	0.686
	¼	1.372
	⅜	2.059
	½	2.746
	⅝	3.432
	¾	4.119
	⅞	4.805
	1	5.492
	1⅛	6.178
	1¼	6.864
	1⅜	7.551
	1½	8.237
1¾	⅛	0.739
	¼	1.479
	⅜	2.218
	½	2.957
	⅝	3.696
	¾	4.435
	⅞	5.178
	1	5.914
	1⅛	6.653
	1¼	7.393
	1⅜	8.132
	1½	8.871
	1⅝	9.610
1⅞	⅛	0.792
	¼	1.584
	⅜	2.376
	½	3.168
	⅝	3.960
	¾	4.752
	⅞	5.544
	1	6.336
	1⅛	7.129
	1¼	7.921
	1⅜	8.713
	1½	9.505
	1⅝	10.297
	1¾	11.089
2	⅛	0.845
	¼	1.689
	⅜	2.534
	½	3.379
	⅝	4.224
	¾	5.069
	⅞	5.914
	1	6.758
	1⅛	7.604
	1¼	8.448
	1⅜	9.294
	1½	10.138
	1⅝	10.983
	1¾	11.828
	1⅞	12.673
2⅛	⅛	0.898
	¼	1.795
	⅜	2.693
	½	3.591
	⅝	4.488
	¾	5.386
	⅞	6.283
	1	7.181
	1⅛	8.079
	1¼	8.977
	1⅜	9.874
	1½	10.772
	1⅝	11.670
	1¾	12.567
	1⅞	13.465
	2	14.362
2¼	⅛	0.950
	¼	1.900
	⅜	2.851
	½	3.802
	⅝	4.752
	¾	5.703
	⅞	6.653
	1	7.604
	1⅛	8.554
	1¼	9.505
	1⅜	10.455
	1½	11.406
	1⅝	12.356
	1¾	13.307
	1⅞	14.257
	2	15.208
	2⅛	16.158
2⅜	⅛	1.003
	¼	2.006
	⅜	3.009
	½	4.013
	⅝	5.016
	¾	6.019
	⅞	7.022
	1	8.025
	1⅛	9.028
	1¼	10.032
	1⅜	11.035
	1½	12.038
	1⅝	13.042
	1¾	14.045
	1⅞	15.048
	2	16.051
	2⅛	17.054
	2¼	18.057
2½	⅛	1.056
	¼	2.112
	⅜	3.168
	½	4.224
	⅝	5.280
	¾	6.336
	⅞	7.392
	1	8.448
	1⅛	9.504
	1¼	10.550
	1⅜	11.616
	1½	12.672
	1⅝	13.728
	1¾	14.784
	1⅞	15.840
	2	16.896
	2⅛	17.952
	2¼	19.008
	2⅜	20.064
2⅝	⅛	1.109
	¼	2.218
	⅜	3.327
	½	4.436
	⅝	5.545
	¾	6.654
	⅞	7.763
	1	8.872
	1⅛	9.981
	1¼	11.090
	1⅜	12.199
	1½	13.308
	1⅝	14.417
	1¾	15.526
	1⅞	16.635
	2	17.744
	2⅛	18.853
	2¼	19.962
	2⅜	21.071
	2½	22.180
2¾	⅛	1.162
	¼	2.323
	⅜	3.485
	½	4.647
	⅝	5.808
	¾	6.979
	⅞	8.132
	1	9.294
	1⅛	10.455
	1¼	11.617
	1⅜	12.779
	1½	13.940
	1⅝	15.102
	1¾	16.264
	1⅞	17.425
	2	18.587
	2⅛	19.749
	2¼	20.910
	2⅜	22.072
	2½	23.234
	2⅝	24.395
2⅞	⅛	1.215
	¼	2.429
	⅜	3.644
	½	4.858
	⅝	6.072
	¾	7.287
	⅞	8.502
	1	9.716
	1⅛	10.931
	1¼	12.145
	1⅜	13.360
	1½	14.574
	1⅝	15.789
	1¾	17.003
	1⅞	18.218
	2	19.432
	2⅛	20.647
	2¼	21.861
	2⅜	23.076
	2½	24.290
	2⅝	25.505
	2¾	26.719
3	⅛	1.267
	¼	2.535

EXAMPLE.—What is the weight of a bar of Iron 4¾ in. in breadth by 1¾ in. thick.

Find 4¾ in. in the column of *breadths*, and below it in the column of *thickness* find 1¾; and opposite to that is 28.092, which is 28 lbs. and 92-1000 of a lb. *Ans.*

NOTE.—The weight of a lineal foot of flat bar iron from three up to six inches in breadth can be ascertained by doubling on the foregoing Table.

EXHIBITING THE WEIGHT OF A LINEAL FOOT OF SQUARE ROLLED IRON, IN LBS., FROM ¼ TO 12 SQUARE INCHES.

Size in Inches	Weight in Pounds
¼	.211
⅜	.475
½	.845
⅝	1.320
¾	1.901
⅞	2.588
1	3.380
1⅛	4.278
1¼	5.280
1⅜	6.390
1½	7.604
1⅝	8.926
1¾	10.352
1⅞	11.883
2	13.520
2⅛	15.263
2¼	17.112
2⅜	19.066
2½	21.120
2⅝	23.292
2¾	25.560
2⅞	27.939
3	30.416
3⅛	33.010
3¼	35.704
3⅜	38.503
3½	41.408
3⅝	44.418
3¾	47.534
3⅞	50.756
4	54.084
4⅛	57.517
4¼	61.055
4⅜	64.700
4½	68.448
4⅝	72.305
4¾	76.264
4⅞	80.333
5	84.480
5⅛	88.784
5¼	93.168
5⅜	97.657
5½	102.240
5⅝	106.253
5¾	111.756
5⅞	116.671
6	121.664
6¼	132.040
6½	142.816
6¾	154.012
7	165.632
7¼	177.672
7½	190.136
7¾	203.024
8	216.336
8¼	230.068
8½	244.220
8¾	258.800
9	273.792
9¼	289.220
9½	305.056
9¾	321.332
10	337.920
10¼	355.136
10½	372.672
10¾	390.628
11	408.960
11¼	427.812
11½	447.024
11¾	466.684
12	486.656

EXAMPLE.—What is the weight of a bar of rolled iron 1¾ inches square, and 1 foot in length?

In column first, find 1¾, and opposite to it is 10,352 lbs., which is 10 lbs. and 352-1000 of a lb.

If the lesser denomination of ounces is required, the result is obtained as follows: Multiply the remainder by 16, pointing off the decimals as in multiplication of decimals, and the figures remaining on the left of the point indicate the number of ounces.

$$\text{Thus, 352-1000 of a lb.} = \begin{array}{r} 352 \\ 16 \\ \hline 2112 \\ 352 \\ \hline 5.632 \end{array}$$

The weight, then, is 10 lbs. 5 and 632-1000 ounces.

If the weight of a piece of iron less than a foot be required, first find the weight for a foot, and then take an aliquot part for the answer.

Thus, the weight of a bar 2¾ inches square, and 8 inches long, is obtained as follows: 2¾ and 12 inches long = 25.560 lbs. And 8 inches = ⅔ of 12 inches; therefore, 25.560 × ⅔ = 17.040 lbs.

EXHIBITING THE WEIGHT OF A LINEAL FOOT OF ROUND ROLLED IRON, FROM ¼ TO 12 INCHES DIAMETER.

Diameter in Inches	Weight in Pounds
¼	.165
⅜	.373
½	.663
⅝	1.043
¾	1.493
⅞	2.032
1	2.654
1⅛	3.360
1¼	4.172
1⅜	5.019
1½	5.972
1⅝	7.010
1¾	8.128
1⅞	9.333
2	10.616
2⅛	11.988
2¼	13.440
2⅜	14.975
2½	16.688
2⅝	18.298
2¾	20.076
2⅞	21.944
3	23.888
3⅛	25.926
3¼	28.040
3⅜	30.240
3½	32.512
3⅝	34.886
3¾	37.332
3⅞	39.864
4	42.464
4⅛	45.174
4¼	47.952
4⅜	50.815
4½	53.760
4⅝	56.788
4¾	59.900
4⅞	63.094
5	66.752
5⅛	69.731
5¼	73.172
5⅜	76.700
5½	80.304
5⅝	84.001
5¾	87.776
5⅞	91.634
6	95.552
6¼	103.704
6½	112.160
6¾	120.960
7	130.048
7¼	139.544
7½	149.328
7¾	159.456
8	169.856
8¼	180.696
8½	191.808
8¾	203.260
9	215.040
9¼	227.152
9½	239.600
9¾	252.376
10	266.288
10¼	278.924
10½	292.688
10¾	306.800
11	321.216
11¼	336.004
11½	351.104
11¾	366.536
12	382.208

NOTE.—The application of this table is the same as the preceding one.

The weight of bar iron being 1, the weight of cast iron = .95
    "   "   steel = 1.02
    "   "   copper = 1.16
    "   "   brass = 1.09
    "   "   lead = 1.48

TABLE SHOWING THE WEIGHT PER FOOT OF EACH SIZE OF MANILLA ROPE.

(800 FEET IN EACH COIL.)

Diameter,	¼	⅜	½	⅝	¾	⅞	1	1⅛	1¼	1½	1¾	2 inch.
	20	15	10	7	5	4	3	2½	2	1½	1	¾ No. of feet to lb.